HEALTH CA

ALMANAC 2019

The only comprehensive
guide to the health care industry

Jack W. Plunkett

Published by:
Plunkett Research®, Ltd., Houston, Texas
www.plunkettresearch.com

PLUNKETT'S HEALTH CARE INDUSTRY ALMANAC 2019

Editor and Publisher:
Jack W. Plunkett

Executive Editor and Database Manager:
Martha Burgher Plunkett

Senior Editor and Researchers:
Isaac Snider
Shuang Zhou

Editors, Researchers and Assistants:
John Brucato
Michael Cappelli
Annie Paynter
Anoosh Saidi
Jorden Smith
Gina Sprenkel

Information Technology Manager:
Rebeca Tijiboy

Special Thanks to:
American Hospital Association
Organisation for Economic Cooperation and Development (OECD)
The World Bank
U.S. Department of Commerce,
Census Bureau,
International Trade Administration,
National Technical Information Service
U.S. Department of Health and Human Services
Centers for Disease Control,
Centers for Medicare and Medicaid Services,
National Center for Health Statistics,
National Institutes of Health
U.S. Department of Labor
Bureau of Labor Statistics
U.S. National Science Foundation

Plunkett Research®, Ltd.
P. O. Drawer 541737, Houston, Texas 77254 USA
Phone: 713.932.0000   Fax: 713.932.7080
www.plunkettresearch.com

Plunkett Research®, Ltd.
P. O. Drawer 541737
Houston, Texas 77254-1737
Phone: 713.932.0000, Fax: 713.932.7080 www.plunkettresearch.com

ISBN13 # 978-1-62831-509-7 (eBook Edition # 978-1-62831-832-6)

Limited Warranty and Terms of Use:

Users' publications in static electronic format containing any portion of the content of this book (and/or the content of any related Plunkett Research, Ltd. online service to which you are granted access, hereinafter collectively referred to as the "Data") or Derived Data (that is, a set of data that is a derivation made by a User from the Data, resulting from the applications of formulas, analytics or any other method) may be resold by the User only for the purpose of providing third-party analysis within an established research platform under the following conditions: (However, Users may not extract or integrate any portion of the Data or Derived Data for any other purpose.)

a) Users may utilize the Data only as described herein. b) User may not export more than an insubstantial portion of the Data or Derived Data, c) Any Data exported by the User may only be distributed if the following conditions are met:

i) Data must be incorporated in added-value reports or presentations, either of which are part of the regular services offered by the User and not as stand-alone products.
ii) Data may not be used as part of a general mailing or included in external websites or other mass communication vehicles or formats, including, but not limited to, advertisements.
iii) Except as provided herein, Data may not be resold by User.

"Insubstantial Portions" shall mean an amount of the Data that (1) has no independent commercial value, (2) could not be used by User, its clients, Authorized Users and/or its agents as a substitute for the Data or any part of it, (3) is not separately marketed by the User, an affiliate of the User or any third-party source (either alone or with other data), and (4) is not retrieved by User, its clients, Authorized Users and/or its Agents via regularly scheduled, systematic batch jobs.

LIMITED WARRANTY; DISCLAIMER OF LIABILITY: While Plunkett Research, Ltd. ("PRL") has made an effort to obtain the Data from sources deemed reliable, PRL makes no warranties, expressed or implied, regarding the Data contained herein. This book and its Data are provided to the End-User "AS IS" without warranty of any kind. No oral or written information or advice given by PRL, its employees, distributors or representatives will create a warranty or in any way increase the scope of this Limited Warranty, and the Customer or End-User may not rely on any such information or advice. Customer Remedies: PRL's entire liability and your exclusive remedy shall be, at PRL's sole discretion, either (a) return of the price paid, if any, or (b) repair or replacement of a book that does not meet PRL's Limited Warranty and that is returned to PRL with sufficient evidence of or receipt for your original purchase.

NO OTHER WARRANTIES: TO THE MAXIMUM EXTENT PERMITTED BY APPLICABLE LAW, PRL AND ITS DISTRIBUTORS DISCLAIM ALL OTHER WARRANTIES AND CONDITIONS, EITHER EXPRESSED OR IMPLIED, INCLUDING, BUT NOT LIMITED TO, IMPLIED WARRANTIES OR CONDITIONS OF MERCHANTABILITY, FITNESS FOR A PARTICULAR PURPOSE, TITLE AND NON-INFRINGEMENT WITH REGARD TO THE BOOK AND ITS DATA, AND THE PROVISION OF OR FAILURE TO PROVIDE SUPPORT SERVICES. LIMITATION OF LIABILITY: TO THE MAXIMUM EXTENT PERMITTED BY APPLICABLE LAW, IN NO EVENT SHALL PRL BE LIABLE FOR ANY SPECIAL, INCIDENTAL OR CONSEQUENTIAL DAMAGES WHATSOEVER (INCLUDING, WITHOUT LIMITATION, DAMAGES FOR LOSS OF BUSINESS PROFITS, BUSINESS INTERRUPTION, ABILITY TO OBTAIN OR RETAIN EMPLOYMENT OR REMUNERATION, ABILITY TO PROFITABLY MAKE AN INVESTMENT, OR ANY OTHER PECUNIARY LOSS) ARISING OUT OF THE USE OF, OR RELIANCE UPON, THE BOOK OR DATA, OR THE INABILITY TO USE THIS DATA OR THE FAILURE OF PRL TO PROVIDE SUPPORT SERVICES, EVEN IF PRL HAS BEEN ADVISED OF THE POSSIBILITY OF SUCH DAMAGES. IN ANY CASE, PRL'S ENTIRE LIABILITY SHALL BE LIMITED TO THE AMOUNT ACTUALLY PAID BY YOU FOR THE BOOK.

PLUNKETT'S HEALTH CARE INDUSTRY ALMANAC 2019

CONTENTS

Continued on next page

Continued from previous page

Continued on next page

Continued from previous page

INTRODUCTION

PLUNKETT'S HEALTH CARE INDUSTRY ALMANAC is designed to be used as a general source for researchers of all types.

The data and areas of interest covered are intentionally broad, ranging from the costs and effectiveness of the American health care system, to emerging technology, to an in-depth look at the major firms (which we call THE HEALTH CARE 500) within the many industry sectors that make up the health care system.

This reference book is designed to be a general source for researchers. It is especially intended to assist with market research, strategic planning, employment searches, contact or prospect list creation and financial research, and as a data resource for executives and students of all types.

PLUNKETT'S HEALTH CARE INDUSTRY ALMANAC takes a rounded approach for the general reader. This book presents a complete overview of the health care field (see "How To Use This Book"). For example, Medicare and Medicaid growth and expenditures are provided in exacting detail, along with easy-to-use charts and tables on all facets of health care in general: from where health care dollars come from to how they are spent.

THE HEALTH CARE 500 is our unique grouping of the biggest, most successful corporations in all segments of the health care industry. Tens of thousands of pieces of information, gathered from a wide variety of sources, have been researched and are presented in a unique form that can be easily understood. This section includes thorough indexes to THE HEALTH CARE 500, by geography, industry, sales, brand names, subsidiary names and many other topics. (See Chapter 4.)

Especially helpful is the way in which PLUNKETT'S HEALTH CARE INDUSTRY ALMANAC enables readers who have no business background to readily compare the financial records and growth plans of health care companies and major industry groups. You'll see the mid-term financial record of each firm, along with the impact of earnings, sales and strategic plans on each company's potential to fuel growth, serve new markets and provide investment and employment opportunities.

No other source provides this book's easy-to-understand comparisons of growth, expenditures, technologies, corporations and many other items of great importance to people of all types who may be studying this, one of the largest and most complex industries in the world today.

By scanning the data groups and the unique indexes, you can find the best information to fit your personal research needs. The major companies in health care are profiled and then ranked using several different groups of specific criteria. Which firms are the biggest employers? Which companies earn the most profits? These things and much more are easy to find.

In addition to individual company profiles, an overview of health care markets and trends is provided. This book's job is to help you sort through easy-to-understand summaries of today's trends in a quick and effective manner.

Whatever your purpose for researching the health care field, you'll find this book to be a valuable guide. Nonetheless, as is true with all resources, this volume has limitations that the reader should be aware of:

- Financial data and other corporate information can change quickly. A book of this type can be no more current than the data that was available as of the time of editing. Consequently, the financial picture, management and ownership of the firm(s) you are studying may have changed since the date of this book. For example, this almanac includes the most up-to-date sales figures and profits available to the editors as of late-2018. That means that we have typically used corporate financial data as of the end of 2017.

- Corporate mergers, acquisitions and downsizing are occurring at a very rapid rate. Such events may have created significant change, subsequent to the publishing of this book, within a company you are studying.

- Some of the companies in THE HEALTH CARE 500 are so large in scope and in variety of business endeavors conducted within a parent organization, that we have been unable to completely list all subsidiaries, affiliations, divisions and activities within a firm's corporate structure.

- This volume is intended to be a general guide to a vast industry. That means that researchers should look to this book for an overview and, when conducting in-depth research, should contact the specific corporations or industry associations in question for the very latest changes and data. Where possible, we have listed contact names, toll-free telephone numbers and Internet site addresses for the companies, government agencies and industry associations involved so that the reader may get further details without unnecessary delay.

- Tables of industry data and statistics used in this book include the latest numbers available at the time of printing, generally through the end of 2017. In a few cases, the only complete data available was for earlier years.

- We have used exhaustive efforts to locate and fairly present accurate and complete data. However, when using this book or any other source for business and industry information, the reader should use caution and diligence by conducting further research where it seems appropriate. We wish you success in your endeavors, and we trust that your experience with this book will be both satisfactory and productive.

Jack W. Plunkett
Houston, Texas
September 2018

HOW TO USE THIS BOOK

The two primary sections of this book are devoted first to the health care industry as a whole and then to the "Individual Data Listings" for THE HEALTH CARE 500. If time permits, you should begin your research in the front chapters of this book. Also, you will find lengthy indexes in Chapter 4 and in the back of the book.

> **Video Tip**
> For our brief video introduction to the HealthCare industry, see www.plunkettresearch.com/video/healthcare.

THE HEALTH CARE INDUSTRY

Chapter 1: Major Trends Affecting the Health Care Industry. This chapter presents an encapsulated view of the major trends that are creating rapid changes in the health care industry today.

Chapter 2: Health Care Industry Statistics. This chapter presents in-depth statistics on payors, patients, Medicare, Medicaid, hospitals, pharmaceuticals, the Affordable Care Act and more.

Chapter 3: Important Health Care Industry Contacts – Addresses, Telephone Numbers and Internet Sites. This chapter covers contacts for important government agencies, health care organizations and trade groups. Included are numerous important Internet sites.

THE HEALTH CARE 500

Chapter 4: THE HEALTH CARE 500: Who They Are and How They Were Chosen. The companies compared in this book were carefully selected from the health care industry, largely in the United States, although many of the firms are global in nature or are headquartered in other nations. For a complete description, see THE HEALTH CARE 500 indexes in this chapter.

Individual Data Listings:

Look at one of the companies in THE HEALTH CARE 500's Individual Data Listings. You'll find the following information fields:

Company Name:

The company profiles are in alphabetical order by company name. If you don't find the company you are seeking, it may be a subsidiary or division of one of the firms covered in this book. Try looking it up in the Index by Subsidiaries, Brand Names and Selected Affiliations in the back of the book.

Industry Code:

Industry Group Code: An NAIC code used to group companies within like segments.

Types of Business:

A listing of the primary types of business specialties conducted by the firm.

Brands/Divisions/Affiliations:

Major brand names, operating divisions or subsidiaries of the firm, as well as major corporate affiliations—such as another firm that owns a significant portion of the company's stock. A complete Index by Subsidiaries, Brand Names and Selected Affiliations is in the back of the book.

Contacts:

The names and titles up to 27 top officers of the company are listed, including human resources contacts.

Growth Plans/ Special Features:

Listed here are observations regarding the firm's strategy, hiring plans, plans for growth and product development, along with general information regarding a company's business and prospects.

Financial Data:

Revenue (2017 or the latest fiscal year available to the editors, plus up to five previous years): This figure represents consolidated worldwide sales from all operations. These numbers may be estimates.

R&D Expense (2017 or the latest fiscal year available to the editors, plus up to five previous years): This figure represents expenses associated with the research and development of a company's goods or services. These numbers may be estimates.

Operating Income (2017 or the latest fiscal year available to the editors, plus up to five previous years): This figure represents the amount of profit realized from annual operations after deducting operating expenses including costs of goods sold, wages and depreciation. These numbers may be estimates.

Operating Margin % (2017 or the latest fiscal year available to the editors, plus up to five previous years): This figure is a ratio derived by dividing operating income by net revenues. It is a measurement of a firm's pricing strategy and operating efficiency. These numbers may be estimates.

SGA Expense (2017 or the latest fiscal year available to the editors, plus up to five previous years): This figure represents the sum of selling, general and administrative expenses of a company, including costs such as warranty, advertising, interest, personnel, utilities, office space rent, etc. These numbers may be estimates.

Net Income (2017 or the latest fiscal year available to the editors, plus up to five previous years): This figure represents consolidated, after-tax net profit from all operations. These numbers may be estimates.

Operating Cash Flow (2017 or the latest fiscal year available to the editors, plus up to five previous years): This figure is a measure of the amount of cash generated by a firm's normal business operations. It is calculated as net income before depreciation and after income taxes, adjusted for working capital. It is a prime indicator of a company's ability to generate enough cash to pay its bills. These numbers may be estimates.

Capital Expenditure (2017 or the latest fiscal year available to the editors, plus up to five previous years): This figure represents funds used for investment in or improvement of physical assets such as offices, equipment or factories and the purchase or creation of new facilities and/or equipment. These numbers may be estimates.

EBITDA (2017 or the latest fiscal year available to the editors, plus up to five previous years): This figure is an acronym for earnings before interest, taxes, depreciation and amortization. It represents a company's financial performance calculated as revenue minus expenses (excluding taxes, depreciation and interest), and is a prime indicator of profitability. These numbers may be estimates.

Return on Assets % (2017 or the latest fiscal year available to the editors, plus up to five previous years): This figure is an indicator of the profitability of a company relative to its total assets. It is calculated by dividing annual net earnings by total assets. These numbers may be estimates.

Return on Equity % (2017 or the latest fiscal year available to the editors, plus up to five previous years): This figure is a measurement of net income as a percentage of shareholders' equity. It is also called the rate of return on the ownership interest. It is a vital indicator of the quality of a company's operations. These numbers may be estimates.

Debt to Equity (2017 or the latest fiscal year available to the editors, plus up to five previous years): A ratio of the company's long-term debt to its shareholders' equity. This is an indicator of the overall financial leverage of the firm. These numbers may be estimates.

Address:
The firm's full headquarters address, the headquarters telephone, plus toll-free and fax numbers where available. Also provided is the internet site address.

Stock Ticker, Exchange: When available, the unique stock market symbol used to identify this firm's common stock for trading and tracking purposes is indicated. Where appropriate, this field may contain "private" or "subsidiary" rather than a ticker symbol. If the firm is a publicly-held company headquartered outside of the U.S., its international ticker and exchange are given.

Total Number of Employees: The approximate total number of employees, worldwide, as of the end of 2017 (or the latest data available to the editors).

Parent Company: If the firm is a subsidiary, its parent company is listed.

Salaries/Bonuses:
(The following descriptions generally apply to U.S. employers only.)

Highest Executive Salary: The highest executive salary paid, typically a 2017 amount (or the latest year available to the editors) and typically paid to the Chief Executive Officer.

Highest Executive Bonus: The apparent bonus, if any, paid to the above person.

Second Highest Executive Salary: The next-highest executive salary paid, typically a 2017 amount (or the latest year available to the editors) and typically paid to the President or Chief Operating Officer.

Second Highest Executive Bonus: The apparent bonus, if any, paid to the above person.

Other Thoughts:
Estimated Female Officers or Directors: It is difficult to obtain this information on an exact basis, and employers generally do not disclose the data in a public way. However, we have indicated what our best efforts reveal to be the apparent number of women who either are in the posts of corporate officers or sit on the board of directors. There is a wide variance from company to company.

Hot Spot for Advancement for Women/Minorities: A "Y" in appropriate fields indicates "Yes." These are firms that appear either to have posted a substantial number of women and/or minorities to high posts or that appear to have a good record of going out of their way to recruit, train, promote and retain women or minorities. (See the Index of Hot Spots For Women and Minorities in the back of the book.) This information may change frequently and can be difficult to obtain and verify. Consequently, the reader should use caution and conduct further investigation where appropriate.

Glossary: A short list of health care industry terms.

Chapter 1

MAJOR TRENDS AND TECHNOLOGIES AFFECTING THE HEALTH CARE INDUSTRY

1) Introduction to the Health Care Industry

Video Tip
For our brief video introduction to the HealthCare industry, see www.plunkettresearch.com/video/healthcare.

Health Expenditures and Services in the U.S.:

Health care expenditures continue to rise in the U.S. and throughout the world. Total U.S. health care expenditures were estimated to be $3.68 trillion in 2018, and are projected to soar to $5.70 trillion in 2026.

The health care market in the U.S. during 2018 included the major categories of hospital care ($1,189.9 billion); dental, physician and clinical services ($969.9 billion); and prescription drugs ($360.2 billion), along with nursing home and home health care ($277.4 billion). Registered U.S. hospitals totaled 5,534 properties in 2016, according to an American Hospital Association survey, containing 894,574 beds serving 35.2 million admitted patients yearly (the latest data available).

Medicare, the U.S. federal government's health care program for Americans 65 years or older, provided coverage to an estimated 59.9 million seniors during 2018. National expenditures on Medicare for fiscal 2018 were projected to be $748.1 billion, including premiums paid by beneficiaries and health care costs covered by Medicare. By 2030, the number of people covered by Medicare will balloon to about 82 million due to the massive number of Americans who will become of eligible age.

Medicaid is the federal government's health care program for low-income and disabled persons (including children), as well as certain groups of seniors in nursing homes. National expenditures on Medicaid totaled an estimated $622.0 billion in 2018. The majority of that expense is paid for by the federal government. However, the states pick up a significant share of the cost, which is a massive burden on state budgets.

Health spending in the U.S., at about 18.2% of Gross Domestic Product (GDP) in 2018, is projected to grow steadily. Health care spending in America accounts for a larger share of GDP than in any other country, by a wide margin. Despite the incredible investment America continues to make in health care, 8.7% of people in the U.S. (28.0 million) lacked health care coverage for the entire year of 2017. For some, insurance was unavailable or unaffordable. In other cases, a lack of insurance was due to a personal decision not to pay for it. According to the Kaiser Family Foundation, most uninsured people are in low-income working families, but a large segment of those counted among America's uninsured are non-U.S. citizens, both lawful and illegal residents.

In March 2010, President Obama signed the Patient Protection and Affordable Care Act (ACA), designed to strengthen insurance company regulation and provide medical coverage to millions of uninsured Americans. The act called for sweeping changes. Provisions taking effect within the first six months of signing included coverage for adult children up to age 26 on their parents' policies; making it unlawful for insurers to place lifetime caps on payouts or deny coverage should a policy holder become ill; and new policies are required to pay the full cost of selected preventive care and exempt such care from deductibles. Effective in 2010, small businesses with fewer than 25 employees and average annual wages of less than $50,000 became eligible for tax credits to cover up to 35% of staff insurance premiums.

Online health care insurance "exchanges" began enabling consumers to shop for health coverage. A 3.8% unearned income tax is levied on individuals earning more than $200,000 per year and families earning more than $250,000 per year, to fund the programs in the act. As of 2016, employers, with the equivalent of 50 full-time employees, which do not offer health benefits will pay a fine per full time staff member if any of the workers receives a tax credit to buy coverage. A similar fine took effect in 2015 for employers with the equivalent of 100 full-time employees. Most businesses with more than 200 employees are required to enroll all staff automatically in health insurance plans. Also, the government began fining citizens who choose not to have health insurance. Consumers whose annual incomes do not exceed set amounts may receive financial assistance if they purchase their own health insurance.

Despite the immense effort and expense, many Americans are greatly disappointed in the results of the Affordable Care Act. Insurance policies sold under the exchanges had 2017 premium increases averaging roughly 25% for mid-level "Silver" coverage plans. Some locales saw massive increases. For example, Birmingham, Alabama's Silver plans increased 71%, while those in Phoenix, Arizona rose by 145%. The number of insurance firms offering coverage via the exchanges plummeted.

Increases in Silver plan premiums for 2018 were forecast to increase by roughly 20%. While the 2017 increases were largely an attempt by insurers to raise premiums sufficiently to cover their surprisingly high health coverage expenses, part of the 2018 increases may have been due to uncertainty on the part of insurers as to whether or not federal government support of coverage for certain categories of individuals would continue. Increases proposed for 2019 are much lower than those of 2017 and 2018, but still may create a substantial burden to some families.

Enough residents of Colorado signed a petition that a Constitutional Amendment 69 was placed on the ballot for November 2016, which would have provided universal healthcare for all Colorado residents. Although the amendment did not gain approval, largely due to unhappiness with the vast state tax increases that would have been be required, the effort was a clear indication of continued consumer discontent with current health market conditions.

The Trump administration has been focused on altering the ACA. The act's mandate that Americans must carry insurance or face penalties has been dropped. More consumer control over care and insurance may be emphasized, while Medicare may be given the power to negotiate drug prices.

Health Expenditures Globally and in OECD Developed Nations:

A comprehensive study published by the Organization for Economic Cooperation & Development (OECD) covering more than 30 nations, including the majority of the world's most developed economies (but excluding Brazil, Russia, India or China), found stark contrasts between health costs in the United States and those of other nations. In 2017 (the latest complete data available), the average of a list that includes, for example, the UK, France, Germany, Mexico, Canada, South Korea, Japan, Australia and the U.S., spent 8.9% of GDP (gross domestic product—a measure of a nation's economy) on health care. The highest figures in this study were in America at 17.1% of GDP, Switzerland at 12.3%, France at 11.5%, Germany at 11.3%, Sweden at 10.9%, Japan at 10.7%, Canada at 10.4, and Norway at 10.4%.

Total health care expenditures around the world are difficult to determine, but $9.6 trillion would be a fair estimate for the formal health care industry for 2018. That would place health care at about 11% of global GDP, with expenditures per capita of about $1,250. This $9.6 trillion breaks down to approximately $3.7 trillion in the U.S., $3.2 trillion in non-U.S. OECD nations and $2.7 trillion elsewhere around the world. Outside the U.S. and the rest of the OECD, that would allow roughly $100 per capita per year. Clearly, there is vast disparity in the availability and cost of care among nations, as there is with personal income and GDP. Health care spending per capita in the U.S. was equal to about $11,193 during 2018, while spending in the world's remotest villages is next to nothing. The trend over the near future is for the modest amount now spent on health care in emerging nations to rise dramatically, while OECD nations like America struggle to contain their own mountainous costs. Globally, the total prescription drug market was over $1 trillion in 2018 and is expected to reach $1.5 trillion by 2021.

Health Care Costs in the U.S.

Particularly in the U.S., continuous increases in the cost of health care, growing at rates far exceeding the rate of inflation in general, have been inflicting financial pain on health consumers and payers of all types. Government agencies are strained by the ever-growing cost of public health care programs such as Medicare, while employers are hit hard by vast increases in the cost of providing coverage to employees and retirees.

Many major employers are utilizing unique new programs in efforts to reduce employee illness, and thereby cut costs. For example, the use of preventive care programs is growing, as is the use of employee education aimed at better managing the effects of diseases such as diabetes. Some very large employers are even hiring in-house physicians and nurses, or contracting with outside providers for on-premises care facilities, to offer primary and preventive care in the workplace.

Patients and insurance companies are also dealing with sticker shock over the nation's prescription drug costs. Other factors edging costs upward include expensive new medical technologies and patients' demands for greater flexibility in choosing doctors and specialists at their own discretion. At the same time, hospitals and health systems write off massive amounts of potential revenues to bad debt, which increases costs for bill-paying patients.

In the wake of the tremendous growth of all aspects of the health care industry from the end of World War II onward, efficiency, competition, price transparency and productivity were, regretfully, largely overlooked. Much of this occurred because employers, plus federal and state governments, pay such a large portion of the health care bill, to the extent that patients were generally not sensitive to health care costs.

As of 2014, according to the National Health Council, 133 million Americans (nearly one-half of all adults) suffered from one or more of the most common chronic diseases, such as cancer, diabetes, heart disease, pulmonary conditions, stroke or hypertension. In addition to the massive cost of health care for these patients, the lost time at work and lost economic output due to these illnesses substantially reduced the nation's GDP. These burdens could be vastly reduced through better consumer health practices and better preventive medicine. For example, obesity, lack of exercise and cigarette smoking are immense contributors to these diseases. The Centers for Disease Control and Prevention reported that medical costs for obesity-related diseases rose as high as $147 billion in 2008, compared to $74 billion in 1998. That number has likely grown to more than $220 billion today.

The American health care industry faces more challenges than ever, due to many significant factors:

- One of the most dramatic results of the Affordable Care act of 2010 has been consolidation within the hospital industry, with mergers creating massive organizations that in many cases have dominant, regional or city-wide market share. A similar effect has been a migration of physicians leaving private practice or small clinics in order to join giant physician practice groups or the staffs of hospitals. Independent physicians are concerned about their ability to meet increased regulatory scrutiny, successfully deploy electronic health records and earn the incomes that they desire. Many older physicians state that they will simply retire earlier than they had planned.
- The U.S. population is aging rapidly. At the same time, the life expectancy of seniors is extending. Senior citizens will place a significant strain on the health care system in coming years. America's 70+ million surviving Baby Boomers began turning 65 in 2011.

- The future obligations of Medicare and Medicaid are enough to cause vast problems for federal and state budgets for decades to come. The number of seniors covered by Medicare will continue to grow at an exceedingly high rate, from 47.4 million people in 2010 to 82 million in 2030.
- Likewise, costs for Medicaid, which is administered at the state level, have grown so rapidly that they are competing fiercely for budget dollars that might otherwise go to education and other vital state-provided services.
- High, and growing, pharmaceutical costs have created a large backlash among health consumers and payers. Some of the newest cancer drugs cost more than $400,000 to cover a treatment period.
- We are now in what will long be remembered as the beginning of the Biotech Era. Breakthroughs in research for targeted drug therapies are occurring at a rapid pace, and highly advanced, genetically-engineered drugs are available for many diseases.
- Due to rising costs, employers large and small are straining under the financial burden of health care coverage expenses for current employees and retirees.
- Physicians, hospitals, medical device makers and pharmaceutical manufacturers face daunting pressure from litigation and claims regarding malpractice. Lawsuit reform legislation has recently been enacted in many states with very promising results.
- Vast numbers of Americans fail to lead healthy lifestyles that would prevent disease and cut both the amount and the cost of medical care. Obesity-related illnesses are adding an immense amount to the nation's health care costs. Large numbers of people smoke cigarettes and/or do not exercise regularly.
- The three biggest causes of death in the U.S. are heart disease, cancer and stroke. Nearly one-fourth of America's annual health expenditures go for treatment of these three killers.
- Only a relatively modest amount of money is spent on preventive medicine and health education. The vast majority of health care funds are spent on the treatment of chronic diseases as well as end-of-life care for dying patients.

Source: Plunkett Research, Ltd.

2) Continued Rise in Health Care Costs

Total Health Care Spending: Total U.S. health care expenditures were projected to increase to $3.68 trillion in 2018, up from $3.54 trillion in 2017 and $3.35 trillion in 2016, according to the U.S. Centers for Medicare and Medicaid Services (CMS). Growth in health care costs has been extraordinary. In 1990, national health expenditures were only $696 billion. By 2005, the amount had tripled to $1.98 trillion. For 2026, the CMS projects spending of $5.70 trillion. Health care costs are so enormous that they are crowding out investment in other vital areas such as infrastructure, transportation and scientific research.

Mid-term projections for health care cost growth far exceed those for overall economic growth. Health spending in the U.S., at an estimated 18.2% of Gross Domestic Product (GDP) in 2018 (compared to only 9% in 1980), could grow to nearly 20% of GDP by 2020. Approximately 59.9 million Americans were enrolled in Medicare in 2018 (up from only 34 million in 1990), patients who have reached a stage in life where they require much higher levels of health care than younger people.

Spending by Employers: Employers have been struggling for years to reduce their health coverage costs. Strategies include a steady shift of costs to employees through co-payments and deductibles, wellness programs and the growing use of generic drugs, which cost much less than branded drugs.

In order to find the average cost to employers who provide coverage to their employees, surveys are conducted by several different organizations each year. Results of the studies vary widely depending on methodology. According to a Kaiser Family Foundation survey, during 2017 (the latest year available) employees were paying, on average, $5,714, or 30% of the total premium (workers at firms with less than 200 employees pay $6,814 on average), for their share of the cost of family coverage (in addition to the $13,049 paid on average by the employer, for a combined total cost of $18,764 for a typical family for one year).

One way in which employers are attempting to control costs is to implement continuous monitoring and preventive care plans for chronic conditions such as diabetes and heart disease.

The U.S. continues to spend more on health care than any other developed nation, whether measured as total spending, spending per capita or spending as a percentage of GDP. Per capita health expenditures in the U.S. were estimated at $11,193 for 2018, compared to only $4,730 during 2000.

Many cash-strapped Americans have bypassed increasingly expensive private health care plans, choosing not to be insured at all. These individuals and families are also avoiding or putting off health care until absolutely necessary, slowing overall health care spending to some extent. Unfortunately, patients who are not covered by insurance are typically charged much higher rates for care, because insurance providers negotiate the rates that they will pay. For example, a hospital might charge a set price of $1,200 for a CT scan procedure when billing an individual not covered by an insurance contract, but discount the cost to $400 for someone who is covered.

Costs are also rising significantly in cases where private medical practices are being taken over by hospitals. In these cases, Medicare pays more for a number of services performed in hospitals than for the same procedures if performed in doctors' offices.

Insurers are working to lower costs by putting pressure on drug manufacturers. Cancer care is an area that is especially hard hit by costs. IMS Health forecasted that spending would reach $79.1 billion in 2020. Some of the newer cancer drugs cost more than $400,000 per round of treatment.

Insurance Premiums Soar: As of late 2018, many health insurance companies that offer insurance coverage via the "exchanges" set up by the Affordable Care Act were seeking lower increases for the 2019 premium year than they had in 2018 and 2017. For example, large insurers in Mississippi and Florida are looking for sing-digit increases, while Blue Cross Blue Shield of Wyoming (the state's only ACA insurer) is hoping for a 0.27% average decrease in 2019, following a 48% hike in its 2018 premiums.

The act does, however, force insurers to accept new enrollees no matter how sick they may be, and to charge standard rates regardless of whether or not a person is ill. A lower number of healthy patients than expected have enrolled. Consequently, the ranks of enrollees include a high ratio of people who are ill and need expensive care. For the most part, insurance companies have incurred huge losses within the exchanges. Many have pulled out altogether or have sharply curtailed their activities. The Kaiser Family Foundation reported that the national average premium for benchmark ACA plans (for a 40-year old person) rose by approximately 34% in 2018 and 20% in 2017.

3) Employers Fight Rapidly Growing Health Care Premiums/Require Employees to Pay a Significant Share of Costs

As employers face continued growth in health care costs, they are shifting more of the burden onto employees. According to the Kaiser Family Foundation, for 2017 (The latest year available) employees were paying, on average, $5,714, or 30% of the total premium, as their share of the cost of covering a typical family (in addition to the $13,049 paid on average by the employer). Employees at firms with less than 200 employees pay $6,814 on average. The Foundation also reported that 81% of covered workers had a general deductible in 2017, up from only 47% in 2009. Approximately 51% had deductibles of at least $1,000 in 2017, up from only 22% in 2009. This means that covered employees are facing a multi-faceted burden: 1) a very expensive personal contribution to the total annual coverage premium, 2) a high deductible that must be met before insurance kicks in, plus 3) costly co-pays (often 20% or more) for most instances of doctor visits, lab or hospital services and pharmacy prescriptions.

Employer-sponsored health plan premiums rose 4% in 2017, after a 3% rise in 2016 and 4% in 2015. While this was relatively modest compared to some recent years, it nonetheless adds up to a huge increase in total expenses. In fact, employer plan premiums rose by 55% from 2007 to 2016, according to Kaiser, and health cost inflation remains much higher than inflation in consumer costs in general.

Another initiative in California is the California Public Employees' Retirement System (Calpers), which set a maximum price that Calpers would pay for a number of procedures such as colonoscopies, joint replacements and cataract removal starting in 2011. For example, the maximum for a knee or hip replacement surgery was set at $30,000, with Calpers' members paying 20%, or up to $3,000. Members selecting hospitals that charged more than Calpers' maximum were forced to pay the difference out-of-pocket. As a result, the knee and hip replacement surgery market share for lower-priced hospitals rose by 28%, with higher-priced institutions lowering their prices to stay competitive. Prices for the surgeries fell overall by an average of more than 20%, saving Calpers and its patients $6 million over two years.

This is part of a long-term trend where employers are attempting to force employees to become better, more knowledgeable, and more cost-conscious consumers of health care. It is hoped that consumers who clearly see the costs of health coverage (and are forced to make choices while paying more out of pocket) will take more personal responsibility for their physical condition and habits. However, a 2016 survey by the Society for Human Resource Management found that employers offering health coaching (counseling to help employees make healthier lifestyle choices) dropped from 50% the previous year to 37%. Employers offering free flu vaccinations fell from 61% to 54%.

Also, many employers have taken measures to decrease health care benefits for retirees in order to cut costs. Whether by raising retirees' share of premiums, capping the total amount paid or cutting benefits either partially or entirely, employers have been steadily placing more of the financial burden of health care onto their retired employees. These trends will likely continue over the mid-term, with more and more of the cost of elderly health care being pushed onto Medicare.

State and local governments face some of the largest cost problems of all. This is because many cities and other government units provided employees with exceptionally generous health care coverage plans, and in many cases continued this coverage after employees retired.

Employees who practice unhealthy lifestyles cost their employers staggering amounts of money due to health complications. Many employers are taking proactive measures. Examples include employer-sponsored wellness or disease management programs, as well as employers increasing certain employees' share of premiums, co-payments or deductibles. Some firms are penalizing employees who practice poor health behaviors such as smoking. Recently, at General Electric, for example, employees who admit to smoking must pay an additional fee per year for health benefits. CVS employees who do not report their weight, body fat and cholesterol levels to the firm's benefits provider are charged a fee. At Michelin, employees with high blood pressure or large waist measurements can be assessed an extra fee for health care benefits.

Another alternative is called reference-based pricing, in which employees have a choice among hospitals, doctors or procedures. Information regarding pricing and quality of care is available to help employees decide. Should the employee choose a procedure or provider that is more expensive that what is offered under the employer health care plan, he or she may be required to make up the difference. Should the employee go with a less costly option, the employer can offer a health care credit against another procedure. Reference-based pricing encourages employees to learn more about their health benefit options and make cost-effective choices.

In 2017, dozens of major corporations, including American Express, Marriott, Macy's, IBM and The Coca-Cola Company, formed the Health Transformation Alliance (HTA) to cut health care spending for employees. The alliance created group contracts to purchase prescription drugs through CVS Health Corp. and UnitedHealth Group, Inc., created specialized physician networks and makes use of IBM's highly advanced Watson software to analyze health care data. As of August 2018, HTA had more than 47 corporate members covering more than 6 million employees and their families, and $25 billion in annual spending power.

4) Medicare and Medicaid Spending Continue to Surge/More Baby Boomers Hit 65+ Years of Age

The term "Baby Boomer" generally refers to people born from 1946 to 1964. The phrase evolved to include the children of soldiers and war industry workers who were involved in World War II. When those veterans and workers returned to civilian life, they started or added to families in large numbers. As a result, the Baby Boom generation, at one time as large as 78 million, is one of the largest demographic segments in U.S. history.

Medicare: Today, roughly millions of Americans reach traditional retirement age (65) yearly, which is also the age that Medicare coverage kicks in for a typical retiree, subject to meeting eligibility rules. The increased load on Medicare is immense. At the same time, this surging senior population will put a greater strain on virtually all sectors of the health care system. Medicare enrollment in 2018 was estimated by the U.S. Centers for Medicare and Medicaid Services to be 59.9 million, up from only 47.4 million in 2010.

Medicare expenditures cover a wide range of patients varying in age and levels of disease, with most spending devoted to the very old and those with a number of chronic conditions. An estimated 25% to 30% of all Medicare spending is for patients in their last year of life. Meanwhile, 21% of Medicare beneficiaries have five or more chronic conditions such as high blood pressure, heart disease or diabetes.

Medicaid: Medicaid was envisioned as a safety net for the poor. Today, while Medicaid covers many of the health needs of low-income households, a vast portion of this program covers nursing home care for seniors and the seriously disabled. In fact, Medicaid pays about 40% of America's total spending on long term care. Medicaid is administered largely at the state level, with major financial support coming from the federal government. The states are straining under costs that have been soaring over the long-term. Total expenditures were expected to reach $622.0 billion in 2018, according to the U.S. Centers for Medicare and Medicaid Services (CMS). While most of the money is provided by the federal government, states are required to provide a significant portion.

A serious problem facing both Medicare and Medicaid is fraud. The former head of the CMS and analysts at the RAND Corporation estimated that fraud, along with the costs associated with rules and inspections to fight it, added as much as $98 billion in a recent year to Medicare and Medicaid spending, and $272 billion in costs across the entire U.S. health care system. Numerous cases, including a Miami doctor who fraudulently billed for 1,000 powered wheelchairs, and a New York clinic that wrote fake prescriptions for approximately 5 million painkillers and then sold them on the street for between $30 and $90 each, have come to light under heightened federal screening. In mid-2016, a nationwide sweep led by the Medicare Fraud Strike Force in 36 federal districts, resulted in criminal and civil charges against 301 individuals, including 61 doctors, nurses and other licensed medical professionals, for their alleged participation in health care fraud schemes involving approximately $900 million in false billings. Fortunately, advanced software based on deep-learning and data mining has the potential to spot fraudulent claims on a much faster basis than in the past. Nonetheless, the system will remain very tempting to criminals due to its lack of effective controls and vast total spending.

5) U.S. Affordable Care Act (ACA) of 2010 Rewrote the Rules and Increased Coverage, But Costs Continue to Rise

In March 2010, President Obama signed the Patient Protection and Affordable Care Act (ACA, sometimes referred to as Obamacare). It was designed to force health insurance firms to provide more coverage (and to provide coverage to people regardless of pre-existing health problems), force more individuals and employers to participate in health care insurance and increase the number of people who qualify for Medicaid.

Provisions that took effect within the first six months of signing included coverage for adult children up to age 26 on their parents' policies; making it unlawful for insurers to place lifetime caps on payouts or deny coverage should a policy holder become ill; and new policies being required to pay the full cost of selected preventive care and exempt that care from deductibles. Effective in 2010, small businesses with fewer than 25 employees and average annual wages of less than $50,000 became eligible for tax credits to cover up to 35% of staff insurance premiums.

A 3.8% income tax on investment income was levied on individuals earning more than $200,000 per year and families earning more than $250,000 per year to fund the programs in the act. Also, the government began fining citizens who choose not to carry health insurance. (This penalty was eliminated by the Trump administration.) Employers with more than 50 employees that do not offer health benefits began paying a fine per full time staff member if any of the workers receives a tax credit to buy coverage. Businesses with more than 200 employees are now required to enroll all staff automatically in health insurance plans. Self-insurance is an option for large companies and is a common practice. Under self-insurance, employers typically hire large outside health insurance firms to manage their plans.

The act is more than 1,000 pages in length and has far too many provisions to cover succinctly; however, there are a number of additional provisions that are little known. These include allowing insurers to charge smokers as much as 50% more for coverage in new polices; and a 30% break for employees who participate in company wellness programs or meet high health standards.

Meanwhile, online health care insurance "exchanges" began enabling consumers to shop for health coverage on a state-by-state basis. However, many major insurers posted substantial losses and pulled out of exchanges. Companies that did continue to offer insurance on the exchanges generally posted massive rate increases for 2017 and 2018, in an effort to shift from losses to profits. Proposed increases for 2019 are generally lower than in previous years. Another shift in 2019 is a small number of insurers who plans to re-enter ACA exchanges, including Centene Corp. and Molina Healthcare in the states of North Carolina, Wisconsin and Utah. There were also some small providers that are planning to enter ACA exchanges for the first time in 2019, including Bright Health, Inc. in Tennessee, Virginia Premier in Virginia and Presbyterian Health Plan in New Mexico.

The Trump administration has been focused on altering the ACA. If reform legislation is enacted over the near term, then more control over Medicaid may be given to the 50 states, streamlining the ACA's massive expansion of Medicaid. More consumer control over care and insurance may be emphasized, while Medicare may be given the power to negotiate drug prices.

Another Trump action was to reduce restrictions on short-term medical insurance which offers low-cost plans for periods of up to one year with options to renew for up to 36 months. Under previous ACA rules, these plans were limited to 90 days.

6) Accountable Care Organizations (ACOs) and Hospital Mergers Result from the Affordable Care Act/Many Hospital Chains Grow Dramatically in Market Share

An additional change in health care delivery, since the passage of the Affordable Care Act, has been the growth of "accountable care organizations," or ACOs. An ACO is a network of doctors, hospitals and other providers that take a coordinated approach to care for patients. The health care reform act offers financial rewards to ACOs that meet targets for quality of care and cost. The hope is that these networks will be able to eliminate duplicated or unnecessary tests and other procedures while developing more efficient electronic health records on their patients. The goal of the electronic records is to enable all caregivers involved in an individual's care to remain fully informed about that patient's unique needs and medical history.

One of the most dramatic results of the health care reform act to date is consolidation within the hospital industry, with mergers creating massive organizations that in many cases have dominant market share in major markets. Hospital firms have been merging aggressively, while also making investments in outpatient clinics and acquiring physician practices at a rapid pace. This consolidation of care providers under one roof means greater pricing power for ever-larger hospital chains while creating an environment of lessened competition in the marketplace and fewer choices for consumers. The Federal Trade Commission (FTC) has been blocking a few of these hospital mergers over concerns that they stifle price competition, but the FTC's response may have been too little and too late.

Meanwhile, post-ACA, physicians in private practice and smaller groups are concerned about their ability to meet increased regulatory scrutiny, successfully deploy electronic health records and continue earning the incomes that they have enjoyed in the past. As a result, large numbers have signed on as hospital employees, or joined massive, multi-office physician practices.

Doctors are going to find themselves in increasing demand. A study in 2015 by the Association of American Medical Colleges predicted that by 2025, the U.S. will have a shortage of between 46,000 and 90,000 physicians. Doctors' practices will be forced to become more efficient in order to meet growing demand, and as a guard against potential reductions in the fees they are paid by insurers, Medicare and Medicaid. Extremely large practices, based within hospitals or within ACOs, may be able to achieve operating efficiencies unattainable by smaller offices.

Arguments for the Formation of Major Hospital and Physician Groups:

1) Large groups may have access to better, more effective technical support for digital health records.
2) Massive organizations are likely to have greater pricing power, leading to higher fees charged to insurers and higher profits for the groups. They also should have better purchasing power, enabling them to obtain lower costs for supplies and services. At the same time, services and procedures provided by the hospitals, where the physicians are now full-time employees rather than third parties, are typically billed at much higher prices than non-hospital-based services.

3) The ACA provides additional payments to hospitals that meet requirements regarding patient outcomes, such as patient satisfaction and reduction in the amount of re-admission of patients to the hospital for a specific illness. Newly enlarged hospital groups may be able to develop best practices that will meet these goals.

Meanwhile, the federal government launched bonus programs that it hopes will lead to better outcomes and lower costs of patient care by ACOs. Initially, 32 "pioneer" ACOs were participating in a study based on their cost of care for Medicare patients. By 2016, 23 of these ACOs had dropped out of the program because they were spending more than they had before the program started. The overall savings were minimal at best, and the program has yet to show that it can have a significant effect on health costs. Other schemes will be attempted and monitored, but cost savings have historically been elusive. By the first quarter of 2018, there were 561 ACOs covering a total of 10.5 million patients.

Hospitals may embrace a new billing procedure in which fees are bundled into one package price. For example, everything involved in a heart bypass, from initial diagnosis to surgery to follow-up care and everything in between, might be billed at a set price. Should the hospital deliver the service efficiently at low internal costs, it earns a significant profit. However, if there are complications and more care is required, then the hospital would absorb the additional costs. By mid-2018 there were 1,025 participants in the Bundled Payments for Care Improvement Initiative, treating a wide variety of conditions.

7) Concierge Care/Direct Primary Care Are on the Rise/New Twists on House Calls

Some physicians are betting on higher demand for private, on-demand health care for those who can afford it. Some refer to this kind of practice as concierge care. MDVIP, for example, is a national network of primary care physicians who provide personalized care to patients for an additional fee of about $1,650 to $1,800 per year. The plan offers an annual physical exam, personal wellness plan and digital health records available online in addition to a personal doctor web site and secure messaging. Patients are guaranteed same-day or next-day appointments that start on time, as well as after-hours availability by phone or pager.

For 2017, *Concierge Medicine Today* estimated there were as many as 20,000 physicians in the U.S. operating concierge practices. In 2014, the American Academy of Private Physicians estimated that there were about 4,400 concierge doctors, up 30% from 2013. A Merritt Hawkins survey found that 7% to 10% of physicians questioned planned to transition to concierge or cash-only practices by 2017. Even in nations where universal health care has been in place for years, such as the UK and Sweden, private health care is extremely popular among those who can afford it.

Health care is taking a page out of the Uber business model in the form of in-person visits on demand. A number of startups are offering health care in the home or office, similar to old fashioned house calls. Treatments run the gamut of minor procedures from flu shots to stitching lacerations to treating strep throat to pregnancy tests. Some firms partner with major insurance companies such as Humana, Anthem and Cigna. California-based Heal sends a doctor in under an hour for a $99 flat fee. As of late 2018, Heal has made more than 53,000 house calls and raised $55 million in Series A financing and from investors including Qualcomm chairman Paul Jacobs. Pager, which is available in New York City and San Francisco, uses Uber drivers to transport doctors or nurses to customers for $200 per urgent care visit and $75-$100 per wellness check, in addition to $25 tele-consultations with Pager staff nurses. Other examples include MedZed (available in Atlanta, Los Angeles, San Francisco and New York City) and DispatchHealth (Denver) which was formerly True North Health Navigation. The companies hire off-duty doctors and nurses looking for extra work and have attracted venture-capital investment and interest from hospital systems and insurers.

8) Insurance Companies Change Strategies Due to Affordable Care Act (ACA) and Rapidly Rising Costs of Care

The Patient Protection and Affordable Care Act (ACA) completely changed the rules for health insurance underwriters as well as care providers. Most of these insurance firms are of massive scale. These are among the largest corporations in the U.S., and they have grown to such size by analyzing care providers, patient needs and treatment outcomes in an effort to provide effective coverage while attempting to control costs. Their business requires enormous computer and data mining power, along with legions of claims administrators and utilization managers. It is an extremely complex business, subject to very exacting regulation. Prior to the ACA, such regulation was primarily at the state level, but it now includes extensive federal oversight.

The health reform act placed significant new requirements and restrictions on insurance underwriters, and they, in turn, have altered their relationships with the doctors, clinics and hospitals that serve the patients they insure. For one thing, the act requires insurance firms to provide certain minimums of preventive care. For example, insurers are no longer allowed to charge co-payments for preventive examinations such as mammograms. Firms are required to spend at least 85% of collected premiums on health care for their clients, and no more than 15% on overhead and profit.

Also, the act set up insurance "exchanges" that enable consumers to compare insurance plans and costs, and then purchase the plans that best suit their individual needs. These exchanges are among the most disappointing outcomes of the act. The ACA cannot force Americans to sign up for insurance. It does, however, force insurers to accept new enrollees no matter how sick they may be, and to charge standard rates regardless of whether or not a person is ill. A lower number of healthy patients than expected have enrolled. Consequently, the ranks of enrollees include a high ratio of people who are ill and need expensive care. For the most part, insurance companies have incurred huge losses within the exchanges. Many have pulled out altogether or have sharply curtailed their activities. Those that remain active have drastically raised their rates. For example, rate increases for 2017 alone averaged about 25%, and in many cases were much higher. Very substantial increases were also announced in many states for 2018. However, 2019 increases are generally lower.

Health insurers are no longer able to refuse a customer (or charge higher fees) due to pre-existing health conditions. Nonetheless, they may charge higher prices to consumers who smoke or participate in certain other unhealthy activities. Healthy people are far cheaper to insure than sick ones.

A radical shift in the way doctors and hospitals are paid by insurers has begun. Incentives are being paid, by insurers such as Medicare and Blue Cross Blue Shield, to providers that improve outcomes. Improved care and lower costs are measured by closely following patients and coordinating care efforts for best results. For example, Horizon Blue Cross Blue Shield of New Jersey recently paid a primary care physician about $5 per patient per month to manage care, and another $11 per patient per month if specified quality and efficiency goals are met. The incentive could afford a 1,000-patient practice between $60,000 and $192,000 per year. These may be relatively small bonuses, but the long-term potential of financial incentives such as these is being studied throughout the industry, including at Medicare.

9) Number of Uninsured Americans Declines But Remains High

The total number of people in America who were without health insurance for the full year of 2012 was 47.95 million, according to the U.S. Census Bureau. At this level, approximately 15.4% of people in the U.S. did not have health care benefits. For all of 2017, the percentage of uninsured had dropped to 8.7% of the population (28.0 million people) after the Affordable Care Act (ACA) expanded coverage through Medicaid and provided subsidies for private insurance for patients whose income was not above certain levels. It is worthwhile to note that the official survey of the uninsured, like the official census count, attempts to include all people residing in the United States, regardless of whether they are in America legally.

In addition to the number of people with no insurance at all, the number of underinsured Americans remains a massive problem. In many cases, consumers can only afford health plans that have very high deductibles. These deductibles often run from $1,000 to $5,000 yearly, and most types of care must be paid for out of the consumer's pocket before the insurer begins to pay. Many consumers simply do not have sufficient cash on hand to deal with this burden. According to the Centers for Disease Control and Prevention, 39.3% of U.S. residents under the age of 65 had high-deductible plans as of the end of 2016.

The Affordable Care Act was designed to force individuals who are uninsured to purchase coverage or pay a penalty, force larger employers to provide coverage or pay a penalty, greatly increase the number of people who qualify for coverage under Medicaid, provide subsidies for coverage to small employers and provide substantial subsidies to lower income families. Under the Trump administration, penalties for people who do not purchase insurance were eliminated.

10) New Blockbuster Drugs Come to Market/Drug Prices Soar

Drug spending in the U.S. reached and estimated $360.1 billion in 2017, up from $342.1 billion in 2016 and $328.4 billion in 2015, according to the Centers for Medicare & Medicaid Services (CMS). Median drug prices rose 8.9% in 2016, far above the U.S. inflation rate of 2%, according to Raymond James & Associates. In 2017, drug price hikes slowed somewhat due to pressure from consumers and the Trump administration. Many drug makers, including AbbieVie, Allergan, Novo Nordisk and Sanofi pledged to keep price increases at 10% or less. After raising prices on almost 100 of its drugs by an average of 20% in 2017, Pfizer announced plans to drop prices back to their previous levels in mid-2018 in response to public pressure and criticism from President Trump. Some drug companies, such as Sanofi SA, reported that their prices actually fell in 2018, but only after accounting for rebates and discounts. Meanwhile, Eli Lilly & Co. said average prices for its drugs rose 6% in 2017.

Consumers' voracious need for drugs will continue to soar, thanks in part to the rapidly aging populations of such nations as the U.S., most of Europe and much of Asia, including Japan and China, and also due to the continuing introduction of new drugs. In coming years, taming pharmaceutical costs will be one of the biggest challenges facing the health care system. Prescription drug costs already account for about 10% of all health care expenditures in the U.S. Managed care must be able to determine which promising new drugs can deliver meaningful clinical benefits proportionate to their costs.

Following a brief period in recent years when a number of extremely lucrative "blockbuster" drugs such as the cholesterol therapy Lipitor went off patent and thus opened the door for exploding sales of generic equivalents, several highly effective and extremely expensive new drugs began to hit the market.

Part of the reason that many new drugs command astronomical prices is the total expense and level of risk that drug companies incur in order to develop medicines, including the investment in drugs that fail to be effective or win regulatory approval, and therefore never make it to market, despite massive investments in research and testing.

Extraordinarily high new drug prices are causing backlash, and attempts are being made to limit pharmaceutical costs. With regard to cancer drugs, for example, the American Society of Clinical Oncology released a "value framework" in 2015. Points are awarded to drugs based on their effectiveness, possible side effects and costs, not only from the patient's point of view, but also the overall cost of the drug to the health system. Roche's Avastin, for example, received a low 16 out of 130 possible points as a lung cancer treatment, largely because its monthly cost was $11,907.87, compared to $182.09 for using chemotherapy as an alternative.

A growing trend has created a new category for blockbuster drugs based on vanity, convenience or personal choices. Historically, pharmaceutical research was focused primarily on curing life-threatening or severely debilitating illnesses. But a segment of drugs, commonly referred to as "lifestyle" drugs, is transforming the pharmaceutical industry. Lifestyle drugs target a variety of human conditions, ranging from the painful to the inconvenient, including obesity, impotence, memory loss, urinary urgency and depression. Drug companies also continue to develop lifestyle treatments for hair loss and skin wrinkles in an effort to capture their share of the huge anti-aging market aimed at older generations. The use of lifestyle drugs dramatically increases the total annual consumer intake of pharmaceuticals, and creates a great deal of controversy over which drugs should be covered by managed care and which should be paid for by the consumer alone.

Factors leading to high expenditures in the American health care system:

- 70+ million surviving Baby Boomers are beginning to enter their senior years. The lifespan of Americans is increasing, and chronic illnesses are increasing as the population ages.
- Obesity-related illnesses, for patients young and old, are estimated by Plunkett Research to cost as much as $200 billion yearly.
- Fraud, abuse and billing errors in the Medicare and Medicaid system cost an estimated $100 billion yearly. Fraud and billing abuse throughout the rest of the health care system could easily cost another $150 billion+ yearly.
- Malpractice insurance, lawsuits and "defensive" treatment practices intended to limit exposure to lawsuits add billions of dollars to overall health care costs each year.
- Drug prices and total drug expenditures are soaring. Breakthroughs in research and development are creating significant new drug therapies, allowing a wide range of popular, but sometimes extraordinarily expensive, treatments that were not previously available.
- The hospital and clinic industry has merged and consolidated to the extent that major metro markets across the U.S. are often served by only two or three very large health care companies. This limits competition and gives these few companies the ability to command high prices.
- A rapid expansion of government-funded health care, particularly through the Affordable Care Act (ACA), has driven demand and expenses while doing very little to lower costs or prices.
- "Lifestyle" drug use is high, as shown by the popularity of such drugs as Viagra (for the treatment of sexual dysfunction), Propecia (for the treatment of male baldness) and Botox (for the treatment of facial wrinkles). Such drugs are often quite expensive.

Source: Plunkett Research, Ltd.

It is clear that the largest pharma companies, such as Pfizer, invest vast sums in their efforts to develop new drugs, and the number of drugs they finally commercialize as a result is very small. Smaller drug firms that are more focused on a particular type of disease or therapy are likely to spend less, as are firms based in lower-cost nations. Exorbitantly high prices paid in the U.S. foot the bill for much of global drug development, marketing and profits, to the benefit of billions of patients worldwide.

In mid-2018, Amazon acquired online pharmacy PillPack, Inc. for $1 billion. The purchase may eventually put the online retail giant in direct competition with CVS Health Corp., Walgreens Boots Alliance, Inc. and Rite Aid Corp., which could possibly result in lower prices for consumers.

11) Generic Drugs Have Biggest Market Share by Unit Volume, but not by Total Revenues

U.S. patent policy grants drug manufacturers the normal 20 years' protection from the date of the original patent (which is most likely filed very early in the research process), plus a period of 14 years after FDA approval. Once the patent on an existing drug expires, competing drug companies may be allowed to market cheaper generic versions which are nearly-identical chemical compounds. (However, the FDA must approve the generic version, which may require several years of effort and a substantial financial investment on the part of the generic manufacturer.) Generic prescriptions as a percentage of all U.S. pharmaceutical sales rose from 49% by volume in 2000 to 91% in 2015 (but accounted for a significantly lower percentage of total drug expenditures), according to PhRMA. Some drugs sell in such low volume that they aren't taken up by generic manufacturers even though they have gone off-patent.

Retailers including Wal-Mart, Target, Walgreens, Kmart and Publix offer a large number of generic drugs for a flat monthly fee. Wal-Mart offers 90-day supplies of hundreds of generic drugs for $10 each, and 30-day supplies for $4, in an effort to undercut mail-order pharmacy businesses while providing a high-value service to the public that brings more consumers into Wal-Mart drug departments.

Some major drug companies are trying to get in on the generic business by quietly creating their own generic drug subsidiaries. Pfizer, for example, has a division called Greenstone, LLC, which produces generic versions of its blockbuster drugs including Zoloft, an antidepressant that brought in upwards of $2 billion in 2006 sales, at which time its patent expired.

There's a wild card where generic drugs are concerned that has some doctors and patients wary of choosing generics over brand-name drugs. The FDA has a broad definition of bioequivalence, stating that a generic's maximum concentration of active ingredient in the blood must not fall more than 20% below or 25% above that of the brand-name equivalent. The result is a significant potential difference to the original, brand name drug. Also, while the generic must contain the same active ingredient as the original, additional ingredients (called "excipients") can be different and may be of lower quality in a generic. Concern is greatest over generic versions of "narrow therapeutic index drugs" which require precise dosing because even minor variations can cause life threatening complications. In 2012, the FDA's advisory committee for pharmaceutical science and clinical pharmacology voted to support the tightening of bioequivalence standards for these narrow therapeutic drugs. In addition, the U.S. Congress passed the Generic Drug User Fee Amendments of 2012, which calls for generic drug manufacturers to pay the FDA $299 million annually to beef up inspections of generic manufacturing plants abroad and speed up the review and approval of generic drug applications at home.

India is the world's largest exporter of generics, fueled by almost 550 manufacturing labs. Major manufacturers include Cipla, Sun Pharmaceutical, Lupin and Dr. Reddy's. Pharma firms in India sold $29.6 billion in generic drugs during 2017. About 1 billion prescriptions written by U.S. doctors each year are fulfilled with drugs made in India.

A number of U.S. hospital chains are hoping to get in on the generic drug market. In early 2018, four large hospital companies (with collectively about 300 hospitals) announced plans to work together to create a nonprofit generic drug manufacturing firm. The result could be greater control of the supply chain for the hospitals, and possibly lower prices for patients.

12) Coupons and Other Marketing Schemes Obscure the Retail Prices of Drugs in the U.S., Which Are Vastly Higher than Prices Paid in Other Nations

Among all the world's nations, the U.S. is in a unique and painfully costly conundrum regarding the retail prices paid for drugs. American universities and corporations discover, test and produce a vast supply of innovative drugs each year. However, while U.S. taxpayers and patients support much of this vital research (through R&D tax credits, cash donations to encourage research and hundreds of billions of dollars in yearly drug purchases), much of the financial benefit (in terms of extremely low drug prices) is passed along to patients everywhere in the world outside of America. Meanwhile patients and payers in the U.S. bear astonishingly high prices, often 10-times the price paid in other nations. Americans spend 44% more on drugs per person than Canadians, the next highest country on the list.

Mail-Order, Discount Drugs, From Canada to a Pacific Island, to U.S. Patients at One-Fifth the Price

Even in generic drugs, which make up most of the volume of drugs sold in America, prices can be dramatically higher in the U.S. than elsewhere. A good example is Tadalafil, the generic version of prostate health and erectile function drug Cialis (developed by GlaxoSmithKline, but developed by Icos Corporation in Washington State in the U.S.) A 2016 search showed typical retail prices at major U.S. stores such as Walgreens of about $300 for a 30-day supply of 5 mg tablets.

At the same time, Canadian online pharmacies typically offered a price of about $60. (It is legal for U.S. patients to order from Canadian pharmacies with a valid doctor's prescription.) The supply chain might go like this: The American patient sends his prescription to an order center in Canada. The Canadian business processes the order, and, seeking to achieve the lowest possible cost, has a pharmacy in the Indian Ocean nation of Mauritius mail the drug to America after obtaining it at wholesale from a manufacturer in India. The total price is about $70 with shipping. An example in higher priced drugs is Nilutamide, used for cancer patients. A 2016 search showed retail prices as high as $6,500 for a 30-day supply of 150 mg tablets at retail American pharmacies. Americans can order the drug from Canadian pharmacies for a typical cost of $332. In one supply chain, pharmaceutical giant Sanofi Aventis makes the drug in its plant in Australia, which supplies it to a pharmacy in the South Pacific island kingdom of Vanuatu, which mails it directly to the U.S. patient.

U.S. government regulations do not regulate drug prices (in most other nations they are highly regulated), and they prohibit Medicare from negotiating drug prices. (The Trump administration has stated that it wants to enable Medicare to negotiate drug prices. In May 2018, 60 House Democrats sponsored legislation that would enable

Medicare to negotiate, but the end-result remains to be seen). Agents for U.S. health insurers negotiate modest discounts on prices, but final prices remain extremely high and the discounts are not necessarily passed along to patients.

In Germany, pricing rules came into effect in 2010 under which any new drug must prove that it has greater efficacy or more benefits than rival medications in order to be priced at a higher level than the rival. In 2014, Germany went even further, announcing plans to publish the discounts agreed to by drug makers. This transparency might be used by payers outside of Germany to drive down prices in other countries.

Norway, which sets maximum drug prices that can be charged within its borders, uses a QALY gauge which describes a drug's cost per quality-adjusted life year. The same system has been adopted by other government health systems to set thresholds for determining coverage, including the National Institute for Health and Care Excellence (NICE) in Great Britain. Should a drug company refuse to lower prices to what Norway deems acceptable, then Norway refuses to cover the drug at all. A number of drug companies have been willing to cut prices in order to market their products in Norway and other countries with government-controlled health care systems.

While retail prices for many non-generic drugs have become astronomical in America (prices of $300,000+ yearly for new cancer drugs are becoming common), the final pricing has become convoluted and confusing as many drug makers attempt to encourage drug purchases using non-traditional methods such as coupons. The high prices may not only boost drug firms' profits, but also generate larger fees for pharmacy benefits management firms. These are companies that negotiate with drug companies over prices, acting as agents for private health care insurers that are clients. The benefits management companies earn gross fees based on a percentage of the retail drug price, then pass any discount on to the insurance companies after deducting their fees. The higher the retail price, the higher the managers' fees. Patients do not always see benefits from these discounts. For example, a patient who has not yet met his yearly insurance deductible threshold may end up paying a full drug retail price out-of-pocket, while the discount nonetheless gets passed along to the insurer. Another issue is the lists (called formularies) of drugs that are approved by various insurers. In many cases, a doctor will prescribe a drug with recent innovations and advantages, although there may be lower-cost alternatives on the market. The insurer refuses to cover the newer drug, so if the patient desires the drug he must pay full retail out-of-pocket.

Drug makers are attempting to help circumvent high deductibles or high co-pays by offering discount coupons to the patient. The coupons are often available online and in magazines. They are also handed out by doctors in an effort to ease patients' financial pain, even though the doctors may strongly disapprove of the drug makers' pricing and marketing schemes. For example, in late 2016 the maker of the EpiPen was offering a coupon that can "be used to reduce the amount of your out-of-pocket expense of up to a maximum of $300 per EpiPen 2-Pak." This scheme may work well in eliminating the effect of the co-pay for privately insured patients. However, this coupon, similar to those of other firms, could not be used by patients in any federal or state-funded plan, including Medicare, Medicaid, VA/TriCare, or "if the patient's insurance plan is paying the entire cost of this prescription." In other words, if the money can be pried out of the government or an insurer, then the discount doesn't apply. Worse still, it doesn't work at all for uninsured patients. Total yearly drug expenditures have been soaring. The total cost will get much worse as more and more Baby Boomers hit their senior years. There can be little change without government action.

13) Biotech and Orphan Drugs Create New Revenues for Drug Firms

Many biotech companies have focused on developing drugs for relatively small patient populations. For example, biotech pioneers Genentech and Biogen Idec developed Rituxan for the treatment of non-Hodgkin's lymphoma, an important but relatively small market.

Drugs such as Rituxan are commonly referred to as "orphan drugs," which means that they treat illnesses that no other drug on the market addresses, which are needed by relatively small patient populations. Technically, a drug designated by the FDA with orphan status provides therapeutic benefit for a disease or condition that affects less than 200,000 people in the U.S. These drugs enjoy a unique status due to the Orphan Drug Act of 1983, which gives pharmaceutical companies a seven-year monopoly on the drug without having to file for patent protection, plus a 50% tax credit for research and development costs.

Plunkett Research estimates that combined biotech revenues for publicly-held firms headquartered in the U.S. and E.U. will be $160 billion during 2018, while the U.S. firms' portion will be $123 billion. Analysts at global accounting firm EY estimate global biotech industry revenues for U.S. and EU companies at $139.4 billion in 2016 (the latest data available), up from $132.7 billion in 2015 and $123.1 billion in 2014.

Orphan drugs, however, receive expedited approval from the FDA, greatly reducing the costs of clinical trials. Long-term profit is also more likely for orphans. While brand-name drugs lose 80% of their market value within one year of patent expiration, biotech and orphan drugs face less generic competition because of the difficulty in developing generic versions once they go off-patent.

The number of new drugs approved by the U.S. FDA in 2017 was 46, of which 18 were orphan drugs. Orphan drugs approved during 2017 included the first-ever treatments for the rare Batten disease, which can cause seizures, visual problems/blindness, personality and behavior changes, dementia and loss of the ability to walk, talk and communicate (Brineura). Another orphan drug breakthrough in 2017 was for the treatment of hemophilia A (Hemlibra).

Commentary: The Challenges Facing the Biopharmaceuticals Industry

- Working with governments to develop methods to safely and effectively speed approval of new drugs. Many observers contend that FDA approval is much too slow and cumbersome.
- Working with the investment community to build confidence and foster patience for the lengthy timeframe required for commercialization of promising new drugs.
- Working with civic, government, religious and academic leaders to deal with ethical questions centered on stem cells, personalized medicine and other new technologies.
- A growing level of discontent with soaring drug prices.
- Fostering payer acceptance, diagnostic practices and physician practices that will harness the full potential of genetically targeted, personalized medicine as the base of potentially expensive but highly effective biopharmaceuticals grows.

Source: Plunkett Research, Ltd.

14) Quality of Care and Health Care Outcomes Data Are Available Online, Creating a New Level of Transparency

From the earliest days of the internet, one of the most popular activities online has been searching for information about illness, disease, pharmaceuticals and their side effects, as well as information related to care and diagnosis, such as options for surgery. Now, online activity about health care has risen to a massive level. With rapidly rising health care costs and concerns about the quality of care received for the dollar spent, many patients, employers and insurance providers are using online databases for information regarding doctors and hospitals—call it comparison shopping for health care. For example, there are growing numbers of web sites that track data on hospitals, such as the U.S. Department of Health and Human Services' web site, Hospital Compare (www.medicare.gov/hospitalcompare/search.html). Hospital Compare uses data from Medicare and Medicaid to track performance at thousands of facilities across the U.S. Also, many insurers make hospital data available to members on their web sites.

These databases typically enable an insurer or patient to compare specific hospitals to the national average on statistics such as mortality rates. For example, the Hospital Compare site compares each hospital in Houston, Texas to the Texas state average and to the national average. Data includes many items concerning patient experiences and satisfaction, surgical outcomes, readmission, hospital-related infections, and time spent waiting for care in emergency rooms. Also, average costs for various types of procedures are now available online on web sites that are attempting to earn profits from such services, although the quality of the data may vary.

The Medicare claims database is a digital record of the bills Medicare pays. It is used by federal investigators to sniff out fraud and for analysis by researchers and consultants for cost and utilization studies. Medicare has begun making some data about payments to individual physicians available. The database covers millions of caregivers and beneficiaries, but it is prohibited by law from disclosing patients' names.

Internet Research Tip:
Top web sites for health care information include:
National Cancer Institute, www.cancer.gov
Centers for Disease Control and Prevention (CDC), www.cdc.gov
FamilyDoctor.org, www.familydoctor.org
Health Finder, www.healthfinder.gov , a service of the U.S. Dept. of Health & Human Services
KidsHealth, www.kidshealth.org
Mayo Clinic, www.mayoclinic.org
NIH National Institute on Aging, www.nia.nih.gov/health
Medscape, www.medscape.com

Internet Research Tip—Checking a Web Site's Accuracy Rating:

When researching health care web sites, look for the seal of approval from the Health on the Net Foundation (www.hon.ch), a nonprofit organization based in Geneva, Switzerland. Founded in 1995 at the behest of international medical experts, the foundation approves medical web sites that meet or exceed its guidelines.

Elsewhere, corporations in various segments of the health industry may publish interesting cost and outcomes information. For example, health diagnostics and monitoring devices firm Alere, formerly Inverness Medical Innovations, Inc., provides an online database giving the exact CPT procedure code and Medicare reimbursement rate for hundreds of procedures such as cholesterol tests at www.codemap.com/alere. The data is sorted geographically as well as by type of care.

Data on individual doctors is becoming available online, at such web sites as www.drscore.com and www.findadoc.com. The quality of the data from such sites may vary, and one should use caution. Nonetheless, the information is intriguing. Findadoc, for example, enables the user to look up doctors by location and specialty, and then view their hospital affiliations, languages spoken and patient ratings for such qualities as bedside manner and wait time.

Quantum Health (www.quantum-health.com), a Columbus, Ohio health care coordinator, offers comparative health care data to its corporate clients, plus a laundry list of services that help employees covered by company insurance navigate the often confusing health care system and get the most out of their health benefits. Quantum Health services include informing patients of what questions they should ask their physicians about their conditions, assistance in finding specialists, advice on medical tests that should or should not be taken and education on disease management and prevention. Quantum reports that its employer clients have enjoyed reduced spending on workers' health care, thanks to reductions in waste and unnecessary care, better results from disease management and a 25% reduction in health benefits-related workload. Two of its most impressive statistics are a 22% reduction in readmissions and a 4% reduction in emergency room usage.

The Affordable Care Act of 2010 (ACA) includes a provision that hospitals and doctors that score poorly on patient surveys can be denied Medicare reimbursement fees. Surveys such as those from Press Ganey, Gallup and National Research Corp., on which patients score health care providers on care experiences (based on patient surveys) including waiting times, pain relief and bedside manner, are becoming powerful arbiters in how patients are treated.

Internet Research Tip:
To compare costs for procedures, try the following site:
www.healthcarebluebook.com

For bill negotiation services, see these sites:
www.medicalcostadvocate.com
www.medliminal.com

To determine whether or not a physician is board certified:
www.abms.org

15) Malpractice Suits Are Blamed for Rising Health Care Costs/Tort Reform Is Capping Awards for Damages

Health care costs have long been a hot political topic, and many people have pointed at malpractice lawsuits as a primary cause of rising costs. For years, punitive lawsuits for pain and suffering have levied huge settlements from doctors, hospitals and their insurers. In reaction, premiums for malpractice insurance have burgeoned, growing far faster than the costs for any other type of insurance. Doctors and hospitals, in order to offset malpractice insurance premiums, may raise their own fees and conduct extensive, and often unnecessary, tests in order to protect themselves from legal claims. These factors contribute significantly to the overall cost of health care in the U.S., and a political battle has ensued, particularly between lobbyists for plaintiffs' lawyers and lobbyists for the health care industry.

There is wide disagreement about the causes and actual yearly combined costs of malpractice insurance, litigation, lawsuit awards and defensive medical procedures and tests intended to lessen the likelihood of a malpractice lawsuit loss. However, a 2010 Gallup poll found that one in four health care dollars in the U.S. can be attributed to defensive medicine (meaning unnecessary tests, medicines or specialist referrals in order to provide malpractice protection). A 2013 Jackson Healthcare survey found that 75% of doctors order more tests, medications and procedures than are medically necessary to protect themselves from lawsuits.

Internet Research Tip: Getting Hospital Ratings Online
Patients and concerned family members can now use any of several web sites to check on the quality of hospitals before checking in for treatment. Available data typically includes patient outcomes, fees and whether the latest in technology is available. For patients needing specialized care, this knowledge can be a real windfall. WebMD Health Services, at www.webmdhealthservices.com, (formerly Subimo) gets high marks for its ease of use. It sells subscriptions to major employers and health plans, whose members can then log in. Other sites include HealthGrades, www.healthgrades.com, Medicare's Hospital Compare at www.medicare.gov/hospitalcompare/search.html and United Healthcare's www.myUHC.com, designed to be used by the millions of patients who are covered by United's health plans.

In addition to adding immense costs to the health care system, malpractice lawsuits have done much to erode the relationship between doctors and their patients. At the same time, fear of malpractice suits can discourage young physicians from pursuing higher-risk specialties, such as obstetrics and emergency room care, rather than fields where they are much less likely to be sued. Relations between doctors and lawyers have also become strained, with many doctors blaming the situation on some lawyers' willingness to take even the most frivolous cases. Malpractice insurance premiums vary widely, according to the type and location of the practice.

Self-interest has caused some physicians to respond. Reports have been published of physicians refusing to treat attorneys, their families or their employees except in cases of emergency. Meanwhile, many would-be patients have learned how hard it can be to get a physician in high-risk fields, such as obstetrics and gynecology, to take a new client.

Many states are tackling the malpractice awards issue through referenda and legislation that limit total damage awards. Texas, after suffering years in which more than 50% of practicing physicians were hit with malpractice suits, passed legislation to limit awards given to plaintiffs for "non-economic" damages, which include pain, inconvenience, suffering and disfigurement. Dozens of states have now limited non-economic damages in medical malpractice cases, generally to amounts between $250,000 and $500,000 dollars. The statutes also generally limit the amount that lawyers can make off such cases via contingency fees, making sure that the plaintiff receives a substantial portion of the reward. Some critics of this move see such laws as contributing to a failure of the justice system. Others feel that a $250,000 to $500,000 award cap is not fair payment for a patient who has been severely disfigured for life.

On the other hand, there may be few limits on the amount of "economic" damages awarded to a patient—that is, loss of earnings due to the inability to function fully at a job or profession. Patients who earn extremely high salaries may seek damages that are proportionately high—even multimillion-dollar amounts. However, attorneys may be discouraged from taking, on contingency, clients who work in low-paying jobs or have very complicated cases.

As in any other legal matter, there are two sides to the story; arguments for and against malpractice award limits abound. California is often named as the poster child for how effective such legislation can be in lowering insurance premiums and health care costs in general.

Texas enjoyed stunning success as a result of its tort reform. Malpractice rates fell with more than 30 malpractice insurance firms competing for business in the state. One of the largest firms, Texas Medical Liability Trust (TMLT), created by the Texas Medical Association, cut rates 10 times between 2004 and 2012, resulting in a 52% decrease overall. Texas has experienced a resurgence in the numbers of practicing physicians as well since malpractice insurance premiums dropped significantly. The number of malpractice lawsuits in Texas has been cut dramatically.

Meanwhile, the costs and challenges of lawsuits are not limited to physicians. Every sector of the health chain, from equipment makers to hospitals to drug makers, is swamped by lawsuits, and they are forced to pass along the costs of insurance and litigation in the form of higher fees charged to patients. Tort reform is beginning to take hold for these sectors as well. It is worth noting that the 2010 Patient Protection and Affordable Care Act (ACA) did not make any provision for limiting malpractice damages.

Internet Research Tip: Malpractice Awards

The National Practitioner Data Bank, www.npdb.hrsa.gov, is a federal initiative that collects data on malpractice lawsuit awards and license revocations, on a state-by-state basis. It publishes annual reports that provide detailed information.

16) Obesity Sparks Government, School and Corporate Initiatives/Snack Foods Get Healthier/Taxes on Unhealthy Foods

Obesity is increasing in countries throughout the world. The problem is acute in the U.S., where obesity is unfortunately very common and has deep links to the high overall cost of health care. Obesity is a much more serious problem than being merely overweight—see the box regarding "Body Mass Index (BMI)" that follows.

A 2013 study by the Institute for Health Metrics and Evaluation at the University of Washington found that, between 1980 and 2013, the number of overweight and obese people worldwide rose by 27.5% for adults and 47.1% for children. The total global count of overweight and obese people in 2013 reached 2.1 billion, or 29% of the population. The World Health Organization (WHO) reported that 3.4 million adults die every year because they are overweight or obese.

Numbers from the U.S. CDC (Centers for Disease Control) show that obesity is a massive problem in America, one capable of generating vast annual expenses for treatment of chronic diseases related to obesity. For 2016, the CDC found that 30.5% of all adults over age 20 were obese.

The overweight portion of a nation's population often soars when household income increases. In mid-2013, a survey published by the Chinese General Administration of Sport found that 34.4% of Chinese between the ages of 20 and 69 were overweight. It also found that 11% of people aged 20 to 39 were obese, up from 9% in 2010.

Body Mass Index (BMI) as an indicator of health status based on weight:

Underweight = less than 18.5 BMI
Normal weight = 18.5 to 24.9
Overweight = 25 to 29.9
Obese = 30 or more

To calculate Body Mass Index:
First: divide weight (pounds) by height (inches)
Second: divide the result by height again
Third: multiply the result by 703

Internet Research Tip:

For an easy-to-use, online calculator and a full discussion of BMI, see www.nhlbi.nih.gov/guidelines/obesity/BMI/bmicalc.htm
Source: National Institutes of Health, National Heart, Lung and Blood Institute

A 2014 report by the McKinsey Global Institute found that the annual global cost for lost productivity and the treatment of conditions such as diabetes, heart disease and certain cancers related to obesity is $2 trillion. An "Obesity Update 2012" published by the OECD estimated that an obese person incurs 25% higher health costs than a person of normal weight in a given year, and that obese people earn up to 18% less than non-obese people.

One of the most critical problems of obesity is the onset of diabetes. The impact of the soaring diabetes problem combined with an accompanying rise in heart disease, cancer, high blood pressure and cholesterol levels may wreak havoc on the global health care system.

The alarming rise in obesity in the U.S. has brought about significant changes in the latest set of dietary guidelines from the U.S. federal government. The 2010 federal dietary guidelines are the result of more than a year's work by an anonymous panel of nutrition experts in the fields of pediatrics, obesity, cardiovascular disease and public health. Panel members remain anonymous to avoid lobbying from food industry groups such as the Soft Drink

Association, the Wheat Foods Council, the National Dairy Council and the United Fresh Produce Association. Final results were presented by the U.S. Department of Health and Human Services.

By law, federal dietary guidelines must be revised every five years based on the latest research. Compared to those of 2005, the 2010 guidelines recommend limiting salt, especially for people who are age 51 or older or who are African American or have high blood pressure. They also recommend eating more fruits and vegetables, filling half of meal plates with them, and consuming more seafood instead of meat.

Even the USDA's food pyramid, which after going through several permutations in the spring of 2005 and again in 2010, has been abandoned in favor of a plate showing representative portions of vegetables, fruit, grains and protein and a nearby glass representing dairy. Launched in mid-2011, the new plate initiative, called MyPlate (www.choosemyplate.gov), was developed by the USDA at a cost of $2.9 million over a three-year period.

The impact of the new guidelines on the food industry is significant. The snack food industry (which tends to make heavily salted snacks) is facing a challenge since the recommended sodium level for about one-half the U.S. population (those who are 51 years of age or older, are African American, or suffer from high blood pressure, diabetes or chronic kidney disease) is only 1,500 milligrams per day, compared to the 2005 limit of 2,300 milligrams per day (about one teaspoon of salt).

Wal-Mart is taking an aggressive approach to reducing salt, fat and sugar in the grocery products it sells. It announced a five-year plan in early 2011 in which sodium would be reduced by 25%, industrially-added trans fats will be eliminated and added sugars will be reduced by 10% in packaged foods manufactured under its Great Value house brand. The company also announced plans to press major suppliers such as Kellogg Co. to adopt these standards over the mid-term. Wal-Mart is not alone in these initiatives (ConAgra Foods, for example, pledged to reduce sodium in its packaged foods by 20% by 2015), but as America's largest retailers, its focus will have a profound effect on the food industry.

PepsiCo, Inc., one of the world's largest makers of snacks as well as soft drinks, beat Wal-Mart to the punch in early 2010, making a similar pledge to lower salt, sugar and saturated fat in its products by 2015. Even PepsiCo's higher fat snacks, such as Lay's potato chips and Rold Gold pretzels, got makeovers, substituting natural flavors such as molasses, paprika and beet juice instead of monosodium glutamate (MSG) and FD&C Red 40 food coloring.

In America's massive Affordable Care Act (ACA) passed in 2010, the U.S. federal government set up a requirement that all restaurant chains with 20 or more restaurants post calorie counts for menu and buffet items. In late 2014, the FDA ruled that restaurants with at least 20 locations (and vending machines that have at least 20 units) must post calorie counts by November 2015.

Early results of posting calorie counts and other health-conscious efforts show that restaurants that increased the number of lower-calorie options saw a 5.5% increase in same store sales, according to a study of 21 fast-food and sit-down restaurant chains between 2006 and 2011 by the Hudson Institute. (The study was funded by the Robert Wood Johnson Foundation.) The study further reported that the number of lower-calorie food and beverage servings sold increased 2.5% to 18.7 billion. The number of higher-calorie servings sold fell 4.2% to 31.2 billion. Restaurants offering healthy choices are growing in number at a fast clip. Healthy Dining Finder, www.healthydiningfinder.com, a web site that promotes restaurants that offer lower-calorie options, estimates that the number of restaurants it lists on its site has grown dramatically since its launch in 2005. A number of food companies are promoting products that are lower in calories and fats, and higher in nutrients such as protein, fiber, calcium and certain vitamins. PepsiCo, Inc. packages such food with a distinctive green label. To have the label, foods must contain no more than 35% of their calories from fat, contain one gram or less of saturated fats and no trans fats as well as meet limits for cholesterol, sodium and sugar. Products include Tropicana and Dole juices, Quaker oatmeal, Baked! LAY'S potato chips and Rold Gold pretzels. Nabisco is also promoting healthier 100 Calorie Packs of many of its popular brands such as Chips Ahoy! and Oreo cookies and Ritz and Teddy Grahams crackers.

McDonald's has enjoyed some success with healthier, lower-fat menu items such as salads, fruit and oatmeal. T.G.I. Friday's, a casual restaurant, offers "Right Portion, Right Price" portions of menu items that are roughly one-third smaller than regular sizes and cost less. The initiative came about in response to industry research stating that 51% of U.S. adults believe that portion sizes in casual restaurants are too large (63% of American women polled believed this to be the case).

The Healthy Weight Commitment Foundation (HWCF) is a U.S. effort designed to help reduce obesity, especially childhood obesity, by 2015. It is a first-of-its-kind coalition that brings together more than 150 retailers, food and beverage manufacturers, restaurants, sporting goods and insurance companies, trade associations and professional sports organizations. The HWCF is helping consumers lead healthier lives by offering healthier nutrition options. According to its five-year anniversary report in 2015, the Foundation reported the removal of 6.4 trillion calories from the food marketplace (400% over its initial goal) and over $1 million in grants and prizes awarded to American schools shown to have the greatest needs.

Meanwhile, as people switch from sugar-heavy soft drinks to water, tea, juice or coffee, soft drink manufacturers are feeling the pinch. Falling sales of juice drinks and sodas are a serious blow.

Along with overeating, sedentary lifestyles are certainly a major contributor to obesity. Vast numbers of people are spending much of their work hours in front of a computer screen, while more and more of their leisure time is spent playing electronic games, watching TV and enjoying digital media—activities that are not burning many calories.

An article that appeared in *The Lancet* medical journal in 2011, written by researchers from the Harvard School of Public Health and Deakin University in Melbourne, Australia called for a 10% tax on unhealthy food and drinks, more obvious nutrition labeling on food packaging and reductions in ads for junk foods and beverages that target children. The article also suggested school-based programs to teach healthy eating and exercise habits and to reduce television watching. In 2011, the nation of Denmark levied new taxes on the purchase of foods with a saturated fat content of more than 2.3%. The tax amounted to about $2.90 per kilogram of saturated fat. However, the tax was dropped after a few months. Critics said it caused consumers to shop across the border in Germany, boosted food costs and resulted in job losses. Many other nations have debated or experimented with taxes in an effort to reduce consumption of unhealthy foods.

Mexico instituted a tax of about 10% per liter of sugar-sweetened beverages and 8% on junk food in 2014. Junk foods are defined as those containing more than 275 calories per 100 grams, or just over three ounces. Early results seemed to show a reduction in the consumption of sugary drinks. France passed a similar tax. Hungary passed a tax on junk foods.

Some countries have national initiatives focused on obesity. Singapore, which requires military service of all adults, has instituted an extended six-week training camp for recruits who are obese in addition to its 10-week basic boot camp. After discharge from the service, most Singaporean men and women remain on reserve status, which requires an annual physical and basic fitness test.

Japan, which has very small numbers of obese citizens, is requiring, under the so-called "metabo" law passed in 2008, waist measurements for men and women ages 40 through 74 as part of annual checkups. Men's waists must measure less than 33.5 inches. The maximum is 35.4 inches for women. Those who exceed the limits will receive dietary guidance and monitoring until excess weight is lost. Rates of obesity are exceptionally low in Japan.

17) Health Care Goes Offshore, Medical Tourism and Clinical Trials Continue in China, India and Elsewhere

Many people might assume that certain professions could never be outsourced, such as the work of health care professionals. This is not entirely true. For example, in a practice called teleradiology, medical technicians and physicians in India and elsewhere are analyzing x-rays and CAT scans performed in the U.S., diagnosing American patients and relaying results back to American hospitals. In fact, telemedicine has advanced greatly in recent years, and certain physicians provide long-distance patient evaluations on a regular basis. While this is typically done for a patient in a difficult-to-reach location, such as a ship at sea or an offshore oil rig, it could just as easily be a pediatrician in Florida discussing a toddler in Omaha's symptoms with the mother via teleconferencing.

Meanwhile, certain less-skilled health care tasks are rapidly moving offshore. Most notably, tens of thousands of jobs in medical record transcription have been moved from the U.S. to offshore centers. Other business process outsourcing (BPO) tasks related to health care include claims processing, human resources and benefits administration, customer relations and supply chain logistics.

Medical trials conducted outside the U.S. continue to grow as well. Since clinical trials for drugs are exceptionally expensive to conduct, the opportunity to offshore the work and reduce costs is hard for drug firms to resist. However, significant concerns arose regarding the number of deaths of patients in trials. Starting in 2013, India created much tighter regulatory laws for clinical trials. These include requiring trials to be performed in good clinical practice (GCP)-compliant facilities, approval by an ethics committee, registration with regulators and random inspections, all of which come at significant cost.

Meanwhile, medical tourism may continue to grow, but it is difficult to measure by how much. Analysts vary widely in their estimations of the number of people seeking medical care abroad, and extremely optimistic forecasts have been made that were unreasonable. However, it is clear that high health care costs in the U.S. and other developed nations are likely contributing to growth in this trade.

A procedure like a hip replacement or a triple bypass can be obtained in nations such as India at as little as 10% to 30% of the cost of the same procedure in the U.S. A heart bypass, for example, may cost only $18,500 in Singapore and $11,000 in Thailand, according to the Thai Public Health Ministry, but could easily cost $60,000 to $100,000 in the U.S. Since many patients in the U.S. are either underinsured or not insured at all, the cost savings sound very appealing. In addition, in nations like Canada and the UK, where medicine is socialized, the wait to get an appointment with and obtain care from a specialist can be months or even years (and some "elective" procedures are not covered by government payment programs). Consequently, such patients are more likely to consider going offshore. Finally, many physicians in India, Thailand, Singapore and elsewhere received their training in the finest clinics and hospitals in the U.S., Canada and the UK. Several of them have returned to their home nations where they are opening clinics specifically for medical tourists. In many offshore clinics that have been adapted to attract foreign patients, surgery and care are of very high quality and outcomes are excellent.

A business sector has opened up that manages medical tourism. For example, MedRetreat (www.medretreat.com), a medical tourism agency based in

Odenton, Maryland, partners with hospitals in Argentina, Brazil, Costa Rica, El Salvador, India, Malaysia, Mexico, South Africa, Thailand and Turkey to provide cosmetic, dental and medical procedures to U.S. patients. The company schedules procedures, arranges flights and hotel stays and assigns guides to facilitate the process.

Another medical tourism company, IndUSHealth (www.indushealth.com), is based in North Carolina and outsources medical procedures to hospitals, clinics and physicians in India. IndUSHealth focuses on companies rather than individual patients. Specifically, these are companies that self-insure or pay employees' health care costs directly instead of contracting with an insurance provider.

Agencies like MedRetreat and IndUSHealth generate most of their revenue from commissions for booking hotel rooms and taking approximately 20% of fees on treatments offered by the providers in exchange for referrals. However, there is no regulation of this practice, and lawsuits or severe medical problems that arise as a result of a mishandled procedure could cripple this relatively new industry. Despite these obstacles, medical tourism agencies are betting that low prices and Western-trained practitioners will insure their success.

Qunomedical (www.qunomedical.com) is an online startup based in Berlin that allows patients to search from 1,000 doctors in 25 countries for a variety of treatments. The company says it arranges for treatment of 4,000 patients per month. Medigo (www.medigo.com) is another Berlin-based startup that offers similar services.

India's famed Dr. Shetty operates a 140-bed acute care hospital in the Cayman Islands, called Health City Cayman Islands, in partnership with the nonprofit health care system Ascension, based in St. Louis, Missouri. Shetty also operates thousands of beds in his respected hospitals in India, and his vision includes expanding this new Cayman Islands location to 2,000 beds over the long term. Shetty is the world's leader in reducing the cost of high-quality surgery. His Narayana Health firm is a system of dozens of hospitals in India (with plans to expand to Kuala Lumpur and Malaysia) that provide excellent outcomes at very low cost. Open heart surgery, for example, is provided at his Indian facilities for about $2,000. The project in the Caribbean, only a quick flight away from Miami, could have a dramatic effect on health care in the nearby nations of North and South America. Fees for surgery at Health City Cayman Islands run about one-half of fees typically charged in the U.S. The patient experience is excellent, as the hospital is attached to a luxury hotel via a convenient pathway. North America's hospital operators will undoubtedly pay close attention to Shetty's methods, which include high-volume, specialized surgery centers, prompt treatment, and proprietary software called iKare that analyzes real-time clinical data for each patient, and then recommends best protocols for treatment.

18) Retail Clinics, Urgent Care Centers and Employer Sites Increase Health Care Options/Reduce Costs

More and more, the delivery of health care is moving away from the hospital into outpatient clinics and surgery centers. The number of hospitals and hospital beds has been falling while outpatient options have increased. Now, consumers in many U.S. cities can go to the local discount store or drug store for basic health care.

Clinics in Retail Stores: As of late 2018, there were approximately 1,100 MinuteClinics in CVS pharmacies and Target stores; 370 Take Care clinics in Walgreens drug stores; 215 The Little Clinics in Kroger, JayC, King Sooper and Fry's supermarkets. Wal-Mart offers a modest number of in-store clinics, typically operated by local hospitals. Wal-Mart is also taking in-store treatment a step further, by providing primary medical care in a few locations. These facilities offer chronic disease management in addition to care for minor health problems. Wal-Mart's huge rural footprint may position the retailer to fill a gap long existent in towns where doctors are hard to find. Another plus is Wal-Mart's low prices.

The in-store clinics offer reasonable costs and great convenience. Also, the setting may seem less intimidating to some consumers than a trip to a medical office center or full-scale clinic building. Visits to these new in-store clinics typically range from about $25 to $75 in cost. Many of the patients will be people with no health insurance coverage—cost will be a major consideration. However, since charges are generally much less than those of traditional doctors' offices, health insurers will also be pleased with these clinics. Procedures provided tend to be basic, such as flu shots, a quick physical required for participation on a sports team, or treatment for a simple infection or a minor illness. However, in-store clinics are adding treatments for more complex illnesses such as asthma and osteoporosis. They tend to be staffed by nurse practitioners. These practitioners have extended educations and special licenses that in many states across the nation allow them to treat minor illnesses and write simple prescriptions. In some states, they must work in conjunction and consultation with MDs, but the MDs need not be present at the time of treatment.

Urgent and Emergency Care Centers: Thousands of urgent care centers, providing a higher level of service than the simple clinics found in retailers, are also growing at a significant rate. These well-equipped clinics are staffed by physicians who can provide emergency care and treat a wide range of conditions, while offering walk-in, no-appointment treatment. Location is a key element, so clinics typically open in high-traffic strip centers close to patients' homes and workplaces. Most are open at least 12 hours a day, including weekends, and many are open 24/7. Total fees are typically much lower than those for a hospital emergency room visit. Some of the clinics are operated as outposts of major hospitals, while others are run by physicians who are owner/operators.

Workplace Care Centers: CHS Health Services and Take Care Employer Solutions merged and then rebranded the company as Premise Health. The firm offers worksite health and wellness centers, serving corporations including Intel, Goldman Sachs, Continental Airlines and Toyota (in addition to its clinics in drug stores). The clinics provide annual check-ups, flu shots, x-rays and simple blood work and are staffed by two doctors, two pharmacists and a dietician, plus a number of nurses and technicians. Client companies typically expect to lower their overall health care costs by as much as 20%; since more employees are able to utilize preventive care, fewer emergency hospital visits are required and costs per visit to the on-site clinic average out to a very reasonable amount. Productivity is also expected to rise for firms with on-site clinics because employees take fewer sick days. The on-site clinics even offer health coaches to provide lifestyle advice to employees considered at risk for health problems.

Services generally include health screenings and immunizations. Some facilities, such as the clinic at Harrah's Entertainment, Inc.'s Las Vegas location, include fully-equipped gyms to promote wellness and preventive health measures. Another leader in worksite clinics is Marathon Health.

19) Health Care Industry Grows Rapidly in China, India and Mexico

Growing Health Expenditures in China: China is in the process of implementing a broad, national boost to health care availability. Today, about 97% of the people in China are covered by some kind insurance (compared to less than one-third of the population in 2003). However, the health facilities and services available will remain relatively limited for some time, particularly in remote villages and towns. China's mid-term plan is to have an affordable health delivery system available throughout the nation by 2020. In other words, China intends to introduce relatively modern health care to more than 1.3 billion consumers for the first time. This is an immense undertaking in a nation with little health care infrastructure and few doctors who have been trained to Western standards. While health care coverage has become widespread, the co-pay for care is very high, as much as 50%, which creates a difficult financial burden for many patients.

Health care expenditures in China are expected to rise substantially over the mid-term. China's health care spending is expected to reach about $1 trillion per year by 2020 ($770 per capita), but will remain very low on a per capita basis compared to that in Europe, Japan and the U.S. This will be a dramatic increase from about $300 billion spent in 2009 and $500 billion in 2014.

Over the longer term, China will face a growing elderly portion of its population, even more dramatic than the aging population facing the U.S. China is also challenged by high cigarette smoking rates.

At the same time, new private clinics are attracting wealthy locals in China. Residents who can afford it may sign up for care via a private health program offered by Beijing Universal Medical Assistance, at a fee equal to a few thousand dollars yearly. While the fees are vastly higher than those at the state-run public clinics, these private clinics feature luxury surroundings and prompt, quality service for basic health care needs. Look for the number of larger private hospitals in China to grow.

Hospital companies are investing heavily in China and in other countries in Asia, especially Malaysia, Thailand, Vietnam and the Philippines. Siloam Hospitals, based in Indonesia, plans to increase the number of hospitals it owns in Indonesia from 16 to 40 by 2017, 39 of which will be private. 2014 was the first year in Indonesia's five-year plan to bring health coverage to about 90% of the population.

Health Care in India: In order to provide advanced health care, such as diagnostics and drugs, at extremely low prices suitable to the Indian and rural Chinese markets, a vast amount of innovation and creativity will be required. Much of this innovation will eventually trickle into the developed world, helping to establish new ways to lower health care costs. While initial steps into modern health care in China and India were based on equipment, procedures and technologies from the West, health care delivery in the future will accelerate quickly based on locally developed efficiencies and technologies.

India, especially, is seeing significant growth in health care initiatives. With its growing middle class clamoring for better and more modern medical care, some health care companies are investing heavily. Indian physicians (many of whom were trained in Western medical schools) are making strides in developing innovative and cost-effective new treatments.

One of the world's most closely watched doctors is India's Devi Shetty, a surgeon trained in London who has become an extremely successful medical entrepreneur. While he gained fame at one time as Mother Teresa's heart surgeon, he is best known today as a builder of highly cost-effective hospitals. Shetty has been compared, by at least one journalist, to America's Henry Ford. Ford, in one of the most important innovations in industrial history, launched the modern automobile manufacturing industry by creating the assembly line to turn out a high volume of quality cars at affordable cost. Before Ford, the car was just a distant, unaffordable dream for most people, and was assembled slowly, by hand, at great cost. Dr. Shetty, in a vaguely similar vein, employs the economies of scale offered by high volume output to deliver high quality surgery at modest cost.

At Shetty's massive, 1,000-bed privately-owned hospital in Bangalore (three to six times larger than a typical American hospital), open heart surgery runs about $2,000 or less, and the outcomes are excellent. The hospital is like a surgery factory. Dozens of theaters give this center the capacity to perform up to 70 heart surgeries in one day. The hospital states that about 30% of its heart surgery is done on children.

Adjacent to his Narayana Hrudayalaya Hospital for heart care, he has built a 1,400-bed cancer center and a 300-bed facility for eye care. Another Shetty unit provides a broad range of dental care; yet another runs a stem cell bank to enable mothers to deposit their babies' umbilical cords for potential use in the future for stem cell therapy. Additional surgical specialties at Shetty's hospitals include neurology and orthopedics. He has raised millions of dollars with the goal of building several more medical centers in India, hoping for 30,000 total beds. As of early 2017, Narayana Hrudayalaya managed or owned a system of 24 hospitals and seven heart centers in India and an international hospital in the Cayman Islands, in addition to a telemedicine practice which links physicians via Skype in facilities in India and in Africa.

Shetty's hospital is also a partner in a "micro health insurance" program called Yeshaswini, which covers nearly 3 million farmers at a monthly premium of 10 rupees each (about 22 cents). The state government of Karnataka contributes an additional five cents per month per person. All told, the program covers surgeries in 400 hospitals across the state. The states of Andhra Pradesh and Tamil Nadu have started similar programs.

SPOTLIGHT: Mexico's Health Insurance Program

Mexico launched a national health care program called Seguro Popular (Popular Insurance) in 2004, which swelled to cover 95% of the country's population. By 2017, the program served 53.5 million people. The Mexican government increased its spending on health care from 5% of GDP to almost 6.5%, and has built more than 200 new hospitals and 2,000 clinics in addition to renovating thousands of existing facilities. Although access to health care is still spotty in rural areas, the country has seen significant improvement in overall health, including the increase in the survival rate for children with leukemia from three in ten to seven in ten.

The Outlook for Health Care Technology

20) Health Care Technology Introduction

In recent years, the health care industry has capitalized on many remarkable advances in medical technology, including breakthroughs in computing, communications, small-incision surgery, drug therapies, diagnostics, advanced radiation and instruments. For example, huge advances are being made in the fields of cardiovascular care, cancer care, diagnostic imaging and testing, organ transplants and minimally invasive surgery.

In the area of drug development, innovative methods, including genome mapping and high-throughput screening, are providing a clearer understanding of the potential of drugs before they are sent into clinical trials. In addition, the FDA has hired legions of employees in recent years to help process applications for new drugs, medical procedures and equipment. Nonetheless, drug development remains a slow, tedious, extremely expensive risk, and very few potential drugs make it through trials and onto the market.

Meanwhile, more emphasis is being placed on the use of computers and advanced telecommunication technology in many phases of hospital operations and patient care, often in conjunction with complex equipment, to diagnose and improve patients' conditions. Investors, well aware of the long term potential growth of the industry, continue to be anxious to fund new health technologies. An extensive use of digitized patient records is slowly becoming a reality.

The first half of the 21st century promises to bring even greater milestones in human health as we begin to reap the benefits of new therapies created through biotechnology and genetic engineering. As our understanding of human biology at the molecular level matures, genetically engineered pharmaceuticals and gene therapies will be developed that target diseases at their molecular origins, thus lessening the need for more costly elements of treatment such as invasive surgery and acute care. If applied during the early stages of disease development, these new biotechnologies will extend and improve the quality of life for the patient. If the disease has already caused the failure or malfunction of vital organs or tissue, it may one day be possible for the patient to receive a fully functioning, engineered replacement, grown from cells harvested from the patient's own tissues.

Gene mapping and proteomics will allow patients to be screened to determine whether they are genetically predisposed to certain diseases. Dramatic breakthroughs are already being made by determining, through personal gene mapping, whether a patient is likely to respond favorably to specific drug therapies for cancer and other diseases. The use of personal genetic profiles in order to avoid adverse reactions to specific drugs will eventually become important as well.

Knowledge obtained from biomedical research will also help to improve the general health of the public by identifying beneficial behavioral changes. Meanwhile, advanced imaging technology, including 320-slice CT scanning (capable of providing incredibly precise, high-resolution scans of the body), will greatly enhance physicians' ability to diagnose patients and lead to earlier intervention and higher rates of cure.

21) RFID Helps Manage Hospital and Pharmacy Inventories

RFID (radio frequency identification) is a huge breakthrough in hospital inventory management. RFID systems are based on the placement of microchips in product packaging. These chips, continuously broadcasting product identification data, are used with special sensors in handheld devices or on shelves that alert a central inventory management system about product usage and the need to restock inventory. From loading docks to stockroom shelves to the hospital floor, radio frequency readers wirelessly track the movement of each and every item, replacing bar codes. These systems lead to fewer out-of-stock situations and the elimination of costly manual inventory counts.

SPOTLIGHT: The Hospital Patient Smart Room

A professional organization, the RFID in Healthcare Consortium, has been formed to promote development in this field. The group has developed a concept called the Hospital Patient Smart Room. It utilizes RFID to validate patient information, reduce errors and optimize patient data.

The Johns Hopkins Hospital adopted RFID in order to track bags of intravenous fluid, one of the thousands of possible applications that could save the medical industry vast sums currently lost due to mistakes in the prescription, storage and delivery of drugs. RFID chips and the scanners that look after them are rapidly becoming smaller and cheaper and are steadily being adopted for more and more items in hospitals and pharmacies as costs fall. Beyond the monetary savings through better inventory control, RFID systems save some of the many people who die every year due to errors in prescription drug delivery.

RFID tags implanted in the wristbands worn by hospital patients also reduce patient identification mistakes, thereby reducing instances of errors in treatment. Data gathered electronically from RFID systems is integrated with enterprise-wide computer systems throughout the hospital, including the pharmacy.

Many medical innovations using RFID are becoming widespread. For example, "med carts" equipped with computers and bar code scanners allow nurses to scan patients' identifying wristbands to verify identity and medication orders, improving safety and efficiency. These carts are evolving to use RFID instead of bar codes. In addition, examination and operating rooms are now often equipped with wireless laptops that transmit on-the-spot notes and evaluations for each patient to a central information system.

22) Electronic Health Records (EHR) Digitize Patient Data at an Accelerating Pace

There is a strong movement in the United States, the UK, Canada and elsewhere to implement widespread use of electronic health records (EHRs, or sometimes EMRs for electronic medical records). A major goal in this movement is to create Continuity of Care Records (CCRs), which would ensure that a patient's health history could be utilized seamlessly by hospitals, primary care physicians and specialists.

Leading Companies in the Electronic Health Records (EHR) Field:

General Electric (GE), Centricity brand
AthenaHealth
Optum
Allscripts, TouchWorks brand
Epic
NextGen
eClinicalWorks
Cerner

In 2009, the U.S. federal government authorized a $787 billion economic stimulus bill which included $19 billion to be spent by hospitals and physicians on the installation of EHRs. Later funding brought the total spending to date on EHR to over $24 billion. Hospitals received up to several million dollars, depending upon their size. A 500-bed hospital, for example, was eligible for about $6 million in federal funds to be used for digital health records. Health care practitioners and organizations that did not adopt electronic records suffered cuts in Medicare and Medicaid reimbursements.

Technology firms both large and small are fiercely competing in the EHR market. Optum and NextGen got a leg up on the competition by securing preferred designation from the American Medical Association (AMA) in 2010. Large or small, most systems are not compatible with any other system, thereby locking out competitors and guaranteeing renewals from existing customers. This use of proprietary systems can be counterproductive by making the sharing of patient records difficult.

Kaiser Permanente HealthConnect links its hundreds of medical offices and Kaiser hospitals, thousands of physicians and more than 9 million members. Kaiser maintains one of the world's largest non-governmental digital medical data depositories.

Proponents of EHRs estimate that they could significantly reduce medical errors, save lives and cut billions in medical spending a year in shortened hospital stays, reduced nursing time, savings on unnecessary drugs (or drugs that could dangerously react with medications already prescribed for a patient) and the reduction of redundant lab tests and paperwork. Physicians, caregivers and researchers could also benefit enormously by tracking clinical data nationwide and learning which treatments are most effective in any given situation.

The Canadian government is investing in health information projects including telemedicine, EHR, electronic prescription systems, laboratory information systems and diagnostic imaging systems. This is done via an agency called Canada Health Infoway.

Several major electronic medical claims processors have been established in the U.S. A pioneer was WebMD. Emdeon One (formerly MedAvant Healthcare Solutions and later Capario) also provides electronic processing services. The company was initially a coalition by Aetna, Anthem, Cigna, Heath Net, Oxford, PacifiCare and

WellPoint Health Systems called MedUnite. Growth in health care transaction processing is still far from over. Billions of transactions occur every year in the U.S., including prescription processing, insurance claims and so on. The 2010 Affordable Care Act (ACA) is greatly boosting the total number of health care transactions in America.

As hospitals and other major health care providers scramble to digitize, concerns about the quality of patient care have been voiced. As a result, caregivers and insurers have combined forces to monitor the changes brought about by the technological boom. The Leapfrog Group, a coalition of companies and private organizations that provides health care benefits, was created to improve, among other things, the flow of patient data and benchmarks for patient outcomes at hospitals. Leapfrog has set exacting standards for the health system to strive for in the creation and utilization of digital data. "Leapfrog compliance" is a catch phrase among hospitals, which are rated on the organization's web site (www.leapfroggroup.org) with regard to compliance issues such as computerized prescription order systems and statistics on staffing and medical procedure success rates.

In addition to Leapfrog, nonprofit HIMMSS formed the Personal Connected Health Alliance (www.pchalliance.org), which includes partners such as AT&T, Eli Lilly & Company, Philips, Samsung, Cisco Systems, Intel and Qualcomm Life. PCHAlliance holds an annual Connected Health Conference to promote the exchange of health research and technologies, and publishes and promotes standards for data exchange to and from personal health devices called the Continua Design Guidelines.

The use of advanced predictive analytics software for the study of patient care outcomes data will attempt to forecast the best possible treatment for specific diseases and ailments. Patient records are kept in increasingly powerful databases, which can be analyzed to find the history of treatment outcomes. For the first time, payers such as insurance companies have vast amounts of data available to them, including answers to questions such as:

- Which procedures and surgeries bring the best results?
- Which drugs are most cost effective?
- Which physicians and hospitals have the highest and lowest rates of cure (or of untimely deaths of patients)?
- What is the average length of stay required for the treatment and recovery of patients undergoing various surgeries?
- How long should it take for the rehabilitation of a patient with a worker's compensation claim for a specific type of injury?

23) Telemedicine and Remote Patient Monitoring Rely on Wireless

The healthcare products business of electronics giant Royal Philips Electronics offers an ICU (intensive care unit) remote monitoring system called eICU. Originally developed by Visicu, Inc., a Baltimore, Maryland medical information technology company that is now part of Phillips, eICU is a combination of software, video and audio feeds and real-time patient vital statistics that hooks patients in ICUs in multiple hospitals to central monitoring facilities manned by ICU specialists. A specialist at the central location mans a standing desk outfitted with a cutting edge graphical dashboard called orb that displays patient data, including real-time video and audio for up to 150 ICU beds at a time. The system ranks patients according to their conditions and flags gravely ill patients in red so that their progress can be more easily monitored. Indications such as changes in blood pressure alert the specialist who then contacts the nurse or physician on duty to treat the patient accordingly. eICU is in use in hundreds of hospitals around the world.

Hospitals that have eICU have experienced significant cost savings since the system cuts the average ICU stay from 4.4 days to 3.6 by lowering the instances of complications such as pneumonia and infections (these conditions generally occur when patients are not closely monitored by ICU specialists). The Leapfrog Group estimates that 54,000 patients per year could be saved if every U.S. ICU were monitored by specialists.

Other remote monitoring systems are allowing patients to be monitored at home or at out-of-the-way care facilities. For example, American Telecare, Inc.'s CareTone Telephonic Stethoscope checks for heart, lung and bowel sounds using a small stethoscope, a phone line and two-way video stations. Cardiocom LLC's Telescale is a telemonitoring device integrated with an electronic scale. The patient steps onto the scale and answers questions using a touch pad about his or her symptoms. The answers and the patient's weight are communicated via two-way messaging to the consulting physician, who is alerted if there is any deterioration in the patient's health. The system also sends alerts back to the patient for follow-up visits or care plan adjustments. Other remote monitoring systems track cardiac patients' vital signs and links them via video chat to a nurse when necessary.

Many of the world's leading technology companies see immense potential in remote home monitoring of elderly and chronically ill patients. One example is the "Health Buddy" from Bosch, which can utilize home monitors for weight, glucose, blood pressure and blood oxygen. Philips, Honeywell and Intel are also developing products. Intel's design includes two-way video between the patient at home and caregivers.

Another slant on telemonitoring is the growing practice of patients connecting with physicians via laptop webcams, video-enabled tablets or smartphones. Rather than an expensive doctor visit, some patients are opting for virtual consultations at much lower costs than office or hospital visits. Insurers including WellPoint, Aetna and United Health are offering virtual visit options in several U.S. states that do not require a face to face meeting before a doctor can prescribe medication. A large number of companies have launched telehealth services, with many of them aimed at saving costs for employee health plans.

Thomas Jefferson University Hospital is investing in video apps that enable physicians to consult with patients from their homes. The hospital began testing video consultations in late 2014, with primary care physicians following up with patients after they went home. The facility hopes to eventually perform triage via video for many of the patients who visit its Emergency Room each year. Video assessments may enable doctors to assess who needs emergency treatment and who would be better served at an urgent care clinic or by calling a regular doctor.

A new player in the wearable sensor arena is Apple's smartwatch which is basically a wearable computer that is part watch, part iPhone, part iPod and much more. With regard to health care, users can download apps to the watch that track readings from external monitors such as those used to measure glucose. DexCom, Inc. has designed just such an app to go with its glucose monitor that displays blood sugar data in a simple, easy to read graph. Watch for apps and sensors that track other medical data to hit the market in the near term such as electrocardiograms (EKGs), blood oxygen levels and respiratory rates, pending FDA approval.

PricewaterhouseCoopers (in partnership with GSM Association) forecasted that global mobile health revenue would reach $23 billion by 2017. Grand View Research projected that the worldwide market would total $49 billion by 2020. This includes mobile operators, device vendors, health-care providers and content makers.

Mobile health apps are extremely popular with consumers, and are adding features and capabilities on a continual basis. Examples include MyFitnessPal, which was acquired by Under Armour, and Runkeeper. Apple released the HealthKit and ResearchKit (in addition to its Health tracking and fitness app) that enable physicians search for health apps according to their medical specialty and leverage health resources. Stanford University found that 11,000 people signed up for a cardiovascular study using ResearchKit less than 24 hours after its release.

In the Finnish city of Oulu, a telemonitoring system called Self Care has users who login to their computers to make appointments, refill prescriptions and exchange messages with doctors. People who test blood pressure or blood sugar levels at home can enter the results online for doctors to view. Lab results are posted within hours. Self Care costs the city $390,000 each year, but has saved millions in reducing expensive, face-to-face doctor's visits.

24) Stem Cells—Multiple Sources Stem from New Technologies

During the 1980s, a biologist at Stanford University, Irving L. Weissman, was the first to isolate the stem cell that builds human blood (the mammalian hematopoietic cell). Later, Weissman isolated a stem cell in a laboratory mouse and went on to co-found SysTemix, Inc. (now part of drug giant Novartis) and StemCells, Inc. to continue this work in a commercial manner.

In November 1998, two different university-based groups of researchers announced that they had accomplished the first isolation and characterization of the human embryonic stem cell (HESC). One group was led by James A. Thomson at the University of Wisconsin at Madison. The second was led by John D. Gearhart at the Johns Hopkins University School of Medicine at Baltimore. The HESC is among the most versatile basic building blocks in the human body. Embryos, when first conceived, begin creating small numbers of HESCs, and these cells eventually differentiate and develop into the more than 200 cell types that make up the distinct tissues and organs of the human body. If scientists can reproduce and then guide the development of these basic HESCs, then they could theoretically grow replacement organs and tissues in the laboratory—even such complicated tissue as brain cells or heart cells.

Ethical and regulatory difficulties arose from the fact that the only source for human "embryonic" stem cells was, as per the name, human embryos. A laboratory can obtain these cells in one of three ways: 1) inserting a patient's DNA into an egg, thus producing a blastocyst that is a clone of the patient—which is then destroyed after only a few days of development; 2) harvesting stem cells from aborted fetuses; or 3) harvesting stem cells from embryos that are left over and unused after an in vitro fertilization of a hopeful mother. (Artificial in vitro fertilization requires the creation of a large number of test tube embryos per instance, but only one of these embryos is used in the final process.)

A rich source of similar but "non-embryonic" stem cells is bone marrow. Doctors have been performing bone marrow transplants in humans for decades. This procedure essentially harnesses the healing power of stem cells, which proliferate to create healthy new blood cells in the recipient. Several other non-embryonic stem cell sources have great promise.

Fortunately, tremendous strides have been made in harvesting stem cells through non-embryonic means. Scientists have discovered that there are stem cells in existence in many diverse places in the adult human body, and they are thus succeeding in creating stem cells without embryos, by utilizing "post-embryonic" cells, such as cells from marrow. Such cells are already showing the ability to differentiate and function in animal and human recipients. Best of all, these types of stem cells may not be plagued by problems found in the use of HESCs, such as the tendency for HESCs to form tumors when they develop into differentiated cells.

Methods of developing "post-embryonic" stem cells without the use of human embryos:

- Adult Skin Cells—Exposure of harvested adult skin cells to viruses that carry specific genes, capable of reprogramming the skin cells so that they act as stem cells.
- Parthenogenesis—manipulation of unfertilized eggs.
- Other Adult Cells—Harvesting adult stem cells from bone marrow or brain tissue.
- Other Cells—harvesting of stem cells from human umbilical cords, placentas or other cells.
- De-Differentiation—use of the nucleus of an existing cell, such as a skin cell, that is altered by an egg that has had its own nucleus removed.
- Transdifferentiation—making a skin cell de-differentiate back to its primordial state so that it can then morph into a useable organ cell, such as heart tissue.
- Pluripotent state cells (iPSCs). Adult cells are drawn from a skin biopsy and treated with reprogramming factors.
- Most recently, researchers have found it possible to harvest stem cells from a wide variety of tissue.

25) Government Support for Stem Cell Research Evolves

Shortly after taking office, U.S. President Barack Obama reversed an eight-year ban on the use of federal funding for embryonic stem cell research. Specifically, Obama issued Executive Order 13505, entitled "Removing Barriers to Responsible Scientific Research Involving Human Stem Cells." This executive order, dated March 9, 2009, charged the National Institutes of Health (NIH) with issuing new guidelines for stem cell research which became effective in July 2009. The order further authorized the NIH to "support and conduct responsible, scientifically worthy human stem cell research, including human embryonic stem cell research, to the extent permitted by law." The important words here are "human embryonic," since the harvesting of stem cells from discarded human embryos is what started the stem cell funding controversy in the first place. Further, this wording clearly eliminates the possibility of funding research projects involving stem cells that result from cloning. Under previous U.S. regulations, federal research funds were granted only for work with 21 specific lines of stem cells that existed in 2001. Harvesting and developing new embryonic lines did not qualify.

By mid-April 2009, the NIH had issued a new policy statement. The issue of funding remains politically charged. The NIH is taking a middle road. Its guidelines state that embryos donated for such research must be given voluntarily and without financial inducement. (Such embryos typically are donated by couples who have completed fertility treatments and have no need for remaining, redundant embryos. This is a common practice in seeking laboratory-aided pregnancies.)

Once a stem cell starts to replicate, a large colony, or line, of self-replenishing cells can theoretically continue to reproduce forever. Unfortunately, only about a dozen of the stem cell lines existing in 2001 were considered to be useful, and some scientists believe that these lines were getting tired.

The use of non-federal funding, however, was not restricted during the eight-year ban, although many groups did want to see further state or federal level restrictions on stem cell research or usage. A major confrontation continued between American groups that advocated the potential health benefits of stem cell therapies and groups that decried the use of stem cells on ethical or religious terms. Meanwhile, stem cell development forged ahead in other technologically advanced nations.

In November 2004, voters in California approved a unique measure that provides $3 billion in state funding for stem cell research. Connecticut, Massachusetts and New Jersey also passed legislation that permits embryonic stem cell research. California already has a massive biotech industry, spread about San Diego and San Francisco in particular. As approved, California's Proposition 71 created an oversight committee that determines how and where grants will be made, and an organization, the California Institute for Regenerative Medicine (CIRM, www.cirm.ca.gov), to issue bonds for funding and to manage the entire program. The money is being invested in research over 10 years.

As of early 2018, CIRM had made 973 grants totaling more than $2.53 billion. These grants are funding dedicated laboratory space for the culture of human embryonic stem cells (HESCs), particularly those that fall outside federal guidelines, in addition to underwriting staff positions, research models, training programs and more.

Corporate investment in stem cells has also been strong. AstraZeneca Pharmaceuticals invested $77 million in a startup firm in San Diego called BrainCells, Inc. to study how antidepressants might be used to spur brain cell growth. In late 2012, Osiris Therapeutics, Inc. received approval in Canada and New Zealand for the world's first stem cell drug Prochymal, which derives cells from the bone marrow of young adults to treat acute graft versus host disease (GvHD). Prochymal was in Phase III trials for treatment of Crohn's disease and acute graft versus host disease (GvHD), and Phase II trials for acute myocardial infarction in early 2016.

26) Stem Cells—Therapeutic Cloning Techniques Advance

There are two distinct types of embryonic cloning: "reproductive" cloning and "therapeutic" cloning. While they have similar beginnings, the desired end results are vastly different.

The clearest path to "therapeutic" cloning may lie in "autologous transplantation." In this method, a tiny amount of a patient's muscle or other tissue is harvested. This sample's genetic material is then de-differentiated; that is, reduced to a simple, unprogrammed state. The patient's DNA sample is then inserted into an egg to grow a blastocyst. The blastocyst is manipulated so that its stem cells differentiate into the desired type of tissue, such as heart tissue. That newly grown tissue would then be transplanted to the patient's body. Many obstacles must be overcome before such a transplant can become commonplace, but there is potential to completely revolutionize healing through such regenerative, stem cell-based processes.

"Reproductive" cloning is a method of reproducing an exact copy of an animal—or potentially an exact copy of a human being. A scientist would remove the nucleus from a donor's unfertilized egg, insert a nucleus from the animal, or human, to be copied, and then stimulate the nucleus to begin dividing to form an embryo. In the case of a mammal, such as a human, the embryo would then be implanted in the uterus of a host female for gestation and birth. The successful birth of a cloned human baby doesn't necessarily mean that a healthy adult human will result. To date, cloned animals have often developed severe health problems. For example, a U.S. firm, Ocata Therapeutics (now a part of the Astellas Institute for Regenerative Medicine (AIRM)), reports that it engineered the birth of cloned cows that appeared healthy at first but developed severe health problems after a few years. Nonetheless, relatively successful cloning of animals is now progressing in many nations.

On the other hand, "therapeutic" cloning is a method of reproducing exact copies of cells needed for research or for the development of replacement tissue. In this case as well, a scientist removes the nucleus from a donor's unfertilized egg, inserts a nucleus from the animal, or human, whose cells are to be copied, and then stimulates the nucleus to begin dividing to form an embryo. However, in therapeutic use, the embryo would never be allowed to grow to any significant stage of development. Instead, it would be allowed to grow for a few hours or days, and stem cells would then be removed from it for use in regenerating tissue.

Because it can provide a source of stem cells, cloning has uses in regenerative medicine that can be vital in treating many types of disease. The main differences between stem cells derived from clones and those derived from aborted fetuses or fertility specimens is that a) they are made from only one source of genes, rather than by mixing sperm and eggs; and b) they are made specifically for scientific purposes, rather than being existing specimens. Although the use of cloning for regeneration has stirred heated debate as well, it has not resulted in universal rejection. Most industrialized countries, including Canada, Russia, most of Western Europe and most of Asia, have made some government-sanctioned allowances for research in this area.

Specifically, researchers are cloning early-stage embryos in search of new treatments for such degenerative diseases as Parkinson's disease, Alzheimer's and diabetes. The embryos are destroyed before they are two weeks old and therefore do not develop beyond a tiny cluster of cells.

Reprogramming has evolved recently to use proteins to manipulate cells to return to embryonic states. In the past, reprogramming was accomplished by using a virus to carry genes into a mature cell. This is problematic since the virus can cause cancer or spark changes in the target cell that are undesirable. One technology uses a wash made of four proteins that are associated with the genes. The wash is absorbed in the target cell where the proteins trigger additional protein changes, causing the reversion to a primitive state.

27) Stem Cells and 3-D Printing—A New Era of Regenerative Medicine Takes Shape

Many firms are conducting product development and research in the areas of skin replacement, vascular tissue replacement and bone grafting or regeneration. Stem cells, as well as transgenic organs harvested from pigs, are under study for use in humans. At its highest and most promising level, regenerative medicine may eventually utilize human stem cells to create virtually any type of replacement organ or tissue.

In one recent, exciting experiment, doctors took stem cells from bone marrow and injected them into the hearts of patients undergoing bypass surgery. The study showed that the bypass patients who received the stem cells were pumping blood 24% better than patients who had not received them.

In another experiment, conducted by Dr. Mark Keating at Harvard, the first evidence was shown that stem cells may be used for regenerating lost limbs and organs. The regenerative abilities of amphibians have long been known, but exactly how they do it, or how it could be applied to mammals, has been little understood. Much of the regenerative challenge lies in differentiation, or the development of stem cells into different types of adult tissue such as muscle and bone. Creatures such as amphibians have the ability to turn their complex cells back into stem cells in order to regenerate lost parts. In the experiment, Dr. Keating made a serum from the regenerating nub (stem cells) of a newt's leg and applied it to adult mouse cells in a petri dish. He observed the mouse cells "de-differentiate," or turn into stem cells. In a later experiment, de-differentiated cells were turned back into muscle, bone and fat. These experiments could be the first steps to true human regeneration. Keating is continuing to make exciting breakthroughs in regenerative research.

The potential of the relatively young science of tissue engineering appears to be unlimited. Transgenics (the use of organs and tissues grown in laboratory animals for transplantation to humans) is considered by many to have great future potential, and improvements in immune system suppression will eventually make it easier for the human body to tolerate foreign tissue instead of rejecting it. There is also increasing theoretical evidence that malfunctioning or defective organs such as livers, bladders and kidneys could be replaced with perfectly functioning "neo-organs" (like spare parts) grown in the laboratory from the patient's own stem cells, with minimal risk of rejection.

The ability of most human tissue to repair itself is a result of the activity of these cells. The potential that cultured stem cells have for transplant medicine and basic developmental biology is enormous.

Diabetics who are forced to cope with daily insulin injection treatments could also benefit from engineered tissues. If they could receive a fully functioning replacement pancreas, diabetics might be able to throw away their hypodermic needles once and for all.

Elsewhere, the harvesting of replacement cartilage, which does not require the growth of new blood vessels, is being used to repair damaged joints and treat urological disorders. Genzyme Corp. won FDA approval for its replacement cartilage product Carticel, the first biologic cell therapy to become licensed. Genzyme's process involves harvesting the patient's own cartilage-forming cells, and, from those cells, re-growing new cartilage in the laboratory. The physician then injects the new cartilage into the damaged area. Full regeneration of the replacement cartilage is expected to take up to 18 months.

The next big thing in tissue replacement is three-dimensional (3D) printers to fabricate a variety of shapes made of living tissue, including tubes suitable for blood vessels, cartilage for use in human joints and patches of skin and muscle. The process takes stem cells harvested from a patient and treats them in the lab to stimulate multiplication, creating cell aggregates. The resulting "bioink" is loaded in cartridges shaped like syringes with extrusion nozzles. Software directs the printer to extrude the bioink in a precise pattern of layers interspersed with hydrogel (a gelatinous water-based substance) used to mold the cells into the desired shape. The printed tissue is then allowed to grow into mature cells suitable for research.

Although in its infancy, one San Diego, California firm called Organovo, Inc. (organovo.com) already produces commercial 3D bioprinters for use in research. In early 2014, Organovo launched its first product, slivers of human liver tissue for use in laboratories to test drug toxicity. Physicians and researchers can find out how a patient's liver will respond to different treatments before going to the expense of clinical trials. As of 2017, the firm was generating kidney tissue, and in 2018 it announced the ability to create functional human liver tissue. In addition to Organovo, industry analysts estimate that 80 teams at research institutions and biotechnology firms are working on the concept. Ultimately, it is hoped that 3D bioprinting will be able to produce viable replacement organs.

Revivicor (www.revivicor.com), a division of United Therapeutics, is working to breed pigs with human genes. Organs from these animals may be transplanted into humans with fewer immune system rejection problems. Researchers at the National Heart, Lung and Blood Institute in Bethesda, Maryland have been testing the specialized pig organs in baboons. Revivicor ultimately plans to breed up to 1,000 pigs per year and ship organs rapidly by helicopter.

Companies to Watch in Replacement Tissues, including 3-D Printing of Tissues:
ViaCord (formerly ViaCell, Inc. before its acquisition by PerkinElmer), in Boston, Massachusetts (www.viacord.com), develops therapies using umbilical cord stems. Also, their ViaCord product enables families to preserve their baby's umbilical cord at the time of birth for possible future use in treating over 40 diseases and genetic disorders.
Cytori Therapeutics, in San Diego, California (www.cytori.com), is focused on the use of adult Adipose-Derived Regenerative Cells (ADRCs). Its goal is to apply these cells as therapies for chronic heart failure, burn care, soft tissue injury and sports medicine.
Allevi (formerly BioBots), in Philadelphia, Pennsylvania (allevi3d.com), offers desktop 3-D bioprinters capable of printing hydrogels such as collagen, hyper-elastic bone and conductive tissues.
Aspect Biosystems Ltd. in Vancouver, British Columbia (www.aspectbiosystems.com) is developing a portfolio of 3-D bioprinted human tissues used in predictive pre-clinical models and implantable tissue therapies.
Materialise NV, in Leuven, Belgium (www.materialise.com) offers 3-D printing technology for many industries including health care, for which it designs implants, surgical guides and other medical devices.

Internet Research Tip:
For an excellent primer on genetics and basic biotechnology techniques, see:
National Center for Biotechnology Information
www.ncbi.nlm.nih.gov

28) Health Care Robotics

While robotics are revolutionizing the manufacturing, fulfillment and hospitality industries, the next revolution may well be in health care, in terms of both service robots for tasks like cleaning and deliveries to patients' rooms and highly advanced devices in the form of surgical robots and robotic limbs for patients who have lost arms or legs.

One company on the forefront is Parker Hannifin Corp. which has a long history of motion and control technologies and systems used in construction, factory equipment and aircraft. Its newest venture is the Indego exoskeleton. Weighing in at about 26 pounds, Indego is a set of motorized braces that help paralyzed or otherwise disabled people walk by supporting, moving and bending their legs. Another firm, ReWalk Robotics, has a similar device called the ReWalk Personal 6.0.

Meanwhile, Johns Hopkins University is working on robotic arms that have 26 joints, can lift up to 45 pounds and are controlled by the wearer's mind. In order to communicate with the devices, patients will likely require surgery to remap nerve endings to allow brain signals to reach the prosthetics. For more on the project, see www.jhuapl.edu/prosthetics.

The International Federation of Robotics (IFR) projected that 14,750 medical service robots would be sold between 2016 and 2019. It states that the most important of these devices are used in robot-assisted surgery and other patient therapies.

Robotic surgery has also become common, especially in minimally-invasive procedures. The technology utilizes cameras and mechanical arms wielding surgical instruments controlled by a human surgeon, typically via a small incision. The surgeon uses a console which displays images from the camera in high-definition, magnified, 3-D view. For example, the da Vinci Surgical System (www.davinicisurgery.com) is used in a variety of procedures to treat cardiac, colorectal, gynecological, head and neck, thoracic and urological problems.

29) Patients' Genetic Profiles Plummet in Price as DNA Sequencing Technologies Advance

Scientists now believe that nearly all diseases have at least some genetic component. For example, some people have a genetic predisposition for breast cancer or heart disease. The understanding of human genetics is hoped to lead to breakthroughs in therapies for many illnesses. Organizations worldwide are experimenting with personalized drugs that are designed to provide appropriate therapies based on a patient's personal genetic makeup or their lack of specific genes.

The DNA sequencing (genetic testing) of the genes within a patient is the process of determining the order of DNA nucleotides, or bases, in the genome—that is, the entire DNA makeup of the patient. The nucleotides are described on the order of A, C, G and T. The human genome consists of about 3 billion of these genetic letters. Once the genome has been sequenced, much work remains to be done for fully understanding human genetics. Scientists must analyze and translate the strings of A, C, G and T into usable knowledge, which requires sophisticated analytical software.

China's Sichuan University in Chengdu is organizing an ambitious plan to decode the genetic makeup of at least 1 million people by 2020. A similar effort in the U.S. is being headed by Regeneron Pharmaceuticals, Inc., and funded by Abbvie, Inc., Alnylam Pharmaceuticals, Inc., AstraZeneca PLC, Biogen, Inc. and Pfizer, Inc. Each company is paying Regeneron $10 million to sequence the genes of 500,000 people. It is targeted for completion by 2022. Saudi Arabia, the U.K. and Qatar are also collecting and analyzing data, but on a smaller scale.

DNA sequencing was first achieved in 2001 at a cost of about $100 million per genome (one patient's entire genetic makeup). However, by 2017, the price had dropped to as little as $795 per genome. Costs may continue to drop. In addition, some companies offer testing of a small, select group of genes within a patient at very modest prices—typically less than $100. The genome sequencing market is led by Illumina, Inc., a San Diego, California-based company. Competitors include Tute Genomics (which acquired Knome in late 2015), Thermo Fisher Scientific, Complete Genomics and BGI, formerly the Beijing Genomics Institute.

The scientific community's improving knowledge of genes and the role they play in disease is leading to several different tracks for improved treatment results. One track is to profile a patient's genetic makeup for a better understanding of a) which drugs a patient may respond to effectively, and b) whether certain defective genes reside in a patient and are causing a patient's disease or illness. Yet another application of genetic profiling is to study how a patient is able to metabolize medication, which could help significantly when deciding upon proper dosage. Since today's widely used drugs often produce desired results in only about 50% of patients who receive them, the use of specific medications based on a patient's genetic profile could greatly boost treatment results while cutting costs. Each year, by one count, 2.2 million Americans suffer side effects from prescription drugs. Of those, more than 100,000 die, making adverse drug reaction a leading cause of death in the U.S. A Journal of the American Medical Association study states that the annual cost of treating these drug reactions totals $4 billion each year.

Drugs that target the genetic origins of tumors may offer more effective, longer-lasting and far less toxic alternatives to conventional chemotherapy and radiation. In other cases, biotech drugs, used in combination with surgery or chemotherapy, can reduce the chance of a cancer recurrence. One of the most noted drugs that target specific genetic action is Herceptin, a monoclonal antibody that was developed by Genentech. Approved by the FDA in 1998, Herceptin, when used in conjunction with chemotherapy, shows great promise in significantly reducing breast cancer for certain patients who are known to "overexpress" the HER2 protein (that is, there is an excess of HER2-related protein on tumor cell surfaces, or there is an excess of the HER2 gene itself). A simple test is used to determine if this gene is present in the patient. Herceptin, which works by blocking genetic signals, thus preventing the growth of cancerous cells, may show potential in treating other types of cancer, such as ovarian, pancreatic or prostate cancer.

Another genetic test is marketed by Genomic Health, based in Redwood City, California, (www.genomichealth.com). Its Oncotype DX test provides breast cancer patients with an assessment of the likelihood of the recurrence of their cancer based on the expression of 21 different genes in a tumor. The test enables patients to evaluate the results they may expect from post-operative therapies such as Tamoxifen or chemotherapy. As of mid-2018, more than 900,000 patients had been tested worldwide. The firm also offers an Oncotype DX test for colon and prostate cancers. Such tests will be standard preventive treatment in coming decades.

The industry has moved onto what is commonly referred to as "Next Generation" sequencing of DNA. That is, highly advanced hardware and software that can determine the DNA of a human sample with extremely rapid output and low cost. This means that scientists worldwide will be able to conduct massive studies of human or other animal genetics at relatively affordable cost compared to the billions of dollars that the first genomic studies required.

A relatively recent entry to the field of biotechnology is epigenetics, a branch of biology focused on gene "silencers," which is used in a technique called "antisense." Scientists involved in epigenetics are studying the function within a gene that regulates whether that gene is operating at full capacity or is toned down to a lower level. The level of operation of a given gene may lead to a higher risk of disease, such as certain types of cancer. Epigenetics may be very effective in combatting abnormal gene expressions that cause cancer. In early 2013, the FDA approved a drug called Kynamro, created by Isis Pharmaceuticals and marketed by Sanofi's Genzyme. Kynamro uses antisense to shut off genes that cause abnormally high blood pressure and heart attacks in young people less than 30 years of age. By mid-2016, there were a number of epigenetic drugs on the market including Azacitidine, Decitabine, Vorinostat, Romidepsin and Ruxolitnub.

Pharmacy benefit managers (PBMs) are organizations that provide administrative services in processing and analyzing prescription claims for pharmacy benefit and coverage programs. Some PBMs are selling services that test patients for genetic variations that might indicate which drugs would be more effective for individual patients. Express Scripts (formerly Medco Health Solutions, Inc.) for example, is a PBM and pharmacy mail order business that is selling tests for patients who take drugs such as the blood thinner warfarin and breast cancer treatment Tamoxifen. CVS Caremark partners with Generation Health, Inc. to offer a similar testing service. PBMs are selling their services to employers who are willing to invest in them for improved health outcomes and lower prescription costs. If personally-tailored prescriptions become a widespread reality, billions of dollars each year could be saved as patients take only those drugs which will do them some good and avoid those which could do them harm.

Meanwhile, the American Society of Clinical Oncology (ASCO) was running a clinical trial in mid-2018 called TAPUR that offers cancer patients a genetic test and then selects drugs that appear to be a good match, even if that drug was developed to treat a different kind of malignancy. In a similar vein, the U.S. National Cancer Institute has a trial named MATCH which sends tumor biopsies to gene-testing laboratories to scan for more than 4,000 possible variants of 143 pertinent genes.

30) Advances for Cancer Patients in Chemotherapy and Radiation, Including Proton Beams and IMRT

Radiation therapy is commonly used in the treatment of cancerous tumors. This technology has been moving toward greater precision in irradiating tumors. Modern x-ray radiation equipment (photon radiation) can focus on and attack tumors while doing less damage to surrounding tissue than previous technologies. State-of-the-art radiation techniques of today involve several different formats. Specific formats have been found to be most effective for specific cancers.

IMRT (Intensity Modulated Radiation Therapy): is a radiation technology that enables the technician to apply narrowly focused radiation directly toward cancerous tumors. IMRT helps to limit the amount of damage to surrounding tissues. The process includes using multiple beams (typically from 7 to 12) aimed at the tumor from various directions. The beams meet at the tumor to administer the desired dosage. Breaking the dose down into multiple beams lessens the level of radiation that healthy tissues are exposed to. The point at which the beams join can be shaped to conform to the exact size, shape and location of the tumor, thus further sparing healthy tissue. Advanced imaging, such as CT, is used to provide precise guidance to the tumor's location.

An important breakthrough in radiation therapy is the ability to provide "respiratory gating," which enables the radiation equipment to accurately track the radiation target while allowing for the natural body motion caused by breathing in and out. This technology was pioneered by Varian.

An enhancement to IMRT is Varian's RapidArc VMAT (Volumetric Modulated Arc Therapy). This technology is able to deliver a radiation dose in a 360-degree rotation that is more targeted in much less time than previous units. Treatments that might take five minutes or more with older technologies can be reduced to two minutes.

Image Guided Radiation Therapy (IGRT): takes advantage of sophisticated imaging technologies in order to best target radiation therapy. Prostate cancer is often treated with IGRT. To treat that disease, tiny metal markers are implanted in the prostate using an outpatient procedure. The IGRT equipment is then able to locate the position of the prostate exactly by determining the location of the markers in real time. Varian is a leading manufacturer of IGRT equipment, as is Accuray, Inc., which makes the TomoTherapy system. The technology is similar to IMRT, but better enables radiation technicians to use ultrasound, CT or X-ray images to line up the radiation beam with the intended target.

Brachytherapy: is a method of internal radiation therapy whereby tiny containers of radioactive material, sometimes referred to as "seeds," are implanted directly in contact with tissue that is afflicted with cancerous tumors. It is a common method of treating prostate cancer and is sometimes used for the treatment of breast cancer. These seeds are never removed from the body. They typically have a radioactive half-life of six months. Eventually, they emit virtually no radiation at all.

An innovation in this field is called HDR, or high dose rate brachytherapy. In this instance, small radioactive seeds are attached to the end of flexible rods and guided into very specific, imaging-defined locations within the cancerous area. The rods are left in-place for a calculated number of seconds and then removed. This may be repeated several times over a series of days or weeks. This method exposes the cancer to a very high dose of radiation, and the results have been excellent in many cases. Leaders in this therapy include the UCLA Medical Center, the University of San Francisco Medical Center and Sloan Kettering.

The *Gamma Knife* is a unique type of radiation therapy with tissue-sparing properties. It involves focusing low-dose gamma radiation on a tumor, while exposing only a small amount of healthy, nearby tissue to radiation. It is often used to treat certain brain cancers.

Patient immobilization is an advancing technology. The point is to hold vital parts of the patient as still as possible so that the radiation beam affects only the desired targets. However, since patients must breathe during treatment, some movement of the body is always going to occur, and this can have an effect on radiation of areas such as the lungs. New technologies enable the radiation beam to allow for and synchronize with a patient's breathing rhythm.

PBRT, or Proton Beam Radiation Therapy is the use of a highly advanced technology to deliver external beam radiation therapy (EBRT) to a patient in order to kill cancerous cells and shrink tumors. While traditional radiation therapies rely on photons delivered by X-rays or gamma rays, Proton Beam Radiation Therapy relies on a particle accelerator to create and deliver protons. Protons are high-energy particles that carry a charge. By varying the velocity of the particles at the time that they enter the body, physicists are able to control the exact spot within the body where the radiation is released. The higher the velocity, the deeper within the body the radiation begins to take effect.

With traditional radiation (based on photons rather than protons), there is a significant entry dose of radiation that can be harmful to healthy tissues. Proton beam therapy has virtually no entry dose or exit dose, plus the ability to better focus the radiation on the exact place of the tumor, significantly cutting down on side effects and damage to surrounding tissues.

In the U.S., centers are in place at locations including Loma Linda (California) University Medical Center, which is considered a pioneer in applying this technology; Massachusetts General Hospital in Boston, Massachusetts; The University of Florida Proton Therapy Institute in Jacksonville, Florida; the M.D. Anderson Cancer Center in Houston, Texas; and the ProCure Proton Therapy Center in Oklahoma City, Oklahoma. As of mid-2018, there were 28 centers in the U.S., with another 23 centers under construction or in development. PBRT is in wide use or under planning in dozens of locations outside the U.S. including Japan, Germany and Korea. Recent new sites under planning or construction include Argentina, Australia, Singapore, Saudi Arabia and Thailand.

The Loma Linda, California facility began operations in 1990. It was the only hospital-based proton radiation center in the U.S. until 2003. Head and neck cancers and pediatric cancers are also treated there in large numbers. Recently, it has been conducting trials in post-lumpectomy breast cancer treatment. The center has treated nearly 50 different types of cancers.

PBRT may eventually be in very wide use worldwide. Its tissue sparing nature makes it ideal for eliminating side effects and for treating tumors in challenging locations, such as the eye and brain. It may be the best possible way to treat small children in order to spare healthy surrounding tissues that are not through growing. And, it has great potential for the treatment of non-cancerous conditions such as macular degeneration.

Major obstacles facing the development of new proton beam facilities include the immense investment required, the complexity of the accelerator and other equipment, the need to acquire and train specialized staff, and the need to educate referring physicians about this revolutionary technology and its high success rate. The high costs of proton facilities and proton treatments have caused considerable controversy. Many private insurers in the U.S. are refusing to pay higher rates for PBRT than they pay for more standard means of radiation. Eventually, advances in design and technology may make it easier and less costly to establish proton centers. Today's proton units typically have four treatment rooms.

Newer, smaller and much cheaper proton beam facilities with a single treatment room, and much less adjoining space needed for equipment, are opening, equipped with systems from Mevion Medical Systems, Inc. Its MEVION S250 Proton Therapy System is in use at the S. Lee Kling Center for Proton Therapy at the Siteman Cancer Center at Barnes-Jewish Hospital and Washington University School of Medicine in St. Louis, Missouri. While the older, larger facilities cost between $100 million and $200 million to build, the Mevion system and others like it cost between $25 million and $30 million. Meanwhile, at Loma Linda and elsewhere, highly automated treatment rooms are in use that increase the number of patients that proton centers are able to handle each day, thus amortizing a proton center's capital cost over a much wider base of patients.

Many insurers, including UnitedHealth Group, Inc. and Aetna, Inc., stopped covering proton beam treatment for prostate cancer treatment. The newer, less expensive facilities may help those firms to reinstate coverage.

For additional information, see The National Association for Proton Therapy, www.proton-therapy.org. Also, see the web site of Loma Linda University Medical Center's proton unit, www.protons.com.

Treating Cancer with Electricity: Another new high-tech tool for treating certain types of cancer is a short burst of electricity directed at the tumor. This process, called electroporation, involves treating the tumor with chemotherapy and then sending short electrical pulses into the tumor with a needle electrode. The electrical pulse allows the tumor to become more porous and thus more susceptible to the chemotherapeutic drugs.

Inovio Biomedical, www.inovio.com, is a leading company in the new field of electroporation therapy. Inovio has clinical trials ongoing for the use of its technology in the treatment of a wide variety of cancers, including breast, head and neck and melanoma.

Radio Frequency Ablation (RFA): RFA is the use of focused radio waves to produce high levels of heat within tumors in order to kill cancer. It is typically applied via needles that have been placed in the tumor, using ultrasound or other imaging techniques to insure correct placement. It is often used in the treatment of cancer of the kidney, and has applications in the treatment of tumors found in the lung, liver, bone, breast and adrenal system.

Carbon Ion Therapy: Already in use in Europe and Asia, carbon ion therapy is a relatively new treatment that promises to have a higher relative effectiveness and linear energy transfer than protons or photons when used to destroy malignant cells. The University of Colorado is working to build a $300 million carbon ion therapy center, the first in the U.S. The technology was pioneered in Japan at the National Institute of Radiological Sciences, and can be utilized in treating human as well as animal cancers.

High-Intensity Focused Ultrasound (HIFU) is an FDA-approved, minimally-invasive procedure typically used for the treatment of prostate cancer. It seeks to destroy malignant cells through the delivery of precisely focused sound waves. Cells are targeted using MRI and confirmed with traditional ultrasound. The sound waves that are aimed at the prostate tissue rapidly increase tissue temperature, hopefully destroying only the cancerous lesions and protecting the healthy surrounding tissue. HIFU system manufacturers include EDAP TMS, Sonacare Medical, Philips Healthcare, Shenzhen Wikkon and Promedica Bioelectronics. HIFU is also utilized in cosmetic procedures to tighten skin tissue.

Improvements in Chemotherapy: Chemotherapy continues to reduce the need for surgical excision of cancers and enable the treatment of cancers that are considered inoperable. Improvements in chemotherapy continue to reduce the number and severity of side effects and the length of treatment, boosting a shift from inpatient to outpatient care. For example, scientists in the Netherlands at the University of Leiden and the University of Utrecht developed new compounds for platinum-based chemotherapy that could alleviate side effects altogether. Although some cancers show resistance to chemotherapy, researchers have recently discovered a unique gene that causes resistance, so compounds may be added to chemotherapy that will block the gene's ability to resist. In many cases, chemotherapy is combined with radiation, other drugs and/or surgery.

31) Better Imaging, including MRI, PET and 320-Slice CT, Creates Advances in Detection

Today, improved diagnostic imaging, diagnostic catheterization and better monitoring procedures have made earlier detection of many diseases possible and reduced the need for exploratory surgery. Over the long-term, highly advanced new imaging systems, eventually utilizing molecular diagnostics, will enable levels of early intervention undreamed of in the past.

Magnetic resonance imaging (MRI) uses a combination of radio waves and a strong magnetic field to gauge the behavior of hydrogen atoms in water molecules within the body. Improvements in hardware and software have made MRI scans faster and more thorough than before. Ultra-fast MRI has many important clinical applications. Recent studies show that MRI may be the best method for determining the extent of a patient's recovery after a heart attack. Rapid-imaging MRI machines also expedite the diagnosis and treatment of heart conditions and strokes, thus reducing the time and money needed to scan the patient.

However, this technology has been extremely expensive, with equipment costs alone running from $1 million to $2 million. Until recently, very heavy shielding was needed to encapsulate the imaging room, which necessitated special construction of new facilities or very costly reinforcement of older building space. Progress in shielding technology and facility design, combined with more cost-effective mid-field and low-field MRI, has dramatically lowered the cost of most new installations. Some of these lighter, less powerful devices can be used in mobile settings, which makes MRI available in rural areas that could never have justified the expense of permanent installations. Low-field MRI technology has also enabled the development of open-MRI devices, which do not require a patient to be completely surrounded by a tunnel-shaped magnet. Open MRIs reduce patient anxiety and claustrophobia. In addition, the lower intensity of the magnetic field allows technicians, physicians and even family members to be present in the room at the time of the test, if the patient prefers.

Whole-body MRI can be useful for checking the entire skeleton or multiple parts of the body for metastasis of cancer. Although not part of routine patient care in the U.S., many health manufacturers such as Siemens, General Electric and Philips, are making scanners with full-body capability. The technology utilizes a gliding table that moves the patient smoothly enough to keep images clear. Related software takes five to six sets of images and weaves them together for a complete picture. The process generally takes about 20 to 45 minutes, the same amount of time used in traditional MRI.

Magnetoencephalography (MEG) is a newer technology derived from both MRI and electroencephalography (EEG). Like EEG, MEG registers brain patterns, but whereas EEG measures electrical activity in the brain, MEG measures magnetic waves, primarily in the cerebral cortex of the brain. Computer enhancement of the generated data is improving EEG as a diagnostic tool. Recent refinements in EEG technology make it possible to use this device to help diagnose various forms of depression and schizophrenia.

Computed tomography (also known as a CT scan or CAT scan) uses a circular pattern of x-rays to produce high-resolution, cross-sectional images, which can help precisely locate tumors, clots, narrowed arteries and aneurysms. Because CT essentially creates images of distinct slices of the body, it can be referred to as multi-slice or multi-row detector imaging. CT can produce three-dimensional images, which are beneficial in reconstructive surgery. However, CT machines cost between $1.5 million and $2 million or more for 64-slice technology. The advanced electronics enabling 64-slice CT (compared to 8- and 16-slice CT) are an immense breakthrough in the evolution of imaging. For example, 64-slice CT can show a higher level of detail in arteries than angiography, which is the traditional method of looking for arterial blockage and plaque when checking cardiovascular health. In fact, 64-slice CT enables the user to see cross-sections of arteries, including the walls. And, this advanced CT can provide vastly improved images of beating hearts, including the interior. (About 1.5 million U.S. patients undergo angiograms yearly. A CT scan does not bring the risk of arterial puncture associated with angiography's wire-guided probes.) 64-slice CT is extremely useful for early detection of heart disease as a preventive measure, and for guiding surgeons during surgery.

There is some concern about the exposure of patients to radiation during CT scans. In response, General Electric Healthcare developed a device that reduces radiation during cardiac CT scans by up to 70%. The system is called SnapShot Pulse, and it pulses with a patient's heartbeat, automatically turning the X-ray on and off at desired times during the heart rate cycle, which reduces the patient's radiation exposure time.

The latest advance is the 320-slice CT (similar to but more powerful than recently-introduced 256-slice CTs), which has the ability to provide astonishing levels of image resolution. Both 256-slice and 320-slice CTs can scan areas as large as 6.3 inches, wide enough to capture almost all human organs. Each scan takes one second or less, compared to the 64-slice CT which takes up to 10 seconds for a scan of an area of 1.3 inches. In addition, the device measures subtle changes in blood flow or minute blockages forming in blood vessels in the heart and brain. The first 320-slice CT scanner in North America was installed at The Johns Hopkins Hospital in late 2007. There are 320-slice scanners installed around the world, including one in Chennai, India. A second-generation 320-detector row CT scanner requires less time and exposes patients to less radiation. Extremely fast scans will mean that large numbers of patients can be processed daily with one of these expensive machines. The cost of scans may drop proportionately.

As with MRIs, there has recently been some interest in whole-body CT scans. Many independent imaging centers have been offering such scans to the public at reasonable cost. However, there is concern among some physicians that whole-body CTs often lead to a large number of questionable findings, or false positives, and that such scans may be of little value.

Two other imaging machines, single photon emission computed tomography (SPECT) and positron emission tomography (PET), use forms of radioisotope imaging to detect and study conditions such as stroke, epilepsy, schizophrenia and Parkinson's and Alzheimer's diseases. PET is a major research tool for understanding the human brain, and has a substantial indirect impact on medical and surgical practices.

PET offers a unique advantage in that it can offer functional imaging. That is, it can show how an area of the body is functioning and responding. Because it is based on safe, short-lived radioactive substances that are injected into the body, PET enables physicians to see metabolic activity. For example, in addition to imaging of brain activity, PET can be used to determine how cancerous tumors react to certain drugs. The FDA is cooperating with the National Cancer Institute to determine whether PET should be used in clinical trials of new cancer treatments to determine whether tumors are responding to therapies.

Other improvements in x-ray technology include digital subtractive angiography (DSA). DSA involves the use of enhanced x-rays to see blood vessels and arteries, while bones and soft tissues are blotted out of the image. It can clearly image aneurysms and can be used in angioplasty, a procedure that reduces the need for heart bypass surgery. However, as advanced CT becomes more widely accepted, DSA may become irrelevant.

Mammography is another x-ray technology that has been refined over the years. While traditional mammography with film offers sufficient x-ray images of older women's breasts, the film lacks the versatility of gray values that radiologists need to interpret mammograms from younger women. A new digital x-ray sensitive camera produces digital images on a computer screen with a higher dynamic range of gray values. Modern mammography equipment gives detailed and precise images of breast tissue, resulting in high detection levels of very small malignant tumors. The sooner a malignancy is discovered, the better the prognosis is for excision and follow-up treatment success. Advanced mammography techniques reduce the chance for misdiagnoses, the amount of radiation needed to develop the image and the time spent in the exam room.

Another improved imaging technique, sonography, uses ultrasound to create images of internal body tissues and fetuses. Ultrasound is a cheaper alternative to many other imaging techniques, and results are available almost immediately. This scanning technique is recommended for pregnant women, since the sound waves apparently cause no harm to human tissue. Refinements in sonography have led to excellent prenatal images, which can be used to detect even small abnormalities in a fetus. Sonography is also being used in other imaging applications. For example, a recent ultrasound device is capable of displaying a three-dimensional image of organs such as the heart. Ultrasound in real time has even become sensitive enough to show blood flow. Ultrasound units are common in all but the very smallest hospitals.

New ultrasound diagnostic devices are now on the market that are small enough to carry and provide doctors with a comprehensive picture of a patient's major organs and possible problems. These devices, which resemble the handheld scanners used on *Star Trek*, use ultrasonic waves to map out the interior features of a patient and then enhance them to provide an accurate and easy-to-read picture. Not only can doctors spot heart murmurs and breathing abnormalities with a simple inspection, but they can also spot objects like kidney stones and gallstones, or the presence of an abnormal amount of fluid surrounding an organ. The machines could potentially save millions in radiology and other diagnostic bills. In addition, these devices will be carried on ambulances or even on a doctor's person, allowing diagnostics to be performed wherever they are needed. The popular SonoSite M-Turbo is the size of a small laptop computer. As of mid-2017, a startup called the Butterfly Network (www.butterflynetinc.com) was investing $100 million to develop a small ultrasound scanner in which ultrasound emitters are etched directly onto a semiconductor chip. The compact, versatile unit costs a few hundred dollars and promises to create 3-D images in real time.

Ultrasound may take a giant leap forward with the advent of photoacoustic tomography, which combines sound waves with optics. Pulses of laser light are projected onto tissue which infinitesimally raises the tissue's temperature. The rise in temperature causes the tissue to expand slightly, and in the process emitting sound waves in the ultrasonic range. Sensors on the patient's skin pick up the waves which are analyzed and triangulated by computer. The resulting image may be as detailed as those derived by MRI or CT scans, but use equipment the size of an ultrasound scanner.

Another exciting monitoring technique involves measuring the levels of the chemical creatine in the heart, which indicate the extent of muscle damage caused by a heart attack. Using a combination of MRI and MRS (magnetic resonance spectroscopy), this noninvasive method allows doctors to pinpoint injured heart tissue by measuring depleted levels of creatine in areas of the heart that were difficult to view using older imaging techniques.

Some patients even carry monitoring equipment on or in their bodies for long-term diagnostic purposes relating to biochemical balances, brain and sleep disorders, heart and vascular diseases and metabolic problems. More accurate, easy-to-use equipment has been introduced. For example, Medtronic has released an implantable heart monitoring device the size of three sticks of gum. Released under the company's Reveal brand, the device can detect brief heart stoppages or other abnormalities and report them to a support network.

Light diagnostic devices have also been showing up to diagnose certain forms of cancer. Similar to spectroscopy, which has been used to analyze chemical compositions for decades, these small diagnostic devices detect cancer by finding abnormalities in the body's reaction to light. In one instance, doctors at the University of Texas at Austin found that cervical cancer could be detected using a small ultraviolet light shown on the cervix. Precancerous cells are distinctly more fluorescent than normal cells. A preliminary study showed that the technique was 50% more accurate than a PAP smear and microscope examination, reducing the need to perform further diagnostic biopsies on healthy women. In another instance of light diagnostics, researchers at the University of California, Irvine found that infrared light could assist in finding breast cancer.

***Internet Research Tip*:**
For descriptions of advanced imaging procedures, see the web site of the Radiological Society of North America at www.rsna.org.

32) Nanotechnology Makes Breakthroughs in Health Care

Nanotech research and development in the health care sector is being conducted in a variety of diagnostics and treatments. For example, Nanosphere developed a diagnostic device that can detect protein concentrations in blood samples in order to indicate cardiac problems or Alzheimer's disease that would otherwise go undetected. The firm's Verigene System is a platform using two instruments that together run a variety of assays on nucleic acids and proteins with greater depth than ever before. Its technology is based on nanoparticles. Nanosphere was acquired by Luminex Corporation in mid-2016.

On the treatment side, there are exciting developments using nanotechnology that may aid cancer treatment by delivering agents that enhance images of tumors in diagnostics, or helping deliver cancer drugs directly to tumor sites. Research at the Sanford-Burnham Institute for Medical Research in La Jolla, California on this technology used iron oxide nanoparticles coated with peptides (protein fragments) that are attracted to protein clots in tumor blood vessels.

Research scientist Rutledge Ellis-Behnke at the University of Heidelberg, Mannheim Faculty of Medicine is developing a clear gel made of nanoscale peptides that stops bleeding almost instantly. The gel forms a protective seal over wounds that provides protection from the air and supplies amino-acid building blocks that promote cell growth and repair. The human body breaks down the peptides within a few weeks so there is no need to remove the gel once the wound has healed. The first use of the technology, once approved, will likely be in operating rooms.

Researchers at Washington University in St. Louis are studying the use of the active element in bee venom (called melittin) to treat cancer. Bee venom alone does too much damage to healthy cells to be a viable treatment, but when combined with nanoparticles, the resulting product, called "nanobees," travel through the blood stream until they reach cancerous cells, which are attacked and killed. Recent tests in mice resulted in positive results for shrinking tumors and reducing precancerous lesions relating to breast cancer and melanoma. Researchers at the Washington University School of Medicine found that the treatment can also effectively destroy the HIV virus while leaving surrounding cells unharmed.

Another promising use of nanoparticles is to lower cholesterol. Northwestern University's Shad Thaxton is developing nanoparticles that are coated with fat and protein molecules that enable them to bind with cholesterol. The process mimics HDL, the so called "good cholesterol" which isolates the lipids that form artery-clogging plaque and carries them to the liver where they are broken down and made ready to excrete from the body. Thaxton's synthetic HDL could be ready for use in humans by 2020.

In 2011, researchers at IBM announced the development of a nanoparticle that has the potential to target and destroy antibiotic-resistant bacteria. IBM, working in collaboration with the Institute of Bioengineering and Nanotechnology, Singapore, is testing the technology in animal studies while it seeks a partnership with a drug company to develop the concept. In early 2013, IBM announced the discovery of a synthetic, bacteria-killing hydrogel, which is undergoing testing and further development. In 2016, the IBM/Institute of Bioengineering and Nanotechnology partnership announced the discovery of a new macromolecule with triple-play action to fight virus infection and drug resistance. The three actions are: attraction, prevention and neutralization.

Google is working on nanoparticles that attach themselves to human cells, proteins or other molecules to seek out cancer and other diseases. One of the challenges in this technology is finding coatings that will help the particles to bind to specific cells.

SPOTLIGHT: Nanopiezotronics

The field of piezoelectricity is finding exciting potential in the use of nanowires. Piezoelectricity is the ability of crystals and some ceramic materials to generate electric current in response to applied mechanical stress. In nanotechnology, tiny zinc oxide nanowires are bent with the probe of an atomic force microscope. As the nanowires spring back to their original shape, electric current is generated. Zhong Lin Wang of Georgia Tech University embedded zinc oxide nanowires in a layer of polymer. When the polymer was flexed, 50 millivolts of current was generated. Possible uses for the technology include clothing embedded with the polymer (the wearer's movement could generate enough power to run portable devices such as music players or cellphones); hearing aids that use the nanowires' current to amplify sound and send it directly to the auditory nerve; and bone loss monitors embedded in patients that would detect bone stress as mechanical strain capable of tripping the embedded nanowires.

33) Artificial Intelligence (AI), Deep Learning and Machine Learning Advance into Commercial Applications, Including Health Care and Robotics

The concept of Artificial Intelligence (often referred to as "AI") continues to evolve, as scientists and software engineers gain a greater understanding of reasonably possible goals for this technology. In 1956, John McCarthy may have been the first to use the phrase, describing artificial intelligence as "the science and engineering of making intelligent machines." This was a pretty dramatic statement, considering the barely advanced state of computers and robotics at the time.

In 1950, computer pioneer Alan Turing proposed, in a paper titled *Computing Machinery and Intelligence,* a test that could determine whether or not a machine could "think." Essentially, he suggested that, in a situation where a person asked the same questions of both a machine and a human being, if he couldn't tell the difference between text answers coming from the machine and the human in blind results, then it might be reasonable to call the machine "intelligence." The Turing Test clearly avoids any discussion of what "consciousness" is.

Gary Marcus, a scientist at New York University, proposed another test, the Ikea Construction Challenge, to see whether or not a machine could assemble a piece of Ikea furniture when provided with a pile of parts and related instructions. Near the end of 2015, a group of well-known Silicon Valley investors, including Elon Musk and Peter Thiel, announced a long-term commitment to raise funds of as much a $1 billion for a new organization to be known as OpenAI, www.openai.com. OpenAI is a nonprofit group, dedicated to moving AI ahead to the point that it "will benefit humanity."

Another well-funded AI organization is the Allen Institute for Artificial Intelligence (AI2). Located in Seattle, the group was co-founded by Paul Allen, one of the co-founders of Microsoft, and scientist Oren Etzioni. AI2 has developed its own complex test for artificial intelligence called a GeoSolver.

While the practical definition and ultimate capabilities of AI are debated, industry has put AI to work and continues to invest very heavily in advanced development. Today, AI has synergies with many highly advanced technologies such as virtual reality, factory automation, robotics, self-driving cars, speech recognition and predictive analytics.

One of the more promising advancements is called "deep learning." In 2014, Google spent nearly $600 million to acquire UK-based DeepMind, an intensive learning research group. Deep learning is sometimes referred to in conjunction with phrases such as "machine learning" and "neural networking." The main point is that software can be trained by being constantly fed data, queried as to its meaning, and receiving feedback to its responses. It is essentially training a machine to respond correctly to data of a given nature or to data within a given set of circumstances.

The most compelling opportunities for the development and use of artificial intelligence software may be in engineering/research, investment analysis and, especially, health care. Simply put, health care is one of the world's largest and fastest-growing industries, and virtually all of the government and private health initiatives that pay for health care are desperately seeking ways to improve patient care outcomes, cut billing fraud, create operating efficiencies and generally slow the growth of costs overall.

IBM, clearly one of the world's top software engineering companies, is betting big on the massive, global opportunity in health care analytics via artificial intelligence. It has created a business unit called Watson Health, based on its advanced "Watson" supercomputing-artificial intelligence hardware/software technology, combined with massive health care database firms that it has aggressively acquired at a cost of several billion dollars. In early 2016, IBM announced the acquisition of Truven Health Analytics, Inc. for $2.6 billion, for the Watson Health unit. This acquisition helped Watson Health soar to a 5,000-employee juggernaut. Truven's databases and experience when combined with IBM's technologies will enable Watson Health to analyze and look for patterns or problems in billing, patient outcomes, insurance claims, drugs and drug usage, pricing and myriad other aspects of the health care system, from a data set covering about 300 million patients. One of Watson Health's competitors in this arena is Enlitic, Inc.

The trend toward "big data," that is, the building of massive databases such as the patient data referred to above, is giving a large boost to the potential of AI. In fact, the lines are blurring between AI and the analytics software used in big data projects.

Chapter 2

HEALTH CARE STATISTICS

Including Medicare & Medicaid

Tables and Charts:

I. Health Care Industry Overview

Contents:

U.S. Health Care Industry Statistics and Market Size Overview

	Amount	Units	Year	Source
Expenditures				
National Health Care Expenditures	3,675.3	Bil. US$	2018*	CMS
In 2025	5,696.2	Bil. US$	2026*	CMS
National Health Care Expenditures per Capita	11,193	US$	2018*	CMS
National Health Care Expenditures as a Percentage of GDP	18.2	%	2018*	CMS
National Health Care Expenditures by Type:				
Hospital Care	1,189.9	Bil. US$	2018*	CMS
Physician & Clinical Services	733.9	Bil. US$	2018*	CMS
Dental Services	134.4	Bil. US$	2018*	CMS
Nursing Home and Home Health Care	277.4	Bil. US$	2018*	CMS
Prescription Drugs & Medical Products	483.9	Bil. US$	2018*	CMS
Research, Structures & Equipment Investments	171.1	Bil. US$	2018*	CMS
Total Health Care Industry Employment	16.0	Million	Jul-18	BLS
Aging				
U.S. Population Less Than 65 Years of Age	274.7	Million	2017*	Census
In 2030	282.0	Million	2030*	Census
In 2060	309.8	Million	2060*	Census
U.S. Population Age 65 Years & Older	50.9	Million	2017*	Census
In 2030	74.1	Million	2030*	Census
In 2060	94.7	Million	2060*	Census
Medicare/Medicaid				
National Health Expenditures from Medicare	748.1	Bil. US$	2018*	CMS
National Health Expenditures from Medicaid	622.0	Bil. US$	2018*	CMS
Medicare Enrollment	59.9	Million	2018*	CMS
Hospital Insurance (HI)	59.5	Million	2018*	CMS
Supplementary Medical Insurance (SMI)	54.7	Million	2018*	CMS
Part D	45.7	Million	2018*	CMS
Medicaid Enrollment	74.8	Million	2018*	CMS
Vital Statistics				
U.S. Fertility Rate	1.87	Children Born/Woman	2017*	WFB
U.S. Birth Rate	12.5	Births/1,000 Pop.	2017*	WFB
U.S. Infant Mortality Rate	5.8	Deaths/1,000 Live Births	2017*	WFB
U.S. Life Expectancy at Birth	80	Years	2017*	WFB
U.S. Death Rate	8.2	Deaths/1,000 Pop.	2017*	WFB
Obesity				
Obesity, All Adults 20 & Older[1]	31.5	%	2017	CDC
Diabetes				
Diagnosed Diabetes, Adults 18 & Older	12.2	%	2015	ADA
Diagnosed Diabetes, Adults 65 & Older	25.2	%	2015	ADA
Hospitals				
Number of U.S. Registered[2] Hospitals	5,534		2016	AHA
Staffed Beds in All U.S. Registered[2] Hospitals	894,574		2016	AHA
Admissions in All U.S. Registered[2] Hospitals	35,158,934		2016	AHA
Uninsured				
Number of People Without Health Insurance for the Entire Year	28.0	Million	2017	Census
Percent of Population	8.7	%	2017	Census

* Estimate, where appropriate includes impact of Affordable Care Act.

BLS = U.S. Bureau of Labor Statistics; CMS = U.S. Ctrs. for Medicare & Medicaid Services; WFB = CIA World Fact Book; Census = U.S. Census Bureau; CDC = U.S. Ctrs. for Disease Control & Prevention; ADA = American Diabetes Association; AHA = American Hospital Association.

[1] Age-adjusted using the projected 2000 U.S. population as the standard population and four age groups.

[2] Registered hospitals are those hospitals that meet the AHA's criteria for registration as a hospital facility and include AHA member and nonmember hospitals. For a complete listing of the criteria used for registration, please see www.aha.org.

Source: Plunkett Research,® Ltd.

Global Health Statistics, 2012-2018

Estimated Global Health Care Expenditures	Amount	Units	Year	Source
Total	9.6	Trillion$	2018	PRE
% of GDP	11.0	%	2018	PRE
Per Capita	1,250	US$	2018	PRE

Health Care Expenditures	(As a % of Total GDP)				
	2012	2013	2014	2015	Source
United States	16.36%	16.32%	16.52%	16.84%	TWB
Euro Area	10.08%	10.16%	10.22%	10.19%	TWB
OECD Members	11.79%	11.90%	12.04%	12.45%	TWB
Latin America & Caribbean	6.73%	6.83%	6.93%	7.39%	TWB
Middle East & North Africa	4.77%	4.74%	5.10%	5.45%	TWB
South Asia	3.24%	3.60%	3.53%	3.72%	TWB
Sub-Saharan Africa	5.13%	5.08%	5.01%	5.35%	TWB
East Asia & Pacific	6.96%	6.70%	6.67%	6.77%	TWB
World	**9.41%**	**9.44%**	**9.54%**	**9.90%**	TWB

Health expenditures per capita, PPP	(In Constant 2011 PPP $)				
	2012	2013	2014	2015	Source
United States	8,432.51	8,634.63	9,059.52	9,535.95	TWB
Euro Area	3,790.77	3,943.55	4,058.54	4,162.58	TWB
OECD Members	4,348.33	4,528.41	4,694.37	4,886.97	TWB
Latin America & Caribbean	961.29	1,008.89	1,052.78	1,081.34	TWB
Middle East & North Africa	825.11	884.01	988.14	1,056.62	TWB
South Asia	149.49	177.57	186.50	211.92	TWB
Sub-Saharan Africa	172.30	180.69	186.91	198.74	TWB
East Asia & Pacific	760.80	818.84	875.76	959.57	TWB
World	**1,123.26**	**1,179.71**	**1,234.02**	**1,300.11**	TWB

Life Expectancy at Birth	(In years)					
	1980	1990	2000	2015	2016	Source
United States	78.74	78.74	78.84	78.69	78.69	TWB
Euro Area	81.23	81.51	81.93	81.56	81.56	TWB
OECD Members	79.72	79.90	80.16	80.07	80.12	TWB
Latin America & Caribbean	74.69	74.91	75.13	75.34	75.54	TWB
Middle East & North Africa	72.68	72.88	73.09	73.29	73.49	TWB
South Asia	67.55	67.88	68.18	68.46	68.71	TWB
Sub-Saharan Africa	58.28	58.88	59.44	59.94	60.39	TWB
East Asia & Pacific	74.74	74.92	75.09	75.25	75.40	TWB
World	**71.22**	**71.46**	**71.69**	**71.86**	**72.04**	TWB

Infant Mortality Rate	(Per 1,000 live births)					
	1980	1990	2000	2015	2016	Source
United States	6.00	5.90	5.80	5.70	5.60	TWB
Euro Area	3.31	3.26	3.18	3.12	3.05	TWB
OECD Members	6.69	6.49	6.30	6.11	5.93	TWB
Latin America & Caribbean	16.95	16.36	15.86	15.33	14.88	TWB
Middle East & North Africa	22.00	21.49	21.02	20.55	20.11	TWB
South Asia	45.50	43.70	42.00	40.30	38.80	TWB
Sub-Saharan Africa	60.66	58.63	56.67	54.92	53.26	TWB
East Asia & Pacific	16.37	15.56	14.82	14.17	13.56	TWB
World	**34.70**	**33.60**	**32.40**	**31.40**	**30.50**	TWB

PPP = Purchasing Power Parity, an equalized price for a basket of goods across different markets. OECD = Organisation for Economic Co-operation & Development.

PRE = Plunkett Research Estimates

TWB = The World Bank: World Development Indicators & Global Development Finance, for terms of use see http://go.worldbank.org/OJC02YMLA0.

Plunkett Research,® Ltd.

www.plunkettresearch.com

Affordable Care Act Overview

In 2010
Insurance companies are no longer allowed to deny coverage to children (individuals 19 years of age and younger) with pre-existing conditions.
Individuals may remain on their parents' policies up until the age of 26.
Insurance companies may no longer charge co-payments for preventative examinations, such as colonoscopies or mammograms.
Small businesses (with under 25 employees) that provide health insurance for employees will be eligible for a 35% tax credit (25% for nonprofits).
States that choose to expand Medicaid programs will be eligible for matching federal funds.
Individuals without insurance for six months become eligible to join state-based high risk pools.
Insurance companies may not drop customers if they become sick.
Lifetime limits on insurance coverage are eliminated, and annual limits are restricted.
Insurance companies are restricted from making "unreasonable" rate hikes, which must now be justified.
In 2011
Medicare recipients will qualify for a free annual checkup.
Insurance companies must spend at least 85% of premium dollars on health care for large employer plans and at least 80% on individual and small employer plans.
A new fee is applied to pharmaceutical companies with sales over $5 million, based on market share.
In 2012
Accountable Care Organizations will be established to try to coordinate doctor-patient care and prevent diseases and reduce unnecessary hospital admissions.
Health care providers will be required to implement electronic health records.
Health care providers will be required to report performance; incentives will be provided to those that improve in quality.
In 2013
New funding becomes available to state Medicaid plans that provide expanded preventive care.
States are required to pay primary care physicians no less than 100% of Medicare payment rates in 2013 and 2014 for primary care services, with the increase fully funded by the federal government.
Payroll taxes for Medicare are increased from 1.45% to 2.35% for individuals with more than $200,000/year in income or couples with more than $250,000.
A 3.8% surtax is implemented on capital gains and dividends earned by individuals with more than $200,000 in modified adjusted gross income (MAGI) and couples with more than $250,000 in MAGI.
In 2014
Coverage under the newly established health insurance exchanges begins.
All individuals must have health coverage or pay a fee of $95 or 1% of personal income, whichever is larger. (Penalty eliminated in 2018.)
Workers meeting certain requirements who are unable to afford their employer's coverage may use the funds the employer would have paid to purchase a more affordable plan in the new insurance exchanges.
Those who earn less than 133% of the poverty level will be eligible for Medicaid, initially funded by the federal government and phasing to 90% federal funding in subsequent years.
Those between 100% and 400% of the poverty level will be eligible for insurance subsidies.
Annual and lifetime limits on insurance coverage will no longer be allowed.
Insurers cannot drop or limit coverage to individuals that choose to participate in clinical trials that treat cancer or other life-threatening diseases.
Insurance companies will no longer be able to deny coverage or charge more based on pre-existing conditions or gender.
Small businesses that wish to purchase insurance for employees will be eligible for a 50% tax credit (35% for nonprofits).
In 2015
Payments to physicians will be tied to quality of care.
Employers with at least 100 or equivalent full-time employee must offer health insurance or be subject to a penalty starting at $2,000 per employee.
The penalty for adults without health insurance increases to $325 or 2% of taxable household income. (Penalty eliminated in 2018.)
In 2016
The penalty for adults without health insurance increases to $695 or 2.5% of taxable household income.
Employers with at least 50 or equivalent full-time employees must offer health insurance or be subject to a penalty starting at $2,000 per employee.
In 2022
So-called "Cadillac Plans," which provide more than $10,200 of coverage for individuals or $27,500 for families, will have a 40% tax applied.

Source: U.S. Department of Health & Human Services
Plunkett Research,® Ltd.
www.plunkettresearch.com

Domestic & Foreign Pharmaceutical Sales, PhRMA Member Companies: 1980-2016

(In Millions of US$)

Year	Domestic Sales	APC	Sales Abroad[1]	APC	Total Sales	APC
2016	218,401.4	7.9%	103,456.8	3.4%	321,858.1	6.4%
2015	202,370.8	13.3%	100,012.5	-6.9%	302,383.3	5.7%
2014	178,645.6	1.6%	107,438.2	0.5%	286,083.9	1.2%
2013	175,759.6	-1.5%	106,880.1	-0.7%	282,639.7	-1.2%
2012	178,437.6	-5.0%	107,677.8	-8.1%	286,115.4	-6.2%
2011	187,870.7	1.7%	117,138.5	9.9%	305,009.2	4.7%
2010	184,660.3	2.0%	106,593.2	12.0%	291,253.5	5.4%
2009	181,116.8	-1.1%	95,162.5	-7.5%	276,279.3	-3.4%
2008	183,167.2	-1.1%	102,842.4	16.6%	286,009.6	4.6%
2007	185,209.2	4.2%	88,213.4	14.8%	273,422.6	7.4%
2006	177,736.3	7.0%	76,870.2	10.0%	254,606.4	7.9%
2005	166,155.5	3.4%	69,881.0	0.1%	236,036.5	2.4%
2004[2]	160,751.0	8.6%	69,806.9	14.6%	230,557.9	10.3%
2003[2]	148,038.6	6.4%	60,914.4	13.4%	208,953.0	8.4%
2002	139,136.4	6.4%	53,697.4	12.1%	192,833.8	8.0%
2001	130,715.9	12.8%	47,886.9	5.9%	178,602.8	10.9%
2000	115,881.8	14.2%	45,199.5	1.6%	161,081.3	10.4%
1999	101,461.8	24.8%	44,496.6	2.7%	145,958.4	17.1%
1998	81,289.2	13.3%	43,320.1	10.8%	124,609.4	12.4%
1997	71,761.9	10.8%	39,086.2	6.1%	110,848.1	9.1%
1996	64,741.4	13.3%	36,838.7	8.7%	101,580.1	11.6%
1995	57,145.5	12.6%	33,893.5	(3)	91,039.0	(3)
1994	50,740.4	4.4%	26,870.7	1.5%	77,611.1	3.4%
1993	48,590.9	1.0%	26,467.3	2.8%	75,058.2	1.7%
1992	48,095.5	8.6%	25,744.2	15.8%	73,839.7	11.0%
1991	44,304.5	15.1%	22,231.1	12.1%	66,535.6	14.1%
1990	38,486.7	17.7%	19,838.3	18.0%	58,325.0	17.8%
1989	32,706.6	14.4%	16,817.9	-4.7%	49,524.5	7.1%
1988	28,582.6	10.4%	17,649.3	17.1%	46,231.9	12.9%
1987	25,879.1	9.4%	15,068.4	15.6%	40,947.5	11.6%
1986	23,658.8	14.1%	13,030.5	19.9%	36,689.3	16.1%
1985	20,742.5	9.0%	10,872.3	4.0%	31,614.8	7.3%
1984	19,026.1	13.2%	10,450.9	0.4%	29,477.0	8.3%
1983	16,805.0	14.0%	10,411.2	-2.4%	27,216.2	7.1%
1982	14,743.9	16.4%	10,667.4	0.1%	25,411.3	9.0%
1981	12,665.0	7.4%	10,658.3	1.4%	23,323.3	4.6%
1980	11,788.6	10.7%	10,515.4	26.9%	22,304.0	17.8%
Average		**8.5%**		**7.2%**		**7.8%**

Notes: Total values may be affected by rounding. APC = Annual Percent Change.

[1] Sales Abroad includes sales generated outside the United States by U.S.-owned PhRMA member companies, and sales generated abroad by the U.S. divisions of foreign-owned PhRMA member companies. Sales generated abroad by the foreign divisions of foreign-owned PhRMA member companies are excluded. Domestic sales, however, includes sales generated within the United States by all PhRMA member companies; [2] Revised in 2007 to reflect updated data; [3] Sales Abroad affected by merger and acquisition activity.

Source: Pharmaceutical Research and Manufacturers of America (PhRMA), *PhRMA Annual Membership Survey*, 2017
Plunkett Research,® Ltd.
www.plunkettresearch.com

Employment in the Health Care Industry, U.S.: 2013-July 2018

(Annual Estimates in Thousands of Employed Workers)

NAICS Code[1]	Industry Sector	2013	2014	2015	2016	2017	Jul-18*
62	**Total health care & social assistance**	**17,731.1**	**18,022.2**	**18,557.4**	**19,068.8**	**19,517.0**	**19,925.8**
621,2,3	**Health care**	**14,491.5**	**14,676.5**	**15,042.3**	**15,413.5**	**15,727.8**	**16,038.1**
621	**Ambulatory health care services**	**6,476.5**	**6,631.5**	**6,855.5**	**7,080.0**	**7,296.9**	**7,501.5**
6211	Offices of physicians	2,378.0	2,411.2	2,471.0	2,526.5	2,587.4	2,638.8
621111	Offices of physicians, except mental health	2,329.2	2,360.9	2,419.6	2,473.0	2,531.7	2,580.7
621112	Offices of mental health physicians	48.8	50.3	51.4	53.4	55.6	58.2
6212	Offices of dentists	870.2	887.0	904.6	922.5	933.1	947.1
6213	Offices of other health practitioners	751.8	779.9	812.7	854.7	889.4	929.0
62131	Offices of chiropractors	126.1	127.0	129.1	133.2	137.1	141.5
62132	Offices of optometrists	120.5	123.4	127.6	132.2	134.5	136.6
62133	Offices of mental health practitioners	66.8	71.1	76.0	82.4	89.4	95.2
62134	Offices of specialty therapists	318.8	332.4	348.1	366.8	381.1	399.7
62139	Offices of all other health practitioners	119.6	126.1	131.8	140.0	147.3	155.8
621391	Offices of podiatrists	36.1	35.3	35.3	35.2	34.4	33.5
621399	Offices of miscellaneous health practitioners	83.5	90.8	96.5	104.8	112.9	122.5
6214	Outpatient care centers	731.1	763.7	805.7	853.0	896.9	933.9
62142	Outpatient mental health centers	197.5	203.7	213.5	223.9	233.9	240.2
62141,9	Outpatient care centers, except mental health	533.7	559.9	592.2	629.1	663.0	693.6
621491	HMO medical centers	174.1	176.2	182.4	193.3	203.7	214.0
621492	Kidney dialysis centers	105.6	113.0	118.7	122.9	129.4	133.4
621493	Freestanding emergency medical centers	111.9	120.3	130.4	141.1	147.7	153.0
621410,98	Miscellaneous outpatient care centers	142.2	150.5	160.7	171.9	182.2	193.1
6215	Medical & diagnostic laboratories	243.1	249.3	260.0	265.9	269.8	282.4
621511	Medical laboratories	175.8	181.4	190.3	194.8	196.3	205.7
621512	Diagnostic imaging centers	67.3	67.9	69.7	71.1	73.5	77.5
6216	Home health care services	1,230.3	1,262.4	1,314.7	1,365.3	1,415.1	1,462.4
6219	Other ambulatory health care services	272.0	278.1	286.9	292.2	305.3	308.0
62191	Ambulance services	162.9	165.1	168.5	171.4	175.1	172.8
62199	All other ambulatory health care services	109.1	113.0	118.4	120.8	130.2	134.6
621991	Blood & organ banks	69.0	69.2	69.2	69.0	72.4	75.2
621999	Miscellaneous ambulatory health care svcs.	40.1	43.8	49.1	51.8	57.8	60.0

(Continued on next page)

Employment in the Health Care Industry, U.S.: 2013-July 2018 (cont'd)

(Annual Estimates in Thousands of Employed Workers)

NAICS Code[1]	Industry Sector	2013	2014	2015	2016	2017	Jul-18*
622	**Hospitals**	**4,785.8**	**4,786.8**	**4,895.8**	**5,015.2**	**5,083.5**	**5,181.1**
6221	General medical & surgical hospitals	4,442.0	4,432.6	4,498.4	4,608.3	4,682.9	4,767.8
6222	Psychiatric & substance abuse hospitals	121.1	126.1	137.9	141.8	136.2	139.9
6223	Other hospitals	222.7	228.2	259.5	265.1	264.4	274.5
623	**Nursing & residential care facilities**	**3,229.2**	**3,258.2**	**3,290.9**	**3,318.3**	**3,347.3**	**3,355.5**
6231	Nursing care facilities	1,653.8	1,650.3	1,648.3	1,641.5	1,628.7	1,608.7
6232	Residential mental health facilities	594.4	603.7	607.0	616.1	629.0	634.1
62321	Residential intellectual & developmental disability facilities	390.2	394.1	392.6	395.3	401.6	399.9
62322	Residential mental & substance abuse care	204.3	209.6	214.3	220.8	227.5	234.7
6233	Community care facilities for the elderly	821.7	843.8	873.3	896.1	921.1	941.3
623311	Continuing care retirement communities	440.1	448.5	465.7	477.1	492.4	504.2
623212	Assisted living facilities for the elderly	381.7	395.3	407.6	419.0	428.7	437.0
6239	Other residential care facilities	159.2	160.4	162.4	164.6	168.5	171.5
624	**Social assistance**	**3,239.6**	**3,345.6**	**3,515.1**	**3,655.3**	**3,789.2**	**3,887.7**
6241	Individual & family services	1,901.2	2,009.1	2,144.1	2,241.7	2,343.5	2,435.1
62411	Child & youth services	178.4	183.0	187.6	189.9	195.2	198.4
62412	Services for the elderly & disabled	1,347.0	1,444.4	1,558.1	1,637.2	1,716.9	1,787.2
62419	Other individual & family services	375.7	381.8	398.3	414.6	431.4	448.8

[1] For a full description of the NAICS codes used in this table, see www.census.gov/eos/www/naics/.

* Preliminary estimate, seasonally adjusted.

Source: U.S. Bureau of Labor Statistics
Plunkett Research,® Ltd.
www.plunkettresearch.com

Employment & Earnings in Health Care Practitioner & Technical Occupations, U.S.: May 2017

(Wage & Salary in US$; Latest Year Available)

	Employment[1]	Median Hourly Wage	Mean Hourly Wage	Mean Annual Salary[2]	Mean Wage RSE[3] (%)
Health Diagnosing and Treating Practitioners	**5,269,630**	**38.21**	**48.45**	**100,780**	**0.3%**
Chiropractors	33,630	33.00	40.07	83,350	1.9%
Dentists, General	110,400	72.81	83.71	174,110	1.2%
Oral and Maxillofacial Surgeons	4,800	(4)	116.70	242,740	3.7%
Orthodontists	5,080	(4)	110.28	229,380	3.7%
Dietitians and Nutritionists	62,980	28.56	28.92	60,150	0.4%
Optometrists	37,240	53.03	57.26	119,100	1.2%
Pharmacists	309,330	59.70	58.52	121,710	0.3%
Anesthesiologists	30,590	(4)	127.88	265,990	1.6%
Family and General Practitioners	126,440	95.55	100.27	208,560	1.0%
Internists, General	42,280	93	95.37	198,370	2.5%
Obstetricians and Gynecologists	18,880	(4)	113.10	235,240	1.4%
Pediatricians, General	28,990	83.00	90.16	187,540	1.4%
Psychiatrists	25,250	-5.00	103.89	216,090	1.6%
Surgeons	38,600	(4)	121.10	251,890	1.3%
Physicians and Surgeons, All Other	355,460	(4)	101.63	211,390	0.8%
Physician Assistants	109,220	50.41	50.37	104,760	0.4%
Podiatrists	9,670	61.41	71.38	148,470	2.2%
Occupational Therapists	126,050	40.00	40.69	84,640	0.4%
Physical Therapists	225,420	41.76	42.34	88,080	0.3%
Radiation Therapists	17,250	38.73	40.96	85,190	0.6%
Respiratory Therapists	128,250	28.71	29.72	61,810	0.3%
Speech-Language Pathologists	142,360	36.83	38.35	79,770	0.5%
Veterinarians	69,370	43.47	48.81	101,530	1.1%
Registered Nurses	2,906,840	33.65	35.36	73,550	0.2%
Audiologists	12,020	36.50	38.48	80,040	1.5%
Health Technologists and Technicians	3,075,910	20.95	22.74	47,310	0.2%
Clinical Laboratory Technologists and Technicians	322,380	24.89	25.59	53,230	0.3%
Dental Hygienists	211,600	35.61	35.91	74,680	0.5%
Cardiovascular Technologists and Technicians	56,130	26.57	27.52	57,250	0.6%
Diagnostic Medical Sonographers	68,750	34.33	35.19	73,200	0.5%
Nuclear Medicine Technologists	18,930	36.38	37.33	77,660	0.4%
Radiologic Technologists	201,200	28.10	29.00	60,320	0.3%
Emergency Medical Technicians and Paramedics	251,860	16.05	17.64	36,700	0.7%
Pharmacy Technicians	417,720	15.26	15.90	33,060	0.3%
Psychiatric Technicians	66,930	15.23	17.34	36,070	1.2%
Respiratory Therapy Technicians	9,600	24.21	24.47	50,900	1.0%
Surgical Technologists	106,470	22.26	23.11	48,060	0.3%
Veterinary Technologists and Technicians	103,430	16.06	16.69	34,710	0.6%
Licensed Practical and Licensed Vocational Nurses	702,700	21.65	21.98	45,710	0.2%
Medical Records and Health Information Technicians	204,220	18.83	20.59	42,820	0.4%
Opticians, Dispensing	75,450	17.43	18.79	39,070	1.0%
Occupational Health and Safety Specialists	81,330	34.51	35.38	73,600	0.3%
Occupational Health and Safety Technicians	17,490	24.02	25.93	53,930	0.7%

[1] Estimates for detailed occupations do not sum to the totals because the totals include occupations not shown separately. Estimates do not include self-employed workers. [2]Annual wages have been calculated by multiplying the hourly mean wage by a "year-round, full-time" hours figure of 2,080 hours; for those occupations where there is not an hourly mean wage published, the annual wage has been directly calculated from the reported survey data. [3]The relative standard error (RSE) is a measure of the reliability of a survey statistic. The smaller the relative standard error, the more precise the estimate. [4]This wage is equal to or greater than $100.00 per hour.

Source: U.S. Bureau of Labor Statistics
Plunkett Research,® Ltd.
www.plunkettresearch.com

Employment & Earnings in Health Care Support Occupations, U.S.: May 2017

(Wage & Salary in US$; Latest Year Available)

	Employ-ment[1]	Median Hourly Wage	Mean Hourly Wage	Mean Annual Salary[2]	Mean Wage RSE[3] (%)
Healthcare Support Occupations	**4,113,410**	**13.80**	**15.05**	**31,310**	**0.2%**
Home Health Aides	820,960	11.16	11.67	24,280	0.4%
Psychiatric Aides	65,770	13.04	14.10	29,330	0.9%
Nursing Assistants	1,453,670	13.23	13.72	28,540	0.2%
Orderlies	52,630	13.07	13.94	28,990	0.6%
Occupational Therapy Assistants	41,650	28.51	28.59	59,470	0.6%
Occupational Therapy Aides	7,740	14.04	16.24	33,780	3.1%
Physical Therapist Assistants	90,170	27.61	27.70	57,620	0.4%
Physical Therapist Aides	49,290	12.37	13.42	27,910	0.8%
Massage Therapists	103,300	19.23	21.61	44,950	1.2%
Dental Assistants	337,160	18.09	18.60	38,690	0.4%
Medical Assistants	646,320	15.61	16.15	33,580	0.2%
Medical Equipment Preparers	53,920	17.00	17.82	37,060	0.4%
Medical Transcriptionists	55,880	16.95	17.50	36,400	1.2%
Pharmacy Aides	35,960	12.56	13.96	29,030	1.2%
Veterinary Assistants and Laboratory Animal Caretakers	84,400	12.57	13.26	27,570	0.6%
Phlebotomists	122,550	16.19	16.69	34,710	0.3%
Healthcare Support Workers, All Other	92,030	17.89	18.56	38,600	0.9%

[1] Estimates for detailed occupations do not sum to the totals because the totals include occupations not shown separately. Estimates do not include self-employed workers.

[2] Annual wages have been calculated by multiplying the hourly mean wage by a "year-round, full-time" hours figure of 2,080 hours; for those occupations where there is not an hourly mean wage published, the annual wage has been directly calculated from the reported survey data.

[3] The relative standard error (RSE) is a measure of the reliability of a survey statistic. The smaller the relative standard error, the more precise the estimate.

Source: U.S. Bureau of Labor Statistics
Plunkett Research,® Ltd.
www.plunkettresearch.com

The U.S. Drug Discovery & Approval Process

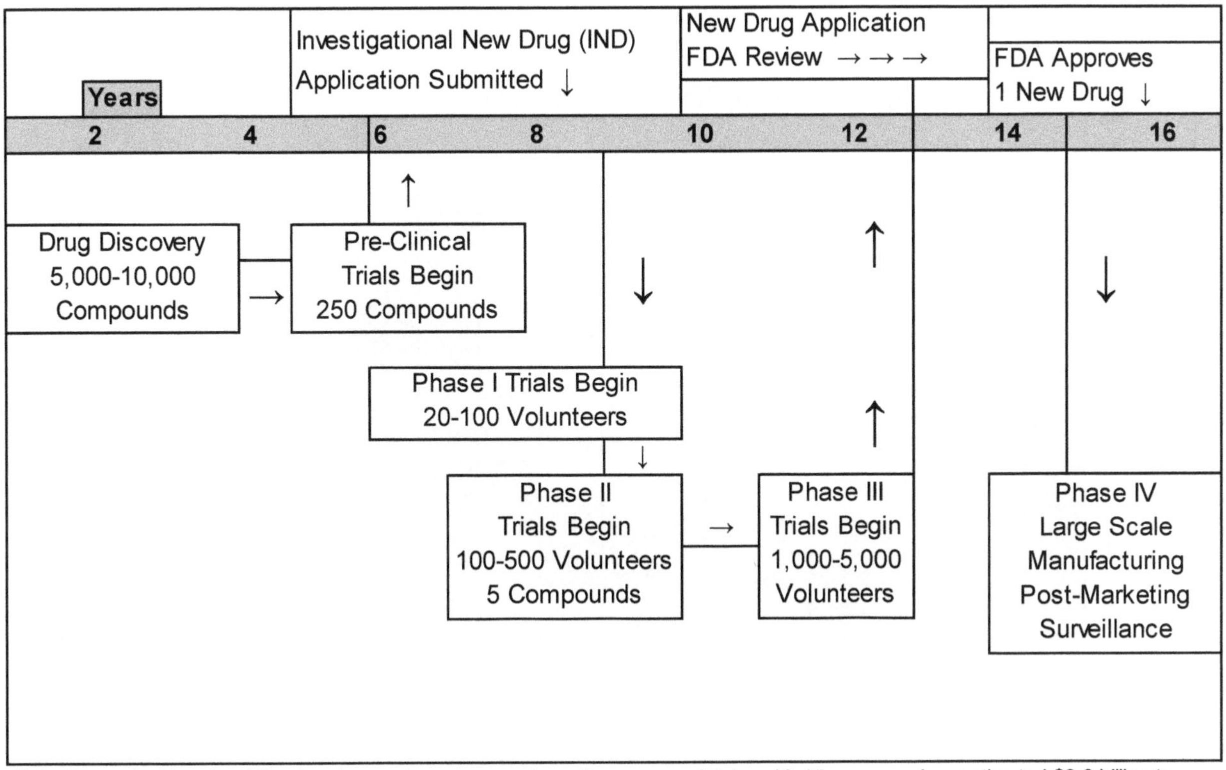

Note: The actual length of the development process varies. On average, it takes 10-15 years and an estimated $2.6 billion to create a successful new medicine (in 2013 dollars). Less than 12% of the candidate medicines that make it into phase I clinical trials will be approved by the FDA.

Source: Pharmaceutical Research and Manufacturers Association (PhRMA)
Plunkett Research, ® Ltd.
www.plunkettresearch.com

U.S. FDA New Drug (NDA) and Biologic (BLA) Approvals, 2017

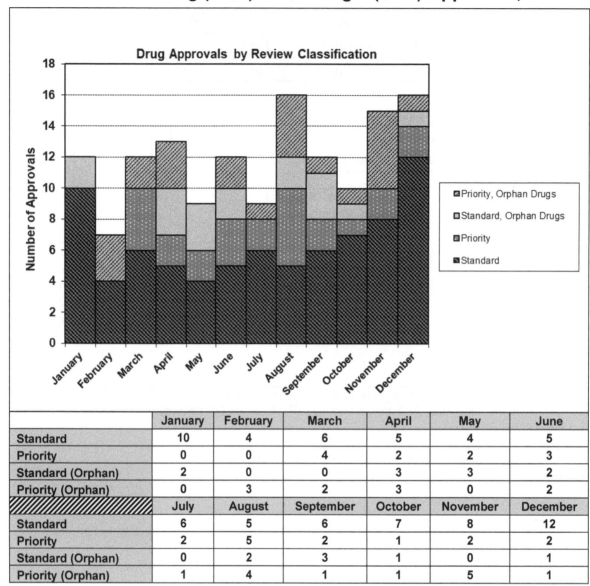

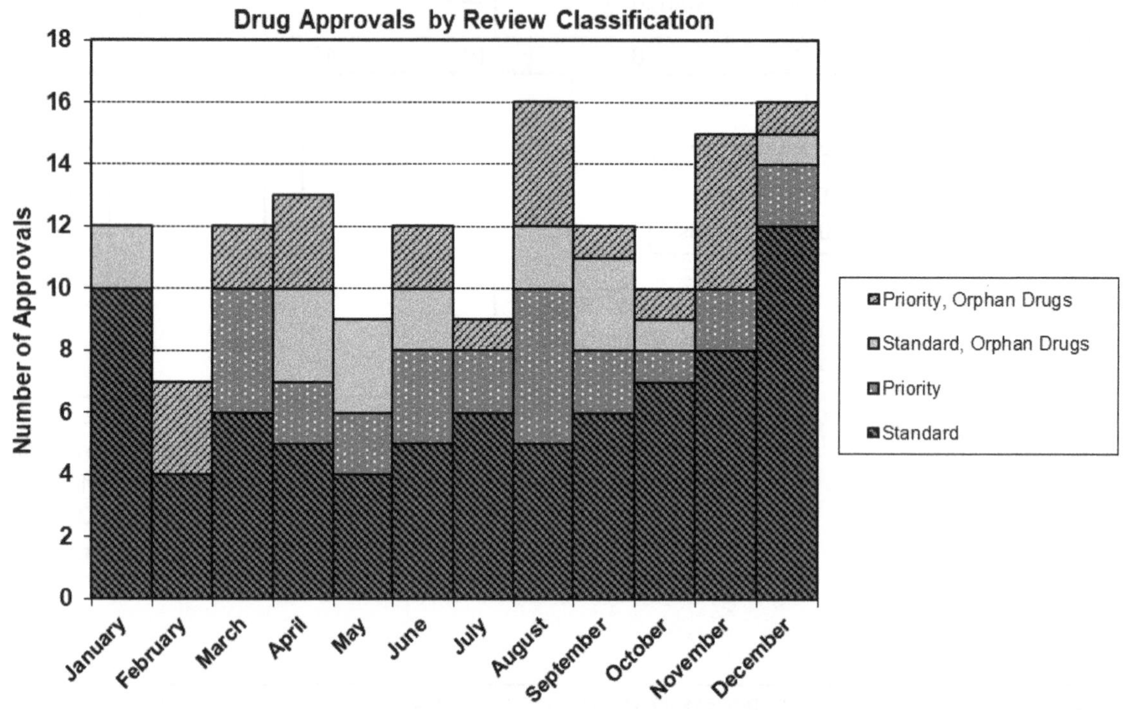

	January	February	March	April	May	June
Standard	10	4	6	5	4	5
Priority	0	0	4	2	2	3
Standard (Orphan)	2	0	0	3	3	2
Priority (Orphan)	0	3	2	3	0	2
	July	August	September	October	November	December
Standard	6	5	6	7	8	12
Priority	2	5	2	1	2	2
Standard (Orphan)	0	2	3	1	0	1
Priority (Orphan)	1	4	1	1	5	1

Notes: Priority Review classifies drugs that are a significant improvement compared to marketed products, in the treatment, diagnosis, or prevention of a disease. Standard Review classifies drugs that do not qualify for priority review. Orphan Designation is assigned to drugs pursuant to Section 526 of the Orphan Drug Act (Public Law 97-414 as amended). Data refers to CDER's approvals of New Drug Applications (NDAs) and Biologic License Applications (BLAs).

An NDA is an application requesting FDA approval, after completion of the all-important Phase III Clinical Trials, to market a new drug for human use in the U.S. The drug may contain chemical compounds that were previously approved by the FDA as distinct molecular entities suitable for use in drug trials (NMEs). Generally, more NDAs are approved yearly than NMEs. A "biologic" is a drug developed through bioengineering of a living organism (biotechnology). The approval to market a new biologic is obtained under a "BLA" or Biologics License Application.

Source: U.S. Food & Drug Administration (FDA)
Plunkett Research,® Ltd.
www.plunkettresearch.com

Federal R&D & R&D Plant Funding for Health and Human Services, U.S.: Fiscal Years 2017-2019

(In Millions of US$; Latest Year Available)

	2017 Actual	2018 Estimated[1]	2019 Proposed	Change, 2018-19	
				Dollar	Percent
Total	34,222	33,772	24,742	–9,030	–27%
Administration for Children and Families	16	5	89	84	1680%
Centers for Disease Control and Prevention	511	464	296	–168	–36%
Centers for Medicare and Medicaid Services	278	19	17	–2	–11%
Departmental Management	116	131	158	27	21%
Food and Drug Administration	390	410	410	0	0%
Health Resources and Services Administration	30	30	22	–8	–27%
National Institutes of Health[2]	32,881	32,713	23,750	–8,963	–27%

Notes: This table shows funding levels for Departments or Independent agencies with more than $200 million in R&D activities in 2019. Detail may not add to total because of rounding.

[1]Because an appropriation for FY 2018 was not passed by the time this chapter went to print, the chapter calculates FY 2018 estimates using an annualized version of the FY 2018 Continuing Resolution.

[2]The FY 2019 Budget proposes to consolidate the activities of the Agency for Healthcare Research and Quality (AHRQ) within NIH. The NIH total includes R&D funding that previously occurred in AHRQ.

Source: EOP, OMB, Analytical Perspectives, Budget of the United States Government, Fiscal Year 2019
Plunkett Research,® Ltd.
www.plunkettresearch.com

II. U.S. Health Care Expenditures & Costs

Contents:

The Nation's Health Dollar: 2018
Where It Came From (Estimated)

($3.68 Trillion Total, Figures in Billions)

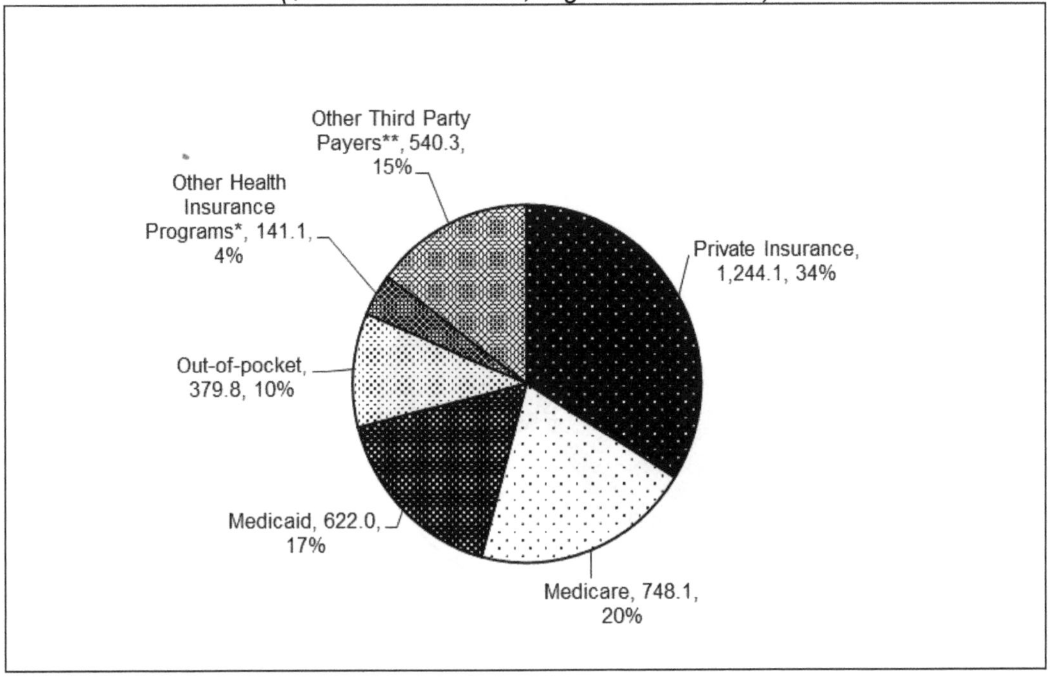

* Includes Children's Health Insurance Program (Titles XIX and XXI), Department of Defense, and Department of Veterans' Affairs. ** Includes worksite health care, other private revenues, Indian Health Service, workers' compensation, general assistance, maternal and child health, vocational rehabilitation, other federal programs, Substance Abuse and Mental Health Services Administration, other state and local programs, and school health.

Source: Centers for Medicare & Medicaid Services, Office of the Actuary
Plunkett Research,® Ltd.
www.plunkettresearch.com

The Nation's Health Dollar: 2018
Where It Went (Estimated)

($3.68 Trillion, Figures in Billions)

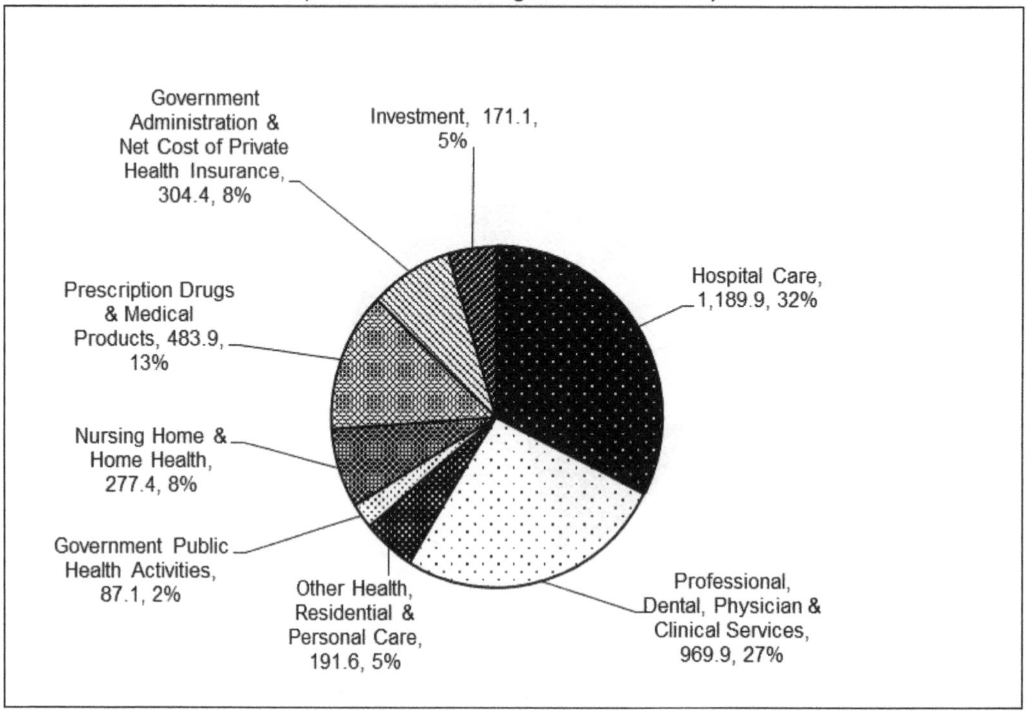

Source: Centers for Medicare & Medicaid Services, Office of the Actuary
Plunkett Research,® Ltd.
www.plunkettresearch.com

National Health Expenditures & Annual Percent Change, U.S.: 2010-2026

(By Source of Funds)

Year	Total	Out-of-Pocket Payments	Health Insurance					Other Third Party Payers[2]
			Total	Private Health Insurance	Medicare	Medicaid	Other Health Insurance[1]	
Amount in Billions of US$ (Historical Estimates)								
2010	2,598.8	299.7	1,876.9	864.3	519.8	397.2	95.6	422.2
2011	2,689.3	310.0	1,950.2	898.6	544.7	406.7	100.1	429.2
2012	2,797.3	318.3	2,022.9	928.2	569.6	422.7	102.4	456.0
2013	2,879.0	325.2	2,087.8	946.4	590.2	445.4	105.9	466.0
2014	3,026.2	330.1	2,228.1	999.9	618.9	496.6	112.7	468.0
2015	3,200.8	339.3	2,382.8	1,068.8	648.8	544.1	121.1	478.7
2016	3,337.2	352.5	2,486.8	1,123.4	672.1	565.5	125.8	497.9
(Projected)								
2017	3,489.2	365.3	2,607.3	1,186.6	705.8	582.0	132.8	516.6
2018	3,675.3	379.8	2,755.2	1,244.1	748.1	622.0	141.1	540.3
2019	3,867.6	398.3	2,898.9	1,286.0	807.6	656.3	149.1	570.4
2020	4,090.9	417.3	3,075.6	1,348.8	873.1	696.4	157.3	598.1
2021	4,322.0	436.7	3,258.3	1,410.9	942.6	738.4	166.4	627.0
2022	4,561.8	459.2	3,446.3	1,472.9	1,015.7	782.4	175.3	656.3
2023	4,818.5	482.0	3,649.4	1,544.4	1,092.5	828.3	184.2	687.1
2024	5,090.9	506.0	3,866.0	1,619.8	1,175.9	877.0	193.3	718.9
2025	5,369.8	530.7	4,086.2	1,697.7	1,253.0	932.8	202.8	752.8
2026	5,696.2	555.3	4,351.9	1,776.0	1,366.0	996.2	213.8	789.0
Annual Percent Change from Previous Year (Historical Estimates)								
2010	—	—	—	—	—	—	—	—
2011	3.5	3.4	3.9	4.0	4.8	2.4	4.8	1.7
2012	4.0	2.7	3.7	3.3	4.6	3.9	2.2	6.3
2013	2.9	2.2	3.2	2.0	3.6	5.4	3.4	2.2
2014	5.1	1.5	6.7	5.7	4.9	11.5	6.4	0.4
2015	5.8	2.8	6.9	6.9	4.8	9.5	7.5	2.3
2016	4.3	3.9	4.4	5.1	3.6	3.9	3.9	4.0
(Projected)								
2017	4.6	3.6	4.8	5.6	5.0	2.9	5.5	3.8
2018	5.3	4.0	5.7	4.8	6.0	6.9	6.2	4.6
2019	5.2	4.9	5.2	3.4	8.0	5.5	5.7	5.6
2020	5.8	4.8	6.1	4.9	8.1	6.1	5.5	4.9
2021	5.6	4.7	5.9	4.6	8.0	6.0	5.8	4.8
2022	5.5	5.2	5.8	4.4	7.8	6.0	5.3	4.7
2023	5.6	5.0	5.9	4.9	7.6	5.9	5.1	4.7
2024	5.7	5.0	5.9	4.9	7.6	5.9	4.9	4.6
2025	5.5	4.9	5.7	4.8	6.6	6.4	4.9	4.7
2026	6.1	4.6	6.5	4.6	9.0	6.8	5.4	4.8

[1] Includes Children's Health Insurance Program (Titles XIX and XXI), Department of Defense, and Department of Veterans' Affairs. [2] Includes worksite health care, other private revenues, Indian Health Service, workers' compensation, general assistance, maternal and child health, vocational rehabilitation, other federal programs, Substance Abuse and Mental Health Services Administration, other state and local programs, and school health.

Source: Centers for Medicare & Medicaid Services, Office of the Actuary

Plunkett Research,® Ltd.

www.plunkettresearch.com

National Health Expenditures by Type of Expenditure with Affordable Care Act Impacts, U.S.: Selected Calendar Years, 2010-2026

(In Billions of US$)

Item	2010	2012	2014	2016	2018	2020	2022	2024	2026
National Health Expenditures	2,598.8	2,797.3	3,026.2	3,337.2	3,675.3	4,090.9	4,561.8	5,090.9	5,696.2
Health Consumption Expenditures	2,456.1	2,644.0	2,876.4	3,179.8	3,504.3	3,901.7	4,351.7	4,858.0	5,437.1
Personal Health Care	2,196.0	2,366.9	2,560.2	2,834.0	3,112.7	3,466.3	3,868.9	4,320.2	4,836.3
Hospital Care	822.3	902.5	978.1	1,082.5	1,189.9	1,326.4	1,478.3	1,645.3	1,848.2
Professional Services	688.3	743.2	792.5	881.2	969.9	1,074.9	1,188.4	1,317.1	1,457.8
Physician & Clinical Services	512.6	557.1	595.7	664.9	733.9	814.2	900.7	999.9	1,110.2
Other Professional Services	69.9	76.4	83.0	92.0	101.6	113.7	126.4	140.7	155.6
Dental Services	105.9	109.7	113.8	124.4	134.4	147.0	161.2	176.5	192.0
Other Health, Residential & Personal Care	129.1	139.1	151.6	173.5	191.6	214.4	240.8	269.5	301.1
Home Health Care	71.6	78.1	84.0	92.4	102.8	117.1	133.3	151.3	172.6
Nursing Care Facilities & Continuing Care Retirement Communities	140.5	147.4	152.4	162.7	174.6	191.9	211.9	234.8	261.0
Retail Sales of Medical Prod.	344.3	356.6	401.7	441.7	483.9	541.6	616.3	702.1	795.6
Prescription Drugs	253.1	259.2	298.0	328.6	360.2	404.4	462.5	530.1	604.8
Other Medical Products	91.2	97.4	103.7	113.2	123.6	137.3	153.8	172.0	190.8
Durable Medical Equipment	39.9	43.7	46.7	51.0	55.7	62.4	70.7	79.7	89.1
Other Non-Durable Medical Prod.	51.2	53.7	57.0	62.2	68.0	74.9	83.1	92.4	101.7
Government Administration	30.0	33.8	41.0	43.8	48.1	54.5	61.9	70.4	81.2
Net Cost of Private Health Insurance	154.4	165.9	195.8	219.8	256.3	288.9	323.4	363.8	408.6
Govt. Public Health Activities	75.6	77.4	79.4	82.2	87.1	92.1	97.5	103.5	110.9
Investment	142.7	153.2	149.7	157.4	171.1	189.2	210.1	232.9	259.2
Research[1]	49.2	48.4	45.9	47.7	52.9	58.1	64.0	70.4	78.4
Structures & Equipment	93.5	104.8	103.8	109.7	118.2	131.2	146.1	162.5	180.7

Note: Numbers may not add to totals because of rounding. Figures for 2018-2026 are forecasts.

[1] Research and development expenditures of drug companies and other manufacturers and providers of medical equipment and supplies are excluded from research expenditures. These research expenditures are implicitly included in the expenditure class in which the product falls, in that they are covered by the payment received for that product.

Source: Centers for Medicare & Medicaid Services, Office of the Actuary
Plunkett Research, ®Ltd.
www.plunkettresearch.com

Hospital Care Expenditures & Annual Percent Change, U.S.: 2010-2026

(By Source of Funds)

Year	Total	Out-of-Pocket Payments	Health Insurance					Other Third Party Payers[2]
			Total	Private Health Insurance	Medicare	Medicaid	Other Health Insurance[1]	
			Amount in Billions of US$ (Historical Estimates)					
2010	822.3	27.8	714.0	300.6	220.3	141.8	51.4	80.5
2011	851.9	29.3	740.8	316.7	226.9	143.9	53.3	81.7
2012	902.5	31.8	780.2	337.8	238.2	149.8	54.3	90.5
2013	937.6	33.8	808.1	349.5	246.0	155.7	56.9	95.7
2014	978.1	32.9	849.3	366.6	252.9	169.0	60.8	95.9
2015	1,033.4	31.2	907.9	400.2	260.0	183.6	64.1	94.4
2016	1,082.5	32.7	951.1	426.7	267.5	189.8	67.1	98.7
				(Projected)				
2017	1,132.6	34.2	995.7	451.1	277.5	196.2	70.8	102.7
2018	1,189.9	35.9	1,046.4	472.3	291.8	206.6	75.7	107.6
2019	1,256.0	38.0	1,102.9	491.4	314.2	216.9	80.5	115.1
2020	1,326.4	39.9	1,165.9	512.9	339.6	228.0	85.4	120.6
2021	1,401.7	41.6	1,234.0	536.0	367.0	240.3	90.7	126.1
2022	1,478.3	43.5	1,303.7	559.3	395.5	253.3	95.7	131.1
2023	1,559.8	45.5	1,378.2	585.5	425.3	266.8	100.6	136.1
2024	1,645.3	47.5	1,456.7	612.7	456.8	281.5	105.6	141.1
2025	1,735.5	49.7	1,539.4	641.4	486.0	301.2	110.9	146.4
2026	1,848.2	51.9	1,644.6	670.0	530.5	327.0	117.0	151.7
			Annual Percent Change from Previous Year (Historical Estimates)					
2010	—	—	—	—	—	—	—	—
2011	3.6	5.5	3.8	5.4	3.0	1.5	3.9	1.5
2012	6.0	8.7	5.3	6.7	5.0	4.1	1.9	10.8
2013	3.9	6.3	3.6	3.5	3.3	3.9	4.6	5.7
2014	4.3	-2.8	5.1	4.9	2.8	8.5	6.8	0.2
2015	5.7	-5.1	6.9	9.2	2.8	8.6	5.5	-1.6
2016	4.7	4.8	4.8	6.6	2.9	3.4	4.7	4.6
				(Projected)				
2017	4.6	4.8	4.7	5.7	3.8	3.4	5.5	4.0
2018	5.1	4.8	5.1	4.7	5.1	5.3	6.8	4.8
2019	5.6	5.9	5.4	4.0	7.7	5.0	6.3	7.0
2020	5.6	4.9	5.7	4.4	8.1	5.1	6.1	4.8
2021	5.7	4.4	5.8	4.5	8.1	5.4	6.2	4.5
2022	5.5	4.6	5.6	4.3	7.8	5.4	5.5	4.0
2023	5.5	4.6	5.7	4.7	7.5	5.4	5.2	3.8
2024	5.5	4.4	5.7	4.6	7.4	5.5	5.0	3.7
2025	5.5	4.5	5.7	4.7	6.4	7.0	5.0	3.7
2026	6.5	4.4	6.8	4.5	9.2	8.6	5.5	3.6

[1] Children's Health Insurance Program (Titles XIX and XXI), Department of Defense, and Department of Veterans' Affairs. [2] Includes worksite health care, other private revenues, Indian Health Service, workers' compensation, general assistance, maternal and child health, vocational rehabilitation, other federal programs, Substance Abuse and Mental Health Services Administration, other state and local programs, and school health.

Source: Centers for Medicare & Medicaid Services, Office of the Actuary
Plunkett Research, ® Ltd.
www.plunkettresearch.com

Nursing Home Care Expenditures & Annual Percent Change, U.S.: 2010-2026

(By Source of Funds)

Year	Total	Out-of-Pocket Payments	Health Insurance					Other Third Party Payers[2]
			Total	Private Health Insurance	Medicare	Medicaid	Other Health Insurance[1]	
Amount in Billions of US$ (Historical Estimates)								
2010	140.5	37.5	93.4	10.7	32.3	46.3	4.1	9.6
2011	145.4	37.1	98.7	11.0	35.8	47.6	4.3	9.5
2012	147.4	39.2	97.7	11.6	34.0	47.7	4.4	10.5
2013	149.0	39.3	99.0	11.7	34.7	48.1	4.5	10.7
2014	152.4	39.6	101.7	12.2	35.6	49.1	4.7	11.2
2015	158.1	41.4	105.5	14.0	37.0	49.5	5.0	11.1
2016	162.7	43.8	107.3	14.8	37.5	50.0	5.1	11.6
(Projected)								
2017	168.1	45.6	110.4	15.5	39.6	50.0	5.4	12.0
2018	174.6	46.8	115.5	16.1	41.8	51.9	5.7	12.3
2019	182.7	48.6	121.3	17.0	45.1	53.5	5.9	12.8
2020	191.9	50.3	128.4	17.8	48.8	55.7	6.1	13.2
2021	201.6	51.9	136.1	18.6	53.0	58.2	6.3	13.6
2022	211.9	53.6	144.2	19.4	57.6	60.7	6.5	14.0
2023	223.0	55.7	152.8	20.4	62.6	63.1	6.7	14.5
2024	234.8	57.9	161.8	21.4	67.8	65.6	6.9	15.1
2025	246.8	60.3	170.8	22.5	72.9	68.2	7.1	15.7
2026	261.0	62.7	182.1	23.5	80.4	70.9	7.3	16.2
Annual Percent Change from Previous Year (Historical Estimates)								
2010	—	—	—	—	—	—	—	—
2011	3.5	-0.9	5.7	2.3	10.8	2.8	6.5	-0.7
2012	1.4	5.4	-1.0	5.6	-4.9	0.2	2.0	10.4
2013	1.1	0.5	1.3	0.8	2.2	0.8	2.3	1.7
2014	2.3	0.5	2.7	4.8	2.5	2.1	5.3	4.4
2015	3.7	4.7	3.8	14.3	4.0	0.9	5.4	-0.6
2016	2.9	5.7	1.7	5.9	1.2	0.9	1.2	4.1
(Projected)								
2017	3.3	4.2	2.9	4.8	5.7	0.0	6.0	3.9
2018	3.9	2.7	4.5	3.9	5.5	3.8	5.9	2.3
2019	4.6	3.8	5.1	5.2	7.8	3.1	3.1	3.7
2020	5.0	3.5	5.8	4.8	8.4	4.2	3.5	3.2
2021	5.1	3.2	6.0	4.5	8.5	4.5	4.4	3.0
2022	5.1	3.3	6.0	4.7	8.7	4.3	3.5	3.2
2023	5.3	3.8	5.9	5.0	8.6	4.1	3.0	3.7
2024	5.3	4.0	5.9	5.1	8.4	4.0	2.6	3.9
2025	5.1	4.1	5.6	5.1	7.6	4.0	2.6	4.0
2026	5.7	3.9	6.6	4.3	10.2	3.8	3.2	3.4

[1] Includes Children's Health Insurance Program (Titles XIX and XXI), Department of Defense, and Department of Veterans' Affairs. [2] Includes worksite health care, other private revenues, Indian Health Service, workers' compensation, general assistance, maternal and child health, vocational rehabilitation, other federal programs, Substance Abuse and Mental Health Services Administration, other state and local programs, and school health.

Source: Centers for Medicare & Medicaid Services, Office of the Actuary
Plunkett Research, ® Ltd.
www.plunkettresearch.com

Home Health Care Expenditures & Annual Percent Change, U.S.: 2010-2026

(By Source of Funds)

Year	Total	Out-of-Pocket Payments	Health Insurance					Other Third Party Payers[2]
			Total	Private Health Insurance	Medicare	Medicaid	Other Health Insurance[1]	
Amount in Billions of US$ (Historical Estimates)								
2010	71.6	6.0	63.3	5.3	31.7	25.9	0.4	2.3
2011	74.6	6.9	65.4	5.8	32.1	27.1	0.4	2.4
2012	78.1	7.2	68.3	6.8	33.4	27.7	0.4	2.5
2013	80.5	7.4	70.6	7.8	33.7	28.7	0.4	2.5
2014	84.0	7.8	73.8	8.8	34.3	30.2	0.5	2.4
2015	88.8	8.0	78.4	9.4	35.8	32.5	0.7	2.4
2016	92.4	8.1	81.7	9.6	37.4	34.0	0.7	2.6
(Projected)								
2017	97.1	8.3	86.0	10.1	39.4	35.7	0.8	2.8
2018	102.8	8.5	91.4	10.5	41.8	38.3	0.8	2.9
2019	109.7	8.8	97.8	11.0	45.2	40.7	0.9	3.1
2020	117.1	9.2	104.6	11.5	48.9	43.3	1.0	3.2
2021	125.0	9.6	112.0	11.9	52.9	46.1	1.0	3.4
2022	133.3	10.0	119.7	12.4	57.0	49.2	1.1	3.6
2023	142.1	10.4	127.9	12.9	61.5	52.3	1.2	3.8
2024	151.3	10.8	136.5	13.4	66.2	55.6	1.3	4.0
2025	160.9	11.2	145.4	13.9	71.0	59.2	1.4	4.3
2026	172.6	11.7	156.4	14.3	77.7	62.8	1.5	4.5
Annual Percent Change from Previous Year (Historical Estimates)								
2010	—	—	—	—	—	—	—	—
2011	4.2	14.4	3.2	8.3	1.3	4.4	9.0	4.7
2012	4.7	4.7	4.5	18.7	3.8	2.4	3.1	7.8
2013	3.1	2.6	3.3	14.2	0.9	3.3	6.9	0.1
2014	4.3	4.9	4.6	12.9	2.0	5.2	8.7	-5.0
2015	5.8	3.1	6.2	6.6	4.3	7.7	45.8	1.1
2016	4.0	0.5	4.3	2.8	4.3	4.6	5.1	6.4
(Projected)								
2017	5.1	2.8	5.3	5.0	5.5	5.1	5.4	6.7
2018	5.9	2.7	6.3	3.9	6.0	7.2	8.9	4.4
2019	6.7	4.1	7.0	5.0	8.1	6.4	7.6	5.5
2020	6.7	4.2	7.0	4.2	8.2	6.4	8.0	5.7
2021	6.7	3.9	7.0	3.8	8.1	6.6	8.5	5.8
2022	6.6	4.0	6.9	3.7	7.9	6.5	8.0	5.6
2023	6.6	4.1	6.8	3.9	7.8	6.4	8.0	5.7
2024	6.5	4.1	6.7	3.9	7.6	6.4	7.9	5.7
2025	6.3	4.0	6.5	3.6	7.2	6.3	8.0	5.6
2026	7.3	3.9	7.6	3.5	9.6	6.2	8.5	5.7

[1] Includes Children's Health Insurance Program (Titles XIX and XXI), Department of Defense, and Department of Veterans' Affairs. [2] Includes worksite health care, other private revenues, Indian Health Service, workers' compensation, general assistance, maternal and child health, vocational rehabilitation, other federal programs, Substance Abuse and Mental Health Services Administration, other state and local programs, and school health.

Source: Centers for Medicare & Medicaid Services, Office of the Actuary

Plunkett Research, ® Ltd.

www.plunkettresearch.com

Prescription Drug Expenditures, U.S.: 1996-2026

(In Billions of US$)

Year	Total	Out-of-Pocket Payments	Health Insurance					Other Third Party Payers[2]
			Total	Private Health Insurance	Medicare	Medicaid	Other Health Insurance Programs[1]	
Historical Estimates								
1996	68.1	24.5	42.3	29.9	1.0	10.8	0.5	1.4
1997	77.6	26.0	50.1	35.9	1.3	12.2	0.7	1.5
1998	88.4	27.8	58.9	42.3	1.6	14.0	1.0	1.7
1999	104.7	30.9	71.9	51.9	1.9	16.6	1.5	1.9
2000	120.9	33.9	84.7	60.7	2.1	19.8	2.1	2.3
2001	138.7	36.6	99.3	70.6	2.4	23.3	2.9	2.7
2002	158.2	40.9	114.1	79.9	2.5	27.4	4.3	3.1
2003	176.0	45.3	127.1	86.5	2.5	32.1	6.0	3.6
2004	192.2	48.0	140.4	94.6	3.4	35.7	6.7	3.7
2005	204.7	51.3	149.5	101.8	3.9	36.3	7.5	3.9
2006	224.1	51.1	168.9	102.2	39.6	18.9	8.2	4.1
2007	235.9	52.1	180.1	107.4	46.0	18.4	8.3	3.8
2008	242.7	49.9	189.2	111.0	50.6	19.2	8.4	3.7
2009	252.7	49.1	200.1	116.1	54.5	20.3	9.1	3.5
2010	253.1	45.2	204.5	116.1	58.9	20.4	9.1	3.4
2011	258.8	45.2	210.7	117.0	63.3	21.0	9.4	2.8
2012	259.2	45.1	211.6	112.9	67.6	21.6	9.5	2.5
2013	265.2	43.5	219.3	113.6	74.1	22.4	9.2	2.4
2014	298.0	44.8	251.2	128.1	84.9	28.0	10.2	2.0
2015	324.5	45.5	277.1	141.5	92.8	31.7	11.1	1.9
2016	328.6	45.0	281.7	142.6	95.4	33.4	10.2	1.9
Projected								
2017	338.1	44.6	291.5	144.3	101.3	35.3	10.6	1.9
2018	360.2	45.9	312.3	153.1	110.2	37.9	11.0	2.1
2019	380.5	47.7	330.5	158.6	119.9	40.5	11.5	2.3
2020	404.4	50.1	351.8	167.0	129.8	43.1	11.8	2.4
2021	432.2	53.1	376.5	177.9	140.3	46.1	12.2	2.6
2022	462.5	56.7	403.0	189.4	151.7	49.3	12.7	2.8
2023	495.1	60.3	431.8	202.3	163.8	52.6	13.1	3.0
2024	530.1	64.2	462.6	216.4	176.5	56.1	13.6	3.2
2025	565.2	68.5	493.3	231.2	188.2	59.8	14.1	3.4
2026	604.8	73.1	528.1	247.2	202.5	63.7	14.6	3.7

[1] Includes Children's Health Insurance Program (Titles XIX and XXI), Department of Defense, and Department of Veterans' Affairs.

[2] Includes worksite health care, other private revenues, Indian Health Service, workers' compensation, general assistance, maternal and child health, vocational rehabilitation, other federal programs, Substance Abuse and Mental Health Services Administration, other state and local programs, and school health.

Source: Centers for Medicare & Medicaid Services (CMS), Office of the Actuary
Plunkett Research,® Ltd.
www.plunkettresearch.com

Prescription Drug Expenditures & Annual Percent Change, U.S.: 2010-2026

(By Source of Funds)

Year	Total	Out-of-Pocket Payments	Health Insurance					Other Third Party Payers[3]
			Total	Private Health Insurance	Medicare	Medicaid	Other Health Insurance[2]	
Amount in Billions of US$ (Historical Estimates)								
2010	253.1	45.2	204.5	116.1	58.9	20.4	9.1	3.4
2011	258.8	45.2	210.7	117.0	63.3	21.0	9.4	2.8
2012	259.2	45.1	211.6	112.9	67.6	21.6	9.5	2.5
2013	265.2	43.5	219.3	113.6	74.1	22.4	9.2	2.4
2014	298.0	44.8	251.2	128.1	84.9	28.0	10.2	2.0
2015	324.5	45.5	277.1	141.5	92.8	31.7	11.1	1.9
2016	328.6	45.0	281.7	142.6	95.4	33.4	10.2	1.9
(Projected)[1]								
2017	338.1	44.6	291.5	144.3	101.3	35.3	10.6	1.9
2018	360.2	45.9	312.3	153.1	110.2	37.9	11.0	2.1
2019	380.5	47.7	330.5	158.6	119.9	40.5	11.5	2.3
2020	404.4	50.1	351.8	167.0	129.8	43.1	11.8	2.4
2021	432.2	53.1	376.5	177.9	140.3	46.1	12.2	2.6
2022	462.5	56.7	403.0	189.4	151.7	49.3	12.7	2.8
2023	495.1	60.3	431.8	202.3	163.8	52.6	13.1	3.0
2024	530.1	64.2	462.6	216.4	176.5	56.1	13.6	3.2
2025	565.2	68.5	493.3	231.2	188.2	59.8	14.1	3.4
2026	604.8	73.1	528.1	247.2	202.5	63.7	14.6	3.7
Annual Percent Change from Previous Year (Historical Estimates)								
2010	—	—	—	—	—	—	—	—
2011	2.2	0.0	3.0	0.8	7.5	2.6	3.3	-15.6
2012	0.2	-0.3	0.4	-3.5	6.6	3.0	1.2	-9.9
2013	2.3	-3.4	3.6	0.6	9.6	3.9	-3.6	-6.3
2014	12.4	2.8	14.6	12.8	14.6	24.6	11.6	-16.0
2015	8.9	1.6	10.3	10.4	9.3	13.4	8.9	-3.2
2016	1.3	-1.0	1.6	0.8	2.8	5.5	-8.2	-3.5
(Projected)[1]								
2017	2.9	-1.0	3.5	1.2	6.2	5.5	3.9	3.6
2018	6.6	2.9	7.1	6.1	8.8	7.5	3.8	6.4
2019	5.6	4.0	5.8	3.6	8.8	6.8	3.9	9.1
2020	6.3	5.1	6.4	5.3	8.3	6.5	2.9	7.7
2021	6.9	5.9	7.0	6.5	8.1	6.9	3.2	7.5
2022	7.0	6.8	7.1	6.5	8.1	6.8	4.0	7.2
2023	7.0	6.4	7.1	6.8	8.0	6.8	3.7	7.2
2024	7.1	6.5	7.1	6.9	7.8	6.7	3.7	7.1
2025	6.6	6.6	6.6	6.8	6.6	6.7	3.7	7.1
2026	7.0	6.8	7.0	6.9	7.6	6.5	3.6	7.0

[1] Includes Children's Health Insurance Program (Titles XIX and XXI), Department of Defense, and Department of Veterans' Affairs. [2] Includes worksite health care, other private revenues, Indian Health Service, workers' compensation, general assistance, maternal and child health, vocational rehabilitation, other federal programs, Substance Abuse and Mental Health Services Administration, other state and local programs, and school health.

Source: Centers for Medicare & Medicaid Services, Office of the Actuary

Plunkett Research, ® Ltd.

www.plunkettresearch.com

III. Medicare & Medicaid

Contents:

Medicare Enrollment, 1975-2092

(In Thousands)

Year	HI (Part A)	SMI		Total[1]
		Part B	Part D	
1975	24,481	23,744	—	24,864
1980	28,002	27,278	—	28,433
1985	30,621	29,869	—	31,081
1990	33,747	32,567	—	34,251
1995	37,175	35,641	—	37,594
2000	39,257	37,335	—	39,688
2005	42,233	39,752	1,841	42,606
2006	43,065	40,361	30,560	43,436
2007	44,010	41,093	31,392	44,368
2008	45,150	41,975	32,589	45,500
2009	46,256	42,908	33,644	46,604
2010	47,365	43,882	34,772	47,720
2011	48,549	44,917	35,720	48,896
2012	50,540	46,477	37,448	50,874
2013	52,169	47,952	39,103	52,504
2014	53,766	49,413	40,499	54,104
2015	55,246	50,753	41,804	55,587
2016	56,740	52,059	43,217	57,090
2017	58,035	53,395	44,455	58,393
2018	59,495	54,704	45,738	59,862
2019	61,118	56,175	47,193	61,495
2020	62,892	57,795	48,793	63,278
2021	64,660	59,418	50,378	65,055
2022	66,450	61,065	51,991	66,855
2023	68,197	62,687	53,536	68,611
2024	69,895	64,252	55,004	70,318
2025	71,625	65,847	56,459	72,058
2030	79,285	72,966	62,588	79,757
2035	84,029	77,325	66,327	84,524
2040	86,430	79,568	68,251	86,935
2045	87,971	80,902	69,395	88,482
2050	90,045	82,799	71,022	90,567
2055	92,846	85,338	73,201	93,379
2060	96,351	88,595	75,994	96,911
2065	99,752	91,714	78,670	100,339
2070	103,470	95,125	81,595	104,092
2075	107,374	98,741	84,697	108,038
2080	109,894	101,068	86,693	110,595
2085	111,950	102,938	88,297	112,689
2090	115,126	105,820	90,769	115,916
2091	115,932	106,560	91,404	116,735
2092	116,768	107,326	92,061	117,583

Note: All data past 2017 are estimated. HI = Hospital Insurance, SMI = Supplementary Medical Insurance.
[1] Number of beneficiaries with HI and/or SMI coverage. [2] Enrollment is not explicitly projected beyond 2040.

Source: The Boards Of Trustees, Federal Hospital Insurance And Federal Supplementary Medical Insurance Trust Funds
Plunkett Research,® Ltd.
www.plunkettresearch.com

Medicare Cost & Non-Interest Income by Source as a Percent of GDP, 1970-2092

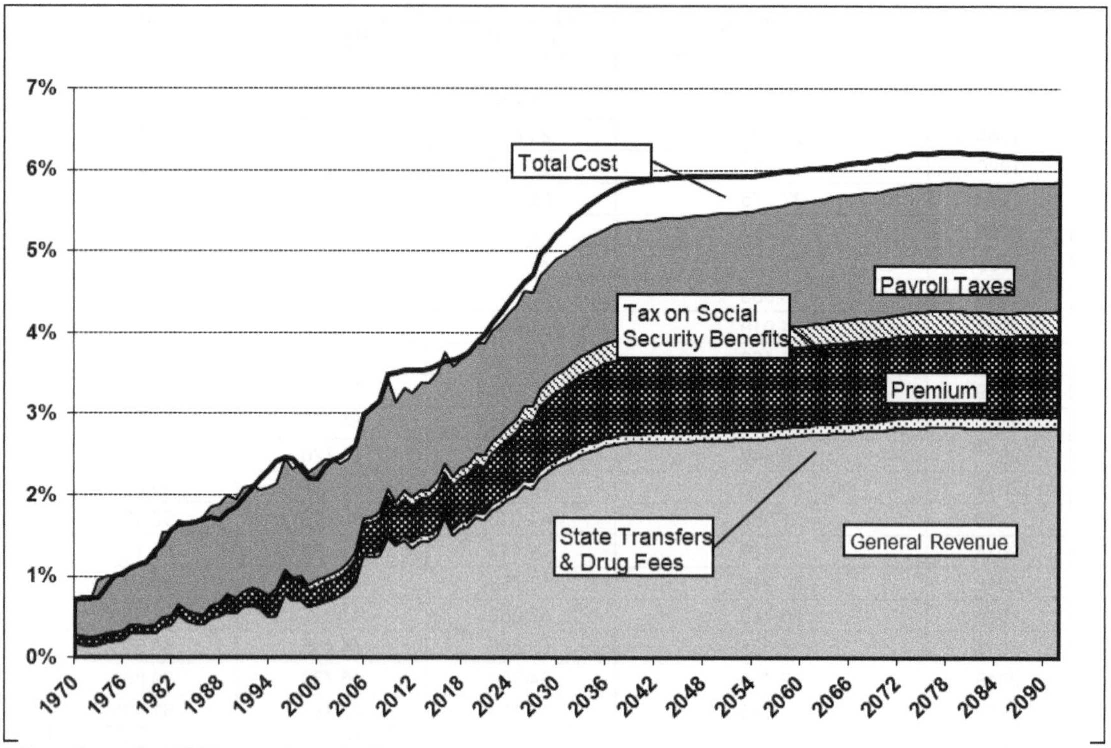

Note: Data after 2017 are estimated. This chart includes impacts of the Affordable Care Act.

Source: Social Security and Medicare Boards of Trustees
Plunkett Research,® Ltd.
www.plunkettresearch.com

Medicare Beneficiaries with Prescription Drug Coverage, Summary Report: August 2018

Current Contract Summary:	# of Contracts	Drug Plan Enrollment		Special Needs Plan (SNP) Enrollment		Employer Plan Enrollees		Total Enrollees
		MA-Only Enrollees	Drug Plan Enrollees	SNP Enrollees	Non-SNP Enrollees	Employer Plan Enrollees (800-Series Plans)	Non-Employer Plan Enrollees	
Total "Prepaid" Contracts[1]	**697**	**2,671,695**	**18,764,577**	**2,755,377**	**18,680,895**	**4,220,389**	**17,215,883**	**21,436,272**
Local CCPs	466	2,069,996	16,741,434	2,411,012	16,400,418	4,157,777	14,653,653	18,811,430
PFFS	6	47,871	100,127	0	147,998	0	147,998	147,998
MSA	3	6,632	0	0	6,632	36	6,596	6,632
Regional PPOs	24	114,394	1,233,046	344,365	1,003,075	6,336	1,341,104	1,347,440
MA Subtotal	**499**	**2,238,893**	**18,074,607**	**2,755,377**	**17,558,123**	**4,164,149**	**16,149,351**	**20,313,500**
Medicare-Medicaid Plan	**50**	**0**	**379,502**	**0**	**379,502**	**0**	**379,502**	**379,502**
1876 Cost	15	361,257	267,551	0	628,808	56,240	572,568	628,808
1833 Cost (HCPP)	9	71,545	0	0	71,545	0	71,545	71,545
PACE	124	0	42,917	0	42,917	0	42,917	42,917
Other Subtotal	198	432,802	689,970	0	1,122,772	56,240	1,066,532	**1,122,772**
Total PDPs	**63**	**0**	**25,523,518**	**0**	**25,523,518**	**4,649,623**	**20,873,895**	**25,523,518**
Employer/Union Only Direct Contract PDP	3	0	112,811	0	112,811	112,811	0	112,811
All Other PDP[1]	60	0	25,410,707	0	25,410,707	4,536,812	20,873,895	25,410,707
TOTAL	**760**	**2,671,695**	**44,288,095**	**2,755,377**	**44,204,413**	**8,870,012**	**38,089,778**	**46,959,790**

Note: Totals reflect enrollment as of the August 1, 2018 payment. The August payment reflects enrollments accepted through July 6, 2018.

MA = Medicare Advantage; CCP = Coordinated Care Plan; PFFS = Private Fee-For-Service Plan; MSA = Medicare Savings Account; PPO = Preferred Provider Organization; 1876 Cost refers to Health Maintenance Organizations (HMOs) and Comprehensive Medical Plans (CMPs); 1833 Cost refers to HCPPs; HCPP = Health Care Prepayment Plan; PACE = Program of All-inclusive Care for the Elderly; PDP = Prescription Drug Plan.

[1] Totals include beneficiaries enrolled in employer/union only group plans (contracts with "800 series" plan IDs). Where a beneficiary is enrolled in both an 1876 cost or PFFS plan and a PDP plan, both enrollments are reflected in these counts.

Source: Centers for Medicare & Medicaid Services
Plunkett Research,® Ltd.
www.plunkettresearch.com

Medicaid Enrollment & Expenditures for Medical Assistance Payments & Administration: Selected Years, 1966-2025

(Enrollment in millions of person-year equivalents; Expenditures in billions of dollars)

Fiscal Year	Enrollment	Total Expenditures	Federal Expenditures	State Expenditures
Historical Data:				
1966	4.0	0.9	0.5	0.4
1970	14.0	5.1	2.8	2.3
1975	20.2	13.1	7.3	5.9
1980	19.6	25.2	14.0	11.2
1985	19.8	41.3	22.8	18.4
1990	22.9	72.2	40.9	31.3
1995	33.4	159.5	90.7	68.8
2000	34.5	206.2	117.0	89.2
2005	46.3	315.9	180.4	135.5
2006	46.7	315.1	179.3	135.8
2007	46.4	332.2	189.0	143.2
2008	47.7	351.9	200.2	151.7
2009	50.9	378.6	246.3	132.3
2010	54.5	401.5	269.8	131.7
2011	56.3	427.4	270.7	156.7
2012	58.9	431.2	248.9	182.3
2013*	59.8	455.6	262.7	192.9
2014*	65.1	494.7	299.3	195.4
2015*	70	552.3	347.7	204.7
Projections (Includes impacts of Affordable Care Act):				
2016	72.2	575.9	363.4	212.5
2017	73.5	595.5	368.9	226.6
2018	74.8	632.9	392.5	240.4
2019	76.0	672.0	415.3	256.7
2020	77.2	713.8	439.0	274.8
2021	78.3	757.4	465.3	292.0
2022	79.2	801.9	492.2	309.7
2023	80.1	850.1	521.8	328.3
2024	80.8	901.5	553.4	348.1
2025	81.6	957.5	587.6	369.8

* Enrollment is estimated for 2013, 2014 and 2015.

Source: Centers for Medicare & Medicaid Services, US Department of Health & Human Services.

Plunkett Research,® Ltd.

www.plunkettresearch.com

Medicaid Enrollment and Expenditures, by Enrollment Group: Fiscal Year 2015

(Latest Year Available)

Eligibility Group	Enrollment[1] (in Millions)	Expenditures (in Billions)	Per Enrollee Spending
Children	28	$95	$3,389
Adults	15	$76	$4,986
Expansion Adults	9	$58	$6,365
Disabled	11	$204	$19,478
Aged	6	$80	$14,323
Total	69	$514	$7,492

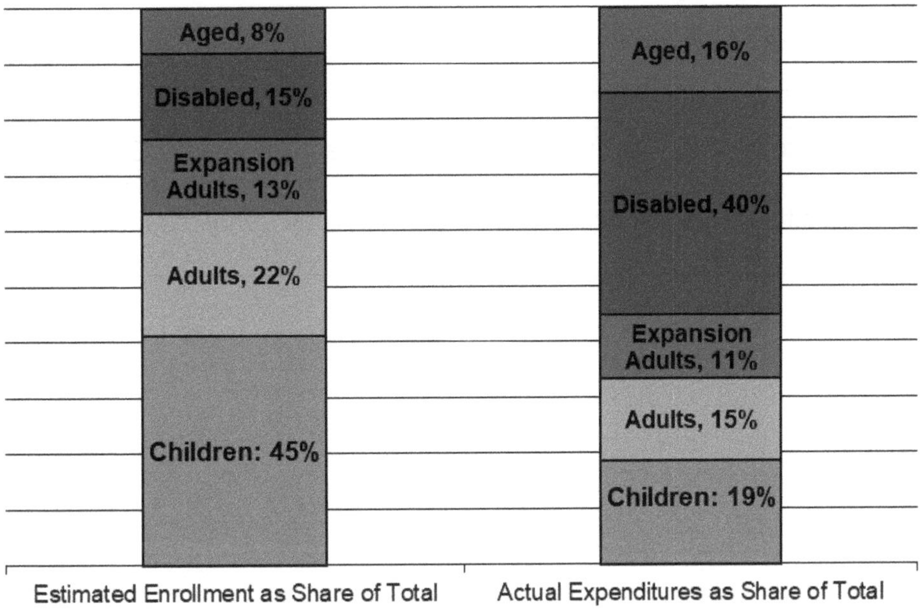

Note: Figures do not include DSH expenditures, territorial enrollees or payments, or adjustments.

[1] Measured in person-year equivalents.

Source: Centers for Medicare & Medicaid Services, US Department of Health & Human Services.

Plunkett Research,® Ltd.

www.plunkettresearch.com

IV. U.S. Health Insurance Coverage & The Uninsured

Contents:

Number & Percent of Persons of All Ages with and without Health Insurance Coverage, U.S.: 1999-2017

(In Thousands; Latest Year Available)

Year	Total Population	Private Health Insurance	%	Public Health Insurance	%	Total Covered	%	Total Uncovered	%
1999	276,804	202,021	73.0	67,103	24.2	239,102	86.4	37,702	13.6
2000	279,517	205,575	73.5	68,183	24.4	242,932	86.9	36,586	13.1
2001	282,082	204,142	72.4	70,330	24.9	244,059	86.5	38,023	13.5
2002	285,933	204,163	71.4	72,825	25.5	246,157	86.1	39,776	13.9
2003	288,280	201,989	70.1	76,116	26.4	246,332	85.4	41,949	14.6
2004	291,166	203,014	69.7	79,480	27.3	249,414	85.7	41,752	14.3
2005	293,834	203,205	69.2	80,283	27.3	250,799	85.4	43,035	14.6
2006	296,824	203,942	68.7	80,343	27.1	251,610	84.8	45,214	15.2
2007	299,106	203,903	68.2	83,147	27.8	255,018	85.3	44,088	14.7
2008	301,483	202,626	67.2	87,586	29.1	256,702	85.1	44,780	14.9
2009	304,280	196,245	64.5	93,245	30.6	255,295	83.9	48,985	16.1
2010	306,553	196,147	64.0	95,525	31.2	256,603	83.7	49,951	16.3
2011	308,827	197,323	63.9	99,497	32.2	260,214	84.3	48,613	15.7
2012	311,116	198,812	63.9	101,493	32.6	263,165	84.6	47,951	15.4
2013	313,400	201,100	64.2	107,600	34.3	271,400	86.6	42,000	13.4
2014	313,890	208,333	66.4	104,228	33.2	277,220	88.3	36,670	11.7
2015	316,451	213,514	67.5	109,874	34.7	286,693	90.6	29,758	9.4
2016	318,176	215,859	67.8	112,688	35.4	290,872	91.4	27,304	8.6
2017	320,775	216,952	67.6	113,720	35.5	292,756	91.3	28,019	8.7

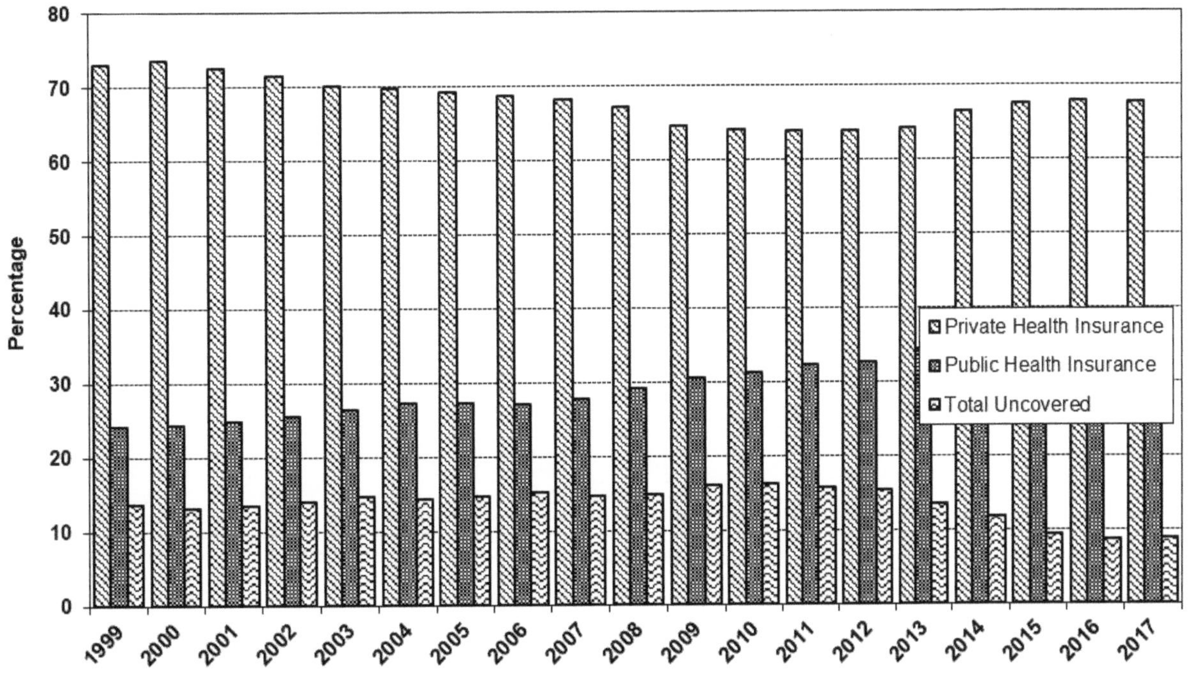

Note: Data are based on household interviews of a sample of the civilian noninstitutionalized population. Numbers as of March of the following year. Uncovered persons includes those not covered by private health insurance (such as employment-based or direct purchase) or public health insurance (such as Medicaid, Medicare, or military health care).

Source: U.S. Census Bureau, American Community Survey Tables for Health Insurance Coverage.
Plunkett Research,® Ltd.
www.plunkettresearch.com

Employers' Costs for Total Compensation and Health Insurance, by Selected Characteristics, U.S.: Selected Years, 2014-2018

(Amount per Employee-Hour Worked in US$)

Characteristic	Total Compensation per Employee-Hour Worked					Health Insurance as Percent of Total Compensation				
	2014	2015	2016	2017	2018	2014	2015	2016	2017	2018
	In US$					*In Percent (%)*				
State and local government	43.10	44.25	45.23	48.24	49.40	11.7	11.6	11.7	11.6	11.9
Total private industry	29.99	31.65	32.06	33.11	34.17	7.9	7.7	7.6	7.6	7.5
Census region:										
Northeast	34.79	38.93	39.06	41.19	41.48	8.2	7.7	7.7	7.6	7.6
Midwest	28.71	29.08	29.40	30.51	31.03	8.6	8.5	8.5	8.2	8.4
South	27.14	29.04	29.48	29.84	30.68	7.3	7.1	7.2	7.3	7.1
West	31.59	32.23	33.13	34.35	37.08	7.5	7.7	7.3	7.3	7.3
Union status:										
Union	43.84	46.62	45.72	48.97	47.65	12.6	12.1	12.6	12.5	32.9
Nonunion	28.63	30.18	30.72	31.58	12.90	7.1	7.0	6.9	6.8	6.8
Establishment employment size:										
1–99 employees	25.03	26.45	27.04	28.16	28.79	6.6	6.4	6.4	6.4	6.3
100 or more	35.76	37.78	38.14	39.05	40.53	8.9	8.7	8.7	8.6	8.6
100–499	29.92	32.07	32.62	32.74	34.76	8.7	8.5	8.3	8.3	8.5
500 or more	44.04	46.19	46.85	48.70	49.16	9.1	8.9	9.1	8.9	8.8

Note: Costs are calculated from March survey data each year.
Total compensation includes wages and salaries, and benefits.

Source: U.S. Department of Labor, Bureau of Labor Statistics, National Compensation Survey, Employer Costs for Employee Compensation, March release

Plunkett Research,® Ltd.

www.plunkettresearch.com

V. U.S. Vital Statistics & Population Indicators

Contents:

Life Expectancy at Age 65, U.S.

(Selected Years, 1940-2095)

Year	Male	Female
1940	11.9	13.4
1950	12.8	15.1
1960	12.9	15.9
1970	13.1	17.1
1980	14.0	18.4
1990	15.1	19.1
2000	15.9	19.0
2010	17.6	20.2
2015	17.8	20.4
2016	18.1	20.6
2017	18.2	20.7
2020	18.4	20.9
2025	18.8	21.2
2030	19.1	21.5
2035	19.5	21.8
2040	19.8	22.1
2045	20.1	22.3
2050	20.4	22.6
2055	20.7	22.9
2060	20.9	23.1
2065	21.2	23.4
2070	21.5	23.6
2075	21.7	23.8
2080	22.0	24.0
2085	22.2	24.3
2090	22.5	24.5
2095	22.7	24.7

Note: Years 2016-2095 are estimated.

Source: Social Security Administration, Office of the Chief Actuary
Plunkett Research,® Ltd.
www.plunkettresearch.com

Prevalence of Obesity Among Adults, by Age, Sex and Race/Ethnicity: U.S., 2017

(Percent of 20 Years and over Population; Latest Year Available)

	Male	Female	Total
Age:			
20-39	24.9	29.1	27.0
40-59	37.4	35.2	36.3
60 and over	30.8	30.4	30.6
Race/Ethnicity[1]:			
Hispanic or Latino	31.9	34.9	--
Not Hispanic or Latino, single race, white	30.1	29.6	--
Not Hispanic or Latino, single race, black	32.5	46.7	--

Note: Obesity is defined as a body mass index of 30 kg/m^2 or more. Data are based on household interviews of a sample of the civilian noninstitutionalized population.

[1] Estimates are age-adjusted using the projected 2000 U.S. population as the standard population and five age groups: 20–24, 25–34, 35–44, 45–64, and 65 and over.

Source: National Center for Health Statistics, *Health, United States, 2018*
Plunkett Research,® Ltd.
www.plunkettresearch.com

Chapter 3

IMPORTANT HEALTH CARE INDUSTRY CONTACTS

Contents:

1) Aging

Administration for Community Living (ACL)
One Massachusetts Ave. NW
Washington, DC 20201 US
Phone: 202-619-0724
Fax: 202-357-3555
Toll Free: 800-677-1116
E-mail Address: *aclinfo@acl.hhs.gov*
Web Address: acl.gov
The Administration for Community Living (ACL), combining the efforts of the Administration on Aging (AOA), the Administration on Intellectual and Developmental Disabilities and the Health and Human Services (HHS) Office on Disability, is the federal focal point and advocate agency for the concerns of older persons and people with disabilities across the lifespan. In this role, the ACL works to heighten awareness among other federal agencies, organizations, groups and the public.

Aging with Dignity
3050 Highland Oaks Terr., Ste. 2
Tallahassee, FL 32301-3841 USA
Phone: 850-681-2010
Fax: 850-681-2481
Toll Free: 888-594-7437
E-mail Address: fivewishes@agingwithdignity.org
Web Address: www.agingwithdignity.org
Aging with Dignity is a nonprofit organization that offers information, advice and legal tools needed to ensure that the wishes of the elderly concerning health and death be respected.

American Society on Aging (ASA)
575 Market St., Ste. 2100
San Francisco, CA 94105-2869 USA
Phone: 415-974-9600
Fax: 415-974-0300
Toll Free: 800-537-9728
E-mail Address: membership@asaging.org
Web Address: www.asaging.org
The American Society on Aging (ASA) is a nonprofit organization committed to enhancing the knowledge and skills of those working with older adults and their families.

LeadingAge
2519 Connecticut Ave. NW
Washington, DC 20008-1520 USA
Phone: 202-783-2242
Fax: 202-783-2255
Toll Free: 888-508-9441
E-mail Address: info@leadingage.org
Web Address: www.leadingage.org
LeadingAge was formerly the American Association of Home Services for the Aging (AAHSA). The LeadingAge membership community includes over 6,000 not-for-profit organizations in the United States, state partners, businesses, research partners, consumer organizations, foundations and a broad global network of aging services organizations that reach over 30 countries. The work of LeadingAge is focused on advocacy, leadership development, and applied research and promotion of effective services, home health, hospice, community services, senior housing, assisted living residences, continuing care communities, nursing homes, as well as technology solutions, to seniors, children, and others with special needs.

National Association of Area Agencies on Aging (N4A)
1730 Rhode Island Ave. NW, Ste. 1200
Washington, DC 20036 USA
Phone: 202-872-0888
Fax: 202-872-0057
E-mail Address: info@n4a.org
Web Address: www.n4a.org
The National Association of Area Agencies on Aging (N4A) is the umbrella organization for the 622 area agencies on aging and more than 256 Title VI Native American aging programs in the U.S.

National Council on Aging (NCOA)
251 18th St. South, Ste. 500
Arlington, VA 22202 USA
Phone: 571-527-3900
Web Address: www.ncoa.org
The National Council on Aging (NCOA) is a group of organizations and professionals promoting the dignity, self-determination and well-being of older persons.

2) AIDS/HIV

AIDS United
1424 K St. NW, Ste. 200
Washington, DC 20005 USA
Phone: 202-408-4848
Fax: 202-408-1818
Web Address: www.aidsunited.org
AIDS United, formed by the 2010 merger of AIDS Action and the National AIDS Fund, is committed to the development, analysis, cultivation, encouragement and implementation of good programs and policies with regard to the HIV/AIDS virus.

CDC National Prevention Information Network (CDCNPIN)
P.O. Box 6003
Rockville, MD 20849-6003 USA
Toll Free: 800-232-4636
E-mail Address: NPIN-info@cdc.gov
Web Address: npin.cdc.gov
The CDC National Prevention Information Network (CDCNPIN) is the U.S. reference, referral and distribution service for information on HIV/AIDS, sexually transmitted diseases and tuberculosis. It is operated by the Centers for Disease Control, a Federal Government agency.

HIV InSite
4150 Clement St., Box 111V
San Francisco, CA 94121 USA
Fax: 415-379-5547
E-mail Address: hivinsite@ucsf.edu
Web Address: hivinsite.ucsf.edu
HIV InSite, which was developed by the Center for HIV Information at the

University of California San Francisco, offers comprehensive, up-to-date information on HIV/AIDS treatment, prevention and policy.

HIV/AIDS Treatment Information Service
P.O. Box 4780
Rockville, MD 20849-6303 USA
Phone: 301-315-2818
Fax: 301-315-2818
Toll Free: 800-448-0440
E-mail Address: contactus@aidsinfo.nih.gov
Web Address: www.aidsinfo.nih.gov
The HIV/AIDS Treatment Information Service is a central resource for federally approved treatment guidelines for HIV and AIDS, HIV treatment and prevention clinical trials and other research information for health care providers and general public.

3) Alzheimer's Disease

Alzheimer's Association
225 N. Michigan Ave., Fl. 17
Chicago, IL 60601 USA
Phone: 312-335-8700
Fax: 866-699-1246
Toll Free: 1-800-272-3900
E-mail Address: info@alz.org
Web Address: www.alz.org
The Alzheimer's Association is the largest national voluntary health organization committed to finding a cure for Alzheimer's and helping those affected by the disease.

Alzheimer's Disease Education and Referral Center (ADEAR)
ADEAR Ctr.
P.O. Box 8250
Silver Spring, MD 20907-8250 USA
Fax: 301-495-3334
Toll Free: 800-438-4380
E-mail Address: adear@nia.nih.gov
Web Address: www.nia.nih.gov/alzheimers
The Alzheimer's Disease Education and Referral Center (ADEAR) provides information about Alzheimer's disease, its impact on families and health professionals and research into possible causes and cures.

Alzheimer's Foundation of America (AFA)
322 8th Ave., Fl. 7
New York, NY 10001 USA
Fax: 646-638-1546
Toll Free: 866-232-8484
Web Address: www.alzfdn.org
From the beginning, AFA's objective has been to unite organizations from coast-to-coast that are dedicated to meeting the educational, social, emotional and practical needs of individuals with Alzheimer's disease and related illnesses, and their caregivers and families. Under AFA's umbrella, these organizations collaborate on education, resources, program design and implementation, fundraising campaigns, and advocacy, all resulting in better care for those affected by the disease.

4) Arthritis

Arthritis Foundation
1355 Peachtree St. NE, Fl. 6
Atlanta, GA 30309 USA
Phone: 404-872-7100
Toll Free: 800-283-7800
Web Address: www.arthritis.org
The Arthritis Foundation is a nonprofit organization providing advocacy, programs, services and research for the treatment of more than 100 types of arthritis and related conditions.

Arthritis Insight
Web Address: www.arthritisinsight.com
Arthritis Insight provides information and education on arthritis, as well as news and referrals.

Arthritis National Research Foundation (ANRF)
5354 E. 2nd St., Ste. 201
Long Beach, CA 90803 USA
Phone: 562-437-6808
Toll Free: 800-588-2873
Web Address: www.curearthritis.org
The Arthritis National Research Foundation (ANRF) provides funding for researchers associated with major research institutes, universities and hospitals throughout the country seeking to discover new knowledge for the prevention, treatment and cure of arthritis and related rheumatic diseases.

Arthritis.com
Web Address: www.arthritis.com
Arthritis.com is an online resource for information on chronic joint symptoms. The web site is operated by Pfizer, Inc.

5) Biotechnology & Biological Industry Associations

BIOCOM
10996 Torreyana Rd., Ste. 200
San Diego, CA 92121 USA
Phone: 858-455-0300
E-mail Address: sandiego@biocom.org
Web Address: www.biocom.org
BIOCOM is a trade organization which seeks to promote the interests of life science industry through advancements in health, energy and agriculture. Its covers a range of areas, including diagnostic, pharmaceuticals, biotechnology, medical device, bio-renewable energy, agriculture and connected health. With over 700 member companies, service providers and research institutions, the organization offers talent development, networking, public policy initiatives and capital development opportunities.

Biomedical Engineering Society (BMES)
8201 Corporate Dr., Ste. 1125
Landover, MD 20785-2224 USA
Phone: 301-459-1999
Fax: 301-459-2444
Toll Free: 877-871-2637
Web Address: www.bmes.org
The Biomedical Engineering Society (BMES) supports and advances the use of engineering and technology for human health and well being. It promotes the development of professionals in the biomedical engineering and bioengineering industry.

Biotechnology Industry Organization (BIO)
1201 Maryland Ave. SW, Ste. 900
Washington, DC 20024 USA
Phone: 202-962-9200
Fax: 202-488-6301
E-mail Address: info@bio.org
Web Address: www.bio.org
The Biotechnology Industry Organization (BIO) represents members involved in the research and development of health care, agricultural, industrial and environmental biotechnology products. BIO has both small and large member organizations.

California Healthcare Institute (CHI)
250 E. Grand Ave., Ste. 26
La Jolla, CA 92037 USA
Phone: 650-871-3250
E-mail Address: info@califesciences.org
Web Address: http://califesciences.org
California Life Sciences Association (CLSA) was formed in 2015 through the merger between California Health Care Institute and Bay Area Bioscience Association. It works to promote California's life sciences industry in collaboration with government, academia as well as other stakeholders to form public policy and business solutions. CLSA membership includes over 750 biotechnology, pharmaceutical, medical device and diagnostics companies, research universities and institutes, investors and service providers.

International Society for Stem Cell Research (ISSCR)
5215 Old Orchard Rd., Ste. 270
Skokie, IL 60077 USA
Phone: 224-592-5700
Fax: 224-365-0004
E-mail Address: info@isscr.org
Web Address: www.isscr.org
The International Society for Stem Cell Research (ISSCR) is an independent, nonprofit organization established to promote the exchange and dissemination of information and ideas relating to stem cells; to encourage the general field of research involving stem cells; and to promote professional and public education in all areas of stem cell research and application.

Society for Biomaterials
1120 Route 73, Ste. 200
Mt. Laurel, NJ 08054 USA
Phone: 856-439-0826
Fax: 856-439-0525
E-mail Address: info@biomaterials.org
Web Address: www.biomaterials.org
The Society for Biomaterials is a professional society that promotes advances in all phases of materials research and development by encouraging cooperative educational programs, clinical applications and professional standards in the biomaterials field.

6) Biotechnology Investing

Burrill & Company
1 Embarcadero Ctr., Ste. 2700
San Francisco, CA 94111 USA
Phone: 415-591-5400
Fax: 415-591-5401
Web Address: www.burrillandco.com
Burrill & Company is a leading private merchant bank concentrated on companies in the life sciences industries: biotechnology, pharmaceuticals, medical technologies, agricultural technologies, animal health and nutraceuticals.

7) Biotechnology Resources

Biospace, Inc.
6465 S. Greenwood Plz., Ste. 400
Centennial, CO 80111 USA
Toll Free: 877-277-7585
E-mail Address: support@biospace.com
Web Address: www.biospace.com
Biospace.com offers information, news and profiles on biotech companies. It also provides an outlet for business and scientific leaders in bioscience to communicate with each other.

Centre for Cellular and Molecular Biology (CCMB)
Habsiguda, Uppal Rd.
Hyderabad, Telangana 500007 India
Phone: 91-40-2716-0222-31
Fax: 91-040-2716-0591
Web Address: www.ccmb.res.in
Centre for Cellular and Molecular Biology (CCMB) is one of the constituent Indian national laboratories of the Council of Scientific and Industrial Research (CSIR), a multidisciplinary research and development organization of the Government of India. CCMB's research is focused on seven areas: Biomedicine and Biotechnology; Genetics, Evolution and Genomics; Cell Biology and Development; Molecular and Structural Biology; Biochemistry and Biophysics; Infectious Diseases; and Computational Biology and Bioinformatics.

Institute for Cellular and Molecular Biology (ICMB)
Moffett Molecular Biology Bldg.
2500 Speedway, A4800
Austin, TX 78712 USA
Phone: 512-471-1156
Fax: 512-471-2149
E-mail Address: icmb@austin.utexas.edu
Web Address: www.icmb.utexas.edu
The Institute for Cellular and Molecular Biology (ICMB) web site offers a comprehensive dictionary of biotech terms, plus extensive research data regarding biotechnology. ICMB is located in The Louise and James Robert Moffett Molecular Biology Building at the University of Texas at Austin.

8) Blindness

American Council of the Blind (ACB)
1703 N. Beauregard St., Ste. 420
Arlington, VA 22201-3354 USA
Phone: 202-467-5081
Fax: 703-465-5085
Toll Free: 800-424-8666
E-mail Address: info@acb.org
Web Address: www.acb.org
The American Council of the Blind (ACB) is a leading membership organization for blind and visually impaired people, which strives to increase the independence, opportunity, security and quality of life of such people.

Guide Dog Foundation for the Blind, Inc.
371 E. Jericho Tpke.
Smithtown, NY 11787-2976 USA
Phone: 631-930-9000
Fax: 631-930-9009
Toll Free: 800-548-4337
E-mail Address: info@guidedog.org
Web Address: www.guidedog.org
The Guide Dog Foundation for the Blind, Inc. strives to be the leading resource and provider of premier services to facilitate the independence of people who are blind or visually impaired.

Helen Keller International Organization (HKI)
352 Park Ave. S, Fl. 12
New York, NY 10010 USA
Phone: 212-532-0544
Toll Free: 877-535-5374
E-mail Address: info@hki.org
Web Address: www.hki.org
The Helen Keller International Organization (HKI) directly addresses the causes of preventable blindness, provides rehabilitation services to blind people and helps reduce micronutrient malnutrition which can cause blindness and death in children.

Learning Ally
20 Roszel Rd.
Princeton, NJ 08540 USA
Phone: 609-750-1830
Toll Free: 800-221-4792
Web Address: www.learningally.org
Learning Ally, formerly Recording for the Blind and Dyslexic (RFB&D), is an educational library serving people who cannot effectively read standard print because of visual impairment, dyslexia or other disabilities.

Lighthouse Guild
15 W. 65th St.
New York, NY 10023 USA
Phone: 212-769-6200
Toll Free: 800-284-4422
Web Address: www.lighthouseguild.org
Lighthouse Guild, formed in 2013 with the merger of Jewish Guild Healthcare and Lighthouse International is a nonprofit vision and healthcare organization. It is dedicated to addressing the needs of blind, visually impaired people, including those with multiple disabilities or chronic medical conditions.

National Eye Institute (NEI)
31 Ctr. Dr., MSC 2510
Bethesda, MD 20892-2510 USA
Phone: 301-496-5248
E-mail Address: 2020@nei.nih.gov
Web Address: www.nei.nih.gov
The National Eye Institute (NEI) conducts and supports research that helps prevent and treat eye diseases and other vision related disorders.

National Federation of the Blind
200 E. Wells St., Jernigan Place
Baltimore, MD 21230 USA

Phone: 410-659-9314
Fax: 410-685-5653
E-mail Address: nfb@nfb.org
Web Address: www.nfb.org
The National Federation of the Blind website lists information about vision loss as well as resources for visual impaired including products, assistive technology and programs for improving lives for blind people. In addition, the site contains information regarding accessibility web certification and access technology tips.

National Library Service for the Blind and Physically Handicapped (NLS)
1291 Taylor St. NW
Washington, DC 20011 USA
Phone: 202-707-5100
Fax: 202-707-0712
Toll Free: 800-424-8567
E-mail Address: nls@loc.gov
Web Address: www.loc.gov/nls
National Library Service for the Blind and Physically Handicapped (NLS), part of the Library of Congress, administers a free library program of Braille and audio materials circulated to eligible borrowers in the United States by postage-free mail.

Prevent Blindness America (PBA)
211 W. Wacker Dr., Ste. 1700
Chicago, IL 60606 USA
Toll Free: 800-331-2020
E-mail Address: info@preventblindness.org
Web Address: www.preventblindness.org
Prevent Blindness America (PBA) is a leading volunteer eye health and safety organization dedicated to fighting blindness and saving sight.

VISIONS
500 Greenwich St., Fl. 3
New York, NY 10013-1354 USA
Phone: 212-625-1616
Fax: 212-219-4078
Toll Free: 888-245-8333
E-mail Address: info@visionsvcb.org
Web Address: www.visionsvcb.org
VISIONS is a nonprofit rehabilitation and social service agency that promotes the independence of people who are blind or visually impaired.

9) Blood Bank Industry Associations

American Association of Blood Banks (AABB)
8101 Glenbrook Rd.
Bethesda, MD 20814-2749 USA
Phone: 301-907-6977
Fax: 301-907-6895
Web Address: www.aabb.org
The American Association of Blood Banks (AABB) promotes high standards of care for blood banking and transfusion medicine.

10) Burns

American Burn Association (ABA)
311 S. Wacker Dr., Ste. 4150
Chicago, IL 60606 USA
Phone: 312-642-9260
Fax: 312-642-9130
E-mail Address: info@ameriburn.org
Web Address: www.ameriburn.org
The American Burn Association (ABA) dedicates its efforts to the problems of burn injuries and burn victims throughout the U.S., Canada and other countries.

11) Canadian Government Agencies-Health Care

Canadian Institutes of Health Research (CIHR)
160 Elgin St., Fl. 9
Ottawa, ON K1A 0W9 Canada
Phone: 613-941-2672
Fax: 613-954-1800
Toll Free: 888-603-4178
E-mail Address: support@cihr-irsc.gc.ca
Web Address: www.cihr-irsc.gc.ca
The Canadian Institutes of Health Research (CIHR) is the government of Canada's agency for health research. CIHR's mission is to create new scientific knowledge and to catalyze its translation into improved health, more effective health services and products, and a strengthened Canadian health-care system. Composed of 13 Institutes, CIHR provides leadership and support to health researchers and trainees across Canada. The agency provides grants for research in the fields of biomedical, clinical, health systems and environmental health.

Federal Healthcare Partnership (FHP)
66 Slater St., Ste. 600
Ottawa, Ontario K1A 0P4 Canada
Phone: 613-947-3585
Web Address: www.fhp-pfss.gc.ca
The Federal Healthcare Partnership (FHP) is a Canadian government agency whose purpose is to promote more efficient and effective healthcare programs between its member departments.

Health Canada (Health Portfolio, Canadian Minister of Health)
Health Canada
Address Locator: 0900C2
Ottawa, ON K1A 0K9 Canada
Phone: 613-957-2991
Fax: 613-941-5366
Toll Free: 866-225-0709
E-mail Address: Info@hc-sc.gc.ca
Web Address: www.hc-sc.gc.ca
The Minister of Health is responsible for maintaining and improving the health of Canadians. This objective is supported by the Health Portfolio, which comprises Health Canada, the Public Health Agency of Canada, the Canadian Institutes of Health Research, the Hazardous Materials Information Review Commission, the Patented Medicine Prices Review Board and Assisted Human Reproduction Canada.

Patented Medicine Prices Review Board (PMPRB)
333 Laurier Ave. W, Ste. 1400
Box L40, Standard Life Ctr.
Ottawa, ON K1P 1C1 Canada
Phone: 613-954-8299
Fax: 613-952-7626
Toll Free: 877-861-2350
E-mail Address: PMPRB.Information-Renseignements.CEPMB@pmprb-cepmb.gc.ca
Web Address: www.pmprb-cepmb.gc.ca
The Patented Medicine Prices Review Board (PMPRB) is an independent quasi-judicial body established by Parliament of Canada in 1987 under the Patent Act. Its role includes the regulation of drug prices. It also publishes a wealth of information about the Canadian drug industry and drug development.

12) Cancer

American Cancer Society (ACS)
250 Williams St. NW
Atlanta, GA 30303 USA
Toll Free: 800-227-2345
Web Address: www.cancer.org
The American Cancer Society (ACS) is a nationwide community-based voluntary health organization dedicated to eliminating cancer as a major health problem by preventing the disease, saving lives and diminishing suffering from cancer.

Association of Cancer Resources Online (ACOR)
173 Duane St., Ste. 3A
New York, NY 10013 USA
Phone: 212-226-5525
E-mail Address: Feedback@acor.org.
Web Address: www.acor.org
The Association of Cancer Online Resources, Inc. (ACOR) is a 501 (c) (3) nonprofit organization. The heart of ACOR is a large collection of cancer-related Internet mailing lists, which has delivered millions of e-mail messages to subscribers across the globe. In addition

to supporting the mailing lists, ACOR develops and hosts state-of-the-art Internet-based knowledge systems that allow the public to find and use credible information. ACOR aims to Provide information and support to cancer patients and those who care for them through the creation and maintenance of cancer-related Internet mailing lists and Web-based resources.

Association of Community Cancer Centers (ACCC)
11600 Nebel St., Ste. 201
Rockville, MD 20852 USA
Phone: 301-984-9496
Fax: 301-770-1949
Web Address: www.accc-cancer.org
The Association of Community Cancer Centers (ACCC) helps oncology professionals adapt to the complex challenges of program management, cuts in reimbursement, hospital consolidation and mergers, and legislation and regulations that threaten to compromise the delivery of quality cancer care.

LIVESTRONG Foundation
2201 E. Sixth St.
Austin, TX 78702 USA
Toll Free: 877-236-8820
Web Address: www.livestrong.org
The LIVESTRONG Foundation, formerly the Lance Armstrong Foundation (LAF), provides cancer patients, their families and caregivers with advocacy, education, public health and research programs relating to the treatment of and possible cures for all forms of cancer.

National Association for Proton Therapy (The)
1155 15th St. NW, Ste. 500
Washington, DC 20005 USA
Phone: 202-495-3133
Fax: 202-530-0659
E-mail Address: info@proton-therapy.org
Web Address: www.proton-therapy.org
The National Association for Proton Therapy (NAPT) promotes the clinical benefits of proton beam radiation therapy for cancer patients and their families. Founded in 1990, NAPT is an independent, nonprofit, public benefit corporation. It serves as a resource center for cancer patients and their families, physicians and health care providers, academic medical centers, cancer centers, the U.S. Centers for Medicare and Medicaid Services (CMS) and other federal health care agencies, members of Congress and staff, and the nation's news media.

National Marrow Donor Program (NMDP)
500 N 5th St.
Minneapolis, MN 55401-1206 USA
Phone: 612-627-5800
Toll Free: 800-627-7692
E-mail Address: foundation@nmdp.org
Web Address: bethematch.org
The National Marrow Donor Program (NMDP) is an international leader in the facilitation of marrow and blood stem cell transplantation through non-family donors.

NCI Contact Center
BG 9609 MSC 9760
9609 Medical Ctr. Dr.
Bethesda, MD 20892-9760 USA
Toll Free: 800-422-6237
Web Address: http://www.cancer.gov/contact/contact-center
The NCI Contact Center, also known as the Cancer Information Service (CIS) is a national information and education network provided by the National Cancer Institute. It offers updated information on a range of topics, including cancer research and clinical trials, cancer prevention, cancer treatment centers, risk factors, symptoms, treatment, early detection and diagnosis.

OncoLink
3400 Spruce St., Ste. 2
Philadelphia, PA 19104 USA
Phone: 215-349-8895
Web Address: www.oncolink.org
OncoLink is the web site maintained by a group of oncology healthcare professionals, which strives to help cancer patients, families, health care professionals and the general public obtain accurate cancer-related information.

Susan G. Komen Breast Cancer Foundation
5005 LBJ Fwy., Ste. 250
Dallas, TX 75244 USA
Toll Free: 877-465-6636
E-mail Address: helpline@komen.org
Web Address: ww5.komen.org
This Susan G. Komen Breast Cancer Foundation strives to eradicate breast cancer as a life-threatening disease by advancing research, education, screening and treatment.

13) Careers-Biotech

Chase Group (The)
10975 Grandview Dr., Ste. 100
Overland Park, KS 66210 USA
Phone: 913-663-3100
Fax: 913-663-3131
E-mail Address: chase@chasegroup.com
Web Address: www.chasegroup.com
The Chase Group is an executive search firm specializing in biomedical and pharmaceutical placement.

14) Careers-First Time Jobs/New Grads

CollegeGrad.com, Inc.
950 Tower Ln., Fl. 6
Foster City, CA 94404 USA
E-mail Address: info@quinstreet.com
Web Address: www.collegegrad.com
CollegeGrad.com, Inc. offers in-depth resources for college students and recent grads seeking entry-level jobs.

MonsterCollege
444 N. Michigan Ave., Ste. 600
Chicago, IL 60611 USA
E-mail Address: info@college.monster.com
Web Address: www.college.monster.com
MonsterCollege provides information about internships and entry-level jobs, as well as career advice and resume tips, to recent college graduates.

National Association of Colleges and Employers (NACE)
62 Highland Ave.
Bethlehem, PA 18017-9085 USA
Phone: 610-868-1421
E-mail Address: customer_service@naceweb.org
Web Address: www.naceweb.org
The National Association of Colleges and Employers (NACE) is a premier U.S. organization representing college placement offices and corporate recruiters who focus on hiring new grads.

15) Careers-General Job Listings

CareerBuilder, Inc.
200 N La Salle St., Ste. 1100
Chicago, IL 60601 USA
Phone: 773-527-3600
Fax: 773-353-2452
Toll Free: 800-891-8880
Web Address: www.careerbuilder.com
CareerBuilder, Inc. focuses on the needs of companies and also provides a database of job openings. The site has over 1 million jobs posted by 300,000 employers, and receives an average 23 million unique visitors monthly. The company also operates online career centers for 140 newspapers and 9,000 online partners. Resumes are sent directly to the company, and applicants can set up

a special e-mail account for job-seeking purposes. CareerBuilder is primarily a joint venture between three newspaper giants: The McClatchy Company, Gannett Co., Inc. and Tribune Company.

CareerOneStop
Toll Free: 877-872-5627
E-mail Address: info@careeronestop.org
Web Address: www.careeronestop.org
CareerOneStop is operated by the employment commissions of various state agencies. It contains job listings in both the private and government sectors, as well as a wide variety of useful career resources and workforce information. CareerOneStop is sponsored by the U.S. Department of Labor.

LaborMarketInfo (LMI)
Employment Development Dept.
P.O. Box 826880, MIC 57
Sacramento, CA 94280-0001 USA
Phone: 916-262-2162
Fax: 916-262-2352
Web Address:
www.labormarketinfo.edd.ca.gov
LaborMarketInfo (LMI) provides job seekers and employers a wide range of resources, namely the ability to find, access and use labor market information and services. It provides statistics for employment demographics on both a local and regional level, as well as career searching tools for California residents. The web site is sponsored by California's Employment Development Office.

Recruiters Online Network
E-mail Address: rossi.tony@comcast.net
Web Address: www.recruitersonline.com
The Recruiters Online Network provides job postings from thousands of recruiters, Careers Online Magazine, a resume database, as well as other career resources.

USAJOBS
USAJOBS Program Office
1900 E St. NW, Ste. 6500
Washington, DC 20415-0001 USA
Phone: 818-934-6600
Web Address: www.usajobs.gov
USAJOBS, a program of the U.S. Office of Personnel Management, is the official job site for the U.S. Federal Government. It provides a comprehensive list of U.S. government jobs, allowing users to search for employment by location; agency; type of work; or by senior executive positions. It also has special employment sections for individuals with disabilities, veterans and recent college graduates; an information center, offering resume and interview tips and other information; and allows users to create a profile and post a resume.

16) Careers-Health Care

Health Care Source
100 Sylvan Rd., Ste. 100
Woburn, MA 01801 USA
Phone: 781-368-1033
Fax: 800-829-6600
Toll Free: 800-869-5200
E-mail Address:
solutions@healthcaresource.com
Web Address: www.healthcaresource.com
Health Care Source is a leading provider of talent management, recruitment and employment services for healthcare providers. It offers a comprehensive suite of solutions, which includes features, such as applicant tracking and onboarding, recruitment optimization, reference checking, behavioral assessments, merit planning, employee performance and eLearning courseware among others.

MedicalWorkers.com
Web Address: www.medicalworkers.com
MedicalWorkers.com is an employment site for medical and health care professionals.

MedJump.com
E-mail Address: info@medjump.com
Web Address: www.medjump.com
MedJump.com is dedicated to empowering health care and medical-related professionals with the necessary tools to market their abilities and skills.

Medzilla, Inc.
P.O. Box 1710
Marysville, WA 98270 USA
Phone: 360-657-5681
Fax: 425-279-5427
E-mail Address: info@medzilla.com
Web Address: www.medzilla.com
Medzilla, Inc.'s web site offers job searches, salary surveys, a search agent and information on employment in the biotech, pharmaceuticals, healthcare and science sectors.

Monster Career Advice-Healthcare
133 Boston Post Rd.
Weston, MA 02493 USA
Phone: 978-461-8000
Fax: 978-461-8100
Toll Free: 800-666-7837
Web Address: career-advice.monster.com/Healthcare/job-category-3975.aspx
Monster Career Advice-Healthcare, a service of Monster Worldwide, Inc., provides industry-related articles, job listings, job searches and search agents for the medical field.

NationJob Network-Medical and Health Care Jobs Page
920 Morgan St., Ste. T
Des Moines, IA 50309 USA
Fax: 515-243-5384
Toll Free: 800-292-7731
E-mail Address:
customerservice@nationjob.com
Web Address:
www.nationjob.com/medical
The NationJob Network-Medical and Health Care Jobs Page offers information and listings for health care employment.

Nurse-Recruiter.com
15500 SW Jay St., Ste. 26760
Beaverton, OR 97006-6018 USA
Toll Free: 877-562-7966
Web Address: www.nurse-recruiter.com
Nurse-Recruiter.com is an online job portal devoted to bringing health care employers and the nursing community together.

PracticeLink
415 2nd Ave.
Hinton, WV 25951 USA
Toll Free: 800-776-8383
E-mail Address:
helpdesk@practicelink.com
Web Address: www.practicelink.com
PracticeLink, one of the largest physician employment web sites, is a free service with over 1.7 million page views each month. There are more than 5,000 hospitals, medical groups, private practices and health systems, posting over 20,000 physician job opportunities on the web site.

RPh on the Go USA, Inc.
8001 N. Lincoln Ave., Ste. 800
Skokie, IL 60077 USA
Phone: 847-588-7170
Fax: 847-588-7060
Toll Free: 800-553-7359
Web Address: www.rphonthego.com
RPh on the Go USA, Inc. places temporary and permanent qualified professionals in the pharmacy community. This pharmacy staffing firm offers access to more than 160,000 pharmacy professionals and matches the right pharmacy personnel to help meet clients' needs.

17) Careers-Job Reference Tools

Vault.com, Inc.
132 W. 31st St., Fl. 17
New York, NY 10001 USA

Fax: 212-366-6117
Toll Free: 800-535-2074
E-mail Address: customerservice@vault.com
Web Address: www.vault.com
Vault.com, Inc. is a comprehensive career web site for employers and employees, with job postings and valuable information on a wide variety of industries. Its features and content are largely geared toward MBA degree holders.

18) Careers-Science

New Scientist Jobs
Quadrant House, Sutton
Surrey, SM2 5AS UK
Phone: 781-734-8770
E-mail Address: nssales@newscientist.com
Web Address: jobs.newscientist.com
New Scientist Jobs is a web site produced by the publishers of New Scientist Magazine that connects jobseekers and employers in the bioscience fields. The site includes a job search engine and a free-of-charge e-mail job alert service.

19) Child Development

Human Growth Foundation
997 Glen Cove Ave., Ste. 5
Glenhead, NY 11545 USA
Fax: 516-671-4055
Toll Free: 800-451-6434
Web Address: www.hgfound.org
The Human Growth Foundation helps children and adults with disorders related to growth or growth hormone through research, education, support and advocacy.

20) Children-Vital Statistics

Federal Interagency Forum on Child and Family Statistics (Childstats)
Web Address: www.childstats.gov
The Forum is a joint effort by 22 U.S. government agencies. Its signature report, America's Children: Key National Indicators of Well-Being, is an annual indicators report that details the status of children and families in the United States. All data are updated annually on the Forum's website. A more detailed report alternates every other year with a condensed version that highlights selected indicators.

21) Chinese Government Agencies-Science & Technology

China Ministry of Science and Technology (MOST)
15B Fuxing Rd.
Beijing, 100862 China
Web Address: www.most.gov.cn
The China Ministry of Science and Technology (MOST) is the PRC's official body for science and technology related activities. It drafts laws, policies and regulations regarding science and technology; oversees budgeting and accounting for funds; and supervises research institutes operating in China, among other duties.

22) Christian Health Coverage Associations

Alliance of Health Care Sharing Ministries
2200 South Babcock St
Melbourne, FL 32901 USA
Phone: 833-997-4273
Web Address: www.healthcaresharing.org
The alliance was established ii 2007 as a 501(c)(6) trade organization to represent the common interests of Christian organizations which are facilitating the sharing of health care needs (financial, emotional, and spiritual) by individuals and families, and their participants. The alliance is comprised of America's three largest health care sharing ministries: Samaritan Ministries, Christian Care Ministry, and Christian Healthcare Ministries.

23) Clinical Trials

Clinical Trials
U.S. National Library of Medicine
8600 Rockville Pike
Bethesda, MD 20894 USA
Phone: 301-594-5983
Toll Free: 888-346-3656
Web Address: www.clinicaltrials.gov
Clinical Trials, a service of the National Library of Medicine (NLM), offers up-to-date information for locating federally and privately supported clinical trials for a wide range of diseases and conditions, both within the U.S. and internationally.

Institute of Clinical Research (ICR)
10 Cedar Ct., Grove Park
White Waltham Rd.
Maidenhead, SL6 3LW UK
Phone: 44-1628-501700
Fax: 44-1628-501709
E-mail Address: icrenquiries@yahoo.co.uk
Web Address: www.icr-global.org
The Institute of Clinical Research (ICR) is a nonprofit professional organization for clinical researchers in the pharmaceutical industry in the U.K. It has over 3,000 members in 49 countries worldwide, which primarily include professionals involved in the design, management and conduct of human clinical trials.

24) Communications Professional Associations

Health and Science Communications Association (HeSCA)
P.O. Box 31323
Omaha, NE 68132 USA
Phone: 402-915-5373
E-mail Address: hesca@hesca.org
Web Address: hesca.net
The Health and Science Communications Association (HeSCA) is an organization of communications professionals committed to sharing knowledge and resources in the health sciences arena.

Health Industry Business Communications Council (HIBCC)
2525 E. Arizona Biltmore Cir., Ste. 127
Phoenix, AZ 85016 USA
Phone: 602-381-1091
Fax: 602-381-1093
E-mail Address: info@hibcc.org
Web Address: www.hibcc.org
The Health Industry Business Communications Council (HIBCC) seeks to facilitate electronic communications by developing appropriate standards for information exchange among all health care trading partners.

25) Consulting Industry Associations

American Association of Legal Nurse Consultants (AALNC)
330 N. Wabash Ave., Ste. 2000
Chicago, IL 60611 USA
Fax: 312-673-6655
Toll Free: 877-402-2562
E-mail Address: info@aalnc.org
Web Address: www.aalnc.org
The American Association of Legal Nurse Consultants (AALNC) is a nonprofit organization dedicated to the professional enhancement of registered nurses practicing in a consulting capacity in the legal field.

National Society of Certified Healthcare Business Consultants (NSCHBC)
12100 Sunset Hills Rd., Ste. 130
Reston, VA 20190 USA
Phone: 703-234-4099
Fax: 703-435-4390
E-mail Address: info@nschbc.org
Web Address: www.nschbc.org
The National Society of Certified Healthcare Business Consultants was founded by the membership of the Institute of Certified Healthcare Business Consultants, the National Association of Healthcare Consultants and the Society of Medical Dental Management Consultants on July 1, 2006. It offers an active platform for sharing best practices, networking and understanding healthcare environment.

26) Corporate Information Resources

bizjournals.com
120 W. Morehead St., Ste. 400
Charlotte, NC 28202 USA
Toll Free: 866-853-3661
E-mail Address: gmurchison@bizjournals.com
Web Address: www.bizjournals.com
Bizjournals.com is the online media division of American City Business Journals, the publisher of dozens of leading city business journals nationwide. It provides access to research into the latest news regarding companies both small and large. The organization maintains 42 websites and 64 print publications and sponsors over 700 annual industry events.

Business Wire
101 California St., Fl. 20
San Francisco, CA 94111 USA
Phone: 415-986-4422
Fax: 415-788-5335
Toll Free: 800-227-0845
E-mail Address: info@businesswire.com
Web Address: www.businesswire.com
Business Wire offers news releases, industry- and company-specific news, top headlines, conference calls, IPOs on the Internet, media services and access to tradeshownews.com and BW Connect On-line through its informative and continuously updated web site.

Edgar Online, Inc.
11200 Rockville Pike, Ste. 310
Rockville, MD 20852 USA
Phone: 301-287-0300
Fax: 301-287-0390
Toll Free: 888-870-2316
Web Address: www.edgar-online.com
Edgar Online, Inc. is a gateway and search tool for viewing corporate documents, such as annual reports on Form 10-K, filed with the U.S. Securities and Exchange Commission.

PR Newswire Association LLC
350 Hudson St., Ste. 300
New York, NY 10014-4504 USA
Fax: 800-793-9313
Toll Free: 800-776-8090
E-mail Address: MediaInquiries@prnewswire.com
Web Address: www.prnewswire.com
PR Newswire Association LLC provides comprehensive communications services for public relations and investor relations professionals, ranging from information distribution and market intelligence to the creation of online multimedia content and investor relations web sites. Users can also view recent corporate press releases from companies across the globe. The Association is owned by United Business Media plc.

Silicon Investor
E-mail Address: si.admin@siliconinvestor.com
Web Address: www.siliconinvestor.com
Silicon Investor is focused on providing information about technology companies. Its web site serves as a financial discussion forum and offers quotes, profiles and charts.

27) Diabetes

American Diabetes Association
1701 N. Beauregard St.
Alexandria, VA 22311 USA
Toll Free: 800-342-2383
Web Address: www.diabetes.org
The American Diabetes Association is a nonprofit health organization providing diabetes research, information and advocacy. It consists of over 1million volunteers, more than 441,000 members with diabetes, their families and caregivers, over 800 staff members and roughly 16,500 healthcare professionals.

Juvenile Diabetes Research Foundation (JDRF)
26 Broadway, Fl.14
New York, NY 10004 USA
Fax: 212-785-9595
Toll Free: 800-533-2873
E-mail Address: info@jdrf.org
Web Address: www.jdrf.org
The Juvenile Diabetes Research Foundation (JDRF) is a major nonprofit, nongovernmental sponsor of type 1 diabetes (T1D) research. JDRF focuses on innovative cure, prevention and treatment of T1D and its complications, which it achieves through funding research, advocating government support of research and new therapies and connecting and engaging the T1D community.

28) Disabling Conditions

Americans with Disabilities Act (ADA)
950 Pennsylvania Ave. NW
Civil Rights Div., Disability Rights Section-NYA
Washington, DC 20530 USA
Phone: 202-307-0663
Fax: 202-307-1197
Toll Free: 800-514-0301
Web Address: www.ada.gov
The Americans with Disabilities Act (ADA) web site provides information and technical assistance on the Americans with Disabilities Act.

Job Accommodation Network (JAN)
P.O. Box 6080
Morgantown, WV 26506-6080 USA
Phone: 304-293-7186
Fax: 304-293-5407
Toll Free: 800-526-7234
E-mail Address: jan@askjan.org
Web Address: askjan.org
The Job Accommodation Network (JAN) is a free consulting service that provides guidance and information about job accommodations, the Americans with Disabilities Act and the employability of people with disabilities.

National Easter Seal Society
233 S. Wacker Dr., Ste. 2400
Chicago, IL 60606 USA
Phone: 312-726-6200
Fax: 312-726-1494
Toll Free: 800-221-6827
Web Address: www.easterseals.com
The National Easter Seal Society provides services to children and adults with disabilities and special needs, as well as assistance to their families. It offers education, outreach, advocacy, child development centers, physical rehabilitation and job training for people with disabilities.

29) Diseases, Rare & Other

American Association on Intellectual and Developmental Disabilities (AAIDD)
501 3rd St. NW, Ste. 200
Washington, DC 20001 USA
Phone: 202-387-1968
Fax: 202-387-2193
E-mail Address: ccarpenter@aaidd.org

Web Address: aaidd.org
The American Association on Intellectual and Developmental Disabilities (AAIDD) promotes progressive policies, sound research, effective practices and universal human rights for people with mental challenges.

American SIDS Institute
528 Raven Way
Naples, FL 34110 USA
Phone: 239-431-5425
Fax: 239-431-5536
Web Address: www.sids.org
The American SIDS Institute is a nonprofit healthcare organization dedicated to the prevention of sudden infant death and the promotion of infant health. It is involved in research and education of both causes and prevention of sudden infant death, as well as offers support for the families affected by it.

Amyotrophic Lateral Sclerosis Association (ALSA)
1275 K St. NW, Ste. 250
Washington, DC 20005 USA
Phone: 202-407-8580
Fax: 202-464-8869
Toll Free: 800-782-4747
E-mail Address: alsinfo@alsa-national.org
Web Address: www.alsa.org
The Amyotrophic Lateral Sclerosis Association (ALSA) seeks to be the primary resource for Lou Gehrig's Disease by providing information about the disease, products and services, physicians and other information.

Angelman Syndrome Foundation (ASF)
75 Executive Dr., Ste. 327
Aurora, IL 60504 USA
Phone: 630-978-4245
Fax: 630-978-7408
Toll Free: 800-432-6435
Web Address: www.angelman.org
The mission of the Angelman Syndrome Foundation (ASF) is to advance the awareness and treatment of Angelman Syndrome through education, information exchange and research.

Autism Society of America (ASA)
4340 E-W Hwy, Ste. 350
Bethesda, MD 20814 USA
Phone: 301-657-0881
Toll Free: 800-328-8476
E-mail Address: info@autism-society.org
Web Address: www.autism-society.org
The Autism Society of America (ASA) seeks to promote lifelong access and opportunity for all individuals affected by autism to be fully participating members of their communities.

Cleft Palate Foundation (CPF)
1504 E. Franklin St., Ste. 102
Chapel Hill, NC 27514-2820 USA
Phone: 919-933-9044
Fax: 919-933-9604
Toll Free: 800-242-5338
E-mail Address: info@cleftline.org
Web Address: www.cleftline.org
The Cleft Palate Foundation (CPF) is a nonprofit organization dedicated to optimizing the quality of life for individuals affected by facial birth defects. It serves individuals and families affected by cleft lip/palate and other craniofacial conditions through team care, education and personal support.

Cystic Fibrosis Foundation (CFF)
6931 Arlington Rd., Fl. 2
Bethesda, MD 20814 USA
Phone: 301-951-4422
Fax: 301-951-6378
Toll Free: 800-344-4823
E-mail Address: info@cff.org
Web Address: www.cff.org
The Cystic Fibrosis Foundation (CFF) assures the development of the means to cure and control cystic fibrosis and to improve the quality of life for those affected with the disease.

Dystonia Medical Research Foundation
One E. Wacker Dr., Ste. 2810
Chicago, IL 60601-1905 USA
Phone: 312-755-0198
Fax: 312-803-0138
Toll Free: 800-377-3978
E-mail Address: dystonia@dystonia-foundation.org
Web Address: www.dystonia-foundation.org
The Dystonia Medical Research Foundation seeks to advance research for treatments and ultimately a cure for dystonia, to promote awareness and education of the disease and to support the needs and well-being of affected individuals and families.

Epilepsy Foundation of America
8301 Professional Place E., Ste. 200
Landover, MD 20785-2353 USA
Fax: 301-577-2684
Toll Free: 800-332-1000
E-mail Address: ContactUs@efa.org
Web Address: www.epilepsyfoundation.org
The Epilepsy Foundation of America is the national nonprofit voluntary agency devoted to the wellbeing of people with epilepsy in the U.S. and their families. It is dedicated to prevent, control and cure epilepsy through community services, public education, federal and local advocacy and research into new treatments and therapies.

Hepatitis B Foundation
3805 Old Easton Rd.
Doylestown, PA 18902 USA
Phone: 215-489-4900
Fax: 215-489-4920
E-mail Address: info@hepb.org
Web Address: www.hepb.org
The Hepatitis B Foundation is a national nonprofit organization dedicated to finding a cure and improving the quality of life of those affected by hepatitis B worldwide through research, education and patient advocacy.

Huntington's Disease Society of America, Inc. (HDSA)
505 8th Ave., Ste. 902
New York, NY 10018 USA
Phone: 212-242-1968
Fax: 212-239-3430
Toll Free: 800-345-4372
E-mail Address: hdsainfo@hdsa.org
Web Address: www.hdsa.org
The Huntington's Disease Society of America, Inc. (HDSA) is dedicated to finding a cure for Huntington's disease (HD) while providing support and services for those living with HD and their families.

International Myeloma Foundation (IMF)
12650 Riverside Dr., Ste. 206
North Hollywood, CA 91607 USA
Phone: 818-487-7455
Fax: 818-487-7454
Toll Free: 800-452-2873
E-mail Address: TheIMF@myeloma.org
Web Address: www.myeloma.org
The International Myeloma Foundation (IMF) is a network dedicated to the treatment of myeloma with over 350,000 members in 140 countries.

Lupus Foundation of America
2000 L St. NW, Ste. 410
Washington, DC 20036 USA
Phone: 202-349-1155
Fax: 202-349-1156
Toll Free: 800-558-0121
E-mail Address: info@lupus.org
Web Address: www.lupus.org
The Lupus Foundation of America is a nonprofit voluntary health organization dedicated to improving the diagnosis and treatment of lupus, supporting individuals and families affected by the disease, increasing awareness of lupus among health professionals and the public, and finding the cure.

Muscular Dystrophy Association (MDA)
222 S. Riverside Plaza, Ste. 1500
Chicago, IL 60606 USA
Toll Free: 800-572-1717
E-mail Address: mda@mdausa.org
Web Address: www.mda.org
The Muscular Dystrophy Association (MDA) is a voluntary health agency aimed at conquering neuromuscular diseases that affect more than 1 million Americans.

Myasthenia Gravis Foundation of America (MGFA)
355 Lexington Ave., 15th Fl.
New York, NY 10017 USA
Fax: 212-297-2159
Toll Free: 800-541-5454
Web Address: www.myasthenia.org
The Myasthenia Gravis Foundation of America (MGFA) is a national volunteer health agency dedicated solely to the fight against myasthenia gravis. It consists of a network of chapters, support groups and programs; and works to find cure, improve treatment options and provide information and support to people living with the disease.

National Down Syndrome Congress (NDSC)
30 Mansell Ct., Ste. 108
Roswell, GA 30076 USA
Phone: 770-604-9500
Fax: 770-604-9898
Toll Free: 800-232-6372
E-mail Address: info@ndsccenter.org
Web Address: www.ndsccenter.org
The National Down Syndrome Congress (NDSC) strives to be the national advocacy organization for Down syndrome and to provide support and leadership in all areas of concern related to persons with Down syndrome.

National Multiple Sclerosis Society (NMSS)
900 S Broadway, Fl. 2
Denver, CO 80209 USA
Phone: 303-698-7400
Fax: 303-698-7421
Toll Free: 800-344-4867
E-mail Address: cowyreceptionist@nmss.org
Web Address: www.nmss.org
The National Multiple Sclerosis Society (NMSS) and its network of chapters nationwide promote research, educate and advocate on critical issues, as well as organize a wide range of programs for those living with multiple sclerosis.

National Organization for Rare Disorders (NORD)
55 Kenosia Ave.
Danbury, CT 06810 USA
Phone: 203-744-0100
Fax: 203-798-2291
Toll Free: 800-999-6673
Web Address: www.rarediseases.org
The National Organization for Rare Disorders (NORD) is a unique federation of voluntary health organizations dedicated to helping people with rare diseases and assisting the organizations that serve them.

National Peticulosis Association (NPA)
1005 Boylston St., Ste. 343
Newton, MA 02461 USA
Phone: 617-905-0176
E-mail Address: npa@headlice.org
Web Address: www.headlice.org
The National Peticulosis Association (NPA) is a nonprofit health and education agency dedicated to protecting children from the misuse and abuse of potentially harmful lice and scabies pesticidal treatments.

National Reye's Syndrome Foundation (NRSF)
426 N. Lewis St.
P.O. Box 829
Bryan, OH 43506 USA
Phone: 419-924-9000
Fax: 419-924-9999
Toll Free: 800-233-7393
E-mail Address: nrsf@reyessyndrome.org
Web Address: www.reyessyndrome.org
The National Reye's Syndrome Foundation (NRSF) attempts to generate a concerted, organized lay movement to eradicate Reye's syndrome. It works to raise awareness, educate public, offer support and guidance and conduct research into the cause, management, treatment and prevention of Reye's Syndrome.

Scleroderma Foundation
300 Rosewood Dr., Ste. 105
Danvers, MA 01923 USA
Phone: 978-463-5843
Fax: 978-777-1313
Toll Free: 800-722-4673
E-mail Address: sfinfo@scleroderma.org
Web Address: www.scleroderma.org
The Scleroderma Foundation seeks to help patients and their families cope with scleroderma, as well as raise public awareness and stimulate research.

Sickle Cell Disease Association of America, Inc. (SCDAA)
3700 Koppers St., Ste. 570
Baltimore, MD 21202 USA
Phone: 410-528-1555
Fax: 410-528-1495
Toll Free: 800-421-8453
E-mail Address: scdaa@sicklecelldisease.org
Web Address: www.sicklecelldisease.org
The Sickle Cell Disease Association of America (SCDAA) is devoted to the care and cure of individuals with sickle cell disease. The group also organizes conferences and prepares and distributes substantive educational materials about the sickle cell disease problem.

Spina Bifida Association (SBA)
1600 Wilson Blvd., Ste. 800
Arlington, VA 22209 USA
Phone: 202-944-3285
Fax: 202-944-3295
Toll Free: 800-621-3141
E-mail Address: sbaa@sbaa.org
Web Address: www.sbaa.org
The Spina Bifida Association is a national voluntary health agency that seeks to promote the prevention of spina bifida and to enhance the lives of all affected. Through its network of chapters, the association is present in over 125 communities across the nation connecting 10,000 people annually.

Tourette Syndrome Association, Inc. (TSA)
42-40 Bell Blvd., Ste. 205
Bayside, NY 11361-2820 USA
Phone: 718-224-2999
E-mail Address: support@tourette.org
Web Address: tourette.org
The Tourette Syndrome Association, Inc. (TSA) is a voluntary, nonprofit membership organization that seeks to identify the cause, find the cure for and control the effects of Tourette syndrome.

United Cerebral Palsy (UCP)
1825 K St. NW, Ste. 600
Washington, DC 20006 USA
Phone: 202-776-0406
Toll Free: 800-872-5827
Web Address: www.ucp.org
United Cerebral Palsy (UCP) is a national organization that strives for change and progress for disabled persons within society. It works to advance the independence, productivity and full citizenship of people with disabilities through an affiliate network.

30) Drug & Alcohol Abuse

Al-Anon/Alateen
1600 Corporate Landing Pkwy.
Virginia Beach, VA 23454-5617 USA
Phone: 757-563-1600
Fax: 757-563-1655

Toll Free: 888-425-2666
E-mail Address: wso@al-anon.org
Web Address: www.al-anon.alateen.org
Al-Anon/Alateen strives to help families and friends of alcoholics recover from the effects of living with the problem drinking of a relative or friend.

Alcoholics Anonymous (AA)
475 Riverside Dr. at W. 120th St., Fl. 11
NY, NY 10115 USA
Phone: 212-870-3400
Web Address: www.aa.org
Alcoholics Anonymous (AA) is a nonprofit international fellowship dedicated to helping alcoholics in defeating their addictions or drinking problems. Its web site offers many useful resources for those who wish to seek help regarding alcohol addiction and related concerns.

Drug Information Association (DIA)
800 Enterprise Rd., Ste. 200
Horsham, PA 19044-3595 USA
Phone: 215-442-6100
Fax: 215-442-6199
E-mail Address:
Americas@DIAglobal.org
Web Address: www.diaglobal.org
The Drug Information Association (DIA) provides a neutral global forum for the exchange and dissemination of information on the discovery, development, evaluation and utilization of medicines and related health care technologies.

National Clearinghouse for Alcohol and Drug Information (NCADI)
P.O. Box 2345
Rockville, MD 20847-2345 USA
Phone: 301-468-2600
Fax: 301-468-6433
Toll Free: 800-729-6686
E-mail Address: info@health.org
Web Address: www.health.org
The National Clearinghouse for Alcohol and Drug Information (NCADI) is the information service of the Center for Substance Abuse Prevention of the Substance Abuse and Mental Health Services Administration in the U.S. Department of Health & Human Services.

Phoenix House Foundation (The)
50 Jay St.
Brooklyn, NY 11201 USA
Phone: 646-505-2080
Fax: 212-595-6365
Toll Free: 888-671-9392
E-mail Address:
jinevins@phoenixhouse.org.
Web Address: www.phoenixhouse.org
The Phoenix House Foundation is a drug awareness and rehabilitation group with operations in California, Florida, New England, New York, Maryland, New Hampshire, Massachusetts, Rhode Island, Vermont, Virginia, Texas and Washington D.C. It conducts more than 130 programs including individualized, holistic drug and alcohol addiction treatment.

31) Economic Data & Research

Centre for European Economic Research (The, ZEW)
L 7, 1
Mannheim, 68161 Germany
Phone: 49-621-1235-01
Fax: 49-621-1235-224
E-mail Address: empfang@zew.de
Web Address: www.zew.de/en
Zentrum fur Europaische Wirtschaftsforschung, The Centre for European Economic Research (ZEW), distinguishes itself in the analysis of internationally comparative data in a European context and in the creation of databases that serve as a basis for scientific research. The institute maintains a special library relevant to economic research and provides external parties with selected data for the purpose of scientific research. ZEW also offers public events and seminars concentrating on banking, business and other economic-political topics.

Economic and Social Research Council (ESRC)
Polaris House
North Star Ave.
Swindon, SN2 1UJ UK
Phone: 44-01793 413000
E-mail Address: esrcenquiries@esrc.ac.uk
Web Address: www.esrc.ac.uk
The Economic and Social Research Council (ESRC) funds research and training in social and economic issues. It is an independent organization, established by Royal Charter. Current research areas include the global economy; social diversity; environment and energy; human behavior; and health and well-being.

Eurostat
5 Rue Alphonse Weicker
Joseph Bech Bldg.
Luxembourg, L-2721 Luxembourg
Phone: 352-4301-1
E-mail Address: eurostat-pressoffice@ec.europa.eu
Web Address: ec.europa.eu/eurostat
Eurostat is the European Union's service that publishes a wide variety of comprehensive statistics on European industries, populations, trade, agriculture, technology, environment and other matters.

Federal Statistical Office of Germany
Gustav-Stresemann-Ring 11
Wiesbaden, D-65189 Germany
Phone: 49-611-75-2405
Fax: 49-611-72-4000
Web Address: www.destatis.de
Federal Statistical Office of Germany publishes a wide variety of nation and regional economic data of interest to anyone who is studying Germany, one of the world's leading economies. Data available includes population, consumer prices, labor markets, health care, industries and output.

India Brand Equity Foundation (IBEF)
Fl. 20, Jawahar Vyapar Bhawan
Tolstoy Marg
New Deli, 110001 India
Phone: 91-11-43845500
Fax: 91-11-23701235
E-mail Address: info.brandindia@ibef.org
Web Address: www.ibef.org
India Brand Equity Foundation (IBEF) is a public-private partnership between the Ministry of Commerce and Industry, the Government of India and the Confederation of Indian Industry. The foundation's primary objective is to build positive economic perceptions of India globally. It aims to effectively present the India business perspective and leverage business partnerships in a globalizing marketplace.

National Bureau of Statistics (China)
57, Yuetan Nanjie, Sanlihe
Xicheng District
Beijing, 100826 China
Fax: 86-10-6878-2000
E-mail Address: info@gj.stats.cn
Web Address: www.stats.gov.cn/english
The National Bureau of Statistics (China) provides statistics and economic data regarding China's economy and society.

Organization for Economic Co-operation and Development (OECD)
2 rue Andre Pascal, Cedex 16
Paris, 75775 France
Phone: 33-1-45-24-82-00
Fax: 33-1-45-24-85-00
E-mail Address: webmaster@oecd.org
Web Address: www.oecd.org
The Organization for Economic Co-operation and Development (OECD) publishes detailed economic, government, population, social and trade statistics on a country-by-country basis for over 30 nations representing the world's largest economies. Sectors covered range from

industry, labor, technology and patents, to health care, environment and globalization.

Statistics Bureau, Director-General for Policy Planning (Japan)
19-1 Wakamatsu-cho
Shinjuku-ku
Tokyo, 162-8668 Japan
Phone: 81-3-5273-2020
E-mail Address: toukeisoudan@soumu.go.jp
Web Address: www.stat.go.jp/english
The Statistics Bureau, Director-General for Policy Planning (Japan) and Statistical Research and Training Institute, a part of the Japanese Ministry of Internal Affairs and Communications, plays the central role of producing and disseminating basic official statistics and coordinating statistical work under the Statistics Act and other legislation.

Statistics Canada
150 Tunney's Pasture Driveway
Ottawa, ON K1A 0T6 Canada
Phone: 514-283-8300
Fax: 514-283-9350
Toll Free: 800-263-1136
E-mail Address: STATCAN.infostats-infostats.STATCAN@canada.ca
Web Address: www.statcan.gc.ca
Statistics Canada provides a complete portal to Canadian economic data and statistics. Its conducts Canada's official census every five years, as well as hundreds of surveys covering numerous aspects of Canadian life.

32) Electronic Health Records/Continuity of Care Records

American Health Information Management Association (AHIMA)
233 N. Michigan Ave., Fl. 21
Chicago, IL 60601-5809 USA
Phone: 312-233-1100
Fax: 312-233-1090
Toll Free: 800-335-5535
Web Address: www.ahima.org
The American Health Information Management Association (AHIMA) is a professional association that consists health information management professionals who work throughout the health care industry.

American Medical Informatics Association (AMIA)
4720 Montgomery Ln., Ste. 500
Bethesda, MD 20814 USA
Phone: 301-657-1291
Fax: 301-657-1296
Web Address: www.amia.org
The American Medical Informatics Association (AMIA) is a membership organization of individuals, institutions and corporations dedicated to developing and using information technologies to improve health care.

College of Healthcare Information Management Executives (CHIME)
710 Avis Dr., Ste. 200
Ann Arbor, MI 48108 USA
Phone: 734-665-0000
Fax: 734-665-4922
E-mail Address: staff@cio-chime.org
Web Address: www.cio-chime.org
College of Healthcare Information Management Executives (CHIME) was formed with the dual objective of serving the professional development needs of health care CIOs and advocating the more effective use of information management within health care.

Healthcare Information and Management Systems Society (HIMSS)
33 W Monroe St., Ste. 1700
Chicago, IL 60603-5616 USA
Phone: 312-664-4467
Fax: 312-664-6143
Web Address: www.himss.org
The Healthcare Information and Management Systems Society (HIMSS) provides leadership in the optimal use of technology, information and management systems for the betterment of health care.

National Association of Health Data Organizations (NAHDO)
124 S. 400 E, Ste. 220
Salt Lake City, UT 84111 USA
Phone: 801-532-2299
Fax: 801-532-2228
E-mail Address: info@nahdo.org
Web Address: www.nahdo.org
The National Association of Health Data Organizations (NAHDO) is a nonprofit membership organization dedicated to strengthening the nation's health information system.

33) Engineering, Research & Scientific Associations

American Association for the Advancement of Science (AAAS)
1200 New York Ave. NW
Washington, DC 20005 USA
Phone: 202-326-6400
Web Address: www.aaas.org
The American Association for the Advancement of Science (AAAS) is the world's largest scientific society and the publisher of Science magazine. It is an international nonprofit organization dedicated to advancing science around the globe.

American Society for Healthcare Engineering (ASHE)
155 N. Wacker Dr., Ste. 400
Chicago, IL 60606 USA
Phone: 312-422-3800
Fax: 312-422-4571
E-mail Address: ashe@aha.org
Web Address: www.ashe.org
The American Society for Healthcare Engineering (ASHE) is the advocate and resource for continuous improvement in the health care engineering and facilities management professions. It is devoted to professionals who design, build, maintain and operate hospitals and other healthcare facilities.

American Society of Safety Engineers (ASSE)
520 N. Northwest Hwy
Park Ridge, IL 60068 USA
Phone: 847-699-2929
E-mail Address: customerservice@asse.org
Web Address: www.asse.org
The American Society of Safety Engineers (ASSE) is the world's oldest and largest professional safety organization. It manages, supervises and consults on safety, health and environmental issues in industry, insurance, government and education.

Association of the Scientific Medical Societies in Germany (AWMF)
Ubierstr. 20
Dusseldorf, D-40223 Germany
Phone: 49-211-31-28-28
Web Address: www.awmf.org
The Association of the Scientific Medical Societies in Germany (AWMF) represents roughly 173 specialty scientific societies in Germany as well as the medical sciences, research and practices in general.

European Commission Research & Innovation
ORBN 2/65
Brussels, B-1049 Belgium
Phone: 32-2-29-911111
Web Address: ec.europa.eu/research/index.cfm?lg=en
The European Commission Research & Innovation site has over 25,000 pages and links of interest to those in research, through many industries including research, business, teaching. The site offers information in more than 11 languages.

German Association of High-Tech Industries (SPECTARIS)
Werderscher Markt 15
Berlin, 10117 Germany
Phone: 49-30-4140-210
Fax: 49-30-4140-2133
E-mail Address: info@spectaris.de
Web Address: www.spectaris.de
The German Association of High-Tech Industries (SPECTARIS) is the trade association for technology and research in the consumer optics, photonics, biotech, laboratory technology and medical technology sectors.

Institute of Biological Engineering (IBE)
446 East High St., Ste. 10
Lexington, KY 40507 USA
Phone: 859-977-7450
Fax: 859-271-0607
E-mail Address: info@ibe.org
Web Address: www.ibe.org
The Institute of Biological Engineering (IBE) is a professional organization encouraging inquiry and interest in biological engineering and professional development for its members.

Institute of Electrical and Electronics Engineers (IEEE)
3 Park Ave., Fl. 17
New York, NY 10016-5997 USA
Phone: 212-419-7900
Fax: 212-752-4929
Toll Free: 800-678-4333
E-mail Address: society-info@ieee.org
Web Address: www.ieee.org
The Institute of Electrical and Electronics Engineers (IEEE) is a nonprofit, technical professional association of more than 430,000 individual members in approximately 160 countries. The IEEE sets global technical standards and acts as an authority in technical areas ranging from computer engineering, biomedical technology and telecommunications, to electric power, aerospace and consumer electronics.

Institute of Physics and Engineering in Medicine (IPEM)
230 Tadcaster Rd.
Fairmount House
York, YO24 1ES UK
Phone: 44-1904-610-821
Fax: 44-1904-612-279
E-mail Address: office@ipem.ac.uk
Web Address: www.ipem.ac.uk
The Institute of Physics and Engineering in Medicine (IPEM) is an organization of scientists applying physics and engineering in medical and biological applications.

International Union of Microbiological Societies (IUMS)
Web Address: www.iums.org
The International Union of Microbiological Societies (IUMS) works to promote the study of microbiological sciences around the world through its three divisions: Bacteriology & Applied Microbiology (BAM); Mycology; and Virology. The association is one of the 31 Scientific Unions of the International Council of Science (ICSU).

National Academy of Science (NAS)
500 5th St. NW
Washington, DC 20001 USA
Phone: 202-334-2000
E-mail Address: worldwidefeedback@nas.edu
Web Address: www.nationalacademies.org
The National Academy of Science (NAS) is a private, nonprofit, self-perpetuating society of scholars engaged in scientific and engineering research. Three organizations comprise the NAS: The National Academy of Engineering, the National Academy of Sciences and the National Academy of Medicine.

National Medical Research Council (NMRC)
11 Biopolis Way
Helios 09-10/11
Singapore, 138667 Singapore
Phone: 65-6325-8130
Fax: 65-6324-3735
E-mail Address: MOH_NMRC@MOH.GOV.SG
Web Address: www.nmrc.gov.sg
National Medical Research Council (NMRC) oversees the development and advancement of medical research in Singapore.

Research in Germany, German Academic Exchange Service (DAAD)
Kennedyallee 50
Bonn, 53175 Germany
Phone: 49-228-882-743
Web Address: www.research-in-germany.de
The Research in Germany portal, German Academic Exchange Service (DAAD), is an information platform and contact point for those looking to find out more about Germany's research landscape and its latest research achievements. The portal is an initiative of the Federal Ministry of Education and Research.

Royal Society (The)
6-9 Carlton House Ter.
London, SW1Y 5AG UK
Phone: 44-20-7451-2500
E-mail Address: science.policy@royalsociety.org
Web Address: royalsociety.org
The Royal Society, originally founded in 1660, is the UK's leading scientific organization and the oldest scientific community in continuous existence. It operates as a national academy of science, supporting scientists, engineers, technologists and researchers. Its web site contains a wealth of data about the research and development initiatives of its fellows and foreign members.

34) Environmental Industry Associations

Air & Waste Management Association (A&WMA)
420 Fort Duquesne Blvd., Fl. 3
Pittsburgh, PA 15222-1435 USA
Phone: 412-232-3444
Fax: 412-232-3450
Toll Free: 800-270-3444
E-mail Address: info@awma.org
Web Address: www.awma.org
The Air & Waste Management Association (A&WMA) is a nonprofit professional organization that provides education and support to more than 5,000 environmental professionals in 65 nations.

35) Fitness Industry Associations

Aerobics and Fitness Association of America (AFAA)
1750 E. Northrop Blvd., Ste. 200
Chandler, AZ 85286 USA
Toll Free: 877-446-2322
E-mail Address: customerservice@afaa.com
Web Address: www.afaa.com
The Aerobics and Fitness Association of America (AFAA) provides certification training for personal trainers, group exercise instructors, kickboxing teachers and others in the fitness instruction field. It also offers workshops and answers questions from the public regarding safe and effective exercise programs and practices.

American Fitness Professionals and Associates (AFPA)
1601 Long Beach Blvd.
P.O. Box 214
Ship Bottom, NJ 08008 USA
Phone: 609-978-7583
Fax: 609-978-7582
Toll Free: 800-494-7782
E-mail Address: afpa@afpafitness.com
Web Address: www.afpafitness.com

American Fitness Professionals and Associates (AFPA) offers health and fitness professionals certification programs, continuing education courses, home correspondence courses and regional conventions.

International Health, Racquet and Sportsclub Association (IHRSA)
70 Fargo St.
Boston, MA 02210 USA
Phone: 617-951-0055
Fax: 617-951-0056
Toll Free: 800-228-4772
E-mail Address: info@ihrsa.org
Web Address: www.ihrsa.org
The International Health, Racquet & Sportsclub Association is the fitness industry's only global trade association. IHRSA represents over 10,000 for profit health and fitness facilities, and over 600 supplier companies in 75 countries.

National Academy of Kinesiology (NAK)
P.O. Box 5076
Champaign, IL 61820-2200 USA
Fax: 217-351-1549
E-mail Address: nak@hkusa.com
Web Address: www.nationalacademyofkinesiology.org
The National Academy of Kinesiology (NAK), formerly the American Academy of Kinesiology and Physical Education (AAKPE), promotes research of human movement and physical activity. NAK's members transmit knowledge about human movement and physical activity through yearly meetings and publications.

North American Society for the Psychology of Sport and Physical Activity (NASPSPA)
E-mail Address: qalmeida@wlu.ca
Web Address: http://naspspa.com
The North American Society for the Psychology of Sport and Physical Activity (NASPSPA) is an association of scholars from the behavioral sciences and related professions that seeks to advance the scientific study of human behavior in sport and physical activity.

SHAPE America-Society of Health and Physical Educators
1900 Association Dr.
Reston, VA 20191-1598 USA
Phone: 703-476-3400
Fax: 703-476-9527
Toll Free: 800-213-7193
Web Address: www.shapeamerica.org
SHAPE America-Society of Health and Physical Educators, formerly the American Alliance for Health, Physical Education, Recreation & Dance (AAHPERD) is an organization of professionals who support and assist those involved in physical education, fitness, leisure, dance, health promotion and education. It works with its 50 state affiliates and national partners to support initiatives, including the Presidential Youth Fitness Program and the Jump Rope For Heart/Hoops For Heart programs.

36) Fitness Resources

President's Council on Physical Fitness, Sports and Nutrition (PCPFSN)
1101 Wootton Pkwy., Ste. 560
Rockville, MD 20852 USA
Phone: 240-276-9567
Fax: 240-276-9860
E-mail Address: fitness@hhs.gov
Web Address: www.fitness.gov
The President's Council on Physical Fitness, Sports and Nutrition (PCPFSN) offers information about exercise, fitness and nutrition for people of all ages and works to promote active, healthy lifestyles.

YMCA of the USA
101 N. Wacker Dr.
Chicago, IL 60606 USA
Phone: 312-977-0031
Toll Free: 800-872-9622
E-mail Address: fulfillment@ymca.net
Web Address: www.ymca.net
The YMCA of the USA is the largest nonprofit community service organization in America, with over 2,700 YMCA locations in the U.S. These locations offer youth development and sports activities, fitness and other community events.

37) Food Service Industry Associations

Association for Healthcare Foodservices (AHF)
8400 Westpark Dr., Fl. 2
McLean, VA 22102 USA
Phone: 703-662-0615
Fax: 703-995-4456
E-mail Address: info@healthcarefoodservice.org
Web Address: www.healthcarefoodservice.org
The Association for Healthcare Foodservices (AHF), born out of the merger of the National Society for Healthcare Foodservice Management (HFM) and the American Society for Healthcare Food Service Administrators (ASHFSA), is a society dedicated to professionals and suppliers in the self-operated healthcare foodservice industry.

38) Genetics & Genomics Industry Associations

American College of Medical Genetics and Genomics (ACMG)
7220 Wisconsin Ave., Ste. 300
Bethesda, MD 20814 USA
Phone: 301-718-9603
Fax: 301-718-9604
E-mail Address: acmg@acmg.net
Web Address: www.acmg.net
The American College of Medical Genetics and Genomics (ACMG) provides education, resources and a voice for the medical genetics profession. The ACMG promotes the development and implementation of methods to diagnose, treat and prevent genetic disease.

39) Headache/Head Injury

American Council for Headache Education (ACHE)
19 Mantua Rd.
Mt. Royal, NJ 08061 USA
Phone: 856-423-0043
Fax: 856-423-0082
E-mail Address: achehq@talley.com
Web Address: www.achenet.org
The American Council for Headache Education (ACHE) is a nonprofit patient-health professional partnership dedicated to advancing the treatment and management of headaches and to raising the public awareness of headaches as valid, biologically based illnesses.

Brain Injury Association of America (BIAA)
1608 Spring Hill Rd., Ste. 110
Vienna, VA 22182 USA
Phone: 703-761-0750
Fax: 703-761-0755
Toll Free: 800-444-6443
E-mail Address: info@biausa.org
Web Address: www.biausa.org
The Brain Injury Association of America (BIAA) works to create a better future through brain injury prevention, research, education and advocacy.

National Headache Foundation (NHF)
820 N. Orleans, Ste. 411
Chicago, IL 60610 USA
Phone: 312-274-2650
Fax: 312-640-9049
Toll Free: 888-643-5552
E-mail Address: info@headaches.org
Web Address: www.headaches.org
The National Headache Foundation (NHF) is a nonprofit organization dedicated to educating headache sufferers and health care professionals about headache causes and treatments.

40) Health & Nutrition Associations

Academy of Nutrition and Dietetics
120 S. Riverside Plz., Ste. 2190
Chicago, IL 60606-6995 USA
Phone: 312-899-0040
Toll Free: 800-877-1600
E-mail Address: foundation@eatright.org
Web Address: www.eatright.org
The Academy of Nutrition and Dietetics, formerly known as the American Dietetic Association (ADA) is the world's largest organization of food and nutrition professionals, with nearly 65,000 members. In addition to services for its professional members, this organization's web site offers consumers a respected source for food and nutrition information.

American College of Nutrition (ACN)
300 S. Duncan Ave., Ste. 225
Clearwater, FL 33755 USA
Phone: 727-446-6086
Fax: 727-446-6202
E-mail Address:
office@americancollegeofnutrition.org
Web Address:
www.americancollegeofnutrition.org
The American College of Nutrition exists to promote knowledge and education on a variety of nutrition-related issues. The organization seeks to bring together professionals from diverse disciplines, including the business, education and medical fields.

Food Allergy Research & Education (FARE)
7925 Jones Branch Dr., Ste. 1100
McLean, VA 22102 USA
Phone: 703-691-3179
Fax: 703-691-2713
Toll Free: 800-929-4040
E-mail Address: info@foodallergy.org
Web Address: www.foodallergy.org
Food Allergy Research & Education (FARE), formed by the merger of the Food Allergy & Anaphylaxis Network (FAAN) and the Food Allergy Initiative, is a leader in food allergy and anaphylaxis awareness and the issues surrounding these conditions.

National Environmental Health Association (NEHA)
720 S. Colorado Blvd., Ste. 1000-N
Denver, CO 80246-1926 USA
Phone: 303-756-9090
Fax: 303-691-9490
Toll Free: 866-956-2258
E-mail Address: staff@neha.org
Web Address: www.neha.org
The National Environmental Health Association (NEHA) strengthens the foundation of food safety training in the United States by establishing a nationwide network of registered food safety trainers and other environmental health practitioners and by providing effective learning materials to trainers, managers and employees.

41) Health Associations-International

World Health Organization (WHO)
Ave. Appia 20, CH-1211
Geneva, 27 Switzerland
Phone: 41-22-791-2111
Fax: 41-22-791-3111
Web Address: www.who.int
The World Health Organization (WHO), the United Nations' specialized agency for health, works for the attainment by all people of the highest possible level of health. Health is defined in WHO's constitution as a state of complete physical, mental and social well-being and not merely the absence of disease or infirmity. It consists of offices in over 150 countries, with more than 7,000 people in its workforce.

42) Health Care Business & Professional Associations

Academy of Laser Dentistry (ALD)
9900 W. Sample Rd., Ste. 400
Coral Springs, FL 33065 USA
Phone: 954-346-3776
Fax: 954-757-2598
Toll Free: 877-527-3776
Web Address: www.laserdentistry.org
The Academy of Laser Dentistry (ALD) is an international professional membership association of dental practitioners and supporting organizations.

Academy of Medical-Surgical Nurses (AMSN)
E. Holly Ave., Box 56
Pitman, NJ 08071-0056 USA
Toll Free: 866-877-2676
E-mail Address: amsn@ajj.com
Web Address: www.amsn.org
The Academy of Medical-Surgical Nurses (AMSN) is dedicated to fostering excellence in adult health and in the medical-surgical nursing practice.

Academy of Spinal Cord Injury Nurses
206 S. Sixth St.
Springfield, IL 62701 USA
Phone: 217-753-1190
Fax: 217-525-1271
E-mail Address: kwinnett@firminc.com
Web Address:
www.academyscipro.org/Public/NursesMain.aspx
The Academy of Spinal Cord Injury Nurses, formerly the American Association of Spinal Cord Injury Nurses, is a division within the Academy of Spinal Cord Injury Professional, Inc. and is dedicated to promoting quality care for individuals with spinal cord impairment.

Advanced Medical Technology Association (AdvaMed)
701 Pennsylvania Ave. NW, Ste. 800
Washington, DC 20004-2654 USA
Phone: 202-783-8700
Fax: 202-783-8750
E-mail Address: info@advamed.org
Web Address: www.advamed.org
The Advanced Medical Technology Association (AdvaMed) strives to be the advocate for a legal, regulatory and economic climate that advances global health care by assuring worldwide access to the benefits of medical technology.

AFT Healthcare
555 New Jersey Ave. NW
Washington, DC 20001 USA
Phone: 202-879-4400
Web Address: www.aft.org/healthcare
AFT Healthcare, a division of the American Federation of Teachers, represents its members in the health professions and seeks to enhance the professional norms and ethics of health care workers.

Aging Life Care Association (ALCA), The
3275 W. Ina Rd., Ste. 130
Tucson, AZ 85741-2198 USA
Phone: 520-881-8008
Fax: 520-325-7925
Web Address: www.aginglifecare.org
The Aging Life Care Association (ALCA), formerly the National Association of Professional Geriatric Care Managers (GCM) is a nonprofit, professional organization of practitioners whose goal is the advancement of dignified care for the elderly and their families through education, professional development and highest ethical standards. It has over 2,000 members.

Air and Surface Transport Nurses Association (ASTNA)
13918 E. Mississippi Ave., Ste. 215
Aurora, CO 80012 USA
Phone: 303-344-0457
Fax: 800-937-9890
E-mail Address: astna@astna.org
Web Address: www.astna.org

The Air and Surface Transport Nurses Association (ASTNA) is a nonprofit member organization whose mission is to represent, promote and provide guidance to professional nurses who practice the unique and distinct specialty of transport nursing.

American Academy of Allergy, Asthma & Immunology (AAAAI)
555 E. Wells St., Ste. 1100
Milwaukee, WI 53202-3823 USA
Phone: 414-272-6071
Web Address: www.aaaai.org
The American Academy of Allergy, Asthma & Immunology (AAAAI) offers information and services to allergy and asthma sufferers and their families and friends.

American Academy of Ambulatory Care Nursing (AAACN)
E. Holly Ave., Box 56
Pitman, NJ 08071-0056 USA
Toll Free: 800-262-6877
E-mail Address: aaacn@aacn.org
Web Address: www.aaacn.org
The American Academy of Ambulatory Care Nursing (AAACN) is the association of professional nurses who identify ambulatory care practice as essential to the continuum of high-quality, cost-effective health care.

American Academy of Child and Adolescent Psychiatry (AACAP)
3615 Wisconsin Ave. NW
Washington, DC 20016-3007 USA
Phone: 202-966-7300
Fax: 202-464-0131
Web Address: www.aacap.org
The American Academy of Child and Adolescent Psychiatry (AACAP) is the leading national professional medical association dedicated to treating and improving the quality of life for children, adolescents and families affected by these disorders.

American Academy of Facial Plastic and Reconstructive Surgery (AAFPRS)
310 S. Henry St.
Alexandria, VA 22314 USA
Phone: 703-299-9291
E-mail Address: info@aafprs.org
Web Address: www.aafprs.org
The American Academy of Facial Plastic and Reconstructive Surgery (AAFPRS) is the world's largest association of facial plastic and reconstructive surgeons. Its membership consists of 2,700 board certified surgeons specializing in surgery of the face, head and neck.

American Academy of Family Physicians (AAFP)
11400 Tomahawk Creek Pkwy.
Leawood, KS 66211-2680 USA
Phone: 913-906-6000
Fax: 913-906-6075
Toll Free: 800-274-2237
Web Address: www.aafp.org
The American Academy of Family Physicians (AAFP) is a member association of family doctors, family medicine residents and medical students nationwide.

American Academy of Hospice and Palliative Medicine (AAHPM)
8735 West Higgins Rd., Ste. 300
Chicago, IL 60631 USA
Phone: 847-375-4712
Fax: 847-375-6475
E-mail Address: info@aahpm.org
Web Address: www.aahpm.org
The American Academy of Hospice and Palliative Medicine (AAHPM) is the only organization in the United States for physicians dedicated to the advancement of hospice and palliative medicine.

American Academy of Nursing (AAN)
1000 Vermont Ave., Ste. 910
Washington, DC 20005 USA
Phone: 202-777-1170
E-mail Address: info@aannet.org
Web Address: www.aannet.org
The American Academy of Nursing (AAN) works to enhance nursing profession by advancing health policy and practice and generate, synthesize and disseminate nursing knowledge.

American Academy of Ophthalmology (AAO)
655 Beach St.
San Francisco, CA 94120-7424 USA
Phone: 415-561-8500
Fax: 415-561-8533
Web Address: www.aao.org
The American Academy of Ophthalmology (AAO) is dedicated to advancing the education and interests of ophthalmologists in order to ensure that the public can obtain the best possible eye care.

American Academy of Orthotics and Prosthetics (AAOP)
1331 H. St. NW, Ste. 501
Washington, DC 20005 USA
Phone: 202-380-3663
Fax: 202-380-3447
E-mail Address: mbhaskar@oandp.org
Web Address: www.oandp.org
The American Academy of Orthotics and Prosthetics (AAOP) promotes high standards of patient care through advocacy, education, collaboration, literature and research.

American Association for Physician Leadership
400 N. Ashley Dr., Ste. 400
Tampa, FL 33602 USA
Phone: 813-287-2000
Fax: 813-287-8993
Toll Free: 800-562-8088
E-mail Address: info@physicianleaders.org
Web Address: www.physicianleaders.org/
The American Association for Physician Leadership, formerly the American College of Physician Executives (ACPE) represents physicians in health care leadership. It offers certification programs, online courses, consulting, physician leadership development programs, as well as career guidance, consulting and mentoring.

American Association of Colleges of Nursing (AACN)
1 Dupont Cir. NW, Ste. 530
Washington, DC 20036 USA
Phone: 202-463-6930
Fax: 202-785-8320
E-mail Address: info@aacn.nche.edu
Web Address: www.aacn.nche.edu
The American Association of Colleges of Nursing (AACN) is the national voice for U.S. nursing education programs, which works to promote excellence in nursing education, research and practice.

American Association of Critical Care Nurses (AACN)
101 Columbia
Aliso Viejo, CA 92656-4109 USA
Phone: 949-362-2000
Fax: 949-362-2020
Toll Free: 800-899-2226
E-mail Address: info@aacn.org
Web Address: www.aacn.org
The American Association of Critical Care Nurses (AACN) is a nonprofit organization which works to promote the interests of 500,000 member nurses caring for acutely and critically ill patients, as well as provides leadership to establish work/care environments that involves respect and healing.

American Association of Immunologists
1451 Rockville Pike, Ste. 650
Rockville, MD 20852 USA
Phone: 301-634-7178
Fax: 301-634-7887
E-mail Address: infoaai@aai.org
Web Address: www.aai.org
The American Association of Immunologists is a nonprofit organization that represents professionals in the

immunology field. Its membership consists of professionally trained scientists, who work to advance the knowledge of immunology and its related disciplines, foster the interchange of ideas and information among investigators and address the potential integration of immunologic principles into clinical practice.

American Association of Medical Assistants (AAMA)
20 N. Wacker Dr., Ste. 1575
Chicago, IL 60606 USA
Phone: 312-899-1500
Fax: 312-899-1259
Toll Free: 800-228-2262
Web Address: www.aama-ntl.org
The American Association of Medical Assistants (AAMA) seeks to promote the professional identity and stature of its members and the medical assisting profession through education and credentialing.

American Association of Neuroscience Nurses (AANN)
8735 W. Higgins Rd., Ste. 300
Chicago, IL 60631 USA
Phone: 847-375-4733
Fax: 847-375-6430
Toll Free: 888-557-2266
E-mail Address: info@aann.org
Web Address: www.aann.org
The American Association of Neuroscience Nurses (AANN) is a national organization of registered nurses and other health care professionals that work to improve the care of neuroscience patients and further the interests of health professionals in the neurosciences.

American Association of Nurse Anesthetists (AANA)
222 S. Prospect Ave.
Park Ridge, IL 60068-4001 USA
Phone: 847-692-7050
Fax: 847-692-6968
Toll Free: 855-526-2262
E-mail Address: info@aana.com
Web Address: www.aana.com
The American Association of Nurse Anesthetists (AANA) is a professional member organization that represents 49,000 registered nurse anesthetists nationwide.

American Association of Nurse Practitioners (AANP)
225 Reinekers Ln., Ste. 525
Alexandria, VA 22314 USA
Phone: 703-740-2529
Fax: 703-740-2533
E-mail Address: admin@aanp.org
Web Address: www.aanp.org
The American Association of Nurse Practitioners (AANP), the result of the merger between the American College of Nurse Practitioners (ACNP) and the American Academy of Nurse Practitioners, is focused on advocacy and keeping nurse practitioners current on legislative, regulatory and clinical practice issues that affect them in the rapidly changing health care arena.

American Association of Occupational Health Nurses (AAOHN)
7794 Grow Dr.
Pensacola, FL 32514 USA
Phone: 850-474-6963
Fax: 850-484-8762
Toll Free: 800-241-8014
E-mail Address:
AAOHN@internationalamc.com
Web Address: www.aaohn.org
The American Association of Occupational Health Nurses (AAOHN) seeks to advance the profession of occupational and environmental health nursing as the authority on health, safety, productivity and disability management for worker populations.

American Board of Facial Plastic and Reconstructive Surgery (ABFPRS)
115C S. St. Asaph St.
Alexandria, VA 22314 USA
Phone: 703-549-3223
Fax: 703-549-3357
E-mail Address: lwirth@abfprs.org
Web Address: www.abfprs.org
The American Board of Facial Plastic and Reconstructive Surgery (ABFPRS) is dedicated to improving the quality of facial plastic surgery available to the public by measuring the qualifications of candidate surgeons against rigorous standards.

American Board of Medical Specialties (ABMS)
353 North Clark St., Ste. 1400
Chicago, IL 60601 USA
Phone: 312-436-2600
Web Address: www.abms.org
The American Board of Medical Specialties (ABMS) is an organization that works with its 24 approved medical specialty boards in the evaluation and certification of physicians.

American Chiropractic Association (ACA)
1701 Clarendon Blvd., Ste. 200
Arlington, VA 22209 USA
Phone: 703-276-8800
Fax: 703-243-2593
E-mail Address:
memberinfo@acatoday.org
Web Address: www.acatoday.org
The American Chiropractic Association (ACA) exists to preserve, protect, improve and promote the chiropractic profession for the benefit of the patients it serves.

American College of Chest Physicians (ACCP)
2595 Patriot Blvd.
Glenview, IL 60026 USA
Phone: 224-521-9800
Fax: 224-521-9801
Toll Free: 800-343-2227
Web Address: www.chestnet.org
The American College of Chest Physicians (ACCP) is the world's largest clinical cardiopulmonary and critical care medical society with 19,000 members in 100 countries. Members include physicians, allied health professionals, and PhDs from the specialties of pulmonology, critical care medicine, thoracic surgery, cardiology, sleep, and other chest-related specialties.

American College of Emergency Physicians (ACEP)
1125 Executive Cir.
Irving, TX 75038-2522 USA
Phone: 972-550-0911
Fax: 972-580-2816
Toll Free: 800-798-1822
E-mail Address: membership@acep.org
Web Address: www.acep.org
The American College of Emergency Physicians (ACEP) exists to support quality emergency medical care and to promote the interests of emergency physicians.

American College of Health Care Administrators (ACHCA)
1101 Connecticut Ave. NW, Ste. 450
Washington, DC 20036 USA
Phone: 202-536-5120
Fax: 866-874-1585
E-mail Address: wodonnell@achca.org
Web Address: www.achca.org
The American College of Health Care Administrators (ACHCA) offers educational programming, professional certification and career development opportunities for health care administrators.

American College of Healthcare Executives (ACHE)
1 N. Franklin St., Ste. 1700
Chicago, IL 60606-3529 USA
Phone: 312-424-2800
Fax: 312-424-0023
E-mail Address: contact@ache.org
Web Address: www.ache.org

The American College of Healthcare Executives (ACHE) is an international professional society of health care executives that offers certification and educational programs.

American College of Legal Medicine (ACLM)
9700 W. Bryn Mawr Ave., Ste. 210
Rosemont, IL 60018 USA
Phone: 847-447-1713
Fax: 847-447-1150
E-mail Address: info@aclm.org
Web Address: www.aclm.org
The American College of Legal Medicine (ACLM) is an organization for healthcare and legal professionals that works to promote interdisciplinary cooperation and an understanding of issues where law and medicine meet.

American College of Medical Quality (ACMQ)
5272 River Rd., Ste. 630
Bethesda, MD 20816 USA
Phone: 301-718-6516
Fax: 301-656-0989
Web Address: www.acmq.org
The American College of Medical Quality (ACMQ) strives to provide leadership and education for professionals in health care quality management.

American College of Physicians (ACP)
190 N. Independence Mall W.
Philadelphia, PA 19106-1572 USA
Phone: 215-351-2400
Toll Free: 800-523-1546
Web Address: www.acponline.org
The American College of Physicians (ACP) exists to enhance the quality and effectiveness of health care by fostering excellence and professionalism in the practice of medicine. It consists of 143,000 members, including internists, internal medicine specialists, medical students, residents and fellows.

American College of Prosthodontists (ACP)
211 E. Chicago Ave., Ste. 1000
Chicago, IL 60611 USA
Phone: 312-573-1260
Web Address: www.gotoapro.org
The American College of Prosthodontists (ACP) is the official sponsoring organization for dentists who specialize in dental implants, dentures, veneers, crowns and teeth whitening.

American College of Rheumatology (ACR)
2200 Lake Blvd. NE
Atlanta, GA 30319 USA
Phone: 404-633-3777
Fax: 404-633-1870
Web Address: www.rheumatology.org
The American College of Rheumatology (ACR) is the professional organization of rheumatologists and associated health professionals dedicated to healing, preventing disability and curing disorders of the joints, muscles and bones.

American College of Sports Medicine (ACSM)
401 W. Michigan St.
Indianapolis, IN 46202-3233 USA
Phone: 317-637-9200
Fax: 317-634-7817
Web Address: www.acsm.org
The American College of Sports Medicine (ACSM) promotes and integrates research, education and applications of sports medicine and exercise science to maintain and enhance quality of life. ACSM has more than 50,000 members and certified professionals from 90 countries worldwide.

American Correctional Health Services Association (ACHSA)
250 Gatsby Pl.
Alpharetta, GA 30022-6161 USA
Toll Free: 855-825-5559
E-mail Address: admin@achsa.org
Web Address: www.achsa.org
The American Correctional Health Services Association (ACHSA) serves as a forum for communications that address the current issues and needs confronting correctional healthcare. Its members include administrators, nurses, physicians, psychiatrists, nurse practitioners and physician assistants, mental health professionals, medical assistants, administrative personnel and ancillary personnel who work in a correctional setting.

American Dental Association (ADA)
211 E. Chicago Ave.
Chicago, IL 60611-2678 USA
Phone: 312-440-2500
Web Address: www.ada.org
The American Dental Association (ADA) is a nonprofit professional association of dentists committed to enhancing public's oral health with a focus on ethics, science and professional advancement.

American Health Care Association (AHCA)
1201 L St. NW
Washington, DC 20005 USA
Phone: 202-842-4444
Fax: 202-842-3860
E-mail Address: mparkinson@ahca.org
Web Address: www.ahcancal.org
The American Health Care Association (AHCA) is a nonprofit federation of affiliated state health organizations that represent assisted living, nursing facility, developmentally-disabled, and subacute care providers.

American Health Lawyers Association (AHLA)
1620 Eye St. NW, Fl. 6
Washington, DC 20006-4010 USA
Phone: 202-833-1100
Fax: 202-833-1105
E-mail Address: msc@healthlawyers.org
Web Address: www.healthlawyers.org
American Health Lawyers Association (AHLA) is an educational organization devoted to legal issues in the health care field. It provides a forum for information exchange and production of quality, non-partisan educational programs, products and services related to health law issues.

American Health Planning Association (AHPA)
7245 Arlington Blvd., Ste. 319
Falls Church, VA 22042 USA
Phone: 703-573-3101
E-mail Address: info@ahpanet.org
Web Address: www.ahpanet.org
The American Health Planning Association (AHPA) is a nonprofit organization committed to the creation of health policies and systems that assure access for all people to quality care at a reasonable cost.

American Health Quality Association (AHQA)
7918 Jones Branch Dr., Ste. 300
McLean, VA 22102 USA
Phone: 202-331-5790
E-mail Address: info@ahqa.org
Web Address: www.ahqa.org
The American Health Quality Association (AHQA) is a nonprofit national association dedicated to community-based, quality evaluation of health care.

American Holistic Nurses Association (AHNA)
2900 SW Plass Court
Topeka, KS 66611-1980 USA
Phone: 785-234-1712
Fax: 785-234-1713
Toll Free: 800-278-2462
E-mail Address: info@ahna.org
Web Address: www.ahna.org
The American Holistic Nurses Association (AHNA) embraces nursing as a lifestyle and a profession by acting as a bridge for nurses between traditional medical philosophy and alternative healing practices.

American Medical Association (AMA)
AMA Plaza
330 N. Wabash Ave.
Chicago, IL 60611 USA
Toll Free: 800-621-8335
Web Address: www.ama-assn.org
The American Medical Association (AMA) is the primary professional society of physicians in the United States, which works to promote sustainable physician practices, smarter medical training and improving professional environment and patient health outcomes. It also provides career support and involvement opportunities for its members.

American Medical Group Association (AMGA)
One Prince St.
Alexandria, VA 22314-3318 USA
Phone: 703-838-0033
Fax: 703-548-1890
E-mail Address: donald.fisher@amga.org
Web Address: www.amga.org
The American Medical Group Association (AMGA) represents medical groups by advancing high-quality, cost-effective, patient-centered and physician-directed health care.

American Medical Society for Sports Medicine (AMSSM)
4000 W. 114th St., Ste. 100
Leawood, KS 66211 USA
Phone: 913-327-1415
Fax: 913-327-1491
E-mail Address: tthompson@amssm.org
Web Address: www.amssm.org
The mission of the American Medical Society for Sports Medicine, Inc. (AMSSM) is to offer a forum that fosters a collegial relationship among dedicated, competent primary care sports medicine physicians as they seek to improve their individual expertise and raise the general level of the sports medicine practice.

American Medical Technologists (AMT)
10700 W. Higgins Rd., Ste. 150
Rosemont, IL 60018 USA
Phone: 847-823-5169
Fax: 847-823-0458
E-mail Address:
mail@americanmedtech.org
Web Address: www.americanmedtech.org
American Medical Technologists (AMT) is a nationally and internationally recognized nonprofit certification agency and professional membership association representing allied health professionals. Its members include laboratory health professionals, as well as medical and dental office professionals.

American Medical Women's Association (AMWA)
12100 Sunset Hills Rd., Ste. 130
Reston, VA 20190 USA
Phone: 703-234-4069
Fax: 703-435-4390
Toll Free: 866-564-2483
E-mail Address:
associatedirector@amwa-doc.org
Web Address: www.amwa-doc.org
The American Medical Women's Association (AMWA) is an organization of women physicians and medical students dedicated to serving as the unique voice for women's health and the advancement of women in medicine.

American Nephrology Nurses Association (ANNA)
E. Holly Ave., Box 56
Pitman, NJ 08071-0056 USA
Phone: 856-256-2320
Fax: 856-589-7463
Toll Free: 888-600-2662
E-mail Address: anna@annanurse.org
Web Address: www.annanurse.org
The American Nephrology Nurses Association (ANNA) is a member organization that seeks to advance the nephrology nursing practice and positively influence outcomes for patients with diseases that require replacement therapies.

American Neurological Association (ANA)
1120 Route 73, Ste. 200
Mount Laurel, NJ 08054 USA
Phone: 856-380-6892
E-mail Address: info@myana.org
Web Address: https://myana.org
The American Neurological Association (ANA) is a professional society of academic neurologists and neuroscientists devoted to advancing the goals and science of neurology.

American Occupational Therapy Association, Inc. (AOTA)
4720 Montgomery Ln., Ste. 200
Bethesda, MD 20814-3449 USA
Phone: 301-652-6611
Fax: 301-652-7711
Toll Free: 800-377-8555
Web Address: www.aota.org
The American Occupational Therapy Association, Inc. (AOTA) advances the quality, availability, use and support of occupational therapy through standard-setting, advocacy, education and research on behalf of its members and the public.

American Organization of Nurse Executives (AONE)
800 10th St. NW
Two City Ctr., Ste. 400
Washington, DC 20001 USA
Phone: 312-422-2800
E-mail Address: aone@aha.org
Web Address: www.aone.org
The American Organization of Nurse Executives (AONE) is a national organization focused on advancing nursing practice and patient care through leadership, professional development, advocacy and research.

American Orthopedic Society for Sports Medicine (AOSSM)
9400 W. Higgins Rd., Ste. 300
Rosemont, IL 60018 USA
Phone: 847-292-4900
Fax: 847-292-4905
Toll Free: 877-321-3500
E-mail Address: mary@aossm.org
Web Address: www.sportsmed.org
The American Orthopedic Society for Sports Medicine (AOSSM) is a trade association for orthopedic doctors and sports medicine practitioners. The AOSSM works to improve the identification, prevention, treatment and rehabilitation of sports injuries.

American Osteopathic Association (AOA)
142 E. Ontario St.
Chicago, IL 60611-2864 USA
Phone: 312-202-8000
Fax: 312-202-8200
Toll Free: 800-621-1773
E-mail Address: crc@osteopathic.org
Web Address: www.osteopathic.org
The American Osteopathic Association (AOA) is organized to advance the philosophy and practice of osteopathic medicine by promoting education, research and the delivery of cost-effective health care.

American Pediatric Surgical Association (APSA)
1 Parkview Plaza, Ste. 800
Oakbrook Terrace, IL 60181 USA
Phone: 847-686-2237
Fax: 847-686-2253
E-mail Address: eapsa@eapsa.org
Web Address: www.eapsa.org
The American Pediatric Surgical Association (APSA) is a surgical specialty organization composed of individuals who have dedicated themselves to the care of pediatric surgical patients.

American Psychiatric Association (APA)
1000 Wilson Blvd., Ste. 1825
Arlington, VA 22209-3901 USA
Phone: 703-907-7300
Toll Free: 888-357-7924

Web Address: www.psychiatry.org
The American Psychiatric Association (APA) seeks to ensure humane care and effective treatment for all persons with mental disorders, including intellectual and developmental disabilities and substance-related disorders.

American Public Health Association (APHA)
800 I St. NW
Washington, DC 20001-3710 USA
Phone: 202-777-2742
Fax: 202-777-2534
Web Address: www.apha.org
The American Public Health Association (APHA) is an association of individuals and organizations working to improve the public's health and to achieve equity in health status for all.

American School Health Association (ASHA)
7918 Jones Branch Dr., Ste. 300
McLean, VA 22102 USA
Phone: 703-506-7675
Fax: 703-506-3266
E-mail Address: info@ashaweb.org
Web Address: www.ashaweb.org
The American School Health Association (ASHA) advocates high-quality school health instruction, health services and a healthy school environment.

American Society for Dermatologic Surgery, Inc. (ASDS)
5550 Meadowbrook Dr., Ste. 120
Rolling Meadows, IL 60008 USA
Phone: 847-956-0900
Fax: 847-956-0999
Web Address: www.asds.net
The American Society for Dermatologic Surgery, Inc. (ASDS) is a member organization for dermasurgeons, which seeks to enhance dermatological surgery and foster the highest standards of patient care.

American Society of Addiction Medicine (ASAM)
4601 N. Park Ave.
Upper Arcade, Ste. 101
Chevy Chase, MD 20815-4520 USA
Phone: 301-656-3920
Fax: 301-656-3815
E-mail Address: email@asam.org
Web Address: www.asam.org
The American Society of Addiction Medicine (ASAM) is dedicated to educating physicians and improving the treatment of individuals suffering from alcoholism and other addictions.

American Society of Clinical Oncology (ASCO)
2318 Mill Rd., Ste. 800
Alexandria, VA 22314 USA
Phone: 571-483-1300
E-mail Address:
customerservice@asco.org
Web Address: www.asco.org
The American Society of Clinical Oncology (ASCO) is a nonprofit organization, founded in 1964, with overarching goals of improving cancer care and prevention and ensuring that all patients with cancer receive care of the highest quality. Nearly 30,000 oncology practitioners belong to ASCO, representing all oncology disciplines.

American Society of Pain Management Nursing (ASPMN)
18000 W. 105th St.
Olathe, KS 66061-7543 USA
Phone: 913-895-4606
Fax: 913-895-4652
Toll Free: 888-342-7766
Web Address: www.aspmn.org
The American Society of Pain Management Nursing (ASPMN) is an organization of professional nurses dedicated to promoting and providing optimal care of patients with pain.

American Society of Peri-Anesthesia Nurses (ASPAN)
90 Frontage Rd.
Cherry Hill, NJ 08034-1424 USA
Fax: 856-616-9601
Toll Free: 877-737-9696
E-mail Address: aspan@aspan.org
Web Address: www.aspan.org
The American Society of Peri-Anesthesia Nurses (ASPAN) advances perianesthesia nursing practice through education, research and standards. It has over 15,000 members, who specialize in preanesthesia and postanesthesia care, ambulatory surgery and pain management.

American Society of Plastic Surgeons (ASPS)
444 E. Algonquin Rd.
Arlington Heights, IL 60005 USA
Phone: 847-228-9900
E-mail Address:
media@plasticsurgery.org
Web Address: www.plasticsurgery.org
The American Society of Plastic Surgeons (ASPS) seeks to support its members in their efforts to provide the highest-quality patient care and maintain professional and ethical standards through education, research and advocacy of socioeconomic and other professional activities.

American Society of Therapeutic Radiology and Oncology (ASTRO)
251 18th St. S., Fl. 8
Arlington, VA 22202 USA
Phone: 703-502-1550
Fax: 703-502-7852
E-mail Address: info@astro.org
Web Address: www.astro.org
The American Society of Therapeutic Radiology and Oncology (ASTRO) works to advance the practice of radiation oncology by promoting excellence in patient care, providing opportunities for educational and professional development, promoting research and disseminating research results and representing radiation oncology in a rapidly evolving healthcare environment.

American Telemedicine Association (ATA)
1100 Connecticut Ave. NW, Ste. 540
Washington, DC 20036 USA
Phone: 202-223-3333
Fax: 202-223-2787
E-mail Address:
info@americantelemed.org
Web Address: www.americantelemed.org
The American Telemedicine Association (ATA) is the leading resource and advocate promoting access to medical care for consumers and health professionals via telecommunications technology.

Association for Applied Sport Psychology (AASP)
8365 Keystone Crossing, Ste. 107
Indianapolis, IN 46240 USA
Phone: 317-205-9225
Fax: 317-205-9481
E-mail Address:
info@appliedsportpsych.org
Web Address: appliedsportpsych.org
The Association for Applied Sport Psychology (AASP) provides information about applied sports psychology to coaches, athletes, students, parents, certified consultants and AASP members.

Association for Dental Sciences of the Republic of China (ADS-ROC)
Hengyang Rd.
Taipei No. 36, 3rd fl.
Taipei City, 10045 Taiwan
Phone: 886-02-2311-6001
Fax: 886-02-2311-6080
E-mail Address: ads.tw@msa.hinet.net
Web Address: www.ads.org.tw
The Association for Dental Sciences of the Republic of China (ADS-ROC) represents the dental industry in the Republic of China.

Association for Healthcare Volunteer Resource Professionals (AHVRP)
155 N. Wacker Dr., Ste. 400
Chicago, IL 60606-1725 USA
Phone: 312-422-3939
Fax: 312-278-0884
E-mail Address: ahvrp@aha.org
Web Address: www.ahvrp.org
The Association for Healthcare Volunteer Resource Professionals (AHVRP), formerly the American Society of Directors of Volunteer Services, exists to strengthen the profession of volunteer services administration, provide opportunities for professional development and promote volunteerism as a resource in serving the health care needs of the nation.

Association for the Healthcare Environment (AHE)
155 N. Wacker Dr., Ste. 400
Chicago, IL 60606 USA
Phone: 312-422-3860
Fax: 312-422-4578
E-mail Address: ahe@aha.org
Web Address: www.ahe.org
The Association for the Healthcare Environment (AHE), formerly the American Society for Healthcare Environmental Services, is the premier health care association for environmental services, housekeeping and textile professionals.

Association of Camp Nurses (ACN)
19006 Hunt County Ln.
Fisherville, KY 40023 USA
Phone: 502-232-2945
E-mail Address: gaslin@campnurse.org
Web Address: www.acn.org
The Association of Camp Nurses (ACN) promotes and develops the practice of camp nursing for a healthy camp community.

Association of Clinicians for the Underserved (ACU)
1420 Spring Hill Rd., Ste. 600
Tysons Corner, VA 22102 USA
Phone: 844-422-8247
Fax: 703-562-8801
E-mail Address: acu@clinicians.org
Web Address: www.clinicians.org
The Association of Clinicians for the Underserved (ACU) is a nonprofit, interdisciplinary organization whose mission is to improve the health of underserved populations by enhancing the development and support of the health care clinicians serving these populations.

Association of Food and Drug Officials (AFDO)
2550 Kingston Rd., Ste. 311
York, PA 17402 USA
Phone: 717-757-2888
Fax: 717-650-3650
E-mail Address: afdo@afdo.org
Web Address: www.afdo.org
The Association of Food and Drug Officials (AFDO) is a trusted resource for building consensus and promoting uniformity on public health and consumer protection issues related to the regulation of foods, drugs, devices, cosmetics and consumer products.

Association of Nurses in AIDS Care (ANAC)
3538 Ridgewood Rd.
Akron, OH 44333-3122 USA
Phone: 330-670-0101
Fax: 330-670-0109
Toll Free: 800-260-6780
E-mail Address: anac@anacnet.org
Web Address: www.nursesinaidscare.org
The Association of Nurses in AIDS Care (ANAC) addresses the specific needs of nurses working in HIV/AIDS. ANAC also publishes a peer-reviewed journal and runs an annual conference on the latest developments in HIV nursing.

Association of periOperative Registered Nurses (AORN), The
2170 S. Parker Rd., Ste. 300
Denver, CO 80231-5711 USA
Phone: 303-755-6300
Fax: 800-847-0045
Toll Free: 800-755-2676
E-mail Address: custsvc@aorn.org
Web Address: www.aorn.org
The Association of periOperative Registered Nurses (AORN) is a nonprofit membership association, which offers nursing education, standards and clinical practice resources to achieve optimal outcomes for patients undergoing operative and other invasive procedures. Its membership includes 41,000 registered nurses, which are engaged in managing, teaching and practicing perioperative nursing.

Association of Rehabilitation Nurses (ARN)
8735 W. Higgins Rd., Ste. 300
Chicago, IL 60631-2738 USA
Toll Free: 800-229-7530
E-mail Address: info@rehabnurse.org
Web Address: www.rehabnurse.org
The Association of Rehabilitation Nurses (ARN) helps nurses stay on top of the skills and knowledge needed to provide quality rehabilitative and restorative care across settings, conditions and age spans.

Association of Women's Health, Obstetric and Neonatal Nurses (AWHONN)
1800 M St. NW, Ste. 7450
Washington, DC 20036 USA
Phone: 202-261-2400
Fax: 202-728-0575
Toll Free: 800-673-8499
E-mail Address: customerservice@awhonn.org
Web Address: www.awhonn.org
The Association of Women's Health, Obstetric and Neonatal Nurses (AWHONN) is nonprofit membership organization, which works to promote the health of women and newborns through advocacy, research, education and provides access to professional and clinical resources to nurses and health care professionals.

British Dental Association
64 Wimpole St.
London, W1G8YS UK
Phone: 44-20-7935-0875
Fax: 44-20-7487-5232
E-mail Address: enquiries@bda.org
Web Address: www.bda.org
The British Dental Association (BDA) is the professional association and trade union for dentists in the United Kingdom. It promotes policies which benefit dental practice and dental care and lobby politicians on issues affecting dentists as business people and clinicians.

British Medical Association
BMA House, Tavistock Sq.
London, WC1H 9JP UK
Phone: 44-20-7387-4499
Web Address: www.bma.org.uk
The British Medical Association is a trade union, which represents over 170,00 doctors in the U.K. It advocates the interests of its members, including employment issues and work with government for improving healthcare system.

Caregivers Action Network (CAN)
1130 Connecticut Ave., Ste. 300
Washington, DC 20036 USA
Phone: 202-454-3970
E-mail Address: info@caregiveraction.org
Web Address: caregiveraction.org
The Caregivers Action Network (CAN), formerly the National Family Caregivers Association (NFCA), is a grass-roots organization created to educate, support, empower and speak for the millions of Americans who care for loved ones that are chronically ill, aged or disabled.

Case Management Society of America (CMSA)
6301 Ranch Dr.
Little Rock, AR 72223 USA
Phone: 501-225-2229
Fax: 501-221-9068
Toll Free: 800-216-2672
E-mail Address: cmsa@cmsa.org
Web Address: www.cmsa.org
Founded in 1990, the Case Management Society of America (CMSA) has grown to be the leading non-profit association dedicated to the support and development of the profession of case management. It serves more than 9,000 members, 20,000 subscribers, 17,000 social community participants and 75 chapters through educational forums, networking opportunities, legislative advocacy and establishing standards to advance the profession.

Chinese Medical Association (CMA)
42 Dongsi Xidajie
Beijing, 100710 China
Phone: 86-10-8515-8136
Fax: 86-10-8515-8551
E-mail Address: intl@cma.org.cn
Web Address: www.cma.org.cn/ensite/
The Chinese Medical Association (CMA) is nonprofit association consisting of Chinese medical science and technology professionals representing the medical industry in China. With roughly 500,000 members, it has 85 specialist societies representing all medical fields; and edits and publishes 125 medical and popular science journals.

Chinese-American Medical Society (CAMS)
265 Canal St., Ste. 515
New York, NY 10013 USA
Phone: 212-334-4760
Fax: 646-304-6373
E-mail Address: jlove@camsociety.org
Web Address: www.camsociety.org
The Chinese-American Medical Society (CAMS) exists to promote the scientific association of medical professionals of Chinese descent, advance medical knowledge and scientific research with emphasis on aspects unique to the Chinese and establish scholarships for medical and dental students.

Clinical Immunology Society (CIS)
555 E. Wells St., Ste. 1100
Milwaukee, WI 53202-3823 USA
Phone: 414-224-8095
Fax: 414-272-6070
E-mail Address: info@clinimmsoc.org
Web Address: www.clinimmsoc.org
The Clinical Immunology Society (CIS) is devoted to fostering developments in the science and practice of clinical immunology through education, translational research and novel approaches to therapy.

Contact Lens Manufacturers Association (CLMA)
P.O. Box 29398
Lincoln, NE 68529 USA
Phone: 402-465-4122
Fax: 402-465-4187
Toll Free: 800-344-9060
Web Address: www.clma.net
The Contact Lens Manufacturers Association (CLMA) seeks to increase awareness and utilization of custom-manufactured contact lenses.

Contact Lens Society of America (CLSA)
2025 Woodlane Dr.
St. Paul, MN 55125-2998 USA
Fax: 651-731-0410
Toll Free: 800-296-9776
E-mail Address: clsa@clsa.info
Web Address: www.clsa.info
The Contact Lens Society of America (CLSA) is a member organization that strives to educate and share knowledge among fitters of contact lenses.

Corporate Angel Network, Inc. (CAN)
One Loop Rd.
Westchester County Airport
White Plains, NY 10604-1215 USA
Phone: 914-328-1313
Fax: 914-328-3938
E-mail Address:
info@corpangelnetwork.org
Web Address:
www.corpangelnetwork.org
The Corporate Angel Network (CAN) exists to ease the emotional stress, physical discomfort and financial burden of travel for cancer patients by arranging free flights to treatment centers, using the empty seats on corporate aircraft flying on routine business.

Cryogenic Society of America, Inc. (CSA)
218 Lake St.
Oak Park, IL 60302-2609 USA
Phone: 708-383-6220
Fax: 708-383-9337
E-mail Address:
csa@cryogenicsociety.org
Web Address: www.cryogenicsociety.org
The Cryogenic Society of America, Inc. (CSA) is a nonprofit organization that brings together those in all disciplines concerned with the applications of cryogenics, which refers to the art and science of achieving extremely low-temperatures. With membership spanning over 47 countries, the organization works to promote information sharing, increase awareness and conduct research in low temperature processes and techniques.

Dental Council of India
Kotla Rd., Temple Ln.
Aiwan-E-Galib Marg
New Delhi, 110 002 India
Phone: 91-11-23238542
E-mail Address: secretary@dciindia.org
Web Address: www.dciindia.org
The Dental Council of India is a statutory body incorporated to regulate the dental education and the profession of dentistry throughout India.

Dental Trade Alliance (DTA)
4350 N. Fairfax Dr., Ste. 220
Arlington, VA 22203 USA
Phone: 703-379-7755
Fax: 703-931-9429
Web Address:
www.dentaltradealliance.org
The Dental Trade Alliance (DTA) represents dental manufacturers, dental dealers and dental laboratories.

Direct Primary Care Coalition
E-mail Address: info@dpcare.org
Web Address: www.dpcare.org
The Direct Primary Care Coalition is an organization representing primary care physicians who operate on a business model whereby patients pay a monthly fee for unlimited access to their doctors. Additional enhanced services, such as preventative care and email access to doctors, are often added in a comprehensive package.

Emergency Nurses Association (ENA)
915 Lee St.
Des Plaines, IL 60016-6569 USA
Phone: 847-460-4095
Toll Free: 800-900-9659
E-mail Address: execoffice@ena.org
Web Address: www.ena.org
The Emergency Nurses Association (ENA) is the specialty nursing association serving the emergency nursing profession through research, publications, professional development and injury prevention.

Federation of American Hospitals (FAH)
750 9th St. NW, Ste. 600
Washington, DC 20001 USA
Phone: 202-624-1500
Fax: 202-737-6462
E-mail Address: info@fah.org
Web Address: www.fah.org
The Federation of American Hospitals (FAH) is the national representative of

privately owned and managed community hospitals and health systems in the U.S.

German Medical Technology Association (BVMed)
Reinhardt Strasse 29b
Berlin, D-10117 Germany
Phone: 49-30-246-255-0
Fax: 49-30-246-255-99
E-mail Address: info@bvmed.de
Web Address: www.bvmed.de
The German Medical Technology Association (BVMed) represents about 200 manufacturers and service providers of medical devices.

Health Industry Distributors Association (HIDA)
310 Montgomery St.
Alexandria, VA 22314-1516 USA
Phone: 703-549-4432
Fax: 703-549-6495
E-mail Address: rowan@hida.org
Web Address: www.hida.org
The Health Industry Distributors Association (HIDA) is the international trade association representing medical products distributors.

Healthcare Financial Management Association (HFMA)
3 Westbrook Corp. Ctr., Ste. 600
Westchester, IL 60154 USA
Phone: 708-531-9600
Fax: 708-531-0032
Toll Free: 800-252-4362
E-mail Address: memberservices@hfma.org
Web Address: www.hfma.org
The Healthcare Financial Management Association (HFMA) is one of the nation's leading personal membership organizations for health care financial management executives and leaders.

Home Healthcare Nurses Association (HHNA)
288 7th St. SE
Washington, DC 20003 USA
Phone: 202-547-7424
Fax: 202-547-3540
Web Address: www.hhna.org
The Home Healthcare Nurses Association (HHNA) is a national professional nursing organization of members involved in home health care practice, education, administration and research.

Hong Kong Dental Association (HKDA)
15 Hennessy Rd.
Fl. 8, Duke of Windsor Social Service Bldg.
Wanchai, Hong Kong Hong Kong
Phone: 852-2528-5327
Fax: 852-2529-0755
E-mail Address: hkda@hkda.org
Web Address: www.hkda.org
The Hong Kong Dental Association represents the dental profession in Hong Kong. It works to promote best interests of dental profession by offering continuing educational opportunities, organizing monthly meetings and workshops for over 1,900 members.

Hong Kong Medical Association
15 Hennessy Rd.
5/F Duke of Windsor Social Service Bldg.
Wanchai, Hong Kong Hong Kong
Phone: 852-2527-8285
Fax: 852-2865-0943
E-mail Address: hkma@hkma.org
Web Address: www.hkma.org
The Hong Kong Medical Association's objective is to promote the welfare of the medical profession and the health of the public of Hong Kong. Its members include over 8,000 professionals across all healthcare sectors in Hong Kong.

Hong Kong Society for Nursing Education
P.O. Box 98898
Tsim Sha Tsui Post Office
Kowloon, New Territories Hong Kong
E-mail Address: info@hksne.org.hk
Web Address: www.hksne.org.hk
The Hong Kong Society for Nursing Education aims to promote the welfare and protect the interests of the nursing profession.

Independent Medical Distributors Association (IMDA)
500 W. Wilson Bridge Rd., Ste. 125
Worthington, OH 43085 USA
Fax: 614-467-2071
Toll Free: 866-463-2937
E-mail Address: imda@imda.org
Web Address: www.imda.org
The Independent Medical Distributors Association (IMDA) is an association of medical product sales and marketing organizations. It advances the business interests of its members by offering education and networking opportunities.

Institute for Diversity in Health Management (IDHM)
155 N. Wacker
Chicago, IL 60606 USA
Phone: 312-422-2630
E-mail Address: institute@aha.org
Web Address: www.diversityconnection.org
The Institute for Diversity in Health Management (IDHM) is a nonprofit organization that collaborates with educators and health services organizations to expand leadership opportunities to ethnic minorities in health services management.

Institute for Health Care Improvement
20 University Rd., Fl. 7
Cambridge, MA 02138 USA
Phone: 617-301-4800
Fax: 617-301-4830
Toll Free: 866-787-0831
E-mail Address: info@ihi.org
Web Address: www.ihi.org
The Institute for Healthcare Improvement (IHI) is a nonprofit organization that strives for the improvement of health by advancing the quality and value of healthcare.

International Association of Flight and Critical Care Paramedics (IAFCCP)
4835 Riveredge Cove
Snellville, GA 30039 USA
Phone: 770-979-6372
Fax: 770-979-6500
Web Address: www.iafccp.org
The International Association of Flight and Critical Care Paramedics (IAFCCP), formerly the International Association of Flight Paramedics (IAFP), provides education and representation to critical care paramedics that transport critical care patients via airborne or ground vehicles.

International Association of Forensic Nurses (IAFN)
6755 Bus. Pkwy., Ste. 303
Elkridge, MD 21075 USA
Phone: 410-626-7805
Fax: 410-626-7804
E-mail Address: info@forensicnurses.org
Web Address: www.forensicnurses.org
The International Association of Forensic Nurses (IAFN) is an international professional organization of registered nurses that develops, promotes and disseminates information about the science of forensic nursing.

International Association of Medical Equipment Remarketers & Servicers (IAMERS)
85 Edgemont Pl.
Teaneck, NJ 07666 USA
Phone: 201-357-5400
Fax: 201-833-2021
E-mail Address: info@iamers.org
Web Address: www.iamers.org
The International Association of Medical Equipment Remarketers & Servicers (IAMERS) works to improve the quality of pre-owned medical equipment, both domestically and internationally.

International Council of Nurses (ICN)
3 Place Jean Marteau
Geneva, 1201 Switzerland

Phone: 41-22-908-01-00
Fax: 41-22-908-01-01
E-mail Address: icn@icn.ch
Web Address: www.icn.ch
The International Council of Nurses (ICN) is a federation of national nurses' associations representing nurses in more than 130 countries.

International Nurses Society on Addiction (IntNSA)
3416 Primm Lane
Birmingham, AL 66285-4846 USA
Phone: 205-823-6106
E-mail Address: intnsa@intnsa.org
Web Address: www.intnsa.org
The International Nurses Society on Addiction (IntNSA) is a global voice for nurses committed to addressing the impact of addictions on society. It is dedicated to advance nursing care for the prevention and treatment of addictions through advocacy, education, research and policy development.

International Transplant Nurses Society (ITNS)
8735 W. Higgins Rd., Ste. 300
Chicago, IL 60631 USA
Phone: 847-375-6340
Fax: 847-375-6341
E-mail Address: info@itns.org
Web Address: www.itns.org
The International Transplant Nurses Society (ITNS) is a member organization that promotes transplant clinical nursing through educational and professional growth opportunities, interdisciplinary networking, collaborative activities and transplant nursing research.

Joint Commission
1 Renaissance Blvd.
Oakbrook Terrace, IL 60181 USA
Phone: 630-792-5100
Fax: 630-792-5005
Toll Free: 800-994-6610
Web Address: www.jointcommission.org
The Joint Commission is an independent, nonprofit organization, which evaluates and accredits health care organizations and programs in the United States.

Medical Council of India
Dwarka Phase 1, Pocket 14, Sector 8
New Delhi, 110 077 India
Phone: 91-11-25367033
Fax: 91-11-25367024
Toll Free: 800-111-1154
E-mail Address: mci@bol.net.in
Web Address: www.mciindia.org
The Medical Council of India establishes uniform standards of higher qualifications in medicine and recognition of medical qualifications in India and abroad.

Medical Device Manufacturers Association (MDMA)
1333 H St., Ste. 400 W.
Washington, DC 20005 USA
Phone: 202-354-7171
Web Address: www.medicaldevices.org
The Medical Device Manufacturers Association (MDMA) is a national trade association that represents independent manufacturers of medical devices, diagnostic products and health care information systems.

Medical Group Management Association (MGMA)
104 Inverness Terrace E.
Englewood, CO 80112-5306 USA
Phone: 303-799-1111
Toll Free: 877-275-6462
E-mail Address: support@mgma.com
Web Address: www.mgma.com
Medical Group Management Association (MGMA) is one of the nation's principal voices for medical group practice. It represents over 33,000 administrators and executives in 18,000 healthcare organizations in which 385,000 physicians practice.

National Association for Healthcare Quality (NAHQ)
8735 W. Higgins Rd., Ste. 300
Chicago, IL 60631 USA
Phone: 847-375-4720
Fax: 847-375-6320
Toll Free: 800-966-9392
E-mail Address: info@nahq.org
Web Address: www.nahq.org
The National Association for Healthcare Quality (NAHQ) is a member organization for quality and safety healthcare professionals offering education, leadership development opportunities and products to its members.

National Association for Home Care & Hospice (NAHC)
228 Seventh St. SE
Washington, DC 20003 USA
Phone: 202-547-7424
Fax: 202-547-3540
Web Address: www.nahc.org
The National Association for Home Care & Hospice(NAHC) is a nonprofit organization committed to representing the interests of the home care and hospice community.

National Association for the Support of Long-Term Care (NASL)
1050 17th St. NW, Ste. 500
Washington, DC 20036-5558 USA
Phone: 202-803-2385
E-mail Address: membership@nasl.org
Web Address: www.nasl.org
The National Association for the Support of Long-Term Care (NASL) provides a task-force-specific committee structure that focuses on payment reform, legislative policy, medical products and medical services for executives and their associated businesses.

National Association of Clinical Nurse Specialists (NACNS)
100 N. 20th St., Fl. 4
Philadelphia, PA 19103 USA
Phone: 215-320-3881
Fax: 215-564-2175
E-mail Address: info@nacns.org
Web Address: www.nacns.org
The National Association of Clinical Nurse Specialists (NACNS) exists to enhance and promote the contributions of clinical nurse specialists to the health of individuals, families, groups and communities.

National Association of Health Services Executives (NAHSE)
1050 Connecticut Ave. NW, Fl. 5
Washington, DC 20036 USA
Phone: 202-772-1030
Fax: 202-772-1072
Web Address: www.nahse.org
The National Association of Health Services Executives (NAHSE) is a nonprofit association of black health care executives who promote the advancement and development of black health care leaders and elevate the quality of health care services rendered to minority and underserved communities.

National Association of Hispanic Nurses (NAHN)
1500 Sunday Dr., Ste.102
Raleigh, NC 27607 USA
Phone: 919-573-5443
Fax: 919-787-4916
E-mail Address: info@thehispanicnurses.org
Web Address: www.thehispanicnurses.org
The National Association of Hispanic Nurses (NAHN) strives to serve the nursing and health care delivery needs of the Hispanic community and the professional needs of Hispanic nurses.

National Association of Neonatal Nurses (NANN)
8735 W. Higgins Rd., Ste. 300
Chicago, IL 60631 USA
Toll Free: 800-451-3795
E-mail Address: info@nann.org
Web Address: www.nann.org
The National Association of Neonatal Nurses (NANN) represents the community of neonatal nurses that

provide evidence-based care to high-risk neonatal patients.

National Association of Orthopedic Nurses (NAON)
330 N. Wabash Ave., Ste. 2000
Chicago, IL 60611 USA
Fax: 312-673-6941
Toll Free: 800-289-6266
E-mail Address: naon@orthonurse.org
Web Address: www.orthonurse.org
The National Association of Orthopedic Nurses (NAON) is a nonprofit organization, which exists to promote education and research related to nursing care of persons with orthopedic conditions, as well as to advance the profession of nursing.

National Association of Pediatric Nurse Practitioners (NAPNAP)
5 Hanover Sq., Ste. 1401
New York, NY 10004 USA
Phone: 917-746-8300
Fax: 212-785-1713
Web Address: www.napnap.org
The National Association of Pediatric Nurse Practitioners (NAPNAP) is the professional organization that advocates for children and provides leadership for pediatric nurse practitioners who deliver primary healthcare in a variety of settings.

National Association of School Nurses (NASN)
1100 Wayne Ave., # 925
Silver Spring, MD 20910 USA
Phone: 240-821-1130
Fax: 301-585-1791
Toll Free: 866-627-6767
E-mail Address: nasn@nasn.org
Web Address: www.nasn.org
The National Association of School Nurses (NASN) improves the health and educational success of children and youth by developing and providing leadership to advance school nursing practice.

National Association of State Mental Health Program Directors (NASMHPD)
66 Canal Ctr. Plz., Ste. 302
Alexandria, VA 22314 USA
Phone: 703-739-9333
Fax: 703-548-9517
Web Address: www.nasmhpd.org
The National Association of State Mental Health Program Directors (NASMHPD) organizes to reflect and advocate for the collective interests of state mental health authorities and their directors at the national level.

National Black Nurses Association (NBNA)
8630 Fenton St., Ste. 330
Silver Spring, MD 20910-3803 USA
Phone: 301-589-3200
Fax: 301-589-3223
E-mail Address: contact@nbna.org
Web Address: www.nbna.org
The National Black Nurses Association (NBNA) is a professional nursing organization representing roughly 150,000 African American nurses from the United States, Canada, Eastern Caribbean and Africa.

National Board of Medical Examiners (NBME)
3750 Market St.
Philadelphia, PA 19104-3102 USA
Phone: 215-590-9500
Web Address: www.nbme.org
The National Board of Medical Examiners (NBME) exists to protect the health of the public through state-of-the-art assessment of health professionals.

National Committee for Quality Assurance (NCQA)
1100 13th St. NW, Ste. 1000
Washington, DC 20005 USA
Phone: 202-955-3500
Fax: 202-955-3599
Toll Free: 888-275-7585
E-mail Address:
customersupport@ncqa.org
Web Address: www.ncqa.org
The National Committee for Quality Assurance (NCQA) is a private, nonprofit organization that seeks to drive improvement throughout the health care industry.

National Hospice and Palliative Care Organization (NHPCO)
1731 King St., Ste. 100
Alexandria, VA 22314 USA
Phone: 703-837-1500
Fax: 703-837-1233
Toll Free: 800-646-6460
E-mail Address: nhpco_info@nhpco.org
Web Address: www.nhpco.org
The National Hospice and Palliative Care Organization (NHPCO) is a nonprofit membership organization representing hospice and palliative care programs and professionals in the United States.

National Student Nurses' Association (NSNA)
45 Main St., Ste. 606
Brooklyn, NY 11201 USA
Phone: 718-210-0705
Fax: 718-797-1186
Web Address: www.nsna.org
The National Student Nurses' Association (NSNA) is a membership organization representing those in programs preparing students for registered nurse licensure, as well as RNs in BSN completion programs.

Nurse Practitioner Associates for Continuing Education (NPACE)
209 W. Central St., Ste. 228
Natick, MA 01760 USA
Phone: 508-907-6424
Fax: 508-907-6425
E-mail Address: npace@npace.org
Web Address: www.npace.org
Nurse Practitioner Associates for Continuing Education (NPACE) seeks to improve health care in the U.S. by providing continuing education and professional support to nurse practitioners and other clinicians in advanced practice.

Oncology Nursing Society (ONS)
125 Enterprise Dr.
Pittsburgh, PA 15275 USA
Phone: 412-859-6100
Fax: 877-369-5497
Toll Free: 866-257-4667
E-mail Address: help@ons.org
Web Address: www.ons.org
The Oncology Nursing Society (ONS) is a national organization of registered nurses and other health care professionals dedicated to excellence in patient care, teaching, research, administration and education in the field of oncology.

Optometrists & Opticians Board, Singapore
16 College Rd., #01-01
College of Medicine Bldg.
Singapore, 169854 Singapore
Phone: 65-6355-2533
Fax: 65-6258-2134
E-mail Address: enquiries@oob.gov.sg
Web Address:
www.healthprofessionals.gov.sg/content/hprof/oob/en.html
The Optometrists & Opticians Board is a professional board established under the Ministry of Health of Singapore which issues guidelines on the standards for the practice of optometry and opticianry.

Regulatory Affairs Professionals Society (RAPS)
5635 Fishers Ln., Ste. 550
Rockville, MD 20852 USA
Phone: 301-770-2920
Fax: 301-841-7956
E-mail Address: raps@raps.org
Web Address: www.raps.org
The Regulatory Affairs Professionals Society (RAPS) is an international professional society representing the

health care regulatory affairs profession and individual professionals worldwide.

Shanghai Medical Instrument Trade Association (SMITA)
Zhao Jia Bang Rd.
701 No. 2 446 Ln.
Shanghai, 200031 China
Phone: 86-21-61248288
Fax: 86-21-54651421
E-mail Address: smia_sh@yahoo.com.cn
Web Address: www.smianet.com
The Shanghai Medical Instrument Trade Association (SMITA) serves the interests of manufacturers and suppliers of medical radio-diagnostic and radio-therapeutic machines, emergency apparatus, equipment for operating room, medical ultrasonic instrument, medical optical instrument, medical physiologic detecting and diagnostic device, artificial organ, surgical instrument, dental equipment, sanitary material etc.

Singapore Dental Association (SDA)
2 College Rd.
Level. 2 Alumni Assoc.
Singapore, 169850 Singapore
Phone: 65-6220 2588
Fax: 65-6224-7967
Web Address: http://sda.org.sg
The Singapore Dental Association (SDA) is the professional association of dentists dedicated to serving both the public and the profession of dentistry.

Singapore Dental Council
81 Kim Keat Rd.
09-00 NKF Building
Singapore, 328836 Singapore
Phone: 65-6355-2405
Fax: 65-6253-3185
E-mail Address: enquiries@dentalcouncil.gov.sg
Web Address: http://www.healthprofessionals.gov.sg/content/hprof/sdc/en.html
The Singapore Dental Council is the self-regulatory body for the dental professions. Its key objectives are to promote the interests of the dental profession in Singapore.

Singapore Medical Association (SMA)
2 College Rd.
Alumni Medical Ctr., 2nd Level.
Singapore, 169850 Singapore
Phone: 65-6223-1264
Fax: 65-6224-7827
E-mail Address: sma@sma.org.sg
Web Address: www.sma.org.sg
Singapore Medical Association (SMA) is the national medical organization representing the majority of medical practitioners in both the public and private sectors. The website contains information and links to medical organizations and hospitals in Singapore.

Society for Social Work Leadership in Health Care (SSWLHC)
100 N. 20th St., Ste. 400
Philadelphia, PA 19103 USA
Phone: 215-599-6134
Toll Free: 866-237-9542
E-mail Address: info@sswlhc.org
Web Address: www.sswlhc.org
The Society for Social Work Leadership in Health Care (SSWLHC) is dedicated to promoting the universal availability, accessibility, coordination and effectiveness of health care that addresses the psychosocial components of health and illness.

Society for Vascular Nursing (SVN)
N83 W13410 Leon Rd.
Menomonee Falls, WI 53051 USA
Phone: 414-376-0001
Fax: 414-359-1671
Web Address: www.svnnet.org
The Society for Vascular Nursing (SVN) is a nonprofit international association dedicated to the compassionate and comprehensive care of persons with vascular disease. The group works to provide quality education, foster clinical expertise and support nursing research.

Society of Critical Care Medicine (SCCM)
500 Midway Dr.
Mount Prospect, IL 60056 USA
Phone: 847-827-6869
Fax: 847-827-6886
E-mail Address: info@sccm.org
Web Address: www.sccm.org
The Society of Critical Care Medicine (SCCM) is a multidisciplinary, multi-professional organization dedicated to ensuring excellence and consistency in the practice of critical care medicine; and to offer highest quality care for all critically ill and injured patients.

Society of Gastroenterology Nurses and Associates (SGNA)
330 N. Wabash Ave., Ste. 2000
Chicago, IL 60611-7621 USA
Phone: 312-321-5165
Fax: 312-673-6694
Toll Free: 800-245-7462
E-mail Address: sgna@smithbucklin.com
Web Address: www.sgna.org
The Society of Gastroenterology Nurses and Associates (SGNA) is a professional organization of nurses and associates dedicated to the safe and effective practice of gastroenterology and endoscopy nursing.

Society of Nuclear Medicine and Molecular Imaging (SNMI)
1850 Samuel Morse Dr.
Reston, VA 20190-5316 USA
Phone: 703-708-9000
Fax: 703-708-9015
Web Address: www.snmmi.org
The Society of Nuclear Medicine and Molecular Imaging (SNMI), formerly The Society of Nuclear Medicine, is a nonprofit international scientific and medical organization founded to promote the science, technology and practical application of nuclear medicine. SNMI works to advance molecular imaging and therapy.

Society of Pediatric Nurses (SPN)
330 N. Wabash Ave., Ste. 2000
Chicago, IL 60611 USA
Phone: 312-321-5154
Fax: 312-673-6754
E-mail Address: info@pednurses.org
Web Address: www.pedsnurses.org
The Society of Pediatric Nurses (SPN) seeks to promote excellence in nursing care of children and their families through support of its members' clinical practice, education, research and advocacy.

Society of Trauma Nurses (STN)
446 E. High St., Ste. 10
Lexington, KY 40507 USA
Phone: 859-977-7456
Fax: 859-271-0607
E-mail Address: info@traumanurses.org
Web Address: www.traumanurses.org
The Society of Trauma Nurses (STN) is a membership-based, nonprofit organization whose members are trauma nurses from around the world. It is dedicated to ensure optimal trauma care to all people by encouraging leadership, mentoring, interdisciplinary collaboration and innovation in the delivery of trauma care.

Society of Urologic Nurses and Associates (SUNA)
E. Holly Ave., Box 56
Pitman, NJ 08071-0056 USA
Toll Free: 888-827-7862
E-mail Address: suna@ajj.com
Web Address: www.suna.org
The Society of Urologic Nurses and Associates (SUNA) is a nonprofit professional membership organization committed to excellence in patient care standards and a continuum of quality care, clinical practice and research through education of its members, patients, families and community. It has over 3,000 urologic healthcare professional members and publishes a professional, peer-

reviewed bi-monthly journal and a newsletter.

Southern Nursing Research Society (SNRS)
10200 W. 44th Ave., Ste. 304
Wheat Ridge, CO 80033 USA
Toll Free: 877-314-7677
E-mail Address: info@snrs.org
Web Address: www.snrs.org
The Southern Nursing Research Society (SNRS) exists to advance nursing research, promote the utilization of research finding and facilitate the career development of nurses as researchers.

Telemedicine Society of India
Sanjay Gandhi Post Graduate Institute of Medical Sciences
Raebareli Road
Lucknow, 226 014 India
Phone: 91-522-2668838
Fax: 91-522-2668839
E-mail Address: contact@tsi.org.in
Web Address: www.tsi.org.in
The Telemedicine Society of India seeks to promote and encourage development, advancement and research in the science of telemedicine and associated fields.

Urgent Care Association of America (UCAOA)
387 Shuman Blvd., Ste. 235W
Naperville, IL 60563 USA
Phone: 331-472-3739
Fax: 331-457-5439
Toll Free: 877-698-2262
E-mail Address: info@ucaoa.org
Web Address: www.ucaoa.org
UCAOA represents the many urgent care centers that provide appropriate and timely alternatives to the more costly and inconvenient hospital emergency departments. True emergencies require hospital emergency services, but urgent care centers meet the need for convenient access for minor injuries and illnesses.

Visiting Nurse Associations of America (VNAA)
2121 Crystal Dr., Ste. 750
Arlington, VA 22202 USA
Phone: 571-527-1520
Fax: 571-527-1521
Toll Free: 888-866-8773
E-mail Address: vnaa@vnaa.org
Web Address: www.vnaa.org
Visiting Nurse Associations of America (VNAA) is the official, national association of freestanding, nonprofit, community-based visiting nurse agencies.

Wound, Ostomy and Continence Nurses Society (WOCN)
1120 Rt. 73, Ste. 200
Mt. Laurel, NJ 08054 USA
Fax: 856-439-0525
Toll Free: 888-224-9626
E-mail Address: wocn_info@wocn.org
Web Address: www.wocn.org
The Wound, Ostomy and Continence Nurses Society (WOCN) is a professional, international nursing society of nurse professionals who are experts in the care of patients with wound, ostomy and continence problems.

43) Health Care Costs

Kaiser Family Foundation (The Henry J.)
2400 Sand Hill Rd.
Menlo Park, CA 94025 USA
Phone: 650-854-9400
Fax: 650-854-4800
Web Address: www.kff.org
The Henry J. Kaiser Family Foundation publishes an annual study on employers' health care coverage costs and the amount of that coverage that is paid for by employees. The foundation also runs a large healthcare public opinion research program and publishes studies on a continuous basis.

44) Health Care Resources

Directory of Indian Government Websites
Nat'l Portal Secretariat, FL. 3, Nat'l Informatics Ctr.
A-Block, CGO Complex, Lodhi Rd.
New Delhi, 110 003 India
E-mail Address: goidirectory@nic.in
Web Address: goidirectory.nic.in/sectors_categories.php?ct=ST016
The Directory of Indian Government Websites is a portal maintained by the National Informatics Centre (NIC) in India. The site lists Indian Government websites at all levels including institutions and organizations relating to the health and medical sector in India.

Health and Medicine Division (HMD), The
500 Fifth St. NW
Washington, DC 20001 USA
Phone: 202-334-2352
E-mail Address: HMD-NASEM@nas.edu
Web Address: www.nationalacademies.org/hmd/About-HMD.aspx
The Health and Medicine Division (HMD), formerly known as Institute of Medicine (IOM), is a division of the National Academies of Sciences, Engineering, and Medicine (the Academies). HMD's network consists of 3,000 volunteers, who offer their time, knowledge, and expertise, in order to furnish evidence to both government and private sectors to make informed health decisions. Many of the studies that the HMD undertakes begin as specific mandates from Congress; still others are requested by federal agencies and independent organizations

Hong Kong Medical Web
18 Cheung Lee St.
Cheung Tang Ctr., Rm. 504-5
Chai Wan, Hong Kong Hong Kong
Phone: 852-2578-3833
Fax: 852-2578-3929
E-mail Address: hkmw@medcom.com.hk
Web Address: www.medicine.org.hk
The Hong Kong Medical Web is a portal to public health information with links to medical societies and continuing medical education in Hong Kong. The site also has a searchable database of doctors in Hong Kong. The portal is maintained by the Hong Kong Medical Association.

Ministry of Health (MOH) Singapore
16 College Rd.
College of Medicine Bldg.
Singapore, 169854 Singapore
Phone: 65-6325-9220
Toll Free: 800-225-4122
E-mail Address: MOH_INFO@moh.gov.sg
Web Address: www.moh.gov.sg
Through the Ministry of Health (MOH), the Singapore Government manages the public healthcare system to ensure that good and affordable basic medical services are available to all Singaporeans. The website provides medical information, statistics, publications, news and other links.

Singapore Medical Council (SMC)
16 College Rd.
01-01 College of Medicine Bldg.
Singapore, 169854 Singapore
Phone: 65-6506-2102
Fax: 65-6258-2134
E-mail Address: enquiries@smc.gov.sg
Web Address: www.healthprofessionals.gov.sg/content/hprof/smc/en.html
The Singapore Medical Council (SMC), a statutory board under the Ministry of Health, maintains the Register of Medical Practitioners in Singapore, administers the compulsory continuing medical education program and also governs and regulates the professional conduct and ethics of registered medical practitioners.

Singapore Nursing Board (SNB)
81 Kim Keat Rd., #08-00
Singapore, 328836 Singapore
Phone: 65-6478-5413
Fax: 65-6353-3460
E-mail Address: snb_contact@snb.gov.sg
Web Address: www.healthprofessionals.gov.sg/content/hprof/snb/en.html
The Singapore Nursing Board (SNB) is the regulatory authority for nurses and midwives in Singapore.

TeleMedIndia.com
Web Address: www.telemedindia.org
The TeleMedIndia.com site includes glossary, overview, links, publications and information regarding the telemedicine field which is an upcoming field in health science arising out of the effective fusion of information and communication technologies with medical Science.

45) Health Care-General

MedicAlert Foundation
5226 Pirrone Court
Salida, CA 95386 USA
Toll Free: 800-432-5378
Web Address: www.medicalert.org
The MedicAlert Foundation is a nonprofit service that protects and saves the lives of its members by providing biunique identification and critical personal health information. Products include wrist bands that contain personal health issue information to be read in the event of a health emergency.

46) Health Facts-Global

Globalhealthfacts.org
Web Address: http://kff.org/globaldata/
Funded by the Kaiser Family Foundation, globalhealthfacts.org provides up-to-date data on HIV/AIDS, TB, Malaria and other diseases, on a country-by-country basis. It also provides data on programs and funding to combat global diseases.

GlobalHealthReporting.org
Web Address: http://kff.org/global-health-policy/
Globalhealthreporting.org, which is operated by the Kaiser Family Foundation with major support from the Bill & Melinda Gates Foundation, provides coverage of worldwide health care news and reporting on diseases and health programs.

Institute for Health Metrics and Evaluation (IHME)
2301 Fifth Ave., Ste. 600
Seattle, WA 98121 USA
Phone: 206-897-2800
Fax: 206-897-2899
E-mail Address: ihme@healthdata.org
Web Address: www.healthdata.org
The Institute for Health Metrics and Evaluation (IHME) was launched with the goal of providing an unbiased, evidence-based picture of global health trends and determinants to inform the work of a broad range of organizations, policymakers, researchers, and funders. A primary backer is the Bill & Melinda Gates Foundation. The IHME publishes a wide range of research on health care practices, funding and outcomes.

Organisation for Economic Co-Operation and Development (OECD) - Health Statistics
2 rue Andre Pascal
Paris, 75775 France
Phone: 33-1-4524-8200
Fax: 33-1-4524-8500
Web Address: www.oecd.org
The Organisation for Economic Co-Operation and Development (OECD) offers extensive health statistics on a country-by-country basis. Data ranges from health expenditures per capita to health expenditures as percent of GDP for over 34 nations with the world's largest economies.

47) Health Insurance Industry Associations

America's Health Insurance Plans (AHIP)
601 Pennsylvania Ave. NW, S. Bldg., Ste. 500
Washington, DC 20004 USA
Phone: 202-778-3200
Fax: 202-331-7487
E-mail Address: ahip@ahip.org
Web Address: www.ahip.org
America's Health Insurance Plans (AHIP) is a prominent trade association representing the health care insurance community. Its members offer health and supplemental benefits through employer-sponsored coverage, the individual insurance market, and public programs such as Medicare and Medicaid.

American Association of Preferred Provider Organizations (AAPPO)
974 Breckenridge Ln., Ste. 162
Louisville, KY 40207 USA
Phone: 502-403-1122
Fax: 502-403-1129
Web Address: www.aappo.org
The American Association of Preferred Provider Organizations (AAPPO) is the leading national association of network-based preferred provider organizations. AAPPO's membership includes payer, network and Workers' Compensation organizations

Blue Cross and Blue Shield Association
225 N. Michigan Ave.
Chicago, IL 60601-7680 USA
Toll Free: 888-630-2583
Web Address: www.bcbs.com
Blue Cross and Blue Shield Association is a nonprofit professional association of health care insurance providers. The 36 local member companies of the Blue Cross and Blue Shield Association provide healthcare coverage for more than nearly 105 million people in the U.S.

International Federation of Health Plans
83 Victoria St.
London, SW1H 0HW UK
Phone: 44-20-3585-5230
Fax: 44-20-3008-6180
E-mail Address: admin@ifhp.com
Web Address: www.ifhp.com
The International Federation of Health Plans was founded in 1968 by a group of health insurance industry leaders, and is now the leading global network of the industry, with 100 member companies in 31 countries. The group publishes a report on comparative prices in several nations for health care procedures.

National Association of Health Underwriters (NAHU)
1212 New York Ave., Ste. 1100
Washington, DC 20005 USA
Phone: 202-552-5060
Fax: 202-747-6820
E-mail Address: info@nahu.org
Web Address: www.nahu.org
The National Association of Health Underwriters (NAHU) is a professional association of licensed health insurance agents, brokers, general agents, consultants and benefit professionals through more than 200 chapters throughout the U.S.

48) Hearing & Speech

Alexander Graham Bell Association for the Deaf and Hard of Hearing (AGBELL)
3417 Volta Pl. NW
Washington, DC 20007 USA
Phone: 202-337-5220
Fax: 202-337-8314
E-mail Address: info@agbell.org
Web Address: nc.agbell.org

The Alexander Graham Bell Association for the Deaf and Hard of Hearing (AGBELL) is an international membership organization and resource center on hearing loss and spoken language approaches and related issues.

American Speech-Language-Hearing Association (ASHA)
2200 Research Blvd.
Rockville, MD 20850-3289 USA
Phone: 301-296-5700
Fax: 301-296-8580
Toll Free: 800-638-8255
Web Address: www.asha.org
The American Speech-Language-Hearing Association (ASHA) is the professional, scientific and credentialing association for audiologists, speech-language pathologists and speech, language and hearing scientists.

Bridges
935 Edgehill Ave.
Nashville, TN 37203 USA
Phone: 615-248-8828
Fax: 615-248-4797
Toll Free: 866-385-6524
E-mail Address: info@hearingbridges.org
Web Address:
http://bridgesfordeafandhh.org
Bridges, formerly the League for the Deaf and Hard of Hearing and the Ear Foundation, is dedicated to the interests of the hearing impaired. The group funds programs to further medical education on the merits of the early detection of hearing loss.

Hearing Industries Association (HIA)
1444 I St. NW, Ste. 700
Washington, DC 20005 USA
Phone: 202-449-1090
Fax: 202-216-9646
E-mail Address: mjones@bostrom.com
Web Address: www.hearing.org
The Hearing Industries Association (HIA) represents and unifies the many aspects of the hearing industry.

National Family Association for Deaf-Blind (NFADB)
141 Middle Neck Rd.
Sands Point, NY 11050 USA
Fax: 516-883-9060
Toll Free: 800-255-0411
E-mail Address: NFADBinfo@gmail.com
Web Address: www.nfadb.org
The National Family Association for Deaf-Blind (NFADB) is the largest nonprofit, volunteer based national network of families focusing on issues surrounding deaf-blindness.

National Institute on Deafness and Other Communication Disorders (NIDCD)
31 Center Dr., MSC 2320
Bethesda, MD 20892-2320 USA
Phone: 301-496-7243
Fax: 301-402-0018
Toll Free: 800-241-1044
E-mail Address: nidcdinfo@nidcd.nih.gov
Web Address: www.nidcd.nih.gov
The National Institute on Deafness and Other Communication Disorders (NIDCD) conducts and supports biomedical and behavioral research and research training in the normal and disordered processes of hearing, balance, smell, taste, voice, speech and language.

49) Heart Disease

American Heart Association (AHA)
7272 Greenville Ave.
Dallas, TX 75231 USA
Phone: 214-570-5978
Toll Free: 800-242-8721
Web Address:
www.heart.org/HEARTORG/
The American Heart Association (AHA) is a national voluntary health agency that seeks to reduce disability and death from cardiovascular diseases and stroke.

50) Hospice Care

Children's Hospice International (CHI)
500 Montgomery St., Ste. 400
Alexandria, VA 22314 USA
Phone: 703-684-0330
E-mail Address: info@chionline.org
Web Address: www.chionline.org
The Children's Hospice International (CHI) is a nonprofit organization founded to promote hospice support through pediatric care facilities, to encourage the inclusion of children in existing and developing hospice and home-care programs and to include the hospice perspectives in all areas of pediatric care, education and the public arena.

Hospice Education Institute
3 Unity Sq.
P.O. Box 98
Machiasport, ME 04655-0098 USA
Phone: 207-255-8800
Fax: 207-255-8008
Toll Free: 800-331-1620
E-mail Address: hospiceall@aol.com
Web Address: www.hospiceworld.org
The Hospice Education Institute is an independent, not-for-profit organization serving members of the public and health care professions with information and education about the many facets of caring for the dying and the bereaved.

51) Hospital Care

American Hospital Association (AHA)
155 N. Wacker Dr.
Chicago, IL 60606 USA
Phone: 312-422-3000
Fax: 312-422-4796
Toll Free: 800-424-4301
Web Address: www.aha.org
The American Hospital Association (AHA) is a national organization that represents and serves all types of hospitals, health care networks, their patients and communities.

Council of Teaching Hospitals and Health Systems (COTH)
655 K St. NW, Ste. 100
Washington, DC 20001-2399 USA
Phone: 202-828-0490
E-mail Address: lford@aamc.org
Web Address:
www.aamc.org/members/coth
The Council of Teaching Hospitals and Health Systems (COTH), part of the Association of American Medical Colleges (AAMC), provides representation and services related to the special needs, concerns and opportunities facing major teaching hospitals in the United States and Canada. The COTH web site offers a listing of member hospitals.

Shriners Hospitals for Children
2900 Rocky Point Dr.
Tampa, FL 33607-1460 USA
Phone: 813-281-0300
Toll Free: 800-237-5055
E-mail Address: shrinepr@shrinenet.org
Web Address:
www.shrinershospitalsforchildren.org
Shriners Hospitals for Children is a one-of-a-kind international health care system of 22 hospitals dedicated to improving the lives of children by providing specialty pediatric care, innovative research and outstanding teaching programs. Children up to the age of 18 with orthopedic conditions, burns, spinal cord injuries and cleft lip and palate are eligible for admission and receive all care in a family-centered environment at no charge, regardless of financial need.

52) Human Resources Professionals Associations

American Society for Healthcare Human Resources Administrators (ASHRM)
155 N. Wacker St., Ste. 400
Chicago, IL 60606 USA
Phone: 312-422-3720
Fax: 312-422-4577
E-mail Address: ashhra@aha.org
Web Address: www.ashrm.org
The American Society for Healthcare Human Resources Administrators (ASHRM) is the professional society for healthcare risk management professionals and those responsible for decisions that will promote quality care, maintain a safe environment and preserve human and financial resources in health care organizations.

International Association of Healthcare Central Service Materiel Management (IAHCSMM)
55 West Wacker Dr., Ste. 501
Chicago, IL 60610 USA
Phone: 312-440-0078
Fax: 312-440-9474
Toll Free: 800-962-8274
E-mail Address: mailbox@iahcsmm.org
Web Address: www.iahcsmm.org
The International Association of Healthcare Central Service Materiel Management (IAHCSMM) exists to provide education, networking, recognition, membership advocacy and professional practices to promote innovative ideas toward the future of the industry.

53) Immunization Resources

CDC National Immunization Program (NIP)
1600 Clifton Rd.
Atlanta, GA 30333 USA
Toll Free: 800-232-4636
Web Address: www.cdc.gov/vaccines/
The CDC National Immunization Program (NIP) offers up-to-date immunization information, including vaccine schedules, side effects, contraindications, recommendations and more.

54) Industry Research/Market Research

Forrester Research
60 Acorn Park Dr.
Cambridge, MA 02140 USA
Phone: 617-613-5730
Toll Free: 866-367-7378
E-mail Address: press@forrester.com
Web Address: www.forrester.com
Forrester Research is a publicly traded company that identifies and analyzes emerging trends in technology and their impact on business. Among the firm's specialties are the financial services, retail, health care, entertainment, automotive and information technology industries.

Gartner, Inc.
56 Top Gallant Rd.
Stamford, CT 06902 USA
Phone: 203-964-0096
E-mail Address: info@gartner.com
Web Address: www.gartner.com
Gartner, Inc. is a publicly traded IT company that provides competitive intelligence and strategic consulting and advisory services to numerous clients worldwide.

MarketResearch.com
11200 Rockville Pike, Ste. 504
Rockville, MD 20852 USA
Phone: 240-747-3093
Fax: 240-747-3004
Toll Free: 800-298-5699
E-mail Address:
customerservice@marketresearch.com
Web Address: www.marketresearch.com
MarketResearch.com is a leading broker for professional market research and industry analysis. Users are able to search the company's database of research publications including data on global industries, companies, products and trends.

Plunkett Research, Ltd.
P.O. Drawer 541737
Houston, TX 77254-1737 USA
Phone: 713-932-0000
Fax: 713-932-7080
E-mail Address:
customersupport@plunkettresearch.com
Web Address: www.plunkettresearch.com
Plunkett Research, Ltd. is a leading provider of market research, industry trends analysis and business statistics. Since 1985, it has served clients worldwide, including corporations, universities, libraries, consultants and government agencies. At the firm's web site, visitors can view product information and pricing and access a large amount of basic market information on industries such as financial services, InfoTech, e-commerce, health care and biotech.

55) Insurance Industry Resources

Center for Risk Management and Insurance Research
35 Broad St.
Georgia State University, 11th Fl.
Atlanta, GA 30303 USA
Phone: 404-413-7471
Fax: 404-413-7516
E-mail Address: rwklein@gsu.edu
Web Address: rmi.robinson.gsu.edu
The Center for Risk Management and Insurance Research in the Robinson College of Business at Georgia State University was established in 1969 through grants and general financial support from the insurance industry through the Educational Foundation, Inc. The Center is established as a leading information source on risk and insurance issues.

56) Internet Usage Statistics

Pew Internet & American Life Project
1615 L St. NW, Ste. 800
Washington, DC 20036 USA
Phone: 202-419-4300
Fax: 202-419-4349
E-mail Address: info@pewinternet.org
Web Address: www.pewinternet.org
The Pew Internet & American Life Project, an initiative of the Pew Research Center, produces reports that explore the impact of the Internet on families, communities, work and home, daily life, education, health care and civic and political life.

57) Learning Disorders

Children and Adults with Attention Deficit Disorder (CHADD)
4601 Presidents Dr., Ste. 300
Landover, MD 20785 USA
Phone: 301-306-7070
Fax: 301-306-7090
Toll Free: 800-233-4050
Web Address: www.chadd.org
Children and Adults with Attention Deficit Disorder (CHADD) is the nation's leading nonprofit membership organization serving individuals with Attention-Deficit/Hyperactivity Disorder (ADHD) through education, advocacy and support. It produces a bi-monthly magazine, Attention, for members and sponsors an annual conference.

58) Libraries-Medical Data

Medical Library Association (MLA)
65 E. Wacker Pl., Ste. 1900
Chicago, IL 60601-7246 USA
Phone: 312-419-9094
Fax: 312-419-8950
E-mail Address:
websupport@mail.mlahq.org
Web Address: www.mlanet.org
The Medical Library Association (MLA) is dedicated to improving the quality and leadership of health information professionals in order to foster the art and science of health information services.

National Library of Medicine (NLM)
8600 Rockville Pike
Bethesda, MD 20894 USA
Phone: 301-594-5983
Toll Free: 888-346-3656
Web Address: www.nlm.nih.gov
The National Library of Medicine (NLM) is the world's largest medical library. The web site offers links to several databases of medical research, as well as a variety of online health information.

Weill Cornell Medical Library
1300 York Ave.
New York, NY 10021-4896 USA
Phone: 646-962-2468
Fax: 212-746-8375
E-mail Address:
infodesk@med.cornell.edu
Web Address: library.weill.cornell.edu/
The Weill Cornell Medical Library houses information on the biomedical sciences, as well as performs data retrieval, management and evaluation.

59) Liver Diseases

American Liver Foundation (ALF)
39 Broadway, Ste. 2700
New York, NY 10006 USA
Phone: 212-668-1000
Fax: 212-483-8179
Toll Free: 800-465-4837
Web Address: www.liverfoundation.org
The American Liver Foundation (ALF) is a national, nonprofit organization dedicated to the prevention, treatment and cure of hepatitis and other liver diseases.

60) Long Term Care, Assisted Living Associations

Argentum
1650 King St., Ste. 602
Alexandria, VA 22314-2747 USA
Phone: 703-894-1805
E-mail Address: jvann@alfa.org
Web Address: www.alfa.org
Argentum, formerly the Assisted Living Federation of America (ALFA) represents for-profit and nonprofit providers of assisted living, continuing care retirement communities, independent living and other forms of housing and services.

National Consumer Voice for Quality Long-Term Care
1001 Connecticut Ave. NW, Ste. 632
Washington, DC 20036 USA
Phone: 202-332-2275
Fax: 866-230-9789
E-mail Address:
info@theconsumervoice.org
Web Address:
www.theconsumervoice.org
The National Consumer Voice for Quality Long-Term Care, formerly the National Citizens' Coalition for Nursing Home Reform (NCCNHR), represents the grassroots membership of concerned advocates of quality long term care nationwide.

61) Managed Care Information

Managed Care Information Center (MCIC)
1913 Atlantic Ave., Ste. 200
Manasquan, NJ 08736 USA
Phone: 732-292-1100
Fax: 732-292-1111
E-mail Address: info@themcic.com
Web Address: www.themcic.com
The Managed Care Information Center (MCIC) is a clearinghouse for health care executives' managed care information needs. MCIC publishes newsletters, advisories, guides, manuals, special reports and books.

Managed Care On-Line (MCOL)
1101 Standiford Ave., Ste. C-3
Modesto, CA 95350 USA
Phone: 209-577-4888
Fax: 209-577-3557
E-mail Address: mcare@mcol.com
Web Address: www.mcol.com
Managed Care On-Line (MCOL) is an Internet-based health care company delivering business-to-business managed care resources. The web site includes a knowledge center and extensive resources.

62) Maternal & Infant Health

Association of Maternal and Child Health Programs (AMCHP)
2030 M St. NW, Ste. 350
Washington, DC 20036 USA
Phone: 202-775-0436
Fax: 202-775-0061
E-mail Address: info@amchp.org
Web Address: www.amchp.org
The Association of Maternal and Child Health Programs (AMCHP) is the national organization representing public health leaders and others working to improve the health and well-being of women, children and youth.

La Leche League International
35 E. Wacker Dr., Ste. 850
Chicago, IL 60601 USA
Phone: 312-646-6260
Fax: 312-644-8557
Toll Free: 877-452-5324
E-mail Address: info@llli.org
Web Address: www.lalecheleague.org
The La Leche League International seeks to help mothers worldwide to breastfeed through mother-to-mother support, encouragement, information and education and to promote a better understanding of breastfeeding.

National Center for Education in Maternal and Child Health (NCEMCH)
2115 Wisconsin Ave. NW, Ste. 601
Washington, DC 20007-2292 USA
Phone: 202-784-9770
Fax: 202-784-9777
E-mail Address:
MCHgroup@georgetown.edu
Web Address: www.ncemch.org
The National Center for Education in Maternal and Child Health (NCEMCH) provides national leadership to the maternal and child health community to improve the health and well-being of the nation's children and families.

63) MBA Resources

MBA Depot
Web Address: www.mbadepot.com
MBA Depot is an online community and information portal for MBAs, potential MBA program applicants and business professionals.

64) Medical & Health Indexes

Medical World Search
TLC Information Services
P.O. Box 944
Yorktown Heights, NY 10598 USA
Phone: 914-248-6770
Fax: 914-248-6429
E-mail Address:
mwsearch@mwsearch.com
Web Address: www.mwsearch.com
Medical World Search is a free medical search engine offered by TLC Information

Service that helps patients to understand medical terms and acronyms.

65) Medicare Information

Medicare Rights Center (MRC)
266 W. 37th St., Fl. 3
New York, NY 10018 USA
Phone: 212-869-3850
Fax: 212-869-3532
Toll Free: 800-333-4114
E-mail Address: info@medicarerights.org
Web Address: www.medicarerights.org
The Medicare Rights Center (MRC) is a nonprofit organization that acts as a source for Medicare consumers and professionals. Its web site is a helpful, independent source of Medicare information.

Medicare.gov
7500 Security Blvd.
Baltimore, MD 21244-1850 USA
Toll Free: 800-633-4227
Web Address: www.medicare.gov
Medicare.gov is the official U.S. Government web site for people with questions or problems relating to Medicare.

66) Mental Health

International Foundation for Research and Education on Depression (IFRED) (The)
P.O. Box 17598
Baltimore, MD 21297-1598 USA
Fax: 443-782-0739
E-mail Address: info@ifred.org
Web Address: www.ifred.org
The International Foundation for Research and Education on Depression (IFRED) is an organization dedicated to researching causes of depression, to support those dealing with depression, and to combat the stigma associated with depression.

International Society for Mental Health Online (ISMHO)
Phone: 608-618-1774
Web Address: www.ismho.org
The International Society for Mental Health Online (ISMHO) strives to promote the use and development of online communication, information and technology for the mental health community.

Mental Health America
500 Montgomery St., Ste. 820
Alexandria, VA 22314 USA
Phone: 703-684-7722
Fax: 703-684-5968
Toll Free: 800-969-6642
Web Address: www.mentalhealthamerica.net
Mental Health America, formerly the National Mental Health Association (NMHA) is a community-based, nonprofit organization addressing all aspects of mental health, mental wellness and mental illness.

67) Nanotechnology Associations

Alliance for NanoHealth
Phone: 713-441-7350
E-mail Address: jhsakamoto@tmhs.org
Web Address: alliancefornanohealth.org
The Alliance for NanoHealth is comprised of eight medical research universities and clinical institutions within the Texas Medical Center, located in Houston. Its purpose is to coordinate efforts to apply advanced research to the use of nanotechnology in health care.

NCI Alliance for Nanotechnology in Cancer
31 Ctr. Dr., Bldg. 31, Rm. 10A52, MSC 2580
Attn. NCI Office of Cancer Nanotechnology Research
Bethesda, MD 20892-2580 USA
Phone: 301-451-8983
Fax: 301-451-7440
Toll Free: 888-422-6237
E-mail Address: cancer.nano@mail.nih.gov
Web Address: nano.cancer.gov
The NCI Alliance for Nanotechnology in Cancer, a service of the National Cancer Institute, is dedicated to using nanotechnology to advance the prevention, treatment and diagnosis of cancer. It especially seeks to lower the barriers preventing commercial development of advanced oncology therapeutics that use nanotechnology.

68) Neurological Disease

American Parkinson's Disease Association (APDA)
135 Parkinson Ave.
Staten Island, NY 10305 USA
Phone: 718-981-8001
Fax: 718-981-4399
Toll Free: 800-223-2732
E-mail Address: apda@apdaparkinson.org
Web Address: www.apdaparkinson.org
The American Parkinson's Disease Association (APDA) seeks to promote a better quality of life for people in the Parkinson's community through a nationwide network of chapters, information and referral centers and support groups. It also funds research and works to enhance patient services and public awareness.

Christopher & Dana Reeve Foundation
636 Morris Tpk., Ste. 3A
Short Hills, NJ 07078 USA
Phone: 973-379-2690
Toll Free: 800-225-0292
Web Address: www.christopherreeve.org
The Christopher & Dana Reeve Foundation is committed to funding research that develops treatments and cures for paralysis caused by spinal cord injury and other central nervous system disorders.

National Rehabilitation Information Center (NARIC)
8400 Corporate Dr., Ste. 500
Landover, MD 20785 USA
Fax: 301-459-4263
Toll Free: 800-346-2742
E-mail Address: naricinfo@heitechservices.com
Web Address: www.naric.com
The National Rehabilitation Information Center (NARIC) collects and disseminates the results of federally funded research projects.

69) Nutrition & Food Research & Education

Center for Nutrition Policy and Promotion (CNPP)
3101 Park Ctr. Dr., Fl. 10
Alexandria, VA 22302-1594 USA
Phone: 703-305-7600
Fax: 703-305-3300
Web Address: www.cnpp.usda.gov
The Center for Nutrition Policy and Promotion (CNPP) is an arm of the U.S. Department of Agriculture's Food, Nutrition and Consumer Services division. The center develops and promotes science-based dietary guidance and economic information for consumers and professionals in health, education, industry and media.

Center for Science in the Public Interest (CSPI)
1220 L St. NW, Ste. 300
Washington, DC 20009 USA
Phone: 202-332-9110
Fax: 202-265-4954
E-mail Address: cspi@cspinet.org
Web Address: www.cspinet.org
The Center for Science in the Public Interest (CSPI) is a nonprofit education and advocacy organization that focuses on improving the safety and nutritional quality of our food supply and on

reducing the incidences of alcohol-related injuries.

70) Online Health Data, General

EverydayHealth
345 Hudson St., Fl. 16
New York, NY 10014 USA
Phone: 646-728-9500
Fax: 646-728-9501
E-mail Address: info@everydayhealth.com
Web Address: www.everydayhealth.com
EverydayHealth.com is a free, comprehensive health and medical information site, specifically designed with the Family's Chief Medical Officer - women and other caregivers - in mind. EverydayHealth.com offers the best health information, treatment advice and more than 125 online tools.

Health Sciences Library
1959 NE Pacific St.
T334 Health Science Bldg., P.O. Box 357155
Seattle, WA 98195-7155 USA
Phone: 206-543-3390
Web Address: hsl.uw.edu
The Health Sciences Library, based at the University of Washington Health Sciences Center, offers health-related information and articles from the center's HealthBeat publication.

Healthfinder
1101 Wootton Parkway
Rockville, MD 20013-113 USA
E-mail Address: healthfinder@nhic.org.
Web Address: www.healthfinder.gov
Healthfinder is a resource for finding government and nonprofit health and human services information on the Internet. It has resources on a range of health topics retrieved from roughly 1,400 government and non-profit organizations.

MedlinePlus
8600 Rockville Pike
Bethesda, MD 20894 USA
Web Address: www.nlm.nih.gov/medlineplus
MedlinePlus offers information from the National Library of Medicine, the world's largest medical library, as well as other governmental and health-related organizations.

Medscape
825 Eighth Ave., Fl. 11
New York, NY 10019 USA
Phone: 212-301-6700
Web Address: www.medscape.com
Medscape, an online resource for better patient care, provides links to journal articles, health care-related sites and health care information. The site is owned by WebMD.

National Women's Health Information Center (NWHIC)
200 Independence Ave. SW
Washington, DC 20201 USA
Phone: 202-690-2650
Fax: 202-205-2631
Toll Free: 800-994-9662
Web Address: womenshealth.gov
The National Women's Health Information Center (NWHIC) provides a gateway to the vast array of federal and other women's health information resources.

PubMed
8600 Rockville Pike
Bethesda, MD 20894 USA
Toll Free: 888-346-3656
Web Address: www.ncbi.nlm.nih.gov/sites/entrez
PubMed provides access to over 26 million citations dating back to the mid-1960s from MEDLINE, online books and life science journals. PubMed includes links to open access full text articles.

RxList
395 Hudson St., Fl. 3
New York, NY 10014 USA
Phone: 212-624-3700
Web Address: www.rxlist.com
RxList is an online portal, which offers detailed and current information on brands and generic drugs. The web site is owned and operated by WebMD.

WebMD
395 Hudson St., Fl. 3
New York, NY 10014 USA
Phone: 212-624-3700
E-mail Address: newstip@webmd.net
Web Address: www.webmd.com
WebMD serves consumers, physicians, employers and health plans as a major provider of health information services through its broad selection of interrelated health topics, current medical news and its own medical search engine.

71) Online Health Information, Reliability & Ethics

Health Internet Ethics (Hi-Ethics)
E-mail Address: Cheryl@DrGreene.com
Web Address: www.hiethics.org
Health Internet Ethics (Hi-Ethics) is an association of companies providing online health information services with adherence to high quality and ethical standards, ensuring that individual customers can fully utilize the Internet to improve the health of their families.

Health on the Net Foundation Code of Conduct
C/o HUG-Belle-Idee
Chemin du Petit-Bel-Air 2
Chene-Bourg, 1225 Switzerland
Phone: 41-22-372-62-50
Fax: 41-22-305-57-28
E-mail Address: honsecretariat@healthonnet.org
Web Address: www.hon.ch/HONcode
The Health on the Net Foundation Code of Conduct defines a set of rules to help standardize the reliability of medical and health information on the Internet.

National Practitioner Data Bank (NPDB)
4094 Majestic Ln., PMB-332
Fairfax, VA 22033 USA
Phone: 703-802-9380
Fax: 703-803-1964
Toll Free: 800-767-6732
E-mail Address: help@npdb.hrsa.gov
Web Address: www.npdb.hrsa.gov
The National Practitioner Data Bank (NPDB) is an alert or flagging system intended to facilitate a comprehensive review of health care practitioners' professional credentials. It is a joint operation of several U.S. federal government agencies, including the Department of Health and Human Services, the Health Resources and Services Administration and the Bureau of Health Professions. Authorized NPDB queries and reporters include State licensing boards, medical malpractice payers (authorized only to report to the NPDB), hospitals and other health care entities, professional societies, and licensed health care practitioners (self-query only). Authorized users and reporters include Federal and State Government agencies, health plans, and health care practitioners, providers and suppliers (self-query only).

72) Organ Donation

Living Bank (The)
P.O. Box 6725
Houston, TX 77265-6725 USA
Phone: 713-961-9431
Toll Free: 800-528-2971
E-mail Address: info@livingbank.org
Web Address: www.livingbank.org
The Living Bank is a national organ donor and transplant education organization that keeps computerized records of organ donor data for future retrieval in case of emergency.

73) Osteoporosis

National Osteoporosis Foundation (NOF)
251 18th St. S, Ste. 630
Arlington, VA 22202 USA
Phone: 202-223-2226
Toll Free: 800-231-4222
E-mail Address: info@nof.org
Web Address: www.nof.org
The National Osteoporosis Foundation (NOF) is a voluntary health organization that works to fight osteoporosis and promote bone health. It also conducts programs of public and clinician awareness, education, advocacy and research.

74) Patent Resources

Patent Docs
E-mail Address: PatentDocs@gmail.com
Web Address: patentdocs.typepad.com/patent_docs/
Patent Docs is an excellent blog about patent law and patent news in the fields of biotechnology and pharmaceuticals.

75) Patients' Rights & Information

Electronic Privacy Information Center (EPIC) - Medical Record Privacy
1718 Connecticut Ave. NW, Ste. 200
Washington, DC 20009 USA
Phone: 202-483-1140
E-mail Address: info@epic.org
Web Address: www.epic.org/privacy/medical
The Medical Record Privacy section of the Electronic Privacy Information Center (EPIC) tracks recent developments in medical privacy legislation.

FamiliesUSA
1201 New York Ave. NW, Ste. 1100
Washington, DC 20005 USA
Phone: 202-628-3030
Fax: 202-347-2417
E-mail Address: info@familiesusa.org
Web Address: www.familiesusa.org
FamiliesUSA is a national nonprofit, non-partisan organization dedicated to the achievement of high-quality, affordable health and long-term care for all Americans.

Society for Healthcare Consumer Advocacy (SHCA)
155 N. Wacker Dr., Ste. 400
Chicago, IL 60606 USA
Phone: 312-422-3700
Fax: 312-278-0881
E-mail Address: hope@aha.org
Web Address: www.hpoe.org/resources/organization-websites/1105
The Society for Healthcare Consumer Advocacy (SHCA), a personal membership group of the American Hospital Association (AHA) strives to advance health care consumer advocacy by supporting professionals that represent and advocate for consumers throughout the health care industry.

76) Pharmaceutical Industry Associations (Drug Industry)

Academy of Physicians in Clinical Research (APCR)
6816 Southpoint Pkwy., Ste. 1000
Jacksonville, FL 32216 USA
Phone: 904-309-6271
Fax: 904-998-0855
E-mail Address: contact@apcrnet.org
Web Address: www.apcrnet.org
The Academy of Physicians in Clinical Research (APCR), formerly the Academy of Pharmaceutical Physicians and Investigators (APPI), is an association that arose when the American Academy of Pharmaceutical Physicians and the Association of Clinical Research Professionals merged. It is a nonprofit, membership organization that provides scientific and educational activities on issues concerning pharmaceutical medicine.

Accreditation Council for Pharmacy Education (ACPE)
135 S. LaSalle St., Ste. 4100
Chicago, IL 60603-4810 USA
Phone: 312-664-3575
Fax: 312-664-4652
E-mail Address: info@acpe-accredit.org
Web Address: www.acpe-accredit.org
The Accreditation Council for Pharmacy Education (ACPE) provides accreditation for pharmaceutical programs. It is the national agency for accreditation of professional degree programs as well as providers of continuing pharmacy education.

American Association of Colleges of Pharmacy (AACP)
1727 King St.
Alexandria, VA 22314 USA
Phone: 703-739-2330
Fax: 703-836-8982
E-mail Address: mail@aacp.org
Web Address: www.aacp.org
The American Association of Colleges of Pharmacy (AACP) is the national organization representing the interests of pharmaceutical education and educators.

American Association of Pharmaceutical Sciences (AAPS)
2107 Wilson Blvd., Ste. 700
Arlington, VA 22201-3042 USA
Phone: 703-243-2800
Fax: 703-243-2800
E-mail Address: aaps@aaps.org
Web Address: www.aaps.org
The American Association of Pharmaceutical Scientists (AAPS) represents scientists in the pharmaceutical field. Members are given access to international forum, scientific programs, ongoing education, opportunities for networking and professional development.

American Pharmacists Association (AphA)
2215 Constitution Ave. NW
Washington, DC 20037 USA
Phone: 202-628-4410
Fax: 202-783-2351
Toll Free: 800-237-4410
E-mail Address: infocenter@aphanet.org
Web Address: www.pharmacist.com
American Pharmaceutical Association (APhA), formerly American Pharmaceutical Association is a national professional society that provides news and information to pharmacists. Its membership includes over 62,000 practicing pharmacists, pharmaceutical scientists, student pharmacists and pharmacy technicians.

American Society for Clinical Pharmacology and Therapeutics (ASCPT)
528 N. Washington St.
Alexandria, VA 22314 USA
Phone: 703-836-6981
E-mail Address: info@ascpt.org
Web Address: www.ascpt.org
The American Society for Clinical Pharmacology and Therapeutics (ASCPT) is a nonprofit organization that is devoted to the discovery, development, regulation and use of safe and effective medications necessary for the prevention and treatment of illness.

American Society for Pharmacology and Experimental Therapeutics (ASPET)
9650 Rockville Pike
Bethesda, MD 20814-3995 USA
Phone: 301-634-7060
Fax: 301-634-7061
Web Address: www.aspet.org
The American Society for Pharmacology and Experimental Therapeutics (ASPET) is a scientific society, with members from

academia, industry and the government, conducting research in basic and clinical pharmacology.

Association of the British Pharmaceutical Industry (ABPI)
105 Victoria St., Southside, Fl. 7
London, SW1E 6QT UK
Phone: 44-20-7930-3477
Fax: 44-20-7747-1447
Web Address: www.abpi.org.uk
The Association of the British Pharmaceutical Industry (ABPI) is a trade association that provides research and information for the British pharmaceuticals industry.

Canadian Pharmacists Association (CPhA)
1785 Alta Vista Dr.
Ottawa, ON K1G 3Y6 Canada
Phone: 613-523-7877
Fax: 613-523-0445
Toll Free: 800-917-9489
E-mail Address: info@pharmacists.ca
Web Address: www.pharmacists.ca
The Canadian Pharmacists Association (CPhA) is a professional organization providing drug information, pharmacy practice support material, patient information and news about the pharmacy industry.

Chinese Pharmaceutical Association (CPA)
No. 4 Jianwai St. Chaoyang District
18/F Twr. 9, Jianwai SOHO
Beijing, 100022 China
Phone: 0086-10-58699271
Fax: 0086-10-58699272
E-mail Address: int@cpa.org.cn
Web Address:
www.cpa.org.cn/Index.html
The Chinese Pharmaceutical Association (CPA) is the national organization of pharmaceutical professionals including scientists, legislators and pharmacists serving in the pharmacies, hospitals/clinics and industry.

Generic Pharmaceutical Association (GPhA)
777 6th St. NW, Ste. 510
Washington, DC 20001 USA
Phone: 202-249-7100
Fax: 202-249-7105
Web Address: www.gphaonline.org
The Generic Pharmaceutical Association (GPhA) represents the manufacturers and distributors of finished generic pharmaceutical products, manufacturers and distributors of bulk active pharmaceutical chemicals and suppliers of other goods and services to the generic pharmaceutical industry.

Indian Drug Manufacturers' Association (IDMA)
102-B, Poonam Chambers, A Wing, FL. 1
Dr. A. B. Rd., Worli
Mumbai, 400 018 India
Phone: 91-22-2494-4624
Fax: 91-22-2495-0723
E-mail Address: ppr@idmaindia.com
Web Address: www.idma-assn.org
The Indian Drug Manufacturers' Association (IDMA) is a wholly Indian association mainly promoting the interests of Indian drug manufacturers, as well as protecting the interest of the Indian consumers.

Innovative Medicines Canada
55 Metcalfe St., Ste. 1220
Ottawa, ON K1P 6L5 Canada
Phone: 613-236-0455
E-mail Address: info@imc-mnc.ca
Web Address: innovativemedicines.ca
Innovative Medicines Canada is dedicated to the discovery and development of new medicines and vaccines. Its 50 member companies are guided by strict code of ethical practices ensuring valued partnership in the Canadian healthcare system.

International Federation of Pharmaceutical Manufacturers & Associations (IFPMA)
Chemin des Mines 9
P.O. Box 195
Geneva 20, 1211 Switzerland
Phone: 41-22-338-32-00
Fax: 41-22-338-32-99
E-mail Address: info@ifpma.org
Web Address: www.ifpma.org
The International Federation of Pharmaceutical Manufacturers & Associations (IFPMA) is a nonprofit organization that represents the world's research-based pharmaceutical and biotech companies.

International Pharmaceutical Excipients Council of the Americas (IPEC-Americas)
3138 N. 10th St., Ste. 500
Arlington, VA 22201 USA
Phone: 571-814-3449
E-mail Address:
ipecamer@ipecamericas.org
Web Address: ipecamericas.org
The International Pharmaceutical Excipients Council of the Americas (IPEC-Americas) is a trade organization that promotes standardized approval criteria for drug inert ingredients, or excipients, among different nations. The organization also works to promote safe and useful excipients in the U.S.

International Pharmaceutical Federation (FIP)
Andries Bickerweg 5
The Hague, AE 2517 JP The Netherlands
Phone: 31-70-3021-970
Fax: 31-70-3021-999
E-mail Address: fip@fip.org
Web Address: www.fip.org
The International Pharmaceutical Federation (FIP) is a global federation of national associations representing 3 million pharmacists and pharmaceutical scientists around the world.

International Society for Pharmacoepidemiology (ISPE)
5272 River Rd., Ste. 630
Bethesda, MD 20816 USA
Phone: 301-718-6500
Fax: 301-656-0989
Web Address: www.pharmacoepi.org
The International Society for Pharmacoepidemiology (ISPE) is a nonprofit international organization dedicated to the health of the public by advancing the study of the effects and determinants of pharmacology on epidemic diseases and to help provide risk benefit assessments on drugs with large scale distributions.

International Society of Regulatory Toxicology & Pharmacology (ISRTP)
21517 Fox Field Cir.
Germantown, MD 20876 USA
E-mail Address:
memberservices@isrtp.org
Web Address: www.isrtp.org
The International Society of Regulatory Toxicology & Pharmacology (ISRTP) is an association of professionals that mediates between policy makers and scientists in order to promote sound toxicologic and pharmacologic science as a basis for regulation affecting the environment and human safety and health.

Korean Research-based Pharmaceutical Industry Association (KRPIA)
832-7 Yeoksam-Dong, Gangnam-Gu
Fl. 6, Hwanghwa Bldg.
Seoul, 143-200 Korea
Phone: 82-2-456-8553
Fax: 82-2-456-8320
Web Address: www.krpia.or.kr
The Korean Research-based Pharmaceutical Industry Association (KRPIA) is an association of research-based pharmaceutical companies operating in Korea.

LEEM (French Pharmaceutical Companies Association)
58 Gouvion Blvd.

Saint Cyr, 75017 France
Phone: 33-1-45-03-88-88
Fax: 33-1-45-04-47-71
Web Address: www.leem.org
LEEM (Les Entreprises du Medicament or the French Pharmaceuticals Association) represents the 270 pharmaceutical companies operating in France engaged in the research and/or development of medicines for human use.

National Pharmacy Association
38-42 St. Peter's St.
St. Albans, Mallinson House
Hertfordshire, AL1 3NP UK
Phone: 44-1727-858687
E-mail Address: npa@npa.co.uk
Web Address: www.npa.co.uk
The National Pharmacy Association (NPA), a nonprofit organization was established in 1921 as the trade association of community pharmacy owners in the UK. It works to support, protect and represent the interests of community pharmacies.

Pharmaceutical Research and Manufacturers of America (PhRMA)
950 F St. NW, Ste. 300
Washington, DC 20004 USA
Phone: 202-835-3400
Web Address: www.phrma.org
Pharmaceutical Research and Manufacturers of America (PhRMA) represents the nation's leading research-based pharmaceutical and biotechnology companies.

Pharmaceutical Society of Hong Kong
12 Tak Hing St.
Rm. 1303, Rightful Ctr., Jordan
Hong Kong, Hong Kong Hong Kong
Phone: 852-2376-3090
Fax: 852-2376-3091
E-mail Address: pharmacist@pshk.hk
Web Address: www.pshk.hk
Pharmaceutical Society of Hong Kong is the official representative body of the pharmaceutical industry in Hong Kong.

Pharmaceutical Society of Singapore (PSS)
2 College Rd.
Alumni Medical Ctr., 2nd Lvl.
Singapore, 169850 Singapore
Phone: 65-6221-1136
Fax: 65-6223-0969
E-mail Address: admin@pss.org.sg
Web Address: www.pss.org.sg
The Pharmaceutical Society of Singapore (PSS) is the professional organization representing pharmacists in Singapore. PSS focuses its efforts in two areas: to upgrade pharmacists professionally and public outreach through health education programs. These programs also attract a large number of participants from nearby regions, including Hong Kong, Brunei and Indonesia.

Pharmacy Council of India
Kotla Rd., Aiwan-E-Ghalib, Marg
Combined Councilsâ€™ Bldg.
New Delhi, 110-002 India
Phone: 91-11-2323-1348
Fax: 91-11-2323-9184
E-mail Address: pci@ndb.vsnl.net.in
Web Address: www.pci.nic.in
The Pharmacy Council of India provides regulation of pharmacists under the Pharmacy Act and is a statutory body working under India's Ministry of Health and Family Welfare.

Royal Pharmaceutical Society
66-68 E. Smithfield
London, E1W 1AW UK
Phone: 44-20-7572-2737
Fax: 44-20-7735-7629
E-mail Address: support@rpharms.com
Web Address: www.rpharms.com
The Royal Pharmaceutical Society is the regulatory agency and professional membership organization for pharmacists in England, Wales and Scotland.

Singapore Association of Pharmaceutical Industries (SAPI)
151 Chin Swee Rd.
02-13A/14 Manhattan House
Singapore, 169876 Singapore
Phone: 65-6738-0966
Fax: 65-6738-0977
E-mail Address: admin@sapi.org.sg
Web Address: www.sapi.org.sg
The Singapore Association of Pharmaceutical Industries (SAPI) represents a wide spectrum of pharmaceutical related businesses, namely the trading houses, manufacturers, representative offices and pharmacies in Singapore.

Society of Infectious Diseases Pharmacists (SIDP)
823 Congress Ave., Ste. 230
Austin, TX 78701 USA
Phone: 512-328-8632
Fax: 512-495-9031
E-mail Address: sbulak@eami.com
Web Address: www.sidp.org
The Society of Infectious Diseases Pharmacists (SIDP) is an association of health professionals dedicated to promoting the appropriate use of antimicrobials. It offers members education, advocacy and leadership in all aspects of the treatment of infectious diseases.

77) Pharmaceutical Industry Resources (Drug Industry)

Pharmabiz.com
1st Dhobi Talao Ln.
Fl. 2, Laura Bldg., Dhobi Talao
Mumbai, 400 002 India
Phone: 91-22-2206-3132
Fax: 91-22-2206-3133
E-mail Address: editorial@saffronmedia.in
Web Address: www.pharmabiz.com
Pharmabiz.com includes links to most pharmaceutical associations and India's leading industry bodies. The site includes news, company profiles and new drug approvals. It is maintained by Saffron Media Pvt. Ltd.

Tufts Center for the Study of Drug Development
75 Kneeland St., Ste. 1100
Boston, MA 02111 USA
Phone: 617-636-2170
Fax: 617-636-2425
E-mail Address: csdd@tufts.edu
Web Address: csdd.tufts.edu
The Tufts Center for the Study of Drug Development, an affiliate of Tuft's University, provides analyses and commentary on pharmaceutical issues. Its mission is to improve the quality and efficiency of pharmaceutical development, research and utilization. It is famous, among other things, for its analysis of the true total cost of developing and commercializing a new drug. Tuft's Center conducts research in areas of drug development, public policy and regulation and biotechnology.

78) Privacy & Consumer Matters

Federal Trade Commission-Privacy and Security
600 Pennsylvania Ave. NW
Washington, DC 20580 USA
Phone: 202-326-2222
Web Address: business.ftc.gov/privacy-and-security
Federal Trade Commission-Privacy and Security is responsible for many aspects of business-to-consumer and business-to-business trade and regulation.

Privacy International
62 Britton St.
London, EC1M 5UY UK
Phone: 44-20-3422-4321
E-mail Address: info@privacy.org
Web Address: www.privacyinternational.org

Privacy International is a government and business watchdog, alerting individuals to wiretapping and national security activities, medical privacy infringement, police information systems and the use of ID cards, video surveillance and data matching.

TRUSTe
835 Market St., Ste. 800, Box 137
San Francisco, CA 94103-1905 USA
Phone: 415-520-3490
Fax: 415-520-3420
Toll Free: 888-878-7830
E-mail Address: eleanor@truste.com
Web Address: www.truste.com
TRUSTe formed an alliance with all major portal sites to launch the Privacy Partnership campaign, a consumer education program designed to raise the awareness of Internet privacy issues. The organization works to meet the needs of business web sites while protecting user privacy.

79) Research & Development, Laboratories

Battelle Memorial Institute
505 King Ave.
Columbus, OH 43201-2693 USA
Phone: 614-424-6424
Toll Free: 800-201-2011
E-mail Address: solutions@battelle.org
Web Address: www.battelle.org
Battelle Memorial Institute serves commercial and governmental customers in developing new technologies and products. The institute adds technology to systems and processes for manufacturers; pharmaceutical and agrochemical industries; trade associations; and government agencies supporting energy, the environment, health, national security and transportation.

Commonwealth Scientific and Industrial Research Organization (CSRIO)
CSIRO Enquiries, Private Bag 10
Clayton South, Victoria 3169 Australia
Phone: 61-3-9545-2176
Toll Free: 1300-363-400
Web Address: www.csiro.au
The Commonwealth Scientific and Industrial Research Organization (CSRIO) is Australia's national science agency and a leading international research agency. CSRIO performs research in Australia over a broad range of areas including agriculture, minerals and energy, manufacturing, communications, construction, health and the environment.

Computational Neurobiology Laboratory
CNL-S c/o The Salk Institute
10010 N. Torrey Pines Rd.
La Jolla, CA 92037 USA
Phone: 858-453-4100
Fax: 858-587-0417
Web Address: www.cnl.salk.edu
The Computational Neurobiology Laboratory at The Salk Institute strives to understand the computational resources of the brain from the biophysical to the systems levels.

Fraunhofer-Gesellschaft (FhG) (The)
Fraunhofer-Gesellschaft zur Forderung der angewandten Forschung e.V.
Postfach 20 07 33
Munich, 80007 Germany
Phone: 49-89-1205-0
Fax: 49-89-1205-7531
Web Address: www.fraunhofer.de
The Fraunhofer-Gesellschaft (FhG) institute focuses on research in health, security, energy, communication, the environment and mobility. FhG includes over 80 research units in Germany. Over 70% of its projects are derived from industry contracts.

German Cancer Research Center
Im Neuenheimer Feld 280
Heidelberg, 69120 Germany
Phone: 49-6221-420
Fax: 49-6221-422-995
Web Address: www.dkfz.de
The German Cancer Research Center (Deutsches Krebsforschungszentrum, DKFZ) is the largest biomedical research institute in Germany and is a member of the Helmholtz Association of National Research Centers. More than 2,700 staff members, including 1,200 scientists, are investigating the mechanisms of cancer and are working to identify cancer risk factors. They provide the foundations for developing novel approaches in the prevention, diagnosis and treatment of cancer. In addition, the staff of the Cancer Information Service (KID) offers information about the widespread disease of cancer for patients, their families and the general public.

Helmholtz Association
Anna-Louisa-Karsch-Strasse 2
Berlin, 10178 Germany
Phone: 49-30-206329-0
E-mail Address: info@helmholtz.de
Web Address: www.helmholtz.de/en
The Helmholtz Association is a community of 18 scientific-technical and biological-medical research centers. Helmholtz Centers perform top-class research in strategic programs in several core fields: energy, earth and environment, health, key technologies, structure of matter, aeronautics, space and transport.

Max Planck Society (MPG)
Hofgartenstr. 8
Munich, 80539 Germany
Phone: 49-89-2108-0
Fax: 49-89-2108-1111
E-mail Address: post@gv.mpg.de
Web Address: www.mpg.de
The Max Planck Society (MPG) currently maintains 83 institutes, research units and working groups that are devoted to basic research in the natural sciences, life sciences, social sciences, and the humanities. Max Planck Institutes work largely in an interdisciplinary setting and in close cooperation with universities and research institutes in Germany and abroad.

National Research Council Canada (NRC)
1200 Montreal Rd., Bldg. M-58
Ottawa, ON K1A 0R6 Canada
Phone: 613-993-9101
Fax: 613-952-9907
Toll Free: 877-672-2672
E-mail Address: info@nrc-cnrc.gc.ca
Web Address: www.nrc-cnrc.gc.ca
National Research Council Canada (NRC) is comprised of 12 government organization, research institutes and programs that carry out multidisciplinary research. It maintains partnerships with industries and sectors key to Canada's economic development.

SRI International
333 Ravenswood Ave.
Menlo Park, CA 94025-3493 USA
Phone: 650-859-2000
Web Address: www.sri.com
SRI International is a nonprofit research organization that offers contract research services to government agencies, as well as commercial enterprises and other private sector institutions. It is organized around broad divisions including biosciences, global partnerships, education, products and solutions division, advanced technology and systems and information and computing sciences division.

80) Respiratory

American Lung Association (ALA)
55 W. Wacker Dr., Ste. 1150
Chicago, IL 60601 USA
Toll Free: 800-548-8252
E-mail Address: info@lung.org
Web Address: www.lung.org

The American Lung Association (ALA) is dedicated to improving lung health and fight lung disease in all its forms, with special emphasis on asthma, tobacco control and environmental health.

Asthma and Allergy Foundation of America (AAFA)
8201 Corp. Dr., Ste. 1000
Landover, MD 20785 USA
Toll Free: 800-727-8462
E-mail Address: info@aafa.org
Web Address: www.aafa.org
The Asthma and Allergy Foundation of America (AAFA) is dedicated to improving the quality of life for people with asthma and allergies through education, advocacy and research.

81) Science & Technology Resources

Life Science Tennessee
217 5th Ave. N, Ste. 200
Nashville, TN 37219 USA
Phone: 615-242-8856
Fax: 615-242-8857
E-mail Address: info@lifesciencetn.org
Web Address: www.lifesciencetn.org
Life Science Tennessee is a statewide, nonprofit, member organization that supports the life science industries in Tennessee through advocacy, partnerships and alignment with economic and workforce development.

Technology Review
1 Main St., Fl. 13
Cambridge, MA 02142 USA
Phone: 617-475-8000
Fax: 617-475-8000
Web Address: www.technologyreview.com
Technology Review, an MIT enterprise, publishes tech industry news, covers innovation and writes in-depth articles about research, development and cutting-edge technologies.

82) Seniors Housing

American Seniors Housing Association (ASHA)
5225 Wisconsin Ave. NW, Ste. 502
Washington, DC 20015 USA
Phone: 202-237-0900
Fax: 202-237-1616
Web Address: www.seniorshousing.org
The American Seniors Housing Association (ASHA) was originally formed as a committee of the National Multi Housing Council in 1991, and became an independent non-profit organization ten years later on January 1, 2001. The group represents building owners and managers who develop housing options, services and amenities for seniors.

National Investment Center for the Seniors Housing & Care Industry (NIC)
1997 Annapolis Exchange Pkwy., Ste. 480
Annapolis, MD 21401 USA
Phone: 410-267-0504
Fax: 410-268-4620
Web Address: www.nic.org
NIC serves as a resource to lenders, investors, developers/operators, and others interested in meeting the housing and healthcare needs of America's seniors. NIC serves the entire industry as an objective purveyor of information: NIC's research and educational efforts are neither association-driven nor company-oriented. As an impartial observer and unbiased source, NIC has become the primary link between the financial markets and seniors housing developers/operators, connecting each side through relevant research and practical information.

83) Sexually Transmitted Diseases

Herpes Resource Center (HRC)
P.O. Box 13827
Research Triangle Park, NC 27709 USA
Phone: 919-361-8400
Toll Free: 800-783-9877
E-mail Address: info@ashasexualhealth.org
Web Address: www.ashasexualhealth.org/stdsstis/herpes
The Herpes Resource Center (HRC), as part of the American Social Health Association, focuses on increasing education, public awareness and support to anyone concerned about herpes.

84) Singaporean Government & Agencies - Health Care

Ministry of Social and Family Development (MSF)
512 Thomson Rd., MSF Building
Singapore, 298136 Singapore
Phone: 65-6355-5000
Fax: 65-6353-6695
E-mail Address: msf_email@msf.gov.sg
Web Address: app.msf.gov.sg
Ministry of Social and Family Development (MSF) develops the social services for Singapore through its policies, community infrastructure, programs and services. Its mission is to nurture a resilient and caring society that can overcome challenges together.

85) Technology Transfer Associations

Association of University Technology Managers (AUTM)
One Parkview Plaza, Ste. 880
Oakbrook Terrace, IL 60015 USA
Phone: 847-686-2244
Fax: 847-686-2253
E-mail Address: info@autm.net
Web Address: www.autm.net
The Association of University Technology Managers (AUTM) is a nonprofit professional association whose members belong to over 300 research institutions, universities, teaching hospitals, government agencies and corporations. The association's mission is to advance the field of technology transfer and enhance members' ability to bring academic and nonprofit research to people around the world.

Federal Laboratory Consortium for Technology Transfer
950 N. Kings Hwy., Ste. 105
Cherry Hill, NJ 08304 USA
Phone: 856-667-7727
E-mail Address: support@federallabs.org
Web Address: www.federallabs.org
In keeping with the aims of the Federal Technology Transfer Act of 1986 and other related legislation, the Federal Laboratory Consortium (FLC) works to facilitate the sharing of research results and technology developments between federal laboratories and the mainstream U.S. economy. FLC affiliates include federal laboratories, large and small businesses, academic and research institutions, state and local governments and various federal agencies. The group has regional support offices and local contacts throughout the U.S.

Licensing Executives Society (USA and Canada), Inc.
11130 Sunrise Valley Dr., Ste. 350
Reston, VA 20191 USA
Phone: 703-234-4058
Fax: 703-435-4390
E-mail Address: info@les.org
Web Address: www.lesusacanada.org
Licensing Executives Society (USA and Canada), Inc., established in 1965, is a professional association composed of about 3,000 members who work in fields related to the development, use, transfer, manufacture and marketing of intellectual property. Members include executives, lawyers, licensing consultants, engineers, academic researchers, scientists and

government officials. The society is part of the larger Licensing Executives Society International, Inc. (same headquarters address), with a worldwide membership of some 12,000 members from approximately 80 countries.

State Science and Technology Institute (SSTI)
5015 Pine Creek Dr.
Westerville, OH 43081 USA
Phone: 614-901-1690
E-mail Address: contactus@ssti.org
Web Address: www.ssti.org
The State Science and Technology Institute (SSTI) is a national nonprofit group that serves as a resource for technology-based economic development. In addition to the information on its web site, the Institute publishes a free weekly digest of news and issues related to technology-based economic development efforts, as well as a members-only publication listing application information, eligibility criteria and submission deadlines for a variety of funding opportunities, federal and otherwise.

86) Textile & Fabric Industry Associations

INDA, Association of the Nonwoven Fabrics Industry
1100 Crescent Gr., Ste. 115
Cary, NC 27518 USA
Phone: 919-459-3700
Fax: 919-459-3701
E-mail Address: info@inda.org
Web Address: www.inda.org
INDA, the Association of the Nonwoven Fabrics Industry, has been representing this sector since 1968. It offers networking events, educational courses, test methods, market data, consultancy and issue advocacy help to its members. Nonwoven textiles are widely used in the health care industry for disposable wipes, drapes, apparel and other items.

87) Trade Associations-General

Associated Chambers of Commerce and Industry of India (ASSOCHAM)
5, Sardar Patel Marg, Chanakyapuri
New Delhi, 110 021 India
Phone: 91-11-4655-0555
Fax: 91-11-2301-7008
E-mail Address: assocham@nic.in
Web Address: www.assocham.org
The Associated Chambers of Commerce and Industry of India (ASSOCHAM) has a membership of more than 300 chambers and trade associations and serves members from all over India. It works with domestic and international government agencies to advocate for India's industry and trade activities.

BUSINESSEUROPE
168 Ave. de Cortenbergh 168
Brussels, 1000 Belgium
Phone: 32-2-237-65-11
Fax: 32-2-231-14-45
E-mail Address: main@businesseurope.eu
Web Address: www.businesseurope.eu
BUSINESSEUROPE is a major European trade federation that operates in a manner similar to a chamber of commerce. Its members are the central national business federations of the 34 countries throughout Europe from which they come. Companies cannot become direct members of BUSINESSEUROPE, though there is a support group which offers the opportunity for firms to encourage BUSINESSEUROPE objectives in various ways.

United States Council for International Business (USCIB)
1212 Ave. of the Americas
New York, NY 10036 USA
Phone: 212-354-4480
Fax: 212-575-0327
E-mail Address: azhang@uscib.org
Web Address: www.uscib.org
The United States Council for International Business (USCIB) promotes an open system of world trade and investment through its global network. Standard USCIB members include corporations, law firms, consulting firms and industry associations. Limited membership options are available for chambers of commerce and sole legal practitioners.

88) Trade Associations-Global

World Trade Organization (WTO)
Centre William Rappard
Rue de Lausanne 154
Geneva 21, CH-1211 Switzerland
Phone: 41-22-739-51-11
Fax: 41-22-731-42-06
E-mail Address: enquiries@wto.og
Web Address: www.wto.org
The World Trade Organization (WTO) is a global organization dealing with the rules of trade between nations. To become a member, nations must agree to abide by certain guidelines. Membership increases a nation's ability to import and export efficiently.

89) U.S. Government Agencies

Agency for Health Care Research and Quality (AHCRQ)
Office of Communications and Knowledge Transfer
5600 Fishers Lane, Fl. 7
Rockville, MD 20857 USA
Phone: 301-427-1104
Web Address: www.ahrq.gov
The Agency for Health Care Research and Quality (AHCRQ) provides evidence-based information on health care outcomes, quality, cost, use and access. Its research helps people make more informed decisions and improve the quality of health care services.

Bureau of Economic Analysis (BEA)
4600 Silver Hill Rd.
Washington, DC 20233 USA
Phone: 301-278-9004
E-mail Address: customerservice@bea.gov
Web Address: www.bea.gov
The Bureau of Economic Analysis (BEA), an agency of the U.S. Department of Commerce, is the nation's economic accountant, preparing estimates that illuminate key national, international and regional aspects of the U.S. economy.

Bureau of Labor Statistics (BLS)
2 Massachusetts Ave. NE
Washington, DC 20212-0001 USA
Phone: 202-691-5200
Fax: 202-691-7890
Toll Free: 800-877-8339
E-mail Address: blsdata_staff@bls.gov
Web Address: stats.bls.gov
The Bureau of Labor Statistics (BLS) is the principal fact-finding agency for the Federal Government in the field of labor economics and statistics. It is an independent national statistical agency that collects, processes, analyzes and disseminates statistical data to the American public, U.S. Congress, other federal agencies, state and local governments, business and labor. The BLS also serves as a statistical resource to the Department of Labor.

Centers for Disease Control and Prevention (CDC)
1600 Clifton Rd.
Atlanta, GA 30333 USA
Toll Free: 800-232-4636
Web Address: www.cdc.gov
The Centers for Disease Control and Prevention (CDC), headquartered in Atlanta, is the federal agency charged with protecting the public health of the nation by providing leadership and direction in the prevention and control of

diseases and other preventable conditions and responding to public health emergencies.

Centers for Medicare and Medicaid Services (CMMS)
7500 Security Blvd.
Baltimore, MD 21244-1850 USA
Phone: 410-786-3000
Toll Free: 877-267-2323
Web Address: www.cms.gov
The Centers for Medicare and Medicaid Services (CMMS) runs the Medicare and Medicaid programs in the U.S., as well as State Children's Health Insurance Program.

Department of Health and Human Services (HHS)
200 Independence Ave. SW
Washington, DC 20201 USA
Phone: 202-619-0257
Toll Free: 877-696-6775
Web Address: www.hhs.gov
The Department of Health and Human Services (HHS) is the principle agency in the United States for safeguarding the health of Americans and for providing necessary health care service programs. Some of the organization's 300 plus programs include Medicare, Medicaid, Head Start, food and drug safety, health information technology and health and social research.

Federal Emergency Management Agency (FEMA)
500 C St. SW
Washington, DC 20472 USA
Phone: 202-646-2500
Toll Free: 800-621-3362
Web Address: www.fema.gov
Federal Emergency Management Agency (FEMA) exists to reduce loss of life and property and protect the nation's infrastructure from all types of unexpected hazards. The site has information regarding floods, fires, storms, terrorism and other disaster information including assistance, recovery and preparation.

Health Resources and Services Administration (HRSA)
5600 Fishers Ln.
Rockville, MD 20857 USA
Phone: 301-443-3376
Toll Free: 888-275-4772
Web Address: www.hrsa.gov
Health Resources and Services Administration (HRSA) is an agency within the U.S. Department of Health and Human Services. Its mission is to improve and expand access to quality health care to low income, uninsured, isolated, vulnerable and special needs populations.

Health.gov
1101 Wootton Parkway, Ste. LL100
Rockville, MD 20852 USA
Phone: 240-453-8280
Fax: 240-453-8282
E-mail Address: odphpinfo@hhs.gov
Web Address: www.health.gov
Health.gov is a portal to the web sites of a number of multi-agency health initiatives and activities of the U.S. Department of Health and Human Services (HHS) and other federal departments and agencies. The web site is coordinated by the Office of Disease Prevention and Health Promotion, Office of the Assistant Secretary for Health, Office of the Secretary, U.S. Department of Health and Human Services

National Cancer Institute (NCI)
9609 Medical Ctr. Dr.
BG 9609 MSC 9760
Bethesda, MD 20892-9760 USA
Toll Free: 800-422-6237
Web Address: www.cancer.gov
The National Cancer Institute (NCI) is the Federal Government's principal agency for cancer research and training.

National Center for Chronic Disease Prevention and Health Promotion (NCCDPHP)
600 Clifton Rd.
Atlanta, GA 30329-4027 USA
Toll Free: 800-232-4636
E-mail Address: ccdinfo@cdc.gov
Web Address:
www.cdc.gov/chronicdisease/index.htm
The National Center for Chronic Disease Prevention and Health Promotion (NCCDPHP), a division of the Center for Disease Control (CDC), provides national leadership in areas of health promotion and chronic disease prevention largely through educational initiatives.

National Center for Complementary and Integrative Health (NCCIH)
31 Center Dr., MSC 2182
Bethesda, MD 20892-2182 USA
Phone: 301-402-4335
Toll Free: 888-644-6226
E-mail Address: info@nccam.nih.gov
Web Address: nccam.nih.gov
The National Center for Complementary and Integrative Health (NCCIH), part of National Institutes of Health (NIH) is a Federal agency for scientific research on the diverse medical and health care systems, practices, and products that are not generally considered part of conventional medicine.

National Center for Health Statistics (NCHS)
1600 Clifton Rd.
Atlanta, GA 30329 USA
Toll Free: 800-232-4636
E-mail Address: cdcinfo@cdc.gov
Web Address: www.cdc.gov/nchs
The National Center for Health Statistics (NCHS), division of the Center for Disease Control and Prevention (CDC), is the federal government's principal vital and health statistics agency.

National Heart, Lung and Blood Institute (NHLBI)
P.O. Box 30105
Bethesda, MD 20824-0105 USA
Phone: 301-592-8573
Fax: 301-592-8563
E-mail Address: nhlbiinfo@nhlbi.nih.gov
Web Address: www.nhlbi.nih.gov
The National Heart, Lung, and Blood Institute (NHLBI) provides leadership for a national program in diseases of the heart, blood vessels, lung and blood; blood resources; and sleep disorders.

National Institute of Allergy and Infectious Diseases (NIAID)
5601 Fishers Ln., MSC 9806
Bethesda, MD 20892-9806 USA
Phone: 301-496-5717
Fax: 301-402-3573
Toll Free: 866-284-4107
E-mail Address:
ocpostoffice@niaid.nih.gov
Web Address: www.niaid.nih.gov
The National Institute of Allergy and Infectious Diseases (NIAID) conducts and supports research that strives for understanding, treatment and prevention of the many infectious, immunologic and allergic diseases that threaten people worldwide.

National Institute of Child Health and Human Development (NICHD)
31 Center Dr., Bldg. 31, Rm. 2A32
Bethesda, MD 20892-2425 USA
Fax: 1-866-760-5947
Toll Free: 800-370-2943
E-mail Address:
NICHDInformationResourceCenter@mail.nih.gov
Web Address: www.nichd.nih.gov
The National Institute of Child Health and Human Development (NICHD) conducts and supports laboratory, clinical and epidemiological research on the reproductive, neurobiological, developmental and behavioral processes that determine and maintain the health of children, adults, families and populations.

National Institute of Diabetes and Digestive and Kidney Disorders (NIDDK)
9000 Rockville Pike
Bethesda, MD 20892 USA
Phone: 301-496-3583
Web Address: www2.niddk.nih.gov
The National Institute of Diabetes and Digestive and Kidney Disorders (NIDDK) conducts and supports basic, translational and clinical research on many of the most serious, chronic diseases and conditions affecting public health.

National Institute of Environmental Health Services (NIEHS)
111 T.W. Alexander Dr.
Research Triangle Park, NC 27709 USA
Phone: 919-541-3345
Fax: 301-480-2978
Web Address: www.niehs.nih.gov
The National Institute of Environmental Health Services (NIEHS) is the segment of the National Institutes of Health that deals with the environmental effects on human health.

National Institute of General Medical Sciences (NIGMS)
45 Center Dr., MSC 6200
Bethesda, MD 20892-6200 USA
Phone: 301-496-7301
E-mail Address: info@nigms.nih.gov
Web Address: www.nigms.nih.gov
The National Institute of General Medical Sciences (NIGMS) supports basic biomedical research that lays the foundation for advances in disease diagnosis, treatment and prevention.

National Institute of Mental Health (NIMH)
6001 Executive Blvd.
Rm. 6200, MSC 9663
Bethesda, MD 20892-9663 USA
Phone: 301-443-4513
Fax: 301-443-4279
Toll Free: 866-615-6464
E-mail Address: nimhinfo@nih.gov
Web Address: www.nimh.nih.gov
The National Institute of Mental Health (NIMH), a part of the U.S. Department of Health and Human Services, acts as the Federal governments principle biomedical and behavioral research agency. The organization strives to reduce the burden of mental illness and behavioral disorders through research on mind, brain, and behavior.

National Institute of Neurological Disorders and Stroke (NINDS)
6001 Executive Blvd., Ste. 3309
Bethesda, MD 20892-9531 USA
Phone: 301-496-5751
Toll Free: 800-352-9424
Web Address: www.ninds.nih.gov
The National Institute of Neurological Disorders and Stroke (NINDS) works to lead the neuroscience community in seeking knowledge about the brain and nervous system. It supports and performs basic, translational, and clinical neuroscience research; funds and conducts research training and career development programs; and promotes timely dissemination of scientific discoveries and their implications for neurological health to the public, health professionals, researchers, and policy-makers.

National Institute of Nursing Research (NINR)
31 Center Dr., Rm. 5B10
Bethesda, MD 20892-2178 USA
Phone: 301-496-0207
Fax: 301-480-8845
E-mail Address: info@ninr.nih.gov
Web Address: www.nih.gov/ninr
The National Institute of Nursing Research (NINR) supports clinical and basic nursing research to establish a scientific basis for the care of individuals of all ages. From management of patients during illness and recovery to the reduction of risks for disease and disability, NINR promotes healthy lifestyles, quality of life for those with chronic illnesses and care for individuals at the end of life.

National Institute on Aging (NIA)
31 Center Dr., Bldg. 31
MSC 2292, Room 5C27
Bethesda, MD 20892-2292 USA
Phone: 301-496-1752
Fax: 301-496-1072
Toll Free: 800-222-2225
E-mail Address: niaic@nia.nih.gov
Web Address: www.nia.nih.gov
The National Institute on Aging (NIA) is one of the 27 institutes and centers of the National Institutes of Health and leads a broad scientific effort to understand the nature of aging and to extend the healthy, active years of life.

National Institute on Alcohol Abuse and Alcoholism (NIAAA)
5635 Fishers Ln.
Rockville, MD 20892 USA
Phone: 301-443-3860
E-mail Address: niaaaweb-r@exchange.nih.gov
Web Address: www.niaaa.nih.gov
The National Institute on Alcohol Abuse and Alcoholism (NIAAA) provides information on alcohol abuse and the advancement of its treatment. It conducts and supports alcohol-related research, coordinates with other research institutes at state, national and international level and translates and disseminates research findings to health care providers, researchers, public and policymakers.

National Institute on Arthritis and Musculoskeletal and Skin Diseases (NIAMS)
1 AMS Cir.
Bethesda, MD 20892-3675 USA
Phone: 301-495-4484
Fax: 301-718-6366
Toll Free: 877-226-4267
E-mail Address: niamsinfo@mail.nih.gov
Web Address: www.niams.nih.gov
The National Institute on Arthritis and Musculoskeletal and Skin Diseases (NIAMS) supports research into the causes, treatment and prevention of arthritis and musculoskeletal and skin diseases, the training of basic and clinical scientists to carry out this research and the dissemination of information on research progress in these diseases.

National Institute on Drug Abuse (NIDA)
6001 Executive Blvd.
Rm. 5213, MSC 9561
Bethesda, MD 20892-9561 USA
Phone: 301-443-1124
Web Address: www.drugabuse.gov
The National Institute on Drug Abuse (NIDA) seeks to lead the nation in bringing the power of science to the advantage of curbing drug abuse and addiction.

National Institutes of Health (NIH)
9000 Rockville Pike
Bethesda, MD 20892 USA
Phone: 301-496-4000
E-mail Address: NIHinfo@od.nih.gov
Web Address: www.nih.gov
The National Institutes of Health (NIH) is the leader of medical and behavioral research in the U.S. and is comprised of 27 institutes and centers ranging from the National Cancer Institute to the National Institute of Mental Health.

National Science Foundation (NSF)
4201 Wilson Blvd.
Arlington, VA 22230 USA
Phone: 703-292-5111
Toll Free: 800-877-8339
E-mail Address: info@nsf.gov
Web Address: www.nsf.gov
The National Science Foundation (NSF) is an independent U.S. government agency responsible for promoting science and engineering. The foundation provides colleges and universities with grants and

funding for research into numerous scientific fields.

Occupational Safety and Health Administration (OSHA)
200 Constitution Ave. NW
Washington, DC 20210 USA
Toll Free: 800-321-6742
Web Address: www.osha.gov
The Occupational Safety and Health Administration (OSHA), regulates safety within the workplace. Its web site provides information on laws and regulations, safety and health, statistics, compliance assistance and news. OSHA is a unit of the U.S. Department of Labor.

Recalls.gov
E-mail Address: webteam@cpsc.gov
Web Address: www.recalls.gov
Recalls.gov is a one-stop website where six different U.S. government agencies post announcements about governmental recalls in consumer products, motor vehicles, boats, food, medicine, cosmetics and environmental products.

Social Security Administration (SSA)
6401 Security Blvd.
Baltimore, MD 21235 USA
Toll Free: 800-772-1213
Web Address: www.ssa.gov
The Social Security Administration (SSA) offers extensive information on social security and retirement through its web site, Social Security Online.

U.S. Census Bureau
4600 Silver Hill Rd.
Washington, DC 20233-8800 USA
Phone: 301-763-4636
Toll Free: 800-923-8282
E-mail Address: pio@census.gov
Web Address: www.census.gov
The U.S. Census Bureau is the official collector of data about the people and economy of the U.S. Founded in 1790, it provides official social, demographic and economic information. In addition to the Population & Housing Census, which it conducts every 10 years, the U.S. Census Bureau numerous other surveys annually.

U.S. Department of Commerce (DOC)
1401 Constitution Ave. NW
Washington, DC 20230 USA
Phone: 202-482-2000
E-mail Address: TheSec@doc.gov
Web Address: www.commerce.gov
The U.S. Department of Commerce (DOC) regulates trade and provides valuable economic analysis of the economy.

U.S. Department of Labor (DOL)
200 Constitution Ave. NW
Washington, DC 20210 USA
Phone: 202-693-4676
Toll Free: 866-487-2365
Web Address: www.dol.gov
The U.S. Department of Labor (DOL) is the government agency responsible for labor regulations.

U.S. Environmental Protection Agency (EPA)
1200 Pennsylvania Ave. NW
Ariel Rios Bldg.
Washington, DC 20460 USA
Phone: 202-272-0167
Web Address: www.epa.gov
The U.S. Environmental Protection Agency (EPA) is a government organization that seeks to protect human health and to safeguard the natural environment by developing and enforcing regulations, performing environmental research, sponsoring voluntary programs and offering financial assistance to state environmental programs.

U.S. Food and Drug Administration (FDA)
10903 New Hampshire Ave.
Room 5377, Bldg. 32
Silver Spring, MD 20993 USA
Toll Free: 888-463-6332
Web Address: www.fda.gov
The U.S. Food and Drug Administration (FDA) promotes and protects the public health by helping safe and effective products reach the market in a timely way and by monitoring products for continued safety after they are in use. It regulates both prescription and over-the-counter drugs as well as medical devices and food products.

U.S. Securities and Exchange Commission (SEC)
100 F St. NE
Washington, DC 20549 USA
Phone: 202-942-8088
Toll Free: 800-732-0330
E-mail Address: help@sec.gov
Web Address: www.sec.gov
The U.S. Securities and Exchange Commission (SEC) is a nonpartisan, quasi-judicial regulatory agency responsible for administering federal securities laws. These laws are designed to protect investors in securities markets and ensure that they have access to disclosure of all material information concerning publicly traded securities. Visitors to the web site can access the EDGAR database of corporate financial and business information.

90) UK Government Agencies

National Institute for Health and Clinical Excellence (NICE)
10 Spring Gardens
London, SW1A 2BU UK
Phone: 44-300 323 0140
Fax: 44-300-323-0148
E-mail Address: nice@nice.org.uk
Web Address: www.nice.org.uk
The National Institute for Health and Clinical Excellence (NICE) is the national organization responsible for providing guidance on the promotion of good health and the prevention and treatment of ill health in the UK.

91) Urological Disorders

National Association for Continence (NAFC)
P.O. Box 1019
Charleston, SC 29402 -1019 USA
Phone: 843-377-0900
Toll Free: 800-252-3337
Web Address: www.nafc.org
The National Association for Continence (NAFC) is a national, private, nonprofit organization dedicated to improving the quality of life of people with incontinence. It aims to offer quality continence care through education, collaboration and advocacy.

National Kidney Foundation
30 E. 33rd St.
New York, NY 10016 USA
Phone: 855-653-2273
Fax: 212-689-9261
Toll Free: 800-622-9010
E-mail Address: info@kidney.org
Web Address: www.kidney.org
The National Kidney Foundation seeks to prevent kidney and urinary tract diseases, improve the health and well-being of individuals and families affected by these diseases and increase the availability of all organs for transplantation.

Urology Care Foundation
1000 Corporate Blvd.
Linthicum, MD 21090 USA
Phone: 410-689-3700
Fax: 410-689-3998
Toll Free: 800-828-7866
E-mail Address: info@urologycarefoundation.org
Web Address: www.urologyhealth.org
The Urology Care Foundation, formerly the American Urological Association Foundation (AUAF), seeks the prevention and cure of urologic disease through the expansion of patient education, public awareness, research and advocacy.

92) Vitamin & Supplement Industry Associations

Council for Responsible Nutrition
1828 L St. NW, Ste. 510
Washington, DC 20036-5114 USA
Phone: 202-204-7700
Fax: 202-204-7701
E-mail Address: jblatman@crnusa.org
Web Address: www.crnusa.org
The Council for Responsible Nutrition (CRN), founded in 1973, is a Washington-based trade association representing ingredient suppliers and manufacturers in the dietary supplement industry. CRN members adhere to a strong code of ethics, comply with dosage limits and manufacture dietary supplements to high quality standards under good manufacturing practices. CRN's mission is to improve the environment for member companies to responsibly market dietary supplements by enhancing confidence among media, healthcare professionals, decision makers and consumers.

93) Wholesale Distributors Associations

Global Market Development Center (GMDC)
1275 Lake Plaza Dr.
Colorado Springs, CO 80906-3583 USA
Phone: 719-576-4260
Fax: 719-576-2661
E-mail Address: info@gmdc.org
Web Address: www.gmdc.org
The Global Market Development Center (GMDC) is an international trade association serving the general merchandise, health and beauty care and pharmacy industries.

Chapter 4

THE HEALTH CARE 500: WHO THEY ARE AND HOW THEY WERE CHOSEN

Includes Indexes by Company Name, Industry & Location,

The companies chosen to be listed in PLUNKETT'S HEALTH CARE INDUSTRY ALMANAC comprise a unique list. THE HEALTH CARE 500 were chosen specifically for their dominance in the many facets of the health care industry in which they operate. Complete information about each firm can be found in the "Individual Profiles," beginning at the end of this chapter. These profiles are in alphabetical order by company name.

THE HEALTH CARE 500 includes leading companies from all parts of the United States as well as many other nations, and from all health care and related industry segments: insurance companies; manufacturers and distributors of health care supplies and products; pharmaceuticals manufacturers; health care providers of all types, including major firms owning clinics, physical rehabilitation centers, hospitals, outpatient surgery centers, nursing homes, home health care offices and other types of health care specialists; specialized service companies that are vital to the health care field, such as medical information management companies; health maintenance organizations and many others.

Simply stated, the list contains the largest, most successful, fastest growing firms in health care and related industries in the world. To be included in our list, the firms had to meet the following criteria:

1) Generally, these are corporations based in the U.S.; however, the headquarters of many firms are located in other nations.
2) Prominence, or a significant presence, in health care and supporting fields. (See the following Industry Codes section for a complete list of types of businesses that are covered).
3) The companies in THE HEALTH CARE 500 do not have to be exclusively in the health care field.
4) Financial data and vital statistics must have been available to the editors of this book, either directly from the company being written about or from outside sources deemed reliable and accurate by the editors. A small number of companies that we would like to have included are not listed because of a lack of sufficient, objective data.

INDEXES TO THE HEALTH CARE 500, AS FOUND IN THIS CHAPTER AND IN THE BACK OF THE BOOK:

INDEX OF COMPANIES WITHIN INDUSTRY GROUPS

The industry codes shown below are based on the 2012 NAIC code system (NAIC is used by many analysts as a replacement for older SIC codes because NAIC is more specific to today's industry sectors, see www.census.gov/NAICS). Companies are given a primary NAIC code, reflecting the main line of business of each firm.

Industry Group/Company	Industry Code	2017 Sales	2017 Profits
Ambulance Services, Air or Ground			
Air Methods Corporation	621910	1,200,000,000	
LogistiCare Solutions LLC	621910	866,000,000	
Medica Sur SAB de CV	621910	180,345,184	12,182,531
Ambulatory Health Care Services, Other			
ActiveCare Inc	621999		
Apollo Medical Holdings Inc	621999	57,427,700	-8,969,816
Horizon Health Corporation	621999		
InfuSystem Holdings Inc	621999	71,077,000	-20,707,000
Magellan Health Inc	621999	5,838,582,784	110,207,000
Nobilis Health Corp	621999	299,716,992	3,797,000
Protech Home Medical Corp	621999	58,745,384	-18,276,154
Ambulatory, Outpatient Surgical Clinics, Urgent Care and Emergency Centers			
Adeptus Health Inc	621493	430,000,000	
AMSURG Corporation	621493	3,000,000,000	
CareSpot Urgent Care	621493		
LCA-Vision Inc	621493	92,580,000	
Surgery Partners Inc	621493	1,341,219,000	-79,032,000
TLC Vision Corporation	621493	210,000,000	
United Surgical Partners International Inc	621493	710,000,000	
Urgent Care MSO LLC (MedExpress)	621493		
US NeuroSurgical Inc	621493	3,414,000	538,000
Blood and Organ Banks			
HemaCare Corporation	621991		
Clinics - General Health			
Concentra Inc	621498	1,120,000,000	
Little Clinic (The)	621498		
MinuteClinic LLC	621498		
Take Care Health Systems LLC	621498		
Clinics - Outpatient Clinics & Surgery			
Fresenius Medical Care AG & Co KGaA	621400	20,680,978,432	1,488,298,752
Fresenius SE & Co KGaA	621400	38,446,092,288	2,058,112,768
Computer Software, Healthcare & Biotechnology			
1Life Healthcare Inc	511210D		
Aeon Global Health Corp	511210D	20,198,772	-32,073,514
Allscripts Healthcare Solutions Inc	511210D	1,806,342,016	-152,608,992
Cerner Corporation	511210D	5,142,272,000	866,977,984
eClinicalWorks	511210D	462,000,000	
Epic Systems Corporation	511210D	2,100,000,000	
Grand Rounds (Consulting Medical Associates Inc)	511210D		
IBM Watson Health	511210D	236,250,000	

Industry Group/Company	Industry Code	2017 Sales	2017 Profits
Indegene Aptilon Inc	511210D		
Medical Information Technology Inc (MEDITECH)	511210D	485,369,291	
Quality Systems Inc	511210D	509,624,000	18,241,000
SHL Telemedicine Ltd	511210D	37,378,000	2,408,000
Welltok Inc	511210D	68,800,000	
Consulting Services, Marketing			
Interpace Diagnostics Group Inc	541613	15,897,000	-12,216,000
Continuing Care Retirement Communities			
Regional Health Properties Inc	623311	25,148,000	-985,000
Data Processing, Business Process Outsourcing (BPO) and Internet Content Hosting Services			
Global Healthcare Exchange LLC	518210		
Health Catalyst	518210	70,000,000	
Dental Equipment and Supplies Manufacturing			
Institut Straumann AG	339114	1,118,691,200	274,534,016
Dentists			
Castle Dental Centers Inc	621210		
Coast Dental Services LLC	621210		
Smile Brands Inc	621210	483,000,000	
Diagnostic Imaging Centers, Including CAT Scan, PET and MRI			
Alliance Healthcare Services Inc	621512	550,000,000	
Medical Imaging Corp	621512	7,224,226	-3,023,024
RadNet Inc	621512	922,185,984	53,000
Dialysis Centers			
DaVita Healthcare Partners Inc	621492	10,876,634,112	663,617,984
Diet and Weight Loss Centers			
Jenny Craig Inc	812191	300,000,000	
Medifast Inc	812191	301,563,008	27,721,000
Weight Watchers International Inc	812191	1,306,910,976	163,514,000
Disease Management & Utilization Management			
CorVel Corporation	524298A	518,686,016	29,479,000
Tivity Health Inc	524298A	556,942,016	63,715,000
Document Preparation, Call Centers, Collection Agencies and Other Business Support Services			
HealthTrust Purchasing Group LP	561400		
Intalere Inc	561400		
Vizient Inc	561400		
Equipment Rental and Leasing, Commercial and Industrial Machinery			
Universal Hospital Services Inc	532490	514,783,000	8,828,000
Factory Automation, Robots (Robotics) Industrial Process, Thermostat, Flow Meter and Environmental Quality Monitoring and Control Manufacturing			
Siemens AG	334513	94,225,031,168	6,859,619,840
Family Planning Centers			
IntegraMed America Inc	621410	350,000,000	
Hazardous Waste Collection			
Stericycle Inc	562112	3,580,699,904	42,400,000

Industry Group/Company	Industry Code	2017 Sales	2017 Profits
Health Care Utilization Management			
MultiPlan Inc	524298		
Health Insurance and Medical Insurance Underwriters (Direct Carriers), including Group Health, Supplemental Health and HMOs			
Aetna Inc	524114	60,535,001,088	1,904,000,000
AFLAC Inc	524114	21,600,000,000	4,604,000,256
Alignment Healthcare LLC	524114	525,000,000	
Amerigroup Corporation	524114	11,000,000,000	
Anthem Inc	524114	90,039,402,496	3,842,800,128
Arkansas Blue Cross and Blue Shield	524114	1,680,000,000	
AvMed Health Plans Inc	524114	1,029,000,000	
AXA PPP Healthcare Limited	524114	2,371,282,523	106,176,000
Blue Care Network of Michigan	524114	3,580,930,000	240,381,000
Blue Cross and Blue Shield Association	524114	568,050,000	
Blue Cross and Blue Shield of Florida Inc	524114	9,100,000,000	
Blue Cross and Blue Shield of Georgia	524114		
Blue Cross and Blue Shield of Louisiana	524114	3,477,600,000	
Blue Cross and Blue Shield of Massachusetts	524114	7,505,175,000	-6,920,000
Blue Cross and Blue Shield of Michigan	524114	26,945,000,000	1,191,000,000
Blue Cross and Blue Shield of Minnesota	524114	12,477,401,000	-62,394,000
Blue Cross and Blue Shield of Montana	524114	682,500,000	
Blue Cross and Blue Shield of Nebraska	524114	1,676,920,966	46,873,985
Blue Cross and Blue Shield of North Carolina	524114	9,400,000,000	734,000,000
Blue Cross and Blue Shield of Oklahoma	524114		
Blue Cross and Blue Shield of Texas	524114		
Blue Cross and Blue Shield of Vermont	524114	578,276,649	7,582,497
Blue Cross and Blue Shield of Wyoming	524114		
Blue Cross Blue Shield of Kansas City (Blue KC)	524114	3,044,207,000	108,863,000
Blue Cross of California	524114		
Blue Cross of Idaho	524114	2,147,481,000	79,835,000
Blue Shield of California	524114	17,684,000,000	296,000,000
BlueCross BlueShield of Tennessee Inc	524114	7,770,000,000	427,000,000
British United Provident Association Limited (BUPA)	524114	16,459,300,000	655,539,000
Cambia Health Solutions Inc	524114	9,500,000,000	
Capital BlueCross	524114	3,815,700,000	
CareFirst Inc	524114	8,800,000,000	240,600,000
Centene Corporation	524114	48,382,001,152	828,000,000
Cigna Behavioral Health	524114		
Cigna Corporation	524114	41,615,998,976	2,236,999,936
Coventry Health Care Inc	524114	15,225,000,000	
Delta Dental Plans Association	524114	21,000,000,000	
Dental Benefits Providers Inc	524114		
EmblemHealth Inc	524114	8,708,250,600	
Envolve Vision Inc	524114		
EyeMed Vision Care LLC	524114		
First Choice Health Network Inc	524114		
First Health Group Corp	524114		
Harvard Pilgrim Health Care Inc	524114	3,000,000,000	-8,700,000

Industry Group/Company	Industry Code	2017 Sales	2017 Profits
Health Care Service Corporation (HCSC)	524114	36,800,000,000	
Health Net Inc	524114	17,850,000,000	
HealthNow New York Inc	524114	2,415,000,000	
Highmark Health	524114	18,261,000,000	1,063,000,000
Horizon Healthcare Services Inc	524114	12,661,596,150	
Humana Inc	524114	53,767,000,064	2,448,000,000
Lifetime Healthcare Companies (The)	524114	6,400,000,000	
Lumeris Inc	524114	682,500,000	
Medical Mutual of Ohio	524114	2,894,850,000	
Metropolitan Health Networks Inc	524114	735,000,000	
Molina Healthcare Inc	524114	19,812,999,168	-512,000,000
Premera Blue Cross	524114	4,704,835,800	
SafeGuard Health Enterprises Inc	524114		
Tufts Associated Health Plans Inc	524114	4,700,000,000	59,400,000
UnitedHealth Group Inc	524114	200,135,999,488	10,558,000,128
UnitedHealthcare Community & State	524114	31,000,000,000	
Vision Service Plan	524114		
WellCare Health Plans Inc	524114	17,007,200,256	373,700,000
Home Health Care Services			
Addus Homecare Corporation	621610	425,715,008	13,608,000
Amedisys Inc	621610	1,533,680,000	30,301,000
American HomePatient Inc	621610	315,249,328	
Apria Healthcare Group Inc	621610	1,377,000,000	
BioScrip Inc	621610	817,190,016	-64,196,000
Chemed Corporation	621610	1,666,723,968	98,177,000
Civitas Solutions Inc	621610	1,474,509,952	6,331,000
Envision Healthcare Corporation	621610	7,819,299,840	-228,000,000
Kindred at Home	621610	2,150,000,000	
LHC Group Inc	621610	1,072,086,016	50,112,000
National Home Health Care Corp	621610		
New York Health Care Inc	621610		
Pediatric Services of America Inc	621610		
Hospitals, General Medical and Surgical			
Adventist Health System	622110	9,699,947,345	229,800,000
Advocate Aurora Health	622110	6,233,413,000	811,343,000
AHMC Healthcare Inc	622110	1,302,000,000	
Allina Health	622110	4,308,729,861	
Ardent Health Services LLC	622110	4,600,000,000	
Ascension	622110	22,600,000,000	1,800,000,000
Avera Health	622110	201,013,260	
Banner Health	622110	7,835,266,000	5,784,480,000
BJC HealthCare	622110	5,000,000,000	
Bon Secours Health System Inc	622110	3,100,000,000	
Cancer Treatment Centers of America Inc (CTCA)	622110	5,250,000,000	
Catholic Health Initiatives	622110	15,547,464,000	128,390,000
Chindex International Inc	622110	194,250,000	
CHRISTUS Health	622110	4,922,429,000	141,369,000
Cleveland Clinic Foundation (The)	622110	8,400,000,000	328,000,000
Community Health Systems Inc	622110	15,352,999,936	-2,459,000,064

Industry Group/Company	Industry Code	2017 Sales	2017 Profits
Detroit Medical Center (DMC)	622110		
Dignity Health	622110	12,900,000,000	384,000,000
Dynacq Healthcare Inc	622110		
Fairview Health Services	622110	5,300,000,000	456,900,000
HCA Holdings Inc	622110	43,613,999,104	2,216,000,000
Healthscope Ltd	622110	1,628,075,136	80,246,024
Henry Ford Health System	622110	5,980,000,000	203,600,000
Houston Methodist	622110	3,045,000,000	
Indiana University Health	622110	6,300,000,000	989,000,000
Intermountain Healthcare	622110	7,236,100,000	655,100,000
Johns Hopkins Medicine	622110	8,400,000,000	
Kaiser Permanente	622110	72,700,000,000	3,800,000,000
KPC Healthcare Inc	622110		
Life Healthcare Group Holdings Ltd	622110	1,457,576,960	57,049,944
LifePoint Health Inc	622110	7,263,099,904	102,400,000
Magee Rehabilitation Hospital	622110	157,500,000	
Main Line Health System	622110	1,785,000,000	
Mayo Clinic	622110	11,993,000,000	707,000,000
Mediclinic International Plc	622110	3,586,197,760	298,741,120
MedStar Health	622110	5,530,000,000	
Memorial Hermann Healthcare System	622110	4,873,050,000	
Mercy	622110	5,500,000,000	
Mercy Health	622110	4,717,297,200	
National Healthcare Group Pte Ltd	622110	1,601,250,000	
National University Health System (NUHS)	622110		
Netcare Limited	622110	2,391,682,304	-34,552,364
New York City Health and Hospitals Corporation	622110	7,293,634,000	
NewYork-Presbyterian Healthcare System	622110	5,600,000,000	
OhioHealth Corporation	622110	3,768,067,800	
Partners HealthCare	622110	13,125,000,000	
Prime Healthcare Services Inc	622110		
Providence St Joseph Health	622110	23,163,000,000	780,000,000
Ramsay Health Care Limited	622110	6,271,475,200	353,796,672
RCCH HealthCare Partners	622110	2,300,000,000	
Rhon Klinikum AG	622110	1,632,700,000	44,005,900
Sentara Healthcare	622110	5,337,579,450	
Spectrum Health	622110	5,681,000,000	282,000,000
SSM Health	622110	6,497,006,000	242,974,000
Steward Health Care System LLC	622110	1,785,000,000	
Surgical Care Affiliates Inc	622110	2,000,000,000	
Sutter Health Inc	622110	12,444,000,000	958,000,000
Tenet Healthcare Corporation	622110	19,178,999,808	-704,000,000
Texas Health Resources	622110	4,746,000,000	
Thomas Jefferson University Hospitals Inc	622110		
Trinity Health	622110	17,627,845,000	1,336,823,000
Universal Health Services Inc	622110	10,409,865,216	752,302,976
UPMC	622110	15,643,000,000	245,000,000
USMD Health System	622110	351,750,000	

Industry Group/Company	Industry Code	2017 Sales	2017 Profits
Hospitals, Psychiatric and Substance Abuse			
Acadia Healthcare Company Inc	622210	2,836,315,904	199,835,008
Hospitals, Specialty			
Centric Health Corporation	622310	129,974,624	1,420,000
MD Anderson Cancer Center	622310	5,000,000,000	
Medical Facilities Corporation	622310	385,328,992	20,637,000
Memorial Sloan Kettering Cancer Center	622310	4,452,793,000	239,765,000
St Jude Children's Research Hospital	622310	1,971,606,000	693,962,000
Insurance Agencies, Risk Management Consultants and Insurance Brokers			
EHealth Inc	524210	172,355,008	-25,412,000
Insurance Claims Administration and Services			
athenahealth Inc	524292	1,220,300,032	53,100,000
Change Healthcare Inc	524292	1,600,000,000	
Express Scripts Holding Co	524292	100,064,600,064	4,517,400,064
HMS Holdings Corp	524292	521,212,000	40,054,000
UnitedHealthcare National Accounts	524292		
Internet Search Engines, Online Publishing, Sharing, Gig and Consumer Services, Online Radio, TV and Entertainment Sites and Social Media			
Everyday Health Inc	519130	266,000,000	
Healthgrades Operating Company Inc	519130	85,050,000	
Ping An Healthcare and Technology Co Ltd	519130	286,825,000	93,970,600
WebMD Health Corp	519130	740,298,321	
Laboratory Instruments and Lab Equipment Manufacturing			
Bruker Corporation	334516	1,765,900,032	78,600,000
Mettler-Toledo International Inc	334516	2,725,052,928	375,972,000
Life Insurance and Annuity Underwriters (Direct Carriers)			
Independence Holding Company	524113	320,494,016	42,042,000
Trustmark Companies	524113	842,777,548	24,801,418
Medical Diagnostics, Reagents, Assays and Test Kits Manufacturing			
Bio Rad Laboratories Inc	325413	2,160,153,088	122,249,000
Bio-Techne Corporation	325413	563,003,008	76,086,000
GenMark Diagnostics Inc	325413	52,519,000	-61,850,000
Hologic Inc	325413	3,058,800,128	755,500,032
Immucor Inc	325413	39,897,060	
Meridian Bioscience Inc	325413	200,771,008	21,557,000
NxStage Medical Inc	325413	393,940,992	-13,992,000
PerkinElmer Inc	325413	2,256,982,016	292,632,992
Quidel Corporation	325413	277,743,008	-8,165,000
Medical Equipment and Supplies Manufacturing			
3M Company	339100	31,657,000,960	4,857,999,872
Abiomed Inc	339100	445,304,000	52,116,000
Acelity LP Inc	339100	1,995,000,000	
Advanced Bionics LLC	339100	210,000,000	
Align Technology Inc	339100	1,473,412,992	231,418,000
AngioDynamics Inc	339100	349,643,008	5,008,000

Industry Group/Company	Industry Code	2017 Sales	2017 Profits
Ansell Limited	339100	1,292,996,736	138,941,888
Arthrex Inc	339100	2,000,000,000	
Atrion Corporation	339100	146,595,008	36,593,000
Auris Health Inc	339100	14,700,000	
Avanos Medical Inc	339100	611,600,000	79,300,000
Avinger Inc	339100	9,934,000	-48,732,000
Bausch & Lomb Inc	339100	4,871,000,000	1,440,000,000
Baxter International Inc	339100	10,561,000,448	717,000,000
Becton Dickinson & Company	339100	12,092,999,680	1,100,000,000
BioTelemetry Inc	339100	286,776,000	-15,956,000
Boston Scientific Corporation	339100	9,048,000,512	104,000,000
Cantel Medical Corporation	339100	770,156,992	71,378,000
CIVCO Medical Instruments Co Ltd	339100	3,600,000,000	
Coloplast AS	339100	2,363,362,304	577,903,552
CONMED Corporation	339100	796,392,000	55,487,000
ConvaTec Inc	339100	1,764,600,000	158,400,000
Cooper Companies Inc (The)	339100	2,139,000,064	372,900,000
Cordis Corporation	339100	861,000,000	
Criticare Technologies Inc	339100		
CryoLife Inc	339100	189,702,000	3,704,000
Dentsply Sirona Inc	339100	3,993,400,064	-1,550,000,000
DePuy Synthes Inc	339100	9,100,000,000	
DexCom Inc	339100	718,499,968	-50,200,000
DJO Global Inc	339100	1,190,000,000	-35,900,000
Draegerwerk AG & Co KGaA	339100	2,918,408,448	83,507,872
EDAP TMS SA	339100	41,569,952	-791,953
Edwards Lifesciences Corporation	339100	3,435,300,096	583,600,000
Electromed Inc	339100	25,861,144	2,229,472
Elekta AB	339100	1,170,744,448	13,671,810
Endologix Inc	339100	181,156,992	-66,400,000
Entellus Medical Inc	339100	78,943,200	
Essilor International SA	339100	8,497,940,992	895,176,960
Ethicon Inc	339100	5,800,000,000	
Exactech Inc	339100	261,000,000	
Fielmann AG	339100	1,572,486,656	190,184,832
GE Healthcare	339100	19,116,000,000	3,448,000,000
Gerresheimer AG	339100	1,567,920,768	117,324,112
Getinge AB	339100	2,460,378,880	150,499,280
Globus Medical Inc	339100	635,977,024	107,348,000
Haemonetics Corporation	339100	886,115,968	-26,268,000
Hill-Rom Holdings Inc	339100	2,743,699,968	133,600,000
ICU Medical Inc	339100	1,292,612,992	68,644,000
Integra Lifesciences Holdings Corporation	339100	1,188,236,032	64,743,000
Intersect ENT Inc	339100	96,301,000	-16,363,000
Intuitive Surgical Inc	339100	3,128,900,096	660,000,000
Invacare Corporation	339100	966,497,024	-76,541,000
K2M Group Holdings Inc	339100	258,031,008	-37,145,000
Keystone Dental Inc	339100		
Lakeland Industries Inc	339100	86,183,000	3,893,000

Industry Group/Company	Industry Code	2017 Sales	2017 Profits
LifeScan Inc	339100		
Lumenis Ltd	339100	316,050,000	
Medical Action Industries Inc	339100	315,000,000	
MEDIVATORS Inc	339100		
Medtronic ENT Surgical Products Inc	339100		
Medtronic MiniMed Inc	339100	1,890,000,000	
Medtronic Vascular Inc	339100	11,000,000,000	
Mentor Worldwide LLC	339100		
Meridian Medical Technologies Inc	339100		
Merit Medical Systems Inc	339100	727,852,032	27,523,000
Mindray Medical International Limited	339100	1,433,250,000	
Misonix Inc	339100	27,269,964	-1,681,179
Molnlycke Health Care AB	339100	1,730,910,000	
MRI Interventions Inc	339100	7,379,525	
MSA Safety Inc	339100	1,196,808,960	26,027,000
National Dentex Corporation	339100		
Natus Medical Incorporated	339100	500,969,984	-20,293,000
NMI Health Inc	339100	588,000	
Nobel Biocare Holding AG	339100		
Nordion (Canada) Inc	339100	12,075,000	
NuVasive Inc	339100	1,029,520,000	83,006,000
Olympus Corporation	339100	6,724,286,464	702,865,728
Opto Circuits (India) Ltd	339100	33,832,700	-78,316,700
Orthofix International NV	339100	433,823,008	6,223,000
Philips Respironics Inc	339100		
Precision Therapeutics Inc	339100	654,836	-7,746,593
Safilo Group SpA	339100	1,187,845,376	-285,420,768
Shandong Weigao Group Medical Polymer Co Ltd	339100	914,003,712	251,270,800
Siemens Healthineers	339100	16,043,725,824	1,659,495,424
Smiths Group plc	339100	4,171,435,776	724,914,112
Span America Medical Systems Inc	339100	71,008,526	
STAAR Surgical Company	339100	90,611,000	-2,139,000
STERIS plc	339100	2,612,755,968	109,965,000
Stryker Corporation	339100	12,444,000,256	1,020,000,000
Sunrise Medical GmbH	339100	570,465,000	
Supreme Products Co Ltd	339100		
Symmetry Surgical Inc	339100	90,300,000	
Teleflex Incorporated	339100	2,146,302,976	152,530,000
Terumo Corporation	339100	4,621,864,960	487,433,248
Theragenics Corporation	339100		
Thoratec Corporation	339100	550,200,000	
Utah Medical Products Inc	339100	41,414,000	8,505,000
Valeritas Inc	339100	20,450,000	-49,301,000
Welch Allyn Inc	339100	753,900,000	
Wright Medical Group NV	339100	744,988,992	-202,598,000
Young Innovations Inc	339100		
Zimmer Biomet Holdings Inc	339100	7,824,099,840	1,813,799,936
Zoll Medical Corporation	339100	997,500,000	

Industry Group/Company	Industry Code	2017 Sales	2017 Profits
Medical Imaging and Electromedical (Medical Devices) Equipment, including MRI, Ultrasound, Pacemakers, EKG and CAT			
Accuray Inc	334510	383,414,016	-29,579,000
Analogic Corporation	334510	486,372,000	-74,237,000
Beckman Coulter Inc	334510	5,100,000,000	
Biosensors International Group Ltd	334510		
Cochlear Limited	334510	907,263,360	161,806,080
Coherent Inc	334510	1,723,310,976	207,122,000
Cynosure Inc	334510	455,208,600	
Danaher Corporation	334510	18,329,700,352	2,492,100,096
Hitachi Healthcare America Corporation	334510	204,750,000	
IDEXX Laboratories Inc	334510	1,969,058,048	263,144,000
Intarcia Therapeutics Inc	334510		
IRIDEX Corporation	334510	41,593,000	-12,867,000
Masimo Corporation	334510	798,108,032	131,616,000
Mazor Robotics Ltd	334510	64,947,000	-12,419,000
MEDITE Cancer Diagnostics Inc	334510	6,813,000	-6,811,000
Medtronic plc	334510	29,710,000,128	4,028,000,000
Novanta Inc	334510	521,289,984	60,051,000
Optos plc	334510	102,900,000	25,100,000
Philips Healthcare	334510	21,298,000,000	2,240,000,000
Precision Optics Corporation	334510	3,154,547	-1,006,457
Proteus Digital Health Inc	334510		
ResMed Inc	334510	2,066,737,024	342,284,000
Semler Scientific Inc	334510	12,452,000	-1,510,000
Sonova Holding AG	334510	2,409,844,224	351,240,832
Tandem Diabetes Care Inc	334510	107,601,000	-73,033,000
TransEnterix Inc	334510	7,111,000	-144,796,000
Varian Medical Systems Inc	334510	2,668,199,936	249,600,000
William Demant Holding Group	334510	2,007,366,400	266,958,880
Medical Laboratories			
21st Century Oncology Holdings Inc	621511	1,125,000,000	
AmeriPath Inc	621511	922,000,000	
Bio-Reference Laboratories Inc	621511	924,000,000	
Hooper Holmes Inc	621511		
iKang Healthcare Group Inc	621511	435,712,992	-11,251,000
Laboratory Corporation of America Holdings	621511	10,441,400,320	1,268,199,936
Quest Diagnostics Inc	621511	7,709,000,192	772,000,000
Sonic Healthcare Limited	621511	3,656,819,200	309,531,840
Specialty Laboratories Inc	621511	388,500,000	
Medical, Dental and Hospital Equipment and Supplies (Medical Devices) Wholesale Distribution			
Amplifon	423450	1,472,257,280	116,964,768
Carl Zeiss Meditec AG	423450	1,350,022,016	152,537,456
Fisher & Paykel Healthcare Limited	423450	574,579,840	111,777,656
Fuse Medical Inc	423450	26,407,206	699,678
Henry Schein Inc	423450	12,461,543,424	406,299,008
Moore Medical LLC	423450		

Industry Group/Company	Industry Code	2017 Sales	2017 Profits
Owens & Minor Inc	423450	9,318,275,072	72,793,000
Patterson Companies Inc	423450	5,593,126,912	170,892,992
Sartorius Stedim Biotech SA	423450	1,226,509,184	182,765,856
Thermo Fisher Scientific Inc	423450	20,917,999,616	2,224,999,936
Nursing Care Facilities (Skilled Nursing Facilities)			
Diversicare Healthcare Services Inc	623110	574,793,984	-4,827,000
Ensign Group Inc (The)	623110	1,849,316,992	40,475,000
Extendicare Inc	623110	844,100,736	1,640,000
Genesis Healthcare LLC	623110	5,373,740,032	-578,982,016
Kindred Healthcare Inc	623110	6,034,122,752	-698,352,000
ManorCare Inc (HCR ManorCare)	623110	3,700,000,000	
National HealthCare Corporation	623110	966,995,968	56,205,000
ORPEA Groupe	623110	3,560,551,168	101,872,048
Office Administrative Services			
Premier Inc	561110	1,454,673,024	113,425,000
Offices of All Other Miscellaneous Health Practitioners			
Hanger Inc	621399	1,040,769,024	-104,671,000
Offices of Physical, Occupational and Speech Therapists, and Audiologists			
HearUSA Inc	621340		
US Physical Therapy Inc	621340	414,051,008	22,256,000
Pharmaceuticals and Druggists' Merchandise Distributors			
Alfresa Holdings Corporation	424210	22,944,784,384	277,764,800
AmerisourceBergen Corp	424210	153,143,820,288	364,484,000
BioMerieux SA	424210	2,596,126,464	270,141,472
BTG plc	424210	725,549,952	42,731,780
Cardinal Health Inc	424210	129,976,000,512	1,288,000,000
Ebos Group Limited	424210	5,003,709,952	87,167,000
McKesson Corporation	424210	198,533,005,312	5,070,000,128
Medipal Holdings Corporation	424210	27,542,931,456	260,782,400
Profarma Distribuidora de Produtos Farmaceuticos SA	424210	1,443,000,000	-34,006,400
Sigma Healthcare Limited	424210	3,347,451,904	40,270,772
Sinopharm Group Co Ltd	424210	40,215,121,920	767,366,976
Suzuken Co Ltd	424210	19,124,940,800	191,584,240
Toho Holdings Co Ltd	424210	11,062,800,000	127,833,000
Pharmaceuticals, Biopharmaceuticals, Generics and Drug Manufacturing			
3SBio Inc	325412	585,649,216	146,695,472
Abbott Laboratories	325412	27,389,999,104	477,000,000
Actelion Pharmaceuticals Ltd	325412	2,603,399,232	
AEterna Zentaris Inc	325412	923,000	-16,796,000
Alcon Inc	325412	13,000,000,000	
Allergan plc	325412	15,940,700,160	-4,125,499,904
Amgen Inc	325412	22,848,999,424	1,979,000,064
Aradigm Corporation	325412	14,465,000	-10,705,000
ArQule Inc	325412	0	-29,203,000
Astellas Pharma Inc	325412	11,790,671,872	1,965,922,432
AstraZeneca plc	325412	22,464,999,424	3,000,999,936

Industry Group/Company	Industry Code	2017 Sales	2017 Profits
Bausch Health Companies Inc	325412	8,723,999,744	2,404,000,000
Bayer AG	325412	39,727,022,080	8,323,216,896
Bayer Corporation	325412	6,350,000,000	
Bayer HealthCare Pharmaceuticals Inc	325412	14,500,000,000	
Biogen Inc	325412	12,273,899,520	2,539,099,904
Bristol-Myers Squibb Co	325412	20,775,999,488	1,007,000,000
China Nuokang Bio-Pharmaceutical Inc	325412		
China Resources Pharmaceutical Group Limited	325412	22,075,000,000	878,616,000
Cipla Limited	325412	1,952,710,656	139,921,744
Cumberland Pharmaceuticals Inc	325412	41,150,132	-7,978,633
Eli Lilly and Company	325412	22,871,300,096	-204,100,000
Endo International PLC	325412	3,468,858,112	-2,035,432,960
Galderma SA	325412	236,250,000	
Galenica Group	325412	4,312,000,000	
Genentech Inc	325412	19,000,000,000	
Gilead Sciences Inc	325412	26,107,000,832	4,627,999,744
GlaxoSmithKline Pharmaceuticals Ltd	325412	404,374,112	46,828,096
GlaxoSmithKline plc	325412	39,379,038,208	1,998,564,992
Incyte Corporation	325412	1,536,216,064	-313,142,016
Jiangsu Hengrui Medicine Co Ltd	325412	2,124,320,000	505,169,000
Johnson & Johnson	325412	76,449,996,800	1,300,000,000
Lupin Limited	325412	2,414,644,736	355,572,192
Medicure Inc	325412	20,871,410	33,400,680
Merck & Co Inc	325412	40,121,999,360	2,393,999,872
Merck Serono SA	325412	7,000,000,000	
Mylan NV	325412	11,907,699,712	696,000,000
Novartis AG	325412	50,134,999,040	7,703,000,064
Novo-Nordisk AS	325412	17,409,302,528	5,943,066,112
Par Pharmaceutical Companies Inc	325412	3,885,000,000	
Pfizer Inc	325412	52,545,998,848	21,308,000,256
Regeneron Pharmaceuticals Inc	325412	5,872,226,816	1,198,510,976
Roche Holding AG	325412	56,076,292,096	8,684,149,760
Sanofi Genzyme	325412	6,796,680,000	
Sanofi SA	325412	42,102,571,008	9,808,117,760
Shire Plc	325412	15,160,599,552	4,271,500,032
Simcere Pharmaceutical Group	325412	546,000,000	
Sun Pharmaceutical Industries Ltd	325412	4,475,788,800	995,621,184
Suven Life Sciences Limited	325412	87,139,900	19,024,100
Takeda Oncology	325412	1,050,000,000	
Takeda Pharmaceutical Company Limited	325412	15,569,557,504	1,033,205,696
Teva Pharmaceutical Industries Limited	325412	22,385,000,448	-16,264,999,936
Yuhan Corporation	325412	1,056,920,000	117,988,000
Pharmacies and Drug Stores			
Accredo Health Group Inc	446110		
CVS Health Corporation	446110	184,765,005,824	6,622,000,128
Duane Reade Inc	446110		
Jean Coutu Group (PJC) Inc (The)	446110	2,360,602,368	158,145,056
Omnicare Inc	446110	6,990,000,000	
PharMerica Corporation	446110	2,140,000,000	

Industry Group/Company	Industry Code	2017 Sales	2017 Profits
Rite Aid Corporation	446110	32,845,072,384	4,053,000
Walgreens Boots Alliance Inc	446110	118,214,000,640	4,078,000,128
Photographic and Photocopying Equipment Manufacturing			
Agfa-Gevaert NV	333316	2,841,028,096	43,028,260
Physicians (except Mental Health Specialists)			
Continucare Corporation	621111	435,750,000	
HealthTronics Inc	621111	210,000,000	
MEDNAX Inc	621111	3,458,311,936	320,372,000
Team Health Holdings Inc	621111	4,200,000,000	
US Oncology Inc	621111		
Professional Employer Organizations			
ATC Healthcare Inc	561330		
Professional Training, Management Development and Corporate Employee Training			
HealthStream Inc	611430	247,662,000	10,004,000
Residential Intellectual and Developmental Disability Facilities			
ResCare Inc	623210	1,875,000,000	
Residential Mental Health and Substance Abuse Facilities			
AAC Holdings Inc	623220	317,640,992	-20,579,000
Catasys Inc	623220	7,717,000	
Retirement Communities and Assisted Living Facilities for the Elderly			
Atria Senior Living Group	623310		
Brookdale Senior Living Inc	623310	4,747,116,032	-571,419,008
Capital Senior Living Corporation	623310	466,996,992	-44,168,000
Five Star Senior Living Inc	623310	1,396,105,984	-20,902,000
Life Care Centers of America	623310	3,200,000,000	
Sunrise Senior Living LLC	623310	1,650,000,000	
Scientific Research and Development (R&D) in Life Sciences, Medical Devices, Biotechnology and Pharmaceuticals (Drugs)			
IQVIA Holdings Inc	541711	9,738,999,808	1,308,999,936
Pharmaceutical Product Development LLC	541711	1,350,000,000	
Semiconductor and Solar Cell Manufacturing, Including Chips, Memory, LEDs, Transistors and Integrated Circuits			
Hoya Corporation	334413	4,402,073,088	779,713,408
Surgical Appliance and Supplies (Medical Devices) Manufacturing			
Smith & Nephew plc	339113	4,765,000,192	767,000,000
Temporary Staffing, Help and Employment Agencies			
Allied Healthcare International Inc	561320	462,000,000	
AMN Healthcare Services Inc	561320	1,988,454,016	132,558,000
Vaccines, Skin Replacement Products and Biologicals Manufacturing			
CSL Behring LLC	325414	5,500,000,000	
CSL Limited	325414	6,223,505,408	1,258,096,640
Grifols SA	325414	5,021,599,232	770,671,040

Industry Group/Company	Industry Code	2017 Sales	2017 Profits
MiMedx Group Inc	325414		
Organogenesis Inc	325414	477,750,000	
Shanghai RAAS Blood Products Co Ltd	325414	296,000,000	127,744,000
Veterinary Services			
VCA Inc	541940	2,700,000,000	
Vitamins, Botanicals, Nutritional Supplements and Medicinal Chemicals Manufacturing			
Yunnan Baiyao Group Co Ltd	325411	3,733,430,000	480,991,000

ALPHABETICAL INDEX

EmblemHealth Inc
Endo International PLC
Endologix Inc
Ensign Group Inc (The)
Entellus Medical Inc
Envision Healthcare Corporation
Envolve Vision Inc
Epic Systems Corporation
Essilor International SA
Ethicon Inc
Everyday Health Inc
Exactech Inc
Express Scripts Holding Co
Extendicare Inc
EyeMed Vision Care LLC
Fairview Health Services
Fielmann AG
First Choice Health Network Inc
First Health Group Corp
Fisher & Paykel Healthcare Limited
Five Star Senior Living Inc
Fresenius Medical Care AG & Co KGaA
Fresenius SE & Co KGaA
Fuse Medical Inc
Galderma SA
Galenica Group
GE Healthcare
Genentech Inc
Genesis Healthcare LLC
GenMark Diagnostics Inc
Gerresheimer AG
Getinge AB
Gilead Sciences Inc
GlaxoSmithKline Pharmaceuticals Ltd
GlaxoSmithKline plc
Global Healthcare Exchange LLC
Globus Medical Inc
Grand Rounds (Consulting Medical Associates Inc)
Grifols SA
Haemonetics Corporation
Hanger Inc
Harvard Pilgrim Health Care Inc
HCA Holdings Inc
Health Care Service Corporation (HCSC)
Health Catalyst
Health Net Inc
Healthgrades Operating Company Inc
HealthNow New York Inc
Healthscope Ltd
HealthStream Inc
HealthTronics Inc
HealthTrust Purchasing Group LP
HearUSA Inc
HemaCare Corporation
Henry Ford Health System
Henry Schein Inc
Highmark Health
Hill-Rom Holdings Inc
Hitachi Healthcare America Corporation
HMS Holdings Corp
Hologic Inc
Hooper Holmes Inc
Horizon Health Corporation
Horizon Healthcare Services Inc
Houston Methodist
Hoya Corporation
Humana Inc
IBM Watson Health
ICU Medical Inc
IDEXX Laboratories Inc
iKang Healthcare Group Inc
Immucor Inc
Incyte Corporation
Indegene Aptilon Inc
Independence Holding Company
Indiana University Health
InfuSystem Holdings Inc
Institut Straumann AG
Intalere Inc
Intarcia Therapeutics Inc
Integra Lifesciences Holdings Corporation
IntegraMed America Inc
Intermountain Healthcare
Interpace Diagnostics Group Inc
Intersect ENT Inc
Intuitive Surgical Inc
Invacare Corporation
IQVIA Holdings Inc
IRIDEX Corporation
Jean Coutu Group (PJC) Inc (The)
Jenny Craig Inc
Jiangsu Hengrui Medicine Co Ltd
Johns Hopkins Medicine
Johnson & Johnson
K2M Group Holdings Inc
Kaiser Permanente
Keystone Dental Inc
Kindred at Home
Kindred Healthcare Inc
KPC Healthcare Inc
Laboratory Corporation of America Holdings
Lakeland Industries Inc
LCA-Vision Inc
LHC Group Inc
Life Care Centers of America
Life Healthcare Group Holdings Ltd
LifePoint Health Inc
LifeScan Inc
Lifetime Healthcare Companies (The)
Little Clinic (The)
LogistiCare Solutions LLC
Lumenis Ltd
Lumeris Inc
Lupin Limited
Magee Rehabilitation Hospital
Magellan Health Inc
Main Line Health System
ManorCare Inc (HCR ManorCare)
Masimo Corporation
Mayo Clinic
Mazor Robotics Ltd
McKesson Corporation
MD Anderson Cancer Center
Medica Sur SAB de CV
Medical Action Industries Inc
Medical Facilities Corporation
Medical Imaging Corp
Medical Information Technology Inc (MEDITECH)
Medical Mutual of Ohio
Mediclinic International Plc
Medicure Inc
Medifast Inc
Medipal Holdings Corporation
MEDITE Cancer Diagnostics Inc
MEDIVATORS Inc
MEDNAX Inc
MedStar Health
Medtronic ENT Surgical Products Inc
Medtronic MiniMed Inc
Medtronic plc
Medtronic Vascular Inc
Memorial Hermann Healthcare System
Memorial Sloan Kettering Cancer Center
Mentor Worldwide LLC
Merck & Co Inc
Merck Serono SA
Mercy
Mercy Health
Meridian Bioscience Inc
Meridian Medical Technologies Inc
Merit Medical Systems Inc
Metropolitan Health Networks Inc
Mettler-Toledo International Inc
MiMedx Group Inc
Mindray Medical International Limited
MinuteClinic LLC
Misonix Inc
Molina Healthcare Inc
Molnlycke Health Care AB
Moore Medical LLC
MRI Interventions Inc
MSA Safety Inc
MultiPlan Inc
Mylan NV
National Dentex Corporation
National HealthCare Corporation
National Healthcare Group Pte Ltd
National Home Health Care Corp
National University Health System (NUHS)
Natus Medical Incorporated
Netcare Limited
New York City Health and Hospitals Corporation
New York Health Care Inc
NewYork-Presbyterian Healthcare System
NMI Health Inc
Nobel Biocare Holding AG
Nobilis Health Corp
Nordion (Canada) Inc
Novanta Inc
Novartis AG
Novo-Nordisk AS
NuVasive Inc
NxStage Medical Inc
OhioHealth Corporation
Olympus Corporation
Omnicare Inc
Opto Circuits (India) Ltd
Optos plc
Organogenesis Inc

ORPEA Groupe
Orthofix International NV
Owens & Minor Inc
Par Pharmaceutical Companies Inc
Partners HealthCare
Patterson Companies Inc
Pediatric Services of America Inc
PerkinElmer Inc
Pfizer Inc
Pharmaceutical Product Development LLC
PharMerica Corporation
Philips Healthcare
Philips Respironics Inc
Ping An Healthcare and Technology Co Ltd
Precision Optics Corporation
Precision Therapeutics Inc
Premera Blue Cross
Premier Inc
Prime Healthcare Services Inc
Profarma Distribuidora de Produtos Farmaceuticos SA
Protech Home Medical Corp
Proteus Digital Health Inc
Providence St Joseph Health
Quality Systems Inc
Quest Diagnostics Inc
Quidel Corporation
RadNet Inc
Ramsay Health Care Limited
RCCH HealthCare Partners
Regeneron Pharmaceuticals Inc
Regional Health Properties Inc
ResCare Inc
ResMed Inc
Rhon Klinikum AG
Rite Aid Corporation
Roche Holding AG
SafeGuard Health Enterprises Inc
Safilo Group SpA
Sanofi Genzyme
Sanofi SA
Sartorius Stedim Biotech SA
Semler Scientific Inc
Sentara Healthcare
Shandong Weigao Group Medical Polymer Co Ltd
Shanghai RAAS Blood Products Co Ltd
Shire Plc
SHL Telemedicine Ltd
Siemens AG
Siemens Healthineers
Sigma Healthcare Limited
Simcere Pharmaceutical Group
Sinopharm Group Co Ltd
Smile Brands Inc
Smith & Nephew plc
Smiths Group plc
Sonic Healthcare Limited
Sonova Holding AG
Span America Medical Systems Inc
Specialty Laboratories Inc
Spectrum Health
SSM Health
St Jude Children's Research Hospital
STAAR Surgical Company
Stericycle Inc
STERIS plc
Steward Health Care System LLC
Stryker Corporation
Sun Pharmaceutical Industries Ltd
Sunrise Medical GmbH
Sunrise Senior Living LLC
Supreme Products Co Ltd
Surgery Partners Inc
Surgical Care Affiliates Inc
Sutter Health Inc
Suven Life Sciences Limited
Suzuken Co Ltd
Symmetry Surgical Inc
Take Care Health Systems LLC
Takeda Oncology
Takeda Pharmaceutical Company Limited
Tandem Diabetes Care Inc
Team Health Holdings Inc
Teleflex Incorporated
Tenet Healthcare Corporation
Terumo Corporation
Teva Pharmaceutical Industries Limited
Texas Health Resources
Theragenics Corporation
Thermo Fisher Scientific Inc
Thomas Jefferson University Hospitals Inc
Thoratec Corporation
Tivity Health Inc
TLC Vision Corporation
Toho Holdings Co Ltd
TransEnterix Inc
Trinity Health
Trustmark Companies
Tufts Associated Health Plans Inc
United Surgical Partners International Inc
UnitedHealth Group Inc
UnitedHealthcare Community & State
UnitedHealthcare National Accounts
Universal Health Services Inc
Universal Hospital Services Inc
UPMC
Urgent Care MSO LLC (MedExpress)
US NeuroSurgical Inc
US Oncology Inc
US Physical Therapy Inc
USMD Health System
Utah Medical Products Inc
Valeritas Inc
Varian Medical Systems Inc
VCA Inc
Vision Service Plan
Vizient Inc
Walgreens Boots Alliance Inc
WebMD Health Corp
Weight Watchers International Inc
Welch Allyn Inc
WellCare Health Plans Inc
Welltok Inc
William Demant Holding Group
Wright Medical Group NV
Young Innovations Inc
Yuhan Corporation
Yunnan Baiyao Group Co Ltd
Zimmer Biomet Holdings Inc
Zoll Medical Corporation

INDEX OF U.S. HEADQUARTERS LOCATION BY STATE

To help you locate members of the firms geographically, the city and state of the headquarters of each company are in the following index.

IOWA
CIVCO Medical Instruments Co Ltd; Kalona

KANSAS
Hooper Holmes Inc; Olathe

KENTUCKY
Atria Senior Living Group; Louisville
Humana Inc; Louisville
Kindred at Home; Louisville
Kindred Healthcare Inc; Louisville
PharMerica Corporation; Louisville
Protech Home Medical Corp; Wilder
ResCare Inc; Louisville

LOUISIANA
Amedisys Inc; Baton Rouge
Blue Cross and Blue Shield of Louisiana; Baton Rouge
LHC Group Inc; Lafayette

MAINE
IDEXX Laboratories Inc; Westbrook

MARYLAND
Bon Secours Health System Inc; Marriottsville
CareFirst Inc; Baltimore
Coventry Health Care Inc; Bethesda
Dental Benefits Providers Inc; Columbia
Johns Hopkins Medicine; Baltimore
Medifast Inc; Baltimore
MedStar Health; Columbia
Meridian Medical Technologies Inc; Columbia
US NeuroSurgical Inc; Rockville

MASSACHUSETTS
Abiomed Inc; Danvers
Analogic Corporation; Peabody
ArQule Inc; Burlington
athenahealth Inc; Watertown
Biogen Inc; Cambridge
Blue Cross and Blue Shield of Massachusetts; Boston
Boston Scientific Corporation; Marlborough
Bruker Corporation; Billerica
Civitas Solutions Inc; Boston
Cynosure Inc; Westford
eClinicalWorks; Westborough
Five Star Senior Living Inc; Newton
Haemonetics Corporation; Braintree
Harvard Pilgrim Health Care Inc; Wellesley
Hologic Inc; Marlborough
Intarcia Therapeutics Inc; Boston
Keystone Dental Inc; Burlington
Medical Information Technology Inc (MEDITECH); Westwood
Novanta Inc; Bedford
NxStage Medical Inc; Lawrence
Organogenesis Inc; Canton
Partners HealthCare; Boston
PerkinElmer Inc; Waltham
Philips Healthcare; Andover
Precision Optics Corporation; Gardner
Sanofi Genzyme; Cambridge
Steward Health Care System LLC; Boston
Takeda Oncology; Cambridge
Thermo Fisher Scientific Inc; Waltham
Tufts Associated Health Plans Inc; Watertown
Zoll Medical Corporation; Chelmsford

MICHIGAN
Blue Care Network of Michigan; Southfield
Blue Cross and Blue Shield of Michigan; Detroit
Detroit Medical Center (DMC); Detroit
Henry Ford Health System; Ann Arbor
InfuSystem Holdings Inc; Madison Heights
Spectrum Health; Grand Rapids
Stryker Corporation; Kalamazoo
Trinity Health; Livonia

MINNESOTA
3M Company; St. Paul
Allina Health; Minneapolis
Bio-Techne Corporation; Minneapolis
Blue Cross and Blue Shield of Minnesota; Eagan
Cigna Behavioral Health; Eden Prairie
Electromed Inc; New Prague
Entellus Medical Inc; Plymouth
Fairview Health Services; Minneapolis
Mayo Clinic; Rochester
MEDIVATORS Inc; Minneapolis
Medtronic ENT Surgical Products Inc; Minneapolis
Patterson Companies Inc; St. Paul
Precision Therapeutics Inc; Eagan
UnitedHealth Group Inc; Minnetonka
Universal Hospital Services Inc; Minneapolis

MISSOURI
Ascension; St. Louis
BJC HealthCare; St. Louis
Blue Cross Blue Shield of Kansas City (Blue KC); Kansas City
Centene Corporation; St. Louis
Cerner Corporation; North Kansas City
Express Scripts Holding Co; St. Louis
Intalere Inc; St. Louis
Lumeris Inc; Maryland Heights
SSM Health; St. Louis

MONTANA
Blue Cross and Blue Shield of Montana; Helena

NEBRASKA
Blue Cross and Blue Shield of Nebraska; Omaha

NEVADA
Medical Imaging Corp; Las Vegas
NMI Health Inc; Reno

NEW JERSEY
Aeon Global Health Corp; Berkeley Heights
Bausch & Lomb Inc; Bridgewater
Bayer Corporation; Whippany
Bayer HealthCare Pharmaceuticals Inc; Wayne
Becton Dickinson & Company; Franklin Lakes
Bio-Reference Laboratories Inc; Elmwood Park
Cantel Medical Corporation; Little Falls
ConvaTec Inc; Bridgewater
Horizon Healthcare Services Inc; Newark
Integra Lifesciences Holdings Corporation; Plainsboro
Interpace Diagnostics Group Inc; Parsippany
Johnson & Johnson; New Brunswick
Merck & Co Inc; Kenilworth
Quest Diagnostics Inc; Madison
Valeritas Inc; Bridgewater

NEW YORK
AngioDynamics Inc; Latham
ATC Healthcare Inc; Lake Success
Bristol-Myers Squibb Co; New York
CONMED Corporation; Utica
Duane Reade Inc; New York
EmblemHealth Inc; New York
Everyday Health Inc; New York
HealthNow New York Inc; Buffalo
Henry Schein Inc; Melville
IntegraMed America Inc; Purchase
Lakeland Industries Inc; Ronkonkoma
Lifetime Healthcare Companies (The); Rochester
Memorial Sloan Kettering Cancer Center; New York
Misonix Inc; Farmingdale
MultiPlan Inc; New York
New York City Health and Hospitals Corporation; New York
New York Health Care Inc; Valley Stream
NewYork-Presbyterian Healthcare System; New York
Par Pharmaceutical Companies Inc; Chestnut Ridge
Pfizer Inc; New York
Regeneron Pharmaceuticals Inc; Tarrytown
WebMD Health Corp; New York
Weight Watchers International Inc; New York
Welch Allyn Inc; Skaneateles Falls

NORTH CAROLINA
Blue Cross and Blue Shield of North Carolina; Durham
Envolve Vision Inc; Rocky Mount
IQVIA Holdings Inc; Durham
Laboratory Corporation of America Holdings; Burlington
Pharmaceutical Product Development LLC; Wilmington
Premier Inc; Charlotte
TransEnterix Inc; Morrisville

OHIO
Cardinal Health Inc; Dublin
Chemed Corporation; Cincinnati
Cleveland Clinic Foundation (The); Cleveland
Ethicon Inc; Cincinnati
EyeMed Vision Care LLC; Mason
Hitachi Healthcare America Corporation; Twinsburg
Invacare Corporation; Elyria
LCA-Vision Inc; Cincinnati
ManorCare Inc (HCR ManorCare); Toledo
Medical Mutual of Ohio; Cleveland
Mercy Health; Cincinnati
Meridian Bioscience Inc; Cincinnati
Mettler-Toledo International Inc; Columbus
OhioHealth Corporation; Columbus
Omnicare Inc; Cincinnati

OKLAHOMA
Blue Cross and Blue Shield of Oklahoma; Tulsa
Mercy; Tishomingo

OREGON
Cambia Health Solutions Inc; Portland
Semler Scientific Inc; Portland

PENNSYLVANIA
AmerisourceBergen Corp; Chesterbrook
BioTelemetry Inc; Malvera
Capital BlueCross; Harrisburg
CSL Behring LLC; King of Prussia
Dentsply Sirona Inc; York
Genesis Healthcare LLC; Kennett Square
Globus Medical Inc; Audubon
Highmark Health; Pittsburgh
Magee Rehabilitation Hospital; Philadelphia
Main Line Health System; Bryn Mawr
MSA Safety Inc; Pittsburgh
Philips Respironics Inc; Murrysville
Rite Aid Corporation; Camp Hill
Take Care Health Systems LLC; Conshohocken
Teleflex Incorporated; Wayne
Thomas Jefferson University Hospitals Inc; Philadelphia
Universal Health Services Inc; King Of Prussia
UPMC; Pittsburgh

RHODE ISLAND
Criticare Technologies Inc; North Kingstown
CVS Health Corporation; Woonsocket
MinuteClinic LLC; Woonsocket

SOUTH CAROLINA
Span America Medical Systems Inc; Greenville

SOUTH DAKOTA
Avera Health; Sioux Falls

TENNESSEE
AAC Holdings Inc; Brentwood
Acadia Healthcare Company Inc; Franklin
Accredo Health Group Inc; Memphis
American HomePatient Inc; Brentwood
AMSURG Corporation; Nashville
Ardent Health Services LLC; Nashville
BlueCross BlueShield of Tennessee Inc; Chattanooga
Brookdale Senior Living Inc; Brentwood
CareSpot Urgent Care; Brentwood
Change Healthcare Inc; Nashville
Community Health Systems Inc; Franklin
Cumberland Pharmaceuticals Inc; Nashville
Diversicare Healthcare Services Inc; Brentwood
Envision Healthcare Corporation; Nashville
HCA Holdings Inc; Nashville
HealthStream Inc; Nashville
HealthTrust Purchasing Group LP; Nashville
Life Care Centers of America; Cleveland
LifePoint Health Inc; Brentwood
Little Clinic (The); Nashville
National HealthCare Corporation; Murfreesboro
RCCH HealthCare Partners; Brentwood
St Jude Children's Research Hospital; Memphis
Surgery Partners Inc; Brentwood
Symmetry Surgical Inc; Antioch
Team Health Holdings Inc; Knoxville
Tivity Health Inc; Franklin

TEXAS
Acelity LP Inc; San Antonio
Adeptus Health Inc; Lewisville
Alcon Inc; Fort Worth
Atrion Corporation; Allen
Blue Cross and Blue Shield of Texas; Richardson
Capital Senior Living Corporation; Dallas
Castle Dental Centers Inc; Houston
CHRISTUS Health; Irving
Concentra Inc; Addison
Dynacq Healthcare Inc; Pasadena
Fuse Medical Inc; Richardson
Hanger Inc; Austin
HealthTronics Inc; Austin
HMS Holdings Corp; Irving
Horizon Health Corporation; Lewisville
Houston Methodist; Houston
MD Anderson Cancer Center; Houston
Memorial Hermann Healthcare System; Houston
Nobilis Health Corp; Houston
Tenet Healthcare Corporation; Dallas
Texas Health Resources; Arlington
United Surgical Partners International Inc; Addison
US Oncology Inc; The Woodlands
US Physical Therapy Inc; Houston
USMD Health System; Irving
Vizient Inc; Irving

UTAH
ActiveCare Inc; Orem
Health Catalyst; Salt Lake City
Intermountain Healthcare; Salt Lake City
Merit Medical Systems Inc; South Jordan
Utah Medical Products Inc; Midvale

VIRGINIA
Amerigroup Corporation; Virginia Beach
K2M Group Holdings Inc; Leesburg
Medical Action Industries Inc; Mechanicsville
Owens & Minor Inc; Mechanicsville
Sentara Healthcare; Norfolk
Sunrise Senior Living LLC; McLean
UnitedHealthcare Community & State; Vienna

VERMONT
Blue Cross and Blue Shield of Vermont; Berlin

WASHINGTON
Danaher Corporation; Washington
First Choice Health Network Inc; Seattle
Premera Blue Cross; Mountlake Terrace
Providence St Joseph Health; Renton

WEST VIRGINIA
Urgent Care MSO LLC (MedExpress); Morgantown

WISCONSIN
Epic Systems Corporation; Verona

WYOMING
Blue Cross and Blue Shield of Wyoming; Cheyenne

INDEX OF NON-U.S. HEADQUARTERS LOCATION BY COUNTRY

GlaxoSmithKline plc; Middlesex
Mediclinic International Plc; London
Mylan NV; Hatfield
Optos plc; Dunfermline
Smith & Nephew plc; London
Smiths Group plc; London
STERIS plc; Chaddesden
Wright Medical Group NV; Middlesex

Individual Profiles
On Each Of
THE HEALTH CARE 500

1Life Healthcare Inc

www.1life.com

NAIC Code: 511210D

TYPES OF BUSINESS:

Computer Software, Healthcare and Biotechnology

BRANDS/DIVISIONS/AFFILIATES:

One Medical Group

GROWTH PLANS/SPECIAL FEATURES:

1Life Healthcare, Inc. is a healthcare technology and management services company affiliated with One Medical Group, which develops enhanced digital health tools and other services. 1Life provides a proprietary technology platform which supports electronic management of health records, online scheduling and patient billing, along with other administrative services. The company's mobile application and technology services includes video visit technology, digital dermatology and nutritional coaching apps. 1Life is headquartered in San Francisco, California, USA.

CONTACTS: *Note: Officers with more than one job title may be intentionally listed here more than once.*

Amir Dan Rubin, CEO
Jenni Vargas, Chief Strategy Officer
Garrick Bernstein, CFO
Doug Sweeny, CMO
Christine Morehead, Chief People Officer
Kimber Lockhart, CTO
Tom X. Lee, Chmn.

FINANCIAL DATA: *Note: Data for latest year may not have been available at press time.*

In U.S. $	2017	2016	2015	2014	2013	2012
Revenue						
R&D Expense						
Operating Income						
Operating Margin %						
SGA Expense						
Net Income						
Operating Cash Flow						
Capital Expenditure						
EBITDA						
Return on Assets %						
Return on Equity %						
Debt to Equity						

CONTACT INFORMATION:

Phone: 415-658-6792 Fax:
Toll-Free:
Address: 130 Sutter St., Fl. 2, San Francisco, CA 94104 United States

STOCK TICKER/OTHER:

Stock Ticker: Private Exchange:
Employees: Fiscal Year Ends:
Parent Company:

SALARIES/BONUSES:

Top Exec. Salary: $ Bonus: $
Second Exec. Salary: $ Bonus: $

OTHER THOUGHTS:

Estimated Female Officers or Directors:
Hot Spot for Advancement for Women/Minorities:

21st Century Oncology Holdings Inc

www.21co.com

NAIC Code: 621,511

TYPES OF BUSINESS:

Integrated Cancer Care Services

BRANDS/DIVISIONS/AFFILIATES:

21st Century Oncology

CONTACTS:
Note: Officers with more than one job title may be intentionally listed here more than once.

Kimberly J. Commins-Tzoumakas, CEO
Odette Bolano, COO
Blake Howard, Interim CFO
Kristin Meyer, VP-Human Resources
Gabe de Paz, Interim CIO

GROWTH PLANS/SPECIAL FEATURES:

21st Century Oncology is a global, physician-led provider of integrated cancer care services. The company's physicians provide comprehensive, academic-quality, cost-effective, coordinated care for cancer patients in personal and convenient community settings. 21st Century operates the largest integrated network of cancer treatment centers and affiliated physicians in the world, which is comprised of more than 947 community-based physicians in the fields of radiation oncology; medical oncology; breast, colorectal, gynecological and general surgery; as well as ear/nose/throat and urology. Headquartered in Florida, the firm operates 167 treatment centers, including 131 centers located in 16 U.S. In addition, the firm also operates 36 centers located in seven countries within Latin America. The company filed for bankruptcy protection in the spring of 2017. In January 2018, 21st Century emerged from Chapter 11 under new owners, including certain funds and accounts managed by Beach Point Capital Management LP; Governors Lane, LP; J.P. Morgan Investment Management, Inc.; Oaktree Capital Management, LP; Roystone Capital Management LP; and HPS Investment Partners LLC.

FINANCIAL DATA:
Note: Data for latest year may not have been available at press time.

In U.S. $	2017	2016	2015	2014	2013	2012
Revenue	1,125,000,000	1,050,000,000	1,079,227,000	1,026,422,016	736,515,968	693,950,976
R&D Expense						
Operating Income						
Operating Margin %						
SGA Expense						
Net Income			-126,842,000	-349,249,984	-80,214,000	-154,208,000
Operating Cash Flow						
Capital Expenditure						
EBITDA						
Return on Assets %						
Return on Equity %						
Debt to Equity						

CONTACT INFORMATION:

Phone: 239 931-7275 Fax:
Toll-Free:
Address: 2270 Colonial Blvd., Fort Myers, FL 33907 United States

STOCK TICKER/OTHER:

Stock Ticker: Private
Employees: 3,930
Parent Company:
Exchange:
Fiscal Year Ends: 12/31

SALARIES/BONUSES:

Top Exec. Salary: $ Bonus: $
Second Exec. Salary: $ Bonus: $

OTHER THOUGHTS:

Estimated Female Officers or Directors:
Hot Spot for Advancement for Women/Minorities:

3M Company

www.3m.com

NAIC Code: 339,100

TYPES OF BUSINESS:

Health Care Products
Specialty Materials & Textiles
Industrial Products
Safety, Security & Protection Products
Display & Graphics Products
Consumer & Office Products
Electronics & Communications Products
Fuel Cell Technology

BRANDS/DIVISIONS/AFFILIATES:

3M Purification Inc
Thinsulate
Scotch
Command
Filtrete
Scott Safety

CONTACTS: *Note: Officers with more than one job title may be intentionally listed here more than once.*

Inge Thulin, Chairman of the Board
Kristen Ludgate, Senior VP, Divisional
Ippocratis Vrohidis, Chief Accounting Officer
John Banovetz, Chief Technology Officer
Michael Roman, COO
James Bauman, Executive VP, Divisional
Ashish Khandpur, Executive VP, Divisional
Joaquin Delgado, Executive VP, Divisional
Julie Bushman, Executive VP, Divisional
Michael Vale, Executive VP, Divisional
Frank Little, Executive VP, Divisional
Hak Shin, Executive VP
Ivan Fong, General Counsel
Mojdeh Poul, General Manager, Subsidiary
Paul Keel, Senior VP, Divisional
Marlene McGrath, Senior VP, Divisional
Jon Lindekugel, Senior VP, Divisional

GROWTH PLANS/SPECIAL FEATURES:

3M Company is involved in the research, manufacturing and marketing of a variety of products. Its operations are organized in five segments: industrial, safety and graphics, electronics and energy, healthcare and consumer. The industrial segment serves the automotive, electronics, appliance, paper, printing, food, beverage and construction markets. Its major industrial products include Thinsulate acoustic insulation and 3M paint finishing and detail products. Also, 3M Purification, Inc. provides a line of filtration products. The safety and graphics segment serves a range of markets, with major product offerings including personal protection, traffic safety, border and civil security solutions, commercial graphics sheeting, architectural surface and lighting solutions, cleaning products and roofing granules for asphalt shingles. The electronics and energy segment serves customers with telecommunications networks, electrical products, power generation and distribution and infrastructure protection. Major products include LCD computers and televisions, hand-held mobile devices, notebook PCs and automotive displays. The healthcare segment serves medical clinics, hospitals, pharmaceuticals, dental and orthodontic practitioners, health information systems and food manufacturing and testing. Products include medical and surgical supplies, skin health, infection prevention, inhalation and transdermal drug delivery systems. The consumer segment serves markets such as consumer retail, office retail, home improvement and building maintenance. Major products include the Scotch tape, Command adhesive and Filtrete filtration family lines of products. During 2017, the firm sold its safety prescription eyewear business, its identity management business, its tolling and automated license/number plate recognition business and its electronic monitoring business. It acquired Scott Safety, a manufacturer of self-contained breathing apparatus systems, gas and flame detection instruments and other safety devices.

The company offers employees medical and dental insurance, domestic partner benefits, tuition reimbursement, flexible spending accounts, disability coverage, 401(k) and adoption assistance.

FINANCIAL DATA: *Note: Data for latest year may not have been available at press time.*

In U.S. $	2017	2016	2015	2014	2013	2012
Revenue	31,657,000,000	30,109,000,000	30,274,000,000	31,821,000,000	30,871,000,000	29,904,000,000
R&D Expense	1,850,000,000	1,735,000,000	1,763,000,000	1,770,000,000	1,715,000,000	1,634,000,000
Operating Income	7,234,000,000	7,223,000,000	6,946,000,000	7,135,000,000	6,666,000,000	6,483,000,000
Operating Margin %	22.85%	23.98%	22.94%	22.42%	21.59%	21.67%
SGA Expense	6,572,000,000	6,111,000,000	6,182,000,000	6,469,000,000	6,384,000,000	6,102,000,000
Net Income	4,858,000,000	5,050,000,000	4,833,000,000	4,956,000,000	4,659,000,000	4,444,000,000
Operating Cash Flow	6,240,000,000	6,662,000,000	6,420,000,000	6,626,000,000	5,817,000,000	5,300,000,000
Capital Expenditure	1,373,000,000	1,420,000,000	1,461,000,000	1,493,000,000	1,665,000,000	1,484,000,000
EBITDA	9,414,000,000	8,726,000,000	8,407,000,000	8,576,000,000	8,078,000,000	7,810,000,000
Return on Assets %	13.70%	15.39%	15.10%	15.29%	13.81%	13.57%
Return on Equity %	44.44%	45.89%	38.94%	32.38%	26.56%	26.93%
Debt to Equity	1.05	1.04	0.75	0.51	0.25	0.28

CONTACT INFORMATION:

Phone: 651 733-1110 Fax: 651 733-9973
Toll-Free: 800-364-3577
Address: 3M Center, St. Paul, MN 55144 United States

STOCK TICKER/OTHER:

Stock Ticker: MMM Exchange: NYS
Employees: 91,584 Fiscal Year Ends: 12/31
Parent Company:

SALARIES/BONUSES:

Top Exec. Salary: $1,526,595 Bonus: $
Second Exec. Salary: $839,575 Bonus: $

OTHER THOUGHTS:

Estimated Female Officers or Directors: 7
Hot Spot for Advancement for Women/Minorities: Y

3SBio Inc

www.3sbio.com

NAIC Code: 325,412

TYPES OF BUSINESS:

Biopharmaceutical Manufacturing & Design
Anemia Treatments
Cancer Treatments
Exporting Biopharmaceuticals

BRANDS/DIVISIONS/AFFILIATES:

TPIAO
Ruisiyi
Wanwei
Etanercept
SEPO
EPIAO
Mandi
BYETTA

CONTACTS: *Note: Officers with more than one job title may be intentionally listed here more than once.*

Jing Lou, CEO
Xiao Weihong, COO
Bo Tan, CFO
Dongmei Su, VP-R&D
Ke Li, Corp. Sec.
Jing Lou, Chmn.

GROWTH PLANS/SPECIAL FEATURES:

3SBio, Inc. is a biotechnology company that researches, develops, manufactures and markets biopharmaceutical products, primarily in China. The company's products are divided into five groups: oncology, autoimmunity, nephrology, dermatology and metabolism. Oncology is comprised of five products, including: TPIAO, for the treatment of certain types of thrombocytopenia, a deficiency of platelets; Ruisiyi (anastrozole), for advanced breast cancer; Wanwei (azasetron hydrochloride) for vomiting cuased by cytotoxic chemotherapy; Intefen, for lymphatic or hematopoietic malignancies and viral infections, hepatitis B, chronic hepatitis C and condyloma acuminate; and Inleusin, for renal cell carcinoma, melanoma, thoracic fluid build-up caused by cancer and tuberculosis. Autoimmunity has one product, Etanercept, to control the inflammation and relieve rheumatic diseases such as rheumatoid arthritis, ankylosing spondylitis, morning stiffness, pain, swelling, low back pain and skin lesions of psoriasis. Nephrology offers four products, including: SEPO, for anemia associated with chronic kidney disease and more; EPIAO, for anemia caused by chronic kidney disease, chemotherapy and more; SPARIN, for prophylaxis and treatment of deep vein thrombosis, and prevention of clotting during hemodialysis; and Jiannipai, for prevention of acute rejection after renal transplantation. Dermatology offers one product, Mandi (minoxidil), for male-pattern alopecia and alopecia areata, a non-prescription drug for hair loss. Last, metabolism offers two products, including: BYETTA (exenatide injection), to improve the glycemic control in patients with type 2 diabetes; and Humulin (recombinant insulin) for the treatment of diabetes. 3SBio's manufacturing bases are located in Shenyang, Shanghai, Shenzhen and Hangzhou, China, as well as in Italy Como.

FINANCIAL DATA: *Note: Data for latest year may not have been available at press time.*

In U.S. $	2017	2016	2015	2014	2013	2012
Revenue	585,649,216	438,694,080	262,393,504	177,349,904	125,000,000	105,066,808
R&D Expense						
Operating Income						
Operating Margin %						
SGA Expense						
Net Income	146,695,472	111,750,192	82,535,600	45,751,208		
Operating Cash Flow						
Capital Expenditure						
EBITDA						
Return on Assets %						
Return on Equity %						
Debt to Equity						

CONTACT INFORMATION:

Phone: 86 2425811820 Fax:
Toll-Free:
Address: Shenyang Development Zone, No. 3 A1, Rd. 10, Shenyang, Liaoning 110027 China

STOCK TICKER/OTHER:

Stock Ticker: Private
Employees: 4,051
Parent Company: Decade Sunshine Limited
Exchange:
Fiscal Year Ends: 12/31

SALARIES/BONUSES:

Top Exec. Salary: $ Bonus: $
Second Exec. Salary: $ Bonus: $

OTHER THOUGHTS:

Estimated Female Officers or Directors: 1
Hot Spot for Advancement for Women/Minorities: Y

AAC Holdings Inc

www.americanaddictioncenters.com

NAIC Code: 623,220

TYPES OF BUSINESS:

Substance Abuse Facilities
Substance Abuse Treatment

BRANDS/DIVISIONS/AFFILIATES:

American Addiction Centers

CONTACTS:

Note: Officers with more than one job title may be intentionally listed here more than once.

Michael Cartwright, CEO
Andrew McWilliams, CFO
Michael Nanko, COO
Kathryn Phillips, General Counsel
Thomas Doub, Other Executive Officer
Michael Blackburn, Senior VP, Divisional

GROWTH PLANS/SPECIAL FEATURES:

AAC Holdings, Inc. provides inpatient and outpatient substance use treatment services for individuals with drug addiction, alcohol addiction and co-occurring mental/behavioral health issues. AAC stands for American Addiction Centers, at which perform clinical diagnostic laboratory services and provide physician services to its clients. As of December 2017, AAC operated nine residential substance abuse treatment facilities, comprising 939 residential beds (including 630 licensed detoxification beds), 19 standalone outpatient centers and five sober living facilities. These facilities are located in California, Florida, Louisiana, Mississippi, New Jersey, Nevada, Rhode Island and Texas. In addition, through AAC's websites Rehabs.com and Recovery.org, the firm serves families and individuals struggling with addiction and seeking treatment options through comprehensive online directories of treatment providers, treatment provider reviews, forums and professional communities. AAC also provides online marketing solutions to other treatment providers such as enhanced facility profiles, audience targeting, lead generation and tools for digital reputation management.

FINANCIAL DATA:

Note: Data for latest year may not have been available at press time.

In U.S. $	2017	2016	2015	2014	2013	2012
Revenue	317,641,000	279,770,000	212,261,000	132,968,000	115,741,000	66,035,000
R&D Expense						
Operating Income	17,026,000	3,347,000	20,008,000	12,032,000	6,927,000	3,239,000
Operating Margin %	5.36%	1.19%	9.42%	9.04%	5.98%	4.90%
SGA Expense	205,888,000	207,625,000	143,595,000	91,365,000	83,246,000	51,780,000
Net Income	-20,579,000	-589,000	11,174,000	7,548,000	786,000	1,504,000
Operating Cash Flow	19,292,000	143,000	6,193,000	8,038,000	3,443,000	69,000
Capital Expenditure	33,041,000	37,304,000	52,065,000	15,584,000	12,975,000	6,264,000
EBITDA	38,530,000	18,900,000	24,565,000	15,455,000	6,500,000	4,515,000
Return on Assets %	-5.06%	-.16%	4.54%	6.02%	2.64%	2.80%
Return on Equity %	-13.02%	-.38%	8.77%	12.97%	39.40%	170.71%
Debt to Equity	1.46	1.08	0.99	0.24	3.31	15.25

CONTACT INFORMATION:

Phone: 615 732-1231 Fax:
Toll-Free:
Address: 200 Powell Pl., Brentwood, TN 37027 United States

STOCK TICKER/OTHER:

Stock Ticker: AAC Exchange: NYS
Employees: 2,100 Fiscal Year Ends: 12/31
Parent Company:

SALARIES/BONUSES:

Top Exec. Salary: $557,500 Bonus: $
Second Exec. Salary: $379,167 Bonus: $159,750

OTHER THOUGHTS:

Estimated Female Officers or Directors:
Hot Spot for Advancement for Women/Minorities:

Abbott Laboratories

www.abbott.com

NAIC Code: 325,412

TYPES OF BUSINESS:

Nutritional Products Manufacturing
Immunoassays
Diagnostics
Consumer Health Products
Medical & Surgical Devices
Generic Pharmaceutical Products
LASIK Devices

BRANDS/DIVISIONS/AFFILIATES:

Zone Perfect
EAS
Alere Inc

CONTACTS: *Note: Officers with more than one job title may be intentionally listed here more than once.*

Miles White, CEO
Sean Shrimpton, Senior VP, Divisional
Brian Yoor, CFO
Robert Funck, Chief Accounting Officer
Stephen Fussell, Executive VP, Divisional
John Capek, Executive VP, Divisional
Robert Ford, Executive VP, Divisional
Daniel Salvadori, Executive VP, Divisional
Brian Blaser, Executive VP, Divisional
Hubert Allen, Executive VP
Roger Bird, Senior VP, Divisional
Jaime Contreras, Senior VP, Divisional
Sharon Bracken, Senior VP, Divisional
Charles Brynelsen, Senior VP, Divisional
Michael Pederson, Senior VP, Divisional

GROWTH PLANS/SPECIAL FEATURES:

Abbott Laboratories develops, manufactures and sells healthcare products and technologies, marketed in over 150 countries. The firm operates in four segments: established pharmaceutical, diagnostics, nutrition and cardiovascular and neuromodulation products. The established pharmaceutical segment includes a broad line of branded generic pharmaceuticals manufactured worldwide and marketed and sold outside the U.S. in emerging markets. These products are primarily sold directly to wholesalers, distributors, government agencies, healthcare facilities, pharmacies and independent retailers from Abbott-owned distribution centers and public warehouses. This segment's principal therapeutic offerings include gastroenterology, women's health, cardiovascular, metabolic, pain, central nervous system, respiratory and vaccination products. The diagnostics segment includes a line of diagnostic systems and tests manufactured, marketed and sold worldwide. These products are primarily marketed and sold directly to blood banks, hospitals, commercial laboratories, clinics, physicians' offices, government agencies, alternate care testing sites and plasma protein therapeutic companies from Abbot-owned distribution centers, public warehouses and third-party distributors. This segment's products include: core laboratory systems in the areas of immunoassay, clinical chemistry, hematology and transfusions; molecular diagnostics systems; point of care systems; rapid diagnostic systems; and informatics and automation solutions for use in laboratories. The nutrition segment offers a line of pediatric and adult nutritional products manufactured, marketed and sold worldwide. This segment's products include: various forms of prepared infant formula and follow-on formula; adult and other pediatric nutritional products; nutritional products used in enteral feeding in healthcare institutions; and Zone Perfect and EAS family of nutritional food brands. In October 2017, Abbott acquired Alere, Inc., a global manufacturer of rapid point-of-care diagnostic tests.

Abbott offers comprehensive insurance benefits and employee assistance programs.

FINANCIAL DATA: *Note: Data for latest year may not have been available at press time.*

In U.S. $	2017	2016	2015	2014	2013	2012
Revenue	27,390,000,000	20,853,000,000	20,405,000,000	20,247,000,000	21,848,000,000	39,873,910,000
R&D Expense	2,235,000,000	1,422,000,000	1,405,000,000	1,345,000,000	1,452,000,000	4,610,182,000
Operating Income	1,726,000,000	3,185,000,000	2,867,000,000	2,599,000,000	2,629,000,000	8,084,515,000
Operating Margin %	6.30%	15.27%	14.05%	12.83%	12.03%	20.27%
SGA Expense	9,117,000,000	6,672,000,000	6,785,000,000	6,530,000,000	6,936,000,000	12,059,500,000
Net Income	477,000,000	1,400,000,000	4,423,000,000	2,284,000,000	2,576,000,000	5,962,920,000
Operating Cash Flow	5,570,000,000	3,203,000,000	2,966,000,000	3,675,000,000	3,324,000,000	9,314,401,000
Capital Expenditure	1,135,000,000	1,121,000,000	1,110,000,000	1,077,000,000	1,145,000,000	1,795,289,000
EBITDA	6,156,000,000	3,197,000,000	4,818,000,000	4,216,000,000	4,397,000,000	9,638,224,000
Return on Assets %	.74%	2.98%	10.71%	5.42%	4.67%	9.35%
Return on Equity %	1.85%	6.70%	20.69%	9.78%	9.92%	23.31%
Debt to Equity	0.88	1.00	0.27	0.15	0.13	0.67

CONTACT INFORMATION:

Phone: 847 937-6100 Fax: 847 937-1511
Toll-Free:
Address: 100 Abbott Park Rd., Abbott Park, IL 60064-6400 United States

STOCK TICKER/OTHER:

Stock Ticker: ABT
Employees: 75,000
Parent Company:
Exchange: NYS
Fiscal Year Ends: 12/31

SALARIES/BONUSES:

Top Exec. Salary: $644,231 Bonus: $5,000,000
Second Exec. Salary: $1,900,000 Bonus: $

OTHER THOUGHTS:

Estimated Female Officers or Directors: 5
Hot Spot for Advancement for Women/Minorities: Y

Abiomed Inc

NAIC Code: 339,100

www.abiomed.com

TYPES OF BUSINESS:

Equipment-Cardiac Assistance
Heart Replacement Technology

BRANDS/DIVISIONS/AFFILIATES:

AbioCor
Impella
BVS 5000
AB5000
Automated Impella Console

CONTACTS: *Note: Officers with more than one job title may be intentionally listed here more than once.*

Michael Minogue, CEO
Ian McLeod, CFO
Todd Trapp, CFO
David Weber, COO
Michael Howley, General Manager, Divisional
Andrew Greenfield, General Manager, Divisional
William Bolt, Senior VP, Divisional

GROWTH PLANS/SPECIAL FEATURES:

Abiomed, Inc. is a global provider of mechanical circulatory support devices, offering a continuum of care in heart support and recovery. The company manufactures advanced medical technologies to assist heart patients and is a leading provider of ventricle assist devices. Abiomed previously manufactured the AbioCor self-contained replacement heart. The firm suspended testing and sales of AbioCor in 2009. Abiomed's surgery suite includes the Impella platforms of catheter-based pumps, intra-aortic balloons (IABs), the BVS 5000 blood pump and the AB5000 ventricular assist devices (VADs). These are designed to support acute heart failure patients in need of more blood flow and longer duration of support for acute myocardial infarction (AMI), cardiogenic shock post-AMI and myocarditis. The IAB is inserted percutaneously into a patient's descending aorta and inflates and deflates in counter pulsation to the patient's heart rhythm. The BVS 5000 is widely used as a mechanical cardiac device in patients with recoverable hearts and provides short-term support without additional surgery. The AB5000 is another temporary support device that allows the patient ease of use and transportability. The Automated Impella Console is an automated control interface designed to support its Impella systems. The controller displays catheter position information, controls catheter performance and monitors for alarms. In early-2018, Abiomed received an expanded US FDA pre-market approval for its Impella 2.5, Impella CP, Impella 5.0 and Impella LD heart pumps to provide treatment for heart failure associated with cardiomyopathy leading to cardiogenic shock; and received the same type of approval for the Impella 2.5 and Impella CP heart pumps during elective urgent high-risk percutaneous coronary intervention procedures.

The firm offers employees medical and dental insurance, life and travel insurance, disability coverage; 401(k) and employee stock purchase plans; tuition reimbursement and employee assistance programs; discounted car and homeowners insurance; and a 529 college savings plan.

FINANCIAL DATA: *Note: Data for latest year may not have been available at press time.*

In U.S. $	2017	2016	2015	2014	2013	2012
Revenue	445,304,000	329,543,000	230,311,000	183,643,000	158,124,000	
R&D Expense	66,386,000	49,759,000	35,973,000	30,707,000	25,647,000	
Operating Income	90,138,000	65,104,000	28,666,000	8,363,000	16,543,000	
Operating Margin %	20.24%	19.75%	12.44%	4.55%	10.46%	
SGA Expense	218,153,000	164,261,000	125,727,000	107,251,000	84,227,000	
Net Income	52,116,000	38,147,000	113,688,000	7,351,000	15,014,000	
Operating Cash Flow	115,116,000	76,795,000	43,290,000	23,466,000	26,399,000	
Capital Expenditure	50,415,000	15,624,000	5,188,000	2,761,000	2,836,000	
EBITDA	96,340,000	68,381,000	31,436,000	10,871,000	19,266,000	
Return on Assets %	10.69%	10.00%	41.81%	3.91%	9.27%	
Return on Equity %	12.69%	11.55%	49.43%	4.81%	11.40%	
Debt to Equity	0.03					

CONTACT INFORMATION:

Phone: 978 646-1400 Fax: 978 777-8411
Toll-Free:
Address: 22 Cherry Hill Dr., Danvers, MA 01923 United States

STOCK TICKER/OTHER:

Stock Ticker: ABMD Exchange: NAS
Employees: 908 Fiscal Year Ends: 02/28
Parent Company:

SALARIES/BONUSES:

Top Exec. Salary: $717,515 Bonus: $
Second Exec. Salary: $413,225 Bonus: $

OTHER THOUGHTS:

Estimated Female Officers or Directors: 1
Hot Spot for Advancement for Women/Minorities:

Acadia Healthcare Company Inc

www.acadiahealthcare.com

NAIC Code: 622,210

TYPES OF BUSINESS:

Psychiatric and Substance Abuse Hospitals
Residential Treatment Facilities
Behavioral Health Care Centers

BRANDS/DIVISIONS/AFFILIATES:

Partnerships in Care (PiC)

CONTACTS: *Note: Officers with more than one job title may be intentionally listed here more than once.*

David Duckworth, CFO
Joey Jacobs, Chairman of the Board
Ronald Fincher, COO
Christopher Howard, Executive VP
Brent Turner, President
Bruce Shear, Vice Chairman
Randall Goldberg, Vice President, Divisional

GROWTH PLANS/SPECIAL FEATURES:

Acadia Healthcare Company, Inc. provides inpatient behavioral health care services via 582 facilities with more than 17,800 licensed beds in 39 U.S. states, the U.K. and Puerto Rico. Acadia provides psychiatric and chemical dependency services in a variety of settings, including psychiatric hospitals, residential treatment centers, outpatient clinics and therapeutic school-based programs. Treatment specializes in helping children, teenagers and adults suffering from mental health disorders and/or alcohol and drug addiction. Acadia operates through four types of facilities: acute inpatient psychiatric facilities, residential treatment centers, outpatient community-based services and specialty. Acute inpatient psychiatric facilities help stabilize patients that are either a threat to themselves or to others, and have 24-hour observation, daily intervention and residential treatment centers. Residential treatment centers treat patients with behavioral disorders in a non-hospital setting, and balance therapy activities with social, academic and other activities. Certain residential treatment centers provide group home and therapeutic foster care programs. Outpatient community-based services are usually divided between children and adolescents (7-18 years of age) and young children (three months to six years old). Community-based programs provide therapeutic treatment to minors who have clinically-defined emotional, psychiatric or chemical dependency disorders while enabling the youth to remain at home and within their community. Specialty treatment facilities include residential recovery facilities, eating disorder facilities and comprehensive treatment centers (CTCs) for addictive disorders, co-occurring mental disorders and detoxification. Acadia's U.K. operations work under the Partnerships in Care (PiC) name.

FINANCIAL DATA: *Note: Data for latest year may not have been available at press time.*

In U.S. $	2017	2016	2015	2014	2013	2012
Revenue	2,836,316,000	2,810,914,000	1,794,492,000	1,004,601,000	713,408,000	407,461,000
R&D Expense						
Operating Income	413,615,000	396,819,000	284,239,000	159,113,000	115,845,000	62,598,000
Operating Margin %	14.58%	14.11%	15.83%	15.83%	16.23%	15.36%
SGA Expense	1,947,864,000	1,966,436,000	1,239,957,000	702,167,000	499,901,000	294,104,000
Net Income	199,835,000	6,143,000	112,554,000	83,040,000	42,579,000	20,403,000
Operating Cash Flow	399,577,000	361,478,000	240,403,000	115,286,000	65,562,000	33,898,000
Capital Expenditure	315,234,000	348,229,000	302,669,000	136,421,000	77,033,000	80,754,000
EBITDA	556,625,000	531,922,000	347,789,000	191,780,000	132,935,000	70,580,000
Return on Assets %	3.21%	.11%	3.46%	4.81%	3.85%	2.92%
Return on Equity %	8.43%	.31%	8.77%	12.19%	9.32%	7.71%
Debt to Equity	1.24	1.50	1.30	1.21	1.25	1.07

CONTACT INFORMATION:

Phone: 615 861-6000 Fax: 615 261-9685
Toll-Free:
Address: 6100 Tower Circle, Ste. 1000, Franklin, TN 37067 United States

STOCK TICKER/OTHER:

Stock Ticker: ACHC
Exchange: NAS
Employees: 40,400
Fiscal Year Ends: 12/31
Parent Company:

SALARIES/BONUSES:

Top Exec. Salary: $1,124,500 Bonus: $
Second Exec. Salary: $676,000 Bonus: $

OTHER THOUGHTS:

Estimated Female Officers or Directors:
Hot Spot for Advancement for Women/Minorities:

Accredo Health Group Inc

www.accredo.com

NAIC Code: 446,110

TYPES OF BUSINESS:

Drug Distribution-Specialty Pharmacy
Reimbursement Assistance Services

BRANDS/DIVISIONS/AFFILIATES:

Express Scripts Inc
Therapeutic Resource Centers

CONTACTS: *Note: Officers with more than one job title may be intentionally listed here more than once.*

Tim Wentworth, CEP
Michael A. James, Sr. VP-Commercial Strategy
Sharon Harris, Dir.-HR & Finance Systems
Michael A. James, Sr. VP-Oper.
George Paz, Chmn. - Express Scripts, Inc.

GROWTH PLANS/SPECIAL FEATURES:

Accredo Health Group, Inc., a wholly-owned subsidiary of Express Scripts, Inc., provides specialty pharmacy and related services to treat certain chronic diseases. Through its Therapeutic Resource Centers (TRC), the company works with patients in a single disease state offering tailored and individualized counseling and education. Through the TRC, the firm provides patients access to 500 specialty-trained pharmacists on the phone; access o 550 specialty-trained infusion nurses that meet patients face-to-face in their homes; nutrition support for oncology; therapy management programs to protect patient health and safety; coordination of care between the medical benefit, pharmacy benefit and physicians; and safe, prompt delivery of medications, including training on administration of the medication. Specialized pharmacy care is provided for patients with chronic illnesses such as cancer, growth hormone deficiency, hemophilia and other bleeding disorders, hepatitis C, HIV/AIDS, infertility, multiple sclerosis, psoriasis, pulmonary arterial hypertension/fibrosis/arthritis and respiratory syncytial virus (RSV). Additionally, Accredo provides services including the collection of medication use and patient compliance information; patient education and monitoring; reimbursement expertise; and overnight, temperature-controlled drug delivery. Accredo also offers comprehensive clinical and reimbursement services for healthcare professionals; and collaborates with pharmaceutical and biotech companies to provide high-touch services to patients based on their needs and therapy.

The company offers employees paid time off, a health and wellness package, an employee stock purchase program and a 401(k) savings plan with company contributions.

FINANCIAL DATA: *Note: Data for latest year may not have been available at press time.*

In U.S. $	2017	2016	2015	2014	2013	2012
Revenue						
R&D Expense						
Operating Income						
Operating Margin %						
SGA Expense						
Net Income						
Operating Cash Flow						
Capital Expenditure						
EBITDA						
Return on Assets %						
Return on Equity %						
Debt to Equity						

CONTACT INFORMATION:

Phone: 901-385-3688 Fax: 901-385-3689
Toll-Free: 877-222-7336
Address: 1640 Century Center Pkwy., Memphis, TN 38134 United States

STOCK TICKER/OTHER:

Stock Ticker: Subsidiary
Exchange:
Employees: 5,000
Fiscal Year Ends: 12/31
Parent Company: Express Scripts Inc

SALARIES/BONUSES:

Top Exec. Salary: $ Bonus: $
Second Exec. Salary: $ Bonus: $

OTHER THOUGHTS:

Estimated Female Officers or Directors: 1
Hot Spot for Advancement for Women/Minorities:

Accuray Inc

www.accuray.com

NAIC Code: 334,510

TYPES OF BUSINESS:

Surgical and Medical Instrument Manufacturing

BRANDS/DIVISIONS/AFFILIATES:

CyberKnife
TomoTherapy
Radixact
TomoHelical
TomoDirect
TomoEdge

CONTACTS: *Note: Officers with more than one job title may be intentionally listed here more than once.*

Joshua Levine, CEO
Kevin Waters, CFO
Louis Lavigne, Chairman of the Board
Shigeyuki Hamamatsu, Chief Accounting Officer
Elizabeth Davila, Director
Alaleh Nouri, General Counsel
Lionel Hadjadjeba, Other Executive Officer
Andy Kirkpatrick, Senior VP, Divisional

GROWTH PLANS/SPECIAL FEATURES:

Accuray, Inc. develops a commercially available intelligent robotic radiosurgery system, the CyberKnife system, designed to treat solid tumors anywhere in the body as an alternative to traditional surgery. CyberKnife represents the next generation of radiosurgery systems, combining continuous image-guidance technology with a compact linear accelerator (linac) which can move in three dimensions according to a patient's treatment plan. Linac uses microwaves to accelerate electrons to create high-energy X-ray beams to destroy the tumor. This combination extends the benefits of radiosurgery to the treatment of tumors anywhere in the body including the head and neck. The CyberKnife system autonomously tracks, detects and corrects tumor and patient movement in real-time during the procedure, enabling delivery of precise, high dose radiation typically with sub-millimeter accuracy. The CyberKnife procedure requires no anesthesia, can be performed on an outpatient basis and allows for the treatment of patients who otherwise would not have been treated with radiation or who may not have been good candidates for surgery. The firm also offers the TomoTherapy and intensity modulated radiation therapy (IMRT) systems, which offer daily imaging and cancer treatment abilities through CT imaging optimized beamlet-based delivery. The latest generation TomoTherapy System is the Radixact that includes the following options: TomoHelical, TomoDirect and TomoEdge dynamic jaws. The CyberKnife and TomoTherapy systems are sold in over 92 countries.

Employees of the firm receive benefits including medical, dental, vision, life, AD&D and disability coverage; a flexible spending account; travel assistance; an employee assistance program; a wellness program; education assistance; a 401(k); and paid time off.

FINANCIAL DATA: *Note: Data for latest year may not have been available at press time.*

In U.S. $	2017	2016	2015	2014	2013	2012
Revenue	383,414,000	398,800,000	379,801,000	369,419,000	315,974,000	
R&D Expense	49,921,000	56,652,000	55,752,000	53,724,000	66,197,000	
Operating Income	-9,823,000	-4,873,000	-19,169,000	-18,144,000	-80,655,000	
Operating Margin %	-2.56%	-1.22%	-5.04%	-4.91%	-25.52%	
SGA Expense	101,243,000	106,934,000	108,819,000	107,220,000	112,098,000	
Net Income	-29,579,000	-25,504,000	-40,209,000	-35,448,000	-103,219,000	
Operating Cash Flow	-380,000	33,538,000	-16,733,000	346,000	-66,177,000	
Capital Expenditure	5,364,000	8,066,000	10,445,000	11,931,000	15,358,000	
EBITDA	6,804,000	13,423,000	324,000	2,420,000	-57,846,000	
Return on Assets %	-6.75%	-5.43%	-8.33%	-7.30%	-21.75%	
Return on Equity %	-55.70%	-37.66%	-46.13%	-34.51%	-68.25%	
Debt to Equity	1.10	2.85	2.67	1.98	1.86	

CONTACT INFORMATION:

Phone: 408 716-4600 Fax: 408 716-4601
Toll-Free:
Address: 1310 Chesapeake Terrace, Sunnyvale, CA 94089 United States

STOCK TICKER/OTHER:

Stock Ticker: ARAY
Exchange: NAS
Employees: 944
Fiscal Year Ends: 06/30
Parent Company:

SALARIES/BONUSES:

Top Exec. Salary: $707,216 Bonus: $
Second Exec. Salary: $551,816 Bonus: $

OTHER THOUGHTS:

Estimated Female Officers or Directors: 3
Hot Spot for Advancement for Women/Minorities: Y

Acelity LP Inc

NAIC Code: 339,100

www.acelity.com/home

TYPES OF BUSINESS:

Equipment-Specialized Mattresses & Beds
Kinetic Therapy Products
Therapeutic Support Surfaces
Wound Closure Devices
Circulatory Devices

BRANDS/DIVISIONS/AFFILIATES:

Kinetic Concepts Inc
Systagenix Wound Management Ltd
Acelity
Crawford Healthcare

CONTACTS: *Note: Officers with more than one job title may be intentionally listed here more than once.*

R. Andrew Eckert, CEO
Joseph F. Woody, Pres.
Tracy Jokinen, CFO
Gaurav Agarwal, Chief Commercial Officer

GROWTH PLANS/SPECIAL FEATURES:

Acelity LP, Inc. is a global medical technology company which designs, develops, manufactures and markets advanced wound therapeutics and regenerative medicine. Acelity combines the strengths of two companies: Kinetic Concepts, Inc. and Systagenix Wound Management Ltd. Available in more than 90 countries, Acelity products include wound management solutions, including treatments for diabetic foot ulcers, pressure ulcers, venous leg ulcers, acute and traumatic wounds and infected wounds; plastic and reconstructive surgery solutions, including technologies used in a wide range of reconstructive procedures such as breast reconstruction, ear/nose/throat surgery, face/head/neck surgery, orthopedic soft tissue repair, skin grafting, dental gum repair and pelvic floor reconstruction; abdominal surgery solutions, such as abdominal wall reconstruction and open abdomen management procedures; incision management solutions, such as advanced negative pressure therapies and post-operative dressings; epidermal harvesting solutions, which produces autologous skin grafts with minimal patient discomfort; and animal health solutions, such as granulation tissue formation therapies and pressure solutions. In June 2018, the firm acquired Crawford Healthcare, an advanced would care and dermatology company, and all its assets.

FINANCIAL DATA: *Note: Data for latest year may not have been available at press time.*

In U.S. $	2017	2016	2015	2014	2013	2012
Revenue	1,995,000,000	1,900,000,000	1,867,173,000	1,866,339,000	1,732,901,000	1,729,503,000
R&D Expense						
Operating Income						
Operating Margin %						
SGA Expense						
Net Income			-47,656,000	-230,473,000	-558,658,000	-141,417,000
Operating Cash Flow						
Capital Expenditure						
EBITDA						
Return on Assets %						
Return on Equity %						
Debt to Equity						

CONTACT INFORMATION:

Phone: 210 524-9000 Fax: 210-255-6998
Toll-Free: 800-275-4524
Address: 12930 Interstate Hwy. 10 W., San Antonio, TX 78249 United States

STOCK TICKER/OTHER:

Stock Ticker: Private
Employees: 5,000
Parent Company:
Exchange:
Fiscal Year Ends: 12/31

SALARIES/BONUSES:

Top Exec. Salary: $ Bonus: $
Second Exec. Salary: $ Bonus: $

OTHER THOUGHTS:

Estimated Female Officers or Directors:
Hot Spot for Advancement for Women/Minorities: Y

Actelion Pharmaceuticals Ltd

www.actelion.com

NAIC Code: 325,412

TYPES OF BUSINESS:

Drugs, Discovery & Development
Pharmaceutical Research
Cardiovascular Treatment
Genetic Disorder Treatment

BRANDS/DIVISIONS/AFFILIATES:

Johnson & Johnson
Janssen Pharmaceutical Companies
Tracleer
Zavesca
Ventavis
Veletri
Opsumit
Uptravi

CONTACTS: *Note: Officers with more than one job title may be intentionally listed here more than once.*

Jean-Paul Clozel, CEO
Otto Schwarz, COO
Andre C. Muller, CFO
Christian Albrich, Sr. VP-Global Human Resources
Martine Clozel, Chief Scientific Officer
Marian Borovsky, General Counsel
Nicholas France, Chief Bus. Dev. Officer
Roland Haefeli, Head-Public Affairs
Roland Haefeli, Head-Investor Rel.
Guy Braunstein, Exec. VP
Jean-Pierre Garnier, Chmn.

GROWTH PLANS/SPECIAL FEATURES:

Actelion Pharmaceuticals Ltd., part of the Janssen Pharmaceutical Companies of Johnson & Johnson, is a biopharmaceutical company that focuses on the discovery, development and marketing of drugs for unaddressed medical needs. Actelion focuses its drug discovery efforts on the design and synthesis of novel low molecular weight, drug-like molecules. Additional drug discovery platforms include G-Protein coupled receptors (GPCRs), aspartic proteinases, anti-infectives and ion channels. The firm's most recognized product is Tracleer, which is an endothelin receptor antagonist used for pulmonary arterial hypertension (PAH). Another marketed drug, Zavesca, is one of the first approved orally available therapy treatments for a genetic lipid metabolic disorder called Gaucher disease. Ventavis is an inhaled formulation of iloprost for the treatment of PAH. Veletri is an injectable epoprostenol, a lipid molecule approved for PAH that remains stable at room temperatures. Opsumit is an orally available endothelin receptor antagonist. Uptravi is the only approved oral, selective IP receptor agonist targeting the prostacyclin pathway in PAH. Actelion has two drugs in Phase III clinical development: Macitentan, a tissue-targeting endothelin receptor antagonist intended for treatment of the cardiovascular system, and Ponesimod, directed for the treatment of multiple sclerosis and plaque psoriasis. Actelion is based in Switzerland and has subsidiaries in more than 30 countries.

Actelion offers its employees performance-based bonuses and a program of restricted stock units.

FINANCIAL DATA: *Note: Data for latest year may not have been available at press time.*

In U.S. $	2017	2016	2015	2014	2013	2012
Revenue	2,603,399,232	2,479,427,840	2,097,069,312	2,007,665,024	1,831,152,640	1,772,350,336
R&D Expense						
Operating Income						
Operating Margin %						
SGA Expense						
Net Income		714,095,552	565,893,184	608,896,576	464,050,464	310,937,216
Operating Cash Flow						
Capital Expenditure						
EBITDA						
Return on Assets %						
Return on Equity %						
Debt to Equity						

CONTACT INFORMATION:

Phone: 41-61-565-65-65 Fax: 41-61-565-65-00
Toll-Free:
Address: Gewerbestrasse 16, Allschwil, CH-4123 Switzerland

STOCK TICKER/OTHER:

Stock Ticker: Subsidiary
Employees: 2,624
Parent Company: Johnson & Johnson
Exchange:
Fiscal Year Ends: 12/31

SALARIES/BONUSES:

Top Exec. Salary: $ Bonus: $
Second Exec. Salary: $ Bonus: $

OTHER THOUGHTS:

Estimated Female Officers or Directors: 1
Hot Spot for Advancement for Women/Minorities:

ActiveCare Inc

www.activecare.com

NAIC Code: 621,999

TYPES OF BUSINESS:

Other Miscellaneous Ambulatory Health Care Services
Remote Patient Monitoring Services

BRANDS/DIVISIONS/AFFILIATES:

CareCenter

CONTACTS:

Note: Officers with more than one job title may be intentionally listed here more than once.

David Boone, CEO
Michael Acton, CFO
James Dalton, Chairman of the Board

GROWTH PLANS/SPECIAL FEATURES:

ActiveCare, Inc. provides remote patient monitoring (RPM) services to individuals with diabetes. Diabetes is a pandemic that affects approximately 9% of the U.S. population or 29 million Americans. Studies have shown that the annual cost of treating an individual with diabetes and the comorbidities associated with the disease is approximately $13,700 per year. This combination costs the U.S. health system up to $245 billion annually. The lack of regular glucose monitoring by diabetics is a major driver of diabetic related claims. It is estimated that as much as 80% of diabetics are non-compliant with their treatment plans, despite physician recommendations. The ActiveCare solution is focused on getting diabetic patients to test and manage their chronic illness on a regular and real-time basis. An ActiveCare member's introduction to the program begins his/her receipt of a state-of-the-art cellular glucometer and testing supplies. The firm's CareSpecialist will then walk the new member through how to use the new device and direct the member to register on a private and secure website that records all of the member's readings. From that point forward, the CareSpecialist establishes a personal working relationship with the diabetic member â€" encouraging testing; helping the member better understand their test results and how to respond to high or low readings â€" all on a real-time basis. It is this relationship that facilitates better health for the members, while ultimately saving the healthcare provider significant amounts in reduced claims. The firm staffs its CareCenter with highly trained CareSpecialists that maintain consistent contact with its members helping them through the ups and downs of managing their glucose levels. The approach of ActiveCare is designed to improve the health and wellness of members while also lowering the overall costs of medical care paid by their employers.

FINANCIAL DATA:

Note: Data for latest year may not have been available at press time.

In U.S. $	2017	2016	2015	2014	2013	2012
Revenue						
R&D Expense						
Operating Income						
Operating Margin %						
SGA Expense						
Net Income						
Operating Cash Flow						
Capital Expenditure						
EBITDA						
Return on Assets %						
Return on Equity %						
Debt to Equity						

CONTACT INFORMATION:

Phone: 877-219-6050 Fax: 855-291-6384
Toll-Free:
Address: 1365 West Business Park Drive, Orem, UT 84058 United States

STOCK TICKER/OTHER:

Stock Ticker: ACARQ
Employees: 38
Parent Company:
Exchange: PINX
Fiscal Year Ends: 09/30

SALARIES/BONUSES:

Top Exec. Salary: $ Bonus: $
Second Exec. Salary: $ Bonus: $

OTHER THOUGHTS:

Estimated Female Officers or Directors:
Hot Spot for Advancement for Women/Minorities:

Addus Homecare Corporation

www.addus.com

NAIC Code: 621,610

TYPES OF BUSINESS:

Home Health Care Services

BRANDS/DIVISIONS/AFFILIATES:

Addus HealthCare Inc
Ambercare Corporation Inc

GROWTH PLANS/SPECIAL FEATURES:

Addus Homecare Corporation is the holding company for home social and medical services provider Addus HealthCare, Inc. Addus HealhCare offers services including skilled nursing, personal aids and rehabilitation therapy. Its primary services assist younger adults with disabilities and aging adults with daily living activities such as bathing, grooming, dressing, personal hygiene and medication reminders. The firm serves over 34,000 consumers in 24 states through over 116 locations. In April 2018, Addus acquired the assets of Arcadia Home Care & Staffing, a Southfield, Michigan-based provider of home care services, for $18.5 million. The following May, the firm completed the purchase of Ambercare Corporation, Inc., a provider of personal care, hospice and home health services, headquartered in Albuquerque, New Mexico, for $40 million.

CONTACTS: *Note: Officers with more than one job title may be intentionally listed here more than once.*

Brian Poff, CFO
James Zoccoli, Chief Information Officer
W. Bickham, COO
Steven Geringer, Director
R. Allison, Director
Darby Anderson, Executive VP
Laurie Manning, Executive VP

FINANCIAL DATA: *Note: Data for latest year may not have been available at press time.*

In U.S. $	2017	2016	2015	2014	2013	2012
Revenue	425,715,000	400,688,000	336,815,000	312,942,000	265,941,000	244,315,000
R&D Expense						
Operating Income	23,772,000	15,235,000	16,154,000	18,071,000	15,461,000	15,168,000
Operating Margin %	5.58%	3.80%	4.79%	5.77%	5.81%	6.20%
SGA Expense	76,902,000	84,213,000	70,452,000	61,834,000	50,118,000	46,362,000
Net Income	13,608,000	12,024,000	11,623,000	12,243,000	19,145,000	7,635,000
Operating Cash Flow	52,771,000	-743,000	4,106,000	7,028,000	27,393,000	15,405,000
Capital Expenditure	3,616,000	1,712,000	2,359,000	6,461,000	887,000	1,114,000
EBITDA	33,185,000	24,900,000	20,788,000	21,919,000	17,809,000	18,362,000
Return on Assets %	5.46%	5.67%	6.22%	7.10%	12.20%	5.01%
Return on Equity %	8.14%	7.99%	8.61%	10.12%	18.38%	8.44%
Debt to Equity	0.22	0.14	0.01	0.02		0.17

CONTACT INFORMATION:

Phone: 630-296-3400 Fax:
Toll-Free: 888-233-8746
Address: 2300 Warrenville Rd., Downers Grove, IL 60515 United States

STOCK TICKER/OTHER:

Stock Ticker: ADUS
Employees: 23,070
Parent Company:
Exchange: NAS
Fiscal Year Ends: 12/31

SALARIES/BONUSES:

Top Exec. Salary: $520,432 Bonus: $
Second Exec. Salary: $337,115 Bonus: $

OTHER THOUGHTS:

Estimated Female Officers or Directors:
Hot Spot for Advancement for Women/Minorities:

Adeptus Health Inc

www.adhc.com

NAIC Code: 621,493

TYPES OF BUSINESS:

Emergency Medical Centers and Clinics, Freestanding
General Medical and Surgical Hospitals

BRANDS/DIVISIONS/AFFILIATES:

Deerfield Management
First Choice Emergency Room

GROWTH PLANS/SPECIAL FEATURES:

Adeptus Health, Inc. is a patient-centered healthcare organization providing emergency medical care through a network of independent freestanding emergency rooms in the U.S. and partnerships with leading healthcare systems. The firm offers its emergency room services through First Choice Emergency Room. These facilities are located in the markets of Houston, San Antonio and Austin, Texas. In October 2017, the reorganized firm emerged from chapter 11 bankruptcy and was acquired by Deerfield Management, a healthcare investment firm.

CONTACTS: *Note: Officers with more than one job title may be intentionally listed here more than once.*

Frank Williams, CFO
Andrew Jordan, Chief Marketing Officer
Gregory Scott, Director
James Muzzarelli, Other Corporate Officer
Andrew Hinkelman, Other Executive Officer
Traci Bowen, Senior VP, Divisional

FINANCIAL DATA: *Note: Data for latest year may not have been available at press time.*

In U.S. $	2017	2016	2015	2014	2013	2012
Revenue	430,000,000	410,000,000	364,687,008	210,694,000	102,883,000	72,601,000
R&D Expense						
Operating Income						
Operating Margin %						
SGA Expense						
Net Income			13,217,000	-3,351,000	-2,212,000	
Operating Cash Flow						
Capital Expenditure						
EBITDA						
Return on Assets %						
Return on Equity %						
Debt to Equity						

CONTACT INFORMATION:

Phone: 972 899-6666 Fax:
Toll-Free:
Address: 2941 S. Lake Vista, Lewisville, TX 75067 United States

STOCK TICKER/OTHER:

Stock Ticker: Private
Exchange:
Employees: 1,869
Fiscal Year Ends: 12/31
Parent Company: Deerfield Management

SALARIES/BONUSES:

Top Exec. Salary: $ Bonus: $
Second Exec. Salary: $ Bonus: $

OTHER THOUGHTS:

Estimated Female Officers or Directors:
Hot Spot for Advancement for Women/Minorities:

Advanced Bionics LLC

www.advancedbionics.com

NAIC Code: 339,100

TYPES OF BUSINESS:

Medical Equipment-Manufacturing
Bionic Devices
Cochlear Implant Technology

BRANDS/DIVISIONS/AFFILIATES:

HiRes Fidelity 120
HiResolution Bionic Ear System
Harmony
Naida CI Q90
Sonova Holding AG
Kinder Clip
T-Mic
Neptune

CONTACTS: *Note: Officers with more than one job title may be intentionally listed here more than once.*

HansjÃ¼rg Emch, Global VP-Cochlear Implants-Sonova Holding AG
Hansjurg Emch, Pres.
Hansjurg Emch, VP-Medical
Mark Downing, Dir.-Product Mgmt. & Surgical Support

GROWTH PLANS/SPECIAL FEATURES:

Advanced Bionics LLC, a subsidiary of hearing aid manufacturer Sonova Holding AG, develops and markets bionic technologies used in implantable neurostimulation devices such as cochlear implants for the restoration of hearing in severe hearing impaired and deaf individuals. Unlike traditional hearing aids, cochlear implants bypass the inner ear to send sounds as electric pulses directly to the brain. The hearing systems consist of implanted receivers and external sound processors. Products in the company's HiResolution Bionic Ear System include the HiRes Fidelity 120 implant, designed to provide hearing that closely resembles how a normal ear hear; Hifocus electrodes for neural targeting; Harmony behind-the-ear processors that produce high-quality sound resolution; Neptune, a waterproof sound processor for swimming and bathing; and Clear Voice Processor, which enhances speech understanding. Advanced Bionics partners with fellow nanotech company Phonak for the development, manufacture and distribution of the Naida CI Q90, a behind the ear sound processor utilizing Phonak's Binaural VoiceStream Technology and wireless bimodal streaming capabilities. In addition to the implant systems, the company produces various accessories for users, including T-Mic microphones; the Kinder Clip, which allows the hearing aid device to be worn on a shirt collar; the Phonal ComPilot, which links the unit to Bluetooth devices, mobile phones, computers, media players, TVs and other devices; and Skinit device covers. The firm maintains corporate offices in California, the U.K., France, Switzerland, Hong Kong, Turkey, Sweden, Spain, Russia, Korea, Jordan, Italy, India, Germany, Finland, Denmark, China, Brazil, Belgium and Australia.

FINANCIAL DATA: *Note: Data for latest year may not have been available at press time.*

In U.S. $	2017	2016	2015	2014	2013	2012
Revenue	210,000,000	200,000,000	188,802,915	196,124,727		
R&D Expense						
Operating Income						
Operating Margin %						
SGA Expense						
Net Income						
Operating Cash Flow						
Capital Expenditure						
EBITDA						
Return on Assets %						
Return on Equity %						
Debt to Equity						

CONTACT INFORMATION:

Phone: 661-362-1400 Fax: 661-362-1500
Toll-Free: 877-829-0026
Address: 28515 Westinghouse Pl., Valencia, CA 91355 United States

STOCK TICKER/OTHER:

Stock Ticker: Subsidiary
Employees: 724
Parent Company: Sonova Holding AG
Exchange:
Fiscal Year Ends: 12/31

SALARIES/BONUSES:

Top Exec. Salary: $ Bonus: $
Second Exec. Salary: $ Bonus: $

OTHER THOUGHTS:

Estimated Female Officers or Directors:
Hot Spot for Advancement for Women/Minorities:

Adventist Health System

www.adventisthealthsystem.com

NAIC Code: 622,110

TYPES OF BUSINESS:

General Medical and Surgical Hospitals
Nursing Homes
Home Health Care Services

BRANDS/DIVISIONS/AFFILIATES:

Florida Hospital
Seventh-day Adventist Church

CONTACTS:

Note: Officers with more than one job title may be intentionally listed here more than once.

Terry D. Shaw, CEO
Lars D. Houmann, COO
Donald L. Jernigan, Pres.
Paul C. Rathbun, CFO
Olesea Azevedo, Chief Human Resources Officer
Brent G. Snyder, CIO
John McLendon, CIO-Information Services
Robert R. Henderschedt, Sr. VP-Admin.
Jeffrey S. Bromme, Chief Legal Officer
Sandra K. Johnson, VP-Bus. Dev., Risk Mgmt. & Compliance
Womack H. Rucker, Jr., VP-Corp. Rel.
Lewis Seifert, Sr. VP-Finance
Amanda Brady, Chief Acct. Officer
Amy L. Zbaraschuk, VP-Finance
T.L. Trimble, VP-Legal Svcs.
Ted Hamilton, VP-Medical Mission
Carlene Jamerson, Sr. VP
John Brownlow, Sr. VP-Managed Care
Celeste M. West, VP-Supply Chain Mgmt.

GROWTH PLANS/SPECIAL FEATURES:

Adventist Health System, sponsored by the Seventh-day Adventist Church, is one of the largest nonprofit Protestant health care organizations in the U.S. The firm operates 46 hospitals in several states and multiple affiliated extended care centers within the long-term care division. The company serves more than 5 million patients annually through its over 80,000 caregivers. Adventist Health's flagship organization, Florida Hospital, is one of the largest health care providers in central Florida and a national leader in cardiac care. The hospital has more than 2,500 beds across 16 campuses and provides care in the areas of cancer, neurosciences, orthopedics, kidney disease, limb replantation, sports medicine, rehabilitation. Adventist Health is a world leader in the use of tissue-sparing radiation based on proton beams, rather than traditional photon-based radiation. The firm is guided by its Christian mission, combining disease treatment, preventative medicine, education and advocacy of a wholesome lifestyle. The hospitals in the Adventist Health group provide a wide range of free or reduced-price services in their communities, including free medical vans and community clinics, free screening and education programs, debt forgiveness, abuse shelters and programs for the homeless and jobless.

FINANCIAL DATA:

Note: Data for latest year may not have been available at press time.

In U.S. $	2017	2016	2015	2014	2013	2012
Revenue	9,699,947,345	9,651,689,000	9,116,187,000	7,955,000,000	7,597,799,000	7,346,597,000
R&D Expense						
Operating Income						
Operating Margin %						
SGA Expense						
Net Income	229,800,000	89,559,000	-131,403,000	600,000,000	578,818,000	504,958,000
Operating Cash Flow						
Capital Expenditure						
EBITDA						
Return on Assets %						
Return on Equity %						
Debt to Equity						

CONTACT INFORMATION:

Phone: 407-357-1000 Fax:
Toll-Free:
Address: 900 Hope Way, Altamonte Springs, FL 32714 United States

STOCK TICKER/OTHER:

Stock Ticker: Nonprofit
Exchange:
Employees: 80,000
Fiscal Year Ends: 12/31
Parent Company:

SALARIES/BONUSES:

Top Exec. Salary: $ Bonus: $
Second Exec. Salary: $ Bonus: $

OTHER THOUGHTS:

Estimated Female Officers or Directors: 6
Hot Spot for Advancement for Women/Minorities: Y

Advocate Aurora Health

www.advocateaurorahealth.org

NAIC Code: 622,110

TYPES OF BUSINESS:

General Medical and Surgical Hospitals
Clinics & Outpatient Centers
Home Health Care
Physician Groups

BRANDS/DIVISIONS/AFFILIATES:

Advocate BroMenn Medical Center
Advocate Christ Medical Center
Advocate Condell Medical Center
Advocate Good Samaritan Hospital
Advocate Good Shepherd Hospital
Advocate Illinois Masonic Medical Center
Advocate Lutheran General Hospital
Advocate Trinity Hospital

CONTACTS: *Note: Officers with more than one job title may be intentionally listed here more than once.*

Jim Skogsbergh, CEO
William P. Santulli, COO
Dominic Nakis, CFO
Kelly Jo Golson, CMO
Kevin R. Brady, Chief Human Resources Officer
Lee Sacks, Chief Medical Officer
Bobbie Byrne, CIO
Gail D. Hasbrouck, General Counsel
Scott Powder, Sr. VP-Strategic Planning & Growth
Dominic Nakis, Treasurer
Lee Sacks, CEO-Advocate Physician Partners
James R. Dan, Pres., Advocate Medical Group
Kathie Bender Schwich, Sr. VP-Mission & Spiritual Care

GROWTH PLANS/SPECIAL FEATURES:

Advocate Aurora Health, a product of the merger of Advocate Health Care and Aurora Health Care, is a nonprofit health care network providing acute care and outpatient services in Illinois. The company's operations have over 784,000 patient portal users, with 500 Outpatient locations, 63 Walgreen's Clinics and 27 hospitals. Advocate-branded hospitals include BroMenn Medical Center, Christ Medical Center, Condell Medical Center, Dreyer, Eureka Hospital, Good Samaritan Hospital, Good Shepherd Hospital, Illinois Masonic Medical Center, Lutheran General Hospital, Sherman Hospital, South Suburban Hospital and Trinity Hospital. Its children's hospital is Advocate Children's Hospital, with campuses located at Oak Lawn and Park Ridge. Advocate's outpatient facilities include sites run by its physician groups as well as Advocate Medical Campus Southwest, Advocate Occupational Health, Midwest Center for Day Surgery, Naperville Surgical Center and Tinley Woods Surgery Center. The company utilizes an Electronic Intensive Care Unit program (eICU) that links real-time monitoring from all adult ICU beds in Advocate's hospitals to a central command center staffed by physicians. Advocate sponsors community outreach programs such as school-based health centers; free and reduced cost clinics; nutritional services; and educational programs. The firm is also affiliated with several medical schools and serves as one of the leading trainers of primary care physicians in Illinois. In 2018, Advocate Health Care and Aurora Health Care finished their purposed merger. The new combined system, called Advocate Aurora Health, is the tenth largest not-for-profit hospital system in the U.S.

Advocate's employees receive benefits including medical, dental and vision plans; education assistance; life and disability insurance; and adoption assistance.

FINANCIAL DATA: *Note: Data for latest year may not have been available at press time.*

In U.S. $	2017	2016	2015	2014	2013	2012
Revenue	6,233,413,000	5,587,420,000	5,329,562,000	5,231,393,000	4,940,000,000	4,599,133,000
R&D Expense						
Operating Income						
Operating Margin %						
SGA Expense						
Net Income	811,343,000	597,604,000	78,605,000	369,607,000	765,300,000	671,656,000
Operating Cash Flow						
Capital Expenditure						
EBITDA						
Return on Assets %						
Return on Equity %						
Debt to Equity						

CONTACT INFORMATION:

Phone: 630-572-9393 Fax:
Toll-Free:
Address: 3075 Highland Pkwy., Ste. 600, Downers Grove, IL 60515 United States

STOCK TICKER/OTHER:

Stock Ticker: Nonprofit
Employees: 70,000
Parent Company:
Exchange:
Fiscal Year Ends: 12/31

SALARIES/BONUSES:

Top Exec. Salary: $ Bonus: $
Second Exec. Salary: $ Bonus: $

OTHER THOUGHTS:

Estimated Female Officers or Directors: 3
Hot Spot for Advancement for Women/Minorities: Y

Aeon Global Health Corp

aeonglobalhealth.com

NAIC Code: 511210D

TYPES OF BUSINESS:

Computer Software, Healthcare & Biotechnology
Software-Referral management
Software-Care Coordination

BRANDS/DIVISIONS/AFFILIATES:

CONTACTS:

Note: Officers with more than one job title may be intentionally listed here more than once.

Hanif Roshan, CEO
Michael Poelking, CFO
David Goldberg, COO

GROWTH PLANS/SPECIAL FEATURES:

Aeon Global Health Corp, formly Authentidate Holding Corporation, reports its business in two segments, the AEON business and the AHC business. AEON's primary business focus is on production of actionable medical information for value-based medicine. This includes the testing of an individual's urine or saliva for the presence of drugs or chemicals and the patient's DNA profile. AEON's four primary testing services include: Medical Toxicology, utilizes HPLC-Tandem Mass Spectrometry testing and provides information about medications and other substances in the patient's system from either urine or oral fluid samples with rapid 48- to 72-hour turnaround time; DNA Pharmacogenomics, a genetic-based testing to determine patient therapy; Cancer Genetic Testing, providing testing for hereditary cancer markers, offering multiple BRCA testing options; and Molecular Microbiology, identifying identifies microorganisms including viruses, bacteria and parasites through DNA or RNA detection versus traditional microbiology procedures which use culture to grow potential microorganisms. The AHC business provides revenue cycle management applications and telehealth products and services that are designed to enable healthcare organizations to increase revenues, improve productivity, reduce costs, coordinate care for patients and enhance related administrative and clinical workflows and compliance with regulatory requirements. The company's products and services address a variety of business needs for customers including enabling health care organizations to increase revenues; improve productivity; enhance patient care and reduce costs by eliminating paper and manual work steps from clinical, administrative and other processes; and enhancing compliance with regulatory requirements.

FINANCIAL DATA:

Note: Data for latest year may not have been available at press time.

In U.S. $	2017	2016	2015	2014	2013	2012
Revenue						
R&D Expense						
Operating Income						
Operating Margin %						
SGA Expense						
Net Income						
Operating Cash Flow						
Capital Expenditure						
EBITDA						
Return on Assets %						
Return on Equity %						
Debt to Equity						

CONTACT INFORMATION:

Phone: 908 787-1700 Fax:
Toll-Free:
Address: 300 Connell Dr., Fl. 5, Berkeley Heights, NJ 07922 United States

STOCK TICKER/OTHER:

Stock Ticker: AGHC
Employees: 148
Parent Company:
Exchange: PINX
Fiscal Year Ends: 06/30

SALARIES/BONUSES:

Top Exec. Salary: $202,725 Bonus: $200,000
Second Exec. Salary: $200,000 Bonus: $5,000

OTHER THOUGHTS:

Estimated Female Officers or Directors:
Hot Spot for Advancement for Women/Minorities:

AEterna Zentaris Inc

www.aezsinc.com

NAIC Code: 325,412

TYPES OF BUSINESS:

Drug Development
Oncology Products
Endocrine Therapy Products

BRANDS/DIVISIONS/AFFILIATES:

Zoptrex
MACRILEN

CONTACTS: *Note: Officers with more than one job title may be intentionally listed here more than once.*

James Clavijo, CFO
Nicola Ammer, Chief Medical Officer
Carolyn Egbert, Director
Michael Ward, President
Brian Garrison, Senior VP, Divisional
Gunther Grau, Vice President, Divisional
Eckhard Guenther, Vice President, Divisional
Michael Teifel, Vice President, Divisional

GROWTH PLANS/SPECIAL FEATURES:

AEterna Zentaris, Inc. is a Canadian specialty biopharmaceutical company focused on serving the unmet medical needs of patients with rare endocrine diseases through acquisition, development and licensing orphan products. The firm's current macimorelin product is an oral growth hormone secretagogue (GHS) receptor agonist used to test for Adult Growth Hormone Deficiency, a rare endocrine disorder. AGHD may occur in an adult subject who has a history of childhood onset GHD or may occur during adulthood as an acquired condition. GHS are potent regulators of lipid, sugar and protein metabolism that directly stimulate growth hormone secretion from the pituitary gland without the involvement of Growth Hormone-Releasing Hormone or somatostatin. Macimorelin stimulates the secretion of GH from the pituitary gland into the circulatory system. Stimulated GH levels are measured in only four blood samples over ninety minutes after oral administration of macimorelin (no intravenous infusions or intramuscular injections involved). In October 2017, Macimorelin was granted orphan drug designation by the U.S. FDA for diagnosis of AGHD. Subsequently, AEterna proposed to market macimorelin under the name Macrilen, which was approved. That December, the FDA granted marketing approval for Macrilen. In January 2018, AEterna sold Macrilen's U.S. and Canadian rights to Strongbridge Biopharma plc for an upfront payment of $24 million, as well as tiered royalties payments and milestone payments.

FINANCIAL DATA: *Note: Data for latest year may not have been available at press time.*

In U.S. $	2017	2016	2015	2014	2013	2012
Revenue	923,000	911,000	545,000	11,000	6,175,000	33,665,000
R&D Expense	10,704,000	16,495,000	17,234,000	23,716,000	21,284,000	20,604,000
Operating Income	-23,074,000	-29,476,000	-34,884,000	-37,395,000	-27,476,000	-27,004,000
Operating Margin %	-2499.89%	-3235.56%	-6400.73%	-339954.54%	-444.95%	-80.21%
SGA Expense	13,293,000	13,892,000	18,195,000	13,690,000	11,367,000	12,110,000
Net Income	-16,796,000	-24,959,000	-50,143,000	-16,564,000	6,815,000	-20,412,000
Operating Cash Flow	-22,913,000	-29,010,000	-33,844,000	-31,082,000	-19,984,000	-30,815,000
Capital Expenditure	4,000	66,000	26,000	127,000	85,000	272,000
EBITDA	-22,980,000	-29,196,000	-34,543,000	-36,517,000	-24,779,000	-18,711,000
Return on Assets %	-62.37%	-60.02%	-101.36%	-31.06%	10.74%	-28.54%
Return on Equity %	-979.64%	-179.38%	-277.80%	-105.00%	131.44%	
Debt to Equity						

CONTACT INFORMATION:

Phone: 418-652-8525 Fax: 418-652-0881
Toll-Free:
Address: 1405 du Parc-Technologique Blvd., Quebec, QC G1P 4P5 Canada

STOCK TICKER/OTHER:

Stock Ticker: AEZS
Employees: 47
Parent Company:
Exchange: NAS
Fiscal Year Ends: 12/31

SALARIES/BONUSES:

Top Exec. Salary: $277,596 Bonus: $
Second Exec. Salary: $273,770 Bonus: $

OTHER THOUGHTS:

Estimated Female Officers or Directors:
Hot Spot for Advancement for Women/Minorities:

Aetna Inc

www.aetna.com

NAIC Code: 524,114

TYPES OF BUSINESS:

Insurance-Medical & Health
Long-Term Care Insurance
Group Insurance
Pension Products
Dental Insurance
Disability Insurance
Life Insurance

BRANDS/DIVISIONS/AFFILIATES:

CONTACTS:
Note: Officers with more than one job title may be intentionally listed here more than once.

Mark Bertolini, CEO
Shawn Guertin, CFO
Heather Dixon, Chief Accounting Officer
Harold Paz, Chief Medical Officer
Francis Soistman, Executive VP, Divisional
Margaret McCarthy, Executive VP, Divisional
Richard Jelinek, Executive VP, Divisional
Thomas Sabatino, Executive VP
Karen Lynch, President
Karen Lynch, President

GROWTH PLANS/SPECIAL FEATURES:

Aetna, Inc. is a health care benefits company, providing a broad range of traditional and consumer-directed health insurance products. These include medical, pharmacy, dental, behavioral health, group life and disability plans and Medicaid health care management capabilities to roughly 46.7 million people. Aetna operates in three segments: health care, group insurance and large case pensions. Health care products include medical insurance plans & products, pharmacy benefits management, dental, behavioral health and vision plans offered on both an insured basis and an employee-funded basis. This division's medical plans include point of service, health maintenance organization, preferred provider organization, health savings accounts and indemnity benefits. Group insurance products primarily include life insurance, including group term life insurance coverage and accidental death and dismemberment coverage; disability insurance, including short- and long-term disability; and long-term care insurance products, including the cost of care in private home settings, adult day care, assisted living or nursing facilities. The large case pensions segment primarily manages retirement products for tax-qualified pension plans. Customers include employer groups, individuals, college students, part-time/hourly workers, governmental units, labor groups and expatriates. In November 2017, the firm sold its domestic group life insurance, group disability insurance and absence management businesses to Hartford Life and Accident Insurance Company. The following December, Aetna agreed to be acquired by drugstore giant CVS Health Corp. for $69 billion, subject to government and share holder approval.

Employee benefits include medical, dental and vision coverage; flexible spending accounts; life and AD&D insurance; short- and long-term disability; employee assistance programs; 401(k) & employee stock purchase plan; and tuition assistance.

FINANCIAL DATA:
Note: Data for latest year may not have been available at press time.

In U.S. $	2017	2016	2015	2014	2013	2012
Revenue	60,535,000,000	63,155,000,000	60,336,500,000	58,003,200,000	47,294,600,000	36,595,900,000
R&D Expense						
Operating Income						
Operating Margin %			6.72%	5.66%	5.37%	5.66%
SGA Expense	12,064,000,000	12,085,000,000	11,649,300,000	10,837,700,000	8,645,400,000	6,876,400,000
Net Income	1,904,000,000	2,271,000,000	2,390,200,000	2,040,800,000	1,913,600,000	1,657,900,000
Operating Cash Flow	-464,000,000	3,719,000,000	3,866,100,000	3,372,800,000	2,278,700,000	1,822,000,000
Capital Expenditure	410,000,000	270,000,000	362,900,000	369,600,000	479,100,000	338,200,000
EBITDA						
Return on Assets %	3.06%	3.70%	4.47%	3.95%	4.18%	4.14%
Return on Equity %	11.38%	13.36%	15.62%	14.31%	15.66%	16.15%
Debt to Equity	0.52	1.06	0.48	0.54	0.56	0.62

CONTACT INFORMATION:

Phone: 860 273-0123 Fax:
Toll-Free: 800-872-3862
Address: 151 Farmington Ave., Hartford, CT 06156 United States

STOCK TICKER/OTHER:

Stock Ticker: AET Exchange: NYS
Employees: 49,500 Fiscal Year Ends: 12/31
Parent Company:

SALARIES/BONUSES:

Top Exec. Salary: $1,200,000 Bonus: $
Second Exec. Salary: $931,500 Bonus: $

OTHER THOUGHTS:

Estimated Female Officers or Directors: 8
Hot Spot for Advancement for Women/Minorities: Y

AFLAC Inc

NAIC Code: 524,114

www.aflac.com

TYPES OF BUSINESS:

Insurance-Supplemental & Specialty Health
Life Insurance
Cancer Insurance
Long-Term Care Insurance
Accident & Disability Insurance
Vision Plans
Dental Plans

BRANDS/DIVISIONS/AFFILIATES:

American Family Life Assurance Company
Continental American Insurance Company
Aflac Group Insurance
AFLAC Japan
EVER

CONTACTS: *Note: Officers with more than one job title may be intentionally listed here more than once.*

Daniel Amos, CEO
June Howard, Chief Accounting Officer
Masatoshi Koide, COO, Divisional
Eric Kirsch, Executive VP, Subsidiary
Frederick Crawford, Executive VP
Audrey Tillman, Executive VP
Koji Ariyoshi, Executive VP
James Daniels, Executive VP
Teresa White, President, Divisional
Charles Lake, President, Subsidiary
Albert Riggieri, Senior VP, Subsidiary
Max Broden, Senior VP

GROWTH PLANS/SPECIAL FEATURES:

AFLAC, Inc. is a holding company whose principle subsidiary, AFLAC (American Family Life Assurance Company of Columbus), insures more than 50 million people worldwide. The subsidiary is a leading writer of supplemental insurance marketed to employers in the U.S., offering policies for payroll accounts through approximately 13,000 sales agencies, with more than 110,000 sales associates employed by those agencies. AFLAC sells supplemental insurance products, including accident/disability plans, cancer plans, short-term disability plans, sickness & hospital indemnity plans, hospital intensive care plans, fixed-benefit dental plans, vision care plans, long-term care plans and life insurance products. In addition, AFLAC offers specified health event coverage for major medical crises such as heart attack and stroke. U.S. insurance products are designed to provide supplemental coverage to individuals who already have major medical or primary insurance coverage. Through Continental American Insurance Company (branded as Aflac Group Insurance), the company also markets and administers group projects. Subsidiary AFLAC Japan is one of the largest foreign-based insurers in that country. AFLAC Japan's insurance products are designed to help consumers pay for medical and non-medical costs that are not reimbursed under Japan's national health insurance system. EVER, AFLAC Japan's stand-alone medical product, offers a basic level of hospitalization coverage with an affordable premium. AFLAC Japan also sells cancer plans, general medical indemnity plans, medical/sickness riders to its cancer plan, care plans, living benefit life plans, ordinary life insurance plans and annuities. AFLAC Japan accounts for about 70% of AFLAC's annual insurance earnings.

Employee benefits include medical and dental coverage, short- and long-term disability, life insurance, flexible spending accounts, an employee assistance program, employee discount programs and Aflac insurance policies including cancer insurance and hospital confinement indemnity.

FINANCIAL DATA: *Note: Data for latest year may not have been available at press time.*

In U.S. $	2017	2016	2015	2014	2013	2012
Revenue	21,600,000,000	22,380,000,000	20,845,000,000	22,606,000,000	23,827,000,000	25,272,000,000
R&D Expense						
Operating Income						
Operating Margin %						
SGA Expense						
Net Income	4,604,000,000	2,659,000,000	2,533,000,000	2,951,000,000	3,158,000,000	2,866,000,000
Operating Cash Flow	6,128,000,000	5,987,000,000	6,776,000,000	6,550,000,000	10,547,000,000	14,952,000,000
Capital Expenditure						
EBITDA						
Return on Assets %	3.44%	2.14%	2.12%	2.44%	2.50%	2.30%
Return on Equity %	20.42%	13.92%	14.05%	17.90%	20.64%	19.44%
Debt to Equity	0.21	0.26	0.28	0.28	0.33	0.27

CONTACT INFORMATION:

Phone: 706 323-3431 Fax:
Toll-Free: 800-235-2667
Address: 1932 Wynnton Rd., Columbus, GA 31999 United States

STOCK TICKER/OTHER:

Stock Ticker: AFL
Employees: 10,212
Parent Company:
Exchange: NYS
Fiscal Year Ends: 12/31

SALARIES/BONUSES:

Top Exec. Salary: $1,441,100 Bonus: $
Second Exec. Salary: $700,000 Bonus: $

OTHER THOUGHTS:

Estimated Female Officers or Directors: 8
Hot Spot for Advancement for Women/Minorities: Y

Agfa-Gevaert NV

www.agfa.com

NAIC Code: 333,316

TYPES OF BUSINESS:

Imaging Equipment
Commercial Printing Equipment & Products
Image Publishing Software
Consumer Photographic Products
Medical Imaging Systems
X-Ray Films

BRANDS/DIVISIONS/AFFILIATES:

Agfa Graphics
Agfa HealthCare
Agfa Specialty Products

CONTACTS: *Note: Officers with more than one job title may be intentionally listed here more than once.*

Christian Reinaudo, CEO
Christian Reinaudo, Pres.
Dirk De Man, CFO
Luc Thijs, Pres., Agfa HealthCare
Luc Delagaye, Pres., Agfa Materials
Stefaan Vanhooren, Pres., Agfa Graphics
Julien De Wilde, Chmn.

GROWTH PLANS/SPECIAL FEATURES:

Agfa-Gevaert NV is a leading imaging equipment company that develops, produces and markets analog and digital systems as well as IT solutions primarily for the printing and healthcare sectors. Agfa has three main divisions: Agfa Graphics, Agfa HealthCare and Agfa Specialty Products. Agfa Graphics provides pre-press services for printing, such as scanning images and designing layouts for anything from books and magazines to billboards and CDs. In addition, the company's commercial printing systems provide commercial, newspaper and packaging printers, including computer-to-film and computer-to-plate systems as well as equipment and consumables. Agfa also supplies digital proofing systems, large-format printing, digital inkjet presses and the professional software that controls the entire prepress process. Agfa HealthCare supplies both analog and digital imaging solutions as well as diagnosis and communications equipment. The company's digital networks and information systems streamline the distribution, storage and management of digital images and optimize the workflow of the entire hospital organization. The Agfa Specialty Products division provides large-scale film-based products and technology solutions for the business-to-business (B2B) market, such as motion picture film, microfilm and film for non-destructive testing as well as materials for smart cards, conductive polymers, synthetic paper and membranes for gas separation. The company also provides solutions for aerial photography, printed circuit boards, identification cards and many other applications.

FINANCIAL DATA: *Note: Data for latest year may not have been available at press time.*

In U.S. $	2017	2016	2015	2014	2013	2012
Revenue	2,841,028,000	2,950,343,000	3,077,102,000	3,046,866,000	3,331,783,000	3,594,604,000
R&D Expense	167,461,300	163,972,600	167,461,300	169,787,200	169,787,200	189,556,900
Operating Income	195,371,600	239,562,800	225,607,600	196,534,500	266,310,000	156,995,000
Operating Margin %	6.87%	8.11%	7.33%	6.45%	7.99%	4.36%
SGA Expense	587,277,600	594,255,200	607,047,400	590,766,400	625,654,100	674,497,100
Net Income	43,028,260	81,404,820	72,101,410	58,146,300	47,679,960	-47,679,960
Operating Cash Flow	45,354,110	165,135,500	173,276,000	175,601,800	124,433,100	37,213,630
Capital Expenditure	53,494,600	51,168,740	43,028,260	43,028,260	46,517,040	51,168,740
EBITDA	188,394,000	227,933,500	187,231,100	189,556,900	229,096,400	109,315,000
Return on Assets %	1.61%	2.94%	2.50%	1.95%	1.51%	-1.41%
Return on Equity %	15.10%	31.60%	38.62%	23.92%	6.59%	-4.36%
Debt to Equity	0.17	0.34	0.60	1.34	0.98	0.44

CONTACT INFORMATION:

Phone: 32 34442111 Fax: 32 34447094
Toll-Free:
Address: Septestraat 27, Mortsel, B-2640 Belgium

STOCK TICKER/OTHER:

Stock Ticker: AFGVF Exchange: GREY
Employees: 10,086 Fiscal Year Ends: 12/31
Parent Company:

SALARIES/BONUSES:

Top Exec. Salary: $ Bonus: $
Second Exec. Salary: $ Bonus: $

OTHER THOUGHTS:

Estimated Female Officers or Directors:
Hot Spot for Advancement for Women/Minorities:

AHMC Healthcare Inc

www.ahmchealth.com

NAIC Code: 622,110

TYPES OF BUSINESS:

General Medical and Surgical Hospitals

BRANDS/DIVISIONS/AFFILIATES:

Alhambra Hospital Medical Center
Anaheim Regional Medical Center
Garfield Medical Center
Greater El Monte Community Hospital
Monterey Park Hospital
San Gabriel Valley Medical Center
Whittier Hospital Medical Center

CONTACTS:

Note: Officers with more than one job title may be intentionally listed here more than once.

Iris Lai, CEO

GROWTH PLANS/SPECIAL FEATURES:

AHMC Healthcare, Inc. operates six comprehensive acute care hospitals that provide healthcare services in the Greater San Gabriel Valley area. AHMC stands for Alhambra Hospital Medical Center. The firm owns and operates the following hospitals: Anaheim Regional Medical Center, Garfield Medical Center, Greater El Monte Community Hospital, Monterey Park Hospital, San Gabriel Valley Medical Center and Whittier Hospital Medical Center. AHMC hospitals offer advanced diagnostic tools such as the MRI GE Signa HDxt1.5TMR system and the Toshiba Aquilon 128-slice CT scanner. Anaheim Regional's heart center has the second largest volume of open heart surgeries in Orange County. The hospitals include about 1,023 total beds and 2,500 physicians. AHMC treats more than 200,000 patients annually.

AHMC offers its employees medical, dental and vision coverage; 401(k) matching; flexible spending accounts, tuition reimbursement; and a wellness program.

FINANCIAL DATA:

Note: Data for latest year may not have been available at press time.

In U.S. $	2017	2016	2015	2014	2013	2012
Revenue	1,302,000,000	1,240,000,000	1,215,000,000	1,100,000,000	1,000,000,000	
R&D Expense						
Operating Income						
Operating Margin %						
SGA Expense						
Net Income						
Operating Cash Flow						
Capital Expenditure						
EBITDA						
Return on Assets %						
Return on Equity %						
Debt to Equity						

CONTACT INFORMATION:

Phone: 626-457-7400 Fax: 626-457-7455
Toll-Free:
Address: 500 E. Main St., Alhambra, CA 91801 United States

STOCK TICKER/OTHER:

Stock Ticker: Private
Employees: 7,000
Parent Company:
Exchange:
Fiscal Year Ends:

SALARIES/BONUSES:

Top Exec. Salary: $ Bonus: $
Second Exec. Salary: $ Bonus: $

OTHER THOUGHTS:

Estimated Female Officers or Directors:
Hot Spot for Advancement for Women/Minorities:

Air Methods Corporation

www.airmethods.com

NAIC Code: 621,910

TYPES OF BUSINESS:

Air Emergency Medical Transport Service
Tourism Services
Helicopter System Design

BRANDS/DIVISIONS/AFFILIATES:

American Services LLC
ASP AMC Intermediate Holdings Inc
American Securities
Sundance Helicopters Inc

CONTACTS: *Note: Officers with more than one job title may be intentionally listed here more than once.*

Aaron Todd, CEO
Peter Csapo, CFO
Sharon Keck, Chief Accounting Officer
JaeLynn Williams, Exec. VP-Sales & Mktg
Heather Dumas, Sr. VP-Human Resources
Doni Perry, VP-IT
David Doerr, Executive VP, Divisional
Crystal Gordon, General Counsel
Michael Allen, President, Divisional

GROWTH PLANS/SPECIAL FEATURES:

Air Methods Corporation provides air medical emergency transport services and systems throughout the U.S. The company also designs, manufactures and installs medical aircraft interiors and other aerospace and medical transport products for domestic and international customers. Air Method's operations consist of three primary divisions: air medical services (AMS), united rotorcraft (UR) and tourism. The AMS division provides air medical transportation services in 48 states to the general population as an independent service and to hospitals or other institutions under exclusive operating agreements. The company's UR division designs, manufactures and certifies modular medical interiors, multi-mission interiors and other aerospace and medical transport products. These interiors and other products range from basic life support to intensive care suites and advanced search and rescue systems. The tourism division was created through the acquisition of Sundance Helicopters, Inc. Sundance provides helicopter tour operations, focusing primarily on Grand Canyon and Hawaiian Island helicopter tours, as well as helicopter services to support firefighting, natural resource agency operations, aerial photography and motion pictures, news gathering and aerial surveying. Its fleet consists of 65 helicopters and two fixed wing aircraft. Air Methods is a wholly-owned subsidiary of ASP AMC Intermediate Holdings, Inc., an indirect wholly-owned subsidiary of affiliated funds managed by American Securities, itself owned American Services, LLC.

FINANCIAL DATA: *Note: Data for latest year may not have been available at press time.*

In U.S. $	2017	2016	2015	2014	2013	2012
Revenue	1,200,000,000	1,170,455,040	1,085,686,016	1,004,772,992	881,601,024	850,812,032
R&D Expense						
Operating Income						
Operating Margin %						
SGA Expense						
Net Income		97,905,000	108,645,000	94,871,000	62,339,000	93,152,000
Operating Cash Flow						
Capital Expenditure						
EBITDA						
Return on Assets %						
Return on Equity %						
Debt to Equity						

CONTACT INFORMATION:

Phone: 303-792-7400 Fax:
Toll-Free:
Address: 5500 S. Quebec St., Ste. 300, Greenwood Village, CO 80111 United States

STOCK TICKER/OTHER:

Stock Ticker: Private
Exchange:
Employees: 5,133
Fiscal Year Ends: 12/31
Parent Company: American Securities LLC

SALARIES/BONUSES:

Top Exec. Salary: $ Bonus: $
Second Exec. Salary: $ Bonus: $

OTHER THOUGHTS:

Estimated Female Officers or Directors: 5
Hot Spot for Advancement for Women/Minorities: Y

Alcon Inc

www.alcon.com

NAIC Code: 325,412

TYPES OF BUSINESS:

Eye Care Products
Ophthalmic Products & Equipment
Contact Lens Care Products
Surgical Instruments

GROWTH PLANS/SPECIAL FEATURES:

Alcon, Inc., a subsidiary of Novartis AG, is a leading eye care products company. Its portfolio spans three key ophthalmic categories: pharmaceutical, surgical and consumer eye care products. The divisions develop, manufacture and market ophthalmic pharmaceuticals, surgical equipment and devices, contact lens care products and other consumer eye care products that treat diseases and conditions of the eye. The company's products include prescription and over-the-counter drugs, contact lens solutions, surgical instruments, intraocular lenses and office systems for ophthalmologists. Its brand names include Pataday solution for eye allergies, AcrySof intraocular lenses, Systane lubricant drops for dry eyes and the Opti-Free system for contact lens care. The firm also has research and development laboratories in Germany, the U.S., Switzerland and Spain.

Alcon offers its employees 401(k) and retirement plans; medical, dental, vision, life, disability and AD&D insurance; paid time off; a wellness program, including onsite or discounted fitness centers, flu shots and Weight Watchers discounts; and an employee assistance program.

BRANDS/DIVISIONS/AFFILIATES:

Novartis AG
Pataday
AcrySof
Systane
Opti-Free

CONTACTS: *Note: Officers with more than one job title may be intentionally listed here more than once.*

Mike Ball, CEO
David Endicott, COO
David Murray, CFO
Kim Adler, VP-Global Communications
Merrick McCracken, Sr. VP-Human Resources
Sabri Markabi, Chief Medical Officer
Ed McGough, Sr. VP-Tech. Oper.
Ed McGough, Sr. VP-Global Mfg.
Christina Ackerman, General Counsel
Bettina Maunz, Head-Comm.
Robert Karsunky, Sr. VP-Finance
Sergio Duplan, Pres., Latin America & Caribbean
Stuart Raetzman, Pres., Europe, Middle East & Africa
Robert Warner, Pres., U.S. & Canada
Roy Acosta, Pres., Asia
Sue Whitfill, Head-Global Quality

FINANCIAL DATA: *Note: Data for latest year may not have been available at press time.*

In U.S. $	2017	2016	2015	2014	2013	2012
Revenue	13,000,000,000	11,000,000,000	10,800,000,000	10,827,000,000	10,496,000,000	10,200,000,000
R&D Expense						
Operating Income						
Operating Margin %						
SGA Expense						
Net Income			1,117,900,000	1,597,000,000	1,232,000,000	
Operating Cash Flow						
Capital Expenditure						
EBITDA						
Return on Assets %						
Return on Equity %						
Debt to Equity						

CONTACT INFORMATION:

Phone: 800-757-9785 Fax:
Toll-Free: 817-568-6725
Address: 6201 S. Freeway, Fort Worth, TX 76134-2001 United States

STOCK TICKER/OTHER:

Stock Ticker: Subsidiary
Employees: 19,000
Parent Company: Novartis AG
Exchange:
Fiscal Year Ends: 12/31

SALARIES/BONUSES:

Top Exec. Salary: $ Bonus: $
Second Exec. Salary: $ Bonus: $

OTHER THOUGHTS:

Estimated Female Officers or Directors: 3
Hot Spot for Advancement for Women/Minorities: Y

Alfresa Holdings Corporation

NAIC Code: 424,210

www.alfresa.com

TYPES OF BUSINESS:

Drugs and Druggists' Sundries Merchant Wholesalers

BRANDS/DIVISIONS/AFFILIATES:

Alfresa Corporation
Alfresa Healthcare Corporation
Alfresa Pharma Corporation
Alfresa System Corporation
Apollo Medical Holdings Inc

CONTACTS:

Note: Officers with more than one job title may be intentionally listed here more than once.

Taizo Kubo, Pres.
Hiroyuki Kanome, Chmn.

GROWTH PLANS/SPECIAL FEATURES:

Alfresa Holdings Corporation, through its subsidiaries, engage in the wholesale, manufacture, marketing and import/export of pharmaceuticals, diagnostic reagents, medical devices and related equipment. Alfresa divides its business into four groups: ethical pharmaceuticals wholesaling, self-medication products wholesaling, manufacturing and medical-related business. The ethical pharmaceuticals wholesaling business group delivers a wide range of products, including diagnostic reagents and medical devices and related equipment. It accomplishes this by distributing the products from its nationwide distribution centers to hospitals, clinics and dispensing pharmacies. The self-medication products wholesaling business group delivers over-the-counter drugs, health foods, supplements and other products to drug stores and pharmacies. The manufacturing business group manufactures and markets high-quality active pharmaceutical ingredients (APIs), pharmaceuticals, diagnostic reagents and medical devices that meet stringent requirements. This division also researches, develops, manufactures and markets distinctive, unique products and undertake contract manufacturing of pharmaceuticals. Last, the medical-related business group engages in expanding business within the healthcare industry primarily to meet the medical needs of Alfresa's dispensing pharmacy and medical-related businesses. Just a few of Aflresa Holdings' many subsidiaries include: Alfresa Corporation, Aflresa Healthcare Corporation, Alfresa Pharma Corporation, Alfresa System Corporation and Apollo Medical Holdings, Inc.

FINANCIAL DATA:

Note: Data for latest year may not have been available at press time.

In U.S. $	2017	2016	2015	2014	2013	2012
Revenue	22,944,780,000	23,164,540,000	21,768,610,000	22,519,100,000	21,465,880,000	
R&D Expense						
Operating Income	298,768,200	407,202,000	262,803,500	314,367,900	211,715,500	
Operating Margin %	1.30%	1.75%	1.20%	1.39%	.98%	
SGA Expense						
Net Income	277,764,800	314,466,800	206,096,000	229,868,700	186,756,000	
Operating Cash Flow	308,775,400	340,190,600	322,001,400	-247,320,600	740,325,400	
Capital Expenditure	122,352,100	128,061,500	142,861,000	187,906,800	61,068,150	
EBITDA	501,753,300	585,011,600	420,131,300	479,931,600	408,325,800	
Return on Assets %	2.46%	2.82%	1.91%	2.16%	1.83%	
Return on Equity %	8.14%	9.72%	6.96%	8.68%	7.93%	
Debt to Equity	0.01	0.01	0.01	0.01	0.01	

CONTACT INFORMATION:

Phone: 81 352195100 Fax: 81 352195102
Toll-Free:
Address: 1-1-3 Otemachi, Tokyo, 100-0004 Japan

STOCK TICKER/OTHER:

Stock Ticker: ALFRY
Exchange: GREY
Employees: 14,629
Fiscal Year Ends:
Parent Company:

SALARIES/BONUSES:

Top Exec. Salary: $ Bonus: $
Second Exec. Salary: $ Bonus: $

OTHER THOUGHTS:

Estimated Female Officers or Directors:
Hot Spot for Advancement for Women/Minorities:

Align Technology Inc

www.aligntech.com

NAIC Code: 339,100

TYPES OF BUSINESS:

Orthodontic Equipment

BRANDS/DIVISIONS/AFFILIATES:

Invisalign
ClinCheck
Vivera Retainers
iTero
OrthoCAD
Invisalign Full
Invisalign G5
Invisalign G6

CONTACTS: *Note: Officers with more than one job title may be intentionally listed here more than once.*

Joseph Hogan, CEO
John Morici, CFO
Charles Larkin, Chairman of the Board
Zelko Relic, Chief Technology Officer
Jennifer Olson, Managing Director, Divisional
Julie Tay, Managing Director, Geographical
Simon Beard, Managing Director, Geographical
Christopher Puco, Managing Director, Geographical
Raphael Pascaud, Other Corporate Officer
Roger George, Other Executive Officer
Emory Wright, Senior VP, Divisional
Stuart Hockridge, Senior VP, Divisional
Sreelakshmi Kolli, Senior VP, Divisional

GROWTH PLANS/SPECIAL FEATURES:

Align Technology, Inc. (ATI) designs, manufactures and markets a system of clear aligner therapy, intra-oral scanners and CAD/CAM (computer-aided design and computer-aided manufacturing) digital services used in dentistry, orthodontics and dental records storage. The company operates in two segments: clear aligner, known as the Invisalign system; and scanners and CAD/CAM services, known as the iTero intra-oral scanner and OrthoCAD services. Clear aligner produces Invisalign for the treatment of malocclusion (misalignment of the teeth). Invisalign is series of doctor prescribed, custom manufactured, clear plastic removable orthodontic aligners. Customized systems are designed in conjunction with the ClinCheck software program, which works off an original mold of the patient's mouth and makes incremental adjustments that eventually lead to total alignment. Upon completion of the treatment, the patient may be prescribed a single clear retainer product or one of the company's Vivera Retainers. Invisalign G5 is designed to treat deep bites; and Invisalign G6 is in clinical tests for first premolar extraction. Scanners and CAD/CAM services utilize intra-oral scanning to create a 3D image of a patient's teeth using a handheld intra-oral scanner inside the mouth, as opposed to the traditional methods of taking a mold or physical impression. The company's iTero scanner is used by dental professionals and/or labs for restorative and orthodontic digital procedures as well as Invisalign digital impression submission. It stands as the only intra-oral scanner system in the market based on parallel confocal imaging, which can capture 100,000 points of laser light in perfect focus. These images are used in the OrthoCAD program, which aid in the fabrication of veneers, inlays, onlays, crowns, bridges and implant abutment; Invisialign digital impressions; and digital records storage. During 2017, 89% of the company's revenues originated from the Invisalign Full product; and scanners and services accounted for 11%.

FINANCIAL DATA: *Note: Data for latest year may not have been available at press time.*

In U.S. $	2017	2016	2015	2014	2013	2012
Revenue	1,473,413,000	1,079,874,000	845,486,000	761,653,000	660,206,000	560,041,000
R&D Expense	97,559,000	75,720,000	61,237,000	52,799,000	44,083,000	42,869,000
Operating Income	353,611,000	248,921,000	188,634,000	193,576,000	161,225,000	125,638,000
Operating Margin %	23.99%	23.05%	22.31%	25.41%	24.42%	22.43%
SGA Expense	665,777,000	490,653,000	390,239,000	332,068,000	292,798,000	247,881,000
Net Income	231,418,000	189,682,000	144,020,000	145,832,000	64,295,000	58,691,000
Operating Cash Flow	438,539,000	247,654,000	237,997,000	226,899,000	185,976,000	133,778,000
Capital Expenditure	195,695,000	70,576,000	53,451,000	24,092,000	19,412,000	38,333,000
EBITDA	391,350,000	272,923,000	206,638,000	211,432,000	178,050,000	143,449,000
Return on Assets %	14.58%	14.84%	13.41%	16.02%	8.09%	8.35%
Return on Equity %	21.56%	20.58%	17.99%	21.03%	10.58%	10.94%
Debt to Equity						

CONTACT INFORMATION:

Phone: 408 470-1000 Fax:
Toll-Free:
Address: 2560 Orchard Pkwy., San Jose, CA 95131 United States

STOCK TICKER/OTHER:

Stock Ticker: ALGN
Employees: 6,060
Parent Company:
Exchange: NAS
Fiscal Year Ends: 12/31

SALARIES/BONUSES:

Top Exec. Salary: $998,077 Bonus: $
Second Exec. Salary: $372,115 Bonus: $400,000

OTHER THOUGHTS:

Estimated Female Officers or Directors: 2
Hot Spot for Advancement for Women/Minorities:

Alignment Healthcare LLC

www.alignmenthealthcare.com

NAIC Code: 524,114

TYPES OF BUSINESS:

Medicare Plans

BRANDS/DIVISIONS/AFFILIATES:

Alignment Health Services

CONTACTS:

Note: Officers with more than one job title may be intentionally listed here more than once.

John E. Kao, CEO
Scott Powers, COO
Thomas Freeman, CFO
Supriya Sood, VP-Human Resources

GROWTH PLANS/SPECIAL FEATURES:

Alignment Healthcare, LLC and its subsidiaries provides population health management to medical partners in California, North Carolina and Florida, USA. Based in Orange, California, Alignment Healthcare focuses on improving the health and wellness of seniors. The firm offers healthcare partners a continuous end-to-end care program, including clinical care coordination, risk management capabilities and IT enablement. The company's offerings include health evaluation, diabetes management, post hospitalization care and wound care services; and a command center solution that allows its clinical care teams to access and stratify large quantities of real time and historical patient data. Management capabilities include risk contracting, revenue optimization, catastrophic case management, care management, Rx management, claims adjustment and much more. Alignment Healthcare operates a Medicare Advantage prescription drug plan organization that provides care and service to its Medicare Advantage members in select areas in California. Alignment Health Services is a business unit that offers the company's proprietary technology to third parties, allowing partner companies to access Alignment's clinical model and population health technology while taking on financial risk themselves. In December 2017, the firm added PrimeCare Medical Network, comprised of 14 PrimeCare independent practice associations (IPAs) including Empire Physicians Medical Group and Valley Physicians Network, to its Alignment Health Plan's Medicare Advantage provider network.

FINANCIAL DATA:

Note: Data for latest year may not have been available at press time.

In U.S. $	2017	2016	2015	2014	2013	2012
Revenue	525,000,000	500,000,000				
R&D Expense						
Operating Income						
Operating Margin %						
SGA Expense						
Net Income						
Operating Cash Flow						
Capital Expenditure						
EBITDA						
Return on Assets %						
Return on Equity %						
Debt to Equity						

CONTACT INFORMATION:

Phone: 844-310-2247 Fax: 844-320-2247
Toll-Free:
Address: 1100 W Town and Country Rd., Ste. 1600, Orange, CA 92868 United States

STOCK TICKER/OTHER:

Stock Ticker: Private
Employees: 400
Parent Company:
Exchange:
Fiscal Year Ends:

SALARIES/BONUSES:

Top Exec. Salary: $ Bonus: $
Second Exec. Salary: $ Bonus: $

OTHER THOUGHTS:

Estimated Female Officers or Directors:
Hot Spot for Advancement for Women/Minorities:

Allergan plc

www.allergan.com

NAIC Code: 325,412

TYPES OF BUSINESS:

Pharmaceutical Development
Eye Care Supplies
Dermatological Products
Neuromodulator Products
Obesity Intervention Products
Urologic Products
Medical Aesthetics

BRANDS/DIVISIONS/AFFILIATES:

Alloderm
Botox
Estrace
Zenpep
Keller Medical Inc
Zeltiq Aesthetics Inc
Coolsculpting
LifeCell Corporation

CONTACTS: *Note: Officers with more than one job title may be intentionally listed here more than once.*

Brenton Saunders, CEO
Maria Hilado, CFO
Paul Bisaro, Chairman of the Board
James DArecca, Chief Accounting Officer
Robert Stewart, COO
William Meury, Executive VP, Divisional
Charles Mayr, Other Executive Officer
Patrick Eagan, Other Executive Officer
Karen Ling, Other Executive Officer
Robert Bailey, Other Executive Officer

GROWTH PLANS/SPECIAL FEATURES:

Allergan plc is a global pharmaceutical company focused on developing, manufacturing and commercializing branded pharmaceutical, device, biologic, surgical and regenerative medicine products. The firm's portfolio features seven franchises in therapeutic categories: dermatology & medical aesthetics, central nervous system, eye care, women's health, urology, gastroenterology and anti-infective. Because of the differences between the types of products Allergan operates its business in three segments: U.S. specialized therapeutics, U.S. general medicine and international. The U.S. specialized therapeutics segment includes sales and expenses relating to branded products within the U.S., including medical aesthetics, medical dermatology, eye care and neuroscience and urology therapeutic products. The U.S. general medicine segment includes sales and expenses relating to branded products within the U.S. that do not fall into the U.S. specialized category, including central nervous system, gastrointestinal, women's health, anti-infectives and diversified brands. The international segment includes sales and expenses relating to products sold outside the U.S. Branded products include: Alloderm, a regenerative medicine; Botox cosmetics, for facial aesthetics; Estrace cream, a hormone cream for women's health; Lumigan/Ganfort, for eye care; Namenda XR, for the central nervous system; and Zenpep, for gastrointestinal purposes. The majority of Allergan's branded drug delivery research and development activities take place in Irvine, California. During 2017, the firm acquired: Keller Medical, Inc., a medical device company and developer of the Keller Funnel; Zeltiq Aesthetics, Inc., which develops and commercializes products utilizing its proprietary controlled-cooling technology platform Coolsculpting; and LifeCell Corporation, a regenerative medicine company.

U.S. employees of the firm receive medical, long-term care, dental, vision and prescription drug coverage; life, AD&D, business travel accident and disability insurance; group legal services; tuition reimbursement; flexible spending accounts; domestic partner coverage; and pet insurance.

FINANCIAL DATA: *Note: Data for latest year may not have been available at press time.*

In U.S. $	2017	2016	2015	2014	2013	2012
Revenue	15,940,700,000	14,570,600,000	15,071,000,000	13,062,300,000	8,677,600,000	5,914,900,000
R&D Expense	2,100,100,000	2,575,700,000	2,358,500,000	1,085,900,000	616,900,000	401,800,000
Operating Income	-541,200,000	-1,076,600,000	-2,230,900,000	-518,100,000	479,500,000	470,300,000
Operating Margin %	-3.39%	-7.38%	-14.80%	-3.96%	5.52%	7.95%
SGA Expense	5,016,700,000	4,740,300,000	4,679,600,000	3,593,200,000	2,047,800,000	1,171,300,000
Net Income	-4,125,500,000	14,973,400,000	3,915,200,000	-1,630,500,000	-750,400,000	97,300,000
Operating Cash Flow	5,873,400,000	1,425,300,000	4,530,000,000	2,243,000,000	1,213,500,000	665,800,000
Capital Expenditure	964,200,000	333,400,000	609,600,000	274,700,000	307,900,000	146,500,000
EBITDA	-1,922,200,000	5,094,600,000	2,758,400,000	1,528,100,000	646,100,000	940,400,000
Return on Assets %	-3.56%	11.09%	3.91%	-4.33%	-4.07%	.93%
Return on Equity %	-6.28%	20.56%	7.36%	-8.61%	-11.22%	2.63%
Debt to Equity	0.37	0.42	0.56	0.52	0.89	1.63

CONTACT INFORMATION:

Phone: 441 295 2244 Fax: 714 246-4971
Toll-Free: 800-347-4500
Address: Clonshaugh Business & Tech Park, Coolock, Dublin, D17 E400 Ireland

STOCK TICKER/OTHER:

Stock Ticker: AGN
Employees: 16,700
Parent Company:
Exchange: NYS
Fiscal Year Ends: 12/31

SALARIES/BONUSES:

Top Exec. Salary: $1,232,822 Bonus: $
Second Exec. Salary: $873,973 Bonus: $

OTHER THOUGHTS:

Estimated Female Officers or Directors: 2
Hot Spot for Advancement for Women/Minorities: Y

Alliance Healthcare Services Inc www.alliancehealthcareservices-us.com

NAIC Code: 621,512

TYPES OF BUSINESS:

Diagnostic Imaging Centers
Diagnostic Imaging Support Services
MRI Imaging
PET Imaging
CT Imaging
Radiation Therapy

BRANDS/DIVISIONS/AFFILIATES:

Tahoe Investment Group Co Ltd
Alliance HealthCare Radiology
Alliance Oncology LLC
Alliance HealthCare Interventional Partners LLC

CONTACTS: *Note: Officers with more than one job title may be intentionally listed here more than once.*

Percy Tomlinson, CEO
Rhonda Longmore-Grund, CFO
Christianna Rosow, Chief Accounting Officer
Richard Johns, COO
Laurie Miller, Executive VP, Divisional
Richard Jones, President, Divisional
Gregory Spurlock, President, Divisional
Steven Siwek, President, Divisional
Larry Buckelew, Vice Chairman of the Board

GROWTH PLANS/SPECIAL FEATURES:

Alliance HealthCare Services, Inc., owned by Tahoe Investment Group Co., Ltd., provides outsourced health care services to hospitals and providers. The company also operates freestanding outpatient radiology, oncology and interventional clinics, as well as ambulatory surgical centers (ASCs) that are not owned by hospitals or providers. Diagnostic radiology services are delivered through Alliance HealthCare Radiology; radiation oncology services through Alliance Oncology, LLC; and interventional and pain management services through Alliance HealthCare Interventional Partners, LLC. The company operates over 600 diagnostic imaging and radiation therapy systems, including 108 fixed-site radiology centers throughout the U.S., as well as 54 radiation therapy centers and stereotactic radiosurgery facilities. Additionally, the firm operates 22 pain management/interventional procedures clinics. Alliance HealthCare provides health care services for more than 1,100 hospitals and health care partners in 46 states, via approximately 2,750 team members.

The firm offers employees medical and dental insurance, life insurance, disability coverage, educational assistance and a 401(k) savings plan.

FINANCIAL DATA: *Note: Data for latest year may not have been available at press time.*

In U.S. $	2017	2016	2015	2014	2013	2012
Revenue	550,000,000	505,548,992	473,054,016	436,387,008	448,831,008	472,257,984
R&D Expense						
Operating Income						
Operating Margin %						
SGA Expense						
Net Income		493,000	6,742,000	10,618,000	-21,483,000	-11,938,000
Operating Cash Flow						
Capital Expenditure						
EBITDA						
Return on Assets %						
Return on Equity %						
Debt to Equity						

CONTACT INFORMATION:

Phone: 949 242-5300 Fax:
Toll-Free: 800-544-3215
Address: 100 Bayview Cir., Ste. 400, Newport Beach, CA 92660 United States

STOCK TICKER/OTHER:

Stock Ticker: Private Exchange:
Employees: 2,450 Fiscal Year Ends: 12/31
Parent Company: Tahoe Investment Group Co Ltd

SALARIES/BONUSES:

Top Exec. Salary: $ Bonus: $
Second Exec. Salary: $ Bonus: $

OTHER THOUGHTS:

Estimated Female Officers or Directors: 1
Hot Spot for Advancement for Women/Minorities:

Allied Healthcare International Inc

www.alliedhealthcare.com

NAIC Code: 561,320

TYPES OF BUSINESS:

Temporary Staffing
Home Health Care
Nursing & Para-Professional Services
Home Medical Equipment & Oxygen
Respiration Therapy
Medical Staffing

BRANDS/DIVISIONS/AFFILIATES:

Saga Group Limited
Allied Nursing Services

CONTACTS: *Note: Officers with more than one job title may be intentionally listed here more than once.*

Alexander (Sandy) Young, CEO

GROWTH PLANS/SPECIAL FEATURES:

Allied Healthcare International, Inc., a subsidiary of Saga Group Limited, is a leading provider of flexible healthcare staffing to the U.K. healthcare industry. The company operates a network of 80 branches in England, Scotland and Wales, providing staff including nurses, nurse aides and home health aides. AHI places its staff in hospitals, nursing homes, care homes, private companies, the prison service, the police service, armed services hospitals and private homes on a per diem basis from a pool of healthcare professionals. A large portion of the company's revenue comes from customers that are U.K. government entities, primarily local social-services departments and National Health Service (NHS) hospitals. Homecare for individuals includes traditional homecare, dementia care, care for those with learning disabilities, as well as children and family services. Live-in care is provided for those who need full-time support and 24-hour care to continue living in their own home. Live-in care can be a short-term solution during recovery periods, or a long-term option. Allied Nursing Services supplies experienced nurses from all specialties to private hospitals and clinics, and is one of the U.K.'s largest providers of healthcare professionals to the public and private sector.

FINANCIAL DATA: *Note: Data for latest year may not have been available at press time.*

In U.S. $	2017	2016	2015	2014	2013	2012
Revenue	462,000,000	440,000,000	430,000,000	425,000,000		
R&D Expense						
Operating Income						
Operating Margin %						
SGA Expense						
Net Income						
Operating Cash Flow						
Capital Expenditure						
EBITDA						
Return on Assets %						
Return on Equity %						
Debt to Equity						

CONTACT INFORMATION:

Phone: Fax:
Toll-Free: 800-542-1078
Address: Cavendish House, Lakhpur Court, Staffordshire Tech Park, Stafford, ST18 0FX United Kingdom

STOCK TICKER/OTHER:

Stock Ticker: Subsidiary
Employees: 8,000
Parent Company: Saga Group Limited
Exchange:
Fiscal Year Ends: 12/31

SALARIES/BONUSES:

Top Exec. Salary: $ Bonus: $
Second Exec. Salary: $ Bonus: $

OTHER THOUGHTS:

Estimated Female Officers or Directors:
Hot Spot for Advancement for Women/Minorities: Y

Allina Health

www.allinahealth.org

NAIC Code: 622,110

TYPES OF BUSINESS:

General Medical and Surgical Hospitals
Clinics
Medical Equipment Rental
Emergency Medical Transportation Services
Hospice Care
Pharmacies
Rehabilitation Services

BRANDS/DIVISIONS/AFFILIATES:

Abbott Northwestern Hospital
Buffalo Hospital
Cambridge Medical Center
New Ulm Medical Center
Phillips Eye Institute
Courage Kenny Rehabilitation Institute
Allina Home Oxygen and Medical Equipment

CONTACTS: *Note: Officers with more than one job title may be intentionally listed here more than once.*

Penny Wheeler, CEO
Penny Ann Wheeler, Chief Clinical Officer
Duncan P. Gallagher, Exec. VP-Admin.
Elizabeth Truesdell Smith, General Counsel
Robert Wieland, Exec. VP-Clinic & Community Div.
Thomas O'Connor, VP
Ben Bache-Wiig, VP
Sara Criger, VP

GROWTH PLANS/SPECIAL FEATURES:

Allina Health is a nonprofit network of hospitals, clinics and other healthcare services located throughout Minnesota and western Wisconsin. The company's operations include hospitals, Allina Health clinics and retail pharmacy sites. The firm's hospitals include Abbott Northwestern Hospital, Buffalo Hospital, Cambridge Medical Center, New Ulm Medical Center, United Hospital and Phillips Eye Institute, one of the largest specialty hospitals in the U.S. dedicated to eye diseases and disorders. Another specialized healthcare facility, the Courage Kenny Rehabilitation Institute, treats patients for conditions such as stroke and back pain as well as sports-related, spinal cord and brain injuries. Allina also offers home care services such as hospice and palliative care. In addition, Allina operates Allina Home Oxygen and Medical Equipment, which supplies oxygen, respiratory and other medical equipment and supplies to a patient's home; and Allina Health Emergency Medical Services, which provides ambulance and medical transport services including priority medical dispatch, emergency and non-emergency medical response, flight care and wheelchair transport in more than 100 communities in Minnesota.

Employee benefits include medical and dental coverage, wellness programs, an employee assistance program, a retirement savings account, a health savings account, life and AD&D insurance, short- and long-term disability, tuition reimbursement, adoption assistance and business travel accident coverage.

FINANCIAL DATA: *Note: Data for latest year may not have been available at press time.*

In U.S. $	2017	2016	2015	2014	2013	2012
Revenue	4,308,729,861	4,103,552,249	3,937,422,813	3,684,954,292	3,541,616,949	3,246,367,863
R&D Expense						
Operating Income						
Operating Margin %						
SGA Expense						
Net Income		30,812,991	199,411,489	141,577,304	323,457,347	154,326,778
Operating Cash Flow						
Capital Expenditure						
EBITDA						
Return on Assets %						
Return on Equity %						
Debt to Equity						

CONTACT INFORMATION:

Phone: 612-262-9000 Fax:
Toll-Free: 800-859-5077
Address: 2925 Chicago Ave., Minneapolis, MN 55407 United States

STOCK TICKER/OTHER:

Stock Ticker: Nonprofit
Employees: 30,500
Parent Company:
Exchange:
Fiscal Year Ends: 12/31

SALARIES/BONUSES:

Top Exec. Salary: $ Bonus: $
Second Exec. Salary: $ Bonus: $

OTHER THOUGHTS:

Estimated Female Officers or Directors: 8
Hot Spot for Advancement for Women/Minorities: Y

Allscripts Healthcare Solutions Inc

www.allscripts.com

NAIC Code: 511210D

TYPES OF BUSINESS:

Computer Software, Healthcare & Biotechnology
Interactive Education Services
Clinical Software
Electronic Records Systems
Care Management Software

BRANDS/DIVISIONS/AFFILIATES:

Sunrise Acute EHR
Revenue Cycle Management Services
HealthGrid Holding Company

CONTACTS: *Note: Officers with more than one job title may be intentionally listed here more than once.*

Paul Black, CEO
Dennis Olis, CFO
Brian Farley, Chief Administrative Officer
Michael Klayko, Director
Lisa Khorey, Executive VP
Richard Poulton, President

GROWTH PLANS/SPECIAL FEATURES:

Allscripts Healthcare Solutions, Inc. provides clinical software, connectivity and information solutions that physicians and health care providers use to improve service delivery. The firm provides software solutions for hospitals, physician practices and post-acute organizations. For hospitals and health systems, these applications include the Sunrise Acute EHR suite of clinical solutions, comprising a full acute care electronic health record (EHR), integrated with financial/administrative solutions including performance management and revenue cycle/access management. Acute care solutions include modules of the Sunrise suite that are available on a stand-alone basis as well as additional stand-alone solutions such as an emergency department information system, care management and discharge management. Allscripts' post-acute tools help smooth the patient transition from hospital to post-acute care facilities, including home health providers, hospices and private duty organizations. For physician practices, the firm's products include integrated EHR and practice management functionality available either via traditional on premise delivery or via Software-as-a-Service; revenue cycle management software and the Revenue Cycle Management Services solution, which enables practices to outsource their full revenue cycle to the firm or address requirements in-house; clearinghouse services; stand-alone electronic prescribing; and document imaging solutions for physician practices. The firm's population health management solution enables hospitals/health systems/ physician practices to connect, transition, analyze, and coordinate care. Additionally, Allscripts offers professional services such as conversion and integration of historical data into its software, training and support services, as well as consulting, remote hosting and IT outsourcing services. In April 2018, the firm sold its OneContent business to Hyland Software, Inc. The following May, Allscripts acquired HealthGrid Holding Company, a mobile, enterprise patient engagement solution.

Allscripts offers its employees medical, dental and vision insurance; flex spending accounts; 401(k); adoption assistance; and education assistance.

FINANCIAL DATA: *Note: Data for latest year may not have been available at press time.*

In U.S. $	2017	2016	2015	2014	2013	2012
Revenue	1,806,342,000	1,549,899,000	1,386,393,000	1,377,873,000	1,373,061,000	
R&D Expense	220,219,000	187,906,000	184,791,000	192,821,000	199,751,000	
Operating Income	41,917,000	64,421,000	33,427,000	-36,798,000	-116,147,000	
Operating Margin %	2.32%	4.15%	2.41%	-2.67%	-8.45%	
SGA Expense	486,271,000	392,865,000	339,175,000	358,681,000	419,599,000	
Net Income	-152,609,000	2,884,000	-2,226,000	-66,453,000	-104,026,000	
Operating Cash Flow	279,415,000	269,004,000	211,579,000	103,496,000	80,987,000	
Capital Expenditure	185,271,000	137,982,000	67,586,000	67,099,000	116,156,000	
EBITDA	96,398,000	220,523,000	191,544,000	133,402,000	50,956,000	
Return on Assets %	-4.87%	-.78%	-.08%	-2.59%	-4.15%	
Return on Equity %	-16.69%	-1.94%	-.16%	-5.10%	-7.99%	
Debt to Equity	1.37	1.05	0.43	0.42	0.41	

CONTACT INFORMATION:

Phone: 866 358-6869 Fax:
Toll-Free: 800-654-0889
Address: 222 Merchandise Mart Plz., Ste. 2024, Chicago, IL 60654 United States

STOCK TICKER/OTHER:

Stock Ticker: MDRX
Employees: 7,500
Parent Company:
Exchange: NAS
Fiscal Year Ends: 12/31

SALARIES/BONUSES:

Top Exec. Salary: $1,030,000 Bonus: $
Second Exec. Salary: $615,000 Bonus: $

OTHER THOUGHTS:

Estimated Female Officers or Directors: 2
Hot Spot for Advancement for Women/Minorities: Y

Amedisys Inc

NAIC Code: 621,610

www.amedisys.com

TYPES OF BUSINESS:

Home Health Care Services
Home Health Care
Hospice Care

BRANDS/DIVISIONS/AFFILIATES:

Home Staff LLC

CONTACTS: *Note: Officers with more than one job title may be intentionally listed here more than once.*

Donald Washburn, Chairman of the Board
Scott Ginn, Chief Accounting Officer
Michael North, Chief Information Officer
Christopher Gerard, COO
Paul Kusserow, Director
David Kemmerly, General Counsel
David Pearce, Other Executive Officer
Susan Sender, Other Executive Officer
Lawrence Pernosky, Other Executive Officer

GROWTH PLANS/SPECIAL FEATURES:

Amedisys, Inc. provides home health and hospice services in 34 U.S. states through its wide range of regional subsidiaries. The firm owns and operates 323 Medicare-certified home health agencies and 83 hospice care centers. Approximately 75% to 80% of the firm's revenue is generated by Medicare payments. Amedisys serves more than 369,000 patients per year, dividing its operations between home healthcare and hospice care. Under the home healthcare operations, Medicare recipients who require ongoing intermittent skilled care are provided services by nurses; nurse practitioners; medical social workers; home health aides; and physical, occupational and speech therapists within the patient's home. The firm's chronic care clinical programs incorporate national clinical standards and use patient education to give patients and their caregivers self-care management skills. Chronic care programs include programs for cardiovascular, respiratory, diabetes, behavioral health, rehabilitative and medical surgical conditions. Under the hospice care operations, the company provides care to patients suffering from a terminal illness. Patients given a life expectancy of six months or less and afflicted with heart disease, pulmonary disease, dementia, Alzheimer's, HIV/AIDS or cancer are eligible for hospice care. This service builds a network of support comprised of the patient's family, physicians, nurses, social workers, home health aids, volunteers, bereavement counselors and spiritual counselors. Amedisys offers palliative care in select markets, for patients not eligible for hospice care. This service provides pain and symptom management to those living with chronic diseases. In 2018, the firm agreed to acquire Bring Care Home, a personal care provider; acquired the personal care provider East Tennessee Personal Care Service; acquired the right to operate in 10 counties in western Kentucky from Christian Care Communities.

Employee benefits include health, dental and vision coverage; supplemental life insurance; flex spending accounts; short-term disability; a 401(k); an employee stock purchase plan; an employee assistance plan; and tuition reimbursement.

FINANCIAL DATA: *Note: Data for latest year may not have been available at press time.*

In U.S. $	2017	2016	2015	2014	2013	2012
Revenue	1,533,680,000	1,437,454,000	1,280,541,000	1,204,554,000	1,249,344,000	1,487,905,000
R&D Expense						
Operating Income	108,559,000	61,772,000	68,102,000	27,154,000	4,521,000	49,898,000
Operating Margin %	7.07%	4.29%	5.31%	2.25%	.36%	3.35%
SGA Expense	482,213,000	503,430,000	452,435,000	441,738,000	474,074,000	535,259,000
Net Income	30,301,000	37,261,000	-3,021,000	12,776,000	-96,178,000	-83,588,000
Operating Cash Flow	105,731,000	62,259,000	107,785,000	-65,534,000	102,263,000	69,494,000
Capital Expenditure	10,707,000	15,717,000	21,429,000	12,008,000	41,736,000	48,262,000
EBITDA	102,955,000	86,408,000	30,511,000	57,540,000	-111,680,000	-66,469,000
Return on Assets %	3.91%	5.25%	-.44%	1.83%	-13.20%	-10.52%
Return on Equity %	6.21%	8.56%	-.74%	3.32%	-23.32%	-17.21%
Debt to Equity	0.15	0.19	0.23	0.26	0.08	0.14

CONTACT INFORMATION:

Phone: 225 292-2031 Fax:
Toll-Free: 800-467-2662
Address: 5959 S. Sherwood Forest Blvd., Baton Rouge, LA 70816 United States

STOCK TICKER/OTHER:

Stock Ticker: AMED Exchange: NAS
Employees: 16,000 Fiscal Year Ends: 12/31
Parent Company:

SALARIES/BONUSES:

Top Exec. Salary: $875,000 Bonus: $
Second Exec. Salary: $439,615 Bonus: $20,000

OTHER THOUGHTS:

Estimated Female Officers or Directors: 3
Hot Spot for Advancement for Women/Minorities: Y

American HomePatient Inc

www.ahom.com

NAIC Code: 621,610

TYPES OF BUSINESS:

Home Health Care Services
Respiratory Therapy Services
Infusion Therapy Services
Equipment Leasing
Home Health Supplies
Enteral Nutrition Products and Services

BRANDS/DIVISIONS/AFFILIATES:

Linde Group (The)
Lincare Holdings Inc

CONTACTS: *Note: Officers with more than one job title may be intentionally listed here more than once.*

Mark L. Lamp, CEO
Mark L. Lamp, Pres.
Stephen L. Clanton, CFO

GROWTH PLANS/SPECIAL FEATURES:

American HomePatient, Inc. provides home healthcare services and products consisting primarily of respiratory and infusion therapies and the rental and sale of home medical equipment and home healthcare supplies. The firm provides products and services to over 250 centers. These products and services are paid for primarily by Medicare, Medicaid and other third-party payers. American HomePatient provides a wide variety of home respiratory services primarily to patients with severe and chronic pulmonary diseases. The firm's respiratory services consist of oxygen systems to assist in breathing, including oxygen concentrators, liquid oxygen systems and high-pressure oxygen cylinders; nebulizers and related inhalation drugs; respiratory assist devices for patients with obstructive sleep apnea; home ventilators; non-invasive positive-pressure ventilation masks; and home respiratory evaluations and related diagnostic equipment. Its home infusion therapy services include pumps and related supplies, infusion pharmacy services and infusion therapies and treatments. Its home medical equipment operations consist principally of the rental and sale of wheelchairs, walking aids, lift chairs, hospital beds and rehabilitation equipment. American HomePatient is owned by Lincare Holdings, Inc., which itself is a subsidiary of industrial gas and engineering company, The Linde Group.

FINANCIAL DATA: *Note: Data for latest year may not have been available at press time.*

In U.S. $	2017	2016	2015	2014	2013	2012
Revenue	315,249,328	300,237,455	292,000,000	280,000,000	270,000,000	260,000,000
R&D Expense						
Operating Income						
Operating Margin %						
SGA Expense						
Net Income		7,148,407				
Operating Cash Flow						
Capital Expenditure						
EBITDA						
Return on Assets %						
Return on Equity %						
Debt to Equity						

CONTACT INFORMATION:

Phone: 615-221-8884 Fax:
Toll-Free: 800-890-7271
Address: 5200 Maryland Way, Ste. 400, Brentwood, TN 37027 United States

STOCK TICKER/OTHER:

Stock Ticker: Subsidiary
Employees: 2,177
Parent Company: Linde Group (The)
Exchange:
Fiscal Year Ends: 12/31

SALARIES/BONUSES:

Top Exec. Salary: $ Bonus: $
Second Exec. Salary: $ Bonus: $

OTHER THOUGHTS:

Estimated Female Officers or Directors:
Hot Spot for Advancement for Women/Minorities:

Amerigroup Corporation

www.amerigroupcorp.com

NAIC Code: 524,114

TYPES OF BUSINESS:

Managed Health Care

BRANDS/DIVISIONS/AFFILIATES:

Anthem Inc

CONTACTS:
Note: Officers with more than one job title may be intentionally listed here more than once.

Gail K. Boudreaux, CEO-Anthem, Inc.
Richard C. Zoretic, Exec. VP
Mary T. McCluskey, Exec. VP
Jack Young, VP
Ken Aversa, Sr. VP-Customer Svc. Oper., Medicaid, WellPoint
Georgia Dodds Foley, Chief Compliance Officer, Medicaid, WellPoint
John E. Little, Interim Sr. VP-Gov't Affairs, WellPoint
Aileen McCormick, CEO-Western Region, Medicaid, WellPoint

GROWTH PLANS/SPECIAL FEATURES:

Amerigroup Corporation, the state-sponsored program services division of health benefits company Anthem, Inc., is a managed health care company focused on serving people who receive benefits through publicly-sponsored programs. These programs include Medicaid, Medicare Advantage, Family Care and the Children's Health Insurance Program (CHIP). Since the company does not offer Medicare or commercial products, people served by Amerigroup are generally younger, tend to access health care in an inefficient manner and have a greater percentage of medical expenses related to obstetrics, diabetes, circulatory and respiratory conditions. The firm reduces costs for families and state governments by combining social and behavioral health services to help members obtain health care. Amerigroup's provider networks consist of approximately 136,000 physicians, including primary care physicians, specialists and ancillary providers, and approximately 800 hospitals across all of its markets. The company currently enrolls 5.6million members in nine states nationwide.

FINANCIAL DATA:
Note: Data for latest year may not have been available at press time.

In U.S. $	2017	2016	2015	2014	2013	2012
Revenue	11,000,000,000	10,500,000,000	10,000,000,000	9,625,000,000	9,125,000,000	
R&D Expense						
Operating Income						
Operating Margin %						
SGA Expense						
Net Income						
Operating Cash Flow						
Capital Expenditure						
EBITDA						
Return on Assets %						
Return on Equity %						
Debt to Equity						

CONTACT INFORMATION:

Phone: 757 490-6900 Fax:
Toll-Free: 800-600-4441
Address: 4425 Corporation Ln., Virginia Beach, VA 23462 United States

STOCK TICKER/OTHER:

Stock Ticker: Subsidiary
Exchange:
Employees: 8,000
Fiscal Year Ends: 12/31
Parent Company: Anthem Inc

SALARIES/BONUSES:

Top Exec. Salary: $ Bonus: $
Second Exec. Salary: $ Bonus: $

OTHER THOUGHTS:

Estimated Female Officers or Directors: 3
Hot Spot for Advancement for Women/Minorities: Y

AmeriPath Inc

www.ameripath.com

NAIC Code: 621,511

TYPES OF BUSINESS:

Anatomic Pathology Practice Management
Cancer Diagnostic Services
Staffing Services
Operations Management
Health Care Information Services

BRANDS/DIVISIONS/AFFILIATES:

Quest Diagnostics Inc
AmeriPath Esoteri Institute
AmeriPath Institute of Gastrointestinal
AmeriPath Institute of Urologic Pathology
Center for Advanced Diagnostics (The)
Dermpath Diagnositics
Nephropathology Diagnostics
Institute of Immunofluorescence (The)

CONTACTS: *Note: Officers with more than one job title may be intentionally listed here more than once.*

Nathan Sherman, VP-Anatomy Pathology
Joan Miller, Pres.

GROWTH PLANS/SPECIAL FEATURES:

AmeriPath, Inc., owned by Quest Diagnostics, Inc., is one of the nation's leading providers of anatomic pathology, molecular diagnostic and healthcare information services to physicians, hospitals, national clinical laboratories, surgical centers and managed care organizations. The company has over 450 working pathologists and provides specialty pathology services at independent pathology practices throughout the U.S. AmeriPath directly offers comprehensive diagnostic, prognostic and therapeutic services in the fields of oncology, gastroenterology, hematology, dermatopathology, nephropathology and women's health. The company's primary business is developing, staffing and operating clinical pathology laboratories, which it does through long-term service management agreements. The company operates major centers through this management model, including: AmeriPath Esoteric Institute, AmeriPath Institute of Gastrointestinal Pathology and Digestive Disease, AmeriPath Institute of Urologic Pathology and Renal Disease, The Center for Advanced Diagnostics, Dermpath Diagnostics, Ameripath's Nephropathology Diagnostics and The Institute for Immunofluorescence. These centers cover fields of medical research and analysis such as hematology and genetics examination; women's health; diagnoses of biopsy specimens for urologic pathology and renal diseases; diagnostic tests and diseases management for leukemia, lymphoma and cancers of the breast, prostate and colon; immunofluorescence testing for autoimmune and inflammatory skin diseases; and dermatopathology services.

AmeriPath offers its employees a wide variety of insurance options, credit union access, movie ticket discounts, an employee assistance program, college fund programs, tuition reimbursement and child and dependent care.

FINANCIAL DATA: *Note: Data for latest year may not have been available at press time.*

In U.S. $	2017	2016	2015	2014	2013	2012
Revenue	922,000,000	900,000,000	875,000,000	870,000,000	850,000,000	800,000,000
R&D Expense						
Operating Income						
Operating Margin %						
SGA Expense						
Net Income						
Operating Cash Flow						
Capital Expenditure						
EBITDA						
Return on Assets %						
Return on Equity %						
Debt to Equity						

CONTACT INFORMATION:

Phone: 561-712-6200 Fax: 561-845-0129
Toll-Free: 800-330-6565
Address: 7111 Fairway Dr., Ste. 400, Palm Beach Gardens, FL 33418 United States

STOCK TICKER/OTHER:

Stock Ticker: Subsidiary
Exchange:
Employees: 3,979
Fiscal Year Ends: 12/31
Parent Company: Quest Diagnostics Inc

SALARIES/BONUSES:

Top Exec. Salary: $ Bonus: $
Second Exec. Salary: $ Bonus: $

OTHER THOUGHTS:

Estimated Female Officers or Directors: 1
Hot Spot for Advancement for Women/Minorities:

AmerisourceBergen Corp

www.amerisourcebergen.com

NAIC Code: 424,210

TYPES OF BUSINESS:

Drug Distribution
Pharmacy Management & Consulting Services
Packaging Solutions
Information Technology
Healthcare Equipment

BRANDS/DIVISIONS/AFFILIATES:

AmerisourceBergen Consulting Services
World Courier
MWI Animal Health
Northeast Veterinary Supply Co
HD Smith
Innomar Strategies
Therapeutic Products Inc

CONTACTS: *Note: Officers with more than one job title may be intentionally listed here more than once.*

Steven Collis, CEO
Tim Guttman, CFO
Lazarus Krikorian, Chief Accounting Officer
Gina Clark, Chief Administrative Officer
Dale Danilewitz, Chief Information Officer
Sun Park, Executive VP, Divisional
John Chou, Executive VP
Kathy Gaddes, Executive VP
Robert Mauch, Executive VP
James Cleary, Executive VP
Peyton Howell, President, Divisional

GROWTH PLANS/SPECIAL FEATURES:

AmerisourceBergen Corp. is one of the largest wholesale distributors of pharmaceutical products and services to a wide variety of health care providers and pharmacies. The firm offers brand name and generic pharmaceuticals, supplies and equipment and serves the U.S., Canada and selected global markets. The company's operations are divided into two segments: pharmaceutical distribution services (PDS) and other. PDS provides drug distributes a comprehensive offering of brand-name, specialty brand-name and generic pharmaceuticals, over-the-counter healthcare products, home healthcare supplies and equipment, outsourced compounded sterile preparations and related services to a wide variety of healthcare providers, including acute care hospitals and health systems, independent and chain retail pharmacies, mail order pharmacies, medical clinics, long-term care and alternate site pharmacies and other customers. Through a number of operating businesses, the PDS reportable segment provides pharmaceutical distribution (including plasma and other blood products, injectible pharmaceuticals, vaccines and other specialty pharmaceutical products) and additional services to physicians who specialize in a variety of disease states, especially oncology, and to other healthcare providers, including hospitals and dialysis clinics. Additionally, the PDS provides data analytics, outcomes research and additional services for biotechnology and pharmaceutical manufacturers. The other segment oversses: AmerisourceBergen Consulting Services (ABCS), which provides commercialization support services such as reimbursement support programs, outcomes research, contract field staffing, patient assistance and copay assistance programs; MWI, a leading animal health distribution company in the U.S. and in the U.K.; and World Courier, which is a global specialty transportation and logistics provider for the biopharmaceutical industry serving more than 50 countries. In December 2017, the firm, through MWI Animal Health, acquired Northeast Veterinary Supply Co. In January 2018, AmerisourceBergen completed its acquisition of H.D. Smith, a pharmaceutical wholesaler. The following May, the firm, through Innomar Strategies, acquired Therapeutic Products, Inc., a regulatory consulting firm.

Employee benefits include health care, retirement, life insurance and disability protection.

FINANCIAL DATA: *Note: Data for latest year may not have been available at press time.*

In U.S. $	2017	2016	2015	2014	2013	2012
Revenue	153,143,800,000	146,849,700,000	135,961,800,000	119,569,100,000	87,959,170,000	79,489,600,000
R&D Expense						
Operating Income	1,974,742,000	1,726,723,000	1,330,094,000	1,201,623,000	988,454,000	1,263,828,000
Operating Margin %	1.28%	1.17%	.97%	1.00%	1.12%	1.58%
SGA Expense	2,166,825,000	2,161,905,000	1,923,381,000	1,589,174,000	1,334,203,000	1,264,216,000
Net Income	364,484,000	1,427,929,000	-134,887,000	276,484,000	433,707,000	718,986,000
Operating Cash Flow	1,504,138,000	3,178,497,000	3,920,379,000	1,463,153,000	788,125,000	1,305,449,000
Capital Expenditure	466,397,000	464,616,000	231,585,000	264,457,000	202,450,000	164,041,000
EBITDA	1,499,260,000	1,927,425,000	625,735,000	943,864,000	1,070,299,000	1,407,550,000
Return on Assets %	1.05%	4.65%	-.54%	1.36%	2.52%	4.72%
Return on Equity %	17.38%	103.36%	-10.41%	12.92%	18.16%	27.01%
Debt to Equity	1.66	1.68	5.51	1.01	0.60	0.58

CONTACT INFORMATION:

Phone: 610 727-7000 Fax: 610 647-0141
Toll-Free: 800-829-3132
Address: 1300 Morris Dr., Chesterbrook, PA 19087 United States

STOCK TICKER/OTHER:

Stock Ticker: ABC
Exchange: NYS
Employees: 19,000
Fiscal Year Ends: 09/30
Parent Company:

SALARIES/BONUSES:

Top Exec. Salary: $1,240,000 Bonus: $
Second Exec. Salary: $710,000 Bonus: $

OTHER THOUGHTS:

Estimated Female Officers or Directors: 7
Hot Spot for Advancement for Women/Minorities: Y

Amgen Inc

www.amgen.com

NAIC Code: 325,412

TYPES OF BUSINESS:

Drugs-Diversified
Oncology Drugs
Nephrology Drugs
Inflammation Drugs
Neurology Drugs

BRANDS/DIVISIONS/AFFILIATES:

Embrel
Neulasta
Aranesp
Prolia
Sensipar
XGEVA
EPOGEN
EVENITY

CONTACTS: *Note: Officers with more than one job title may be intentionally listed here more than once.*

Robert Bradway, CEO
David Meline, CFO
David Reese, Executive VP, Divisional
Anthony Hooper, Executive VP, Divisional
Esteban Santos, Executive VP, Divisional
Cynthia Patton, Other Executive Officer
Lori Johnston, Senior VP
David Piacquad, Senior VP, Divisional
Jonathan Graham, Senior VP

GROWTH PLANS/SPECIAL FEATURES:

Amgen, Inc. is a global biotechnology medicines company that discovers, develops, manufactures and markets human therapeutics based on cellular and molecular biology. Its products are used for treatment in the fields of supportive cancer care, nephrology and inflammation. Amgen's current (early-2018) primary pipeline products include: Prolia (denosumab), XGEVA (denosumab) and EVENITY (romosozumab), each for bone health; Repatha (evolucumab), for cardiovascular purposes; Aimovig (erenumab), for the prevention of migraines; Aranesp (darbepoetin alfa), BLINCYTO (blinatumomab), KYPROLIS (carfilzomib) and Vectibix (panitumumab), for oncology/hematology purposes; and Sensipar/Mimpara (cinacalcet), AMJEVITA (adalimumab-atto), AMGEVITA (biosimilar adalimumab), ABP 980 and MVASI (bevacizumab-awwb), each for nephrology purposes. Primary marketed products include: Embrel, for the treatment of adults with rheumatoid arthritis, psoriatic arthritis and plaque psoriasis; Neulasta, to help reduce the chance of infection due to a low white blood cell count in patients with certain types of cancer; Aranesp, to treat a lower-than-normal number of red blood cells caused by chronic kidney disease (CKD); Prolia, to treat postmenopausal women with osteoporosis at high risk for fracture; Sensipar/Mimpara, to treat secondary hyperparathyroidism (sHPT); XGEVA, to prevent skeletal-related events (SREs) in patients with bone metastases from solid tumors; and EPOGEN, to treat anemia caused by CKD. Amgen's product sales to three large wholesalers, AmerisourceBergen Corporation, McKesson Corporation and Cardinal Health, Inc. Each individually accounted for more than 10% of total revenues in 2017. On a combined basis, they accounted for 96% of U.S. gross product sales, and 81% of worldwide gross revenue (in 2017).

Amgen offers its employees health, disability and life insurance; paid time off; home and auto insurance; tuition reimbursement; childcare services; telecommuting options; and recreation/fitness classes.

FINANCIAL DATA: *Note: Data for latest year may not have been available at press time.*

In U.S. $	2017	2016	2015	2014	2013	2012
Revenue	22,849,000,000	22,991,000,000	21,662,000,000	20,063,000,000	18,676,000,000	17,265,000,000
R&D Expense	3,562,000,000	3,840,000,000	4,070,000,000	4,297,000,000	4,083,000,000	3,380,000,000
Operating Income	9,973,000,000	9,794,000,000	8,470,000,000	6,191,000,000	5,867,000,000	5,577,000,000
Operating Margin %	43.64%	42.59%	39.10%	30.85%	31.41%	32.30%
SGA Expense	4,870,000,000	5,062,000,000	4,846,000,000	4,699,000,000	5,184,000,000	4,801,000,000
Net Income	1,979,000,000	7,722,000,000	6,939,000,000	5,158,000,000	5,081,000,000	4,345,000,000
Operating Cash Flow	11,177,000,000	10,354,000,000	9,077,000,000	8,555,000,000	6,291,000,000	5,882,000,000
Capital Expenditure	664,000,000	837,000,000	649,000,000	1,003,000,000	693,000,000	689,000,000
EBITDA	12,856,000,000	12,528,000,000	11,181,000,000	8,748,000,000	7,573,000,000	7,150,000,000
Return on Assets %	2.51%	10.35%	9.87%	7.63%	8.43%	8.42%
Return on Equity %	7.18%	26.64%	25.76%	21.54%	24.69%	22.81%
Debt to Equity	1.35	1.01	1.04	1.17	1.34	1.26

CONTACT INFORMATION:

Phone: 805 447-1000 Fax: 805 447-1010
Toll-Free: 800-772-6436
Address: 1 Amgen Center Dr., Thousand Oaks, CA 91320 United States

STOCK TICKER/OTHER:

Stock Ticker: AMGN Exchange: NAS
Employees: 19,200 Fiscal Year Ends: 12/31
Parent Company:

SALARIES/BONUSES:

Top Exec. Salary: $1,555,962 Bonus: $
Second Exec. Salary: $1,050,173 Bonus: $

OTHER THOUGHTS:

Estimated Female Officers or Directors: 4
Hot Spot for Advancement for Women/Minorities: Y

AMN Healthcare Services Inc

www.amnhealthcare.com

NAIC Code: 561,320

TYPES OF BUSINESS:

Temporary Medical Staffing
Employment Placement Agencies
Recruiting and Placement
Vendor Management

BRANDS/DIVISIONS/AFFILIATES:

American Mobile
Onward Healthcare
O'Grady-Peyton
NurseChoice
Locum Leaders
MedPartners
Phillips DiPisa
Leaders For Today

CONTACTS: *Note: Officers with more than one job title may be intentionally listed here more than once.*

Susan Salka, CEO
Brian Scott, CFO
Douglas Wheat, Director
Denise Jackson, Other Executive Officer
Ralph Henderson, President, Divisional

GROWTH PLANS/SPECIAL FEATURES:

AMN Healthcare Services, Inc. is a healthcare staffing company in the U.S. As a nationwide provider of travel nurse and allied staffing services, locum tenens (temporary physician staffing) and physician permanent placement services, the firm recruits physicians, nurses and allied healthcare professionals nationally and internationally, and places them on assignments of variable lengths and in permanent positions at acute-care hospitals, physician practice groups and other healthcare settings. AMN Healthcare also offers a managed services program in which it manages clinical vendors for clients, as well as recruitment process outsourcing services, where it provides recruitment for permanent clinical positions. The company's hospital and healthcare facility clients utilize its temporary staffing services to cost-effectively manage both short and long-term shortages in their staff due to a variety of circumstances such as a lack of qualified, specialized local healthcare professionals, attrition, leave schedules, new unit openings, and to identify candidates for permanent positions. The firm's staffing services are marketed to healthcare professionals, as well as to hospitals, physician practice groups and other healthcare centers. AMN Healthcare uses distinct brands to market its differentiated services throughout the healthcare staffing spectrum. These brands include, but are not limited to, American Mobile, Nursefinders, NurseChoice, NursesRx, HealthSource Global Staffing, Med Travelers, Club Staffing, Onward Healthcare, B.E. Smith, The First String Healthcare, O'Grady Peyton International, Staff Care and Locum Leaders. In April 2018, AMN Healthcare acquired MedPartners, a leading national mid-revenue cycle firm; and two related brands in healthcare leadership solutions, Phillips DiPisa and Leaders For Today.

FINANCIAL DATA: *Note: Data for latest year may not have been available at press time.*

In U.S. $	2017	2016	2015	2014	2013	2012
Revenue	1,988,454,000	1,902,225,000	1,463,065,000	1,036,027,000	1,011,816,000	953,951,000
R&D Expense						
Operating Income	212,440,000	191,632,000	128,879,000	67,903,000	65,502,000	53,342,000
Operating Margin %	10.68%	10.07%	8.80%	6.55%	6.47%	5.59%
SGA Expense	399,700,000	398,472,000	319,531,000	232,221,000	218,233,000	202,904,000
Net Income	132,558,000	105,838,000	81,891,000	33,217,000	32,933,000	17,136,000
Operating Cash Flow	115,262,000	131,851,000	56,313,000	27,678,000	58,637,000	60,512,000
Capital Expenditure	26,529,000	21,956,000	27,010,000	19,134,000	9,047,000	5,472,000
EBITDA	244,719,000	221,252,000	149,832,000	83,896,000	79,047,000	67,493,000
Return on Assets %	10.86%	10.23%	10.48%	5.21%	5.93%	3.25%
Return on Equity %	26.19%	26.55%	27.09%	14.00%	16.47%	10.78%
Debt to Equity	0.56	0.79	0.52	0.53	0.68	0.86

CONTACT INFORMATION:

Phone: 866 871-8519 Fax: 800 282-0328
Toll-Free:
Address: 12400 High Bluff Dr., San Diego, CA 92130 United States

STOCK TICKER/OTHER:

Stock Ticker: AMN
Employees: 2,990
Parent Company:
Exchange: NYS
Fiscal Year Ends: 12/31

SALARIES/BONUSES:

Top Exec. Salary: $835,577 Bonus: $
Second Exec. Salary: $464,423 Bonus: $

OTHER THOUGHTS:

Estimated Female Officers or Directors:
Hot Spot for Advancement for Women/Minorities:

Amplifon

corporate.amplifon.com

NAIC Code: 423,450

TYPES OF BUSINESS:

Medical, Dental, and Hospital Equipment and Supplies Merchant Wholesalers

BRANDS/DIVISIONS/AFFILIATES:

Beter Horen
Miracle Ear
Naitonal Hearing Care
Bay Audiology
Amplifon Medtechnica Orthphone
Maxtone
Amplifon
MiniSom

CONTACTS: *Note: Officers with more than one job title may be intentionally listed here more than once.*

Enrico Vita, CEO
Gabriele Galli, CFO
Alessandro Bonacina, CMO
Giovanni Caruso, Chief Human Resources Officer
Alberto Baroli, Chief Innovation & Dev. Officer
Massimiliano Gerli, CIO
Paul Mirabelle, Regional Market Dir.-Asia Pacific
Heinz Ruch, Regional Market Dir.-North America
Gilbert Ferraroli, Regional Market Dir.-Europe
Enrico Bortesi, Chief Supply Chain & Purchasing Officer

GROWTH PLANS/SPECIAL FEATURES:

Amplifon is an Italian company that distributes, fits and personalizes hearing systems to the needs of clients with hearing impairment. The firm has operations in 21 countries through 10,000 points of sale (consisting of direct and indirect channels), more than 3,800 service centers and 1,900 affiliates. Amplifon's brands include: Amplifon, the flagship global brand; Dutch brand Beter Horen; Portuguese brand MiniSom; Amplifon Medtechnica Orthphone in Israel; Maxtone in Turkey; Miracle Ear, Elite Hearing Network and Amplifon Hearing Health Care in the U.S.; National Hearing Care in Australia; and Bay Audiology and Dilworth Hearing in New Zealand. The firm's products use state-of-the-art receiver-in-canal (RIC) technology, including the incorporation of Bluetooth technology to integrate users' hearing aids with the environment around them.

FINANCIAL DATA: *Note: Data for latest year may not have been available at press time.*

In U.S. $	2017	2016	2015	2014	2013	2012
Revenue	1,472,257,000	1,317,708,000	1,202,439,000	1,036,087,000	963,637,600	984,545,900
R&D Expense						
Operating Income	175,373,900	156,299,600	133,067,800	106,096,100	82,225,840	114,795,900
Operating Margin %	11.91%	11.86%	11.06%	10.24%	8.53%	11.65%
SGA Expense						
Net Income	116,964,800	73,985,350	54,430,750	54,046,980	14,941,270	50,217,470
Operating Cash Flow	196,474,000	167,099,700	146,646,100	134,712,200	100,973,400	116,560,100
Capital Expenditure	83,929,530	72,699,150	55,937,900	49,924,410	38,839,400	41,152,460
EBITDA	246,391,500	209,626,700	190,622,200	157,630,000	131,565,300	166,874,100
Return on Assets %	7.00%	4.72%	3.68%	3.88%	1.11%	3.70%
Return on Equity %	17.55%	12.03%	9.94%	11.27%	3.16%	10.52%
Debt to Equity	0.21	0.71	0.78	0.99	1.09	0.66

CONTACT INFORMATION:

Phone: 39 2574721 Fax: 39 257300033
Toll-Free:
Address: Via B. Ripamonti 131/133, Milano, MI 20141 Italy

STOCK TICKER/OTHER:

Stock Ticker: AMFPF
Exchange: GREY
Employees: 13,802
Fiscal Year Ends: 12/31
Parent Company:

SALARIES/BONUSES:

Top Exec. Salary: $ Bonus: $
Second Exec. Salary: $ Bonus: $

OTHER THOUGHTS:

Estimated Female Officers or Directors: 3
Hot Spot for Advancement for Women/Minorities: Y

AMSURG Corporation

www.amsurg.com

NAIC Code: 621,493

TYPES OF BUSINESS:

Practice-Based Ambulatory Surgery Centers
Physician Services

BRANDS/DIVISIONS/AFFILIATES:

Envision Healthcare Corporation
Envision Healthcare

CONTACTS:

Note: Officers with more than one job title may be intentionally listed here more than once.

Phillip A. Clendenin, Pres.
Steven Geringer, Chairman of the Board
Thomas Sloan, CFO
Sandy Clingan Smith, VP-ASC Mktg.
Katie Lamb, VP-Human Resources
Eric Thrailkill, CIO
Phillip Clendenin, Executive VP, Divisional
Robert Coward, Other Executive Officer
Christopher Holden, President
Kevin Eastridge, Senior VP, Divisional

GROWTH PLANS/SPECIAL FEATURES:

AMSURG Corporation, a subsidiary of Envision Healthcare Corporation and operating under the name Envision Healthcare, is a leading physician-centric surgical center and physician services firm. The company operates in two business segments: ambulatory services and physician services. Ambulatory services acquire, develop and operate ambulatory surgery centers (ASCs) in partnerships with physicians. This segment operates more than 245 ASCs in 34 states and the District of Columbia, in partnership with approximately 2,000 physicians. The typical size of a single-specialty ASC is 3,000 to 6,000 square feet; and the size of a multi-specialty ASC is approximately 8,000 to 12,000 square feet. Each center has two or three operating/procedure rooms with areas for reception, preparation, recovery and administration. Each surgery center is specifically tailored to meet the needs of physician partners. Surgery centers perform an average of 7,200 procedures each year. The physician services segment provides outsourced physician services in multiple specialties to hospitals, ASCs and other healthcare facilities, primarily in the areas of anesthesiology, radiology, children's services and emergency medicine.

Employee benefits include medical, vision and dental coverage; a flexible spending account; a health savings account; life and AD&D insurance; short- and long-term disability; long-term care insurance; a 401(k); a wellness program; and employee discounts.

FINANCIAL DATA:

Note: Data for latest year may not have been available at press time.

In U.S. $	2017	2016	2015	2014	2013	2012
Revenue	3,000,000,000	2,800,000,000	2,566,884,096	1,621,949,056	1,079,342,976	928,508,992
R&D Expense						
Operating Income						
Operating Margin %						
SGA Expense						
Net Income			162,947,008	53,701,000	72,703,000	62,563,000
Operating Cash Flow						
Capital Expenditure						
EBITDA						
Return on Assets %						
Return on Equity %						
Debt to Equity						

CONTACT INFORMATION:

Phone: 615 665-1283 Fax: 615 665-0755
Toll-Free: 800-945-2301
Address: 1A Burton Hills Blvd., Nashville, TN 37215 United States

STOCK TICKER/OTHER:

Stock Ticker: Subsidiary Exchange:
Employees: 10,500 Fiscal Year Ends: 12/31
Parent Company: Envision Healthcare Corporation

SALARIES/BONUSES:

Top Exec. Salary: $ Bonus: $
Second Exec. Salary: $ Bonus: $

OTHER THOUGHTS:

Estimated Female Officers or Directors: 2
Hot Spot for Advancement for Women/Minorities: Y

Analogic Corporation

www.analogic.com

NAIC Code: 334,510

TYPES OF BUSINESS:

Equipment-Medical Image Processing
Signal Processing Equipment
Patient Monitoring Equipment
Computed Tomography Imaging Systems
Explosive Detection Security Systems

BRANDS/DIVISIONS/AFFILIATES:

Altaris Capital Partners LLC
eXaminer
FlexFocus

CONTACTS: *Note: Officers with more than one job title may be intentionally listed here more than once.*

Peter Granick, VP-Oper.
Bernard Bailey, Chairman of the Board
Will Rousmaniere, CFO
Katia Bejan, VP-Human Resources
Fred Parks, Director
John Fry, General Counsel
Mervat Faltas, General Manager, Divisional
Brooks West, General Manager, Divisional

GROWTH PLANS/SPECIAL FEATURES:

Analogic Corp. designs, manufactures and sells image-processing-based medical and security systems and subsystems. The company primarily focuses on advanced technology in the areas of automated explosives detection, computed tomography (CT), digital radiography, ultrasound, MRI, patient monitoring and advance signal processing. Its operations are divided into three segments: medical imaging, which accounted for 57% of 2017 revenue; security technology, 13%; and ultrasound, 30%. The medical imaging segment primarily includes systems and subsystems for CT and MRI medical imaging equipment as well as state-of-the-art, selenium-based detectors for screening and diagnostic applications in mammography. The firm's CT systems and subsystems include X-ray detectors, data acquisition systems, data management systems and integrated gantries. For OEM producers of MRI equipment, the firm supplies two key components: gradient amplifiers and Radio Frequency (RF) amplifiers. Gradient amplifiers are high power systems that drive a set of coils located inside the MRI system and around the patient. RF amplifiers are used to control another set of the coils within the MRI system that are used to read-back the signals from the anatomy generated by the gradient coils. The security technology segment provides advanced explosives and weapons detection systems for checked luggage and carry-on luggage at airport checkpoints. The segment designs and manufactures the eXaminer family of scanners, capable of generating data for full three-dimensional images of every object contained within passenger baggage. The ultrasound segment designs and manufactures ultrasound systems and probes primarily for urology, surgery and anesthesia. The flagship ultrasound product is the FlexFocus, a portable ultrasound unit that can be used for multiple applications in a variety of settings. In June 2018, Analogic was acquired by Altaris Capital Partners, LLC, a leading private investment firm with expertise in Analogic's end markets, for approximately $1.1 billion.

Analogic offers its employees tuition reimbursement; medical, dental and vision coverage; life insurance; a 401(k); and an employee stock purchase plan.

FINANCIAL DATA: *Note: Data for latest year may not have been available at press time.*

In U.S. $	2017	2016	2015	2014	2013	2012
Revenue	486,372,000	508,848,000	540,291,008	517,548,000	550,363,008	516,571,008
R&D Expense						
Operating Income						
Operating Margin %						
SGA Expense						
Net Income	-74,237,000	12,127,000	33,481,000	34,480,000	31,121,000	43,071,000
Operating Cash Flow						
Capital Expenditure						
EBITDA						
Return on Assets %						
Return on Equity %						
Debt to Equity						

CONTACT INFORMATION:

Phone: 978 326-4000 Fax: 978 977-6811
Toll-Free:
Address: 8 Centennial Dr., Peabody, MA 01960 United States

STOCK TICKER/OTHER:

Stock Ticker: Private
Employees: 1,510
Parent Company: Altaris Capital Partners LLC
Exchange:
Fiscal Year Ends: 07/31

SALARIES/BONUSES:

Top Exec. Salary: $ Bonus: $
Second Exec. Salary: $ Bonus: $

OTHER THOUGHTS:

Estimated Female Officers or Directors: 3
Hot Spot for Advancement for Women/Minorities: Y

AngioDynamics Inc

www.angiodynamics.com

NAIC Code: 339,100

TYPES OF BUSINESS:

Medical Device Manufacturing
Catheters
Ablation Products

BRANDS/DIVISIONS/AFFILIATES:

NAMIC
VenaCure EVLT
Asclera
AngioVac
NanoKnife

CONTACTS: *Note: Officers with more than one job title may be intentionally listed here more than once.*

Michael Greiner, CFO
Howard Donnelly, Director
Stephen Trowbridge, General Counsel
Chad Campbell, General Manager, Divisional
Robert Simpson, General Manager, Divisional
Richard Stark, General Manager, Divisional
James Clemmer, President
Warren Nighan, Senior VP, Divisional
Barbara Kucharczyk, Senior VP, Divisional
Benjamin Davis, Senior VP, Divisional
Heather Daniels-Cariveau, Senior VP, Divisional

GROWTH PLANS/SPECIAL FEATURES:

AngioDynamics, Inc. is a provider of medical devices used in minimally invasive, image-guided procedures to treat peripheral vascular disease and local oncology therapy options for treating cancer. These devices are intended to be used once and then discarded, or they may be temporarily implanted for short- or long-term use. The company designs, develops, manufactures and markets a broad line of therapeutic and diagnostic devices that enable interventional physicians (interventional radiologists, vascular surgeons, surgical oncologists and others) to treat PVD, tumors and other non-coronary diseases. The firm's products are grouped into three categories: peripheral vascular, vascular access and oncology/surgery. Peripheral vascular products include fluid management, comprising AngioDynamics' NAMIC brand of fluid management devices; venous products which focus on the treatment of varicose veins, and comprise the firm's VenaCure EVLT laser system and Asclera injection; and thrombus management products, including AngioVac venous draining system, thrombolytic catheters, and other drainage accessories, micro access kits and related products. Vascular access products involve the use of advanced imaging equipment to guide the placement of catheters that deliver primarily short-term drug therapies, such as chemotherapeutic agents and antibodies, into the central venous system. Oncology/surgery offerings include the company's microwave ablation systems, its radio-frequency ablation products and its NanoKnife product lines. The NanoKnife ablation system is for the surgical ablation of soft tissue, used to permanently open pores in target cell membranes. AngioDynmaics conducts its manufacturing and assembly at facilities in Queensbury and Glens Falls, New York; Manchester, Georgia; and Denmead, England.

FINANCIAL DATA: *Note: Data for latest year may not have been available at press time.*

In U.S. $	2017	2016	2015	2014	2013	2012
Revenue	349,643,000	353,890,000	356,974,000	354,455,000	342,026,000	
R&D Expense	25,269,000	25,053,000	26,931,000	27,510,000	26,319,000	
Operating Income	25,216,000	14,557,000	17,410,000	22,490,000	22,477,000	
Operating Margin %	7.21%	4.11%	4.87%	6.34%	6.57%	
SGA Expense	110,225,000	114,326,000	110,494,000	109,235,000	102,248,000	
Net Income	5,008,000	-43,590,000	-3,268,000	3,088,000	-612,000	
Operating Cash Flow	55,745,000	45,216,000	26,242,000	25,280,000	26,883,000	
Capital Expenditure	3,001,000	5,594,000	13,293,000	13,206,000	12,920,000	
EBITDA	50,027,000	28,258,000	25,690,000	34,935,000	29,852,000	
Return on Assets %	.69%	-5.80%	-.41%	.38%	-.08%	
Return on Equity %	.97%	-8.28%	-.60%	.58%	-.11%	
Debt to Equity	0.17	0.20	0.23	0.25	0.25	

CONTACT INFORMATION:

Phone: 518 795-1400 Fax: 518 795-1401
Toll-Free: 800-772-6446
Address: 14 Plaza Dr., Latham, NY 12110 United States

STOCK TICKER/OTHER:

Stock Ticker: ANGO
Employees: 1,250
Parent Company:
Exchange: NAS
Fiscal Year Ends: 05/31

SALARIES/BONUSES:

Top Exec. Salary: $643,269 Bonus: $
Second Exec. Salary: $399,231 Bonus: $

OTHER THOUGHTS:

Estimated Female Officers or Directors: 2
Hot Spot for Advancement for Women/Minorities:

Ansell Limited

www.ansell.com

NAIC Code: 339,100

TYPES OF BUSINESS:

Protective Wear Manufacture
Latex Gloves
Condoms

BRANDS/DIVISIONS/AFFILIATES:

AlphaTec
HyFlex
EDGE
ActivArmr
Solvex
GAMMEX
MicroFlex
TouchNTuff

CONTACTS: *Note: Officers with more than one job title may be intentionally listed here more than once.*

Magnus Nicolin, CEO
Neil Salmon, CFO
William Reilly, General Counsel
Steve Genzer, Sr. VP-Oper.
Craig Cameron, Sec.
Scott Corriveau, Pres./Gen. Mgr.-Industrial Solutions
Thomas Draskovics, Pres./Gen. Mgr.-Specialty Markets
Peter Carroll, Pres./Gen. Mgr.-Sexual Wellness
Glenn LL Barnes, Chmn.
Peter Dobbelsteijn, Sr. VP

GROWTH PLANS/SPECIAL FEATURES:

Ansell Limited is an Australian advanced solutions provider specializing in the manufacture of rubber latex products. The company operates through two business units: the industrial global business unit and the healthcare global business unit. The industrial global business unit manufactures and markets high-performance hand and body protection solutions for a wide range of industrial applications. This division's products protect workers in almost every industry, including automotive, chemical, metal fabrication, machinery/equipment, food, construction and mining. Primary brands within this business unit include AlphaTec, HyFlex, EDGE, ActivArmr, Solvex and MicroGard. The healthcare global business unit manufactures and markets surgical and exam globes for healthcare and industrial applications. Its customer base in the medical vertical includes acute care hospitals, emergency services, alternate care, dentistry and veterinary clinics. This division also distributes a range of high-performance single-use gloves used in industrial applications, including chemical, food services, life sciences, electronics and automotive aftermarket. Primary brands within this business unit include GAMMEX, MicroFlex, TouchNTuff, Sandel, Encore, BioClean and EDGE. In September 2017, Ansell sold its sexual wellness business unit.

FINANCIAL DATA: *Note: Data for latest year may not have been available at press time.*

In U.S. $	2017	2016	2015	2014	2013	2012
Revenue						
R&D Expense						
Operating Income						
Operating Margin %						
SGA Expense						
Net Income						
Operating Cash Flow						
Capital Expenditure						
EBITDA						
Return on Assets %						
Return on Equity %						
Debt to Equity						

CONTACT INFORMATION:

Phone: 61 3 9270 7270 Fax: 61 3 9270 7300
Toll-Free:
Address: 678 Victoria St., Level 3, Richmond, VIC 3121 Australia

STOCK TICKER/OTHER:

Stock Ticker: ANSLY Exchange: PINX
Employees: 12,482 Fiscal Year Ends: 06/30
Parent Company:

SALARIES/BONUSES:

Top Exec. Salary: $ Bonus: $
Second Exec. Salary: $ Bonus: $

OTHER THOUGHTS:

Estimated Female Officers or Directors: 2
Hot Spot for Advancement for Women/Minorities:

Anthem Inc

www.antheminc.com

NAIC Code: 524,114

TYPES OF BUSINESS:

Health Insurance
Health Maintenance Organizations (HMOs)
Point-of-Service Plans
Dental and Vision Plans
Plan Management (ASO) for Self-Insured Organizations
Prescription Plans
Wellness Programs
Medicare Administrative Services

BRANDS/DIVISIONS/AFFILIATES:

Blue Cross and Blue Shield Association
HealthLink
UniCare
CareMore Health Groups Inc
Blue Cross of California
Anthem Blue Cross Blue Shield
Blue Cross Blue Shield of Georgia
Amerigroup Corporation

CONTACTS: *Note: Officers with more than one job title may be intentionally listed here more than once.*

John Gallina, CFO
Ronald Penczek, Chief Accounting Officer
Gloria McCarthy, Chief Administrative Officer
Deepti Jain, COO, Subsidiary
Elizabeth Tallett, Director
Gail Boudreaux, Director
Thomas Zielinski, Executive VP
Jacquelyn Wolf, Executive VP
Craig Samitt, Executive VP
Peter Haytaian, President, Divisional

GROWTH PLANS/SPECIAL FEATURES:

Anthem, Inc. is a health benefits company, serving roughly 40.2 million medical members through its subsidiaries. The firm is an independent licensee of the Blue Cross and Blue Shield Association, an association of independent health benefit plans, and also serves customers throughout the country under the HealthLink and UniCare brands. Anthem serves certain Arizona, California, Nevada, New York and Virginia markets through subsidiary CareMore Health Group, Inc. The firm offers network-based managed care plans to the large and small employer, individual, Medicaid and senior markets. The managed care plans include preferred provider organizations (PPO), health maintenance organizations (HMO), point-of-service (POS) plans, traditional indemnity plans and other hybrid plans including consumer-driven health plans, hospital-only and limited benefit products. In addition, Anthem provides managed care services to self-insured organizations, including claims processing, underwriting, stop loss insurance, actuarial services, provider network access, medical cost management and other administrative services. The company also provides specialty and other products and services, including life and disability insurance benefits; dental, vision and behavioral health benefit services; long-term care insurance; and flexible spending accounts. Subsidiaries include Blue Cross of California, Anthem Blue Cross Blue Shield and Blue Cross Blue Shield of Georgia as well as non-Blue Cross subsidiaries such as HealthLink, Amerigroup Corporation and HealthCore, Inc. In December 2017, the firm acquired HealthSun, an integrated Medicare Advantage health plans and health care delivery networks in Florida. In February 2018, Anthem acquired America's 1st Choice, a privatelyâ€ held, forâ€ profit Medicare Advantage organization that offers HMO products. The next June, the firm acquired Aspire Health, a major provider of non-hospice, community-based palliative care for people facing a serious illness.

The firm offers employees tuition assistance; a 401(k) plan; stock purchase plan; paid time off; long-term care coverage; adoption assistance; an employee assistance program; life insurance; medical, dental and vision coverage; and flexible spending accounts.

FINANCIAL DATA: *Note: Data for latest year may not have been available at press time.*

In U.S. $	2017	2016	2015	2014	2013	2012
Revenue	90,039,400,000	84,863,000,000	79,156,500,000	73,874,100,000	71,023,500,000	61,711,700,000
R&D Expense						
Operating Income						
Operating Margin %						
SGA Expense	12,649,600,000	12,557,900,000	12,534,800,000	11,748,400,000	9,952,900,000	8,738,300,000
Net Income	3,842,800,000	2,469,800,000	2,560,000,000	2,569,700,000	2,489,700,000	2,655,500,000
Operating Cash Flow	4,184,800,000	3,204,500,000	4,116,000,000	3,369,300,000	3,052,300,000	2,744,600,000
Capital Expenditure	799,500,000	583,600,000	638,200,000	714,600,000	646,500,000	544,900,000
EBITDA						
Return on Assets %	5.66%	3.89%	4.13%	4.22%	4.20%	4.78%
Return on Equity %	14.89%	10.25%	10.82%	10.48%	10.25%	11.27%
Debt to Equity	0.65	0.57	0.66	0.58	0.54	0.59

CONTACT INFORMATION:

Phone: 317 488-6000 Fax:
Toll-Free:
Address: 120 Monument Cir., Indianapolis, IN 46204 United States

STOCK TICKER/OTHER:

Stock Ticker: ANTM Exchange: NYS
Employees: 53,000 Fiscal Year Ends: 12/31
Parent Company:

SALARIES/BONUSES:

Top Exec. Salary: $1,540,385 Bonus: $
Second Exec. Salary: $768,173 Bonus: $

OTHER THOUGHTS:

Estimated Female Officers or Directors: 1
Hot Spot for Advancement for Women/Minorities: Y

Apollo Medical Holdings Inc

www.apollomed.net

NAIC Code: 621,999

TYPES OF BUSINESS:

Ambulatory Health Care Services

BRANDS/DIVISIONS/AFFILIATES:

Apollo Medical Management Inc
Network Medical Management Inc
APAACO Inc
Apollo Palliative Services LLC
Best Choice Hospice Care LLC
Holistic Care Home Health Care Inc
Apollo Care Connect Inc
Allied Pacific of California

CONTACTS: *Note: Officers with more than one job title may be intentionally listed here more than once.*

Mihir Shah, CFO
Thomas Lam, Co-CEO
Warren Hosseinion, Co-CEO
Hing Ang, COO
Kenneth Sim, Director
Adrian Vazquez, Other Executive Officer
Albert Young, Other Executive Officer

GROWTH PLANS/SPECIAL FEATURES:

Apollo Medical Holdings, Inc. is an integrated population health management company. It works to provide coordinated, outcome-based medical care in an economical manner. The company's operations include: hospitalists, which includes contracted physicians who provide comprehensive medical care to hospitalized patients; accountable care organization, which provides care to Medicare fee-for-service patients; independent practice association, which contracts with physicians and provides care to Medicare, Medicaid, commercial and dual-eligible patients on a risk- and value-based fee basis; three clinics, which the firm owns or operates, and which provides specialty care in the Los Angeles region; palliative care, home health and hospice services, including Apollo's at-home and end-of-life services; and a cloud-based population health management IT platform, which includes digital care plans, a case management module, connectivity with multiple healthcare tracking devices and also integrates clinical data. Apollo operates its businesses through the following subsidiaries: Apollo Medical Management, Inc.; Network Medical Management, Inc. (NMM); APAACO, Inc.; Apollo Palliative Care Services, LLC; Best Choice Hospice Care, LLC; Holistic Care Home Health Care, Inc.; and Apollo Care Connect, Inc. In December 2017, Apollo merged NMM with and into itself, bringing together two leading, complementary healthcare organizations to form one of the nation's largest population health management companies. In July 2018, the firm, through affiliates NMM and Allied Pacific of California, acquired a 50% stake in the 128-bed French Hospital, the oldest hospital in Los Angeles, for $17 million.

FINANCIAL DATA: *Note: Data for latest year may not have been available at press time.*

In U.S. $	2017	2016	2015	2014	2013	2012
Revenue	357,747,400	44,048,740	32,989,740	10,484,310	7,776,131	
R&D Expense						
Operating Income	37,577,760	-7,266,129	-694,334	-3,909,879	-2,078,487	
Operating Margin %		-16.49%	-2.10%	-37.29%	-26.72%	
SGA Expense	26,437,600	16,962,690	11,282,220	5,286,610	3,517,536	
Net Income	25,801,840	-9,344,044	-1,802,601	-4,558,874	-8,904,564	
Operating Cash Flow	51,929,380	-1,839,125	-271,910	-1,478,205	57,956	
Capital Expenditure	2,084,770	262,108	44,509	22,931	45,799	
EBITDA	68,866,150	-7,350,734	476,676	-3,828,816	-7,948,670	
Return on Assets %		-54.07%	-12.02%	-126.93%	-388.24%	
Return on Equity %						
Debt to Equity						

CONTACT INFORMATION:

Phone: 818 396-8050 Fax: 818 291-6444
Toll-Free:
Address: 700 N. Brand Blvd., Ste. 1400, Glendale, CA 91203 United States

STOCK TICKER/OTHER:

Stock Ticker: AMEH
Employees: 149
Parent Company:
Exchange: NAS
Fiscal Year Ends: 01/31

SALARIES/BONUSES:

Top Exec. Salary: $500,492 Bonus: $350,000
Second Exec. Salary: $489,550 Bonus: $350,000

OTHER THOUGHTS:

Estimated Female Officers or Directors:
Hot Spot for Advancement for Women/Minorities:

Apria Healthcare Group Inc

www.apria.com

NAIC Code: 621,610

TYPES OF BUSINESS:

Home Health Care Services
Home Medical Equipment Distribution
Respiratory Therapy
Infusion Therapy
Patient Travel Programs

BRANDS/DIVISIONS/AFFILIATES:

Blackstone Group LP (The)
Apria Pharmacy Network
HeartAssist
Apria Great Escapes

CONTACTS:

Note: Officers with more than one job title may be intentionally listed here more than once.

Dan Starck, CEO
Debra L. Morris, CFO
Celina M. Scally, SVP-Human Resources
Mark Litkovitz, CIO
Robert S. Holcombe, General Counsel
Cameron Thompson, Exec. VP-Oper.
Lisa M. Getson, Exec. VP-Gov't Rel. & Corp. Compliance
Peter A. Reynolds, Chief Acct. Officer
Nichola Denney, Exec. VP-Revenue Mgmt.
Daniel E. Greenleaf, Pres., Coram Specialty Infusion Svcs.
Bradley R. Kreick, Exec. VP-Payor & Provider Arrangements
John G. Figueroa, Chmn.

GROWTH PLANS/SPECIAL FEATURES:

Apria Healthcare Group, Inc., owned by The Blackstone Group LP, is one of the largest providers of home health care services in the U.S. The firm offers a wide range of clinical services and equipment. Its services are divided into three groups: therapies, clinical programs and services, and home medical equipment. The therapies group includes the following: oxygen therapy, including concentrators, gas cylinders and various ambulatory options; nebulized respiratory medications, with the company's licensed pharmacy (Apria Pharmacy Network) shipping prescribed respiratory medications directly to patients' homes; sleep management, including positive airway pressure therapies, equipment training and comprehensive follow-up protocols; negative pressure wound therapy; and non-invasive ventilation, which serves to manage the treatment and care of non-invasive ventilation patients in their own homes. The clinical programs and services group includes COPD (chronic obstructive pulmonary disease) care, including screenings, first-dose nebulizer kits, one-on-one education and more; overnight oximetry, a testing service for adult COPD and congestive heart failure (CHF) patients to identify the potential need for long-term oxygen therapy; HeartAssist, which offers education and assistance for patients with CHF who self-manage their disease; and Apria Great Escapes, which assists patents concerning their oxygen and medical equipment when planning to travel within the U.S. Last, the home medical equipment group comprises a comprehensive product line, including hospital beds, ambulatory aids, patient room equipment and bathroom safety items.

The firm offers employees benefits including medical, dental and vision coverage; life, accident and disability insurance; health care flexible spending and savings accounts; and an educational assistance program.

FINANCIAL DATA:

Note: Data for latest year may not have been available at press time.

In U.S. $	2017	2016	2015	2014	2013	2012
Revenue	1,377,000,000	1,325,000,000	1,300,000,000	1,250,000,000	2,467,000,000	2,436,236,000
R&D Expense						
Operating Income						
Operating Margin %						
SGA Expense						
Net Income						
Operating Cash Flow						
Capital Expenditure						
EBITDA						
Return on Assets %						
Return on Equity %						
Debt to Equity						

CONTACT INFORMATION:

Phone: 949-639-2000 Fax: 949-587-9363
Toll-Free: 800-277-4288
Address: 26220 Enterprise Ct., Lake Forest, CA 92630 United States

STOCK TICKER/OTHER:

Stock Ticker: Private Exchange:
Employees: 13,200 Fiscal Year Ends: 12/31
Parent Company: Blackstone Group LP (The)

SALARIES/BONUSES:

Top Exec. Salary: $ Bonus: $
Second Exec. Salary: $ Bonus: $

OTHER THOUGHTS:

Estimated Female Officers or Directors: 4
Hot Spot for Advancement for Women/Minorities: Y

Aradigm Corporation

www.aradigm.com

NAIC Code: 325,412

TYPES OF BUSINESS:

Drug Delivery Systems
Pulmonary Drug Delivery Systems

BRANDS/DIVISIONS/AFFILIATES:

AERx
Lipoquin
Linhaliq
ARD-3100
ARD-3150

CONTACTS: *Note: Officers with more than one job title may be intentionally listed here more than once.*

John Siebert, CEO
Juergen Froehlich, Chief Medical Officer
Lisa Thomas, Controller

GROWTH PLANS/SPECIAL FEATURES:

Aradigm Corporation is a specialty pharmaceutical company focused on the development and commercialization of a selection of drugs, delivered by inhalation, for the treatment of severe respiratory disease. Aradigm's operations are centered on its hand-held AERx pulmonary drug delivery system, which creates aerosols from liquid drug formulations. This system is marketed as a replacement for medical devices such as nebulizers, metered-dose inhalers and dry powder inhalers, and is particularly suitable for drugs where highly-efficient and precise delivery to the respiratory tract is advantageous or essential. Its therapeutic development efforts are focused on the treatment of respiratory disease, including identifying potential drug candidates that it can develop and commercialize in the U.S., without a partner. In selecting its development programs, Aradigm primarily seeks drugs approved by the FDA that can be reformulated for existing and new indications in respiratory disease. The firm is actively developing inhaled liposomal ciprofloxacin for the treatment of cystic fibrosis (Lipoquin, ARD-3100) and bronchiectasis (Linhaliq, ARD-3150). In collaboration with other companies, Aradigm is additionally developing treatments for pain management, pulmonary arterial hypertension, asthma and other chronic obstructive diseases of airways.

Aradigm offers its employees medical, dental, life and disability insurance; a 529 college savings plan; tuition reimbursement; and an educational rewards program.

FINANCIAL DATA: *Note: Data for latest year may not have been available at press time.*

In U.S. $	2017	2016	2015	2014	2013	2012
Revenue	14,465,000	195,000	23,429,000	33,561,000	9,717,000	1,007,000
R&D Expense	13,815,000	24,387,000	35,276,000	31,172,000	8,884,000	3,781,000
Operating Income	-6,942,000	-30,020,000	-17,141,000	-3,837,000	-19,885,000	-6,670,000
Operating Margin %	-47.99%	-15394.87%	-73.16%	-11.43%	-204.64%	-662.36%
SGA Expense	7,592,000	5,828,000	5,294,000	6,226,000	20,718,000	3,896,000
Net Income	-10,705,000	-32,938,000	-17,209,000	4,652,000	-21,564,000	-8,226,000
Operating Cash Flow	-16,498,000	-28,480,000	-16,703,000	107,000	264,000	-6,651,000
Capital Expenditure	154,000	75,000		412,000	43,000	5,000
EBITDA	-6,717,000	-30,411,000	-16,938,000	5,250,000	-19,545,000	-6,305,000
Return on Assets %	-64.64%	-108.56%	-38.41%	8.91%	-72.61%	-84.27%
Return on Equity %		-273.37%	-55.31%	12.78%	-133.76%	
Debt to Equity		13.39			0.27	

CONTACT INFORMATION:

Phone: 510 265-9000 Fax: 510 265-0277
Toll-Free:
Address: 3929 Point Eden Way, Hayward, CA 94545 United States

STOCK TICKER/OTHER:

Stock Ticker: ARDM
Employees: 23
Parent Company:
Exchange: NAS
Fiscal Year Ends: 12/31

SALARIES/BONUSES:

Top Exec. Salary: $436,720 Bonus: $341,355
Second Exec. Salary: $424,000 Bonus: $136,448

OTHER THOUGHTS:

Estimated Female Officers or Directors: 2
Hot Spot for Advancement for Women/Minorities:

Ardent Health Services LLC

www.ardenthealth.com

NAIC Code: 622,110

TYPES OF BUSINESS:

General Medical and Surgical Hospitals

BRANDS/DIVISIONS/AFFILIATES:

BSA Health System
Hilcrest Healthcare System
Lovelace Health System
UT Health East Texas
BSA Hospital
Hillcrest Medical Center
Lovelace Medical Center
Bay Medical Center

CONTACTS:

Note: Officers with more than one job title may be intentionally listed here more than once.

David T. Vandewater, Pres.
Paul Kappelman, Exec. VP
Clint Adams, Exec. VP
Tyra Palmer, VP-Mktg. & Govt. Relations
Neil Hemphil, Sr. VP-HR
Richard Keller, CIO

GROWTH PLANS/SPECIAL FEATURES:

Ardent Health Services, LLC is the parent of several subsidiaries which operate in the health care field. The firm owns and operates three health systems with more than 30 hospitals in seven U.S. states, comprising over 4,800 licensed beds. The three health systems include: BSA Health System, Hillcrest Healthcare System and Lovelace Health System. BSA Health System is located in Amarillo, Texas, and consists of: the BSA Hospital, with 445 beds; the Harrington Cancer Center; the Quail Creek Surgical Hospital, with 20 beds. Hillcrest Healthcare System is located in Oklahoma and consists of: Hillcrest Medical Center, the system's flagship facility in downtown Tulsa; other Hillcrest hospitals throughout the state; investments such as in the Spine and Orthopedic Institute, the Tulsa Spine & Special Hospital, the Oklahoma Heart Institute and the Bailey Medical Center. Last, the Lovelace Health System is located in New Mexico, and consists of: the St. Joseph's Healthcare System; the Northeast Heights Medical Center; West Mesa Medical Center; the Lovelace Medical Center; and the Roswell Regional Hospital. Other hospitals and health systems within Ardent's group include: Bay Medical Center-Sacred Heart, HackensackUMC at Pascack Valley, HackensackUMC Mountainside, Harrington Cancer Center, Heart Hospital of New Mexico at Lovelace Medical Center, Oklahoma Heart Institute, Physicians Surgical Hospitals, Portneuf Medical Center and Seton Medical Center Harker Heights, among others. In March 2018, Ardent Health and The University of Texas Health Science Center at Tyler purchased East Texas Medical Center Regional Healthcare System, with will be combined with UT Health Northeast to form a 10-hospital system known as UT Health East Texas.

Ardent offers its employees certification assistance, tuition assistance, a leadership development program, wellness initiatives and discounts on insurance premiums.

FINANCIAL DATA:

Note: Data for latest year may not have been available at press time.

In U.S. $	2017	2016	2015	2014	2013	2012
Revenue	4,600,000,000	3,000,000,000	1,985,000,000	1,865,000,000	1,800,000,000	1,740,000,000
R&D Expense						
Operating Income						
Operating Margin %						
SGA Expense						
Net Income						
Operating Cash Flow						
Capital Expenditure						
EBITDA						
Return on Assets %						
Return on Equity %						
Debt to Equity						

CONTACT INFORMATION:

Phone: 615-296-3000 Fax:
Toll-Free:
Address: 1 Burton Hills Blvd., Ste. 250, Nashville, TN 37215 United States

STOCK TICKER/OTHER:

Stock Ticker: Private
Employees: 25,000
Parent Company:
Exchange:
Fiscal Year Ends: 12/31

SALARIES/BONUSES:

Top Exec. Salary: $ Bonus: $
Second Exec. Salary: $ Bonus: $

OTHER THOUGHTS:

Estimated Female Officers or Directors:
Hot Spot for Advancement for Women/Minorities:

Arkansas Blue Cross and Blue Shield

www.arkbluecross.com

NAIC Code: 524,114

TYPES OF BUSINESS:

Insurance-Medical & Health, HMOs & PPOs
Charitable Foundation

BRANDS/DIVISIONS/AFFILIATES:

CONTACTS:

Note: Officers with more than one job title may be intentionally listed here more than once.

Curtis Barnett, CEO
David Bridges, Pres.
Gray Dillard, Sr. VP-Financial Svcs.
Eric Paczewitz, VP-Corp. Mktg.
Richard Cooper, VP-Human Resources
Robert Griffin, Chief Medical Officer
Melvin Hardy, VP-IT
Karen Raley, VP-Prod. Dev.
Lee Douglass, Chief Legal Officer
David Bridges, Exec. VP-Internal Oper.
Calvin Kellogg, Exec. VP
Karen Raley, VP-Comm.
Steve Abell, VP-Strategic Svcs.
Jim Bailey, Sr. VP-National Bus. & Inter-Plan Rel.
Ron DeBerry, Sr. VP-Statewide Bus.
Bob Heard, VP-IT Infrastructure
Kathy Ryan, Sr. VP

GROWTH PLANS/SPECIAL FEATURES:

Arkansas Blue Cross and Blue Shield (ABCBS) is a nonprofit mutual insurance company providing comprehensive health insurance and related services to members throughout Arkansas. The company offers insurance for individuals and families, including medical, dental and vision plans for Arkansas residents under age 65 and their families who are not on Medicare. ABCBS also provides Medicare health and prescription drug plans for Medicare-eligible Arkansas residents. For employer groups, the firm offers health and dental plans for companies of all sizes. Other options include just dental insurance, or dental and vision plans for individuals and/or businesses, as well as customizable short- and long-term health plans for people living and traveling abroad. In addition, ABCBS offers a federal employee program that includes dental, vision, pharmacy, maternity-related depression, substance abuse treatment and other benefits, as well as hearing aids and speech-generating devices.

Employee benefits include an onsite gym, employee health clinic, wellness incentives and tuition reimbursement.

FINANCIAL DATA:

Note: Data for latest year may not have been available at press time.

In U.S. $	2017	2016	2015	2014	2013	2012
Revenue	1,680,000,000	1,600,000,000	1,500,000,000	1,400,000,000	1,350,000,000	1,300,000,000
R&D Expense						
Operating Income						
Operating Margin %						
SGA Expense						
Net Income						
Operating Cash Flow						
Capital Expenditure						
EBITDA						
Return on Assets %						
Return on Equity %						
Debt to Equity						

CONTACT INFORMATION:

Phone: 501-378-2000 Fax: 501-378-3258
Toll-Free: 800-238-8379
Address: 601 S. Gaines St., Little Rock, AR 72201 United States

STOCK TICKER/OTHER:

Stock Ticker: Nonprofit
Employees: 2,800
Parent Company:
Exchange:
Fiscal Year Ends: 12/31

SALARIES/BONUSES:

Top Exec. Salary: $ Bonus: $
Second Exec. Salary: $ Bonus: $

OTHER THOUGHTS:

Estimated Female Officers or Directors: 7
Hot Spot for Advancement for Women/Minorities: Y

ArQule Inc

www.arqule.com

NAIC Code: 325,412

TYPES OF BUSINESS:

Research-Drug Discovery
Small-Molecule Compounds
Systems & Software
Predictive Modeling

BRANDS/DIVISIONS/AFFILIATES:

Tivantinib (ARQ 197)
ARQ 761
Derazantinib (ARQ 087)
Miransertib (ARQ 092)
ARQ 751
ARQ 531

CONTACTS: *Note: Officers with more than one job title may be intentionally listed here more than once.*

Patrick Zenner, Chairman of the Board
Robert Weiskopf, Chief Accounting Officer
Brian Schwartz, Chief Medical Officer
Peter Lawrence, Co-CFO
Paolo Pucci, Director

GROWTH PLANS/SPECIAL FEATURES:

ArQule, Inc. is a clinical-stage biotechnology company engaged in the research and development of cancer drugs, with a focus on kinases (enzymes that transmit signals between cells). ArQule's current drug discovery research efforts are built on the design of kinase inhibitors that are powerful, selective and do not interfere with ATP (adenosine triphosphate, a crucial element in normal cell metabolism). The company's early stage R&D pipeline includes: ARQ 761, a potential NQ01 inhibitor; Derazantinib (ARQ 087), a fibroblast growth factor receptor inhibitor; Miransertib (ARQ 092), an AKT (or protein kinase B) inhibitor; ARQ 751, a next-generation inhibitor of AKT; and ARQ 531, a beta lapachone analog being evaluated as a promoter cancer cell death. Tivantinib (ARQ 197), an orally administered, small molecule inhibitor of the c-Met receptor tyrosine kinase and its biological pathway is no longer being developed. The firm licensed commercial rights to tivantinib for human cancer indications to Daiichi Sankyo Co., Ltd. in the U.S., Europe, South America and the rest of the world, excluding Japan and certain other Asian countries, where the firm licensed commercial rights to Kyowa Hakko Kirin Co., Ltd. In February 2018, Roivant Sciences and ArQule, Inc. announced the initiation of a collaboration to pursue the development of derazantinib, a pan-FGFR (fibroblast growth factor receptor) inhibitor, in Greater China. As part of the collaboration, ArQule has granted a Roivant subsidiary an exclusive license to develop and commercialize derazantinib in the People's Republic of China, Hong Kong, Macau, and Taiwan.

ArQule offers its employees tuition reimbursement; a 401(k) and employee stock purchase plan; credit union membership; an employee assistance program; flexible spending accounts; and medical, dental, vision and disability insurance.

FINANCIAL DATA: *Note: Data for latest year may not have been available at press time.*

In U.S. $	2017	2016	2015	2014	2013	2012
Revenue		4,709,000	11,239,000	11,254,000	15,914,000	36,414,000
R&D Expense	19,468,000	20,042,000	15,561,000	22,271,000	27,555,000	33,966,000
Operating Income	-27,019,000	-22,896,000	-14,152,000	-23,171,000	-24,477,000	-11,404,000
Operating Margin %		-486.21%	-125.91%	-205.89%	-153.80%	-31.31%
SGA Expense	7,551,000	7,563,000	9,830,000	12,154,000	12,836,000	13,852,000
Net Income	-29,203,000	-22,718,000	-13,774,000	-23,391,000	-24,600,000	-10,872,000
Operating Cash Flow	-25,175,000	-22,937,000	-22,160,000	-31,782,000	-33,680,000	-34,204,000
Capital Expenditure		15,000	315,000			117,000
EBITDA	-27,618,000	-22,617,000	-13,991,000	-22,753,000	-23,704,000	-9,782,000
Return on Assets %	-71.85%	-62.77%	-26.64%	-28.95%	-21.17%	-8.65%
Return on Equity %	-201.27%	-85.95%	-39.51%	-46.24%	-34.73%	-19.63%
Debt to Equity	2.73					

CONTACT INFORMATION:

Phone: 781 994-0300 Fax: 781 376-6019
Toll-Free:
Address: 1 Wall St., Burlington, MA 01803 United States

STOCK TICKER/OTHER:

Stock Ticker: ARQL
Exchange: NAS
Employees: 35
Fiscal Year Ends: 12/31
Parent Company:

SALARIES/BONUSES:

Top Exec. Salary: $498,718 Bonus: $
Second Exec. Salary: $447,140 Bonus: $

OTHER THOUGHTS:

Estimated Female Officers or Directors: 1
Hot Spot for Advancement for Women/Minorities:

Arthrex Inc

www.arthrex.com

NAIC Code: 339,100

TYPES OF BUSINESS:

Surgical Appliance and Supplies Manufacturing

BRANDS/DIVISIONS/AFFILIATES:

Arthrex Manufacturing Inc
Arthrex California Inc
Arthrex Canada
Arthrex Ltd
Arthrex Swiss AG
Arthrex Japan KK
Arthrex (Shanghai) Co Ltd

CONTACTS: *Note: Officers with more than one job title may be intentionally listed here more than once.*

Reinhold D. Schmieding, Pres.
Karen Gallen, Dir.-Eng. (Distal Extremities)
John Schmieding, VP-Legal Counsel
Lisa Gardiner, Mgr.-Comm.
Andy Stewart, VP-North America
Randy Hacker, Dir.-Eng. (Pump & RF)
Peter Dreyfuss, Dir.-Eng.(Shoulder & Elbow)
Ken Adams, Dir.-Eng. (Powered Resection)
Alex Seifert, VP-Iberoamerica, Africa, Middle East & AsiaPacific
Peter Russano, Dir.-Supply Chain

GROWTH PLANS/SPECIAL FEATURES:

Arthrex, Inc. is a private medical device company specializing in the manufacturing of orthopedic surgical supplies. Over the course of its history, the firm has developed thousands of innovative products and procedures that have helped to advance minimally invasive orthopedics. Arthrex divides its products and procedures into eight specialized groups: shoulder, knee, elbow, hand/wrist, foot/ankle, hip, orthobiologics, and imaging and resection. The shoulder, knee, hand, wrist, foot, ankle and hip groups contain products and procedures specifically developed to treat those anatomical regions. Procedures in these groups include acromioclavicular reconstruction, distal bicep repair, ACL (anterior cruciate ligament) reconstruction, carpal tunnel release, ankle arthritis and labral reconstruction. The ortrhobiologics group contains products and procedures that are used in tissue, bone and soft tissue grafting and cartilage repair. The imaging and resection group encompasses the firm's endoscopes, camera systems, pumps, punches and arthroscopic instrument sets. The firm is headquartered in Florida but has offices in Mexico, Canada, Germany, France, Belgium, Austria, England, Switzerland, Sweden, Netherlands, Denmark, Belgium, Croatia, Poland, Spain, China, Korea and Japan. Arthrex's many subsidiaries include Arthrex Manufacturing, Inc.; Arthrex California, Inc.; Arthrex Canada; Arthrex Ltd.; Arthrex Swiss AG; Arthrex Japan K.K.; and Arthrex (Shanghai) Co., Ltd.

Arthrex Inc provides for its employees medical and dental insurance, catered lunches, short- and long-term disability, an annual performance/profit sharing bonus and a 401(k) with company match.

FINANCIAL DATA: *Note: Data for latest year may not have been available at press time.*

In U.S. $	2017	2016	2015	2014	2013	2012
Revenue	2,000,000,000	1,800,000,000	1,600,000,000	1,556,000,000	1,500,000,000	1,400,000,000
R&D Expense						
Operating Income						
Operating Margin %						
SGA Expense						
Net Income						
Operating Cash Flow						
Capital Expenditure						
EBITDA						
Return on Assets %						
Return on Equity %						
Debt to Equity						

CONTACT INFORMATION:

Phone: 239-643-5553 Fax: 239-598-5534
Toll-Free: 800-933-7001
Address: 1370 Creekside Blvd., Naples, FL 34108-1945 United States

STOCK TICKER/OTHER:

Stock Ticker: Private
Employees: 3,192
Parent Company:
Exchange:
Fiscal Year Ends:

SALARIES/BONUSES:

Top Exec. Salary: $ Bonus: $
Second Exec. Salary: $ Bonus: $

OTHER THOUGHTS:

Estimated Female Officers or Directors: 4
Hot Spot for Advancement for Women/Minorities: Y

Ascension

ascension.org

NAIC Code: 622,110

TYPES OF BUSINESS:

General Medical and Surgical Hospitals
Acute Care Hospitals
Rehabilitation Hospitals
Psychiatric Hospitals
Pharmacy Management

BRANDS/DIVISIONS/AFFILIATES:

Ascension Health
Providence Hospital
St. Vincent's Health System
Sacred Heart's Health System
Peyton Manning Children's Hospital
Alexian Brothers
Lourdes Hospital
Nazareth Living Care Center

CONTACTS: *Note: Officers with more than one job title may be intentionally listed here more than once.*

Anthony R. Tersigni, CEO
Dennis H. Holtschneider, COO
Robert J. Henkel, Pres.
Anthony J. Speranzo, Exec. VP
Nick Ragone, Chief Mktg. & Communications Officer
Herbert J. Vallier, Chief Human Resources Officer
Ziad Haydar, Chief Medical Officer
Christine Kocot McCoy, General Counsel
Patricia A. Maryland, Pres., Health Care Oper.
Eric S. Engler, Sr. VP-Strategic Planning & Dev.
Jon Glaudemans, Chief Advocacy & Communications Officer
Ann Espoito, Sr. VP
Bonnie Phipps, CEO., St. Agnes HealthCare
Susan L. Davis, New York
Scott Caldwell, Chief Supply Chain Officer

GROWTH PLANS/SPECIAL FEATURES:

Ascension, formerly Ascension Health, is a faith-based, nonprofit health organization in the U.S. Its headquarters are in St. Louis, Missouri, and is comprised of 153 hospitals in 22 states as well as in Washington D.C. It has more than 2,600 sites of care and more than 30 senior care facilities. Ascension's facilities include Providence Hospital and St. Vincent's Health System of healthcare facilities in Alabama; Sacred Heart's Health System and St. Vincent's Health facilities in Florida; Peyton Manning Children's Hospital at St. Vincent in Indiana; Saint Thomas Health in Kentucky; St. Mary's of Michigan; Alexian Brothers of Missouri; Lourdes Hospital in New York; Seton Manor in Pennsylvania; Nazareth Living Care Center in Texas; and Ministry Health Care facilities in Wisconsin. Other Ascension subsidiaries provide services and solutions such as physician practice management, venture capital investing, treasury management, biomedical engineering, clinical care management, information services, risk management and contracting. Ascension was formed in 1999 when the four provinces of the Daughters of Charity of St. Vincent de Paul that were sponsors of the Daughters of Charity National Health System (now combined into one, the Province of St. Louise) and the Sisters of St. Joseph of Nazareth brought their health systems together. In December 2017, the firm's subsidiary, Ascension Living, agreed to acquire Shorelight Memory Care. In March 2018, Presence Health merged with Ascension and became part of AMITA Health, a joint venture between Ascension's Alexian Brothers Health System and Adventist Midwest Health, part of Adventist Health System. Later that same month, the firm agreed to sell its St. Vincent's Medical Center in Bridgeport, Connecticut, and all its related operations, to Hartford HealthCare. The following July, Ascension and Centene Corporation, a multi-line healthcare enterprise, signed a letter of intent to explore a joint venture to establish a leading Medicare Advantage plan.

Ascension Health offers employee benefits such as medical, dental, vision and life insurance; health care and dependent care reimbursement accounts; a retirement savings program and a pension plan; tuition reimbursement; and an employee assistance program.

FINANCIAL DATA: *Note: Data for latest year may not have been available at press time.*

In U.S. $	2017	2016	2015	2014	2013	2012
Revenue	22,600,000,000	21,900,000,000	20,538,803,000	19,901,657,000	16,537,000,000	15,293,000,000
R&D Expense						
Operating Income						
Operating Margin %						
SGA Expense						
Net Income	1,800,000,000	477,700,000	562,596,000	1,803,615,000	451,000,000	931,000,000
Operating Cash Flow						
Capital Expenditure						
EBITDA						
Return on Assets %						
Return on Equity %						
Debt to Equity						

CONTACT INFORMATION:

Phone: 314-733-8000 Fax: 314-733-8013
Toll-Free:
Address: 101 S. Hanley Rd., Ste. 450, St. Louis, MO 63105 United States

STOCK TICKER/OTHER:

Stock Ticker: Nonprofit
Employees: 153,000
Parent Company:
Exchange:
Fiscal Year Ends: 06/30

SALARIES/BONUSES:

Top Exec. Salary: $ Bonus: $
Second Exec. Salary: $ Bonus: $

OTHER THOUGHTS:

Estimated Female Officers or Directors: 9
Hot Spot for Advancement for Women/Minorities: Y

Astellas Pharma Inc

www.astellas.com

NAIC Code: 325,412

TYPES OF BUSINESS:

Drugs, Manufacturing
Immunological Pharmaceuticals
Over-the-Counter Products
Reagents
Genomic Research
Venture Capital
Drug Licensing

BRANDS/DIVISIONS/AFFILIATES:

Ocata Therapeutics Inc

CONTACTS: *Note: Officers with more than one job title may be intentionally listed here more than once.*

Kenjl Yasukawa, CEO
Yoshihiko Hantanaka, Pres.
Yoshiro Miyokawa, Exec. VP
Shinichi Tsukamoto, Sr. Corp. Exec. Officer
Masao Yoshida, Sr. Corp. Exec. Officer
Masaru Imahori, Sr. Corp. Exec. VP
Yoshihiko Hatanaka, Chmn.

GROWTH PLANS/SPECIAL FEATURES:

Astellas Pharma, Inc. is one of the largest pharmaceutical manufacturers in Japan. The company's business comprises research, development, manufacturing, technology and medical representatives. The research department explores, optimizes and develops global research activities. The development department engages in clinical trials. The activities within manufacturing and technology department include the industrialization of research, and the manufacturing of products. The medical department supplies information on drug usage. Wholly-owned Ocata Therapeutics, Inc. is a clinical stage biotechnology company focused on the development and commercialization of new therapies in the field of regenerative medicine. Regenerative medicine is the process of replacing or regenerating human cells, tissues or organs to restore or establish normal function. Astellas has more than 35 new molecular/biological entities in its pipeline (as of 2017), and over 100 ongoing collaborative research projects. The firm has its own distribution channels in more than 50 countries worldwide, and develops business across the four main regions of Japan, the Americas, Europe/Middle East/Africa, and Asia/Oceania. Japan derives 36.7% of annual sales; the Americas derive 31.4%; EMEA derives 25.2%; and Asia/Oceania derives 6.7%. In April 2018, Astellas sold certain Agensys research facilities located in Santa Monica, California, USA, to Kite, a Gilead company.

FINANCIAL DATA: *Note: Data for latest year may not have been available at press time.*

In U.S. $	2017	2016	2015	2014	2013	2012
Revenue						
R&D Expense						
Operating Income						
Operating Margin %						
SGA Expense						
Net Income						
Operating Cash Flow						
Capital Expenditure						
EBITDA						
Return on Assets %						
Return on Equity %						
Debt to Equity						

CONTACT INFORMATION:

Phone: 81-3-3244-3000 Fax:
Toll-Free:
Address: 2-5-1 Nihonbashi-Honcho, Chuo-ku, Tokyo, 103-8411 Japan

STOCK TICKER/OTHER:

Stock Ticker: ALPMY
Employees: 16,617
Parent Company:
Exchange: PINX
Fiscal Year Ends: 03/31

SALARIES/BONUSES:

Top Exec. Salary: $ Bonus: $
Second Exec. Salary: $ Bonus: $

OTHER THOUGHTS:

Estimated Female Officers or Directors:
Hot Spot for Advancement for Women/Minorities:

AstraZeneca plc

www.astrazeneca.com

NAIC Code: 325,412

TYPES OF BUSINESS:

Drugs-Diversified
Pharmaceutical Research & Development

BRANDS/DIVISIONS/AFFILIATES:

Viela Bio Inc

CONTACTS:

Note: Officers with more than one job title may be intentionally listed here more than once.

Pascal Soriot, CEO
Marc Dunoyer, CFO
Fiona Cicconi, Exec. VP-Human Resources
Briggs Morrison, Chief Medical Officer
Jeff Pott, General Counsel
David Smith, Exec. VP-Global Oper.
Katarina Ageborg, Chief Compliance Officer
Menelas (Mene) Pangalos, Exec. VP-Innovative Medicines & Early Dev.
Bahija Jallal, Exec. VP-MedImmune
Briggs Morrison, Exec. VP-Global Medicines Dev.
Leif Johansson, Chmn.
Mark Mallon, Exec. VP-Intl

GROWTH PLANS/SPECIAL FEATURES:

AstraZeneca plc is a leading global pharmaceutical company that discovers, develops, manufactures and markets prescription pharmaceuticals, biologics and vaccines. The firm's products are utilized for the treatment or prevention of diseases in the cardiovascular, renal, metabolism, oncology, respiratory, inflammation, autoimmunity, neuroscience and infection categories. AstraZeneca's cardiovascular, renal and metabolism (CVRM) division addresses metabolic risks in relation to CVRM. It focuses on unmet needs concerning atherosclerosis, heart failure, chronic kidney disease (CKD) and diabetes. The oncology division seeks to redefine the treatment paradigm to eliminate cancer as a cause of death, with a concentration on four scientific platforms: haematology, WEE1 inhibition, AKT inhibition and selective oestrogen receptor downregulation. These platforms concentrate on four key diseases: haematologic cancer, ovarian cancer, lung cancer and breast cancer. The respiratory division focuses on the unmet medical needs of those with asthma and chronic obstructive pulmonary disease (COPD) via tailored therapies, devices and support tools. The inflammation and autoimmunity division develops novel treatments for a wide range of related diseases, including lupus. The neuroscience division is committed to discovering and developing compounds that improve patient care in relation to neurodegenerative diseases, analgesia and psychiatry, including Alzheimer's disease and opioid-induced constipation. Last, the infection and vaccines division develops and implements scientific advancement in relation to infections and vaccines, primarily to protect patients against the burdens of influenza, respiratory syncytial virus (RSV) and bacterial infections (primarily those resistant to current antibiotics). In February 2018, AstraZeneca announced plans to spin off six molecules from its early-stage inflammation and autoimmunity programs into an independent biotech company to be called Viela Bio, Inc. The new firm will focus on developing medicines for severe autoimmune diseases by targeting the underlying causes of each disease.

FINANCIAL DATA:

Note: Data for latest year may not have been available at press time.

In U.S. $	2017	2016	2015	2014	2013	2012
Revenue	22,465,000,000	23,002,000,000	24,708,000,000	26,095,000,000	25,711,000,000	27,973,000,000
R&D Expense	5,757,000,000	5,890,000,000	5,997,000,000	5,579,000,000	4,821,000,000	5,243,000,000
Operating Income	2,052,000,000	3,572,000,000	2,614,000,000	1,350,000,000	3,712,000,000	7,178,000,000
Operating Margin %	9.13%	15.52%	10.57%	5.17%	14.43%	25.66%
SGA Expense	10,543,000,000	9,739,000,000	11,451,000,000	13,324,000,000	12,512,000,000	10,159,000,000
Net Income	3,001,000,000	3,499,000,000	2,825,000,000	1,233,000,000	2,556,000,000	6,297,000,000
Operating Cash Flow	3,578,000,000	4,145,000,000	3,324,000,000	7,058,000,000	7,400,000,000	6,948,000,000
Capital Expenditure	1,620,000,000	2,314,000,000	2,788,000,000	2,752,000,000	2,058,000,000	4,619,000,000
EBITDA	5,976,000,000	6,589,000,000	6,390,000,000	4,946,000,000	8,345,000,000	11,194,000,000
Return on Assets %	4.76%	5.70%	4.75%	2.15%	4.67%	11.84%
Return on Equity %	20.13%	20.98%	14.82%	5.75%	10.88%	26.80%
Debt to Equity	1.04	0.97	0.76	0.42	0.36	0.39

CONTACT INFORMATION:

Phone: 44 2037495000 Fax: 44 1223352858
Toll-Free:
Address: 1 Francis Crick Ave., Cambridge, CB2 0AA United Kingdom

STOCK TICKER/OTHER:

Stock Ticker: AZN
Employees: 61,100
Parent Company:
Exchange: NYS
Fiscal Year Ends: 12/31

SALARIES/BONUSES:

Top Exec. Salary: $1,591,547 Bonus: $2,499,511
Second Exec. Salary: $945,796 Bonus: $1,337,160

OTHER THOUGHTS:

Estimated Female Officers or Directors: 3
Hot Spot for Advancement for Women/Minorities: Y

ATC Healthcare Inc

www.atchealthcare.com

NAIC Code: 561,330

TYPES OF BUSINESS:

Health Care Staffing
Management Consulting Services
Medical Staffing
Medical Administrative Staffing

BRANDS/DIVISIONS/AFFILIATES:

ATC Travelers
ATC Physicians
CareBuilders At Home

CONTACTS:

Note: Officers with more than one job title may be intentionally listed here more than once.

David Savitsky, CEO
Stephen Savitsky, Pres.

GROWTH PLANS/SPECIAL FEATURES:

ATC Healthcare, Inc. is a national provider of supplemental staffing and management consulting services to health care institutions through its network of company-owned and franchised offices across the U.S. The company offers medical staffing, outsourcing and human resource solutions to hospitals, nursing homes, health maintenance organizations (HMOs), physician groups, government healthcare and industrial facilities. Healthcare institutions use supplemental staffing to cover permanent positions for which they have openings, for peak periods and for vacations and emergencies. ATC Healthcare takes care of the payment of wages, benefits, payroll taxes, workers' compensation and unemployment insurance for supplemental staff. The company also operates ATC Travelers, a travel nurse program whereby nurses and other health care professionals are placed throughout the U.S. to perform services on a long-term basis with contracts generally ranging from four to 26 weeks; and ATC Physicians, a service that places doctors in doctors' offices, hospitals and health care facilities. ATC, through CareBuilders At Home, places non-medical and skilled nursing care for the elderly and others who may need assistance in their daily lives. ATC provides screening-matching services, using real-time technology and healthcare tracking tools to keep both clients and health care professionals on course.

Employees of the firm receive benefits that include a competitive pay rate, bonus programs, recognition programs, choice of health care settings, medical/dental/vision coverage, flexible savings account and a 401(k) savings plan.

FINANCIAL DATA:

Note: Data for latest year may not have been available at press time.

In U.S. $	2017	2016	2015	2014	2013	2012
Revenue						
R&D Expense						
Operating Income						
Operating Margin %						
SGA Expense						
Net Income						
Operating Cash Flow						
Capital Expenditure						
EBITDA						
Return on Assets %						
Return on Equity %						
Debt to Equity						

CONTACT INFORMATION:

Phone: 516-750-1660 Fax: 516-750-1683
Toll-Free:
Address: 1983 Marcus Ave., Lake Success, NY 11042 United States

STOCK TICKER/OTHER:

Stock Ticker: Private
Exchange:
Employees: 7,074
Fiscal Year Ends: 02/28
Parent Company:

SALARIES/BONUSES:

Top Exec. Salary: $ Bonus: $
Second Exec. Salary: $ Bonus: $

OTHER THOUGHTS:

Estimated Female Officers or Directors:
Hot Spot for Advancement for Women/Minorities:

athenahealth Inc

www.athenahealth.com

NAIC Code: 524,292

TYPES OF BUSINESS:

Outsourced Health Reimbursement Services
Patient Information Management
Billing & Collection Services for Health Care Providers
Automated Messaging

BRANDS/DIVISIONS/AFFILIATES:

athenaNet
athenaCollector
athenaClinicals
athenaCommunicator
athenaCoordinator
Epocrates
Population Health

CONTACTS: *Note: Officers with more than one job title may be intentionally listed here more than once.*

Marc Levine, CFO
Jeffrey Immelt, Chairman of the Board
Dan Haley, Chief Administrative Officer
Tim O'Brien, Chief Marketing Officer
Prakash Khot, Chief Technology Officer
Jeffrey Immelt, Director
Stephen Kahane, Other Corporate Officer
Kyle Armbrester, Other Executive Officer
Jonathan Porter, Senior VP, Divisional

GROWTH PLANS/SPECIAL FEATURES:

Athenahealth, Inc. is a provider of cloud-based business services to physician practices to reduce their administrative work by combining three components: cloud-based software, networked knowledge and back-office work. The firm offers services through its integrated platform, athenaNet. This platform is comprised of four principal tools: athenaCollector, athenaClinicals, athenaCommunicator and athenaCoordinator. AthenaCollector, the company's flagship product, is a revenue cycle management service that includes a management platform and automates and manages billing-related functions for physicians' practices. The athenaCollector system tracks, controls and executes claims and billing processes. AthenaClinicals, aimed at simplifying electronic medical record (EMR) handling, provides a wholly integrated system for managing the processes of providing and receiving pay for care. AthenaCommunicator is an automated message offering that includes automated patient messaging services, live operator services and a patient web portal. AthenaCoordinator is designed to streamline the order process between practices and hospitals, optimizing order transmission, pre-certification and pre-registration. The firm's Population Health services identifies patients in need of care and analyzes the clinical and financial results of that care to drive improvements in outcomes and costs. Epocrates branded services provide a variety of clinical information & decision support offerings through health care providers' mobile devices, including drug & disease information, medical calculator, tools, clinical guidelines & messaging, market research and formulary hosting.

Employee benefits include medical, vision and dental coverage; flexible spending accounts; an employee assistance program; life and AD&D insurance; short- and long-term disability; 401(k); and an employee stock purchase plan.

FINANCIAL DATA: *Note: Data for latest year may not have been available at press time.*

In U.S. $	2017	2016	2015	2014	2013	2012
Revenue	1,220,300,000	1,082,900,000	924,728,000	752,599,000	595,003,000	422,271,000
R&D Expense	173,600,000	134,500,000	94,254,000	69,461,000	57,639,000	33,792,000
Operating Income	70,600,000	26,600,000	-4,056,000	955,000	5,853,000	34,627,000
Operating Margin %	5.78%	2.45%	-.43%	.12%	.98%	8.20%
SGA Expense	397,600,000	388,300,000	374,478,000	314,880,000	249,264,000	161,325,000
Net Income	53,100,000	21,000,000	14,027,000	-3,119,000	2,594,000	18,732,000
Operating Cash Flow	241,100,000	182,600,000	163,844,000	149,105,000	93,308,000	70,213,000
Capital Expenditure	162,900,000	158,500,000	184,975,000	129,569,000	67,383,000	39,561,000
EBITDA	217,200,000	169,600,000	142,704,000	94,637,000	67,989,000	63,771,000
Return on Assets %	4.21%	1.81%	1.36%	-.36%	.42%	4.82%
Return on Equity %	7.45%	3.56%	2.75%	-.71%	.73%	6.83%
Debt to Equity	0.31	0.43	0.52	0.33	0.44	

CONTACT INFORMATION:

Phone: 617 402-1000 Fax: 617 402-1099
Toll-Free: 800-981-5084
Address: 311 Arsenal St., Watertown, MA 02472 United States

STOCK TICKER/OTHER:

Stock Ticker: ATHN
Employees: 5,305
Parent Company:
Exchange: NAS
Fiscal Year Ends: 12/31

SALARIES/BONUSES:

Top Exec. Salary: $598,846 Bonus: $
Second Exec. Salary: $466,673 Bonus: $

OTHER THOUGHTS:

Estimated Female Officers or Directors: 1
Hot Spot for Advancement for Women/Minorities:

Atria Senior Living Group

www.atriaseniorliving.com

NAIC Code: 623,310

TYPES OF BUSINESS:

Assisted Living Facilities
Assisted Living Centers
Alzheimer Care
Short-Term Health Care

BRANDS/DIVISIONS/AFFILIATES:

Fremont Group
Fremont Realty Capital
Ventas Inc
Engage Life
A Dash & A Dollop

CONTACTS: *Note: Officers with more than one job title may be intentionally listed here more than once.*

John A. Moore, CEO
Mark Jessee, Pres.

GROWTH PLANS/SPECIAL FEATURES:

Atria Senior Living Group is one of the nation's largest operators of facilities the provide assisted living services for the country's senior population. Atria currently operates more than 200 communities across 27 states and seven Canadian provinces, which provide housing and support services for over 21,000 seniors. Each program that Atria offers is tailored to the individual, with residents free to bring their own furnishings and pets. Atria provides seniors with the following programs: The Independent Living program, which is a retirement lifestyle that frees seniors from the worries of home maintenance, encourages them to engage in activities and hobbies and allows them to choose their own degree of privacy or sociability; the Assisted Living program, which is available to help seniors with daily activities such as bathing, eating, dressing and medication management; the Life Guidance program, which is available at some communities to provide a separate and secure environment for seniors with Alzheimer's disease and other forms of memory impairment; and short-term retreat programs, which are tailored for seniors on a temporary basis for seasonal stays, hospital recovery or trial-period stays. The firm's Engage Life program works to provide residents with other interesting and meaningful activities, such as book clubs, exercise classes, gardening, arts and crafts, bingo and card games which are coordinated by Engage Life directors that spend individual time with each resident to help them plan activities according to their interests. Atria also released a cookbook, titled A Dash & A Dollop, which includes dishes and stories from Atria residents. It can be purchased online or at any Barnes and Noble store. In late-2017, Atria sold 50% of its own stake to Fremont Realty Capital, the real estate private equity unit of the Fremont Group. Ventas, Inc. owns a 34% stake and Atria holds the remainder.

FINANCIAL DATA: *Note: Data for latest year may not have been available at press time.*

In U.S. $	2017	2016	2015	2014	2013	2012
Revenue						
R&D Expense						
Operating Income						
Operating Margin %						
SGA Expense						
Net Income						
Operating Cash Flow						
Capital Expenditure						
EBITDA						
Return on Assets %						
Return on Equity %						
Debt to Equity						

CONTACT INFORMATION:

Phone: 502-779-4700 Fax: 502-779-4701
Toll-Free: 877-719-1600
Address: 300 East Market Street, Ste 100, Louisville, KY 40202 United States

STOCK TICKER/OTHER:

Stock Ticker: Private
Employees: 14,600
Parent Company:
Exchange:
Fiscal Year Ends: 12/31

SALARIES/BONUSES:

Top Exec. Salary: $ Bonus: $
Second Exec. Salary: $ Bonus: $

OTHER THOUGHTS:

Estimated Female Officers or Directors: 1
Hot Spot for Advancement for Women/Minorities:

Atrion Corporation

www.atrioncorp.com

NAIC Code: 339,100

TYPES OF BUSINESS:

Equipment-Ophthalmic, Diagnostic & Cardiovascular
Fluid Delivery Devices
Medical Device Components
Contract Manufacturing

BRANDS/DIVISIONS/AFFILIATES:

Quest Medical Inc
MPS2 Myocardial Protection System
LacriCATH
Atrion Medical Products Inc

CONTACTS: *Note: Officers with more than one job title may be intentionally listed here more than once.*

David Battat, CEO
Jeffery Strickland, CFO
Emile Battat, Chairman of the Board

GROWTH PLANS/SPECIAL FEATURES:

Atrion Corporation develops and manufactures products for the medical and health care industries. The company sells components to other equipment manufacturers and finished products to physicians, hospitals, clinics and other treatment centers. Its cardiovascular products, which accounted for 33% of its 2017 revenues, are manufactured by subsidiary Quest Medical, Inc. These include cardiac surgery vacuum relief valves and other tools used in cardiac surgery, such as the MPS2 Myocardial Protection System, a proprietary system used for the delivery of solutions to the heart during open-heart surgery, mixing drugs into the bloodstream without diluting the blood. The company's fluid delivery products (44% of revenues) include proprietary valves for use in various intubation, catheter and other applications. Medical tubing clamps in a variety of materials and colors are also manufactured under this section. Atrion's ophthalmic products and services (9%) include soft contact lens storage and disinfection cases and the LacriCATH line of balloon catheters used in the treatment of nasolacrimal duct obstruction as well as custom packaging, warehousing and inventory management offered as part of its pharmaceutical reselling business. The company's other medical and non-medical products (14%), many of which are manufactured by subsidiary Atrion Medical Products, Inc., include inflation devices, oral inflation tubes, right angle connectors, valves and closures for life vests, life rafts, inflatable boats, survival equipment and other inflatable structures. Other products include valves for use on electronics or munitions cases, pressure vessels and transportation container cases.

Employees are offered medical, dental, prescription, life and short-and long-term disability; paid vacation; and retirement plans.

FINANCIAL DATA: *Note: Data for latest year may not have been available at press time.*

In U.S. $	2017	2016	2015	2014	2013	2012
Revenue	146,595,000	143,487,000	145,733,000	140,762,000	131,993,000	119,062,000
R&D Expense	5,799,000	6,574,000	6,346,000	5,286,000	4,288,000	3,766,000
Operating Income	41,274,000	39,126,000	42,510,000	40,817,000	37,944,000	33,626,000
Operating Margin %	28.15%	27.26%	29.16%	28.99%	28.74%	28.24%
SGA Expense	23,681,000	21,930,000	22,125,000	22,415,000	20,830,000	18,748,000
Net Income	36,593,000	27,581,000	28,925,000	27,808,000	26,582,000	23,629,000
Operating Cash Flow	47,037,000	37,403,000	40,427,000	31,223,000	36,576,000	29,369,000
Capital Expenditure	9,677,000	10,639,000	9,323,000	12,671,000	9,653,000	10,347,000
EBITDA	49,951,000	48,079,000	51,333,000	49,540,000	46,536,000	41,236,000
Return on Assets %	18.94%	15.90%	17.22%	16.18%	16.21%	14.87%
Return on Equity %	21.06%	17.96%	19.69%	18.62%	18.73%	17.28%
Debt to Equity						

CONTACT INFORMATION:

Phone: 972 390-9800 Fax:
Toll-Free:
Address: 1 Allentown Pkwy., Allen, TX 75002 United States

STOCK TICKER/OTHER:

Stock Ticker: ATRI
Employees: 520
Parent Company:
Exchange: NAS
Fiscal Year Ends: 12/31

SALARIES/BONUSES:

Top Exec. Salary: $620,000 Bonus: $
Second Exec. Salary: $600,000 Bonus: $

OTHER THOUGHTS:

Estimated Female Officers or Directors:
Hot Spot for Advancement for Women/Minorities:

Auris Health Inc

www.aurishealth.com

NAIC Code: 339,100

TYPES OF BUSINESS:

Surgical Equipment-Robotics
Medical Robotics
Micro-Instrumentation
Endoscopes
Data Science

BRANDS/DIVISIONS/AFFILIATES:

Monarch Platform

GROWTH PLANS/SPECIAL FEATURES:

Auris Health, Inc. creates platforms that enhance physician capabilities and evolve minimally-invasive techniques. The company engages in transforming medical intervention by integrating robotics, micro-instrumentation, endoscope design, sensing and data science into a single platform called the Monarch Platform. This platform enables physicians to accurately access small and hard-to-reach peripheral nodules for diagnosing and targeting treatment for a multitude of diseases, including lung cancer. All of Auris' technology is driven by a patient-specific approach for maintaining the integrity of the human body. Auris is backed by leading technology investors such as Mithril Capital Management, Lux Capital, Coatue Management and Highland Capital.

Auris offers employees comprehensive health, dental, vision and pet insurance; and 401k options.

CONTACTS: *Note: Officers with more than one job title may be intentionally listed here more than once.*

Fred Moll, CEO
Dan Bradford, VP-Operations
Christopher Lowe, CFO
David M. Styka, CFO
Eric Davidson, VP-Mktg. & Sales
Michael Eagle, Director
Robert Cathcart, Senior VP, Divisional
Brian Sheahan, Vice President, Divisional

FINANCIAL DATA: *Note: Data for latest year may not have been available at press time.*

In U.S. $	2017	2016	2015	2014	2013	2012
Revenue	14,700,000	14,000,000	16,068,000	19,495,000	16,982,000	17,636,000
R&D Expense						
Operating Income						
Operating Margin %						
SGA Expense						
Net Income			-46,207,000	-54,246,000	-55,722,000	-22,145,000
Operating Cash Flow						
Capital Expenditure						
EBITDA						
Return on Assets %						
Return on Equity %						
Debt to Equity						

CONTACT INFORMATION:

Phone: 650-610-0750 Fax:
Toll-Free:
Address: 150 Shoreline Dr., Redwood City, CA 94065 United States

STOCK TICKER/OTHER:

Stock Ticker: Private
Employees: 169
Parent Company:
Exchange:
Fiscal Year Ends:

SALARIES/BONUSES:

Top Exec. Salary: $ Bonus: $
Second Exec. Salary: $ Bonus: $

OTHER THOUGHTS:

Estimated Female Officers or Directors: 3
Hot Spot for Advancement for Women/Minorities: Y

Avanos Medical Inc

avanos.com

NAIC Code: 339,100

TYPES OF BUSINESS:

Medical Equipment and Supplies Manufacturing
Surgical Products
Infection Prevention
Pain Management
Respiratory Products
Gastronomy Products
Infusion Systems
Wound Care

BRANDS/DIVISIONS/AFFILIATES:

On-Q
COOLIEF
MIC-KEY
Cortrak
CLOtest
Microcuff
Homepump
Halyard Health Inc

CONTACTS: *Note: Officers with more than one job title may be intentionally listed here more than once.*

Joseph F. Woody, CEO
Steven Voskuil, CFO
Steve Voskul, Sr. VP
Rhonda Gibby, Sr. VP-Human Resources Officer
John Wesley, General Counsel
Rhonda Gibby, Other Executive Officer
John Tushar, President, Divisional
Warren Machan, Senior VP, Divisional

GROWTH PLANS/SPECIAL FEATURES:

Avanos Medical, Inc. (formerly Halyard Health, Inc.) is a medical technology company that operates through its medical devices segment. The firm's medical device solutions aim to improve patients' quality of life, including the reduction of opioid use while helping patients move from surgery to recovery. Avanos' digestive health solutions include: the On-Q pain relief system, offering surgical site and regional anesthesia pain management; the COOLIEF cooled radiofrequency treatment line of products for the relief of degenerative osteoarthritis (OA) knee pain; the MIC-KEY line of enteral feeding tubes; the Cortrak enteral access system; CLOtest diagnostic and endoscopic accessories; and paracentesis procedure kits and trays. Respiratory health solutions include: Microcuff endotracheal tubes; CHG oral rinse; HALYARD oral care kits and components; closed-suction systems; and Mini-BAL sampling catheters. Last, Avanos' intravenous therapy solutions include its Homepump infusion systems for drug delivery. Based in Georgia, USA the company has operations in California, as well as internationally in Australia, Japan, Singapore and Belgium. In April 2018, Avanos sold its surgical and infection prevention business, including the Halyard Health name, and subsequently changed its corporate name to Avanos Medical. Avanos publicly-trades on the New York Stock Exchange under ticker symbol AVNS.

FINANCIAL DATA: *Note: Data for latest year may not have been available at press time.*

In U.S. $	2017	2016	2015	2014	2013	2012
Revenue	611,600,000	1,592,300,000	1,574,400,000	1,672,100,000	1,677,500,000	1,684,000,000
R&D Expense	38,200,000	41,100,000	32,300,000	33,600,000	37,900,000	33,000,000
Operating Income	-43,100,000	87,400,000	96,300,000	94,300,000	225,300,000	228,000,000
Operating Margin %	-7.04%	5.48%	6.40%	5.63%	13.43%	13.53%
SGA Expense	321,700,000	411,100,000	398,500,000	424,500,000	351,400,000	343,000,000
Net Income	79,300,000	39,800,000	-426,300,000	27,100,000	154,600,000	152,600,000
Operating Cash Flow	144,200,000	188,800,000	97,600,000	147,900,000	223,800,000	202,600,000
Capital Expenditure	43,200,000	29,100,000	70,400,000	78,500,000	49,000,000	40,800,000
EBITDA	18,900,000	153,200,000	-312,000,000	182,600,000	297,100,000	288,200,000
Return on Assets %	3.71%	1.95%	-18.83%	1.08%	4.93%	6.02%
Return on Equity %	6.84%	3.68%	-33.48%	1.51%	5.99%	7.42%
Debt to Equity	0.44	0.52	0.54	0.42		

CONTACT INFORMATION:

Phone: 678 425-9273 Fax:
Toll-Free:
Address: 5405 Windward Parkway, Ste. 100, Alpharetta, GA 30004 United States

STOCK TICKER/OTHER:

Stock Ticker: AVNS
Employees: 12,000
Parent Company:
Exchange: NYS
Fiscal Year Ends: 02/28

SALARIES/BONUSES:

Top Exec. Salary: $496,589 Bonus: $250,000
Second Exec. Salary: $664,566 Bonus: $

OTHER THOUGHTS:

Estimated Female Officers or Directors:
Hot Spot for Advancement for Women/Minorities:

Avera Health

www.avera.org

NAIC Code: 622,110

TYPES OF BUSINESS:

General Medical and Surgical Hospitals
Nursing Homes
HMO
Health Insurance Consultation

BRANDS/DIVISIONS/AFFILIATES:

Avera eCARE
Avera Marshall Regional Medical Center

CONTACTS: *Note: Officers with more than one job title may be intentionally listed here more than once.*

Bob Sutton, CEO
Fred Slunecka, COO
John T. Porter, Pres.
James J. Breckenridge, Exec. VP-Finance
Kendra Calhoun, Sr. VP-Mktg.
Kim Jensen, Interim Exec. VP-Human Resources
Jim Veline, SVP
Daniel D. Eisenbraun, Chmn.

GROWTH PLANS/SPECIAL FEATURES:

Avera Health was created by, and is currently sponsored through, an agreement between the Benedictine Sisters of Yankton, South Dakota and the Presentation Sisters of Aberdeen, South Dakota. The partnership is comprised of 33 hospitals, 208 primary and specialty care clinics, 40 senior living facilities, as well as home care, hospice, sports/wellness facilities and home medical equipment outlets via 330 locations in South Dakota, Minnesota, Iowa and Nebraska. The organization is divided into six regional centers in Aberdeen, Mitchell, Pierre, Sioux Falls and Yankton, South Dakota, and Marshall, Minnesota. Within these regions, Avera Health serves a population of nearly 1 million throughout 72,000 square miles and 86 counties. Residents can access a wide range of specialists through the company's Avera eCARE telemedicine services, available at more than 150 Avera clinics and doctor offices. In November 2017, Avera Health's Avera Marshall Regional Medical Center announced plans for a new hospital Emergency Department. In March 2018, the firm announced plans to build an Avera Addiction Care Center in Sioux Falls.

Employee benefits include time off, insurance coverage, a retirement plan, flexible spending accounts and employee discounts.

FINANCIAL DATA: *Note: Data for latest year may not have been available at press time.*

In U.S. $	2017	2016	2015	2014	2013	2012
Revenue	201,013,260	191,441,200	169,384,234	134,809,969	125,047,257	84,380,282
R&D Expense						
Operating Income						
Operating Margin %						
SGA Expense						
Net Income		20,048,913	19,283,729	15,354,369	37,424,271	10,248,917
Operating Cash Flow						
Capital Expenditure						
EBITDA						
Return on Assets %						
Return on Equity %						
Debt to Equity						

CONTACT INFORMATION:

Phone: 605-322-4700 Fax: 605-322-4799
Toll-Free:
Address: 3900 W. Avera Dr., Sioux Falls, SD 57108 United States

STOCK TICKER/OTHER:

Stock Ticker: Nonprofit
Employees: 16,000
Parent Company:
Exchange:
Fiscal Year Ends: 06/30

SALARIES/BONUSES:

Top Exec. Salary: $ Bonus: $
Second Exec. Salary: $ Bonus: $

OTHER THOUGHTS:

Estimated Female Officers or Directors:
Hot Spot for Advancement for Women/Minorities:

Avinger Inc

www.avinger.com

NAIC Code: 339,100

TYPES OF BUSINESS:

Catheters Manufacturing

BRANDS/DIVISIONS/AFFILIATES:

Lightbox
Wildcat
Kittycat
Ocelot
Pantheris
Lumivascular

CONTACTS: *Note: Officers with more than one job title may be intentionally listed here more than once.*

Jeffrey Soinski, CEO
Matthew Ferguson, CFO
James Cullen, Chairman of the Board
Himanshu Patel, Chief Technology Officer

GROWTH PLANS/SPECIAL FEATURES:

Avinger, Inc. is a commercial-stage medical device company that designs, manufactures and sells image-guided, catheter-based systems that are used by physicians to treat patients with peripheral artery disease (PAD). The firm manufactures and sells a suite of products in the U.S. and select European markets based on its Lumivascular platform, the only intravascular image-guided system available in those markets. Avinger's Lumivascular platform combines interventional devices with optical coherence tomography (OCT) a high resolution, light-based, radiation-free intravascular imaging technology. The platform provides physicians with real-time OCT images from the inside of an artery. Avinger's current products include its Lightbox imaging console, as well as its Wildcat, Kittycat and the Ocelot family of catheters, which are designed to allow physicians to penetrate a total blockage in an artery, known as a chronic total occlusion (CTO), and Pantheris, its image-guided atherectomy device, designed to allow physicians to precisely remove arterial plaque in PAD patients.

FINANCIAL DATA: *Note: Data for latest year may not have been available at press time.*

In U.S. $	2017	2016	2015	2014	2013	2012
Revenue	9,934,000	19,214,000	10,713,000	11,213,000	12,964,000	8,560,000
R&D Expense	11,319,000	15,536,000	15,694,000	11,224,000	15,973,000	15,416,000
Operating Income	-39,507,000	-50,717,000	-40,690,000	-25,027,000	-36,972,000	-33,855,000
Operating Margin %	-397.69%	-263.95%	-379.81%	-223.19%	-285.18%	-395.50%
SGA Expense	25,120,000	39,950,000	29,231,000	18,503,000	25,758,000	22,848,000
Net Income	-48,732,000	-56,128,000	-47,344,000	-31,964,000	-39,901,000	-33,864,000
Operating Cash Flow	-34,476,000	-53,069,000	-40,883,000	-21,801,000	-40,655,000	-35,234,000
Capital Expenditure	45,000	971,000	577,000	117,000	496,000	288,000
EBITDA	-40,957,000	-49,098,000	-40,877,000	-24,483,000	-35,455,000	-33,077,000
Return on Assets %	-141.98%	-104.26%	-126.07%	-128.40%	-144.22%	-111.67%
Return on Equity %		-566.09%				
Debt to Equity			1.89			

CONTACT INFORMATION:

Phone: 650 241-7900 Fax: 800 229-2696
Toll-Free:
Address: 400 Chesapeake Drive, Redwood City, CA 94063 United States

STOCK TICKER/OTHER:

Stock Ticker: AVGR
Exchange: NAS
Employees: 197
Fiscal Year Ends: 12/31
Parent Company:

SALARIES/BONUSES:

Top Exec. Salary: $390,000 Bonus: $
Second Exec. Salary: $363,500 Bonus: $

OTHER THOUGHTS:

Estimated Female Officers or Directors:
Hot Spot for Advancement for Women/Minorities:

AvMed Health Plans Inc

www.avmed.org

NAIC Code: 524,114

TYPES OF BUSINESS:

Insurance-Medical & Health, HMOs & PPOs
HMO & POS Plans
Health Education Services
Disease Management

BRANDS/DIVISIONS/AFFILIATES:

SantaFe Healthcare Inc
Nurse On-Call

CONTACTS: *Note: Officers with more than one job title may be intentionally listed here more than once.*

Michael P. Gallagher, CEO
James M. Repp, Pres.
Randall L. Stuart, CFO
Kay Ayers, Sr. VP-Human Resources
Ann O. Wehr, Sr. VP
Jim Simpson, CIO
Steven M. Ziegler, General Counsel
Susan Knapp Pinnas, Sr. VP-Provider & Service Oper.
Michael P. Gallagher, CEO
Kay Ayers, Sr. VP-Member Svcs.
Brad Bentley, Sr. VP-Underwriting, Actuarial & Regulatory Affair

GROWTH PLANS/SPECIAL FEATURES:

AvMed Health Plan, Inc. is a statewide nonprofit company and one of Florida's leading HMO (health maintenance organization) providers, serving more than 290,000 members with a network of over 35,000 physicians, specialists and hospitals. AvMed is owned by SantaFe HealthCare, Inc. The firm's policies include employer group HMO, Medicare HMO, point-of-service (POS) and self-funded plans. The company offers tailored plans for small businesses, with fewer than 50 employees, or large businesses, with over 50 employees. In addition, the company offers health promotion opportunities, smoking cessation programs and a number of onsite health-related seminars. For members with chronic conditions, AvMed offers care management programs that focus on education and individualized attention. These offerings include asthma, diabetes care, high-risk obstetrics, neonatal management, congestive heart failure, chronic obstructive pulmonary disease, oncology care, wound care, catastrophic cases, end-stage renal disease and organ/bone marrow transplant. Such programs aim to help patients navigate the health care systems to actively manage their health. In addition, the firm provides Nurse On-Call, a free, 24-hour phone service staffed by Florida-based registered nurses who help members make informed health care decisions. Beyond standard care options, AvMed offers a range of alternative health and wellness programs in fields such as massage therapy, acupuncture, nutrition, relaxation/meditation training, Yoga, Tai Chi, biofeedback, holistic medicine, Chinese herbal medicine, homeopathy, fitness and spa services.

Employee benefits include medical, dental and vision coverage; health savings account; life & AD&D insurance; short- and long-term disability; a 401(k); tuition assistance; credit union membership; flex time; dry cleaning service; and discounts.

FINANCIAL DATA: *Note: Data for latest year may not have been available at press time.*

In U.S. $	2017	2016	2015	2014	2013	2012
Revenue	1,029,000,000	980,000,000	977,000,000	960,000,000	920,000,000	908,800,000
R&D Expense						
Operating Income						
Operating Margin %						
SGA Expense						
Net Income				-49,000,000	20,400,000	
Operating Cash Flow						
Capital Expenditure						
EBITDA						
Return on Assets %						
Return on Equity %						
Debt to Equity						

CONTACT INFORMATION:

Phone: 305-671-5437 Fax: 305-671-4782
Toll-Free: 800-882-8633
Address: 9400 S. Dadeland Blvd., Ste. 120, Miami, FL 33156 United States

STOCK TICKER/OTHER:

Stock Ticker: Subsidiary
Employees: 765
Parent Company: SantaFe HealthCare Inc
Exchange:
Fiscal Year Ends: 12/31

SALARIES/BONUSES:

Top Exec. Salary: $ Bonus: $
Second Exec. Salary: $ Bonus: $

OTHER THOUGHTS:

Estimated Female Officers or Directors: 3
Hot Spot for Advancement for Women/Minorities: Y

AXA PPP Healthcare Limited

www.axappphealthcare.co.uk

NAIC Code: 524,114

TYPES OF BUSINESS:

Insurance-Medical & Health, HMOs & PPOs
Health Information Services
Dental & Travel Insurance
Employee Assistance

BRANDS/DIVISIONS/AFFILIATES:

AXA Group

CONTACTS: *Note: Officers with more than one job title may be intentionally listed here more than once.*

Keith George Gibbs, CEO
Richard Turner, Dir.-Strategy
Nicola Bell, Financial Dir.
Nick Groom, Dir.-Distribution

GROWTH PLANS/SPECIAL FEATURES:

AXA PPP Healthcare Limited, a subsidiary of the AXA Group, is one of the U.K.'s largest private managed healthcare companies, providing service through a network of hospitals and scanning centers. The firm divides its coverage options into three divisions: personal, business and health and wellbeing. Through its personal division, AXA PPP provides private health coverage to individuals and families in the U.K. Products in this division include private medical insurance; a cancer cash cover program that offers tax-free cash payment on first diagnosis of cancer and other benefits; child healthcare insurance; dental insurance; and international health cover for individuals living or working abroad on short-or long-term basis. The company's business division includes small to medium business healthcare; corporate health cover for over 225 employees; dental plans; health cash plans; travel cover; and a business health center which offers professional counseling, employee health engagement and stress management. The division also offers occupational health insurance services, including a fixed-cost package of occupational health and safety services, on-call expert support, executive care health assessment for key employees, safety services that manage the risk of work-related accidents or illnesses, a free health information service, a tailored package of health and fitness services for employees, an independent referral review service for patients with long-term health problems, attendance management and pre-employment medical clearance services. AXA PPP's health and wellbeing division includes centers that provide information about medical conditions and illnesses. Its online channel, Ask the Expert, comprises nurses, pharmacists and midwives on hand. Topics or concerns can be related to aging, allergies, cancer, dental health, diabetes, diet/nutrition, fitness/exercise, healthy living, heart, mental health, musculoskeletal, pregnancy and childcare.

FINANCIAL DATA: *Note: Data for latest year may not have been available at press time.*

In U.S. $	2017	2016	2015	2014	2013	2012
Revenue	2,371,282,523	2,258,364,308	2,150,823,150	2,048,403,000	1,950,860,000	1,830,490,000
R&D Expense						
Operating Income						
Operating Margin %						
SGA Expense						
Net Income	106,176,000	92,139,000	87,459,200	68,962,100	11,954,000	83,028,000
Operating Cash Flow						
Capital Expenditure						
EBITDA						
Return on Assets %						
Return on Equity %						
Debt to Equity						

CONTACT INFORMATION:

Phone: 44-0189-251-2345 Fax: 44-0189-251-5143
Toll-Free:
Address: Phillips House, Crescent Rd., Turnbridge Wells, Kent TN1 2PL United Kingdom

STOCK TICKER/OTHER:

Stock Ticker: Subsidiary
Employees:
Parent Company: AXA Group
Exchange:
Fiscal Year Ends: 12/31

SALARIES/BONUSES:

Top Exec. Salary: $ Bonus: $
Second Exec. Salary: $ Bonus: $

OTHER THOUGHTS:

Estimated Female Officers or Directors: 1
Hot Spot for Advancement for Women/Minorities:

Banner Health

NAIC Code: 622,110

www.bannerhealth.com

TYPES OF BUSINESS:

General Medical and Surgical Hospitals
Long-Term Care Centers
Home Care Services
Home Medical Equipment Services
Family Clinics
Nursing Registry
Medical Research

BRANDS/DIVISIONS/AFFILIATES:

Banner Good Samaritan Medical Center
Banner Health Foundation
Banner Alzheimer's Foundation
Banner-University Medicine
Banner MD Anderson Cancer Center

CONTACTS: *Note: Officers with more than one job title may be intentionally listed here more than once.*

Peter S. Fine, CEO
Becky Kuhn, COO
Dennis Laraway, CFO
Naomi Cramer, Chief Human Resources Officer
John Hensing, Chief Medical Officer
Ron Bunnell, Chief Admin. Officer
David Bixby, General Counsel
Jim Ferando, Pres., Western Region
Rebecca Kuhn, Pres., Arizona East Region
Kathy Bollinger, Pres., Arizona West Region
Andy Kramer, CEO

GROWTH PLANS/SPECIAL FEATURES:

Banner Health, based in Phoenix, Arizona, is one of the nation's largest nonprofit health care systems. The company's hospitals and facilities are located in Arizona, California, Colorado, Nebraska, Nevada and Wyoming. Banner Health offers services such as home care, inpatient/outpatient care, hospice care, surgery centers and a nursing registry. Banner Health's major programs include cancer, critical care, emergency medicine, heart care, medical imaging, neurosciences, obstetrics, pediatrics, rehabilitation and surgery. In addition to basic medical and emergency services, the firm's hospitals provide specialized services such as burn care, organ transplants, cancer treatment, multiple-birth deliveries, rehabilitation services and behavioral health services. Additional specialized services include Alzheimer's research and treatment, spinal cord injury research, behavioral health, blood conservation medicine, high-risk obstetrics, home care, hospice, level one trauma and organ and bone marrow transplants. The company is active in physician training through programs such as the medical education program at Banner Good Samaritan Medical Center in Phoenix. Its Banner Health Foundation is a charity that contributes toward supporting patient care in Arizona; and Banner Alzheimer's Foundation secures charitable contributions to support research initiatives, family outreach, counseling and support services for Alzheimer's care and prevention. Banner Health's partnership with the University of Arizona Health Network in Tucson formed Banner-University Medicine, which provides academic medicine, comprising research, teaching and patient care via three academic medical centers. And during 2018, its partnership with University of Texas MD Anderson Cancer Center created Banner MD Anderson Cancer Center at North Colorado Medical Center as well as Banner MD Anderson Cancer Center at McKee Medical Center in Loveland, Colorado.

Banner Health offers employees medical, dental, vision and prescription coverage; flexible spending accounts; employee assistance program; tuition reimbursement; and 401(k).

FINANCIAL DATA: *Note: Data for latest year may not have been available at press time.*

In U.S. $	2017	2016	2015	2014	2013	2012
Revenue	7,835,266,000	7,633,205,000	6,971,132,000	4,769,437,583	4,462,552,866	4,252,663,741
R&D Expense						
Operating Income						
Operating Margin %						
SGA Expense						
Net Income	5,784,480,000	551,992,949	444,821,035	416,333,313	482,263,859	412,425,223
Operating Cash Flow						
Capital Expenditure						
EBITDA						
Return on Assets %						
Return on Equity %						
Debt to Equity						

CONTACT INFORMATION:

Phone: 602-495-4000 Fax:
Toll-Free:
Address: 2901 N. Central Ave, Phoenix, AZ 85012 United States

STOCK TICKER/OTHER:

Stock Ticker: Nonprofit
Employees: 49,740
Parent Company:
Exchange:
Fiscal Year Ends: 12/31

SALARIES/BONUSES:

Top Exec. Salary: $ Bonus: $
Second Exec. Salary: $ Bonus: $

OTHER THOUGHTS:

Estimated Female Officers or Directors: 3
Hot Spot for Advancement for Women/Minorities: Y

Bausch & Lomb Inc

www.bausch.com

NAIC Code: 339,100

TYPES OF BUSINESS:

Supplies-Eye Care
Contact Lens Products
Ophthalmic Pharmaceuticals
Surgical Products

BRANDS/DIVISIONS/AFFILIATES:

Valeant Pharmaceuticals International Inc
Biotrue
Bausch + Lomb
PureVision
ReNu
Alaway
Alrex
PreserVision

CONTACTS: *Note: Officers with more than one job title may be intentionally listed here more than once.*

Robert Bertolini, Pres.
John R. Barr, Pres., Surgical Bus.
Mariano Garcia-Valino, Corp. VP
Sheila A. Hopkins, Pres., Vision Care Bus.
Rodney William Unsworth, Pres., Asia Pacific
Joseph C. Papa, Chmn.-Valeant

GROWTH PLANS/SPECIAL FEATURES:

Bausch & Lomb, Inc. (B&L), owned by Valeant Pharmaceuticals International, Inc., is a world leader in the development, marketing and manufacturing of eye care products. The firm's products are marketed in more than 100 countries, and include contact lenses, contact lens care, dry eye products, allergy/redness relief, Rx pharmaceutical, eye vitamins, surgical products and vision accessories. B&L's contact lenses are for people who are nearsighted, farsighted, have astigmatism or presbyopia; they are soft hydrophilic discs that float on the cornea of the eye. Brands include Biotrue, Bausch + Lomb, PureVision, SofLens and Boston Multivision GP. Lens care products include Biotrue eye solution, PeroxiClear cleaning solution, ReNu solution and drops and Boston One Step cleaner and drops as well as Sensitive Eyes solutions. Dry eye product brands include Soothe eye drops, THERA PEARL Eye mask, Advanced Eye Relief and Muro 128 solutions. Allergy and redness relief product brands include Alaway, Opcon and Advanced Relief. Rx pharmaceutical product brands include Alrex, Lotemax, Retisert, BEPREVE, TIMOPTIC, PROLENSA, Vyzulta, Besivance, Zylet, LACRISERT,Istalol, Macugen Visudyne and Zirgan. Eye wash brands include Advanced and Collyrium. Eye vitamins are marketed under the PreserVision brand. Surgical product brands include enVista, Crystalens, Trulign, Akreos and SofPort. Last, vision accessories include magnifiers, cleaning kits, eyewear cleaning products and lens cases, all under the B&L name.

The company offers employees medical and dental coverage, a 401(k) account plan, a vacation buy/sell program, flexible spending accounts and education reimbursement.

FINANCIAL DATA: *Note: Data for latest year may not have been available at press time.*

In U.S. $	2017	2016	2015	2014	2013	2012
Revenue	4,871,000,000	4,927,000,000	4,603,000,000	3,160,000,000	3,100,000,000	3,040,000,000
R&D Expense						
Operating Income						
Operating Margin %						
SGA Expense						
Net Income	1,440,000,000	1,483,000,000				
Operating Cash Flow						
Capital Expenditure						
EBITDA						
Return on Assets %						
Return on Equity %						
Debt to Equity						

CONTACT INFORMATION:

Phone: 585-338-6000 Fax: 585-338-6896
Toll-Free: 800-553-5340
Address: 400 Somerset Corporate Blvd, Bridgewater, NJ 08807 United States

STOCK TICKER/OTHER:

Stock Ticker: Subsidiary Exchange:
Employees: 12,000 Fiscal Year Ends: 12/31
Parent Company: Valeant Pharmaceuticals International Inc

SALARIES/BONUSES:

Top Exec. Salary: $ Bonus: $
Second Exec. Salary: $ Bonus: $

OTHER THOUGHTS:

Estimated Female Officers or Directors: 1
Hot Spot for Advancement for Women/Minorities: Y

Bausch Health Companies Inc

www.bauschhealth.com

NAIC Code: 325,412

TYPES OF BUSINESS:

Prescription & Non-Prescription Pharmaceuticals
Neurology Drugs
Dermatology Drugs
Infectious Diseases Drugs

BRANDS/DIVISIONS/AFFILIATES:

Valeant Pharmaceuticals International Inc
Bausch + Lomb
Salix

CONTACTS: *Note: Officers with more than one job title may be intentionally listed here more than once.*

Joseph Papa, CEO
Paul Herendeen, CFO
William Humphries, Chairman of the Board, Divisional
Thomas Appio, Chairman of the Board, Geographical
Sam Eldessouky, Chief Accounting Officer
Christina Ackermann, Executive VP

GROWTH PLANS/SPECIAL FEATURES:

Bausch Health Companies, Inc., formerly Valeant Pharmaceuticals International, Inc., is a specialty pharmaceutical and medical device company that develops, manufactures and markets its products in over 100 countries. These products include a range of branded, generic and branded generic pharmaceuticals, over-the-counter (OTC) products and medical devices such as contact lenses, intraocular lenses, ophthalmic surgical equipment and aesthetic devices. Bausch Health Companies' products fall into three segments: Bausch + Lomb/international, branded Rx and U.S. diversified products. The Bausch + Lomb/international segment sells: pharmaceuticals, OTCs and medical devices with a focus on four product offerings in the U.S. (vision care, surgical, consumer and ophthalmology Rx) and branded, branded generic pharmaceuticals, OTCs, medical devices and Bausch + Lomb products sold in Europe, Asia, Australia, New Zealand, Latin America, Africa and the Middle East. The branded Rx segment sells pharmaceutical products and medical devices within the Salix portfolio in the U.S.; the dermatological portfolio in the U.S., branded and branded generic pharmaceuticals, OTCs, medical devices and Bausch + Lomb products sold in Canada; and oncology, dentistry and women's health products sold in the U.S. Last, the U.S. diversified products segment sells pharmaceuticals, OTCs and medical devices in the areas of neurology and certain other therapeutic classes, as well as generic products in the U.S. During 2017, Bausch Health Companies, then known as Valeant, sold Dendreon Pharmaceuticals, LLC to Sanpower for $845 million; sold its Australian-based iNoval Pharmaceuticals business for $938 million; sold its Obagi business for $190 million; and sold its Sprout business in exchange for a 6% royalty on global sales of Addyi (flibanserin 100mg) beginning June 2019. In July 2018, Valeant completed its name change to Bausch Health Companies, Inc.

Valeant offers employees a 401(k) plan; medical, dental and vision insurance; life and disability insurance; and group legal and long-term care benefits.

FINANCIAL DATA: *Note: Data for latest year may not have been available at press time.*

In U.S. $	2017	2016	2015	2014	2013	2012
Revenue	8,724,000,000	9,674,000,000	10,446,500,000	8,263,500,000	5,769,605,000	3,546,626,000
R&D Expense	366,000,000	455,000,000	334,400,000	246,000,000	156,783,000	79,052,000
Operating Income	538,000,000	1,125,000,000	2,153,200,000	2,454,600,000	266,119,000	744,090,000
Operating Margin %						
SGA Expense	2,582,000,000	2,810,000,000	2,699,800,000	2,026,300,000	1,305,164,000	756,083,000
Net Income	2,404,000,000	-2,409,000,000	-291,700,000	913,500,000	-866,142,000	-116,025,000
Operating Cash Flow	2,290,000,000	2,087,000,000	2,200,400,000	2,294,700,000	1,041,957,000	656,578,000
Capital Expenditure	336,000,000	291,000,000	303,300,000	470,600,000	184,955,000	181,133,000
EBITDA	2,957,000,000	2,267,000,000	4,035,400,000	3,801,200,000	1,545,670,000	1,065,390,000
Return on Assets %						
Return on Equity %						
Debt to Equity						

CONTACT INFORMATION:

Phone: 514 744-6792 Fax: 514 744-6272
Toll-Free: 800-361-1448
Address: 2150 St. Elzear Blvd. W., Laval, QC H7L 4A8 Canada

STOCK TICKER/OTHER:

Stock Ticker: BHC
Employees: 21,500
Parent Company:
Exchange: NYS
Fiscal Year Ends: 12/31

SALARIES/BONUSES:

Top Exec. Salary: $750,000 Bonus: $3,000,000
Second Exec. Salary: $1,500,000 Bonus: $

OTHER THOUGHTS:

Estimated Female Officers or Directors: 3
Hot Spot for Advancement for Women/Minorities: Y

Baxter International Inc

www.baxter.com

NAIC Code: 339,100

TYPES OF BUSINESS:

Medical Equipment Manufacturing
Supplies-Intravenous & Renal Dialysis Systems
Medication Delivery Products & IV Fluids
Biopharmaceutical Products
Plasma Collection & Processing
Vaccines
Software
Contract Research

BRANDS/DIVISIONS/AFFILIATES:

RECOTHROM
PREVELEAK

CONTACTS: *Note: Officers with more than one job title may be intentionally listed here more than once.*

Jose Almeida, CEO
James Saccaro, CFO
Caroline Karp, Chief Accounting Officer
Sean Martin, General Counsel
Andrew Frye, President, Divisional
Giuseppe Accogli, President, Divisional
Cristiano Franzi, President, Divisional
Brik Eyre, President, Geographical
Jeanne Mason, Senior VP, Divisional
Scott Pleau, Senior VP, Divisional

GROWTH PLANS/SPECIAL FEATURES:

Baxter International, Inc., through its subsidiaries, provides a broad portfolio of essential healthcare products. These offerings include: acute and chronic dialysis therapies; sterile intravenous (IV) solutions; infusion systems and devices; parenteral nutrition therapies; inhaled anesthetics; generic injectable pharmaceuticals; and surgical hemostat and sealant products. In addition, Baxter's renal portfolio addresses the needs of patients with kidney failure or kidney disease. This portfolio includes innovative technologies and therapies for peritoneal dialysis, in-center and home hemodialysis, continuous renal replacement therapy, multi-organ extracorporeal support therapy, and additional dialysis services. Baxter's scientists are currently pursuing a range of next-generation monitors, dialyzers, devices, dialysis solutions and connectivity technology for home patients. Baxter manufactures its products in over 20 countries, and sells them in more than 100 countries. The firm's business is organized into the following geographic regions of: Americas (North and South), EMEA (Europe, Middle East and Africa) and APAC (Asia-Pacific). Each of these regions provide a wide range of essential healthcare products across the company's entire portfolio, with approximately 60% of annual revenue generated outside the U.S. Baxter maintains approximately 50 manufacturing facilities in the U.S., Europe, Asia-Pacific, Latin America and Canada (as of December 2017). In March 2018, the firm acquired two hemostat and sealant products from Mallinckrodt plc: RECOTHROM, a stand-alone recombinant thrombin; and PREVELEAK, a surgical sealant used in vascular reconstruction.

FINANCIAL DATA: *Note: Data for latest year may not have been available at press time.*

In U.S. $	2017	2016	2015	2014	2013	2012
Revenue	10,561,000,000	10,163,000,000	9,968,000,000	16,671,000,000	15,259,000,000	14,190,000,000
R&D Expense	617,000,000	647,000,000	603,000,000	1,421,000,000	1,246,000,000	1,156,000,000
Operating Income	1,258,000,000	724,000,000	449,000,000	2,707,000,000	2,668,000,000	2,821,000,000
Operating Margin %	11.91%	7.12%	4.50%	16.23%	17.48%	19.88%
SGA Expense	2,587,000,000	2,739,000,000	3,094,000,000	4,029,000,000	3,681,000,000	3,324,000,000
Net Income	717,000,000	4,965,000,000	968,000,000	2,497,000,000	2,012,000,000	2,326,000,000
Operating Cash Flow	1,837,000,000	1,654,000,000	1,647,000,000	3,215,000,000	3,198,000,000	3,106,000,000
Capital Expenditure	634,000,000	719,000,000	911,000,000	1,898,000,000	1,525,000,000	1,161,000,000
EBITDA	2,063,000,000	5,843,000,000	1,333,000,000	3,611,000,000	3,527,000,000	3,714,000,000
Return on Assets %	4.39%	27.18%	4.12%	9.64%	8.69%	11.78%
Return on Equity %	8.23%	57.94%	11.41%	30.11%	26.12%	34.40%
Debt to Equity	0.38	0.33	0.44	0.93	0.96	0.80

CONTACT INFORMATION:

Phone: 847 948-2000 Fax: 847 948-2964
Toll-Free: 800-422-9837
Address: 1 Baxter Pkwy., Deerfield, IL 60015 United States

STOCK TICKER/OTHER:

Stock Ticker: BAX
Employees: 48,000
Parent Company:
Exchange: NYS
Fiscal Year Ends: 12/31

SALARIES/BONUSES:

Top Exec. Salary: $1,300,000 Bonus: $
Second Exec. Salary: $521,479 Bonus: $500,000

OTHER THOUGHTS:

Estimated Female Officers or Directors: 6
Hot Spot for Advancement for Women/Minorities: Y

Bayer AG

www.bayer.com

NAIC Code: 325,412

TYPES OF BUSINESS:

Chemicals Manufacturing
Pharmaceuticals
Animal Health Products
Health Care Products
Crop Science
Plant Biotechnology
Over-the-Counter Drugs
Personal Care Products

BRANDS/DIVISIONS/AFFILIATES:

Claritin
Bayer Aspirin
Aleve
Bepanthen/Bepanthol
Canesten
Dr. Scholl's
Coppertone

CONTACTS: *Note: Officers with more than one job title may be intentionally listed here more than once.*

Johannes Dietsch, CFO
Hartmut Klusik, Human Resources
Werner Baumann, Chmn.

GROWTH PLANS/SPECIAL FEATURES:

Bayer AG is a German life science company with core competencies in the areas of healthcare and agriculture. With the company's innovative products, Bayer contributes to finding solutions to some of the major challenges confronting these sectors. It seeks to improve quality of life by preventing, alleviating and treating diseases; and the firm helps to provide a reliable supply of high-quality food, feed and plant-based raw materials. Bayer develops new molecules for use in innovative products. Its research and development activities are based on the biochemical processes in living organisms. The company groups its business into four divisions. The pharmaceuticals division focuses on prescription products, especially for cardiology and women's healthcare, and on specialty therapeutics in the areas of oncology, hematology and ophthalmology. This division also includes a radiology unit, which markets contrast-enhanced diagnostic imaging equipment together with contrast agents. The consumer health division markets non-prescription products in dermatology, dietary supplement, analgesic, gastrointestinal, allergy, cold and flu, foot care, sun protection and cardiovascular risk prevention categories. These products include globally-known brands such as Claritin, Bayer Aspirin, Aleve, Bepanthen/Bepanthol, Canesten, Dr. Scholl's and Coppertone. The crop science division comprises businesses in seeds, crop protection and non-agricultural pest control. Last, the animal health division offers products and services for the prevention and treatment of diseases in companion and farm animals. In October 2017, the firm agreed to sell its seed and herbicide businesses to BASF SE for approximately $7 billion. As for the proposed Bayer and Monsanto merger, in December 2017, the Committee on Foreign Investment in the U.S. concluded that there were no unresolved national security concerns related to the transaction; therefore, the merger was expected to be complete in early-2018.

FINANCIAL DATA: *Note: Data for latest year may not have been available at press time.*

In U.S. $	2017	2016	2015	2014	2013	2012
Revenue						
R&D Expense						
Operating Income						
Operating Margin %						
SGA Expense						
Net Income						
Operating Cash Flow						
Capital Expenditure						
EBITDA						
Return on Assets %						
Return on Equity %						
Debt to Equity						

CONTACT INFORMATION:

Phone: 49 214301 Fax: 49 2143066328
Toll-Free: 800-269-2377
Address: Bayerwerk Gebaeude W11, Leverkusen, GM D-51368 Germany

STOCK TICKER/OTHER:

Stock Ticker: BAYRY
Exchange: PINX
Employees: 99,820
Fiscal Year Ends: 12/31
Parent Company: Capital Group International Inc

SALARIES/BONUSES:

Top Exec. Salary: $1,363,000 Bonus: $1,828,000
Second Exec. Salary: $899,000 Bonus: $1,051,000

OTHER THOUGHTS:

Estimated Female Officers or Directors: 1
Hot Spot for Advancement for Women/Minorities:

Bayer Corporation

www.bayer.us

NAIC Code: 325,412

TYPES OF BUSINESS:

Chemicals Manufacturing
Animal Health Products
Over-the-Counter Drugs
Diagnostic Products
Coatings, Adhesives & Sealants
Polyurethanes & Plastics
Herbicides, Fungicides & Insecticides

BRANDS/DIVISIONS/AFFILIATES:

Capital Group International Inc
Bayer AG
Elmiron
Aleve
Bayer
Alka-Seltzer Plus
Bactine
One-A-Day

CONTACTS: *Note: Officers with more than one job title may be intentionally listed here more than once.*

Philip Blake, CEO
Dan Apel, CFO
Lars Benecke, General Counsel
Stefan Scholz, VP-Corp. Auditing
Philip Blake, Head-Bayer Representative, U.S.
Mark Torsten Minuth, VP-Mergers & Acquisitions
Tracy Spagnol, VP
Marjin Dekkers, Chmn.

GROWTH PLANS/SPECIAL FEATURES:

Bayer Corporation., the U.S. subsidiary of chemical and pharmaceutical giant Bayer AG, operates through four divisions: pharmaceuticals, consumer health, crop science and animal health. The pharmaceuticals division consists of women's healthcare, general medicine, diagnostic imaging, hematology/neurology and oncology. Products within this division include Elmiron, Angeliq and Refludan. The consumer health unit manufactures analgesics (Aleve and Bayer), cold and cough treatments (Alka-Seltzer Plus and Neo-Synephrine), digestive relief products (Phillips' Milk of Magnesia), topical skin preparations (Domeboro and Bactine) and vitamins (One-A-Day and Flintstones). The crop science manufactures crop protection, environmental science and bioscience products, such as herbicides, fungicides and insecticides. The animal health unit focuses on research and development of animal health and pest control products, both for companion animals and farm animals. Parent Bayer AG itself is a subsidiary of Capital Group International, Inc.

The company offers its employees life, disability, medical, dental and vision coverage; prescription drug reimbursement; a 401(k); and adoption assistance.

FINANCIAL DATA: *Note: Data for latest year may not have been available at press time.*

In U.S. $	2017	2016	2015	2014	2013	2012
Revenue	6,350,000,000	6,300,000,000	6,150,000,000	6,100,000,000	6,050,000,000	6,000,000,000
R&D Expense						
Operating Income						
Operating Margin %						
SGA Expense						
Net Income						
Operating Cash Flow						
Capital Expenditure						
EBITDA						
Return on Assets %						
Return on Equity %						
Debt to Equity						

CONTACT INFORMATION:

Phone: 862-404-3000 Fax: 781-356-0165
Toll-Free:
Address: 100 Bayer Blvd., Whippany, NJ 07981-0915 United States

STOCK TICKER/OTHER:

Stock Ticker: Subsidiary Exchange:
Employees: 13,450 Fiscal Year Ends: 12/31
Parent Company: Capital Group International Inc

SALARIES/BONUSES:

Top Exec. Salary: $ Bonus: $
Second Exec. Salary: $ Bonus: $

OTHER THOUGHTS:

Estimated Female Officers or Directors: 1
Hot Spot for Advancement for Women/Minorities:

Bayer HealthCare Pharmaceuticals Inc

www.pharma.bayer.com

NAIC Code: 325,412

TYPES OF BUSINESS:

Pharmaceuticals Discovery, Development & Manufacturing
Gynecology & Andrology Treatments
Contraceptives
Cancer Treatments
Multiple Sclerosis Treatments
Circulatory Disorder Treatments
Diagnostic & Radiopharmaceutical Agents
Proteomics

BRANDS/DIVISIONS/AFFILIATES:

Bayer AG
Betaferon
Glucobay
Kogenare
Adalat
Nexavar
Avalox
Seresto

CONTACTS: *Note: Officers with more than one job title may be intentionally listed here more than once.*

Habib J. Dable, Pres.
Michael Devoy, Head-Medical Affairs & Pharmacovigilance
Oliver Renner, Head-Global Corp. Comm.

GROWTH PLANS/SPECIAL FEATURES:

Bayer HealthCare Pharmaceuticals, Inc. is the pharmaceutical division and subsidiary of Bayer AG. With operations in over 100 countries, the firm manufactures prescription drugs and therapeutic products for seven main disease groups: cardiovascular and blood disorders, cancer, eye conditions, women's health, men's health, other treatment areas and radiology. Cardiovascular and blood disorders include high blood pressure, pulmonary hypertension, heart attack, stroke, hemophilia and thrombosis. Cancer includes gastrointestinal stromal tumors, colorectal cancer, liver cancer, prostate cancer, renal cell carcinoma and thyroid cancer. Eye conditions include age-related macular degeneration, diabetic macular edema, myopic choroidal neovascularization and retinal vein occlusion. Women's health includes contraception, gynecological therapy, endometriosis, menopausal complaints and premenstrual dysphoric disorder. Men's health includes erectile dysfunction and testosterone deficiency. Other treatment areas include multiple sclerosis, diabetes and infectious diseases. Last, the radiology group studies medical images in order to provide a formal assessment and recommendation to the treating doctor who then discusses the results with the patient during a follow-up appointment. Radiology's diagnostic imaging techniques include computer tomography (CT), magnetic resonance imaging (MRI), contrast agents and injectors. Bayer HealthCare has research and development facilities in Germany, the U.S., Norway and Finland; production facilities in the U.S., Europe, Latin America and Asia; and innovation centers in the U.S., China, Singapore and Japan. The firm has developed the following drugs: Betaferon, which reduces the frequency of MS episodes; Glucobay, used to regulate blood sugar control for diabetes; Kogenare, used for the treatment of hemophilia; Adalat, used for treating high blood pressure; Nexavar, a kidney and liver cancer fighting therapy; Avalox/Avelox, a respiratory tract infection treatment; Yasmin, birth control; Xarelto, for venous and arterial thrombosis; and Mirena, a hormonal contraceptive intrauterine delivery system. Bayer HealthCare has also developed Seresto, a flea and tick collar for cats and dogs in the U.S.

FINANCIAL DATA: *Note: Data for latest year may not have been available at press time.*

In U.S. $	2017	2016	2015	2014	2013	2012
Revenue	14,500,000,000	14,000,000,000	15,473,026,160	22,641,486,063	15,489,765,000	13,000,000,000
R&D Expense						
Operating Income						
Operating Margin %						
SGA Expense						
Net Income						
Operating Cash Flow						
Capital Expenditure						
EBITDA						
Return on Assets %						
Return on Equity %						
Debt to Equity						

CONTACT INFORMATION:

Phone: 973-694-4100 Fax: 973-487-2003
Toll-Free:
Address: 6 West Belt Rd., Wayne, NJ 07470-6806 United States

STOCK TICKER/OTHER:

Stock Ticker: Subsidiary
Employees: 39,000
Parent Company: Bayer AG
Exchange:
Fiscal Year Ends: 12/31

SALARIES/BONUSES:

Top Exec. Salary: $ Bonus: $
Second Exec. Salary: $ Bonus: $

OTHER THOUGHTS:

Estimated Female Officers or Directors:
Hot Spot for Advancement for Women/Minorities:

Beckman Coulter Inc

www.beckmancoulter.com

NAIC Code: 334,510

TYPES OF BUSINESS:

Electromedical and Electrotherapeutic Apparatus Manufacturing
Chemistry Systems
Genetic Analysis/Nucleic Acid Testing
Biomedical Research Supplies
Immunoassay Systems
Cellular Systems
Discovery & Automation Systems

BRANDS/DIVISIONS/AFFILIATES:

Danaher Corporation
DxM MicroScan WalkAway
DxH 520 Closed Tube
Early Sepsis Indicator
Access hsTnI

CONTACTS: *Note: Officers with more than one job title may be intentionally listed here more than once.*

J. Robert Hurley, CEO
Pedro Diaz, Dir.-Research
John Blackwood, Sr. VP-Product Mgmt.
Jeff Linton, Sr. VP
Ken Hyek, Dir.-Service Oper.
Allan Harris, Sr. VP-Strategy & Bus. Dev.
Jerry Battenberg, VP-Finance
Clair O'Donovan, Sr. VP-Quality & Regulatory Affairs
Jennifer Honeycutt, Pres., Life Sciences
Richard Creager, Sr. VP
Michael K. Samoszuk, VP
Brian Burnett, Sr. VP-Global Oper.

GROWTH PLANS/SPECIAL FEATURES:

Beckman Coulter, Inc., a wholly-owned subsidiary of Danaher Corporation, designs, develops, manufactures and markets biomedical testing instrument systems, tests and supplies that automate complex biomedical tests. The company operates two divisions: diagnostics and life sciences. The diagnostics division offers diagnostic systems for use in laboratories, hospitals and critical care settings to make treatment decisions, monitor patients and help physicians diagnose many diseases including cancer, HIV and heart conditions. The company's installed base systems provide essential biomedical information to enhance healthcare all around the world. The life sciences division manufactures research instruments used to study complex biological problems including causes of disease and potential new therapies or drugs. The firm operates in over 130 countries worldwide. Its customer base predominately consists of hospital and laboratories, scientists and large biopharma companies. In August 2018, Beckman Coulter announced the commercialization of its DxM MicroScan WalkAway system, a diagnostic solution for bacterial identification and antibiotic susceptibility testing for microbiology laboratories. That same year, the firm received the following: CE Mark of the DxH 520 Closed Tube, 5-part differential hematology analyzer for small-volume labs; CE Mark for its Early Spesis Indicator; and Health Canada clearance and U.S. FDA 510(k) clearance for Access hsTnI, a high-sensitivity troponin assay.

Employee benefits include medical, dental and vision coverage; a wellness program; a 401(k) and company retirement plan; life insurance; disability income protection; credit union membership; and employee discounts.

FINANCIAL DATA: *Note: Data for latest year may not have been available at press time.*

In U.S. $	2017	2016	2015	2014	2013	2012
Revenue	5,100,000,000	5,050,000,000	5,000,000,000	4,700,000,000	4,100,000,000	3,750,000,000
R&D Expense						
Operating Income						
Operating Margin %						
SGA Expense						
Net Income						
Operating Cash Flow						
Capital Expenditure						
EBITDA						
Return on Assets %						
Return on Equity %						
Debt to Equity						

CONTACT INFORMATION:

Phone: 714-993-5321 Fax: 800-232-3828
Toll-Free: 800-526-3821
Address: 250 S. Kraemer Blvd., Brea, CA 92821 United States

STOCK TICKER/OTHER:

Stock Ticker: Subsidiary
Exchange:
Employees: 11,900
Fiscal Year Ends: 12/31
Parent Company: Danaher Corporation

SALARIES/BONUSES:

Top Exec. Salary: $ Bonus: $
Second Exec. Salary: $ Bonus: $

OTHER THOUGHTS:

Estimated Female Officers or Directors: 5
Hot Spot for Advancement for Women/Minorities: Y

Becton Dickinson & Company

www.bd.com

NAIC Code: 339,100

TYPES OF BUSINESS:

Medical Equipment-Injection/Infusion
Drug Delivery Systems
Infusion Therapy Products
Diabetes Care Products
Surgical Products
Microbiology Products
Diagnostic Products
Consulting Services

BRANDS/DIVISIONS/AFFILIATES:

BD Medical
BD Life Sciences
BD Hypak
Alaris
BD Vacutainer
CR Bard Inc

CONTACTS:

Note: Officers with more than one job title may be intentionally listed here more than once.

Vincent Forlenza, CEO
Nabil Shabshab, President, Divisional
Charles Bodner, CFO, Divisional
Christopher Reidy, CFO
John Gallagher, Chief Accounting Officer
James Borzi, Executive VP, Divisional
Linda Tharby, Executive VP
Alberto Mas, Executive VP
Roland Goette, Executive VP
James Lim, Executive VP
Thomas Polen, President
Alexandre Conroy, President, Divisional
Gary DeFazio, Secretary

GROWTH PLANS/SPECIAL FEATURES:

Becton, Dickinson & Company (BD) is a global medical technology company engaged in the development, manufacture and sale of medical supplies, devices, laboratory equipment and diagnostic products. These offerings are primarily used by healthcare institutions, life science researchers, clinical laboratories, the pharmaceutical industry and the general public. The company operates in two worldwide business segments: BD Medical and BD Life Sciences. BD Medical offers products, including specially designed devices for diabetes care; pre-fillable drug delivery systems; and infusion therapy products. It also offers anesthesia and surgical products, ophthalmic surgery devices, critical care systems, elastic support products, respiratory ventilation and diagnostic equipment and thermometers. BD Life Sciences offers products for safe collection and transport of diagnostics specimens; instruments and reagent systems to detect a broad range of infectious diseases; and research and clinical tools that facilitate the study of cells in order to get a comprehensive understanding of normal and disease processes. Some of the products are integrated systems for specimen collection, molecular testing systems for infectious diseases and fluorescence-activated cell sorters and analyzers. BD's most popular international products include: BD Hypak pre-fillable syringe systems; Alaris infusion pumps; and BD Vacutainer blood-collection products. Manufacturing operations outside the U.S. include Bosnia/Herzegovina, Brazil, Canada, China, Dominican Republic, France, Germany, Hungary, India, Ireland, Israel, Italy, Japan, Mexico, Netherlands, Singapore, Spain and the U.K. Products are marketed and distributed in the U.S. and internationally through distribution channels, and directly to end-users by BD and independent sales representatives. In December 2017, BD acquired C.R. Bard, Inc., a medical supplies manufacturer.

The firm offers employees medical, dental, vision and prescription drug coverage; a flexible spending account; an employee assistance program; and at select locations, onsite services such as fitness centers, walking trails, banks and cafeterias.

FINANCIAL DATA:

Note: Data for latest year may not have been available at press time.

In U.S. $	2017	2016	2015	2014	2013	2012
Revenue	12,093,000,000	12,483,000,000	10,282,000,000	8,446,000,000	8,054,000,000	7,708,382,000
R&D Expense	774,000,000	828,000,000	632,000,000	550,000,000	494,000,000	471,755,000
Operating Income	1,833,000,000	2,158,000,000	1,500,000,000	1,606,000,000	1,255,000,000	1,557,885,000
Operating Margin %	15.15%	17.28%	14.58%	19.01%	15.58%	20.21%
SGA Expense	2,925,000,000	3,005,000,000	2,563,000,000	2,145,000,000	2,422,000,000	1,923,354,000
Net Income	1,100,000,000	976,000,000	695,000,000	1,185,000,000	1,293,000,000	1,169,927,000
Operating Cash Flow	2,550,000,000	2,559,000,000	1,730,000,000	1,746,000,000	1,505,000,000	1,760,228,000
Capital Expenditure	727,000,000	718,000,000	633,000,000	653,000,000	588,000,000	553,644,000
EBITDA	2,585,000,000	2,576,000,000	2,001,000,000	2,219,000,000	1,849,000,000	2,118,004,000
Return on Assets %	3.25%	3.72%	3.53%	9.63%	10.99%	10.73%
Return on Equity %	10.01%	13.19%	11.37%	23.47%	28.17%	26.10%
Debt to Equity	1.44	1.38	1.58	0.74	0.74	0.90

CONTACT INFORMATION:

Phone: 201 847-6800 Fax:
Toll-Free: 800-284-6845
Address: 1 Becton Dr., Franklin Lakes, NJ 07417 United States

STOCK TICKER/OTHER:

Stock Ticker: BDX
Employees: 50,928
Parent Company:
Exchange: NYS
Fiscal Year Ends: 09/30

SALARIES/BONUSES:

Top Exec. Salary: $1,153,750 Bonus: $
Second Exec. Salary: $778,230 Bonus: $

OTHER THOUGHTS:

Estimated Female Officers or Directors: 6
Hot Spot for Advancement for Women/Minorities: Y

Bio Rad Laboratories Inc

www.bio-rad.com

NAIC Code: 325,413

TYPES OF BUSINESS:

Clinical Diagnostics Products
Medical Equipment
Analytical Instruments
Laboratory Devices
Biomaterials
Imaging Products
Assays
Software

BRANDS/DIVISIONS/AFFILIATES:

RainDance Technologies Inc

CONTACTS:
Note: Officers with more than one job title may be intentionally listed here more than once.

Norman Schwartz, CEO
Christine Tsingos, CFO
James Stark, Chief Accounting Officer
Michael Crowley, Executive VP, Divisional
Timothy Ernst, Executive VP
Giovanni Magni, Executive VP
John Hertia, Executive VP
Annette Tumolo, Executive VP
Ronald Hutton, Executive VP

GROWTH PLANS/SPECIAL FEATURES:

Bio-Rad Laboratories, Inc. supplies the research, healthcare and analytical chemistry markets with a broad range of life science research and clinical diagnostic products and systems. These are used to separate complex chemical and biological materials and to identify, analyze and purify components. Bio-Rad operates in two segments: clinical diagnostics and life science. The clinical diagnostics division encompasses an array of technologies incorporated into a variety of tests used to detect, identify and quantify substances in blood or other body fluids and tissues. The test results are used as aids for medical diagnosis, detection, evaluation, monitoring and treatment of diseases and other conditions. This division is known for diabetes monitoring products, quality control systems, blood virus testing, blood typing, toxicology, genetic disorders products, molecular pathology and Internet-based software. The firm's life science division develops, manufactures and markets more than 5,000 products for applications including electrophoresis, image analysis, molecular detection, chromatography, gene transfer, sample preparation and amplification. Products include a range of laboratory instruments, apparatuses and consumables used for research in genomics, proteomics and food safety. The life science division provides its services to universities, medical schools, pharmaceutical manufacturers, industrial research organizations, food testing laboratories, government agencies and biotechnology researchers. In 2017, Bio-Rad acquired RainDance Technologies, Inc., the producer of a proprietary droplet technology that enables research in areas such as non-invasive liquid biopsy, for approximately $72.7 million.

FINANCIAL DATA:
Note: Data for latest year may not have been available at press time.

In U.S. $	2017	2016	2015	2014	2013	2012
Revenue	2,160,153,000	2,068,172,000	2,019,441,000	2,175,044,000	2,132,694,000	2,069,235,000
R&D Expense	250,301,000	205,864,000	192,972,000	220,333,000	210,952,000	214,040,000
Operating Income	128,156,000	115,499,000	166,708,000	149,984,000	169,456,000	257,200,000
Operating Margin %	5.93%	5.58%	8.25%	6.89%	7.94%	12.42%
SGA Expense	808,942,000	816,724,000	761,990,000	808,200,000	798,070,000	682,898,000
Net Income	122,249,000	28,125,000	113,093,000	88,845,000	77,790,000	163,778,000
Operating Cash Flow	103,900,000	216,400,000	186,200,000	273,300,000	175,500,000	278,900,000
Capital Expenditure	115,127,000	141,571,000	113,372,000	136,478,000	113,698,000	154,197,000
EBITDA	268,419,000	206,402,000	299,339,000	303,588,000	320,856,000	404,443,000
Return on Assets %	3.00%	.74%	3.20%	2.64%	2.27%	5.01%
Return on Equity %	4.43%	1.10%	4.83%	4.06%	3.70%	8.72%
Debt to Equity	0.14	0.16	0.17	0.19	0.19	0.36

CONTACT INFORMATION:

Phone: 510 724-7000 Fax: 510 741-5817
Toll-Free: 800-424-6723
Address: 1000 Alfred Nobel Dr., Hercules, CA 94547 United States

STOCK TICKER/OTHER:

Stock Ticker: BIO Exchange: NYS
Employees: 8,250 Fiscal Year Ends: 12/31
Parent Company:

SALARIES/BONUSES:

Top Exec. Salary: $922,022 Bonus: $
Second Exec. Salary: $689,500 Bonus: $

OTHER THOUGHTS:

Estimated Female Officers or Directors: 3
Hot Spot for Advancement for Women/Minorities: Y

Biogen Inc

www.biogen.com

NAIC Code: 325,412

TYPES OF BUSINESS:

Drugs-Immunology, Neurology & Oncology
Autoimmune & Inflammatory Disease Treatments
Drugs-Multiple Sclerosis
Drugs-Cancer

BRANDS/DIVISIONS/AFFILIATES:

TECFIDERA
AVONEX
PLEGRIDY
SPINRAZA
FUMADERM
RITUXAN
GAZYVA
OCREVUS

CONTACTS: *Note: Officers with more than one job title may be intentionally listed here more than once.*

Michel Vounatsos, CEO
Jeffrey Capello, CFO
Gregory Covino, Chief Accounting Officer
Alfred Sandrock, Chief Medical Officer
Stelios Papadopoulos, Director
Kenneth Dipietro, Executive VP, Divisional
Adriana Karaboutis, Executive VP, Divisional
Michael Ehlers, Executive VP, Divisional
Paul McKenzie, Executive VP, Divisional
Chirfi Guindo, Executive VP
Ginger Gregory, Executive VP
Susan Alexander, Executive VP

GROWTH PLANS/SPECIAL FEATURES:

Biogen, Inc. is a biotechnology company focused on discovering, developing, manufacturing and marketing therapies for people living with serious neurological and neurodegenerative diseases. The company's core growth areas in relation to these diseases include multiple sclerosis (MS), neuroimmunology, Alzheimer's disease, dementia, movement disorders, and neuromuscular disorders such as spinal muscular atrophy (SMA) and amyotrophic lateral sclerosis (ALS). Biogen announced plans to invest in emerging growth areas such as pain, ophthalmology, neuropsychiatry and acute neurology, as well as discovering potential treatments for rare and genetic disorders. The firm also manufactures and commercializes biosimilars of advanced biologics. Biogen's marketed products include: TECFIDERA, AVONEX, PLEGRIDY, TYSABRI, ZINBRYTA and FAMPRYA for the treatment of MS; SPINRAZA for the treatment of SMA; and FUMADERM for the treatment of severe plaque psoriasis. In addition, the company has certain business and financial rights with respect to: RITUXAN for the treatment of non-Hodgkin's lymphoma, chronic lymphocytic leukemia (CLL) and other conditions; GAZYVA for the treatment of CLL and follicular lymphoma; OCREVUS for the treatment of primary progressive MS and relapsing MS and other potential anti-CD20 therapies under a collaboration agreement with Genentech, Inc., which is wholly-owned by Roche Group.

Biogen offers employees medical, dental and vision insurance; tuition reimbursement; flexible spending accounts; and an employee assistance program.

FINANCIAL DATA: *Note: Data for latest year may not have been available at press time.*

In U.S. $	2017	2016	2015	2014	2013	2012
Revenue	12,273,900,000	11,448,800,000	10,763,800,000	9,703,324,000	6,932,199,000	5,516,461,000
R&D Expense	2,373,600,000	1,973,300,000	2,012,800,000	1,893,422,000	1,444,053,000	1,334,919,000
Operating Income	5,407,800,000	5,653,100,000	5,014,900,000	3,916,763,000	2,490,064,000	1,838,484,000
Operating Margin %	44.05%	49.37%	46.59%	40.36%	35.92%	33.32%
SGA Expense	1,935,500,000	1,947,900,000	2,113,100,000	2,232,342,000	1,712,051,000	1,277,465,000
Net Income	2,539,100,000	3,702,800,000	3,547,000,000	2,934,784,000	1,862,341,000	1,380,033,000
Operating Cash Flow	4,551,000,000	4,522,400,000	3,716,100,000	2,942,115,000	2,345,078,000	1,879,897,000
Capital Expenditure	1,962,800,000	727,700,000	643,000,000	287,751,000	3,509,000,000	261,182,000
EBITDA	6,460,600,000	5,875,700,000	5,463,200,000	4,664,283,000	3,044,219,000	2,257,253,000
Return on Assets %	10.91%	17.47%	20.97%	22.42%	16.93%	14.39%
Return on Equity %	20.51%	34.42%	35.15%	30.21%	23.90%	20.61%
Debt to Equity	0.47	0.53	0.69	0.05	0.06	0.09

CONTACT INFORMATION:

Phone: 617-679-2000   Fax: 619 679-2617
Toll-Free:
Address: 225 Binney St., Cambridge, MA 02142 United States

STOCK TICKER/OTHER:

Stock Ticker: BIIB   Exchange: NAS
Employees: 7,400   Fiscal Year Ends: 12/31
Parent Company:

SALARIES/BONUSES:

Top Exec. Salary: $519,231   Bonus: $1,500,000
Second Exec. Salary: $491,827   Bonus: $1,170,177

OTHER THOUGHTS:

Estimated Female Officers or Directors: 4
Hot Spot for Advancement for Women/Minorities: Y

BioMerieux SA

www.biomerieux.com

NAIC Code: 424,210

TYPES OF BUSINESS:

Diagnostic Reagents Merchant Wholesalers

BRANDS/DIVISIONS/AFFILIATES:

BioFire FilmArray
BacT/ALERT VIRTUAL
VIDAS BRAHMS PCT
Astute Medical Inc
NEPHROCHECK

CONTACTS: *Note: Officers with more than one job title may be intentionally listed here more than once.*

Alexandre Merieux, CEO
Guillaume Bouhours, CFO
Alain Pluquet, VP
Michel Baguenault, Corp. VP-Human Resources
Mark Miller, Chief Medical Officer
Kirk Ririe, VP
Stefan Willemsen, Corp. VP-Legal
Stefan Willemsen, Corp. VP-Bus. Dev.
Michel Baguenault, Corp. VP-Comm.
Thierry Bernard, Corp. VP-Investor Rel.
Marc Mackowiak, CEO-bioMerieux, Inc.
Nicolas Cartier, Corp. VP-Industrial Microbiology Unit
Francois Lacoste, Corp. VP-Immunoassay Unity & Quality
Alain Pluquet, Corp. VP-Innovation & Systems Unit
Thierry Bernard, Exec. VP-Greater China

GROWTH PLANS/SPECIAL FEATURES:

BioMerieux SA has been engaged in the field of in vitro diagnostics for more than 50 years. The firm develops tests that bring high medical value for clinical decisions in the areas of infectious diseases, cardiovascular emergencies and targeted cancers. BioMerieux provides diagnostic solutions, reagents, instruments, services and software that determine the source of disease and contamination in order to improve patient health and ensure consumer safety. The firm has operations in over 150 countries through 43 subsidiaries, with 18 production sites and 17 research and development sites. Its two main focuses are: clinical diagnostics, accounting for 80% of annual sales; and industrial microbiology, accounting for 20% of annual sales. The firm's microbiology solutions serve the agri-food, cosmetics and biopharmaceutical industries, providing solutions for the cataloguing of microbial flora, detection of pathogenic bacteria, monitoring of air and surface quality and sterility testing. During 2017, the firm received U.S. FDA clearance for BioFire FilmArray respiratory panel 2, which reduces sample-to-result time to only 45 minutes while enhancing pathogen coverage and overall sensitivity; received FDA 510(k) clearance for BacT/ALERT VIRTUO fully-automated blood culture system; and received FDA clearance for VIDAS B.R.A.H.M.S PCT, an automated assay measuring procalcitonin (PCT) levels, to help clinicians make decisions regarding the optimal use of antibiotics in two common clinical situations: lower respiratory tract infections and sepsis. During 2018, it submitted its Biofire Filmarray pneumonia panel for FDA 510(k) clearance. In April 2018, BioMerieux acquired Astute Medical, Inc., a company dedicated to improving the diagnosis of high-risk medical conditions and diseases through the identification and validation of protein biomarkers, the FDA-cleared NEPHROCHECK test in particular, for the early risk assessment of acute kidney injuries.

FINANCIAL DATA: *Note: Data for latest year may not have been available at press time.*

In U.S. $	2017	2016	2015	2014	2013	2012
Revenue						
R&D Expense						
Operating Income						
Operating Margin %						
SGA Expense						
Net Income						
Operating Cash Flow						
Capital Expenditure						
EBITDA						
Return on Assets %						
Return on Equity %						
Debt to Equity						

CONTACT INFORMATION:

Phone: 33 478872000 Fax: 33 478872090
Toll-Free:
Address: Chemin de l'Orme, Marcy l'Etoile, 69280 France

STOCK TICKER/OTHER:

Stock Ticker: BMXMF Exchange: PINX
Employees: 10,400 Fiscal Year Ends: 12/31
Parent Company:

SALARIES/BONUSES:

Top Exec. Salary: $ Bonus: $
Second Exec. Salary: $ Bonus: $

OTHER THOUGHTS:

Estimated Female Officers or Directors: 2
Hot Spot for Advancement for Women/Minorities:

Bio-Reference Laboratories Inc

www.bioreference.com

NAIC Code: 621,511

TYPES OF BUSINESS:

Medical Laboratories & Testing
Clinical Laboratory Services
Clinical Knowledge Database
Online Practice Management Services
Drug Testing

BRANDS/DIVISIONS/AFFILIATES:

OPKO Health Inc
Bio-Reference Laboratories
GenPath Oncology
GenPath Women's Health
GeneDX
Laboratorio Bueno Salud

CONTACTS: *Note: Officers with more than one job title may be intentionally listed here more than once.*

Geoff Monkas, Gen. Mgr.
Warren Erdmann, COO
Kevin Feeley, VP-Accounting & Finance
Greg Cahill, VP-Human Resources
John Mooney, CIO
Marc Grodman, Founder

GROWTH PLANS/SPECIAL FEATURES:

Bio-Reference Laboratories, Inc. (BRLI), a subsidiary of OPKO Health, Inc., offers comprehensive laboratory testing services. These services are utilized by health care providers in the detection, diagnosis, evaluation, monitoring and treatment of diseases, including esoteric testing, molecular diagnostics, anatomical pathology, genetics, women's health and correctional health care. BRLI markets and sells these services to physician offices, clinics, hospitals, employers and governmental units nationally, with the largest concentration of business in the larger metropolitan areas across New York, New Jersey, Maryland, Pennsylvania, Delaware, Washington D.C., Florida, California, Texas, Illinois and Massachusetts. The company operates a network of more than 180 patient service centers for collection of patient specimens. Laboratory divisions within the firm include Bio-Reference Laboratories, constituting the company's core clinical testing laboratory offering automated, high volume routine testing services, STAT testing, informatics, HIV, Hep C and other molecular tests; GenPath Oncology, specializing in cancer pathology and diagnostics, as well as molecular diagnostics; GenPath Women's Health, an innovative technology platform for sexually-transmitted infections; GeneDx, which tests rare and ultra-rare genetic diseases with international reach; and Laboratorio Bueno Salud, a national testing laboratory dedicated to serving the Spanish-speaking population in the U.S., where all business is conducted in Spanish including patient and physician interaction.

FINANCIAL DATA: *Note: Data for latest year may not have been available at press time.*

In U.S. $	2017	2016	2015	2014	2013	2012
Revenue	924,000,000	880,000,000	865,640,000	832,281,984	715,353,984	661,660,992
R&D Expense						
Operating Income						
Operating Margin %						
SGA Expense						
Net Income				46,758,000	45,825,000	42,156,000
Operating Cash Flow						
Capital Expenditure						
EBITDA						
Return on Assets %						
Return on Equity %						
Debt to Equity						

CONTACT INFORMATION:

Phone: 201 791-2600 Fax:
Toll-Free: 800-229-5227
Address: 481 Edward H. Ross Dr., Elmwood Park, NJ 07407 United States

STOCK TICKER/OTHER:

Stock Ticker: Subsidiary
Exchange:
Employees: 5,000
Fiscal Year Ends: 10/31
Parent Company: OPKO Health Inc

SALARIES/BONUSES:

Top Exec. Salary: $ Bonus: $
Second Exec. Salary: $ Bonus: $

OTHER THOUGHTS:

Estimated Female Officers or Directors: 3
Hot Spot for Advancement for Women/Minorities: Y

BioScrip Inc

www.bioscrip.com

NAIC Code: 621,610

TYPES OF BUSINESS:

Home Health Care and Infusion Services
Retail, Online & Mail-Order Pharmacies
Disease Management
Specialty Pharmacy Services
Pharmacy Benefits Management

BRANDS/DIVISIONS/AFFILIATES:

HS Infusion Holdings Inc

CONTACTS: *Note: Officers with more than one job title may be intentionally listed here more than once.*

Daniel Greenleaf, CEO
Stephen Deitsch, CFO
R. Pate, Chairman of the Board
Alex Schott, Chief Accounting Officer
Harriet Booker, COO
Jody Kepler, Other Executive Officer
Danny Claycomb, Senior VP, Divisional

GROWTH PLANS/SPECIAL FEATURES:

BioScrip, Inc. is a national provider of infusion solutions. The company partners with physicians, hospital systems, skilled nursing facilities, healthcare payors and pharmaceutical manufacturers to provide patients access to post-acute care services. BioScrip brings customer-focused pharmacy and related healthcare infusion therapy services into the home or alternative-site setting. Its core services are provided in coordination with, and under the direction of, the patient's physician. The firm provides products, services and condition-specific clinical management programs tailored to improve the care of individuals with complex health conditions such as gastrointestinal abnormalities, infectious diseases, cancer, multiple sclerosis, organ and blood transplants, bleeding disorders, immune deficiencies and heart failure. BioScrip operates through a total of 66 service locations in 27 U.S. states.

The firm offers employees health, dental, short- and long-term disability, AD&D and long-term care coverage; pharmacy benefits; health savings accounts; and a 401(k) plan.

FINANCIAL DATA: *Note: Data for latest year may not have been available at press time.*

In U.S. $	2017	2016	2015	2014	2013	2012
Revenue	817,190,000	935,589,000	982,223,000	984,055,000	842,195,000	662,637,000
R&D Expense						
Operating Income	38,619,000	34,137,000	29,650,000	-64,873,000	11,142,000	22,477,000
Operating Margin %	4.72%	3.64%	3.01%	-6.59%	1.32%	3.39%
SGA Expense	39,625,000	39,225,000	42,524,000	239,810,000	233,038,000	184,491,000
Net Income	-64,196,000	-41,506,000	-299,707,000	-147,468,000	-69,654,000	64,707,000
Operating Cash Flow	-763,000	-42,769,000	-64,742,000	-31,416,000	-54,553,000	26,884,000
Capital Expenditure	8,680,000	9,642,000	11,544,000	13,829,000	25,626,000	10,986,000
EBITDA	12,364,000	55,688,000	-267,744,000	-74,473,000	-4,931,000	34,947,000
Return on Assets %	-12.26%	-8.76%	-45.14%	-16.74%	-8.82%	9.80%
Return on Equity %			-455.41%	-51.61%	-21.49%	25.44%
Debt to Equity				1.92	1.05	0.76

CONTACT INFORMATION:

Phone: 720-697-5200 Fax:
Toll-Free:
Address: 1600 Broadway, Ste. 950, Denver, CO 80202 United States

STOCK TICKER/OTHER:

Stock Ticker: BIOS Exchange: NAS
Employees: 2,540 Fiscal Year Ends: 12/31
Parent Company:

SALARIES/BONUSES:

Top Exec. Salary: $725,000 Bonus: $
Second Exec. Salary: $331,500 Bonus: $25,000

OTHER THOUGHTS:

Estimated Female Officers or Directors: 3
Hot Spot for Advancement for Women/Minorities: Y

Biosensors International Group Ltd

www.biosensors.com

NAIC Code: 334,510

TYPES OF BUSINESS:

Electromedical and Electrotherapeutic Apparatus Manufacturing

BRANDS/DIVISIONS/AFFILIATES:

Blue Sail Medical Co Ltd
BioFreedom
BioMatrix
Chroma
BioStream
Powerline
BioPath
Biolimus A9

CONTACTS: *Note: Officers with more than one job title may be intentionally listed here more than once.*

Jose Calle Gordo, CEO
Hao Xi Ede, CFO
Jeffrey B. jump, Pres., Cardiovascular Bus. Unit.

GROWTH PLANS/SPECIAL FEATURES:

Biosensors International Group Ltd. is an international group of companies which develop, manufacture and market innovative medical devices for interventional cardiology and endovascular procedures. The cardiovascular division focuses on the development, manufacture and commercialization of drug-eluting stents, drug-coated stents and bare metal stents, as well as angioplasty catheters for the treatment of coronary artery disease. Branded products within this segment include BioFreedom, BioMatrix, Chroma, BioStream and Powerline. The endovascular division offers interventional devices to treat peripheral arterial disease, and also offers stenting and ballooning solutions for superficial femoral artery and below-the-knee interventions. Branded products in this segment includes BioStream and BioPath. Biosensors developed its own proprietary technology in Biolimus A9, a limus drug designed specifically for coronary stent applications. The firm is a subsidiary of Blue Sail Medical Co., Ltd., a global manufacturer and marketer of health protection gloves.

FINANCIAL DATA: *Note: Data for latest year may not have been available at press time.*

In U.S. $	2017	2016	2015	2014	2013	2012
Revenue					336,187,008	292,140,992
R&D Expense						
Operating Income						
Operating Margin %						
SGA Expense						
Net Income			-224,812,992	40,586,000	115,377,000	364,268,000
Operating Cash Flow						
Capital Expenditure						
EBITDA						
Return on Assets %						
Return on Equity %						
Debt to Equity						

CONTACT INFORMATION:

Phone: 65 6213-5777 Fax: 65 6213-5737
Toll-Free:
Address: 36 Jalan Tukang, Singapore, 619266 Singapore

STOCK TICKER/OTHER:

Stock Ticker: Private
Exchange:
Employees:
Fiscal Year Ends: 03/31
Parent Company: Blue Sail Medical Co Ltd

SALARIES/BONUSES:

Top Exec. Salary: $ Bonus: $
Second Exec. Salary: $ Bonus: $

OTHER THOUGHTS:

Estimated Female Officers or Directors:
Hot Spot for Advancement for Women/Minorities:

Bio-Techne Corporation

www.techne-corp.com

NAIC Code: 325,413

TYPES OF BUSINESS:

Biotechnology Products
Reagents, Antibodies & Assay Kits
Hematology Products

BRANDS/DIVISIONS/AFFILIATES:

R&D Systems
Novus Bilogicals
Tocris Bioscience
ProteinSimple
Atlanta Biologicals Inc
Scientific Ventures Inc

CONTACTS: *Note: Officers with more than one job title may be intentionally listed here more than once.*

Charles Kummeth, CEO
James Hippel, CFO
Robert Baumgartner, Chairman of the Board
J. Bazan, Chief Technology Officer
Robert Gavin, Senior VP, Divisional
Kevin Gould, Senior VP, Divisional
N. Eansor, Senior VP, Divisional
Brenda Furlow, Senior VP

GROWTH PLANS/SPECIAL FEATURES:

Bio-Techne Corporation and its subsidiaries develop, manufacture and sell biotechnology reagents and instruments for research and clinical diagnostic markets worldwide. The firm operates through three segments: biotechnology, protein platforms and diagnostics. The biotechnology segment derived 65% of 2017 net sales, and provides high-quality proteins and antibodies, related immunoassays, biologically-active small molecules and other reagents under the brands of R&D Systems, Novus Biologicals and Tocris Bioscience. The protein platforms segment (16%) develops and supplies instrumentation and related consumables designed to simplify protein analysis processes along with single cell protein analysis under the ProteinSimple brand. Last, the diagnostics segment (19%) serves clinical markets with regulated products such as controls, calibrators, reagents and immunoassays for diagnostic users. In total, Bio-Techne has produced more than 500,000 products. Its distribution network spans the Americas, Europe, Africa and Asia-Pacific. In January 2018, Bio-Techne acquired Atlanta Biologicals, Inc., along with its affiliated company, Scientific Ventures, Inc. That June, the firm agreed to acquire Exosome Diagnostics, Inc. for $250 million; and agreed to acquire QT Holdings Corporation (dba Quad Technologies).

FINANCIAL DATA: *Note: Data for latest year may not have been available at press time.*

In U.S. $	2017	2016	2015	2014	2013	2012
Revenue	563,003,000	499,023,000	452,246,000	357,763,000	310,575,000	
R&D Expense	53,514,000	45,187,000	40,853,000	30,945,000	29,257,000	
Operating Income	120,584,000	150,593,000	147,023,000	159,750,000	158,469,000	
Operating Margin %	21.41%	30.17%	32.50%	44.65%	51.02%	
SGA Expense	200,443,000	140,879,000	119,401,000	60,716,000	43,384,000	
Net Income	76,086,000	104,476,000	107,735,000	110,948,000	112,561,000	
Operating Cash Flow	143,448,000	143,870,000	139,359,000	136,762,000	123,562,000	
Capital Expenditure	15,179,000	16,898,000	19,905,000	13,821,000	22,454,000	
EBITDA	179,358,000	191,993,000	192,932,000	178,925,000	170,790,000	
Return on Assets %	5.66%	9.52%	11.18%	13.52%	15.03%	
Return on Equity %	8.32%	12.10%	13.12%	14.47%	15.94%	
Debt to Equity	0.36	0.10	0.08			

CONTACT INFORMATION:

Phone: 612 379-8854 Fax: 612 379-6580
Toll-Free:
Address: 614 McKinley Place NE, Minneapolis, MN 55413 United States

STOCK TICKER/OTHER:

Stock Ticker: TECH
Exchange: NAS
Employees: 1,800
Fiscal Year Ends: 06/30
Parent Company:

SALARIES/BONUSES:

Top Exec. Salary: $911,000 Bonus: $
Second Exec. Salary: $476,100 Bonus: $

OTHER THOUGHTS:

Estimated Female Officers or Directors:
Hot Spot for Advancement for Women/Minorities:

BioTelemetry Inc

www.gobio.com

NAIC Code: 339,100

TYPES OF BUSINESS:

Mobile Cardiac Monitoring Equipment
Mobile Cardiac Monitoring Services

BRANDS/DIVISIONS/AFFILIATES:

CardioNet LLC
LifeWatch AG
Heartcare Corporation of America Inc
Braemar Manufacturing LLC
Telcare Inc
Cardiocore LLC
VirtualScopics Inc

CONTACTS: *Note: Officers with more than one job title may be intentionally listed here more than once.*

Joseph Capper, CEO
Heather Getz, CFO
Kirk Gorman, Chairman of the Board
Peter Ferola, General Counsel
Fred Broadway, President, Divisional
Daniel Wisniewski, Senior VP, Divisional

GROWTH PLANS/SPECIAL FEATURES:

BioTelemetry, Inc. provides cardiac monitoring services, cardiac monitoring device manufacturing and centralized cardiac core laboratory services. The company operates under three segments: healthcare, technology and research. The healthcare segment generated 81% of 2017 revenue and focuses on the diagnosis and monitoring of cardiac arrhythmias or heart rhythm disorders. It operates as CardioNet, LLC; LifeWatch AG; and Heartcare Corporation of America, Inc., and offers cardiologists and electrophysiologists a full spectrum of solutions, providing them with a single source of cardiac monitoring services, ranging from mobile cardiac telemetry service to wireless and trans telephonic event monitoring. The technology segment generated 5% of 2017 revenue, and focuses on the development, manufacturing, testing and marketing of medical devices to medical companies, clinics and hospitals. This division operates as Braemar Manufacturing, LLC; Telcare, Inc.; and to a small extent LifeWatch. The research segment generated 14% of 2017 revenue and is engaged in central core laboratory services which provide cardiac monitoring, scientific consulting and data management services for drug and medical device trials. This division operates as Cardiocore, LLC and VirtualScopics, Inc. In July 2017, BioTelemetry acquire all the shares of LifeWatch.

Employee benefits include medical, dental and vision coverage; flexible spending accounts; a 401(k); an employee stock purchase plan; short- and long-term disability; and life insurance and AD&D.

FINANCIAL DATA: *Note: Data for latest year may not have been available at press time.*

In U.S. $	2017	2016	2015	2014	2013	2012
Revenue	286,776,000	208,332,000	178,513,000	166,578,000	129,501,000	111,494,000
R&D Expense	11,101,000	8,355,000	7,111,000	7,396,000	7,338,000	4,664,000
Operating Income	29,673,000	18,110,000	9,518,000	-4,313,000	1,101,000	-8,923,000
Operating Margin %	10.34%	8.69%	5.33%	-2.58%	.85%	-8.00%
SGA Expense	118,305,000	93,054,000	81,881,000	81,034,000	62,844,000	58,248,000
Net Income	-15,956,000	53,437,000	7,428,000	-9,793,000	-7,319,000	-12,202,000
Operating Cash Flow	23,782,000	38,851,000	14,350,000	8,811,000	11,259,000	5,743,000
Capital Expenditure	13,697,000	10,899,000	13,600,000	12,781,000	8,169,000	5,962,000
EBITDA	23,062,000	32,379,000	22,006,000	8,237,000	13,419,000	-3,430,000
Return on Assets %	-4.41%	33.07%	5.96%	-9.22%	-8.24%	-13.19%
Return on Equity %	-8.18%	49.74%	10.64%	-15.00%	-10.69%	-16.48%
Debt to Equity	0.79	0.17	0.29	0.36		

CONTACT INFORMATION:

Phone: 610 729-7000 Fax: 610 828-8048
Toll-Free: 888-312-2328
Address: 1000 Cedar Hollow Rd., Malvera, PA 19355 United States

STOCK TICKER/OTHER:

Stock Ticker: BEAT
Employees: 1,087
Parent Company:
Exchange: NAS
Fiscal Year Ends: 12/31

SALARIES/BONUSES:

Top Exec. Salary: $577,089 Bonus: $
Second Exec. Salary: $371,101 Bonus: $

OTHER THOUGHTS:

Estimated Female Officers or Directors: 3
Hot Spot for Advancement for Women/Minorities: Y

BJC HealthCare

www.bjc.org

NAIC Code: 622,110

TYPES OF BUSINESS:

General Medical and Surgical Hospitals
Home Health Services
Physical Rehab Center
Physician Groups
Long-Term Health Care
Occupational Health Services
Hospice Services
Teaching Hospitals

BRANDS/DIVISIONS/AFFILIATES:

Barnes-Jewish Hospital
St Louis Children's Hospital
BJC Home Care Services
BarnesCare Occupational Medicine
BJC Community Health Services
BJC Employee Assistance Program

CONTACTS: *Note: Officers with more than one job title may be intentionally listed here more than once.*

Richard J. Liekweg, CEO
Lee F. Fetter, Pres.
June McAllister Fowler, Sr. VP-Mktg. & Communications
John r. Beatty, Sr. VP
Jerry Fox, Chief Information Officer
Michael A. DeHaven, General Counsel
Robert W. Cannon, Group Pres., Strategic Planning
June McAllister Fowler, VP-Corp. & Public Comm.
Larry Tracy, Pres., Barnes-Jewish St. Peters Hospital
JoAnn M. Shaw, Chief Learning Officer
Richard J. Liekweg, VP
Lee F. Fetter, Group Pres., Clinical Quality
Robert W. Cannon, Group Pres., Supply Chain Oper.

GROWTH PLANS/SPECIAL FEATURES:

BJC HealthCare is a nonprofit healthcare organization primarily serving the areas of St. Louis, Missouri, mid-Missouri and southern Illinois. The firm operates 15 hospitals as well as long-term care facilities, physician offices and rehabilitation and imaging centers. BJC has over 4,350 physicians and over 3,400 staffed beds. Two of the company's hospitals, Barnes-Jewish Hospital and St. Louis Children's Hospital, are ranked highly among America's elite medical centers and teaching hospitals. Both are affiliated with Washington University in St. Louis' School of Medicine. The company's services include inpatient and outpatient care, primary care, community health, workplace health, home health, mental health, rehabilitation, long-term care and hospice. BJC Home Care Services offers patients in Missouri and Illinois a wide range of in-home services, including skilled nursing, adult and pediatric supportive care, rehabilitation therapy, respiratory care, infusion therapy and hospice services. Through the BarnesCare Occupational Medicine service, BJC provides occupational health services to the St. Louis metropolitan business community. The company provides a variety of preventive and early detection services for employers and community members through its BJC Community Health Services program, which includes screenings, wellness coaching and other services. The BJC Employee Assistance Program assists in the identification and resolution of health, behavioral and productivity problems.

FINANCIAL DATA: *Note: Data for latest year may not have been available at press time.*

In U.S. $	2017	2016	2015	2014	2013	2012
Revenue	5,000,000,000	4,800,000,000	4,300,000,000	4,100,000,000	4,000,000,000	3,849,400,000
R&D Expense						
Operating Income						
Operating Margin %						
SGA Expense						
Net Income						
Operating Cash Flow						
Capital Expenditure						
EBITDA						
Return on Assets %						
Return on Equity %						
Debt to Equity						

CONTACT INFORMATION:

Phone: 314-286-2000 Fax: 314-286-2060
Toll-Free:
Address: 4901 Forest Park Ave., St. Louis, MO 63108 United States

STOCK TICKER/OTHER:

Stock Ticker: Nonprofit
Employees: 31,340
Parent Company:
Exchange:
Fiscal Year Ends: 12/31

SALARIES/BONUSES:

Top Exec. Salary: $ Bonus: $
Second Exec. Salary: $ Bonus: $

OTHER THOUGHTS:

Estimated Female Officers or Directors: 5
Hot Spot for Advancement for Women/Minorities: Y

Blue Care Network of Michigan www.bcbsm.com/index/about-us/our-company/about-bcn.html

NAIC Code: 524,114

TYPES OF BUSINESS:

Insurance-Medical & Health, HMOs & PPOs
Online Health Resources & Information

BRANDS/DIVISIONS/AFFILIATES:

Blue Cross and Blue Shield of Michigan
BlueHealthConnection
OneBlue
Personal Plus
MyBlue Medigap
BCN 65
Blue Elect Self-Referral Option
Healthy Blue Living

CONTACTS: *Note: Officers with more than one job title may be intentionally listed here more than once.*

Tiffany A. Albert, CEO
Marc Keshishian, Chief Medical Officer
James P. Kallas, VP-Finance & Treasurer
David Nelson, Sr. VP
Carla Chambers, VP-Health & Medical Affairs
William H. Black, Chmn.

GROWTH PLANS/SPECIAL FEATURES:

Blue Care Network of Michigan (BCN), a subsidiary of Blue Cross and Blue Shield of Michigan (BCBSM), is one of the largest health maintenance organization (HMO) networks in the state, with over 860,000 members. The company works together with BCBSM by sharing resources to identify and fight fraud, protect member privacy and support common technology infrastructures. BCN offers its members traditional indemnity and Medicare as well as supplementary management and care services. BCN works closely with its physician network and provides services and technology tools to support its partners. The company's network is one of the largest in the state, including over 6,000 primary care physicians and over 23,000 specialists. Its BlueHealthConnection service, in collaboration with BCBSM, combines diverse programs to assist members with chronic or complex illnesses. The company's products include coverage options for individuals and groups as well as extended coverage after having left a group. Its individual coverage options consist of the following programs: OneBlue and Personal Plus, designed for individuals under the age of 65; BCN Advantage for the individual, which replaces Medicare coverage with comprehensive HMO coverage; MyBlue Medigap, which provides additional coverage for individuals enrolled in Medicare; and BCN 65, which works with Medicare to cover more healthcare costs. The company's group coverage options include the BCN HMO; the Blue Elect Self-Referral Option for employer groups of two or more in size; Healthy Blue Living, which has decreased co-payment and deductibles for members who live a healthy lifestyle; the Self-funded Option, which lets the employer assume the claims cost risk; BCN Advantage for groups; and BCN 65 for groups.

FINANCIAL DATA: *Note: Data for latest year may not have been available at press time.*

In U.S. $	2017	2016	2015	2014	2013	2012
Revenue	3,580,930,000	3,399,338,000	3,252,461,000	2,992,076,000		
R&D Expense						
Operating Income						
Operating Margin %						
SGA Expense						
Net Income	240,381,000	93,756,000	18,045,000	17,317,000		
Operating Cash Flow						
Capital Expenditure						
EBITDA						
Return on Assets %						
Return on Equity %						
Debt to Equity						

CONTACT INFORMATION:

Phone: 248-799-6400 Fax: 248-799-6979
Toll-Free: 800-662-6667
Address: 20500 Civic Center Dr., Southfield, MI 48076 United States

STOCK TICKER/OTHER:

Stock Ticker: Subsidiary
Employees: 400
Parent Company: Blue Cross and Blue Shield of Michigan
Exchange:
Fiscal Year Ends: 12/31

SALARIES/BONUSES:

Top Exec. Salary: $ Bonus: $
Second Exec. Salary: $ Bonus: $

OTHER THOUGHTS:

Estimated Female Officers or Directors: 2
Hot Spot for Advancement for Women/Minorities: Y

Blue Cross and Blue Shield Association

www.bcbs.com

NAIC Code: 524,114

TYPES OF BUSINESS:

Insurance-Medical & Health, HMOs & PPOs

BRANDS/DIVISIONS/AFFILIATES:

Blue Cross and Blue Shield
BCBS Federal Employee Program
BlueCard
BCBSA National Labor Office

CONTACTS: *Note: Officers with more than one job title may be intentionally listed here more than once.*

Scott P. Serota, CEO
Maureen E. Sullivan, Chief Strategy & Innovation Officer
Scott P. Serota, Pres.
Robert Kolodgy, CFO
Kari Hedges, Sr. VP-Commercial Markets & Enterprise Data Solutions
Maureen A. Cahill, Sr. VP-Human Resources
Trent Haywood, Chief Medical Officer
Petar Naumovski, Chief Information Security Officer
William J. Colbourne, Sr. VP-Admin. Svcs.
Roger G. Wilson, General Counsel
Doug Porter, Sr. VP-Oper.
Maureen E. Sullivan, Chief Strategy Officer
Paul Gerrard, VP-Strategic Comm.
William A. Breskin, VP-Gov't Programs
Jennifer Vachon, Chief of Staff
Cynthia Rolfe, VP-Consumer Brand Strategy
Shirley S. Lady, VP-Informatics & Data Oper.

GROWTH PLANS/SPECIAL FEATURES:

Blue Cross and Blue Shield Association (BCBSA) oversees a national federation of 36 independent and locally operated Blue Cross and Blue Shield (BCBS) companies across the U.S. Together these health insurance and care providers constitute the BCBS System, the oldest and largest group of healthcare companies in the country. The Association owns and manages the Blue Cross and Blue Shield trademarks and names in more than 170 countries; and grants licenses to independent companies to use the trademark's and names. Throughout the U.S., more than 96% of hospitals and 95% of physicians contract with BCBSA plans. BCBSA National Labor Office works with organized labor to cover working Americans with health coverage that insures one in three Americans. BCBSA serves more than 17 million unionized workers, retirees and their families. The BCBS Federal Employee Program is among the largest privately underwritten health insurance contracts in the world, covering roughly 5.6 million people. The firm's BlueCard program electronically links independent Blue Plans through a single electronic network for claims processing and reimbursement, allowing employees of corporations nationwide to participate and allowing individuals with local plans to file claims while traveling outside their region. The BlueCard worldwide program provides members with access to coverage when traveling or living abroad.

BCBSA employees receive benefits including medical, vision and dental insurance; flexible spending accounts; domestic partner coverage; tuition reimbursement; maternity and paternity leave; onsite fitness centers; transportation and parking benefits; credit union membership; various complementary health care programs; and a 401(k) plan.

FINANCIAL DATA: *Note: Data for latest year may not have been available at press time.*

In U.S. $	2017	2016	2015	2014	2013	2012
Revenue	568,050,000	541,000,000	504,178,349	457,383,677	413,909,483	402,665,404
R&D Expense						
Operating Income						
Operating Margin %						
SGA Expense						
Net Income			-5,511,767	7,748,316	-11,233,072	1,074,233
Operating Cash Flow						
Capital Expenditure						
EBITDA						
Return on Assets %						
Return on Equity %						
Debt to Equity						

CONTACT INFORMATION:

Phone: 312-297-6000 Fax: 312-297-6609
Toll-Free:
Address: 225 N. Michigan Ave., Chicago, IL 60601 United States

STOCK TICKER/OTHER:

Stock Ticker: Nonprofit
Employees: 1,293
Parent Company:
Exchange:
Fiscal Year Ends: 12/31

SALARIES/BONUSES:

Top Exec. Salary: $ Bonus: $
Second Exec. Salary: $ Bonus: $

OTHER THOUGHTS:

Estimated Female Officers or Directors: 9
Hot Spot for Advancement for Women/Minorities: Y

Blue Cross and Blue Shield of Florida Inc

www.bcbsfl.com

NAIC Code: 524,114

TYPES OF BUSINESS:

Insurance-Medical & Health, HMOs & PPOs
Life Insurance
Dental Insurance
Medicare & Medicaid Services
Staffing
Administrative Services
Information Technology Services

BRANDS/DIVISIONS/AFFILIATES:

GuideWell Mutual Holding Corporation
Florida Blue
Health Options Inc
Florida Combined Life Insurance Company Inc

CONTACTS: *Note: Officers with more than one job title may be intentionally listed here more than once.*

Patrick J. Geraghty, CEO
Jonathan B. Gavras, Chief Medical Officer
R. Chris Doerr, Chief Admin. Officer
Charlie Joseph, General Counsel
Joyce Kramzer, Sr. VP-Bus. Oper.
Craig Thomas, Chief Strategy & Mktg. Officer
Sharon Wamble-King, Sr. VP-Enterprise Comm.
R. Chris Doerr, Exec. VP-Finance
Camille Harrison, Chief Customer Experience Officer
Elizabeth Strombom, Sr. VP-Gov't Markets
Steven T. Halverson, Chmn.

GROWTH PLANS/SPECIAL FEATURES:

Blue Cross and Blue Shield of Florida, Inc. (BCBSF) is a nonprofit mutual health insurance company providing comprehensive health insurance and related services to a membership of more than 4 million. The company does business as Florida Blue, offering PPO (preferred provider organization) and HMO (health maintenance organization) group healthcare plans for both small and large companies. For individuals under 65 years of age, offerings include PPOs; and individuals over 65 have several plans to choose from, involving a combination of Medicare supplements, HMOs and other services. BCBSF also provides multiple options for pharmacy coverage, dental coverage, life insurance, accidental death and dismemberment, disability, long-term care and workers' compensation. The company's website provides health-related resources and information, as well as support services to help members make educated healthcare choices. The site also offers members access to detailed information about hospitals, such as success rates in medical procedures, complication and infection rates and technological capabilities. Independent licensees of the Blue Cross and Blue Shield Association include Health Options, Inc., which offers HMO coverage; and Florida Combined Life Insurance Company, Inc., which offers dental, life and disability coverage. BCBSF itself operates as a subsidiary of GuideWell Mutual Holding Corporation.

The firm offers employees comprehensive health coverage, flexible spending accounts, an employee assistance program, a 401(k) plan and tuition reimbursement, among other benefits.

FINANCIAL DATA: *Note: Data for latest year may not have been available at press time.*

In U.S. $	2017	2016	2015	2014	2013	2012
Revenue	9,100,000,000	8,750,000,000	8,100,000,000	7,500,000,000	7,000,000,000	6,564,698,595
R&D Expense						
Operating Income						
Operating Margin %						
SGA Expense						
Net Income		242,000,370	270,500,550	255,000,000	225,000,000	159,093,937
Operating Cash Flow						
Capital Expenditure						
EBITDA						
Return on Assets %						
Return on Equity %						
Debt to Equity						

CONTACT INFORMATION:

Phone: 904-791-6111 Fax:
Toll-Free: 800-352-2583
Address: 4800 Deerwood Campus Pkwy., Jacksonville, FL 32246 United States

STOCK TICKER/OTHER:

Stock Ticker: Nonprofit
Exchange:
Employees: 7,600
Fiscal Year Ends: 12/31
Parent Company: GuideWell Mutual Holding Corporation

SALARIES/BONUSES:

Top Exec. Salary: $ Bonus: $
Second Exec. Salary: $ Bonus: $

OTHER THOUGHTS:

Estimated Female Officers or Directors: 8
Hot Spot for Advancement for Women/Minorities: Y

Blue Cross and Blue Shield of Georgia

www.bcbsga.com

NAIC Code: 524,114

TYPES OF BUSINESS:

Insurance-Medical & Health, HMOs & PPOs
Dental & Vision Plans
Pharmacy Programs
POS
Life Insurance
Health Insurance

BRANDS/DIVISIONS/AFFILIATES:

Anthem Inc
Blue Cross and Blue Shield Association
HealthyExtensions

CONTACTS: *Note: Officers with more than one job title may be intentionally listed here more than once.*

Jeff Fusile, Pres.
Mark Kishel, Dir.-Medical
Doris Anderson, Staff VP-Oper.
Dan Pearson, Dir.-Special Acct.

GROWTH PLANS/SPECIAL FEATURES:

Blue Cross and Blue Shield of Georgia (BCBSGa) provides comprehensive health insurance and related services to a membership of more than 3.3 million, making it one of the largest healthcare coverage providers in the state. The company is a subsidiary of Anthem, Inc.; and is an independent licensee of the include Blue Cross and Blue Shield Association, which includes BCBSGa and Blue Cross and Blue Shield Healthcare Plan of Georgia, Inc., a health maintenance organization (HMO). BCBSGa offers a range of plans for individuals, seniors and small and large groups to choose from. Its individual and small group plans offer HMO, POS (Point-Of Service), PPO (preferred provider organization), HSA (health saving account), HDHP (high deductible health plan), dental plans, pharmacy programs and a range of life insurance options. The company currently serves hundreds of thousands of people who purchase medical insurance as individuals or through employers with 50 or fewer employees. For seniors, the firm offers Medicare Part A supplements; dental plans; vision plans; and HealthyExtensions, a program for discounts in vitamins, wellness books and prescription discount programs. The large groups division (51 or more employees) offers products aimed toward its various customers, including key accounts (51-250 employees), major accounts (251-2,000 employees) and special accounts (more than 2,000 employees). BCBSGa operates as a subsidiary of Anthem, Inc.

Employees of the firm receive medical, dental and vision coverage; flexible spending accounts; life and disability insurance; a 401(k) plan; tuition assistance; and an employee assistance program.

FINANCIAL DATA: *Note: Data for latest year may not have been available at press time.*

In U.S. $	2017	2016	2015	2014	2013	2012
Revenue						
R&D Expense						
Operating Income						
Operating Margin %						
SGA Expense						
Net Income						
Operating Cash Flow						
Capital Expenditure						
EBITDA						
Return on Assets %						
Return on Equity %						
Debt to Equity						

CONTACT INFORMATION:

Phone: 404-842-8000 Fax: 404-842-8100
Toll-Free:
Address: 3350 Peachtree Rd., Atlanta, GA 30326 United States

STOCK TICKER/OTHER:

Stock Ticker: Subsidiary
Exchange:
Employees: 1,605
Fiscal Year Ends: 12/31
Parent Company: Anthem Inc

SALARIES/BONUSES:

Top Exec. Salary: $ Bonus: $
Second Exec. Salary: $ Bonus: $

OTHER THOUGHTS:

Estimated Female Officers or Directors: 2
Hot Spot for Advancement for Women/Minorities: Y

Blue Cross and Blue Shield of Louisiana

www.bcbsla.com

NAIC Code: 524,114

TYPES OF BUSINESS:

Insurance-Medical & Health, HMOs & PPOs
Life Insurance

BRANDS/DIVISIONS/AFFILIATES:

HMO Louisiana Inc
Louisiana 2 Step

CONTACTS:
Note: Officers with more than one job title may be intentionally listed here more than once.

I. Steven Udvarhelyi, CEO/Pres.
B. Vindell Washington, Chief Medical Officer
Bryan Camerlinck, CFO
Brian Keller, CMO
John E. Brown Jr., Chief Human Resources Officer
Sue Kozik, CIO
Michele Calandro, General Counsel
John Maginnis, VP-Corp. Comm.
Adam Short, VP-Finance
Brian Small, Chief Actuary
Dawn Cantrell, VP-Network Admin.
Sabrina Heltz, Sr. VP-Health Care System, Quality
Allison Young, Sr. VP-Benefits Admin.
Dan Borne, Chmn.

GROWTH PLANS/SPECIAL FEATURES:

Blue Cross and Blue Shield of Louisiana (BCBSLA) and its subsidiary, HMO Louisiana, Inc., provide health insurance and services to more than 1.6 million members in Louisiana. BCBSLA offers various coverage plans, including HMO (health maintenance organization); PPO (preferred provider organization); POS (point-of-service); senior plans; group plans; HSA (health saving plan); dental, vision and hearing; life and disability; wellness; travel insurance; and small group coverage. Wellness and preventative services for healthy customers, as well as disease management programs for chronically ill policyholders, are available on the company's website. The firm's Louisiana 2 Step program, operated in partnership with the Pennington Biomedical Research Center, provides information related to obesity, metabolic syndromes, nutrition, chronic diseases and preventive medicine.

The firm offers its employees medical, dental, vision, life and disability coverage; health and dependent care spending accounts; long-term care coverage; an employee assistance program; wellness programs; a bonus program; 401(k) and retirement plans; access to a credit union; paid time off; volunteer options; and a charitable gift matching program.

FINANCIAL DATA:
Note: Data for latest year may not have been available at press time.

In U.S. $	2017	2016	2015	2014	2013	2012
Revenue	3,477,600,000	3,312,000,000	3,250,000,000	3,000,000,000	2,900,000,000	2,800,000,000
R&D Expense						
Operating Income						
Operating Margin %						
SGA Expense						
Net Income						
Operating Cash Flow						
Capital Expenditure						
EBITDA						
Return on Assets %						
Return on Equity %						
Debt to Equity						

CONTACT INFORMATION:

Phone: 225-295-3307 Fax: 225-295-2054
Toll-Free: 800-599-2583
Address: 5525 Reitz Ave., Baton Rouge, LA 70809 United States

STOCK TICKER/OTHER:

Stock Ticker: Private
Employees: 2,500
Parent Company:
Exchange:
Fiscal Year Ends: 12/31

SALARIES/BONUSES:

Top Exec. Salary: $ Bonus: $
Second Exec. Salary: $ Bonus: $

OTHER THOUGHTS:

Estimated Female Officers or Directors: 19
Hot Spot for Advancement for Women/Minorities: Y

Blue Cross and Blue Shield of Massachusetts www.bcbsma.com

NAIC Code: 524,114

TYPES OF BUSINESS:

Insurance-Medical & Health, HMOs & PPOs
Indemnity Insurance
Insurance-Dental
Medicare Extension Programs

BRANDS/DIVISIONS/AFFILIATES:

Associated Hospital Service Corporation

CONTACTS: *Note: Officers with more than one job title may be intentionally listed here more than once.*

Andrew Dreyfus, CEO
Deborah Devaux, COO
Andrew Dreyfus, Pres.
Andreana Santagelo, CFO
Patrick Gilligan, Exec. VP-Sales, Mktg. & Products
Susan L. Sgroi, Chief Human Resources Officer
John A. Fallon, Chief Physician Exec.
Stephanie Lovell, General Counsel
Sarah Iselin, Chief Strategy Officer
Jay McQuaide, Sr. VP-Corp. Comm.
Phyllis R. Yale, Chmn.

GROWTH PLANS/SPECIAL FEATURES:

Blue Cross and Blue Shield of Massachusetts (BCBSMA) is an independent, nonprofit healthcare company that provides health services and insurance in Massachusetts. The firm began as the Associated Hospital Service Corporation of Massachusetts in 1937 and is now one of New England's largest health plan providers, including primary care providers, specialists, hospitals, dentists, ancillary providers and behavioral health providers. BCBSMA has approximately 2.8 million members, including approximately 783,000 health maintenance organization (HMO) members, 1.8 million preferred provider organization (PPO) members and 335,000 senior products/Medicare members. More than 26,800 businesses across the state are customers of BCBSMA, as well as 79% of the state's cities and towns, and nearly 115,000 federal employees.

The company offers employees medical, dental and vision coverage; life and disability insurance; a 529 college savings plan; 401(k) and pension plans; work/life benefits; flexible spending accounts; and tuition reimbursement.

FINANCIAL DATA: *Note: Data for latest year may not have been available at press time.*

In U.S. $	2017	2016	2015	2014	2013	2012
Revenue	7,505,175,000	7,111,253,000	6,797,415,000	6,500,692,000	6,284,021,000	6,296,714,000
R&D Expense						
Operating Income						
Operating Margin %						
SGA Expense						
Net Income	-6,920,000	78,091,000	15,058,000	7,948,000	69,085,000	163,861,000
Operating Cash Flow						
Capital Expenditure						
EBITDA						
Return on Assets %						
Return on Equity %						
Debt to Equity						

CONTACT INFORMATION:

Phone: 617-246-5000 Fax: 617-246-4832
Toll-Free: 800-262-2583
Address: 101 Huntington Ave., Ste 1300, Boston, MA 02199-7611 United States

STOCK TICKER/OTHER:

Stock Ticker: Nonprofit
Exchange:
Employees: 3,766
Fiscal Year Ends: 12/31
Parent Company:

SALARIES/BONUSES:

Top Exec. Salary: $ Bonus: $
Second Exec. Salary: $ Bonus: $

OTHER THOUGHTS:

Estimated Female Officers or Directors: 6
Hot Spot for Advancement for Women/Minorities: Y

Blue Cross and Blue Shield of Michigan

www.bcbsm.com

NAIC Code: 524,114

TYPES OF BUSINESS:

Insurance-Medical & Health, HMOs & PPOs
Workers Compensation
Dental & Vision Insurance
Health Care Management Services
Prescription Drug Plans

BRANDS/DIVISIONS/AFFILIATES:

Blue Care Network of Michigan
Blue Cross Blue Shield of Michigan Foundation
AF Group
LifeSecure Insurance Company
Tessellate LLC
Visiant Holdings Inc
Dearborn National Life Insurance
LifeSecure Insurance Company

CONTACTS: *Note: Officers with more than one job title may be intentionally listed here more than once.*

Daniel J. Loepp, CEO
Mark R. Bartlett, CFO
Thomas L. Simmer, Chief Medical Officer
William M Frandrich, Sr. VP
Lynda M. Rossi, Chief of Staff
Tricia A. Keith, Corp. Sec.
Darrell E. Middleton, Exec. VP-Oper. & Bus. Performance
David A. Share, Sr. VP-Value Partnerships
Lynda M. Rossi, Sr. VP-Public Affairs
Carolynn Walton, Treas.
Elizabeth R. Haar, CEO
Darrell E. Middleton, Sr. VP-Bus. Performance
Mark R. Bartlett, Pres., Emerging Markets
Elizabeth R. Haar, Sr. VP-Subsidiary Oper.
Gregory A. Sudderth, Chmn.

GROWTH PLANS/SPECIAL FEATURES:

Blue Cross and Blue Shield of Michigan (BCBSM) is a nonprofit organization providing healthcare plans. It is one of the nation's top Blue Cross Blue Shield health insurance associations, serving nearly 4.5 million in state members and 1.6 million more in other states. The firm offers individual and family health plans, dental and vision plans, Medicare and Medicaid coverage, group plans, specialty benefits and international plans. Plans include traditional, Affordable Care Act, wellness, preferred provider organization (PPO), health maintenance organization (HMO), and state-supported. BCBSM's network in Michigan comprises 152 hospitals and more than 33,00 doctors. Subsidiaries of the firm include Blue Care Network of Michigan; Blue Cross Blue Shield of Michigan Foundation; AF Group; LifeSecure Insurance Company; Tessellate, LLC; and Visiant Holdings, Inc. Specialty benefits are provided through Dearborn National Life Insurance, Assurity Life Insurance Company and LifeSecure Insurance Company.

BCBSM offers employees medical, dental and vision plans; 401(k) matching; long- and short-term disability; and tuition reimbursement.

FINANCIAL DATA: *Note: Data for latest year may not have been available at press time.*

In U.S. $	2017	2016	2015	2014	2013	2012
Revenue	26,945,000,000	25,902,000,000	24,222,000,000	23,131,000,000	21,260,000,000	20,971,900,000
R&D Expense						
Operating Income						
Operating Margin %						
SGA Expense						
Net Income	1,191,000,000	122,000,000	-68,000,000	272,000,000	265,000,000	-2,500,000
Operating Cash Flow						
Capital Expenditure						
EBITDA						
Return on Assets %						
Return on Equity %						
Debt to Equity						

CONTACT INFORMATION:

Phone: 313-225-9000 Fax: 313-225-6764
Toll-Free:
Address: 600 E. Lafayette Blvd., Detroit, MI 48226 United States

STOCK TICKER/OTHER:

Stock Ticker: Nonprofit
Employees: 8,100
Parent Company:
Exchange:
Fiscal Year Ends: 04/01

SALARIES/BONUSES:

Top Exec. Salary: $ Bonus: $
Second Exec. Salary: $ Bonus: $

OTHER THOUGHTS:

Estimated Female Officers or Directors: 6
Hot Spot for Advancement for Women/Minorities: Y

Blue Cross and Blue Shield of Minnesota

www.bluecrossmn.com

NAIC Code: 524,114

TYPES OF BUSINESS:

Insurance-Medical & Health, HMOs & PPOs
Managed Care
Insurance-Life
Investment Management
Pharmacy Benefit Management
Behavioral Health Services
Workers' Compensation

BRANDS/DIVISIONS/AFFILIATES:

Aware Integrated Inc
Blue Cross Blue Shield Association
InstaCare
Basic Blue
BlueSave
Blue Cross and Blue Shield of Minnesota Foundation

CONTACTS: *Note: Officers with more than one job title may be intentionally listed here more than once.*

Craig E. Smith, CEO
Cain A. Hayes, Exec. VP
Jay Matushak, CFO
Ruth Hafoka, Chief Human Resources Officer
Tina Holmes, Chief of Staff
Scott Lynch, Chief Legal Officer
James Egan, Sr. VP-Corp. Oper.
Rochelle Myers, VP-Strategic Planning & Portfolio Mgmt.
Patricia Riley, Chief Gov't Officer
Garrett Black, Sr. VP-Health Mgmt.

GROWTH PLANS/SPECIAL FEATURES:

Blue Cross and Blue Shield of Minnesota (BCBSM), a subsidiary of Aware Integrated, Inc., operates health insurance plans to Minnesotans. The firm is a member of the Blue Cross Blue Shield Association and offers medical, dental, life, indemnity and short-term insurance. Insurance plans include health maintenance organizations (HMOs), preferred provider organizations (PPOs) and Medicare supplemental. The firm's InstaCare plan is short-term coverage for people who are out of work, between jobs and just out of school. BCBSM's Basic Blue plan is a high-deductible health plan with a financial account, health management services and an online member service center. The firm also offers BlueSave, a plan tailored for young adults, leaving out family and childbirth labor coverage, resulting in lower monthly rates. The Blue Cross and Blue Shield of Minnesota Foundation is one of the largest grant-making foundations in Minnesota, focused on early childhood development, housing, social connectedness and the environment. The company offers wellness information on its website focused on addressing general health, stress management, behavioral choices and nutrition.

The firm offers employees medical, dental and life insurance; flexible spending accounts; disability protection; a 401(k) company match; seniority tiered paid time off; flexible work schedule; and wellness programs.

FINANCIAL DATA: *Note: Data for latest year may not have been available at press time.*

In U.S. $	2017	2016	2015	2014	2013	2012
Revenue	12,477,401,000	12,090,953,000	10,692,369,000	10,139,500,000	10,073,887,000	9,530,201,000
R&D Expense						
Operating Income						
Operating Margin %						
SGA Expense						
Net Income	-62,394,000	-322,400,000	-153,549,000	61,531,000	47,689,000	688,369,000
Operating Cash Flow						
Capital Expenditure						
EBITDA						
Return on Assets %						
Return on Equity %						
Debt to Equity						

CONTACT INFORMATION:

Phone: 615-662-8000 Fax:
Toll-Free: 800-382-2000
Address: 3535 Blue Cross Rd., Eagan, MN 55122 United States

STOCK TICKER/OTHER:

Stock Ticker: Subsidiary
Exchange:
Employees: 3,500
Fiscal Year Ends: 12/31
Parent Company: Aware Integrated Inc

SALARIES/BONUSES:

Top Exec. Salary: $ Bonus: $
Second Exec. Salary: $ Bonus: $

OTHER THOUGHTS:

Estimated Female Officers or Directors: 7
Hot Spot for Advancement for Women/Minorities: Y

Blue Cross and Blue Shield of Montana

www.bcbsmt.com

NAIC Code: 524,114

TYPES OF BUSINESS:

Insurance-Medical & Health, HMOs & PPOs

BRANDS/DIVISIONS/AFFILIATES:

Health Care Services Corporation

CONTACTS:

Note: Officers with more than one job title may be intentionally listed here more than once.

Michael Frank, CEO
Sheila Shapiro, COO
Michael Frank, Pres.
Mark Burzynski, CFO
Monica Berner, Chief Medical Officer
Mary Belcher, General Counsel
Deb Thompson, Sr. Dir.-Corp. Affairs & Compliance Officer
Jim Spencer, Chief Actuary

GROWTH PLANS/SPECIAL FEATURES:

Blue Cross and Blue Shield of Montana (BCBSMT), a division of Health Care Services Corporation, provides approximately 250,000 members with a full spectrum of healthcare coverage, including prepaid health plans that cover hospital expenses and plans that cover physician services. The firm's individual health insurance products include the Affordable Care Act's three plan levels: Bronze (member pays 40%, insurer pays 60%), Silver (member-30%, insurer-70%) and Gold (member-20%, insurer-80%). Other plans include student health insurance, travel medical coverage, expatriate coverage, essential health benefits, preventive services, dental and prescription drug coverage and 24/7 non-emergency care options.

BCBSMT offers its employees health coverage, flexible spending accounts, life and disability insurance, tuition reimbursement, an employee assistance program, a defined contribution retirement plan and a 401(k) savings plan, among other benefits.

FINANCIAL DATA:

Note: Data for latest year may not have been available at press time.

In U.S. $	2017	2016	2015	2014	2013	2012
Revenue	682,500,000	650,000,000	632,000,000	625,000,000	610,000,000	593,200,000
R&D Expense						
Operating Income						
Operating Margin %						
SGA Expense						
Net Income						
Operating Cash Flow						
Capital Expenditure						
EBITDA						
Return on Assets %						
Return on Equity %						
Debt to Equity						

CONTACT INFORMATION:

Phone: 406-437-5000 Fax:
Toll-Free: 800-447-7828
Address: 3645 Alice St., P.O. Box 4309, Helena, MT 59604-4309 United States

STOCK TICKER/OTHER:

Stock Ticker: Subsidiary
Exchange:
Employees: 460
Fiscal Year Ends: 12/31
Parent Company: Health Care Service Corporation

SALARIES/BONUSES:

Top Exec. Salary: $ Bonus: $
Second Exec. Salary: $ Bonus: $

OTHER THOUGHTS:

Estimated Female Officers or Directors: 5
Hot Spot for Advancement for Women/Minorities: Y

Blue Cross and Blue Shield of Nebraska

www.nebraskablue.com

NAIC Code: 524,114

TYPES OF BUSINESS:

Insurance-Medical & Health, HMOs & PPOs
POS
Dental Insurance
Medicare Supplemental Insurance
Alternative Healing Benefits

BRANDS/DIVISIONS/AFFILIATES:

BluePreferred
RX Nebraska Pharmacy Network

CONTACTS: *Note: Officers with more than one job title may be intentionally listed here more than once.*

Steven H. Grandfield, CEO
Dale Mackel, Exec. VP-Finance
Timothy McGill, CMO
Rama Kolli, CIO
Lee Handke, Sr. VP-Prod. & Providers
Sarah A. Waldman, Sr. VP-Admin.
Russell Collins, General Counsel
Jennifer Richardson, Sr. VP-Oper.
Brian Pickering, Sr. VP-Comm. & Mktg.
Jerry Byers, Sr. VP-Finance
Dan Alm, Chief Underwriting Officer
Dave Anderson, VP-Finance
Dan Archuleta, VP-Member Svcs.
David Filipi, VP-Quality Advancement
George G. Beattie, Chmn.

GROWTH PLANS/SPECIAL FEATURES:

Blue Cross and Blue Shield of Nebraska (BCBSNE) provides health services to over 700,000 Nebraskans. Its network of BluePreferred hospitals, physicians and other healthcare professionals is one of the state's largest, encompassing every non-governmental acute care hospital in the state. The company's Rx Nebraska Pharmacy Network includes hundreds of pharmacies across Nebraska as well as thousands of pharmacies nationwide that can fill member prescriptions without additional claims and paperwork to be processed. BCBSNE offers individual and family health and dental plans, Medicare coverage, dental plans and travel health insurance. It offers employer and business health and dental plans, group health insurance for travelers, health savings account plan, high deductible health plan, identification protection services, Medicare supplement plan, telehealth and home care offerings. In December 2017, the firm announced that it was going to reorganize itself into a mutual insurance holding company. The proposed reorganization will create a new mutual insurance holding company called GoodLife Partners, Inc. If approved, this new mutual insurance holding company will become the overall parent company for Blue Cross and Blue Shield of Nebraska and its subsidiaries.

The firm offers employees a health, vision and dental plan; flexible spending accounts; a 401(k) plan; tuition reimbursement; access to a free wellness center; and a smoke-free campus.

FINANCIAL DATA: *Note: Data for latest year may not have been available at press time.*

In U.S. $	2017	2016	2015	2014	2013	2012
Revenue	1,676,920,966	1,744,144,657	1,648,177,433	1,636,041,465	1,578,061,382	
R&D Expense						
Operating Income						
Operating Margin %						
SGA Expense						
Net Income	46,873,985	-21,564,221	-31,513,777	5,421,470	24,547,085	
Operating Cash Flow						
Capital Expenditure						
EBITDA						
Return on Assets %						
Return on Equity %						
Debt to Equity						

CONTACT INFORMATION:

Phone: 402-982-7000 Fax: 402-392-4153
Toll-Free: 800-422-2763
Address: 1919 Aksarben Dr., Omaha, NE 68180 United States

STOCK TICKER/OTHER:

Stock Ticker: Nonprofit
Employees:
Parent Company:
Exchange:
Fiscal Year Ends: 12/31

SALARIES/BONUSES:

Top Exec. Salary: $ Bonus: $
Second Exec. Salary: $ Bonus: $

OTHER THOUGHTS:

Estimated Female Officers or Directors: 5
Hot Spot for Advancement for Women/Minorities: Y

Blue Cross and Blue Shield of North Carolina

www.bcbsnc.com

NAIC Code: 524,114

TYPES OF BUSINESS:

Insurance-Medical & Health, HMOs & PPOs
Dental Insurance
Life Insurance

BRANDS/DIVISIONS/AFFILIATES:

BlueCard Program
BCBSNC Foundation

CONTACTS:

Note: Officers with more than one job title may be intentionally listed here more than once.

Patrick Conway, CEO
Gerald Petkau, COO
J. Bradley Wilson, Pres.
Mitch Perry, CFO
John T. Roos, Chief Growth Officer
Fara M. Palumbo, Chief People Officer
Don W. Bradley, Chief Medical Officer
Jo Abernathy, CIO
N. King Prather, General Counsel
Maureen K. O'Connor, Chief Strategy Officer
Don W. Bradley, Sr. VP-Health Care
Frank B. Holding Jr, Chmn.

GROWTH PLANS/SPECIAL FEATURES:

Blue Cross and Blue Shield of North Carolina (BCBSNC) is a nonprofit mutual insurance company providing comprehensive health insurance and related services. It has a membership of more than 3.89 million members throughout North Carolina. The company offers short- and long-term care; Medicare supplements; plans for individuals interested in low co-payments for doctor visits with the freedom to choose between doctors; health maintenance organization (HMO) plans; preferred provider organization (PPO) plans; health savings account (HSA) plans; small group coverage; dental plans; and life insurance plans. The firm contracts with approximately 96% of medical doctors and 99% of hospitals in North Carolina. BCBSNC's BlueCard Program allows members to submit claims while traveling outside of their plan's area, including a network of participating hospitals around the world. The BCBSNC Foundation has invested more than $100 million into the community through over 750 grants.

The firm offers employees fitness programs and services, paid time off and ten paid holidays throughout the year, onsite cafeterias and child care, an onsite BCBSNC credit union, continuing education opportunities with Blue University and a matching 401(k) with immediate vesting/company match.

FINANCIAL DATA:

Note: Data for latest year may not have been available at press time.

In U.S. $	2017	2016	2015	2014	2013	2012
Revenue	9,400,000,000	7,880,000,000	8,200,000,000	8,000,000,000	6,400,000,000	5,700,000,000
R&D Expense						
Operating Income						
Operating Margin %						
SGA Expense						
Net Income	734,000,000	185,000,000	500,000	-50,600,000	92,600,000	57,700,000
Operating Cash Flow						
Capital Expenditure						
EBITDA						
Return on Assets %						
Return on Equity %						
Debt to Equity						

CONTACT INFORMATION:

Phone: 919-489-7431 Fax: 919-765-7818
Toll-Free:
Address: 4615 University Dr., Durham, NC 27707 United States

STOCK TICKER/OTHER:

Stock Ticker: Nonprofit
Exchange:
Employees: 4,700
Fiscal Year Ends: 12/31
Parent Company:

SALARIES/BONUSES:

Top Exec. Salary: $ Bonus: $
Second Exec. Salary: $ Bonus: $

OTHER THOUGHTS:

Estimated Female Officers or Directors:
Hot Spot for Advancement for Women/Minorities: Y

Blue Cross and Blue Shield of Oklahoma

www.bcbsok.com

NAIC Code: 524,114

TYPES OF BUSINESS:

Insurance-Medical & Health, HMOs & PPOs
Managed Care
Life Insurance
Property & Casualty Insurance
Prescription & Dental Insurance

BRANDS/DIVISIONS/AFFILIATES:

Health Care Service Corporation
Oklahoma Caring Foundation (The)
Oklahoma Caring Van Program (The)
Caring Program for Children (The)

CONTACTS: *Note: Officers with more than one job title may be intentionally listed here more than once.*

Ted Haynes, Pres.
Nicole Amend, Chief of Staff
Ashley Hudgeons, Media Contact

GROWTH PLANS/SPECIAL FEATURES:

Blue Cross and Blue Shield of Oklahoma (BCBSOK), a subsidiary of Health Care Service Corporation, is one of the oldest private health insurers in Oklahoma and provides benefits plans for over 700,000 customers across the state. BCBSOK offers dental plans, individual and family healthcare plans and group plans. The firm's individual health insurance products include the Affordable Care Act's three plan levels: Bronze (member pays 40%, insurer pays 60%), Silver (member-30%, insurer-70%) and Gold (member-20%, insurer-80%). It also provides Medicare, short-term, travel, expatriate and student health plans. Group plans offers employers the choice of several health plans including a preferred provider organization (PPO), a health maintenance organization (HMO) or a self-funded employer plan. Another group option is the consumer directed health plans (CDHPs), which pairs a high deductible PPO plan with a tax-advantaged account. The Oklahoma Caring Foundation, administered by the firm as an in-kind donation, provides vaccinations, education and basic healthcare access to children in Oklahoma through The Oklahoma Caring Van Program and The Caring Program for Children. The Oklahoma Caring Foundation is funded by community contributions.

Employees of the firm receive medical, vision, dental and life insurance; a flexible spending account; long- and short-term disability; dependent life coverage; company wellness programs; a pension plan; 401(k); credit union access; paid time off; paid company holidays; tuition reimbursement; an employee assistance program; adoption assistance; military leave; and onsite cafeterias and lunchrooms.

FINANCIAL DATA: *Note: Data for latest year may not have been available at press time.*

In U.S. $	2017	2016	2015	2014	2013	2012
Revenue						
R&D Expense						
Operating Income						
Operating Margin %						
SGA Expense						
Net Income						
Operating Cash Flow						
Capital Expenditure						
EBITDA						
Return on Assets %						
Return on Equity %						
Debt to Equity						

CONTACT INFORMATION:

Phone: 918-560-3500 Fax: 918-560-3060
Toll-Free: 800-942-5837
Address: 1400 S. Boston, Tulsa, OK 74102 United States

STOCK TICKER/OTHER:

Stock Ticker: Subsidiary Exchange:
Employees: 970 Fiscal Year Ends: 12/31
Parent Company: Health Care Service Corporation

SALARIES/BONUSES:

Top Exec. Salary: $ Bonus: $
Second Exec. Salary: $ Bonus: $

OTHER THOUGHTS:

Estimated Female Officers or Directors: 2
Hot Spot for Advancement for Women/Minorities:

Blue Cross and Blue Shield of Texas

www.bcbstx.com

NAIC Code: 524,114

TYPES OF BUSINESS:

Insurance-Medical & Health, HMOs & PPOs
POS
Behavioral Health & Dental Insurance
Medicare Supplement Plan

BRANDS/DIVISIONS/AFFILIATES:

Health Care Service Corporation

CONTACTS: *Note: Officers with more than one job title may be intentionally listed here more than once.*

Dan McCoy, Pres.
Darrell Beckett, Sr. VP-Sales & Mktg.
Paul B. Handel, Chief Medical Officer

GROWTH PLANS/SPECIAL FEATURES:

Blue Cross and Blue Shield of Texas (BCBSTX), a division of Health Care Service Corporation, is a not-for-profit insurer providing members with health maintenance organization (HMO) networks. The firm emphasizes preventive medicine through education outreach programs in order to control operating costs. BCBSTX's group health insurance products are offered to employers based on staff levels and include HMO Blue Texas, a point-of-sale (POS) plan and consumer choice plans. The firm's individual health insurance products include three plan levels: Bronze (member pays 40%, insurer pays 60%), Silver (member-30%, insurer-70%) and Gold (member-20%, insurer-80%). BCBSTX also offers Medicare coverage, a health insurance plan developed by the Federal government with two parts: Part A, which refers to hospital coverage; and Part B, which refers to medical coverage. The firm's website offers the ability to compare plans and to obtain resources.

Employee benefits include medical, vision and dental coverage; flexible spending accounts; short- and long-term disability; life insurance; dependent life coverage; a wellness program; a pension plan; 401(k); credit union memberships; tuition reimbursement; an employee assistance program; adoption assistance; and group legal service.

FINANCIAL DATA: *Note: Data for latest year may not have been available at press time.*

In U.S. $	2017	2016	2015	2014	2013	2012
Revenue						
R&D Expense						
Operating Income						
Operating Margin %						
SGA Expense						
Net Income						
Operating Cash Flow						
Capital Expenditure						
EBITDA						
Return on Assets %						
Return on Equity %						
Debt to Equity						

CONTACT INFORMATION:

Phone: 972-766-6900 Fax:
Toll-Free: 800-451-0287
Address: 1001 E. Lookout Dr., Richardson, TX 75082 United States

STOCK TICKER/OTHER:

Stock Ticker: Subsidiary Exchange:
Employees: 6,630 Fiscal Year Ends: 12/31
Parent Company: Health Care Service Corporation

SALARIES/BONUSES:

Top Exec. Salary: $ Bonus: $
Second Exec. Salary: $ Bonus: $

OTHER THOUGHTS:

Estimated Female Officers or Directors:
Hot Spot for Advancement for Women/Minorities:

Blue Cross and Blue Shield of Vermont

www.bcbsvt.com

NAIC Code: 524,114

TYPES OF BUSINESS:

Insurance-Medical & Health, HMOs & PPOs
POS
Administrative Services
Case Management

BRANDS/DIVISIONS/AFFILIATES:

Comprehensive Benefits Administrators Inc
Blue HealthSolutions
Healthwise Knowledgebase

CONTACTS: *Note: Officers with more than one job title may be intentionally listed here more than once.*

Don George, CEO
Don C. George, Pres.
Ruth K. Greene, VP
Ellen Yakubik, CMO
Robert Wheeler, Chief Medical Dir.
Chris Gannon, Chief Admin. Officer
Chris Gannon, General Counsel
Doug Warren, VP-Oper.
Catherine Hamilton, VP-Corp. Planning
Kevin Goddard, VP-External Affairs & Sales
Chris Gannon, Treas.

GROWTH PLANS/SPECIAL FEATURES:

Blue Cross and Blue Shield of Vermont (BCBSVT), a nonprofit organization, is one of the largest health insurance providers in Vermont. It is the only health insurance provider based in the state to serve clients of all medical statuses and age. BCBSVT's subsidiary, Comprehensive Benefits Administrator, Inc. (CBA Blue), is a third-party administrator that provides an online directory to preferred providers. It also offers risk and disease assessment, predictive modeling and case management of health-related issues for employers. In addition to offering Medicare supplement, vision and dental plans, the company offers PPO, HMO, Point-Of-Sale (POS) and high deductible (HMO, PPO, out of state) plans. The company's Blue HealthSolutions division focuses on reducing healthcare costs through specialty case management, focused inpatient review, tiered and incentive programs for purchasing pharmacy drugs and decision support. BCBSVT's Healthwise Knowledgebase is an online resource center for members only, offering up-to-date medical information. In April 2018, the firm partnered with American Well to give its members 24/7/365 access to doctors via telemedicine. Telemedicine provides online video consultation access with a provider via a computer, or an app on a smartphone or tablet.

Employee benefits include medical, vision and dental coverage; a worksite wellness program; a 401(k) and company pension plan; life insurance; short- and long-term disability; and tuition reimbursement.

FINANCIAL DATA: *Note: Data for latest year may not have been available at press time.*

In U.S. $	2017	2016	2015	2014	2013	2012
Revenue	578,276,649	547,330,815	539,866,593			
R&D Expense						
Operating Income						
Operating Margin %						
SGA Expense						
Net Income	7,582,497	-9,714,555	12,220,330			
Operating Cash Flow						
Capital Expenditure						
EBITDA						
Return on Assets %						
Return on Equity %						
Debt to Equity						

CONTACT INFORMATION:

Phone: 802-223-6131 Fax: 802-223-4229
Toll-Free: 800-247-2583
Address: 445 Industrial Ln., Berlin, VT 05602 United States

STOCK TICKER/OTHER:

Stock Ticker: Nonprofit
Employees: 400
Parent Company:
Exchange:
Fiscal Year Ends: 12/31

SALARIES/BONUSES:

Top Exec. Salary: $ Bonus: $
Second Exec. Salary: $ Bonus: $

OTHER THOUGHTS:

Estimated Female Officers or Directors: 7
Hot Spot for Advancement for Women/Minorities: Y

Blue Cross and Blue Shield of Wyoming

www.bcbswy.com

NAIC Code: 524,114

TYPES OF BUSINESS:

Insurance-Medical & Health, HMOs & PPOs
Life Insurance

BRANDS/DIVISIONS/AFFILIATES:

BlueChoice Business
Caring Foundation of Wyoming

CONTACTS: *Note: Officers with more than one job title may be intentionally listed here more than once.*

Rick Schum, CEO
Dave Keiter, Dir.-Operations
Tim J. Crilly, Pres.
Diane Gore, CFO
Lee Shannon, VP-Mktg. & Sales
Tom Lockhart, Vice Chmn.
Cliff Kirk, Chmn.

GROWTH PLANS/SPECIAL FEATURES:

Blue Cross Blue Shield of Wyoming (BCBSWY) is a nonprofit insurance company and a Blue Cross Blue Shield Association member serving approximately 100,000 members across Wyoming. The firm provides medical, vision and dental insurance to groups, employers and individuals as well as Medicare supplemental coverage, group life insurance, cancer and critical illness coverage, flexible benefits administration, worksite benefits and a prescription drug program. The firm's BlueChoice Business program is a comprehensive health insurance plan, providing benefits to small-, medium- and large-sized companies. BlueChoice Business provides a wide range of administrative services for both partially and fully self-funded plans. Some of the benefits include a choice of prescription drug coverage, life and disability insurance, dental and vision coverage, flexible spending accounts, accidental death insurance and short- and long-term disability. BCBSWY covers all administrative costs for the Caring Foundation of Wyoming, Inc., which provides basic healthcare services to uninsured children, meets the healthcare needs of uninsured women and aids in the prevention of domestic violence. The company is also the carrier for the Wyoming Department of Health's Kid Care CHIP program, which offers health insurance coverage for uninsured children from lower-income families.

The firm offers employees an extended illness time bank, a wellness program, health insurance, life insurance, flexible spending accounts, long-term disability, paid time off and educational assistance, among other benefits.

FINANCIAL DATA: *Note: Data for latest year may not have been available at press time.*

In U.S. $	2017	2016	2015	2014	2013	2012
Revenue						
R&D Expense						
Operating Income						
Operating Margin %						
SGA Expense						
Net Income						
Operating Cash Flow						
Capital Expenditure						
EBITDA						
Return on Assets %						
Return on Equity %						
Debt to Equity						

CONTACT INFORMATION:

Phone: 307-634-1393 Fax: 307-634-5742
Toll-Free: 800-442-2376
Address: 4000 House Ave., Cheyenne, WY 82001 United States

STOCK TICKER/OTHER:

Stock Ticker: Nonprofit
Employees: 200
Parent Company:
Exchange:
Fiscal Year Ends: 12/31

SALARIES/BONUSES:

Top Exec. Salary: $ Bonus: $
Second Exec. Salary: $ Bonus: $

OTHER THOUGHTS:

Estimated Female Officers or Directors: 1
Hot Spot for Advancement for Women/Minorities: Y

Blue Cross Blue Shield of Kansas City (Blue KC) www.bluekc.com

NAIC Code: 524,114

TYPES OF BUSINESS:

Insurance-Medical & Health, HMOs & PPOs

BRANDS/DIVISIONS/AFFILIATES:

Spira Care
Spira Care Center

CONTACTS:
Note: Officers with more than one job title may be intentionally listed here more than once.

Danette Wilson, CEO

GROWTH PLANS/SPECIAL FEATURES:

Blue Cross Blue Shield of Kansas City (Blue KC) is an independent licensee of the Blue Cross Blue Shield Association and a nonprofit health insurance provider with more than 1 million members. Blue KC serves people in more than 30 counties of greater Kansas City and northwestern Missouri, as well as Johnson and Wyandotte counties in Kansas. The company offers individual and family health insurance plans and offers a Blue & U product that provides a range of plan options for customers to choose from. Blue KC also offers dental insurance through several plans with various price options. Short-term security plans are provided as well and is an option for individuals and families who are temporarily without health insurance. Long-term care insurance is offered for home care, assisted living and nursing home facilities; this coverage can be tailored to fit individual needs concerning coverage and budget. In November 2017, Blue KC and Shawnee Mission Health announced the launch of Spira Care, a combined primary care and insurance offering available exclusively to eligible Blue KC members. In May 2018, the firm and Shawnee Mission Health announced the opening of the newest Spira Care Center, located in Shawnee, Kansas. The following August, Blue KC announced that Spira Care will expand to Missouri with the opening of three new Care Centers in the Crossroads District (1916 Grand Boulevard), Lee's Summit (760 N.W. Blue Parkway) and Liberty (8350 N. Church Road).

FINANCIAL DATA:
Note: Data for latest year may not have been available at press time.

In U.S. $	2017	2016	2015	2014	2013	2012
Revenue	3,044,207,000	2,869,020,000	2,649,500,000	2,530,830,000	2,400,000,000	2,375,000,000
R&D Expense						
Operating Income						
Operating Margin %						
SGA Expense						
Net Income	108,863,000	63,361,000	40,737,000	-73,525,000		
Operating Cash Flow						
Capital Expenditure						
EBITDA						
Return on Assets %						
Return on Equity %						
Debt to Equity						

CONTACT INFORMATION:

Phone: 816-395-3558 Fax:
Toll-Free: 888-989-8842
Address: One Pershing Sq., 2301 Main St., Kansas City, MO 64108 United States

STOCK TICKER/OTHER:

Stock Ticker: Nonprofit
Employees: 1,596
Parent Company:
Exchange:
Fiscal Year Ends:

SALARIES/BONUSES:

Top Exec. Salary: $ Bonus: $
Second Exec. Salary: $ Bonus: $

OTHER THOUGHTS:

Estimated Female Officers or Directors:
Hot Spot for Advancement for Women/Minorities:

Blue Cross of California

www.anthem.com/ca/

NAIC Code: 524,114

TYPES OF BUSINESS:

Insurance-Medical & Health, HMOs & PPOs
Point of Service Plans
Indemnity Plans

BRANDS/DIVISIONS/AFFILIATES:

Anthem Inc
Anthem Blue Cross
Anthem Blue Cross Life and Health Insurance
Healthy Generations

CONTACTS: *Note: Officers with more than one job title may be intentionally listed here more than once.*

J. Brian Ternan, Pres.
Kevin Hayden, Pres. State Sponsored Bus. Div.
Michael C. Higgins, Sr. VP-Large Group Div.

GROWTH PLANS/SPECIAL FEATURES:

Blue Cross of California, doing business as Anthem Blue Cross, is a subsidiary of Anthem, Inc. that provides health insurance and related care services to members in California. Along with affiliate Anthem Blue Cross Life and Health Insurance, the company provides health maintenance organizations (HMOs), preferred provider organizations (PPOs), traditional indemnity plans and point-of-service (POS) plans as well as Medicare and Medicaid. The company's large business segment serves groups with over 51 employees. The small group division serves businesses with 2-50 employees. The seniors division offers Medicare supplemental plans and Medicare risk plans, including Medicare Advantage and Medicare Part D coverage. The company is involved in raising funds for the Healthy Generations program through its parent company Anthem, Inc.

The firm, through parent company Anthem Inc., offers its employees tuition assistance, flexible spending account, medical/dental/vision coverage, a 401(k) plan, an employee stock purchase plan, life insurance and long-term disability.

FINANCIAL DATA: *Note: Data for latest year may not have been available at press time.*

In U.S. $	2017	2016	2015	2014	2013	2012
Revenue						
R&D Expense						
Operating Income						
Operating Margin %						
SGA Expense						
Net Income						
Operating Cash Flow						
Capital Expenditure						
EBITDA						
Return on Assets %						
Return on Equity %						
Debt to Equity						

CONTACT INFORMATION:

Phone: 805-557-6655 Fax: 805-557-6872
Toll-Free: 800-393-6130
Address: P.O. Box 272540, Chico, CA 95927-2540 United States

STOCK TICKER/OTHER:

Stock Ticker: Subsidiary
Exchange:
Employees: 5,000
Fiscal Year Ends: 12/31
Parent Company: Anthem Inc

SALARIES/BONUSES:

Top Exec. Salary: $ Bonus: $
Second Exec. Salary: $ Bonus: $

OTHER THOUGHTS:

Estimated Female Officers or Directors: 2
Hot Spot for Advancement for Women/Minorities: Y

Blue Cross of Idaho

www.bcidaho.com

NAIC Code: 524,114

TYPES OF BUSINESS:

Insurance-Medical & Health, HMOs & PPOs
Dental & Vision Insurance
Life Insurance
Health Savings Accounts

BRANDS/DIVISIONS/AFFILIATES:

Bronze
Silver
Gold
True Blue
Secure Blue
Deductible Dental
Incentive Dental
HealthySmiles

CONTACTS: *Note: Officers with more than one job title may be intentionally listed here more than once.*

Charlene Maher, CEO
Zelda Geyer-Sylvia, Pres.
Steve Tobiason, General Counsel
Laurie Heyer, Sr. VP-Oper.
Debra M. Henry, Sr. VP-Organizational Dev.
Rex Warwick, VP-Sales
David J. Hutchins, VP-Actuarial Svcs. & Underwriting
Drew S. Forney, VP-Benefits Mgmt. & Member Svcs.
Jeanie Phillips, VP-Medicare & Medicaid Programs
Jo Anne Stringfield, Chmn.

GROWTH PLANS/SPECIAL FEATURES:

Blue Cross of Idaho (BCI) is a nonprofit health insurer that provides insurance to Idaho residents through six plan options: bronze plans, silver plans, gold plans, platinum plans, short-term PPO and catastrophic plans. For employers that provide coverage to their employees, Blue Cross offers three plans: Bronze, which covers about 60% of a year's medical costs; Silver, covering 70%; and Gold, covering 80%.. These programs have both small group (2-50 employees) and large group (51 and over) options. Additionally, BCI offers Medicare Advantage plans, including True Blue, an HMO; Secure Blue, a PPO; and True Blue HMO SNP, for those enrolled in both Medicare and Idaho Medicaid. Beyond health insurance, the company has several group dental plans: Deductible Dental, a service for basic and preventative care; Incentive Dental, which rewards employees for regular dental service; Preferred Dental, which gives employees flexible options; and Voluntary Dental, which provides optional coverage. The firm also offers an individual dental plan, HealthySmiles, which is a flexible PPO network service. Customers can enroll in value-added services through the firm's discount programs, which offer discounted rates for fitness club memberships, hearing and vision services, natural medicine and orthodontia rate reductions.

BCI offers its employees medical, dental, vision, pharmacy and life insurance; disability coverage; flexible spending accounts; an employee assistance program; a 401(k) or Roth 401(k); a retirement plan; paid time off; paid holidays; an onsite fitness center; education assistance program; and merit increases.

FINANCIAL DATA: *Note: Data for latest year may not have been available at press time.*

In U.S. $	2017	2016	2015	2014	2013	2012
Revenue	2,147,481,000	2,090,508,000	1,985,982,600	1,886,683,470		
R&D Expense						
Operating Income						
Operating Margin %						
SGA Expense						
Net Income	79,835,000	11,019,000				
Operating Cash Flow						
Capital Expenditure						
EBITDA						
Return on Assets %						
Return on Equity %						
Debt to Equity						

CONTACT INFORMATION:

Phone: 208-345-4550 Fax: 208-331-7311
Toll-Free: 800-274-4018
Address: 3000 E. Pine Ave., Meridian, ID 83642 United States

STOCK TICKER/OTHER:

Stock Ticker: Nonprofit
Employees: 995
Parent Company:
Exchange:
Fiscal Year Ends: 12/31

SALARIES/BONUSES:

Top Exec. Salary: $ Bonus: $
Second Exec. Salary: $ Bonus: $

OTHER THOUGHTS:

Estimated Female Officers or Directors: 9
Hot Spot for Advancement for Women/Minorities: Y

Blue Shield of California

www.blueshieldca.com

NAIC Code: 524,114

TYPES OF BUSINESS:

Insurance-Medical & Health, HMOs & PPOs
Managed Care
Life Insurance
Dental Insurance

BRANDS/DIVISIONS/AFFILIATES:

BSC Life & Health Insurance Company
Blue Shield of California Foundation

CONTACTS: *Note: Officers with more than one job title may be intentionally listed here more than once.*

Paul Markovich, CEO
Paul Markovich, Pres.
Michael Murray, CFO
Jeff Robertson, Sr. VP
Mary O'Hara, Chief Human Resources Officer
Marcus Thygeson, Chief Health Officer
Michael Mathias, CIO
Seth A. Jacobs, General Counsel
Steve Shivinsky, VP-Corp. Comm.
Tom Brophy, VP-Finance & Treas. Svcs.
Ed Cymerys, Chief Actuary
Juan Davila, Exec. VP-Health Care Quality & Affordability
Rob Geyer, Sr. VP-Customer Quality
Kirsten Gorsuch, Sr. VP-External Affairs
Doug Busch, Chmn.

GROWTH PLANS/SPECIAL FEATURES:

Blue Shield of California (BSC) is a nonprofit mutual benefit corporation. BSC is a Blue Cross Blue Shield Association member servicing just shy of 4 million members. The firm offers insurance packages including health maintenance organizations (HMOs), and preferred provider organizations (PPOs) and dental and Medicare supplemental through its offices in California. BSC works with HMO physicians and specialists, PPO physicians and specialists, HMO hospitals and PPO hospitals. The company also offers executive medical reimbursement, life and vision insurance and short-term health plans through Blue Shield of California Life & Health Insurance Company (Blue Shield Life). The Blue Shield of California Foundation provides charitable contributions and conducts research and supports programs with an emphasis on domestic violence prevention and medical technology assessments. BSC also offers plans for self-employed California workers not covered by employer-sponsored health plans, as well as low cost PPO plans for individuals. The company offers an enhanced small group dental benefit for pregnant women to reduce risks of periodontal disease and pregnancy gingivitis and is expanding dental coverage options with four new dental PPO plans for small groups.

The firm offers employees medical, dental and vision coverage; life insurance; disability insurance; tuition reimbursement; flexible spending accounts; discounts on entertainment and chiropractic and massage therapy; income protection benefits; a 401(k) savings plan; and a pension.

FINANCIAL DATA: *Note: Data for latest year may not have been available at press time.*

In U.S. $	2017	2016	2015	2014	2013	2012
Revenue	17,684,000,000	17,598,000,000	14,836,000,000	13,349,000,000	11,000,000,000	10,500,000,000
R&D Expense						
Operating Income						
Operating Margin %						
SGA Expense						
Net Income	296,000,000	67,000,000	115,000,000	162,000,000	171,000,000	500,000,000
Operating Cash Flow						
Capital Expenditure						
EBITDA						
Return on Assets %						
Return on Equity %						
Debt to Equity						

CONTACT INFORMATION:

Phone: 415-229-5000 Fax: 800-329-2742
Toll-Free: 888-800-2742
Address: 315 Montgomery St., San Francisco, CA 94104 United States

STOCK TICKER/OTHER:

Stock Ticker: Nonprofit
Employees: 6,800
Parent Company:
Exchange:
Fiscal Year Ends: 12/31

SALARIES/BONUSES:

Top Exec. Salary: $ Bonus: $
Second Exec. Salary: $ Bonus: $

OTHER THOUGHTS:

Estimated Female Officers or Directors: 14
Hot Spot for Advancement for Women/Minorities: Y

BlueCross BlueShield of Tennessee Inc

www.bcbst.com

NAIC Code: 524,114

TYPES OF BUSINESS:

Insurance-Medical & Health, HMOs & PPOs
Health & Disease Management

BRANDS/DIVISIONS/AFFILIATES:

Blue Cross Blue Shield Association

CONTACTS:

Note: Officers with more than one job title may be intentionally listed here more than once.

J.D. Hickey, CEO
Inga Himelright, Chief Medical Officer
Michael Lawley, VP-Tech.
Bob Worthington, Chief Strategy Officer
Roy Vaughn, VP-Corp. Comm.
Steven Coulter, Pres., Gov't Bus. & Emerging Markets
Sherri Zink, VP-Medical Informatics

GROWTH PLANS/SPECIAL FEATURES:

BlueCross BlueShield of Tennessee, Inc. (BCBST) is one of the largest health benefits companies in Tennessee. As part of the nationwide Blue Cross Blue Shield Association, it offers customers the full range of Blue Cross and Blue Shield insurance products. BCBST serves over 3.5 million members and provides benefits to more than 11,000 employer groups. Plans include individual health plans, group plans, dental plans, vision plans and Medicare coverage. The firm's website offers links to locate doctors, hospitals and pharmacies; price a drug; read about claims and coverage; getting fit and living healthy; food and nutrition; health conditions; and pregnancy/birthing.

The firm offers employees health, dental, vision and life insurance; short- and long-term disability coverage; long-term care; domestic partner benefits; a health savings plan; flexible spending accounts; health coaching; biometric screenings and personal health analysis; flu shots; onsite fitness centers; employee assistance program; paid time-off; a 401(k) matching plan; company-funded retirement program; financial planning classes; tuition reimbursement for college-level coursework; corporate incentive programs; employee discounts; and access to a credit union.

FINANCIAL DATA:

Note: Data for latest year may not have been available at press time.

In U.S. $	2017	2016	2015	2014	2013	2012
Revenue	7,770,000,000	7,400,000,000	7,273,097,000	6,720,921,000	5,836,110,000	5,603,230,000
R&D Expense						
Operating Income						
Operating Margin %						
SGA Expense						
Net Income	427,000,000	118,000,000	6,028,000	199,721,000	256,195,000	221,497,000
Operating Cash Flow						
Capital Expenditure						
EBITDA						
Return on Assets %						
Return on Equity %						
Debt to Equity						

CONTACT INFORMATION:

Phone: 423-755-5600 Fax:
Toll-Free: 800-565-9140
Address: 1 Cameron Hill Cir., Chattanooga, TN 37402 United States

STOCK TICKER/OTHER:

Stock Ticker: Nonprofit
Employees: 6,082
Parent Company:
Exchange:
Fiscal Year Ends: 12/31

SALARIES/BONUSES:

Top Exec. Salary: $ Bonus: $
Second Exec. Salary: $ Bonus: $

OTHER THOUGHTS:

Estimated Female Officers or Directors: 3
Hot Spot for Advancement for Women/Minorities: Y

Bon Secours Health System Inc

www.bshsi.com

NAIC Code: 622,110

TYPES OF BUSINESS:

General Medical and Surgical Hospitals
Assisted Living Facilities
Psychiatric Facilities
Hospice Care

BRANDS/DIVISIONS/AFFILIATES:

Bon Secours Ministries
Bon Secours Baltimore Health System
Urban Medical Institute
Bon Secours New York Health System
Bon Secours Charity Health System
Bon Secours St Francis Health System
Roper St Francis Healthcare System
Bon Secours Hampton Roads Health System

CONTACTS: *Note: Officers with more than one job title may be intentionally listed here more than once.*

Richard J. Statuto, CEO
Richard J. Statuto, Pres.
Janice Burnett, CFO
Peter J. Bernard, CEO-Bon Secours Virginia Health System
Terence O'Brien, CEO-Bon Secours Charity Health System
Michael K. Kerner, CEO-Bon Secours Hampton Roads Heath System
Kevin Halter, CEO-Bon Secours Kentucky Health System

GROWTH PLANS/SPECIAL FEATURES:

Bon Secours Health System, Inc. (BSHSI) is a Catholic healthcare ministry operated by of Bon Secours Ministries. Formed in 1983, the BSHSI system includes 19 acute-care hospitals, 14 home care and hospice services, five nursing care facilities, four assisted living facilities and one psychiatric hospital. Its facilities consist of regional health systems in New York, Maryland, Virginia, Kentucky, South Carolina and Florida. In addition to providing traditional hospital care, these systems provide specialized services depending on the needs of the communities in which its facilities are located. The Bon Secours Baltimore Health System, with its Urban Medical Institute, addresses the economic needs of patients in high-need, urban areas. The Bon Secours New York Health System specializes in caring for elderly, homebound patients. The Bon Secours Charity Health System is a leader in offering grief counseling and healing to those who have lost unborn/newborn children. The Bon Secours St. Francis Health System offers oral healthcare to low-income and uninsured individuals. The Roper St. Francis Healthcare System is a specialist in HIV/AIDS care. The Bon Secours Hampton Roads Health System focuses on fostering healthy childhood development, and the Bon Secours Richmond Health System is an asthma specialist. The Bon Secours Kentucky Health System offers specialized orthopedic care through its Human Motion OrthoCare unit. In February 2018, the hospital system agreed to merge with the Cincinnati based, nonprofit hospital system, Mercy Health. The merger of the two Catholic healthcare ministries would create a hospital system with 43 hospitals in seven states. The transaction was expected to close by year's end.

BSHSI offers its employees medical, prescription, dental, vision, life and disability coverage; a retirement plan; tuition reimbursement account; wellness incentives; paid time off; and a flexible spending account.

FINANCIAL DATA: *Note: Data for latest year may not have been available at press time.*

In U.S. $	2017	2016	2015	2014	2013	2012
Revenue	3,100,000,000	3,300,000,000	3,500,000,000	3,500,000,000	3,400,000,000	3,400,000,000
R&D Expense						
Operating Income						
Operating Margin %						
SGA Expense						
Net Income		117,000,000	116,000,000	123,600,000	123,900,000	118,000,000
Operating Cash Flow						
Capital Expenditure						
EBITDA						
Return on Assets %						
Return on Equity %						
Debt to Equity						

CONTACT INFORMATION:

Phone: 410-442-5511 Fax: 410-442-1082
Toll-Free:
Address: 1505 Marriottsville Rd., Marriottsville, MD 21104 United States

STOCK TICKER/OTHER:

Stock Ticker: Nonprofit
Employees: 25,000
Parent Company:
Exchange:
Fiscal Year Ends: 08/31

SALARIES/BONUSES:

Top Exec. Salary: $ Bonus: $
Second Exec. Salary: $ Bonus: $

OTHER THOUGHTS:

Estimated Female Officers or Directors: 1
Hot Spot for Advancement for Women/Minorities: Y

Boston Scientific Corporation

www.bostonscientific.com

NAIC Code: 339,100

TYPES OF BUSINESS:

Supplies-Surgery
Interventional Medical Products
Catheters
Guide wires
Stents
Oncology Research

BRANDS/DIVISIONS/AFFILIATES:

Emcision Limited
Securus Medical Group Inc
nVision Medical Corporation

CONTACTS: *Note: Officers with more than one job title may be intentionally listed here more than once.*

Michael Mahoney, CEO
John Sorenson, Senior VP, Divisional
Daniel Brennan, CFO
Edward Mackey, Executive VP, Divisional
Ian Meredith, Executive VP
Joseph Fitzgerald, Executive VP
Michael Phalen, Executive VP
Kevin Ballinger, Executive VP
Desiree Ralls-Morrison, General Counsel
Arthur Butcher, President, Divisional
Jeffrey Mirviss, President, Divisional
David Pierce, President, Divisional
Maulik Nanavaty, President, Divisional
Warren Wang, President, Geographical
Eric Thepaut, President, Geographical
Wendy Carruthers, Senior VP, Divisional

GROWTH PLANS/SPECIAL FEATURES:

Boston Scientific Corporation is a global developer, manufacturer and marketer of medical devices used in a broad range of interventional medical specialties. The firm comprises seven core businesses organized into three segments: cardiovascular, rhythm management and MedSurg. The cardiovascular segment has two business units: the interventional cardiology business develops and manufactures technologies for diagnosing and treating coronary artery disease and other cardiovascular disorders, including structural heart conditions; and the peripheral interventions business develops and manufactures products to diagnose and treat peripheral arterial diseases, including a broad line of medical devices used in percutaneous transluminal angioplasty (PTA) and peripheral vascular diseases, as well as products to diagnose, treat and ease various forms of cancer. The rhythm management segment has two business units: the cardiac rhythm management business develops and manufactures a variety of implantable devices that monitor the heart and deliver electricity to treat cardiac abnormalities; and the electrophysiology business develops and manufactures less-invasive medical technologies used in the diagnosis and treatment of rate and rhythm disorders of the heart, including a broad portfolio of therapeutic and diagnostic catheters and a variety of equipment used in the electrophysiology lab. Last, the MedSurg segment has three business units: the endoscopy business develops and manufactures devices to diagnose and treat a range of gastrointestinal and pulmonary conditions with innovative, less-invasive technologies; the urology and pelvic health business develops and manufactures devices to treat various urological and pelvic conditions for both male and female anatomies; and the neuromodulation business develops and manufactures devices to treat various neurological movement disorders and manage chronic pain. In early-2018, Boston Scientific acquired EMcision Limited; Securus Medical Group, Inc.; and nVision Medical Corporation. It agreed to acquire NxThera.

The firm offers employees medical, dental, vision and life insurance; educational assistance; and flexible spending accounts.

FINANCIAL DATA: *Note: Data for latest year may not have been available at press time.*

In U.S. $	2017	2016	2015	2014	2013	2012
Revenue	9,048,001,000	8,386,000,000	7,477,000,000	7,380,000,000	7,143,000,000	7,249,000,000
R&D Expense	997,000,000	920,000,000	876,000,000	817,000,000	861,000,000	886,000,000
Operating Income	1,531,000,000	1,319,000,000	990,000,000	902,000,000	884,000,000	931,000,000
Operating Margin %	16.92%	15.72%	13.24%	12.22%	12.37%	12.84%
SGA Expense	3,294,000,000	3,099,000,000	2,873,000,000	2,902,000,000	2,674,000,000	2,535,000,000
Net Income	104,000,000	347,000,000	-239,000,000	-119,000,000	-121,000,000	-4,068,000,000
Operating Cash Flow	1,426,000,000	972,000,000	600,000,000	1,269,000,000	1,082,000,000	1,260,000,000
Capital Expenditure	319,000,000	376,000,000	247,000,000	259,000,000	245,000,000	226,000,000
EBITDA	2,006,000,000	1,225,000,000	403,000,000	432,000,000	790,000,000	-3,163,000,000
Return on Assets %	.56%	1.91%	-1.35%	-.70%	-.71%	-21.16%
Return on Equity %	1.51%	5.31%	-3.74%	-1.83%	-1.80%	-44.64%
Debt to Equity	0.54	0.80	0.89	0.59	0.64	0.61

CONTACT INFORMATION:

Phone: 508 683-4000 Fax: 508 647-2200
Toll-Free: 888-272-1001
Address: 300 Boston Scientific Way, Marlborough, MA 01752-1234 United States

STOCK TICKER/OTHER:

Stock Ticker: BSX
Employees: 27,000
Parent Company:
Exchange: NYS
Fiscal Year Ends: 12/31

SALARIES/BONUSES:

Top Exec. Salary: $1,179,452 Bonus: $
Second Exec. Salary: $652,998 Bonus: $

OTHER THOUGHTS:

Estimated Female Officers or Directors: 5
Hot Spot for Advancement for Women/Minorities: Y

Bristol-Myers Squibb Co

www.bms.com

NAIC Code: 325,412

TYPES OF BUSINESS:

Drugs-Diversified
Medical Imaging Products
Nutritional Products

BRANDS/DIVISIONS/AFFILIATES:

Opdivo
Eliquis
Orencia
Sprycel
Yervoy
Empliciti
Baraclude
Reyataz

CONTACTS: *Note: Officers with more than one job title may be intentionally listed here more than once.*

Giovanni Caforio, CEO
Charles Bancroft, CFO
Joseph Caldarella, Chief Accounting Officer
Paul von Autenried, Chief Information Officer
Thomas Lynch, Chief Scientific Officer
Murdo Gordon, Executive VP
Sandra Leung, General Counsel
Ann Judge, Other Executive Officer
Louis Schmukler, President, Divisional
John Elicker, Senior VP, Divisional

GROWTH PLANS/SPECIAL FEATURES:

Bristol-Myers Squibb Company (BMS) discovers, develops, licenses, manufactures, markets, distributes and sells pharmaceuticals and other healthcare-related products. The company manufactures drugs across multiple therapeutic classes, including: cardiovascular; virology, including immunodeficiency virus infection; oncology; and immunoscience. The firm's pharmaceutical products include chemically-synthesized drugs, or small molecules, and an increasing portion of products produced from biological processes typically involving recombinant DNA technology, or biologics. Small molecule drugs are typically administered orally in the form of a pill, although there are other drug delivery mechanisms that are also used. Biologics are typically administered to patients through injections or by intravenous infusion. BMS' approved indications include: Opdivo, for several anti-cancer indications; Eliquis, for stroke prevention in atrial fibrillation and the prevention and treatment of venous thromboembolism (VTE) disorders; Orencia, a fusion protein with novel immunosuppressive activity for adult patients with active rheumatoid arthritis and prostate specific antigen; Sprycel, a multi-targeted tyrosine kinase inhibitor for adults with Philadelphia chromosome-positive chronic myelogenous leukemia (CML); Yervoy, a monoclonal antibody for adults and pediatric patients with unresectable or metastatic melanoma; Empliciti, a humanized monoclonal antibody for multiple myeloma; Baraclude, a selective inhibitor of the hepatitis B virus; Sustiva, a non-nucleoside reverse transcriptase inhibitor for human immunodeficiency virus (HIV), as well as bulk efavirenz; Reyataz, a protease inhibitor for HIV; Daklinza, an oral small molecule NS5A replication complex inhibitor for hepatitis C virus (HCV); and Sunvepra, an oral small molecule NS3 protease inhibitor for HCV. 2017 revenues included 55% being derived from the U.S., 24% from Europe, 7% from Japan and 14% from other countries.

BMS offers employees medical and dental insurance; pension and 401(k) plans; short- and long-term disability coverage; travel accident insurance; an employee assistance plan; and adoption assistance.

FINANCIAL DATA: *Note: Data for latest year may not have been available at press time.*

In U.S. $	2017	2016	2015	2014	2013	2012
Revenue	20,776,000,000	19,427,000,000	16,560,000,000	15,879,000,000	16,385,000,000	17,621,000,000
R&D Expense	6,411,000,000	4,940,000,000	5,920,000,000	4,534,000,000	3,731,000,000	3,904,000,000
Operating Income	3,450,000,000	4,539,000,000	1,730,000,000	1,714,000,000	2,931,000,000	3,932,000,000
Operating Margin %	16.60%	23.36%	10.44%	10.79%	17.88%	22.31%
SGA Expense	4,849,000,000	5,002,000,000	5,001,000,000	5,699,000,000	5,104,000,000	5,175,000,000
Net Income	1,007,000,000	4,457,000,000	1,565,000,000	2,004,000,000	2,563,000,000	1,960,000,000
Operating Cash Flow	5,275,000,000	2,850,000,000	1,832,000,000	3,148,000,000	3,545,000,000	6,941,000,000
Capital Expenditure	1,055,000,000	1,215,000,000	820,000,000	526,000,000	537,000,000	548,000,000
EBITDA	6,116,000,000	6,464,000,000	2,637,000,000	3,051,000,000	3,853,000,000	3,203,000,000
Return on Assets %	2.99%	13.61%	4.77%	5.54%	6.88%	5.69%
Return on Equity %	7.21%	29.28%	10.74%	13.35%	17.81%	13.25%
Debt to Equity	0.59	0.35	0.45	0.48	0.52	0.48

CONTACT INFORMATION:

Phone: 212 546-4000 Fax: 212 546-4020
Toll-Free:
Address: 345 Park Ave., New York, NY 10154 United States

STOCK TICKER/OTHER:

Stock Ticker: BMY
Employees: 25,000
Parent Company:
Exchange: NYS
Fiscal Year Ends: 12/31

SALARIES/BONUSES:

Top Exec. Salary: $796,154 Bonus: $1,400,000
Second Exec. Salary: $1,587,500 Bonus: $

OTHER THOUGHTS:

Estimated Female Officers or Directors: 4
Hot Spot for Advancement for Women/Minorities: Y

British United Provident Association Limited (BUPA)

www.bupa.co.uk

NAIC Code: 524,114

TYPES OF BUSINESS:

Insurance-Medical & Health, HMOs & PPOs
Life & Disability Insurance
Long-Term Health Care
Hospitals, Clinics & Health Screening Centers
Travel Insurance
Child Care Services
Cosmetic Surgery

BRANDS/DIVISIONS/AFFILIATES:

Bupa Health Insurance
Bupa Centres
Bupa Dental Centres
Bupa Cromwell Hospital

CONTACTS: *Note: Officers with more than one job title may be intentionally listed here more than once.*

David Hynam, CEO
Charles Richardson, CFO
Paul Zollinger-Read, Chief Medical Officer
Theresa Heggie, Chief Strategy & Mktg. Dir.
Steve John, Corp. Affairs Dir.
Alison Platt, Managing Dir.-Int'l Dev. Markets
Robert Lang, Managing Dir.-Int'l Private Medical Insurance
Dean Holden, Managing Dir.-Australia & New Zealand
Inaki Ereno, Managing Dir.-Spain & Latin America

GROWTH PLANS/SPECIAL FEATURES:

British United Provident Association (Bupa) is a leading international healthcare company that provides service to over 31 million customers in in the U.K. and other countries. Bupa is one of the largest private health insurance companies in the U.K., both for individuals and corporations. Bupa Health Insurance provides medical insurance in the U.K., while Bupa International provides international health insurance, offering access to more than 7,500 hospitals and clinics worldwide. The company has care homes throughout the U.K., including long-term nursing, residential care, short-term respite care and specialist dementia care. Insurance is not required to stay in these care homes. Bupa Centres are located throughout the U.K., offering a range of health services such as physiotherapy and cosmetic treatment, or even guidance when physically training for a big event, recovering from an illness or desiring a checkup. Bupa Dental Centres offer a range of preventive and specialist treatments, including general dentistry, dental examinations, hygiene treatment and cosmetic dentistry. Bupa Cromwell Hospital is a 128-bed London hospital that provides patients with access to over 400 consultants, up-to-date technology and equipment. For businesses, Bupa offers healthcare and insurance solutions for those with two to more than 250 employees. Solutions include health insurance, business mental health, dental plans, travel plans, cash plans, flu vaccinations, employee assistance programs, health assessments and private general practitioner and nurse services. The company also offers a range of products for intermediates to offer their clients, whether looking for a health insurance product on behalf of an individual, for a company startup or a corporate client considering to offer health and wellbeing options for their employees. For health care professionals, Bupa's facilities, products, solutions and services are also available to them and their patients. Pay-as-you-go treatments are available to all.

FINANCIAL DATA: *Note: Data for latest year may not have been available at press time.*

In U.S. $	2017	2016	2015	2014	2013	2012
Revenue	16,459,300,000	14,345,049,146	12,817,392,334	12,750,942,157	11,848,394,849	10,920,171,904
R&D Expense						
Operating Income						
Operating Margin %						
SGA Expense						
Net Income	655,539,000	504,432,802	362,936,011	681,780,923	536,504,728	585,213,479
Operating Cash Flow						
Capital Expenditure						
EBITDA						
Return on Assets %						
Return on Equity %						
Debt to Equity						

CONTACT INFORMATION:

Phone: 44-20-7656-2000 Fax: 44-20-7656-2700
Toll-Free:
Address: 15-19 Bloomsbury Way, Bupa House, London, WC1A 2BA United Kingdom

STOCK TICKER/OTHER:

Stock Ticker: Private
Employees: 78,000
Parent Company:
Exchange:
Fiscal Year Ends: 12/31

SALARIES/BONUSES:

Top Exec. Salary: $ Bonus: $
Second Exec. Salary: $ Bonus: $

OTHER THOUGHTS:

Estimated Female Officers or Directors: 5
Hot Spot for Advancement for Women/Minorities: Y

Brookdale Senior Living Inc

www.brookdaleliving.com

NAIC Code: 623,310

TYPES OF BUSINESS:

Assisted Living Facilities
Retirement Communities
Assisted Living Communities
Continued Care Retirement Communities (CCRCs)
Managed Facilities

BRANDS/DIVISIONS/AFFILIATES:

CONTACTS:

Note: Officers with more than one job title may be intentionally listed here more than once.

Lucinda Baier, CEO
Teresa Sparks, CFO
Lee Wielansky, Chairman of the Board
Dawn Kussow, Chief Accounting Officer
Bryan Richardson, Chief Administrative Officer
Mary Patchett, Executive VP, Divisional
H. Kaestner, Executive VP, Divisional
George Hicks, Executive VP, Divisional
Cedric Coco, Executive VP
Jonathan Litt, Founder
Chad White, General Counsel

GROWTH PLANS/SPECIAL FEATURES:

Brookdale Senior Living, Inc. is one of the largest senior living facility operators in the U.S. It operates 1,023 owned, leased or managed senior living facilities in 46 states that can serve approximately 101,000 residents (as of December 2017). Brookdale operates independent living, assisted living and dementia-care communities, as well as continuing care retirement centers (CCRCs). The facilities strive to offer residents a home-like setting and typically feature assistance with daily living, multiple forms of therapy and various home health services. Brookdale offers a full spectrum of care options, including independent living, personalized assisted living, rehabilitation and skilled nursing. It operates memory care communities, which are freestanding assisted living communities designed for residents with Alzheimer's disease and other dementias. Through the firm's ancillary services programs, it also offers a range of home health, hospice and outpatient therapy services to residents of many Brookdale communities and to seniors living outside of Brookdale communities. The company maintains its own culinary arts institute, which offers a training ground for chefs and dining staff. Leased communities generated the largest share (46.9%) of 2017 revenues, followed by owned communities (39.5%), ancillary services (11.6%) and communities Brookdale operates on behalf of third parties or unconsolidated ventures (2%). Brookdale generated 82.1% of 2017 revenue from private pay customers, with the remainder from government reimbursement programs (primarily Medicare).

FINANCIAL DATA:

Note: Data for latest year may not have been available at press time.

In U.S. $	2017	2016	2015	2014	2013	2012
Revenue	4,747,116,000	4,976,980,000	4,960,608,000	3,831,706,000	2,891,966,000	2,770,085,000
R&D Expense						
Operating Income	176,586,000	232,535,000	-22,870,000	-7,964,000	144,179,000	99,015,000
Operating Margin %	3.71%	4.67%	-.46%	-.20%	4.98%	3.57%
SGA Expense	595,167,000	687,044,000	738,153,000	604,097,000	461,277,000	462,854,000
Net Income	-571,419,000	-404,397,000	-457,477,000	-148,990,000	-3,584,000	-65,645,000
Operating Cash Flow	366,664,000	365,732,000	292,366,000	242,652,000	366,121,000	290,969,000
Capital Expenditure	213,887,000	333,647,000	411,051,000	304,245,000	257,527,000	208,412,000
EBITDA	219,936,000	506,583,000	570,768,000	451,781,000	405,308,000	335,099,000
Return on Assets %	-6.76%	-4.19%	-4.44%	-1.95%	-.07%	-1.43%
Return on Equity %	-31.66%	-17.82%	-17.13%	-7.63%	-.35%	-6.42%
Debt to Equity	2.96	2.80	2.52	2.07	2.38	2.16

CONTACT INFORMATION:

Phone: 615 221-2250 Fax: 615 221-2289
Toll-Free: 866-785-9025
Address: 111 Westwood Place, Ste. 400, Brentwood, TN 37027 United States

STOCK TICKER/OTHER:

Stock Ticker: BKD
Employees: 77,600
Parent Company:
Exchange: NYS
Fiscal Year Ends: 12/31

SALARIES/BONUSES:

Top Exec. Salary: $950,000 Bonus: $
Second Exec. Salary: $550,000 Bonus: $

OTHER THOUGHTS:

Estimated Female Officers or Directors: 1
Hot Spot for Advancement for Women/Minorities:

Bruker Corporation

www.bruker.com

NAIC Code: 334,516

TYPES OF BUSINESS:

Scientific Equipment Manufacturing

BRANDS/DIVISIONS/AFFILIATES:

Bruker Scientific Instrument
Bruker Energy & Supercon Technologies
Active Spectrum Inc
Invivo Biotech Services GmbH
SCiLS GmbH
Luxendo
MERLIN Diagnostika GmbH
Sierra Sensors GmbH

CONTACTS:

Note: Officers with more than one job title may be intentionally listed here more than once.

Burkhard Prause, CEO, Subsidiary
Frank Laukien, CEO
Gerald Herman, CFO
Mark Munch, Executive VP
Juergen Srega, President, Divisional

GROWTH PLANS/SPECIAL FEATURES:

Bruker Corporation is a developer, manufacturer and marketer of proprietary life science and materials research systems/products. The firm serves clients involved in life science, pharmaceutical, nanotechnology, biotechnology and molecular diagnostics research. It also offers materials and chemical analysis for use in various industries and government applications. Bruker operates in two segments: Bruker Scientific Instrument (BSI) and Bruker Energy & Supercon Technologies (BEST). The BSI segment is further divided into three groups: Bruker BioSpin, Bruker CALID and Bruker Nano. Bruker BioSpin designs, manufactures and distributes life science tools based on magnetic resonance technology; and also manufactures and sells single and multiple modality systems using MRI (magnetic resonance imaging), PET (positron emission tomography), SPECT (single photon emission tomography), CT (computed tomography), MPI (magnetic particle imaging) and optical imaging technologies to preclinical markets. Bruker CALID designs, manufactures and distributes life science mass spectrometry (MS) instruments that can be integrated and used along with other sample preparation or chromatography instruments, which are both used in research and clinical diagnostic settings. Bruker Nano designs, manufactures and distributes advanced X-ray instruments that use electromagnetic radiation with extremely short wavelengths to determine the characteristics of matter and the three-dimensional structure of molecules, including a product portfolio that comprises instruments based on X-ray fluorescence spectroscopy, X-ray diffraction and X-ray micro computed tomography. The BEST segment purchases materials and components from suppliers used in the development of its products, such as semiconducting products, various accelerators and radio frequency couplers. Bruker's manufacturing facilities are located worldwide, including Switzerland, France, Germany and the U.S. In 2017, the firm acquired: Active Spectrum, Inc.; Invivo Biotech Services GmbH; SCiLS GmbH; MERLIN Diagnostika GmbH; and Luxendo. In 2018, Bruker acquired: JPK Instruments AG; the business of Lactotronic B.V.; Sierra Sensors GmbH; Hain Lifescience GmbH; and Anasys Instruments Corp.

FINANCIAL DATA:

Note: Data for latest year may not have been available at press time.

In U.S. $	2017	2016	2015	2014	2013	2012
Revenue	1,765,900,000	1,611,300,000	1,623,800,000	1,808,900,000	1,839,400,000	1,791,400,000
R&D Expense	162,700,000	149,000,000	145,700,000	174,200,000	190,500,000	195,300,000
Operating Income	230,000,000	196,800,000	161,400,000	116,900,000	170,700,000	182,200,000
Operating Margin %	13.02%	12.21%	9.31%	6.46%	9.28%	10.17%
SGA Expense	416,100,000	390,500,000	392,600,000	451,000,000	444,000,000	453,500,000
Net Income	78,600,000	153,600,000	101,600,000	56,700,000	80,100,000	77,500,000
Operating Cash Flow	154,400,000	130,800,000	229,200,000	114,300,000	145,000,000	133,100,000
Capital Expenditure	43,700,000	37,100,000	34,200,000	33,800,000	50,300,000	72,800,000
EBITDA	277,100,000	245,100,000	194,300,000	174,300,000	199,300,000	211,700,000
Return on Assets %	4.18%	8.67%	5.65%	2.94%	4.16%	4.34%
Return on Equity %	11.13%	21.74%	13.61%	7.03%	10.31%	11.67%
Debt to Equity	0.57	0.57	0.36	0.46	0.41	0.47

CONTACT INFORMATION:

Phone: 978 663-3660 Fax: 978 663-2471
Toll-Free:
Address: 40 Manning Rd., Billerica, MA 01821 United States

STOCK TICKER/OTHER:

Stock Ticker: BRKR Exchange: NAS
Employees: 6,000 Fiscal Year Ends: 12/31
Parent Company:

SALARIES/BONUSES:

Top Exec. Salary: $704,269 Bonus: $
Second Exec. Salary: $523,141 Bonus: $

OTHER THOUGHTS:

Estimated Female Officers or Directors: 1
Hot Spot for Advancement for Women/Minorities:

BTG plc

NAIC Code: 424,210

www.btgplc.com

TYPES OF BUSINESS:

Drugs and Druggists Sundries Merchant Wholesalers
Pharmaceutical Preparation Manufacturing

BRANDS/DIVISIONS/AFFILIATES:

CONTACTS:

Note: Officers with more than one job title may be intentionally listed here more than once.

Louise Makin, CEO
Duncan Kennedy, CFO
Yvonne Rogers, Head-Human Resources
Guenter R. Janhofer, Chief Medical Officer
Anthony Higham, Head-Mfg.
Paul Mussenden, General Counsel
Guenter R. Janhofer, Head-Dev.
Duncan Kennedy, Group Dir.-Finance
Peter Stratford, CTO-Interventional Medicine
John Sylvester, Chief Commercial Officer-Interventional Medicine
Garry Watts, Chmn.
Matthew Gantz, Exec. VP-U.S.
Anthony Higham, Head-Supply

GROWTH PLANS/SPECIAL FEATURES:

BTG plc is involved in the development and commercialization of life science technologies. The firm in-licenses, develops and commercializes pharmaceuticals, and has a broad pipeline of research and development programs targeting oncology, interventional pulmonology and interventional vascular. The firm manufactures and sells pharmaceutical products and potential drugs for use in the treatment of human diseases. BTG's four reportable segments are specialty pharmaceuticals, interventional medicine, licensed products and named patient supplies. The specialty pharmaceutical segment focuses on antidote products used in emergency rooms and intensive care units. It provides antidotes to counteract snake venom and the toxicity associated with some heart and cancer medications. The interventional medicine segment aims to pinpoint the problem inside the body and deliver treatments in target areas. This division's products include treatments for cancer, severe emphysema, severe blood clots and varicose veins. The licensed products segment earns revenue from selling BTG products, and earns royalties on products sold by the company's partners. Last, the named patient supplies segment enables healthcare professionals, on behalf of their patients, to access medicines approved or nearing approval in other countries before marketing authorization has been granted in their home country. BTG's radiopaque imageable bead technology is used for the embolization of hypervascular tumors and arteriovenous malformations; its imageable microscopic beads are being experimented to guide an effective dose of anticancer drug vandetanib to tumors in the liver; and the EKOS advanced endovascular system is portable, comprises a touch screen user interface as well as increased power to control two catheters. The firm has operations worldwide, including North America, Europe, Asia and Australia.

The firm offers employees a competitive compensation package including an employee share option plan.

FINANCIAL DATA:

Note: Data for latest year may not have been available at press time.

In U.S. $	2017	2016	2015	2014	2013	2012
Revenue	725,549,952	569,121,152	467,760,384	369,451,840	297,214,784	250,540,496
R&D Expense						
Operating Income						
Operating Margin %						
SGA Expense						
Net Income	42,731,780	76,942,640	42,731,780	30,904,234	20,857,178	18,567,976
Operating Cash Flow						
Capital Expenditure						
EBITDA						
Return on Assets %						
Return on Equity %						
Debt to Equity						

CONTACT INFORMATION:

Phone: 44 2075750000 Fax: 44 2075750010
Toll-Free:
Address: 5 Fleet Pl., London, EC4M 7RD United Kingdom

STOCK TICKER/OTHER:

Stock Ticker: BTGGF
Exchange: PINX
Employees: 1,631
Fiscal Year Ends: 03/31
Parent Company:

SALARIES/BONUSES:

Top Exec. Salary: $ Bonus: $
Second Exec. Salary: $ Bonus: $

OTHER THOUGHTS:

Estimated Female Officers or Directors: 3
Hot Spot for Advancement for Women/Minorities: Y

Cambia Health Solutions Inc

www.cambiahealth.com

NAIC Code: 524,114

TYPES OF BUSINESS:

Insurance-Medical & Health, HMOs & PPOs
Life Insurance
Disability Insurance

BRANDS/DIVISIONS/AFFILIATES:

Hubbub
Asuris Northwest Health
HealthSparq
LifeMap
MedSavvy
Cambia Health Foundation
Cambia Grove
Echo Health Ventures

CONTACTS: *Note: Officers with more than one job title may be intentionally listed here more than once.*

Mark B. Ganz, CEO
Jared L. Short, COO
Vince Price, Exec. VP
Carol Kruse, Sr. VP
Mark Stimpson, Sr. VP-Human Resources
Richard Popiel, Exec. VP-Health Care Svcs.
Laurent Rotival, CIO
Scott Power, Sr. VP-Health Insurance Operations
Jonathan Hensley, Pres., Regence BlueShield of Washington
Jared L. Short, Pres., Health Insurance Svcs.
Scott Kreiling, Pres., Regence BlueShield of Idaho
Jennifer Danielson, Pres., Regence BlueCross BlueShield of Utah

GROWTH PLANS/SPECIAL FEATURES:

Cambia Health Solutions, Inc. is a nonprofit health solutions company comprised of more than 20 companies in the health industry. The organization's companies provide health solutions and health insurance options to businesses, families and individuals in select U.S. states. Cambia's group of companies include: Hubbub, a technology-driven wellness solution which aims to inspire employees to exercise and live healthy lives; Asuris Northwest Health, a community-based, nonprofit health plan which serves residents in eastern Washington; HealthSparq, which provides healthcare solutions for health plans, employers and employees; LifeMap, a provider of ancillary benefits plans offering financial protection; MedSavvy, which provides online transparency tools and reviews to find the most effective medication at the lowest cost; Cambia Health Foundation, which utilizes a strategic philanthropy for palliative care and for improving the experience of individuals with serious illnesses; Cambia Grove, an innovation center in Seattle for its regional health care community to connect with like-minded innovators and solve problems; Echo Health Ventures, an investment firm engaged in building and growing healthcare companies; BridgeSpan Health, which offers medical coverage, member benefits/discounts, a 24/7 nurse line and health coaches; Regional Health Plans, which serves members in Oregon, Washington, Idaho and Utah, with a focus on affordable, high-quality care; and Healthcare Management Administrators (HMA), a leading administrator of health plans for employers who choose to self-fund their health care. Other investments include GNS Healthcare, True Link, LifeImage, TytoCare, MPulse, MDsave, Circulation, Phreesia, abacus insights, Avizia, Livongo, springbuk, UpFront, AccessOne, Pokitdok, Octave Health, CareMerge, Maxwell Health and Wildflower Health.

Cambia offers employees medical, dental, life, AD&D and short/long-term disability insurance coverage; 401(k); and various employee assistance programs.

FINANCIAL DATA: *Note: Data for latest year may not have been available at press time.*

In U.S. $	2017	2016	2015	2014	2013	2012
Revenue	9,500,000,000	9,000,000,000	8,800,000,000	8,400,000,000		
R&D Expense						
Operating Income						
Operating Margin %						
SGA Expense						
Net Income						
Operating Cash Flow						
Capital Expenditure						
EBITDA						
Return on Assets %						
Return on Equity %						
Debt to Equity						

CONTACT INFORMATION:

Phone: 503-225-5221 Fax: 503-225-5274
Toll-Free: 800-452-7278
Address: 100 SW Market St., Portland, OR 97201 United States

STOCK TICKER/OTHER:

Stock Ticker: Nonprofit
Employees: 4,900
Parent Company:
Exchange:
Fiscal Year Ends: 12/31

SALARIES/BONUSES:

Top Exec. Salary: $ Bonus: $
Second Exec. Salary: $ Bonus: $

OTHER THOUGHTS:

Estimated Female Officers or Directors: 1
Hot Spot for Advancement for Women/Minorities: Y

Cancer Treatment Centers of America Inc (CTCA)

www.cancercenter.com

NAIC Code: 622,110

TYPES OF BUSINESS:

General Medical and Surgical Hospitals
Cancer Treatment

BRANDS/DIVISIONS/AFFILIATES:

GROWTH PLANS/SPECIAL FEATURES:

Cancer Treatment Centers of America (CTCA) operates a network of fully-accredited cancer hospitals and offers advanced technology and a personalized approach to effectively fight cancer. Each hospital provides state-of-the-art cancer treatment by a team of oncologists, surgeons and other health experts that offer cancer treatments as well as evidence-informed supportive therapies that target cancer-related side effects. The comprehensive services are delivered under one roof. CTCA is made up of five hospitals and treats over 125 different types of cancers, including breast, lung, prostate, colorectal, melanoma, throat, cervical, ovarian, pancreatic and lymphomas. The hospitals are located in Atlanta, Georgia; Chicago, Illinois; Philadelphia, Pennsylvania; Phoenix, Arizona; and Tulsa, Oklahoma. Outpatient care centers are located in Chicago, Phoenix and Scottsdale.

CONTACTS: *Note: Officers with more than one job title may be intentionally listed here more than once.*

Rajesh K. Garg, CEO
Adesh Ramchandran, Chief Enterprise Operations Officer
Ben Seib, Interim CFO
Richard Stephenson, Chmn.

FINANCIAL DATA: *Note: Data for latest year may not have been available at press time.*

In U.S. $	2017	2016	2015	2014	2013	2012
Revenue	5,250,000,000	5,000,000,000	4,415,000,000	4,130,000,000	4,000,000,000	3,850,000,000
R&D Expense						
Operating Income						
Operating Margin %						
SGA Expense						
Net Income						
Operating Cash Flow						
Capital Expenditure						
EBITDA						
Return on Assets %						
Return on Equity %						
Debt to Equity						

CONTACT INFORMATION:

Phone: 844-278-2477 Fax:
Toll-Free: 800-615-3055
Address: 5900 Broken Sound Pkwy. NW, Boca Raton, FL 33487 United States

STOCK TICKER/OTHER:

Stock Ticker: Private
Employees:
Parent Company:
Exchange:
Fiscal Year Ends:

SALARIES/BONUSES:

Top Exec. Salary: $ Bonus: $
Second Exec. Salary: $ Bonus: $

OTHER THOUGHTS:

Estimated Female Officers or Directors:
Hot Spot for Advancement for Women/Minorities:

Cantel Medical Corporation

www.cantelmedical.com

NAIC Code: 339,100

TYPES OF BUSINESS:

Equipment-Disinfection & Disposable Equipment
Infection Control Products
Diagnostic Medical Equipment
Precision Instruments
Industrial Equipment
Water Treatment Equipment & Services
Maintenance Services
Dental Care Products

BRANDS/DIVISIONS/AFFILIATES:

Medivators Inc
Crosstex International Inc
Aexis Medical BVBA
Ecode Lanka

CONTACTS: *Note: Officers with more than one job title may be intentionally listed here more than once.*

Peter Clifford, CFO
Charles Diker, Chairman of the Board
Brian Capone, Chief Accounting Officer
George Fotiades, Director
Seth Yellin, Executive VP, Divisional
Eric Nodiff, General Counsel
Dottie Donnelly-Brienza, Other Executive Officer
Jorgen Hansen, President
Lawrence Conway, Senior VP, Divisional

GROWTH PLANS/SPECIAL FEATURES:

Cantel Medical Corporation provides products and services for the control and prevention of infection. Its operations consist of four primary segments: endoscopy, dialysis, water purification and filtration, and healthcare disposables. The endoscopy and dialysis segments are operated through Medivators, Inc., which develops, manufactures and markets disinfection and reprocessing systems and dialysate concentrates for renal dialysis; hollow fiber membrane filtration and separation technologies for medical applications; and medical device reprocessing systems, disinfectants, detergents and other supplies used to clean flexible endoscopes. The water purification and filtration segment designs, develops, manufactures, sells and installs water purification systems for medical, pharmaceutical and other bacteria controlled applications. This division also provides filtration/separation and disinfectant technologies to the medical and life science markets through a worldwide distributor network. Products and services include dialysis water purification systems, bicarbonate systems, hollow fiber filters and other filtration and separation products, liquid disinfectants, cold sterilization products, dry fog products and room temperature sterilizers. The healthcare disposables segment, operated through Crosstex International, Inc., produces single-use infection control products primarily for the dental market, such as face masks, towels and bibs, tray covers, saliva ejectors, germicidal wipes, plastic cups, sterilization pouches and disinfectants. During 2018, Cantel acquired Aexis Medical BVBA and its affiliate, Ecode Lanka, which specialize in advanced software solutions that track and monitor instrument reprocessing workflows in the hospital; and acquired Stericycle, Inc.'s controlled environment solutions business for $17 million.

FINANCIAL DATA: *Note: Data for latest year may not have been available at press time.*

In U.S. $	2017	2016	2015	2014	2013	2012
Revenue	770,157,000	664,755,000	565,004,000	488,749,000	425,026,000	386,490,000
R&D Expense	18,367,000	15,410,000	14,022,000	10,813,000	9,320,000	9,254,000
Operating Income	110,410,000	97,251,000	80,761,000	70,928,000	63,188,000	52,124,000
Operating Margin %	14.33%	14.62%	14.29%	14.51%	14.86%	13.48%
SGA Expense	238,383,000	196,525,000	158,684,000	131,558,000	110,968,000	102,789,000
Net Income	71,378,000	59,953,000	47,953,000	43,265,000	39,239,000	31,337,000
Operating Cash Flow	108,193,000	80,268,000	59,070,000	64,272,000	51,494,000	50,580,000
Capital Expenditure	27,065,000	18,889,000	12,760,000	13,541,000	6,745,000	5,502,000
EBITDA	143,988,000	122,423,000	102,580,000	89,877,000	80,512,000	67,526,000
Return on Assets %	9.58%	9.30%	8.48%	8.33%	8.37%	8.28%
Return on Equity %	14.50%	13.81%	12.31%	12.43%	12.94%	12.28%
Debt to Equity	0.24	0.25	0.19	0.22	0.26	0.28

CONTACT INFORMATION:

Phone: 973 890-7220 Fax: 973 890-7270
Toll-Free:
Address: 150 Clove Rd., 9/Fl, Little Falls, NJ 07424 United States

STOCK TICKER/OTHER:

Stock Ticker: CMD
Employees: 2,337
Parent Company:
Exchange: NYS
Fiscal Year Ends: 07/31

SALARIES/BONUSES:

Top Exec. Salary: $600,000 Bonus: $
Second Exec. Salary: $386,817 Bonus: $

OTHER THOUGHTS:

Estimated Female Officers or Directors: 1
Hot Spot for Advancement for Women/Minorities:

Capital BlueCross

www.capbluecross.com

NAIC Code: 524,114

TYPES OF BUSINESS:

Insurance-Medical & Health, HMOs & PPOs
Administrative Services
Life Insurance

BRANDS/DIVISIONS/AFFILIATES:

Capital Advantage Insurance Company
Capital Advantage Assurance Company
Keystone Health Plan Central

CONTACTS: *Note: Officers with more than one job title may be intentionally listed here more than once.*

Gary St. Hilaire, CEO
Gary St. Hilaire, Pres.
Harvey Littman, CFO
Donna K. Lencki, CMO
Steven J. Krupinski, Sr. VP-Human Resources
Brian L. Sullivan, General Counsel
Aji M. Abraham, VP-Bus. Dev.
David B. Skerpon, VP-Retail Strategies & Brand Mgmt.
William B. Reineberg, Chief Internal Auditor
Anne Baum, VP-Lehigh Valley
Sherry E. Baskin, Corp. Sec.
Jennifer Chambers, Chief Medical Officer
Glenn Heisey, Sr. VP-Strategy & Network
Tracy Onorofsky, Sr. VP-Commercial Group Sales

GROWTH PLANS/SPECIAL FEATURES:

Capital BlueCross provides health insurance and related services to 1.3 million members throughout 21 counties in central Pennsylvania and the Lehigh Valley. The company offers a comprehensive range of products for groups and individuals, including a choice of several PPOs and dental, vision and pharmacy benefit programs. The firm also offers the Children's Health Insurance Program (CHIP), a low-cost or free health insurance program for uninsured children and adolescents who do not qualify for medical assistance through the Department of Public Welfare and who meet certain guidelines with respect to family size and income. Wholly-owned subsidiaries Capital Advantage Insurance Company and Capital Advantage Assurance Company offer comprehensive health coverage alone or in combination with Capital BlueCross. Wholly-owned Keystone Health Plan Central administers Capital BlueCross' family health plans under the brand KHP Central. Other offerings include pet heath, trip protection (for when plans change) and travel coverage (while traveling) as well as hearing discounts.

The firm offers employees medical, dental and vision insurance; disability coverage; life insurance; travel accident insurance; auto and homeowner's insurance; a 401(k) savings plan; flexible spending accounts; a retirement plan; credit union membership; an employee assistance program; and educational reimbursement.

FINANCIAL DATA: *Note: Data for latest year may not have been available at press time.*

In U.S. $	2017	2016	2015	2014	2013	2012
Revenue	3,815,700,000	3,634,000,000	3,530,000,000	3,426,162,000	3,350,000,000	3,200,000,000
R&D Expense						
Operating Income						
Operating Margin %						
SGA Expense						
Net Income						
Operating Cash Flow						
Capital Expenditure						
EBITDA						
Return on Assets %						
Return on Equity %						
Debt to Equity						

CONTACT INFORMATION:

Phone: 717-541-7000 Fax: 717-541-6915
Toll-Free: 800-962-2242
Address: 2500 Elmerton Ave., Harrisburg, PA 17177 United States

STOCK TICKER/OTHER:

Stock Ticker: Nonprofit
Employees: 1,850
Parent Company:
Exchange:
Fiscal Year Ends: 12/31

SALARIES/BONUSES:

Top Exec. Salary: $ Bonus: $
Second Exec. Salary: $ Bonus: $

OTHER THOUGHTS:

Estimated Female Officers or Directors: 11
Hot Spot for Advancement for Women/Minorities: Y

Capital Senior Living Corporation

www.capitalsenior.com

NAIC Code: 623,310

TYPES OF BUSINESS:

Assisted Living Facilities
Nursing Homes
Assisted Living Services
Home Care Services

BRANDS/DIVISIONS/AFFILIATES:

CONTACTS:
Note: Officers with more than one job title may be intentionally listed here more than once.

Lawrence Cohen, CEO
Carey Hendrickson, CFO
Brett Lee, COO
Michael Reid, Director
Kimberly Lody, Independent Director
Robert Hollister, Other Corporate Officer
Donald Beasley, Other Corporate Officer
David Beathard, Senior VP, Divisional
David Brickman, Senior VP
Gloria Holland, Vice President, Divisional
Christopher Lane, Vice President, Divisional
Kevin Wilbur, Vice President, Divisional
Joseph Solari, Vice President, Divisional
Glen Campbell, Vice President, Divisional

GROWTH PLANS/SPECIAL FEATURES:

Capital Senior Living Corporation is one of the nation's largest operators and developers of residential communities for seniors. The firm operates 129 communities in 23 states, including 83 senior housing communities that it owns and 46 that it leases. Its combined facilities can support 16,500 residents. Approximately 94.4% of the company's annual revenue is generated through private pay parties at these communities. The firm provides senior living services to the elderly in four categories of assistance: independent living, assisted living, continuing care retirement communities and home care services. Its independent living communities provide residents with daily meals, transportation, social and recreational activities, laundry, housekeeping and 24-hour staffing. The firm's assisted living communities, with residents that require additional assistance over independent residents, provide personal care services, such as walking, eating, personal hygiene and medication assistance; and special care services for residents with certain forms of dementia. The continuing care retirement communities provide traditional long-term care through 24-hour-per-day skilled nursing care by registered nurses. The company provides home care services to residents at one senior living community through its home care agency and through third-party providers at a majority of its senior living communities. Many of CSL's communities offer a continuum of care to meet its residents' needs as they change over time. This continuum of care, which integrates independent living, assisted living and home care, sustains residents' autonomy and independence based on their physical and mental abilities.

The firm offers employees medical and dental insurance, life insurance and a 401(k) plan.

FINANCIAL DATA:
Note: Data for latest year may not have been available at press time.

In U.S. $	2017	2016	2015	2014	2013	2012
Revenue	466,997,000	447,448,000	412,177,000	383,925,000	350,362,000	310,536,000
R&D Expense						
Operating Income	20,700,000	14,390,000	18,835,000	13,900,000	11,250,000	13,655,000
Operating Margin %	4.43%	3.21%	4.56%	3.62%	3.21%	4.39%
SGA Expense	87,688,000	97,034,000	90,397,000	89,326,000	87,633,000	78,716,000
Net Income	-44,168,000	-28,017,000	-14,284,000	-24,126,000	-16,504,000	-3,119,000
Operating Cash Flow	55,594,000	52,279,000	48,895,000	46,312,000	42,644,000	46,395,000
Capital Expenditure	39,959,000	62,371,000	42,430,000	18,742,000	13,562,000	12,302,000
EBITDA	73,998,000	75,023,000	75,365,000	57,341,000	56,260,000	49,002,000
Return on Assets %	-3.79%	-2.58%	-1.49%	-2.93%	-2.38%	-.56%
Return on Equity %	-44.76%	-22.17%	-10.31%	-16.13%	-10.10%	-1.84%
Debt to Equity	12.27	7.86	5.84	4.51	3.21	2.28

CONTACT INFORMATION:

Phone: 972-770-5600 Fax: 972 770-5666
Toll-Free:
Address: 14160 Dallas Pkwy., Ste. 300, Dallas, TX 75254 United States

STOCK TICKER/OTHER:

Stock Ticker: CSU
Exchange: NYS
Employees: 7,658
Fiscal Year Ends: 12/31
Parent Company:

SALARIES/BONUSES:

Top Exec. Salary: $772,712 Bonus: $
Second Exec. Salary: $327,913 Bonus: $131,165

OTHER THOUGHTS:

Estimated Female Officers or Directors: 2
Hot Spot for Advancement for Women/Minorities:

Cardinal Health Inc

www.cardinalhealth.com

NAIC Code: 424,210

TYPES OF BUSINESS:

Healthcare Products & Services
Supply Chain Services
Medical Products

BRANDS/DIVISIONS/AFFILIATES:

Cardinal.com
Cardinal Health at Home
NaviHealth

CONTACTS:
Note: Officers with more than one job title may be intentionally listed here more than once.

Jon Giacomin, CEO, Divisional
Michael Kaufmann, CEO
Jorge Gomez, CFO
George Barrett, Chairman of the Board
Stuart Laws, Chief Accounting Officer
Patricia Morrison, Chief Information Officer
Michele Holcomb, Executive VP, Divisional
Pamela Kimmet, Other Executive Officer
Craig Morford, Other Executive Officer

GROWTH PLANS/SPECIAL FEATURES:

Cardinal Health, Inc. is a provider of products and services that improve the safety and productivity of health care. The company operates in two segments: pharmaceuticals and medical products. The pharmaceutical segment distributes a broad line of branded and generic pharmaceutical products, specialty pharmaceutical, over-the-counter health care products and consumer products. It is also a full-service wholesale distributor to retail customers, hospitals and alternate care providers located throughout the U.S. In addition, this segment operates nuclear pharmacies and cyclotron facilities, provides pharmacy operations, medication therapy management and patient outcomes services to hospitals and other healthcare providers. The segment offers a broad range of support services including computerized order entry provided through Cardinal.com; generic sourcing programs; product movement, inventory and management reports; and consultation on store operations and merchandising. Through its medical products segment, the company distributes a broad range of medical, surgical and laboratory products to hospitals, ambulatory surgery centers, clinical laboratories, physician offices and other health care providers in the U.S. and Canada, and to patients in the home in the U.S. through its Cardinal Health at Home division. This segment also manufactures, sources and develops its own line of private brand medical and surgical products which include: single-use surgical drapes, gowns and apparel, exam and surgical gloves and fluid suction and collection systems; and manufactures extravascular closure devices. In early-2018, Cardinal Health sold its Cardinal Health China business to Shanghai Pharmaceuticals Holding Co., Ltd. That August, the firm sold 55% of its stake in NaviHealth to Clayton, Dubilier & Rice, and will retain a 45% interest in the business. NaviHealth manages post-acute care through value-based programs.

Employee benefits include medical, dental, vision short/long-term disability and life insurance; a 401(k); and various employee assistance programs.

FINANCIAL DATA:
Note: Data for latest year may not have been available at press time.

In U.S. $	2017	2016	2015	2014	2013	2012
Revenue	129,976,000,000	121,546,000,000	102,531,000,000	91,084,000,000	101,093,000,000	
R&D Expense						
Operating Income	2,242,000,000	2,436,000,000	2,191,000,000	1,910,000,000	1,888,000,000	
Operating Margin %	1.72%	2.00%	2.13%	2.09%	1.86%	
SGA Expense	3,775,000,000	3,648,000,000	3,240,000,000	3,028,000,000	2,875,000,000	
Net Income	1,288,000,000	1,427,000,000	1,215,000,000	1,166,000,000	334,000,000	
Operating Cash Flow	1,184,000,000	2,971,000,000	2,540,000,000	2,524,000,000	1,727,000,000	
Capital Expenditure	387,000,000	465,000,000	300,000,000	249,000,000	195,000,000	
EBITDA	2,959,000,000	3,077,000,000	2,642,000,000	2,369,000,000	2,285,000,000	
Return on Assets %	3.47%	4.44%	4.32%	4.49%	1.33%	
Return on Equity %	19.27%	22.27%	19.19%	18.84%	5.46%	
Debt to Equity	1.33	0.75	0.83	0.49	0.61	

CONTACT INFORMATION:

Phone: 614 757-5000 Fax:
Toll-Free: 800-234-8701
Address: 7000 Cardinal Pl., Dublin, OH 43017 United States

STOCK TICKER/OTHER:

Stock Ticker: CAH
Employees: 49,800
Parent Company:
Exchange: NYS
Fiscal Year Ends: 06/30

SALARIES/BONUSES:

Top Exec. Salary: $1,320,000 Bonus: $
Second Exec. Salary: $746,438 Bonus: $186,609

OTHER THOUGHTS:

Estimated Female Officers or Directors: 8
Hot Spot for Advancement for Women/Minorities: Y

CareFirst Inc

www.carefirst.com

NAIC Code: 524,114

TYPES OF BUSINESS:

Insurance-Medical & Health, HMOs & PPOs
Claims Processing
Administrative Services

BRANDS/DIVISIONS/AFFILIATES:

Group Hospitalization and Medical Services Inc
CareFirst of Maryland Inc
CareFirst BlueCross BlueShield
Service Benefit Plan Administrative Services Corp
Federal Employee Program Operations Center
Capital Area Services Company Inc

CONTACTS: *Note: Officers with more than one job title may be intentionally listed here more than once.*

Brian D. Pieninck, CEO
Chester Burrell, Pres.
G. Mark Chaney, CFO
Jon Shematek, Chief Medical Officer
John A. Picciotto, General Counsel
Kenny W. Kan, Chief Actuary
Kevin O'Neill, Sr. VP-Strategic Managed Care Initiatives
Fred. Plumb, Sr. VP-Federal Employee Program
Gwendolyn D. Skillern, Gen. Auditor
Stephen L. Waechter, Chmn.

GROWTH PLANS/SPECIAL FEATURES:

CareFirst, Inc. is one of the largest healthcare insurers in the Mid-Atlantic, with approximately 3.2 million members. CareFirst is the nonprofit parent company of Group Hospitalization and Medical Services, Inc. (GHMSI) and CareFirst of Maryland, Inc., which collectively do business as CareFirst BlueCross BlueShield. GHMSI's subsidiary Service Benefit Plan Administrative Services Corporation operates the Federal Employee Program (FEP) Operations Center, serving over 640,000 FEP members. The company also operates West Virginia-based subsidiary Capital Area Services Company, Inc. (CASCI), which annually processes over 5 million claims from federal government subscribers and dependents as part of FEP. CareFirst offers individual as well as corporate customer health plans such as individual and family medical plans, Medigap plans, prescription drug plans, dental plans and vision plans. More than 80% of healthcare providers in the firm's operating region participate in one or more of its provider networks. CareFirst has corporate office locations and licensed affiliates throughout Maryland, Washington, D.C. and Northern Virginia; and maintains regional offices in Annapolis, Frederick, Cumberland, Hagerstown, Easton and Salisbury, Maryland.

CareFirst offers its employees medical, dental, vision and prescription drug coverage; a 401(k) plan; paid holidays; college savings plans; short- and long-term disability; tuition reimbursement; paid time off; and flexible spending accounts.

FINANCIAL DATA: *Note: Data for latest year may not have been available at press time.*

In U.S. $	2017	2016	2015	2014	2013	2012
Revenue	8,800,000,000	8,800,000,000	8,600,000,000	7,800,000,000	7,600,000,000	8,518,951,000
R&D Expense						
Operating Income						
Operating Margin %						
SGA Expense						
Net Income	240,600,000	9,400,000	38,600,000		82,000,000	100,000,000
Operating Cash Flow						
Capital Expenditure						
EBITDA						
Return on Assets %						
Return on Equity %						
Debt to Equity						

CONTACT INFORMATION:

Phone: 410-581-3000 Fax:
Toll-Free:
Address: 1501 South Clinton St., Baltimore, MD 21224 United States

STOCK TICKER/OTHER:

Stock Ticker: Nonprofit
Exchange:
Employees: 5,000
Fiscal Year Ends: 12/31
Parent Company:

SALARIES/BONUSES:

Top Exec. Salary: $ Bonus: $
Second Exec. Salary: $ Bonus: $

OTHER THOUGHTS:

Estimated Female Officers or Directors: 18
Hot Spot for Advancement for Women/Minorities: Y

CareSpot Urgent Care

NAIC Code: 621,493

www.carespot.com

TYPES OF BUSINESS:

Freestanding Ambulatory Surgical and Emergency Centers
Urgent Care Centers

BRANDS/DIVISIONS/AFFILIATES:

Tenet Healthcare Corporation
United Surgical Partners International
MedPost Urgent Care
www.CareSpot.com

CONTACTS: *Note: Officers with more than one job title may be intentionally listed here more than once.*

Eric Enderle, CEO
Michael D. Klein, Pres.
Dan Murphy, CFO
Fran J. Coyne, VP-Sales
Susie Hardin, VP-Human Resources
Frank J. Campbell, Chief Medical Officer
Ben Goodman, VP-Mktg.
Jon Sundock, General Counsel
Clay Bittner, VP-Dev.
Fran J. Coyne, VP-Sales & Occupational Health Services

GROWTH PLANS/SPECIAL FEATURES:

CareSpot Urgent Care provides walk-in urgent care, health check and occupational health services through more than 100 locations in nine U.S. states. CareSpot is operated and managed together with MedPost Urgent Care, with both brands expanding together across the nation to provide immediate medical attention and treatment. Core service offerings include urgent care, wellness, in-house lab work and X-rays, seasonal care and occupational health. Appointments are never required, but are available online at www.CareSpot.com as well as through the CareSpot mobile app. Most locations are open 7 days a week, including weekends and holidays. Many common prescriptions can be filled at the center during visits (narcotics are not stocked). Electronic records systems provide each CareSpot location access to the same information so that patients can visit any location within a region. In addition, at most locations the firm is affiliated with a large hospital system, in which case records can be sent to primary care providers if they are associated with that system. CareSpot is owned by United Surgical Partners International, which itself is a division of Tenet Healthcare Corporation.

The firm offers its employees medical, dental, vision and prescription coverage; AD&D insurance; 401(k) retirement savings and Roth 401(k)s; flexible spending accounts; health savings account; and continuing medical education and tuition reimbursement.

FINANCIAL DATA: *Note: Data for latest year may not have been available at press time.*

In U.S. $	2017	2016	2015	2014	2013	2012
Revenue						
R&D Expense						
Operating Income						
Operating Margin %						
SGA Expense						
Net Income						
Operating Cash Flow						
Capital Expenditure						
EBITDA						
Return on Assets %						
Return on Equity %						
Debt to Equity						

CONTACT INFORMATION:

Phone: 904-223-2320 Fax: 904-223-3149
Toll-Free:
Address: 115 E. Park Dr., Ste. 300, Brentwood, TN 37027 United States

STOCK TICKER/OTHER:

Stock Ticker: Private
Employees: 552
Parent Company: United Surgical Partners International
Exchange:
Fiscal Year Ends:

SALARIES/BONUSES:

Top Exec. Salary: $ Bonus: $
Second Exec. Salary: $ Bonus: $

OTHER THOUGHTS:

Estimated Female Officers or Directors: 1
Hot Spot for Advancement for Women/Minorities:

Carl Zeiss Meditec AG

www.meditec.zeiss.com

NAIC Code: 423,450

TYPES OF BUSINESS:

Medical, Dental, and Hospital Equipment and Supplies Merchant Wholesalers

BRANDS/DIVISIONS/AFFILIATES:

Carl Zeiss AG
Swept-Source OCT
IOLMaster 700

CONTACTS: *Note: Officers with more than one job title may be intentionally listed here more than once.*

Ludwin Monz, CEO
Ludwin Monz, Pres.
Justus Felix Wehmer, CFO
Christian Muller, Manager-Legal & Taxes
Christian Muller, Manager-Investor Relations

GROWTH PLANS/SPECIAL FEATURES:

Carl Zeiss Meditec AG is a German supplier of medical technology. The firm offers complete diagnostic and treatment solutions for ophthalmic diseases; and in the field of microsurgery, provides innovative visualization solutions. For example, Meditec's U.S. FDA-approved SWEPT Source OCT (optical coherence tomography) posterior ocular imaging technology enables clinical researchers to open new frontiers of discovery in diseases affecting the retina; and IOLMaster 700, along with SWEPT Source OCT technology, enables professionals to directly measure the posterior corneal surface and to incorporate these measurements in classic intraocular lens (IOL) power calculation formulas. Its medical disciplines include ophthalmology, neurosurgery, plastic and reconstructive surgery, spine surgery, surgery of the ear/nose/throat, dentistry, gynecology and oncology. The firm is majority-owned by Carl Zeiss AG, and has subsidiaries worldwide, including the U.S. and Europe

FINANCIAL DATA: *Note: Data for latest year may not have been available at press time.*

In U.S. $	2017	2016	2015	2014	2013	2012
Revenue						
R&D Expense						
Operating Income						
Operating Margin %						
SGA Expense						
Net Income						
Operating Cash Flow						
Capital Expenditure						
EBITDA						
Return on Assets %						
Return on Equity %						
Debt to Equity						

CONTACT INFORMATION:

Phone: 49-3641220-0 Fax: 49-3641220-112
Toll-Free:
Address: Goeschwitzer Strasse 51-52, Jena, 07745 Germany

STOCK TICKER/OTHER:

Stock Ticker: CZMWF
Employees: 2,958
Parent Company: Carl Zeiss AG
Exchange: PINX
Fiscal Year Ends: 09/30

SALARIES/BONUSES:

Top Exec. Salary: $ Bonus: $
Second Exec. Salary: $ Bonus: $

OTHER THOUGHTS:

Estimated Female Officers or Directors:
Hot Spot for Advancement for Women/Minorities:

Castle Dental Centers Inc

www.castledental.com

NAIC Code: 621,210

TYPES OF BUSINESS:

Dental Practice Management

BRANDS/DIVISIONS/AFFILIATES:

Smile Brands Group Inc
Smiles for Everyone Foundation

CONTACTS:

Note: Officers with more than one job title may be intentionally listed here more than once.

Steve Bilt, CEO-Smile Brands
Roy D. Smith, Chief Oper. Officer
Steven C. Bilt, CEO

GROWTH PLANS/SPECIAL FEATURES:

Castle Dental Centers, Inc. develops, manages and operates integrated dental networks through contracts with general, orthodontic and multi-specialty dental practices in the U.S. The company operates dental centers in California, Oregon, Washington, Arizona, Utah, Colorado, Texas, Arkansas, Tennessee, Indiana, Ohio, Pennsylvania, Virginia and Florida. The typical Castle Dental Center provides general dentistry, preventive care, cosmetic dental care, as well as a full range of dental specialties, including orthodontics, pedodontics, periodontics, endodontics, oral surgery and implantology. Bringing together multi-specialty dental services within a single practice allows Castle Dental Centers to operate more efficiently, use facilities more completely and share dental specialists among multiple locations. Its operating model also incorporates quality assurance and quality control programs, such as peer review and continuing education. Castle Dental Centers establishes regional dental care networks in order to centralize its advertising, billing and collections, payroll and accounting systems. The firm offers a discount program for patients without insurance, and provides communication access to deaf, hard-of-hearing and communication-disabled patients. Castle Dental is a wholly-owned subsidiary of Smile Brands Group, Inc. The Smiles for Everyone Foundation is a nonprofit organization that provides free dental care for those in need, both in the U.S. as well as throughout the world.

FINANCIAL DATA:

Note: Data for latest year may not have been available at press time.

In U.S. $	2017	2016	2015	2014	2013	2012
Revenue						
R&D Expense						
Operating Income						
Operating Margin %						
SGA Expense						
Net Income						
Operating Cash Flow						
Capital Expenditure						
EBITDA						
Return on Assets %						
Return on Equity %						
Debt to Equity						

CONTACT INFORMATION:

Phone: 281-999-9999 Fax:
Toll-Free: 800-867-6453
Address: 3701 Kirby Dr., Ste. 550, Houston, TX 77098 United States

STOCK TICKER/OTHER:

Stock Ticker: Subsidiary Exchange:
Employees: 1,025 Fiscal Year Ends: 12/31
Parent Company: Smile Brands Group Inc

SALARIES/BONUSES:

Top Exec. Salary: $ Bonus: $
Second Exec. Salary: $ Bonus: $

OTHER THOUGHTS:

Estimated Female Officers or Directors: 1
Hot Spot for Advancement for Women/Minorities:

Catasys Inc

www.catasys.com

NAIC Code: 623,220

TYPES OF BUSINESS:

Substance Abuse Treatment Program
Substance Abuse Treatments

BRANDS/DIVISIONS/AFFILIATES:

OnTrak

CONTACTS:

Note: Officers with more than one job title may be intentionally listed here more than once.

Rick Anderson, COO
Susan Etzel, CFO
Richard Anderson, Director

GROWTH PLANS/SPECIAL FEATURES:

Catasys, Inc. is a data-based analytics and predictive modeling driven behavioral health management services company, providing specialized healthcare services for substance abuse. The Catasys substance dependence program, known as OnTrak, was designed to address substance dependence as a chronic disease. The program seeks to lower costs and improve member health through the delivery of integrated medical and psychosocial interventions in combination with long-term care coaching. The firm uses multiple components to treat patient's suffering from substance abuse, including psychosocial behavioral therapy, nutritional counseling and medical treatment. Initiation of the program involves the oral and intravenous administration of pharmaceuticals in an outpatient clinic, hospital or other in-patient facilities. Following this treatment, patients receive one month of prescription medication, nutritional supplements and nutritional guidelines designed to assist in recovery as well as continuing care in the form of group counseling. The entire process is 52 weeks long. The company provides its services to health plans, employers and unions through a network of licensed and company-managed health care providers. The treatment program is also available on a private-pay basis through licensed treatment providers. Catasys currently operates OnTrak in Connecticut, Florida, Georgia, Illinois, Kansas, Kentucky, Louisiana, Massachusetts, Missouri, New Jersey, North Carolina, Oklahoma, Pennsylvania, South Carolina, Tennessee, Texas, Virginia, West Virginia and Wisconsin.

FINANCIAL DATA:

Note: Data for latest year may not have been available at press time.

In U.S. $	2017	2016	2015	2014	2013	2012
Revenue	7,717,000	7,075,000	2,705,000	2,030,000	866,000	541,000
R&D Expense						
Operating Income						
Operating Margin %						
SGA Expense						
Net Income			-7,223,000	-27,346,000	-4,679,000	-11,643,000
Operating Cash Flow						
Capital Expenditure						
EBITDA						
Return on Assets %						
Return on Equity %						
Debt to Equity						

CONTACT INFORMATION:

Phone: 310 444-4300 Fax: 888 975-7712
Toll-Free: 866-517-1414
Address: 11601 Wilshire Blvd., Ste.1100, Los Angeles, CA 90025 United States

STOCK TICKER/OTHER:

Stock Ticker: CATS Exchange: OTC
Employees: 73 Fiscal Year Ends: 12/31
Parent Company:

SALARIES/BONUSES:

Top Exec. Salary: $ Bonus: $
Second Exec. Salary: $ Bonus: $

OTHER THOUGHTS:

Estimated Female Officers or Directors: 2
Hot Spot for Advancement for Women/Minorities:

Catholic Health Initiatives

www.catholichealthinitiatives.org

NAIC Code: 622,110

TYPES OF BUSINESS:

General Medical and Surgical Hospitals
Long-Term Care
Assisted & Independent Living Facilities
Community Health Organizations
Home Care Services
Occupational Health Clinic
Cancer Prevention Institute

BRANDS/DIVISIONS/AFFILIATES:

CHI
Centura Health
Mercy Health
KentuckyOne Health
TriHealth

CONTACTS: *Note: Officers with more than one job title may be intentionally listed here more than once.*

Kevin E. Lofton, CEO
Anthony Jones, Interim-Operations
Kevin E. Lofton, Pres.
J. Dean Swindle, CFO
Joyce M. Ross, Sr. VP-Mktg. & Communications
Patricia G. Webb, Chief Human Resource Officer
Stephen L. Moore, Chief Medical Officer
Mitch H. Melfi, General Counsel
John F. DiCola, Sr. VP-Strategy & Bus. Dev.
Joyce M. Ross, Sr. VP-Comm.
Philip L. Foster, Sr. VP
A. Michelle Cooper, Corp. Responsibility Officer
Kathleen Sanford, Chief Nursing Officer
Joseph W. Wilczek, Sr. VP-Div. Oper.
Christopher Lowney, Chmn.
Steven C. Kehrberg, Sr. VP-Supply Chain

GROWTH PLANS/SPECIAL FEATURES:

Catholic Health Initiatives (CHI) is a national faith-based, nonprofit healthcare organization focused on strengthening and advancing the Catholic health ministry. The organization operates 100 hospitals in 18 states, including academic medical centers and teaching hospitals, critical-access facilities, community health services organizations, accredited nursing colleges, home-health agencies, and other facilities that span the inpatient/outpatient continuum of care. CHI's family of hospitals and facilities comprise the following names: CHI, Centura Health, Mercy Health, KentuckyOne Health, TriHealth, St. Anthony, St. Catherine, St. Mary-Corwin, St. Thomas, St. Rose, and many more. In August 2018, Catholic Health Initiatives and Dignity Health announced that they were combining their healthcare ministries to create a new, nonprofit Catholic health system to advance quality of care and access across 28 U.S. states.

Employee benefits include medical, dental and vision coverage; flexible spending accounts; life and AD&D insurance; short- and long-term disability; a retirement plan; 403(b) and 457(b) plans; and tuition and adoption assistance.

FINANCIAL DATA: *Note: Data for latest year may not have been available at press time.*

In U.S. $	2017	2016	2015	2014	2013	2012
Revenue	15,547,464,000	15,189,587,000	15,713,280,000	13,888,673,000	10,708,225,000	9,844,271,000
R&D Expense						
Operating Income						
Operating Margin %						
SGA Expense						
Net Income	128,390,000	-575,571,000	137,793,000	633,967,000	-54,943,000	311,818,000
Operating Cash Flow						
Capital Expenditure						
EBITDA						
Return on Assets %						
Return on Equity %						
Debt to Equity						

CONTACT INFORMATION:

Phone: 303-298-9100 Fax:
Toll-Free:
Address: 198 Inverness Dr. West, Englewood, CO 80112 United States

STOCK TICKER/OTHER:

Stock Ticker: Nonprofit
Employees: 95,968
Parent Company:
Exchange:
Fiscal Year Ends: 06/30

SALARIES/BONUSES:

Top Exec. Salary: $ Bonus: $
Second Exec. Salary: $ Bonus: $

OTHER THOUGHTS:

Estimated Female Officers or Directors: 6
Hot Spot for Advancement for Women/Minorities: Y

Centene Corporation

www.centene.com

NAIC Code: 524,114

TYPES OF BUSINESS:

Insurance-Medical & Health, HMOs & PPOs
Medicaid Managed Care
Specialty Services
Behavioral Health
Disease Management
Managed Vision
Nurse Triage
Pharmacy Benefit Management

BRANDS/DIVISIONS/AFFILIATES:

CentAccount
MemberConnections
Smart For Your Baby
Fidelis Care

CONTACTS: *Note: Officers with more than one job title may be intentionally listed here more than once.*

Michael Neidorff, CEO
Jeffrey Schwaneke, CFO
Cynthia Brinkley, Chief Administrative Officer
Mark Brooks, Chief Information Officer
Christopher Bowers, Executive VP, Divisional
Claudio Abreu, Executive VP, Divisional
Brandy Burkhalter, Executive VP, Divisional
Keith Williamson, Executive VP
Jesse Hunter, Executive VP
Brent Layton, Other Executive Officer
Chris Koster, Senior VP, Divisional
Christopher Isaak, Senior VP

GROWTH PLANS/SPECIAL FEATURES:

Centene Corporation is a multi-line healthcare plan firm operating in two segments: managed care and specialty services. In the managed care segment, the company provides programs and services to people receiving benefits from foster care, Medicaid, the State Children's Health Insurance Program (CHIP), Medicare special needs plans, supplemental security income (SSI), dual eligible individuals (Duals), long term care (LTC) and federally-facilitated and state-based Marketplaces. This segment accounted for 95% of total revenue in 2017. Centene's specialty services segment provides healthcare services to state programs, correctional facilities, healthcare organizations, and to the firm's own subsidiaries. Specialty Services accounted for 5% of total revenue in 2017. The firm's CentAccount program offers financial incentives to members for achieving healthy behavior. Additionally, the company offers a number of education and outreach programs, including MemberConnections, which is designed to create face-to-face links between members and care providers; Start Smart For Your Baby, a prenatal and infant health program; EPSDT (early and periodic screening, diagnostic and treatment) case management, which encourages early and periodic screening, diagnosis and treatment services; and life and health management programs, designed to educate patients on the best and most cost effective treatment options for specific diseases. During 2018, Centene acquired Fidelis Care, making Fidelis Care its health plan in New York State; and Centene signed a letter of intent with Ascension to explore a joint venture to establish a leading Medicare Advantage plan for multiple geographic markets beginning in 2020.

The company offers employees health, vision and dental coverage; flexible spending accounts; short- and long-term disability; life and supplemental life insurance; 401(k); an employee stock purchase plan; an employee assistance program; tuition reimbursement; a wellness program; an onsite fitness center; and employee discounts.

FINANCIAL DATA: *Note: Data for latest year may not have been available at press time.*

In U.S. $	2017	2016	2015	2014	2013	2012
Revenue	48,382,000,000	40,607,000,000	22,760,000,000	16,560,000,000	10,863,330,000	8,667,612,000
R&D Expense						
Operating Income	1,199,000,000	1,260,000,000	705,000,000	464,000,000	277,417,000	912,000
Operating Margin %	2.47%	3.10%	3.09%	2.80%	2.55%	.01%
SGA Expense	4,446,000,000	3,676,000,000	1,826,000,000	1,314,000,000	931,137,000	704,604,000
Net Income	828,000,000	562,000,000	355,000,000	271,000,000	165,099,000	1,859,000
Operating Cash Flow	1,489,000,000	1,851,000,000	658,000,000	1,223,000,000	382,526,000	278,691,000
Capital Expenditure	422,000,000	306,000,000	150,000,000	103,000,000	67,835,000	82,144,000
EBITDA	1,750,000,000	1,652,000,000	851,000,000	581,000,000	363,294,000	74,702,000
Return on Assets %	3.93%	4.08%	5.38%	5.78%	5.26%	.07%
Return on Equity %	12.99%	13.95%	18.20%	18.19%	15.09%	.19%
Debt to Equity	0.68	0.78	0.56	0.50	0.53	0.56

CONTACT INFORMATION:

Phone: 314 725-4477 Fax: 314 725-5180
Toll-Free:
Address: 7700 Forsyth Blvd., Centene Plz., St. Louis, MO 63105 United States

STOCK TICKER/OTHER:

Stock Ticker: CNC
Employees: 30,500
Parent Company:
Exchange: NYS
Fiscal Year Ends: 12/31

SALARIES/BONUSES:

Top Exec. Salary: $1,500,000 Bonus: $
Second Exec. Salary: $725,000 Bonus: $

OTHER THOUGHTS:

Estimated Female Officers or Directors: 4
Hot Spot for Advancement for Women/Minorities: Y

Centric Health Corporation

www.centrichealth.ca

NAIC Code: 622,310

TYPES OF BUSINESS:

Specialty (except Psychiatric and Substance Abuse) Hospitals
Pharmacies
Home Health Care
Medical Device Sales
Surgical Centers

BRANDS/DIVISIONS/AFFILIATES:

CONTACTS: *Note: Officers with more than one job title may be intentionally listed here more than once.*

Leslie Cho, CFO
Jack Shevel, Chairman of the Board
Paul Rakowski, General Counsel
Diane Mason, Other Executive Officer
Yehoshua Cole, Vice President, Divisional

GROWTH PLANS/SPECIAL FEATURES:

Centric Health Corporation provides a wide range of health care and wellness services throughout Canada for both patients and health care professionals. Centric Health has large national networks that offer orthotics, surgical services, as well as specialty pharmacy services. The firm's orthotics division offers lower extremity care in more than 45 clinics across North America. Its clinicians help relieve lower extremity discomfort by correcting its underlying causes. The surgical services division provides state-of-the-art surgical facilities to patients seeking immediate access to Canada's health care offerings. Centric Health's surgical centers offer a broad range of procedures, including bariatric/lap band weight loss surgery, cardiology, dermatology, general surgery, neurology/neuropathology, orthopedic surgery, otolaryngology, plastic surgery, urology and gynecology. This division also provides diagnostic services such as cardiac CT (computed tomography) angiography, colonoscopy, diagnostic ultrasound and gastroscopy; and specialty programs such as executive health, interventional pain management/migraine treatment and medi-spa. The pharmacy segment provides traditional pharmacy services such as compounding and dispensing medications, as well as innovative clinical and specialty services for long-term care and retirement communities. This division also provides chronic disease management, diabetic support and other retail pharmacy services

Centric Health offers employees medical and dental insurance, life insurance, long-term disability, paid vacations and holidays, an employee assistance program, discounted gym memberships and wellness reimbursements, an employee referral bonus program and product and service discounts.

FINANCIAL DATA: *Note: Data for latest year may not have been available at press time.*

In U.S. $	2017	2016	2015	2014	2013	2012
Revenue	129,974,600	128,740,800	124,939,200	236,980,000	350,664,600	335,885,400
R&D Expense						
Operating Income	5,464,616	1,477,692	-4,716,154	133,077	-6,070,000	1,988,462
Operating Margin %	4.20%	1.14%	-3.77%	.05%	-1.73%	.59%
SGA Expense	34,356,920	19,705,380	20,595,380	42,123,080	99,399,230	89,925,380
Net Income	1,420,000	-15,136,150	35,448,460	-44,190,000	-70,070,000	-5,583,077
Operating Cash Flow	12,363,850	1,307,692	22,651,540	15,168,460	15,541,540	11,780,000
Capital Expenditure	5,884,616	2,263,846	3,941,539	5,955,385	7,186,154	6,492,308
EBITDA	13,402,310	2,510,000	15,666,920	17,976,150	-15,973,850	39,893,850
Return on Assets %	1.23%	-7.38%	13.34%	-16.30%	-20.76%	-1.57%
Return on Equity %	16.58%	-233.34%			-169.05%	-9.38%
Debt to Equity		23.91	15.06		18.17	1.97

CONTACT INFORMATION:

Phone: 416-927-8400 Fax: 416-927-8405
Toll-Free: 800-265-9197
Address: 20 Eglinton Ave. W., Ste. 2100, Toronto, ON M4R 1K8 Canada

STOCK TICKER/OTHER:

Stock Ticker: CHH
Exchange: TSE
Employees: 952
Fiscal Year Ends: 12/31
Parent Company:

SALARIES/BONUSES:

Top Exec. Salary: $ Bonus: $
Second Exec. Salary: $ Bonus: $

OTHER THOUGHTS:

Estimated Female Officers or Directors: 3
Hot Spot for Advancement for Women/Minorities: Y

Cerner Corporation

www.cerner.com

NAIC Code: 511210D

TYPES OF BUSINESS:

Computer Software, Healthcare & Biotechnology
Medical Information Systems
Application Hosting
Integrated Delivery Networks
Access Management
Consulting Services
Safety & Risk Management

BRANDS/DIVISIONS/AFFILIATES:

Cerner Millennium
HealtheIntent
Cerner Health Services
CernerWorks

CONTACTS: *Note: Officers with more than one job title may be intentionally listed here more than once.*

Marc Naughton, CFO
David Shafer, Chairman of the Board
Michael Battaglioli, Chief Accounting Officer
Michael Nill, COO
Jeffrey Townsend, Executive VP
Julia Wilson, Other Executive Officer
Randy Sims, Other Executive Officer
Zane Burke, President
Clifford Illig, Vice Chairman of the Board

GROWTH PLANS/SPECIAL FEATURES:

Cerner Corporation designs, develops, installs and supports information technology and content applications for health care organizations, consumers and physicians. Cerner's applications are designed to help eliminate error, variance and waste in the care process as well as provide appropriate health information and knowledge to care givers, clinicians and consumers, and appropriate management information to healthcare administrations. Cerner solutions are offered on the unified Cerner Millennium architecture and on the HealtheIntent cloud-based platform. The Millennium framework combines clinical, financial and management information systems and provides secure access to an individual's electronic medical record at the point of care, and organizes and proactively delivers information to meet the specific needs of the physician, nurse, laboratory technician, pharmacist or other care provider, front- and back-office professionals as well as consumers. The HealtheIntent platform offers EHR-agnostic (electronic health record) solutions based on sophisticated, statistical algorithms to help providers predict and improve outcomes, control costs, improve quality and manage the health of their patients. Cerner also offers a broad range of services including implementation and training, remote hosting, operational management services, revenue cycle services, support and maintenance, healthcare data analysis, clinical process optimization, transaction processing, employer health centers, employee wellness programs and third-party administrator (TPA) services for employer-based health plans. Cerner Health Services offers a portfolio of enterprise-level clinical and financial healthcare information technology solutions, as well as departmental, connectivity, population health and care coordination solutions globally. CernerWorks is the company's remote-hosting business. Roughly more than 27,000 facilities around the world license Cerner's products. These facilities include hospitals; physician practices; ambulatory facilities such as laboratories, ambulatory centers, cardiac facilities, radiology clinics and surgery centers; home health facilities; and retail pharmacies.

FINANCIAL DATA: *Note: Data for latest year may not have been available at press time.*

In U.S. $	2017	2016	2015	2014	2013	2012
Revenue	5,142,272,000	4,796,473,000	4,425,267,000	3,402,703,000	2,910,748,000	2,665,436,000
R&D Expense	605,046,000	551,418,000	539,799,000	392,805,000	338,786,000	301,370,000
Operating Income	960,471,000	911,013,000	781,136,000	763,084,000	576,012,000	571,662,000
Operating Margin %	18.67%	18.99%	17.65%	22.42%	19.78%	21.44%
SGA Expense	2,632,088,000	2,464,380,000	2,262,024,000	1,642,437,000	1,481,228,000	1,184,207,000
Net Income	866,978,000	636,484,000	539,362,000	525,433,000	398,354,000	397,232,000
Operating Cash Flow	1,307,675,000	1,155,612,000	947,526,000	847,027,000	695,865,000	708,314,000
Capital Expenditure	665,877,000	771,595,000	648,220,000	467,901,000	584,331,000	306,488,000
EBITDA	1,555,864,000	1,427,149,000	1,245,425,000	1,080,520,000	855,818,000	815,356,000
Return on Assets %	14.33%	11.37%	10.68%	12.17%	10.21%	11.84%
Return on Equity %	19.90%	16.32%	14.50%	15.60%	13.27%	15.44%
Debt to Equity	0.10	0.13	0.14	0.01	0.03	0.04

CONTACT INFORMATION:

Phone: 816 221-1024 Fax:
Toll-Free:
Address: 2800 Rockcreek Pkwy., North Kansas City, MO 64117 United States

STOCK TICKER/OTHER:

Stock Ticker: CERN
Exchange: NAS
Employees: 24,400
Fiscal Year Ends: 12/31
Parent Company:

SALARIES/BONUSES:

Top Exec. Salary: $665,000 Bonus: $
Second Exec. Salary: $665,000 Bonus: $

OTHER THOUGHTS:

Estimated Female Officers or Directors: 13
Hot Spot for Advancement for Women/Minorities: Y

Change Healthcare Inc

www.changehealthcare.com/

NAIC Code: 524,292

TYPES OF BUSINESS:

Healthcare Business & Administration Management
Claims Processing & Billing

BRANDS/DIVISIONS/AFFILIATES:

InterQual
InterQual AutoReview
InterQual Connect

CONTACTS: *Note: Officers with more than one job title may be intentionally listed here more than once.*

Neil de Crescenzo, CEO
August Calhoun, Exec. VP-Oper. & Sales
Fredrik Eliasson, CFO
W. Thomas McEnery, CMO
Linda Whitley-Taylor, Chief People Officer
Alex Choy, CIO
Miriam Paramore, Exec. VP-Prod. Mgmt. & Strategy
Gregory T. Stevens, General Counsel
Frank Manzella, Sr. VP-Corp. Dev.
Kevin Mahoney, Exec. VP-Pharmacy Svcs.
Gary D. Stuart, Exec. VP-Payer Svcs.
Sajid Khan, Exec. VP-Ambulatory Svcs.
T. Ulrich Brechbuhl, Exec. VP-Revenue Cycle Solutions

GROWTH PLANS/SPECIAL FEATURES:

Change Healthcare, Inc. is a healthcare information technology company. The firm works alongside customers and partners to enable better patient care, choice and outcomes at scale. Change Healthcare provides software, analytics, network solutions and technology-enabled services to serve the needs of stakeholders in the healthcare system, including commercial and governmental payers, employers, hospitals, physicians, providers, laboratories and consumers. The company comprises a 15,000-member team to help customers improve efficiency, reduce costs, increase cash flow and manage complex workflows. Change Healthcare has 2,100 payer connections reaching nearly all U.S. government and commercial payers. It serves 5,500 hospitals, 800,000 physicians, 130,000 dentists and 600 laboratories. The firm's Intelligent Healthcare Network has the capability of processing more than 12 billion healthcare-related transactions annually. Change Healthcare's InterQual offering aligns payers and providers with actionable, evidence-based clinical intelligence to support appropriate care and foster optimal utilization of resources. InterQual AutoReview and InterQual Connect builds on this technology to automate the creation of medical review and automate the prior authorization process, enabling exception-based utilization management. Change Healthcare's imaging strategy leverages image management, workflow, enterprise viewer and data analytics in a unified, patient-centric manner. It is used in over 3,300 facilities across the U.S. and internationally, and provides imaging workflow efficiency, data silo consolidation and reduces turnaround times.

FINANCIAL DATA: *Note: Data for latest year may not have been available at press time.*

In U.S. $	2017	2016	2015	2014	2013	2012
Revenue	1,600,000,000	1,500,000,000	1,477,083,000	1,350,413,000	1,242,567,000	1,152,313,000
R&D Expense						
Operating Income						
Operating Margin %						
SGA Expense						
Net Income			-96,069,000	-75,854,000	-74,458,000	-78,335,000
Operating Cash Flow						
Capital Expenditure						
EBITDA						
Return on Assets %						
Return on Equity %						
Debt to Equity						

CONTACT INFORMATION:

Phone: 615-932-3000 Fax:
Toll-Free:
Address: 3055 Lebanon Pike, Nashville, TN 37214 United States

STOCK TICKER/OTHER:

Stock Ticker: Private
Employees: 4,100
Parent Company:
Exchange:
Fiscal Year Ends: 12/31

SALARIES/BONUSES:

Top Exec. Salary: $ Bonus: $
Second Exec. Salary: $ Bonus: $

OTHER THOUGHTS:

Estimated Female Officers or Directors: 1
Hot Spot for Advancement for Women/Minorities:

Chemed Corporation

www.chemed.com

NAIC Code: 621,610

TYPES OF BUSINESS:

Home Health Care Services
Plumbing Services

BRANDS/DIVISIONS/AFFILIATES:

VITAS Healthcare Corporation
Roto-Rooter Corporation

CONTACTS: *Note: Officers with more than one job title may be intentionally listed here more than once.*

Nicholas Westfall, CEO, Subsidiary
Kevin Mcnamara, CEO
David Williams, CFO
George Walsh, Chairman of the Board
Michael Witzeman, Chief Accounting Officer
Thomas Hutton, Director
Spencer Lee, Executive VP
Naomi Dallob, Secretary

GROWTH PLANS/SPECIAL FEATURES:

Chemed Corporation, through its wholly-owned subsidiaries VITAS Healthcare Corporation and Roto-Rooter Corporation, offers hospice care and plumbing services, respectively. VITAS is one of the largest national providers of hospice care and end-of-life services. Its team members include registered nurses, licensed practical nurses, home health aides, physicians, social workers, chaplains and other caregiving professionals. VITAS provides hospice care services in the patient's home, including music therapy and pet visits. Additionally, the firm manages inpatient hospice units, providing service in hospitals, nursing homes and assisted living communities/residential care facilities. Approximately 92% of VITAS' service revenues consist of payments from Medicare (as of fiscal 2017-18). Roto-Rooter supports the maintenance needs of residential and commercial markets by providing services such as plumbing, drain cleaning, high-pressure water jetting, underground leak and line detection, video camera pipe inspections, grease trap and liquid waste pumping, backflow protection, emergency services, automated drain care programs and pipe repair and replacement. One of the largest businesses of its type in North America, Roto-Rooter operates hundreds of company-owned and franchises throughout the U.S. Concerning revenues, Roto-Rooter's largest share is generated by plumbing repair and maintenance, followed by sewer and drain cleaning, HVAC (heating, ventilation and air conditioning) repair and other products and services.

Employee benefits include medical, prescription and dental coverage; life insurance; short- and long-term disability; a 401(k); profit sharing; flexible spending accounts; and tuition reimbursement.

FINANCIAL DATA: *Note: Data for latest year may not have been available at press time.*

In U.S. $	2017	2016	2015	2014	2013	2012
Revenue	1,666,724,000	1,576,881,000	1,543,388,000	1,456,282,000	1,413,329,000	1,430,043,000
R&D Expense						
Operating Income	211,207,000	180,810,000	184,606,000	171,537,000	164,597,000	159,918,000
Operating Margin %	12.67%	11.46%	11.96%	11.77%	11.64%	11.18%
SGA Expense	268,222,000	241,511,000	237,673,000	217,000,000	207,536,000	205,157,000
Net Income	98,177,000	108,743,000	110,274,000	99,317,000	77,227,000	89,304,000
Operating Cash Flow	162,495,000	135,393,000	171,500,000	110,279,000	150,847,000	131,768,000
Capital Expenditure	64,300,000	39,772,000	44,135,000	43,571,000	29,324,000	35,252,000
EBITDA	156,814,000	215,407,000	217,270,000	204,012,000	171,252,000	191,063,000
Return on Assets %	10.90%	12.55%	12.88%	11.32%	8.80%	10.78%
Return on Equity %	18.44%	20.96%	22.86%	22.06%	17.12%	20.60%
Debt to Equity	0.16	0.19	0.16	0.31		0.38

CONTACT INFORMATION:

Phone: 513 762-6900 Fax: 513 762-6919
Toll-Free:
Address: 255 E. 5th St., Ste. 2600, Cincinnati, OH 45202 United States

STOCK TICKER/OTHER:

Stock Ticker: CHE Exchange: NYS
Employees: 14,613 Fiscal Year Ends: 12/31
Parent Company:

SALARIES/BONUSES:

Top Exec. Salary: $1,094,990 Bonus: $
Second Exec. Salary: $607,000 Bonus: $

OTHER THOUGHTS:

Estimated Female Officers or Directors: 3
Hot Spot for Advancement for Women/Minorities: Y

China Nuokang Bio-Pharmaceutical Inc

www.lnnk.com

NAIC Code: 325,412

TYPES OF BUSINESS:

Pharmaceutical Preparation Manufacturing
Pharmaceutical Manufacturer
Pharmaceutical Marketing

BRANDS/DIVISIONS/AFFILIATES:

China Yuanda Group Co Ltd
Liaoning Nuokang Pharmaceutical Co Ltd

GROWTH PLANS/SPECIAL FEATURES:

China Nuokang Bio-Pharmaceutical, Inc. is a biopharmaceutical company engaged in the research, development, manufacture, marketing and sale of hospital-based medical products in China. The company's products include blood and hematopoietic drugs and systems, cardiovascular drugs and systems, diabetic medications, allergy medicines, over-the-counter drugs, health supplements and related supplies such as gauzes. China Nuokang Bio-Pharmaceutical has an international standard production facility and R&D center. Product marketing is provided by subsidiary Liaoning Nuokang Pharmaceutical Co., Ltd., offering GSP-certified (graduate safety practitioner) pharmaceutical product management solutions. It is a member company of China Yuanda Group Co., Ltd.

CONTACTS: *Note: Officers with more than one job title may be intentionally listed here more than once.*

Baizhong Xue, Managing Dir.

FINANCIAL DATA: *Note: Data for latest year may not have been available at press time.*

In U.S. $	2017	2016	2015	2014	2013	2012
Revenue						
R&D Expense						
Operating Income						
Operating Margin %						
SGA Expense						
Net Income						
Operating Cash Flow						
Capital Expenditure						
EBITDA						
Return on Assets %						
Return on Equity %						
Debt to Equity						

CONTACT INFORMATION:

Phone: 86 2424696033 Fax: 86 2424696133
Toll-Free:
Address: No. 18-1 East Nanping Rd., Shenyang, Liaoning 110171 China

STOCK TICKER/OTHER:

Stock Ticker: Subsidiary Exchange:
Employees: 634 Fiscal Year Ends: 12/31
Parent Company: China Yuanda Group Co Ltd

SALARIES/BONUSES:

Top Exec. Salary: $ Bonus: $
Second Exec. Salary: $ Bonus: $

OTHER THOUGHTS:

Estimated Female Officers or Directors:
Hot Spot for Advancement for Women/Minorities:

China Resources Pharmaceutical Group Limited

www.crpharm.com/EN/

NAIC Code: 325,412

TYPES OF BUSINESS:

Pharmaceutical Preparation Manufacturing
Pharmaceutical Manufacture
Pharmaceutical Distribution
Health Care Products

BRANDS/DIVISIONS/AFFILIATES:

China Resources Company Limited
China Resources Pharmaceutical Commercial Group
China Resources Sanjiu Medical & Pharmaceutical
China Resources Double-Crane Pharmaceutical Co Ltd

CONTACTS: *Note: Officers with more than one job title may be intentionally listed here more than once.*

Chuncheng Wang, CEO
Yuning Fu, Chmn.

GROWTH PLANS/SPECIAL FEATURES:

China Resources Pharmaceutical Group Limited (CR Pharma) is the flagship subsidiary of China Resources Company Limited, and is engaged in the research and development, manufacturing, distribution and retail of a broad range of pharmaceutical and health care products. CR Pharma owns 26 manufacturing facilities in China, with nearly 200 production lines GMP-compliant for oral solid dosage, oral liquid dosage, large infusion bags, powder vials, injections, topical preparations and other formats. The company's R&D site provides a platform for international partnering, with a focus on innovation, incubation, pilot plant testing, manufacturing, warehousing and logistics services. Collaborations are a fundamental part of CR Pharma's strategy, engaging in all stages of a drug's life, from development to market. The firm currently focuses on 12 categories, but is open to others. These categories include cardiovascular, diabetes, pediatrics, respiratory, central nervous system, oncology, ophthalmology, anti-infection, dermatology, women's health, enteral nutrition and herb medicine. Distribution-wise, CR Pharma is one of the largest distributors in the Chinese pharmaceutical market for sales and distribution. The company covers 29 provinces, supplying 46,000 different drugs as well as medical equipment and various health/nutrition products. CR Pharma also offers marketing, sales, logistics, academic seminars and supply chain added value services to its clients. These clients include hospitals, community health centers, clinics, manufacturers, distributors and retailers, among others. Just a few of the company's many subsidiaries include: China Resources Pharmaceutical Commercial Group Co. Ltd.; China Resources Sanjiu Medical & Pharmaceutical Co. Ltd.; and China Resources Double-Crane Pharmaceutical Co. Ltd.

FINANCIAL DATA: *Note: Data for latest year may not have been available at press time.*

In U.S. $	2017	2016	2015	2014	2013	2012
Revenue	22,075,000,000	20,206,800,000	18,910,400,000	17,514,500,000	15,081,100,000	
R&D Expense						
Operating Income						
Operating Margin %						
SGA Expense						
Net Income	878,616,000	769,562,000	784,732,000	708,583,000	703,433,000	
Operating Cash Flow						
Capital Expenditure						
EBITDA						
Return on Assets %						
Return on Equity %						
Debt to Equity						

CONTACT INFORMATION:

Phone: 852-2593-8991 Fax: 852-259-38992
Toll-Free:
Address: 26 Harbour Rd., China Resources Bldg., 41/Fl, Wanchai, Hong Kong, Hong Kong

STOCK TICKER/OTHER:

Stock Ticker: 3320 Exchange: Hong Kong
Employees: 56,000 Fiscal Year Ends: 12/31
Parent Company: China Resources Company Limited

SALARIES/BONUSES:

Top Exec. Salary: $ Bonus: $
Second Exec. Salary: $ Bonus: $

OTHER THOUGHTS:

Estimated Female Officers or Directors:
Hot Spot for Advancement for Women/Minorities:

Chindex International Inc

www.chindex.com

NAIC Code: 622,110

TYPES OF BUSINESS:

Hospitals
Healthcare Services

BRANDS/DIVISIONS/AFFILIATES:

Healthy Harmony Holdings LP
United Family Healthcare
Chindex Medical Limited

CONTACTS:

Note: Officers with more than one job title may be intentionally listed here more than once.

Roberta Lipson, CEO
Roberta Lipson, Pres.
Walter Xue, Sr. VP-Finance
Xiao Yan Shen, Chief Nursing Officer
Daniel Fulton, VP-IT Svcs.
Pin Qing Zhang, VP-Tech. Svcs.
Elyse Beth Silverberg, Sec.
Alex Carson, VP-Revenue Oper.
Ming Xie, Sr. VP-Hospital Systems Dev.
Simon Hou, VP-UFH Financial Controller
Elyse Beth Silverberg, Exec. VP
Walter Xue, Sr. VP-Finance
Judy Zakreski, VP-U.S. Oper., Chindex Medical Ltd.
Wai Ho Leung, VP-Medical Diagnostic & Imaging Prod.
Walter Stryker, Sr. VP-China Admin.

GROWTH PLANS/SPECIAL FEATURES:

Chindex International, Inc. is an American health care company providing services to Beijing, Shanghai, Tianjin, Qingdao and Guangzhou, China, as well as Ulaanbaatar, Mongolia. The firm provides these services through subsidiary United Family Healthcare (UHF), a network of private primary care hospitals and affiliated ambulatory clinics. These hospitals are staffed by a mix of Western and Chinese physicians. UHF operates on an international-standard healthcare network, managing its business according to international principles in regards to transparency, infection control, medical records, patient confidentiality and peer review. UHF facilities in Beijing, Shanghai and Guangzhou are accredited by the Joint Commission International. These facilities offer services in wellness care, including check-ups and preventive services (routine visits in the absence of illness), diagnostics and patient-centered care for chronic and acute diseases. The hospitals offer premium quality healthcare services, such as 24/7 emergency rooms, intensive care units and neonatal intensive care units, operating rooms, clinical laboratories, radiology and blood banking services. The patient base includes expatriate communities and China's upper-middle class. Services provided to patients who are not covered by insurance are on a fee-for-services cash basis. Under a joint venture with Shanghai Fosun Pharmaceutical (Group) Co., Ltd., Chindex operates Chindex Medical Limited, a Hong Kong company, for the purpose of marketing, distribution and servicing of medical equipment in China and Hong Kong. The company is privately-held by Healthy Harmony Holdings, LP.

FINANCIAL DATA:

Note: Data for latest year may not have been available at press time.

In U.S. $	2017	2016	2015	2014	2013	2012
Revenue	194,250,000	185,000,000	180,000,000	175,000,000	160,000,000	152,442,000
R&D Expense						
Operating Income						
Operating Margin %						
SGA Expense						
Net Income						
Operating Cash Flow						
Capital Expenditure						
EBITDA						
Return on Assets %						
Return on Equity %						
Debt to Equity						

CONTACT INFORMATION:

Phone: 86-10-5927-7000 Fax: 86-10-5927-7220
Toll-Free:
Address: No. 2 Jiangtai Lu, Chaoyang Distr., Beijing, 100016 China

STOCK TICKER/OTHER:

Stock Ticker: Private
Exchange:
Employees: 1,749
Fiscal Year Ends: 03/31
Parent Company: Healthy Harmony Holdings LP

SALARIES/BONUSES:

Top Exec. Salary: $ Bonus: $
Second Exec. Salary: $ Bonus: $

OTHER THOUGHTS:

Estimated Female Officers or Directors: 6
Hot Spot for Advancement for Women/Minorities: Y

CHRISTUS Health

www.christushealth.org

NAIC Code: 622,110

TYPES OF BUSINESS:

General Medical and Surgical Hospitals
Long-Term & Hospice Care
Behavioral Health
Orthopedic Medicine
Online Health Information

BRANDS/DIVISIONS/AFFILIATES:

Sisters of Charity of the Incarnate Word
CHRISTUS SINERGIA Salud

CONTACTS: *Note: Officers with more than one job title may be intentionally listed here more than once.*

Ernie Sadau, CEO
Jeffrey M. Puckett, COO
Ernie Sadau, Pres.
Randolph Safady, CFO
Marty Margetts, SVP
George S. Conklin, CIO
John Gillean, Sr. VP-Physician Integration Svcs.

GROWTH PLANS/SPECIAL FEATURES:

CHRISTUS Health is a faith-based, not-for-profit organization formed from the combination of two Catholic charities, Sisters of Charity of the Incarnate Word in Houston and Sisters of Charity of the Incarnate Word in San Antonio. Today, CHRISTUS is one of the Top 10 Catholic health systems in the U.S. as ranked by size, comprised of almost 600 services and facilities, with more than 60 hospitals, 350 clinics and outpatient centers and numerous other clinics and physician offices. The firm has approximately 45,000 associates and more than 15,000 physicians on staff. CHRISTUS operates in Texas, Arkansas, Iowa, Louisiana, Georgia and New Mexico, U.S., and operates as CHRISTUS SINERGIA Salud in Colombia, South America. Some of the services provided by CHRISTUS's facilities include hospice, long-term and assisted care, emergency and outpatient treatment, surgical, cardiology, emergency, rehabilitation, orthopedics and women's and children's health. The group's website provides a support and resource site for physicians, information on healthy recipes, health news and information and a section on miracles and success stories connected with the organization. The group also operates an advocacy program on both the state and federal levels in the healthcare field with the hope of providing its patients with a healthcare system that can better serve them. Community outreach, especially focusing on the underserved, is a priority for CHRISTUS. In Colombia, CHRISTUS SINERGIA is a health care network that includes 88 ambulatory care facilities, a home care company, a health provider network, two partially-owned hospitals and two wholly-owned hospitals.

CHRISTUS offers employees health, dental, life, long-term care and AD&D insurance; a flexible spending account and other benefits.

FINANCIAL DATA: *Note: Data for latest year may not have been available at press time.*

In U.S. $	2017	2016	2015	2014	2013	2012
Revenue	4,922,429,000	4,212,413,000	3,599,712,000	3,551,631,000	3,701,272,000	3,802,335,000
R&D Expense						
Operating Income						
Operating Margin %						
SGA Expense						
Net Income	141,369,000	220,630,000	13,269,000	143,102,000	159,679,000	-41,395,000
Operating Cash Flow						
Capital Expenditure						
EBITDA						
Return on Assets %						
Return on Equity %						
Debt to Equity						

CONTACT INFORMATION:

Phone: 469-282-2000 Fax:
Toll-Free:
Address: 919 Hidden Ridge, Irving, TX 75038 United States

STOCK TICKER/OTHER:

Stock Ticker: Nonprofit Exchange:
Employees: 45,000 Fiscal Year Ends: 06/30
Parent Company:

SALARIES/BONUSES:

Top Exec. Salary: $ Bonus: $
Second Exec. Salary: $ Bonus: $

OTHER THOUGHTS:

Estimated Female Officers or Directors: 5
Hot Spot for Advancement for Women/Minorities: Y

Cigna Behavioral Health

apps.cignabehavioral.com/web/consumer.do#/findAtherapist

NAIC Code: 524,114

TYPES OF BUSINESS:

Insurance-Supplemental & Specialty Health
Employee Assistance Programs
Behavioral Healthcare

BRANDS/DIVISIONS/AFFILIATES:

Cigna Corporation
Disaster Resource Center (The)

CONTACTS: *Note: Officers with more than one job title may be intentionally listed here more than once.*

David Cordani, CEO
Keith Dixon, Pres.
Rhonda Robinson Beale, Chief Medical Officer
Jodi Prohofsky, Sr. VP-Oper.
Julie Vayer, VP-Provider Network Oper.

GROWTH PLANS/SPECIAL FEATURES:

Cigna Behavioral Health (CBH), a subsidiary of Cigna Corporation, provides various behavioral health care services that include employee assistance plan (EAP) administration, support coping with life events, behavioral care services and productivity solutions. It addresses problems such as stress, personal crisis, family conflict, bereavement, mental illness, alcohol/drug abuse, eating concerns, domestic violence/child abuse, sexual assault/sexual health, suicide, bullying, disability management and disease management. In addition, CBH offers assistance programs for students and for employees deployed internationally. CBH's customers in the U.S. receive benefits through health plans offered by large U.S. employers, unions, national and regional health maintenance organizations (HMOs), Taft-Hartley trusts and disability insurers. Its large employer and HMO plans provide behavioral health management, utilization review, employee assistance program services, life event programs and disability management programs. Taft-Hartley trusts specialize in services for stress, substance abuse and other treatable behavioral problems. CBH also operates Cigna Corporation's various health management services. Its website offers educational information on such topics as autism, eating disorders, bipolar disease and drug and alcohol abuse. The Disaster Resource Center offers resources to help members cope in times of trouble, including literature and links to state-run websites that update the public on disaster situations and management. Cigna maintains sales centers in 30 countries and jurisdictions.

The company offers employees medical, dental, life, disability, long-term care and mental health coverage; education reimbursement; elder-and child-care assistance; 401(k); wellness and fitness programs; and adoption assistance.

FINANCIAL DATA: *Note: Data for latest year may not have been available at press time.*

In U.S. $	2017	2016	2015	2014	2013	2012
Revenue						
R&D Expense						
Operating Income						
Operating Margin %						
SGA Expense						
Net Income						
Operating Cash Flow						
Capital Expenditure						
EBITDA						
Return on Assets %						
Return on Equity %						
Debt to Equity						

CONTACT INFORMATION:

Phone: 952-996-2000 Fax: 952-996-2579
Toll-Free: 800-433-5768
Address: 11095 Viking Dr., Ste. 350, Eden Prairie, MN 55344 United States

STOCK TICKER/OTHER:

Stock Ticker: Subsidiary
Employees:
Parent Company: Cigna Corporation
Exchange:
Fiscal Year Ends: 12/31

SALARIES/BONUSES:

Top Exec. Salary: $ Bonus: $
Second Exec. Salary: $ Bonus: $

OTHER THOUGHTS:

Estimated Female Officers or Directors: 3
Hot Spot for Advancement for Women/Minorities: Y

Cigna Corporation

www.cigna.com

NAIC Code: 524,114

TYPES OF BUSINESS:

Insurance-Medical & Health, HMOs & PPOs
Indemnity Insurance
Investment Management Services
Group Life, Accident & Disability

BRANDS/DIVISIONS/AFFILIATES:

CONTACTS: *Note: Officers with more than one job title may be intentionally listed here more than once.*

David Cordani, CEO
Eric Palmer, CFO
Isaiah Harris, Chairman of the Board
Mary Hoeltzel, Chief Accounting Officer
Mark Boxer, Chief Information Officer
Lisa Bacus, Chief Marketing Officer
John Murabito, Executive VP, Divisional
Alan Muney, Executive VP
Nicole Jones, Executive VP
Jason Sadler, President, Divisional
Christopher Hocevar, President, Divisional
Michael Triplett, President, Divisional
Brian Evanko, President, Divisional

GROWTH PLANS/SPECIAL FEATURES:

Cigna Corporation is a global health services organization. Along with its insurance subsidiaries, the company is a major provider of medical, dental, disability, life and accident insurance and related products and services, the majority of which are offered through employers and other groups. Cigna operates in three segments: global healthcare, global supplemental benefits, and group disability and life. The global healthcare segment accounts for 80% of annual revenue, and is comprised of two divisions: commercial and government. The commercial division consists of global health benefits, products and services designed to meet the needs of local and multinational companies and organizations, along with their domestic and globally mobile employees and dependents. The government division offers Medicare Advantage and Medicare Part D plans to seniors, as well as Medicaid plans. The global supplemental benefits segment accounts for 9% of annual revenue, and offers supplemental health, life and accident insurance products mainly in Asia, Europe and the United States. In addition, it offers services to globally mobile individuals and local citizens through partnerships and local licensing. In China, India and Turkey, products are offered through joint ventures. The group disability and life segment accounts for 11% of annual revenue, and provides group long-term and short-term disability insurance, group life insurance and accident and specialty insurance. These products and services are provided by the firm's subsidiaries. Cigna's other operations include corporate-owned life insurance, deferred gains, run-off reinsurance and its run-off settlement annuity business. In March 2018, Cigna entered into a definitive agreement with Express Scripts Holding Company whereby Cigna will acquire Express Scripts in a cash and stock transaction valued at approximately $54 billion. That August, both companies obtained shareholder approval.

Employee benefits include child/dependent care, adoption assistance, onsite health centers and an employee assistance program.

FINANCIAL DATA: *Note: Data for latest year may not have been available at press time.*

In U.S. $	2017	2016	2015	2014	2013	2012
Revenue	41,616,000,000	39,668,000,000	37,876,000,000	34,914,000,000	32,380,000,000	29,119,000,000
R&D Expense						
Operating Income						
Operating Margin %						
SGA Expense						
Net Income	2,237,000,000	1,867,000,000	2,094,000,000	2,102,000,000	1,476,000,000	1,623,000,000
Operating Cash Flow	4,086,000,000	4,026,000,000	2,717,000,000	1,994,000,000	719,000,000	2,350,000,000
Capital Expenditure	471,000,000	461,000,000	510,000,000	473,000,000	527,000,000	408,000,000
EBITDA						
Return on Assets %	3.69%	3.20%	3.70%	3.81%	2.73%	3.09%
Return on Equity %	16.29%	14.49%	18.36%	19.69%	14.51%	17.92%
Debt to Equity	0.37	0.34	0.41	0.46	0.47	0.51

CONTACT INFORMATION:

Phone: 860 226-6000 Fax: 215 761-3596
Toll-Free: 800-997-1654
Address: 900 Cottage Grove Rd., Bloomfield, CT 06002 United States

STOCK TICKER/OTHER:

Stock Ticker: CI
Exchange: NYS
Employees: 41,000
Fiscal Year Ends: 12/31
Parent Company:

SALARIES/BONUSES:

Top Exec. Salary: $1,284,615 Bonus: $
Second Exec. Salary: $634,615 Bonus: $

OTHER THOUGHTS:

Estimated Female Officers or Directors: 4
Hot Spot for Advancement for Women/Minorities: Y

Cipla Limited

www.cipla.com

NAIC Code: 325,412

TYPES OF BUSINESS:

Pharmaceuticals Manufacturing
Artificial Flavors & Fragrances Manufacturing
Pesticides Manufacturing
Technology Services

BRANDS/DIVISIONS/AFFILIATES:

Meditab Specialties Private Limited
Cipla BioTec
CipTec Discovery Engine
Chase Pharmaceuticals
Cipla Consumer Healthcare
Stempeutics Research
Stempeucel

CONTACTS: *Note: Officers with more than one job title may be intentionally listed here more than once.*

Umang Vohra, CEO
R. Ananthanarayanan, COO
Kedar Upadhye, CFO
Prabir Kumar Jha, Chief People Officer
S. Radhakrishnan, Whole-Time Dir.

GROWTH PLANS/SPECIAL FEATURES:

Cipla Limited, founded in 1935, is a leading Indian pharmaceutical company, selling more than 1,500 products in various therapeutic categories. The company operates through several subsidiaries. Cipla New Ventures is the firm's investment arm to nurture and build innovation-led business streams for Cipla. Its investments range across diverse areas such as biologicals, small-molecule innovation, consumer healthcare and regenerative medicine. Wholly-owned Meditab Specialties Private Limited and Cipla BioTec focus on research, development, manufacturing and marketing of biosimilars, in the fields of cancer, auto-immune diseases, respiratory diseases and diabetes. CipTec Discovery Engine is the company's small-molecule innovation division that utilizes smart delivery technology and modern repurposing tools to add new value to currently-used drugs. CipTec's pipeline consists of early-stage studies in relation to central nervous system and oncology therapies. CipTec's Chase Pharmaceuticals R&D subsidiary (based in the U.S.) has two lead assets in the pipeline to treat Alzheimer's disease. Cipla Consumer Healthcare produces over-the-counter medicines. Last, Stempeutics Research is a group company of Manipal Education and Medical Group and a joint venture with Cipla Limited. Stimpeutics received its novel pool technology granted in the U.S. It also received an Advanced Therapy Medicinal Product classification from the European Medicines Agency for its lead product, Stempeucel, for the treatment of various indications including Buerger's disease, critical limb ischemia and osteoarthritis. Cipla Limited is a pioneer in active pharmaceutical ingredients (APIs), manufacturing APIs in India for more than 50 years. The firm currently manufactures more than 200 generic and complex APIs, and has a pipeline of over 50 APIs at various stages of development. Cipla has also been at the forefront of innovation for inhalation therapy in India. Its respiratory products are available in over 100 countries, with inhalation products comprising 27 molecules and combinations across a range of devices.

FINANCIAL DATA: *Note: Data for latest year may not have been available at press time.*

In U.S. $	2017	2016	2015	2014	2013	2012
Revenue	1,952,711,000	1,899,669,000	1,577,394,000	1,404,291,000	1,151,103,000	
R&D Expense	38,966,870	30,405,200	15,568,950	14,715,290	6,007,630	
Operating Income	229,767,900	277,307,600	259,561,300	253,407,700	296,978,000	
Operating Margin %	11.65%	14.59%	16.21%	18.04%	25.12%	
SGA Expense	200,163,500	164,589,100	146,936,000	119,438,000	103,958,000	
Net Income	139,921,700	209,373,100	164,166,400	193,035,300	214,785,600	
Operating Cash Flow	331,228,800	249,407,700	163,145,900	217,268,800	194,324,100	
Capital Expenditure	157,939,100	149,723,600	89,844,730	79,186,430	105,210,700	
EBITDA	366,044,200	364,031,000	310,076,300	320,943,200	341,107,200	
Return on Assets %	4.80%	8.22%	8.10%	11.08%	14.70%	
Return on Equity %	8.25%	13.29%	11.33%	14.56%	18.54%	
Debt to Equity	0.29	0.01	0.02	0.03		

CONTACT INFORMATION:

Phone: 91 2223082891 Fax: 91 2223070013
Toll-Free:
Address: Cipla House, Peninsula Bus. Park, Ganpatrao Kadam Marg, Lower Parel, Mumbai, 400 013 India

STOCK TICKER/OTHER:

Stock Ticker: CPLFY
Employees: 23,610
Parent Company:
Exchange: GREY
Fiscal Year Ends: 03/31

SALARIES/BONUSES:

Top Exec. Salary: $ Bonus: $
Second Exec. Salary: $ Bonus: $

OTHER THOUGHTS:

Estimated Female Officers or Directors:
Hot Spot for Advancement for Women/Minorities:

CIVCO Medical Instruments Co Ltd

www.civco.com

NAIC Code: 339,100

TYPES OF BUSINESS:

Diagnostic & Therapeutic Medical Equipment
Ultrasound Products
Minimally Invasive Surgical Products
Medical Monitors
Needle & Biopsy Instruments
Disinfectants
Medical Printers & Print Supplies
Custom Design Services

BRANDS/DIVISIONS/AFFILIATES:

Roper Technologies Inc
CIVCO Medical Solutions
AccuCARE
eTRAX

CONTACTS: *Note: Officers with more than one job title may be intentionally listed here more than once.*

Robin Therme, Pres.
Lisa Jonshon, VP-Finance
Jen Segura, Sr. Mgr-Human Resources
Mike Marshall, VP-Prod. Dev.
David S. Schultz, VP-Oper.
Lisa Johnson, Corp. Controller
Nat Geissel, Sr. VP
Robin Therme, Sr. VP
Michael McVey, VP
Hap Peterson, VP-North American Sales, Radiation Oncology

GROWTH PLANS/SPECIAL FEATURES:

CIVCO Medical Instruments Co., Ltd., which does business as CIVCO Medical Solutions, designs, manufactures and markets specialty products for the medical industry. The company's specialties include radiology, anesthesia, vascular access, men's health, women's health, surgery and echocardiography (ECG). CIVCO operates in two business segments: multi-modality imaging (MMI) and radiation oncology. The MMI division manufactures and markets guidance and infection control products for diagnostic and therapeutic imaging and interventional procedures, which includes endocavity and general purpose needle guides, surgical covers, AccuCARE transperineal solutions, eTRAX needle tracking technology, needle computed tomography and accessories. The radiation oncology segment designs, manufactures and markets comprehensive motion management solutions to improve patient outcome and increase clinical productivity. There are approximately 10 product categories, which range from couchtops and overlays for linear accelerators and imaging systems; robotic patient positioning; advances fiducial markers; advanced patient immobilization solutions and consumables. These products are sold worldwide through CIVCO's partners in Europe, Asia, Australia, the Middle East and Central and South America. The company supplies original equipment manufacturers (OEMs). CIVCO operates as a wholly-owned subsidiary of Roper Technologies, Inc.

CIVCO offers medical, dental, vision and prescription coverage; life and AD&D insurance; flexible spending account; short-and long-term disability; and an employee assistance program.

FINANCIAL DATA: *Note: Data for latest year may not have been available at press time.*

In U.S. $	2017	2016	2015	2014	2013	2012
Revenue	3,600,000,000					
R&D Expense						
Operating Income						
Operating Margin %						
SGA Expense						
Net Income						
Operating Cash Flow						
Capital Expenditure						
EBITDA						
Return on Assets %						
Return on Equity %						
Debt to Equity						

CONTACT INFORMATION:

Phone: 319-656-4447 Fax: 319-656-4451
Toll-Free: 800-445-6741
Address: 102 First St. S., Kalona, IA 52247 United States

STOCK TICKER/OTHER:

Stock Ticker: Subsidiary
Exchange:
Employees:
Fiscal Year Ends:
Parent Company: Roper Technologies Inc

SALARIES/BONUSES:

Top Exec. Salary: $ Bonus: $
Second Exec. Salary: $ Bonus: $

OTHER THOUGHTS:

Estimated Female Officers or Directors: 3
Hot Spot for Advancement for Women/Minorities: Y

Civitas Solutions Inc

civitas-solutions.com/

NAIC Code: 621,610

TYPES OF BUSINESS:

Home Health Care Services

BRANDS/DIVISIONS/AFFILIATES:

MENTOR Network (The)
CareMeridian
NeuroRestorative
Creative Connections Inc

CONTACTS: *Note: Officers with more than one job title may be intentionally listed here more than once.*

Bruce Nardella, CEO
Denis Holler, CFO
Jeffrey Cohen, Chief Information Officer
Dwight Robson, Chief Marketing Officer
Brett Cohen, COO
Gina Martin, General Counsel
Gerald Morrissey, Other Executive Officer
David Petersen, President, Divisional

GROWTH PLANS/SPECIAL FEATURES:

Civitas Solutions, Inc. is a provider of home- and community-based health and human services to must-serve individuals with intellectual, developmental, physical or behavioral disabilities and other special needs. The company's clinicians and caregivers develop customized service plans, delivered in non-institutional settings, designed to address a broad range of often life-long conditions and to enable them to thrive in less restrictive settings. Civitas markets its services nationally as The MENTOR Network. This network of local health and human services providers are located in 35 U.S. states, offering its services to both adults and children, as well as their families. The company divides its business offerings into six segments. Human services is comprised of home- and community-based services to adults and children with intellectual and developmental disabilities (I/DD), as well as to at-risk youth (ARY) with emotional, behavioral and medically-complex challenges. The social and rehabilitation services (SRS) segment delivers healthcare and community-based rehabilitation services to individuals who have experienced brain and spinal cord injuries, as well as to individuals with other catastrophic injuries and illnesses. The I/DD segment includes programs for adults and children with intellectual and developmental disabilities in small group homes, intermediate care facilities, host homes and in-home settings. CareMeridian provides a continuum of high-quality, cost-effective, post-acute care and rehabilitation options to people of all ages with brain, spinal cord and other life-threatening injuries and illnesses. ARY services include therapeutic and medically-complex foster care, family preservation services, school-based services, juvenile offender programs, early intervention and adoption services. Last, the NeuroRestorative segment provides post-acute rehabilitation services for people with brain and spinal cord injuries and other neurological challenges in a variety of locations and settings. In July 2018, Civitas acquired Creative Connections, Inc., a provider of community-based services for individuals with intellectual and developmental disabilities.

FINANCIAL DATA: *Note: Data for latest year may not have been available at press time.*

In U.S. $	2017	2016	2015	2014	2013	2012
Revenue	1,474,510,000	1,407,587,000	1,366,946,000	1,255,838,000	1,198,653,000	1,107,351,000
R&D Expense						
Operating Income	71,893,000	57,696,000	62,571,000	60,266,000	53,324,000	46,043,000
Operating Margin %	4.87%	4.09%	4.57%	4.79%	4.44%	4.15%
SGA Expense	166,376,000	184,649,000	162,839,000	145,041,000	146,040,000	139,630,000
Net Income	6,331,000	9,187,000	3,072,000	-22,815,000	-18,296,000	-14,269,000
Operating Cash Flow	96,920,000	107,122,000	90,478,000	83,916,000	55,738,000	29,251,000
Capital Expenditure	46,649,000	43,356,000	42,793,000	35,295,000	31,901,000	29,995,000
EBITDA	117,314,000	129,888,000	126,388,000	103,941,000	117,177,000	106,051,000
Return on Assets %	.59%	.85%	.27%	-2.04%	-1.77%	-1.36%
Return on Equity %	4.10%	6.88%	2.59%	-66.10%		
Debt to Equity	3.83	4.37	5.30	5.55		

CONTACT INFORMATION:

Phone: 617 790-4800 Fax:
Toll-Free:
Address: 313 Congress St., Boston, MA 02210 United States

STOCK TICKER/OTHER:

Stock Ticker: CIVI
Employees: 22,300
Parent Company:
Exchange: NYS
Fiscal Year Ends: 09/30

SALARIES/BONUSES:

Top Exec. Salary: $575,000 Bonus: $
Second Exec. Salary: $375,000 Bonus: $

OTHER THOUGHTS:

Estimated Female Officers or Directors:
Hot Spot for Advancement for Women/Minorities:

Cleveland Clinic Foundation (The)

www.clevelandclinic.org

NAIC Code: 622,110

TYPES OF BUSINESS:

General Medical and Surgical Hospitals

BRANDS/DIVISIONS/AFFILIATES:

Lerner Research Institute
Lerner College of Medicine
Health Education Campus

CONTACTS: *Note: Officers with more than one job title may be intentionally listed here more than once.*

Delos M. Cosgrove, CEO
William M. Peacock, III, Chief-Oper.
Steven C. Glass, CFO
Paul Matsen, CMO
Linda McHugh, Chief Human Resources Officer
Robert Wyllie, Chief Medical Oper. Officer
Doug Smith, Interim CIO
Cindy Hundorfean, Chief Admin. Officer-Clinical Svcs.
David W. Rowan, Chief Legal Officer
Michael Harrington, Chief Acct. Officer
Kristen D.W. Morris, Chief Gov't. & Community Rel. Officer
Linda McHugh, Exec. Admin.-CEO & Board of Governors
K. Kelly Hancock, Interim Exec. Chief Nursing Officer
Ann Huston, Chief Strategy Officer
Robert E. Rich, Jr., Chmn.

GROWTH PLANS/SPECIAL FEATURES:

The Cleveland Clinic Foundation is a nonprofit clinic in Ohio that combines medical care with education and research. It is noted for very advanced surgical techniques and advanced care. Founded in 1921, it serves more than 7.5 million patients per year across the nation and internationally. The Cleveland Clinic has over 4,500 beds across its system, and over 3,675 scientists and physicians work within the system. Facilities include 19 full-service family health centers and 11 regional hospitals. The main campus features 59 buildings on 170 acres, offering tertiary care and comprising 101 operating rooms and seven hybrid surgical suites. Regional clinics and care centers specialize in cardiology, urology, gastroenterology, nephrology, rheumatology, orthopedics, pulmonology, diabetes, endocrinology, neurology, neurosurgery, cancer, geriatrics, gynecology, ophthalmology ear/nose/throat, pediatrics and more. Cleveland's Lerner Research Institute is home to all laboratory-based research by the firm, as well as many translational and clinical studies. The institute comprises 2,000 scientists and support personnel, and is actively involved in programs such as cardiovascular, oncologic, neurologic, allergic, immunologic, musculoskeletal, metabolic, infectious diseases and eye diseases. The Lerner College of Medicine has 160 students enrolled, and offers a tuition-free MD degree with emphasis on clinical research skills. In addition, The Cleveland Clinic Foundation is constructing a 475,115-square-foot Health Education Campus slated to open in 2019 in collaboration with Case Western Reserve University, and will include the Cleveland Clinic Lerner College of Medicine, Case Western Reserve University School of Medicine, School of Dental Medicine, Francis Payne Bolton School of Nursing and a new program for physician assistants.

Employee benefits include pension and savings plans; health, dental and vision insurance; life insurance; short- and long-term disability; adoption assistance; and an employee wellness program.

FINANCIAL DATA: *Note: Data for latest year may not have been available at press time.*

In U.S. $	2017	2016	2015	2014	2013	2012
Revenue	8,400,000,000	8,037,207,000	7,156,972,000	6,687,379,000	6,450,159,000	6,187,137,000
R&D Expense						
Operating Income						
Operating Margin %						
SGA Expense						
Net Income	328,000,000	139,352,000	480,224,000	467,543,000	293,995,000	157,069,000
Operating Cash Flow						
Capital Expenditure						
EBITDA						
Return on Assets %						
Return on Equity %						
Debt to Equity						

CONTACT INFORMATION:

Phone: 216-444-2200 Fax:
Toll-Free: 800-223-2273
Address: 9500 Euclid Ave., Cleveland, OH 44195 United States

STOCK TICKER/OTHER:

Stock Ticker: Nonprofit
Exchange:
Employees: 52,082
Fiscal Year Ends: 12/31
Parent Company:

SALARIES/BONUSES:

Top Exec. Salary: $ Bonus: $
Second Exec. Salary: $ Bonus: $

OTHER THOUGHTS:

Estimated Female Officers or Directors: 22
Hot Spot for Advancement for Women/Minorities: Y

Coast Dental Services LLC

NAIC Code: 621,210

www.coastdental.com

TYPES OF BUSINESS:

Dental Practice Management

BRANDS/DIVISIONS/AFFILIATES:

Dental Technology Inc
Community Dental Services Inc
Coast Dental
SmileCare
Koda Digital Radiography
Smile Plus
Coast Comprehensive Care
ViziLite

CONTACTS: *Note: Officers with more than one job title may be intentionally listed here more than once.*

Terek Diasti, CEO
Adam Diasti, Pres.

GROWTH PLANS/SPECIAL FEATURES:

Coast Dental Services, LLC is a provider of dental practice management services to affiliated general dentists and support staffs across Florida, Georgia, California, Nevada and Texas. The company serves more than 180 dental centers under the Coast Dental and SmileCare brands. Its operating model allows dentists to focus on providing high quality dentistry, while the company's system takes care of aspects of office administration, including human resources, training, insurance processing and marketing. Coast Dental has a revolving credit program for its patients, which has the backing of a financial institution. Programs offered by the company include Kodak Digital Radiography, a replacement of traditional X-rays with digital imaging; Smile Plus, a discounted dental service for patients with no insurance; the Coast Comprehensive Care program, which diagnoses and manages periodontal disease; ViziLite, a non-invasive oral cancer screening exam; and Coast Dental Advantage, a payment plan with monthly payments starting at $25 and no annual fee. The company also owns Dental Technology, Inc., operating as SmileCare; and Community Dental Services, Inc., a California licensed healthcare service plan.

Coast Dental offers its employees credit union membership; an employee assistance program; paid holidays and time off; a 401(k); a dental discount program; and medical, life and disability insurance.

FINANCIAL DATA: *Note: Data for latest year may not have been available at press time.*

In U.S. $	2017	2016	2015	2014	2013	2012
Revenue						
R&D Expense						
Operating Income						
Operating Margin %						
SGA Expense						
Net Income						
Operating Cash Flow						
Capital Expenditure						
EBITDA						
Return on Assets %						
Return on Equity %						
Debt to Equity						

CONTACT INFORMATION:

Phone: 813-288-1999 Fax: 813-289-4500
Toll-Free:
Address: 5706 Benjamin Center Dr., Ste. 103, Tampa, FL 33634 United States

STOCK TICKER/OTHER:

Stock Ticker: Private
Employees: 677
Parent Company:
Exchange:
Fiscal Year Ends: 12/31

SALARIES/BONUSES:

Top Exec. Salary: $ Bonus: $
Second Exec. Salary: $ Bonus: $

OTHER THOUGHTS:

Estimated Female Officers or Directors: 2
Hot Spot for Advancement for Women/Minorities: Y

Cochlear Limited

www.cochlear.com

NAIC Code: 334,510

TYPES OF BUSINESS:

Audiological Equipment, Electromedical, Manufacturing
Auditory Devices & Hearing Aids
Cochlear Implants

BRANDS/DIVISIONS/AFFILIATES:

Cochlear Nucleus
Kanso
Cochlear Baha
Cochlear Carina
Cochlear Vistafix

CONTACTS:

Note: Officers with more than one job title may be intentionally listed here more than once.

Dig Howitt, CEO
Chris Roberts, Pres.
Brent Cubis, CFO
Dean Phizacklea, Sr. VP-Global Mktg.
Jennifer Hornery, Sr. VP-People & Culture
Jim Patrick, Sr. VP
David Hackshall, CIO
Jan Janssen, Sr. VP-Design & Dev.
Dig Howitt, Sr. VP-Mfg.
Neville Mitchell, Corp. Sec.
Bronwyn Evans, Sr. VP-Quality & Regulatory
Mark Salmon, Pres., Asia Pacific Region
Chris Smith, Pres., Americas Region
Rick Holliday-Smith, Chmn.
Richard Brook, Pres., European Region
Dig Howitt, Sr. VP-Logistics

GROWTH PLANS/SPECIAL FEATURES:

Cochlear Limited is an Australian developer of multi-channel hearing aid implant devices. The company's products use electrical stimulation to allow deaf or hard-of-hearing users to clearly hear sound. Its most advanced products include Cochlear Nucleus system, the Kanso sound processor, the Cochlear Baha system and the Cochlear Carina middle-ear implant. The Cochlear Nucleus 7 sound processor helps severely hearing impaired individuals to detect and understand sounds. The Kanso sound processor is small, light and comfortable, without compromising hearing performance technology. It comprises smart sound ability via dual microphones, and wireless connectivity options. The Baha bone product uses bone conduction to alleviate mixed hearing loss, conductive hearing loss or single-sided deafness. The Corina system is a fully implantable middle-ear implant that is 100% invisible, meaning that all the technology is hidden under-the-skin. In addition, the Cochlear True Wireless product offers a wireless phone clip, television streamer and next-generation mini microphones that allow cochlear implant wearers to listen to media without neckloops or wires. The Cochlear Vistafix is a bone-anchored facial prosthetic solution designed to improve the attachment and cosmetic outcome of facial prostheses. The company's manufacturing operations are primarily located in Australia and Sweden, while research operations are conducted in collaboration with more than 100 research partners in 20 countries. The firm controls more than 1,000 issued and pending patents.

FINANCIAL DATA:

Note: Data for latest year may not have been available at press time.

In U.S. $	2017	2016	2015	2014	2013	2012
Revenue	907,263,360	818,055,040	669,775,680	582,442,816	544,660,672	563,672,896
R&D Expense						
Operating Income						
Operating Margin %						
SGA Expense						
Net Income	161,806,080	136,701,152	105,528,224	67,806,800	95,921,128	41,102,028
Operating Cash Flow						
Capital Expenditure						
EBITDA						
Return on Assets %						
Return on Equity %						
Debt to Equity						

CONTACT INFORMATION:

Phone: 61 294286555 Fax: 61 294286539
Toll-Free:
Address: 1 University Ave., Macquarie University, Lane Cove, NSW 2109 Australia

STOCK TICKER/OTHER:

Stock Ticker: CHEOY
Employees: 3,000
Parent Company:
Exchange: PINX
Fiscal Year Ends: 06/30

SALARIES/BONUSES:

Top Exec. Salary: $ Bonus: $
Second Exec. Salary: $ Bonus: $

OTHER THOUGHTS:

Estimated Female Officers or Directors: 1
Hot Spot for Advancement for Women/Minorities:

Coherent Inc

www.coherent.com

NAIC Code: 334,510

TYPES OF BUSINESS:

Equipment-Lasers & Laser Systems
Precision Optics
Laser Accessories

BRANDS/DIVISIONS/AFFILIATES:

OR Lasertechnologie GmbH

CONTACTS: *Note: Officers with more than one job title may be intentionally listed here more than once.*

John Ambroseo, CEO
Kevin Palatnik, CFO
Garry Rogerson, Chairman of the Board
Paul Sechrist, Executive VP, Divisional
Bret DiMarco, Executive VP
Mark Sobey, Executive VP
Thomas Merk, Executive VP

GROWTH PLANS/SPECIAL FEATURES:

Coherent, Inc. designs, manufactures, services and markets lasers and related accessories for a diverse group of customers. The company operates through two business segments: OEM laser sources (OLS) and industrial lasers and systems (ILS). The OLS segment focuses on high-performance laser sources and complex optical sub-systems typically used in microelectronics manufacturing, medical diagnostics and therapeutic applications, as well as in scientific research. This division's offerings are utilized in commercial applications such as bio-instrumentation, medical OEMs (original equipment manufacturers), graphic arts and displays, machine vision and defense. The ILS segment delivers high-performance laser sources, sub-systems and tools primarily used for industrial laser materials processing, serving important end markets like automotive, machine tool, consumer goods and medical device manufacturing. In October 2017, Coherent sold its U.K.-based Hull business. In May 2018, the firm acquired O.R. Lasertechnologie GmbH, which produces a range of compact, high-precision tools for laser additive manufacturing, including both direct metal deposition and selective layer melting technologies as well as systems for cutting, welding, marking and engraving. Their products are used in diverse applications such as dental, medical, jewelry, automotive and aerospace.

The firm offers employees medical, dental, life, accident and vision insurance; educational assistance and tuition reimbursement; 401(k); a flexible spending account; an employee stock purchase plan; an employee assistance program; and credit union membership.

FINANCIAL DATA: *Note: Data for latest year may not have been available at press time.*

In U.S. $	2017	2016	2015	2014	2013	2012
Revenue	1,723,311,000	857,385,000	802,460,000	794,639,000	810,126,000	769,088,000
R&D Expense	119,166,000	81,801,000	81,455,000	79,070,000	82,785,000	78,260,000
Operating Income	322,995,000	127,614,000	101,448,000	76,866,000	84,899,000	88,830,000
Operating Margin %	18.74%	14.88%	12.64%	9.67%	10.47%	11.55%
SGA Expense	292,084,000	169,138,000	149,829,000	154,030,000	149,513,000	138,519,000
Net Income	207,122,000	87,502,000	76,409,000	59,106,000	66,355,000	62,962,000
Operating Cash Flow	384,116,000	105,299,000	124,458,000	91,379,000	115,522,000	64,771,000
Capital Expenditure	63,774,000	49,327,000	22,163,000	23,390,000	21,988,000	36,051,000
EBITDA	440,662,000	158,597,000	132,675,000	115,492,000	119,783,000	120,357,000
Return on Assets %	11.83%	8.21%	7.76%	6.01%	7.18%	7.30%
Return on Equity %	19.97%	10.25%	9.45%	7.49%	9.27%	9.76%
Debt to Equity	0.50					

CONTACT INFORMATION:

Phone: 408 764-4000 Fax: 408 764-4800
Toll-Free: 800-527-3786
Address: 5100 Patrick Henry Dr., Santa Clara, CA 95054 United States

STOCK TICKER/OTHER:

Stock Ticker: COHR
Employees: 2,787
Parent Company:
Exchange: NAS
Fiscal Year Ends: 09/30

SALARIES/BONUSES:

Top Exec. Salary: $766,358 Bonus: $
Second Exec. Salary: $426,747 Bonus: $

OTHER THOUGHTS:

Estimated Female Officers or Directors: 2
Hot Spot for Advancement for Women/Minorities:

Coloplast AS

www.coloplast.com

NAIC Code: 339,100

TYPES OF BUSINESS:

Ostomy Supplies

BRANDS/DIVISIONS/AFFILIATES:

SenSura
Brava
Conveen Active
SpeediCath
Peristeen
Biatain
Coloplast
IncoCare Gunhild Vieler GmbH

CONTACTS: *Note: Officers with more than one job title may be intentionally listed here more than once.*

Lars Rasmussen, CEO
Allan Rasmussen, Exec. VP-Global Oper.
Lars Rasmussen, Pres.
Anders Lonning-Skovgaard, CFO
Oliver Johansen, Sr. VP-Global R&D
Peter Volkers, Sr. VP-Corp. Legal
Anders Monrad Rendtorff, Sr. VP-People & Communications
Lars Einar Hansen, Sr. VP-Corp. Finance
Claus Bjerre, Sr. VP-Sales, North America, Japan & Australia
Jesper Kalenberg, VP-Corp. Procurement
Kristian Villumsen, Sr. VP-Emerging Markets
Nicolas Nemery, Sr. VP-Global Mktg.
Michael Pram Rasmussen, Chmn.
Allan Rasmussen, Sr. VP-Global Oper.

GROWTH PLANS/SPECIAL FEATURES:

Coloplast A/S is a Denmark-based medical device manufacturer that designs products for ostomy care, continence, wound care, skin care and urology care. The company's ostomy segment offers appliances for people with stomas under the brand name SenSura and Brava. Stomas are a result of surgery to correct an intestinal dysfunction resulting from disease, accident or birth defects, where a part of the intestine is surgically redirected through the abdominal wall. Due to the sensitivity of stomas, ostomy bags must be manufactured with extreme care and quality. Coloplast's continence segment sells intermittent catheters, urine bags, urisheaths and anal irrigation systems, which are marketed under the Conveen Active, SpeediCath and Peristeen brands. The wound care segment offers Biatain, a bandage dressing line that provides mobility and function to people with injuries and also have been shown to kill mature biofilms and prevent them from forming. This division's Comfeel Plus dressing product encompasses hydrocolloid, providing moist wound healing and protection for wounds and skin at risk. Coloplast's skin care division offers products such as cleansers, moisturizers, skin protectants, antifungals, hand cleansers and odor control solutions through brands such as Coloplast, Isagel, InterDry and Hex-On. Last, the urology care segment develops, produces and markets products for surgical treatment of urological and gynecological disorders such as urinary stone disease, benign prostate hyperplasia, voiding dysfunctions, erectile dysfunction and urinary incontinence (male and female). Products within this division include prostatic catheters, bladder evacuators, post-operative bags, stone extractors, ureteral stents, access sheaths, guidewires, balloon dilators, irrigation lines, slings, meshes and penile/malleable implants. Brands within this segment inlcude Dormia, N.Stone, Vortek, Orchestra, In-Ka, Restorelle, Virtue, Titan Touch, Genesis and more. In February 2018, Coloplast acquired IncoCare Gunhild Vieler GmbH, a German direct-to-consumer homecare company.

FINANCIAL DATA: *Note: Data for latest year may not have been available at press time.*

In U.S. $	2017	2016	2015	2014	2013	2012
Revenue						
R&D Expense						
Operating Income						
Operating Margin %						
SGA Expense						
Net Income						
Operating Cash Flow						
Capital Expenditure						
EBITDA						
Return on Assets %						
Return on Equity %						
Debt to Equity						

CONTACT INFORMATION:

Phone: 45 49111111 Fax:
Toll-Free:
Address: Holtedam 1-3, Humlebaek, 3050 Denmark

STOCK TICKER/OTHER:

Stock Ticker: CLPBY
Exchange: PINX
Employees: 10,905
Fiscal Year Ends: 09/30
Parent Company:

SALARIES/BONUSES:

Top Exec. Salary: $ Bonus: $
Second Exec. Salary: $ Bonus: $

OTHER THOUGHTS:

Estimated Female Officers or Directors:
Hot Spot for Advancement for Women/Minorities:

Community Health Systems Inc

www.chs.net

NAIC Code: 622,110

TYPES OF BUSINESS:

General Medical and Surgical Hospitals
Surgical & Emergency Services
Acute Care Services
Internal Medicine
Obstetrics
Emergency Room Services
Diagnostic Services
Ambulatory Surgery Centers

BRANDS/DIVISIONS/AFFILIATES:

GROWTH PLANS/SPECIAL FEATURES:

Community Health Systems, Inc. is one of the largest operators of general acute care hospitals in the U.S. As of August 2018, the company owned, leased or operated 118 hospitals in 20 states, with an aggregate of approximately 20,000 licensed beds. Community Health Systems provides health care for local residents, offering a wide range of diagnostic, medical and surgical services in in-patient and out-patient settings. During 2017, Community Health Systems divested 30 hospitals for approximately $1.7 billion in total. In 2018, the firm sold seven hospitals; agreed to sell Oklahoma City Hospital to INTEGRIS Health (in June); and agreed to sell Arkansas-based Sparks Health System to Baptist Health (in July).

The company offers employees medical, dental and vision insurance; flexible spending accounts; life and disability insurance; and a 401(k) savings plan.

CONTACTS: *Note: Officers with more than one job title may be intentionally listed here more than once.*

Benjamin Fordham, Assistant Secretary
Wayne Smith, CEO
Kevin Hammons, Chief Accounting Officer
Lynn Simon, Chief Medical Officer
Thomas Aaron, Executive VP
P. Smith, President, Divisional
Beryl Ramsey, President, Divisional
Tim Hingtgen, President

FINANCIAL DATA: *Note: Data for latest year may not have been available at press time.*

In U.S. $	2017	2016	2015	2014	2013	2012
Revenue	15,353,000,000	18,438,000,000	19,437,000,000	18,639,000,000	12,997,690,000	13,028,980,000
R&D Expense			68,000,000			
Operating Income	217,000,000	1,005,000,000	1,181,000,000	1,222,000,000	835,386,000	1,083,390,000
Operating Margin %	1.41%	5.45%	6.07%	6.55%	6.42%	8.31%
SGA Expense	7,739,000,000	9,074,000,000	9,447,999,000	9,052,000,000	6,505,159,000	6,376,760,000
Net Income	-2,459,000,000	-1,721,000,000	158,000,000	92,000,000	141,203,000	265,640,000
Operating Cash Flow	773,000,000	1,137,000,000	921,000,000	1,615,000,000	1,088,719,000	1,280,120,000
Capital Expenditure	564,000,000	867,000,000	1,010,000,000	3,944,000,000	613,992,000	768,790,000
EBITDA	-1,030,000,000	361,000,000	2,355,000,000	2,501,000,000	1,703,684,000	1,852,262,000
Return on Assets %	-12.48%	-7.05%	.58%	.41%	.83%	1.66%
Return on Equity %	-579.95%	-61.09%	3.93%	2.60%	4.86%	10.35%
Debt to Equity		9.15	4.18	4.16	3.02	3.46

CONTACT INFORMATION:

Phone: 615 465-7000 Fax: 615 645-7001
Toll-Free:
Address: 4000 Meridian Blvd., Franklin, TN 37067 United States

STOCK TICKER/OTHER:

Stock Ticker: CYH
Employees: 120,000
Parent Company:
Exchange: NYS
Fiscal Year Ends: 12/31

SALARIES/BONUSES:

Top Exec. Salary: $1,600,000 Bonus: $
Second Exec. Salary: $800,000 Bonus: $

OTHER THOUGHTS:

Estimated Female Officers or Directors: 18
Hot Spot for Advancement for Women/Minorities: Y

Concentra Inc

www.concentra.com

NAIC Code: 621,498

TYPES OF BUSINESS:

Health Clinics
Workplace Injury Treatment & Management
Group Health & Automobile Claims Management
Claims Cost Control
Case Management
Medical Advisory Services
Workplace-Based Clinics

BRANDS/DIVISIONS/AFFILIATES:

Select Medical Holdings Corporation
Welsh Carson Anderson & Stowe XII LP
MJ Acquisition Corporation
Valor Healthcare

CONTACTS: *Note: Officers with more than one job title may be intentionally listed here more than once.*

Keith Newton, CEO
Su Zan Nelson, CFO
John deLorimier, Sr. VP-Sales
Dani Kendall, VP-Human Resources
W. Tom Fogarty, Chief Medical Officer
Jim Talalai, CIO
William R. Lewis, Sr. VP-Medical Oper.
Daryl Risinger, Sr. VP-Service & Dev. Management
Gregory M. Gilbert, Sr. VP-Reimbursement
Kate Blackmon, VP-Primary Care Oper. & Integration

GROWTH PLANS/SPECIAL FEATURES:

Concentra, Inc. is a national healthcare company that operates over 500 medical centers in 44 states. The firm also serves patients at more than 140 on-site workplace clinics that it establishes at employer sites as well as programs in which it travels to its customers. Concentra divides its business into six segments: occupational health, physical therapy services, health and wellness, urgent care, Valor Healthcare and first dose observation (FDO) services. The firm's occupational health segment offers a vast array of services such as mobile medical services, drug testing and screening, specialist care, clinical and forensic services, medical advisory services, health risk assessments, biometric screenings, vaccinations, health coaching and medical compliance administration. The physical therapy services segment offers specialized treatments with a focus on early intervention for trauma, repetitive stress, chronic and orthopedic injuries. The health and wellness segment focuses on preventative services, combining primary, preventive and occupational and environment health services to reduce employee illness and injury and cut employer health costs. Urgent care runs several urgent care clinics which provide treatment for immediate medical emergencies that are not life threatening enough to merit the emergency room. Subsidiary Valor Healthcare operates more than 30 VA community-based outpatient clinics as a contractor for the U.S. Department of Veteran Affairs. Valor provides a full range of medical services at its VA medical centers, including primary care, diagnostics, laboratory, telehealth, behavioral health and more. Last, in partnership with Novartis, Concentra provides a clinical network that administers FDO services required for patients starting therapy on Gilenya (finglimod). The Gilenya assessment network has more than 300 sites nationwide. Concentra is owned by MJ Acquisition Corporation, a joint venture between Select Medical Holdings Corporation and Welsh, Carson, Anderson & Stowe XII, LP.

FINANCIAL DATA: *Note: Data for latest year may not have been available at press time.*

In U.S. $	2017	2016	2015	2014	2013	2012
Revenue	1,120,000,000	1,050,000,000	1,000,000,000			
R&D Expense						
Operating Income						
Operating Margin %						
SGA Expense						
Net Income						
Operating Cash Flow						
Capital Expenditure						
EBITDA						
Return on Assets %						
Return on Equity %						
Debt to Equity						

CONTACT INFORMATION:

Phone: 972-364-8211 Fax:
Toll-Free: 800-232-3550
Address: 5080 Spectrum Dr., Ste. 1200 W., Addison, TX 75001 United States

STOCK TICKER/OTHER:

Stock Ticker: Subsidiary Exchange:
Employees: 9,000 Fiscal Year Ends: 12/31
Parent Company: Select Medical Holdings Corporation

SALARIES/BONUSES:

Top Exec. Salary: $ Bonus: $
Second Exec. Salary: $ Bonus: $

OTHER THOUGHTS:

Estimated Female Officers or Directors: 3
Hot Spot for Advancement for Women/Minorities: Y

CONMED Corporation

www.conmed.com

NAIC Code: 339,100

TYPES OF BUSINESS:

Equipment-Surgical & Medical Procedure
Patient Care Products
Sports Medicine Equipment
Arthroscopic surgery devices

BRANDS/DIVISIONS/AFFILIATES:

Hall
CONMED Linvatec
Concept
Shutt
AirSeal
VCARE

CONTACTS: *Note: Officers with more than one job title may be intentionally listed here more than once.*

Todd Garner, CFO
Terence Berge, Controller
Curt Hartman, Director
Mark Tryniski, Director
Peter Shagory, Executive VP, Divisional
Wilfredo Ruiz-Caban, Executive VP, Divisional
Heather Cohen, Executive VP, Divisional
Daniel Jonas, Executive VP
Nathan Folkert, General Manager, Divisional
Stanley Peters, General Manager, Divisional
John Kennedy, General Manager, Divisional
Patrick Beyer, President, Divisional
Johonna Pelletier, Vice President, Divisional

GROWTH PLANS/SPECIAL FEATURES:

CONMED Corporation is a medical technology company focused on surgical devices and equipment for minimally-invasive procedures. The company's products are used by surgeons and physicians in a variety of specialties, including orthopedics, general surgery, gynecology, neurosurgery and gastroenterology. Orthopedic surgery products derived 54% of CONMED's 2017 net sales, and general surgery products derived the remaining 46%. Orthopedic surgery products include sports medicine, powered surgical instruments, sports biologics and tissue. These products are marketed under a number of brands, including Hall, CONMED Linvatec, Concept and Shutt. The general surgery division offers a large range of products in the areas of advanced surgical, endoscopic technologies and critical care. Advanced surgical products include the AirSeal clinical insufflation system, which encompasses valve-less access ports. Electrosurgical offerings consist of monopolar and bipolar generators, beam coagulation generators, handpieces, smoke management systems and other accessories. Endomechanical products include tissue retrieval bags, trocars, suction irrigation devices, graspers, scissors and dissectors. CONMED's uterine manipulator, VCARE, is used for laparoscopic hysterectomies and other gynecologic laparoscopic procedures. The firm's endoscopic technologies include a comprehensive line of minimally-invasive diagnostic and therapeutic products used in conjunction with procedures which utilize flexible endoscopy. These include mucosal management devices, forceps, scope management accessories, bronchoscopy devices, dilation, stricture management devices, hemostasis, biliary devices and polypectomy. Critical care products include ECG electrodes and accessories, cardiac defibrillation and pacing pads and a line of suction instruments and tubing. CONMED's products are sold in more than 100 foreign countries, and sales are coordinated through local country dealers.

FINANCIAL DATA: *Note: Data for latest year may not have been available at press time.*

In U.S. $	2017	2016	2015	2014	2013	2012
Revenue	796,392,000	763,520,000	719,168,000	740,055,000	762,704,000	767,140,000
R&D Expense	32,307,000	32,254,000	27,436,000	27,779,000	25,831,000	28,214,000
Operating Income	46,935,000	37,676,000	51,175,000	76,748,000	69,907,000	65,210,000
Operating Margin %	5.89%	4.93%	7.11%	10.37%	9.16%	8.50%
SGA Expense	351,799,000	338,400,000	303,091,000	293,942,000	310,730,000	312,419,000
Net Income	55,487,000	14,664,000	30,498,000	32,192,000	35,939,000	40,481,000
Operating Cash Flow	65,566,000	38,222,000	48,068,000	65,176,000	80,949,000	95,199,000
Capital Expenditure	12,842,000	14,753,000	15,009,000	15,411,000	18,445,000	21,532,000
EBITDA	105,483,000	90,043,000	95,054,000	98,520,000	104,112,000	111,826,000
Return on Assets %	4.13%	1.20%	2.75%	2.94%	3.30%	4.00%
Return on Equity %	9.15%	2.51%	5.22%	5.42%	5.92%	6.86%
Debt to Equity	0.74	0.84	0.46	0.41	0.35	0.26

CONTACT INFORMATION:

Phone: 315 797-8375 Fax: 315 797-0321
Toll-Free:
Address: 525 French Rd., Utica, NY 13502 United States

STOCK TICKER/OTHER:

Stock Ticker: CNMD
Employees: 3,300
Parent Company:
Exchange: NAS
Fiscal Year Ends: 12/31

SALARIES/BONUSES:

Top Exec. Salary: $753,237 Bonus: $
Second Exec. Salary: $392,966 Bonus: $23,713

OTHER THOUGHTS:

Estimated Female Officers or Directors: 2
Hot Spot for Advancement for Women/Minorities:

Continucare Corporation

www.continucare.com

NAIC Code: 621,111

TYPES OF BUSINESS:

Physicians Offices
Managed Health Care
Practice Management Services
Sleep Diagnostic Centers

BRANDS/DIVISIONS/AFFILIATES:

Humana Inc
Seredor Corporation

CONTACTS: *Note: Officers with more than one job title may be intentionally listed here more than once.*

Joe Jasser, Pres.
Yogi Hernandez, Chief Medical Officer
Tom Aponte, VP-Center Oper.
Holly Lopez, VP-Support Svcs.
Dora Rodriguez-Duran, Sr. VP-Support Svcs.
Jose R. Borges, VP-Utilization Mgmt.

GROWTH PLANS/SPECIAL FEATURES:

Continucare Corporation, a subsidiary of Humana, Inc., is a provider of primary senior care physician services. Through a network of 18 medical centers, the company provides primary health care services on an outpatient basis. Continucare also provides practice management services to independent physician affiliates (IPAs). All of Continucare's medical centers and IPAs are located in Miami-Dade, Broward, Pasco and Hillsborough counties, Florida. The firm's medical centers provide facilities for physicians practicing in the areas of general, family and internal medicine. Services provided to independent physician associate clinics enrolled in Humana health plans include assistance with medical utilization management, pharmacy management, specialist network development and financial reports. The company has managed care agreements with a number of HMOs. Under these agreements, Continucare receives monthly payments per patient (at a rate established by the contract) in return for providing all medical care required by patients. Subsidiary Seredor Corporation conducts sleep service facilities and operates sleep diagnostic centers in Florida, South Carolina, North Carolina, West Virginia and Ohio.

FINANCIAL DATA: *Note: Data for latest year may not have been available at press time.*

In U.S. $	2017	2016	2015	2014	2013	2012
Revenue	435,750,000	415,000,000	410,000,000	380,000,000	370,000,000	355,000,000
R&D Expense						
Operating Income						
Operating Margin %						
SGA Expense						
Net Income						
Operating Cash Flow						
Capital Expenditure						
EBITDA						
Return on Assets %						
Return on Equity %						
Debt to Equity						

CONTACT INFORMATION:

Phone: 305-500-2000 Fax: 305-500-2080
Toll-Free:
Address: 6101 Blue Lagoon Dr., Ste. 401, Miami, FL 33126 United States

STOCK TICKER/OTHER:

Stock Ticker: Subsidiary
Employees: 870
Parent Company: Humana Inc
Exchange:
Fiscal Year Ends: 06/30

SALARIES/BONUSES:

Top Exec. Salary: $ Bonus: $
Second Exec. Salary: $ Bonus: $

OTHER THOUGHTS:

Estimated Female Officers or Directors: 3
Hot Spot for Advancement for Women/Minorities: Y

ConvaTec Inc

www.convatec.com

NAIC Code: 339,100

TYPES OF BUSINESS:

Wound Care Products
Skin Care Products
Ostomy Products

BRANDS/DIVISIONS/AFFILIATES:

ConvaTec Group PLC
AQUACEL
Hydrofiber
Ostomy Care
Continence & Critical Care
Flexi-Seal
Unometer Safeti
AbViser AutoValve

CONTACTS: *Note: Officers with more than one job title may be intentionally listed here more than once.*

Paul Moraviec, CEO
Frank Schulkes, CFO
Robbie Heginbotham, Sr. VP-Oper.
Jorgen B. Hansen, Sr. VP-Bus. Dev.
Robert McKee, Sr. VP-Comm.
John Lindskog, Pres., Global Infusion Devices & Asia Pacific
Todd Brown, CEO-180 Medical
Mark Valentine, Pres., Americas
Paul Moraviec, Pres., EMEA

GROWTH PLANS/SPECIAL FEATURES:

ConvaTec, Inc. is a U.S.-based global medical products and technologies company. The firm focuses on therapies for the management of chronic conditions, with leading positions in advanced wound care, ostomy care, continence and critical care, and infusion devices. ConvaTec's products provide a range of clinical and economic benefits including infection prevention, protection of at-risk skin, improved patient outcomes and reduced total cost of care. In July 2018, ConvaTec, Inc. received U.S. FDA 510(k) clearance for its most advanced and innovative antimicrobial dressing: AQUACEL Ag Advantage. AQUACEL Ag Advantage is an enhanced Hydrofiber dressing with silver and strengthening fiber features, which absorbs and retains excess exudate to maintain a moist wound environment to support the healing process. AQUACEL and Hydrofiber are trademarks of ConvaTec, Inc. The company's Ostomy Care franchise specializes in devices, accessories and services for individuals with a stoma (a surgically-created opening where bodily waste is discharged) commonly resulting from colorectal cancer, inflammatory bowel disease, bladder cancer, obesity and other causes. Its Continence & Critical Care franchise distributes disposable, intermittent (single-use) urological catheters directly to patients in the U.S. This division also distributes the Flexi-Seal line of fecal management systems, the Unometer Safeti urine meter and the AbViser AutoValve intra-abdominal pressure monitoring device. The infusion devices franchise specializes in providing disposable infusion sets to manufacturers of insulin pumps for diabetes and similar pumps used in continuous infusion treatments for other conditions. ConvaTec operates as a subsidiary of U.K.-based ConvaTec Group PLC.

FINANCIAL DATA: *Note: Data for latest year may not have been available at press time.*

In U.S. $	2017	2016	2015	2014	2013	2012
Revenue	1,764,600,000	1,688,300,000	1,650,400,000	1,725,000,000	1,700,700,000	1,646,200,000
R&D Expense						
Operating Income						
Operating Margin %						
SGA Expense						
Net Income	158,400,000	-202,800,000	-93,400,000	-286,500,000	-173,700,000	-161,100,000
Operating Cash Flow						
Capital Expenditure						
EBITDA						
Return on Assets %						
Return on Equity %						
Debt to Equity						

CONTACT INFORMATION:

Phone: 908-904-2500 Fax: 908-904-2780
Toll-Free: 800-422-8811
Address: CenterPoint II, 1160 Route 22 East, Ste. 201, Bridgewater, NJ 08807 United States

STOCK TICKER/OTHER:

Stock Ticker: CTEC
Employees: 9,549
Parent Company: ConvaTec Group PLC
Exchange:
Fiscal Year Ends: 12/31

SALARIES/BONUSES:

Top Exec. Salary: $ Bonus: $
Second Exec. Salary: $ Bonus: $

OTHER THOUGHTS:

Estimated Female Officers or Directors: 1
Hot Spot for Advancement for Women/Minorities:

Cooper Companies Inc (The)

www.coopercos.com

NAIC Code: 339,100

TYPES OF BUSINESS:

Medical Devices
Contact Lenses
Gynecological Instruments
Diagnostic Products

BRANDS/DIVISIONS/AFFILIATES:

CooperVision Inc
CooperSurgical Inc
Proclear
Phosphorylcholine (PC) Technology
LifeGlobal Group (The)

CONTACTS: *Note: Officers with more than one job title may be intentionally listed here more than once.*

Albert White, CEO
A. Bender, Chairman of the Board
Agostino Ricupati, Chief Accounting Officer
Carol Kaufman, Chief Administrative Officer
Daniel McBride, COO
Allan Rubenstein, Director
Randal Golden, General Counsel
Brian Andrews, Senior VP

GROWTH PLANS/SPECIAL FEATURES:

The Cooper Companies, Inc. develops, manufactures and markets healthcare products, primarily medical devices. The company operates through two business units: CooperVision, Inc. (CVI) and CooperSurgical, Inc. (CSI). CVI develops, manufactures and markets a broad range of contact lenses, including disposable spherical and specialty contact lenses. It is a leading manufacturer of toric lenses, which correct astigmatism; multifocal lenses for presbyopia, the blurring of vision due to advancing age; and spherical lenses, including hydrogel lenses, which correct the most common near- and far-sighted visual defects. CVI offers single-use, two-week, monthly and quarterly disposable sphere and toric lenses as well as custom toric lenses to correct a high degree of astigmatism. CVI's Proclear line of spherical, toric and multifocal lenses are manufactured with omafilcon, a material that incorporates its proprietary Phosphorylcholine (PC) Technology to enhance tissue-device compatibility. CVI's products are primarily manufactured at its facilities in the U.S., the U.K., Hungary, Costa Rico and Puerto Rico. It distributes its products out of West Henrietta, New York; Fareham, U.K.; Liege, Belgium; and various smaller international distribution facilities. CSI develops, manufactures and markets medical devices, diagnostic products and surgical instruments and accessories used primarily by gynecologists and obstetricians. The subsidiary manufactures and distributes its products at its facilities in Trumbull, Connecticut; Malov, Denmark; Pasadena, California; Stafford, Texas; and Berlin, Germany. In April 2018, The Cooper Companies acquired the assets of The LifeGlobal Group and its affiliates, a global provider of in-vitro fertilization devices.

FINANCIAL DATA: *Note: Data for latest year may not have been available at press time.*

In U.S. $	2017	2016	2015	2014	2013	2012
Revenue	2,139,000,000	1,966,814,000	1,797,060,000	1,717,776,000	1,587,725,000	1,445,136,000
R&D Expense	69,200,000	65,411,000	69,589,000	66,259,000	58,827,000	51,730,000
Operating Income	429,100,000	324,080,000	236,671,000	306,486,000	327,007,000	283,398,000
Operating Margin %	20.06%	16.47%	13.16%	17.84%	20.59%	19.61%
SGA Expense	799,100,000	722,798,000	712,543,000	683,115,000	610,735,000	564,903,000
Net Income	372,900,000	273,917,000	203,523,000	269,856,000	296,151,000	248,339,000
Operating Cash Flow	593,600,000	509,637,000	390,970,000	454,823,000	415,925,000	315,121,000
Capital Expenditure	127,200,000	152,640,000	243,023,000	238,065,000	178,127,000	99,779,000
EBITDA	615,800,000	520,097,000	424,991,000	442,700,000	446,788,000	398,437,000
Return on Assets %	7.98%	6.13%	4.56%	7.10%	9.74%	8.92%
Return on Equity %	12.69%	10.20%	7.77%	10.84%	12.88%	12.02%
Debt to Equity	0.36	0.41	0.41	0.49	0.12	0.15

CONTACT INFORMATION:

Phone: 925 460-3600 Fax: 949 597-0662
Toll-Free:
Address: 6140 Stoneridge Mall Rd., Ste. 590, Pleasanton, CA 94588 United States

STOCK TICKER/OTHER:

Stock Ticker: COO
Employees: 10,600
Parent Company:
Exchange: NYS
Fiscal Year Ends: 10/31

SALARIES/BONUSES:

Top Exec. Salary: $925,000 Bonus: $284,669
Second Exec. Salary: $525,000 Bonus: $112,902

OTHER THOUGHTS:

Estimated Female Officers or Directors: 2
Hot Spot for Advancement for Women/Minorities: Y

Cordis Corporation

www.cordis.com

NAIC Code: 339,100

TYPES OF BUSINESS:

Vascular Treatment Products
Guidewires & Balloons
Stents & Catheters

BRANDS/DIVISIONS/AFFILIATES:

Cardinal Health Inc
AVANTI
EMERALD
INFINITI
EXOSEAL
AQUATRACK
ELITECROSS
FRONTRUNNER

CONTACTS: *Note: Officers with more than one job title may be intentionally listed here more than once.*

David J. Wilson, Pres.
Tico Blumenthal, Dir.-Global Mktg.
Campbell Rogers, Chief Scientific Officer
Charles McDowell, VP-Corp. Rel.
Barbara G. Ramseyer, VP-Regulatory Affairs & Quality Assurance
Paul I. Chang, VP-Worldwide Clinical Research & Oper.

GROWTH PLANS/SPECIAL FEATURES:

Cordis Corporation develops and manufactures interventional vascular technology. Its business and products are divided into two segments: cardiology and endovascular. The cardiology segment develops and manufactures products to treat patients who suffer from cardiovascular disease. These products include sheaths, diagnostic guidewires, diagnostic catheters, steerable guidewires and PTCA balloons. Brands within this segment include AVANTI, EMERALD, INFINITI, EXOSEAL, MYNX ACE and MYNXGRIP. The endovascular segment produces sheaths, access accessories, diagnostic guidewires, crossing devices, diagnostic catheters, steerable guidewires, guiding catheters, PTA balloons, specialty balloons, self-expanding stents, balloon expandable stents, vena cava filters and vascular closure devices. Brands within this segment include AVANTI, EMERALD, AQUATRACK, TEMPO AQUA, ELITECROSS, OUTBACK, FRONTRUNNER, EXOSEAL, RAILWAY AND MYNX. Cordis' range of self-expanding and balloon expandable biliary stents include flex biliary stents, transhepatic biliary stents and carotid stents. Cordis operates as a wholly-owned subsidiary of Cardinal Health, Inc.

FINANCIAL DATA: *Note: Data for latest year may not have been available at press time.*

In U.S. $	2017	2016	2015	2014	2013	2012
Revenue	861,000,000	820,000,000	800,000,000	780,000,000	760,000,000	
R&D Expense						
Operating Income						
Operating Margin %						
SGA Expense						
Net Income						
Operating Cash Flow						
Capital Expenditure						
EBITDA						
Return on Assets %						
Return on Equity %						
Debt to Equity						

CONTACT INFORMATION:

Phone: 408-273-3700 Fax:
Toll-Free:
Address: 1820 McCarthy Blvd., Milpitas, CA 95035 United States

STOCK TICKER/OTHER:

Stock Ticker: Subsidiary
Exchange:
Employees: 5,000
Fiscal Year Ends: 12/31
Parent Company: Cardinal Health Inc

SALARIES/BONUSES:

Top Exec. Salary: $ Bonus: $
Second Exec. Salary: $ Bonus: $

OTHER THOUGHTS:

Estimated Female Officers or Directors: 1
Hot Spot for Advancement for Women/Minorities:

CorVel Corporation

www.corvel.com

NAIC Code: 524298A

TYPES OF BUSINESS:

Utilization Management and Claims Administration
Managed Care Services
Preferred Provider Networks
Payment Processing
Workers' Compensation Services
Claims Cost Control Services

BRANDS/DIVISIONS/AFFILIATES:

24/7 Nurse Triage

CONTACTS:

Note: Officers with more than one job title may be intentionally listed here more than once.

V. Clemons, CEO
Kenneth Cragun, CFO
Maxim Shishin, Chief Information Officer
Diane Blaha, Chief Marketing Officer
Michael Saverien, Executive VP, Divisional
Michael Combs, President
Richard Schweppe, Vice President, Divisional

GROWTH PLANS/SPECIAL FEATURES:

CorVel Corporation is an independent nationwide provider of medical cost containment and managed care services, designed to manage the medical costs of workers' compensation and other liability claims management, primarily for coverage under group health and auto insurance policies. The company offers services in two categories: network solutions and patient management. Its network solution services provide savings and management solutions for employee medical bills; services include preferred provider organization (PPO) management, medical bill re-pricing, provider reimbursement, pharmacy services, true line item review, professional nurse review, Medicare services, directed care services, clearinghouse services and automated adjudication. Through its patient management solution category, the firm administers claims to its managed care customers. Claims administration services include automated first notice of loss, three-point contact within 24 hours, prompt claims investigations, claim history data and litigation management. This segment also offers case management; a 24/7 Nurse Triage system, where injured workers can speak with a registered nurse with expertise in occupational injuries; and utilization review services, which address disability management and recovery, vocational rehabilitation services, utilization management, life care planning, liability claims management and auto claims management. CorVel's services are sold as a bundled solution, as a standalone service and as additional services for existing customers. The firm offers its services to insurers, third-party administrators, self-administered employers, government agencies, municipalities and state funds to help them manage the medical costs and monitor the quality of care associated with health care claims.

FINANCIAL DATA:

Note: Data for latest year may not have been available at press time.

In U.S. $	2017	2016	2015	2014	2013	2012
Revenue	518,686,000	503,584,000	492,625,000	478,816,000	429,310,000	
R&D Expense						
Operating Income	47,549,000	46,060,000	45,564,000	56,507,000	43,895,000	
Operating Margin %	9.16%	9.14%	9.24%	11.80%	10.22%	
SGA Expense	57,243,000	58,484,000	54,405,000	51,974,000	47,765,000	
Net Income	29,479,000	28,525,000	28,590,000	34,392,000	26,730,000	
Operating Cash Flow	52,052,000	51,311,000	44,316,000	54,800,000	54,819,000	
Capital Expenditure	31,041,000	16,756,000	22,868,000	18,344,000	14,887,000	
EBITDA	68,497,000	66,012,000	63,559,000	72,918,000	59,634,000	
Return on Assets %	12.93%	12.99%	13.19%	17.33%	15.09%	
Return on Equity %	21.78%	21.95%	22.47%	28.91%	24.10%	
Debt to Equity						

CONTACT INFORMATION:

Phone: 949 851-1473 Fax: 949 851-1469
Toll-Free: 888-726-7835
Address: 2010 Main St., Ste. 600, Irvine, CA 92614 United States

STOCK TICKER/OTHER:

Stock Ticker: CRVL
Exchange: NAS
Employees: 3,629
Fiscal Year Ends: 03/31
Parent Company:

SALARIES/BONUSES:

Top Exec. Salary: $400,000 Bonus: $
Second Exec. Salary: $335,256 Bonus: $

OTHER THOUGHTS:

Estimated Female Officers or Directors: 3
Hot Spot for Advancement for Women/Minorities: Y

Coventry Health Care Inc

www.coventryhealthcare.com

NAIC Code: 524,114

TYPES OF BUSINESS:

Health Plans
Insurance
Managed Care Products

BRANDS/DIVISIONS/AFFILIATES:

Aetna Inc
CoventryOne
Coventry Health Care Medicare Prescription Drug
Coventry Workers' Compensation Network
Coventry MHNet Behavioral Health

CONTACTS: *Note: Officers with more than one job title may be intentionally listed here more than once.*

Mark T. Bertolini, CEO-Aetna, Inc.
Mark T. Bertolini, Chmn.-Aetna

GROWTH PLANS/SPECIAL FEATURES:

Coventry Health Care, Inc. is a diversified national managed health care company operating health plans, insurance companies and network rental and workers' compensation services companies. The firm's plans for individuals and families are branded under the CoventryOne line, offering low co-pays and deductibles, no specialist referrals necessary, and wellness and preventive programs. Coventry's group plans deliver products and services that give employer customers access to healthcare at affordable prices. Medicare coverage is offered by Coventry, along with Coventry Health Care Medicare Prescription Drug and Medicare Advantage plans, via affordable monthly plan premiums and coverage options. Coventry Workers' Compensation Network offers integrated continuum of cost containment services for workers' comp payors, including 24/7 nurse triage, clinical resources, telephone case managers, medical bill review services, network solutions that manage total spend (medical, pharmacy, physical medicine, durable medical equipment, home health, diagnostics), outcome-based networks, pharmacy benefit management, national network of field-based case managers and an integrated data warehouse. The firm's First Health network solutions offers national PPO (preferred provider organization) network solutions with deep discounts and broad access in urban, suburban and rural markets throughout the U.S., as well as in Puerto Rico. Last, Coventry MHNet Behavioral Health provides behavioral health and EAP/work-life services for health plans, employer groups and public programs. MHNet offers support and treatment for mental health and substance abuse, including conditions such as depression, severe stress/anxiety, alcohol/drug dependency, eating disorders, grief/loss, anger management, mood disorders, gambling problems, impatient care, acute rehab, day treatment, medication management, group therapy and more. Coventry is a subsidiary of Aetna, Inc.

FINANCIAL DATA: *Note: Data for latest year may not have been available at press time.*

In U.S. $	2017	2016	2015	2014	2013	2012
Revenue	15,225,000,000	14,500,000,000	14,000,000,000	13,317,000,000	14,400,000,000	14,113,363,000
R&D Expense						
Operating Income						
Operating Margin %						
SGA Expense						
Net Income						
Operating Cash Flow						
Capital Expenditure						
EBITDA						
Return on Assets %						
Return on Equity %						
Debt to Equity						

CONTACT INFORMATION:

Phone: 301 581-0600 Fax: 301 493-0742
Toll-Free:
Address: 6730-B Rockledge Dr., Ste 700, Bethesda, MD 20817 United States

STOCK TICKER/OTHER:

Stock Ticker: Subsidiary
Employees: 14,400
Parent Company: Aetna Inc
Exchange:
Fiscal Year Ends: 12/31

SALARIES/BONUSES:

Top Exec. Salary: $ Bonus: $
Second Exec. Salary: $ Bonus: $

OTHER THOUGHTS:

Estimated Female Officers or Directors: 1
Hot Spot for Advancement for Women/Minorities: Y

Criticare Technologies Inc

www.criticare.com

NAIC Code: 339,100

TYPES OF BUSINESS:

Equipment-Vital Sign Monitors
Anesthesia Monitors
Vital Signs Monitors
Pulse Oximeters

BRANDS/DIVISIONS/AFFILIATES:

Opto Circuits (India) Ltd
ComfortCuff
DOX Digital Oximetry
UltraSync ECG
High IQ
WaterChek

CONTACTS: *Note: Officers with more than one job title may be intentionally listed here more than once.*

Neeraj Jha, CEO
Deborah A. Zane, VP-OEM & Bus. Dev.

GROWTH PLANS/SPECIAL FEATURES:

Criticare Technologies, Inc. is a developer, marketer and distributor of a variety of patient monitoring devices, including vital sign devices, patient monitors and anesthesia and respiratory monitors. Vital sign devices record basic to advanced patient data ranging from pulse oximetry to invasive blood pressure. Criticare has developed ComfortCuff for fast, comfortable blood pressure readings measured on-inflation; DOX Digital Oximetry, a digital pulse oximetry technology providing high performance in high motion, low perfusion and ambient noise; a hospital-grade ambulatory telemetry monitor that simultaneously transmits real-time electrocardiogram (ECG), NIBP (non-invasive blood pressure) and SpO2 (peripheral capillary oxygen saturation, which estimates the amount of oxygen in the blood) data; a handheld pulse oximeter for spot-checks and continuous monitoring; the patented UltraSync ECG synchronization for monitoring oxygen saturation in highly active and poorly perfused patients; the patented far-infrared technology, High IQ, to automatically identify and quantify five agent gases; and WaterChek, a water separation system for monitoring inspired and expired gases in high humidity environments. Criticare Technologies operates as a subsidiary of India-based Opto Circuits (India) Ltd.

FINANCIAL DATA: *Note: Data for latest year may not have been available at press time.*

In U.S. $	2017	2016	2015	2014	2013	2012
Revenue						
R&D Expense						
Operating Income						
Operating Margin %						
SGA Expense						
Net Income						
Operating Cash Flow						
Capital Expenditure						
EBITDA						
Return on Assets %						
Return on Equity %						
Debt to Equity						

CONTACT INFORMATION:

Phone: 401-667-3837 Fax: 401-294-7541
Toll-Free:
Address: 125 Commerce Park Rd., North Kingstown, RI 02852 United States

STOCK TICKER/OTHER:

Stock Ticker: Subsidiary
Exchange:
Employees:
Fiscal Year Ends: 06/30
Parent Company: Opto Circuits (India) Ltd

SALARIES/BONUSES:

Top Exec. Salary: $ Bonus: $
Second Exec. Salary: $ Bonus: $

OTHER THOUGHTS:

Estimated Female Officers or Directors: 1
Hot Spot for Advancement for Women/Minorities:

CryoLife Inc

NAIC Code: 339,100

www.cryolife.com

TYPES OF BUSINESS:

Surgical Implants Manufacturing
Surgical Adhesives
Heart Valves
Medical Implants
Biomedical Research

BRANDS/DIVISIONS/AFFILIATES:

JOTECH GmbH
On-X Life Technologies Holdings Inc
BioGlue
BioForm
PerClot
CardioGenesis
PhotoFix
SynerGraft

CONTACTS: *Note: Officers with more than one job title may be intentionally listed here more than once.*

Amy Horton, Chief Accounting Officer
David Lee, Executive VP
Jean Holloway, General Counsel
James McDermid, Other Executive Officer
James Mackin, President
John Davis, Senior VP, Divisional
Scott Capps, Vice President, Divisional

GROWTH PLANS/SPECIAL FEATURES:

CryoLife, Inc. manufactures, processes and distributes medical devices, as well as implantable human tissues for use in cardiac and vascular surgeries. The company's surgical sealants and hemostats include BioGlue surgical adhesive, BioFoam surgical matrix and PerClot absorbable powered hemostat. CryoLife distributes these products internationally for Starch Medical, Inc. The firm's CardioGenesis cardiac laser therapy product line is used for the treatment of coronary artery disease in patients with severe angina. CryoLife also distributes PhotoFix, a bovine pericardial patch stabilized using a dye-mediated photo-fixation process that requires no glutaraldehyde. The cardiac and vascular human tissues distributed by the company include the CryoValve SG pulmonary heart valve and the CryoPatch SG pulmonary cardiac patch tissue, both of which are processed using CryoLife's proprietary SynerGraft decellularization technology. Other products include On-X prosthetic heart valves; Chord-X mitral chordal replacement products; cardiac and vascular allografts; and CarbonAid, a carbon dioxide diffuser that reduces air embolism during open heart surgery. Primary operating subsidiaries include: JOTEC GmbH, a Germany-based endovascular and surgical products firm; On-X Life Technologies Holdings, Inc., a Texas-based mechanical heart valve company; CryoLife Europa Ltda., a provider of marketing and distribution support services in Europe, the Middle East and Africa; CryoLife France SAS, which provides direct sales operations in France; CryoLife Canada, Inc., which provides direct sales operations in Canada; and CryoLife Asia Pacific Pte. Ltd., which provides sales and marketing support for the Asia Pacific region. CyroLife itself is headquartered in Georgia, U.S., and markets and sells its products in approximately 95 countries worldwide.

The firm offers its employees medical, prescription and dental coverage; life insurance; long-term disability; paid vacation; a 401(k) plan; an employee stock purchase plan; and tuition reimbursement.

FINANCIAL DATA: *Note: Data for latest year may not have been available at press time.*

In U.S. $	2017	2016	2015	2014	2013	2012
Revenue	189,702,000	180,380,000	145,898,000	144,641,000	140,763,000	
R&D Expense	19,461,000	13,446,000	10,436,000	8,699,000	8,454,000	
Operating Income	7,970,000	13,905,000	5,354,000	8,838,000	13,820,000	
Operating Margin %	4.20%	7.70%	3.66%	6.11%	9.81%	
SGA Expense	101,211,000	91,548,000	74,929,000	73,754,000	68,112,000	
Net Income	3,704,000	10,778,000	4,005,000	7,322,000	16,172,000	
Operating Cash Flow	10,803,000	19,719,000	11,442,000	8,118,000	16,772,000	
Capital Expenditure	6,632,000	7,424,000	4,103,000	5,320,000	4,338,000	
EBITDA	18,187,000	29,839,000	11,793,000	14,906,000	29,206,000	
Return on Assets %	.80%	4.25%	2.19%	4.08%	9.74%	
Return on Equity %	1.49%	5.80%	2.57%	4.88%	11.85%	
Debt to Equity	0.81	0.32				

CONTACT INFORMATION:

Phone: 770 419-3355   Fax: 770 426-0031
Toll-Free: 800-438-8285
Address: 1655 Roberts Blvd. NW, Kennesaw, GA 30144 United States

STOCK TICKER/OTHER:

Stock Ticker: CRY   Exchange: NYS
Employees: 655   Fiscal Year Ends: 12/31
Parent Company:

SALARIES/BONUSES:

Top Exec. Salary: $640,000   Bonus: $108,800
Second Exec. Salary: $402,771   Bonus: $72,499

OTHER THOUGHTS:

Estimated Female Officers or Directors: 3
Hot Spot for Advancement for Women/Minorities: Y

CSL Behring LLC

www.cslbehring.com

NAIC Code: 325,414

TYPES OF BUSINESS:

Plasma Products
Coagulants
Anticoagulants
Immunoglobulins
Surgical Wound Healers
Plasma Expanders
Plasma Collection

BRANDS/DIVISIONS/AFFILIATES:

CSL Limited

CONTACTS: *Note: Officers with more than one job title may be intentionally listed here more than once.*

Paul Perreault, CEO
David Lamont, CFO
Andrew Cuthbertson, Chief Scientific Officer
Mary Sontrop, Exec. VP-Manufacturing
Greg Boss, General Counsel
Ingolf Sieper, Exec. VP-Commercial Oper.
Mary Sontrop, Exec. VP-Planning
Dennis Jackman, Sr. VP-Public Affairs
Karen Etchberger, Exec. VP-Quality & Bus. Svcs.

GROWTH PLANS/SPECIAL FEATURES:

CSL Behring, LLC, a subsidiary of CSL Limited, specializes in the manufacture of plasma-based products. The company researches, develops, manufactures and markets biotherapies used to treat serious and rare conditions. Users of the firm's therapies rely on them for quality of life and even for life itself. Conditions treated include coagulation (bleeding) disorders such as hemophilia and von Willebrand disease, immune deficiencies and genetic emphysema (inherited respiratory disease). Biotherapies are also used in critical care settings to treat shock, sepsis and severe burns; to prevent hemolytic disease in the newborn resulting from Rh factor incompatibilities; during cardiac surgery; and for wound healing. CSL has manufacturing facilities located in Switzerland, Germany, Australia and the U.S. Research and development centers are located in Germany, Switzerland, the U.S., Japan and Australia. During 2018, CSL Behring was constructing a new, leading-edge manufacturing site in Lengnau, Switzerland for the manufacture of medicines for rare disease patients worldwide. The facility will create 300 new jobs.

FINANCIAL DATA: *Note: Data for latest year may not have been available at press time.*

In U.S. $	2017	2016	2015	2014	2013	2012
Revenue	5,500,000,000	5,259,800,000	5,049,000,000	4,947,400,000	4,500,900,000	3,762,800,000
R&D Expense						
Operating Income						
Operating Margin %						
SGA Expense						
Net Income		1,802,600,000	1,776,500,000	1,643,800,000	1,562,200,000	1,184,700,000
Operating Cash Flow						
Capital Expenditure						
EBITDA						
Return on Assets %						
Return on Equity %						
Debt to Equity						

CONTACT INFORMATION:

Phone: 610-878-4000 Fax: 610-878-4009
Toll-Free:
Address: 1020 First Ave., King of Prussia, PA 19406 United States

STOCK TICKER/OTHER:

Stock Ticker: Subsidiary
Employees: 14,000
Parent Company: CSL Limited
Exchange:
Fiscal Year Ends: 12/31

SALARIES/BONUSES:

Top Exec. Salary: $ Bonus: $
Second Exec. Salary: $ Bonus: $

OTHER THOUGHTS:

Estimated Female Officers or Directors: 8
Hot Spot for Advancement for Women/Minorities: Y

CSL Limited

www.csl.com.au

NAIC Code: 325,414

TYPES OF BUSINESS:

Human Blood-Plasma Collection
Plasma Products
Immunohematology Products
Vaccines
Pharmaceutical Marketing
Antivenom
Drugs-Cancer

BRANDS/DIVISIONS/AFFILIATES:

CSL Plasma
Seqirus

CONTACTS:

Note: Officers with more than one job title may be intentionally listed here more than once.

Paul Perreault, CEO
Andrew Cuthbertson, Chief Scientific Officer
Mary Sontrop, Exec. VP-Mfg. & Planning
Greg Boss, General Counsel
Ingolf Sieper, Exec. VP-Commercial Oper.
Karen Etchberger, Exec. VP-Quality & Bus. Svcs.
John Shine, Chmn.

GROWTH PLANS/SPECIAL FEATURES:

CSL Limited develops, manufactures and markets pharmaceutical products of biological origin in 30 countries worldwide. The company focuses on rare and serious diseases and influenza vaccines. Within the rare and serious diseases division, CSL's innovations are used around the world to treat immunodeficiencies, bleeding disorders, hereditary angioedema, Alpha-1 antitrypsin deficiency and neurological disorders. The CSL Plasma division is one of the world's largest and most efficient plasma collection networks, with more than 140 centers in the U.S. and Europe, as well as production facilities in the U.S., Germany, Switzerland and Australia. Within the influenza vaccines division, joint venture Seqirus (with Novartis), is a leading influenza company with corporate offices in the U.K., and manufacturing plants in the U.S., the U.K., Germany and Australia. Seqirus is a transcontinental partner in pandemic preparedness and a major contributor to the prevention and control of influenza globally. CSL's current product pipeline (as of April 2018) includes 14 research/pre-clinical products, 12 clinical development products and 11 registration/post-launch products. These products include immunoglobulins, specialty products, breakthrough medicines, vaccines, inactivated polio vaccines, hemophilia products and transplant products.

CSL Limited offers its employees flexible work arrangements, an employee share plan, tuition reimbursement and technology training.

FINANCIAL DATA:

Note: Data for latest year may not have been available at press time.

In U.S. $	2017	2016	2015	2014	2013	2012
Revenue	6,223,505,408	5,758,213,120	5,142,946,816	4,097,879,808	3,862,053,888	3,207,814,912
R&D Expense						
Operating Income						
Operating Margin %						
SGA Expense						
Net Income	1,258,096,640	1,210,593,792	1,299,256,832	1,003,960,512	948,896,320	710,998,528
Operating Cash Flow						
Capital Expenditure						
EBITDA						
Return on Assets %						
Return on Equity %						
Debt to Equity						

CONTACT INFORMATION:

Phone: 61-3-9389-1911 Fax: 61-3-9389-1434
Toll-Free:
Address: 45 Poplar Rd., Parkville, VIC 3052 Australia

STOCK TICKER/OTHER:

Stock Ticker: CMXHF
Exchange: PINX
Employees: 16,000
Fiscal Year Ends: 06/30
Parent Company:

SALARIES/BONUSES:

Top Exec. Salary: $ Bonus: $
Second Exec. Salary: $ Bonus: $

OTHER THOUGHTS:

Estimated Female Officers or Directors: 4
Hot Spot for Advancement for Women/Minorities: Y

Cumberland Pharmaceuticals Inc

www.cumberlandpharma.com

NAIC Code: 325,412

TYPES OF BUSINESS:

Prescription Drugs Manufacturing

BRANDS/DIVISIONS/AFFILIATES:

Acetadote
Kristalose
Caldolor
Omeclamox-Pak
Vaprisol
Hepatoren
Boxaban
Cumberland Emerging Technologies Inc

CONTACTS: *Note: Officers with more than one job title may be intentionally listed here more than once.*

A. Kazimi, CEO
Michael Bonner, CFO
Martin Cearnal, Director
Leo Pavliv, Executive VP, Divisional
James Herman, Other Executive Officer

GROWTH PLANS/SPECIAL FEATURES:

Cumberland Pharmaceuticals, Inc. is a specialty pharmaceutical company that focuses on hospital acute care and gastroenterology. The firm primarily concentrates on the acquisition, development and commercialization of late-stage and FDA-approved branded prescription drugs. Cumberland has five actively marketed products: Acetadote, Kristalose, Caldolor, Omeclamox-Pak, Vaprisol, Ethyol and Totect. Acetadote is an intravenous formulation of N-acetylcysteine created to protect against hepatoxic overdoses of acetaminophen, a relatively common cause of drug toxicity. Kristalose is a prescription-based orally administered laxative used to treat acute or chronic constipation. Caldolor is an intravenous ibuprofen variation used to treat pain and fever. Omeclamox-Pak is a triple therapy combination medication for Helicobacter pylori infection and duodenal ulcer disease. Vaprisol is an intravenous formulation to raise serum sodium levels in hospitalized patients with euvolemic and hypervolemic hyponatremia. Ethyol is administered through an injection for the reduction of xerostomia (dry mouth) in patients undergoing post-operative radiation treatment for head and neck cancer. Totect is an injection for emergency oncology intervention, to reverse the toxic effects of anthracycline chemotherapy in case of extravasation. Additionally, the company is currently involved in the Phase 2 clinical trials of Hepatoren, an injection being investigated as a possible treatment for critically ill hospitalized patients with hepatorenal syndrome; Vasculan, an oral capsule for the treatment of patients with systemic scleroris; Portaban, an oral formulation for the treatment of patients with portal hypertension associated with liver disease; REdiTrex, an injection for the treatment of active rheumatoid, juvenile idiopathic and severe psoriatic arthritis; and Boxaban, an oral capsule in Phase 2 for the treatment of patients with aspirin-exacerbated respiratory disease. Through its majority owned subsidiary Cumberland Emerging Technologies, Inc. (CET), the company partners with research institutions and universities to produce early-stage drug product candidates. Cumberland relies on government grants to fund CET's research and development activities.

FINANCIAL DATA: *Note: Data for latest year may not have been available at press time.*

In U.S. $	2017	2016	2015	2014	2013	2012
Revenue	41,150,130	33,025,560	33,519,050	36,901,870	32,027,460	48,851,240
R&D Expense	3,901,365	3,190,700	3,847,651	3,389,419	5,615,501	5,095,172
Operating Income	-4,081,348	-1,433,131	1,111,610	3,558,836	-3,801,338	8,818,102
Operating Margin %	-9.91%	-4.33%	3.31%	9.64%	-11.86%	18.05%
SGA Expense	31,523,310	23,115,290	21,602,360	23,303,760	23,877,720	29,425,660
Net Income	-7,978,633	-944,683	731,351	2,423,723	-2,104,614	5,842,492
Operating Cash Flow	-557,714	569,478	5,876,865	6,693,431	746,126	7,135,182
Capital Expenditure	1,489,070	2,131,098	2,699,430	3,264,823	7,559,492	2,536,819
EBITDA	-1,134,269	1,168,438	3,567,602	5,799,847	-2,269,212	10,024,620
Return on Assets %	-8.54%	-1.01%	.78%	2.64%	-2.26%	6.01%
Return on Equity %	-11.61%	-1.25%	.92%	3.02%	-2.54%	6.92%
Debt to Equity	0.15	0.05	0.02			0.05

CONTACT INFORMATION:

Phone: 615 255-0068 Fax: 615 255-0094
Toll-Free: 877-484-2700
Address: 2525 West End Ave., Ste. 950, Nashville, TN 37203 United States

STOCK TICKER/OTHER:

Stock Ticker: CPIX
Employees: 82
Parent Company:
Exchange: NAS
Fiscal Year Ends: 12/31

SALARIES/BONUSES:

Top Exec. Salary: $523,000 Bonus: $260,000
Second Exec. Salary: $376,400 Bonus: $80,000

OTHER THOUGHTS:

Estimated Female Officers or Directors: 4
Hot Spot for Advancement for Women/Minorities: Y

CVS Health Corporation

cvshealth.com

NAIC Code: 446,110

TYPES OF BUSINESS:

Drug Stores
Pharmacy Benefits Management
Online Pharmacy Services

BRANDS/DIVISIONS/AFFILIATES:

CVS.com
Navarro.com
Onofre.com.br
CVS Pharmacy
Longs Drugs
Navarro Discount Pharmacy
CVS Pharmacy Y mas
SilverScript Insurance Company

CONTACTS: *Note: Officers with more than one job title may be intentionally listed here more than once.*

Colleen McIntosh, Assistant General Counsel
Larry Merlo, CEO
David Denton, CFO
David Dorman, Chairman of the Board
Eva Boratto, Chief Accounting Officer
Troyen Brennan, Chief Medical Officer
Jonathan Roberts, Executive VP
Thomas Moriarty, Executive VP
Lisa Bisaccia, Other Executive Officer

GROWTH PLANS/SPECIAL FEATURES:

CVS Health Corporation is a leading provider of prescription and related healthcare services in the U.S. It operates in three segments: corporate, retail/LTC and pharmacy services. The corporate segment provides management and administrative services to support the company's overall operations. The retail/LTC (long-term care) segment includes over 9,800 retail stores, of which 8,060 are stores that operated a pharmacy and 1,695 are CVS pharmacies located within Target Corporation stores. This division also includes CVS online retail pharmacy websites (CVS.com, Navarro.com and Onofre.com.br), 37 on-site pharmacy stores, LTC pharmacy operations and retail healthcare clinics. The retail stores are located in 49 states, the District of Columbia, Puerto Rico and Brazil operating under the CVS Pharmacy, CVS, Longs Drugs, Navarro Discount Pharmacy, CVS Pharmacy Y mas and Drogaria Onofre names. The pharmacy services segment provides a full range of pharmacy benefit management services, including mail order pharmacy services, plan design and administration, formulary management, claims processing and health management programs. Through subsidiary SilverScript Insurance Company, the division is a national provider of drug benefits to eligible beneficiaries under Medicare Part D. The segment operates a national retail pharmacy network with 23 retail specialty pharmacy stores; 18 specialty mail order pharmacies; four mail order dispensing services; and 83 branches with 73 ambulatory infusion suites. In December 2017, CVS agreed to purchase health insurance giant Aetna Inc. for $69 billion. In July 2018, the U.S. Justice Department reported that it would not challenge the planned merger, and as of August 29, 2018, the transaction was not yet finalized.

Employee benefits include medical, dental, vision and prescription coverage; free health screenings at MinuteClinic; a 401(k); employee stock purchase plan; short- and long-term disability; employee discounts; education reimbursement; an employee assistance program; and flexible spending accounts.

FINANCIAL DATA: *Note: Data for latest year may not have been available at press time.*

In U.S. $	2017	2016	2015	2014	2013	2012
Revenue	184,765,000,000	177,526,000,000	153,290,000,000	139,367,000,000	126,761,000,000	123,133,000,000
R&D Expense						
Operating Income	9,517,000,000	10,338,000,000	9,454,000,000	8,799,000,000	8,037,000,000	7,228,000,000
Operating Margin %	5.15%	5.82%	6.16%	6.31%	6.34%	5.87%
SGA Expense						
Net Income	6,622,000,000	5,317,000,000	5,237,000,000	4,644,000,000	4,592,000,000	3,877,000,000
Operating Cash Flow	8,007,000,000	10,069,000,000	8,412,000,000	8,137,000,000	5,783,000,000	6,671,000,000
Capital Expenditure	1,918,000,000	2,224,000,000	2,367,000,000	2,136,000,000	1,984,000,000	2,030,000,000
EBITDA	11,809,000,000	12,190,000,000	11,567,000,000	10,224,000,000	9,915,000,000	8,637,000,000
Return on Assets %	6.98%	5.65%	6.23%	6.37%	6.68%	5.94%
Return on Equity %	17.77%	14.36%	13.93%	12.23%	12.14%	10.23%
Debt to Equity	0.58	0.69	0.70	0.30	0.33	0.24

CONTACT INFORMATION:

Phone: 401 765-1500 Fax: 401 762-2137
Toll-Free: 888-746-7287
Address: 1 CVS Dr., Woonsocket, RI 02895 United States

STOCK TICKER/OTHER:

Stock Ticker: CVS
Employees: 202,000
Parent Company:
Exchange: NYS
Fiscal Year Ends: 12/31

SALARIES/BONUSES:

Top Exec. Salary: $1,630,000 Bonus: $
Second Exec. Salary: $1,033,333 Bonus: $

OTHER THOUGHTS:

Estimated Female Officers or Directors: 4
Hot Spot for Advancement for Women/Minorities: Y

Cynosure Inc

www.cynosure.com

NAIC Code: 334,510

TYPES OF BUSINESS:

Electromedical and Electrotherapeutic Apparatus Manufacturing

BRANDS/DIVISIONS/AFFILIATES:

Hologic Inc
Accolade
Cynergy
Pelleve
Vectus
Apogee+
ReveLite SI
TempSure Envi

CONTACTS:

Note: Officers with more than one job title may be intentionally listed here more than once.

Stephen P. MacMillan, Pres.
Stephen Webber, CFO
Douglas Delaney, Other Executive Officer
Peter Anastos, Senior VP

GROWTH PLANS/SPECIAL FEATURES:

Cynosure, Inc. develops and markets light-based aesthetic and medical treatment systems used by physicians and other practitioners to perform non- and minimally-invasive procedures. Treatments include hair removal, skin revitalization, vascular lesions and scar reduction, as well as tattoo removal, and addressing cellulite and wrinkles. Products include: the Accolade, a high-powered, Q-switched Alexandrite laser that provides fast treatment for removing benign epidermal and dermal pigmented lesions such as freckles, acquired dermal melanocytosis and multi-colored tattoos; the Cynergy vascular workstation, which treats all types of vascular lesions, including facial and leg telangiectasias, spider veins, hemangiomas, and rosacea; the Pelleve radio-frequency system, for the treatment of wrinkles head-to-toe; and the Vectus laser system, for high-volume hair removal. Other product lines by the firm include Apogee+, Cellulaze, Elite, Emerge, MedLite C6, MonaLisa Touch, Icon, PelleFirm, PicoSure, PinPointe FootLaser, PrecisionTx, RevLite SI, SculpSure, Smartlipo Triplex and Smartskin+. In March 2017, the firm was acquired by Hologic, Inc., and was subsequently delisted from being publicly-traded and operates as a wholly-owned subsidiary of Hologic.

FINANCIAL DATA:

Note: Data for latest year may not have been available at press time.

In U.S. $	2017	2016	2015	2014	2013	2012
Revenue	455,208,600	433,532,000	339,462,016	292,368,992	226,010,000	153,492,992
R&D Expense						
Operating Income						
Operating Margin %						
SGA Expense						
Net Income		14,201,000	15,807,000	31,338,000	-1,647,000	10,961,000
Operating Cash Flow						
Capital Expenditure						
EBITDA						
Return on Assets %						
Return on Equity %						
Debt to Equity						

CONTACT INFORMATION:

Phone: 978 256-4200 Fax:
Toll-Free:
Address: 5 Carlisle Rd., Westford, MA 01886 United States

STOCK TICKER/OTHER:

Stock Ticker: Subsidiary
Employees: 982
Parent Company: Hologic Inc
Exchange:
Fiscal Year Ends: 12/31

SALARIES/BONUSES:

Top Exec. Salary: $ Bonus: $
Second Exec. Salary: $ Bonus: $

OTHER THOUGHTS:

Estimated Female Officers or Directors:
Hot Spot for Advancement for Women/Minorities:

Danaher Corporation

www.danaher.com

NAIC Code: 334,510

TYPES OF BUSINESS:

Medical Diagnostic Equipment
Environmental Management Products
Test & Calibration Equipment
Automotive Components & Repair Equipment
Motors & Drives
Bar Code Equipment
Security & Defense Products

BRANDS/DIVISIONS/AFFILIATES:

Fortiv Corporation
DentalCo

CONTACTS: *Note: Officers with more than one job title may be intentionally listed here more than once.*

Thomas Joyce, CEO
Matthew McGrew, CFO, Divisional
Steven Rales, Chairman of the Board
Robert Lutz, Chief Accounting Officer
Mitchell Rales, Co-Founder
Joakim Weidemanis, Executive VP
Rainer Blair, Executive VP
William Daniel II, Executive VP
Daniel Comas, Executive VP
Brian Ellis, General Counsel
William King, Senior VP, Divisional
Daniel Raskas, Senior VP, Divisional
Angela Lalor, Senior VP, Divisional

GROWTH PLANS/SPECIAL FEATURES:

Danaher Corporation designs, manufactures and markets professional, medical, industrial and commercial products. The company operates through four segments: life sciences, deriving 31% of annual sales; diagnostics, 32%; dental, 15%; and environmental & applied solutions, 22%. The life sciences segment offers a range of research tools that scientists use to study genes, proteins, metabolites and cells in an effort to understand the cause of disease and identify new therapies and test new drugs and vaccines. The diagnostics segment offers analytical instruments, reagents, consumables, software and services that hospitals, physicians' offices, reference laboratories and other critical care settings use to diagnose disease and make treatment decisions. The dental segment provides products used to diagnose, treat and prevent disease and ailments of the teeth, gums and supporting bone, as well as to improve the aesthetics of the human smile. These products include implant systems, dental prosthetics, treatment planning software, orthodontic bracket systems, endodontic systems, restorative materials and instruments, infection prevention solutions, digital imaging systems and software, air and electric powered handpieces and treatment units. Last, the environmental & applied solutions segment offers products and services that help protect resources and keep global food and water supplies safe. This division's products include a wide range of analytical instruments, software and related equipment that detect and measure water; ultraviolet disinfection systems; and industrial water treatment solutions. Danaher's manufacturing locations and worldwide presence include North America, Europe, Asia, Australia and Latin America. Recently, Danaher separated its test & measurement segment, industrial technologies segment and retail/commercial petroleum platform through the spin-off of Fortive Corporation. Fortive is now a standalone company trading on the NASDAQ under the symbol FTV. In July 2018, the firm announced its intention to spin off its Dental segment into an independent, publicly-traded company, DentalCo.

FINANCIAL DATA: *Note: Data for latest year may not have been available at press time.*

In U.S. $	2017	2016	2015	2014	2013	2012
Revenue	18,329,700,000	16,882,400,000	20,563,100,000	19,913,800,000	19,118,000,000	18,260,400,000
R&D Expense	1,128,800,000	975,100,000	1,239,100,000	1,314,200,000	1,249,900,000	1,137,900,000
Operating Income	3,021,200,000	2,750,900,000	3,469,100,000	3,431,300,000	3,274,900,000	3,095,200,000
Operating Margin %	16.48%	16.29%	16.87%	17.23%	17.12%	16.95%
SGA Expense	6,042,500,000	5,608,600,000	6,054,300,000	5,697,000,000	5,432,800,000	5,181,200,000
Net Income	2,492,100,000	2,553,700,000	3,357,400,000	2,598,400,000	2,695,000,000	2,392,200,000
Operating Cash Flow	3,477,800,000	3,521,800,000	3,801,800,000	3,758,400,000	3,585,300,000	3,415,000,000
Capital Expenditure	619,600,000	589,600,000	633,000,000	597,500,000	551,500,000	458,300,000
EBITDA	4,339,800,000	3,923,800,000	4,538,100,000	4,543,000,000	4,606,900,000	4,008,100,000
Return on Assets %	5.42%	5.46%	7.87%	7.25%	7.97%	7.60%
Return on Equity %	10.09%	10.93%	14.26%	11.35%	13.01%	13.31%
Debt to Equity	0.39	0.42	0.50	0.14	0.15	0.27

CONTACT INFORMATION:

Phone: 202 828-0850 Fax: 202 828-0860
Toll-Free:
Address: 2200 Pennsylvania Ave. NW, Ste. 800W, Washington, WA 20006 United States

STOCK TICKER/OTHER:

Stock Ticker: DHR
Employees: 62,000
Parent Company:
Exchange: NYS
Fiscal Year Ends: 12/31

SALARIES/BONUSES:

Top Exec. Salary: $1,200,000 Bonus: $
Second Exec. Salary: $905,476 Bonus: $

OTHER THOUGHTS:

Estimated Female Officers or Directors: 2
Hot Spot for Advancement for Women/Minorities: Y

DaVita Healthcare Partners Inc

www.davita.com

NAIC Code: 621,492

TYPES OF BUSINESS:

Renal Care Services
Clinical Research

BRANDS/DIVISIONS/AFFILIATES:

CONTACTS:

Note: Officers with more than one job title may be intentionally listed here more than once.

Javier Rodriguez, CEO, Divisional
Kent Thiry, CEO
Joel Ackerman, CFO
James Hilger, Chief Accounting Officer
Kathleen Waters, Other Executive Officer
James Hearty, Other Executive Officer
Leanne Zumwalt, Vice President, Divisional

GROWTH PLANS/SPECIAL FEATURES:

DaVita HealthCare Partners, Inc. is a leading provider of dialysis services in the U.S. for patients suffering from chronic kidney failure, also known as end stage renal disease (ESRD). The company operates through a network of 2,510 outpatient dialysis centers located in 46 states and Washington, D.C., serving approximately 197,800 patients. The firm also provides acute inpatient dialysis services in approximately 900 hospitals and related laboratory services. The loss of kidney function is normally irreversible, and kidney failure is typically caused by Type 1 and 2 diabetes, high blood pressure, polycystic kidney disease, long-term autoimmune attack on the kidney and prolonged urinary tract obstruction. ESRD is the stage of advanced kidney impairment that requires continued dialysis treatment or a kidney transplant to sustain life. Dialysis removes toxins, fluids and salt from the blood of patients via artificial means, and patients generally require dialysis at least three times a week for the rest of their lives. In December 2017, DaVita agreed to sell its medical group division (DMG) to Collaborative Care Holdings, LLC (Optum), which continued to move forward while seeking regulatory approval requirements as of mid-2018; hence, DaVita reports the division as discontinued. DMG is a patient- and physician-focused integrated healthcare delivery and management company that provides coordinated, outcomes-based medical care in a cost-effective manner.

The firm offers employees medical, dental and vision insurance; short- and long-term disability insurance; life insurance; a 401(k) plan; tuition reimbursement; flexible spending accounts; and an employee assistance program.

FINANCIAL DATA:

Note: Data for latest year may not have been available at press time.

In U.S. $	2017	2016	2015	2014	2013	2012
Revenue	10,876,630,000	14,745,110,000	13,781,840,000	12,795,110,000	11,764,050,000	8,186,280,000
R&D Expense						
Operating Income	1,619,725,000	1,773,742,000	1,362,604,000	1,791,907,000	1,515,576,000	1,280,707,000
Operating Margin %	14.89%	12.02%	9.88%	14.00%	12.88%	15.64%
SGA Expense	1,064,026,000	1,592,698,000	1,452,135,000	1,261,506,000	1,176,485,000	894,575,000
Net Income	663,618,000	879,874,000	269,732,000	723,114,000	633,446,000	536,017,000
Operating Cash Flow	1,907,449,000	1,963,444,000	1,557,200,000	1,459,407,000	1,773,341,000	1,100,848,000
Capital Expenditure	905,250,000	829,095,000	707,998,000	642,348,000	617,597,000	550,146,000
EBITDA	2,607,905,000	2,623,529,000	1,769,540,000	2,310,902,000	2,083,658,000	1,633,766,000
Return on Assets %	3.52%	4.72%	1.47%	4.12%	3.82%	4.30%
Return on Equity %	14.21%	18.48%	5.37%	15.06%	15.45%	18.15%
Debt to Equity	1.95	1.92	1.84	1.62	1.83	2.21

CONTACT INFORMATION:

Phone: 303 405-2100 Fax: 310 792-8928
Toll-Free:
Address: 2000 16th St., Denver, CO 80202 United States

STOCK TICKER/OTHER:

Stock Ticker: DVA
Employees: 41,000
Parent Company:
Exchange: NYS
Fiscal Year Ends: 12/31

SALARIES/BONUSES:

Top Exec. Salary: $1,300,000 Bonus: $
Second Exec. Salary: $500,000 Bonus: $540,000

OTHER THOUGHTS:

Estimated Female Officers or Directors: 3
Hot Spot for Advancement for Women/Minorities: Y

Delta Dental Plans Association

www.deltadental.com

NAIC Code: 524,114

TYPES OF BUSINESS:

Dental Insurance & Dental Care
Dental PPO & HMO

GROWTH PLANS/SPECIAL FEATURES:

Delta Dental Plans Association, a nonprofit organization, is one of the largest dental benefits systems and dental service corporations in the U.S. The firm offers dental insurance coverage in all 50 states, Puerto Rico and other U.S. territories to individuals and employers. Delta Dental Plans is comprised of 39 independent Dental Delta companies. For Delta Dental customers who have a Delta Dental PPO (preferred provider organization), a Delta Dental Premier or a Delta Dental PPO Plus Premier plan, can choose any dentist they want, but are offered additional advantages if they choose a dentist within Delta Dental's own network. For those with a DeltaCare USA plan, must select a primary care dentist from the DeltaCare network. The company's website offers a cost estimation link for information on the price range for particular dental care needs. It will display what the member's plan covers as well as out-of-pocket costs; but the estimate is just an estimate, and does not guarantee the exact overall fees for the procedures.

BRANDS/DIVISIONS/AFFILIATES:

Delta Dental Premier
Delta Dental PPO
Delta Dental PPO Plus Premier
DeltaCare USA
DeltaCare

CONTACTS: *Note: Officers with more than one job title may be intentionally listed here more than once.*

Fred Kwong, CIO
Stefany Currier, Dir.-Admin

FINANCIAL DATA: *Note: Data for latest year may not have been available at press time.*

In U.S. $	2017	2016	2015	2014	2013	2012
Revenue	21,000,000,000	20,000,000,000	19,800,000,000	19,500,000,000		
R&D Expense						
Operating Income						
Operating Margin %						
SGA Expense						
Net Income			139,432,000	36,389,000		
Operating Cash Flow						
Capital Expenditure						
EBITDA						
Return on Assets %						
Return on Equity %						
Debt to Equity						

CONTACT INFORMATION:

Phone: 630-574-6001 Fax: 630-574-6999
Toll-Free:
Address: 1515 W. 22nd St., Ste. 450, Oak Brook, IL 60523 United States

STOCK TICKER/OTHER:

Stock Ticker: Nonprofit
Exchange:
Employees: 3,200
Fiscal Year Ends: 12/31
Parent Company:

SALARIES/BONUSES:

Top Exec. Salary: $ Bonus: $
Second Exec. Salary: $ Bonus: $

OTHER THOUGHTS:

Estimated Female Officers or Directors: 2
Hot Spot for Advancement for Women/Minorities:

Dental Benefits Providers Inc

www.dbp.com

NAIC Code: 524,114

TYPES OF BUSINESS:

Insurance-Supplemental & Specialty Health
Dental Benefits
Dental HMOs, PPOs & EPOs
Administrative Services

BRANDS/DIVISIONS/AFFILIATES:

United Healthcare Services Inc

CONTACTS:

Note: Officers with more than one job title may be intentionally listed here more than once.

Ralph Foxman, CEO
Paul Hebert, Pres.

GROWTH PLANS/SPECIAL FEATURES:

Dental Benefits Providers, Inc. (DBP), a subsidiary of United Healthcare Services, Inc., is a leading private-label dental benefit company. The firm's members are located throughout the U.S., Washington, D.C., Puerto Rico and the Virgin Islands. DBP serves these members through participating dentists and distributor clients. The company subcontracts dental health maintenance organization plans (DHMOs), PPOs, exclusive provider organization (EPO) plans, in-network PPOs, indemnity plans, preventive plans, dental plus vision plans, Medicaid and Medicare plans as well as private label dental programs. Such plans can be customized depending on clients' needs. DBP offers full benefits plans and limited benefits plans; net rate plans that have the ability to offer a risk- or profit-sharing arrangement; lock-in, gatekeeper networks and open access point-of-service (POS) networks; commercial, government or federal employee plans; and either interlocking dental and medical plans or freestanding dental plans. DBP members, dentists and clients have access to online tools such as a dentist directory, plan and claim information, eligibility verification and claim forms. The company's website also offers voluminous dental education resources.

The company offers employees vision, medical, dental, life and disability coverage; flexible spending accounts; an employee stock purchase plan; 401(k); paid time off; paid company holidays; an employee assistance program; tuition reimbursement; and adoption assistance.

FINANCIAL DATA:

Note: Data for latest year may not have been available at press time.

In U.S. $	2017	2016	2015	2014	2013	2012
Revenue						
R&D Expense						
Operating Income						
Operating Margin %						
SGA Expense						
Net Income						
Operating Cash Flow						
Capital Expenditure						
EBITDA						
Return on Assets %						
Return on Equity %						
Debt to Equity						

CONTACT INFORMATION:

Phone: Fax:
Toll-Free: 800-638-3895
Address: 6220 Old Dobbin Ln., Columbia, MD 21045 United States

STOCK TICKER/OTHER:

Stock Ticker: Subsidiary Exchange:
Employees: Fiscal Year Ends: 12/31
Parent Company: United Healthcare Services Inc

SALARIES/BONUSES:

Top Exec. Salary: $ Bonus: $
Second Exec. Salary: $ Bonus: $

OTHER THOUGHTS:

Estimated Female Officers or Directors: 1
Hot Spot for Advancement for Women/Minorities:

Dentsply Sirona Inc

www.dentsplysirona.com/en-us

NAIC Code: 339,100

TYPES OF BUSINESS:

Dental Device Manufacturing

BRANDS/DIVISIONS/AFFILIATES:

CONTACTS:

Note: Officers with more than one job title may be intentionally listed here more than once.

Betsy Holden,
Leslie Varon,
Nick Alexos, CFO
Donald Casey, Director
Eric Brandt, Director
Keith Ebling, Executive VP
Maureen MacInnis, Other Executive Officer
Markus Boehringer, Senior VP, Divisional
Dominique Legros, Senior VP, Divisional
William Newell, Senior VP, Divisional
Gregory Sheehan, Vice President, Divisional
Henning Mueller, Vice President, Divisional

GROWTH PLANS/SPECIAL FEATURES:

Dentsply Sirona, Inc. is a world-leading manufacturer of professional dental products and technologies. With a 130-year history of innovation and service to the dental industry and to patients worldwide, the firm's products and solutions include dental and oral health products as well as other consumable medical devices under a strong portfolio of renowned brands. Dentsply's products provide innovative, high-quality and effective solutions for the purpose of advancing patient care and for delivering better, safer and faster dentistry. The company's primary products consist of: dental technology and equipment, including imaging equipment, computer aided design and machining (CAD/CAM) systems, dental implants, scanning equipment, treatment software, orthodontic appliances and a variety of dental restoration products; dental consumables, including endodontic (root canal) instruments and materials, dental anesthetics, prophylaxis paste, dental sealants, impression materials, restorative materials, tooth whiteners, topical fluoride, dental handpieces, intraoral curing light systems, dental diagnostic systems and ultrasonic scalers and polishers; and healthcare consumables, including urology catheters, surgical products, medical drills and other non-medical products. Dentsply Sirona's global headquarters are based in York, Pennsylvania, and its international headquarters are located in Salzburg, Austria. Approximately two-thirds of the company's sales are derived from regions outside the U.S.

FINANCIAL DATA:

Note: Data for latest year may not have been available at press time.

In U.S. $	2017	2016	2015	2014	2013	2012
Revenue	3,993,400,000	3,745,300,000	2,674,300,000	2,922,620,000	2,950,770,000	2,928,429,000
R&D Expense						
Operating Income	513,800,000	477,900,000	439,900,000	456,683,000	432,522,000	407,656,000
Operating Margin %	12.86%	12.75%	16.44%	15.62%	14.65%	13.92%
SGA Expense	1,674,700,000	1,523,000,000	1,077,300,000	1,143,106,000	1,144,890,000	1,148,731,000
Net Income	-1,550,000,000	429,900,000	251,200,000	322,854,000	313,192,000	314,213,000
Operating Cash Flow	601,900,000	563,400,000	497,400,000	560,401,000	417,846,000	369,685,000
Capital Expenditure	151,000,000	126,100,000	72,000,000	105,767,000	101,421,000	95,401,000
EBITDA	-1,248,800,000	748,500,000	508,500,000	580,360,000	546,863,000	516,729,000
Return on Assets %	-14.07%	5.35%	5.54%	6.63%	6.23%	6.46%
Return on Equity %	-21.04%	8.22%	10.78%	13.29%	13.20%	15.49%
Debt to Equity	0.24	0.18	0.48	0.49	0.46	0.55

CONTACT INFORMATION:

Phone: 717-845-7511 Fax:
Toll-Free: 800-877-0020
Address: 221 W. Philadelphia St., Ste. 60W, York, PA 17401 United States

STOCK TICKER/OTHER:

Stock Ticker: XRAY
Exchange: NAS
Employees: 15,700
Fiscal Year Ends: 09/30
Parent Company:

SALARIES/BONUSES:

Top Exec. Salary: $780,822 Bonus: $2,500,000
Second Exec. Salary: $727,616 Bonus: $

OTHER THOUGHTS:

Estimated Female Officers or Directors: 1
Hot Spot for Advancement for Women/Minorities:

DePuy Synthes Inc

NAIC Code: 339,100

www.depuy.com

TYPES OF BUSINESS:

Orthopedic Devices
Fixative Products
Implants

BRANDS/DIVISIONS/AFFILIATES:

Johnson & Johnson
DePuy Synthes Joint Reconstruction
DePuy Synthes Trauma
DePuy Synthes Spine
DePuy Synthes Mitek Sports Medicine
DePuy Synthes Power Tools
DePuy Synthes Neuro
DePuy Synthes CMF

CONTACTS: *Note: Officers with more than one job title may be intentionally listed here more than once.*

Robert E. Morel, Pres.
Steven L. Artusi, Sec.
Robert E. Morel, Pres., Depuy Ace Medical Company
Max Reinhardt, Pres., Depuy Synthes Spine

GROWTH PLANS/SPECIAL FEATURES:

DePuy Synthes, Inc., a subsidiary of Johnson & Johnson, is a designer, manufacturer and distributor of orthopedic joint reconstruction, neuro, spine, cranio-maxillofacial and sports medicine devices and supplies. The firm is comprised of seven business divisions. DePuy Synthes Joint Reconstruction is one of the largest orthopaedics companies in the world, with products for hip, knee and shoulder replacement. DePuy Synthes Trauma provides orthopaedic trauma devices for internal and external fixation. DePuy Synthes Spine provides spinal care solutions for both traditional and minimally-invasive spine surgery. DePuy Synthes Mitek Sports Medicine develops and manufactures pain management and minimally-invasive solutions, including sports medicine and soft-tissue repair products. DePuy Synthes Power Tools produces a range of power instrument systems, reamers and saws to meet a wide range of clinical needs. DePuy Synthes Neuro provides a range of solutions for the diagnosis and treatment of neurological disorders focusing on neurovascular, neurosurgery and neuromodulation solutions. Last, DePuy Synthes CMF (craniomaxillofacial) offers systems that provide an array of implants and instruments for the treatment of facial trauma, tumor resection and reconstruction. In May 2018, DePuy agreed to acquire assets of Medical Enterprises Distribution, LLC to strengthen its portfolio and to enhance surgeon's capabilities via automation.

Employee benefits include medical, dental, vision, life, disability, accident, auto and home insurance; and flexible spending accounts.

FINANCIAL DATA: *Note: Data for latest year may not have been available at press time.*

In U.S. $	2017	2016	2015	2014	2013	2012
Revenue	9,100,000,000	9,003,500,000	9,320,000,000	9,675,000,000	9,509,000,000	7,799,000,000
R&D Expense						
Operating Income						
Operating Margin %						
SGA Expense						
Net Income						
Operating Cash Flow						
Capital Expenditure						
EBITDA						
Return on Assets %						
Return on Equity %						
Debt to Equity						

CONTACT INFORMATION:

Phone: 574-267-8143 Fax: 574-371-4865
Toll-Free: 800-473-3789
Address: 700 Orthopaedic Dr., Warsaw, IN 46582 United States

STOCK TICKER/OTHER:

Stock Ticker: Subsidiary
Exchange:
Employees: 18,000
Fiscal Year Ends: 12/31
Parent Company: Johnson & Johnson

SALARIES/BONUSES:

Top Exec. Salary: $ Bonus: $
Second Exec. Salary: $ Bonus: $

OTHER THOUGHTS:

Estimated Female Officers or Directors:
Hot Spot for Advancement for Women/Minorities:

Detroit Medical Center (DMC)

www.dmc.org

NAIC Code: 622,110

TYPES OF BUSINESS:

General Medical and Surgical Hospitals
Children's Hospital
Emergency Care
Cancer Care
Women's Health
Orthopedic Services
Teaching Facilities
Ophthalmic Services

BRANDS/DIVISIONS/AFFILIATES:

Tenet Healthcare Corporation
Children's Hospital of Michigan
DMC Detroit Receiving Hospital
DMC Harper University Hospital
DMC Huron Valley-Sinai Hospital
DMC Hutzel Women's Hospital
DMC Sinai-Grace Hospital
DMC Heart Hospital

CONTACTS: *Note: Officers with more than one job title may be intentionally listed here more than once.*

Tony Tedeschi, CEO
Joseph Mullany, Co-Pres.
Suzanne R. White, Chief Medical Officer
Conrad L. Mallett, Jr., Chief Admin. Officer
Shawn Levitt, Chief Nursing Officer

GROWTH PLANS/SPECIAL FEATURES:

Detroit Medical Center (DMC), part of Tenet Healthcare Corporation, is a healthcare provider in southeast Michigan. DMC comprises seven hospitals, a cardiovascular institute, a cancer institute, imaging and surgery centers, rehabilitation outpatient centers, emergency care, clinics and outpatient centers, pediatric outpatient centers and a MedPost Urgent Care. DMC's hospitals are as follows. The Children's Hospital of Michigan is an international leader in pediatric neurology, neonatal and prenatal care, cardiology, rehabilitation and pediatric critical care. DMC Detroit Receiving Hospital trains almost 50% of Michigan's emergency physicians in the southeast; and provides back and spine, brain and neurology, diagnostics, digestive disorder, DMC, elderly care, emergency, same-day surgery and urology services. DMC Harper University Hospital is a teaching institution offering neurological, hypertension and heart failure treatments as well as vascular and organ transplants. DMC Huron Valley-Sinai Hospital covers every stage of life from birthing to senior services and includes surgical suites, cardiac services and the Charach Cancer Treatment Center. DMC Hutzel Women's Hospital's offerings include high-risk obstetrics, infertility treatment, reproductive genetics and gynecology. DMC Sinai-Grace Hospital's general medical services include family medicine, heart and cancer care, emergency medicine, obstetrics and gynecology. DMC Heart Hospital is Michigan's first and only heart hospital and provides immediate care to patients suffering from all forms of heart disease and vascular disease. The Rehabilitation Institute of Michigan (RIM) is one of the nation's largest hospitals that specializes in rehabilitation medicine and research. RIM provides spinal cord injury, brain injury, stroke, complex trauma and orthopedics and catastrophic injury care. It also serves sports injury patients. The Karmanos Cancer Institute at McLaren Bay offers medical oncology, radiation oncology, chemotherapy, interventional radiology, screening, counseling and many other services.

FINANCIAL DATA: *Note: Data for latest year may not have been available at press time.*

In U.S. $	2017	2016	2015	2014	2013	2012
Revenue						
R&D Expense						
Operating Income						
Operating Margin %						
SGA Expense						
Net Income						
Operating Cash Flow						
Capital Expenditure						
EBITDA						
Return on Assets %						
Return on Equity %						
Debt to Equity						

CONTACT INFORMATION:

Phone: 313-745-5111 Fax: 313-578-3225
Toll-Free: 888-362-2500
Address: 3990 John R. St., Detroit, MI 48201 United States

STOCK TICKER/OTHER:

Stock Ticker: Subsidiary Exchange:
Employees: 10,700 Fiscal Year Ends: 12/31
Parent Company: Tenet Healthcare Corporation

SALARIES/BONUSES:

Top Exec. Salary: $ Bonus: $
Second Exec. Salary: $ Bonus: $

OTHER THOUGHTS:

Estimated Female Officers or Directors: 3
Hot Spot for Advancement for Women/Minorities: Y

DexCom Inc

www.dexcom.com

NAIC Code: 339,100

TYPES OF BUSINESS:

Surgical and Medical Instrument Manufacturing
Continuous Glucose Monitoring Systems Manufacturing

BRANDS/DIVISIONS/AFFILIATES:

DexCom G6
G4 Platinum
G5 Mobile

CONTACTS: *Note: Officers with more than one job title may be intentionally listed here more than once.*

Quentin Blackford, CFO
Terrance Gregg, Chairman of the Board
Kevin Sayer, Director
Steven Pacelli, Executive VP, Divisional
Donald Abbey, Executive VP, Divisional
Andrew Balo, Executive VP, Divisional
Richard Doubleday, Executive VP
Patrick Murphy, General Counsel
Jake Leach, Senior VP, Divisional
Heather Ace, Senior VP, Divisional
Jeffrey Moy, Senior VP, Divisional
Kevin Sun, Vice President, Divisional

GROWTH PLANS/SPECIAL FEATURES:

DexCom, Inc. is a medical device company primarily focused on the design, development and commercialization of continuous glucose monitoring. These CGM systems are used by people with diabetes and by healthcare providers. DexCom is currently commercializing its sixth generation of CGM systems, the DexCom G6, which sends glucose readings to the receiver's compatible smart device every five minutes with no fingersticks necessary. With the built-in Share functionality, the Dexcom G6 can keep loved ones and caregivers informed about the glucose levels as well. Other CGM models currently being manufactured include the G4 Platinum and the G5 Mobile. DexCom plans to develop future generations of technologies focused on improved performance and convenience that will enable intelligent insulin administration. The company is also exploring how to extend its product portfolio to other categories of people with diabetes, including those with Type 2 diabetes that are non-insulin using, people with pre-diabetes and people who are obese. DexCom manufactures its products at its headquarters in San Diego, California, which includes more than 28,000 square feet of laboratory space and approximately 18,000 square feet of controlled environment rooms. Recently, the firm opened a second manufacturing facility in Mesa, Arizona, providing about 500 jobs.

FINANCIAL DATA: *Note: Data for latest year may not have been available at press time.*

In U.S. $	2017	2016	2015	2014	2013	2012
Revenue	718,500,000	573,300,000	402,000,000	259,200,000	160,000,000	99,900,000
R&D Expense	185,400,000	156,100,000	137,500,000	69,400,000	44,800,000	39,500,000
Operating Income	-42,500,000	-63,900,000	-57,100,000	-21,500,000	-28,900,000	-55,700,000
Operating Margin %	-5.91%	-11.14%	-14.20%	-8.29%	-18.06%	-55.75%
SGA Expense	349,200,000	286,200,000	198,000,000	128,400,000	84,200,000	62,800,000
Net Income	-50,200,000	-65,600,000	-57,600,000	-22,400,000	-29,800,000	-54,500,000
Operating Cash Flow	92,000,000	56,200,000	49,000,000	23,600,000	2,400,000	-33,100,000
Capital Expenditure	66,000,000	55,700,000	33,300,000	16,200,000	7,900,000	9,500,000
EBITDA	-19,700,000	-49,200,000	-46,300,000	-13,100,000	-21,900,000	-49,000,000
Return on Assets %	-7.68%	-18.88%	-24.17%	-14.58%	-26.08%	-48.12%
Return on Equity %	-14.27%	-25.98%	-31.87%	-19.97%	-36.99%	-60.05%
Debt to Equity	0.79			0.01	0.05	0.08

CONTACT INFORMATION:

Phone: 855 200-0200 Fax: 858 200-0201
Toll-Free:
Address: 6340 Sequence Dr., San Diego, CA 92121 United States

STOCK TICKER/OTHER:

Stock Ticker: DXCM Exchange: NAS
Employees: 2,300 Fiscal Year Ends: 12/31
Parent Company:

SALARIES/BONUSES:

Top Exec. Salary: $546,250 Bonus: $
Second Exec. Salary: $355,300 Bonus: $

OTHER THOUGHTS:

Estimated Female Officers or Directors:
Hot Spot for Advancement for Women/Minorities:

Dignity Health

www.dignityhealth.org

NAIC Code: 622,110

TYPES OF BUSINESS:

General Medical and Surgical Hospitals
Skilled Nursing Facilities
Medical Centers

BRANDS/DIVISIONS/AFFILIATES:

Foundation for International Health
Concentra Group Holdings LLC

CONTACTS: *Note: Officers with more than one job title may be intentionally listed here more than once.*

Lloyd H. Dean, CEO
Marvin O'Quinn, Sr Exec. VP-
Lloyd H. Dean, Pres.
Daniel Morissette, CFO
Darryl Robinson, Chief Human Resources Officer
Robert Wiebe, Chief Medical Officer
Deanna Wise, CIO
Elizabeth Shih, Chief Admin. Officer
Derek F. Covert, General Counsel
Charles P. Francis, Chief Strategy Officer
Bernita McTernan, Exec. VP-Sponsorship & Mission Integrity
Michael D. Blaszyk, Chief Corp. Officer

GROWTH PLANS/SPECIAL FEATURES:

Dignity Health, a nonprofit healthcare provider based in San Francisco, was founded in 1986, when the Sisters of Mercy Burlingame Regional Community and the Sisters of Mercy Auburn Regional Community Catholic Healthcare merged their respective healthcare ministries into one. The group consists of 39 hospitals and 400+ care centers with 60,000 caregivers in 21 states. The organization is one of the largest hospital systems in the country and one of the largest nonprofit hospital providers in California. Dignity Health's Foundation for International Health promotes self-sustaining communities in developing countries by raising funds to expand emergency departments, purchase equipment, recruit more nurses, develop recycling campaigns, expand educational outreach and provide affordable housing for the elderly. The organization is the official healthcare provider for the San Francisco Giants. In February 2018, Dignity Health and Select Medical Holdings Corporation merged U.S. HealthWorks, Inc. (a subsidiary of Dignity Health) into Concentra Group Holdings, LLC (a subsidiary of Select Medical), with Dignity owning a 20% equity interest in the combined entity and Select Medical owning 80%. The newly-combined organization comprises more than 700 medical centers in 44 states.

Employees of the firm are offered medical, dental, vision and life insurance; employee assistance programs; paid time off; holidays; paid vacation time; family and military leave; disability coverage; recognition programs; tuition reimbursement; performance-based cash awards; a retirement plan; and learning opportunities.

FINANCIAL DATA: *Note: Data for latest year may not have been available at press time.*

In U.S. $	2017	2016	2015	2014	2013	2012
Revenue	12,900,000,000	12,600,000,000	12,400,000,000	10,677,351,000	10,411,879,000	9,496,266,000
R&D Expense						
Operating Income						
Operating Margin %						
SGA Expense						
Net Income	384,000,000	-238,000,000	558,000,000	912,680,000	812,000,000	132,500,000
Operating Cash Flow						
Capital Expenditure						
EBITDA						
Return on Assets %						
Return on Equity %						
Debt to Equity						

CONTACT INFORMATION:

Phone: 415-438-5500 Fax: 415-438-5724
Toll-Free:
Address: 185 Berry St., Ste. 300, San Francisco, CA 94107 United States

STOCK TICKER/OTHER:

Stock Ticker: Nonprofit
Employees: 63,000
Parent Company:
Exchange:
Fiscal Year Ends: 06/30

SALARIES/BONUSES:

Top Exec. Salary: $ Bonus: $
Second Exec. Salary: $ Bonus: $

OTHER THOUGHTS:

Estimated Female Officers or Directors: 7
Hot Spot for Advancement for Women/Minorities: Y

Diversicare Healthcare Services Inc

www.dvcr.com

NAIC Code: 623,110

TYPES OF BUSINESS:

Nursing Care Facilities
Assisted Living Facilities

BRANDS/DIVISIONS/AFFILIATES:

GROWTH PLANS/SPECIAL FEATURES:

Diversicare Healthcare Services, Inc. provides post-acute care services to skilled nursing facilities, patients and residents in 10 U.S. states. The firm serves aging, infirmed or disabled individuals who require extensive assistance and intensive care. These services include skilled nursing, comprehensive rehabilitation, memory care and other specialty care offerings. As of December 31, 2017, Diversicare's operations consisted of 76 nursing centers, with 8,456 licensed skilled nursing beds, of which 1,607 were owned and 6,849 were leased. The nursing centers range in size from 48 to 320 licensed nursing beds, which does not include the 489 licensed assisted living beds. The centers are located in Alabama, Florida, Indiana, Kansas, Kentucky, Mississippi, Missouri, Ohio, Tennessee and Texas.

CONTACTS: *Note: Officers with more than one job title may be intentionally listed here more than once.*

James McKnight, CEO
Leslie Campbell, COO
Chad McCurdy, Director

FINANCIAL DATA: *Note: Data for latest year may not have been available at press time.*

In U.S. $	2017	2016	2015	2014	2013	2012
Revenue	574,794,000	426,063,000	387,595,000	344,192,000	281,919,000	308,072,000
R&D Expense						
Operating Income	6,707,000	740,000	7,431,000	6,009,000	-3,213,000	-1,875,000
Operating Margin %	1.16%	.17%	1.91%	1.74%	-1.13%	-.60%
SGA Expense	99,063,000	74,099,000	61,605,000	55,500,000	49,818,000	60,313,000
Net Income	-4,827,000	-1,811,000	1,624,000	4,733,000	-8,534,000	-3,046,000
Operating Cash Flow	12,060,000	-5,618,000	3,277,000	2,981,000	-1,226,000	3,639,000
Capital Expenditure	9,730,000	13,572,000	4,646,000	5,494,000	5,293,000	4,850,000
EBITDA	17,609,000	9,032,000	15,294,000	13,082,000	3,759,000	4,888,000
Return on Assets %	-2.92%	-1.20%	1.21%	3.38%	-7.02%	-2.92%
Return on Equity %	-53.98%	-14.67%	12.98%	45.39%	-70.16%	-17.61%
Debt to Equity	11.54	6.31	4.09	3.62	6.00	1.63

CONTACT INFORMATION:

Phone: 615-771-7575 Fax:
Toll-Free:
Address: 1621 Galleria Blvd., Brentwood, TN 37027 United States

STOCK TICKER/OTHER:

Stock Ticker: DVCR
Employees: 7,400
Parent Company:
Exchange: NAS
Fiscal Year Ends: 12/31

SALARIES/BONUSES:

Top Exec. Salary: $515,100 Bonus: $
Second Exec. Salary: $339,966 Bonus: $

OTHER THOUGHTS:

Estimated Female Officers or Directors: 2
Hot Spot for Advancement for Women/Minorities:

DJO Global Inc

www.djoglobal.com

NAIC Code: 339,100

TYPES OF BUSINESS:

Clinical Orthopedic Rehabilitation Products & Devices
Electrotherapy Products
Rehabilitation Products

BRANDS/DIVISIONS/AFFILIATES:

Blackstone Capital Partners
Cefar
Empi
Ormed
Compex
Aircast
SpinaLogic
CMF OL1000

CONTACTS: *Note: Officers with more than one job title may be intentionally listed here more than once.*

Brady R. Shirley, CEO
Michael P. Mogul, Pres.
Michael C. Eklund, CFO
Stephen J. Murphy, Pres.-Sales & Mktg.
Jeanine Kestler, Exec. VP-Human Resources
Donald M. Roberts, General Counsel
Gerry McDonnell, Exec. VP-Global Oper.
Matt Simmons, Sr. VP-Bus. Dev.
Matt Simmons, Sr. VP-Investor Rel.
Vickie L. Capps, Treas.
Stephen Murphy, Exec. VP-Sales & Mktg., Int'l Commercial Bus.

GROWTH PLANS/SPECIAL FEATURES:

DJO Global, Inc. designs, manufactures, markets and distributes orthopedic devices, sports medicine equipment and other related products for the orthopedic industry worldwide. Its products are used to treat patients with musculoskeletal conditions resulting from degenerative diseases, deformities and acute injuries. DJO Global is the largest non-surgical orthopedic rehabilitation device company in the U.S. The company's products are used by orthopedic specialists, spine surgeons, primary care physicians, pain management specialists, physical therapists, podiatrists, chiropractors, athletic trainers and other healthcare professionals. In addition, many of DJO Global's non-surgical medical devices and accessories are used by athletes and patients for injury prevention and at-home physical therapy treatment. Some of the company's brands and trademarks include Encore, Cefar, Empi, Ormed, Chattanooga, Compex, Aircast, DonJoy, OfficeCare, ProCare, SpinaLogic, CMF (combined magnetic field) OL1000. Partners of the firm include the American Association of Hip and Knee Surgeons, The American Orthopaedic Foot & Ankle Society, American Orthopaedic Society for Sports Medicine, Orthopaedic Research and Education Foundation, Texas A&M University Geoservices, U.S. Ski Team, U.S. Freeskiing Team, U.S. Snowboard Team, Professional Football Athletic Trainers Society, the Federation Internationale de Ski (FIS), and Justin Sportsmedicine Team. DJO Global is owned by Blackstone Capital Partners.

The company offers employees benefits such as medical, dental, vision, home, life, AD&D, auto, pet and disability insurance; a 401(k); a stock purchase program; and an employee assistance program.

FINANCIAL DATA: *Note: Data for latest year may not have been available at press time.*

In U.S. $	2017	2016	2015	2014	2013	2012
Revenue	1,190,000,000	1,155,288,000	1,113,627,000	1,200,000,000	1,175,457,000	1,129,420,000
R&D Expense						
Operating Income						
Operating Margin %						
SGA Expense						
Net Income	-35,900,000	-286,303,000	-340,927,000	-90,534,000	-202,562,000	-118,368,000
Operating Cash Flow						
Capital Expenditure						
EBITDA						
Return on Assets %						
Return on Equity %						
Debt to Equity						

CONTACT INFORMATION:

Phone: 760-727-1280 Fax: 800-936-6569
Toll-Free:
Address: 1430 Decision St., Vista, CA 92081 United States

STOCK TICKER/OTHER:

Stock Ticker: Private
Exchange:
Employees: 5,470
Fiscal Year Ends: 12/31
Parent Company: Blackstone Capital Partners

SALARIES/BONUSES:

Top Exec. Salary: $ Bonus: $
Second Exec. Salary: $ Bonus: $

OTHER THOUGHTS:

Estimated Female Officers or Directors: 2
Hot Spot for Advancement for Women/Minorities:

Draegerwerk AG & Co KGaA

www.draeger.com/en_corp/Home

NAIC Code: 339,100

TYPES OF BUSINESS:

Surgical and Medical Instrument Manufacturing
Clinical Software and IT Solutions

BRANDS/DIVISIONS/AFFILIATES:

Drager BabylogVN500
Carina
Oxylog 3000 plus
MonoLead ECG
Innovian Anesthesia

CONTACTS:

Note: Officers with more than one job title may be intentionally listed here more than once.

Stefan Drager, CEO
Gert-Hartwig Lescow, CFO
Reine Piske, Dir.-Human Resources
Herbert Fehrecke, Head-R&D
Gert-Hartwig Lescow, Head-Finance
Anton Schrofner, Head-Production & Logistics
Herbert Fehrecke, Head-Purchasing

GROWTH PLANS/SPECIAL FEATURES:

Draegerwerk AG & Co KGaA is an international enterprise active in the fields of medical and safety technology. The firm's products include fire and gas detectors; medical gas management systems; ventilation systems for pediatric, adult and neonatal care; anesthesia workstations; warming therapy and neonatal care systems; jaundice management; patient monitoring systems; accessories and consumables such as expiration valves, breathing masks and peep valves; maintenance and training services; clinical IT and software solutions; and architectural systems and lights. Some of the firm's ventilation products include Drager BabylogVN500, Carina and Oxylog3000 plus. Patient monitoring systems include range of Infinity brands and the MonoLead ECG lead-wire set. Clinical software and solutions consists of Innovian Anesthesia and the Infinity suite. The enterprise is represented in 190 countries, with sales and service subsidiaries in over 50 countries. The firm's development and production facilities are based in Germany, the U.K., Norway, Sweden, South Africa, the U.S., Brazil, Chile, Czech Republic and China.

The firm offers its employees a work/life balance schedule, retirement plans and an employee assistance program. Other benefits vary by region.

FINANCIAL DATA:

Note: Data for latest year may not have been available at press time.

In U.S. $	2017	2016	2015	2014	2013	2012
Revenue						
R&D Expense						
Operating Income						
Operating Margin %						
SGA Expense						
Net Income						
Operating Cash Flow						
Capital Expenditure						
EBITDA						
Return on Assets %						
Return on Equity %						
Debt to Equity						

CONTACT INFORMATION:

Phone: 49 4518820 Fax: 49 4518822080
Toll-Free:
Address: Moislinger Allee 53-55, Lubeck, 23558 Germany

STOCK TICKER/OTHER:

Stock Ticker: DGWPF Exchange: PINX
Employees: 13,739 Fiscal Year Ends: 12/31
Parent Company:

SALARIES/BONUSES:

Top Exec. Salary: $ Bonus: $
Second Exec. Salary: $ Bonus: $

OTHER THOUGHTS:

Estimated Female Officers or Directors:
Hot Spot for Advancement for Women/Minorities:

Duane Reade Inc

www.duanereade.com

NAIC Code: 446,110

TYPES OF BUSINESS:

Drug Stores
Retail Pharmacies
Nutraceuticals & Cosmetics
Photo Processing

BRANDS/DIVISIONS/AFFILIATES:

Walgreens Boots Alliance Inc
DuaneReade.com

CONTACTS: *Note: Officers with more than one job title may be intentionally listed here more than once.*

John K. Henry, CFO
Charles R. Newsom, VP-Store Operations
Greg D. Wasson, CEO

GROWTH PLANS/SPECIAL FEATURES:

Duane Reade, Inc., owned by Walgreens Boots Alliance, Inc., is one of the largest retail drug store chains in New York City. The drugstore chain operates throughout Manhattan's business and residential districts; New York's outer boroughs; and in the surrounding New York and New Jersey suburbs, including the Hudson River communities of northeastern New Jersey. Products and services offered include prescription and over-the-counter medications, vitamins, food & beverages, health aids, beauty products, greeting cards and photo processing. Duane Reade's extensive network of conveniently located pharmacies, strong local market position, pricing policies and reputation for high-quality healthcare products and services provide it with a competitive advantage in attracting pharmacy business from individual customers as well as managed care organizations, insurance companies and employers. The company's pharmacies employ computer systems that link all Duane Reade stores and enable them to provide customers with a broad range of services. The network profiles customer medical and other relevant information, supplies customers with information concerning their drug purchases for income tax and insurance purposes and prepares prescription labels and receipts. Duane Reade also has an interactive web site, DuaneReade.com, which customers may use to access company information, refill prescriptions and purchase over-the-counter medications as well as health and beauty care products and other non-pharmacy items.

FINANCIAL DATA: *Note: Data for latest year may not have been available at press time.*

In U.S. $	2017	2016	2015	2014	2013	2012
Revenue						
R&D Expense						
Operating Income						
Operating Margin %						
SGA Expense						
Net Income						
Operating Cash Flow						
Capital Expenditure						
EBITDA						
Return on Assets %						
Return on Equity %						
Debt to Equity						

CONTACT INFORMATION:

Phone: 212-273-5700 Fax: 212-244-6527
Toll-Free:
Address: 440 9th Ave., New York, NY 10001 United States

STOCK TICKER/OTHER:

Stock Ticker: Subsidiary
Exchange:
Employees: 7,000
Fiscal Year Ends: 12/31
Parent Company: Walgreens Boots Alliance Inc

SALARIES/BONUSES:

Top Exec. Salary: $ Bonus: $
Second Exec. Salary: $ Bonus: $

OTHER THOUGHTS:

Estimated Female Officers or Directors:
Hot Spot for Advancement for Women/Minorities:

Dynacq Healthcare Inc

www.dynacq.com

NAIC Code: 622,110

TYPES OF BUSINESS:

Acute Care Hospital
Outpatient Surgery Facilities
Freestanding Ambulatory Surgical and Emergency Centers
Fertility Treatments
Orthopedic Surgery
Bariatric Surgery

BRANDS/DIVISIONS/AFFILIATES:

Sino Bond Inc Limited
Surgery Specialty Hospitals of America

CONTACTS: *Note: Officers with more than one job title may be intentionally listed here more than once.*

Eric Chan, CEO
Hemant Khemka, CFO
Hemant Khemka, CFO
Ringo Cheng, Dir.-IT

GROWTH PLANS/SPECIAL FEATURES:

Dynacq Healthcare, Inc. is a holding company that develops and manages a general and acute care hospital that provides specialized general surgeries. It has operations in the U.S. and China. Within the U.S., Dynacq owns and operates a general acute care hospital, the Surgery Specialty Hospitals of America in Pasadena, Texas. This hospital is designed to handle surgical procedures such as bariatric, transvaginal mesh, orthopedic and neuro-spine surgeries. The hospital contains operating rooms, pre- and post-operative space, intensive care units, nursing units and diagnostic facilities, as well as adjacent medical office buildings that lease space to physicians and other healthcare providers. The company, through its affiliates, owns or leases 100% of the real estate and equipment in its facilities; it has a 100% ownership interest in its Pasadena facility. In Hong Kong, Dynacq invests in debt and equity securities. The company's foreign subsidiary Sino Bond, Inc. Limited is the only subsidiary classified as continuing operations in the corporate division. This subsidiary holds and manages investments in Hong Kong and invests in debt and equity securities in Europe and Asia, including initial public offerings and pre-initial public offerings.

FINANCIAL DATA: *Note: Data for latest year may not have been available at press time.*

In U.S. $	2017	2016	2015	2014	2013	2012
Revenue			6,997,884	10,218,310	6,057,411	5,531,233
R&D Expense						
Operating Income			-6,514,152	-5,190,246	-7,541,260	-8,153,266
Operating Margin %			-93.08%	-50.79%	-124.49%	-147.40%
SGA Expense			6,408,232	6,305,898	5,514,147	
Net Income			-3,838,375	-3,793,349	-3,305,084	-12,151,500
Operating Cash Flow			-6,412,099	2,426,478	-6,944,770	-13,695,790
Capital Expenditure			384,162	267,362	35,108	159,919
EBITDA			-3,067,596	-2,974,798	-2,434,712	-5,414,932
Return on Assets %			-9.15%	-8.48%	-7.52%	-21.62%
Return on Equity %			-16.38%	-13.40%	-11.16%	-32.83%
Debt to Equity						0.03

CONTACT INFORMATION:

Phone: 713 378-2000 Fax: 713 944-0201
Toll-Free:
Address: 4301 Vista Rd., Pasadena, TX 77504 United States

STOCK TICKER/OTHER:

Stock Ticker: DYII Exchange: GREY
Employees: 126 Fiscal Year Ends: 08/31
Parent Company:

SALARIES/BONUSES:

Top Exec. Salary: $630,000 Bonus: $
Second Exec. Salary: $160,000 Bonus: $

OTHER THOUGHTS:

Estimated Female Officers or Directors:
Hot Spot for Advancement for Women/Minorities:

Ebos Group Limited

www.ebos.co.nz

NAIC Code: 424,210

TYPES OF BUSINESS:

Drugs and Druggists' Sundries Merchant Wholesalers
Healthcare Products
Medical Products
Pharmaceuticals
Pet Care Products

BRANDS/DIVISIONS/AFFILIATES:

MedAdvisor Limited

CONTACTS: *Note: Officers with more than one job title may be intentionally listed here more than once.*

John Cullity, CEO
Shaun Hughes, CFO
Andrea Bell, CIO

GROWTH PLANS/SPECIAL FEATURES:

Ebos Group Limited is a diversified Australian marketer, wholesaler and distributor of healthcare, medical and pharmaceutical products. The firm also markets and distributes animal care products. Ebos' business is divided into four categories: community pharmacy, institutional health care, contract logistics and animal care. The community pharmacy business delivers pharmaceutical, over-the-counter medicines and related consumer products to pharmacies across Australia and New Zealand. Product brands include Symbion, TerryWhite Chemmart, ProPharma, Pharmacy Wholesalers Russells, HealthSAVE Pharmacy, Pharmacy+ Choice, Minfos, IntelliPharm, Group Pharmacy Warehouse, DoseAid, Vantage Gold Club, Endeavor, Faulding, Red Seal, Anti-Flamme and Floradix. The institutional healthcare business supplies a range of products and services to public and private hospitals, doctors' surgeries and aged care facilities. Product brands include Symbion, HPS, Ebos Healthcare, OneLink and Zest. The contract logistics business offers services to pharmaceutical manufacturers, medical device suppliers and consumer healthcare companies. These services primarily include warehousing, distribution and logistics support, but also includes specialized logistics services for the clinical research industry. Last, animal care business provides sales, marketing, wholesale and distribution support to pet retailers, veterinarians and grocery stores. It also holds a retail presence in New Zealand. Animal care brands include BlackHawk, VitaPet, MasterPet, Lyppard and Animates. In late-2017, Ebos acquired a 14.1% share in MedAdvisor Limited, a digital medication management company in Australia.

FINANCIAL DATA: *Note: Data for latest year may not have been available at press time.*

In U.S. $	2017	2016	2015	2014	2013	2012
Revenue	5,003,710,000	4,659,625,000	3,981,575,000	3,777,614,000	1,195,488,000	
R&D Expense						
Operating Income	144,345,300	134,182,200	113,571,800	103,049,100	83,636,910	
Operating Margin %	2.88%	2.87%	2.85%	2.72%	6.99%	
SGA Expense	193,952,300	173,189,000	155,681,000	152,185,000	57,982,080	
Net Income	87,167,000	83,329,180	69,513,260	60,411,140	18,508,040	
Operating Cash Flow						
Capital Expenditure	9,626,388	7,299,677	10,131,620	23,166,710	2,024,225	
EBITDA	155,183,600	149,587,900	130,570,100	116,953,000	38,216,190	
Return on Assets %	4.15%	4.42%	4.36%	3.80%	1.76%	
Return on Equity %	11.97%	11.87%	10.43%	14.34%	10.98%	
Debt to Equity	0.38	0.23	0.25	0.25	0.50	

CONTACT INFORMATION:

Phone: 613-9918-5555 Fax: 613-9918-5599
Toll-Free:
Address: Level 7, 737 Bourke St., Docklands, Victoria 3008 Australia

STOCK TICKER/OTHER:

Stock Ticker: EBOSY Exchange: GREY
Employees: Fiscal Year Ends: 06/30
Parent Company:

SALARIES/BONUSES:

Top Exec. Salary: $ Bonus: $
Second Exec. Salary: $ Bonus: $

OTHER THOUGHTS:

Estimated Female Officers or Directors:
Hot Spot for Advancement for Women/Minorities:

eClinicalWorks

www.eclinicalworks.com

NAIC Code: 511210D

TYPES OF BUSINESS:

Computer Software, Healthcare & Biotechnology
Electronic Prescription Filing
Patient Flow Management
Claims Submission & Management Software
Business Optimization Software

BRANDS/DIVISIONS/AFFILIATES:

Enterprise Business Optimizer

CONTACTS: *Note: Officers with more than one job title may be intentionally listed here more than once.*

Girish Kumar Navani, CEO

GROWTH PLANS/SPECIAL FEATURES:

eClinicalWorks is a private company operating in the ambulatory clinical systems market. The company primarily provides electronic health record (EHR) and practice management tools for its clients, including physicians; large and small health systems; large and medium medical group practices, including federally qualified health centers and community health centers; and small, solo provider practices. The firm's customer base consists of more than 130,000 physicians and over 850,000 medical professionals in all 50 states and 24 countries. eClinicalWorks' EHR cloud solution provides patient flow management, patient record access, registry reporting, electronic prescription request, referring physician communication and clinical data transfers, all while keeping the data private. When used with the firm's patient management system, the solution enables clients to: review patient history, current medications, allergies and diagnostic tests; streamline medical billing management; check patient insurance eligibility; electronically submit and manage claims; and perform clinical and financial analyses through its Enterprise Business Optimizer (eBO) tool. eClincialWorks's population health solution covers the population health across all functional accountable care organization (ACO) categories; and the revenue cycle management console assists in processing claims, financial analytics, reimbursement evaluation and six levels of clearinghouse integrations. The company's cloud platform keeps private data private, and each client's database cannot be affected by another practice's upgrades.

eClinicalWorks offers its employees health, dental, vision, life and disability insurance; flexible spending accounts; and a 401(k) plan.

FINANCIAL DATA: *Note: Data for latest year may not have been available at press time.*

In U.S. $	2017	2016	2015	2014	2013	2012
Revenue	462,000,000	440,000,000	358,000,000	333,000,000	300,000,000	255,000,000
R&D Expense						
Operating Income						
Operating Margin %						
SGA Expense						
Net Income						
Operating Cash Flow						
Capital Expenditure						
EBITDA						
Return on Assets %						
Return on Equity %						
Debt to Equity						

CONTACT INFORMATION:

Phone: 508-836-2700 Fax: 508-836-4466
Toll-Free: 866-888-6929
Address: 2 Technology Dr., Westborough, MA 01581 United States

STOCK TICKER/OTHER:

Stock Ticker: Private
Employees: 4,500
Parent Company:
Exchange:
Fiscal Year Ends: 12/31

SALARIES/BONUSES:

Top Exec. Salary: $ Bonus: $
Second Exec. Salary: $ Bonus: $

OTHER THOUGHTS:

Estimated Female Officers or Directors:
Hot Spot for Advancement for Women/Minorities:

EDAP TMS SA

www.edap-tms.com

NAIC Code: 339,100

TYPES OF BUSINESS:

Ultrasound Equipment
High Intensity Focused Ultrasound Equipment
Prostate Cancer Treatment Technology

BRANDS/DIVISIONS/AFFILIATES:

Ablatherm
Focal One
Sonolith
Holmium

CONTACTS:

Note: Officers with more than one job title may be intentionally listed here more than once.

Marc Oczachowski, CEO
Francois Dietsch, CFO
Philippe Chauveau, Chmn.

GROWTH PLANS/SPECIAL FEATURES:

EDAP TMS SA is a French holding company engaged in developing therapeutic ultrasound technology. The company serves patients and medical professionals worldwide. Its operations are grouped into three divisions: high-intensity focused ultrasound (HIFU), extracorporeal shockwave lithotripsy (ESWL) and stone laser. The HIFU division offers a range of robotic HIFU devices, including the Ablatherm and Focal One HIFU devices for the non-invasive treatment of prostate cancer. Treatment by these devices offers optimal efficacy and minimal side effects as compared to surgery and radiotherapy. The ESWL division provides electronoconductive technology, the latest generation of shockwave source, as well as stone localization via the company's Sonolith family of ESWL integrated lithotripter systems (Sonolith i-sys and Sonolith i-move). Sonolith i-sys and i-move are extracorporeal medical devices designed to fragment stones located in the urinary tract. The stone laser division offers a range of minimally-invasive stone solutions covering urinary tract stone indications. This includes the Holmium line of laser surgical systems for the treatment of urinary stones and other urological procedures. In June 2018, EDAP announced that it received 510(k) clearance from the U.S. FDA for its Focal One device for the ablation of prostate tissue.

FINANCIAL DATA:

Note: Data for latest year may not have been available at press time.

In U.S. $	2017	2016	2015	2014	2013	2012
Revenue	41,569,950	41,412,960	37,507,850	31,148,970	28,003,260	30,311,670
R&D Expense	4,513,316	4,498,198	3,128,271	3,409,699	3,017,793	3,092,220
Operating Income	-2,357,251	454,704	566,345	-2,020,002	-3,203,861	-2,360,740
Operating Margin %	-5.67%	1.09%	1.50%	-6.48%	-11.44%	-7.78%
SGA Expense	15,064,540	14,131,880	12,336,320	11,636,240	11,023,380	11,401,330
Net Income	-791,953	4,467,962	-1,938,598	-595,418	-5,839,051	-8,692,872
Operating Cash Flow	-3,557,391	1,301,314	1,555,995	-1,179,207	-2,901,500	-188,394
Capital Expenditure	2,409,583	1,542,040	755,902	1,187,347	883,824	755,902
EBITDA	1,539,714	6,426,329	184,905	661,705	-3,263,170	-5,071,520
Return on Assets %	-1.45%	9.02%	-4.71%	-1.73%	-17.51%	-23.73%
Return on Equity %	-2.74%	19.76%	-11.27%	-4.19%	-57.56%	-88.59%
Debt to Equity	0.05	0.02	0.06	0.04	0.06	0.65

CONTACT INFORMATION:

Phone: 33 472153150 Fax: 33 472153150
Toll-Free: 800-541-8414
Address: 4/6 rue du Dauphine, Vaulx-en-Velin, 69120 France

STOCK TICKER/OTHER:

Stock Ticker: EDAP
Employees: 197
Parent Company:
Exchange: NAS
Fiscal Year Ends: 12/31

SALARIES/BONUSES:

Top Exec. Salary: $ Bonus: $
Second Exec. Salary: $ Bonus: $

OTHER THOUGHTS:

Estimated Female Officers or Directors:
Hot Spot for Advancement for Women/Minorities:

Edwards Lifesciences Corporation

www.edwards.com

NAIC Code: 339,100

TYPES OF BUSINESS:

Supplies-Cardiovascular Disease Related
Cardiac Surgery Products
Critical Care Products
Vascular Products
Heart Valve Implants

BRANDS/DIVISIONS/AFFILIATES:

PERIMOUNT
Edwards Intuity Valve System
Edwards SAPIEN
Swan-Ganz
FloTrac
ClearSight
EV1000

CONTACTS: *Note: Officers with more than one job title may be intentionally listed here more than once.*

Michael Mussallem, CEO
Scott Ullem, CFO
Donald Bobo, Vice President
Larry Wood, Vice President, Divisional
Catherine Szyman, Vice President, Divisional
Jean-Luc Lemercier, Vice President, Geographical
Huimin Wang, Vice President, Geographical

GROWTH PLANS/SPECIAL FEATURES:

Edwards Lifesciences Corporation designs products for cardiovascular diseases, such as heart valve disease, coronary artery disease, peripheral vascular disease (PVD) and congestive heart failure. The firm operates in three main areas: surgical heart valve therapy (21% of 2017 net sales), transcatheter heart valves (59%) and critical care (10%). Surgical heart valve products include the PERIMOUNT line of pericardial heart valves made from biologically inert porcine tissue, often on a wire-form stent; and valve repair therapies, such as the Edwards Intuity Valve System, a minimally-invasive aortic system designed to enable a faster procedure and a smaller incision. Transcatheter heart valves are designed to treat heart valves disease using catheter-based approaches. Its main products are the Edwards SAPIEN, Sapien XT and Sapien 3 transcatheter aortic heart valves and delivery systems used to treat heart valve disease using catheter-based approaches for patients deemed at high risk for traditional open-heart surgery. The aortic heart valves are available for sale in more than 65 countries. The company's critical care products include the Swan-Ganz brand hemodynamic monitoring devices used during surgery; FloTrac, a minimally invasive continuous cardiac output monitoring system; ClearSight hemodynamic monitor that provides real-time, beat-to-beat information; and EV1000 clinical monitoring platform which displays a patient's physiological status and integrates many of the firm's sensors and catheters into one platform. The firm sells its products in approximately 100 countries, including Canada, China, France, Germany, Italy, Japan, Spain and the U.K.

Employee benefits include medical, dental and vision coverage; 401(k); an employee stock purchase plan; short- and long-term disability; and adoption assistance.

FINANCIAL DATA: *Note: Data for latest year may not have been available at press time.*

In U.S. $	2017	2016	2015	2014	2013	2012
Revenue	3,435,300,000	2,963,700,000	2,493,700,000	2,322,900,000	2,045,500,000	1,899,600,000
R&D Expense	552,600,000	477,800,000	383,100,000	356,700,000	323,000,000	291,300,000
Operating Income	1,022,700,000	783,800,000	642,700,000	482,600,000	454,500,000	408,400,000
Operating Margin %	29.77%	26.44%	25.77%	21.21%	22.21%	21.49%
SGA Expense	984,700,000	904,700,000	850,700,000	858,000,000	745,600,000	705,300,000
Net Income	583,600,000	569,500,000	494,900,000	811,100,000	391,700,000	293,200,000
Operating Cash Flow	1,000,700,000	704,400,000	549,700,000	1,022,300,000	472,700,000	373,800,000
Capital Expenditure	175,500,000	217,400,000	106,500,000	93,700,000	110,100,000	127,700,000
EBITDA	1,140,000,000	828,300,000	705,400,000	1,229,800,000	593,800,000	452,800,000
Return on Assets %	11.43%	13.29%	13.05%	25.95%	15.83%	13.95%
Return on Equity %	20.93%	22.23%	21.08%	43.25%	25.78%	20.81%
Debt to Equity	0.14	0.31	0.23	0.27	0.38	0.12

CONTACT INFORMATION:

Phone: 949 250-2500 Fax: 949 250-2525
Toll-Free: 800-424-3278
Address: 1 Edwards Way, Irvine, CA 92614 United States

STOCK TICKER/OTHER:

Stock Ticker: EW
Exchange: NYS
Employees: 11,100
Fiscal Year Ends: 12/31
Parent Company:

SALARIES/BONUSES:

Top Exec. Salary: $995,385 Bonus: $
Second Exec. Salary: $573,506 Bonus: $2,000

OTHER THOUGHTS:

Estimated Female Officers or Directors: 3
Hot Spot for Advancement for Women/Minorities: Y

EHealth Inc

NAIC Code: 524,210

www.ehealthinsurance.com

TYPES OF BUSINESS:

Health Insurance Brokerage-Online
Health Insurance
Student Health Insurance
Short-term Health Insurance
Health Savings Accounts
Dental Insurance
Term Life Insurance
Dental Discount Cards

BRANDS/DIVISIONS/AFFILIATES:

eHealthInsurance Services Inc
eHealth.com
eHealthInsurance.com
eHealthMedicare.com
Medicare.com
GoMedigap.com
PlanPrescriber.com

CONTACTS: *Note: Officers with more than one job title may be intentionally listed here more than once.*

Scott Flanders, CEO
Derek Yung, CFO
Timothy Hannan, Chief Marketing Officer
Ian Kalin, Chief Technology Officer
David Francis, COO
Ellen Tauscher, Director
Robert Hurley, President, Divisional
Jay Jennings, Senior VP, Divisional

GROWTH PLANS/SPECIAL FEATURES:

EHealth, Inc. is a leading private health insurance exchange where individuals, families and small businesses can compare health insurance products from leading insurers side-by-side and purchase and enroll in coverage online through its websites or by phone. Websites include eHealth.com, eHealthInsurance.com, eHealthMedicare.com, Medicare.com, GoMedigap.com and PlanPrescriber.com. The company, along with wholly-owned subsidiary eHealthInsurance Services, Inc., are licensed to market and sell health insurance in all 50 states and Washington, D.C. EHealth organizes and presents health insurance online in a user-friendly format, enabling its customers to choose from a variety of health insurance products. The firm generates revenue primarily from commissions it receives from health insurance carriers, generally based on a percentage of the premium its members have paid to the carrier. It also, in some instances, receives commission override payments for achieving certain sales volume thresholds. In addition to the revenue the company derives from the sale of health insurance products, it generates revenue from its online sponsorship advertising program and from licensing the use of its ecommerce technology. Products offered by eHealth include preferred provider organization (PPO), health maintenance organization (HMO), indemnity plans, short-term medical insurance, student health insurance, health savings account (HSA) eligible health insurance plans and ancillary products such as dental, vision and life insurance. Elements of its platform include online rate quoting, comprehensive plan information, plan comparison, recommendations and online application and enrollment forms. The platform also uses Electronic Processing Interchange technology to integrate its online application process with health insurance carriers' technology systems. Members are able to enroll in select plans online through subsidiary PlanPrescriber.com. Revenue derived from carriers owned by Humana, UnitedHealthcare and Aetna represent approximately 22%, 16% and 9% of eHealth's revenue, respectively.

FINANCIAL DATA: *Note: Data for latest year may not have been available at press time.*

In U.S. $	2017	2016	2015	2014	2013	2012
Revenue	172,355,000	186,960,000	189,541,000	179,677,000	179,180,000	155,473,000
R&D Expense	32,889,000	32,749,000	36,351,000	40,390,000	32,579,000	21,406,000
Operating Income	-28,873,000	-6,152,000	-1,110,000	-6,762,000	3,732,000	13,429,000
Operating Margin %	-16.75%	-3.29%	-.58%	-3.76%	2.08%	8.63%
SGA Expense	165,026,000	156,147,000	148,969,000	140,026,000	135,994,000	114,240,000
Net Income	-25,412,000	-4,882,000	-4,763,000	-16,205,000	1,723,000	7,082,000
Operating Cash Flow	-15,541,000	4,083,000	13,696,000	1,779,000	20,947,000	24,891,000
Capital Expenditure	5,078,000	3,726,000	2,996,000	8,104,000	7,326,000	3,853,000
EBITDA	-23,532,000	-637,000	4,818,000	-1,041,000	8,412,000	17,455,000
Return on Assets %	-25.72%	-4.39%	-4.33%	-11.86%	.94%	3.78%
Return on Equity %	-36.63%	-6.33%	-6.35%	-15.69%	1.13%	4.33%
Debt to Equity						

CONTACT INFORMATION:

Phone: 650 584-2700 Fax: 650 961-2153
Toll-Free: 800-977-8860
Address: 440 E. Middlefield Rd., Mountain View, CA 94043 United States

STOCK TICKER/OTHER:

Stock Ticker: EHTH
Employees: 944
Parent Company:
Exchange: NAS
Fiscal Year Ends: 12/31

SALARIES/BONUSES:

Top Exec. Salary: $600,000 Bonus: $
Second Exec. Salary: $390,769 Bonus: $

OTHER THOUGHTS:

Estimated Female Officers or Directors: 1
Hot Spot for Advancement for Women/Minorities:

Electromed Inc

www.smartvest.com

NAIC Code: 339,100

TYPES OF BUSINESS:

Medical Device Manufacturing

BRANDS/DIVISIONS/AFFILIATES:

SmartVest Airway Clearance System
SmartVest Connect
SmartVest Wrap
Aerobika

CONTACTS: *Note: Officers with more than one job title may be intentionally listed here more than once.*

Kathleen Skarvan, CEO
Jeremy Brock, CFO
Stephen Craney, Chairman of the Board
George Winn, Director

GROWTH PLANS/SPECIAL FEATURES:

Electromed, Inc. is a medical device company that develops, manufactures, markets and sells products that provide airway clearance therapy to patients with compromised pulmonary functioning. Its principal product is the SmartVest Airway Clearance System. The SmartVest System generates high frequency chest wall oscillation (HFCWO), a technique for airway clearance therapy, also known as High Frequency Chest Compression. The vest, which is FDA approved to treat the condition of excess lung secretions, is worn over the torso and repeatedly compresses and releases the chest at frequencies from 5 to 20 cycles per second. Each compression (or oscillation) produces pulsations within the lungs that shear secretions from the surfaces of the airways and propels them toward the mouth where they can be removed by normal coughing. Consequently, it may be prescribed to patients suffering from cystic fibrosis, chronic obstructive pulmonary disease (COPD), muscular dystrophy, post-surgical airway complications and a variety of other diseases and conditions associated with impaired lung and airway capacity. By clearing airways, patients are able to rid their lungs of retained secretions and are therefore less likely to develop lung infections such as pneumonia. The SmartVest System is a doctor-prescribed therapy and, depending on the circumstances of the patient, its cost to an individual is generally reimbursable by Medicare, Medicaid and private insurance, or a combination of the three. Therapy can be tracked via SmartVest Connect wireless technology, providing collaboration between patient and healthcare professionals in treatment decisions. Additionally, Electromed markets the SmartVest Wrap, which functions in the same manner as the full system, but lacks a vest outer shell, making it more suitable for patients recovering from surgery and short-term illnesses. Its Aerobika oscillating positive expiratory pressure (OPEP) device is an airway clearance therapy for patients with compromised pulmonary function that may not need high-frequency chest wall oscillation.

FINANCIAL DATA: *Note: Data for latest year may not have been available at press time.*

In U.S. $	2017	2016	2015	2014	2013	2012
Revenue	25,861,140	22,992,000	19,408,380	15,487,880	15,104,420	19,524,490
R&D Expense	596,876	380,392	315,647	466,063	603,375	920,769
Operating Income	3,569,339	3,109,308	1,310,196	-740,592	-1,827,393	606,337
Operating Margin %	13.80%	13.52%	6.75%	-4.78%	-12.09%	3.10%
SGA Expense	16,402,210	14,386,560	11,974,380	10,908,530	11,673,070	12,617,970
Net Income	2,229,472	2,212,502	1,092,486	-1,288,594	-1,329,276	186,606
Operating Cash Flow	1,191,121	2,166,903	2,781,214	2,062,661	1,876,657	-1,171,777
Capital Expenditure	687,148	579,521	624,507	935,799	1,053,372	853,751
EBITDA	4,341,510	3,848,010	2,048,739	-32,653	-1,220,857	1,147,365
Return on Assets %	10.21%	11.64%	6.58%	-7.72%	-6.90%	.89%
Return on Equity %	12.58%	14.61%	8.20%	-9.67%	-9.16%	1.25%
Debt to Equity	0.05	0.07	0.08	0.09	0.09	0.09

CONTACT INFORMATION:

Phone: 952 758-9299 Fax:
Toll-Free: 800-462-1045
Address: 500 Sixth Ave. NW, New Prague, MN 56071 United States

STOCK TICKER/OTHER:

Stock Ticker: ELMD
Employees: 115
Parent Company:
Exchange: ASE
Fiscal Year Ends: 06/30

SALARIES/BONUSES:

Top Exec. Salary: $285,120 Bonus: $
Second Exec. Salary: $200,000 Bonus: $

OTHER THOUGHTS:

Estimated Female Officers or Directors: 1
Hot Spot for Advancement for Women/Minorities: Y

Elekta AB

NAIC Code: 339,100

www.elekta.com

TYPES OF BUSINESS:

Radiation Technology
Radiosurgery Equipment
Medical Software

BRANDS/DIVISIONS/AFFILIATES:

Leksell Gamma Knife Icon
Leksell Gamma Knife Perfexion
Versa HD
MOSAIQ
Elekta Neuromag TRIUX
XiO

CONTACTS: *Note: Officers with more than one job title may be intentionally listed here more than once.*

Richard Hausmann, CEO
Steven Wort, COO
Thomas Puusepp, Pres.
Gustaf Salford, CFO
Ioannis Panagiotelis, CMO
Karin Svenske Nyberg, VP-Human Resources
Asa Hedin, Exec. VP-Neuroscience
John Lapre, Chief Technology Officer
Michelle Joiner, Dir.-Global Public Rel.
Johan Andersson Melbi, Dir.-Investor Rel.
Gilbert Wai, Exec. VP-Asia Pacific
Ian Alexander, Exec. VP-Latin America & EMEA
Bill Yaeger, Exec. VP-Oncology
John Lapre, Exec. VP-Brachytherapy
James P. Hoey, Exec. VP-North America

GROWTH PLANS/SPECIAL FEATURES:

Elekta AB is a global developer of medical technology for oncology and the management of brain disorders. Products are divided into seven categories: radiotherapy, stereotactic radiosurgery, oncology informatics, brachytherapy, neurosurgery, particle therapy and MR/RT. Radiotheray products include treatment delivery systems and solutions such as imaging, motion management, quality assurance solutions, beam shaping and patient positioning. Stereotactic radiosurgery (also referred to as Gamma Knife surgery) products include: the Leksell Gamma Knife Icon device, which limits radiation dose to healthy tissue and allows for precise treatment target areas during brain surgery; Leksell Gamma Knife Perfexion, for extreme accuracy during cranial radiosurgery; and Versa HD, an advanced linear accelerator capable of delivering dose conformance for an expanded range of targets. Oncology informatics include: the MOSAIQ Oncology line, which provides access to clinical and patient information; tools for sharing, analyzing and applying information; and treatment management for planning, delivery and assessment. Brachytherapy products include treatment delivery systems and solutions for precise, targeted treatment of various cancers such as prostate, breast, skin and surface, rectum and gynecological anatomy. Brachytherapy is suited as a single modality or in combination with other treatments such as external beam radiation. Neurosurgery diagnostic solutions include magnetoencephalography (MEG), a neuroimaging technique for mapping brain activity via magnetic signals. This division's Elekta Neuromag TRIUX addresses key MEG requirements critical for mapping studies. Particle therapy products include integrated software, services and treatment tools for building a proton therapy practice. This includes the MOSAIQ oncology information system, for care management; the XiO treatment planning software, with automated tools and dose calculation algorithms; patient positioning, immobilization and motion management tools; and support services. Last, MR/RT (magnetic resonance/radiation therapy) products enable clinicians to see and track difficult-to-visualize soft-tissue anatomies. Over 6,000 hospitals worldwide rely on Elekta technology.

FINANCIAL DATA: *Note: Data for latest year may not have been available at press time.*

In U.S. $	2017	2016	2015	2014	2013	2012
Revenue						
R&D Expense						
Operating Income						
Operating Margin %						
SGA Expense						
Net Income						
Operating Cash Flow						
Capital Expenditure						
EBITDA						
Return on Assets %						
Return on Equity %						
Debt to Equity						

CONTACT INFORMATION:

Phone: 46 858725400 Fax: 46 858725500
Toll-Free:
Address: Kungstensgatan 18, Box 7593, Stockholm, 103 93 Sweden

STOCK TICKER/OTHER:

Stock Ticker: EKTAF
Exchange: PINX
Employees: 3,702
Fiscal Year Ends: 04/30
Parent Company:

SALARIES/BONUSES:

Top Exec. Salary: $ Bonus: $
Second Exec. Salary: $ Bonus: $

OTHER THOUGHTS:

Estimated Female Officers or Directors: 4
Hot Spot for Advancement for Women/Minorities: Y

Eli Lilly and Company

www.lilly.com

NAIC Code: 325,412

TYPES OF BUSINESS:

Pharmaceuticals Discovery & Development
Veterinary Products

BRANDS/DIVISIONS/AFFILIATES:

Humulin
Trajenta
Alimta
Cyramza
Effient
Rumensin
Coban
Interceptor Plus

CONTACTS: *Note: Officers with more than one job title may be intentionally listed here more than once.*

David Ricks, CEO
Leigh Pusey, Senior VP, Divisional
Joshua Smiley, CFO
Donald Zakrowski, Chief Accounting Officer
Michael Harrington, General Counsel
Melissa Barnes, Other Executive Officer
Alfonso Zulueta, President, Divisional
Susan Mahony, President, Divisional
Enrique Conterno, President, Divisional
Jeffrey Simmons, President, Divisional
Myles ONeill, President, Divisional
Johna Norton, Senior VP, Divisional
Stephen Fry, Senior VP, Divisional
Aarti Shah, Senior VP, Divisional

GROWTH PLANS/SPECIAL FEATURES:

Eli Lilly and Company discovers, develops, manufactures and markets human pharmaceutical and animal health products. Human pharmaceutical products are grouped into five divisions: endocrinology, neuroscience, oncology, immunology and cardiovascular. Endocrinology products include: Humalog, Humulin, Basaglar, Trajenta, Jentadueto, Jardiance, Trulicity and Glyxambi, for the treatment of diabetes; Forteo and Evista, for osteoporosis in women; and Humatrope, for human growth hormone deficiency. Neuroscience products include: Cymbalta and Prozac, for major depressive disorder; Zyprexa, for schizophrenia; Strattera, for attention-deficit hyperactivity disorder; and Amyvid, a radioactive diagnostic agent for brain imaging of people with cognitive decline. Oncology products include: Alimta, for non-small cell lung cancer; Erbitux, for colorectal cancers; Gemzar, for pancreatic cancer/metastatic breast cancer/ovarian cancer/bladder cancer; Cyramza, for advanced or metastatic gastric cancer; Portrazza, to treat epidermal growth factor receptor expressing squamous non-small cell lung cancer; Lartruvo, for soft tissue carcinoma; and Verzenio, for advanced/metastatic breast cancer. Immunology products include: Olumiant, for adults with moderately-to-severe active rheumatoid arthritis; and Taltz, for moderate-to-severe plaque psoriasis and active psoriatic arthritis. Cardiovascular products include: Cialis, for erectile dysfunction; and Effient, for reduction of thrombotic cardiovascular events. Animal health products are grouped into two divisions: food animals and companion animals. Food animal products include: Rumensin, a cattle feed additive; Coban, Maxiban and Monteban, anticoccidial agents for use in poultry; Posilac, a protein supplement; Paylean and Optaflexx, leanness and/or performance enhancers; and Tylan and Denagard, antibiotics. Companion animal products include Trifexis and Comfortis chewable tablets are manufactured for flea prevention; Interceptor Plus, a chewable for the prevention of heartworm disease; and Duramune, Bronchi-Shield, Fel-O and Rabvac, vaccines.

Eli Lilly offers employees life, health, prescription drug and dental insurance; domestic partner benefits; an employee assistance program; paid maternity leave; a 401(k); flexible spending accounts; adoption assistance; and tuition reimbursement.

FINANCIAL DATA: *Note: Data for latest year may not have been available at press time.*

In U.S. $	2017	2016	2015	2014	2013	2012
Revenue	22,871,300,000	21,222,100,000	19,958,700,000	19,615,600,000	23,113,100,000	22,603,400,000
R&D Expense	6,394,400,000	5,273,900,000	5,331,400,000	4,933,800,000	5,588,400,000	5,278,100,000
Operating Income	3,121,200,000	3,714,600,000	2,916,100,000	2,903,000,000	5,400,400,000	4,940,800,000
Operating Margin %	13.64%	17.50%	14.61%	14.79%	23.36%	21.85%
SGA Expense	7,285,500,000	6,578,700,000	6,674,000,000	6,846,300,000	7,216,200,000	7,588,000,000
Net Income	-204,100,000	2,737,600,000	2,408,400,000	2,390,500,000	4,684,800,000	4,088,600,000
Operating Cash Flow	5,615,600,000	4,851,000,000	2,772,800,000	4,367,100,000	5,735,000,000	5,304,800,000
Capital Expenditure	2,163,600,000	1,092,000,000	1,626,200,000	1,565,900,000	1,093,300,000	1,044,200,000
EBITDA	3,989,700,000	5,055,800,000	4,378,900,000	4,528,100,000	7,495,000,000	7,048,200,000
Return on Assets %	-.48%	7.36%	6.62%	6.60%	13.45%	12.01%
Return on Equity %	-1.59%	19.15%	16.08%	14.48%	28.92%	28.88%
Debt to Equity	0.85	0.59	0.54	0.34	0.23	0.37

CONTACT INFORMATION:

Phone: 317 276-2000 Fax:
Toll-Free:
Address: Lilly Corporate Center, Indianapolis, IN 46285 United States

STOCK TICKER/OTHER:

Stock Ticker: LLY
Employees: 41,975
Parent Company:
Exchange: NYS
Fiscal Year Ends: 12/31

SALARIES/BONUSES:

Top Exec. Salary: $1,400,000 Bonus: $
Second Exec. Salary: $1,089,134 Bonus: $

OTHER THOUGHTS:

Estimated Female Officers or Directors: 8
Hot Spot for Advancement for Women/Minorities: Y

EmblemHealth Inc

www.emblemhealth.com

NAIC Code: 524,114

TYPES OF BUSINESS:

Insurance-Medical & Health, HMOs & PPOs

BRANDS/DIVISIONS/AFFILIATES:

ConnectiCare
EmblemHealth Administrators

CONTACTS:

Note: Officers with more than one job title may be intentionally listed here more than once.

Karen M. Ignagni, CEO
William A. Gillespie, Chief Medical Officer
William Mastro, Corp. Sec.
Anne R. Cooke, Sr. VP-Corp. Oper.
Michael Palmateer, Sr. VP-Finance
Shawn M. Fitzgibbon, Sr. VP-Network Mgmt.
George Babitsch, Sr. VP-Underwriting & Account Management
David S. Abernethy, Sr. VP-Gov't Rel.
Jeffrey D. Chansler, Sr. VP
John D. Feerick, Chmn.

GROWTH PLANS/SPECIAL FEATURES:

EmblemHealth, Inc. offers a range of commercial and government-sponsored health plans for large and small groups, individuals and families. The company primarily serves the state of New York, but also operates a ConnectiCare facility in Connecticut, and an EmblemHealth Administrators facility in Florida. EmblemHealth's healthcare plans include Medicare Advantage options with low monthly premiums; the firm is one of the largest Medicare providers in the New York area. Other options include: health and wellness and pharmacy plans for large groups with more than 100 full-time eligible employees, including labor unions and higher education institutions; health and wellness and pharmacy plans for small groups, with less than 100 full-time eligible employees; standard and non-standard plans, catastrophic options and an essential plan that includes dental and vision options for individuals and families; and Medicaid, Enhanced Care Plus (HARP) and Child Health Plus government-sponsored plans. EmblemHealth offers supplements to its traditional health insurance options with a range of programs and discounts for alternative medical practices such as acupuncture, massage therapy and nutritional counseling; mental health services and chemical dependency treatments; pharmacy services; dental plans; and women's wellness programs.

The firm offers its employees reduced-cost medical, dental, optical and life insurance; short- and long-term disability; AD&D coverage; a pension plan; a 401(k) plan; commuter benefits; college savings plans; discounted health club memberships; tuition reimbursement; onsite health screenings; an employee assistance program; and access to discount tickets.

FINANCIAL DATA:

Note: Data for latest year may not have been available at press time.

In U.S. $	2017	2016	2015	2014	2013	2012
Revenue	8,708,250,600	8,293,572,000	8,163,969,000	7,000,000,000	10,400,000,000	10,208,182,000
R&D Expense						
Operating Income						
Operating Margin %						
SGA Expense						
Net Income		-180,246,000	-240,371,000	-485,800,000		
Operating Cash Flow						
Capital Expenditure						
EBITDA						
Return on Assets %						
Return on Equity %						
Debt to Equity						

CONTACT INFORMATION:

Phone: 646-447-5000 Fax:
Toll-Free:
Address: 55 Water St., New York, NY 10041 United States

STOCK TICKER/OTHER:

Stock Ticker: Private
Employees: 4,700
Parent Company:
Exchange:
Fiscal Year Ends: 12/31

SALARIES/BONUSES:

Top Exec. Salary: $ Bonus: $
Second Exec. Salary: $ Bonus: $

OTHER THOUGHTS:

Estimated Female Officers or Directors: 5
Hot Spot for Advancement for Women/Minorities: Y

Endo International PLC

www.endo.com

NAIC Code: 325,412

TYPES OF BUSINESS:

Drugs-Pain Management
Pharmaceutical Preparations

BRANDS/DIVISIONS/AFFILIATES:

Auxilium Pharmaceuticals Inc
Paladin Labs Inc

CONTACTS: *Note: Officers with more than one job title may be intentionally listed here more than once.*

Paul V. Campanelli, CEO
Terrance J. Coughlin, Exec. VP
Daniel Rudio, Controller
Blaise Coleman, Exec. VP
Patrick Barry, Exec. VP
Roger Kimmel, Director
Rajiv De Silva, Director
Susan Hall, Executive VP
Caroline Manogue, Executive VP
Camille Farhat, President, Divisional
Brian Lortie, President, Divisional

GROWTH PLANS/SPECIAL FEATURES:

Endo International PLC is a specialty pharmaceutical company focused on generic and branded pharmaceuticals. Endo operates through three business segments: U.S. generic pharmaceuticals, U.S. branded pharmaceuticals and international pharmaceuticals. The U.S. generic pharmaceuticals segment accounted for 66% of 2017 revenues, focuses on high-barrier-to-entry products, including first-to-file or first-to-market opportunities that are difficult to formulate or manufacture or face complex legal and regulatory challenges. Products in this division include solid oral extended-release, solid oral immediate-release, abuse-deterrent products, liquids, semi-solids, patches, powders, ophthalmics, sprays and sterile injectables, and include products in the pain management, urology, central nervous system (CNS) disorders, immunosuppression, oncology, women's health and cardiovascular disease markets, among others. The U.S. branded pharmaceuticals segment (28%) includes a variety of branded prescription products to treat and manage conditions in urology, urologic oncology, endocrinology, pain and orthopedics. This division includes subsidiary Auxilium Pharmaceuticals, Inc., a fully-integrated specialty pharmaceutical company that develops and commercializes innovative products for specific patients' needs in orthopedics, dermatology and other therapeutic areas. Last, the international pharmaceuticals segment (7%) includes a variety of specialty pharmaceutical products sold outside the U.S., primarily in Canada, through subsidiary Paladin Labs, Inc. This division's products serve growing therapeutic areas such as attention deficit hyperactivity disorder (ADHD), pain, women's health and oncology. During 2017, Endo sold its South African-based operations, Litha Healthcare Group, to Acino Pharma AG for approximately $100 million. In April 2018, the firm agreed to acquire Somerset Therapeutics, LLC, a New Jersey-based specialty pharmaceutical company, along with Somerset's India-based affiliate Wintac Limited, a contract developer and manufacturer.

Employees of the firm receive medical, dental, vision, life and disability coverage; flexible spending accounts; a 401(k); legal assistance; a financial planning plan; educational assistance; an employee assistance program; and flexible time off.

FINANCIAL DATA: *Note: Data for latest year may not have been available at press time.*

In U.S. $	2017	2016	2015	2014	2013	2012
Revenue	3,468,858,000	4,010,274,000	3,268,718,000	2,877,188,000	2,616,907,000	3,027,363,000
R&D Expense	172,067,000	183,372,000	102,197,000	154,203,000	142,472,000	226,120,000
Operating Income	438,387,000	421,201,000	349,566,000	526,575,000	585,580,000	641,303,000
Operating Margin %	12.63%	10.50%	10.69%	18.30%	22.37%	21.18%
SGA Expense	629,874,000	770,728,000	741,304,000	795,855,000	849,339,000	898,847,000
Net Income	-2,035,433,000	-3,347,066,000	-1,495,042,000	-721,319,000	-685,339,000	-740,337,000
Operating Cash Flow	553,985,000	524,439,000	62,026,000	337,776,000	298,517,000	733,879,000
Capital Expenditure	125,654,000	158,062,000	125,742,000	85,425,000	108,483,000	99,818,000
EBITDA	-4,545,000	1,404,510,000	-426,207,000	-562,886,000	-128,976,000	-272,819,000
Return on Assets %	-15.71%	-19.90%	-9.88%	-8.25%	-10.43%	-10.68%
Return on Equity %	-127.75%	-77.21%	-35.84%	-49.73%	-85.72%	-48.53%
Debt to Equity	16.99	3.01	1.38	1.76	6.31	2.83

CONTACT INFORMATION:

Phone: 353 12682000 Fax: 877-329-3636
Toll-Free: 800-462-3636
Address: 1/Fl, Minerva House, Simmonscourt Rd., Ballsbridge, Dublin 4 Ireland

STOCK TICKER/OTHER:

Stock Ticker: ENDP Exchange: NAS
Employees: 4,894 Fiscal Year Ends: 12/31
Parent Company:

SALARIES/BONUSES:

Top Exec. Salary: $950,000 Bonus: $
Second Exec. Salary: $545,833 Bonus: $165,000

OTHER THOUGHTS:

Estimated Female Officers or Directors: 3
Hot Spot for Advancement for Women/Minorities: Y

Endologix Inc

NAIC Code: 339,100

www.endologix.com/

TYPES OF BUSINESS:

Surgical and Medical Instrument Manufacturing

BRANDS/DIVISIONS/AFFILIATES:

AFX Endovascular AAA System
VELA Proximal Endograft
Ovation Abdominal Stent Graft System
Nellix Endovascular Aneurysm Sealing System

CONTACTS:

Note: Officers with more than one job title may be intentionally listed here more than once.

John Onopchenko, CEO
Vaseem Mahboob, CFO
Matthew Thompson, Chief Medical Officer
Michael Chobotov, Chief Technology Officer
Daniel Lemaitre, Director
Jeremy Hayden, General Counsel

GROWTH PLANS/SPECIAL FEATURES:

Endologix, Inc. develops, manufactures, markets and sells innovative devices for aortic disorders. The firm's products are intended for the minimally-invasive endovascular treatment of abdominal aortic aneurysms (AAA). Endologixes' AAA products are built on one of two platforms: traditional minimally-invasive endovascular aneurysm repair (EVAR), or endovascular aneurysm sealing (EVAS), which is the company's innovative solution for sealing the aneurysm sac while maintaining blood flow through two blood flow lumens. Current EVAR products include the AFX Endovascular AAA System, the VELA Proximal Endograft and the Ovation Abdominal Stent Graft System. The firm's current EVAS product is the Nellix Endovascular Aneurysm Sealing System. EVAR and EVAS products, including extensions and accessories, are primarily sold to hospitals in the U.S., Canada, New Zealand, South Korea and 14 European countries, as well as to independent distributors.

FINANCIAL DATA:

Note: Data for latest year may not have been available at press time.

In U.S. $	2017	2016	2015	2014	2013	2012
Revenue	181,157,000	192,925,000	153,612,000	147,588,000	132,257,000	105,946,000
R&D Expense	21,019,000	32,337,000	26,421,000	21,616,000	16,199,000	16,571,000
Operating Income	-40,343,000	-78,213,000	-52,913,000	-29,146,000	-10,368,000	-21,891,000
Operating Margin %	-22.26%	-40.54%	-34.44%	-19.74%	-7.83%	-20.66%
SGA Expense	140,653,000	169,668,000	128,283,000	113,317,000	93,676,000	85,984,000
Net Income	-66,400,000	-154,677,000	-50,424,000	-32,418,000	-16,068,000	-35,774,000
Operating Cash Flow	-38,525,000	-74,808,000	-31,092,000	-26,334,000	1,494,000	-18,529,000
Capital Expenditure	1,170,000	2,796,000	4,191,000	13,461,000	2,862,000	2,338,000
EBITDA	-35,684,000	-129,189,000	-46,399,000	-23,488,000	-13,406,000	-33,053,000
Return on Assets %	-18.32%	-44.47%	-17.26%	-12.85%	-7.62%	-24.22%
Return on Equity %	-70.69%	-143.15%	-44.33%	-28.33%	-16.13%	-41.83%
Debt to Equity	2.77	1.57	1.66	0.56	0.64	

CONTACT INFORMATION:

Phone: 949 595-7200 Fax: 949 457-9561
Toll-Free:
Address: 2 Musick, Irvine, CA 92618 United States

STOCK TICKER/OTHER:

Stock Ticker: ELGX
Employees: 782
Parent Company:
Exchange: NAS
Fiscal Year Ends: 12/31

SALARIES/BONUSES:

Top Exec. Salary: $572,000 Bonus: $
Second Exec. Salary: $390,500 Bonus: $

OTHER THOUGHTS:

Estimated Female Officers or Directors:
Hot Spot for Advancement for Women/Minorities:

Ensign Group Inc (The)

www.ensigngroup.net

NAIC Code: 623,110

TYPES OF BUSINESS:

Nursing Care Facilities
Skilled Nursing
Assisted Living
Home Health
Hospice

BRANDS/DIVISIONS/AFFILIATES:

CONTACTS:
Note: Officers with more than one job title may be intentionally listed here more than once.

Christopher Christensen, CEO
Suzanne Snapper, CFO
Roy Christensen, Chairman of the Board
Barry Port, COO, Subsidiary
Chad Keetch, Executive VP
Beverly Wittekind, General Counsel

GROWTH PLANS/SPECIAL FEATURES:

Ensign Group, Inc., through its subsidiaries, provides skilled nursing, assisted living and home health and hospice services. The company operates through three business segments: transitional and skilled services; assisted living and independent living services; and home health and hospice services. The transitional and skilled services segment provides skilled nursing care at 181 operations, with 18,870 beds located in Arizona, California, Colorado, Idaho, Iowa, Kansas, Nebraska, Nevada, South Carolina, Texas, Utah, Washington and Wisconsin. This division provides short- and long-stay patients with medical, nursing, rehabilitative, pharmacy and routine services. The assisted and independent living services segment provides services at 70 operations, of which 21 are located on the same site locations as the skilled nursing care operations. This division has 5,011 assisted and independent living units located in all the states mentioned above, except for South Carolina. These locations offer residential accommodations, activities, meals, security, housekeeping and assistance in the activities of daily living to seniors who are independent or who require some support, but not the level of nursing care provided in a skilled nursing operations. Last, the home health and hospice services segment provides services in Arizona, California, Colorado, Idaho, Iowa, Oklahoma, Oregon, Texas, Utah and Washington. Home healthcare services consist of nursing, speech, occupational and physical therapists, medical social workers and certified home health aide services. Hospice care focuses on the physical, spiritual and psychosocial needs of terminally ill individuals and their families, and consists primarily of palliative and clinical care, education and counseling.

FINANCIAL DATA:
Note: Data for latest year may not have been available at press time.

In U.S. $	2017	2016	2015	2014	2013	2012
Revenue	1,849,317,000	1,654,864,000	1,341,826,000	1,027,406,000	904,556,000	824,719,000
R&D Expense						
Operating Income	94,606,000	80,622,000	93,082,000	72,924,000	57,942,000	91,047,000
Operating Margin %	5.11%	4.87%	6.93%	7.09%	6.40%	11.03%
SGA Expense	80,617,000	69,165,000	64,163,000	56,895,000	40,103,000	31,819,000
Net Income	40,475,000	49,990,000	55,432,000	35,950,000	24,040,000	40,591,000
Operating Cash Flow	72,952,000	73,888,000	33,369,000	84,880,000	37,424,000	82,050,000
Capital Expenditure	57,166,000	65,699,000	60,018,000	53,693,000	29,759,000	38,853,000
EBITDA	127,366,000	131,636,000	122,038,000	99,948,000	92,390,000	104,766,000
Return on Assets %	3.84%	5.71%	8.92%	5.73%	3.31%	6.30%
Return on Equity %	8.53%	11.31%	16.15%	11.69%	7.04%	13.44%
Debt to Equity	0.61	0.60	0.23	0.26	0.70	0.61

CONTACT INFORMATION:

Phone: 949-487-9500 Fax:
Toll-Free:
Address: 27101 Puerta Real, Ste. 450, Mission Viejo, CA 92691 United States

STOCK TICKER/OTHER:

Stock Ticker: ENSG
Exchange: NAS
Employees: 19,482
Fiscal Year Ends: 12/31
Parent Company:

SALARIES/BONUSES:

Top Exec. Salary: $416,364 Bonus: $375,000
Second Exec. Salary: $490,483 Bonus: $

OTHER THOUGHTS:

Estimated Female Officers or Directors: 3
Hot Spot for Advancement for Women/Minorities: Y

Entellus Medical Inc

www.entellusmedical.com

NAIC Code: 339,100

TYPES OF BUSINESS:

Surgical and Medical Instrument Manufacturing

BRANDS/DIVISIONS/AFFILIATES:

Stryker Corporation
XprESS Pro
XprESS LoProfile
XprESS Ultra
PathAssist
XeroGel

CONTACTS:

Note: Officers with more than one job title may be intentionally listed here more than once.

Spencer Stiles, Pres.
Michael Harry Rosenthal, COO

GROWTH PLANS/SPECIAL FEATURES:

Entellus Medical, Inc. is a medical technology company focused on delivering superior patient and physician experiences through products designed for the minimally invasive treatment of chronic and recurrent sinusitis patients. The firm's XprESS family of products is used by ear, nose and throat (ENT) physicians to treat patients with symptomatic inflammation of the nasal sinuses by opening narrowed or obstructed sinus drainage pathways using balloon sinus dilation. When used as a stand-alone therapy in the doctor's office, the balloon sinus dilation products are the only devices proven in a sufficiently powered prospective, multicenter, randomized, controlled trial to be as effective as functional endoscopic sinus surgery (FESS) the primary surgical treatment for chronic and recurrent sinusitis. Minimally invasive balloon sinus dilation devices have enabled a shift towards office-based treatment of chronic sinusitis patients who are candidates for sinus surgery in the operating room. The XprESS Multi-Sinus Dilation family of devices and PathAssist tools represent a broad product line of FDA-cleared, minimally invasive products for treating chronic sinusitis patients. The XprESS family of products consists of the XprESS Pro device, the XprESS LoProfile device and the XprESS Ultra device. These disposable devices open an obstructed or narrowed drainage pathway of a sinus cavity by means of trans-nasal balloon sinus dilation. The PathAssist tools provide ENT physicians with an easy way to confirm sinus location and XprESS device placement. Additionally, through an exclusive license, the firm manufactures and sells XeroGel nasal packing material to hospitals, physician offices and ambulatory surgery centers. In February 2018, Entellus was acquired by Stryker Corporation, a world-leading medical technology company. Entellus subsequently ceased from public trading on the Nasdaq and operates as Stryker's wholly-owned subsidiary.

FINANCIAL DATA:

Note: Data for latest year may not have been available at press time.

In U.S. $	2017	2016	2015	2014	2013	2012
Revenue	78,943,200	75,184,000	61,570,000	48,820,000	32,545,000	17,559,000
R&D Expense						
Operating Income						
Operating Margin %						
SGA Expense						
Net Income		-28,730,000	-18,300,000	-6,929,000	-13,396,000	-18,996,000
Operating Cash Flow						
Capital Expenditure						
EBITDA						
Return on Assets %						
Return on Equity %						
Debt to Equity						

CONTACT INFORMATION:

Phone: 763 463-1595 Fax:
Toll-Free:
Address: 3600 Holly Ln. N., Plymouth, MN 55447 United States

STOCK TICKER/OTHER:

Stock Ticker: Subsidiary
Exchange:
Employees: 280
Fiscal Year Ends: 12/31
Parent Company: Stryker Corporation

SALARIES/BONUSES:

Top Exec. Salary: $ Bonus: $
Second Exec. Salary: $ Bonus: $

OTHER THOUGHTS:

Estimated Female Officers or Directors:
Hot Spot for Advancement for Women/Minorities:

Envision Healthcare Corporation

www.evhc.net

NAIC Code: 621,610

TYPES OF BUSINESS:

Home Health Care Services
Other Human Health Activities

BRANDS/DIVISIONS/AFFILIATES:

KKR & Co LP

GROWTH PLANS/SPECIAL FEATURES:

Envision Healthcare Corporation is a provider of physician-led services, post-acute care and ambulatory surgery services. The company's physician services include the areas of emergency department and hospitalist services, anesthesiology services, radiology/tele-radiology services and children's services to more than 1,800 clinical departments in health care facilities in 45 U.S. states and the District of Columbia. Post-acute care is delivered through an array of clinical professionals and integrated technologies. Envision owns and operates 261 surgery centers and one surgical hospital, with medical specialties ranging from gastroenterology to ophthalmology and orthopedics. In June 2018, the firm agreed to be wholly-acquired by private equity firm KKR & Co. LP for $5.5 billion.

CONTACTS: *Note: Officers with more than one job title may be intentionally listed here more than once.*

Kevin Eastridge, CFO
William Sanger, Chairman of the Board
Karey Witty, Executive VP
Phillip Clendenin, Executive VP
Brian Jackson, Executive VP
Craig Wilson, General Counsel
Patrick Solomon, Other Executive Officer
Christopher Holden, President
Kenneth Zongor, Senior VP

FINANCIAL DATA: *Note: Data for latest year may not have been available at press time.*

In U.S. $	2017	2016	2015	2014	2013	2012
Revenue	7,819,300,000	3,696,000,000	2,566,884,000	1,621,949,000	1,079,343,000	928,509,000
R&D Expense						
Operating Income	669,700,000	568,200,000	564,659,000	383,915,000	332,677,000	280,381,000
Operating Margin %	8.56%	15.37%	21.99%	23.66%	30.82%	30.19%
SGA Expense	144,200,000	90,500,000				
Net Income	-228,000,000	-18,600,000	162,947,000	53,701,000	72,703,000	62,563,000
Operating Cash Flow	797,400,000	419,800,000	537,959,000	412,371,000	332,824,000	295,652,000
Capital Expenditure	208,900,000	99,500,000	60,305,000	40,217,000	28,856,000	28,864,000
EBITDA	1,103,700,000	718,100,000	662,152,000	444,259,000	365,705,000	310,459,000
Return on Assets %	-1.39%	- .23%	2.54%	1.27%	3.44%	3.45%
Return on Equity %	-3.50%	- .62%	8.45%	4.32%	10.00%	9.58%
Debt to Equity	0.95	0.86	1.13	1.47	0.76	0.90

CONTACT INFORMATION:

Phone: 615-665-1283 Fax:
Toll-Free:
Address: 1A Burton Hills Blvd., Nashville, TN 37215 United States

STOCK TICKER/OTHER:

Stock Ticker: EVHC
Exchange: NYS
Employees: 65,200
Fiscal Year Ends: 12/31
Parent Company:

SALARIES/BONUSES:

Top Exec. Salary: $1,670,131 Bonus: $
Second Exec. Salary: $1,040,000 Bonus: $

OTHER THOUGHTS:

Estimated Female Officers or Directors:
Hot Spot for Advancement for Women/Minorities:

Envolve Vision Inc

www.opticare.com

NAIC Code: 524,114

TYPES OF BUSINESS:

Managed Vision Care Plans
Eye Health Centers

BRANDS/DIVISIONS/AFFILIATES:

Centene Corporation
Envolve Benefit Options Inc

CONTACTS: *Note: Officers with more than one job title may be intentionally listed here more than once.*

David Lavely, CEO
David Lavely, Pres.
Mark Ruchman, Nat'l Dir.-Medical
Tara Price, VP-Oper.
Annie Mayo, VP-Bus. Dev.
George Verrastro, Sr. VP-Finance
Tara Price, Sr. VP-Quality Mgmt.
Larry Keeley, Sr. VP-Regulatory Affairs & Account Svcs.
Connie Cook, Sr. Bus. Analyst
Shaheen Chaudhry, VP-Member & Provider Svcs.

GROWTH PLANS/SPECIAL FEATURES:

Envolve Vision, Inc. provides managed vision care plans. The company collaborates with national and local managed care organizations, providers and benefit managers to design and administer eye care programs. Envolve administers various vision benefits directly for health plans, employer groups, unions and associations. The firm offers a wide range of benefit options that cover routine eye exams, eyeglasses (lenses and frames), contacts and prescription sunglasses. Envolve's offerings include discounts on routine eye exams and optical hardware, discounts on laser surgery in select markets, complete coverage of routine exams with choice of hardware allowances and full medical surgical eye care carve outs. In addition, the firm also offers an online health manager where providers can submit and research claims, verify member benefits and enter and view authorizations. Envolve Vision is a subsidiary of Envolve Benefit Options, Inc., which itself is a subsidiary of Centene Corporation.

FINANCIAL DATA: *Note: Data for latest year may not have been available at press time.*

In U.S. $	2017	2016	2015	2014	2013	2012
Revenue						
R&D Expense						
Operating Income						
Operating Margin %						
SGA Expense						
Net Income						
Operating Cash Flow						
Capital Expenditure						
EBITDA						
Return on Assets %						
Return on Equity %						
Debt to Equity						

CONTACT INFORMATION:

Phone: Fax:
Toll-Free: 800-334-3937
Address: 112 Zebulon Ct., Rocky Mount, NC 27804 United States

STOCK TICKER/OTHER:

Stock Ticker: Subsidiary
Employees:
Parent Company: Centene Corporation
Exchange:
Fiscal Year Ends: 12/31

SALARIES/BONUSES:

Top Exec. Salary: $ Bonus: $
Second Exec. Salary: $ Bonus: $

OTHER THOUGHTS:

Estimated Female Officers or Directors: 1
Hot Spot for Advancement for Women/Minorities: Y

Epic Systems Corporation

www.epic.com

NAIC Code: 511210D

TYPES OF BUSINESS:

Computer Software, Healthcare & Biotechnology
Information Networks
Support Services

BRANDS/DIVISIONS/AFFILIATES:

Epicenter
EpicCare
Epic Europe BV
Lucy
Community Library Exchange

CONTACTS: *Note: Officers with more than one job title may be intentionally listed here more than once.*

Judy Faulkner, CEO
Carl D. Dvorak, COO
Robert M. Fahrenbach, CFO
Carl Dvorak, Exec. VP

GROWTH PLANS/SPECIAL FEATURES:

Epic Systems Corporation is a developer of health industry clinical, access and revenue software for mid-and large-sized medical groups, hospitals, academic facilities, children's organizations, multi-hospital systems and integrated health care organizations. All Epic software applications are designed to share a single database, called Epicenter, so that each viewer can access available patient data through a single interface from anywhere in the organization. The firm's clinical software products include integrated inpatient and ambulatory systems under the EpicCare brand as well as health information management tools and specialty information systems. The firm's interoperability service, Lucy, personal health record that allows patients to organize and access their medical history independently of any one facility. Other products offer access services, including scheduling, inpatient and ambulatory registration, call management and nurse triage; revenue cycle services, such as hospital and professional billing; health plan and managed care administration systems; clinical and financial data repositories; enterprise reporting; patient medical record access systems; and connectivity tools, including voice recognition, interfacing and patient monitoring devices. In conjunction with its software applications, the company provides extensive client services, including training, process engineering, tailoring of applications to the client's situation and access to network specialists who plan and implement client systems. In addition, Epic hosts Community Library Exchange, an online collection of application tools and pre-made content that allows clients to share report and registration templates, custom forms, enterprise report formats and documentation shortcuts. Epic also operates in the Netherlands under Epic Europe BV.

Employees of the firm are offered medical, dental, vision, life and disability insurance; a 401(k) plan; and flexible spending accounts.

FINANCIAL DATA: *Note: Data for latest year may not have been available at press time.*

In U.S. $	2017	2016	2015	2014	2013	2012
Revenue	2,100,000,000	2,000,000,000	1,978,000,000	1,856,000,000	1,750,000,000	1,526,000,000
R&D Expense						
Operating Income						
Operating Margin %						
SGA Expense						
Net Income						
Operating Cash Flow						
Capital Expenditure						
EBITDA						
Return on Assets %						
Return on Equity %						
Debt to Equity						

CONTACT INFORMATION:

Phone: 608-271-9000 Fax: 608-271-7237
Toll-Free:
Address: 1979 Milky Way, Verona, WI 53593 United States

STOCK TICKER/OTHER:

Stock Ticker: Private
Employees: 9,000
Parent Company:
Exchange:
Fiscal Year Ends: 12/31

SALARIES/BONUSES:

Top Exec. Salary: $ Bonus: $
Second Exec. Salary: $ Bonus: $

OTHER THOUGHTS:

Estimated Female Officers or Directors: 1
Hot Spot for Advancement for Women/Minorities:

Essilor International SA

www.essilor.com

NAIC Code: 339,100

TYPES OF BUSINESS:

Supplies-Ophthalmic Products
Corrective Lenses
Lens Treatments
Ophthalmic Instruments
Technical Consulting

BRANDS/DIVISIONS/AFFILIATES:

Eyezen
Essilor
Varilux
Crizal
Xperio
Optifog
Transitions
Bolon

CONTACTS: *Note: Officers with more than one job title may be intentionally listed here more than once.*

Hubert Sagnieres, CEO
Laurent Vacherot, Pres.
Jean-Luc Schuppiser, Corp. Sr. VP-R&D
Patrick Poncin, Corp. Sr. VP-Global Eng.
Kevin Rupp, Exec. VP-Admin., Essilor Of America
Carol Xueref, Corp. Sr. VP-Legal Affairs & Dev.
Claude Brignon, Corp. Sr. VP-Worldwide Oper.
Kate Philipps, VP-Corp. Comm.
Veronique Gillet, Sr. VP-Investor Rel.
Kevin Rupp, Exec. VP-Finance, Essilor Of America
Eric Bernard, Pres., Essilor China
Norbert Gorny, Pres., Satisloh
Jean Carrier-Guillomet, Pres., Essilor of America
Eric Leonard, Pres., European Region
Hubert Sagnieres, Chmn.
Tadeu Alves, Pres., Latin America

GROWTH PLANS/SPECIAL FEATURES:

Essilor International SA is a global designer, manufacturer and distributor of ophthalmic and optical products. The firm divides its operations into three segments: corrective lenses, sunglasses and readers and equipment and instruments. Corrective lenses treat common sight problems such as myopia, hyperopia, astigmatism and presbyopia. This segment's innovations include the e-SPF index, the Eyezen range of lenses and technologies that filter blue-violet light, all of which also benefit Essilor's other activities. The sunglasses and readers segment sells more than 140 million pairs of sunglasses, readers and eyewear annually. Its technologies enable the company to offer sunlenses worldwide, with or without prescription. The equipment and instrument segment contributes to Essilor's technical advances by mastering technologies in lens manufacturing and the instruments used for taking measurements. This division designs, manufactures and distributes innovative products, technologies and services for opticians, optometrists and ophthalmologists in relation to optical and vision care instruments, measurement, edging/mounting tools. In addition, this segment provides a range of diagnostic equipment for preventive healthcare organizations. Primary brands of the firm include Essilor, Varilux, Crizal, Eyezen, Xperio, Optifog, Transitions, Bolon, Costa, Foster Grant, Kodak Lens and Osse. Essilor operates in more than 100 countries, supplies products through a global network of 490 prescription laboratories and 33 production sites, producing millions of lenses annually. In January 2017, Luxottica Group SpA, a manufacturer and retailer of prescription and fashion eyeglass frames and sunglasses, agreed to be merged with and into Essilor. Essilor would become a holding company under new name EssilorLuxottica via a hive-down of all of its operating activities into a wholly-owned company called Essilor International. In March 2018, the proposed merger had been cleared by the U.S. Federal Trade Commission without conditions, and had already been unconditionally approved in the EU and 13 other countries.

FINANCIAL DATA: *Note: Data for latest year may not have been available at press time.*

In U.S. $	2017	2016	2015	2014	2013	2012
Revenue						
R&D Expense						
Operating Income						
Operating Margin %						
SGA Expense						
Net Income						
Operating Cash Flow						
Capital Expenditure						
EBITDA						
Return on Assets %						
Return on Equity %						
Debt to Equity						

CONTACT INFORMATION:

Phone: 33-1-49-77-42-16 Fax: 33-1-49-77-44-20
Toll-Free:
Address: 147 rue de Paris,, Paris, 94220 France

STOCK TICKER/OTHER:

Stock Ticker: ESLOF
Employees: 66,918
Parent Company:
Exchange: PINX
Fiscal Year Ends: 12/31

SALARIES/BONUSES:

Top Exec. Salary: $ Bonus: $
Second Exec. Salary: $ Bonus: $

OTHER THOUGHTS:

Estimated Female Officers or Directors: 5
Hot Spot for Advancement for Women/Minorities: Y

Ethicon Inc

www.ethicon.com

NAIC Code: 339,100

TYPES OF BUSINESS:

Medical Equipment & Supplies
Sutures, Surgical Mesh, Needles & Skin Adhesives
Wound Management Products
Burn & Skin Care Products
Women's Health Surgical Products
Cardiovascular Surgery Products

BRANDS/DIVISIONS/AFFILIATES:

Johnson & Johnson
SURGICEL
SURGIFLO
SURGIFOAM
ENDOPATH

CONTACTS: *Note: Officers with more than one job title may be intentionally listed here more than once.*

Alex Gorsky, CEO-Johnson & Johnson
Jeffrey Hammond, Group Dir.-Medical Affairs

GROWTH PLANS/SPECIAL FEATURES:

Ethicon, Inc., a Johnson & Johnson subsidiary, develops and markets medical devices, products and solutions for surgical procedures to healthcare professionals worldwide. Ethicon's biosurgical products include hemostatic solutions (used during surgery to control blood loss) such as the SURGICEL family of absorbable hemostats as well as the SURGIFLO and SURGIFOAM product lines. The company also develops endo devices for minimally-invasive procedures and surgical products for ligation. Ethicon's wound closure portfolio includes traditional wound care products, such as sponges, bandages, dressings, transparent films and tapes as well as sutures, topical adhesives, surgical meshes and wound drains. The firm also designs technology for wound stapling such as endocutters, linear cutters and circular staplers. Through Ethicon's bariatric and metabolic surgery division, the company provides adjustable gastric bands and ancillary devices to resolve weight-related health conditions. Its hernia solutions portfolio includes mesh hernia repair products for inguinal, ventral and umbilical hernias. For hepato-biliary surgery, Ethicon develops flexible solutions for every aspect of cancer procedures; for uterine and pelvic procedures, it offers adhesion barriers, repair devices, incontinence slings and hysterectomy operative devices; and for thoracic surgery, it develops tools to enable positive outcomes and provides training in relation to its products. The firm's ENDOPATH line of trocars offer surgeons flexibility across surgical specialties.

FINANCIAL DATA: *Note: Data for latest year may not have been available at press time.*

In U.S. $	2017	2016	2015	2014	2013	2012
Revenue	5,800,000,000	5,600,000,000	5,500,000,000	5,600,000,000	5,400,000,000	5,100,000,000
R&D Expense						
Operating Income						
Operating Margin %						
SGA Expense						
Net Income						
Operating Cash Flow						
Capital Expenditure						
EBITDA						
Return on Assets %						
Return on Equity %						
Debt to Equity						

CONTACT INFORMATION:

Phone: 908-218-0707 Fax: 908-218-2471
Toll-Free: 800-255-2500
Address: 4545 Creek Rd., Cincinnati, OH 45242 United States

STOCK TICKER/OTHER:

Stock Ticker: Subsidiary Exchange:
Employees: 8,500 Fiscal Year Ends: 12/31
Parent Company: Johnson & Johnson

SALARIES/BONUSES:

Top Exec. Salary: $ Bonus: $
Second Exec. Salary: $ Bonus: $

OTHER THOUGHTS:

Estimated Female Officers or Directors: 2
Hot Spot for Advancement for Women/Minorities:

Everyday Health Inc

www.everydayhealth.com

NAIC Code: 519,130

TYPES OF BUSINESS:

Online Health Information Services

BRANDS/DIVISIONS/AFFILIATES:

J2 Global Inc

CONTACTS:
Note: Officers with more than one job title may be intentionally listed here more than once.

Maureen Connolly, VP-Editor in Chief
Jeff Blatt, Exec. VP-Gen. Mgr.
Brian Cooper, CFO
Scott Wolf, Executive VP
Jed Savage, Executive VP
Alan Shapiro, General Counsel

GROWTH PLANS/SPECIAL FEATURES:

Everyday Health, Inc. operates a digital marketing and communications platform for health care marketers primarily in the U.S. The platform combines digital content from leading health brands with data and analytics technology to present updated, informed content for users. The content can be accessed by Everyday Health's consumers and professionals anytime, anywhere, across multiple channels, including the web, mobile devices, video and social media. The multi-brand, multi-channel content experience helps with decision making, and allows companies to engage with consumers and healthcare professionals. Its portfolio of properties consists of websites, mobile applications and social media destinations, reaching approximately 50 million consumers every month. Consumers use Everyday Health's tools to manage health and wellness needs such as weight loss, exercise, healthy pregnancy, nutrition and medical conditions. The company also provides health care professionals with news, tools and information needed to keep in touch with current industry, legislative and regulatory developments in major medical specialties. More than 700,000 practicing U.S. physicians can be reached, ranging across numerous specialty areas. Everyday Health's website offers links and access to free newsletters, a symptom checker, drug finder, calorie counter, meal planner and recipes. Everyday Health operates as a wholly-owned subsidiary of j2 Global, Inc., an American technology company based in California.

FINANCIAL DATA:
Note: Data for latest year may not have been available at press time.

In U.S. $	2017	2016	2015	2014	2013	2012
Revenue	266,000,000	250,000,000	231,991,008	184,324,992	155,850,000	138,492,000
R&D Expense						
Operating Income						
Operating Margin %						
SGA Expense						
Net Income			-11,640,000	12,683,000	-18,236,000	-22,454,000
Operating Cash Flow						
Capital Expenditure						
EBITDA						
Return on Assets %						
Return on Equity %						
Debt to Equity						

CONTACT INFORMATION:

Phone: 646-728-9500 Fax: 646-728-9501
Toll-Free:
Address: 345 Hudson St., 16/Fl, New York, NY 10014 United States

STOCK TICKER/OTHER:

Stock Ticker: Subsidiary
Exchange:
Employees: 560
Fiscal Year Ends:
Parent Company: j2 Global Inc

SALARIES/BONUSES:

Top Exec. Salary: $ Bonus: $
Second Exec. Salary: $ Bonus: $

OTHER THOUGHTS:

Estimated Female Officers or Directors: 4
Hot Spot for Advancement for Women/Minorities: Y

Exactech Inc

www.exac.com

NAIC Code: 339,100

TYPES OF BUSINESS:

Equipment-Joint Replacement
Orthopedic Implant Devices
Surgical Instruments
Biologic Products
Bone Fusion Materials

BRANDS/DIVISIONS/AFFILIATES:

TPG Capital

CONTACTS: *Note: Officers with more than one job title may be intentionally listed here more than once.*

David Petty, CEO
Joel Phillips, CFO
Jeffrey Binder, Co-Chmn.
Gary Miller, Executive VP, Divisional
Betty Petty, Founder
Donna Edwards, General Counsel
Bruce Thompson, General Manager, Divisional
William Petty, Co-Chmn.

GROWTH PLANS/SPECIAL FEATURES:

Exactech, Inc. develops, manufactures, distributes and sells orthopedic implant devices, surgical instrumentation and biologic services to hospitals and physicians in the U.S. and in more than 35 international markets across Europe, Latin America, Asia and the Pacific. The company's innovative bone and joint restoration products help surgeons make patients more mobile. Exactech's devices and systems are used for hip, knee, ankle and shoulder restoration and replacements, and other products are used to strengthen, line and stabilize bone structures. Products include stems, systems, prosthesis, liners, spacers, bone cement, cartilage processors, autologous platelet concentrating systems, collagen wraps and grafting material. Exactech manufactures many of its orthopedic devices at its Gainesville, Florida facility. In early-2018, Exactech became privately-held by TPG Capital, and subsequently ceased from trading on the Nasdaq.

Exactech offers employees comprehensive health benefits, life insurance, paid time off and retirement benefits.

FINANCIAL DATA: *Note: Data for latest year may not have been available at press time.*

In U.S. $	2017	2016	2015	2014	2013	2012
Revenue	261,000,000	257,572,992	241,838,000	248,372,992	237,088,000	224,336,992
R&D Expense						
Operating Income						
Operating Margin %						
SGA Expense						
Net Income		162,000	14,767,000	16,488,000	15,372,000	12,741,000
Operating Cash Flow						
Capital Expenditure						
EBITDA						
Return on Assets %						
Return on Equity %						
Debt to Equity						

CONTACT INFORMATION:

Phone: 352 377-1140 Fax: 352 378-2617
Toll-Free: 800-266-7883
Address: 2320 NW 66th Ct., Gainesville, FL 32653 United States

STOCK TICKER/OTHER:

Stock Ticker: Private
Employees: 733
Parent Company: TPG Capital
Exchange:
Fiscal Year Ends: 12/31

SALARIES/BONUSES:

Top Exec. Salary: $ Bonus: $
Second Exec. Salary: $ Bonus: $

OTHER THOUGHTS:

Estimated Female Officers or Directors: 3
Hot Spot for Advancement for Women/Minorities: Y

Express Scripts Holding Co

www.express-scripts.com

NAIC Code: 524,292

TYPES OF BUSINESS:

Pharmacy Benefits Management
Mail & Internet Pharmacies
Formulary Management
Integrated Drug & Medical Data Analysis
Market Research Programs
Medical Information Management
Workers' Compensation Programs
Informed-Decision Counseling

BRANDS/DIVISIONS/AFFILIATES:

Accredo Health Group
CuraScript Specialty Distribution
CareCore National Group LLC

CONTACTS: *Note: Officers with more than one job title may be intentionally listed here more than once.*

John Arlotta, CEO, Subsidiary
David Queller, Senior VP, Divisional
James Havel, CFO
George Paz, Chairman of the Board
Bradley Phillips, Chief Accounting Officer
Steven Miller, Chief Medical Officer
Neal Sample, COO
Christine Houston, Executive VP
Everett Neville, Executive VP, Divisional
Martin Akins, General Counsel
Sara Wade, Other Executive Officer
Glen Stettin, Other Executive Officer
Timothy Wentworth, President
Brian Seiz, Senior VP, Divisional
Phyllis Anderson, Senior VP

GROWTH PLANS/SPECIAL FEATURES:

Express Scripts Holding Co. is one of the largest independent pharmacy benefit managers in the U.S. The firm provides pharmacy service and pharmacy benefit plan design consultation for clients including HMOs, health insurers, third-party administrators, employers, unions and government health care plans. The company operates in two segments: pharmacy benefit management (PBM) and other business operations. The PBM division offers retail network pharmacy management and retail drug card programs; home delivery and specialty pharmacy services; patient care contact centers; rebate programs; electronic claims processing and drug utilization review; information reporting and analysis programs; consumer health and drug information; assistance programs for low-income patients; benefit plan design and consultation; and drug formulary management, compliance and therapy management programs. It dispenses drugs to patients from several home delivery fulfillment pharmacies and maintains partnerships with over 68,000 retail pharmacies. Subsidiary Accredo Health Group focuses on dispensing injectable, infused, oral or inhaled drugs that require a higher level of clinical service and support. Express Scripts' other business operations includes the following brands that service patients through multiple paths: subsidiary CuraScript Specialty Distribution offers specialty medical supplies and pharmaceuticals to treat rare and orphan diseases directly to providers, hospitals and clinics in the U.S.; and CareCore National Group, LLC (d/b/a eviCore) is a leading provider of integrated medical benefit management solutions that focus on driving adherence to evidence-based guidelines and improve quality of patient outcomes and cost of care reductions for clients. In March 2018, Cigna Corp. agreed to acquire Express Scripts for approximately $67 billion. The transaction is expected to close in December 2018.

The firm offers employees a comprehensive health package, a 401(k), a stock purchase plan, financial counseling and paid time off.

FINANCIAL DATA: *Note: Data for latest year may not have been available at press time.*

In U.S. $	2017	2016	2015	2014	2013	2012
Revenue	100,064,600,000	100,287,500,000	101,751,800,000	100,887,100,000	104,098,800,000	93,858,100,000
R&D Expense						
Operating Income	5,494,000,000	5,087,800,000	4,339,300,000	3,602,400,000	3,551,700,000	2,784,500,000
Operating Margin %	5.49%	5.07%	4.26%	3.57%	3.41%	2.96%
SGA Expense	3,268,100,000	3,532,700,000	4,062,600,000	4,322,700,000	4,580,700,000	4,545,700,000
Net Income	4,517,400,000	3,404,400,000	2,476,400,000	2,007,600,000	1,844,600,000	1,312,900,000
Operating Cash Flow	5,351,300,000	4,919,400,000	4,848,300,000	4,549,000,000	4,757,500,000	4,781,600,000
Capital Expenditure	267,400,000	330,400,000	295,900,000	436,600,000	423,000,000	160,200,000
EBITDA	7,338,900,000	7,276,500,000	6,723,200,000	5,892,000,000	6,073,400,000	4,682,600,000
Return on Assets %	8.52%	6.48%	4.62%	3.74%	3.30%	3.56%
Return on Equity %	26.29%	20.25%	13.23%	9.58%	8.15%	10.15%
Debt to Equity	0.82	0.91	0.80	0.54	0.56	0.64

CONTACT INFORMATION:

Phone: 314-996-0900 Fax: 314-770-0303
Toll-Free:
Address: 1 Express Way, St. Louis, MO 63121 United States

STOCK TICKER/OTHER:

Stock Ticker: ESRX
Employees: 25,600
Parent Company:
Exchange: NAS
Fiscal Year Ends: 12/31

SALARIES/BONUSES:

Top Exec. Salary: $1,436,539 Bonus: $
Second Exec. Salary: $741,077 Bonus: $

OTHER THOUGHTS:

Estimated Female Officers or Directors: 3
Hot Spot for Advancement for Women/Minorities: Y

Extendicare Inc

www.extendicare.com

NAIC Code: 623,110

TYPES OF BUSINESS:

Long-Term Care
Assisted Living Facilities
Sub-Acute Care
Rehabilitative Services

BRANDS/DIVISIONS/AFFILIATES:

ParaMed Home Health Care
Silver Group Purchasing
Nutritional Support System
Extendicare Assist
Lynde Creek Retirement Community

CONTACTS: *Note: Officers with more than one job title may be intentionally listed here more than once.*

Timothy Lukenda, CEO
Elaine Everson, CFO
Brandon Parent, General Counsel
Christopher Dennis, President, Subsidiary
Jillian Fountain, Secretary
Christina McKey, Vice President
Karen Scanlan, Vice President, Divisional
Tracey Mulcahy, Vice President, Divisional
Michael Harris, Vice President, Subsidiary
Gary Loder, Vice President, Subsidiary
A. Paula Neves, Vice President, Subsidiary
Mark Lugowski, Vice President, Subsidiary

GROWTH PLANS/SPECIAL FEATURES:

Extendicare, Inc. is a leading provider of long-term care and related services in Canada. Through its subsidiaries, the firm owns and manages 118 senior care centers. The company's long-term care provides long-stay services, short-stay services and complex continuing care for patients with complex health issues. This division includes a chronic care unit and 96 long-term care homes providing support to approximately 13,000 residents across Ontario, Manitoba, Alberta and Saskatchewan. The retirement living segment provides services such as daily personal care, medication reminders, housekeeping, meals and planned social opportunities. Through ParaMed Home Health Care, the firm delivers care directly to the clients and families living within ParaMed communities. These services include in-home personal care, and homemaking and nursing services such as wound and palliative care. ParaMed's workplace health and wellness division meets the health and wellness needs of companies and their employees. These services include health and wellness clinics, mask fit test clinics, immunization clinics, seminars, education, consultation and customized health/wellness programs targeted to the needs of specific workplaces. Through Silver Group Purchasing, Extendicare provides cost saving measures concerning brand product standards and specifications, as well as menu development, nutritional analysis and costing through its Nutritional Support System. Subsidiary Extendicare Assist provides management and consulting services. In April 2018, Extendicare acquired Lynde Creek Retirement Community for $34.5 million, which is located in Whitby, Ontario and consists of the Lynde Creek Manor Retirement Residence (93 suites), the Lynde Creek Life Lease Village (113 townhomes) and 3.7 acres of adjacent land for expansion.

Extendicare offers its employees and their children educational assistance programs as well as scholarship programs for those pursuing health care professions.

FINANCIAL DATA: *Note: Data for latest year may not have been available at press time.*

In U.S. $	2017	2016	2015	2014	2013	2012
Revenue	844,100,700	815,967,700	753,545,400	627,783,800	1,557,281,000	1,567,241,000
R&D Expense						
Operating Income	48,773,850	47,504,620	45,511,540	41,315,380	65,792,310	88,563,080
Operating Margin %	5.77%	5.82%	6.03%	6.22%	3.84%	5.76%
SGA Expense	726,469,200	28,616,150	32,163,080	566,453,100	1,428,943,000	1,417,826,000
Net Income	1,640,000	27,270,770	178,521,500	-14,425,390	4,040,000	48,196,920
Operating Cash Flow	36,276,920	-216,154	40,613,850	65,851,540	75,320,000	83,682,310
Capital Expenditure	31,643,850	29,874,620	27,290,770	28,591,540	42,886,920	64,694,620
EBITDA	78,480,770	75,562,310	73,123,850	84,529,230	115,338,500	138,696,900
Return on Assets %	.22%	3.51%	15.77%	-.99%	.28%	3.44%
Return on Equity %	1.40%	20.44%	273.63%	-106.06%	11.35%	121.68%
Debt to Equity	3.69	2.56	2.49		26.85	19.00

CONTACT INFORMATION:

Phone: 905-470-4000 Fax: 905-470-4003
Toll-Free:
Address: 3000 Steeles Ave. E., Ste. 700, Markham, ON L3R 9W2 Canada

STOCK TICKER/OTHER:

Stock Ticker: EXE Exchange: TSE
Employees: 23,700 Fiscal Year Ends: 12/31
Parent Company:

SALARIES/BONUSES:

Top Exec. Salary: $ Bonus: $
Second Exec. Salary: $ Bonus: $

OTHER THOUGHTS:

Estimated Female Officers or Directors: 7
Hot Spot for Advancement for Women/Minorities: Y

EyeMed Vision Care LLC

portal.eyemedvisioncare.com

NAIC Code: 524,114

TYPES OF BUSINESS:

Vision Plans

BRANDS/DIVISIONS/AFFILIATES:

Luxottica Group SpA
OneSight

CONTACTS:

Note: Officers with more than one job title may be intentionally listed here more than once.

Lukas Ruecker, Pres.
John Lahr, Dir.-Medical
Troy Hall, Associate VP-Mktg. & Strategic Planning
Maury Williams, Dir.-Comm.

GROWTH PLANS/SPECIAL FEATURES:

EyeMed Vision Care, LLC administers vision care plans for over 47 million members in large- and medium-sized companies and government entities and through insurance companies in the U.S. The company is comprised of more includes private optometrists, ophthalmologists and opticians. EyeMed offers a network with vision care and eyewear services from well-known optical retailers such as LensCrafters, Sears Optical and Pearle Vision. The company's member website offers self-service tools that are available any day or night, and can be accessed via desktop or smartphone. Benefit information can be retrieved from the web site, with access to view/print ID cards, explanation of benefits, locate a provider, check claim status and schedule appointments options. In addition, EyeMed is the Platinum Sponsor of OneSight, bringing onsite vision care services such as comprehensive eye exams and new prescription eyewear to more than 11,000 underserved across the nation. EyeMed is a wholly-owned subsidiary of Italian eyewear designer Luxottica Group SpA.

FINANCIAL DATA:

Note: Data for latest year may not have been available at press time.

In U.S. $	2017	2016	2015	2014	2013	2012
Revenue						
R&D Expense						
Operating Income						
Operating Margin %						
SGA Expense						
Net Income						
Operating Cash Flow						
Capital Expenditure						
EBITDA						
Return on Assets %						
Return on Equity %						
Debt to Equity						

CONTACT INFORMATION:

Phone: 513-765-6000 Fax: 513-765-6388
Toll-Free: 800-521-3605
Address: 4000 Luxottica Pl., Mason, OH 45040 United States

STOCK TICKER/OTHER:

Stock Ticker: Subsidiary
Exchange:
Employees:
Fiscal Year Ends: 12/31
Parent Company: Luxottica Group SpA

SALARIES/BONUSES:

Top Exec. Salary: $ Bonus: $
Second Exec. Salary: $ Bonus: $

OTHER THOUGHTS:

Estimated Female Officers or Directors: 1
Hot Spot for Advancement for Women/Minorities:

Fairview Health Services

www.fairview.org

NAIC Code: 622,110

TYPES OF BUSINESS:

General Medical and Surgical Hospitals
Specialty Clinics
Home Care
Hospice Services
Children's Services
Cancer Care
Senior Care
Academic Teaching Hospital

BRANDS/DIVISIONS/AFFILIATES:

www.fairview.org

CONTACTS: *Note: Officers with more than one job title may be intentionally listed here more than once.*

James Hereford, CEO
Osman Akhtar, COO
Daniel Fromm, CFO
Cindy Fruitrail, VP-Mktg., Branding & Communications
Carolyn Jacobson, Chief Human Resources Officer
Brent Asplin, Chief Clinical Officer
Alistair Jacques, CIO
Mark Hansberry, VP-Strategic Planning
Mark Hansberry, VP-Comm.
Brent Asplin, Pres., Fairview Medical Group
Daniel K. Anderson, Pres., Fairview Community Hospitals
Bob Beacher, Pres., Fairview Pharmacy Services
Richard Howard, Pres., Fairview Foundation
Mark Thomas, Pres., Senior Services

GROWTH PLANS/SPECIAL FEATURES:

Fairview Health Services is a nonprofit health care system with numerous primary care and specialty clinics in 30 cities across Minnesota. The company's network is comprised of nearly 4,000 doctors and providers, 12 academic and community hospitals, 110 primary and specialty care clinics and 36 pharmacy locations. Fairview's services and specialties include family medicine, obstetrics, gynecology, urgent care, pharmacy, pediatrics, orthopedics, sports medicine, weight loss, caregiver assurance, acupuncture, aquatic therapy, audiology, bone marrow transplant, cancer care, counseling, dermatology, ear/nose/throat, home infusion, imaging, kidney care, laboratory/diagnostic, neonatal intensive care, pain management and many more. For employers, Fairview offers a portfolio of services that include: an employee assistance program; a single-day, comprehensive annual physical and wellness consultation performed at the University of Minnesota Health Clinics and Surgery Center; an online clinic available 24/7 for the treatment of routine health conditions such as cold, flu, allergies, ear infections, pink eye and more; a customized onsite clinic solution that offers convenient access to high-quality care for employees and dependents; and sleep health. Fairview's website, www.fairview.org, offers patients the capability to pay their related health bills, obtain a prescription refill, pre-register for a hospital visit, obtain personal medical records and request for an appointment. Ebenezer is a part of Fairview's health services and is focused on serving senior adults. For medical professionals, Fairview offers continuing medical education and credentialing services.

Fairview offers employees life, disability, health and dental insurance; various employee assistance programs; and 403(b) and other retirement options.

FINANCIAL DATA: *Note: Data for latest year may not have been available at press time.*

In U.S. $	2017	2016	2015	2014	2013	2012
Revenue	5,300,000,000	4,363,540,000	3,867,550,000	3,560,832,000	3,318,513,000	3,218,081,000
R&D Expense						
Operating Income						
Operating Margin %						
SGA Expense						
Net Income	456,900,000	213,786,000	64,908,000	166,695,000	244,300,000	108,039,000
Operating Cash Flow						
Capital Expenditure						
EBITDA						
Return on Assets %						
Return on Equity %						
Debt to Equity						

CONTACT INFORMATION:

Phone: 612-672-7272 Fax: 612-672-7186
Toll-Free: 800-824-1953
Address: 2450 Riverside Ave., Minneapolis, MN 55454 United States

STOCK TICKER/OTHER:

Stock Ticker: Nonprofit
Employees: 32,000
Parent Company:
Exchange:
Fiscal Year Ends: 12/31

SALARIES/BONUSES:

Top Exec. Salary: $ Bonus: $
Second Exec. Salary: $ Bonus: $

OTHER THOUGHTS:

Estimated Female Officers or Directors: 9
Hot Spot for Advancement for Women/Minorities: Y

Fielmann AG

www.fielmann.de

NAIC Code: 339,100

TYPES OF BUSINESS:

Ophthalmic Goods Manufacturing

BRANDS/DIVISIONS/AFFILIATES:

Korva SE

GROWTH PLANS/SPECIAL FEATURES:

Fielmann AG is engaged in the manufacture, retail and trade of optical products. The company is 71%-owned by the Fielmann family's holding company, Korva SE. It conducts operations in Germany, Switzerland, Austria, Luxembourg, the Netherlands, Italy and Poland. Fielmann is a market leader in eyewear sales, operating more than 720 retail optical stores as well as eCommerce sites, and selling more than 25 million pairs of glasses to date. Products include spectacles, contact lenses and other optical products. Its spectacles include bifocal and varifocal optical glasses, sunglasses, prescription sunglasses, computer glasses and contact lenses. To customers, the company offers free eye exams as well as online eye tests. For current and future employees, Fielmann provides optician training in Germany. Moreover, in several stores, Fielmann also sells hearing aids and related accessories.

CONTACTS: *Note: Officers with more than one job title may be intentionally listed here more than once.*

Gunther Fielmann, Co-CEO
Marc Fielmann, Co-CEO
Gunter Schmid, Head-Material Mgmt. & Production
Mark Binz, Chmn.

FINANCIAL DATA: *Note: Data for latest year may not have been available at press time.*

In U.S. $	2017	2016	2015	2014	2013	2012
Revenue						
R&D Expense						
Operating Income						
Operating Margin %						
SGA Expense						
Net Income						
Operating Cash Flow						
Capital Expenditure						
EBITDA						
Return on Assets %						
Return on Equity %						
Debt to Equity						

CONTACT INFORMATION:

Phone: 49 4027076-0 Fax: 49 4027076-150
Toll-Free:
Address: Weidestrasse 118a, Hamburg, 22083 Germany

STOCK TICKER/OTHER:

Stock Ticker: FLMNF
Employees: 18,522
Parent Company: Korva SE
Exchange: PINX
Fiscal Year Ends: 12/31

SALARIES/BONUSES:

Top Exec. Salary: $ Bonus: $
Second Exec. Salary: $ Bonus: $

OTHER THOUGHTS:

Estimated Female Officers or Directors:
Hot Spot for Advancement for Women/Minorities:

First Choice Health Network Inc

www.fchn.com

NAIC Code: 524,114

TYPES OF BUSINESS:

Insurance-Medical & Health, HMOs & PPOs
Medical Management Services
Third Party Administration
Employee Assistance Program
Physician Assistance Program

BRANDS/DIVISIONS/AFFILIATES:

CONTACTS:

Note: Officers with more than one job title may be intentionally listed here more than once.

Jaja Okigwe, CEO
Kenneth A. Hamm, Pres.
James Cassel, Dir.-Sales & Mktg.

GROWTH PLANS/SPECIAL FEATURES:

First Choice Health Network, Inc. is a Seattle-based physician- and hospital-owned health care company. The firm offers preferred provider organization (PPO) and health benefits management services to large self-funded plan sponsors. The company's principal business is the development and operation of a preferred provider network of hospitals, practitioners and ancillary facilities. The network serves more than 1 million people through contracts with insurers, third-party administrators, union trusts and employers. First Choice's network is primarily in Washington, with additional healthcare providers in Oregon, Alaska, Idaho, Wyoming and Montana, as well as select areas of North and South Dakota. The firm also contracts with self-insured employers, indemnity insurers, health maintenance organizations (HMOs), union trusts and third-party administrators to provide subscribers with access to the PPO, for which it receives a fee. Additionally, hospitals participating in the PPO pay the network an administrative fee. First Choice's health benefits management business segment offers benefits management and administration services to self-funded employers and insurance carriers.

First Choice offers its employees medical, dental and vision insurance; short-and long-term disability; flexible spending accounts; a 401(k) with company match; profit sharing; tuition reimbursement; an employee assistance program; and free public transportation.

FINANCIAL DATA:

Note: Data for latest year may not have been available at press time.

In U.S. $	2017	2016	2015	2014	2013	2012
Revenue						
R&D Expense						
Operating Income						
Operating Margin %						
SGA Expense						
Net Income						
Operating Cash Flow						
Capital Expenditure						
EBITDA						
Return on Assets %						
Return on Equity %						
Debt to Equity						

CONTACT INFORMATION:

Phone: 206-292-8255 Fax: 206-667-8062
Toll-Free: 800-467-5281
Address: 600 University St., 1 Union Sq., Ste. 1400, Seattle, WA 98101 United States

STOCK TICKER/OTHER:

Stock Ticker: Private
Employees: 156
Parent Company:
Exchange:
Fiscal Year Ends:

SALARIES/BONUSES:

Top Exec. Salary: $ Bonus: $
Second Exec. Salary: $ Bonus: $

OTHER THOUGHTS:

Estimated Female Officers or Directors: 2
Hot Spot for Advancement for Women/Minorities:

First Health Group Corp

firsthealth.coventryhealthcare.com

NAIC Code: 524,114

TYPES OF BUSINESS:

Insurance-Medical & Health, PPOs

BRANDS/DIVISIONS/AFFILIATES:

Aetna Inc
Institues of Excellence Transplant Access Network
Aetna Dental Access Network

CONTACTS: *Note: Officers with more than one job title may be intentionally listed here more than once.*

Paul Lavin, COO
Kara Dornig, VP-Bus. Dev.
Susan Korth, VP-Account Mgmt.
John Bryan, Dir.-Sales
Darlene Colyer, Dir.-Oper. Support

GROWTH PLANS/SPECIAL FEATURES:

First Health Group Corp., an indirect wholly-owned subsidiary of Aetna, Inc., provides national preferred provider organization (PPO) and other cost containment programs to help clients manage employee benefit plans. The company's network serves over 2 million people, and includes more than 5,000 hospitals, over 1 million healthcare professional locations and 90,000 ancillary facilities across all 50 states, Washington, D.C. and Puerto Rico. Doctors and hospital administrators can apply for membership in First Health's network by filing an application online. The company also works to provide insurance providers, third party administrators (TPA) and self-insured payers with services designed to achieve optimal cost savings. The firm's non-network claims and fee schedule management achieve savings by combining the most favorable rates and services both in and out of the network, including geography-specific considerations. Its medical management services, including utilization management, early medical assessment and case management, are designed to reduce unnecessary procedures and admissions that may lead to inflated costs. Through its alliance with Aetna, First Health offers Institutes of Excellence Transplant Access Network, which provides pre-transplant, transplant and postoperative care management. The network connects clients with experienced physicians at negotiated rates in order to match good outcomes with minimal cost. First Health's dental solutions program is designed to provide alternative, cost effective solutions for oral care through a network of access points. The Aetna Dental Access Network consists of over 226,000 available dental practice locations nationwide. The vision solutions program offers custom plans for employer-paid and voluntary eye care coverage. These services are supported by an online portal that aims to provide easy and secure access for account management and customer service.

The company offers its employees medical, dental, vision, life, AD&D and short/long-term disability insurance; 401(k); and various employee assistance plans.

FINANCIAL DATA: *Note: Data for latest year may not have been available at press time.*

In U.S. $	2017	2016	2015	2014	2013	2012
Revenue						
R&D Expense						
Operating Income						
Operating Margin %						
SGA Expense						
Net Income						
Operating Cash Flow						
Capital Expenditure						
EBITDA						
Return on Assets %						
Return on Equity %						
Debt to Equity						

CONTACT INFORMATION:

Phone: 630-737-7900 Fax:
Toll-Free:
Address: 3200 Highland Ave., Downers Grove, IL 60515 United States

STOCK TICKER/OTHER:

Stock Ticker: Subsidiary
Employees:
Parent Company: Aetna Inc
Exchange:
Fiscal Year Ends: 12/31

SALARIES/BONUSES:

Top Exec. Salary: $ Bonus: $
Second Exec. Salary: $ Bonus: $

OTHER THOUGHTS:

Estimated Female Officers or Directors: 4
Hot Spot for Advancement for Women/Minorities: Y

Fisher & Paykel Healthcare Limited

www.fphcare.com

NAIC Code: 423,450

TYPES OF BUSINESS:

Medical, Dental, and Hospital Equipment and Supplies Merchant Wholesalers

BRANDS/DIVISIONS/AFFILIATES:

CONTACTS:
Note: Officers with more than one job title may be intentionally listed here more than once.

Lewis Gradon, CEO
Nicholas Fourie, VP-IT & ICT
Andrea Blackie, Acting CFO
Paul Shearer, Sr. VP-Sales & Mktg.
Debra Lumsden, VP-Human Resources
Andrew Somervell, VP-IT & Products
Lewis Gradon, Sr. VP-Products & Technology
Anthony Barclay, Company Secretary
Paul Adreassi, VP-Quality & Regulatory
Tony Carter, Chmn.

GROWTH PLANS/SPECIAL FEATURES:

Fisher & Paykel Healthcare Limited designs, manufactures and markets heated humidification products and systems for respiratory care, acute care, surgery and treatment of obstructive sleep apnea. Exporting to over 120 countries, Fisher & Paykel's head office is located in New Zealand, with manufacturing operations located in New Zealand and Mexico. 99% of revenue is derived overseas. The firm's major clients include hospitals, home health care providers, distributors and manufacturers of medical devices. Products are divided into two major groups: respiratory and acute care and obstructive sleep apnea. Respiratory and acute care offers products for the treatment of respiratory conditions by ventilation or oxygen therapy. These products include humidifiers, single-use and reusable chambers and breathing circuits, infant resuscitators, infant warmers; and accessories. This division also offers special humidification systems for the surgical room, which conditions dry carbon dioxide gas to normal physiological level of temperature and humidity. Obstructive sleep apnea offers a range of products utilizing continuous positive airway pressure therapy (CPAP). The group primarily sells a range of CPAP devices, masks and humidifiers.

FINANCIAL DATA:
Note: Data for latest year may not have been available at press time.

In U.S. $	2017	2016	2015	2014	2013	2012
Revenue						
R&D Expense						
Operating Income						
Operating Margin %						
SGA Expense						
Net Income						
Operating Cash Flow						
Capital Expenditure						
EBITDA						
Return on Assets %						
Return on Equity %						
Debt to Equity						

CONTACT INFORMATION:

Phone: 649 574 0100 Fax: 649 574 0158
Toll-Free:
Address: 15 Maurice Paykel Pl., Auckland, New Zealand 2013 New Zealand

STOCK TICKER/OTHER:

Stock Ticker: FSPKF
Exchange: PINX
Employees: 4,112
Fiscal Year Ends: 03/31
Parent Company:

SALARIES/BONUSES:

Top Exec. Salary: $ Bonus: $
Second Exec. Salary: $ Bonus: $

OTHER THOUGHTS:

Estimated Female Officers or Directors: 2
Hot Spot for Advancement for Women/Minorities:

Five Star Senior Living Inc

www.fivestarseniorliving.com

NAIC Code: 623,310

TYPES OF BUSINESS:

Assisted Living Facilities
Senior Living Communities
Rehabilitation Facilities

BRANDS/DIVISIONS/AFFILIATES:

Five Star Quality Care Inc

CONTACTS: *Note: Officers with more than one job title may be intentionally listed here more than once.*

Gerard Martin, Director
Adam Portnoy, Director
Richard Doyle, Executive VP
Katherine Potter, Executive VP
Bruce Mackey, President
R. Herzig, Senior VP, Divisional

GROWTH PLANS/SPECIAL FEATURES:

Five Star Senior Living, Inc. (formerly Five Star Quality Care, Inc.) operates senior living communities, including independent living, assisted living communities and skilled nursing facilities. As of December 2017, the company operated 283 communities located in 32 U.S. states, with 31,785 living units. Five Star owns and operates 24 of these communities, leases and operates 189 of them and manages-only 70 of them. Independent living communities provide high levels of privacy to residents and require residents to be capable of relatively high degrees of independence. Assisted living communities usually are comprised of one-bedroom units which include private bathrooms and efficiency kitchens. Services bundled within one charge usually include three meals per day in a central dining room, daily housekeeping, laundry, medical reminders and 24-hour availability of assistance with the activities of daily living such as dressing and bathing. Professional nursing and healthcare services are usually available at the community as requested, or at regularly-scheduled times. Skilled nursing facilities generally provide extensive nursing and healthcare services similar to those available in hospitals, without the high costs associated with operating theaters, emergency rooms or intensive care units. Units usually include one or two beds per room with a separate bathroom in each, as well as shared dining facilities. During 2017, Five Star Quality Care changed its corporate name to Five Star Senior Living to represent its shift from a clinical care focus to a full-service healthcare, hospitality and senior lifestyle service company.

Five Star Quality Care offers employees health, dental and vision; life insurance; paid time off; and tuition reimbursement.

FINANCIAL DATA: *Note: Data for latest year may not have been available at press time.*

In U.S. $	2017	2016	2015	2014	2013	2012
Revenue	1,396,106,000	1,378,108,000	1,365,410,000	1,328,075,000	1,296,787,000	1,350,878,000
R&D Expense						
Operating Income	-28,200,000	-15,470,000	-11,535,000	-18,591,000	10,448,000	20,858,000
Operating Margin %	-2.01%	-1.12%	-.84%	-1.39%	.80%	1.54%
SGA Expense	832,845,000	820,786,000	808,918,000	803,293,000	783,062,000	811,404,000
Net Income	-20,902,000	-21,813,000	-43,083,000	-85,406,000	-2,340,000	24,945,000
Operating Cash Flow	17,119,000	-23,442,000	38,389,000	27,856,000	28,777,000	50,737,000
Capital Expenditure	71,095,000	55,419,000	57,671,000	49,916,000	53,766,000	57,386,000
EBITDA	16,454,000	23,171,000	-1,375,000	15,549,000	38,367,000	50,402,000
Return on Assets %	-4.24%	-4.18%	-8.07%	-15.18%	-.40%	4.32%
Return on Equity %	-13.51%	-12.51%	-20.95%	-31.79%	-.75%	8.49%
Debt to Equity	0.05	0.35	0.32	0.21	0.11	0.12

CONTACT INFORMATION:

Phone: 617 796-8387 Fax: 617 796-8385
Toll-Free:
Address: 400 Centre St., Newton, MA 02458 United States

STOCK TICKER/OTHER:

Stock Ticker: FVE Exchange: NAS
Employees: 24,500 Fiscal Year Ends: 12/31
Parent Company:

SALARIES/BONUSES:

Top Exec. Salary: $300,000 Bonus: $600,000
Second Exec. Salary: $300,000 Bonus: $425,000

OTHER THOUGHTS:

Estimated Female Officers or Directors: 3
Hot Spot for Advancement for Women/Minorities: Y

Fresenius Medical Care AG & Co KGaA

www.freseniusmedicalcare.com/en/home/

NAIC Code: 621,400

TYPES OF BUSINESS:

Dialysis Products & Services

BRANDS/DIVISIONS/AFFILIATES:

FMC Austria GmbH
FMC France SAS
FMC de Mexico SA de CV
FMC Australia Pty Ltd
FMC (Shanghai) Co Ltd
Biocare Technology Company Limited
FMC India Private Ltd
FMC Holdings Inc

CONTACTS: *Note: Officers with more than one job title may be intentionally listed here more than once.*

Rice Powell, CEO
Michael Brosnan, CFO
Olaf Schermeier, CEO-Global R&D
Kent Wanzek, CEO-Global Mfg. Oper.
Rainer Runte, Dir.-Law, Compliance & Intellectual Property
Emanuele Gatti, Global Chief Strategist
Ronald Kuerbitz, CEO-North America
Emanuele Gatti, CEO-Latin America & EMEA
Roberto Fuste, CEO-Asia Pacific

GROWTH PLANS/SPECIAL FEATURES:

Fresenius Medical Care AG & Co. KGaA is a provider of dialysis products and services. The company operates in two segments: North America, and international, which includes operations in Europe/Middle East/Africa, the Asia Pacific and Latin America. Within each of its geographical segments, Fresenius Medical divides its activities into dialysis care services and dialysis products. The firm's dialysis care services business provides dialysis treatment and related laboratory and diagnostic services through a network of more than 3,800 outpatient dialysis clinics in approximately 50 countries worldwide. The company provides treatments to more than 325,100 patients throughout its network. In the U.S., it also provides inpatient dialysis services and other services under contract to hospitals. Fresenius Medical also develops and manufactures a full range of dialysis products, including equipment, systems and disposable products for chronic hemodialysis, acute therapy, home therapies and therapeutic apheresis (in which blood is treated and cleansed of undesirable and pathogenic substances outside the patient's body and then transfused back to the patient). Products include hemodialyzers and hemofilters, plasma filters, pediatric therapies and Automated Peritoneal Dialysis (APD) products. Just a few of Fresenius' primary subsidiaries include: FMC Austria GmbH, FMC France SAS, FMC (U.K.) Ltd., ZAO Frsenius SP (Russia), FMC de Mexico SA de CV, FMC Argentina SA, FMC Australia Pty Ltd., FMC (Shanghai) Co. Ltd., Biocare Technology Company Limited (Hong Kong), FMC India Private Ltd., Asia Renal Care (SEA) Pte. Ltd., FMC Vietnam LLC, and FMC Holdings, Inc. (USA).

Fresenius offers its employees a health plan, subsidized childcare, risk insurance, a pension plan and profit-sharing programs.

FINANCIAL DATA: *Note: Data for latest year may not have been available at press time.*

In U.S. $	2017	2016	2015	2014	2013	2012
Revenue	20,680,980,000	19,804,970,000	17,803,460,000	15,140,460,000	12,303,840,000	12,135,070,000
R&D Expense	151,999,100	179,535,100	149,236,700	116,783,000	105,948,900	98,161,020
Operating Income	2,669,194,000	2,844,686,000	2,441,448,000	2,131,759,000	1,870,172,000	1,903,678,000
Operating Margin %	12.90%	14.36%	13.71%	14.07%	15.19%	15.68%
SGA Expense	4,160,689,000	3,366,656,000	3,079,977,000	2,529,204,000	2,014,404,000	1,956,269,000
Net Income	1,488,299,000	1,374,751,000	1,095,002,000	999,633,700	934,713,500	1,043,602,000
Operating Cash Flow	2,548,914,000	2,366,189,000	2,084,866,000	1,780,131,000	1,713,647,000	1,793,019,000
Capital Expenditure	1,098,337,000	1,138,920,000	1,013,628,000	890,955,700	629,889,200	593,823,600
EBITDA	3,653,000,000	3,826,041,000	3,361,904,000	2,905,469,000	2,478,805,000	2,642,879,000
Return on Assets %	5.15%	4.82%	4.25%	4.56%	4.78%	5.61%
Return on Equity %	12.73%	12.23%	11.20%	11.89%	11.95%	13.96%
Debt to Equity	0.59	0.66	0.79	0.96	0.83	0.87

CONTACT INFORMATION:

Phone: 49 61726090 Fax: 49 61726082488
Toll-Free:
Address: Else-Kroener Strasse 1, Bad Homburg, 61352 Germany

STOCK TICKER/OTHER:

Stock Ticker: FMS Exchange: NYS
Employees: 109,319 Fiscal Year Ends: 12/31
Parent Company:

SALARIES/BONUSES:

Top Exec. Salary: $1,415,281 Bonus: $2,671,241
Second Exec. Salary: $854,751 Bonus: $1,529,248

OTHER THOUGHTS:

Estimated Female Officers or Directors:
Hot Spot for Advancement for Women/Minorities:

Fresenius SE & Co KGaA

www.fresenius.com

NAIC Code: 621,400

TYPES OF BUSINESS:

Dialysis Clinics
Dialysis Products & Services
Nutrition, Infusion Therapy & Transfusion Products
Hospital Management & Engineering
Management & Consulting Services
Pharmaceutical Plant Engineering
Information Technology Services

BRANDS/DIVISIONS/AFFILIATES:

Fresenius Medical Care
Fresenius Kabi
Fresenius Helios
Fresenius Vamed
Quironsalud

CONTACTS: *Note: Officers with more than one job title may be intentionally listed here more than once.*

Stephan Sturm, CEO
Ulf M. Schneider, Pres.
Rachel Empey, CFO
Jurgen Gotz, Chief Legal & Compliance Officer
Mats Henriksson, CEO-Fresenius Kabi
Francesco De Meo, CEO-Fresenius Helios
Rice Powell, CEO-Fresenius Medical Care
Ernst Wastler, CEO-Fresenius Vamed
Gerd Krick, Chmn.

GROWTH PLANS/SPECIAL FEATURES:

Fresenius SE & Co. KGaA is an international healthcare group offering products and services primarily for dialysis, with operations in approximately 100 countries. The company is comprised of four business segments: Fresenius Medical Care (FMC), Fresenius Kabi, Fresenius Helios and Fresenius Vamed. FMC is a leading manufacturer of chronic kidney failure products, such as hemodialysis machines, dialyzers and related disposable products as well as renal pharmaceuticals to support patients with chronic kidney failure. It owns and operates more than 3,500 dialysis clinics in Asia-Pacific, Latin America, North America, Europe and Africa. Fresenius Kabi provides parenteral nutrition products that supply nutrients to patients while bypassing the gastro-intestinal tract; enteral nutrition products that artificially feed a patient via the intestinal tract; infusion therapy products, blood replacement and rinsing solutions as well as carrier solutions for drugs; transfusion technology products; and ambulatory care outpatient services. Helios is one of Germany's largest private hospital managers. Fresenius Helios is Germany's largest hospital operator, with the firm owning and operating 110 clinics, including seven maximum care hospitals in Erfurt, Berlin-Buch, Duisburg, Wuppertal, Schwerin, Krefeld and Wiesbaden. Helios also operates 23 post-acute care clinics in Germany, as well as 45 hospitals, 56 outpatient centers and 300 occupational risk centers in Spain via subsidiary Quironsalud. Fresenius Vamed operates in the project and management business of healthcare facilities worldwide. These include hospitals and healthcare centers as well as spas and wellness centers. The company has completed more than 800 health care projects in about 80 countries since its founding in 1982.

FINANCIAL DATA: *Note: Data for latest year may not have been available at press time.*

In U.S. $	2017	2016	2015	2014	2013	2012
Revenue						
R&D Expense						
Operating Income						
Operating Margin %						
SGA Expense						
Net Income						
Operating Cash Flow						
Capital Expenditure						
EBITDA						
Return on Assets %						
Return on Equity %						
Debt to Equity						

CONTACT INFORMATION:

Phone: 49 61726080 Fax: 49 61726082294
Toll-Free:
Address: Else-Kroener-Strasse 1, Bad Homburg, 61352 Germany

STOCK TICKER/OTHER:

Stock Ticker: FSNUF
Exchange: PINX
Employees: 273,249
Fiscal Year Ends: 12/31
Parent Company:

SALARIES/BONUSES:

Top Exec. Salary: $ Bonus: $
Second Exec. Salary: $ Bonus: $

OTHER THOUGHTS:

Estimated Female Officers or Directors:
Hot Spot for Advancement for Women/Minorities:

Fuse Medical Inc

www.fusemedical.com

NAIC Code: 423,450

TYPES OF BUSINESS:

Medical Supplies & Equipment Distribution

BRANDS/DIVISIONS/AFFILIATES:

CPM Medical Consultants LLC
Palm Springs Partners LLC (Maxim Surgical)

CONTACTS:

Note: Officers with more than one job title may be intentionally listed here more than once.

Christopher Reeg, CEO
William McLaughlin, CFO
Mark Brooks, Chmn.
Randall Dei, Director
Rusty Shelton, Director
Jonathan Brown, President

GROWTH PLANS/SPECIAL FEATURES:

Fuse Medical, Inc. markets, distributes and sells internal fixation, durable bone materials, biologics, tissues, surgical and other related products for use in a variety of surgical procedures. The company's products are used in various types of facilities (ambulatory surgical centers, hospitals, physician offices and medical facilities) where surgeons and doctors treat patients and operate. Its products are FDA-approved and/or state-licensed, and consist of plates and screws for recurring bone fractures; upper extremity plating for elective orthopedic trauma, soft tissue fixation and augmentation for sports medicine procedures; total joint reconstruction for both upper and lower extremities; full spinal implants for trauma, degenerative disc disease and deformity indications; allografts for bone chips and tendons; and amniotic products. Amniotic products are derived from the inner layer of the human amniotic tissue and then processed by the manufacturer which results in an FDA-approved allograft. Fuse Medical holds no intellectual property, patents or trademarks. During 2018, Fuse Medical acquired CPM Medical Consultants, LLC, a distributor of medical device implants and biologics; and Palm Springs Partners, LLC (dba Maxim Surgical), a manufacturing company in the spinal fusion device market, and a full-service medical device and distribution company.

FINANCIAL DATA:

Note: Data for latest year may not have been available at press time.

In U.S. $	2017	2016	2015	2014	2013	2012
Revenue						
R&D Expense						
Operating Income						
Operating Margin %						
SGA Expense						
Net Income						
Operating Cash Flow						
Capital Expenditure						
EBITDA						
Return on Assets %						
Return on Equity %						
Debt to Equity						

CONTACT INFORMATION:

Phone: 469-862-3030 Fax: 469-862-3035
Toll-Free:
Address: 1565 N. Central Expressway, Ste. 220, Richardson, TX 75080 United States

STOCK TICKER/OTHER:

Stock Ticker: FZMD
Employees: 3
Parent Company:
Exchange: PINX
Fiscal Year Ends: 08/31

SALARIES/BONUSES:

Top Exec. Salary: $22,500 Bonus: $
Second Exec. Salary: $ Bonus: $

OTHER THOUGHTS:

Estimated Female Officers or Directors:
Hot Spot for Advancement for Women/Minorities:

Galderma SA

www.nestleskinhealth.com/galderma-medical-solutions

NAIC Code: 325,412

TYPES OF BUSINESS:

Dermatological Pharmaceuticals
Dermatological Product Research & Development

BRANDS/DIVISIONS/AFFILIATES:

Nestle SA
Nestle Skin Health SA
Epiduo
Differin
Soolantra
Mirvaso
Cetaphil
Proactiv

CONTACTS: *Note: Officers with more than one job title may be intentionally listed here more than once.*

Stuart Raetzman, CEO-Nestle Skin Health
Humberto C. Antunes, Pres.

GROWTH PLANS/SPECIAL FEATURES:

Galderma SA is the medical solutions business within Nestle Skin Health SA, which itself is the pharmaceutical division and subsidiary of Nestle SA. Galerdma provides prescription drugs and aesthetics solutions, not just for treating skin problems, but also for protecting, enhancing and rejuvenating skin. The firm's business is divided into three groups: prescription, aesthetics and community. The prescription business provides medicines and treatments in relation to skin diseases. This business unit's medical brands include: Epiduo, Differin, Soolantra, Mirvaso, Oracea, Metvix, Benzac, Loceryl, Restylane, Azzalure, Dysport and Sculptra. Its consumer brands include Cetaphil and Proactiv. The aesthetics business provides medical aesthetic solutions for skin health. Its products and services are also utilized by healthcare providers. The community business works closely with healthcare professionals to provide innovative solutions to skin health needs for all patients, of all ages. Whether it is a skin disease (including rare diseases with current unmet needs), for skin protection or for aging skin to research, develop and produce solutions. This division also provides healthcare professionals with tools and resources to help meet their patients' skin health needs.

FINANCIAL DATA: *Note: Data for latest year may not have been available at press time.*

In U.S. $	2017	2016	2015	2014	2013	2012
Revenue	236,250,000	225,000,000	215,000,000	208,000,000	201,000,000	195,160,000
R&D Expense						
Operating Income						
Operating Margin %						
SGA Expense						
Net Income						
Operating Cash Flow						
Capital Expenditure						
EBITDA						
Return on Assets %						
Return on Equity %						
Debt to Equity						

CONTACT INFORMATION:

Phone: 41-21-642-78-00 Fax: 41-21-642-78-01
Toll-Free:
Address: 2 Ave. de Gratta-Paille, World Trade Center, Lausanne, 1018 Switzerland

STOCK TICKER/OTHER:

Stock Ticker: Joint Venture
Employees: 6,000
Parent Company: Nestle SA
Exchange:
Fiscal Year Ends:

SALARIES/BONUSES:

Top Exec. Salary: $ Bonus: $
Second Exec. Salary: $ Bonus: $

OTHER THOUGHTS:

Estimated Female Officers or Directors: 1
Hot Spot for Advancement for Women/Minorities:

Galenica Group

www.galenica.com

NAIC Code: 325,412

TYPES OF BUSINESS:

Drugs (Pharmaceuticals), Discovery & Manufacturing
Retail Pharmacies
Pharmaceutical Logistics Services
Pharmaceutical Databases

BRANDS/DIVISIONS/AFFILIATES:

Amativa
Verfora
Alloga
Galexis
Unione Farmaceutica Distribuzione
Pharmapool
Medifilm
HCI Solutions

CONTACTS: *Note: Officers with more than one job title may be intentionally listed here more than once.*

Jean-Claude Clemencon, CEO
Felix Burkhard, CFO
Gianni Zampieri, Head-Pharma Oper.
Gianni Zampieri, CEO-Vifor Pharma
Jorg Kneubuhler, Chmn.
Jean-Claude Clemencon, Head-Logistics

GROWTH PLANS/SPECIAL FEATURES:

Galenica Group is a fully-integrated health care provider in Switzerland. The company organizes its business in two segments: health and beauty, and services. The health and beauty segment is further divided into two units. The retail unit manages a pharmaceutical network and a distribution network for selling Galenica's own brands, as well as exclusive and partner brands. This unit's retail network consists of nearly 500 pharmacies that serve more than 100,000 customer transactions each day. Retail brands include Amativa, Sun Store, Coop Vitality, Winconcept, Mediservice and Careproduct. The products and brands unit develops and markets Galenica's own brands and products, as well as the exclusive brands and products of its business partners. This division's services include marketing, distribution and supply chain management of over-the-counter pharmaceutical and health and beauty products. Through Verfora, this unit also supports specialist retail trade in Switzerland. The services segment provides specialized pre-wholesale and wholesale distribution, including integrated logistics and IT solutions that ensure that medicines reach patients throughout the entire country of Switzerland. Alloga is this division's pre-wholesale company, which offers storage, logistics and distribution services for the pharmaceutical industry. Galexis is a healthcare wholesaler that supplies pharmacies, medical practices, drugstores, nursing homes and hospitals with a range of more than 100,000 products. Unione Farmaceutica Distribuzione solely serves as a medical wholesaler. Pharmapool is a wholesaler that supplies and supports physicians and medical practices with medicines, consumables, laboratory products and furnishings. In addition, Medifilm prepares medicines and food supplements individually on behalf of pharmacies and according to the treatment plan for permanent and long-term patients; and HCI Solutions is a master data company for the Swiss health market, and develops management solutions for pharmacies as well as tools to securely manage, communicate and distribute sensitive health data.

FINANCIAL DATA: *Note: Data for latest year may not have been available at press time.*

In U.S. $	2017	2016	2015	2014	2013	2012
Revenue	4,312,000,000	4,234,653,440	4,056,550,656	3,774,571,520	3,454,287,616	3,387,357,952
R&D Expense						
Operating Income						
Operating Margin %						
SGA Expense						
Net Income		250,505,888	309,560,512	292,483,584	304,524,224	260,620,640
Operating Cash Flow						
Capital Expenditure						
EBITDA						
Return on Assets %						
Return on Equity %						
Debt to Equity						

CONTACT INFORMATION:

Phone: 41 588528111 Fax: 41 588528112
Toll-Free:
Address: Untermattweg 8, Bern, 3027 Switzerland

STOCK TICKER/OTHER:

Stock Ticker: GALE
Employees: 8,661
Parent Company:
Exchange: SWISS
Fiscal Year Ends: 12/31

SALARIES/BONUSES:

Top Exec. Salary: $ Bonus: $
Second Exec. Salary: $ Bonus: $

OTHER THOUGHTS:

Estimated Female Officers or Directors: 2
Hot Spot for Advancement for Women/Minorities:

GE Healthcare

www3.gehealthcare.com/en

NAIC Code: 339,100

TYPES OF BUSINESS:

Medical Imaging & Information Technology
Magnetic Resonance Imaging Systems
Patient Monitoring Systems
Clinical Information Systems
Nuclear Medicine
Surgery & Vascular Imaging
X-Ray & Ultrasound Bone Densitometers
Clinical & Business Services

BRANDS/DIVISIONS/AFFILIATES:

General Electric Company (GE)
Puridify

CONTACTS:

Note: Officers with more than one job title may be intentionally listed here more than once.

Kieran Murphy, CEO/Pres.
Monish Patolawala, CFO
Raghu Krishnamoorthy, VP-Human Resources
Jorg Debatin, VP
Michael Harsh, CTO
Keith Newman, General Counsel
Markus Ewert, Exec. VP-Bus. Dev.
Jeff DeMarrais, Chief Comm. Officer
Dee Miller, Chief Quality Officer
Rachel Duan, CEO/Pres., China
Tom Gentile, CEO-Health Care Systems
Terri Bresenham, CEO/Pres., India
Brian Masterson, VP-Supply Chain

GROWTH PLANS/SPECIAL FEATURES:

GE Healthcare is the healthcare business of General Electric Company (GE), harnessing data and analytics across hardware, software and biotechnology. The firm is a leading provider of medical imaging equipment, with a track record of more than 100 years in the industry across 100 countries. GE Healthcare products include the health cloud, bone and metabolic health, advanced visualization, anesthesia delivery, applied intelligence, computed tomography, diagnostics, EP recording, healthcare IT, hemodynamic recording, interventional image guided systems, life sciences, magnetic resonance imaging, mammography, maternal-infant care, molecular imaging, nuclear imaging agents, patient monitoring, radiography, fluoroscopy, surgical imaging, ultrasound and ventilators. Specialties include: cardiology, offering a suite of solutions that diagnose and fight cardiovascular disease; orthopedics, offering tools and technologies that cover each stage of patient care, from assessment and diagnosis through treatment and follow-up; and an ambulatory surgery center, which provides single source solutions regarding anesthesia delivery, patient monitoring, point-of-care ultrasound, financial and U.S. government supporting services. Other services by GE Healthcare include education and training, healthcare technology management, research, equipment financing and more. In November 2017, GE Healthcare acquired Puridify, a bioprocessing startup that is developing a nanofiber-based platform purification technology for biopharmaceutical production. In April 2018, the firm announced plans to sell its IT business to private equity firm Veritas Capital for $1.05 billion in order to focus on smart diagnostics and connected devices.

FINANCIAL DATA:

Note: Data for latest year may not have been available at press time.

In U.S. $	2017	2016	2015	2014	2013	2012
Revenue	19,116,000,000	18,291,000,000	17,639,000,000	18,299,000,000	18,200,000,000	18,500,000,000
R&D Expense						
Operating Income						
Operating Margin %						
SGA Expense						
Net Income	3,448,000,000	3,161,000,000	2,882,000,000	3,047,000,000	3,048,000,000	2,920,000,000
Operating Cash Flow						
Capital Expenditure						
EBITDA						
Return on Assets %						
Return on Equity %						
Debt to Equity						

CONTACT INFORMATION:

Phone: 44-1494-544-000 Fax:
Toll-Free:
Address: Nightingales Ln., Pollards Wood, Chalfont St. Giles, HP8 4SP United Kingdom

STOCK TICKER/OTHER:

Stock Ticker: Subsidiary
Exchange:
Employees: 55,125
Fiscal Year Ends: 12/31
Parent Company: General Electric Company (GE)

SALARIES/BONUSES:

Top Exec. Salary: $ Bonus: $
Second Exec. Salary: $ Bonus: $

OTHER THOUGHTS:

Estimated Female Officers or Directors: 4
Hot Spot for Advancement for Women/Minorities: Y

Genentech Inc

www.gene.com

NAIC Code: 325,412

TYPES OF BUSINESS:

Drug Development & Manufacturing
Genetically Engineered Drugs

BRANDS/DIVISIONS/AFFILIATES:

Roche Holding AG
www.gene.com
HEMLIBRA
Lucentis
TECENTRIQ

CONTACTS:

Note: Officers with more than one job title may be intentionally listed here more than once.

Bill Anderson, CEO
Ed Harrington, CFO
Nancy Vitale, Sr. VP-Human Resources
Richard H. Scheller, Exec. VP-Research
Frederick C. Kentz, Sec.
Timothy Moore, Head-Pharmaceutical Technical Operation Biologics
Severin Schwan, Chmn.

GROWTH PLANS/SPECIAL FEATURES:

Genentech, Inc., a wholly-owned subsidiary of Roche Holding AG, is a biotechnology company that discovers, develops, manufactures and commercializes medicines to treat patients with serious or life-threatening medical conditions. The firm makes medicines by splicing genes into fast-growing bacteria that then produce therapeutic proteins and combat diseases on a molecular level. Genentech uses cutting-edge technologies such as computer visualization of molecules, micro arrays and sensitive assaying techniques to develop, manufacture and market pharmaceuticals for unmet medical needs. For patients, the company's website (www.gene.com) provides access for viewing medicine information, investigational medicines, finding open clinical trials and information on diseases in general. Genentech's range of programs and services help make sure that price is not a barrier for patients. For medical professionals, the website offers information on the medicines that are on the market by Genentech, as well as what is on the current pipeline, compliance, product security and various types of medical resources. As of April 2018, there were 38 medicines on the market by the company, and 46 molecules in the pipeline. These medicines and molecules are in various phases in relation to oncology, metabolism, immunology, infectious disease, neuroscience, ophthalmology or other conditions. Approximately half of Genentech's marketed and pipeline products are derived from collaborations with companies and institutions worldwide; therefore, the firm is open to having partners. In early 2018, the U.S. FDA granted breakthrough therapy designation for Genentech's HEMLIBRA (emicizumab-kxwh) in Hemophilia A without inhibitors; the FDA approvedthe Lucentis (ranibizumab injection) 0.3mg pre-filled syringe for diabetic macular edema and diabetic retinopathy; and a Phase III IMpower150 study showed Genentech's TECENTRIQ (atezolizumab) and Avastin (bevacizumab) plus carboplatin and paclitaxel helped people with advanced lung cancer live longer.

Genentech provides employees benefits including a 401(k); disability, life, AD&D, medical, dental and vision coverage; flexible spending accounts; and paid vacations.

FINANCIAL DATA:

Note: Data for latest year may not have been available at press time.

In U.S. $	2017	2016	2015	2014	2013	2012
Revenue	19,000,000,000	18,000,000,000	17,000,000,000	16,300,000,000		
R&D Expense						
Operating Income						
Operating Margin %						
SGA Expense						
Net Income						
Operating Cash Flow						
Capital Expenditure						
EBITDA						
Return on Assets %						
Return on Equity %						
Debt to Equity						

CONTACT INFORMATION:

Phone: 650-225-1000 Fax: 650-225-6000
Toll-Free: 800-626-3553
Address: 1 DNA Way, South San Francisco, CA 94080-4990 United States

STOCK TICKER/OTHER:

Stock Ticker: Subsidiary
Employees: 14,717
Parent Company: Roche Holding AG
Exchange:
Fiscal Year Ends: 12/31

SALARIES/BONUSES:

Top Exec. Salary: $ Bonus: $
Second Exec. Salary: $ Bonus: $

OTHER THOUGHTS:

Estimated Female Officers or Directors: 1
Hot Spot for Advancement for Women/Minorities: Y

Genesis Healthcare LLC

www.genesishcc.com

NAIC Code: 623,110

TYPES OF BUSINESS:

Nursing Care Facilities
Assisted Living Communities
Rehabilitation Services

BRANDS/DIVISIONS/AFFILIATES:

GROWTH PLANS/SPECIAL FEATURES:

Genesis Healthcare, LLC owns and operates more than 450 skilled nursing centers and assisted/senior living communities in 30 U.S. states. In addition to short-stay and long-term care services, Genesis offers memory support, orthopedic rehabilitation, ventilator care, dialysis care and assisted/senior living services. Internationally, Genesis operates facilities in China through affiliates, which include: three rehabilitation clinics in Guangzhou, Shanghai and Hong Kong; a rehabilitation facility; and one nursing home. Genesis also provides inpatient and outpatient rehabilitation services via seven hospital joint ventures in China. In April 2018, Genesis Healthcare agreed to sell 51% of its subsidiary in China (GRS-HS), to Riswein Health Industry Investment Co., Ltd. for $30 million, and expected to close in early 2019.

CONTACTS: *Note: Officers with more than one job title may be intentionally listed here more than once.*

Michael Sherman, Assistant Treasurer
George Hager, CEO
Thomas Divittorio, CFO
Stephen Young, Chief Accounting Officer
Paul Bach, COO, Subsidiary
Robert Fish, Director
JoAnne Reifsnyder, Executive VP, Divisional

FINANCIAL DATA: *Note: Data for latest year may not have been available at press time.*

In U.S. $	2017	2016	2015	2014	2013	2012
Revenue	5,373,740,000	5,732,430,000	5,619,224,000	833,256,000	842,272,000	872,623,000
R&D Expense						
Operating Income	182,729,000	254,498,000	306,118,000	28,081,000	41,184,000	73,493,000
Operating Margin %	3.40%	4.43%	5.44%	3.37%	4.88%	8.42%
SGA Expense	3,354,422,000	3,702,019,000	3,615,985,000	45,989,000	26,619,000	24,249,000
Net Income	-578,982,000	-64,013,000	-426,195,000	-907,000	-10,484,000	21,597,000
Operating Cash Flow	120,455,000	68,361,000	8,618,000	26,321,000	47,921,000	42,676,000
Capital Expenditure	64,106,000	201,417,000	85,723,000	12,981,000	13,436,000	19,522,000
EBITDA	-214,431,000	647,490,000	392,547,000	54,144,000	49,791,000	97,195,000
Return on Assets %	-10.95%	-1.07%	-12.64%	-.14%	-1.58%	3.13%
Return on Equity %				-.96%	-10.91%	24.39%
Debt to Equity				4.18	4.46	4.36

CONTACT INFORMATION:

Phone: 610-444-6350 Fax: 610-925-4000
Toll-Free:
Address: 101 E. State St., Kennett Square, PA 19348 United States

STOCK TICKER/OTHER:

Stock Ticker: GEN
Exchange: NYS
Employees: 82,000
Fiscal Year Ends:
Parent Company:

SALARIES/BONUSES:

Top Exec. Salary: $888,908 Bonus: $
Second Exec. Salary: $515,526 Bonus: $

OTHER THOUGHTS:

Estimated Female Officers or Directors: 2
Hot Spot for Advancement for Women/Minorities:

GenMark Diagnostics Inc

www.genmarkdx.com

NAIC Code: 325,413

TYPES OF BUSINESS:

Diagnostic Instruments

BRANDS/DIVISIONS/AFFILIATES:

XT-8
eSensor
ePlex

CONTACTS:

Note: Officers with more than one job title may be intentionally listed here more than once.

Scott Mendel, CFO
James Fox, Chairman of the Board
Hany Massarany, Director
Eric Stier, General Counsel
James McNally, Senior VP, Divisional
Brian Mitchell, Senior VP, Divisional
Jennifer Williams, Senior VP, Divisional
Mike Gleeson, Senior VP, Divisional

GROWTH PLANS/SPECIAL FEATURES:

GenMark Diagnostics, Inc. is a molecular diagnostics company primarily involved in the development and commercialization of its proprietary eSensor detection technology. The firm's products detect and measure DNA and RNA targets to diagnose disease and to optimize patient treatment. The eSensor detection technology uses electrochemical technology to enable fast, accurate and highly sensitive detection of up to 72 distinct segments of target DNA, referred to as biomarkers, in a single sample. GenMark's XT-8 supports a range of molecular diagnostic tests with a compact workstation and self-contained, disposable test cartridges, offering results in as little as 30 minutes. Four of the firm's diagnostic tests have received U.S. Food and Drug Administration (FDA) clearance: its cycstic fibrosis genotyping test, its Warfarin sensitivity test, its Thrombophilia risk test and its respiratory viral panel. GenMark has also developed several hepatitis C virus (HCV) genotyping tests and custom manufactured reagents. In addition, the firm has designed the ePlex system, which is a sample-to-answer instrument that integrates automated nucleic acid extraction and amplification with its eSensor detection technology to enable operators using ePlex to place a raw or a minimally-prepared patient sample directly into the company's test cartridge and obtain results without any additional steps. Development programs for seven assays of the ePlex instrument includes a respiratory panel, gram-positive and gram-negative blood culture ID panels, a gastrointestinal pathogen panel, an HCV genotyping test, a central nervous system panel and a fungal panel. GenMark's manufacturing operations are located at its Carlsbad, California facility.

FINANCIAL DATA:

Note: Data for latest year may not have been available at press time.

In U.S. $	2017	2016	2015	2014	2013	2012
Revenue	52,519,000	49,274,000	39,411,000	30,594,000	27,404,000	20,469,000
R&D Expense	42,760,000	49,458,000	37,472,000	31,823,000	22,060,000	13,536,000
Operating Income	-59,517,000	-48,981,000	-41,535,000	-39,054,000	-34,880,000	-21,891,000
Operating Margin %	-113.32%	-99.40%	-105.38%	-127.65%	-127.28%	-106.94%
SGA Expense	36,762,000	29,097,000	28,157,000	24,698,000	24,330,000	17,184,000
Net Income	-61,850,000	-50,601,000	-42,197,000	-38,263,000	-33,643,000	-22,103,000
Operating Cash Flow	-53,422,000	-35,637,000	-31,915,000	-29,572,000	-23,796,000	-16,243,000
Capital Expenditure	5,315,000	8,500,000	4,306,000	6,076,000	5,152,000	4,803,000
EBITDA	-53,390,000	-45,049,000	-37,872,000	-36,160,000	-31,050,000	-20,708,000
Return on Assets %	-61.27%	-67.02%	-51.89%	-35.80%	-35.45%	-41.62%
Return on Equity %	-113.93%	-116.66%	-66.65%	-40.88%	-40.62%	-50.76%
Debt to Equity	0.28	0.31	0.20			

CONTACT INFORMATION:

Phone: 760 448-4300 Fax: 760 448-4301
Toll-Free: 800-373-6767
Address: 5964 La Place Ct., Carlsbad, CA 92008 United States

STOCK TICKER/OTHER:

Stock Ticker: GNMK Exchange: NAS
Employees: 308 Fiscal Year Ends: 12/31
Parent Company:

SALARIES/BONUSES:

Top Exec. Salary: $490,345 Bonus: $
Second Exec. Salary: $344,142 Bonus: $

OTHER THOUGHTS:

Estimated Female Officers or Directors: 2
Hot Spot for Advancement for Women/Minorities:

Gerresheimer AG

www.gerresheimer.com

NAIC Code: 339,100

TYPES OF BUSINESS:

Surgical and Medical Instrument Manufacturing

BRANDS/DIVISIONS/AFFILIATES:

Sensile Medical AG

CONTACTS:

Note: Officers with more than one job title may be intentionally listed here more than once.

Rainer Beaujean, CFO
Andreas Schutte, Head-Plastics Systems Div.
Stefan Grote, Head-Tubular Glass Div.

GROWTH PLANS/SPECIAL FEATURES:

Gerresheimer AG is a German manufacturer of specialty products made of glass and plastic for the global pharmacy and healthcare industry. The company's pharma and healthcare segment manufactures bottles, vials, ampoules, cartridges, syringes, other drug delivery devices, and medical and diagnostic products for the pharmaceutical, medical, cosmetic, fragrance, food/beverage and life science research industries. Its services include: development and innovation of business products and processes; quality management systems, specifications and objectives; engineering and development of materials made with glass and/or plastic; business process improvement solutions to the Gerresheimer organization, with a focus on quality and customer centricity; and global manufacturing, with production sites in 15 countries, including the U.S., Brazil, India, Spain, Denmark and Germany. In July 2018, Gerresheimer acquired Sensile Medical AG, which develops innovative drug delivery products and platforms, including digital connected capabilities.

FINANCIAL DATA:

Note: Data for latest year may not have been available at press time.

In U.S. $	2017	2016	2015	2014	2013	2012
Revenue	1,567,921,000	1,599,558,000	1,601,619,000	1,500,193,000	1,472,184,000	1,417,686,000
R&D Expense	4,079,544	3,678,335	2,147,924	1,744,389	2,497,965	
Operating Income	210,124,400	212,345,600	177,140,400	168,974,300	162,132,800	150,053,500
Operating Margin %	13.40%	13.27%	11.06%	11.26%	11.01%	10.58%
SGA Expense	297,207,800	296,981,100	304,699,400	250,875,700	268,819,600	256,743,800
Net Income	117,324,100	141,456,000	121,196,700	77,143,860	72,281,660	69,997,680
Operating Cash Flow	254,870,400	201,752,500	236,976,400	184,074,900	170,573,300	201,844,400
Capital Expenditure	135,503,000	128,760,300	146,294,900	146,119,300	138,444,000	138,233,500
EBITDA	355,037,800	356,649,600	356,945,000	276,370,500	254,333,100	266,393,800
Return on Assets %	4.18%	5.07%	5.11%	4.05%	3.91%	3.91%
Return on Equity %	13.64%	17.98%	17.81%	12.64%	11.94%	11.50%
Debt to Equity	0.90	1.00	1.16	0.68	0.75	0.78

CONTACT INFORMATION:

Phone: 49 0211618100 Fax: 49 02116181295
Toll-Free:
Address: Klaus-Bunger-Strasse 4, Duesseldorf, 40468 Germany

STOCK TICKER/OTHER:

Stock Ticker: GRRMF
Employees: 9,749
Parent Company:
Exchange: GREY
Fiscal Year Ends: 12/31

SALARIES/BONUSES:

Top Exec. Salary: $ Bonus: $
Second Exec. Salary: $ Bonus: $

OTHER THOUGHTS:

Estimated Female Officers or Directors: 3
Hot Spot for Advancement for Women/Minorities: Y

Getinge AB

www.getingegroup.com

NAIC Code: 339,100

TYPES OF BUSINESS:

Medical Equipment Manufacturing

BRANDS/DIVISIONS/AFFILIATES:

CONTACTS:

Note: Officers with more than one job title may be intentionally listed here more than once.

Mattias Perjos, CEO/Pres.
Lars Sandstrom, CFO
Magnus Lundback, Exec. VP-Human Resources
Heinz Jacqui, Exec. VP-Medical Systems
Anders Grahn, Exec. VP-Infection Control
Alex Myers, Exec. VP-Extended Care
Carl Bennet, Chmn.

GROWTH PLANS/SPECIAL FEATURES:

Getinge AB was founded in 1904 in Sweden, and provides products and solutions to health care and life science organizations. For hospital departments, Getinge offers complete settings for operating rooms, intensive care units, emergency rooms, catheter labs, flexible endoscope reprocessing, hybrid operating rooms, recovery rooms and central sterile services departments, when it comes to integrated solutions and patient outcomes. The firm offers acute care therapies for clinical professionals practicing in a hospital setting, as well as sterilization and hygiene solutions for practices of all sizes-whether a single clinician studio or a multi-unit clinic. Acute care solutions include beating heart surgery, dialysis access, endoscopic vessel harvesting, hernia repair, mechanical ventilation, on-pump surgery, peripheral stenting and more. Getinge's life science solutions include a comprehensive line of equipment, technical expertise and consultative services to meet both common and highly-specialized process needs for contamination prevention in biopharmaceutical production, biomedical research, medical device manufacturing and laboratory applications. Besides hospitals and acute care facilities, the company also serves clinics and dental facilities. Getinge builds workplaces with the ability to keep up with current demands while also adapting to future growth. The company's integrated workflow solutions include patient flow management, operating room integration and sterile supply management.

FINANCIAL DATA:

Note: Data for latest year may not have been available at press time.

In U.S. $	2017	2016	2015	2014	2013	2012
Revenue						
R&D Expense						
Operating Income						
Operating Margin %						
SGA Expense						
Net Income						
Operating Cash Flow						
Capital Expenditure						
EBITDA						
Return on Assets %						
Return on Equity %						
Debt to Equity						

CONTACT INFORMATION:

Phone: 46 103350000 Fax: 46 103355640
Toll-Free:
Address: Theres Svenssons gata 7, Gothenburg, 402 72 Sweden

STOCK TICKER/OTHER:

Stock Ticker: GNGBF
Exchange: PINX
Employees: 10,558
Fiscal Year Ends: 12/31
Parent Company:

SALARIES/BONUSES:

Top Exec. Salary: $ Bonus: $
Second Exec. Salary: $ Bonus: $

OTHER THOUGHTS:

Estimated Female Officers or Directors: 2
Hot Spot for Advancement for Women/Minorities:

Gilead Sciences Inc

www.gilead.com

NAIC Code: 325,412

TYPES OF BUSINESS:

Viral & Bacterial Infections Drugs
Respiratory & Cardiopulmonary Diseases Drugs

BRANDS/DIVISIONS/AFFILIATES:

Kite Pharma Inc
Cell Design Labs Inc
Sovaldi
Harvoni
Vemlidy
Yescarta
synNotch
Throttle

CONTACTS: *Note: Officers with more than one job title may be intentionally listed here more than once.*

John Milligan, CEO
Robin Washington, CFO
John Martin, Chairman of the Board
Kevin Young, COO
Gregg Alton, Executive VP, Divisional
Norbert Bischofberger, Executive VP, Divisional

GROWTH PLANS/SPECIAL FEATURES:

Gilead Sciences, Inc. is a research-based biopharmaceutical company that discovers, develops and commercializes innovative medicines in the areas of unmet medical need. The firm's primary areas of focus include human immunodeficiency virus (HIV), acquired immunodeficiency syndrome (AIDS), liver diseases, hematology/oncology and inflammation/respiratory diseases. In relation to HIV/AIDS, Gilead has six single tablet regimens available for treatment. In relation to liver diseases, the company provides products that meet the needs of almost all hepatitis C virus (HCV) patients regardless of disease severity, genotype or prior treatment, and include Sovaldi, Harvoni, Epclusa and Vemlidy, with others in various phases of study. In relation to hematology/oncology, subsidiary Kite Pharma, Inc. is a leader in cellular therapy and provides a foundation from which it will drive continued innovation for people with advanced cancers. Kite's cell therapies express either a CAR (chimeric antigen receptor) or an engineered T cell receptor, depending on the type of cancer. Its Yescarta cell therapy was recently approved by the FDA for the treatment of adult patients with relapsed or refractory large B-cell lymphoma after two or more lines of systemic therapy. EC approval of Yescarta was expected by mid-2018. This segment also oversees Cell Design Labs, Inc., a pre-clinical stage company with expertise in custom cell engineering. Cell Design is developing two proprietary technology platforms: synNotch, a synthetic gene expression system that responds to external cues which can be deployed to engineer CAR T cells that require dual antigen recognition for activation; and Throttle, an on-switch that modulates CAR T cell activity using small molecules. Last, the inflammation/respiratory disease segment is engaged in advancing five ongoing Phase 3 clinical trials of filgotinib, a JAK1 inhibitor for the potential treatment of rheumatoid arthritis; and a Phase 2 study of andecaliximab in combination with nivolumab.

Gilead offers its employees comprehensive benefits.

FINANCIAL DATA: *Note: Data for latest year may not have been available at press time.*

In U.S. $	2017	2016	2015	2014	2013	2012
Revenue	26,107,000,000	30,390,000,000	32,639,000,000	24,890,000,000	11,201,690,000	9,702,517,000
R&D Expense	3,734,000,000	5,098,000,000	3,014,000,000	2,854,000,000	2,119,756,000	1,759,945,000
Operating Income	14,124,000,000	17,633,000,000	22,193,000,000	15,265,000,000	4,523,999,000	4,010,175,000
Operating Margin %	54.10%	58.02%	67.99%	61.32%	40.38%	41.33%
SGA Expense	3,878,000,000	3,398,000,000	3,426,000,000	2,983,000,000	1,699,431,000	1,461,034,000
Net Income	4,628,000,000	13,501,000,000	18,108,000,000	12,101,000,000	3,074,808,000	2,591,566,000
Operating Cash Flow	11,898,000,000	16,669,000,000	20,329,000,000	12,818,000,000	3,104,988,000	3,194,716,000
Capital Expenditure	590,000,000	748,000,000	747,000,000	557,000,000	190,782,000	397,046,000
EBITDA	15,933,000,000	19,219,000,000	23,445,000,000	16,318,000,000	4,859,817,000	4,251,102,000
Return on Assets %	7.27%	24.81%	41.86%	42.34%	14.06%	13.44%
Return on Equity %	23.53%	72.15%	106.64%	90.32%	29.73%	32.29%
Debt to Equity	1.50	1.39	1.14	0.77	0.34	0.75

CONTACT INFORMATION:

Phone: 650 574-3000 Fax: 650 578-9264
Toll-Free: 800-445-3235
Address: 333 Lakeside Dr., Foster City, CA 94404 United States

STOCK TICKER/OTHER:

Stock Ticker: GILD
Employees: 9,000
Parent Company:
Exchange: NAS
Fiscal Year Ends: 12/31

SALARIES/BONUSES:

Top Exec. Salary: $1,539,462 Bonus: $
Second Exec. Salary: $1,253,208 Bonus: $

OTHER THOUGHTS:

Estimated Female Officers or Directors: 4
Hot Spot for Advancement for Women/Minorities: Y

GlaxoSmithKline Pharmaceuticals Ltd

www.gsk-india.com

NAIC Code: 325,412

TYPES OF BUSINESS:

Pharmaceuticals, Manufacturing & Distribution

BRANDS/DIVISIONS/AFFILIATES:

GlaxoSmithKline plc

CONTACTS:

Note: Officers with more than one job title may be intentionally listed here more than once.

A. Vaidheesh, Managing Dir.
Meenakshi Priyam, Exec. VP-Human Resources
S. Joglekar, Exec. VP-Medical & Clinical Research
Kaizad Hazari, Head-Legal & Corp. Affairs, South Asia
S. Khanna, VP-Finance
M.B. Kapadia, Sr. Exec. Dir.
R. Krishnaswamy, Dir.-Tech
H. M. Buch, Exec. VP-Pharmaceuticals
R. Bartaria, VP-Pharmaceuticals
D.S. Parekh, Chmn.

GROWTH PLANS/SPECIAL FEATURES:

GlaxoSmithKline Pharmaceuticals Ltd. (GSK India), a subsidiary of GlaxoSmithKline plc, is a leading Indian pharmaceutical company. The firm operates its business in three segments: pharmaceuticals, vaccines and consumer health. The pharmaceuticals segment has served the health care needs of India for more than 90 years, and offers a wide range of prescription medicines across areas such as anti-infectives, dermatology, gynecology, diabetes, oncology, cardiovascular disease and respiratory diseases. The vaccines segment develops, produces and distributes more than 2.5 million vaccines every day to people across 170 countries. This division's global vaccines help fight critical diseases such as pneumococcal disease, meningitis, hepatitis, rotavirus, whooping cough, small pox and influenza. It is also a long-standing leader in the private vaccines market in India. The consumer health segment provides everyday health care products such as health-food beverages, over-the-counter analgesics, biscuits and other food products, vitamin and mineral supplements, and toothpaste.

FINANCIAL DATA:

Note: Data for latest year may not have been available at press time.

In U.S. $	2017	2016	2015	2014	2013	2012
Revenue	404,374,100	384,218,800	459,342,300		355,197,300	369,032,600
R&D Expense						
Operating Income	56,192,080	66,512,100	81,791,230		72,246,160	111,144,900
Operating Margin %	13.47%	17.28%			20.27%	30.16%
SGA Expense	40,146,030	40,640,710	47,641,230		39,259,830	35,475,310
Net Income	46,828,100	52,391,360	66,236,990		66,967,740	78,120,100
Operating Cash Flow	32,811,360	19,352,150	46,943,680		39,112,050	43,599,820
Capital Expenditure	42,325,790	32,300,270	22,679,510		8,094,757	5,432,908
EBITDA	74,769,730	84,068,830	108,654,900		101,725,600	118,530,700
Return on Assets %	11.13%	12.01%			15.49%	18.26%
Return on Equity %	18.19%	18.20%			24.10%	28.50%
Debt to Equity						

CONTACT INFORMATION:

Phone: 91-22-2495-9595 Fax: 91-22-2494-9494
Toll-Free:
Address: Dr. Annie Besant Rd., Worli, Mumbai, 400 030 India

STOCK TICKER/OTHER:

Stock Ticker: GLXKY
Exchange: GREY
Employees: 4,620
Fiscal Year Ends: 12/31
Parent Company: GlaxoSmithKline plc

SALARIES/BONUSES:

Top Exec. Salary: $ Bonus: $
Second Exec. Salary: $ Bonus: $

OTHER THOUGHTS:

Estimated Female Officers or Directors: 2
Hot Spot for Advancement for Women/Minorities:

GlaxoSmithKline plc

www.gsk.com

NAIC Code: 325,412

TYPES OF BUSINESS:

Prescription Medications
Asthma Drugs
Respiratory Drugs
Antibiotics
Antivirals
Dermatological Drugs
Over-the-Counter & Nutritional Products

BRANDS/DIVISIONS/AFFILIATES:

Sensodyne
Panadol
Horlicks
ViiV Healthcare
Stiefel Laboratories Inc

CONTACTS: *Note: Officers with more than one job title may be intentionally listed here more than once.*

Emma Walmsley, CEO
David Redfern, Chief Strategy Officer
Simon Dingemans, CFO
Claire Thomas, Sr. VP-Human Resources
Moncef Slaoui, Chmn.-Global R&D & Vaccines
Karenann Terrell, CTO
Roger Connor, Pres., Global Mfg. & Supply
Dan Troy, General Counsel
David Redfern, Chief Strategy Officer
Phil Thomson, Sr. VP-Global Comm.
Simon Bicknell, Sr. VP-Governance, Ethics & Assurance
Deirdre Connelly, Pres., North American Pharmaceuticals
Bill Louv, Sr. VP-Core Bus. Svcs.
Emma Walmsley, Pres., Consumer Health Care Worldwide
Philip Hampton, Chmn.
Abbas Hassain, Pres., Europe, Japan & EMAP
Roger Connor, Pres., Global Mfg. & Supply

GROWTH PLANS/SPECIAL FEATURES:

GlaxoSmithKline plc (GSK) is a leading research-based pharmaceutical company. Its subsidiaries consist of global drug and health companies engaged in the creation, discovery, development, manufacturing and marketing of pharmaceuticals and consumer health products. GSK researches and develops a broad range of innovative products in three primary areas: pharmaceuticals, vaccines and consumer healthcare. The pharmaceuticals division (representing 57% of the firm's net revenue in 2017) develops and makes medicines to treat a broad range of acute and chronic diseases. These medicines are made up of both patent-protected and off patent medicines. The vaccines division (17% of revenue) produces pediatric and adult vaccines against a range of infectious diseases. In 2017, it distributed more than 2 million vaccine doses per day to people in over 160 countries. The consumer healthcare division (26%) develops and markets a range of consumer healthcare products based on scientific innovation. Its brands fall within four main categories, wellness, oral health, skin health and nutrition, and include names such as Sensodyne, Panadol and Horlicks. In addition to its primary areas, the firm also researches new options for the care and treatment of people living with HIV/AIDS through subsidiary ViiV Healthcare. Through Stiefel Laboratories, Inc., GSK also offers a portfolio of dermatological products for such conditions as psoriasis, eczema, atopic dermatitis and superficial skin infections. In early 2018, GSK agreed to buy out Novartis' 36.5% stake in their consumer healthcare joint venture for $13 billion, in order to hold full ownership of the business; and GSK agreed to transfer its rare disease gene therapy portfolio to Orchard Therapeutics, enabling GSK to continue to invest in the development of its cell and gene therapies, with a focus on oncology.

FINANCIAL DATA: *Note: Data for latest year may not have been available at press time.*

In U.S. $	2017	2016	2015	2014	2013	2012
Revenue	39,379,040,000	36,382,490,000	31,208,660,000	30,012,390,000	34,577,000,000	34,480,460,000
R&D Expense	5,839,150,000	4,732,894,000	4,644,185,000	4,500,685,000	5,117,735,000	5,176,440,000
Operating Income	7,906,856,000	7,861,196,000	3,428,348,000	5,617,376,000	7,678,560,000	8,043,833,000
Operating Margin %	20.07%	21.60%	10.98%	18.71%	22.20%	23.32%
SGA Expense	12,617,570,000	12,218,380,000	12,043,570,000	10,757,290,000	11,062,550,000	11,400,430,000
Net Income	1,998,565,000	1,189,746,000	10,986,890,000	3,595,330,000	7,091,514,000	5,955,254,000
Operating Cash Flow	9,024,852,000	8,475,638,000	3,351,379,000	6,752,332,000	9,421,434,000	5,707,390,000
Capital Expenditure	2,872,611,000	3,068,293,000	2,479,943,000	2,284,261,000	2,219,033,000	1,982,910,000
EBITDA	8,045,137,000	5,758,268,000	16,796,030,000	6,705,368,000	11,463,050,000	11,586,980,000
Return on Assets %	2.65%	1.62%	17.90%	6.66%	13.01%	11.05%
Return on Equity %	290.15%	29.24%	179.63%	48.95%	84.89%	65.95%
Debt to Equity		13.04	2.99	3.71	2.20	2.52

CONTACT INFORMATION:

Phone: 44 20-8047-5000 Fax: 44 20-8047-7807
Toll-Free: 888-825-5249
Address: 980 Great W. Rd., Brentford, Middlesex, TW8 9GS United Kingdom

STOCK TICKER/OTHER:

Stock Ticker: GSK
Employees: 98,462
Parent Company:
Exchange: NYS
Fiscal Year Ends: 12/31

SALARIES/BONUSES:

Top Exec. Salary: $1,258,887 Bonus: $2,009,001
Second Exec. Salary: $1,017,546 Bonus: $1,470,224

OTHER THOUGHTS:

Estimated Female Officers or Directors: 8
Hot Spot for Advancement for Women/Minorities: Y

Global Healthcare Exchange LLC

www.ghx.com

NAIC Code: 518,210

TYPES OF BUSINESS:

Healthcare Supply Chain Management
Consulting Services
Data Management

BRANDS/DIVISIONS/AFFILIATES:

Temasek Holdings PL
Thoma Bravo LLC

CONTACTS:

Note: Officers with more than one job title may be intentionally listed here more than once.

Bruce Johnson, CEO
Rob Gillespie, CFO
Scott Kelley, VP-Mktg. & Sales
Steve Cochran, CTO
Christopher McManus, General Counsel
Paul Feicht, VP-Customer Oper.
Tina Vatanka Murphy, Sr. VP-Global Markets

GROWTH PLANS/SPECIAL FEATURES:

Global Healthcare Exchange LLC (GHX) improves health care efficacy through automation, cost reductions and improved decision making. The firm was founded by various top medical products manufacturers such as Johnson & Johnson, GE Healthcare, Abbott Laboratories, Baxter International, Inc. and Medtronic, Inc. At present, GHX operates its business electronically through more than 4,100 healthcare providers and 600 manufacturer divisions in North America, and another 1,500 provider organizations and 350 suppliers in Europe. GHX delivers a cloud-based technology and healthcare consulting services. Its products and services help automate and eliminated manual supply chain processes. For healthcare providers, solutions include purchasing automation, contract and price management, item master management, requisition and workflow control, invoice and payment automation, supply chain optimization, implantable device supply chain and credentialing. For healthcare suppliers, solutions include sales data analytics, e-Commerce, master data management, pricing alignment, order-to-case optimization, implantable device supply chain, UDI (unique device identification) data distribution and invoice and payment automation. GHX is headquartered in Colorado, USA, with offices in Nebraska and Georgia, as well as internationally in Canada and five European countries. During 2017, Temasek Holdings PL acquired a majority stake in GHX from Thoma Bravo, LLC, which continues to retain a minority position (as of August 2018).

The firm offers its employees medical, dental, vision, life, AD&D and short/long-term disability coverage; a 401(k), flexible spending and health savings accounts; and an employee assistance program.

FINANCIAL DATA:

Note: Data for latest year may not have been available at press time.

In U.S. $	2017	2016	2015	2014	2013	2012
Revenue						
R&D Expense						
Operating Income						
Operating Margin %						
SGA Expense						
Net Income						
Operating Cash Flow						
Capital Expenditure						
EBITDA						
Return on Assets %						
Return on Equity %						
Debt to Equity						

CONTACT INFORMATION:

Phone: 720-887-7000 Fax: 720-887-7200
Toll-Free: 800-968-7449
Address: 1315 W. Century Dr., Ste. 100, Louisville, CO 80027 United States

STOCK TICKER/OTHER:

Stock Ticker: Private
Employees: 600
Parent Company: Temasek Holdings PL
Exchange:
Fiscal Year Ends: 12/31

SALARIES/BONUSES:

Top Exec. Salary: $ Bonus: $
Second Exec. Salary: $ Bonus: $

OTHER THOUGHTS:

Estimated Female Officers or Directors: 1
Hot Spot for Advancement for Women/Minorities: Y

Globus Medical Inc

www.globusmedical.com

NAIC Code: 339,100

TYPES OF BUSINESS:

Surgical and Medical Instrument Manufacturing
Surgical Implants and Fixation Systems
Surgical Technologies
Orthopedic Trauma Systems

BRANDS/DIVISIONS/AFFILIATES:

CAPTIVATE
ANTHEM
ARBOR
QUARTEX
ELSA
KINEX
CONDUCT
ExcelsiusGPS

CONTACTS: *Note: Officers with more than one job title may be intentionally listed here more than once.*

David Demski, CEO
David Paul, Chairman of the Board
Steven Payne, Chief Accounting Officer
David Davidar, Director
A. Murphy, Executive VP, Divisional
Eric Schwartz, General Counsel
Anthony Williams, President
Daniel Scavilla, Senior VP

GROWTH PLANS/SPECIAL FEATURES:

Globus Medical, Inc. is a musculoskeletal solutions company with a focus on spinal surgery via advanced engineering and technological products. The firm develops and commercializes treatments for musculoskeletal disorders. Since 2003, Globus has launched more than 185 products and solutions that address an array of musculoskeletal pathologies, anatomies and surgical approaches. The company's infusion products include a range of implant and surgical options to treat degenerative, deformity, tumor and trauma conditions along the entire spine. Disruptive technologies and related products include expandable cages, minimally-invasive surgical (MIS) technologies, imaging/navigational/robotic (INR) technologies, motion preservation technologies, regenerative biologic technologies and interventional pain management solutions. Orthopedic trauma products include the U.S. FDA-cleared CAPTIVATE compression screws, ANTHEM fixation plates, AUTOBAHN intramedullary nails and ARBOR external fixation system. Other brands and trademarks by Globus include: QUARTEX stabilization systems, ELSA expandable devices, KINEX bone void fillers, CONDUCT ceramic collagen, and the ExcelsiusGPS robotic guidance/navigation system. A significant portion of Globus' implant products are manufactured at its facilities in Eagleville, Pennsylvania, and most of its regenerative biologics products are processed at its facilities in San Antonio, Texas and in Audubon, Pennsylvania. The ExcelsiusGPS is assembled at its Methuen, Massachusetts facility. Other products are manufactured through a network of more than 100 third-party suppliers. As of December 31, 2017, Globus owned 291 U.S. issued patents, 227 foreign issued patents and had nearly 800 U.S. and foreign patent applications pending. The firm's trademark portfolio contains 188 registered trademarks with 102 pending.

Globus offers employees comprehensive health coverage, a 401(k) and various incentives.

FINANCIAL DATA: *Note: Data for latest year may not have been available at press time.*

In U.S. $	2017	2016	2015	2014	2013	2012
Revenue	635,977,000	563,994,000	544,753,000	474,371,000	434,459,000	385,994,000
R&D Expense	43,679,000	44,532,000	36,982,000	31,687,000	26,870,000	27,926,000
Operating Income	163,451,000	155,967,000	172,222,000	138,362,000	101,673,000	114,793,000
Operating Margin %	25.70%	27.65%	31.61%	29.16%	23.40%	29.73%
SGA Expense	267,817,000	222,156,000	214,014,000	187,798,000	182,518,000	168,862,000
Net Income	107,348,000	104,341,000	112,784,000	92,485,000	68,612,000	73,831,000
Operating Cash Flow	159,535,000	171,893,000	121,957,000	79,172,000	93,471,000	76,519,000
Capital Expenditure	51,303,000	40,909,000	50,760,000	24,754,000	23,680,000	24,684,000
EBITDA	205,518,000	194,738,000	196,306,000	160,116,000	121,070,000	132,901,000
Return on Assets %	10.70%	11.84%	14.66%	14.56%	13.54%	19.01%
Return on Equity %	11.92%	13.48%	17.34%	17.48%	15.97%	22.07%
Debt to Equity						

CONTACT INFORMATION:

Phone: 610 930-1800 Fax:
Toll-Free:
Address: 2560 General Armistead Ave., Audubon, PA 19403 United States

STOCK TICKER/OTHER:

Stock Ticker: GMED
Employees: 1,400
Parent Company:
Exchange: NYS
Fiscal Year Ends: 12/31

SALARIES/BONUSES:

Top Exec. Salary: $396,483 Bonus: $
Second Exec. Salary: $374,290 Bonus: $

OTHER THOUGHTS:

Estimated Female Officers or Directors:
Hot Spot for Advancement for Women/Minorities:

Grand Rounds (Consulting Medical Associates Inc)

www.grandrounds.com

NAIC Code: 511210D

TYPES OF BUSINESS:

Computer Software, Healthcare & Biotechnology

BRANDS/DIVISIONS/AFFILIATES:

Consulting Medical Associates Inc
www.grandrounds.com
Grand Rounds

CONTACTS:

Note: Officers with more than one job title may be intentionally listed here more than once.

Owen Tripp, CEO
Gabe Cortes, CFO
Nupur Srivastava, VP-Product
Wade Chambers, CTO

GROWTH PLANS/SPECIAL FEATURES:

Grand Rounds, owned and operated by Consulting Medical Associates, Inc., is an online platform which provides an employer-based solution that gives employees and their families the technology, information and support needed to make health care decisions. The www.grandrounds.com website and Grand Rounds mobile app are divided into three categories: patient members, employers and providers. For patients, physicians can provide second opinions on a current diagnosis and treatment plan, with no travel required and the process is completed in a matter of days. Appointments can be made, medical records forwarded, as well as insurance compatibility verified. If a loved one is admitted to a hospital, the platform can connect family members with that loved one as well as with his/her hospital care team. Experts who consult on second opinions include leading physicians that are quality-verified, as are those who perform in-person office visits. For employers, the platform provides a comprehensive health benefit that meets patient needs throughout their health care journey, including expert opinions, in-hospital treatment decision support, records collection, long-term patient follow-up, patient/physician matching, concierge-style office visits and scheduling, as well as patient preparation for interactions with physicians. For providers, the platform enables patients to request appointments, a care team reviews patient history and matches the patients with appropriate physicians, and then books appointments. Since not everyone knows where to go or what kind of physician to contact, Grand Rounds' solutions can reduce unnecessary appointments and hassles.

FINANCIAL DATA:

Note: Data for latest year may not have been available at press time.

In U.S. $	2017	2016	2015	2014	2013	2012
Revenue						
R&D Expense						
Operating Income						
Operating Margin %						
SGA Expense						
Net Income						
Operating Cash Flow						
Capital Expenditure						
EBITDA						
Return on Assets %						
Return on Equity %						
Debt to Equity						

CONTACT INFORMATION:

Phone: Fax:
Toll-Free: 800-929-0926
Address: 360 3rd St., San Francisco, CA 94107 United States

STOCK TICKER/OTHER:

Stock Ticker: Private
Employees: 400
Parent Company: Consulting Medical Associates Inc
Exchange:
Fiscal Year Ends:

SALARIES/BONUSES:

Top Exec. Salary: $ Bonus: $
Second Exec. Salary: $ Bonus: $

OTHER THOUGHTS:

Estimated Female Officers or Directors:
Hot Spot for Advancement for Women/Minorities:

Grifols SA

www.grifols.com

NAIC Code: 325,414

TYPES OF BUSINESS:

Biotherapeutics Research, Development & Manufacturing
Plasma Derivatives
Diagnostics

BRANDS/DIVISIONS/AFFILIATES:

Grifols Engineering SA
GigaGen Inc
Biotest US Corporation
Biotest Pharmaceuticals Corporation

CONTACTS: *Note: Officers with more than one job title may be intentionally listed here more than once.*

Victor Grifols Roura, CEO
Victor Grifols Roura, Pres.
Gregory Gene Rich, Pres., U.S. Oper.
Albert Grifols Roura, VP

GROWTH PLANS/SPECIAL FEATURES:

Grifols SA develops, manufactures and distributes a broad range of biological medicines on plasma-derived proteins. Plasma derivatives are proteins found in human plasma, which once isolated and purified, have therapeutic value. The firm operates its business in four segments: bioscience, diagnostic, hospital and raw materials and others. The bioscience segment includes activities relating to the manufacture of plasma derivatives for therapeutic use, including the reception, analysis, quarantine, classification, fractionation and purification of plasma, as well as the sale and distribution of end products. Primary plasma products manufactured by Grifols are IVIG, Factor VIII, A1PI and Albumin. The diagnostic segment researches, develops, manufactures and markets in vitro diagnostic products, including analytical instruments, reagents, software and associated products for use in clinical and blood bank laboratories. This division covers the entire chain, from donation to transfusion. The hospital segment manufactures and installs products used by hospitals, including parental solutions and enteral and parenteral nutritional fluids, which are sold almost exclusively in Spain and Portugal. This division also includes products not manufactured by Grifols, but are marketed as supplementary to the products the company does manufacture. Last, the raw materials and other segment includes subsidiary Grifols Engineering SA, which specializes in biopharmaceutical engineering, providing applied engineering services and machine development for industrial pharmaceutical manufacturing. It is a strategic partner for biotechnology and diagnostic companies. During 2017, Grifols acquired a 44% stake in GigaGen, Inc., a biopharmaceutical company based in San Francisco, California. In August 2018, the firm acquired Biotest U.S. Corporation for $286 million, which included 24 plasma donation centers in the U.S. operated by Biotest Pharmaceuticals Corporation, a wholly-owned subsidiary of Biotest U.S. Corporation.

FINANCIAL DATA: *Note: Data for latest year may not have been available at press time.*

In U.S. $	2017	2016	2015	2014	2013	2012
Revenue	5,021,599,000	4,709,652,000	4,575,606,000	3,902,063,000	3,188,431,000	3,047,964,000
R&D Expense	335,294,800	229,813,900	260,719,900	210,202,400	143,355,000	144,718,000
Operating Income	1,166,814,000	1,092,462,000	1,128,468,000	997,428,800	856,053,100	767,628,800
Operating Margin %	23.23%	23.19%	24.66%	25.56%	26.84%	25.18%
SGA Expense	1,000,521,000	901,577,000	856,419,400	768,428,900	649,448,800	633,878,400
Net Income	770,671,000	634,324,900	618,845,200	546,869,400	401,850,200	298,506,800
Operating Cash Flow	978,888,300	643,421,400	863,795,800	1,138,421,000	688,465,000	589,740,700
Capital Expenditure	375,593,700	340,376,800	659,402,300	333,805,100	201,010,600	193,194,600
EBITDA	1,349,860,000	1,329,719,000	1,284,588,000	1,149,721,000	978,434,800	894,828,500
Return on Assets %	6.29%	5.52%	5.89%	6.58%	6.02%	4.48%
Return on Equity %	18.03%	15.54%	17.87%	19.76%	17.37%	14.50%
Debt to Equity	1.61	1.25	1.38	1.53	1.16	1.37

CONTACT INFORMATION:

Phone: 34 935710165 Fax: 34 935710267
Toll-Free:
Address: Avinguda de la Generalitat, 152-158 Parc de Negocis, Barcelona, 08174 Spain

STOCK TICKER/OTHER:

Stock Ticker: GRFS
Employees: 14,877
Parent Company:
Exchange: NAS
Fiscal Year Ends: 12/31

SALARIES/BONUSES:

Top Exec. Salary: $ Bonus: $
Second Exec. Salary: $ Bonus: $

OTHER THOUGHTS:

Estimated Female Officers or Directors:
Hot Spot for Advancement for Women/Minorities:

Haemonetics Corporation

www.haemonetics.com

NAIC Code: 339,100

TYPES OF BUSINESS:

Equipment-Blood-Recovery Systems
Surgical Blood Salvage Equipment
Blood Component Therapy Equipment
Automated Blood Collection Equipment

BRANDS/DIVISIONS/AFFILIATES:

Haemoscope Corporation

CONTACTS: *Note: Officers with more than one job title may be intentionally listed here more than once.*

Christopher Simon, CEO
William Burke, CFO
Richard Meelia, Chairman of the Board
Dan Goldstein, Chief Accounting Officer
Said Bolorforosh, Executive VP
Michelle Basil, Executive VP
Jacqueline Scanlan, Senior VP, Divisional

GROWTH PLANS/SPECIAL FEATURES:

Haemonetics Corporation manufactures automated systems for the collection, processing and surgical salvage of blood. Haemonetics' customers include hospitals, commercial plasma fractionators and national health organizations in 100 countries. The firm divides its products into four categories: plasma, hemostasis management, blood center and cell processing. Plasma products consist of plasma collection devices and disposables, plasma donor management software, and anticoagulant and saline sold to plasma customers. Hemostasis management includes devices and methodologies for measuring coagulation characteristics of blood, such as Haemonetics' TEG (thrombelastograph hemostasis) analyzer. Blood center includes blood collection and processing devices and disposables for red cells, platelets and whole blood, as well as related donor management software. Last, cell processing includes surgical blood salvage systems, specialized blood cell processing systems, disposables and blood transfusion management software. Subsidiary Haemoscope Corporation develops and sells hemostasis analyzers. The firm primarily operates throughout North America, Europe, the Middle East, Africa and Japan, as well as in other countries to a lesser extent.

Haemonetics offers its employees life, disability, medical, dental and vision insurance; onsite child care; a flexible spending program; an employee stock purchase plan; a 401(k) plan; and tuition reimbursement.

FINANCIAL DATA: *Note: Data for latest year may not have been available at press time.*

In U.S. $	2017	2016	2015	2014	2013	2012
Revenue	886,116,000	908,832,000	910,373,000	938,509,000	891,990,000	
R&D Expense	37,556,000	44,965,000	54,187,000	54,200,000	44,394,000	
Operating Income	39,212,000	48,453,000	45,981,000	49,038,000	60,684,000	
Operating Margin %	4.42%	5.33%	5.05%	5.22%	6.80%	
SGA Expense	301,726,000	317,223,000	334,250,000	365,127,000	323,053,000	
Net Income	-26,268,000	-55,579,000	16,897,000	35,148,000	38,800,000	
Operating Cash Flow	159,738,000	121,865,000	127,178,000	139,524,000	85,074,000	
Capital Expenditure	76,135,000	102,405,000	122,220,000	73,648,000	62,188,000	
EBITDA	128,945,000	138,364,000	132,034,000	130,778,000	126,165,000	
Return on Assets %	-2.05%	-3.96%	1.12%	2.36%	3.27%	
Return on Equity %	-3.59%	-7.18%	2.03%	4.37%	5.16%	
Debt to Equity	0.34	0.50	0.49	0.46	0.59	

CONTACT INFORMATION:

Phone: 781 848-7100 Fax: 781 356-3558
Toll-Free: 800-225-5242
Address: 400 Wood Rd., Braintree, MA 02184 United States

STOCK TICKER/OTHER:

Stock Ticker: HAE Exchange: NYS
Employees: 3,136 Fiscal Year Ends: 02/28
Parent Company:

SALARIES/BONUSES:

Top Exec. Salary: $858,462 Bonus: $
Second Exec. Salary: $425,818 Bonus: $150,000

OTHER THOUGHTS:

Estimated Female Officers or Directors: 2
Hot Spot for Advancement for Women/Minorities: Y

Hanger Inc

www.hanger.com

NAIC Code: 621,399

TYPES OF BUSINESS:

Orthotic & Prosthetic Patient Care Centers
Orthotic & Prosthetic Devices & Components Distribution

BRANDS/DIVISIONS/AFFILIATES:

Hanger Clinic

CONTACTS:

Note: Officers with more than one job title may be intentionally listed here more than once.

Vinit Asar, CEO
Gabrielle Adams, Chief Accounting Officer
Samuel Liang, COO, Subsidiary
Thomas Cooper, Director Emeritus
Christopher Begley, Director
Thomas Kiraly, Executive VP
Thomas Hartman, General Counsel
Lucinda Baily, Other Executive Officer
Scott Ranson, Other Executive Officer
Rebecca Hast, Senior VP, Divisional

GROWTH PLANS/SPECIAL FEATURES:

Hanger, Inc. provides services and products that enhance human physical capabilities via orthotic and prosthetic (O&P) devices and components. Hanger is built on the legacy of James Edward Hanger, the first amputee of the American Civil War. The company operates through two segments: patient care and products and services. The patient care segment is comprised of Hanger Clinic, which designs, fabricates and delivers custom O&P devices through more than 680 patient care clinics and 112 satellite locations in 44 U.S. states and the District of Columbia (as of December 2017). This division also provides payor network contracting services to other O&P providers. The products and services segment includes Hanger's distribution and rehabilitative solutions businesses. It coordinates the procurement and distribution of a broad catalog of O&P parts, componentry and devices to independent O&P providers nationwide. These products are delivered from one of five distribution facilities located in Nevada, Georgia, Illinois, Pennsylvania and Texas. The products and services segment also comprises the firm's rehabilitative solutions business, which develops specialized rehabilitation technologies and provides evidence-based clinical programs for post-acute rehabilitation to patients at approximately 4,000 skilled nursing, long-term care and other sub-acute rehabilitation facilities throughout the U.S.

Employees are offered medical, dental, vision, prescription and life insurance; a 401(k); disability coverage; and flexible spending accounts.

FINANCIAL DATA:

Note: Data for latest year may not have been available at press time.

In U.S. $	2017	2016	2015	2014	2013	2012
Revenue	1,040,769,024	1,042,054,016	1,067,171,968	1,012,099,968	1,046,438,016	985,550,016
R&D Expense						
Operating Income						
Operating Margin %						
SGA Expense						
Net Income	-104,671,000	-106,471,000	-327,091,008	-18,966,000	63,584,000	63,692,000
Operating Cash Flow						
Capital Expenditure						
EBITDA						
Return on Assets %						
Return on Equity %						
Debt to Equity						

CONTACT INFORMATION:

Phone: 512 777-3800 Fax: 301 986-0702
Toll-Free:
Address: 10910 Domain Dr., Ste. 300, Austin, TX 78758 United States

STOCK TICKER/OTHER:

Stock Ticker: HNGR
Exchange: PINX
Employees: 4,900
Fiscal Year Ends: 12/31
Parent Company:

SALARIES/BONUSES:

Top Exec. Salary: $ Bonus: $
Second Exec. Salary: $ Bonus: $

OTHER THOUGHTS:

Estimated Female Officers or Directors: 3
Hot Spot for Advancement for Women/Minorities: Y

Harvard Pilgrim Health Care Inc

www.harvardpilgrim.org

NAIC Code: 524,114

TYPES OF BUSINESS:

Insurance-Medical & Health, HMOs & PPOs
Indemnity Insurance

BRANDS/DIVISIONS/AFFILIATES:

Health Plans Inc
Harvard Pilgrim Health Care Institute
Harvard Pilgrim Health Care Foundation

CONTACTS: *Note: Officers with more than one job title may be intentionally listed here more than once.*

Eric H. Schultz, CEO
Eric H. Schultz, Pres.
Charles Goheen, CFO
Beth Roberts, Sr. VP-Mktg. & Sales
Cynthia Ring, Chief Human Resources Officer
Michael Sherman, Chief Medical Officer
Deborah A. Norton, CIO
Pranav Mehta, Sr. VP-Prod. Dev.
Maura Lapping, Dir.-Admin.
William J. Graham, VP-Policy & Gov't Affairs
Beth Roberts, VP-Regional Markets
Bill Breidenbach, CEO-Health Plans, Inc.
Rick Weisblatt, Sr. VP-Provider Network

GROWTH PLANS/SPECIAL FEATURES:

Harvard Pilgrim Health Care, Inc. is a nonprofit health services company with a network of more than 70,000 doctors and clinicians and 182 hospitals. The firm provides health coverage in Massachusetts, Maine, New Hampshire and Connecticut. Harvard Pilgrim offers a variety of plan choices, including HMOs (health maintenance organizations), PPOs (preferred provider organizations) and point-of-service (POS) plans. The company also enrolls Medicare beneficiaries through its Medicare Advantage Plan, Stride (HMO) and Stride of NH (HMO), offered in select counties in Massachusetts, Maine and New Hampshire. Subsidiary Health Plans, Inc. provides integrated care management, health coaching and plan administration solutions to self-funded employers nationwide. Health coaching support includes smoking cessation, stress reduction, life balance, lowering cholesterol, dealing with back pain, blood pressure control, weight management, exercise and nutrition. Alternative medicine support is also provided, and includes coverage for acupuncture, yoga practitioners, tai chi and more. The Harvard Pilgrim Health Care Institute, which is affiliated with the Harvard Medical School, focuses on medical research and teaching as well as research geared toward patient populations and the healthcare system. Harvard Pilgrim Health Care Foundation provides tools, training and leadership to people in an effort to build healthy communities. It works to increase access to fresh, affordable food to communities and families, and addresses health disparities affecting diverse populations.

The firm offers employees medical and dental insurance, flexible spending accounts, life insurance, short- and long-term disability insurance, a 401(k) plan, tuition reimbursement, an onsite fitness center, long-term care insurance, access to credit unions, employee discounts and adoption assistance.

FINANCIAL DATA: *Note: Data for latest year may not have been available at press time.*

In U.S. $	2017	2016	2015	2014	2013	2012
Revenue	3,000,000,000	3,100,000,000	2,733,898,000	2,545,722,000	2,632,821,000	2,660,539,000
R&D Expense						
Operating Income						
Operating Margin %						
SGA Expense						
Net Income	-8,700,000	-48,500,000	-54,774,000	8,354,000	19,807,000	22,453,000
Operating Cash Flow						
Capital Expenditure						
EBITDA						
Return on Assets %						
Return on Equity %						
Debt to Equity						

CONTACT INFORMATION:

Phone: 617-509-1000 Fax:
Toll-Free: 888-888-4742
Address: 93 Worcester St., Wellesley, MA 02481 United States

STOCK TICKER/OTHER:

Stock Ticker: Nonprofit
Exchange:
Employees: 28,000
Fiscal Year Ends: 12/31
Parent Company:

SALARIES/BONUSES:

Top Exec. Salary: $ Bonus: $
Second Exec. Salary: $ Bonus: $

OTHER THOUGHTS:

Estimated Female Officers or Directors: 8
Hot Spot for Advancement for Women/Minorities: Y

HCA Holdings Inc

www.hcahealthcare.com

NAIC Code: 622,110

TYPES OF BUSINESS:

General Medical and Surgical Hospitals
Outpatient Surgery Centers
Sub-Acute Care
Psychiatric Hospitals
Rehabilitation Services
Hospital Management Services

BRANDS/DIVISIONS/AFFILIATES:

CONTACTS:
Note: Officers with more than one job title may be intentionally listed here more than once.

R. Johnson, CEO
Charles Hall, President, Geographical
William Rutherford, CFO
Martin Paslick, Chief Information Officer
Jonathan Perlin, Chief Medical Officer
Samuel Hazen, COO
Robert Waterman, General Counsel
Joseph Sowell, Other Executive Officer
Alan Yuspeh, Other Executive Officer
John Steele, Other Executive Officer
Jane Englebright, Other Executive Officer
A. Moore, President, Divisional
Michael Cuffe, President, Divisional
Jon Foster, President, Geographical
Victor Campbell, Senior VP
Ravi Chari, Senior VP, Divisional
Sandra Morgan, Senior VP, Divisional

GROWTH PLANS/SPECIAL FEATURES:

HCA Holdings, Inc. owns and operates 179 hospitals and 120 freestanding surgery centers in 20 U.S. states and in London, England (as of August 2018). The company's acute care hospitals provide a full range of services, including internal medicine, general surgery, neurosurgery, orthopedics, obstetrics, cardiac care, diagnostic services, emergency services, radiology, respiratory therapy, cardiology and physical therapy. The psychiatric hospitals provide therapeutic programs including child, adolescent and adult psychiatric care and adult and adolescent alcohol and drug abuse treatment and counseling. The outpatient healthcare facilities operated by HCA include surgery centers, diagnostic and imaging centers, comprehensive outpatient rehabilitation and physical therapy centers. The company's hospitals do not engage in extensive medical research and education programs; however, some facilities are affiliated with medical schools and may participate in the clinical rotation of medical interns and residents. In addition, HCA provides a variety of management services to healthcare facilities such as patient safety programs; ethics and compliance programs; national supply contracts; equipment purchasing and leasing contracts; and accounting, financial and clinical systems. Other services include governmental reimbursement assistance, construction planning and coordination, information technology systems, legal counsel, human resource services and internal audit.

Employee benefits include medical, vision and dental coverage; a 401(k); life insurance; disability; and financial education resources.

FINANCIAL DATA:
Note: Data for latest year may not have been available at press time.

In U.S. $	2017	2016	2015	2014	2013	2012
Revenue	43,614,000,000	41,490,000,000	39,678,000,000	36,918,000,000	34,182,000,000	33,013,000,000
R&D Expense						
Operating Income	6,057,000,000	6,198,000,000	5,965,000,000	5,565,000,000	4,792,000,000	4,816,000,000
Operating Margin %	13.88%	14.90%	14.91%	14.73%	13.38%	13.57%
SGA Expense						
Net Income	2,216,000,000	2,890,000,000	2,129,000,000	1,875,000,000	1,556,000,000	1,605,000,000
Operating Cash Flow	5,426,000,000	5,653,000,000	4,734,000,000	4,448,000,000	3,680,000,000	4,175,000,000
Capital Expenditure	3,015,000,000	2,760,000,000	2,375,000,000	2,176,000,000	1,943,000,000	1,862,000,000
EBITDA	8,202,000,000	8,483,000,000	7,526,000,000	7,044,000,000	6,547,000,000	6,371,000,000
Return on Assets %	6.29%	8.69%	6.65%	6.24%	5.46%	5.83%
Return on Equity %						
Debt to Equity						

CONTACT INFORMATION:

Phone: 615 344-9551 Fax: 615 320-2266
Toll-Free:
Address: 1 Park Plaza, Nashville, TN 37203 United States

STOCK TICKER/OTHER:

Stock Ticker: HCA
Employees: 241,000
Parent Company:
Exchange: NYS
Fiscal Year Ends: 12/31

SALARIES/BONUSES:

Top Exec. Salary: $1,427,500 Bonus: $
Second Exec. Salary: $1,091,667 Bonus: $

OTHER THOUGHTS:

Estimated Female Officers or Directors: 2
Hot Spot for Advancement for Women/Minorities:

Health Care Service Corporation (HCSC)

www.hcsc.com

NAIC Code: 524,114

TYPES OF BUSINESS:

Insurance-Medical & Health, HMOs & PPOs
Traditional Indemnity Plans
Medicare Supplemental Health
Life Insurance
Dental & Vision Insurance
Electronic Claims & Information Network
Workers' Compensation
Retirement Services

BRANDS/DIVISIONS/AFFILIATES:

Blue Cross and Blue Shield
Dental Network of America Inc
Availity LLC
Dearborn National
Medecision Inc
HCSC Insurance Service Company
Prime Therapeutics LLC
TriWest Healthcare Alliance

CONTACTS: *Note: Officers with more than one job title may be intentionally listed here more than once.*

Paula Steiner, CEO
Eric Feldstein, Sr. VP
Nazneen Razi, Sr. VP
Stephen Ondra, Chief Medical Officer
Steve Betts, Sr. VP
John Cannon, Chief Admin. Officer
Deborah Dorman-Rodriguez, Corp. Sec.
Martin G. Foster, Pres., Plan Oper.
Paula A. Steiner, Chief Strategy Officer
Ross Blackstone, Contact-Media
Ted Haynes, Pres., Oklahoma Div.
Kurt Shipley, Pres., New Mexico Div.
Karen M. Atwood, Pres., Illinois Div.
Bert E. Marshall, Pres., Texas Div.

GROWTH PLANS/SPECIAL FEATURES:

Health Care Service Corporation (HCSC) is a customer-owned health insurer which operates through its Blue Cross and Blue Shield divisions in Illinois, Montana, Texas, New Mexico, Oklahoma and Texas. HCSC is a legal reserve company, meaning that it maintains policy reserves according to the standards established by the insurance laws of the various states it serves. The firm provides preferred provider organizations (PPOs), health maintenance organizations (HMOs), point of service (POS), traditional indemnity and Medicare supplemental health plans to over 15 million members. The company also has several subsidiaries that offer a variety of health and life insurance products and related services to employers and individuals. Through its non-Blue Cross and Blue Shield subsidiaries, HCSC offers prescription drug plans, Medicare supplemental insurance, dental and vision coverage, life and disability insurance, workers' compensation, retirement services and medical financial services. One such subsidiary, Dental Network of America, Inc., functions as a third-party administrator for all company dental programs and is registered in every state except Florida. It also offers a dental discount card program. Availity, LLC, a partially-owned subsidiary, operates a health care clearinghouse and provides internet-based health information services. Dearborn National operates as the brand name for HCSC's ancillary benefits subsidiaries, offering group life, disability, dental, worksite and voluntary products. Other subsidiaries include Medecision, Inc.; HCSC Insurance Service Company; Prime Therapeutics, LLC; and TriWest Healthcare Alliance. In August 2017, HCSC launched the Customer First (C1) Innovation Lab in Dallas, Texas, a 32,000-square-foot facility that serves as the company's primary hub for collaboration, incubation and development of new products and services. In March 2018, HCSC sold wholly-owned subsidiary Academic HealthPlans, Inc.

Employee benefits include: medical, short/long-term disability, AD&D and life insurance; 401(k) and pension plans; and various employee assistance programs.

FINANCIAL DATA: *Note: Data for latest year may not have been available at press time.*

In U.S. $	2017	2016	2015	2014	2013	2012
Revenue	36,800,000,000	33,000,000,000	35,000,000,000	31,200,000,000	22,690,000,000	20,714,282,000
R&D Expense						
Operating Income						
Operating Margin %						
SGA Expense						
Net Income		106,300,000	-65,800,000	-281,000,000	684,300,000	1,007,066,000
Operating Cash Flow						
Capital Expenditure						
EBITDA						
Return on Assets %						
Return on Equity %						
Debt to Equity						

CONTACT INFORMATION:

Phone: 312-653-6000 Fax: 312-819-1220
Toll-Free: 800-654-7385
Address: 300 E. Randolph St., Chicago, IL 60601 United States

STOCK TICKER/OTHER:

Stock Ticker: Mutual Company
Employees: 21,000
Parent Company:
Exchange:
Fiscal Year Ends: 12/31

SALARIES/BONUSES:

Top Exec. Salary: $ Bonus: $
Second Exec. Salary: $ Bonus: $

OTHER THOUGHTS:

Estimated Female Officers or Directors: 6
Hot Spot for Advancement for Women/Minorities: Y

Health Catalyst

www.healthcatalyst.com

NAIC Code: 518,210

TYPES OF BUSINESS:

Data Processing, Hosting, and Related Services

BRANDS/DIVISIONS/AFFILIATES:

Adaptive Data Architecture
Medicity

CONTACTS:

Note: Officers with more than one job title may be intentionally listed here more than once.

Dan Burton, CEO
Brent Dover, Pres.
Patrick Nelli, CFO
LInda Llewelyn, Chief People Officer
Dale Sanders, Pres.-Technology
Paul Horstmeier, COO

GROWTH PLANS/SPECIAL FEATURES:

Health Catalyst provides a comprehensive, fully-integrated suite of health care data warehousing and process improvement solutions which enable organizations to improve care. The company was formed by a group of health care veterans with data warehousing and quality improvement experience, and collaborated to revolutionize clinical process models using analytics. The firm's Adaptive Data Architecture platform utilizes a late-binding bus architecture which is agile, flexible and can be implemented in a matter of weeks. The platform helps healthcare organizations to spot trends, map out plans and implement processes, as well as organizational changes, in order to make sustainable improvements in a relatively swift and convenient manner. Examples of the unified data involved includes patient records, patient conditions, co-morbidities and even changes in scientific flow. Health Catalyst's mission-driven data warehousing, analytics and outcomes-improvement capabilities help healthcare organizations of all sizes improve clinical, financial and operational outcomes. More than 75 million patients are impacted by the company's platform. Investors of the firm include, but are not limited to, HB Ventures, CHV Capital, Sorenson Capital, Sequoia Capital, Tenaya Capital, Epic Ventures, Leavitt Group, Cougar Capital and Leerink Capital Partners. Some of the company's clients include Stanford Hospital & Clinics, AllinaHealth, Crystal Run Healthcare, John Muir Health, Kaiser Permanente Thrive, MedStar Health, Nicklaus Children's Hospital. Orlando Health, The University of Kansas Hospital, and many more. Health Catalyst is headquartered in Salt Lake City, Utah. In July 2018, Health Catalyst acquired Medicity, a leading U.S. health population management company.

FINANCIAL DATA:

Note: Data for latest year may not have been available at press time.

In U.S. $	2017	2016	2015	2014	2013	2012
Revenue	70,000,000	66,700,000	41,000,000			
R&D Expense						
Operating Income						
Operating Margin %						
SGA Expense						
Net Income						
Operating Cash Flow						
Capital Expenditure						
EBITDA						
Return on Assets %						
Return on Equity %						
Debt to Equity						

CONTACT INFORMATION:

Phone: 801-708-6800 Fax:
Toll-Free:
Address: 3165 Millrock Dr., Ste. 400, Salt Lake City, UT 84121 United States

STOCK TICKER/OTHER:

Stock Ticker: Private
Employees: 400
Parent Company:
Exchange:
Fiscal Year Ends:

SALARIES/BONUSES:

Top Exec. Salary: $ Bonus: $
Second Exec. Salary: $ Bonus: $

OTHER THOUGHTS:

Estimated Female Officers or Directors:
Hot Spot for Advancement for Women/Minorities:

Health Net Inc

www.healthnet.com

NAIC Code: 524,114

TYPES OF BUSINESS:

Insurance-Medical & Health, HMOs & PPOs
Utilization Management
Health Care Services Management
Administrative Services
Health Insurance Underwriting
Life Insurance Underwriting

BRANDS/DIVISIONS/AFFILIATES:

Centene Corporation
Managed Health Network Inc
MHN Government Services
Health Net Federal Services
California Correctional Health Care Services
Health Net Access

CONTACTS: *Note: Officers with more than one job title may be intentionally listed here more than once.*

Jay Gellert, CEO
Roger Greaves, Chairman of the Board
Scott Law, Other Corporate Officer
Andy Ortiz, Other Executive Officer
Steven Tough, President, Divisional
Steven Sell, President, Divisional
Karin Mayhew, Senior VP, Divisional
Kathleen Waters, Senior VP

GROWTH PLANS/SPECIAL FEATURES:

Health Net, Inc. provides and administers health benefits through group, individual, Medicare, Medi-Cal and dual eligible programs. Medicare benefits include the prescription drug benefit known as Part D. The company also offers access to behavioral health, substance abuse and employee assistance programs, as well as managed healthcare products related to prescription drugs. Subsidiary Managed Health Network, Inc. provides behavioral health solutions for individuals and organizations, working with more than 55,000 credentialed practitioners and 1,400 hospitals and care facilities. MHN Government Services is a behavioral health and wellness provider and contractor to the U.S. government. It offers active service members, guard and reserve components, their families and veterans with coping skills, behavioral techniques and psycho-education to thrive in the face of the challenges presented by the military lifestyle. Health Net Federal Services provides counseling and behavioral health services to military personnel and their families. California Correctional Health Care Services provides healthcare in all adult prisons operated by the California Department of Corrections and Rehabilitation throughout California. Last, Health Net Access provides medical coverage to members in Maricopa County, Arizona. Health Net, Inc. is a wholly-owned subsidiary of Medicaid insurer Centene Corporation.

FINANCIAL DATA: *Note: Data for latest year may not have been available at press time.*

In U.S. $	2017	2016	2015	2014	2013	2012
Revenue	17,850,000,000	17,000,000,000	16,243,587,072	14,008,586,240	11,053,743,104	11,289,092,096
R&D Expense						
Operating Income						
Operating Margin %						
SGA Expense						
Net Income			185,676,992	145,628,992	170,126,000	122,063,000
Operating Cash Flow						
Capital Expenditure						
EBITDA						
Return on Assets %						
Return on Equity %						
Debt to Equity						

CONTACT INFORMATION:

Phone: 818 676-6000 Fax: 818 676-6000
Toll-Free: 800-291-6911
Address: 21650 Oxnard St., Woodland Hills, CA 91367 United States

STOCK TICKER/OTHER:

Stock Ticker: Subsidiary
Exchange:
Employees: 8,014
Fiscal Year Ends: 12/31
Parent Company: Centene Corporation

SALARIES/BONUSES:

Top Exec. Salary: $ Bonus: $
Second Exec. Salary: $ Bonus: $

OTHER THOUGHTS:

Estimated Female Officers or Directors: 8
Hot Spot for Advancement for Women/Minorities: Y

Healthgrades Operating Company Inc

www.healthgrades.com

NAIC Code: 519,130

TYPES OF BUSINESS:

Online Health Information
Health Providers Ratings Data
Consulting Services
Marketing Assistance Services

BRANDS/DIVISIONS/AFFILIATES:

Vestar Capital Partners
HealthGrades.com
BetterMedicine.com
CPM Healthgrades
Patient Direct Connect
Physician Relationship Management
Patient Advocate Center

CONTACTS: *Note: Officers with more than one job title may be intentionally listed here more than once.*

Rob Draughon, CEO
Kate Hyatt, Chief People Officer
James Hallick, Exec. VP-R&D
C.J. Singh, Chief Technology Officer
James Hallick, Exec. VP-Prod. Dev.
Rob Draughon, Chief Admin. Officer
Erick J. Hallick, Exec. VP-Bus. Oper.
Joel Liffmann, Exec. VP-Corp. Dev.
Andrea Pearson, Exec. VP-Internet Prod. Strategy & Oper.
Kurt Blasena, Chief Revenue Officer
Brad Graner, Pres., inHealth Div.
Evan Marks, Exec. VP-Informatics & Strategy
M. John Neal, Exec. VP-Corp. Strategy & Dev.

GROWTH PLANS/SPECIAL FEATURES:

Healthgrades Operating Company, Inc. is a health care ratings and consulting company that provides the means to assess and compare the quality or qualifications of health care providers, including hospitals, nursing homes, home health agencies, hospice programs and fertility clinics. The firm currently offers ratings or profile information on more than 1 million physicians in over 100 specialties. This information is available on websites HealthGrades.com and BetterMedicine.com free of charge to consumers, employers and health plans, with detailed reports available for a fee. Over one million users utilize Healthgrades' services every day. Hospitals with high ratings are given the opportunity to license their ratings and trademarks. The company also provides marketing assistance. CPM Healthgrades offers hospitals business intelligence and communication platform services designed to facilitate a change in behavior among patients and physicians. CPM Healthgrades' suite of products includes: Patient Direct Connect, designed to connect appointment-ready patients with hospitals; customer relationship management (CRM) marketing campaigns; a Physician Relationship Management system, designed to help identify, recruit and maintain high-value physicians; and a Patient Advocate Center, allowing patients to navigate the health care system from before the doctor appointment through the billing process, and includes guidance on how to avoid common medical mistakes and lower health care costs. For physicians, Healthgrades' physician portal allows physicians to sponsor their own profile as an alternative form of marketing. Healthgrades is owned by Vestar Capital Partners.

The firm offers employee benefits including life, medical, dental, vision and AD&D insurance as well as a 401(k) plan.

FINANCIAL DATA: *Note: Data for latest year may not have been available at press time.*

In U.S. $	2017	2016	2015	2014	2013	2012
Revenue	85,050,000	81,000,000	80,000,000	71,500,000	70,000,000	60,000,000
R&D Expense						
Operating Income						
Operating Margin %						
SGA Expense						
Net Income						
Operating Cash Flow						
Capital Expenditure						
EBITDA						
Return on Assets %						
Return on Equity %						
Debt to Equity						

CONTACT INFORMATION:

Phone: 303-716-0041 Fax: 303-716-1298
Toll-Free:
Address: 999 18th St., Ste. 600, Denver, CO 80202 United States

STOCK TICKER/OTHER:

Stock Ticker: Private
Employees: 210
Parent Company: Vestar Capital Partners
Exchange:
Fiscal Year Ends: 12/31

SALARIES/BONUSES:

Top Exec. Salary: $ Bonus: $
Second Exec. Salary: $ Bonus: $

OTHER THOUGHTS:

Estimated Female Officers or Directors: 2
Hot Spot for Advancement for Women/Minorities: Y

HealthNow New York Inc

www.healthnowny.com

NAIC Code: 524,114

TYPES OF BUSINESS:

Insurance-Medical & Health, HMOs & PPOs

BRANDS/DIVISIONS/AFFILIATES:

HealthNow Systems Inc
www.healthnowny.com
BlueCross BlueShield of Western New York

CONTACTS:

Note: Officers with more than one job title may be intentionally listed here more than once.

David W. Anderson, CEO
David W. Anderson, Pres.
Cheryl A. Howe, Exec. VP
Linda Kramer, Dir.-Bus. Intelligence & Enterprise Architecture
Karen Merkel-Liberatore, Sr. Dir.-Public Rel. & Comm.

GROWTH PLANS/SPECIAL FEATURES:

HealthNow New York, Inc. provides diversified health benefits. The company offers its innovative products, services and technologies to individuals, families, employers and organizations to help improve the availability, quality and cost of health care. Coverage for members includes $0 co-pay on 140 services; discounts at health facilities; and online tools for personal health management. Products and services include a personal health concierge to advocate for members, worksite wellness programs, health promotion services, behavioral health services, disease and care management services, pharmacy benefit management, as well as a nationally-recognized physician and hospital quality incentive plan. Medicare & HIPAA (Health Insurance Portability and Accountability Act of 1996) information and forms are available on the company's website, www.healthnowny.com. Subsidiary BlueCross BlueShield of Western New York offers commercial health plans, Medicare Advantage plans, individual and family plans, dental plans, vision plans, Medicaid and Child Health Plus benefits. In addition, it offers personal health advocate services and a BlueCross BlueShield wellness debit card. HealthNow New York itself is a subsidiary of HealthNow Systems, Inc.

Healthnow New York provides its employees life, medical and dental insurance; AD&D and disability insurance; a 401(k) savings plan with company match; spending accounts; short- and long-term disability insurance; term life insurance; and tuition assistance.

FINANCIAL DATA:

Note: Data for latest year may not have been available at press time.

In U.S. $	2017	2016	2015	2014	2013	2012
Revenue	2,415,000,000	2,300,000,000	2,250,000,000	2,635,000,000	2,500,000,000	2,460,000,000
R&D Expense						
Operating Income						
Operating Margin %						
SGA Expense						
Net Income		4,200,000	350,000,000	-52,300,000	310,000,000	31,500,000
Operating Cash Flow						
Capital Expenditure						
EBITDA						
Return on Assets %						
Return on Equity %						
Debt to Equity						

CONTACT INFORMATION:

Phone: 716-887-9380 Fax: 716-887-8981
Toll-Free:
Address: 257 West Genesee St., Buffalo, NY 14202 United States

STOCK TICKER/OTHER:

Stock Ticker: Private
Exchange:
Employees: 1,350
Fiscal Year Ends: 12/31
Parent Company: HealthNow Systems Inc

SALARIES/BONUSES:

Top Exec. Salary: $ Bonus: $
Second Exec. Salary: $ Bonus: $

OTHER THOUGHTS:

Estimated Female Officers or Directors:
Hot Spot for Advancement for Women/Minorities: Y

Healthscope Ltd

www.healthscope.com.au

NAIC Code: 622,110

TYPES OF BUSINESS:

General Medical and Surgical Hospitals
Health Care Services
Rehabilitation
Maternity
Mental Health
Residential Care

GROWTH PLANS/SPECIAL FEATURES:

Healthscope Ltd. is a health care services provider in Australia. The company provides medical and surgical services at more than 30 acute care hospitals, rehabilitation services at six rehab hospitals and maternity services at 12 maternity units throughout the country. Medical and surgical services include bariatric surgery, cardiology, cardiothoracic surgery, colorectal surgery, ear/nose/throat, endocrinology, gastroenterology, general surgery, gynecology, hematology, internal medicine, neurology, neurosurgery, obstetrics, oncology, oral/maxillo surgery, orthopedic surgery, pediatric surgery, plastic/reconstructive surgery, respiratory medicine, urology and vascular surgery. Other services include rehabilitation, mental health, maternity, emergency care, post-hospital care, attendant care and residential care for those with acquired brain injuries and disabilities. Healthscope's international pathology division offers human pathology services across New Zealand, Malaysia, Singapore and Vietnam, as well as veterinary pathology services throughout New Zealand via Gribbles Veterinary.

BRANDS/DIVISIONS/AFFILIATES:

CONTACTS: *Note: Officers with more than one job title may be intentionally listed here more than once.*

Gordon Ballantyne, CEO
Michael Sammells, CFO

FINANCIAL DATA: *Note: Data for latest year may not have been available at press time.*

In U.S. $	2017	2016	2015	2014	2013	2012
Revenue						
R&D Expense						
Operating Income						
Operating Margin %						
SGA Expense						
Net Income						
Operating Cash Flow						
Capital Expenditure						
EBITDA						
Return on Assets %						
Return on Equity %						
Debt to Equity						

CONTACT INFORMATION:

Phone: 61 399267500 Fax: 61 399267599
Toll-Free:
Address: Level 1, 312 St Kilda Rd, Melbourne, VIC 3004 Australia

STOCK TICKER/OTHER:

Stock Ticker: HHCSY Exchange: PINX
Employees: 18,113 Fiscal Year Ends: 06/30
Parent Company:

SALARIES/BONUSES:

Top Exec. Salary: $ Bonus: $
Second Exec. Salary: $ Bonus: $

OTHER THOUGHTS:

Estimated Female Officers or Directors:
Hot Spot for Advancement for Women/Minorities:

HealthStream Inc

www.healthstream.com

NAIC Code: 611,430

TYPES OF BUSINESS:

Educational & Training Content
Internet-based Educational Programs

BRANDS/DIVISIONS/AFFILIATES:

Echo

CONTACTS:
Note: Officers with more than one job title may be intentionally listed here more than once.

Gerard Hayden, CFO
Jeffrey Doster, Chief Information Officer
Jeffrey Cunningham, Chief Technology Officer
J. Pearson, COO
Robert Frist, Founder
Michael Collier, General Counsel
Michael Sousa, President, Subsidiary

GROWTH PLANS/SPECIAL FEATURES:

HealthStream, Inc. provides internet-based training, learning management, talent management, performance assessment, credentialing and managing simulation-based programs. The company's solutions are divided into two groups: workforce solutions and provider solutions. HealthStream's workforce solutions are primarily comprised of software-as-a-service, subscription-based products used by healthcare organizations to meet a broad range of talent management, training, certification, competency, assessment, performance appraisal and development needs. The firm's provider solutions are branded as Echo, and enable healthcare organizations to launch paperless credentialing processes, reduce provider enrollment timelines, accelerate provider onboarding processes, and drive improvement through validated provider profiles. More than 2,400 hospitals and 1,000 medical groups in the U.S. use one or more Echo products. HealthStream markets its products and services through direct sales teams based in Nashville, Tennessee (corporate headquarters), as well as in additional offices in Maryland, New York, California, Illinois and Florida. HealthStream has more than 4.7 million subscribers.

FINANCIAL DATA:
Note: Data for latest year may not have been available at press time.

In U.S. $	2017	2016	2015	2014	2013	2012
Revenue	247,662,000	225,974,000	209,002,000	170,690,000	132,274,000	103,732,000
R&D Expense	27,899,000	28,897,000	24,214,000	16,463,000	11,757,000	8,610,000
Operating Income	9,800,000	5,567,000	13,557,000	16,375,000	14,666,000	13,459,000
Operating Margin %	3.95%	2.46%	6.48%	9.59%	11.08%	12.97%
SGA Expense	77,680,000	72,669,000	64,848,000	52,776,000	42,394,000	33,344,000
Net Income	10,004,000	3,755,000	8,621,000	10,394,000	8,418,000	7,645,000
Operating Cash Flow	46,712,000	24,234,000	34,917,000	34,256,000	26,283,000	22,514,000
Capital Expenditure	17,873,000	14,806,000	15,359,000	10,202,000	8,711,000	8,751,000
EBITDA	36,083,000	27,774,000	30,554,000	27,306,000	22,518,000	20,120,000
Return on Assets %	2.47%	.96%	2.70%	4.42%	4.34%	4.65%
Return on Equity %	3.41%	1.32%	3.84%	6.55%	5.97%	6.04%
Debt to Equity						

CONTACT INFORMATION:

Phone: 615 301-3100 Fax: 615 301-3200
Toll-Free: 800-521-0574
Address: 209 10th Ave. S., Ste. 450, Nashville, TN 37203 United States

STOCK TICKER/OTHER:

Stock Ticker: HSTM Exchange: NAS
Employees: 1,120 Fiscal Year Ends: 12/31
Parent Company:

SALARIES/BONUSES:

Top Exec. Salary: $319,300 Bonus: $
Second Exec. Salary: $299,536 Bonus: $

OTHER THOUGHTS:

Estimated Female Officers or Directors:
Hot Spot for Advancement for Women/Minorities:

HealthTronics Inc

www.healthtronics.com

NAIC Code: 621,111

TYPES OF BUSINESS:

Urologists' offices
Prostate Cancer Treatment
Urologic Staffing

BRANDS/DIVISIONS/AFFILIATES:

HT Intermediate Company LLC
HS Amica

CONTACTS: *Note: Officers with more than one job title may be intentionally listed here more than once.*

Russel Newman, Pres.
Gary J. Kozen, VP-Operations
Richard A. Rusk, CFO
Jose E. Martinez, Sr. Dir.-Human Resources
Argil J. Wheelock, Chief Medical Advisor
Scott Eden, VP-Mfg. Oper.
Clint B. Davis, General Counsel
Richard A. Rusk, Treas.
Cornelius J. Merlini, Sr. VP
Joanna K. Napp, Compliance Officer
Russell Newman, VP

GROWTH PLANS/SPECIAL FEATURES:

HealthTronics, Inc. is a health care service provider and medical device manufacturer. HealthTronics offers urological and lithotripsy services and products in the U.S., serving a network of over 3,000 physicians with over 50,000 procedures done annually. Lithotripsy is the non-invasive treatment of kidney stones using shockwaves to break up the stones and allow them to pass painlessly from the body with a short recovery period, usually a matter of hours. The company's lithotripsy services include scheduling, staffing, training, quality assurance, regulatory compliance and contracting with payers, hospitals and surgery centers. HealthTronics also provides benign and cancerous prostate disease treatment services. In treating benign prostate disease, the company uses three technologies: photo-selective vaporization of the prostate, trans-urethral needle ablation and trans-urethral microwave therapy. For treating cancerous conditions, the firm uses cryosurgery, a process that uses a double freeze thaw cycle to destroy cancers cells. For health care providers needing microwave ablation technology, HealthTronic's HS Amica system works by applying heat directly into the tissue through a probe, which agitates water molecules in the tissue, generates heat and causes ablation of the tissue. The system is FDA-cleared for thermal ablation of soft tissue other than cardiac tissue and is typically used for ablation of liver, lung and kidney tissue. HealthTronics also provides related services such as equipment operation, scheduling, training, quality assurance, regulatory compliance and contracting. HealthTronics is owned by HT Intermediate Company, LLC.

FINANCIAL DATA: *Note: Data for latest year may not have been available at press time.*

In U.S. $	2017	2016	2015	2014	2013	2012
Revenue	210,000,000	200,000,000	230,000,000	225,000,000	221,000,000	205,000,000
R&D Expense						
Operating Income						
Operating Margin %						
SGA Expense						
Net Income						
Operating Cash Flow						
Capital Expenditure						
EBITDA						
Return on Assets %						
Return on Equity %						
Debt to Equity						

CONTACT INFORMATION:

Phone: 512-328-2892 Fax: 512-328-8303
Toll-Free: 888-252-6575
Address: 9825 Spectrum Dr., Bldg. 3, Austin, TX 78717 United States

STOCK TICKER/OTHER:

Stock Ticker: Subsidiary
Exchange:
Employees: 600
Fiscal Year Ends: 12/31
Parent Company: HT Intermediate Company LLC

SALARIES/BONUSES:

Top Exec. Salary: $ Bonus: $
Second Exec. Salary: $ Bonus: $

OTHER THOUGHTS:

Estimated Female Officers or Directors: 2
Hot Spot for Advancement for Women/Minorities:

HealthTrust Purchasing Group LP

healthtrustpg.com

NAIC Code: 561,400

TYPES OF BUSINESS:

Group Buying Programs for Medical Supplies
Group Purchasing Organization (GPO)

BRANDS/DIVISIONS/AFFILIATES:

Hospital Corporation of America
Parallon Business Solutions LLC

CONTACTS: *Note: Officers with more than one job title may be intentionally listed here more than once.*

Ed Jones, CEO
Michael Berryhill, COO

GROWTH PLANS/SPECIAL FEATURES:

HealthTrust Purchasing Group LP provides consulting, managed and/or outsourcing services to health care providers. More than 1,500 hospitals and health systems, and over 31,000 other member locations such as ambulatory surgery centers, physician practices, long-term care and alternate care sites have partnered with HealthTrust to strengthen performance and clinical excellence through its total spend management advisory solutions. HealthTrust specializes in optimizing operations across the healthcare continuum via sourcing, value analysis, spend analytics, collections, payments and healthcare IT. The company's supply chain solutions provide significant savings on products and supplies through its group purchasing capabilities. Members are also offered the flexibility to customize contracts for preferred health care items when demand is high within local markets. The firm's physician advisory program consists of a group of more than 150 physician advisors nationwide that combine HealthTrust's clinical research and data capabilities to: present reviews, study and analyze drug- and device-utilization trends, and identify ways to drive value for partners and members across physician-preferred product categories. For the health care workforce, HealthTrust offers labor management solutions that improve patient care and employee satisfaction, enhance operational performance and save money. Workforce management solutions include staffing, recruiting, credentialing and advisory services. HealthTrust Purchasing Group operates as a subsidiary of Parallon Business Solutions, LLC, itself a subsidiary of Hospital Corporation of America.

HealthTrust offers employees medical, dental, vision, life and disability insurance; 401(k); and various employee assistance programs.

FINANCIAL DATA: *Note: Data for latest year may not have been available at press time.*

In U.S. $	2017	2016	2015	2014	2013	2012
Revenue						
R&D Expense						
Operating Income						
Operating Margin %						
SGA Expense						
Net Income						
Operating Cash Flow						
Capital Expenditure						
EBITDA						
Return on Assets %						
Return on Equity %						
Debt to Equity						

CONTACT INFORMATION:

Phone: 615-344-3000 Fax:
Toll-Free:
Address: 1100 Charlotte Ave., Ste. 1100, Nashville, TN 37203 United States

STOCK TICKER/OTHER:

Stock Ticker: Private Exchange:
Employees: Fiscal Year Ends:
Parent Company: Hospital Corporation of America

SALARIES/BONUSES:

Top Exec. Salary: $ Bonus: $
Second Exec. Salary: $ Bonus: $

OTHER THOUGHTS:

Estimated Female Officers or Directors:
Hot Spot for Advancement for Women/Minorities:

HearUSA Inc

www.hearusa.com

NAIC Code: 621,340

TYPES OF BUSINESS:

Hearing Care Centers
Hearing Benefits Management
Hearing Aids
Hearing Care Devices

BRANDS/DIVISIONS/AFFILIATES:

Siemens Hearing Instruments Inc
Audiology Distribution LLC
HearUSA Hearing Care Network
Total Care Program

CONTACTS: *Note: Officers with more than one job title may be intentionally listed here more than once.*

Scott Klein, CEO
Scott Davis, CEO-Siemens Hearing Instruments, Inc

GROWTH PLANS/SPECIAL FEATURES:

HearUSA, Inc. owns and manages a network of HearUSA hearing care centers that provide a full range of audiological products and services for the hearing impaired. HearUSA is a wholly-owned subsidiary of Audiology Distribution, LLC, which is itself a wholly-owned subsidiary of Siemens Hearing Instruments, Inc. The company serves customers through more than 220 company-owned hearing centers throughout the U.S. HearUSA also sponsors the HearUSA Hearing Care Network, consisting of approximately 4,000 credentialed audiologist providers that participate in selected hearing benefit programs contracted by the company with employer groups, health insurers and benefit sponsors in 49 states. Through the network, the company can pursue national hearing care contracts and offer managed hearing benefits in areas outside its center markets. HearUSA services over 400 benefit programs for hearing care with various health maintenance organizations (HMOs), preferred provider organizations (PPOs), insurers, benefit administrators and healthcare providers. Each HearUSA center is staffed by a licensed audiologist or hearing instrument specialist, and most are located in shopping or medical centers. The centers offer a complete range of high quality hearing aids, with emphasis on the latest digital technology along with assessment and evaluation of hearing. In addition, HearUSA offers other products related to hearing care, such as telephone and television amplifiers, telecaptioners and decoders, pocket talkers, specially adapted telephones, alarm clocks, doorbells and fire alarms. It also offers online information about hearing loss, hearing aids, assistive listening devices and the services offered by hearing healthcare professionals. The company's Total Care Program includes a hearing assessment, explanation of results, assistance in selecting products and technologies, hearing aid fitting and adjustments, measurable improvement outcomes and ongoing support.

The firm offers employees medical benefits, a 401(k) plan, access to rehabilitation programs and continuing education programs.

FINANCIAL DATA: *Note: Data for latest year may not have been available at press time.*

In U.S. $	2017	2016	2015	2014	2013	2012
Revenue						
R&D Expense						
Operating Income						
Operating Margin %						
SGA Expense						
Net Income						
Operating Cash Flow						
Capital Expenditure						
EBITDA						
Return on Assets %						
Return on Equity %						
Debt to Equity						

CONTACT INFORMATION:

Phone: 561-478-8770 Fax: 888-888-0009
Toll-Free: 800-323-3277
Address: 10455 Riverside Dr., Palm Beach Gardens, FL 33410 United States

STOCK TICKER/OTHER:

Stock Ticker: Subsidiary Exchange:
Employees: Fiscal Year Ends: 12/31
Parent Company: Siemens Hearing Instruments Inc

SALARIES/BONUSES:

Top Exec. Salary: $ Bonus: $
Second Exec. Salary: $ Bonus: $

OTHER THOUGHTS:

Estimated Female Officers or Directors: 1
Hot Spot for Advancement for Women/Minorities:

HemaCare Corporation

www.hemacare.com

NAIC Code: 621,991

TYPES OF BUSINESS:

Blood and Organ Banks
Blood Products
Stem-Cell Collection
Therapeutics
Temporary Equipment & Staffing

BRANDS/DIVISIONS/AFFILIATES:

CONTACTS:
Note: Officers with more than one job title may be intentionally listed here more than once.

Peter van der Wal, CEO
Lisa Bacerra, CFO
Anna Stock, COO
Steven Gerber, Director

GROWTH PLANS/SPECIAL FEATURES:

HemaCare Corporation provides human blood products and services in support of the field of immune therapy, including stem cell therapy. The firm is engaged in blood, tissue and cell collection, processing and storage, with a robust donor recruitment and management system that supports an extensive registry of repeat donors. HemaCare's procedures ensure a readily-available inventory of high-quality, consistent and selectable primary human cells and biological products for advanced biomedical research. The company, along with participating customers, contribute to basic research and development of clinical therapies designed to manipulate the immune system for the treatment and cure of cancer, degenerative diseases and immune and genetic disorders. HemaCare's products and services address several key markets: immune therapy research, cell manufacturing for clinical therapy; and clinical laboratory instrument development. The firm specializes in custom cell collections for customers who may require donors with specific attributes or sub-sets of immune cells that can be selected in the company's laboratory.

FINANCIAL DATA:
Note: Data for latest year may not have been available at press time.

In U.S. $	2017	2016	2015	2014	2013	2012
Revenue						
R&D Expense						
Operating Income						
Operating Margin %						
SGA Expense						
Net Income						
Operating Cash Flow						
Capital Expenditure						
EBITDA						
Return on Assets %						
Return on Equity %						
Debt to Equity						

CONTACT INFORMATION:

Phone: 877-310-0717 Fax: 818-251-5300
Toll-Free:
Address: 15350 Sherman Way, Ste. 423, Van Nuys, CA 91406 United States

STOCK TICKER/OTHER:

Stock Ticker: HEMA
Employees: 120
Parent Company:
Exchange: PINX
Fiscal Year Ends: 12/31

SALARIES/BONUSES:

Top Exec. Salary: $244,000 Bonus: $50,000
Second Exec. Salary: $189,000 Bonus: $35,000

OTHER THOUGHTS:

Estimated Female Officers or Directors: 2
Hot Spot for Advancement for Women/Minorities: Y

Henry Ford Health System

www.henryford.com

NAIC Code: 622,110

TYPES OF BUSINESS:

General Medical and Surgical Hospitals
Nursing Homes
Home Health Care
Medical Equipment
Insurance
Psychiatric Services
Research & Education
Osteopathy

BRANDS/DIVISIONS/AFFILIATES:

Henry Ford Hospital
Henry Ford Kingswood Hospital
Henry Ford Wyandotte Hospital
Henry Ford Macomb Hospital in Clinton Township
Henry Ford West Bloomfield Hospital
Henty Ford Allegiance Health

CONTACTS: *Note: Officers with more than one job title may be intentionally listed here more than once.*

Wright L. Lassiter III, Pres.
Robert G. Riney, COO
Robert G. Riney, Pres.
Nina Ramsey, Sr. VP
John Popovich, Chief Medical Officer
Paul Browne, CIO
James M. Connelly, Exec. VP-Admin.
David Lee, General Counsel
William Schramm, Sr. VP-Strategic Bus. Dev.
Rose Glenn, Sr. VP-Comm.
James M. Connelly, Exec. VP-Finance
Edie Eisenmann, VP
Susan S. Hawkins, Sr. VP-Performance Excellence
Barbara Rossman, Pres.
Veronica Hall, Chief Nursing Officer

GROWTH PLANS/SPECIAL FEATURES:

Henry Ford Health System is a not-for-profit collection of hospitals and other healthcare facilities in southeastern Michigan. Hospitals include: Henry Ford Hospital, which provides bariatric surgery, cancer care and cancer surgery, heart and vascular care, neuroscience care, organ transplantation, orthopedic surgery, urology care, dialysis, nursing care at home, hospice and eye care; Henry Ford Kingswood Hospital, a 100-bed facility providing inpatient treatment for acute episodes of mental illness; Henry Ford Wyandotte Hospital, which provides bariatric surgery, heart and vascular care, neurosurgery, orthopedics, radiology, robotic surgery, women's healthcare, dialysis, eye care and home care services; Henry Ford Macomb Hospital in Clinton Township, which provides bariatric surgery, cancer care, heart and vascular care, joint replacement services, stroke care, weight management, women's healthcare, business health, dialysis, at-home care services, eye care, radiology, spine care and wound care; Henry Ford West Bloomfield Hospital, which provides cancer care, emergency room services, heart and vascular care, neurology and neurosurgery services, orthopedic surgery, stroke services, urology care, women's healthcare services, dialysis, at-home care services, eye care and pharmacy services; and Henry Ford Allegiance Health, providing cancer care, hearth and vascular care, prevention care, surgery, family and internal medicine, orthopedics and joint replacement, spine/stroke/neurology care and women and children care. Henry Ford Health System is one of the largest group practices in the U.S., with more than 1,200 physicians and researchers in 40 specialties.

Employee benefits include medical, vision and dental coverage; employee and dependent life insurance; AD&D insurance; long-term disability; flexible spending accounts; domestic partner benefits; adoption assistance; tuition assistance, a 403(b) retirement plan; and an employee assistance program.

FINANCIAL DATA: *Note: Data for latest year may not have been available at press time.*

In U.S. $	2017	2016	2015	2014	2013	2012
Revenue	5,980,000,000	5,700,000,000	5,100,000,000	4,700,000,000	4,520,000,000	4,480,000,000
R&D Expense						
Operating Income						
Operating Margin %						
SGA Expense						
Net Income	203,600,000	95,100,000	111,900,000	27,800,000	-12,000,000	28,361,000
Operating Cash Flow						
Capital Expenditure						
EBITDA						
Return on Assets %						
Return on Equity %						
Debt to Equity						

CONTACT INFORMATION:

Phone: 734-973-3090 Fax: 313-876-9243
Toll-Free: 800-436-7936
Address: 27555 Carpenter Rd., Ann Arbor, MI 48108 United States

STOCK TICKER/OTHER:

Stock Ticker: Nonprofit
Employees: 31,000
Parent Company:
Exchange:
Fiscal Year Ends: 12/31

SALARIES/BONUSES:

Top Exec. Salary: $ Bonus: $
Second Exec. Salary: $ Bonus: $

OTHER THOUGHTS:

Estimated Female Officers or Directors: 10
Hot Spot for Advancement for Women/Minorities: Y

Henry Schein Inc

www.henryschein.com

NAIC Code: 423,450

TYPES OF BUSINESS:

Health Care Products Distribution
Dental Supplies Distribution
Veterinary Products Distribution
Electronic Catalogs

BRANDS/DIVISIONS/AFFILIATES:

Henry Schein Animal Health
Oasis
Dentrix
EXACT
Easy Dental
DVM Manager
AVImark
ABASE

CONTACTS: *Note: Officers with more than one job title may be intentionally listed here more than once.*

James Breslawski, CEO, Divisional
Paul Rose, Senior VP, Divisional
Stanley Bergman, CEO
Steven Paladino, CFO
Gerald Benjamin, Chief Administrative Officer
James Harding, Chief Technology Officer
Mark Mlotek, Director
Walter Siegel, General Counsel
David McKinley, Other Executive Officer
Michael Racioppi, Other Executive Officer
Robert Minowitz, President, Divisional
Peter McCarthy, President, Divisional
Michael Ettinger, Secretary
Lorelei McGlynn, Senior VP, Divisional

GROWTH PLANS/SPECIAL FEATURES:

Henry Schein, Inc. distributes products and services to office-based health care practitioners in North America and Europe. The firm serves more than 1 million customers worldwide and distributes more than 120,000 national and Henry Schein private-brand products and 180,000 special order items. The company operates in two segments: health care distribution and technology. The health care distribution segment, which accounts for roughly 96.5% of annual revenue, aggregates the dental, medical and animal health divisions. This segment distributes branded and generic pharmaceuticals, small equipment, laboratory products, large dental equipment, consumable products, infection-control products, vaccines, diagnostic tests, surgical products and vitamins. Through Henry Schein Animal Health, a majority-owned subsidiary, the firm distributes animal health products in Europe as well as the U.S., Australia and New Zealand. The technology segment provides software, technology and other value-added services to health care practitioners, primarily in the U.S. and Canada. Value-added solutions include practice-management software systems for dental and medical practitioners and animal health clinics. Practice-management software solutions include Oasis, Dentrix, EXACT and Easy Dental for dental practices; DVM Manager and AVImark for veterinary clinics; and MicroMD for physician usage. The technology group also provides financial services and continuing education for practitioners. In early-2018, Henry Schein acquired a 60% stake in ABASE, a family-owned distributor of veterinary health care products with a strong presence in Brazil's Campinas region in the state of Sao Paulo.

The company offers employees medical, dental, vision, life, AD&D and disability insurance; flexible spending accounts; 401(k); college savings plan; tuition assistance; and paid time off.

FINANCIAL DATA: *Note: Data for latest year may not have been available at press time.*

In U.S. $	2017	2016	2015	2014	2013	2012
Revenue	12,461,540,000	11,571,670,000	10,629,720,000	10,371,390,000	9,560,647,000	8,939,967,000
R&D Expense						
Operating Income	859,369,000	817,465,000	768,903,000	715,142,000	677,054,000	634,153,000
Operating Margin %	6.89%	7.06%	7.23%	6.89%	7.08%	7.09%
SGA Expense	2,539,734,000	2,416,504,000	2,243,356,000	2,196,173,000	1,978,960,000	1,873,360,000
Net Income	406,299,000	506,778,000	479,058,000	466,077,000	431,554,000	388,076,000
Operating Cash Flow	545,515,000	615,461,000	586,841,000	592,504,000	664,175,000	408,099,000
Capital Expenditure	81,501,000	70,179,000	71,684,000	82,116,000	60,215,000	51,237,000
EBITDA	1,069,574,000	957,508,000	905,893,000	885,607,000	820,267,000	760,412,000
Return on Assets %	5.58%	7.65%	7.57%	7.92%	7.87%	7.70%
Return on Equity %	14.49%	17.85%	16.81%	16.64%	15.98%	15.38%
Debt to Equity	0.32	0.25	0.16	0.19	0.16	0.18

CONTACT INFORMATION:

Phone: 631 843-5500 Fax: 631 843-5665
Toll-Free:
Address: 135 Duryea Rd., Melville, NY 11747 United States

STOCK TICKER/OTHER:

Stock Ticker: HSIC Exchange: NAS
Employees: 21,000 Fiscal Year Ends: 12/31
Parent Company:

SALARIES/BONUSES:

Top Exec. Salary: $665,000 Bonus: $800,000
Second Exec. Salary: $1,382,654 Bonus: $

OTHER THOUGHTS:

Estimated Female Officers or Directors: 6
Hot Spot for Advancement for Women/Minorities: Y

Highmark Health

www.highmarkhealth.org/hmk/index.shtml

NAIC Code: 524,114

TYPES OF BUSINESS:

Insurance-Medical & Health, HMOs & PPOs
Health Care Networks
Dental Care
Vision Care
Home Health
Eyeglasses Manufacturing
Risk Management and Insurance

BRANDS/DIVISIONS/AFFILIATES:

Highmark Inc
Allgheny Health Network
HM Health Solutions
United Concordia Dental
HM Insurance Group
Visionworks
HM Home & Community Services

CONTACTS: *Note: Officers with more than one job title may be intentionally listed here more than once.*

David L. Holmberg, CEO/Pres.
Deborah L. Rice-Johnson, Pres., Highmark Health Plan
Karen L. Hanlon, COO
Cindy Donohoe, Exec. VP
Nanette DeTurk, Chief Admin. Officer
Thomas L. VanKirk, Chief Legal Officer
Jayanth Godla, Chief Strategy Officer
Nanette DeTurk, Treas.
David L. Holmberg, Pres., Diversified Services
John W. Paul, Pres., Integrated Delivery Network
Joseph C. Guyaux, Chmn.

GROWTH PLANS/SPECIAL FEATURES:

Highmark Health and its subsidiaries and affiliates comprise a national, nonprofit health and wellness organization that serves nearly 50 million Americans in all 50 states and the District of Columbia. The organization includes businesses in health insurance, health care delivery, managed vision care, retail eyewear and eye care services, eyewear manufacturing, dental solutions, health risk solutions, and innovative, technology-based solutions. Highmark Health is the parent of seven health care companies, including: Highmark Inc., Allegheny Health Network, HM Health Solutions, United Concordia Dental, HM Insurance Group, Visionworks and HM Home & Community Services. Highmark, Inc. is an independent licensee of the Blue Cross and Blue Shield Association. Highmark, together with its Blue-branded affiliates, collectively comprise the third-largest Blue Cross and Blue Shield-affiliated organization and one of the nation's 10 largest health insurance organizations. Allegheny Health Network provides health care delivery, research, medical education and wellness services through an integrated delivery network of eight hospitals, more than 2,400 staff physicians and clinical and research partnerships. HM Health Solutions provides innovative, technology-based solutions that support the multiple product lines of health plans, with more than 10 million health plan members on its platform. United Concordia provides dental solutions to nearly 8.6 million members, and is licensed in all 50 states, Washington D.C. and Puerto Rico. HM Insurance focuses on protecting businesses from financial risks associated with catastrophic health care costs, and holds insurance licenses in 50 states and D.C. Visionworks is the third-largest retail optical chain in the U.S., operating over 700 locations in 40 states and D.C. Last, HM Home & Community Services provides health care organizations that are accountable for post-acute spend with customized solutions for the entire process following hospitalization, including lower costs, improved health outcomes and improved patient experience.

FINANCIAL DATA: *Note: Data for latest year may not have been available at press time.*

In U.S. $	2017	2016	2015	2014	2013	2012
Revenue	18,261,000,000	18,233,000,000	18,231,900,000	17,000,000,000	14,877,700,000	14,994,300,000
R&D Expense						
Operating Income						
Operating Margin %						
SGA Expense						
Net Income	1,063,000,000	58,500,000	-84,700,000			
Operating Cash Flow						
Capital Expenditure						
EBITDA						
Return on Assets %						
Return on Equity %						
Debt to Equity						

CONTACT INFORMATION:

Phone: 412-544-7000 Fax:
Toll-Free:
Address: 120 Fifth Ave., Pittsburgh, PA 15222-3099 United States

STOCK TICKER/OTHER:

Stock Ticker: Nonprofit
Employees: 40,000
Parent Company:
Exchange:
Fiscal Year Ends: 12/31

SALARIES/BONUSES:

Top Exec. Salary: $ Bonus: $
Second Exec. Salary: $ Bonus: $

OTHER THOUGHTS:

Estimated Female Officers or Directors: 5
Hot Spot for Advancement for Women/Minorities: Y

Hill-Rom Holdings Inc

www.hill-rom.com

NAIC Code: 339,100

TYPES OF BUSINESS:

Equipment-Hospital Beds & Related Products
Specialized Therapy Products
Rentals

BRANDS/DIVISIONS/AFFILIATES:

Vest
VitalCough
MetaNeb
Monarch

CONTACTS: *Note: Officers with more than one job title may be intentionally listed here more than once.*

John Groetelaars, CEO
William Dempsey, Chairman of the Board
Richard Wagner, Controller
Kenneth Meyers, Other Executive Officer
Deborah Rasin, Other Executive Officer
Alton Shader, President, Divisional
Francisco Vega, President, Divisional
Paul Johnson, President, Divisional
Andreas Frank, Senior VP, Divisional
Steven Strobel, Senior VP
Carlos Alonso-Marum, Senior VP
Jason Richardson, Treasurer

GROWTH PLANS/SPECIAL FEATURES:

Hill-Rom Holdings, Inc. is a global medical technology company. Hill-Rom partners with healthcare providers in more than 100 countries, with a focus on patient care solutions that improve clinical and economic outcomes. The firm operates through three segments: patient support systems, front line care and surgical solutions. The patient support systems segment globally provides the following products: surgical beds, intensive care unit beds and bariatric patient beds; mobility lifts and other devices to safely move patients; non-invasive therapeutic products and surfaces; and clinical workflow solutions such as software and information technologies to improve care and deliver actionable insight to caregivers and patients. The front line care segment globally provides respiratory care products, sells medical diagnostic monitoring equipment, and sells a diversified portfolio of physical assessment tolls that asses, diagnose, treat and manage a wide variety of illnesses and diseases. This division's products include patient monitoring and diagnostics products from Welch Allyn, Inc. and Mortara Instruments, Inc., and Hill-Rom's own respiratory health products. Patient monitoring and diagnostics products include blood pressure, physical assessment, vital signs monitoring, diagnostic cardiopulmonary, diabetic retinopathy screening and thermometry products; and respiratory health products include the Vest, VitalCough, MetaNeb and Monarch systems. Respiratory health products are designed to assist patients in the mobilization of retained blockages that, if not removed, may lead to increased rates of respiratory infection, hospitalization and reduced lung function. Last, the surgical solutions segment provides products that improve surgical safety and efficiency in the operating room, including tables, lights, pendants, positioning devices and various other surgical products and accessories. This division also offers operating room surgical safety and accessory products such as scalpels, blades, light handle systems, skin markers and disposable products.

FINANCIAL DATA: *Note: Data for latest year may not have been available at press time.*

In U.S. $	2017	2016	2015	2014	2013	2012
Revenue	2,743,700,000	2,655,200,000	1,988,200,000	1,686,100,000	1,716,200,000	1,634,300,000
R&D Expense	133,700,000	133,500,000	91,800,000	71,900,000	70,200,000	66,900,000
Operating Income	310,800,000	270,200,000	124,300,000	159,700,000	160,600,000	191,400,000
Operating Margin %	11.32%	10.17%	6.25%	9.47%	9.35%	11.71%
SGA Expense	876,100,000	853,300,000	664,200,000	548,300,000	549,500,000	496,400,000
Net Income	133,600,000	124,100,000	47,700,000	60,600,000	105,000,000	120,800,000
Operating Cash Flow	311,100,000	281,200,000	213,800,000	210,300,000	263,200,000	261,700,000
Capital Expenditure	97,500,000	83,300,000	121,300,000	62,700,000	65,300,000	77,800,000
EBITDA	482,700,000	437,700,000	201,700,000	231,400,000	270,300,000	281,700,000
Return on Assets %	3.03%	2.84%	1.53%	3.62%	6.53%	8.25%
Return on Equity %	10.33%	10.45%	4.88%	7.27%	12.56%	15.54%
Debt to Equity	1.56	1.57	1.89	0.45	0.26	0.29

CONTACT INFORMATION:

Phone: 3120819-7200 Fax:
Toll-Free:
Address: 130 E. Randolph St., Ste. 1000, Chicago, IL 60601 United States

STOCK TICKER/OTHER:

Stock Ticker: HRC
Employees: 10,000
Parent Company:
Exchange: NYS
Fiscal Year Ends: 09/30

SALARIES/BONUSES:

Top Exec. Salary: $1,047,692 Bonus: $
Second Exec. Salary: $502,269 Bonus: $

OTHER THOUGHTS:

Estimated Female Officers or Directors: 1
Hot Spot for Advancement for Women/Minorities: Y

Hitachi Healthcare America Corporation

www.hitachimed.com

NAIC Code: 334,510

TYPES OF BUSINESS:

Marketing-Medical Imaging Systems

BRANDS/DIVISIONS/AFFILIATES:

Hitachi Ltd
Oasis
ProSound
LISENDO
SOFIA
Scenaria
SUPRIA
ETG-4000

CONTACTS: *Note: Officers with more than one job title may be intentionally listed here more than once.*

Donald Broomfield, CEO
John Hahn, VP-Operations
Donald Broomfield, Pres.
Richard Kurz, CFO
Sheldon Schaffer, VP-Mktg.
Richard Katz, General Counsel
Richard Kurz, Controller
Sheldon Schaffer, VP
Douglas Thistlethwaite, Mgr.-Regulatory Affairs
James Confer, VP-Service

GROWTH PLANS/SPECIAL FEATURES:

Hitachi Healthcare America Corporation, a wholly-owned subsidiary of Hitachi Ltd., provides marketing and support for all of Hitachi's medical diagnostic imaging equipment in the U.S. Hitachi Healthcare markets several types of imaging products, from a line of magnetic resonance imaginging (MRI) systems to ultrasound and computed tomography (CT) systems. MRI systems include the Oasis model, which combines fast gradients and multi-channel RF technology with Hitachi's 1.2T open architecture vertical-field magnet. Its other MRI models include the Echelon brand. Hitachi Healthcare's ultrasound imaging systems include the ProSound, LISENDO, ARIETTA, Noblus and SOFIA brands. Its CT imaging system includes the Scenaria, a 128-slice CT that enhances patient access and comfort by combining a wider 75cm aperture, wide 48cm tabletop, 88cm thin gantry and a unique standard lateral shift table for easier positioning and lower dose. This division also includes the SUPRIA 16-slice CT. In addition, the firm's ETG-4000 optical topography system is a non-invasive tool for the investigation of cerebral hemodynamics using near-infrared spectroscopy. The system makes it possible to see the brain via absorption spectra of oxygenated and deoxygenated hemoglobin in the near-infrared region of light. This technology provides access to real-time measurements of brain activity, simultaneously measuring up to 52 brain site channels of one's choice. Hitachi Healthcare provides assistance for its marketed products, including installation, accreditation support, systematic preventive maintenance and other services. In partnership with Agfa Healthcare, Hitachi Healthcare also promotes Agfa's portfolio of direct radiography and computed radiography solutions to its MRI and CT customers in the U.S., including hospitals, imaging centers and orthopedic clinics.

The firm offers employees medical and dental insurance, a 401(k) plan, short- and long-term disability coverage, life insurance and tuition reimbursement.

FINANCIAL DATA: *Note: Data for latest year may not have been available at press time.*

In U.S. $	2017	2016	2015	2014	2013	2012
Revenue	204,750,000	195,000,000	190,000,000	185,000,000	175,000,000	164,758,079
R&D Expense						
Operating Income						
Operating Margin %						
SGA Expense						
Net Income						
Operating Cash Flow						
Capital Expenditure						
EBITDA						
Return on Assets %						
Return on Equity %						
Debt to Equity						

CONTACT INFORMATION:

Phone: 330-425-1313 Fax: 330-425-1410
Toll-Free: 800-800-3106
Address: 1959 Summit Commerce Park, Twinsburg, OH 44087 United States

STOCK TICKER/OTHER:

Stock Ticker: Subsidiary
Exchange:
Employees: 400
Fiscal Year Ends: 03/31
Parent Company: Hitachi Ltd

SALARIES/BONUSES:

Top Exec. Salary: $ Bonus: $
Second Exec. Salary: $ Bonus: $

OTHER THOUGHTS:

Estimated Female Officers or Directors:
Hot Spot for Advancement for Women/Minorities:

HMS Holdings Corp

www.hms.com

NAIC Code: 524,292

TYPES OF BUSINESS:

Health Care Benefit Management

BRANDS/DIVISIONS/AFFILIATES:

Health Management Systems Inc

CONTACTS:

Note: Officers with more than one job title may be intentionally listed here more than once.

William Lucia, CEO
Tracy South, Chief Administrative Officer
Emmet OGara, Executive VP, Divisional
Semone Neuman, Executive VP, Divisional
Jeffrey Sherman, Executive VP
Cynthia Nustad, Executive VP
Meredith Bjorck, Executive VP
Douglas Williams, President, Divisional
Greg Aunan, Senior VP

GROWTH PLANS/SPECIAL FEATURES:

HMS Holdings Corp. offers cost management services for government-sponsored health and human services programs. The firm, which acts as a holding company for Health Management Systems, Inc., serves customers such as state and federal healthcare agencies, group and individual health lines of business, government and private employers, and other healthcare payers and sponsors. HMS Holdings serves 38 state Medicaid programs and the District of Columbia, federal government health agencies and approximately 250 health plans. The company's services include: the coordination of benefits services such as cost avoidance services, in which it provides validated insurance coverage information that is used by government-sponsored payers to coordinate benefits properly for incoming claims; payment integrity services, which are services designed to review claims paid by government programs, identify payment errors and then recover any erroneous payments and eligibility verification services, which are designed to ensure that individuals meet qualifying criteria for enrollment in a health care program; and analytical services, offering actionable insights to manage quality, risk, cost and compliance across all lines of business, and for providing consumer engagement services.

Employee benefits include medical, dental and vision coverage; flex spending accounts; life and AD&D insurance; short- and long-term disability; a 401(k); prepaid legal services; transportation reimbursement; and an employee assistance program.

FINANCIAL DATA:

Note: Data for latest year may not have been available at press time.

In U.S. $	2017	2016	2015	2014	2013	2012
Revenue	521,212,000	489,720,000	474,216,000	443,225,000	491,762,000	473,696,000
R&D Expense						
Operating Income	50,431,000	57,669,000	47,572,000	34,204,000	77,178,000	99,512,000
Operating Margin %	9.67%	11.77%	10.03%	7.71%	15.69%	21.00%
SGA Expense	105,654,000	89,381,000	83,121,000	78,963,000	68,701,000	55,274,000
Net Income	40,054,000	37,636,000	24,527,000	13,947,000	39,997,000	50,516,000
Operating Cash Flow	86,464,000	88,639,000	70,716,000	98,761,000	101,181,000	83,039,000
Capital Expenditure	33,043,000	21,019,000	11,817,000	26,201,000	25,783,000	27,466,000
EBITDA	100,796,000	103,036,000	98,219,000	87,859,000	136,118,000	154,742,000
Return on Assets %	4.31%	4.32%	2.82%	1.58%	4.43%	5.65%
Return on Equity %	6.88%	6.96%	4.63%	2.69%	8.28%	11.82%
Debt to Equity	0.39	0.35	0.37	0.37	0.46	0.64

CONTACT INFORMATION:

Phone: 214-453-3000 Fax:
Toll-Free:
Address: 5615 High Point Dr., Irving, TX 75038 United States

STOCK TICKER/OTHER:

Stock Ticker: HMSY
Employees: 2,315
Parent Company:
Exchange: NAS
Fiscal Year Ends: 12/31

SALARIES/BONUSES:

Top Exec. Salary: $690,385 Bonus: $
Second Exec. Salary: $515,000 Bonus: $

OTHER THOUGHTS:

Estimated Female Officers or Directors: 8
Hot Spot for Advancement for Women/Minorities: Y

Hologic Inc

NAIC Code: 325,413

www.hologic.com

TYPES OF BUSINESS:

Medical Diagnostic & Imaging Equipment
Mammography Systems
X-Ray Bone Densitometers
Radiography Systems
Biopsy Systems

BRANDS/DIVISIONS/AFFILIATES:

Cynosure Inc
Aptima
SculpSure
PicoSure
MonaLisa Touch
NovaSure
MyoSure

CONTACTS: *Note: Officers with more than one job title may be intentionally listed here more than once.*

Stephen Macmillan, CEO
Karleen Oberton, CFO
Benjamin Cohn, Chief Accounting Officer
John Griffin, General Counsel
Peter Valenti, President, Divisional
Thomas West, President, Divisional
Allison Bebo, Senior VP, Divisional

GROWTH PLANS/SPECIAL FEATURES:

Hologic, Inc. develops, manufactures and supplies diagnostic products, medical imaging systems and surgical products primarily serving women's healthcare. Hologic operates through five segments: diagnostics, breast health, medical aesthetics, GYN surgical and skeletal health. The diagnostics segment produces the Aptima family of assays used to detect the infectious microorganisms that cause common sexually-transmitted diseases, chlamydia and gonorrhea, certain high-risk strains of human papillomavirus (HPV) and Trichomonas vaginalis. This division also offers viral load assays for the quantitation of hepatitis B and C viruses (HBV, HCV) as well as immunodeficiency virus (HIV-1) for use on Hologic's Panther instrument system. All of these viral load assays are CE-marked and currently marketed in Europe; and the HCV and HIV-1 viral load assays are approved for sale and marketing in the U.S. Other diagnostic products include various assay technologies, screening systems, instrumentation, software and applications. Breast health products include digital mammography systems, a breast tomosynthesis dimension platform, a synthesized 2D system, computer-aided detection systems, stereotactic breast biopsy systems and minimally-invasive breast biopsy products. Medical aesthetics' primary products include: the SculpSure laser system for non-invasive body contouring; the PicoSure laser system for the removal of tattoos, benign pigmented lesions and the reduction of wrinkles; and the MonaLisa Touch CO2 laser for vaginal rejuvenation for postmenopausal women, breast cancer survivors and women who have undergone hysterectomies and who may suffer from changes to their gynecologic health. GYN surgical products include the NovaSure endometrial ablation system, and the MyoSure fibroid/tissue removal system. Skeletal health products include bone densitometry systems and mini C-arm imaging systems. In addition, subsidiary Cynosure, Inc. develops, manufactures and supplies a broad array of light-based aesthetic and medical treatment systems.

Hologic offers comprehensive medical, dental, vision, life and disability insurance; 401(k); and various employee assistance programs.

FINANCIAL DATA: *Note: Data for latest year may not have been available at press time.*

In U.S. $	2017	2016	2015	2014	2013	2012
Revenue	3,058,800,000	2,832,700,000	2,705,000,000	2,530,700,000	2,492,279,000	2,002,652,000
R&D Expense	232,800,000	232,100,000	214,900,000	203,200,000	197,646,000	130,962,000
Operating Income	483,800,000	559,100,000	483,600,000	337,000,000	281,328,000	244,583,000
Operating Margin %	15.81%	19.73%	17.87%	13.31%	11.28%	12.21%
SGA Expense	841,900,000	682,400,000	624,000,000	591,500,000	569,817,000	542,356,000
Net Income	755,500,000	330,800,000	131,600,000	17,300,000	-1,172,838,000	-73,634,000
Operating Cash Flow	8,300,000	787,200,000	786,100,000	508,400,000	493,822,000	370,222,000
Capital Expenditure	107,600,000	98,500,000	89,400,000	80,200,000	90,130,000	83,273,000
EBITDA	1,832,900,000	1,036,000,000	874,100,000	791,900,000	-395,876,000	428,877,000
Return on Assets %	9.87%	4.41%	1.63%	.19%	-12.04%	-.89%
Return on Equity %	30.66%	15.67%	6.35%	.86%	-47.84%	-2.49%
Debt to Equity	0.78	1.42	1.56	2.01	2.18	1.67

CONTACT INFORMATION:

Phone: 508-263-2900 Fax:
Toll-Free:
Address: 250 Campus Dr., Marlborough, MA 01752 United States

STOCK TICKER/OTHER:

Stock Ticker: HOLX
Exchange: NAS
Employees: 5,333
Fiscal Year Ends: 09/30
Parent Company:

SALARIES/BONUSES:

Top Exec. Salary: $1,048,077 Bonus: $
Second Exec. Salary: $555,000 Bonus: $

OTHER THOUGHTS:

Estimated Female Officers or Directors: 4
Hot Spot for Advancement for Women/Minorities: Y

Hooper Holmes Inc

www.provanthealth.com

NAIC Code: 621,511

TYPES OF BUSINESS:

Services-Testing (Health & Life Insurance Prospects)
Health Information Underwriting Services
Medical Examinations
Outsourced Information Services

BRANDS/DIVISIONS/AFFILIATES:

Provant Health

CONTACTS: *Note: Officers with more than one job title may be intentionally listed here more than once.*

Henry Dubois, CEO
Mark Clermont, Pres.
Steven Balthazor, CFO
Jay Zollinger, Secretary

GROWTH PLANS/SPECIAL FEATURES:

Hooper Holmes, Inc. does business as Provant Health and provides on-site health screenings, laboratory testing, risk assessment and sample collection services to individuals as part of comprehensive health and wellness programs offered through corporate and government employers. The company is engaged by the organizations sponsoring such programs, including health and wellness and care management companies, broker and wellness companies, disease management organizations, reward administrators, third party administrators, clinical research organizations and health plans. Provant Health provides these services through a national network of health professionals. The firm's screening services include: scheduling screenings, organizing health/wellbeing events, end-to-end screening management, provision and fulfillment of needed screening supplies, e-documentation for participants, performing biometric health screenings, administering flu shots and other tests, coordinating lab testing of blood specimens and other fluids, onsite health and wellbeing coaching, onsite health consultation services, data processing and transmission, analytics in relation to lab tests, notification services, in-home services and data collection for academic and clinical research organizations. During 2017, Provant Health delivered nearly 1 million screenings. Based in Olathe, Kansas, the company has an additional office location in East Greenwich, Rhode Island. During 2017, the firm merged with Provant.

FINANCIAL DATA: *Note: Data for latest year may not have been available at press time.*

In U.S. $	2017	2016	2015	2014	2013	2012
Revenue		34,271,000	32,115,000	28,524,000	49,160,000	146,255,008
R&D Expense						
Operating Income						
Operating Margin %						
SGA Expense						
Net Income		-10,324,000	-10,874,000	-8,475,000	-11,275,000	-17,598,000
Operating Cash Flow						
Capital Expenditure						
EBITDA						
Return on Assets %						
Return on Equity %						
Debt to Equity						

CONTACT INFORMATION:

Phone: 913-764-1045 Fax:
Toll-Free:
Address: 560 N. Rogers Rd., Olathe, KS 66062 United States

STOCK TICKER/OTHER:

Stock Ticker: HPHW
Employees: 200
Parent Company:
Exchange: ASE
Fiscal Year Ends: 12/31

SALARIES/BONUSES:

Top Exec. Salary: $ Bonus: $
Second Exec. Salary: $ Bonus: $

OTHER THOUGHTS:

Estimated Female Officers or Directors: 1
Hot Spot for Advancement for Women/Minorities:

Horizon Health Corporation

www.horizonhealth.com

NAIC Code: 621,999

TYPES OF BUSINESS:

Managed Health Care Services
Hospital Consulting Services

BRANDS/DIVISIONS/AFFILIATES:

Universal Health Services Inc
Psychiatric Solutions Inc
CQI+

CONTACTS:

Note: Officers with more than one job title may be intentionally listed here more than once.

Anne Constantino, CEO
Mark Blakeney, Dir.-Professional Recruitment

GROWTH PLANS/SPECIAL FEATURES:

Horizon Health Corporation provides contract management services to healthcare facilities, with a focus on behavioral health clinical services. Horizon Health builds, manages and improves psychiatric programs within hospital settings. The company provides its expertise in best practicing, policies, procedures, education and training to help hospitals become effective quickly and improve outcomes. Its services include inpatient care, outpatient care, tele-psychiatry, emergency department, contract management and consulting. The firm utilizes advanced technology and analytics to provide insights into the data collected and analyzed by its systems. Its CQI+ (continuous quality improvement) outcomes measurement system provides a combination of standardized, proprietary and custom clinical case-mix data tools to provide a behavioral outcome benchmarking and performance improvement database. Horizon Health is a wholly-owned subsidiary of Psychiatric Solutions, Inc., which in turn is owned by Universal Health Services, Inc.

FINANCIAL DATA:

Note: Data for latest year may not have been available at press time.

In U.S. $	2017	2016	2015	2014	2013	2012
Revenue						
R&D Expense						
Operating Income						
Operating Margin %						
SGA Expense						
Net Income						
Operating Cash Flow						
Capital Expenditure						
EBITDA						
Return on Assets %						
Return on Equity %						
Debt to Equity						

CONTACT INFORMATION:

Phone: 972-420-8300 Fax: 972-420-8252
Toll-Free: 800-931-4646
Address: 1965 Lakepointe Dr., Ste 100, Lewisville, TX 75057 United States

STOCK TICKER/OTHER:

Stock Ticker: Subsidiary
Exchange:
Employees:
Fiscal Year Ends: 12/31
Parent Company: Universal Health Services Inc

SALARIES/BONUSES:

Top Exec. Salary: $ Bonus: $
Second Exec. Salary: $ Bonus: $

OTHER THOUGHTS:

Estimated Female Officers or Directors:
Hot Spot for Advancement for Women/Minorities:

Horizon Healthcare Services Inc

www.horizon-bcbsnj.com

NAIC Code: 524,114

TYPES OF BUSINESS:

Insurance-Medical & Health, HMOs & PPOs
Workers' Compensation
Utilization Management
Insurance-Dental
Insurance-Behavioral Health
Insurance-Casualty
Insurance-Life

BRANDS/DIVISIONS/AFFILIATES:

Horizon Blue Cross Blue Shield of New Jersey
Horizon BCBSNJ Dental
Horizon Casualty Services
Horizon NJ Health
OMNIA Health Alliance
HorizonBlue.com/OMNIA

CONTACTS: *Note: Officers with more than one job title may be intentionally listed here more than once.*

Kevin P. Conlin, CEO
Mark L. Barnard, VP-Operations
Robert J. Marino, Pres.
Dave R. Huber, CFO
Margaret M. Coons, -Human Resources
Douglas E. Blackwell, CIO
David R. Huber, Sr. VP-Admin.
Linda Willet, General Counsel
Mark Bernard, Sr. VP
Christopher M. Lepre, Sr. VP-Market Bus. Units
Kevin P. Conlin, Exec. VP-Health Care Mgmt.
Kevin P. Conlin, Chmn.

GROWTH PLANS/SPECIAL FEATURES:

Horizon Healthcare Services, Inc., doing business as Horizon Blue Cross Blue Shield of New Jersey (HBCBSNJ), is the only licensed Blue Cross Blue Shield plan in New Jersey. The firm serves over 3.8 million members throughout the state and is a not-for-profit health service corporation. HBCBSNJ provides a wide array of medical, dental, vision and prescription insurance products and services. Its family of companies include: Horizon BCBSNJ Dental, providing oral health; Horizon Casualty Services, providing administrative services to the workers' compensation and personal injury protection business sectors; and Horizon NJ Health, providing healthcare management to publicly-insured individuals in the Medicaid and NJ FamilyCare programs. HBCBSNJ's OMNIA Health Alliance platform aims to benefit New Jersey residents by accelerating the move from traditional fee-for-service healthcare to free-for-value healthcare. Via the OMNIA Health Alliance, members that purchase its health plans have access to all of Horizon's current New Jersey hospitals and physicians with lower premiums, as well as the ability to save significant out-of-pocket costs. This alliance, comprising Atlantic Health System, Barnabas Health, Hackensack University Health Network, Hunterdon Healthcare, Inspira Health Network, Robert Wood Johnson Health System and Summit Medical Group, represents multiple hospitals, their aligned physicians and a multispecialty physician group. Information can be located at HorizonBlue.com/OMNIA.

Employees of the firm receive health coverage, onsite childcare, gym access, retirement benefits, a 401(k) plan and paid time off.

FINANCIAL DATA: *Note: Data for latest year may not have been available at press time.*

In U.S. $	2017	2016	2015	2014	2013	2012
Revenue	12,661,596,150	12,058,663,000	11,331,172,000	10,390,815,000	9,859,477,000	9,369,601,000
R&D Expense						
Operating Income						
Operating Margin %						
SGA Expense						
Net Income		84,635,000	106,707,000	147,481,000	214,086,000	200,415,000
Operating Cash Flow						
Capital Expenditure						
EBITDA						
Return on Assets %						
Return on Equity %						
Debt to Equity						

CONTACT INFORMATION:

Phone: 973-466-4000 Fax: 973-466-4317
Toll-Free: 800-224-4426
Address: 3 Penn Plaza East, Newark, NJ 07105 United States

STOCK TICKER/OTHER:

Stock Ticker: Nonprofit
Employees: 5,000
Parent Company:
Exchange:
Fiscal Year Ends: 12/31

SALARIES/BONUSES:

Top Exec. Salary: $ Bonus: $
Second Exec. Salary: $ Bonus: $

OTHER THOUGHTS:

Estimated Female Officers or Directors: 2
Hot Spot for Advancement for Women/Minorities: Y

Houston Methodist

NAIC Code: 622,110

www.houstonmethodist.org

TYPES OF BUSINESS:

General Medical and Surgical Hospitals

BRANDS/DIVISIONS/AFFILIATES:

Houston Methodist Hospital Central
Houston Methodist Sugar Land Hospital
Houston Methodist West Hospital
Houston Methodist Willowbrook Hospital
Houston San Jacinto Methodist Hospital
Houston Methodist St John Hospital
Houston Methodist The Woodlands Hospital
Houston Methodist Specialty Physician Group

CONTACTS: *Note: Officers with more than one job title may be intentionally listed here more than once.*

Marc L. Boom, CEO
Marc L. Boom, Pres.
Gregory Nelson, Sec.
Carlton Caucum, Treas.
Joseph Walter III, Assistant Treas.
Robert K. Moses, Jr., Assistant Sec.
Ewing Werlein, Jr., Chmn.

GROWTH PLANS/SPECIAL FEATURES:

Houston Methodist is a nonprofit healthcare organization that owns and operates several hospitals and facilities located in Houston. Its hospitals include Houston Methodist Hospital Central, Houston San Jacinto Methodist Hospital, Houston Methodist St. John Hospital, Houston Methodist Sugar Land Hospital, Houston Methodist West Hospital, Houston Methodist Willowbrook Hospital, Houston Methodist St. Catherine Hospital and Houston Methodist The Woodlands Hospital. Each campus is staffed by highly-trained specialists who provide advanced treatment as well as follow-up care. Some of the Methodist hospital's areas of focus include breast care, heart care, neuroscience, orthopedics and oncology. Houston Methodist Hospital, the system's flagship, is among U.S. News & World Report's best hospitals. Houston Methodist Research Institute is home to physicians that collaborate on more than 800 clinical trials. The Houston Methodist Institute for Technology, Innovation and Education is a 35,000-square-foot surgical training center and virtual hospital which provides ongoing education. Houston Methodist Hospital Foundation accepts all gifts on Houston Methodist's behalf and views donor contribution as essential to its growth and success. Houston Methodist Community Benefits support individuals and organizations that provide financial and medical assistance to more than 150,000 patients on an annual basis. Houston Methodist Specialty Physician Group are physicians employed by Houston Methodist that are rooted in an academic and research environment where teaching and continued education are encouraged. Houston Methodist Primary Care Group is dedicated to providing patient care for the entire family. Other centers include long-term acute care hospitals, emergency care centers and a comprehensive care center.

FINANCIAL DATA: *Note: Data for latest year may not have been available at press time.*

In U.S. $	2017	2016	2015	2014	2013	2012
Revenue	3,045,000,000	2,900,000,000	2,800,000,000	2,616,170,000	2,616,169,000	2,331,041,000
R&D Expense						
Operating Income						
Operating Margin %						
SGA Expense						
Net Income						
Operating Cash Flow						
Capital Expenditure						
EBITDA						
Return on Assets %						
Return on Equity %						
Debt to Equity						

CONTACT INFORMATION:

Phone: 713-790-3311 Fax:
Toll-Free:
Address: 6565 Fannin St., Houston, TX 77030 United States

STOCK TICKER/OTHER:

Stock Ticker: Nonprofit Exchange:
Employees: 20,000 Fiscal Year Ends: 12/31
Parent Company:

SALARIES/BONUSES:

Top Exec. Salary: $ Bonus: $
Second Exec. Salary: $ Bonus: $

OTHER THOUGHTS:

Estimated Female Officers or Directors: 5
Hot Spot for Advancement for Women/Minorities: Y

Hoya Corporation

www.hoya.co.jp

NAIC Code: 334,413

TYPES OF BUSINESS:

Semiconductor Manufacturing Equipment
Glass Semiconductor Components
Medical Equipment
Eyeglass Lenses
Optical Glass
Bio-Compatible Bone Replacement
Laser & UV Light Sources
Nanoimprint Technology

BRANDS/DIVISIONS/AFFILIATES:

GROWTH PLANS/SPECIAL FEATURES:

HOYA Corporation, established in 1941, primarily manufactures innovative high-tech and healthcare products. HOYA operates through two segments: life care and information technology. Life care encompasses healthcare products such as eyeglass lenses; medical related products such as intraocular lenses for cataract surgery, medical endoscopes, surgical equipment and artificial bones and implants; and the operation of HOYA's contact lens retail stores. Information technology focuses on electronics products for the semiconductor industry; LCD panels, glass disks for hard disk drives (HDDs); and optical lenses for digital cameras and smart phones. HOYA comprises more than 100 subsidiaries and affiliates worldwide.

CONTACTS: *Note: Officers with more than one job title may be intentionally listed here more than once.*

Hiroshi Suzuki, CEO
Eiichiro Ikeda, COO
Hiroshi Suzuki, Pres.
Ryo Hirooka, CFO
Taro Hagiwara, CTO

FINANCIAL DATA: *Note: Data for latest year may not have been available at press time.*

In U.S. $	2017	2016	2015	2014	2013	2012
Revenue						
R&D Expense						
Operating Income						
Operating Margin %						
SGA Expense						
Net Income						
Operating Cash Flow						
Capital Expenditure						
EBITDA						
Return on Assets %						
Return on Equity %						
Debt to Equity						

CONTACT INFORMATION:

Phone: 81339521151 Fax: 81,339,520,726
Toll-Free:
Address: 20/Fl Nittochi Nishishinjuku Bldg, 6-10-1 Nishi-Shinjuku, Tokyo, 160-8347 Japan

STOCK TICKER/OTHER:

Stock Ticker: HOCPY
Exchange: PINX
Employees: 37,812
Fiscal Year Ends: 03/31
Parent Company:

SALARIES/BONUSES:

Top Exec. Salary: $ Bonus: $
Second Exec. Salary: $ Bonus: $

OTHER THOUGHTS:

Estimated Female Officers or Directors:
Hot Spot for Advancement for Women/Minorities:

Humana Inc

NAIC Code: 524,114

www.humana.com

TYPES OF BUSINESS:

Insurance-Medical & Health, HMOs & PPOs
Insurance-Dental
Employee Benefit Plans
Insurance-Group Life
Wellness Programs

BRANDS/DIVISIONS/AFFILIATES:

Curo Health Services

CONTACTS:

Note: Officers with more than one job title may be intentionally listed here more than once.

Bruce Broussard, CEO
William Fleming, President, Divisional
Brian Kane, CFO
Kurt Hilzinger, Chairman of the Board
Cynthia Zipperle, Chief Accounting Officer
Brian LeClaire, Chief Information Officer
Roy Beveridge, Chief Medical Officer
Samir Deshpande, Chief Risk Officer
Christopher Todoroff, Other Executive Officer
Jody Bilney, Other Executive Officer
Heidi Margulis, Other Executive Officer
Timothy Huval, Other Executive Officer
Christopher Hunter, Other Executive Officer
Elizabeth Bierbower, President, Divisional
Alan Wheatley, President, Divisional

GROWTH PLANS/SPECIAL FEATURES:

Humana, Inc. is a leading health benefits company in the U.S., serving approximately 14 million medical benefit plan members and 7 million specialty products members in the U.S. and Puerto Rico. It operates in three segments: retail, group and specialty and healthcare services. The retail segment consists of Medicare and commercial fully-insured medical and specialty health insurance benefits, including dental, vision and other supplemental health and financial protection products, marketed directly to individuals. The group and specialty segment consist of employer group commercial fully-insured medical and specialty health insurance benefits marketed to individuals and employer groups, including dental, vision, and other supplemental health and voluntary insurance benefits, as well as administrative services only (ASO) products marketed to employer groups. Humana provides health benefits and related services to companies ranging from fewer than 10 to over 10,000 employees. The healthcare services segment includes services offered to health plan members as well as to third parties that promote health and wellness, including provider services, pharmacies, integrated wellness and home care services. Other businesses consist of military services, primarily the TRICARE South Region, Medicaid and closed-block long-term care businesses as well as the firm's contract with the Centers for Medicare and Medicaid Services to administer the Limited Income Newly Eligible Transition program, known as LI-NET. Many of its products are offered through HMOs (health maintenance organizations), private fee-for-service (PFFS) and preferred provider organizations (PPOs). In July 2018, Humana, with TPG Capital and Welsh, Carson, Anderson & Stowe, announced the completion of the acquisition of Curo Health Services, a hospital operator with 245 locations in 22 states, from Thomas H. Lee Partners. The following August, the firm completed its sell of KMG Capital America Company to Continental General Insurance Company, owned by HC2 Holdings, Inc.

The firm offers employees an array of comprehensive benefits.

FINANCIAL DATA:

Note: Data for latest year may not have been available at press time.

In U.S. $	2017	2016	2015	2014	2013	2012
Revenue	53,767,000,000	54,379,000,000	54,289,000,000	48,500,000,000	41,313,000,000	39,126,000,000
R&D Expense						
Operating Income						
Operating Margin %						
SGA Expense	6,567,000,000	7,277,000,000	7,318,000,000	7,639,000,000	6,355,000,000	5,830,000,000
Net Income	2,448,000,000	614,000,000	1,276,000,000	1,147,000,000	1,231,000,000	1,222,000,000
Operating Cash Flow	4,051,000,000	1,936,000,000	868,000,000	1,618,000,000	1,716,000,000	1,923,000,000
Capital Expenditure	526,000,000	527,000,000	523,000,000	528,000,000	441,000,000	410,000,000
EBITDA						
Return on Assets %	9.31%	2.45%	5.29%	5.18%	6.04%	6.48%
Return on Equity %	23.85%	5.83%	12.76%	12.09%	13.55%	14.45%
Debt to Equity	0.48	0.35	0.36	0.39	0.27	0.29

CONTACT INFORMATION:

Phone: 502 580-1000 Fax: 502 580-1441
Toll-Free:
Address: 500 W. Main St., Louisville, KY 40202 United States

STOCK TICKER/OTHER:

Stock Ticker: HUM Exchange: NYS
Employees: 54,200 Fiscal Year Ends: 12/31
Parent Company:

SALARIES/BONUSES:

Top Exec. Salary: $1,272,367 Bonus: $
Second Exec. Salary: $698,779 Bonus: $

OTHER THOUGHTS:

Estimated Female Officers or Directors: 3
Hot Spot for Advancement for Women/Minorities: Y

IBM Watson Health

www.merge.com

NAIC Code: 511210D

TYPES OF BUSINESS:

Computer Software, Healthcare & Biotechnology
Custom-Designed Medical Products
Engineering Services

BRANDS/DIVISIONS/AFFILIATES:

International Business Machines Corporation
Merge Cardio
Merge Hemo

CONTACTS:

Note: Officers with more than one job title may be intentionally listed here more than once.

Anne Le Grand, Managing Dir.
Steve Oreskovich, CFO
Jen Naylor, CFO
Michael Klozotsky, Dir.-Global Mktg.
Monica Chambers, Dir.-Human Resources
Steven Tolle, Other Executive Officer
Kurt Hammond, Other Executive Officer
Antonia Wells, Other Executive Officer

GROWTH PLANS/SPECIAL FEATURES:

IBM Watson Health is a leading provider of innovative artificial intelligence, enterprise imaging and interoperability solutions that seek to advance health care. The company's innovative solutions improve the healthcare experience for patients, providers and payers, and meet the unique needs of specialties such as radiology, cardiology, orthopedics and enterprise systems. Watson Health's artificial intelligence solutions provide contextual relevance by quickly interpreting billions of data points (both text and image data), improve clinical reliability by aggregating and displaying information that may otherwise be easily overlooked, and ensure communication between physicians via structured and unstructured patient data. The firm's interoperability solutions provide capabilities to seamlessly ingest, manage, store, view, share and exchange imaging related healthcare data. The physician referral process can be streamlined, pre-authorization can be automated, patient information can be accessed from point-of-care locations, image viewing is capable from anywhere, data storage capacity requirements can be conveniently managed and retinal screening can be efficiently enabled. Watson Health's radiology solutions provide a suite of products designed to meet the specific needs of hospitals and imaging centers, from workflow to image and document management. The company's cardiology solutions comprise Merge Cardio and Merge Hemo, which together offer a single web-based view of a patient's complete record from all cardiology modalities, access to reporting tools and integration with leading health information systems. Watson Health's ophthalmic image and informatics solutions enable eye care specialists to break down silos so they can better manage clinical images, improve workflow and speed the detection of eye conditions for quality care purposes. Last, the firm's orthopedic solutions provide image management and digital templating for access and storage efficiency. IBM Watson Health is a business unit of International Business Machines Corporation (IBM).

IBM offers employees comprehensive medical, dental, vision and other insurance coverage; and a 401(k) retirement plan.

FINANCIAL DATA:

Note: Data for latest year may not have been available at press time.

In U.S. $	2017	2016	2015	2014	2013	2012
Revenue	236,250,000	225,000,000	215,000,000	212,304,000	231,667,008	248,904,000
R&D Expense						
Operating Income						
Operating Margin %						
SGA Expense						
Net Income				-447,000	-38,980,000	-28,802,000
Operating Cash Flow						
Capital Expenditure						
EBITDA						
Return on Assets %						
Return on Equity %						
Debt to Equity						

CONTACT INFORMATION:

Phone: 312 565-6868 Fax: 312 565-6870
Toll-Free: 877-446-3743
Address: 71 South Wacker Dr., 20/Fl., Chicago, IL 60606 United States

STOCK TICKER/OTHER:

Stock Ticker: Subsidiary Exchange:
Employees: 800 Fiscal Year Ends: 12/31
Parent Company: International Business Machines Corporation

SALARIES/BONUSES:

Top Exec. Salary: $ Bonus: $
Second Exec. Salary: $ Bonus: $

OTHER THOUGHTS:

Estimated Female Officers or Directors: 2
Hot Spot for Advancement for Women/Minorities:

ICU Medical Inc

www.icumed.com

NAIC Code: 339,100

TYPES OF BUSINESS:

Equipment-Intravenous Connection Devices
Custom IV Systems

BRANDS/DIVISIONS/AFFILIATES:

CLAVE
MicroClave
MicroClave Clear
NanoClave
ChemoCLAVE
ChemoLock

CONTACTS: *Note: Officers with more than one job title may be intentionally listed here more than once.*

Vivek Jain, CEO
Scott Lamb, CFO
Kevin McGrody, Chief Accounting Officer
Christian Voigtlander, COO
Thomas McCall, General Manager, Divisional
Alison Burcar, Vice President, Divisional

GROWTH PLANS/SPECIAL FEATURES:

ICU Medical, Inc. develops, manufactures and sells innovative medical devices, categorized into three main lines: infusion therapy, critical care and oncology. Infusion therapy products are used in hospitals and ambulatory clinics and consist of a tube running from a bottle or plastic bag containing an IV solution to a catheter inserted in a patient's vein. The company's largest selling product, the CLAVE, is a one-piece, needleless connection device and includes the products The MicroClave and MicroClave Clear, which are smaller versions of the standard Clave, and The NanoClave, which is smaller than the MicroClave and designed for use on neonatal and pediatric patients. The Neutron catheter device is also a part of Clave technology and includes a bi-directional valve that helps prevent blood reflux into a catheter to minimize blocking of the catheter. The CLAVE allows protected, secure and sterile IV connections without needles. Critical care products are used to monitor vital signs as well as specific physiological functions of key organ systems. These products include Hemodynamic monitoring systems, catheters and custom angiography and interventional radiology kits. Oncology products are used to prepare and deliver hazardous medications such as those used in chemotherapy which, if released, can have harmful effects to the health care worker and environment. These products include the ChemoCLAVE and ChemoLock closed system transfer devices, custom preparation and administration sets and accessories and the DIANA hazardous drug compounding system. ICU sells substantially all of its products to medical product manufacturers, independent distributors and directly to end users. Products are marketed and sold domestically as well as internationally through subsidiaries and other international distributors.

FINANCIAL DATA: *Note: Data for latest year may not have been available at press time.*

In U.S. $	2017	2016	2015	2014	2013	2012
Revenue	1,292,613,000	379,372,000	341,668,000	309,260,000	313,716,000	316,869,000
R&D Expense	51,253,000	12,955,000	15,714,000	18,332,000	12,407,000	10,630,000
Operating Income	62,889,000	99,017,000	81,867,000	44,130,000	51,949,000	61,276,000
Operating Margin %	4.86%	26.10%	23.96%	14.26%	16.55%	19.33%
SGA Expense	303,953,000	89,426,000	83,216,000	88,939,000	90,376,000	84,604,000
Net Income	68,644,000	63,084,000	44,985,000	26,335,000	40,418,000	41,281,000
Operating Cash Flow	154,423,000	89,941,000	54,865,000	60,640,000	65,726,000	66,271,000
Capital Expenditure	79,682,000	24,553,000	13,935,000	17,593,000	19,495,000	20,305,000
EBITDA	119,899,000	118,067,000	99,940,000	63,577,000	71,455,000	80,277,000
Return on Assets %	6.23%	9.47%	7.70%	5.06%	8.70%	10.45%
Return on Equity %	7.38%	10.17%	8.26%	5.41%	9.44%	11.60%
Debt to Equity						

CONTACT INFORMATION:

Phone: 949 366-2183 Fax:
Toll-Free: 800-824-7890
Address: 951 Calle Amanecer, San Clemente, CA 92673 United States

STOCK TICKER/OTHER:

Stock Ticker: ICUI
Exchange: NAS
Employees: 2,803
Fiscal Year Ends: 12/31
Parent Company:

SALARIES/BONUSES:

Top Exec. Salary: $650,000 Bonus: $
Second Exec. Salary: $395,150 Bonus: $

OTHER THOUGHTS:

Estimated Female Officers or Directors: 1
Hot Spot for Advancement for Women/Minorities:

IDEXX Laboratories Inc

www.idexx.com

NAIC Code: 334,510

TYPES OF BUSINESS:

Veterinary Laboratory Testing Equipment
Point-of-Care Diagnostic Products
Veterinary Pharmaceuticals
Information Management Software
Food & Water Testing Products
Laboratory Testing Services
Consulting

BRANDS/DIVISIONS/AFFILIATES:

IDEXX VetLab
VetLyte
VetStat
Catalyst Dx
SNAPshot DX
SNAP Beta-Lactam
Colilert
SNAP Lepto

CONTACTS: *Note: Officers with more than one job title may be intentionally listed here more than once.*

Jonathan Ayers, CEO
Brian Mckeon, CFO
Jay Mazelsky, Executive VP
Giovani Twigge, Other Executive Officer
Jacqueline Studer, Vice President

GROWTH PLANS/SPECIAL FEATURES:

IDEXX Laboratories, Inc. develops, manufactures and distributes products and provides services for the veterinary and the food and water testing markets. The company operates in three business segments: companion animal group, which provides diagnostic and information technology-based products and services for the veterinary markets; livestock, poultry and dairy, which provides diagnostic products and services for animal health, and to ensure the quality and safety of milk and food; and water quality products. IDEXX markets an integrated and flexible suite of in-house laboratory analyzers for use in veterinary practices, which is referred to as the IDEXX VetLab suite. The suite includes in-clinic chemistry, hematology, immunoassay, urinalysis and coagulation analyzers such as the VetTest, VetLyte, VetStat, LaserCyte Dx, Catalyst One, Catalyst Dx, Coag Dx and ProCyte Dx; and the hand-held IDEXX SNAPshot Dx rapid assay test kits which provide quick, accurate and convenient point-of-care diagnostic test results. Catalyst SDMA allows customers to use the Catalyst One and Catalyst Dx to screen for symmetrical dimethyl arginine (SDMA), a biomarker that detects kidney disease. In addition, the company provides assay kits, software and instrumentation for accurate assessment of infectious disease in production animals, such as cattle, swine and poultry. IDEXX's principal product for use in testing for antibiotic residue in milk is the SNAP Beta-Lactam test, which detects penicillin, amoxicillin, ampicillin, ceftiofur and cephapirin residues. SNAPduo Beta-Tetra ST detects certain tetracycline antibiotic residues in addition to those detected by the Beta-Lactam test kits. Last, water quality products include Colilert, Colilert-18 and Colisure tests, which simultaneously detect total coliforms and E. coli in water. SNAP Giardia is a fecal test for soluble Giardia antigens, a common cause of water-born infection; and SNAP Lepto tests for leptospirosis, a bacterial infection spread through contact with water or soil contaminated by the urine of infected animals.

FINANCIAL DATA: *Note: Data for latest year may not have been available at press time.*

In U.S. $	2017	2016	2015	2014	2013	2012
Revenue	1,969,058,000	1,775,423,000	1,601,892,000	1,485,807,000	1,377,058,000	1,293,338,000
R&D Expense	109,182,000	101,122,000	99,681,000	98,263,000	88,003,000	82,014,000
Operating Income	413,028,000	350,239,000	308,124,000	260,255,000	266,762,000	262,563,000
Operating Margin %	20.97%	19.72%	19.23%	17.51%	19.37%	20.30%
SGA Expense	575,172,000	524,075,000	482,465,000	457,598,000	401,353,000	354,571,000
Net Income	263,144,000	222,045,000	192,078,000	181,906,000	187,800,000	178,267,000
Operating Cash Flow	373,276,000	334,571,000	216,364,000	235,846,000	245,996,000	230,282,000
Capital Expenditure	76,704,000	64,787,000	82,921,000	60,698,000	78,636,000	66,392,000
EBITDA	501,422,000	432,113,000	371,336,000	320,872,000	323,243,000	316,873,000
Return on Assets %	16.22%	14.77%	13.43%	13.91%	16.09%	16.70%
Return on Equity %			1150.47%	57.23%	32.53%	30.32%
Debt to Equity				2.97	0.29	

CONTACT INFORMATION:

Phone: 207 556-0300 Fax: 207 856-0346
Toll-Free: 800-548-6733
Address: 1 Idexx Dr., Westbrook, ME 04092 United States

STOCK TICKER/OTHER:

Stock Ticker: IDXX
Employees: 7,365
Parent Company:
Exchange: NAS
Fiscal Year Ends: 12/31

SALARIES/BONUSES:

Top Exec. Salary: $800,000 Bonus: $
Second Exec. Salary: $549,538 Bonus: $

OTHER THOUGHTS:

Estimated Female Officers or Directors: 2
Hot Spot for Advancement for Women/Minorities: Y

iKang Healthcare Group Inc

www.ikanggroup.com

NAIC Code: 621,511

TYPES OF BUSINESS:

Medical Services
Medical Examinations
Health Screening
Dental Services

BRANDS/DIVISIONS/AFFILIATES:

CONTACTS:
Note: Officers with more than one job title may be intentionally listed here more than once.

Ligang Zhang, CEO
Feiyan Huang, COO
Yang Chen, CFO
Ligang Zhang, Chmn.

GROWTH PLANS/SPECIAL FEATURES:

iKang Healthcare Group, Inc. provides comprehensive and high quality preventive healthcare solutions to individuals throughout China. The company's services include a wide range of medical examinations, disease screening, dental services and more. iKang's nationwide network is comprised of 110 self-owned medical centers which cover 33 of the most affluent cities in the country. iKang also contracts with approximately 400 third-party service provider facilities, including independent medical examination centers and hospitals across all of China's provinces, creating a nationwide network that allows the firm to serve customers in markets in which it does not own medical centers. The company's medical examinations typically include internal, gynecology, ophthalmology, ear/nose/throat, dental, lab testing, electrocardiogram, ultrasound and X-ray examination services and solutions. Disease screening focuses on cancer screening, cardiovascular disease screening, certain chronic disease screening and functional medicine testing. Dental care includes oral health services, pediatric dentistry, cosmetic dentistry, orthodontics and dental implants. Outpatient services include acupuncture, Chinese medicine, gynecology, internal medicine, obstetrics, ophthalmology, pediatrics, urology and minor surgery. On-site healthcare management is provided by the firm, as well as clinics at certain locations in which iKang assigns small medical teams to provide scheduling services or operate primary care clinics on the customer's premises. iKang performed approximately 6.4 million medical examinations in 2017. In March 2018, the entered into a merger agreement with IK Healthcare Investment Limited, a special purpose vehicle wholly-owned by one or more affiliates of Yunfeng Capital and Alibaba Group Holding Limited, where the firm would become a privately held company.

FINANCIAL DATA:
Note: Data for latest year may not have been available at press time.

In U.S. $	2017	2016	2015	2014	2013	2012
Revenue	435,713,000	370,812,000	290,781,000	202,304,000	133,871,000	
R&D Expense	3,194,000	3,716,000	1,401,000	1,603,000	1,270,000	
Operating Income	13,298,000	26,002,000	41,047,000	33,364,000	19,589,000	
Operating Margin %	3.05%	7.01%	14.11%	16.49%	14.63%	
SGA Expense	157,087,000	130,185,000	93,390,000	60,932,000	41,933,000	
Net Income	-11,251,000	18,325,000	27,113,000	21,607,000	12,111,000	
Operating Cash Flow	50,043,000	43,602,000	41,097,000	34,303,000	16,314,000	
Capital Expenditure	63,389,000	37,181,000	40,106,000	35,838,000	9,979,000	
EBITDA	51,650,000	59,055,000	62,533,000	44,273,000	27,399,000	
Return on Assets %	-1.46%	2.81%	7.15%	-2.95%	-59.37%	
Return on Equity %	-3.43%	5.53%	27.90%			
Debt to Equity	0.32	0.66				

CONTACT INFORMATION:

Phone: 86 10-5320-6688 Fax: 86 10-5320-6689
Toll-Free:
Address: Tower B, No. 92 (A) Jianguo Rd., Fl. 6, Chaoyang District, Beijing, 100022 China

STOCK TICKER/OTHER:

Stock Ticker: KANG
Exchange: NAS
Employees: 15,918
Fiscal Year Ends: 12/31
Parent Company:

SALARIES/BONUSES:

Top Exec. Salary: $ Bonus: $
Second Exec. Salary: $ Bonus: $

OTHER THOUGHTS:

Estimated Female Officers or Directors:
Hot Spot for Advancement for Women/Minorities:

Immucor Inc

www.immucor.com

NAIC Code: 325,413

TYPES OF BUSINESS:

Diagnostic Products
Automated Blood Bank Instruments
Blood Reagents

BRANDS/DIVISIONS/AFFILIATES:

TPG Capital
NEO
Capture
Echo
PreciseType HEA
ELISA
xMAP
LIFECODES KIR Genotyping

CONTACTS: *Note: Officers with more than one job title may be intentionally listed here more than once.*

Avi Pelossof, CEO
Dominique Petitgenet, COO
Dominique Petitgenet, CFO

GROWTH PLANS/SPECIAL FEATURES:

Immucor, Inc., owned by firm TPG Capital, develops, manufactures and markets immunological diagnostic medical products, primarily reagents and automated systems used by hospitals, clinical laboratories and blood banks in tests performed to detect and identify certain properties of human blood prior to blood transfusions. Transfusion blood potentially contains antigens, which can cause a recipient's body to produce antibodies. The interaction between antigens and antibodies can cause severe complications. To protect against these potential complications, the firm produces an automated blood testing instrument, NEO, which allows technicians to analyze samples for potentially life-threatening foreign agents. NEO is capable of performing all routine blood bank tests, including blood grouping, antibody screening, crossmatch, direct antiglobulin test (DAT) and antibody identification. A high-volume output instrument, NEO processes up to 224 different samples at once and can perform approximately 60 type-and-screen tests an hour. Other products include Capture, a semi-automated device marketed as a back-up system for NEO or a stand-alone system for small laboratories; Echo, a device geared toward the small- to medium-sized hospital market that is able to perform up to 14 type-and-screen tests an hour; the PreciseType HEA (human erythrocyte antigens) test, an FDA-approved in-vitro diagnostic for molecular typing of red blood cell antigens; and ELISA and xMAP technology, which evaluate human leukocyte antigens (HLA) compatibility between donors and recipients. Immucor's transplant products include LIFECODES KIR Genotyping kits, which are based on the xMAP technology, for identifying HLA alleles present in samples; antibody detection products; and KIR (killer cell immunoglobulin-like receptors) and serology-based HLA typing trays, which identify the presence or absence of various genes.

FINANCIAL DATA: *Note: Data for latest year may not have been available at press time.*

In U.S. $	2017	2016	2015	2014	2013	2012
Revenue	39,897,060	379,972,000	389,300,000	388,056,000	347,788,000	261,814,000
R&D Expense						
Operating Income						
Operating Margin %						
SGA Expense						
Net Income		-43,767,000	-60,725,000	-182,257,000	-39,142,000	-49,647,000
Operating Cash Flow						
Capital Expenditure						
EBITDA						
Return on Assets %						
Return on Equity %						
Debt to Equity						

CONTACT INFORMATION:

Phone: 770-441-2051 Fax: 770-441-3807
Toll-Free: 800-829-2553
Address: 3130 Gateway Dr., Norcross, GA 30091 United States

STOCK TICKER/OTHER:

Stock Ticker: Private
Employees: 1,125
Parent Company: TPG Capital
Exchange:
Fiscal Year Ends: 05/31

SALARIES/BONUSES:

Top Exec. Salary: $ Bonus: $
Second Exec. Salary: $ Bonus: $

OTHER THOUGHTS:

Estimated Female Officers or Directors:
Hot Spot for Advancement for Women/Minorities:

Incyte Corporation

NAIC Code: 325,412

www.incyte.com

TYPES OF BUSINESS:

Drug Discovery & Development
Drug Development
Drug Research

BRANDS/DIVISIONS/AFFILIATES:

JAKAFI
ICLUSIG
JAK
IDO1
PD-1
PD13K-delta
FGER 1/2/3/

CONTACTS: *Note: Officers with more than one job title may be intentionally listed here more than once.*

Herve Hoppenot, CEO
David Gryska, CFO
Paul Trower, Chief Accounting Officer
Reid Huber, Chief Scientific Officer
Vijay Iyengar, Executive VP, Divisional
Paula Swain, Executive VP, Divisional
Steven Stein, Executive VP
Barry Flannelly, Executive VP
Wenqing Yao, Executive VP

GROWTH PLANS/SPECIAL FEATURES:

Incyte Corporation is a biopharmaceutical company focused on the discovery, development and commercialization of proprietary therapeutics. The firm's two marketed indications include JAKAFI (ruxolitinib) and ICLUSIG (ponatinib). JAKAIF is Incyte's first product to be approved for sale in the U.S. for the treatment of patients with intermediate or high-risk myelofibrosis, as well as for patients with polycythemia vera who have had an inadequate response to first-line therapies such as hydroxyurea. Myelofibrosis and polycythemia vera are both rare blood cancers. ICLUSIG is a kinase inhibitor which primarily targets BCR-ABL, an abnormal tyrosine kinase that is expressed in chronic myeloid leukemia (CML) and Philadelphia-chromosome positive acute lymphoblastic leukemia (Ph+ALL). Incyte's clinical programs in oncology seeks to recruit the patient's own immune system to tackle cancer, and targets therapies to block the effects of cancer-causing mutations. The firm's most advanced programs include: JAK inhibition for patients with acute graft-versus-host-disease (GVHD); IDO1 inhibition against specific cells so they are no longer able to attack a person's cancer cells; PD-1 antagonism, an investigational monoclonal antibody that inhibits PD-1 immune cells; P13K-delta inhibition, a potential therapeutic utility in the treatment of patients with lymphoma; and FGER 1/2/3 inhibition, a family of receptor tyrosine kinases that can act as oncogenic drivers in a number of liquid and solid tumor types. Clinical programs outside of oncology include an atopic dermatitis indication and a vitiligo indication, each of which are in Phase two studies and utilizing topical ruxolitinib (JAK1/JAK2). Incyte has operations in the U.S., Europe and Japan.

Incyte offers its employees medical, vision and dental plans; life insurance; disability coverage; a 401(k) plan; tuition reimbursement; employee discounts; referral and spot bonuses; and variable compensation plans.

FINANCIAL DATA: *Note: Data for latest year may not have been available at press time.*

In U.S. $	2017	2016	2015	2014	2013	2012
Revenue	1,536,216,000	1,105,719,000	753,751,000	511,495,000	354,947,000	297,059,000
R&D Expense	1,326,361,000	581,861,000	479,514,000	347,523,000	260,436,000	210,391,000
Operating Income	-236,030,000	162,420,000	50,651,000	-4,804,000	-16,102,000	1,148,000
Operating Margin %	-15.36%	14.68%	6.71%	-.93%	-4.53%	.38%
SGA Expense	366,406,000	303,251,000	196,614,000	165,772,000	109,983,000	85,363,000
Net Income	-313,142,000	104,222,000	6,531,000	-48,481,000	-83,147,000	-44,320,000
Operating Cash Flow	-92,988,000	304,756,000	86,536,000	26,256,000	9,180,000	-94,830,000
Capital Expenditure	111,021,000	120,277,000	26,003,000	27,876,000	4,267,000	2,839,000
EBITDA	-253,212,000	204,574,000	53,159,000	-1,719,000	-44,196,000	1,912,000
Return on Assets %	-15.89%	7.87%	.71%	-6.64%	-17.32%	-13.44%
Return on Equity %	-30.54%	35.29%	14.58%			
Debt to Equity	0.01	1.55	3.62			

CONTACT INFORMATION:

Phone: 302 498-6700 Fax: 302 425-2750
Toll-Free: 855-446-2983
Address: 1801 Augustine Cut-Off, Wilmington, DE 19803 United States

STOCK TICKER/OTHER:

Stock Ticker: INCY Exchange: NAS
Employees: 980 Fiscal Year Ends: 12/31
Parent Company:

SALARIES/BONUSES:

Top Exec. Salary: $966,505 Bonus: $
Second Exec. Salary: $473,070 Bonus: $100,000

OTHER THOUGHTS:

Estimated Female Officers or Directors: 2
Hot Spot for Advancement for Women/Minorities: Y

Indegene Aptilon Inc

www.indegene.com

NAIC Code: 511210D

TYPES OF BUSINESS:

Computer Software, Healthcare & Biotechnology

BRANDS/DIVISIONS/AFFILIATES:

Indegene Lifesystems Pvt Ltd
Medsn Inc
Medcases LLC
Aptilon
Total Therapeutic Management

CONTACTS: *Note: Officers with more than one job title may be intentionally listed here more than once.*

Manish Gupta, CEO
Rajesh Nair, Pres.
Suhas Prabhu, VP-Finance
Sridhar V, Sr. VP-Mktg.
Bina Patil, VP-Human Resources
Manish gupta, CEO-Indegene Lifesystems

GROWTH PLANS/SPECIAL FEATURES:

Indegene Aptilon, Inc. connects pharmaceutical, biotech and medical device companies through video and mobile detailing, digital access channels and permission-based email services. It helps global healthcare organizations address complex challenges by seamlessly integrating analytics, technology, operations and medical expertise. The firm offers medical, marketing, risk, healthcare quality, clinical effectiveness and care management solutions through its comprehensive portfolio of solutions and technology platforms. Indegene works with more than 85 global customers, including biotechnology companies, medical device manufacturers, life science organizations, health plans, accountable care organizations and healthcare co-ops, as well as provider organizations. With offices located in the U.S., the U.K., China, India and Australia, Indegene is able to help solve complex industry challenges by partnering with clients; leveraging global talent pool of clinicians, technologies, specialists, domain experts and business process specialists; deploying global infrastructure assets; and harnessing global healthcare knowledge. Partners of the firm include: The Abacus Group; Corporate Call Center, Inc.; and TranScrip. Indegene subsidiaries include Medsn, Inc., a medical education and marketing firm; Medcases, LLC, a provider of continuing medical education for students, residents and practicing physicians in multiple specialties; Aptilon, based in Canada, which enables life science companies to effectively reach, message, connect and interact with U.S. physicians and healthcare providers via multiple channels; and Total Therapeutic Management, a physician-focused quality improvement company that provides health information management, research and education support to healthcare organizations. Indegene Aptilon itself is a subsidiary of Indegene Lifesystems Pvt. Ltd.

FINANCIAL DATA: *Note: Data for latest year may not have been available at press time.*

In U.S. $	2017	2016	2015	2014	2013	2012
Revenue						
R&D Expense						
Operating Income						
Operating Margin %						
SGA Expense						
Net Income						
Operating Cash Flow						
Capital Expenditure						
EBITDA						
Return on Assets %						
Return on Equity %						
Debt to Equity						

CONTACT INFORMATION:

Phone: 514-422-0777 Fax: 514-422-0733
Toll-Free:
Address: 455 Fenelon Blvd., Ste. 104, Montreal, QC H9S 5T8 Canada

STOCK TICKER/OTHER:

Stock Ticker: Subsidiary Exchange:
Employees: 35 Fiscal Year Ends: 12/31
Parent Company: Indegene Lifesystems Pvt Ltd

SALARIES/BONUSES:

Top Exec. Salary: $ Bonus: $
Second Exec. Salary: $ Bonus: $

OTHER THOUGHTS:

Estimated Female Officers or Directors:
Hot Spot for Advancement for Women/Minorities:

Independence Holding Company

www.ihcgroup.com

NAIC Code: 524,113

TYPES OF BUSINESS:

Insurance Underwriting
Medical Stop-Loss
Group Disability & Life Insurance
Individual Life Insurance
Pet Insurance

BRANDS/DIVISIONS/AFFILIATES:

Standard Security Life Insurance of New York
Independence American Insurance Company
Madison National Life Insurance Company Inc
AMIC Holdings Inc

CONTACTS: *Note: Officers with more than one job title may be intentionally listed here more than once.*

Roy Thung, CEO
Teresa Herbert, CFO
David Kettig, COO
Larry Graber, Director
Steven Lapin, Director
Gary Balzofiore, Vice President, Subsidiary

GROWTH PLANS/SPECIAL FEATURES:

Independence Holding Company (IHC) is a holding company principally engaged in the life and health insurance business. IHC primarily provides specialized disability and health coverages and related services to commercial customers and individuals. Wholly-owned insurance company subsidiaries include: Standard Security Life Insurance of New York, Independence American Insurance Company and Madison National Life Insurance Company, Inc. These subsidiaries market their products through independent and affiliated brokers, producers and agents. Independence American also distributes to consumers through dedicated controlled distribution companies and through company-owned websites. Specialty health benefits include ancillary benefits such as dental, vision, short-term medical, supplemental products (fixed indemnity, critical illness and hospital indemnity); pet insurance; and non-subscriber occupational accident and injured on duty coverage. IHC's administrative companies underwrite, market, administer and/or price life and health insurance business for the company's owned and affiliated carriers, and to a lesser extent, for non-affiliated insurance companies. In addition, wholly-owned AMIC Holdings, Inc. (formerly American Independence Corp.) is an independent, private insurance holding company engaged in the insurance and reinsurance business.

FINANCIAL DATA: *Note: Data for latest year may not have been available at press time.*

In U.S. $	2017	2016	2015	2014	2013	2012
Revenue	320,494,000	311,004,000	532,868,000	533,933,000	575,044,000	428,061,000
R&D Expense						
Operating Income						
Operating Margin %						
SGA Expense	157,104,000	132,174,000	172,180,000	177,848,000	179,553,000	149,999,000
Net Income	42,042,000	123,298,000	29,944,000	16,293,000	13,779,000	19,661,000
Operating Cash Flow	28,604,000	-30,998,000	-164,724,000	27,331,000	-162,316,000	-115,394,000
Capital Expenditure						
EBITDA						
Return on Assets %	3.86%	10.57%	2.51%	1.32%	1.08%	1.50%
Return on Equity %	9.68%	32.45%	9.74%	5.81%	4.97%	7.19%
Debt to Equity			0.13	0.14	0.16	0.16

CONTACT INFORMATION:

Phone: 203 358-8000 Fax: 203 348-3103
Toll-Free: 877-442-4467
Address: 96 Cummings Point Rd., Stamford, CT 06902 United States

STOCK TICKER/OTHER:

Stock Ticker: IHC
Employees: 270
Parent Company:
Exchange: NYS
Fiscal Year Ends: 12/31

SALARIES/BONUSES:

Top Exec. Salary: $106,184 Bonus: $1,102,209
Second Exec. Salary: $374,946 Bonus: $775,000

OTHER THOUGHTS:

Estimated Female Officers or Directors: 1
Hot Spot for Advancement for Women/Minorities:

Indiana University Health

www.iuhealth.org

NAIC Code: 622,110

TYPES OF BUSINESS:

General Medical and Surgical Hospitals
Children's Services
Medical Research

BRANDS/DIVISIONS/AFFILIATES:

IU Health Cancer
IU Health Cardiovascular
IU Health Neuroscience
IU Health Orthopedics
Riley Hospital for Children
IU Health Transplant
Video Visits

CONTACTS: *Note: Officers with more than one job title may be intentionally listed here more than once.*

Dennis Murphy, CEO
Daniel F. Evans, Jr., Pres.
John C. Kohne, Chief Medical Officer
Linda Q. Everett, Chief Nurse Exec.

GROWTH PLANS/SPECIAL FEATURES:

Indiana University Health (IU Health) is one of the largest network of physicians in the state of Indiana. IU Health partners with Indiana University School of Medicine, and is comprised of hospitals, physicians and allied services dedicated to providing preeminent care throughout Indiana and beyond. Its care services for children and adults include the areas of: cancer, via its IU Health Cancer centers; cardiovascular, via IU Health Cardiovascular, which treats some of the most complex cases; neuroscience, via IU Health Neuroscience, providing a range of neurological and neurosurgical services; orthopedics, via IU Health Orthopedics, which is Indiana's only nationally-ranked orthopedics program, providing comprehensive joint, spine, bone and muscle care; pediatrics, via Riley Hospital for Children, providing routine care as well as complex care; and transplant, via IU Health Transplant, providing organ transplant such as kidney, lung and liver. In total, the firm's hospitals have approximately 2,683 beds, 119,908 inpatient admissions and more than 2.87 million outpatient visits. IU Health also offers access to health care through its telemedicine program, Video Visits, in which patients connect via live video with a highly-skilled IU Health or IU Health affiliated physician to diagnose low-intensity complaints such as bronchitis, flu, pink eye or similar ailments. Most visits take less than 20 minutes, including registration and wait times, and the program is available via tablet, smartphone or computer. In August 2018, IU Health's North Hospital broke ground on the Joe and Shelly Schwarz Cancer Center, which is expected to open in 2020 and offer radiation oncology spaces and infusion rooms, a pharmacy and laboratory under a single roof.

FINANCIAL DATA: *Note: Data for latest year may not have been available at press time.*

In U.S. $	2017	2016	2015	2014	2013	2012
Revenue	6,300,000,000	6,233,578,000	6,100,815,000	5,726,583,000	5,246,882,000	5,578,276,000
R&D Expense						
Operating Income						
Operating Margin %						
SGA Expense						
Net Income	989,000,000	260,095,000	612,676,000	725,529,000	447,985,000	651,498,000
Operating Cash Flow						
Capital Expenditure						
EBITDA						
Return on Assets %						
Return on Equity %						
Debt to Equity						

CONTACT INFORMATION:

Phone: 317-962-2000 Fax: 317-962-4533
Toll-Free:
Address: 340 West 10th St., Ste. 5200, Indianapolis, IN 46206 United States

STOCK TICKER/OTHER:

Stock Ticker: Nonprofit
Employees: 33,000
Parent Company:
Exchange:
Fiscal Year Ends: 12/31

SALARIES/BONUSES:

Top Exec. Salary: $ Bonus: $
Second Exec. Salary: $ Bonus: $

OTHER THOUGHTS:

Estimated Female Officers or Directors: 4
Hot Spot for Advancement for Women/Minorities: Y

InfuSystem Holdings Inc

www.infusystem.com

NAIC Code: 621,999

TYPES OF BUSINESS:

Infusion Pump Management Services

BRANDS/DIVISIONS/AFFILIATES:

InfuSystem Holdings USA Inc
InfuSystem Inc
First Biomedical Inc
IFC LLC

CONTACTS:

Note: Officers with more than one job title may be intentionally listed here more than once.

Trent Smith, Chief Accounting Officer
Michael McReynolds, Chief Information Officer
Richard DiIorio, Director
Gregg Lehman, Director
Greg Schulte, Executive VP

GROWTH PLANS/SPECIAL FEATURES:

InfuSystem Holdings, Inc. is a provider of ambulatory infusion pump management services for oncologists in the United States. Ambulatory infusion pumps are small, lightweight electronic pumps designed to be worn by patients and which allow patients the freedom to move about while receiving chemotherapy treatments. The pumps are battery powered and attached to intravenous administration tubing, which is in turn attached to a reservoir or plastic cassette that contains the chemotherapy drug. InfuSystem supplies electronic ambulatory infusion pumps and associated disposable supply kits to physicians' offices, infusion clinics and hospital outpatient chemotherapy clinics to be utilized by patients who receive continuous chemotherapy infusions. It provides pump management services for the pumps and associated disposable supply kits to oncology practices in the United States. In addition, the company sells safety devices for cytotoxic drug transfer and administration and rents pole-mounted or ambulatory infusion pumps for use within the oncology practice. InfuSystem purchases electronic ambulatory infusion pumps from a variety of suppliers on a non-exclusive basis, including Smiths Medical, Inc. and WalkMed Infusion, LLC. The pumps are currently used mainly for continuous infusion of chemotherapy drugs for patients with colorectal cancer, as well as for pain management. Subsidiaries of the company include InfuSystem Holdings USA, Inc.; InfuSystem, Inc.; First Biomedical, Inc.; and IFC, LLC.

FINANCIAL DATA:

Note: Data for latest year may not have been available at press time.

In U.S. $	2017	2016	2015	2014	2013	2012
Revenue	71,077,000	70,497,000	72,125,000	66,487,000	62,280,000	58,828,000
R&D Expense						
Operating Income	-2,819,000	974,000	8,864,000	9,331,000	5,896,000	2,000,000
Operating Margin %	-3.96%	1.38%	12.28%	14.03%	9.46%	3.39%
SGA Expense	34,979,000	34,286,000	34,202,000	29,733,000	28,631,000	32,926,000
Net Income	-20,707,000	-222,000	3,743,000	3,357,000	1,669,000	-1,489,000
Operating Cash Flow	7,583,000	7,909,000	7,054,000	7,255,000	7,463,000	5,452,000
Capital Expenditure	3,595,000	8,795,000	10,245,000	9,705,000	5,962,000	6,542,000
EBITDA	8,598,000	11,724,000	15,521,000	15,486,000	14,230,000	9,590,000
Return on Assets %	-25.06%	-.23%	4.23%	4.26%	2.15%	-1.93%
Return on Equity %	-50.72%	-.43%	7.65%	7.52%	4.03%	-3.71%
Debt to Equity	0.82	0.57	0.58	0.40	0.50	0.68

CONTACT INFORMATION:

Phone: 248 291-1210 Fax:
Toll-Free:
Address: 31700 Research Park Dr., Madison Heights, MI 48071 United States

STOCK TICKER/OTHER:

Stock Ticker: INFU
Exchange: ASE
Employees: 250
Fiscal Year Ends: 12/31
Parent Company:

SALARIES/BONUSES:

Top Exec. Salary: $350,000 Bonus: $
Second Exec. Salary: $268,613 Bonus: $52,666

OTHER THOUGHTS:

Estimated Female Officers or Directors:
Hot Spot for Advancement for Women/Minorities:

Institut Straumann AG

www.straumann.com

NAIC Code: 339,114

TYPES OF BUSINESS:

Dental Implants
Dental Tissue Regeneration
CAD/CAM Elements & Equipment

BRANDS/DIVISIONS/AFFILIATES:

Straumann Holding AG
Roxolid
SLActive
Emdogain
BoneCeramic
Createch Medical
botiss medical AG

CONTACTS: *Note: Officers with more than one job title may be intentionally listed here more than once.*

Beat Spalinger, Pres.
Peter Hackel, CFO
Gerhard Bauer, Head-Research, Dev. & Oper.
Sandro Matter, Head-Strategic Projects & Alliances
Wolfgang Becker, Head-Sales, Central Europe
Guillaume Daniellot, Head-Sales, Western Europe
Andy Molnar, Head-Sales, North America
Alexander Ochsner, Head-Sales-Asia Pacific

GROWTH PLANS/SPECIAL FEATURES:

Institut Straumann AG (Straumann) is a world leader in implant and restorative dentistry products and a major provider of dental tissue regeneration products. It is a subsidiary of Straumann Holding AG. Straumann operates four geographical segments: Europe, North America, Asia/Pacific and the rest of the world. It maintains subsidiaries and distributors in more than 70 countries, with its most important markets being Germany and the U.S. The company offers three basic products: implants, regenerative systems and computer aided design and manufacturing (CAD/CAM) technology. Implants are designed to mimic natural teeth as closely as possible, being more durable and supporting themselves better than conventional bridges. They include devices inserted at the bone or soft tissue level, surgical tools and 3D modeling software used to plan surgery. Straumann's product, Roxolid, is a high-performance implant material combining high tensile and fatigue strengths with osseointegration. The firm also offers SLActive, an implant surface technology that decreases the healing time after surgery and increases general stability of the dental implants. Regenerative systems include products that support or repair oral structures, such as Emdogain. This product, along with BoneCeramic, a synthetic bone graft substitute that augments the patient's jaw bone, provides stability for synthetic implants. Last, CAD/CAM products, are divided into prosthetic elements (crowns, inlays, overlays or bridges) and manufacturing equipment (software, scanners and milling units). Also within Straumann's CAD/CAM line are ceramic-based prosthetics, which provides increased durability and aesthetic design. Principal production sites for implant components and instruments are in Switzerland, the U.S., Brazil and Germany; CAD/CAM prosthetics are milled in Germany, the U.S., Japan and Brazil; and biomaterials are manufactured in Sweden. During 2018, Straumann increased its stake in Createch Medical to 100%; and acquired a 30% stake in its biomaterials partner botiss medical AG.

FINANCIAL DATA: *Note: Data for latest year may not have been available at press time.*

In U.S. $	2017	2016	2015	2014	2013	2012
Revenue						
R&D Expense						
Operating Income						
Operating Margin %						
SGA Expense						
Net Income						
Operating Cash Flow						
Capital Expenditure						
EBITDA						
Return on Assets %						
Return on Equity %						
Debt to Equity						

CONTACT INFORMATION:

Phone: 41 619651111 Fax: 41 619651101
Toll-Free:
Address: Peter Merian-Weg 12, Basel, 4002 Switzerland

STOCK TICKER/OTHER:

Stock Ticker: SAUHF
Exchange: PINX
Employees: 4,881
Fiscal Year Ends: 12/31
Parent Company: Straumann Holding AG

SALARIES/BONUSES:

Top Exec. Salary: $ Bonus: $
Second Exec. Salary: $ Bonus: $

OTHER THOUGHTS:

Estimated Female Officers or Directors:
Hot Spot for Advancement for Women/Minorities:

Intalere Inc

NAIC Code: 561,400

www.intalere.com

TYPES OF BUSINESS:

Group Buying Programs for Medical Supplies
Health Care Consultation Services and Solutions
Healthcare Provider Insurance
Pharmacy Solutions

BRANDS/DIVISIONS/AFFILIATES:

Intalere Choice
Intalere Insurance Services
DataBay Resources
Tempest Med

CONTACTS: *Note: Officers with more than one job title may be intentionally listed here more than once.*

Julius Heil, CEO
Steve Schoch, Interim CFO
Steve Kiewiet, Chief Commercial Officer
Jim Wilson, Chief Strategy Officer
Bert R. Zimmerli, Chmn.

GROWTH PLANS/SPECIAL FEATURES:

Intalere, Inc. provides tailored smart solutions and consultation services for health care providers. The company offers its solutions and services through four subsidiaries: Intalere Choice, Intalere Insurance Services, DataBay Resources and Tempest Med. Intalere Choice identifies actionable opportunities for contract savings and product standardization within health care facilities, from assessment and strategic expense reduction to on-site contact utilization management and operational benchmarking. Intalere Choice's expertise in supply chain management strategies help to maximize operating margins. Intalere Insurance Services offers benefit and risk cost containment strategies that provide long-term insurance solutions for health care providers. It partners with Gallagher and Myron Steves, healthcare industry insurance leaders, to help solve the challenges of operating a sustainable health care organization while meeting the needs of employees and the community. Insurance solutions by Gallagher include ancillary, risk management, health, pharmacy, human resources, consulting, health care analytics and retirement planning; and insurance solutions by Myron Steves focus on catastrophic occurrences. DataBay Resources offers business intelligence tools to assist providers with the overall analysis of their service areas. This information helps determine the best strategies for improving market share within the communities each facility serves and also highlights opportunities for market growth. Last, Tempest Med offers solutions to health care organizations dedicated to the non-acute, alternate site marketplace. For independent pharmacies, Tempest Med provides products, tools and services such as: revenue cycle management, for maximizing reimbursement and enhance profitability; a comprehensive portfolio of contracts and services; and insurance contracts with prescription drug plans and pharmacy benefit management providers. As of mid-2018, Intalere's membership includes 3,800 acute care hospitals, 42,274 clinics, 13,009 long-term care facilities, 133 physicians (hospital-based), 3,754 ambulatory surgery centers, 1,266 emergency services and 39,366 other types of related members.

FINANCIAL DATA: *Note: Data for latest year may not have been available at press time.*

In U.S. $	2017	2016	2015	2014	2013	2012
Revenue						
R&D Expense						
Operating Income						
Operating Margin %						
SGA Expense						
Net Income						
Operating Cash Flow						
Capital Expenditure						
EBITDA						
Return on Assets %						
Return on Equity %						
Debt to Equity						

CONTACT INFORMATION:

Phone: Fax:
Toll-Free: 877-711-5700
Address: Two CityPlace Dr., Ste. 400, St. Louis, MO 63141 United States

STOCK TICKER/OTHER:

Stock Ticker: Subsidiary
Employees:
Parent Company: Intermountain Healthcare
Exchange:
Fiscal Year Ends:

SALARIES/BONUSES:

Top Exec. Salary: $ Bonus: $
Second Exec. Salary: $ Bonus: $

OTHER THOUGHTS:

Estimated Female Officers or Directors:
Hot Spot for Advancement for Women/Minorities:

Intarcia Therapeutics Inc

www.intarcia.com

NAIC Code: 334,510

TYPES OF BUSINESS:

Electromedical and Electrotherapeutic Apparatus Manufacturing

BRANDS/DIVISIONS/AFFILIATES:

ITCA 650

CONTACTS: *Note: Officers with more than one job title may be intentionally listed here more than once.*

Kurt Graves, CEO
James Ahlers, CFO
James P. Brady, VP-Human Resources
Anthony Hurley, VP-Global Technical Operations
Kurt Graves, Chmn.

GROWTH PLANS/SPECIAL FEATURES:

Intarcia Therapeutics, Inc. is a biopharmaceutical company that develops innovative therapies which merge medicine with technology and have the potential to transform therapeutic categories. Intarcia focuses on serious diseases that are prevalent and poorly controlled. The firm's goal is to provide a new level of freedom for patients with type 2 diabetes (T2D). Intarcia's lead product, ITCA 650 (continuous subcutaneous delivery of exenatide), is an advanced clinical drug for the treatment of T2D. This platform technology system comprises a small, matchstick-sized osmotic pump placed sub-dermally (just beneath the skin) to deliver a slow and consistent flow of medication. Each device contains an appropriate volume of drug product to treat a patient for a predetermined extended duration of time. The device can be sub-dermally placed in various locations in the abdomen in as little as five minutes by a physician or physician's assistant. As of August 2018, all Phase 3 trials for ITCA 650 have been completed and the New Drug Application has been submitted to the U.S. FDA. In addition, Intarcia and the Bill & Melinda Gates Foundation are collaborating to prevent the spread of HIV in Sub-Saharan Africa and other areas where the HIV epidemic is most severe. The collaboration focuses on combining the Medici Drug Delivery System with preventive medicine capable of significantly lowering the epidemic rate of new infections in these areas. Intarcia also collaborates with Numab, which has a discovery and optimization platform offering great potential to identify promising antibody based therapeutic candidates suitable for the Medici Drug Delivery System formulation and delivery technology. In September 2017, the selection of a multi-specific antibody construct targeting autoimmune and inflammatory diseases marked a major milestone in the Intarcia/Numab partnership. Intarcia's manufacturing site is located in Hayward, California, and its R&D site is located in Durham, North Carolina.

FINANCIAL DATA: *Note: Data for latest year may not have been available at press time.*

In U.S. $	2017	2016	2015	2014	2013	2012
Revenue						
R&D Expense						
Operating Income						
Operating Margin %						
SGA Expense						
Net Income						
Operating Cash Flow						
Capital Expenditure						
EBITDA						
Return on Assets %						
Return on Equity %						
Debt to Equity						

CONTACT INFORMATION:

Phone: 617-936-2500 Fax:
Toll-Free:
Address: One Marina Park Dr., 13/F, Boston, MA 02210 United States

STOCK TICKER/OTHER:

Stock Ticker: Private
Employees:
Parent Company:
Exchange:
Fiscal Year Ends:

SALARIES/BONUSES:

Top Exec. Salary: $ Bonus: $
Second Exec. Salary: $ Bonus: $

OTHER THOUGHTS:

Estimated Female Officers or Directors:
Hot Spot for Advancement for Women/Minorities:

Integra Lifesciences Holdings Corporation

www.integralife.com

NAIC Code: 339,100

TYPES OF BUSINESS:

Medical Equipment Manufacturing
Implants & Biomaterials
Absorbable Medical Products
Tissue Regeneration Technology
Neurosurgery Products
Skin Replacement Products

BRANDS/DIVISIONS/AFFILIATES:

AccuDrain
Capture
DigiFuse
Integra
Redmond
SurgiMend
Titan
Uni-CP

CONTACTS: *Note: Officers with more than one job title may be intentionally listed here more than once.*

Peter Arduini, CEO
Glenn Coleman, CFO
Richard Caruso, Chairman Emeritus
Stuart Essig, Chairman of the Board
Richard Gorelick, General Counsel
Lisa Evoli, Other Executive Officer
Daniel Reuvers, President, Divisional
Robert Davis, President, Divisional
Joseph Vinhais, Vice President, Divisional
Judith OGrady, Vice President, Divisional
John Mooradian, Vice President, Divisional
Kenneth Burhop, Vice President
Jeffrey Mosebrook, Vice President

GROWTH PLANS/SPECIAL FEATURES:

Integra Lifesciences Holdings Corporation develops, manufactures and markets surgical implants and medical instruments primarily for use in neurosurgery, orthopedics and general surgery. The company operates through two business segments: Codman specialty surgical solutions and orthopedics & tissue technologies. Codman specialty surgical solutions offers global, market-leading technologies, brands and instrumentation. The product portfolio represents a continuum of care from pre-operative, to the neurosurgery operating room, to the neuro-critical care unit and post care for both adult and pediatric patients suffering from brain tumors, brain injury, cerebrospinal fluid pressure complications and other neurological conditions. The orthopedics & tissue technologies segment offers differentiated soft tissue repair and tissue regeneration products, as well as small bone fixation and joint replacement solutions. This division sells regenerative technology products that can be used to provide treatment for acute and chronic wounds, as well as for surgical tissue repair, including hernia repair, peripheral nerve repair and tendon repair. For extremity bone and joint reconstruction procedures, Integra sells hardware products such as bone and joint fixation and replacement devices, implants and instruments that provide orthopedic reconstruction of bone. A few of the many trademarks of the company include AccuDrain, Capture, DigiFuse, Integra, Movement, Redmond, SafeGuard, SurgiMend, Titan and Uni-CP. In September 2017, Integra agreed to sell certain neurosurgery assets to Natus Medical for $47.5 million. The following October, the firm acquired the Johnson & Johnson Codman Neurosurgery business, which offers devices focused on hydrocephalus, neuro-critical care and operative neurosurgery.

Employee benefits include medical, dental and vision coverage; flexible spending accounts; life and AD&D insurance; a stock purchase plan; a 401(k); short- and long-term disability; and employee/educational assistance programs.

FINANCIAL DATA: *Note: Data for latest year may not have been available at press time.*

In U.S. $	2017	2016	2015	2014	2013	2012
Revenue	1,188,236,000	992,075,000	882,734,000	928,305,000	836,214,000	830,871,000
R&D Expense	63,455,000	58,155,000	50,895,000	51,596,000	52,088,000	51,012,000
Operating Income	44,804,000	115,340,000	79,587,000	65,541,000	-3,644,000	73,782,000
Operating Margin %	3.77%	11.62%	9.01%	7.06%	-.43%	8.88%
SGA Expense	624,096,000	455,629,000	415,757,000	445,967,000	394,250,000	373,114,000
Net Income	64,743,000	74,564,000	-3,519,000	34,004,000	-16,977,000	41,204,000
Operating Cash Flow	114,544,000	116,405,000	94,483,000	79,463,000	53,268,000	58,715,000
Capital Expenditure	43,503,000	47,328,000	33,413,000	42,396,000	47,851,000	69,031,000
EBITDA	135,349,000	188,874,000	143,051,000	126,074,000	42,008,000	126,877,000
Return on Assets %	2.57%	4.16%	-.20%	2.45%	-1.43%	3.57%
Return on Equity %	7.18%	9.37%	-.48%	4.94%	-2.85%	8.15%
Debt to Equity	1.85	0.79	0.93	0.88	0.58	1.00

CONTACT INFORMATION:

Phone: 609-275-0500 Fax:
Toll-Free:
Address: 311 Enterprise Dr., Plainsboro, NJ 08536 United States

STOCK TICKER/OTHER:

Stock Ticker: IART
Employees: 3,700
Parent Company:
Exchange: NAS
Fiscal Year Ends: 12/31

SALARIES/BONUSES:

Top Exec. Salary: $905,024 Bonus: $
Second Exec. Salary: $536,250 Bonus: $

OTHER THOUGHTS:

Estimated Female Officers or Directors: 4
Hot Spot for Advancement for Women/Minorities: Y

IntegraMed America Inc

www.integramed.com

NAIC Code: 621,410

TYPES OF BUSINESS:

Fertility Treatments
Physician Practice Management-Reproductive Services
Treatment Financing Programs
Fertility-Related Pharmaceutical Distribution

BRANDS/DIVISIONS/AFFILIATES:

Sagard Capital Partners LP
Attain IVF
Attain Fertility Network

CONTACTS: *Note: Officers with more than one job title may be intentionally listed here more than once.*

Chris Throckmorton, CEO
Mark Attarian, Interim CFO
Shannon Delage, Exec. VP-Mktg. & Technology
Tom Miller, Chief Technology Officer
Scott Soifer, Chief Admin. Officer
Claude E. White, General Counsel
David Collins, Managing Dir.-Investor Rel.
Daniel P. Doman, Exec. VP
Pamela Schumann, Exec. VP-Attain Fertility Centers

GROWTH PLANS/SPECIAL FEATURES:

IntegraMed America, Inc. develops, markets and manages specialty outpatient healthcare facilities, with a current focus on the fertility markets. The firm is privately-held by Sagard Capital Partners, LP. It helps practices grow faster and more profitably through proprietary programs, tools and expertise such as clinical and market leadership solutions, and patient experience solutions. IntegraMed's fertility division provides a range of services that can include clinical and business information systems, marketing and sales, facilities and operations management, finance and accounting, human resources, legal, risk management, quality assurance and fertility management financing programs. Its Attain IVF programs are offered exclusively at practices that are members of IntegraMed's Attain Fertility Network, which is comprised of 39 centers at more than 150 locations across 32 U.S. states and the District of Columbia. Attain Fertility's website offers information and support, including a social media community for fertility patients.

FINANCIAL DATA: *Note: Data for latest year may not have been available at press time.*

In U.S. $	2017	2016	2015	2014	2013	2012
Revenue	350,000,000	340,000,000	330,000,000	325,000,000	310,000,000	300,000,000
R&D Expense						
Operating Income						
Operating Margin %						
SGA Expense						
Net Income						
Operating Cash Flow						
Capital Expenditure						
EBITDA						
Return on Assets %						
Return on Equity %						
Debt to Equity						

CONTACT INFORMATION:

Phone: 914-253-8000 Fax: 914-253-8008
Toll-Free: 800-458-0044
Address: 2 Manhattanville Rd., 3/Fl, Purchase, NY 10577 United States

STOCK TICKER/OTHER:

Stock Ticker: Private
Exchange:
Employees: 2,200
Fiscal Year Ends: 12/31
Parent Company: Sagard Capital Partners LP

SALARIES/BONUSES:

Top Exec. Salary: $ Bonus: $
Second Exec. Salary: $ Bonus: $

OTHER THOUGHTS:

Estimated Female Officers or Directors: 3
Hot Spot for Advancement for Women/Minorities: Y

Intermountain Healthcare

www.intermountainhealthcare.org

NAIC Code: 622,110

TYPES OF BUSINESS:

General Medical and Surgical Hospitals
Surgical Centers
Emergency Air Transport
Pharmacies
Counseling Services
Rehabilitation Centers
Home Care
Health Insurance

BRANDS/DIVISIONS/AFFILIATES:

Life Flight
Intermountain Home Care
Intermountain Medical Group
InstaCare
KidsCare
WorkMed
Intermountain Medical Center Campus
LiVe

CONTACTS: *Note: Officers with more than one job title may be intentionally listed here more than once.*

A. Marc Harrison, CEO
Robert W. Allen, COO
Charles Sorensen, Pres.
Bert Zimmerli, CFO
Joseph E. Fournier, Chief People Officer
Greg Poulsen, Chief Strategy Officer

GROWTH PLANS/SPECIAL FEATURES:

Intermountain Healthcare is a nonprofit healthcare provider for Utah and southeastern Idaho. The firm operates 22 hospitals and approximately 185 physician clinic sites throughout the region. Intermountain Healthcare runs Life Flight, an emergency air transport system; a collection of pharmacies; and counseling, dialysis and rehabilitation centers. Additionally, the company runs a variety of subsidiaries for additional patient assistance. Intermountain Home Care offers adult and pediatric skilled home nursing, rehabilitation therapies and certified Home Health Aide services. Intermountain Medical Group offers services through a multi-specialty network of more than 1,400 physicians, with clinics such as InstaCare and KidsCare, ExpressCare clinics located in grocery stores and WorkMed clinics. SelectHealth, with 750,000 members, supplies medical, prescription and dental insurance to corporate and individual clients. The Intermountain Medical Center Campus, in addition to a central laboratory, physician offices and medical education and research facilities, includes five specialized hospitals: a heart and lung hospital, a women's and newborn hospital, a cancer treatment hospital, an ambulatory and outpatient diagnostics hospital and a critical care and trauma hospital. IHC also maintains a child obesity public service program, LiVe, to encourage youth fitness.

The firm offers employees health, dental, life, disability and vision insurance; flexible spending accounts; an employee assistance program; an employee discount program; credit union membership; group home and auto insurance; education assistance; adoption assistance; 401(k) and 403(b) savings plans; paid time off; and a pension plan.

FINANCIAL DATA: *Note: Data for latest year may not have been available at press time.*

In U.S. $	2017	2016	2015	2014	2013	2012
Revenue	7,236,100,000	6,954,100,000	6,109,200,000	5,573,400,000	5,041,500,000	4,918,700,000
R&D Expense						
Operating Income						
Operating Margin %						
SGA Expense						
Net Income	655,100,000	495,400,000	279,100,000	431,000,000	766,300,000	475,000,000
Operating Cash Flow						
Capital Expenditure						
EBITDA						
Return on Assets %						
Return on Equity %						
Debt to Equity						

CONTACT INFORMATION:

Phone: 801-442-2000 Fax: 801-442-3327
Toll-Free: 800-888-3134
Address: 36 S. State St., Salt Lake City, UT 84111 United States

STOCK TICKER/OTHER:

Stock Ticker: Nonprofit
Exchange:
Employees: 37,000
Fiscal Year Ends: 12/31
Parent Company:

SALARIES/BONUSES:

Top Exec. Salary: $ Bonus: $
Second Exec. Salary: $ Bonus: $

OTHER THOUGHTS:

Estimated Female Officers or Directors: 3
Hot Spot for Advancement for Women/Minorities: Y

Interpace Diagnostics Group Inc

www.interpacediagnostics.com

NAIC Code: 541,613

TYPES OF BUSINESS:

Marketing & Advertising-Medical & Pharmaceutical Products
Contract Sales Organization
Pharmaceutical Sales Support
Marketing Research

BRANDS/DIVISIONS/AFFILIATES:

PancraGEN
PathFinderTG
ThyGenX
ThyraMIR
RespriDX
BarreGen

GROWTH PLANS/SPECIAL FEATURES:

Interpace Diagnostics Group, Inc., formerly PDI, Inc., develops and commercializes molecular diagnostic tests primarily for early detection of high potential progressors to cancer. The company leverages the latest technology and personalized medicine for patient diagnosis and management. Interpace currently has commercialized molecular tests: PancraGEN, a pancreatic cyst molecular test utilizing the firm's PathFinderTG platform; ThyGenX, which assess thyroid nodules for risk of malignancy; ThyraMIR, which assesses thyroid nodules risk of malignancy utilizing a proprietary gene expression assay; and RespriDX, a molecular test that helps physicians differentiate metastatic or recurrent lung cancer from the presence of a newly formed primary lung cancer. Interpace is also in the process of soft launching BarreGen, an esophageal cancer risk classifier for Barrett's Esophagus, while we gather additional market data. BarreGen also utilizes o PathFinderTG platform.

CONTACTS: *Note: Officers with more than one job title may be intentionally listed here more than once.*

James Early, CFO
Thomas Freeburg, Chief Accounting Officer
Jack Stover, Director
Stephen Sullivan, Director
Gregory Richard, Other Executive Officer

FINANCIAL DATA: *Note: Data for latest year may not have been available at press time.*

In U.S. $	2017	2016	2015	2014	2013	2012
Revenue	15,897,000	13,085,000	9,432,000	119,935,000	150,842,000	126,899,000
R&D Expense	1,461,000	1,647,000	2,292,000			
Operating Income	-11,895,000	-14,939,000	-30,862,000	-11,384,000	-4,277,000	-1,009,000
Operating Margin %	-74.82%	-114.16%	-327.20%	-9.49%	-2.83%	-.79%
SGA Expense	15,720,000	15,966,000	27,280,000	29,152,000	28,687,000	27,869,000
Net Income	-12,216,000	-8,332,000	-11,356,000	-16,073,000	-4,565,000	-25,527,000
Operating Cash Flow	-15,263,000	-8,940,000	-19,842,000	-16,378,000	-3,512,000	-10,286,000
Capital Expenditure	29,000		353,000	11,351,000	1,818,000	1,112,000
EBITDA	-9,009,000	-1,945,000	-35,471,000	-11,147,000	-2,852,000	1,025,000
Return on Assets %	-25.61%	-15.21%	-12.36%	-17.37%	-6.18%	-26.61%
Return on Equity %	-52.65%	-85.15%	-68.49%	-61.11%	-13.40%	-53.65%
Debt to Equity		1.21	0.55	1.34		

CONTACT INFORMATION:

Phone: 862 207-7800 Fax:
Toll-Free: 800-242-7494
Address: 300 Interpace Pkwy., Morris Corp. Ctr. 1, Bldg. A, Parsippany, NJ 07054 United States

STOCK TICKER/OTHER:

Stock Ticker: IDXG
Employees: 1,129
Parent Company:
Exchange: NAS
Fiscal Year Ends: 12/31

SALARIES/BONUSES:

Top Exec. Salary: $535,300 Bonus: $
Second Exec. Salary: $318,500 Bonus: $92,000

OTHER THOUGHTS:

Estimated Female Officers or Directors: 4
Hot Spot for Advancement for Women/Minorities: Y

Intersect ENT Inc

NAIC Code: 339,100

www.intersectent.com

TYPES OF BUSINESS:

Surgical and Medical Instrument Manufacturing

BRANDS/DIVISIONS/AFFILIATES:

PROPEL
PROPEL mini
PROPEL Contour
SINUVA

CONTACTS:

Note: Officers with more than one job title may be intentionally listed here more than once.

Lisa Earnhardt, CEO
Jeryl Hilleman, CFO
Richard Kaufman, COO
David Lehman, General Counsel
Drake Parker, Other Executive Officer
Gwen Carscadden, Other Executive Officer

GROWTH PLANS/SPECIAL FEATURES:

Intersect ENT, Inc. is a commercial stage drug-device company focusing on patients with ear, nose and throat conditions. The firm has developed a drug releasing bioabsorbable implant technology that enables targeted and sustained release of therapeutic agents. FDA approved products of Intersect ENT include PROPEL, PROPEL mini and PROPEL Contour. PROPEL and PROPEL mini are inserted by a physician into the ethmoid sinuses following sinus surgery. The self-expanding implants are designed to conform to and hold open the surgically enlarged sinus, while gradually releasing an anti-inflammatory steroid over a period of approximately 30 days, before being fully absorbed into the body. PROPEL Contour is a steroid releasing implant designed to fit the ostia, or openings, of the dependent sinuses following enlargement of the sinuses. When used with balloon openings, PROPEL Contour provides a less invasive procedure performed in the physician's office for patients with primary chronic sinusitis who have not had sinus surgery. The firm's product still undergoing clinical trials is SINUVA. SINUVA is a steroid releasing implant designed to provide a cost-effective, less invasive solution for patients that have had ethmoid sinus surgery yet suffer from recurrent sinus obstruction due to polyps. The SINUVA implant is designed to be placed in the ethmoid sinus in a procedure conducted in the physician's office as an alternative to other treatment options such as further medical therapy or revision surgery. Currently, Intersect ENT has approximately 2,400 accounts that have stocked PROPEL implants for use by ENT physicians.

FINANCIAL DATA:

Note: Data for latest year may not have been available at press time.

In U.S. $	2017	2016	2015	2014	2013	2012
Revenue	96,301,000	78,708,000	61,593,000	38,587,000	17,931,000	5,863,000
R&D Expense	18,360,000	18,890,000	16,608,000	10,331,000	9,518,000	9,260,000
Operating Income	-17,603,000	-26,111,000	-26,940,000	-18,078,000	-17,966,000	-16,485,000
Operating Margin %	-18.27%	-33.17%	-43.73%	-46.84%	-100.19%	-281.17%
SGA Expense	80,045,000	72,926,000	59,637,000	36,111,000	18,229,000	9,251,000
Net Income	-16,363,000	-25,222,000	-26,634,000	-18,362,000	-18,369,000	-16,365,000
Operating Cash Flow	-8,041,000	-20,059,000	-20,087,000	-17,954,000	-19,101,000	-16,148,000
Capital Expenditure	2,281,000	2,069,000	1,524,000	367,000	467,000	1,413,000
EBITDA	-16,139,000	-24,945,000	-26,114,000	-17,370,000	-17,375,000	-15,978,000
Return on Assets %	-12.33%	-18.38%	-25.66%	-43.72%	-129.99%	-226.44%
Return on Equity %	-14.12%	-20.62%	-28.94%			
Debt to Equity						

CONTACT INFORMATION:

Phone: 650 641-2100 Fax:
Toll-Free:
Address: 1555 Adams Dr., Menlo Park, CA 94025 United States

STOCK TICKER/OTHER:

Stock Ticker: XENT
Exchange: NAS
Employees: 303
Fiscal Year Ends: 12/31
Parent Company:

SALARIES/BONUSES:

Top Exec. Salary: $539,721 Bonus: $
Second Exec. Salary: $367,713 Bonus: $

OTHER THOUGHTS:

Estimated Female Officers or Directors:
Hot Spot for Advancement for Women/Minorities:

Intuitive Surgical Inc

www.intuitivesurgical.com

NAIC Code: 339,100

TYPES OF BUSINESS:

Endoscopic Surgery Products
Operative Surgical Robots

BRANDS/DIVISIONS/AFFILIATES:

da Vinci Surgical System
EndoWrist
da Vinci S HD Surgical System
da Vinci Si HD Surgical System
da Vinci SP Surgical System

CONTACTS: Note: Officers with more than one job title may be intentionally listed here more than once.

Gary Guthart, CEO
Marshall Mohr, CFO
Lonnie Smith, Chairman of the Board
Jamie Samath, Chief Accounting Officer
Myriam Curet, Chief Medical Officer
Salvatore Brogna, Executive VP
David Rosa, Executive VP
Mark Meltzer, General Counsel

GROWTH PLANS/SPECIAL FEATURES:

Intuitive Surgical, Inc. manufactures operative surgical robotics, including the da Vinci Surgical System, which consists of a surgeon's console, a patient-side cart, a high-performance vision system and Intuitive's proprietary wristed instruments. The system provides the surgeon with the control, range of motion, fine tissue manipulation capability and 3-D visualization characteristics of open surgery, but utilizes the small ports of minimally invasive surgery (MIS). The da Vinci Surgical System controls Intuitive's endoscopic instruments. Surgeons operate while seated at a console viewing a 3-D high definition (HD) vision system, which enhances visualization of tissue planes and critical anatomy and has a digital zoom feature, allowing surgeons to magnify the surgical field of view without adjusting endoscope position. The system also includes a motorized patient cart. In addition, Intuitive manufactures a variety of EndoWrist instruments; each incorporates a wrist joint with tips customized for various surgical procedures. The firm's da Vinci S HD Surgical System offers, in addition to 3-D high-definition vision, better resolution and 20% more viewing area than the original design. The company's da Vinci Si HD Surgical System is a more efficient, higher resolution version of the da Vinci HD Surgical System. In May 2018, the FDA cleared the da Vinci SP surgical system for urologic surgical procedures that are appropriate for a single port approach. Within the same month, Intuituve Surgical began direct operations in India, opening an international office in Bengaluru.

Intuitive offers its employees a dependent care plan; a medical expenses reimbursement plan; a commuter check program; an employee assistance program; a patent bonus program; onsite dry cleaning and oil change services; company events; a 401(k) plan; a employee stock purchase plan; and prescription, dental and vision coverage.

FINANCIAL DATA: Note: Data for latest year may not have been available at press time.

In U.S. $	2017	2016	2015	2014	2013	2012
Revenue	3,128,900,000	2,704,400,000	2,384,400,000	2,131,700,000	2,265,100,000	2,178,800,000
R&D Expense	328,600,000	239,600,000	197,400,000	178,000,000	167,700,000	170,000,000
Operating Income	1,054,600,000	945,200,000	740,000,000	544,800,000	852,500,000	878,100,000
Operating Margin %	33.70%	34.95%	31.03%	25.55%	37.63%	40.30%
SGA Expense	810,900,000	705,300,000	640,500,000	691,000,000	574,000,000	522,200,000
Net Income	660,000,000	735,900,000	588,800,000	418,800,000	671,000,000	656,600,000
Operating Cash Flow	1,143,900,000	1,042,900,000	771,900,000	665,100,000	880,000,000	814,200,000
Capital Expenditure	190,700,000	53,900,000	81,000,000	105,600,000	104,600,000	141,800,000
EBITDA	1,153,700,000	1,037,300,000	829,500,000	619,200,000	919,800,000	935,900,000
Return on Assets %	10.77%	12.91%	13.28%	10.58%	16.75%	18.43%
Return on Equity %	12.56%	14.57%	15.29%	12.17%	18.95%	21.09%
Debt to Equity						

CONTACT INFORMATION:

Phone: 408 523-2100 Fax: 408 523-1390
Toll-Free: 888-868-4647
Address: 1020 Kifer Rd., Sunnyvale, CA 94086 United States

SALARIES/BONUSES:

Top Exec. Salary: $744,188 Bonus: $
Second Exec. Salary: Bonus: $
$531,563

STOCK TICKER/OTHER:

Stock Ticker: ISRG Exchange: NAS
Employees: 3,755 Fiscal Year Ends: 12/31
Parent Company:

OTHER THOUGHTS:

Estimated Female Officers or Directors: 3
Hot Spot for Advancement for Women/Minorities: Y

Sales, profits and employees may be estimates. Financial information, benefits and other data can change quickly and may vary from those stated here.

Invacare Corporation

www.invacare.com

NAIC Code: 339,100

TYPES OF BUSINESS:

Supplies-Wheelchairs
Home Health Care Equipment
Home Respiratory Products
Medical Supplies

BRANDS/DIVISIONS/AFFILIATES:

Invacare Continuing Care Inc
Storm Series
SureStep
Motion Concepts ROVI
TDX
Invacare Top End
Invacare HomeFill Oxygen Systems
Perfecto2

CONTACTS: *Note: Officers with more than one job title may be intentionally listed here more than once.*

Matthew Monaghan, CEO
Ralf Ledda, General Manager, Geographical
Dean Childers, General Manager, Geographical
Kathleen Leneghan, Senior VP
Anthony LaPlaca, Senior VP

GROWTH PLANS/SPECIAL FEATURES:

Invacare Corporation is a leading manufacturer and distributor of healthcare products for the non-acute care environment, including the home healthcare, retail and extended care markets. The firm sells its products through a network of associates in over 100 countries including locations in the U.S., Australia, New Zealand, Canada, Europe and Asia. Invacare's product line includes power and manual wheelchairs, motorized scooters, seating and positioning products, walkers, home care beds, mattress overlays, home respiratory products, bathing equipment, lifts and sling and patient aids. Invacare's power wheelchair line includes the Storm Series, SureStep, Motion Concepts ROVI and TDX brand names. The firm also manufactures and markets custom manual wheelchairs for every day, sports and recreational uses, marketed under the Invacare and Invacare Top End brand names. The company's home respiratory products include non-delivery oxygen concentrators, such as the Invacare HomeFill Oxygen System; and stationary oxygen concentrators, manufactured under the Perfecto2 and Platinum brand names. The firm, through Invacare Continuing Care, Inc., also sells and distributes healthcare furniture such as beds, bedside rails, mattresses, overbed tables and traction equipment for the long-term care markets.

Invacare offers its employees medical, dental and vision plans; life insurance optional plan; short- and long-term disability insurance; an employee assistance program; weight loss and smoking cessation programs; and a 401(k).

FINANCIAL DATA: *Note: Data for latest year may not have been available at press time.*

In U.S. $	2017	2016	2015	2014	2013	2012
Revenue	966,497,000	1,047,474,000	1,142,338,000	1,270,163,000	1,352,359,000	1,455,461,000
R&D Expense						
Operating Income	-27,565,000	-20,154,000	-7,023,000	-36,525,000	-24,357,000	30,399,000
Operating Margin %	-2.85%	-1.92%	-.61%	-2.87%	-1.80%	2.08%
SGA Expense	296,816,000	303,781,000	319,847,000	383,913,000	401,823,000	414,502,000
Net Income	-76,541,000	-42,856,000	-26,190,000	-56,070,000	33,051,000	1,827,000
Operating Cash Flow	-25,774,000	-56,613,000	-5,378,000	8,892,000	10,054,000	62,291,000
Capital Expenditure	14,569,000	10,151,000	7,522,000	12,327,000	14,158,000	20,091,000
EBITDA	-28,712,000	953,000	10,601,000	-27,382,000	1,957,000	57,688,000
Return on Assets %	-7.77%	-4.92%	-2.90%	-5.44%	2.80%	.14%
Return on Equity %	-18.10%	-9.68%	-5.09%	-9.07%	5.11%	.29%
Debt to Equity	0.57	0.34	0.09	0.03	0.04	0.36

CONTACT INFORMATION:

Phone: 440 329-6000 Fax: 440 366-9008
Toll-Free: 800-333-6900
Address: 1 Invacare Way, Elyria, OH 44036 United States

STOCK TICKER/OTHER:

Stock Ticker: IVC
Employees: 4,600
Parent Company:
Exchange: NYS
Fiscal Year Ends: 12/31

SALARIES/BONUSES:

Top Exec. Salary: $780,778 Bonus: $
Second Exec. Salary: $445,668 Bonus: $

OTHER THOUGHTS:

Estimated Female Officers or Directors: 3
Hot Spot for Advancement for Women/Minorities: Y

IQVIA Holdings Inc

www.iqvia.com

NAIC Code: 541,711

TYPES OF BUSINESS:

Contract Research
Pharmaceutical, Biotech & Medical Device Research
Consulting & Training Services
Sales & Marketing Services

BRANDS/DIVISIONS/AFFILIATES:

IQVIA CORE
Quintiles IMS Holdings Inc

CONTACTS: *Note: Officers with more than one job title may be intentionally listed here more than once.*

Michael Mcdonnell, CFO
Ari Bousbib, Chairman of the Board
Robert Parks, Controller
Eric Sherbet, Executive VP
W. Staub, President, Divisional
Kevin Knightly, President, Divisional

GROWTH PLANS/SPECIAL FEATURES:

IQVIA Holdings, Inc. (formerly Quintiles IMS Holdings, Inc.) provides integrated information and technology-enabled healthcare services. The company's offerings help clients improve clinical, scientific and commercial results, with operations in more than 100 countries. IQVIA Holdings' range of healthcare information, technology and service solutions span the entire product lifecycle, from clinical to commercial operations. Its information includes more than 530 million comprehensive and anonymous patient records spanning sales, prescription and promotional data; medical claims; electronic medical records; and social media. The firm's proprietary assets develop clinical and commercial capabilities. These assets and capabilities include: healthcare-specific global IT infrastructure, data-enriched clinical development, real-world insights ecosystem and proprietary commercial applications. In November 2017, Quintiles IMS Holdings changed its name to IQVIA Holdings. The company continues to trade on the NYSE, but under a new ticker symbol: IQV.

FINANCIAL DATA: *Note: Data for latest year may not have been available at press time.*

In U.S. $	2017	2016	2015	2014	2013	2012
Revenue	9,739,000,000	6,878,000,000	5,737,619,000	5,459,998,000	5,099,545,000	4,865,513,000
R&D Expense						
Operating Income	822,000,000	828,000,000	679,848,000	599,378,000	476,404,000	415,176,000
Operating Margin %	8.44%	12.03%	11.84%	10.97%	9.34%	8.53%
SGA Expense	1,605,000,000	1,011,000,000	920,985,000	882,338,000	860,510,000	817,755,000
Net Income	1,309,000,000	115,000,000	387,205,000	356,383,000	226,591,000	177,546,000
Operating Cash Flow	970,000,000	860,000,000	475,691,000	431,754,000	397,370,000	335,701,000
Capital Expenditure	369,000,000	164,000,000	78,391,000	82,650,000	92,346,000	71,336,000
EBITDA	1,688,000,000	912,000,000	768,529,000	723,791,000	554,128,000	500,087,000
Return on Assets %	5.95%	.91%	10.70%	11.18%	8.14%	7.36%
Return on Equity %	15.63%	2.85%				
Debt to Equity	1.24	0.82				

CONTACT INFORMATION:

Phone: 919-998-2000 Fax:
Toll-Free: 866-267-4479
Address: 4820 Emperor Blvd., Durham, NC 27703 United States

STOCK TICKER/OTHER:

Stock Ticker: IQV
Employees: 50,000
Parent Company:
Exchange: NYS
Fiscal Year Ends: 12/31

SALARIES/BONUSES:

Top Exec. Salary: $1,600,000 Bonus: $
Second Exec. Salary: $650,000 Bonus: $

OTHER THOUGHTS:

Estimated Female Officers or Directors: 3
Hot Spot for Advancement for Women/Minorities: Y

IRIDEX Corporation

www.iridex.com

NAIC Code: 334,510

TYPES OF BUSINESS:

Equipment-Laser Systems
Ophthalmological & Dermatological Laser Systems

BRANDS/DIVISIONS/AFFILIATES:

IQ
OcuLight
Cyclo G6
MicroPulse P3
G-Probe
EndoProbe

GROWTH PLANS/SPECIAL FEATURES:

IRIDEX Corporation develops, manufactures and markets innovative and versatile laser-based medical systems, delivery devices and consumable instrumentation for the ophthalmology and otolaryngology market. The company's products are sold in the U.S. through a direct sales force, and internationally through a combination of direct sales forces and a network of approximately 60 independent distributors into more than 100 countries. Laser products include the IQ family of laser systems for repeatable, tissue-sparing glaucoma and retinal therapies; the OcuLight family of surgical retina laser systems, which are often used in vitrectomy procedures to treat proliferative diabetic, retinopathy, macular holes, retinal tears and detachments; and the Cyclo G6 laser system used for the treatment of glaucoma. Probes used in the company's glaucoma product line include its patented MicroPulse P3 probe and G-Probe; and surgical retina probes include the EndoProbe family of products used in vitrectomy procedures.

CONTACTS: *Note: Officers with more than one job title may be intentionally listed here more than once.*

William Moore, CEO
Atabak Mokari, CFO
Romeo Dizon, Chief Accounting Officer

FINANCIAL DATA: *Note: Data for latest year may not have been available at press time.*

In U.S. $	2017	2016	2015	2014	2013	2012
Revenue	41,593,000	46,158,000	41,757,000	42,814,000	38,273,000	33,859,000
R&D Expense	5,730,000	5,365,000	5,214,000	4,629,000	3,684,000	4,385,000
Operating Income	-13,028,000	-2,445,000	288,000	2,587,000	2,160,000	-860,000
Operating Margin %	-31.32%	-5.29%	.68%	6.04%	5.64%	-2.53%
SGA Expense	22,801,000	17,919,000	14,451,000	14,189,000	12,743,000	12,821,000
Net Income	-12,867,000	-11,713,000	474,000	10,038,000	2,231,000	1,438,000
Operating Cash Flow	-3,565,000	-144,000	-593,000	4,014,000	767,000	-443,000
Capital Expenditure	575,000	1,062,000	875,000	568,000	380,000	394,000
EBITDA	-12,170,000	-1,797,000	810,000	3,007,000	3,123,000	367,000
Return on Assets %	-28.66%	-26.03%	1.13%	26.59%	7.12%	4.71%
Return on Equity %	-36.93%	-32.15%	1.40%	33.69%	9.34%	6.48%
Debt to Equity						

CONTACT INFORMATION:

Phone: 650 940-4700 Fax: 650 940-4710
Toll-Free: 800-388-4747
Address: 1212 Terra Bella Ave., Mountain View, CA 94043 United States

STOCK TICKER/OTHER:

Stock Ticker: IRIX
Employees: 121
Parent Company:
Exchange: NAS
Fiscal Year Ends: 12/31

SALARIES/BONUSES:

Top Exec. Salary: $501,347 Bonus: $
Second Exec. Salary: $336,132 Bonus: $

OTHER THOUGHTS:

Estimated Female Officers or Directors:
Hot Spot for Advancement for Women/Minorities:

Jean Coutu Group (PJC) Inc (The)

www.jeancoutu.com

NAIC Code: 446,110

TYPES OF BUSINESS:

Drug Stores
Pharmaceuticals
Warehousing
Distribution

BRANDS/DIVISIONS/AFFILIATES:

Metro Inc

GROWTH PLANS/SPECIAL FEATURES:

The Jean Coutu Group (PJC), Inc. is a leading Canadian distributor and retailer of pharmaceuticals and over-the-counter drugs. The company, a wholly-owned subsidiary of Metro, Inc., oversees Metro's pharmaceutical operations and provides its more than 400 franchise stores with a range of professional and technical support services. Jean Coutu Group also supplies, warehouses and delivers pharmaceuticals, pharmaceutical products and consumer goods. Distribution centers are located in Quebec and Ontario. In May 2018, Jean Coutu Group was acquired by Metro, Inc.

CONTACTS: *Note: Officers with more than one job title may be intentionally listed here more than once.*

Francois Coutu, CEO
Jean Coutu, Chairman of the Board
Nicolle Forget, Director
Alain Lafortune, Executive VP, Divisional
Andre Belzile, Executive VP, Divisional
Normand Messier, Executive VP, Divisional
Richard Mayrand, Executive VP, Divisional
Jean-Michel Coutu, Executive VP, Divisional
Marcel Raymond, President, Subsidiary
Brigite Dufour, Secretary
Louis Coutu, Vice President, Divisional
Marie-Chantal Lamothe, Vice President, Divisional
Daniel Cote, Vice President, Divisional

FINANCIAL DATA: *Note: Data for latest year may not have been available at press time.*

In U.S. $	2017	2016	2015	2014	2013	2012
Revenue	2,360,602,368	2,263,020,032	2,230,360,576	2,166,706,176	2,171,621,120	2,166,547,712
R&D Expense						
Operating Income						
Operating Margin %						
SGA Expense						
Net Income	158,145,056	169,401,504	173,523,584	346,412,992	442,647,648	182,322,624
Operating Cash Flow						
Capital Expenditure						
EBITDA						
Return on Assets %						
Return on Equity %						
Debt to Equity						

CONTACT INFORMATION:

Phone: 450 646-9760 Fax:
Toll-Free:
Address: 245, Jean Coutu St., Varennes, QC J3X 0E1 Canada

STOCK TICKER/OTHER:

Stock Ticker: PJC.A Exchange: TSE
Employees: 1,074 Fiscal Year Ends: 03/31
Parent Company: Metro Inc

SALARIES/BONUSES:

Top Exec. Salary: $ Bonus: $
Second Exec. Salary: $ Bonus: $

OTHER THOUGHTS:

Estimated Female Officers or Directors: 13
Hot Spot for Advancement for Women/Minorities: Y

Jenny Craig Inc

NAIC Code: 812,191

www.jennycraig.com

TYPES OF BUSINESS:

Weight Management Programs
Packaged Food
Video Production
Franchising
Online Sales & Services

BRANDS/DIVISIONS/AFFILIATES:

North Castle Partners LLC

CONTACTS: *Note: Officers with more than one job title may be intentionally listed here more than once.*

Monty Sharma, CEO
Peter Noverr, COO
Michael Schantz, CFO
Michelle Hodges, Chief Human Resources Officer
Yash Muralidharan, VP-IT
Kim Matthews, General Counsel
Andy Henton, VP-Oper.
Corrinne Peritano, VP-North America Bus.

GROWTH PLANS/SPECIAL FEATURES:

Jenny Craig, Inc., owned by private equity firm North Castle Partners, LLC, is a weight management, diet and nutrition company. The firm has franchised locations throughout the U.S., Canada and Puerto Rico, with operating consultants available worldwide. Jenny Craig offers clients personalized diet programs with the help of one-on-one consultations with weight loss counselors. Weight loss is achieved via personalized diet plans, which include Jenny's Cuisine food products and fresh foods prepared using Jenny Craig recipes; exercise plans; and counseling and support available online, by phone or in person at Jenny Craig centers. In a given week, around 75,000 unique customers follow a Jenny Craig program. The firm provides options for clients with significant weight loss goals as well as for clients who wish to track daily calorie intake and expenditure. Both options can be conducted either from home, supplemented by weekly phone consultations, or in-center, with regular visits to Jenny Craig locations. Once a weight goal is achieved, the firm offers weight maintenance programs with consultations and menu planning. Information is available for members on personal weight tracking, lifestyle planning and selected recipes through the company's online service. The website also features 100 popular food products such as Jenny's Cuisine breakfast, lunch, dinner and snack items as well as sauces, dressings, cookbooks and exercise videos. In addition, the company produces and markets DVDs, journals, CDs and workout accessories.

The company offers its employees life and AD&D insurance; an employee assistance program; medical, dental, prescription and vision insurance; long-term disability insurance; a 401(k) plan; and company discounts.

FINANCIAL DATA: *Note: Data for latest year may not have been available at press time.*

In U.S. $	2017	2016	2015	2014	2013	2012
Revenue	300,000,000	298,000,000	300,000,000	325,000,000	352,000,000	360,000,000
R&D Expense						
Operating Income						
Operating Margin %						
SGA Expense						
Net Income						
Operating Cash Flow						
Capital Expenditure						
EBITDA						
Return on Assets %						
Return on Equity %						
Debt to Equity						

CONTACT INFORMATION:

Phone: 760-696-4000 Fax: 760-696-4009
Toll-Free: 800-597-5366
Address: 5770 Fleet St., Carlsbad, CA 92008 United States

STOCK TICKER/OTHER:

Stock Ticker: Private
Exchange:
Employees: 3,510
Fiscal Year Ends: 12/31
Parent Company: North Castle Partners LLC

SALARIES/BONUSES:

Top Exec. Salary: $ Bonus: $
Second Exec. Salary: $ Bonus: $

OTHER THOUGHTS:

Estimated Female Officers or Directors: 3
Hot Spot for Advancement for Women/Minorities: Y

Jiangsu Hengrui Medicine Co Ltd

www.hrs.com.cn

NAIC Code: 325,412

TYPES OF BUSINESS:

Pharmaceutical Preparation Manufacturing
Pharmaceuticals
Raw Materials

BRANDS/DIVISIONS/AFFILIATES:

GROWTH PLANS/SPECIAL FEATURES:

Jiangsu Hengrui Medicine Co., Ltd. develops, manufactures and markets a variety of pharmaceutical medicines, raw materials and related packaging materials. The company's products include anti-neoplastic drugs, angiomyocardiac drugs, drugs for surgery, pain management medicines, antibiotics, specialty infusions, contrast agents, aluminum foil and other related products. Hengrui Medicine distributes its medicines both domestically and overseas. The firm's pharmaceutical business engages in the research, development, production and marketing of medicines. The company has applied for more than 400 domestic invention patents and more than 100 Patent Cooperation Treaty (PCT) applications for international protection. Hengrui Medicine has research and development centers located in China and the U.S.

CONTACTS: *Note: Officers with more than one job title may be intentionally listed here more than once.*

Zhou Yunshu, Pres.
Sun Piaoyang, Chmn.

FINANCIAL DATA: *Note: Data for latest year may not have been available at press time.*

In U.S. $	2017	2016	2015	2014	2013	2012
Revenue	2,124,320,000	1,596,280,000	1,475,460,000	1,193,000,000		
R&D Expense						
Operating Income						
Operating Margin %						
SGA Expense						
Net Income	505,169,000	378,457,000	345,510,000	245,966,000		
Operating Cash Flow						
Capital Expenditure						
EBITDA						
Return on Assets %						
Return on Equity %						
Debt to Equity						

CONTACT INFORMATION:

Phone: 86-518-8122-0983 Fax:
Toll-Free:
Address: 38 Huanghe Rd., Eco & Tech Dev. Park, Lianyungang, Jiangsu 222000 China

STOCK TICKER/OTHER:

Stock Ticker: 600276
Employees:
Parent Company:
Exchange: Shanghai
Fiscal Year Ends:

SALARIES/BONUSES:

Top Exec. Salary: $ Bonus: $
Second Exec. Salary: $ Bonus: $

OTHER THOUGHTS:

Estimated Female Officers or Directors:
Hot Spot for Advancement for Women/Minorities:

Johns Hopkins Medicine

www.hopkinsmedicine.org

NAIC Code: 622,110

TYPES OF BUSINESS:

General Medical and Surgical Hospitals
Medical Research
Medical School
Home Care Services
Physician Network Management

BRANDS/DIVISIONS/AFFILIATES:

Johns Hopkins University School of Medicine
Johns Hopkins Hospital
Johns Hopkins Health System
Johns Hopkins Bayview Medical Center
Johns Hopkins Medicine International

CONTACTS: *Note: Officers with more than one job title may be intentionally listed here more than once.*

Paul B. Rothman, CEO
Robert Kasdin, COO
Ronald J. Daniels, Pres., The Johns Hopkins University
Ronald J. Werthman, CFO
Inez Stewart, Sr. VP-Human Resources
Joanne E. Pollak, Sr. VP
Judy A. Reitz, Exec. VP
Ronald R. Peterson, Exec. VP

GROWTH PLANS/SPECIAL FEATURES:

Johns Hopkins Medicine is a nonprofit organization that includes Johns Hopkins University School of Medicine, the Johns Hopkins Hospital and the Johns Hopkins Health System. Johns Hopkins Medicine operates six academic and community hospitals, four suburban healthcare and surgery centers and 39 primary and specialty care outpatient sites. The university has a multitude of academic departments ranging from anesthesiology to urology. The Johns Hopkins Hospital is a partner with the University medical school and faculty, with a training school for nurses and comprises 33 state-of-the-art operating rooms (14 neurosurgery/general surgery, 10 pediatric, six cardiac and three obstetric), 355 private inpatient rooms for adults, 205 private inpatient rooms for children, and emergency departments for adults and children. The Johns Hopkins Health System provides comprehensive healthcare services, operating clinics and hospitals in and around Baltimore. Johns Hopkins Bayview Medical Center, in eastern Baltimore, is a teaching hospital housing a neonatal intensive care unit, sleep disorders center, area-wide trauma center, a regional burn center and a nationally regarded geriatrics center. The organization also maintains a home care group that provides visits by nurses, physical and occupational therapists, home health aides and social workers; a network of physicians providing community-based healthcare; several facilities at which faculty physicians practice; and programs to assist patients and families from foreign countries or other U.S. cities with physician appointments, lodging, transportation, interpreter services, financial arrangements, daycare centers and sightseeing. Johns Hopkins Medicine International offers hospital management, healthcare consulting and clinical education services through alliances and affiliations in North America, Latin America, Europe, the Middle East and Asia.

FINANCIAL DATA: *Note: Data for latest year may not have been available at press time.*

In U.S. $	2017	2016	2015	2014	2013	2012
Revenue	8,400,000,000	8,000,000,000	7,700,000,000	6,700,000,000	6,500,000,000	7,000,000,000
R&D Expense						
Operating Income						
Operating Margin %						
SGA Expense						
Net Income			1,820,000,000			
Operating Cash Flow						
Capital Expenditure						
EBITDA						
Return on Assets %						
Return on Equity %						
Debt to Equity						

CONTACT INFORMATION:

Phone: 410-955-5000 Fax: 410-955-4452
Toll-Free:
Address: 1800 Orleans St, Baltimore, MD 21287 United States

STOCK TICKER/OTHER:

Stock Ticker: Nonprofit
Exchange:
Employees: 41,000
Fiscal Year Ends: 06/30
Parent Company:

SALARIES/BONUSES:

Top Exec. Salary: $ Bonus: $
Second Exec. Salary: $ Bonus: $

OTHER THOUGHTS:

Estimated Female Officers or Directors: 18
Hot Spot for Advancement for Women/Minorities: Y

Johnson & Johnson

www.jnj.com

NAIC Code: 325,412

TYPES OF BUSINESS:

Personal Health Care & Hygiene Products
Sterilization Products
Surgical Products
Pharmaceuticals
Skin Care Products
Baby Care Products
Contact Lenses
Medical Equipment

BRANDS/DIVISIONS/AFFILIATES:

Motrin
Band-Aid
Listerine
Tylenol
Neosporin
Risperdal Consta
Actelion Ltd
Idorsia Ltd

CONTACTS: *Note: Officers with more than one job title may be intentionally listed here more than once.*

Alex Gorsky, CEO
Kathy Wengel, Vice President, Divisional
Dominic Caruso, CFO
Jorge Mesquita, Chairman of the Board, Divisional
Sandra Peterson, Chairman of the Board, Divisional
Joaquin Duato, Chairman of the Board, Divisional
Ashley McEvoy, Chairman, Divisional
Jennifer Taubert, Chairman, Divisional
Ronald Kapusta, Chief Accounting Officer
Paulus Stoffels, Executive VP
Peter Fasolo, Executive VP
Michael Ullmann, General Counsel
Michael Sneed, Other Executive Officer
Joseph Wolk, Vice President, Divisional

GROWTH PLANS/SPECIAL FEATURES:

Johnson & Johnson, founded in 1886, is one of the world's most comprehensive and well-known researchers, developers and manufacturers of healthcare products. Johnson & Johnson's worldwide operations are divided into three segments: consumer, pharmaceuticals and medical devices. The company's principal consumer goods are personal care and hygiene products, including baby care, skin care, oral care, wound care and women's healthcare products as well as nutritional and over-the-counter pharmaceutical products. Major consumer brands include Motrin, Band-Aid, Listerine, Tylenol, Neosporin, Aveeno and Pepcid AC. The pharmaceutical segment covers a wide spectrum of health fields, including anti-infective, antipsychotic, contraceptive, dermatology, gastrointestinal, hematology, immunology, neurology, oncology, pain management and virology. Among its pharmaceutical products are Risperdal Consta, an antipsychotic used to treat schizophrenia, and Remicade for the treatment of immune mediated inflammatory diseases. In the medical devices segment, Johnson & Johnson makes a number of products including orthopedic joint reconstruction devices, surgical care, advanced sterilization products, blood glucose monitoring devices, diagnostic products and disposable contact lenses. The firm owns more than 260 companies in virtually all countries of the world, and is headquartered in New Brunswick, New Jersey. During 2017, Johnson & Johnson acquired Actelion Ltd., Europe's largest biotech firm by sales and market capitalization, for $30 billion. The deal included the spin-off of Actelion's drug discovery operations and early-stage development assets into a newly-created, Swiss-based biopharmaceutical company, Idorsia Ltd. Johnson & Johnson controls 16% of Idorsia, with the ability to raise the stake to 32% through convertible notes. In March 2018, Johnson & Johnson agreed to sell its LifeScan, Inc. business to Platinum Equity LLC for approximately $2.1 billion.

FINANCIAL DATA: *Note: Data for latest year may not have been available at press time.*

In U.S. $	2017	2016	2015	2014	2013	2012
Revenue	76,450,000,000	71,890,000,000	70,074,000,000	74,331,000,000	71,312,000,000	67,224,000,000
R&D Expense	10,962,000,000	9,124,000,000	9,270,000,000	8,672,000,000	8,763,000,000	8,828,000,000
Operating Income	18,714,000,000	21,136,000,000	18,065,000,000	20,959,000,000	18,377,000,000	15,869,000,000
Operating Margin %	24.47%	29.40%	25.77%	28.19%	25.76%	23.60%
SGA Expense	21,420,000,000	19,945,000,000	21,203,000,000	21,954,000,000	21,830,000,000	20,869,000,000
Net Income	1,300,000,000	16,540,000,000	15,409,000,000	16,323,000,000	13,831,000,000	10,853,000,000
Operating Cash Flow	21,056,000,000	18,767,000,000	19,279,000,000	18,471,000,000	17,414,000,000	15,396,000,000
Capital Expenditure	3,513,000,000	3,349,000,000	3,566,000,000	4,013,000,000	3,861,000,000	2,934,000,000
EBITDA	24,249,000,000	24,283,000,000	23,494,000,000	24,991,000,000	20,057,000,000	17,973,000,000
Return on Assets %	.87%	12.04%	11.65%	12.37%	10.88%	9.23%
Return on Equity %	1.99%	23.36%	21.87%	22.70%	19.91%	17.80%
Debt to Equity	0.50	0.31	0.18	0.21	0.17	0.17

CONTACT INFORMATION:

Phone: 732 524-0400 Fax: 732 214-0332
Toll-Free:
Address: 1 Johnson & Johnson Plaza, New Brunswick, NJ 08933 United States

STOCK TICKER/OTHER:

Stock Ticker: JNJ
Employees: 126,400
Parent Company:
Exchange: NYS
Fiscal Year Ends: 12/31

SALARIES/BONUSES:

Top Exec. Salary: $1,600,000 Bonus: $
Second Exec. Salary: $1,173,023 Bonus: $

OTHER THOUGHTS:

Estimated Female Officers or Directors: 4
Hot Spot for Advancement for Women/Minorities: Y

K2M Group Holdings Inc

NAIC Code: 339,100

www.k2m.com

TYPES OF BUSINESS:

Technologies for Spinal Surgery
3D Printing of Spinal Devices

BRANDS/DIVISIONS/AFFILIATES:

Balance ACS
Lamellar 3D Titanium Technology

CONTACTS: *Note: Officers with more than one job title may be intentionally listed here more than once.*

Eric Major, CEO
Gregory Cole, CFO
George Moratis, Chief Accounting Officer
John Kostuik, Chief Medical Officer
Lane Major, COO

GROWTH PLANS/SPECIAL FEATURES:

K2M Group Holdings, Inc. is a global leader of complex spine and minimally-invasive solutions, with a focus on achieving three-dimensional total body balance. The company has designed, developed and commercialized innovative technologies and techniques used by spine surgeons to treat complicated spinal pathologies. It has leveraged these core competencies into Balance ACS, a platform of products, services and research to help surgeons achieve three-dimensional spinal balance across the axial, coronal and sagittal (ACS) planes, with the goal of supporting the full continuum of care to facilitate quality patient outcomes. Many of K2M's spinal devices comprise its Lamellar 3D Titanium Technology, which utilizes an advanced 3D-printing method to create structures considered impractical when using traditional manufacturing techniques. Starting with a titanium powder, the spinal devices are grown through a selective application of a high-energy laser beam, allowing for the incorporation of a porosity and surface roughness that K2M believes have associated with bone growth activity. The Balance ACS platform, in combination with K2M's technologies and techniques in the 3D-printing of spinal devices, enable the firm to compete in the global spinal surgery market. Products within K2M's portfolio include fixation spinal systems, retractor systems, cage systems, plate systems, connectors, interbody systems (including 3D), access systems, bone graft systems, osteobiologic systems and allograft systems. Quality control inspections, in-process inspections and packaging and labeling inspections all take place at K2M's headquarters facility.

K2M offers medical, dental, vision, life and disability insurance packages; 401(k); and tuition reimbursement.

FINANCIAL DATA: *Note: Data for latest year may not have been available at press time.*

In U.S. $	2017	2016	2015	2014	2013	2012
Revenue	258,031,000	236,634,000	216,007,000	186,672,000	157,584,000	135,145,000
R&D Expense	22,247,000	21,547,000	19,868,000	16,302,000	12,402,000	9,031,000
Operating Income	-33,457,000	-34,731,000	-36,270,000	-47,969,000	-44,921,000	-45,832,000
Operating Margin %	-12.96%	-14.67%	-16.79%	-25.69%	-28.50%	-33.91%
SGA Expense	180,592,000	167,640,000	160,618,000	155,539,000	139,941,000	127,984,000
Net Income	-37,145,000	-41,660,000	-39,216,000	-59,637,000	-37,913,000	-32,655,000
Operating Cash Flow	-12,813,000	-13,298,000	-18,310,000	-30,162,000	-19,090,000	-16,447,000
Capital Expenditure	6,878,000	18,746,000	14,280,000	3,023,000	1,611,000	1,432,000
EBITDA	-4,870,000	-7,949,000	-13,143,000	-24,222,000	-6,668,000	-2,650,000
Return on Assets %	-9.81%	-10.99%	-11.58%	-17.59%	-19.22%	-14.22%
Return on Equity %	-14.74%	-15.19%	-14.38%	-23.65%	-33.97%	-28.39%
Debt to Equity	0.30	0.27	0.11		0.10	0.17

CONTACT INFORMATION:

Phone: 703 777-3155 Fax:
Toll-Free:
Address: 600 Hope Pkwy. SE, Leesburg, VA 20175 United States

STOCK TICKER/OTHER:

Stock Ticker: KTWO
Exchange: NAS
Employees: 457
Fiscal Year Ends: 12/31
Parent Company:

SALARIES/BONUSES:

Top Exec. Salary: $573,491 Bonus: $
Second Exec. Salary: $434,178 Bonus: $

OTHER THOUGHTS:

Estimated Female Officers or Directors:
Hot Spot for Advancement for Women/Minorities:

Kaiser Permanente

www.kaiserpermanente.org

NAIC Code: 622,110

TYPES OF BUSINESS:

General Medical and Surgical Hospitals
General & Specialty Hospitals
Outpatient Facilities
HMO
Health Insurance
Integrated Health Care System
Physician Networks
Clinical Record Management

BRANDS/DIVISIONS/AFFILIATES:

Kaiser Foundation Health Plan Inc
Kaiser Foundation Hospitals
Permanente Medical Groups
Kaiser Permanente Center for Health Research
KP HealthConnect

CONTACTS: *Note: Officers with more than one job title may be intentionally listed here more than once.*

Bernard J. Tyson, CEO
Kathy Lancaster, CFO
Chuck Columbus, Chief Human Resources Officer
Raymond J. Baxter, Sr. VP-Community Benefit, Research & Health Policy
Richard D. Daniels, CIO
Mark S. Zemelman, General Counsel
Arthur M. Southam, Exec. VP-Health Plan Oper.
Chris Grant, Sr. VP-Corp. Dev. & Care Delivery Strategy
Diane Gage Lofgren, Sr. VP
Cynthia Powers Overmyer, Sr. VP-Internal Audit Svcs.
Daniel P. Garcia, Chief Compliance Officer
Anthony Barrueta, Sr. VP-Gov't Rel.
Amy Compton-Phillips, Associate Exec. Dir.-Quality, Permanente
Bernard J.Tyson, Chmn.

GROWTH PLANS/SPECIAL FEATURES:

Kaiser Permanente is a nonprofit company dedicated to providing integrated health care coverage. The firm operates in California, Colorado, Georgia, Hawaii, Maryland, Washington D.C., Oregon, Virginia and Washington. It serves 12.2 million members, most of which are in California (more than 8.7 million). Kaiser has three main operating divisions: Kaiser Foundation Health Plan, Inc., which contracts with individuals and groups to provide medical coverage; Kaiser Foundation Hospitals and their subsidiaries, operating community hospitals and outpatient facilities in several states; and Permanente Medical Groups, the company's network of physicians providing healthcare to its members. The company's resources include approximately 39 medical centers, including hospitals and outpatient facilities; 684 medical offices; and 22,000 physicians. Kaiser Permanente is one of the largest health plans serving the Medicare program. Kaiser Foundation Hospitals also fund medical- and health-related research. The Kaiser Permanente Center for Health Research, founded in 1964, is a single research center that spans two regions of Kaiser Permanente: Northwest and Hawaii. The center pursues a vigorous agenda of public health research within large, diverse populations, and specializes in the disciplines of biostatistics, clinical research support services, data resources, evidence-based practices and qualitative research. In addition, the company's KP HealthConnect platform integrates clinical records with appointments, registration and billing, thereby significantly improving care delivery and patient satisfaction.

Employees of the firm are offered medical, vision, dental and life insurance; a prescription plan; paid time off for vacations; designated holidays; sick leave; disability benefits; retirement plans; tuition reimbursement; employee assistance programs; and transit spending account options. Kaiser Permanente's employee health care coverage extends to spouses, domestic partners and unmarried children.

FINANCIAL DATA: *Note: Data for latest year may not have been available at press time.*

In U.S. $	2017	2016	2015	2014	2013	2012
Revenue	72,700,000,000	64,600,000,000	60,700,000,000	56,400,000,000	53,100,000,000	50,600,000,000
R&D Expense						
Operating Income						
Operating Margin %						
SGA Expense						
Net Income	3,800,000,000	3,100,000,000	1,900,000,000	3,100,000,000	2,700,000,000	2,600,000,000
Operating Cash Flow						
Capital Expenditure						
EBITDA						
Return on Assets %						
Return on Equity %						
Debt to Equity						

CONTACT INFORMATION:

Phone: 510-271-5910 Fax:
Toll-Free:
Address: 1 Kaiser Plaza, 19/Fl., Oakland, CA 94612 United States

STOCK TICKER/OTHER:

Stock Ticker: Nonprofit
Employees: 186,497
Parent Company:
Exchange:
Fiscal Year Ends: 12/31

SALARIES/BONUSES:

Top Exec. Salary: $ Bonus: $
Second Exec. Salary: $ Bonus: $

OTHER THOUGHTS:

Estimated Female Officers or Directors: 9
Hot Spot for Advancement for Women/Minorities: Y

Keystone Dental Inc

NAIC Code: 339,100

www.keystonedental.com

TYPES OF BUSINESS:

Dental Device Manufacturing

BRANDS/DIVISIONS/AFFILIATES:

Genesis
TILOBEMAXX
Tri-Nex
Accell Connexus
DynaBlast
InOss
DynaMatrix
Cytoplast

CONTACTS:

Note: Officers with more than one job title may be intentionally listed here more than once.

Michael Kehoe, Pres.
Mark Oppenheim, CFO

GROWTH PLANS/SPECIAL FEATURES:

Keystone Dental, Inc. is a developer and manufacturer of dental devices. The company delivers advanced, easy-to-use implants, biomaterials and planning software for dental professionals focused on providing functional and aesthetically-pleasing outcomes for patients. Keystone's products fall in three categories: implant systems, bone grafting and membrane. Dental implant systems allow for immediate placement into a multi-rooted molar extraction site. This alternative treatment maximizes bone preservation, minimizes the need for bone grafting and reduces treatment time. Implant systems include the Genesis, TILOBEMAXX, PrimaConnex, Prima Plus, Restore, Stage-1, OT-F2, Digital Dentistry, Tri-Nex and OCT brands. Bone grafting products combine human bone and proprietary technology and materials to create a moldable substance used to adhere to the mouth, providing immediate and sustained accessibility to the patient's bone proteins. The bone graft substance can be shaped and packed into the mouth defect, thickens at body temperature and holds the graft in place. Once the graft has taken hold, dental implants can be implemented. Bone graft brands used by the firm include Accell Connexus, DynaBlast, DynaGraft-D, Particulate, In'Oss, MBCP and OCS-B. Membrane materials include porcine small intestine submucosa used as a barrier membrane for guided bone and guided tissue regeneration procedures. Membranes are designed to remodel soft tissue, communicate with the body to help stimulate the natural healing process via the body's proteins and molecules and facilitate the recruitment of the body's own cells to restore itself. This process remodels into strong, fully vascularized tissue, becomes undetectable once the healing process is complete and adjoins with the patient's natural gingival tissue. Keystone's membrane products include the DynaMatrix and Cytoplast brand lines.

Keystone offers its employees life and health insurance, short- and long-term disability coverage, dental and vision benefits and a 401(k) plan.

FINANCIAL DATA:

Note: Data for latest year may not have been available at press time.

In U.S. $	2017	2016	2015	2014	2013	2012
Revenue						
R&D Expense						
Operating Income						
Operating Margin %						
SGA Expense						
Net Income						
Operating Cash Flow						
Capital Expenditure						
EBITDA						
Return on Assets %						
Return on Equity %						
Debt to Equity						

CONTACT INFORMATION:

Phone: 781-328-3300 Fax: 781-328-3400
Toll-Free: 866-902-9272
Address: 154 Middlesex Turnpike, Burlington, MA 01803 United States

STOCK TICKER/OTHER:

Stock Ticker: Private
Exchange:
Employees:
Fiscal Year Ends: 12/31
Parent Company:

SALARIES/BONUSES:

Top Exec. Salary: $ Bonus: $
Second Exec. Salary: $ Bonus: $

OTHER THOUGHTS:

Estimated Female Officers or Directors: 1
Hot Spot for Advancement for Women/Minorities:

Kindred at Home

www.kindredhealthcare.com/our-services/home-care/about/affiliates/gentiva

NAIC Code: 621,610

TYPES OF BUSINESS:

Home Health Care Services
Administrative Services

BRANDS/DIVISIONS/AFFILIATES:

TPG Capital
Welsh Carson Anderson & Stowe
Humana Inc
Gentiva Health Services Inc

CONTACTS: *Note: Officers with more than one job title may be intentionally listed here more than once.*

David Causby, CEO
Tom Dolan, CFO
John Camperlengo, General Counsel
Charlotte Weaver, Other Executive Officer
Jeff Shaner, President, Divisional
R. Hicks, Vice Chairman of the Board

GROWTH PLANS/SPECIAL FEATURES:

Kindred at Home (formerly Gentiva Health Services, Inc.) provides in-home skilled nursing, hospice and rehabilitation therapy services. The firm's care focuses on helping patients manage a chronic condition or recover from acute illness, surgery, accident or a change in medical condition. Kindred at Home's services are delivered according to a plan of treatment developed by patients, their family members, physicians and the company's home health staff to maximize independent functioning and reduce re-hospitalizations. In-home care includes medication management/instruction/administration, illness assessment/instruction, dementia/Alzheimer's care, fall prevention, stroke/brain injury care, low vision care, bathing, personal care assistance, assessment at each visit, blood pressure measurement, lung sound assessment, blood glucose measurement or pulse oximetry, along with related care ordered by the patient's doctor. In July 2018, Humana, Inc. acquired a 40% stake in Kindred Healthcare's hospice and in-home business, Gentiva Health Services, which was separated from Kindred Healthcare and renamed Kindred at Home. Private equity companies TPG Capital and Welsh, Carson, Anderson & Stowe own the remaining 60%, though Humana has an option to buy the remaining ownership over time.

FINANCIAL DATA: *Note: Data for latest year may not have been available at press time.*

In U.S. $	2017	2016	2015	2014	2013	2012
Revenue	2,150,000,000	2,000,000,000	1,904,825,000	1,969,688,000	1,726,643,968	1,712,803,968
R&D Expense						
Operating Income						
Operating Margin %						
SGA Expense						
Net Income			-1,950,000	-432,492,000	-598,993,984	26,796,000
Operating Cash Flow						
Capital Expenditure						
EBITDA						
Return on Assets %						
Return on Equity %						
Debt to Equity						

CONTACT INFORMATION:

Phone: 855-865-5894 Fax:
Toll-Free:
Address: 680 S. Fourth St., Louisville, KY 40202 United States

STOCK TICKER/OTHER:

Stock Ticker: Subsidiary
Employees: 17,200
Parent Company: TPG Capital
Exchange:
Fiscal Year Ends: 12/31

SALARIES/BONUSES:

Top Exec. Salary: $ Bonus: $
Second Exec. Salary: $ Bonus: $

OTHER THOUGHTS:

Estimated Female Officers or Directors: 1
Hot Spot for Advancement for Women/Minorities:

Kindred Healthcare Inc

www.kindredhealthcare.com

NAIC Code: 623,110

TYPES OF BUSINESS:

Nursing Care Facilities
Nursing Centers
Contract Rehabilitation Services

GROWTH PLANS/SPECIAL FEATURES:

Kindred Healthcare, Inc. is a specialty hospital company. In July 2018, the firm sold its skilled nursing facility business to BM Eagle Holdings, LLC for $700 million. Then, Kindred's long-term acute care hospitals, inpatient rehabilitation facilities and contract rehabilitation services business were separated from its home health, hospice and community care businesses. Kindred Healthcare became a separate specialty hospital company privately held by TPG Capital and Welsh, Carson, Anderson & Stowe (WCAS), and subsequently ceased from being publicly-traded on the New York Stock Exchange. The acute care hospitals, inpatient rehabilitation facilities and contract rehabilitation services businesses are operated by Kindred Healthcare. The home health, hospice and community care businesses collectively operate as a standalone company operated by Kindred at Home, and is 40%-owned by Humana, Inc. The remaining 60% is owned by TPG and WCAS.

BRANDS/DIVISIONS/AFFILIATES:

TPG Capital
Welsh Carson Anderson & Stowe
Humana Inc
Kindred at Home

CONTACTS: *Note: Officers with more than one job title may be intentionally listed here more than once.*

Benjamin A. Breier, CEO
Stephen Cunanan, Chief Administrative Officer
Phyllis Yale, Director
William Altman, Executive VP
David Causby, Executive VP
Joseph Landenwich, General Counsel
Pete Kalmey, President, Divisional
Jason Zachariah, President, Divisional
Benjamin Breier, President
John Lucchese, Senior VP
Paul Diaz, Vice Chairman of the Board

FINANCIAL DATA: *Note: Data for latest year may not have been available at press time.*

In U.S. $	2017	2016	2015	2014	2013	2012
Revenue	6,034,122,752	7,219,518,976	7,054,906,880	5,027,598,848	4,900,510,208	6,181,291,008
R&D Expense						
Operating Income						
Operating Margin %						
SGA Expense						
Net Income	-698,352,000	-664,230,016	-93,384,000	-79,837,000	-168,492,000	-40,367,000
Operating Cash Flow						
Capital Expenditure						
EBITDA						
Return on Assets %						
Return on Equity %						
Debt to Equity						

CONTACT INFORMATION:

Phone: 502 596-7300 Fax: 502 596-4170
Toll-Free: 800-545-0749
Address: 680 S. Fourth St., Louisville, KY 40202 United States

STOCK TICKER/OTHER:

Stock Ticker: Private
Employees: 100,100
Parent Company:
Exchange:
Fiscal Year Ends: 12/31

SALARIES/BONUSES:

Top Exec. Salary: $ Bonus: $
Second Exec. Salary: $ Bonus: $

OTHER THOUGHTS:

Estimated Female Officers or Directors: 4
Hot Spot for Advancement for Women/Minorities: Y

KPC Healthcare Inc

kpchealth.com/

NAIC Code: 622,110

TYPES OF BUSINESS:

General Medical and Surgical Hospitals

BRANDS/DIVISIONS/AFFILIATES:

Anaheim Global Medical Center
Chapman Global Medical Center
Hemet Valley Medical Center
Menifee Valley Medical Center
Orange County Global Medical Center
South Coast Global Medical Center
Victor Valley Global Medical Center

GROWTH PLANS/SPECIAL FEATURES:

KPC Healthcare, Inc. is engaged in healthcare, pharmaceuticals, education, engineering and real estate, with more than $10 billion in assets. These assets include hospitals, clinics, schools, commercial real estate properties and agricultural research centers. KPC's healthcare division comprises a group of integrated healthcare delivery systems made up of acute care hospitals, independent physicians associations (IPAs), medical groups, urgent care facilities and multi-specialty facilities throughout the western portion of the U.S. California facilities include: Anaheim Global Medical Center, Chapman Global Medical Center, Hemet Valley Medical Center, Menifee Valley Medical Center, Orange County Global Medical Center, South Coast Global Medical Center and Victor Valley Global Medical Center. These facilities collectively serve some of California's most densely populated areas in the southern region, totaling nearly 10 million people.

CONTACTS: *Note: Officers with more than one job title may be intentionally listed here more than once.*

Peter Baronoff, CEO
Kenneth K. Westbrook, Pres.
Jeremiah R. Kanaly, Chief Acct. Officer

FINANCIAL DATA: *Note: Data for latest year may not have been available at press time.*

In U.S. $	2017	2016	2015	2014	2013	2012
Revenue						
R&D Expense						
Operating Income						
Operating Margin %						
SGA Expense						
Net Income						
Operating Cash Flow						
Capital Expenditure						
EBITDA						
Return on Assets %						
Return on Equity %						
Debt to Equity						

CONTACT INFORMATION:

Phone: 714 953-3652 Fax:
Toll-Free:
Address: 1301 N. Tustin Ave., Santa Ana, CA 92705 United States

STOCK TICKER/OTHER:

Stock Ticker: Private
Employees: 3,225
Parent Company:
Exchange:
Fiscal Year Ends: 03/31

SALARIES/BONUSES:

Top Exec. Salary: $ Bonus: $
Second Exec. Salary: $ Bonus: $

OTHER THOUGHTS:

Estimated Female Officers or Directors:
Hot Spot for Advancement for Women/Minorities:

Laboratory Corporation of America Holdings

www.labcorp.com

NAIC Code: 621,511

TYPES OF BUSINESS:

Clinical Laboratory Testing
Diagnostics
Urinalyses
Blood Cell Counts
Blood Chemistry Analysis
HIV Tests
Genetic Testing
Specialty & Niche Tests

BRANDS/DIVISIONS/AFFILIATES:

Covance Inc
LabCorp Diagnositcs
Covance Drug Development

CONTACTS: *Note: Officers with more than one job title may be intentionally listed here more than once.*

John Ratliff, CEO, Divisional
Gary Huff, CEO, Divisional
David King, CEO
Lance Berberian, Chief Information Officer
Brian Caveney, Chief Medical Officer
Glenn Eisenberg, Executive VP
Lisa Uthgenannt, Other Executive Officer
F. Eberts, Other Executive Officer
Edward Dodson, Senior VP

GROWTH PLANS/SPECIAL FEATURES:

Laboratory Corporation of America Holdings (LabCorp) is a leading independent clinical laboratory company based in the U.S. LabCorp serves customers in approximately 60 countries, providing diagnostic, drug development and technology-enabled solutions for more than 110 million patient encounters annually. The firm operates in two business segments: LabCorp Diagnostics, a clinical laboratory business; and Covance Drug Development, a division of subsidiary Covance, Inc. and a provider of end-to-end drug development, medical device and diagnostic services, from early-stage research to regulatory approval and beyond. LabCorp processes tests on more than 2.5 million patient specimens weekly, and has clinical laboratory locations throughout the U.S. and other countries, including Canada and the U.K. It offers a menu of nearly 5,000 tests, with several hundred used in general patient care by physicians to establish or support a diagnosis, to monitor treatment or to search for an otherwise undiagnosed condition. Most frequent tests include blood chemistry analysis, blood cell counts, thyroid tests, Pap tests, Hemoglobin A1C, prostate-specific antigen, tests for sexually-transmitted diseases, hepatitis C, Vitamin D and substance-abuse tests. Covance collaborated on more than 90% of the novel drugs approved by the U.S. FDA in 2017, including over 90% of the novel rare and orphan disease drugs and two-thirds of the novel oncology drugs. LabCorp Diagnostics derived 70.3% of 2017 net revenues, and Covance derived 29.7%. In April 2018, LabCorp agreed to sell Covance's food solutions business to Eurofins Scientific for about $670 million.

Employee benefits include medical, dental and vision coverage; flexible spending accounts; 401(k) and stock purchase plan; life and AD&D insurance; and short- and long-term disability.

FINANCIAL DATA: *Note: Data for latest year may not have been available at press time.*

In U.S. $	2017	2016	2015	2014	2013	2012
Revenue	10,441,400,000	9,641,800,000	8,680,100,000	6,011,600,000	5,808,300,000	5,671,400,000
R&D Expense						
Operating Income	1,435,100,000	1,370,800,000	1,116,800,000	928,200,000	1,012,700,000	1,048,800,000
Operating Margin %	13.74%	14.21%	12.86%	15.44%	17.43%	18.49%
SGA Expense	1,812,400,000	1,630,200,000	1,622,000,000	1,198,200,000	1,128,800,000	1,114,600,000
Net Income	1,268,200,000	732,100,000	436,900,000	511,200,000	573,800,000	583,100,000
Operating Cash Flow	1,459,400,000	1,175,900,000	982,400,000	739,000,000	818,700,000	841,400,000
Capital Expenditure	315,400,000	278,900,000	255,800,000	203,500,000	202,200,000	176,300,000
EBITDA	1,903,200,000	1,823,800,000	1,464,800,000	1,181,700,000	1,242,200,000	1,268,500,000
Return on Assets %	8.23%	5.14%	4.05%	7.16%	8.33%	9.01%
Return on Equity %	20.56%	14.01%	11.25%	19.24%	22.03%	22.33%
Debt to Equity	0.92	0.96	1.21	0.95	1.15	0.80

CONTACT INFORMATION:

Phone: 336 229-1127 Fax: 336 229-7717
Toll-Free:
Address: 358 S. Main St., Burlington, NC 27215 United States

STOCK TICKER/OTHER:

Stock Ticker: LH
Employees: 52,000
Parent Company:
Exchange: NYS
Fiscal Year Ends: 12/31

SALARIES/BONUSES:

Top Exec. Salary: $1,150,000 Bonus: $
Second Exec. Salary: $666,474 Bonus: $

OTHER THOUGHTS:

Estimated Female Officers or Directors: 3
Hot Spot for Advancement for Women/Minorities: Y

Lakeland Industries Inc

www.lakeland.com

NAIC Code: 339,100

TYPES OF BUSINESS:

Safety Clothing
Reusable Industrial & Medical Apparel
Chemical Protection Clothing
Specialty Safety Gloves
Heat Resistant Clothing
Disposable Protective Garments

BRANDS/DIVISIONS/AFFILIATES:

Nomex
Kevlar

CONTACTS:

Note: Officers with more than one job title may be intentionally listed here more than once.

Christopher Ryan, CEO
Teri Hunt, CFO
Alfred Kreft, Chairman of the Board
Charles Roberson, COO
Daniel Edwards, Senior VP, Divisional

GROWTH PLANS/SPECIAL FEATURES:

Lakeland Industries, Inc. manufactures and sells a comprehensive line of safety garments and accessories for industrial safety and protective clothing industries. In North America, the firm's products are sold through a network of over 1,200 safety and mill supply distributors. Lakeland's products are sold in over 40 countries internationally. The company's major product areas include disposable and limited-use protective clothing, chemical protective suits, fire-fighting and heat protective apparel, gloves and arm guards for the food service market, reusable woven garments and high visibility clothing for traffic and public safety officials. The firm's disposable and reusable garments protect the wearer from contaminants or irritants, such as chemicals, pesticides, fertilizers, paint, grease and dust; from viruses and bacteria; and from limited exposure to hazardous waste and toxic chemicals, including acids, asbestos, lead and hydro-carbons. Lakeland's products are also used to prevent human contamination of manufacturing processes in clean-room environments. Disposable clothing products include coveralls, lab coats, hoods, aprons, sleeves and smocks. Lakeland's heat protective gear is used by firefighters as well as for maintenance of extreme high-temperature industrial equipment and for crash and rescue operations. The company's high-end chemical protective suits protect wearers from highly concentrated and powerful chemical and biological toxins such as toxic wastes at Super fund sites, accidental toxic chemical spills or biological discharges, the handling of chemical or biological warfare weapons and the cleaning and maintenance of chemical, petrochemical and nuclear facilities. Lakeland buys most of its raw materials for manufacturing from DuPont, including those required for the Nomex and Kevlar brands.

FINANCIAL DATA:

Note: Data for latest year may not have been available at press time.

In U.S. $	2017	2016	2015	2014	2013	2012
Revenue	86,183,000	99,646,000	99,733,740	91,384,700	95,117,540	
R&D Expense						
Operating Income	6,847,000	11,812,000	4,957,402	-359,009	-1,030,168	
Operating Margin %	7.94%	11.85%	4.97%	-.39%	-1.08%	
SGA Expense			28,754,550	25,192,350	28,357,600	
Net Income	3,893,000	3,854,000	8,398,704	-119,501	-26,288,670	
Operating Cash Flow	11,493,000	-518,000	3,328,912	-3,881,374	2,187,373	
Capital Expenditure	413,000	840,000	904,703	828,894	1,384,539	
EBITDA	8,087,000	12,678,000	3,748,166	822,551	-18,266,890	
Return on Assets %	4.50%	4.24%	9.49%	-.14%	-28.30%	
Return on Equity %	5.60%	5.89%	15.23%	-.25%	-44.08%	
Debt to Equity	0.01	0.01	0.01	0.05	0.02	

CONTACT INFORMATION:

Phone: 631 981-9700 Fax: 631 981-9751
Toll-Free: 800-645-9291
Address: 3555 Veterans Memorial Highway, Ste. C, Ronkonkoma, NY 11779 United States

STOCK TICKER/OTHER:

Stock Ticker: LAKE
Employees: 993
Parent Company:
Exchange: NAS
Fiscal Year Ends: 01/31

SALARIES/BONUSES:

Top Exec. Salary: $400,000 Bonus: $175,000
Second Exec. Salary: $215,000 Bonus: $35,000

OTHER THOUGHTS:

Estimated Female Officers or Directors:
Hot Spot for Advancement for Women/Minorities:

LCA-Vision Inc

www.lasikplus.com

NAIC Code: 621,493

TYPES OF BUSINESS:

Services-Laser Vision Correction Surgery Centers
PRK (photo-refractive keratectomy)
LASIK (Laser-In-Situ Keratomileusis)

BRANDS/DIVISIONS/AFFILIATES:

Vision Acquisitions LLC
LasikPlus

CONTACTS: *Note: Officers with more than one job title may be intentionally listed here more than once.*

Craig P. R. Joffe, CEO
Bharat Kakar, Sr. VP-Oper. & Mktg.

GROWTH PLANS/SPECIAL FEATURES:

LCA-Vision, Inc. is a provider of fixed-site laser vision correction services at its LasikPlus vision centers. The company's vision centers help correct nearsightedness, farsightedness and astigmatism. Treatments are done by using one of two methods, PRK (photo-refractive keratectomy) and LASIK (laser-in-situ keratomileusis). PRK removes the thin layer of cell covering the outer surface of the cornea (the epithelium) and treats it with excimer laser pulses. LASIK reshapes the cornea with an excimer laser by cutting a flap in the top of the cornea to expose the inner cornea. The corneal flap is then treated with excimer laser pulses according to the patient's prescription. The LASIK procedure now accounts for virtually all of the procedures performed by LCA, as recovery time is significantly shorter and patient discomfort is negligible. The company operates more than 50 LasikPlus vision correction centers in the U.S., including full-service LasikPlus fixed site laser vision correction centers as well as pre- and post-operative LasikPlus satellite centers. LCA-Vision is owned by Vision Acquisitions, LLC.

FINANCIAL DATA: *Note: Data for latest year may not have been available at press time.*

In U.S. $	2017	2016	2015	2014	2013	2012
Revenue	92,580,000	92,500,000	92,000,000	90,000,000	92,185,000	101,493,000
R&D Expense						
Operating Income						
Operating Margin %						
SGA Expense						
Net Income						
Operating Cash Flow						
Capital Expenditure						
EBITDA						
Return on Assets %						
Return on Equity %						
Debt to Equity						

CONTACT INFORMATION:

Phone: 513 792-9292 Fax: 513 792-5620
Toll-Free: 800-688-4550
Address: 7840 Montgomery Rd., Cincinnati, OH 45236 United States

STOCK TICKER/OTHER:

Stock Ticker: Subsidiary
Exchange:
Employees: 380
Fiscal Year Ends: 12/31
Parent Company: Vision Acquisitions LLC

SALARIES/BONUSES:

Top Exec. Salary: $ Bonus: $
Second Exec. Salary: $ Bonus: $

OTHER THOUGHTS:

Estimated Female Officers or Directors: 2
Hot Spot for Advancement for Women/Minorities:

LHC Group Inc

www.lhcgroup.com

NAIC Code: 621,610

TYPES OF BUSINESS:

Home Health Care Services
Hospices
Long-Term Acute Care Hospitals

BRANDS/DIVISIONS/AFFILIATES:

CONTACTS:

Note: Officers with more than one job title may be intentionally listed here more than once.

Keith Myers, CEO
Joshua Proffitt, CFO
Jeffrey Reibel, Chief Accounting Officer
Donald Stelly, COO
C. Guenthner, Other Executive Officer

GROWTH PLANS/SPECIAL FEATURES:

LHC Group, Inc. provides post-acute health care services to patients through its home nursing agencies, community-based service agencies, hospice agencies and long-term acute care hospitals (LTACHs). Through its subsidiaries, LHC operates 780 locations in 37 U.S. states, all of which are either wholly-owned, majority-owned or under lease agreements (most are wholly- or majority-owned). The company operates through four segments: home health services, hospice services, community-based services and facility-based services (via LTACHs). Home health services include skilled nursing, medically-oriented social services, as well as physical, occupational and speech therapy. Hospice services provides end-of-life care to patients with terminal illnesses through interdisciplinary teams of physicians, nurses, home health aides, counselors and volunteers. Community-based services provides assistance with activities of daily living to elderly, chronically ill and disabled patients. LTACH/facility-based services are provided to patients with complex medical conditions who have transitioned out of a hospital intensive care unit but whose conditions remain too severe for treatment in a non-acute setting. This division owns and operates LTACHs (most located within host hospitals), a pharmacy, a family health center, a family health clinic and physical therapy clinics. In August 2018, LHC announced two equity partnership agreements to purchase and share ownership of home health and hospice services locations with regional health system providers in the Reno, Nevada and Jefferson City, Missouri markets.

FINANCIAL DATA:

Note: Data for latest year may not have been available at press time.

In U.S. $	2017	2016	2015	2014	2013	2012
Revenue	1,072,086,000	914,823,000	816,366,000	733,632,000	658,283,000	637,569,000
R&D Expense						
Operating Income	76,253,000	71,761,000	67,616,000	49,132,000	46,757,000	54,305,000
Operating Margin %	7.11%	7.84%	8.28%	6.69%	7.10%	8.51%
SGA Expense	310,539,000	270,622,000	248,629,000	233,945,000	214,133,000	205,637,000
Net Income	50,112,000	36,583,000	32,335,000	21,837,000	22,342,000	27,440,000
Operating Cash Flow	32,326,000	67,472,000	59,934,000	38,657,000	45,915,000	74,772,000
Capital Expenditure	10,176,000	16,009,000	13,283,000	8,105,000	8,343,000	8,415,000
EBITDA	88,628,000	83,214,000	78,755,000	55,322,000	55,325,000	62,295,000
Return on Assets %	7.11%	6.19%	6.11%	4.77%	5.52%	7.00%
Return on Equity %	11.87%	9.75%	9.60%	7.14%	7.96%	10.31%
Debt to Equity	0.32	0.22	0.27	0.19	0.07	0.07

CONTACT INFORMATION:

Phone: 337 233-1307 Fax: 337 235-8037
Toll-Free:
Address: 901 Hugh Wallis Rd. S., Lafayette, LA 70508 United States

STOCK TICKER/OTHER:

Stock Ticker: LHCG
Exchange: NAS
Employees: 11,598
Fiscal Year Ends: 12/31
Parent Company:

SALARIES/BONUSES:

Top Exec. Salary: $735,000 Bonus: $
Second Exec. Salary: $575,000 Bonus: $

OTHER THOUGHTS:

Estimated Female Officers or Directors: 6
Hot Spot for Advancement for Women/Minorities: Y

Life Care Centers of America

www.lcca.com

NAIC Code: 623,310

TYPES OF BUSINESS:

Assisted Living Facilities
Home Care
Respite Care
Alzheimer's Care
Hospice
Rehabilitation
Physical Therapy

BRANDS/DIVISIONS/AFFILIATES:

Century Park

CONTACTS:

Note: Officers with more than one job title may be intentionally listed here more than once.

Forrest L. Preston, CEO
Beecher Hunter, Pres.
Steve Ziegler, CFO
Terry Henry, Sr. VP-Acct.
Forrest L. Preston, Chmn.
John Kitterman, Dir.-Purchasing

GROWTH PLANS/SPECIAL FEATURES:

Life Care Centers of America (LCCA) operates more than 200 skilled nursing, rehabilitation, senior living and Alzheimer's centers in 28 states. Life Care inpatient and outpatient rehabilitation services help patients return lost skills and bring back strength and mobility. Its skilled therapy services offer physical occupational and speech therapy, as well as rehab gyms. Skilled nursing communities provide post-operative recovery, short-term rehab, long-term care and in- and outpatient services. The company's senior living campuses provide various types of facilities in one location, offering retirement, assisted living and nursing care depending on the changing needs of the patients. Services range from intermittent to live-in and may include administration of medication as well as physical, occupational and speech therapy. Many of LCCA's locations also provide specialty care such as Alzheimer's and dementia care, respite care, sub-acute medical care, wound care, adult day care and hospice care. The firm's home care services range from skilled nursing care, therapy and extended live-in workers to private services such as light housekeeping, running errands and shopping. Century Park, an affiliate of LCCA, operates over 40 additional independent and assisted living communities in 20 states. Century Park facilities offer accommodations that include laundry service, internet cafes, indoor swimming pools, putting greens, trained chefs and transportation.

FINANCIAL DATA:

Note: Data for latest year may not have been available at press time.

In U.S. $	2017	2016	2015	2014	2013	2012
Revenue	3,200,000,000	3,100,000,000	3,050,000,000	2,950,000,000	2,900,000,000	2,750,000,000
R&D Expense						
Operating Income						
Operating Margin %						
SGA Expense						
Net Income						
Operating Cash Flow						
Capital Expenditure						
EBITDA						
Return on Assets %						
Return on Equity %						
Debt to Equity						

CONTACT INFORMATION:

Phone: 423-472-9585 Fax:
Toll-Free:
Address: 3570 Keith St. NW, Cleveland, TN 37320 United States

STOCK TICKER/OTHER:

Stock Ticker: Private
Exchange:
Employees: 40,500
Fiscal Year Ends: 12/31
Parent Company:

SALARIES/BONUSES:

Top Exec. Salary: $ Bonus: $
Second Exec. Salary: $ Bonus: $

OTHER THOUGHTS:

Estimated Female Officers or Directors: 2
Hot Spot for Advancement for Women/Minorities:

Life Healthcare Group Holdings Ltd

www.lifehealthcare.co.za

NAIC Code: 622,110

TYPES OF BUSINESS:

Hospitals & Clinics
Higher Education

BRANDS/DIVISIONS/AFFILIATES:

Life Employee Health Solutions
Life Esidimeni
Life College of Learning
Alliance Medical
Scanmed SA
Max Healthcare

CONTACTS: *Note: Officers with more than one job title may be intentionally listed here more than once.*

Shrey Viranna, CEO
Pieter van der Westhuizen, CFO

GROWTH PLANS/SPECIAL FEATURES:

Life Healthcare Group Holdings Ltd. is a leading private health care services provider and hospital operator in South Africa. The company operates in three divisions: hospital, out-of-hospital services and international business. In addition to its 66 hospital facilities, most of which comprise emergency units, the hospital division oversees specialized units for physical rehabilitation, mental health treatment, renal dialysis, maternity, cardiac treatment and radiotherapy. The out-of-hospital services division consists of three units: Life Employee Health Solutions, which supports more than 365 clinics and cares for over 471,000 employees; Life Esidimeni, a wholly-owned subsidiary with 11 healthcare facilities and 3,080 beds, two of which are non-governmental organizations in partnership with the Department of Social Development; and Life College of Learning, which comprises seven learning centers across South Africa where students are trained in nursing and healthcare sciences. Last, the international business division comprises three units: Alliance Medical, one of Western Europe's leading providers of complex molecular and diagnostic imaging services across the U.K., Italy and Ireland, with participation in eight European markets; Scanmed SA, which provides primary care, ambulatory care and acute care services in Poland; and Max Healthcare, an acute care hospital in India.

FINANCIAL DATA: *Note: Data for latest year may not have been available at press time.*

In U.S. $	2017	2016	2015	2014	2013	2012
Revenue						
R&D Expense						
Operating Income						
Operating Margin %						
SGA Expense						
Net Income						
Operating Cash Flow						
Capital Expenditure						
EBITDA						
Return on Assets %						
Return on Equity %						
Debt to Equity						

CONTACT INFORMATION:

Phone: 27 112199000 Fax: 27 112199001
Toll-Free:
Address: 21 Chaplin Rd., Oxford Manor, Illovo, 2196 South Africa

STOCK TICKER/OTHER:

Stock Ticker: LTGHY Exchange: PINX
Employees: 20,499 Fiscal Year Ends: 09/30
Parent Company:

SALARIES/BONUSES:

Top Exec. Salary: $ Bonus: $
Second Exec. Salary: $ Bonus: $

OTHER THOUGHTS:

Estimated Female Officers or Directors: 5
Hot Spot for Advancement for Women/Minorities: Y

LifePoint Health Inc

NAIC Code: 622,110

www.lifepointhealth.net

TYPES OF BUSINESS:

General Medical and Surgical Hospitals

BRANDS/DIVISIONS/AFFILIATES:

CONTACTS:

Note: Officers with more than one job title may be intentionally listed here more than once.

William Carpenter, CEO
Michael Coggin, CFO
J. Grooms, Chief Accounting Officer
John Bumpus, Chief Administrative Officer
Russell Holman, Chief Medical Officer
David Dill, COO
Jennifer Peters, General Counsel
Jeffrey Seraphine, Other Executive Officer
Victor Giovanetti, President, Divisional
Melissa Waddey, President, Divisional
Robert Klein, President, Divisional
R. Raplee, President, Divisional

GROWTH PLANS/SPECIAL FEATURES:

LifePoint Health, Inc. is a holding company that owns and operates community hospitals, regional health systems, physician practices, outpatient centers and post-acute facilities throughout the U.S. The firm operates approximately 70 hospitals comprising about 9,000 beds, which are primarily located in non-urban communities. These hospitals typically offer a range of medical and surgical services, including: internal medicine; obstetrics; general surgery; emergency room, psychiatric, diagnostic and coronary care; radiology; oncology; rehabilitation and pediatric services; and, in some hospitals, specialized services such as open-heart surgery, skilled nursing and neuro-surgery. In many markets, LifePoint also provides outpatient services such as one-day surgery, laboratory, x-ray, respiratory therapy, imaging, sports medicine and lithotripsy. Post-acute services and facilities include long-term care services, nursing homes and assisted living establishments. Outpatient centers and services include urgent care centers, diagnostic imaging centers, ambulatory surgery centers and radiation oncology programs. In July 2018, LifePoint sold its ownership interest in three Louisiana hospital campuses and associated assets to Allegiance Health Management. That same month, LifePoint Health agreed to be acquired and absorbed by RegionalCare Hospital Partners Holdings, Inc., which does business as RCCH HealthCare Partners.

The company offers its employees medical, dental, vision, life and disability insurance; adoption assistance; flexible spending accounts; a wellness program; a Wells Fargo Employee Home Mortgage Program; and a 401(k) plan.

FINANCIAL DATA:

Note: Data for latest year may not have been available at press time.

In U.S. $	2017	2016	2015	2014	2013	2012
Revenue	7,263,100,000	7,273,600,000	6,014,400,000	5,300,900,000	4,428,700,000	4,016,200,000
R&D Expense						
Operating Income	317,700,000	377,200,000	426,700,000	383,700,000	308,800,000	352,500,000
Operating Margin %	4.37%	5.18%	7.09%	7.23%	6.97%	8.77%
SGA Expense	520,000,000	552,600,000	423,200,000	367,700,000	316,200,000	280,300,000
Net Income	102,400,000	121,900,000	181,900,000	126,100,000	128,200,000	151,900,000
Operating Cash Flow	471,600,000	435,200,000	627,100,000	412,300,000	354,000,000	382,200,000
Capital Expenditure	474,200,000	399,500,000	274,700,000	207,100,000	185,200,000	221,400,000
EBITDA	668,300,000	721,800,000	705,700,000	634,200,000	537,000,000	545,600,000
Return on Assets %	1.62%	1.97%	3.17%	2.28%	2.48%	3.34%
Return on Equity %	4.63%	5.48%	8.23%	5.77%	6.01%	7.60%
Debt to Equity	1.28	1.32	1.16	1.02	0.81	0.82

CONTACT INFORMATION:

Phone: 615 920-7000 Fax:
Toll-Free:
Address: 330 Seven Springs Way, Brentwood, TN 37027 United States

STOCK TICKER/OTHER:

Stock Ticker: LPNT
Employees: 47,000
Parent Company:
Exchange: NAS
Fiscal Year Ends: 12/31

SALARIES/BONUSES:

Top Exec. Salary: $1,179,000 Bonus: $
Second Exec. Salary: $687,000 Bonus: $

OTHER THOUGHTS:

Estimated Female Officers or Directors: 1
Hot Spot for Advancement for Women/Minorities: Y

LifeScan Inc

www.lifescan.com

NAIC Code: 339,100

TYPES OF BUSINESS:

Medical Testing Products
Blood Glucose Monitoring Products

BRANDS/DIVISIONS/AFFILIATES:

Johnson & Johnson
OneTouch
PatternAlert
OneTouch Delica
OneTouch UltraSoft
OneTouch Reveal

CONTACTS: *Note: Officers with more than one job title may be intentionally listed here more than once.*

Val Asbury, Pres.
Alan Cariski, VP-Worldwide Medical Affairs & Safety
Ashley McEvoy, Chmn.-Johnson & Johnson

GROWTH PLANS/SPECIAL FEATURES:

LifeScan, Inc., a subsidiary of Johnson & Johnson, is a provider of systems and procedures for diabetic blood glucose monitoring. The company's OneTouch technology eliminates wiping and timing procedures, making it easier for patients to test their own blood glucose levels. OneTouch systems include: a meter that allows users to see the effect of food on their blood sugar results; a small, simple testing meter designed for quick testing; a meter with PatternAlert technology designed to notice patterns in patients' blood sugar levels and offer solutions. The OneTouch Delica lancing system is designed to provide a more comfortable solution for blood glucose testing; and OneTouch UltraSoft lancets allow for a less painful stick. LifeScan also sells OneTouch test strips and control solutions; and OneTouch Reveal mobile and web application and logbook, which help users manage diabetes in the moment and on-the-go. LThe firm's website offers resources on food, fitness, medications, tracking and prevention, as well as insurance and Medicare information. In June 2018, parent Johnson & Johnson agreed to sell LifeScan to Platinum Equity, LLC for approximately $2.1 billion. The transaction was expected to close by year's end, subject to regulatory clearances and closing conditions.

FINANCIAL DATA: *Note: Data for latest year may not have been available at press time.*

In U.S. $	2017	2016	2015	2014	2013	2012
Revenue						
R&D Expense						
Operating Income						
Operating Margin %						
SGA Expense						
Net Income						
Operating Cash Flow						
Capital Expenditure						
EBITDA						
Return on Assets %						
Return on Equity %						
Debt to Equity						

CONTACT INFORMATION:

Phone: 408-263-9789 Fax: 408-942-6070
Toll-Free: 800-227-8862
Address: 1000 Gibraltar Dr., Milpitas, CA 95035 United States

STOCK TICKER/OTHER:

Stock Ticker: Subsidiary
Exchange:
Employees:
Fiscal Year Ends:
Parent Company: Johnson & Johnson

SALARIES/BONUSES:

Top Exec. Salary: $ Bonus: $
Second Exec. Salary: $ Bonus: $

OTHER THOUGHTS:

Estimated Female Officers or Directors:
Hot Spot for Advancement for Women/Minorities:

Lifetime Healthcare Companies (The)

www.lifethc.com

NAIC Code: 524,114

TYPES OF BUSINESS:

Insurance-Medical & Health, HMOs & PPOs
Insurance-Group Life
Insurance-Property/Casualty
Insurance-Long-Term Care
Health Care Services
Employee Benefits Services
Medical Centers
Medical Equipment Distribution

BRANDS/DIVISIONS/AFFILIATES:

Excellus BlueCross BlueShield
Univera Healthcare
Lifetime Benefit Solutions Inc
Lifetime Care
MedAmerica Insurance Company

GROWTH PLANS/SPECIAL FEATURES:

The Lifetime Healthcare Companies is a nonprofit family of companies which provide health coverage and health care services to more than 1.5 million upstate New Yorkers. The family of companies include: Excellus BlueCross BlueShield, a nonprofit independent licensee of the Blue Cross Blue Shield Association, serving upstate New York; Univera Healthcare, which offers managed care, indemnity and dental plans to individuals and groups; Lifetime Benefit Solutions Inc., a provider of flexible benefit programs; Lifetime Care, a provider of home health services, hospice, durable medical equipment and nursing services; and MedAmerica Insurance Company, which offers long-term care insurance to both individuals and employer groups.

CONTACTS: *Note: Officers with more than one job title may be intentionally listed here more than once.*

Christopher C. Booth, CEO
Philip J. Puchalski, Sr. VP-Corp. Comm.
Marie Y. Philippe, Chief Diversity Officer

FINANCIAL DATA: *Note: Data for latest year may not have been available at press time.*

In U.S. $	2017	2016	2015	2014	2013	2012
Revenue	6,400,000,000	6,125,000,000	5,923,166,000	5,272,005,000	6,290,443,000	6,000,833,000
R&D Expense						
Operating Income						
Operating Margin %						
SGA Expense						
Net Income			57,923,000	24,190,000	52,557,000	105,743,000
Operating Cash Flow						
Capital Expenditure						
EBITDA						
Return on Assets %						
Return on Equity %						
Debt to Equity						

CONTACT INFORMATION:

Phone: 585-454-1700 Fax:
Toll-Free:
Address: 165 Court St., Rochester, NY 14647 United States

STOCK TICKER/OTHER:

Stock Ticker: Nonprofit
Exchange:
Employees: 5,600
Fiscal Year Ends: 12/31
Parent Company:

SALARIES/BONUSES:

Top Exec. Salary: $ Bonus: $
Second Exec. Salary: $ Bonus: $

OTHER THOUGHTS:

Estimated Female Officers or Directors: 1
Hot Spot for Advancement for Women/Minorities: Y

Little Clinic (The)

www.thelittleclinic.com

NAIC Code: 621,498

TYPES OF BUSINESS:

Health Clinics
In-Store Clinics

BRANDS/DIVISIONS/AFFILIATES:

Kroger Co (The)

CONTACTS:

Note: Officers with more than one job title may be intentionally listed here more than once.

Colleen Lindholz, Pres.
Chance Cole, COO
Russell Scott, CFO
Tom Shelly, VP-Human Resources
Kenneth Patric, Chief Medical Officer
William D. Wright, Chief Legal Officer

GROWTH PLANS/SPECIAL FEATURES:

The Little Clinic, a wholly-owned subsidiary of retail grocer The Kroger Co., manages small, family healthcare facilities primarily within select Kroger locations. Staffed with certified nurse practitioners, physician assistants and dietician nutritionists (who receive contracted consultation from outside collaborating physicians), the clinics offer treatment for minor illnesses for patients 12 months and up (18 months and up in Mississippi, and 24 months and up in Kentucky), as well as vaccinations, health screenings, physical evaluations and nutrition counseling. In addition to offering telephone consultation to the nursing staff, contracted physicians are expected to provide chart and script reviews, as well as occasional onsite rounds. Each clinic accepts numerous forms of health insurance, including Medicare, Cigna, Aetna, Humana and Blue Cross Blue Shield. As of early-2018, the firm operated 220 Little Clinics in select Kroger, Fry's, JayC, Dillons and King Soopers stores in Ohio, Kansas, Kentucky, Tennessee, Arizona, Georgia, Indiana, Virginia, Mississippi and Colorado.

Employee benefits include medical, prescription, dental and vision coverage: flexible spending accounts; term life/voluntary life/dependent life/personal accident insurance; a 401(k) plan; stock ownership; employee discounts; and an employee assistance program.

FINANCIAL DATA:

Note: Data for latest year may not have been available at press time.

In U.S. $	2017	2016	2015	2014	2013	2012
Revenue						
R&D Expense						
Operating Income						
Operating Margin %						
SGA Expense						
Net Income						
Operating Cash Flow						
Capital Expenditure						
EBITDA						
Return on Assets %						
Return on Equity %						
Debt to Equity						

CONTACT INFORMATION:

Phone: 877-852-2677 Fax:
Toll-Free:
Address: 2620 Elm Hill Pike, Nashville, TN 37214 United States

STOCK TICKER/OTHER:

Stock Ticker: Subsidiary
Employees:
Parent Company: Kroger Co (The)
Exchange:
Fiscal Year Ends:

SALARIES/BONUSES:

Top Exec. Salary: $ Bonus: $
Second Exec. Salary: $ Bonus: $

OTHER THOUGHTS:

Estimated Female Officers or Directors: 1
Hot Spot for Advancement for Women/Minorities:

LogistiCare Solutions LLC

www.logisticare.com

NAIC Code: 621,910

TYPES OF BUSINESS:

Medical Transportation Management Services
Outsourced Logistics Services

BRANDS/DIVISIONS/AFFILIATES:

Providence Service Corporation
LogistiCAD
EMTrack

CONTACTS: *Note: Officers with more than one job title may be intentionally listed here more than once.*

Jeff Felton, CEO
Richard Boland, Jr., COO
Jenny Southern, Sr. VP-Human Resources
Neil Singer, CTO
Albert Cortina, Chief Admin. Officer
Chinta Gaston, General Counsel
Gregg Bryars, Sr. VP-Oper.
Steven D. Linowes, Exec. VP-Corp. Dev.
Chuck DeZearn, Sr. VP-Oper.
Chris Echols, Sr. VP-Oper.
Sandy Reifel, VP-Managed Care Accounts
Bill Walter, VP-Bus. Dev.

GROWTH PLANS/SPECIAL FEATURES:

LogistiCare Solutions, LLC, a subsidiary of Providence Service Corporation, is an outsourced scheduler of non-emergency patient transport services for insurance companies, managed care organizations and government health agencies. Instead of owning its own vehicles, the firm manages call centers, patient eligibility screening, scheduling, dispatch, billing and quality assurance. It also manages transportation provider networks of local, commercial, nonprofit and public transportation companies. LogistiCare recruits and accredits local firms for its network of providers. In sum, the company brokers non-emergency medical transportation (NEMT) services through a network of transportation providers. LogistiCare routes transportation requests through one of its call centers. All calls are recorded digitally and archived in the system database. The firm developed its integrated software system, known as LogistiCAD, in order to automatically coordinate all of its data and to and generate scheduling, routing, quality assurance reporting, transportation cost estimates and billing verification. It processes transportation requests and dispatches drivers through its network of carriers using its proprietary EMTrack system, which tracks all of the company's vehicles. LogistiCare is able to use its LogistiCAD system in conjunction with sophisticated GPS navigation to gain improved transportation access and service delivery in rural and remote areas. LogistiCare and Lyft have a three-year (2017-2020) nationwide partnership to improve solutions for private-, commercial- and government-assisted riders seeking healthcare appointments and social programs. The partnership utilizes LogistiCare's proprietary platform and Lyft's application program interface (API) to address riders' needs. Additionally, the firm provides finance and consulting services, including billing management, customer reimbursement, medical services billing, fraud detection and risk management. The company's government clients include state Medicaid agencies, school boards and Americans with Disabilities Act (ADA) paratransit authorities. Healthcare sector clients include hospital systems and many of the nation's largest managed care organizations.

FINANCIAL DATA: *Note: Data for latest year may not have been available at press time.*

In U.S. $	2017	2016	2015	2014	2013	2012
Revenue	866,000,000	840,000,000	830,000,000	824,000,000	800,000,000	750,658,000
R&D Expense						
Operating Income						
Operating Margin %						
SGA Expense						
Net Income						
Operating Cash Flow						
Capital Expenditure						
EBITDA						
Return on Assets %						
Return on Equity %						
Debt to Equity						

CONTACT INFORMATION:

Phone: 404-888-5800 Fax:
Toll-Free:
Address: 1275 Peachtree St NE #600, Atlanta, GA 30309 United States

STOCK TICKER/OTHER:

Stock Ticker: Subsidiary
Employees:
Parent Company: Providence Service Corporation
Exchange:
Fiscal Year Ends: 12/31

SALARIES/BONUSES:

Top Exec. Salary: $ Bonus: $
Second Exec. Salary: $ Bonus: $

OTHER THOUGHTS:

Estimated Female Officers or Directors: 2
Hot Spot for Advancement for Women/Minorities: Y

Lumenis Ltd

www.lumenis.com

NAIC Code: 339,100

TYPES OF BUSINESS:

Laser Surgery Products
Aesthetic Laser Products
Ophthalmic Laser Products

BRANDS/DIVISIONS/AFFILIATES:

XIO Group
Intense Pulsed Light
UltraPulse Encore
LightSheer
VersaPulse
UltraPulse SurgiTouch
SCAAR FX
MOSES

CONTACTS: *Note: Officers with more than one job title may be intentionally listed here more than once.*

Tzipi Ozer-Armon, CEO
Shlomi Cohen, CFO
Amir Lichter, VP-Global R&D
Amir Lichter, VP-Technology & Ventures
Shlomo Alkalay, VP-Corp. Projects
William Weisel, General Counsel
Eran Cohen, Head-Oper.
Kfir Azoulay, VP
Ido Ben-Tov, VP-Global Service
Rick Gaykowski, VP-Regulatory Affairs & Quality Systems
Kordt Griepenkerl, Pres.
Qiying Zhai, Pres., China & Asia Pacific
Elad Benjamin, VP
Roy Ramati, Sr. VP
Robert Di Silvio, Pres., Americas
Toshio Fukuda, Pres., Lumenis Japan

GROWTH PLANS/SPECIAL FEATURES:

Lumenis, Ltd. is a world leader in laser and light-based technologies for medical and aesthetic applications. The firm holds over 220 registered patents in and outside the U.S., and numerous FDA clearances. Lumenis has more than 80,000 installed systems in medical facilities across 100+ countries. Aesthetic applications include tattoo and hair removal; wrinkle treatment; removal of benign pigmented lesions, including brown spots, age spots, sunspots, scars and stretch marks; reducing the damage from sun, aging or environmental exposure; and removing vascular lesions such as spider veins and other red spots. Products include Intense Pulsed Light (IPL) technology systems that generate high temperature broad band light pulses, including UltraPulse Encore; and various laser systems, including the LightSheer hair removal laser. Surgical systems have a wide variety of applications in urology, neurosurgery, podiatry, gynecology, gastroenterology, otolaryngology (ear, nose and throat), thoracic and pulmonary surgery and general surgery. Its laser systems may be used to resurface skin, ablate (or remove) tissue, vaporize tissue and treat fungal infections. Lasers include VersaPulse and UltraPulse SurgiTouch. The ophthalmic segment develops systems for non-invasive and minimally invasive treatments for conditions such as diabetic retinopathy and retinal detachment; and pioneered the use of selective laser trabeculoplasty (SLT) in the glaucoma market with a demonstrated success rate of 93% as primary therapy and clinical efficacy. The company's SCAAR FX laser treatment solution treats scars up to four millimeters deep. Technology-wise, Leminis' patent-protected MOSES technology is used for holmium laster treatments in both urinary stones and benign prostatic hyperplasia, enabling less stone migration and a more efficient procedure. Lumenis is owned by global alternative investments firm, XIO Group.

FINANCIAL DATA: *Note: Data for latest year may not have been available at press time.*

In U.S. $	2017	2016	2015	2014	2013	2012
Revenue	316,050,000	301,000,000	300,000,000	289,719,008	265,356,000	248,590,000
R&D Expense						
Operating Income						
Operating Margin %						
SGA Expense						
Net Income				12,725,000	17,393,000	6,997,000
Operating Cash Flow						
Capital Expenditure						
EBITDA						
Return on Assets %						
Return on Equity %						
Debt to Equity						

CONTACT INFORMATION:

Phone: 972-4-959-9000 Fax: 972-4-959-9050
Toll-Free:
Address: Yokneam Industrial Park, Hakidma 6, PO Box 240, Yokneam, 2069204 Israel

STOCK TICKER/OTHER:

Stock Ticker: Private
Employees: 1,137
Parent Company: XIO Group
Exchange:
Fiscal Year Ends: 12/31

SALARIES/BONUSES:

Top Exec. Salary: $ Bonus: $
Second Exec. Salary: $ Bonus: $

OTHER THOUGHTS:

Estimated Female Officers or Directors: 2
Hot Spot for Advancement for Women/Minorities:

Lumeris Inc

lumeris.com

NAIC Code: 524,114

TYPES OF BUSINESS:

Supplementary Health Insurance Coverage
Electronic Medical Record Management
Insurance
Patient Care Accountability Services
Software

BRANDS/DIVISIONS/AFFILIATES:

Essence Group Holdings Corporation

CONTACTS: *Note: Officers with more than one job title may be intentionally listed here more than once.*

W. Michael Long, CEO
Chris McGinnis, CFO
Ross Armstrong, Sr. VP-Mktg.
Stephanie Pimmel, Sr. VP-Human Resources
Deborah Zimmerman, Chief Medical Officer
Gail Halterman, General Counsel
Terry Snyder, Sr. VP-Oper.
Lou Anne Gilmore, VP-Dev.
Glenda Holmstrom, VP-Client Svcs.
Jeff Smith, Pres., Mid-Atlantic Initiative
Terry Snyder, Sr. VP-Worldwide Sales

GROWTH PLANS/SPECIAL FEATURES:

Lumeris, Inc. provides strategic advising and cloud-based technology to help providers and payers, via seamless transitions, to deliver improved and more affordable care across populations. The firm works collaboratively with clients to align contracts and engage physicians in programs that drive high-quality, cost-effective care. For health systems and medical groups, Lumeris creates value-based payment arrangements, launches provider-sponsored health plans, optimizes care models, develops population health management strategies, engages physicians and consumers, manages performance and reimbursements, spearheads value-based care transformation and more. For payers, it aligns care delivery models and incentives, deploys population health tools and services, assess provider capabilities, creates empowered networks, retains and optimizes networks, engages physicians and consumers and aims to grow membership. Premier customers of the company include: Essence Healthcare, a Lumeris-operated Medicare Advantage plan with a customer management system rating of 4.5 to 5 stars for the past six years; and Accountable Delivery System Institute, an educational resource for accountable care. Lumeris is privately-held by Essence Group Holdings Corporation.

FINANCIAL DATA: *Note: Data for latest year may not have been available at press time.*

In U.S. $	2017	2016	2015	2014	2013	2012
Revenue	682,500,000	650,000,000	600,000,000	565,000,000	550,000,000	500,000,000
R&D Expense						
Operating Income						
Operating Margin %						
SGA Expense						
Net Income						
Operating Cash Flow						
Capital Expenditure						
EBITDA						
Return on Assets %						
Return on Equity %						
Debt to Equity						

CONTACT INFORMATION:

Phone: 888-586-3747 Fax:
Toll-Free:
Address: 13900 Riverport Dr., Maryland Heights, MO 63043 United States

STOCK TICKER/OTHER:

Stock Ticker: Private Exchange:
Employees: 450 Fiscal Year Ends:
Parent Company: Essence Group Holdings Corporation

SALARIES/BONUSES:

Top Exec. Salary: $ Bonus: $
Second Exec. Salary: $ Bonus: $

OTHER THOUGHTS:

Estimated Female Officers or Directors: 6
Hot Spot for Advancement for Women/Minorities: Y

Lupin Limited

www.lupinworld.com

NAIC Code: 325,412

TYPES OF BUSINESS:

Pharmaceutical Preparation Manufacturing
Pharmaceuticals
Active Pharmaceutical Ingredients
Biotechnology

BRANDS/DIVISIONS/AFFILIATES:

Lupifil
Cephalexin
Cefaclor
Ethambutol

CONTACTS: *Note: Officers with more than one job title may be intentionally listed here more than once.*

Desh Bandhu Gupta, Chmn.

GROWTH PLANS/SPECIAL FEATURES:

Lupin Limited is an India-based, innovation-led transnational pharmaceutical company developing and delivering a range of branded and generic formulations, biotechnology products and active pharmaceutical ingredients (APIs). Lupin is a leading player in the cardiovascular, diabetology, asthma, pediatric, central nervous system, gastrointestinal, anti-infective and non-steroidal anti-inflammatory drug (NSAID) space. Moreover, the firm holds a global leadership position in the anti-tuberculosis segment. Lupin comprises 18 global formulations manufacturing facilities, with its key markets being India, the U.S., Europe, Japan and Commonwealth of Independent States (CIS). Lupin's biotechnology division is based out of Pune, and comprises advanced capabilities such as development, manufacturing and pre-clinical studies to clinical programs in biotech products required for approval in both regulated as well as semi-regulated markets. This division's current pipeline (as of August 2018) includes 10 biosimilars in various stages of development, two of which were commercialized: Lupifil and Lupifil-P. These are biosimilars for molecules Filgrastim and Peg-Filgrastim. A biosimilar for Etanercept is being developed for global markets. Lupin includes a mix of products across indications such as rheumatoid arthritis, oncology, ophthalmology and osteoporosis. Lupin's company name is congruent with a Lupin flower's inherent qualities for nourishing the land and soil it grows in; it is capable of pioneering change even in barren and poor climates. The flower and bean pods are also used as food and sources of nourishment. Lupin's API business serves customers in more than 50 countries, and its flagship products include Cephalexin, Cefaclor and Ethambutol, which are anti-infective and anti-TB treatments. The API division has six manufacturing sites located in Ankleshwar, Tarapur, Vadodara, Mandideep, Indore and Vishakapatnam, India. Lupin's advanced drug delivery division creates and leverages technologies that not only provide clinical advantage but also transforms and facilitates better patient convenience and experience.

FINANCIAL DATA: *Note: Data for latest year may not have been available at press time.*

In U.S. $	2017	2016	2015	2014	2013	2012
Revenue	2,414,645,000	1,972,676,000	1,773,549,000	1,566,931,000	1,338,841,000	
R&D Expense						
Operating Income	540,660,300	465,195,800	463,423,100	396,371,500	275,352,700	
Operating Margin %	22.39%	23.58%	26.12%	25.29%	20.56%	
SGA Expense	238,453,300	215,690,800	169,980,800	171,336,300	149,922,400	
Net Income	355,572,200	315,701,600	334,130,500	255,316,600	182,712,000	
Operating Cash Flow	572,087,400	-51,299,130	379,985,100	278,613,100	173,934,900	
Capital Expenditure	366,601,700	808,578,900	121,123,100	73,498,580	76,622,660	
EBITDA	636,807,400	545,992,300	535,990,200	431,353,700	317,110,000	
Return on Assets %	10.42%	12.76%	20.58%	19.20%	15.60%	
Return on Equity %	20.89%	22.86%	30.40%	30.26%	28.51%	
Debt to Equity	0.41	0.48	0.01	0.02	0.04	

CONTACT INFORMATION:

Phone: 91 2266402222 Fax: 91 2266402130
Toll-Free:
Address: B/4 Laxmi Towers, Bandra Kurla Complex, Mumbai, Maharashtra 400051 India

STOCK TICKER/OTHER:

Stock Ticker: LUPNY
Employees: 17,042
Parent Company:
Exchange: GREY
Fiscal Year Ends: 03/31

SALARIES/BONUSES:

Top Exec. Salary: $ Bonus: $
Second Exec. Salary: $ Bonus: $

OTHER THOUGHTS:

Estimated Female Officers or Directors:
Hot Spot for Advancement for Women/Minorities:

Magee Rehabilitation Hospital

www.mageerehab.org/

NAIC Code: 622,110

TYPES OF BUSINESS:

General Medical and Surgical Hospital

BRANDS/DIVISIONS/AFFILIATES:

Magee Riverfront
Magee at Oxford Valley
Magee at Watermark
Magee Outpatient Physician Practice
Thomas Jefferson University
Jefferson Health

CONTACTS: *Note: Officers with more than one job title may be intentionally listed here more than once.*

Jack A. Carroll, Pres.

GROWTH PLANS/SPECIAL FEATURES:

Magee Rehabilitation Hospital is a nonprofit hospital serving the city of Philadelphia. This flagship hospital is a 96-bed specialty medical rehabilitation facility that provides physical and cognitive rehabilitation. This main campus is located in Center City Philadelphia, and offers comprehensive services for spinal cord injury, brain injury, stroke, orthopedic replacement, amputation, pain management, ventilator services, Guillain Barre Syndrome therapy, Multiple Sclerosis therapy and work injury therapy. Magee is a founding member of The Christopher Reeve Foundation NeuroRecovery Network. The firm's objectives include clinical service, education, research and community Involvement. Additional Magee locations include four therapy and/or outpatient services facilities: Magee Riverfront, Magee at Oxford Valley, Magee at Watermark and Magee Outpatient Physician Practice, all of which are in Philadelphia and in close proximity to the hospital. In January 2018, Magee Rehabilitation Hospital and Thomas Jefferson University integrated their acute and post-acute patient-care delivery systems. The Jefferson Health enterprise includes 14 hospitals, more than 2,900 licensed beds, and over 50 outpatient and urgent care locations across Pennsylvania and New Jersey.

The firm offers employees medical, dental, vision, prescription, life and disability coverage; a legal plan; funeral leave; access to a credit union; and tuition assistance.

FINANCIAL DATA: *Note: Data for latest year may not have been available at press time.*

In U.S. $	2017	2016	2015	2014	2013	2012
Revenue	157,500,000	150,000,000	147,542,467			
R&D Expense						
Operating Income						
Operating Margin %						
SGA Expense						
Net Income			6,033,497			
Operating Cash Flow						
Capital Expenditure						
EBITDA						
Return on Assets %						
Return on Equity %						
Debt to Equity						

CONTACT INFORMATION:

Phone: 215-587-3000 Fax: 215-568-3736
Toll-Free: 800-96-MAGEE
Address: 1513 Race St., Philadelphia, PA 19102 United States

STOCK TICKER/OTHER:

Stock Ticker: Nonprofit
Employees: 510
Parent Company:
Exchange:
Fiscal Year Ends: 06/30

SALARIES/BONUSES:

Top Exec. Salary: $ Bonus: $
Second Exec. Salary: $ Bonus: $

OTHER THOUGHTS:

Estimated Female Officers or Directors:
Hot Spot for Advancement for Women/Minorities:

Magellan Health Inc

www.magellanhealth.com

NAIC Code: 621,999

TYPES OF BUSINESS:

Specialty Managed Health Care Services
Psychiatric Hospitals
Residential Treatment Centers

BRANDS/DIVISIONS/AFFILIATES:

Magellan Complete Care

CONTACTS: *Note: Officers with more than one job title may be intentionally listed here more than once.*

Sanjeev Srivastava, CEO, Divisional
Mostafa Kamal, CEO, Subsidiary
Barry Smith, CEO
Jonathan Rubin, CFO
Caskie Lewis-Clapper, Other Executive Officer
Daniel Gregoire, Secretary
Jeffrey West, Senior VP

GROWTH PLANS/SPECIAL FEATURES:

Magellan Health, Inc. is engaged in the healthcare management business. Magellan develops innovative solutions that combine advanced analytics, agile technology and clinical excellence to promote best decision-making capabilities for its clients. The firm serves health plans, managed care organizations, employers, labor unions, various military and governmental agencies and third-party administrators. Magellan operates in two business segments: Magellan healthcare and Magellan Rx management. Magellan healthcare includes the firm's management of behavioral healthcare services and employee assistance program services; management of specialty areas such as diagnostic imaging and musculoskeletal management; and the integrated management of physical, behavioral and pharmaceutical health care for special populations delivered via Magellan Complete Care. Special populations include individuals with serious mental illness, dual eligible, long-term services and supports and other populations with unique and often complex health care needs. Magellan Rx management comprises products and solutions that provide clinical and financial management of pharmaceuticals paid under medical and pharmacy benefit programs. Its services include pharmacy benefit management, pharmacy benefit administration for state Medicaid and other government-sponsored programs, pharmaceutical dispensing operations, clinical and formulary management programs, medical pharmacy management programs, as well as programs for the integrated management of specialty drugs across both the medical and pharmacy benefit that treat complex conditions. In July 2017, the firm entered into a definitive agreement to acquire Senior Whole Health (SWH), a healthcare company focused on serving complex, high-risk populations, providing both Medicare and Medicaid dual-eligible benefits to more than 22,000 members in Massachusetts and New York.

Magellan offers employees medical, dental, disability, AD&D and life insurance; an employee assistance program; a 401(k); educational assistance; adoption assistance; telecommuting; and flexible spending accounts.

FINANCIAL DATA: *Note: Data for latest year may not have been available at press time.*

In U.S. $	2017	2016	2015	2014	2013	2012
Revenue	5,838,583,000	4,836,884,000	4,597,400,000	3,760,118,000	3,546,317,000	3,207,397,000
R&D Expense						
Operating Income	155,314,000	152,892,000	75,532,000	124,006,000	166,200,000	189,093,000
Operating Margin %	2.66%	3.16%	1.64%	3.29%	4.68%	5.89%
SGA Expense						
Net Income	110,207,000	77,879,000	31,413,000	79,404,000	125,261,000	151,027,000
Operating Cash Flow	162,273,000	66,699,000	239,185,000	211,044,000	183,161,000	181,293,000
Capital Expenditure	57,232,000	60,881,000	71,584,000	62,337,000	64,542,000	69,549,000
EBITDA	276,907,000	261,756,000	180,541,000	216,377,000	240,179,000	251,600,000
Return on Assets %	4.08%	3.45%	1.50%	4.12%	7.65%	10.58%
Return on Equity %	9.27%	7.19%	2.85%	6.93%	11.52%	16.21%
Debt to Equity	0.58	0.19	0.22	0.22	0.02	

CONTACT INFORMATION:

Phone: 602-572-6050 Fax:
Toll-Free: 800-410-8312
Address: 4800 Scottsdale Rd, Ste. 4000, Scottsdale, AZ 85251 United States

STOCK TICKER/OTHER:

Stock Ticker: MGLN Exchange: NAS
Employees: 9,700 Fiscal Year Ends: 12/31
Parent Company:

SALARIES/BONUSES:

Top Exec. Salary: $1,150,000 Bonus: $
Second Exec. Salary: $630,375 Bonus: $

OTHER THOUGHTS:

Estimated Female Officers or Directors: 3
Hot Spot for Advancement for Women/Minorities: Y

Main Line Health System

www.mainlinehealth.org

NAIC Code: 622,110

TYPES OF BUSINESS:

General Medical and Surgical Hospital

BRANDS/DIVISIONS/AFFILIATES:

Lankenau Medical Center
Bryn Mawr Hospital
Paoli Hospital
Riddle Hospital
Bryn Mawr Rehab Hospital
Mirmont Treatment Center
Lankenau Institute for Medical Research
Main Line HealthCare

CONTACTS: *Note: Officers with more than one job title may be intentionally listed here more than once.*

John J. Lynch III, Pres.
Mike Buongiorno, Exec. VP
Paul Yakulis, Sr. VP-HR
Kay Carr, Sr. VP
Elizabeth (Betsy) Balderston, Chmn.

GROWTH PLANS/SPECIAL FEATURES:

Main Line Health, Inc. (MLH) is a nonprofit health system serving the Philadelphia area. MLH is comprised of four acute care hospitals: Lankenau Medical Center, Bryn Mawr Hospital, Paoli Hospital and Riddle Hospital. The firm also maintains a leading rehabilitative hospital, Bryn Mawr Rehabilitation Hospital. Other facilities include: Mirmont Treatment Center for drug and alcohol recovery; Main Line health centers in Broomall, Collegeville, Concordville, Exton and Newtown Square; Lankenau Institute for Medical Research, a non-profit biomedical research organization dedicated to understanding the causes of cancer, diabetes and heart disease; and Main Line HealthCare, a multi-specialty physician network. MLH's health care services focus on the areas of cancer, heart care, orthopedics, maternity care, women's health, homecare and hospice, imaging/radiology and lab testing. In June 2018, MLH broke ground on a new Women's Specialty Center in collaboration with Axia Women's Health. The 94,000-square-foot facility is scheduled to open in late-2019, and will serve as a destination for enhancing health and wellness of those in the region. Its services will include breast health, digestive health, heart and vascular care, infertility services, integrative medicine, obstetrics, gynecology, pelvic floor care, rheumatology, autoimmune treatment, skin care, weight management, emotional wellness and more.

The firm offers its employees medical, dental, vision, life, AD&D and disability coverage; a 403(b) retirement savings plan; pension plan; tuition reimbursement; and grant programs.

FINANCIAL DATA: *Note: Data for latest year may not have been available at press time.*

In U.S. $	2017	2016	2015	2014	2013	2012
Revenue	1,785,000,000	1,700,000,000	1,586,313,000	1,487,954,000	1,431,775,000	
R&D Expense						
Operating Income						
Operating Margin %						
SGA Expense						
Net Income			201,155,000	171,798,000	183,003,000	
Operating Cash Flow						
Capital Expenditure						
EBITDA						
Return on Assets %						
Return on Equity %						
Debt to Equity						

CONTACT INFORMATION:

Phone: 610-647-2400 Fax: 610-409-6210
Toll-Free:
Address: 130 South Bryn Mawr Ave., Bryn Mawr, PA 19010 United States

STOCK TICKER/OTHER:

Stock Ticker: Nonprofit
Employees: 11,123
Parent Company:
Exchange:
Fiscal Year Ends: 05/30

SALARIES/BONUSES:

Top Exec. Salary: $ Bonus: $
Second Exec. Salary: $ Bonus: $

OTHER THOUGHTS:

Estimated Female Officers or Directors:
Hot Spot for Advancement for Women/Minorities:

ManorCare Inc (HCR ManorCare)

www.hcr-manorcare.com

NAIC Code: 623,110

TYPES OF BUSINESS:

Nursing Care Facilities
Home Health Care
Short-Term Care Facilities
Assisted Living Facilities
Rehabilitation Clinics

BRANDS/DIVISIONS/AFFILIATES:

ProMedica
Welltower Inc

CONTACTS:

Note: Officers with more than one job title may be intentionally listed here more than once.

Randy Oostra, CEO
Steve Cavanaugh, Pres.
Spencer C. Moler, Principal Acct. Officer

GROWTH PLANS/SPECIAL FEATURES:

ManorCare, Inc., doing business as HCR ManorCare, provides a range of health care services, including skilled nursing care, assisted living, post-acute medical care, hospice care, home health care and rehabilitation therapy. ManorCare operates more than 500 properties in over 32 states. The firm's long-term care services consist of skilled nursing centers, assisted living services, post-hospital centers and rehabilitation care and Alzheimer's care. The skilled nursing centers use interdisciplinary teams of experienced medical professionals, including registered nurses, licensed practical nurses and certified nursing assistants, to provide services prescribed by physicians. Other services include quality of life programs to give the highest practicable level of functional independence to patients; physical, speech, respiratory and occupational therapy; quality nutrition services; social services; housekeeping and laundry services; and activities. ManorCare's assisted living services provide personal care services and assistance with general activities of daily living such as dressing, bathing, meal preparation and medication management. In July 2018, ManorCare was acquired out of bankruptcy by becoming a joint venture company between ProMedica and Welltower, Inc.

FINANCIAL DATA:

Note: Data for latest year may not have been available at press time.

In U.S. $	2017	2016	2015	2014	2013	2012
Revenue	3,700,000,000	5,250,000,000	5,300,000,000	5,200,000,000	5,000,000,000	4,800,000,000
R&D Expense						
Operating Income						
Operating Margin %						
SGA Expense						
Net Income						
Operating Cash Flow						
Capital Expenditure						
EBITDA						
Return on Assets %						
Return on Equity %						
Debt to Equity						

CONTACT INFORMATION:

Phone: 419-252-5500 Fax: 419-252-6404
Toll-Free:
Address: 333 N. Summit St., Toledo, OH 43604 United States

STOCK TICKER/OTHER:

Stock Ticker: Joint Venture
Employees: 50,000
Parent Company:
Exchange:
Fiscal Year Ends: 12/31

SALARIES/BONUSES:

Top Exec. Salary: $ Bonus: $
Second Exec. Salary: $ Bonus: $

OTHER THOUGHTS:

Estimated Female Officers or Directors:
Hot Spot for Advancement for Women/Minorities:

Masimo Corporation

www.masimo.com

NAIC Code: 334,510

TYPES OF BUSINESS:

Medical Equipment
Patient Monitoring Devices
Circuit Boards
Patient Sensors
Software

BRANDS/DIVISIONS/AFFILIATES:

Masimo SET
uSp02
SofTouch
Rainbow
Radical-7
Radius
SafetyNet
Eve

CONTACTS: *Note: Officers with more than one job title may be intentionally listed here more than once.*

Joseph Kiani, CEO
Micah Young, CFO
David Van Ramshorst, Chief Accounting Officer
Yongsam Lee, Chief Information Officer
Anand Sampath, COO
Tao Levy, Executive VP, Divisional
Bilal Muhsin, Executive VP, Divisional
Thomas McClenahan, Executive VP
Jon Coleman, President, Divisional

GROWTH PLANS/SPECIAL FEATURES:

Masimo Corporation is a medical technology company that develops, manufactures and markets noninvasive patient monitoring products. Patient monitoring products are based on its Masimo Signal Extraction Technology (Masimo SET), which provides the capabilities of measure-through motion and low perfusion pulse oximetry to address the primary limitations of conventional pulse oximetry. The firm markets patient monitoring circuit boards, which are incorporated into its proprietary devices or sold to original equipment manufacturer (OEM) customers for incorporation into their monitors; sensors and patient cables; and standalone patient monitoring devices. Its circuit boards include the Masimo SET; the Masimo rainbow SET; and the uSp02 cable/board, which incorporates SET technology-in-a-cable. The firm has developed a broad line of single-patient use (disposable), reusable and ReSposable sensors and cables. These include SofTouch sensors, used for patients with compromised skin conditions; trauma and newborn sensors; blue sensors, which monitor arterial blood oxygen saturation levels in cyanotic infants; and Rainbow Acoustic Sensors, which measure respiration rate using an acoustic sensor placed on the patient's neck. Masimo's primary patient monitoring device, Radical-7, incorporates the firm's MX circuit boards and is capable of functioning as a standalone device for bedside monitoring; as a detachable, battery-operated handheld unit for portable monitoring; and as an interface that allows it to work with third-party products. Other monitors include the Rad and Radius lines of wearable wireless monitors. In addition, Masimo offers remote alarm/monitoring solutions and software such as its Root product. SafetyNet, the company's remote monitoring and clinician notification system, routes bedside-generated alarms through a server to a clinician's handheld paging device in real-time and supports up to 200 individual bedside monitors. In early-2018, Masimo received CE marking of Eve, a critical congenital heart disease newborn application for the Rad-97 pulse CO-oximeter.

FINANCIAL DATA: *Note: Data for latest year may not have been available at press time.*

In U.S. $	2017	2016	2015	2014	2013	2012
Revenue	798,108,000	694,625,000	630,111,000	586,643,000	547,245,000	493,233,000
R&D Expense	61,953,000	59,362,000	56,617,000	56,581,000	55,631,000	47,077,000
Operating Income	197,361,000	150,770,000	100,641,000	93,182,000	87,727,000	85,226,000
Operating Margin %	24.72%	21.70%	15.97%	15.88%	16.03%	17.27%
SGA Expense	275,786,000	253,667,000	252,725,000	241,016,000	215,469,000	193,948,000
Net Income	131,616,000	300,666,000	83,300,000	72,518,000	58,381,000	62,272,000
Operating Cash Flow	56,062,000	416,842,000	114,209,000	95,459,000	54,317,000	75,434,000
Capital Expenditure	46,763,000	24,351,000	54,594,000	78,414,000	13,016,000	14,492,000
EBITDA	217,422,000	167,587,000	116,325,000	106,000,000	99,148,000	94,595,000
Return on Assets %	15.20%	42.28%	14.27%	14.45%	14.33%	16.78%
Return on Equity %	20.77%	71.95%	28.65%	22.93%	19.47%	22.64%
Debt to Equity			0.67	0.40		

CONTACT INFORMATION:

Phone: 949 297-7000 Fax: 949 297-7001
Toll-Free: 800-326-4890
Address: 52 Discovery, Irvine, CA 92618 United States

STOCK TICKER/OTHER:

Stock Ticker: MASI
Exchange: NAS
Employees: 4,293
Fiscal Year Ends: 12/31
Parent Company:

SALARIES/BONUSES:

Top Exec. Salary: $1,045,450 Bonus: $
Second Exec. Salary: $439,089 Bonus: $

OTHER THOUGHTS:

Estimated Female Officers or Directors:
Hot Spot for Advancement for Women/Minorities:

Mayo Clinic

www.mayo.edu

NAIC Code: 622,110

TYPES OF BUSINESS:

General Medical and Surgical Hospitals
Physician Practice Management
Medical Research
Health Care Education

BRANDS/DIVISIONS/AFFILIATES:

Mayo Clinic
Mayo Clinic Hospital
Saint Mary's Campus
Mayo Clinic Building
Samuel C Johnson Research
Mayo Clinic Collaborative Research
Mayo Clinic Specialty

CONTACTS: *Note: Officers with more than one job title may be intentionally listed here more than once.*

John H. Noseworthy, CEO
Shirley A. Weis, Chief Admin. Officer
Jonathan J. Oviatt, Chief Legal Officer
Harry N. Hoffman, Treas.
William C. Rupp, VP
Wyatt W. Decker, VP
Robert F. Brigham, Assistant Sec.
Sherry L. Hubert, Assistant Sec.
Samuel A. Di Piazza Jr., Chmn.

GROWTH PLANS/SPECIAL FEATURES:

Mayo Clinic is a nonprofit health care organization founded in 1864, and part of the Mayo Foundation for Medical Education and Research. Mayo Clinic provides medical treatment, physician management, healthcare education, research and other specialized medical services through a network of clinics and hospitals in Minnesota, Arizona and Florida. The organization's primary clinics, which house physician group practices, are located in Rochester, Minnesota; Jacksonville, Florida; and Scottsdale and Phoenix, Arizona. The Rochester campus has been in business for more than 100 years, and includes the Mayo Clinic, the Mayo Clinic Hospital, Saint Mary's Campus and Mayo Clinic Hospital-Methodist Campus, which together provide comprehensive diagnosis and treatment in virtually every medical and surgical specialty. The Mayo Clinic Hospital, located on the Jacksonville campus, offers 261 beds and represents more than 40 medical and surgical specialties. In Arizona, Mayo Clinic serves more than 100,000 patients every year, and focuses on adult specialty and surgical disciplines, supported by programs in medical education and research. The original Scottsdale campus opened in 1987, and includes the Mayo Clinic Building, the Samuel C. Johnson Research building and the Mayo Clinic Collaborative Research building. The Phoenix campus includes the Mayo Clinic Specialty building and Mayo Clinic Hospital.

Doctors are paid by salary, rather than fee for service. Employees of the firm are offered medical, dental, vision, AD&D, life, disability and prescription drug plans; employee and tuition assistance; flexible spending accounts; and pension plans.

FINANCIAL DATA: *Note: Data for latest year may not have been available at press time.*

In U.S. $	2017	2016	2015	2014	2013	2012
Revenue	11,993,000,000	10,990,000,000	10,315,000,000	9,760,600,000	9,420,800,000	8,843,900,000
R&D Expense						
Operating Income						
Operating Margin %						
SGA Expense						
Net Income	707,000,000	475,000,000	526,000,000	834,800,000	612,100,000	395,400,000
Operating Cash Flow						
Capital Expenditure						
EBITDA						
Return on Assets %						
Return on Equity %						
Debt to Equity						

CONTACT INFORMATION:

Phone: 507-284-2511 Fax: 507-284-0161
Toll-Free: 800-660-4582
Address: 200 First St. SW, Rochester, MN 55905 United States

STOCK TICKER/OTHER:

Stock Ticker: Nonprofit
Employees: 63,134
Parent Company:
Exchange:
Fiscal Year Ends: 12/31

SALARIES/BONUSES:

Top Exec. Salary: $ Bonus: $
Second Exec. Salary: $ Bonus: $

OTHER THOUGHTS:

Estimated Female Officers or Directors: 5
Hot Spot for Advancement for Women/Minorities: Y

Mazor Robotics Ltd

www.mazorrobotics.com

NAIC Code: 334,510

TYPES OF BUSINESS:

Electromedical and Electrotherapeutic Apparatus Manufacturing

BRANDS/DIVISIONS/AFFILIATES:

Renaissance
Mazor X

CONTACTS: *Note: Officers with more than one job title may be intentionally listed here more than once.*

Ori Hadomi, CEO
Sharon Levita, CFO & Bus. Operations
Doron Dinstein, CMO
Moshe Shoham, CTO
Jonathan Adereth, Chmn.

GROWTH PLANS/SPECIAL FEATURES:

Mazor Robotics Ltd. develops and markets surgical guidance systems for spine and brain surgery and complementary products that provide a safer environment for patients, surgeons, and operating room staff. The company's flagship product, the Renaissance surgical guidance system, enables surgeons to conduct spine surgeries in a more accurate and secure manner. It does this by transforming spine surgery from freehand procedures to state-of-the-art procedures, increasing both accuracy and favorable outcomes. Renaissance's intuitive interface allows surgeons to plan operations in a virtual 3D environment, creating a surgical blueprint for accuracy. Procedures in a spine program include minimally-invasive and percutaneous degenerative repair, pedicle screw fixation for complex spinal deformity, as well as vertebral augmentation. In recent years, Mazor completed a two-stage (in 2016), multi-faceted commercial agreement with Medtronic plc, for co-promotion, co-development and potential global distribution of certain Mazor products (stage one), as well as a minority equity investment by Medtronic in Mazor (stage two). As a result, the company presented its Mazor X system, a transformative surgical assurance platform which enhances the predictability of spine surgeries for the benefit of patients and those who treat them. By early-2017, 15 Mazor X systems had been commercially supplied, with an additional 19 orders by mid-2017. Mazor Robotics' core technology was utilized in both the Renaissance and Mazor X surgical guidance systems. In August 2017, Medtronic assumed exclusive worldwide distribution of the Mazor X system for spinal surgeries.

FINANCIAL DATA: *Note: Data for latest year may not have been available at press time.*

In U.S. $	2017	2016	2015	2014	2013	2012
Revenue	64,947,000	36,379,000	26,096,000	21,208,000	19,983,000	12,175,000
R&D Expense	8,192,000	5,736,000	6,324,000	5,776,000	4,174,000	2,760,000
Operating Income	-13,803,000	-19,021,000	-15,307,000	-14,708,000	-6,929,000	-4,210,000
Operating Margin %	-21.25%	-52.28%	-58.65%	-69.35%	-34.67%	-34.57%
SGA Expense	46,423,000	39,075,000	28,731,000	25,307,000	18,019,000	10,589,000
Net Income	-12,419,000	-18,668,000	-15,385,000	-15,272,000	-20,529,000	-7,064,000
Operating Cash Flow	-5,891,000	-10,102,000	-11,572,000	-14,290,000	-5,050,000	-1,820,000
Capital Expenditure	2,364,000	2,361,000	702,000	503,000	272,000	372,000
EBITDA	-12,281,000	-18,199,000	-14,780,000	-14,587,000	-19,751,000	-5,815,000
Return on Assets %	-11.62%	-27.92%	-27.55%	-23.21%	-44.52%	-33.76%
Return on Equity %	-13.90%	-34.79%	-31.83%	-25.80%	-53.38%	-53.60%
Debt to Equity						

CONTACT INFORMATION:

Phone: 972 46187100 Fax: 972 46187111
Toll-Free:
Address: 5 Shacham St., North Industrial Park, Caesarea, 3088900 Israel

STOCK TICKER/OTHER:

Stock Ticker: MZOR
Employees: 204
Parent Company:
Exchange: NAS
Fiscal Year Ends: 12/31

SALARIES/BONUSES:

Top Exec. Salary: $384,525 Bonus: $
Second Exec. Salary: $362,786 Bonus: $

OTHER THOUGHTS:

Estimated Female Officers or Directors:
Hot Spot for Advancement for Women/Minorities:

McKesson Corporation

www.mckesson.com

NAIC Code: 424,210

TYPES OF BUSINESS:

Pharmaceutical Distribution
Medical-Surgical Products Distribution
Health Care Management Software
Consulting
Outsourcing

BRANDS/DIVISIONS/AFFILIATES:

RelayHealth Pharmacy Solutions
Macro Helix
McKesson High Volume Solutions
McKesson Pharmacy Systems
Supplylogix
McKesson Canada
McKesson Europe
Medical Specialties Distributors LLC

CONTACTS: *Note: Officers with more than one job title may be intentionally listed here more than once.*

John Hammergren, CEO
Britt Vitalone, CFO
Brian Tyler, Chairman of the Board, Geographical
Erin Lampert, Chief Accounting Officer
Kathleen McElligott, Chief Information Officer
Jorge Figueredo, Executive VP, Divisional
Bansi Nagji, Executive VP, Divisional
Lori Schechter, Executive VP
Sundeep Reddy, Other Corporate Officer
Michele Lau, Secretary
Paul Smith, Senior VP, Divisional
Brian Moore, Senior VP

GROWTH PLANS/SPECIAL FEATURES:

McKesson Corporation provides medicines, pharmaceutical supplies, information and care management products and services to the healthcare industry. The company's business is divided into six divisions: U.S. pharmaceutical, medical-surgical, specialty health, pharmacy technology, McKesson Canada and McKesson Europe. The U.S. pharmaceutical division supplies branded, generic and over-the-counter pharmaceuticals to more than 40,000 customers. It also provides supply chain technology, marketing programs, managed care and repackaging products and services to retail chains, independent retail pharmacies, hospitals, health systems, integrated delivery networks and long-term care providers. The medical-surgical division offers a range of related supplies and equipment to physicians' offices, post-acute care agencies and surgery centers. Supplies and equipment range from bandages to exam tables. This division's catalogue comprises more than 150,000 national brand products, along with its own proprietary products. The specialty health division unites independent provides with manufactures and payers. The pharmacy technology division provides solutions to pharmaceutical companies, health systems, clinics and payers across the healthcare industry. The technology and connectivity solutions help them stay competitive, compliant and focused on patient outcomes. This division's businesses include RelayHealth Pharmacy Solutions, Macro Helix, McKesson High Volume Solutions, McKesson Pharmacy Systems and Supplylogix. The McKesson Canada division delivers vital medicines, supplies and information technology to pharmacies, manufacturers, hospitals and other health care institutions. Last, the McKesson Europe division is a pharmaceutical wholesale and retail pharmacy leader, providing service to more than 2 million patients annually. This division comprises more than 115 pharmaceutical distribution centers. In June 2018, McKesson acquired Medical Specialties Distributors, LLC.

Employee benefits include medical, dental, vision, AD&D and dependent life insurance; an employee assistance program; and flexible spending accounts.

FINANCIAL DATA: *Note: Data for latest year may not have been available at press time.*

In U.S. $	2017	2016	2015	2014	2013	2012
Revenue	198,533,000,000	190,884,000,000	179,045,000,000	137,609,000,000	122,455,000,000	
R&D Expense	341,000,000	392,000,000	392,000,000	456,000,000	480,000,000	
Operating Income	3,464,000,000	3,748,000,000	3,118,000,000	2,435,000,000	2,306,000,000	
Operating Margin %	1.74%	1.96%	1.74%	1.76%	1.88%	
SGA Expense	7,466,000,000	7,276,000,000	7,901,000,000	5,418,000,000	4,198,000,000	
Net Income	5,070,000,000	2,258,000,000	1,476,000,000	1,263,000,000	1,338,000,000	
Operating Cash Flow	4,744,000,000	3,672,000,000	3,112,000,000	3,136,000,000	2,483,000,000	
Capital Expenditure	562,000,000	677,000,000	545,000,000	415,000,000	406,000,000	
EBITDA	8,109,000,000	4,488,000,000	4,048,000,000	3,103,000,000	2,750,000,000	
Return on Assets %	8.62%	4.08%	2.79%	2.91%	3.94%	
Return on Equity %	50.65%	26.68%	17.86%	16.20%	19.25%	
Debt to Equity	0.65	0.73	1.02	1.05	0.63	

CONTACT INFORMATION:

Phone: 415 983-8300 Fax: 415 983-8453
Toll-Free: 800-826-9360
Address: 1 Post St., San Francisco, CA 94104 United States

STOCK TICKER/OTHER:

Stock Ticker: MCK Exchange: NYS
Employees: 78,000 Fiscal Year Ends: 03/31
Parent Company:

SALARIES/BONUSES:

Top Exec. Salary: $1,680,000 Bonus: $
Second Exec. Salary: $620,839 Bonus: $500,000

OTHER THOUGHTS:

Estimated Female Officers or Directors: 4
Hot Spot for Advancement for Women/Minorities: Y

MD Anderson Cancer Center

NAIC Code: 622,310

www.mdanderson.org

TYPES OF BUSINESS:

Cancer Hospital

BRANDS/DIVISIONS/AFFILIATES:

University of Texas Medical School at Houston
Baylor College of Medicine
MD Anderson Children's Cancer Hospital
International Center
Baptist MD Anderson Cancer Center

CONTACTS:

Note: Officers with more than one job title may be intentionally listed here more than once.

Peter WT Pisters, Pres.

GROWTH PLANS/SPECIAL FEATURES:

The University of Texas MD Anderson Cancer Center is both a degree-granting academic institution and a cancer treatment and research center located in Houston, Texas. MD Anderson Cancer Center is affiliated with two major research-based medical schools: The University of Texas Medical School at Houston and Baylor College of Medicine. The cancer center aims to eliminate cancer in Texas, the nation and the world through outstanding programs that integrate patient care, research and prevention, as well as through education for undergraduate and graduate students, trainees, professionals, employees and the public. More than 1.3 million patients have been treated since 1944, and the center employs and utilizes more than 1,740 faculty, 3,200 onsite and offsite volunteers and more than 7,000 trainees. During 2017, MD Anderson Cancer Center cared for approximately 137,000 patients, more than 44,000 were new; and over 10,800 participants were enrolled in 1,250+ clinical trials exploring innovative treatments. Other group centers include: MD Anderson Children's Cancer Hospital, for children with cancer; and the International Center, which helps patients travel to Houston from all over the world for cancer treatment via patient admissions, travel arrangements and language assistance. In August 2018, the 9-story, 330,000-square-foot Baptist MD Anderson Cancer Center opened in Jacksonville, Florida, with its first patient scheduled for a September 4, 2018 visit; and Texas MD Anderson Cancer Center launched a multidisciplinary partnership with the University of Houston to address cancer health disparities among black and Hispanic populations in the city.

MD Anderson Cancer Center offers employees medical, dental and vision coverage; prescriptions; disability, life and accidental death insurances; flexible spending accounts; and long-term care.

FINANCIAL DATA:

Note: Data for latest year may not have been available at press time.

In U.S. $	2017	2016	2015	2014	2013	2012
Revenue	5,000,000,000	4,012,043,122	4,086,291,840	4,413,000,000		
R&D Expense						
Operating Income						
Operating Margin %						
SGA Expense						
Net Income		207,532,713	566,878,526			
Operating Cash Flow						
Capital Expenditure						
EBITDA						
Return on Assets %						
Return on Equity %						
Debt to Equity						

CONTACT INFORMATION:

Phone: 713-792-2121 Fax:
Toll-Free: 877-632-6789
Address: 1515 Holcombe Blvd., Houston, TX 77030 United States

STOCK TICKER/OTHER:

Stock Ticker: Nonprofit
Exchange:
Employees: 19,530
Fiscal Year Ends: 08/31
Parent Company:

SALARIES/BONUSES:

Top Exec. Salary: $ Bonus: $
Second Exec. Salary: $ Bonus: $

OTHER THOUGHTS:

Estimated Female Officers or Directors:
Hot Spot for Advancement for Women/Minorities:

Medica Sur SAB de CV

www.medicasur.com.mx

NAIC Code: 621,910

TYPES OF BUSINESS:

Ambulance Services

BRANDS/DIVISIONS/AFFILIATES:

Medical-University Complex
Medica Sur Loma Hospital
Holiday Inn & Suites Mexico - Medica Sur

CONTACTS:
Note: Officers with more than one job title may be intentionally listed here more than once.

Misael Uribe Esquivel, Chmn.

GROWTH PLANS/SPECIAL FEATURES:

Medica Sur SAB de CV is a medical care company engaged in medical attention, research, diagnostic, teaching and community service. The group's Medical-University Complex in Mexico City is a high specialty center, and secondary level care is provided at Medica Sur Loma Hospital, also in Mexico City. Medica Sur medical units include behavioral disorders, blood bank and transfusional medicine, cardiology, check-ups, emergencies, foot/ankle, gastroenterology, imaging, magnetic resonance, weight control, neonatology, neurophysiology, nuclear medicine, obstetrics/gynecology, pediatrics, physical therapy medicine, radiotherapy, short-stay surgery, urology and women's health. Specialized centers include comprehensive diagnostics and treatment, cancer care, radiotherapy, Gamma Knife radiosurgery and laboratory. Holiday Inn & Suites Mexico - Medica Sur comprises hotel facilities strategically located within the company's hospital complex, offering 72 rooms (including 12 luxury suites), restaurants and banks. Medica Sur is a hospital member of the Mayo Clinic Care Network, working together with international physicians for the best interest of patients.

FINANCIAL DATA:
Note: Data for latest year may not have been available at press time.

In U.S. $	2017	2016	2015	2014	2013	2012
Revenue	180,345,200	136,136,000	119,763,500	120,464,800	118,588,700	109,842,100
R&D Expense						
Operating Income	28,221,820	11,260,250	19,097,190	24,331,520	25,969,680	20,983,170
Operating Margin %		8.27%	15.94%	20.19%	21.89%	19.10%
SGA Expense	34,854,770	30,913,950	18,832,770	16,714,590	15,767,680	15,210,560
Net Income	12,182,530	7,496,362	12,667,120	18,346,690	19,959,170	15,793,970
Operating Cash Flow	11,246,370	10,447,320	17,228,440	24,942,300	25,967,970	18,085,120
Capital Expenditure	13,984,250	12,105,120	12,001,580	16,643,980	11,384,290	176,272
EBITDA	38,837,080	29,003,660	24,775,610	31,022,540	32,413,970	27,775,460
Return on Assets %		3.09%	6.49%	9.99%	11.34%	9.41%
Return on Equity %		4.35%	7.59%	11.90%	14.21%	12.62%
Debt to Equity		0.38				

CONTACT INFORMATION:

Phone: 52 54247200 Fax:
Toll-Free:
Address: Puente de Piedra 150, Toriello Guerra, Mexico DF, 14050 Mexico

STOCK TICKER/OTHER:

Stock Ticker: MEDICA B
Employees: 3,895
Parent Company:
Exchange: MEX
Fiscal Year Ends: 12/31

SALARIES/BONUSES:

Top Exec. Salary: $ Bonus: $
Second Exec. Salary: $ Bonus: $

OTHER THOUGHTS:

Estimated Female Officers or Directors:
Hot Spot for Advancement for Women/Minorities:

Medical Action Industries Inc

www.medical-action.com

NAIC Code: 339,100

TYPES OF BUSINESS:

Supplies-Laparoscopy Sponges & Operating Room Towels
Operating Room Disposables
Containment Systems for Medical Waste
Patient Bedside Products
Laboratory Products
Minor Procedure Kits & Trays
Sterilization Products
Dressings and Surgical Sponges

BRANDS/DIVISIONS/AFFILIATES:

Owens & Minor Inc

GROWTH PLANS/SPECIAL FEATURES:

Medical Action Industries, Inc. (MAI) develops, manufactures, markets and distributes disposable medical products primarily to: acute care facilities as well as long-term care facilities; physician, dental and veterinary offices; and out-patient surgery centers. MAI specializes in the provision of medical supplies in six categories: customer procedure trays; minor procedure kits and trays, including infusion therapy, instrument kits and endoscopy kits; operating room supplies; medical products such as wound care; patient apparel such as slippers; and sterilization products such as seal pouches, sterility monitoring products, integrators, bowie dick tests, indicator tape, foam pouches, tray liners, basin separators and foam aligners. MAI is owned by healthcare logistics company Owens & Minor, Inc.

Employee benefits include medical, dental and vision coverage; wellness programs; 401(k); life insurance; flexible spending accounts; short- and long-term disability; and cancer and accident protection.

CONTACTS: *Note: Officers with more than one job title may be intentionally listed here more than once.*

P. Cody Phipps, CEO-Owens & Minor
Paul D. Meringolo, Pres.
John Sheffield, Corp. Sec.
Eric Liu, VP-Oper.

FINANCIAL DATA: *Note: Data for latest year may not have been available at press time.*

In U.S. $	2017	2016	2015	2014	2013	2012
Revenue	315,000,000	300,000,000	290,000,000	287,849,000	284,763,000	272,734,000
R&D Expense						
Operating Income						
Operating Margin %						
SGA Expense						
Net Income				4,192,000	-54,856,000	181,000
Operating Cash Flow						
Capital Expenditure						
EBITDA						
Return on Assets %						
Return on Equity %						
Debt to Equity						

CONTACT INFORMATION:

Phone: Fax:
Toll-Free: 800-488-8850
Address: 9120 Lockwood Blvd., Mechanicsville, VA 23116 United States

STOCK TICKER/OTHER:

Stock Ticker: Subsidiary
Exchange:
Employees: 525
Fiscal Year Ends: 03/31
Parent Company: Owens & Minor Inc

SALARIES/BONUSES:

Top Exec. Salary: $ Bonus: $
Second Exec. Salary: $ Bonus: $

OTHER THOUGHTS:

Estimated Female Officers or Directors: 1
Hot Spot for Advancement for Women/Minorities: Y

Medical Facilities Corporation

www.medicalfc.com

NAIC Code: 622,310

TYPES OF BUSINESS:

Specialty (except Psychiatric and Substance Abuse) Hospitals

BRANDS/DIVISIONS/AFFILIATES:

Black Hills Surgical Hospital
Oklahoma Spine Hospital
Arkansas Surgical Hospital
Sioux Falls Specialty Hospital
Unity Medical and Surgical Hospital
Newport Center Surgical

CONTACTS: *Note: Officers with more than one job title may be intentionally listed here more than once.*

R. Curd, CEO, Subsidiary
Carrie Helm, CEO, Subsidiary
Tyler Murphy, CFO
Robert Horrar, Director
Marilynne Day-Linton, Director
James Rolfe, Other Executive Officer
Jimmy Porter, Vice President, Divisional

GROWTH PLANS/SPECIAL FEATURES:

Medical Facilities Corporation (MFC) owns controlling interests in five specialty surgical hospitals located in South Dakota, Oklahoma, Indiana and Arkansas, as well as an ambulatory surgery center in California. In addition, through a partnership with NueHealth, LLC, Medical Facilities owns controlling interests in seven ambulatory surgery centers in Arkansas, Michigan, Missouri, Nebraska, Ohio, Oregon and Pennsylvania. The firm's specialty surgical hospitals perform scheduled surgery, imaging and diagnostic procedures. MFC's focus is to be different from regular hospitals by creating a five-star hotel environment and service. Black Hills Surgical Hospital in South Dakota, focuses primarily on orthopaedic, neurosurgical and pain management procedures and features 11 operating rooms and 26 overnight rooms. Oklahoma Spine Hospital in Oklahoma, focuses on neurosurgery and pain management procedures and has a total of 7 operating rooms and 25 overnight rooms. Arkansas Surgical Hospital is nationally acclaimed and physician-owned, specializing in orthopedic and spine surgery, with 11 operating rooms and 41 overnight rooms. Sioux Falls Specialty Hospital in South Dakota specializes in orthopedics, ear/nose/throat, pain management, gastroenterology and urology procedures, and comprises 14 operating rooms and 34 overnight rooms. Unity Medical and Surgical Hospital in Indiana is a 29-bed Medicare-certified surgical hospital, with four operating rooms and 29 overnight rooms. It specializes in orthopedics, pain management and spine surgery. Last, Newport Center Surgical is a licensed ambulatory surgery center in California, with two operating rooms and one procedure room. It specializes in orthopedics, obstetrics/gynecology, pain management, gastroenterology and urology. In June 2018, MFC sold its 51%-stake in Integrated Medical Delivery, LLC to N. Harris Computer Corporation.

FINANCIAL DATA: *Note: Data for latest year may not have been available at press time.*

In U.S. $	2017	2016	2015	2014	2013	2012
Revenue	385,329,000	339,472,000	308,778,000	311,834,000	309,162,000	239,380,000
R&D Expense						
Operating Income	66,901,000	68,073,000	74,692,000	71,236,000	91,072,000	65,977,000
Operating Margin %	17.36%	20.05%	24.18%	22.84%	29.45%	27.56%
SGA Expense	175,722,000	149,136,000	125,218,000	127,117,000	122,200,000	92,950,000
Net Income	20,637,000	9,754,000	47,127,000	23,308,000	11,239,000	32,815,000
Operating Cash Flow	79,986,000	78,290,000	80,240,000	88,000,000	85,275,000	77,145,000
Capital Expenditure	11,190,000	43,704,000	7,385,000	8,297,000	13,325,000	10,633,000
EBITDA	95,692,000	74,199,000	131,687,000	108,080,000	74,568,000	74,399,000
Return on Assets %	4.33%	2.22%	11.89%	5.49%	2.56%	8.47%
Return on Equity %	14.21%	6.20%	29.99%	15.24%	7.68%	24.44%
Debt to Equity	0.57	0.91	0.35	0.48	0.37	0.51

CONTACT INFORMATION:

Phone: 416 848-7380 Fax:
Toll-Free: 877-42-7162
Address: 45 St. Clair Ave. W., Ste. 200, Toronto, ON M4V 1K6 Canada

STOCK TICKER/OTHER:

Stock Ticker: DR
Employees: 1,544
Parent Company:
Exchange: TSE
Fiscal Year Ends: 12/31

SALARIES/BONUSES:

Top Exec. Salary: $ Bonus: $
Second Exec. Salary: $ Bonus: $

OTHER THOUGHTS:

Estimated Female Officers or Directors: 1
Hot Spot for Advancement for Women/Minorities:

Medical Imaging Corp

www.medimagingcorp.com

NAIC Code: 621,512

TYPES OF BUSINESS:

Diagnostic Imaging Centers

BRANDS/DIVISIONS/AFFILIATES:

Canadian Teleradiology Services Inc
Custom Teleradiology Services
Schuylkill Open MRI Inc
Schuylkill Medical Imaging
Partners Imaging Center of Venice LLC
Partners Imaging Center of Naples LLC
Partners Imaging Center of Charlotte LLC

GROWTH PLANS/SPECIAL FEATURES:

Medical Imaging Corp. is a U.S.-based healthcare services company with a specific focus on medical diagnostic imaging. The company currently owns and operates five wholly-owned subsidiaries: Canadian Teleradiology Services, Inc., which operates as Custom Teleradiology Services; Schuylkill Open MRI, Inc., which operates as Schuylkill Medical Imaging; Partners Imaging Center of Venice LLC; Partners Imaging Center of Naples LLC; and Partners Imaging Center of Charlotte LLC. With operations in the U.S. and Canada, the company is executing a growth strategy centered on acquiring and operating profitable medical diagnostic imaging facilities and imaging services businesses with a goal of profitably increasing revenues.

CONTACTS: *Note: Officers with more than one job title may be intentionally listed here more than once.*

Mitchell Geisler, CEO
Richard Jagodnik, CFO

FINANCIAL DATA: *Note: Data for latest year may not have been available at press time.*

In U.S. $	2017	2016	2015	2014	2013	2012
Revenue						
R&D Expense						
Operating Income						
Operating Margin %						
SGA Expense						
Net Income						
Operating Cash Flow						
Capital Expenditure						
EBITDA						
Return on Assets %						
Return on Equity %						
Debt to Equity						

CONTACT INFORMATION:

Phone: 877 331-3444 Fax:
Toll-Free:
Address: 848 N. Rainbow Blvd., Las Vegas, NV 89107 United States

STOCK TICKER/OTHER:

Stock Ticker: MEDD
Exchange: PINX
Employees: 41
Fiscal Year Ends: 12/31
Parent Company:

SALARIES/BONUSES:

Top Exec. Salary: $75,715 Bonus: $4,854
Second Exec. Salary: $15,143 Bonus: $

OTHER THOUGHTS:

Estimated Female Officers or Directors:
Hot Spot for Advancement for Women/Minorities:

Medical Information Technology Inc (MEDITECH)

www.meditech.com

NAIC Code: 511210D

TYPES OF BUSINESS:

Computer Software, Healthcare & Biotechnology

BRANDS/DIVISIONS/AFFILIATES:

Web EHR
Expanse

CONTACTS:

Note: Officers with more than one job title may be intentionally listed here more than once.

Howard Messing, CEO
Michelle O'Connor, COO
Howard Messing, Pres.
Barbara A. Manzolillo, CFO
Helen Waters, VP-Mktg. & Sales
Scott Radner, VP-Advanced Technology
Chris Anschuetz, VP-Tech.
Michelle O'Connor, Exec. VP-Prod. Dev.
Hoda Sayed-Friel, Exec. VP-Strategy & Mktg.
Barbara A. Manzolillo, Treas.
Robert Gale, Sr. VP-Prod. Dev.
Leah Farina, VP-Client Svcs. & Int'l
Scott Radner, VP-Advanced Tech.
A. Neil Pappalardo, Chmn.
Steven Koretz, Sr. VP- Int'l & Client Svcs.

GROWTH PLANS/SPECIAL FEATURES:

Medical Information Technology, Inc. (MEDITECH) develops and markets information system software for the health care industry. MEDITECH's software products automate a variety of hospital functions, and offer various solutions for long-term care facilities, ambulatory care centers, acute-care hospitals, emergency rooms and pharmacies, as well as imaging, therapeutic service and behavioral health facilities. The company specifies aggregate components for each hospital and suggests typical configurations from selected hardware vendors pertaining to software needs. The firm's solutions are accessible via desktop and mobile devices anywhere, any time. MEDITECH'S Web EHR (electronic health record) product offers a cohesive set of software designed to work in conjunction with the overall operation of the hospital. Web EHR facilitates over 300 billion data transactions per year. The firm's software products will automate clinical laboratory departments, which perform diagnostic tests; and automate hospital billing, accounts receivable and general accounting. MEDITECH has more than 2,400 customers worldwide. Its primary international subsidiary locations are based in Asia Pacific, South Africa, the U.K. and Ireland. During 2018, MEDITECH launched its contemporary, cloud-based subscription model, MEDITECH as a Services (MaaS), to power the firm's Expanse next-generation EHR web platform.

The firm offers employees benefits such as medical, dental, AD&D, life and long-term disability insurance; educational assistance; paid time off; a profit sharing plan; and an annual bonus.

FINANCIAL DATA:

Note: Data for latest year may not have been available at press time.

In U.S. $	2017	2016	2015	2014	2013	2012
Revenue	485,369,291	462,256,468	475,525,581	517,002,274	579,645,457	597,838,787
R&D Expense						
Operating Income						
Operating Margin %						
SGA Expense						
Net Income		72,890,198	70,066,792	123,508,355	133,328,172	130,546,535
Operating Cash Flow						
Capital Expenditure						
EBITDA						
Return on Assets %						
Return on Equity %						
Debt to Equity						

CONTACT INFORMATION:

Phone: 781-821-3000 Fax: 781-821-2199
Toll-Free:
Address: Meditech Circle, Westwood, MA 02090 United States

STOCK TICKER/OTHER:

Stock Ticker: Private
Employees: 3,700
Parent Company:
Exchange:
Fiscal Year Ends: 12/31

SALARIES/BONUSES:

Top Exec. Salary: $ Bonus: $
Second Exec. Salary: $ Bonus: $

OTHER THOUGHTS:

Estimated Female Officers or Directors: 10
Hot Spot for Advancement for Women/Minorities: Y

Medical Mutual of Ohio

www.medmutual.com

NAIC Code: 524,114

TYPES OF BUSINESS:

Insurance-Medical & Health, HMOs & PPOs
Workers' Compensation Insurance
Life Insurance
Dental Insurance
Vision Insurance

BRANDS/DIVISIONS/AFFILIATES:

SuperMed

CONTACTS:

Note: Officers with more than one job title may be intentionally listed here more than once.

Rick Chiricosta, CEO
Rick Chiricosta, Pres.
Ray Mueller, CFO
Andrea Hogben, CMO
John Kish, CIO
Pat Dugan, Chief Legal Officer
Jared Chaney, Chief Comm. Officer
Sue Tyler, Chief Experience Officer
Steffany Matticola, Chief of Staff
Rick Chiricosta, Chmn.

GROWTH PLANS/SPECIAL FEATURES:

Medical Mutual of Ohio is a nonprofit healthcare company that provides health insurance to individual and group customers through individual and corporate plans. The firm has numerous locations throughout Ohio. As a mutual company, the firm is owned by its policyholders. Medical Mutual's insurance programs include health maintenance organization (HMO), preferred provider organization (PPO), point of service (POS), indemnity and Medicare supplemental and Advantage plans. Medial Mutual also provides dental, vision, life and workers' compensation insurance. The company sells its insurance under the SuperMed brand. Medical Mutual's website offers information on individual insurance policies as well as healthcare planning, special information on accounts for retirement and general health information. The company also offers a health and wellness section that offers resources for preventative information, smoking cessation, diet/nutrition, mental health, financial health, medications, family/relationships and fitness.

The company offers employees a comprehensive wellness program, tuition assistance and a rewards program.

FINANCIAL DATA:

Note: Data for latest year may not have been available at press time.

In U.S. $	2017	2016	2015	2014	2013	2012
Revenue	2,894,850,000	2,757,000,000	2,462,000,000	2,700,000,000	2,634,400,000	2,500,000,000
R&D Expense						
Operating Income						
Operating Margin %						
SGA Expense						
Net Income		40,400,000	120,000,000			
Operating Cash Flow						
Capital Expenditure						
EBITDA						
Return on Assets %						
Return on Equity %						
Debt to Equity						

CONTACT INFORMATION:

Phone: 216-687-7000 Fax: 216-687-6044
Toll-Free: 800-382-5729
Address: 2060 E. 9th St., Cleveland, OH 44115 United States

STOCK TICKER/OTHER:

Stock Ticker: Nonprofit
Exchange:
Employees: 2,500
Fiscal Year Ends: 12/31
Parent Company:

SALARIES/BONUSES:

Top Exec. Salary: $ Bonus: $
Second Exec. Salary: $ Bonus: $

OTHER THOUGHTS:

Estimated Female Officers or Directors: 3
Hot Spot for Advancement for Women/Minorities: Y

Mediclinic International Plc

www.mediclinic.com

NAIC Code: 622,110

TYPES OF BUSINESS:

General Medical and Surgical Hospitals

BRANDS/DIVISIONS/AFFILIATES:

Hirslanden
Spire Healthcare Group plc

GROWTH PLANS/SPECIAL FEATURES:

Mediclinic International Plc operates multidisciplinary private hospitals in South Africa, Switzerland and the Middle East. The company's core purpose is to enhance the quality of life of patients by providing cost-effective acute care services. Mediclinic's combined group comprises 74 hospitals and 30 clinics, with more than 10,600 inpatient beds. Within South Africa, Mediclinic Southern Africa operates 48 private acute care hospitals and two day clinics; and Mediclinic operates three hospitals in Namibia, with more than 8,100 inpatient beds. Within Switzerland, the Hirslanden hospital group operates 17 private acute care facilities and four clinics, with more than 1,800 inpatient bed. Within the Middle East, Mediclinic operates six private acute care hospitals and 24 clinics, with more than 700 inpatient beds in the United Arab Emirates. In addition, Mediclinic holds a 29.9% stake in Spire Healthcare Group plc, a U.K.-based private healthcare group.

CONTACTS: *Note: Officers with more than one job title may be intentionally listed here more than once.*

Ronnie van der Merwe, CEO
Jurgens Myburgh, CFO
Magnus Oetiker, Chief Human Resources Officer
Dirk le Roux, CIO
Ronnie van der Merwe, Chief Clinical Officer
Gert Hattingh, Exec.-Group Svcs.
Koert Pretorius, CEO-Mediclinic Southern Africa
Ole Wiesinger, CEO-Hirslanden
Edwin Hertzog, Chmn.

FINANCIAL DATA: *Note: Data for latest year may not have been available at press time.*

In U.S. $	2017	2016	2015	2014	2013	2012
Revenue	3,586,198,000	2,748,679,000	2,556,140,000	2,253,801,000	2,282,034,000	
R&D Expense						
Operating Income	474,854,900	377,013,900	415,142,500	406,859,200	392,355,300	
Operating Margin %	13.24%	13.71%	16.24%	18.05%	17.36%	
SGA Expense	898,832,400	722,718,700	588,729,000	484,979,200	506,726,400	
Net Income	298,741,100	229,600,200	320,986,400	259,414,300	-87,613,310	
Operating Cash Flow			435,816,200	341,081,800	330,199,000	
Capital Expenditure	324,832,000	242,645,600	248,737,300	192,897,800	189,627,500	
EBITDA	476,159,400	375,709,300	530,552,500	496,360,900	191,207,000	
Return on Assets %	3.27%	3.23%	5.68%	4.77%	-1.75%	
Return on Equity %	6.03%	6.68%	15.07%	14.61%	-6.92%	
Debt to Equity	0.43	0.43	0.87	1.17	1.45	

CONTACT INFORMATION:

Phone: 44 207954-9600 Fax: 44 207954-9886
Toll-Free:
Address: 65 Gresham St., 6/Fl, London, EC2V 7NQ United Kingdom

STOCK TICKER/OTHER:

Stock Ticker: ALNRF Exchange: GREY
Employees: 31,504 Fiscal Year Ends: 03/31
Parent Company:

SALARIES/BONUSES:

Top Exec. Salary: $730,546 Bonus: $666,623
Second Exec. Salary: $486,596 Bonus: $396,582

OTHER THOUGHTS:

Estimated Female Officers or Directors: 1
Hot Spot for Advancement for Women/Minorities:

Medicure Inc

NAIC Code: 325,412

www.medicure.com

TYPES OF BUSINESS:

Pharmaceutical Preparation Manufacturing

BRANDS/DIVISIONS/AFFILIATES:

AGGRASTAT
Medicure International Inc (Barbados)
Medicure Pharma Inc
Tardoxal
Zypitamag
Prexxartan
ANDA

CONTACTS: *Note: Officers with more than one job title may be intentionally listed here more than once.*

Albert Friesen, CEO
James Kinley, CFO

GROWTH PLANS/SPECIAL FEATURES:

Medicure, Inc. is a specialty pharmaceutical company involved in research, clinical development and commercialization of human therapeutics. The company is dedicated to exclusively marketing its FDA approved small molecule, AGGRASTAT. The drug is indicated to reduce the rate of thrombotic cardiovascular events (combined endpoint of death, myocardial infarction or refractory ischemia/repeat cardiac procedure) in patients with non-ST elevation acute coronary syndrome (NSTE-ACS). Medicure's business is generating revenue to support operations and to make selected investments in the clinical advancement of AGGRASTAT. The U.S. rights to AGGRASTAT are owned by Medicure's subsidiary, Medicure International, Inc. (Barbados), and the product is distributed in the USA by subsidiary Medicure Pharma, Inc. Medicure's transdermal delivery formulation of AGGRASTAT (tirofiban HCl) has many benefits over intravenous delivery, including being non-invasive, ease of administration and possible reduction of length of hospital stay. The firm's recent AGGRASTAT High-Dose Bolus (HDB) dose regimen achieves greater than 90% inhibition of platelet aggregation within 10 minutes of bolus administration. Currently, Medicure is developing a modified formulation of Tardoxal, a naturally-occurring molecule drug to treat neurological conditions such as Tardive Dyskinesia (TD); received approval for Zypitamag for primary hyperlipidemia or mixed dyslipidemia (expected to launch commercially during 2018); is developing Prexxartan to treat hypertension; and is developing generic ANDA to treat acute cardiology. In October 2017, Medicure sold its interests in the Apicore business.

FINANCIAL DATA: *Note: Data for latest year may not have been available at press time.*

In U.S. $	2017	2016	2015	2014	2013	2012
Revenue	20,871,410			3,885,201	2,002,077	3,689,855
R&D Expense	3,960,179			529,747	1,308,061	803,455
Operating Income	2,809,445			126,475	-1,605,012	7,166
Operating Margin %	13.46%			3.25%	-80.16%	.19%
SGA Expense	11,436,640			2,561,193	1,786,800	2,056,712
Net Income	33,400,680			-1,260,732	-1,980,234	17,989,060
Operating Cash Flow	16,863,950			85,292	-761,906	320,992
Capital Expenditure	1,016,805			4,241	5,690	75,317
EBITDA	7,949,186			-509,114	-1,208,382	19,090,050
Return on Assets %	25.26%			-46.61%	-63.03%	471.60%
Return on Equity %	73.85%					
Debt to Equity						

CONTACT INFORMATION:

Phone: 204 487-7412 Fax: 204 488-9823
Toll-Free:
Address: 2-1250 Waverley Street, Winnipeg, MB R3T 6C6 Canada

STOCK TICKER/OTHER:

Stock Ticker: MPH
Employees: 303
Parent Company:
Exchange: TSX
Fiscal Year Ends: 05/31

SALARIES/BONUSES:

Top Exec. Salary: $ Bonus: $
Second Exec. Salary: $ Bonus: $

OTHER THOUGHTS:

Estimated Female Officers or Directors:
Hot Spot for Advancement for Women/Minorities:

Medifast Inc

www.medifast1.com

NAIC Code: 812,191

TYPES OF BUSINESS:

Weight Management Programs
Diet Products
Online Retail
Direct Marketing

BRANDS/DIVISIONS/AFFILIATES:

Jason Pharmaceuticals Inc
Performance Products LLC
Jason Properties LLC
Jason Enterprises Inc
Seven Crondall Associates LLC
Medifast Nutrition Inc
Optavia LLC
Medifast Franchise Systems Inc

CONTACTS: *Note: Officers with more than one job title may be intentionally listed here more than once.*

Daniel Chard, CEO
Timothy Robinson, CFO
Michael Macdonald, Chairman of the Board
Joseph Kelleman, Controller
Jason Groves, Executive VP

GROWTH PLANS/SPECIAL FEATURES:

Medifast, Inc. produces, distributes and sells weight loss, weight management and healthy living products. Medifast conducts the majority of its business through eight wholly-owned subsidiaries: Jason Pharmaceuticals, Inc.; Performance Products, LLC; Jason Properties, LLC; Jason Enterprises, Inc.; Seven Crondall Associates, LLC; Medifast Nutrition, Inc.; Optavia, LLC; and Medifast Franchise Systems, Inc. Jason Pharmaceuticals produces approximately 42% of the Medifast products at its facility in Maryland, USA (as of fiscal 2017-18). Medifast product lines include weight loss, weight management and healthy living meal replacements, snacks, hydration products and vitamins under the Medifast, OPTAVIA, Thrive by Medifiast, Optimal Health by OPTAVIA, Flavors of Home and Essential 1 brands. The Thrive by Medifast and Optimal Health by OPTAVIA lines include a variety of specially-formulated bars, shakes and smoothies. The company's nutritional products are formulated with high-quality, low-calorie and low-fat ingredients. Its meals are individually portioned, calorie- and carbohydrate-controlled which provide a balance of protein and good carbohydrates, including fiber. The meals replacements are also fortified to contain vitamins and minerals, as well as other nutrients essential for good health. Current franchised centers and reseller locations include the following U.S. states: Arizona, California, Louisiana, Minnesota, Maryland, Pennsylvania and Wisconsin.

FINANCIAL DATA: *Note: Data for latest year may not have been available at press time.*

In U.S. $	2017	2016	2015	2014	2013	2012
Revenue	301,563,000	274,534,000	272,773,000	285,285,000	356,886,000	356,706,000
R&D Expense						
Operating Income	39,632,000	26,859,000	28,684,000	30,246,000	33,590,000	23,262,000
Operating Margin %	13.14%	9.78%	10.51%	10.60%	9.41%	6.52%
SGA Expense	188,180,000	178,805,000	172,631,000	178,961,000	234,256,000	244,773,000
Net Income	27,721,000	17,835,000	20,058,000	13,181,000	23,969,000	15,876,000
Operating Cash Flow	43,237,000	25,350,000	29,411,000	25,536,000	42,360,000	40,264,000
Capital Expenditure	3,242,000	2,876,000	2,819,000	7,024,000	11,606,000	11,383,000
EBITDA	43,841,000	32,264,000	35,799,000	38,298,000	44,972,000	34,467,000
Return on Assets %	20.75%	14.95%	17.19%	10.60%	18.23%	13.45%
Return on Equity %	27.09%	19.32%	23.72%	14.73%	25.33%	19.33%
Debt to Equity						0.04

CONTACT INFORMATION:

Phone: 410 581-8042 Fax: 410 581-8070
Toll-Free:
Address: 100 International Dr., Baltimore, MD 21201 United States

STOCK TICKER/OTHER:

Stock Ticker: MED
Employees: 422
Parent Company:
Exchange: NYS
Fiscal Year Ends: 12/31

SALARIES/BONUSES:

Top Exec. Salary: $650,000 Bonus: $
Second Exec. Salary: $434,402 Bonus: $

OTHER THOUGHTS:

Estimated Female Officers or Directors: 3
Hot Spot for Advancement for Women/Minorities: Y

Medipal Holdings Corporation

www.medipal.co.jp

NAIC Code: 424,210

TYPES OF BUSINESS:

Drugs and Druggists' Sundries Merchant Wholesalers

BRANDS/DIVISIONS/AFFILIATES:

Mediceo Corporation
MM Corporation
EVERLTH Co Ltd
ATOL Co Ltd
MVC Co Ltd
Paltac Corporation
MP Agro Co Ltd
Medipal Foods Corporation

CONTACTS: *Note: Officers with more than one job title may be intentionally listed here more than once.*

Shuichi Watanabe, CEO
Shuichi Watanabe, Pres.
Nobuaki Nozawa, Deputy Gen. Mgr.-Admin. Div.
Kenichi Takase, Mgr.-Corp. Planning Dept.
Toshio Hirasawa, Sr. Managing Exec. Officer-Finance & Acct.
Masanori Kawahara, VP-OrphanPacific, Inc.
Kimio Nakamura, Deputy Gen. Mgr.-Admin. Div.

GROWTH PLANS/SPECIAL FEATURES:

Medipal Holdings Corporation is engaged in the wholesale of pharmaceutical products, cosmetics and daily miscellaneous goods. The company has three business segments: prescription pharmaceutical wholesale, accounting for approximately 68% of fiscal 2017-18 revenues; cosmetics, daily necessities and over the counter (OTC) pharmaceutical wholesale, 30%; and animal health products and food processing wholesale, 2%. Medipal's subsidiaries include: Mediceo Corporation; MM Corporation; M.I.C. (Medical Information College), Inc.; EVERLTH Co., Ltd.; ASTEC Co., Ltd.; ATOL Co., Ltd.; MVC Co., Ltd.; Trim Co., Ltd.; SPLine Corporation; MEDE Co., Ltd.; Paltac Corporation; MP Agro Co., Ltd.; and Medipal Foods Corporation. These companies distribute products to the wholesale market, including: prescription pharmaceuticals, medical equipment, medical supplies, clinical diagnostics, cosmetics, daily necessities, over-the-counter pharmaceuticals, animal health products and raw ingredients for food processing. Medipal's joint ventures and affiliates include: Sinopharm Group Beijing Huahong Co. Ltd. (China); Beijing Tianxingpuxin Bio-med Sinopharm Holding Co. Ltd. (China); MC Healthcare, Inc.; Shikoku Yakugyo Co., Ltd.; Yakuju Corporation; Presuscube Corporation; and Kuraya (USA) Corporation.

FINANCIAL DATA: *Note: Data for latest year may not have been available at press time.*

In U.S. $	2017	2016	2015	2014	2013	2012
Revenue						
R&D Expense						
Operating Income						
Operating Margin %						
SGA Expense						
Net Income						
Operating Cash Flow						
Capital Expenditure						
EBITDA						
Return on Assets %						
Return on Equity %						
Debt to Equity						

CONTACT INFORMATION:

Phone: 81 335175800 Fax:
Toll-Free:
Address: 2-7-15, Yaesu, Chuo-ku, Tokyo, 1048461 Japan

STOCK TICKER/OTHER:

Stock Ticker: MAHLY
Employees: 22,068
Parent Company:
Exchange: PINX
Fiscal Year Ends: 03/31

SALARIES/BONUSES:

Top Exec. Salary: $ Bonus: $
Second Exec. Salary: $ Bonus: $

OTHER THOUGHTS:

Estimated Female Officers or Directors:
Hot Spot for Advancement for Women/Minorities:

MEDITE Cancer Diagnostics Inc

www.medite-group.com

NAIC Code: 334,510

TYPES OF BUSINESS:

Electromedical and Electrotherapeutic Apparatus Manufacturing
Surgical and Medical Instrument Manufacturing

BRANDS/DIVISIONS/AFFILIATES:

MEDITE
TPC15 Duo
TPC15 Trio
TES99
TES Valida
A550
SoftPAP
SoftKit

CONTACTS: *Note: Officers with more than one job title may be intentionally listed here more than once.*

W. Lewis, Chairman of the Board
Stephen Von Rump, Director

GROWTH PLANS/SPECIAL FEATURES:

MEDITE Cancer Diagnostics, Inc. is a medical technology company specializing in the development, engineering, manufacturing and marketing of premium medical devices and consumables for detection, risk assessment and diagnosis in the histology and cytology cancer diagnostics segment. Most of the firm's devices, sold under the brand name MEDITE, and some consumables are manufactured at its German facility. A direct sales force is employed in Germany, Poland and the US, while about 80 more countries worldwide are covered with an existing and continuously expanding network of independent distributors. A general goal of MEDITE in sales is to act as a one- stop-shop for its customers. Instrument purchases are usually bigger investments, with prices often above the $50,000 level, which are more seasonal and depend significantly on investment budgets. Therefore, the firm also offers to sell the day to day consumables and sees its brand not just on the devices but also on the supply products. Products of the firm include a comprehensive range of histology laboratory devices for processing tissue, from receiving the tissue in the laboratory to the final diagnosis, as well as cytology products for the whole process, from cell collection over processing to diagnosis. Individual histology devices include the USE33, an ultrasonic decalcification instrument; TPC15 Duo or Trio, a biopsy processing instrument; TES99 and TES Valida, a paraffin block embedding center; and A550, an automatic mirotome. Cytology products include the SoftPAP, a cervical cell collection device, SoftKit, a disposable device for the self-collection of a sample that can be evaluated to provide an assessment of the health of the entire female genital tract.

FINANCIAL DATA: *Note: Data for latest year may not have been available at press time.*

In U.S. $	2017	2016	2015	2014	2013	2012
Revenue						
R&D Expense						
Operating Income						
Operating Margin %						
SGA Expense						
Net Income						
Operating Cash Flow						
Capital Expenditure						
EBITDA						
Return on Assets %						
Return on Equity %						
Debt to Equity						

CONTACT INFORMATION:

Phone: 312 222-9550 Fax: 312 222-9580
Toll-Free:
Address: 4203 SW 34th St., Orlando, IL 32811 United States

STOCK TICKER/OTHER:

Stock Ticker: MDIT
Employees: 80
Parent Company:
Exchange: PINX
Fiscal Year Ends: 12/31

SALARIES/BONUSES:

Top Exec. Salary: $108,462 Bonus: $62,850
Second Exec. Salary: $79,846 Bonus: $17,140

OTHER THOUGHTS:

Estimated Female Officers or Directors:
Hot Spot for Advancement for Women/Minorities:

MEDIVATORS Inc

NAIC Code: 339,100

www.medivators.com

TYPES OF BUSINESS:

Supplies-Kidney Dialysis Products
Sterilants
Filtration & Separation Products

BRANDS/DIVISIONS/AFFILIATES:

Cantel Medical Corporation
ENDOCUFF
EndoStratus CO2
JET PREP
MicroCam
EG SCAN II
Endo SmartCap
UK Scientific

CONTACTS: *Note: Officers with more than one job title may be intentionally listed here more than once.*

Dave Hemink, Pres.
Paul Helms, Exec. VP-Global Oper.
Shaun Blakeman, VP-Finance
Bill Haydon, VP-Global Mktg.
Robin Borg, VP-Human Resources
Michael P. Petersen, VP-R&D
Kevin B. Finkle, Sr. VP-Admin.
Kevin B. Finkle, Sr. VP-Finance
Don Byrne, Pres., Endoscopy Bus. Group
Craig B. Smith, Sr. VP-Corp. Regulatory Affairs & Quality
Paul E. Helms, Exec. VP
Terrence S. Mistalski, VP-Education & Training
Javier Henao, Gen. Mgr.-Cantel Int'l Bus.
LuAnn M. Petersen, VP-Supply Chain Logistics

GROWTH PLANS/SPECIAL FEATURES:

MEDIVATORS, Inc., a subsidiary of Cantel Medical Corporation, designs, develops, manufactures and sells medical devices critical to endoscopy and infection prevention and control. The company's products and services are divided into eight categories. Its endoscope reprocessing line includes equipment, detergents, disinfectants and related supplies, providing bedside pre-cleaning, leak testing, manual cleaning, disinfection and storage solutions. GI physician products are suited for the needs of gastrointestinal physicians and practitioners, such as bowel site cleaning, disposable scopes and tools that enable effective endoscopy procedures, including the ENDOCUFF overtube, Endo Stratus CO2 insufflator, fecal transplant donor and processing kits, JET PREP flushing device, MicroCam capsule endoscope and E.G. SCAN II disposable endoscope. Endoscopy procedure products include the Endo SmartCap disposable water bottle; EndoGator disposable irrigation tubing; and DEFENDO disposable biopsy valves, which are available for Olympus, Fujinon and Pentax endoscopes. U.K. products are comprised of endoscopes, clean air equipment and surgical products for endoscopy procedures through three subsidiaries: U.K. Endoscopy, U.K. Scientific and U.K. Surgical. The renal systems product line includes hemodialysis concentrates, dialyzer reprocessing, cold sterilants, test strips and kits, cleaners/disinfectants, autodilutors, recirculation connectors and clamps. Therapeutic Technologies consists of MEDIVATORS' non-glycerin polysulfone hollow fiber technology for filter applications such as its hemoconcentrator/congestive heart failure, hemofilter, diafilter and non-extracorporeal applications. REVOX sterilization solutions provides sterilization services for medical devices, biologicals, tissue material and orthopedic implantable items. BIOREDOX decontamination service is a solution to provide safe environments via its proprietary dry fog technology. Last, the custom development unit manufactures products with private labeling and customized packaging for the medical device and filtration industries. In March 2018, MEDIVATORS acquired Aexis Medical BVBA, which specializes in advanced software solutions focused on the tracking and monitoring of instrument reprocessing workflows for hospitals and healthcare professionals.

FINANCIAL DATA: *Note: Data for latest year may not have been available at press time.*

In U.S. $	2017	2016	2015	2014	2013	2012
Revenue						
R&D Expense						
Operating Income						
Operating Margin %						
SGA Expense						
Net Income						
Operating Cash Flow						
Capital Expenditure						
EBITDA						
Return on Assets %						
Return on Equity %						
Debt to Equity						

CONTACT INFORMATION:

Phone: 763-553-3300 Fax: 763-553-3387
Toll-Free: 800-328-3345
Address: 14605 28th Ave. N., Minneapolis, MN 55447 United States

STOCK TICKER/OTHER:

Stock Ticker: Subsidiary
Exchange:
Employees: 1,680
Fiscal Year Ends: 07/31
Parent Company: Cantel Medical Corporation

SALARIES/BONUSES:

Top Exec. Salary: $ Bonus: $
Second Exec. Salary: $ Bonus: $

OTHER THOUGHTS:

Estimated Female Officers or Directors: 2
Hot Spot for Advancement for Women/Minorities:

MEDNAX Inc

www.mednax.com

NAIC Code: 621,111

TYPES OF BUSINESS:

Hospital-Based Pediatrician Practice Management
Pediatric Intensive Care Unit Management
Neonatal Intensive Care Unit Management
Perinatal Physician Services
Staffing Services
Laboratory Services

BRANDS/DIVISIONS/AFFILIATES:

Women's Radiology Associates LLP
Children's Eye Care LLC
Children's Urology Associates PA

CONTACTS: *Note: Officers with more than one job title may be intentionally listed here more than once.*

Roger Medel, CEO
Vivian Lopez-Blanco, CFO
Cesar Alvarez, Chairman of the Board
John Pepia, Chief Accounting Officer
Joseph Calabro, COO
Dominic Andreano, General Counsel
David Clark, President, Divisional

GROWTH PLANS/SPECIAL FEATURES:

MEDNAX, Inc. is a leading provider of physician services including newborn, maternal-fetal, teleradiology, pediatric cardiology and other pediatric subspecialty care. The MEDNAX network comprises over 4,100 affiliated physicians in 50 U.S. states, primarily within hospital-based neonatal intensive care units (NICUs), to babies born prematurely or with medical complications. Approximately 1,400 affiliated physicians provide anesthesia care to patients in connection with surgical and other procedures, as well as pain management. In addition, 325 affiliated physicians provide maternal-fetal and obstetrical medical care to expectant mothers experiencing complicated pregnancies primarily in areas where MEDNAX neonatal physicians practice. Approximately 175 physicians provide pediatric intensive care, 110 physicians provide pediatric cardiology care, 130 physicians provide hospital-based pediatric care, 20 physicians provide pediatric surgical care and eight physicians provide pediatric ear, nose and throat and pediatric ophthalmology services. MEDNAX also provides radiology services, including diagnostic imaging, interventional radiology and nuclear medicine through a network of 285 affiliated physicians; and provides teleradiology services through a network of 445 affiliated radiologists. During 2018, MEDNAX acquired the following: Women's Radiology Associates LLP, a private radiology physician group based in Houston, Texas; Children's Eye Care LLC, a private pediatric ophthalmology practice in Kirkland, Washington; and Children's Urology Associates PA, a private pediatric urology practice in Miami, Florida.

The firm offers employees medical, dental and vision insurance; life insurance; short- and long-term disability; long-term care; a 401(k); tuition reimbursement; an employee assistance program; employee stock purchase plans; and flexible spending accounts.

FINANCIAL DATA: *Note: Data for latest year may not have been available at press time.*

In U.S. $	2017	2016	2015	2014	2013	2012
Revenue	3,458,312,000	3,183,159,000	2,779,996,000	2,438,913,000	2,154,012,000	1,816,612,000
R&D Expense						
Operating Income	480,076,000	571,687,000	557,868,000	512,999,000	452,131,000	389,520,000
Operating Margin %	13.88%	17.95%	20.06%	21.03%	20.99%	21.44%
SGA Expense	2,754,839,000	2,403,792,000	2,059,420,000	1,790,922,000	1,579,527,000	1,324,453,000
Net Income	320,372,000	324,914,000	336,320,000	317,281,000	280,517,000	240,907,000
Operating Cash Flow	511,378,000	443,778,000	368,701,000	422,641,000	405,398,000	325,692,000
Capital Expenditure	49,309,000	39,264,000	27,073,000	18,061,000	15,654,000	14,495,000
EBITDA	587,860,000	666,155,000	627,067,000	563,497,000	493,793,000	422,232,000
Return on Assets %	5.71%	6.57%	8.24%	9.53%	9.67%	9.59%
Return on Equity %	10.99%	12.50%	14.30%	13.77%	12.81%	12.79%
Debt to Equity	0.60	0.60	0.51	0.24	0.01	0.07

CONTACT INFORMATION:

Phone: 954 384-0175 Fax:
Toll-Free: 800-243-3839
Address: 1301 Concord Terrace, Sunrise, FL 33323 United States

STOCK TICKER/OTHER:

Stock Ticker: MD
Employees: 3,617
Parent Company:
Exchange: NYS
Fiscal Year Ends: 12/31

SALARIES/BONUSES:

Top Exec. Salary: $1,000,000 Bonus: $
Second Exec. Salary: $600,000 Bonus: $

OTHER THOUGHTS:

Estimated Female Officers or Directors: 3
Hot Spot for Advancement for Women/Minorities: Y

MedStar Health

www.medstarhealth.org

NAIC Code: 622,110

TYPES OF BUSINESS:

General Medical and Surgical Hospitals
Assisted Living Services
Home Health Services
Ambulatory Centers
Rehabilitation Centers
Nursing Homes
Physician Network Management
Research

BRANDS/DIVISIONS/AFFILIATES:

MedStar Franklin Square Medical Center
MedStar Good Samaritan Hospital
MedStar Harbor Hospital
MedStar Montgomery Medical Center
MedStar Southern Maryland Hospital Center
MedStar National Rehabilitation Hospital
MedStar Physician Partners
MedStar Health Research Institute

CONTACTS: *Note: Officers with more than one job title may be intentionally listed here more than once.*

Kenneth A. Samet, CEO
Joy Drass, COO
Kenneth A. Samet, Pres.
Susan K. Nelson, CFO
Kevin P. Kowalski, Exec. VP-Mktg.
Loretta Young Walker, VP-Chief Human Resources Officer
Stephen R.T. Evans, Chief Medical Officer
Michael J. Curran, Chief Admin. Officer
Oliver M. Johnson, II, General Counsel
Eric R. Wagner, Exec. VP-Diversified Oper. & External Affairs
Christine M. Swearingen, Exec. VP-Planning & Community Rel.
Jean Hitchcock, VP-Public Affairs & Mktg.
Susan K. Nelson, VP-Finance & Acct. Oper.
Carl Schindelar, Exec. VP-Oper., Baltimore Region
Jennie P. McConagha, Chief of Staff
Joel N. Bryan, Treas.
Pegeen Townsend, VP-Gov't Affairs
William J. Martorana, Chmn.

GROWTH PLANS/SPECIAL FEATURES:

MedStar Health is a nonprofit, community-based health care organization primarily composed of several integrated businesses, including 10 major hospitals, with 31,000 associates and 5,400 affiliated physicians (as of fiscal 2017). The hospitals are located within proximity of the Baltimore/Washington, D.C. area and include the following: MedStar Franklin Square Medical Center, MedStar Good Samaritan Hospital, MedStar Harbor Hospital, MedStar Montgomery Medical Center, MedStar Southern Maryland Hospital Center, MedStar St. Mary's Hospital, MedStar Union Memorial Hospital, MedStar Georgetown University Hospital, MedStar Washington Hospital Center and MedStar National Rehabilitation Hospital. The hospitals' services include primary, urgent and sub-acute care; behavioral health and psychiatric services; medical education; and research. MedStar also provides assisted living, home health, hospice and long-term care and operates nursing homes, senior housing, adult day care, rehabilitation and ambulatory centers. MedStar serves roughly 1436,800 inpatients, over 4.6 million outpatients and conducts 294,500 home health visits annually. The organization manages MedStar Physician Partners, a comprehensive physician network serving in the region. Its MedStar Health Research Institute conducts research and clinical trials; and MedStar Health has one of the largest graduate medical education programs in the country, training more than 1,100 medical residents annually, and is the medical education and clinical partner of Georgetown University.

MedStar's employees are offered health, dental and vision insurance; flexible spending accounts; an employee assistance program; paid leave; a tax deferred retirement savings plan; life & disability insurance; and tuition assistance.

FINANCIAL DATA: *Note: Data for latest year may not have been available at press time.*

In U.S. $	2017	2016	2015	2014	2013	2012
Revenue	5,530,000,000	5,125,000,000	5,030,000,000	4,628,100,000	4,200,000,000	4,175,900,000
R&D Expense						
Operating Income						
Operating Margin %						
SGA Expense						
Net Income			359,000,000	304,700,000	185,700,000	69,900,000
Operating Cash Flow						
Capital Expenditure						
EBITDA						
Return on Assets %						
Return on Equity %						
Debt to Equity						

CONTACT INFORMATION:

Phone: 410-772-6500 Fax: 410-715-3905
Toll-Free: 877-772-6505
Address: 10980 Grantchester Way, Columbia, MD 21044 United States

STOCK TICKER/OTHER:

Stock Ticker: Nonprofit
Exchange:
Employees: 31,198
Fiscal Year Ends: 06/30
Parent Company:

SALARIES/BONUSES:

Top Exec. Salary: $ Bonus: $
Second Exec. Salary: $ Bonus: $

OTHER THOUGHTS:

Estimated Female Officers or Directors: 15
Hot Spot for Advancement for Women/Minorities: Y

Medtronic ENT Surgical Products Inc www.medtronic.com/us-en/healthcare-professionals/products/ear-nose-throat/powered-ent-instruments/powered-ent-instruments/related-products.html

NAIC Code: 339,100

TYPES OF BUSINESS:

Supplies-Ear, Nose & Throat Surgery
Wound Dressings
Plastic Surgery Equipment
Endoscopy & Image Guidance Equipment
Computed Tomography (CT) Scanners

BRANDS/DIVISIONS/AFFILIATES:

Medtronic Plc

CONTACTS: *Note: Officers with more than one job title may be intentionally listed here more than once.*

Gerard Bussell, VP-Global Oper.
Jacob Paul, VP-Strategy
Jacob Paul, VP-Finance
Omar Ishrak, Chmn.

GROWTH PLANS/SPECIAL FEATURES:

Medtronic ENT Surgical Products, Inc. is a leading developer, manufacturer and marketer of surgical products for use by ear, nose and throat (ENT) specialists. It is a subsidiary of Medtronic Plc, operating in Medtronic's ENT division. The firm carries over 5,000 ENT products, both powered and manual instruments for surgeries and other needs. These products include fusion ENT navigation systems, integrated power consoles, microdebriders, otologic drills, otologic burs, automated tracking blades, nerve monitoring systems, endoscopic sinus irrigation systems, scope cleaners, nasal packing solutions and sinus stents. The firm's website offers information and education for ENT patients and healthcare professionals. Medtronic ENT's full product catalog is also available online.

Employees of Medtronic, Inc. receive health care and disability coverage, adoption and elder care assistance, stock ownership opportunities and retirement plans.

FINANCIAL DATA: *Note: Data for latest year may not have been available at press time.*

In U.S. $	2017	2016	2015	2014	2013	2012
Revenue						
R&D Expense						
Operating Income						
Operating Margin %						
SGA Expense						
Net Income						
Operating Cash Flow						
Capital Expenditure						
EBITDA						
Return on Assets %						
Return on Equity %						
Debt to Equity						

CONTACT INFORMATION:

Phone: 763-514-4000 Fax:
Toll-Free: 800-874-5797
Address: 710 Medtronic Pkwy., Minneapolis, MN 55432-5604 United States

STOCK TICKER/OTHER:

Stock Ticker: Subsidiary
Employees:
Parent Company: Medtronic Plc
Exchange:
Fiscal Year Ends: 04/30

SALARIES/BONUSES:

Top Exec. Salary: $ Bonus: $
Second Exec. Salary: $ Bonus: $

OTHER THOUGHTS:

Estimated Female Officers or Directors:
Hot Spot for Advancement for Women/Minorities:

Medtronic MiniMed Inc

www.medtronicdiabetes.com

NAIC Code: 339,100

TYPES OF BUSINESS:

Equipment-Diabetes Management Products
Drug Delivery Microinfusion Systems
External Insulin Pumps & Related Products

BRANDS/DIVISIONS/AFFILIATES:

Medtronic Plc
MiniMed 670G
MiniMed 630G
MiniMed 530G
Sugar.IQ
MiniMed Revel

CONTACTS:

Note: Officers with more than one job title may be intentionally listed here more than once.

Hooman Hakami, Pres.-Diabetes

GROWTH PLANS/SPECIAL FEATURES:

Medtronic MiniMed, Inc., a subsidiary of Medtronic Plc, designs, develops, manufactures and markets advanced microinfusion systems for the delivery of a variety of drugs, with a primary focus on insulin for the intensive management of diabetes. The company sells external insulin pumps and related disposables designed to deliver small quantities of insulin in a controlled, programmable manner. Medtronic MiniMed operates three global business units: the advanced insulin management business unit serves patients in need of insulin pump therapy; the multiple daily injection solutions business unit delivers innovative solutions that address unmet needs for people with both type 1 and 2 diabetes who rely on multiple daily injections to manage their diabetes; and the non-intensive diabetes therapies business unit addresses the needs of patients with type 2 diabetes who do not use intensive insulin regimens and provides solutions along the diabetes care continuum. The MiniMed family of products include: MiniMed 670G, which automatically pumps insulin to a diabetic patient's body on sensing its absence or reduction; 630G, which is user-friendly, wireless, waterproof, features airplane mode for traveling and is small and worn on the body, continuously delivering insulin, with required tubing changes every 2-3 days; and 530G, which is worn on the body, delivers tiny drops of rapid-acting insulin which meets individual needs, presents readings every five minutes and requires tubing changes every 2-3 days. Other products include glucose monitoring systems, the Sugar.IQ diabetes assistant, the MiniMed Revel insulin pump, infusion sets, injection ports and related software and accessories.

Medtronic MiniMed offers employees tuition reimbursement, flexible spending accounts, a savings plan and credit union membership.

FINANCIAL DATA:

Note: Data for latest year may not have been available at press time.

In U.S. $	2017	2016	2015	2014	2013	2012
Revenue	1,890,000,000	1,800,000,000	1,740,000,000	1,726,000,000	1,526,000,000	1,481,000,000
R&D Expense						
Operating Income						
Operating Margin %						
SGA Expense						
Net Income						
Operating Cash Flow						
Capital Expenditure						
EBITDA						
Return on Assets %						
Return on Equity %						
Debt to Equity						

CONTACT INFORMATION:

Phone: Fax:
Toll-Free: 866-948-6633
Address: 18000 Devonshire St., Northridge, CA 91325 United States

STOCK TICKER/OTHER:

Stock Ticker: Subsidiary
Employees:
Parent Company: Medtronic Plc
Exchange:
Fiscal Year Ends: 04/30

SALARIES/BONUSES:

Top Exec. Salary: $ Bonus: $
Second Exec. Salary: $ Bonus: $

OTHER THOUGHTS:

Estimated Female Officers or Directors:
Hot Spot for Advancement for Women/Minorities: Y

Medtronic plc

www.medtronic.com

NAIC Code: 334,510

TYPES OF BUSINESS:

Equipment-Defibrillators & Pacing Products
Neurological Devices
Diabetes Management Devices
Ear, Nose & Throat Surgical Equipment
Pain Management Devices
Cardiac Surgery Equipment

BRANDS/DIVISIONS/AFFILIATES:

CONTACTS: *Note: Officers with more than one job title may be intentionally listed here more than once.*

Omar Ishrak, CEO
Mark Ploof, Sr. VP-Global Operations
Karen Parkhill, CFO
Karen L. Parkhill, CFO
Carol A. Surface, -Chief Human Resources Officer
Michael Coyle, Executive VP
Hooman Hakami, Executive VP
Robert Hoedt, Executive VP
Bradley Lerman, General Counsel
Richard Kuntz, Other Executive Officer
Carol Surface, Other Executive Officer
Geoffrey Martha, President, Divisional
Bob White, President, Divisional
Chris Lee, President, Geographical
Omar Ishrak, Chmn.

GROWTH PLANS/SPECIAL FEATURES:

Medtronic plc is a global leader in medical device technology, serving physicians, clinicians and patients in approximately 160 countries worldwide. Its operations consist of four primary segments: the cardiac and vascular group, which includes the cardiac rhythm and heart failure disease management (CRHF), as well as coronary, structural heart and endovascular therapies; the restorative therapies group, which includes the spinal, brain, specialty and pain therapies; the minimally invasive therapies group, which includes surgical and patient monitoring and recovery solutions; and the diabetes group, which includes intensive insulin management, non-intensive diabetes therapies and diabetes services and solutions. Products in the CRHF division manage cardiac rhythm disorders and include pacemakers, implantable defibrillators, ablation products and products for the treatment of atrial fibrillation (AF). The coronary, structural heart and endovascular therapies makes technology that supports the interventional treatment of coronary artery disease to help improve blood flow, and includes products such as stents, guide wires, and catheters. The spinal division offers medical devices used to treat spinal and cranial conditions. The neuromodulation division develops devices for the treatment of neurological, urological and gastroenterological disorders. The surgical technologies division develops and manufactures minimally invasive products to treat ear, nose and throat and neurological diseases. The patient monitoring and recovery develops and markets sensors, monitors and temperature management products, as well as products and therapies for complication-free recovery. The diabetes unit develops integrated diabetes management systems, insulin pump therapies, continuous glucose monitoring systems and therapy management software.

The firm offers employees health care and disability, adoption and elder care assistance, retirement plans and stock options.

FINANCIAL DATA: *Note: Data for latest year may not have been available at press time.*

In U.S. $	2017	2016	2015	2014	2013	2012
Revenue	29,710,000,000	28,833,000,000	20,261,000,000	17,005,000,000	16,590,000,000	
R&D Expense	2,193,000,000	2,224,000,000	1,640,000,000	1,477,000,000	1,557,000,000	
Operating Income	6,313,000,000	5,960,000,000	4,557,000,000	4,818,000,000	4,770,000,000	
Operating Margin %	21.24%	20.67%	22.49%	28.33%	28.75%	
SGA Expense	9,711,000,000	9,469,000,000	6,904,000,000	5,847,000,000	5,698,000,000	
Net Income	4,028,000,000	3,538,000,000	2,675,000,000	3,065,000,000	3,467,000,000	
Operating Cash Flow	6,880,000,000	5,218,000,000	4,902,000,000	4,959,000,000	4,883,000,000	
Capital Expenditure	1,254,000,000	1,046,000,000	571,000,000	396,000,000	457,000,000	
EBITDA	8,613,000,000	8,542,000,000	5,458,000,000	4,934,000,000	5,458,000,000	
Return on Assets %	4.03%	3.42%	3.69%	8.42%	10.20%	
Return on Equity %	7.87%	6.72%	7.36%	16.08%	19.37%	
Debt to Equity	0.51	0.57	0.63	0.52	0.50	

CONTACT INFORMATION:

Phone: 3531-438-1700 Fax:
Toll-Free:
Address: 20 On Hatch, Lower Hatch St., Dublin, 2 Ireland

STOCK TICKER/OTHER:

Stock Ticker: MDT
Employees: 91,000
Parent Company:
Exchange: NYS
Fiscal Year Ends: 04/30

SALARIES/BONUSES:

Top Exec. Salary: $1,641,583 Bonus: $
Second Exec. Salary: $896,923 Bonus: $

OTHER THOUGHTS:

Estimated Female Officers or Directors: 5
Hot Spot for Advancement for Women/Minorities: Y

Medtronic Vascular Inc

www.medtronic.com/us-en/healthcare-professionals/products/cardiovascular.html

NAIC Code: 339,100

TYPES OF BUSINESS:

Medical Instruments-Stents & Catheters
Coronary Products
Perfusion Systems
Peripheral Products
Endovascular Products
Catheters

BRANDS/DIVISIONS/AFFILIATES:

Medtronic Plc

CONTACTS:

Note: Officers with more than one job title may be intentionally listed here more than once.

Omar Isharak, CEO

GROWTH PLANS/SPECIAL FEATURES:

Medtronic Vascular, Inc., a subsidiary of Medtronic Plc, is a global health care solutions company that offers medical technologies, services and solutions for improving the lives of people. The company's business is divided into four groups: cardiac and vascular, diabetes, minimally-invasive therapies and restorative therapies. The cardiac and vascular group addresses aortic and peripheral vascular issues, cardiac rhythm, heart failure and coronary and structural heart procedures. The diabetes group offers related services and solutions, as well as intensive insulin management solutions and non-intensive therapies. The minimally-invasive therapies group is engaged in developing early technologies, renal care solutions, respiratory solutions, monitoring solutions and surgical innovations. The restorative therapies group addresses brain therapies, pain therapies, specialty therapies and spine issues. The company's products include: ablation systems, aortic stent grafts, blood management, diagnostics, cannulae (adult and pediatric), cardiopulmonary, cardiothoracic, catheters (balloon, guide, aspiration and diagnostic), coronary stents, electrosurgical hardware and instruments, embolic protection systems, heart valves (surgical and transcatheter), interventional accessories/guidewires, pediatric perfusion products, revascularization products, therapy management software, monitoring systems, digestive testing products, bone grafting products and many more.

FINANCIAL DATA:

Note: Data for latest year may not have been available at press time.

In U.S. $	2017	2016	2015	2014	2013	2012
Revenue	11,000,000,000	10,200,000,000				
R&D Expense						
Operating Income						
Operating Margin %						
SGA Expense						
Net Income						
Operating Cash Flow						
Capital Expenditure						
EBITDA						
Return on Assets %						
Return on Equity %						
Debt to Equity						

CONTACT INFORMATION:

Phone: 763-514-4000 Fax:
Toll-Free: 800-633-8766
Address: 3576 Unocal Pl., Fountaingrove A, Santa Rosa, CA 95403 United States

STOCK TICKER/OTHER:

Stock Ticker: Subsidiary
Exchange:
Employees:
Fiscal Year Ends: 04/30
Parent Company: Medtronic Plc

SALARIES/BONUSES:

Top Exec. Salary: $ Bonus: $
Second Exec. Salary: $ Bonus: $

OTHER THOUGHTS:

Estimated Female Officers or Directors:
Hot Spot for Advancement for Women/Minorities: Y

Memorial Hermann Healthcare System

www.memorialhermann.org

NAIC Code: 622,110

TYPES OF BUSINESS:

General Medical and Surgical Hospitals
Long-Term Care
Retirement & Nursing Homes
Wellness Centers
Rehabilitation Services
Home Health Services
Air Ambulance Services
Sports Medicine

BRANDS/DIVISIONS/AFFILIATES:

Heart & Vascular Institute
Memorial Hermann-Texas Medical Center
TIRR Memorial Hermann
Children's Memorial Hermann Hospital
IRONMAN Sports Medicine Institute at Memorial
Memorial Hermann Surgical Hospital First Colony
Memorial Hermann Surgical Hospital Kingwood
Life Flight

CONTACTS: *Note: Officers with more than one job title may be intentionally listed here more than once.*

Charles D. Stokes, CEO
Daniel J. Wolterman, Pres.
Brian Dean, CFO
M. Michael Shabot, Chief Medical Officer
Craig Cordola, CEO-Children's Memorial Hermann Hospital
Sean L. Richardson, COO-Memorial Hermann Northeast Hospital

GROWTH PLANS/SPECIAL FEATURES:

Memorial Hermann Healthcare System is a leading provider of healthcare in greater Houston and southeast Texas. Memorial Hermann owns and operates 15 hospitals, including 11 acute care centers, a children's hospital, an orthopedic hospital and two rehabilitation hospitals. Prominent names among these are the Heart & Vascular Institute, Memorial Hermann-Texas Medical Center, Memorial Hermann, TIRR Memorial Hermann, Children's Memorial Hermann Hospital, IRONMAN Sports Medicine Institute at Memorial Hermann, Women's Memorial Hermann and Mischer Neuroscience Institute. In addition, Memorial Hermann has joint ventures with four other hospital facilities, including Memorial Hermann Surgical Hospital First Colony, Memorial Hermann Surgical Hospital Kingwood, Memorial Hermann Tomball Hospital and Memorial Hermann First Colony Hospital. Together, these hospitals offer a full range of health care services, including radiology, chemical dependency programs, nutrition programs, infertility services, hospice, diabetes self-management programs and cancer treatment. The system operates: Life Flight, an air ambulance service; sports medicine centers; ambulatory surgery centers; convenient care centers; institutes; substance abuse treatment center; diagnostic laboratories; imaging centers; a senior living community; a home health agency; and urgent care facilities.

Employee benefits include medical, dental and vision coverage; AD&D insurance; a pharmacy plan; tuition reimbursement; an employee assistance program; a 403(b)/401(k) plan; flexible spending accounts; short- and long-term disability; basic and supplemental life insurance; adoption assistance; a critical illness plan; and access to a credit union.

FINANCIAL DATA: *Note: Data for latest year may not have been available at press time.*

In U.S. $	2017	2016	2015	2014	2013	2012
Revenue	4,873,050,000	4,641,000,000	4,420,000,000	3,940,000,000	3,578,490,000	3,351,343,000
R&D Expense						
Operating Income						
Operating Margin %						
SGA Expense						
Net Income						
Operating Cash Flow						
Capital Expenditure						
EBITDA						
Return on Assets %						
Return on Equity %						
Debt to Equity						

CONTACT INFORMATION:

Phone: 713-448-5555 Fax: 713-448-5665
Toll-Free:
Address: 929 Gessner Dr., Ste 2600, Houston, TX 77024 United States

STOCK TICKER/OTHER:

Stock Ticker: Nonprofit
Employees: 24,000
Parent Company:
Exchange:
Fiscal Year Ends: 06/30

SALARIES/BONUSES:

Top Exec. Salary: $ Bonus: $
Second Exec. Salary: $ Bonus: $

OTHER THOUGHTS:

Estimated Female Officers or Directors:
Hot Spot for Advancement for Women/Minorities:

Memorial Sloan Kettering Cancer Center

www.mskcc.org

NAIC Code: 622,310

TYPES OF BUSINESS:

Cancer Hospitals
Cancer Research

BRANDS/DIVISIONS/AFFILIATES:

Sloan-Kettering Institute
Rockefeller Outpatient Pavilion
Sidney Kimmel Center
Evelyn H Lauder Breast Cancer

CONTACTS: *Note: Officers with more than one job title may be intentionally listed here more than once.*

Ned Groves, Exec. VP
Kathryn Martin, COO
Craig B. Thompson, Pres.
Michael Gutnick, Exec. VP
Kerry Bessey, Sr. VP
Patricia Skarulis, CIO
Norman C. Selby, Sec.
Clifton S. Robbins, Treas.

GROWTH PLANS/SPECIAL FEATURES:

Memorial Sloan-Kettering Cancer Center (MSKCC), a nonprofit organization, provides cancer treatment, research and education. The organization can accurately screen for mutations in more than 400 genes. MSKCC operates one hospital, several outpatient facilities, as well as three research facilities, all located in New York. Today, MSKCC is one of 47 National Cancer Institute-designated comprehensive cancer centers, with more than 470 inpatient beds, a 72,000-square-foot surgical center, as well as a state-of-the-art treatment hub for outpatient procedures. The Sloan-Kettering Institute is the hospital's research arm, with specific focus on cell biology, cancer biology genetics, biochemistry, molecular biology, structural biology, computational and developmental biology, immunology and therapeutics. The institute provides research training in conjunction with Louis V. Gerstner, Jr. Graduate School of Biomedical Sciences, Rockefeller University, Cornell University and Weill Medical College of Cornell University for PhD and MD students. Several of the firm's leading researchers are members of the Institute of Medicine and the National Academy of Science, and some are Howard Hughes Medical Institute investigators. MSKCC also operates the Rockefeller Outpatient Pavilion for the provision of outpatient services, including medical consultation, diagnostic imaging, chemotherapy, pharmacy services, cancer screening and integrative medicine services; and the Sidney Kimmel Center for Prostate and Urologic Cancers, which provides treatment for genitourinary cancers. MSKCC's Evelyn H. Lauder Breast Cancer center provides breast and cervical cancer screening.

The firm offers employees medical, dental and vision coverage; long-term disability; AD&D coverage; life insurance; health and dependent care flexible spending accounts; a retirement savings plan with matching eligibility; paid holidays and vacations; sick leave; tuition reimbursement; a commuter spending account program; backup child care options; backup adult/elder care (in-home only); adoption reimbursement program; employee assistance program; wellness programs; and employee discounts on retail and entertainment.

FINANCIAL DATA: *Note: Data for latest year may not have been available at press time.*

In U.S. $	2017	2016	2015	2014	2013	2012
Revenue	4,452,793,000	3,980,362,000	3,675,485,000	3,391,083,000	3,078,065,000	2,859,277,000
R&D Expense						
Operating Income						
Operating Margin %						
SGA Expense						
Net Income	239,765,000	189,937,000	169,169,000	242,655,000	178,492,000	114,601,000
Operating Cash Flow						
Capital Expenditure						
EBITDA						
Return on Assets %						
Return on Equity %						
Debt to Equity						

CONTACT INFORMATION:

Phone: 212-639-2000 Fax: 212-639-3576
Toll-Free: 800-525-2225
Address: 1275 York Ave., New York, NY 10065 United States

STOCK TICKER/OTHER:

Stock Ticker: Nonprofit
Exchange:
Employees: 17,301
Fiscal Year Ends: 12/31
Parent Company:

SALARIES/BONUSES:

Top Exec. Salary: $ Bonus: $
Second Exec. Salary: $ Bonus: $

OTHER THOUGHTS:

Estimated Female Officers or Directors: 1
Hot Spot for Advancement for Women/Minorities: Y

Mentor Worldwide LLC

www.mentorwwllc.com

NAIC Code: 339,100

TYPES OF BUSINESS:

Supplies-Plastic Surgery Products
Breast Implants
Liposuction

BRANDS/DIVISIONS/AFFILIATES:

Johnson & Johnson
MemoryShape
MemoryGel
Mentor
Artoura
Contour Profile

CONTACTS:

Note: Officers with more than one job title may be intentionally listed here more than once.

Alex Gorsky, CEO - Johnson & Johnson
Alex Gorsky, CEO-Johnson & Johnson

GROWTH PLANS/SPECIAL FEATURES:

Mentor Worldwide, LLC develops, manufactures, licenses and markets breast implants and related accessories. The company's breast implant products includes: MemoryShape teardrop shape implants; MemoryGel, its silicone gel-filled implant brand; Mentor volume sizing system, which enables physicians and patients to select implant volume; Artoura, a breast tissue expander that provides precise control pocket formation; and Contour Profile, a breast tissue expander intended for breast reconstruction after mastectomy, correction of underdeveloped breast, scar revision and tissue defect procedures. All of these mammary prostheses are used in augmentation procedures to enhance breast size and shape, correct breast asymmetries, help restore fullness after breast-feeding and reconstruct breasts following a mastectomy. In addition, Mentor's smooth tissue expander has a Dacron reinforced base with a firm platform for directional expansion capabilities. The firm is owned by Johnson & Johnson.

FINANCIAL DATA:

Note: Data for latest year may not have been available at press time.

In U.S. $	2017	2016	2015	2014	2013	2012
Revenue						
R&D Expense						
Operating Income						
Operating Margin %						
SGA Expense						
Net Income						
Operating Cash Flow						
Capital Expenditure						
EBITDA						
Return on Assets %						
Return on Equity %						
Debt to Equity						

CONTACT INFORMATION:

Phone: Fax:
Toll-Free: 800-636-8678
Address: 33 Technology Dr., Irvine, CA 92618 United States

STOCK TICKER/OTHER:

Stock Ticker: Subsidiary
Exchange:
Employees: 1,250
Fiscal Year Ends: 12/31
Parent Company: Johnson & Johnson

SALARIES/BONUSES:

Top Exec. Salary: $ Bonus: $
Second Exec. Salary: $ Bonus: $

OTHER THOUGHTS:

Estimated Female Officers or Directors:
Hot Spot for Advancement for Women/Minorities: Y

Merck & Co Inc

www.merck.com

NAIC Code: 325,412

TYPES OF BUSINESS:

Drugs-Diversified
Anti-Infective & Anti-Cancer Drugs
Dermatologicals
Cardiovascular Drugs
Animal Health Products

BRANDS/DIVISIONS/AFFILIATES:

Merck Sharp & Dohme Corp

CONTACTS: *Note: Officers with more than one job title may be intentionally listed here more than once.*

Kenneth Frazier, CEO
Robert Davis, CFO
Rita Karachun, Chief Accounting Officer
Mirian Graddick-Weir, Executive VP, Divisional
Julie Gerberding, Executive VP
Sanat Chattopadhyay, Executive VP
Adam Schechter, Executive VP
Roger Perlmutter, Executive VP
Richard DeLuca, Executive VP
Ashley Watson, Other Executive Officer

GROWTH PLANS/SPECIAL FEATURES:

Merck & Co., Inc., known as Merck Sharp & Dohme Corp. outside of the U.S. and Canada, is a global healthcare company that develops and manufactures medicines, vaccines and biologics. The firm operates through four segments: pharmaceutical, animal health, healthcare services and alliances. Pharmaceutical, the company's primary segment, markets human health pharmaceutical and vaccine products either directly or through joint ventures. Merck & Co. markets and develops human health pharmaceutical products for the treatment of bone, respiratory, dermatology, immunology, cardiovascular, diabetes, obesity, infectious disease, neurological, ophthalmology and oncology conditions. These products are sold primarily to drug wholesalers and retailers, hospitals, government agencies and managed healthcare providers such as health maintenance organizations (HMOs), pharmacy benefit managers and other institutions. Vaccine products are primarily sold to physicians, wholesalers, physician distributors and government entities. This segment also offers certain women's health products, including contraceptives and fertility treatments. The animal health segment offers vaccine, anti-infective and anti-parasitic products for disease prevention, treatment and control in farm and companion animals. The healthcare services segment provides services and solutions that focus on engagement, health analytics and clinical services to improve the value of care delivered to patients. The alliances segment consists of revenue derived from the company's relationship with AstraZeneca LP. Merck continues to pursue opportunities for establishing external alliances to complement its internal research capabilities, including research collaborations as well as licensing preclinical and clinical compounds and technology platforms. In February 2018, Merck agreed to acquire Viralytics, an Australian public company focused on oncolytic immunotherapy treatments for a range of cancers.

FINANCIAL DATA: *Note: Data for latest year may not have been available at press time.*

In U.S. $	2017	2016	2015	2014	2013	2012
Revenue	40,122,000,000	39,807,000,000	39,498,000,000	42,237,000,000	44,033,000,000	47,267,000,000
R&D Expense	10,208,000,000	10,124,000,000	6,704,000,000	7,180,000,000	7,503,000,000	8,168,000,000
Operating Income	7,309,000,000	6,030,000,000	7,547,000,000	6,683,000,000	7,665,000,000	9,877,000,000
Operating Margin %	18.21%	15.14%	19.10%	15.82%	17.40%	20.89%
SGA Expense	9,830,000,000	9,762,000,000	10,313,000,000	11,606,000,000	11,911,000,000	12,776,000,000
Net Income	2,394,000,000	3,920,000,000	4,442,000,000	11,920,000,000	4,404,000,000	6,168,000,000
Operating Cash Flow	6,447,000,000	10,376,000,000	12,421,000,000	7,860,000,000	11,654,000,000	10,022,000,000
Capital Expenditure	1,888,000,000	1,614,000,000	1,283,000,000	2,317,000,000	1,548,000,000	1,954,000,000
EBITDA	11,912,000,000	10,793,000,000	12,448,000,000	24,706,000,000	13,334,000,000	16,431,000,000
Return on Assets %	2.61%	3.97%	4.43%	11.68%	4.15%	5.83%
Return on Equity %	6.43%	9.24%	9.51%	24.22%	8.56%	11.46%
Debt to Equity	0.62	0.60	0.53	0.38	0.41	0.30

CONTACT INFORMATION:

Phone: 908 423-1000 Fax: 908 735-1253
Toll-Free:
Address: 2000 Galloping Hill Rd., Kenilworth, NJ 07033 United States

STOCK TICKER/OTHER:

Stock Ticker: MRK
Exchange: NYS
Employees: 68,000
Fiscal Year Ends: 12/31
Parent Company:

SALARIES/BONUSES:

Top Exec. Salary: $1,572,212 Bonus: $
Second Exec. Salary: $1,083,750 Bonus: $

OTHER THOUGHTS:

Estimated Female Officers or Directors: 4
Hot Spot for Advancement for Women/Minorities: Y

Merck Serono SA

www.merckserono.com

NAIC Code: 325,412

TYPES OF BUSINESS:

Biopharmaceuticals Development
Fertility Drugs
Neurology Drugs
Growth & Metabolism Drugs
Dermatology Drugs
Oncology Research

BRANDS/DIVISIONS/AFFILIATES:

Merck KGaA
EMD Serono Inc
Rebif
GONAL-f
Ovidrel
Cetrotide
Saizen
Serostim

CONTACTS: *Note: Officers with more than one job title may be intentionally listed here more than once.*

Belen Garijo Lopez, Pres.
Thierry Hulot, Head-Global Mfg. & Supply
Thomas Gunning, Head-Legal
Meeta Gulyani, Head-Strategy & Global Franchises
Patrice Grand, Head-Communications
Susan Herbert, Head-Global Bus. Dev. & Strategy
Sascha Becker, Sr. VP
Elchin Ergun, Head-Global Commercial
Annalisa Jenkins, Head-Global Dev. & Medical

GROWTH PLANS/SPECIAL FEATURES:

Merck Serono SA is a biopharmaceutical company, and an operating subsidiary of Merck KGaA. The firm discovers, develops, manufactures and commercializes prescription medicines of chemical and biological origin in specialist indications. For neurodegenerative diseases, the company has developed drugs such as Rebif, a modifying drug that treats relapsing forms of multiple sclerosis; and Erbitux, an antibody that targets the epidermal growth factor receptor for treating squamous cell carcinoma of the head and neck, and metastatic colorectal cancer. Merck Serono also develops fertility drugs for various stages of the reproductive cycle and recombinant versions of various hormones to treat infertility, such as GONAL-f (follitropin alfa for injection), Ovidrel pre-filled syringe (choriogonadotropin alfa injection) and Cetrotide (cetrorelix acetate for injection). For metabolic endocrinology, products include Saizen (somatropin-rDNA origin-for injection), and Serostim (somatropin-rDNA origin-for injection). For oncology, BAVENCIO (avelumab) is indicated for the treatment of adults and pediatric patients 12 years and older with metastatic Merkel cell carcinoma, as well as patients with locally-advanced or metastatic urothelial carcinoma. EMD Serono's diversified pipeline includes multiple, high-priority projects currently in development to deliver new and innovative products to people living with unmet patient needs. The company's research and development translational innovation platforms focus on using emerging science and tools to apply precision medicine to develop personalized therapies for patients. Merck Serono is headquartered in Darmstadt, Germany, with additional offices in Boston, Massachusetts, and markets its products in more than 150 countries. In Canada and the U.S., Merck Serono operates as EMD Serono, Inc.

FINANCIAL DATA: *Note: Data for latest year may not have been available at press time.*

In U.S. $	2017	2016	2015	2014	2013	2012
Revenue	7,000,000,000	6,900,000,000	6,800,000,000	6,690,000,000		
R&D Expense						
Operating Income						
Operating Margin %						
SGA Expense						
Net Income						
Operating Cash Flow						
Capital Expenditure						
EBITDA						
Return on Assets %						
Return on Equity %						
Debt to Equity						

CONTACT INFORMATION:

Phone: 49-6151-72-0 Fax: 49-6151-72-2000
Toll-Free:
Address: Frankfurter St. 250, Darmstadt, 64293 Germany

STOCK TICKER/OTHER:

Stock Ticker: Subsidiary
Employees: 4,775
Parent Company: Merck KGaA
Exchange:
Fiscal Year Ends: 12/31

SALARIES/BONUSES:

Top Exec. Salary: $ Bonus: $
Second Exec. Salary: $ Bonus: $

OTHER THOUGHTS:

Estimated Female Officers or Directors: 5
Hot Spot for Advancement for Women/Minorities: Y

Mercy

www.mercy.net

NAIC Code: 622,110

TYPES OF BUSINESS:

General Medical and Surgical Hospitals
Outpatient Care
Health Classes
Long-Term Care
Community Service & Outreach

BRANDS/DIVISIONS/AFFILIATES:

International Business Machines Corporation (IBM)
IBM Watson Health
Mercy Virtual Care Center
MyMercy
Mercy SafeWatch

CONTACTS: *Note: Officers with more than one job title may be intentionally listed here more than once.*

Lynn Britton, Pres.
Michael McCurry, COO
Shannon Sock, Exec. VP
Donn Sorensen, Regional Pres., East Communities
Diana Smalley, Regional Pres., West Communities
Shannon Sock, Exec. VP-Organizational Effectiveness
Kim Day, Regional Pres., Central Communities
Donn Sorenson, Exec. VP-Operations

GROWTH PLANS/SPECIAL FEATURES:

Mercy, established in 1986, is one of the largest health systems in the U.S., serving millions of people annually. Mercy comprises more than 40 acute care and specialty hospitals (heart, children's, orthopedic and rehabilitation), 800 physician practices and outpatient facilities, 44,000 co-workers and 2,100 Mercy Clinic physicians in Arkansas, Kansas, Missouri and Oklahoma. It also has outreach ministries in Arkansas, Louisiana, Mississippi and Texas. The Mercy Virtual Care Center monitors patients 24/7/365 using high-speed data and video connections. MyMercy is a free service that allows patients to connect online with their doctors; provides access to their medical information and test results; renew subscriptions; and schedule office appointments as well as schedule e-visits via personal computer, tablet or smartphone. Mercy SafeWatch is an electronic intensive care unit (ICU) that provides 24-hour vigilance to critically-ill patients. Mercy's IT division provides technology services, supply chain organization solutions, return on investment solutions and system-wide virtual solutions. Mercy operates as a wholly-owned subsidiary of IBM Watson Health, itself a business unit within International Business Machines Corporation (IBM).

Mercy offers employees medical, dental, vision, life and long-term disability coverage; a retirement program; tuition reimbursement; and a co-worker assistance plan for full- and part-time employees and their immediate family members.

FINANCIAL DATA: *Note: Data for latest year may not have been available at press time.*

In U.S. $	2017	2016	2015	2014	2013	2012
Revenue	5,500,000,000	5,250,000,000	5,000,000,000	4,510,184,000	4,380,885,000	4,200,000,000
R&D Expense						
Operating Income						
Operating Margin %						
SGA Expense						
Net Income						
Operating Cash Flow						
Capital Expenditure						
EBITDA						
Return on Assets %						
Return on Equity %						
Debt to Equity						

CONTACT INFORMATION:

Phone: 580-371-2592 Fax:
Toll-Free:
Address: 1000 S. Byrd St., Tishomingo, OK 73460 United States

STOCK TICKER/OTHER:

Stock Ticker: Subsidiary Exchange:
Employees: 44,000 Fiscal Year Ends: 06/30
Parent Company: International Business Machines Corporation (IBM)

SALARIES/BONUSES:

Top Exec. Salary: $ Bonus: $
Second Exec. Salary: $ Bonus: $

OTHER THOUGHTS:

Estimated Female Officers or Directors: 10
Hot Spot for Advancement for Women/Minorities: Y

Mercy Health

www.mercy.com

NAIC Code: 622,110

TYPES OF BUSINESS:

General Medical and Surgical Hospitals
Long-Term Care
Hospice Programs
Home Health Services
Low-Income Housing

BRANDS/DIVISIONS/AFFILIATES:

CONTACTS:
Note: Officers with more than one job title may be intentionally listed here more than once.

John M. Starcher, Jr., CEO
Brian Smith, COO
Michael D. Connelly, Pres.
Deborah Bloomfield, CFO
Sandra Mackey, CMO
Joe Gage, Chief Human Resources Officer
Michael A. Bezney, General Counsel
Jane Durney Crowley, Exec. VP-Bus. Dev. & Clinical Integration
Doris Gottemoeller, Sr. VP-Mission & Values Integrity
R. Jeffrey Copeland, Sr. VP-Insurance & Physician Svcs.
Stephen R. Grossbart, Chief Quality Officer
Brian Smith, Exec. VP-Networks

GROWTH PLANS/SPECIAL FEATURES:

Mercy Health is a non-profit health system serving Ohio and Kentucky, with 23 hospitals and 450 places where patients can receive care. In Ohio, care is provided in the cities of Cincinnati, Defiance, Lima, Lorain, Springfield, Tiffin, Toledo, Willard and Youngstown. In Kentucky, care is provided in Irvine, Northern Kentucky and Paducah. Mercy Health offers more than 34 specialties, which includes medication management, bariatrics, behavioral/mental health, cancer care, breast health, cardiovascular/thoracic surgery, cholesterol, clinical trials/research, diabetes care, dermatology, ear/nose/throat, emergency care, Gamma Knife surgery, heart care, imaging services, laboratory services, liver/pancreas center, orthopedics/sports medicine, pain medicine, palliative care/hospice, rehabilitation, rheumatology and wound care. Mercy Health serves approximately 6 million patients annually. In February 2018, the non-profit health system agreed to merge with the Marriottsville, Maryland based, non-profit hospital system, Bon Secours Health System, Inc. The merger of the two Catholic healthcare ministries, if approved by both the Federal Trade Commission and the Vatican, would create a hospital system with 43 hospitals in seven states.

FINANCIAL DATA:
Note: Data for latest year may not have been available at press time.

In U.S. $	2017	2016	2015	2014	2013	2012
Revenue	4,717,297,200	4,492,664,000	4,275,353,000	4,040,341,000	3,955,601,000	3,752,654,000
R&D Expense						
Operating Income						
Operating Margin %						
SGA Expense						
Net Income		152,669,000	-13,020,000	198,137,000	128,004,000	122,616,000
Operating Cash Flow						
Capital Expenditure						
EBITDA						
Return on Assets %						
Return on Equity %						
Debt to Equity						

CONTACT INFORMATION:

Phone: 513-952-5000 Fax: 513-639-2700
Toll-Free:
Address: 1701 Mercy Health Place, Cincinnati, OH 45237 United States

STOCK TICKER/OTHER:

Stock Ticker: Nonprofit
Employees: 33,000
Parent Company:
Exchange:
Fiscal Year Ends: 12/31

SALARIES/BONUSES:

Top Exec. Salary: $ Bonus: $
Second Exec. Salary: $ Bonus: $

OTHER THOUGHTS:

Estimated Female Officers or Directors: 15
Hot Spot for Advancement for Women/Minorities: Y

Meridian Bioscience Inc

www.meridianbioscience.com/default.aspx

NAIC Code: 325,413

TYPES OF BUSINESS:

Diagnostic Test Kits
Contract Manufacturing
Bulk Antigens, Antibodies & Reagents

BRANDS/DIVISIONS/AFFILIATES:

MyTaq
SensiFAST
Curian

CONTACTS: *Note: Officers with more than one job title may be intentionally listed here more than once.*

Amy Winslow, CEO, Subsidiary
Jack Kenny, CEO
Melissa Lueke, CFO
John Kraeutler, Director
Susan Rolih, Executive VP, Divisional
Lawrence Baldini, Executive VP
Marco Calzavara, Managing Director, Subsidiary

GROWTH PLANS/SPECIAL FEATURES:

Meridian Bioscience, Inc. is a life science company that develops, manufactures, sells and distributes diagnostic test kits, primarily for respiratory, gastrointestinal, viral and parasitic infectious diseases. The firm also manufactures and distributes bulk antigens, antibodies and reagents; and contract manufactures proteins and other biologicals. The company operates in two segments: diagnostics and life science. The diagnostics segment focuses on the development, manufacture, sale and distribution of diagnostic test kits, which utilize immunodiagnostic technologies that test samples of body fluids or tissue for the presence of antigens and antibodies of specific infectious diseases. This division includes FDA-cleared products for the testing of blood to diagnose lead poisoning in children and adults. Products also include transport media that store and preserve specimen samples from patient collection to laboratory testing. Its sales and distribution network consists of direct sales forces in the U.S, Belgium, France, Holland, Singapore, Italy and Australia; and independent distributors in other European, African and Middle Eastern countries. The life sciences segment focuses on the development, manufacture, sale and distribution of bulk antigens, antibodies and reagents as well as contract development and manufacturing services. These products are marketed primarily to diagnostic manufacturing customers as a source of raw materials for their immunoassay products, or as an outsourced step in their manufacturing processes. Molecular biology products such as PCR/qPCR (polymerase chain reaction) reagents, nucleotides and competent cells are marketed to academic/research and industrial customers. Products such as MyTaq and SensiFAST are examples of this type of PCR/qPCR reagent. Meridian's current R&D pipeline for immunoassay products includes an instrumentation that utilizes fluorescent chemistry and has colorimetric capabilities; it is branded under the Curian name. In mid-2018, the company expects to submit a 501(k) to the U.S. FDA for one or more of its existing rapid immunoassay tests using the Curian instrument.

FINANCIAL DATA: *Note: Data for latest year may not have been available at press time.*

In U.S. $	2017	2016	2015	2014	2013	2012
Revenue	200,771,000	196,082,000	194,830,000	188,832,000	188,686,000	173,542,000
R&D Expense	15,680,000	13,815,000	12,605,000	12,552,000	10,787,000	10,275,000
Operating Income	44,010,000	52,859,000	56,060,000	52,392,000	57,314,000	49,296,000
Operating Margin %	21.92%	26.95%	28.77%	27.74%	30.37%	28.40%
SGA Expense	65,143,000	61,113,000	53,217,000	52,299,000	52,943,000	50,307,000
Net Income	21,557,000	32,229,000	35,540,000	34,743,000	38,032,000	33,371,000
Operating Cash Flow	41,355,000	37,223,000	42,809,000	38,262,000	44,436,000	42,446,000
Capital Expenditure	4,467,000	4,004,000	4,764,000	7,002,000	3,277,000	4,835,000
EBITDA	46,189,000	58,168,000	61,278,000	57,954,000	62,937,000	55,893,000
Return on Assets %	8.59%	14.81%	19.73%	19.64%	22.49%	21.06%
Return on Equity %	12.82%	19.39%	21.74%	21.98%	25.54%	23.72%
Debt to Equity	0.29	0.32				

CONTACT INFORMATION:

Phone: 513 271-3700 Fax: 513 271-3762
Toll-Free: 800-543-1980
Address: 3471 River Hills Dr., Cincinnati, OH 45244 United States

STOCK TICKER/OTHER:

Stock Ticker: VIVO
Employees: 440
Parent Company:
Exchange: NAS
Fiscal Year Ends: 09/30

SALARIES/BONUSES:

Top Exec. Salary: $655,942 Bonus: $
Second Exec. Salary: $404,904 Bonus: $

OTHER THOUGHTS:

Estimated Female Officers or Directors: 4
Hot Spot for Advancement for Women/Minorities: Y

Meridian Medical Technologies Inc

www.meridianmeds.com

NAIC Code: 339,100

TYPES OF BUSINESS:

Supplies-Allergic Reaction Auto-Injectors
Cardiopulmonary Diagnostics

BRANDS/DIVISIONS/AFFILIATES:

Pfizer Inc
Antidote Treatment Nerve Agent, Auto-Injector

GROWTH PLANS/SPECIAL FEATURES:

Meridian Medical Technologies, Inc., a subsidiary of Pfizer, Inc., is a worldwide developer and manufacturer of antidotes for chemical weapons. The company's drug delivery systems unit participates in the rapidly-developing home and emergency markets for drugs using innovative technology. This technology allows for rapid intramuscular administration, including self-administration, even through clothing and protective gear. Meridian currently markets the Antidote Treatment Nerve Agent, Auto-Injector (ATNAA), which injects atropine and pralidoxime chloride for the treatment of poisoning by susceptible organophosphorous nerve agents having anticholinesterase activity. This product is only available for use by U.S. military personnel.

CONTACTS: *Note: Officers with more than one job title may be intentionally listed here more than once.*

Ian Read, CEO
Ian Read, Chmn.

FINANCIAL DATA: *Note: Data for latest year may not have been available at press time.*

In U.S. $	2017	2016	2015	2014	2013	2012
Revenue						
R&D Expense						
Operating Income						
Operating Margin %						
SGA Expense						
Net Income						
Operating Cash Flow						
Capital Expenditure						
EBITDA						
Return on Assets %						
Return on Equity %						
Debt to Equity						

CONTACT INFORMATION:

Phone: 443-259-7800 Fax: 443-259-7801
Toll-Free: 800-638-8093
Address: 6350 Steven Forest Rd.,Ste 301, Columbia, MD 21046 United States

STOCK TICKER/OTHER:

Stock Ticker: Subsidiary
Employees:
Parent Company: Pfizer Inc
Exchange:
Fiscal Year Ends:

SALARIES/BONUSES:

Top Exec. Salary: $ Bonus: $
Second Exec. Salary: $ Bonus: $

OTHER THOUGHTS:

Estimated Female Officers or Directors:
Hot Spot for Advancement for Women/Minorities:

Merit Medical Systems Inc

NAIC Code: 339,100

www.merit.com

TYPES OF BUSINESS:

Disposable Products-Cardiology & Radiology

BRANDS/DIVISIONS/AFFILIATES:

QuadraSphere
HeRO Graf
DFINE
CentrosFLO
CorVocet

CONTACTS:

Note: Officers with more than one job title may be intentionally listed here more than once.

Fred Lampropoulos, CEO
Raul Parra, CFO
Ronald Frost, COO
Brian Lloyd, Other Executive Officer
Anne-Marie Wright, President, Divisional

GROWTH PLANS/SPECIAL FEATURES:

Merit Medical Systems, Inc. designs, manufactures and markets medical devices used in an array of interventional and diagnostic medical procedures. The company's products offer a high level of quality, value and safety to customers, and are used in the following clinical areas: diagnostic & interventional cardiology, interventional radiology, vascular/general/thoracic surgery, electrophysiology, cardiac rhythm management, interventional pulmonology, interventional nephrology, oncology, pain management, outpatient access centers, computed tomography, ultrasound and interventional gastroenterology. Merit manufactures and sells various products designed to alleviate patient suffering from peripheral vascular and non-vascular disease. Its line of peripheral catheters meet the growing trends of transradial access, a procedure which uses the wrist as the entry point for cardiac catheterization and peripheral procedures rather than the femoral artery approach. Its FDA-approved QuadraSphere microspheres provide another treatment option for patients and physicians with primary liver cancer. HeRO Graf is a fully subcutaneous vascular access system intended for use in maintaining long-term vascular access for chronic hemodialysis in patients who have exhausted peripheral venous access sites suitable for fistulas or grafts. The DFINE line of vertebral augmentation products are used for the treatment of vertebral compression fractures, as well as medical devices used to treat metastatic spine tumors. CentrosFLO catheters anchor the company's chronic dialysis line. And Merit's CorVocet biopsy system is designed to cut full-core of tissue, providing large specimens for pathological examination. The company owns or has a license to more than 1,000 U.S. and international patents and patent applications. During 2017, Merit acquired proprietary bone and spine biopsy products from Laurane Medical SAS (of France), and transferred the manufacturing processes to its Irish facility.

The firm offers employees medical and dental coverage, (flexible spending) plan, 401(k), employee stock purchase plan, employee assistance program, employee wellness initiatives, group life insurance and paid time off.

FINANCIAL DATA:

Note: Data for latest year may not have been available at press time.

In U.S. $	2017	2016	2015	2014	2013	2012
Revenue	727,852,000	603,838,000	542,149,000	509,689,000	449,049,000	394,288,000
R&D Expense	63,539,000	45,690,000	41,810,000	36,632,000	33,886,000	30,245,000
Operating Income	33,580,000	34,937,000	37,623,000	40,696,000	31,839,000	29,641,000
Operating Margin %	4.61%	5.78%	6.93%	7.98%	7.09%	7.51%
SGA Expense	229,134,000	184,398,000	156,348,000	147,894,000	128,642,000	122,106,000
Net Income	27,523,000	20,121,000	23,802,000	22,974,000	16,570,000	19,710,000
Operating Cash Flow	62,727,000	53,599,000	69,458,000	53,325,000	51,373,000	46,938,000
Capital Expenditure	41,200,000	35,054,000	52,915,000	35,895,000	61,122,000	66,103,000
EBITDA	97,199,000	77,939,000	74,854,000	76,330,000	60,425,000	50,756,000
Return on Assets %	2.67%	2.33%	3.11%	3.11%	2.31%	3.42%
Return on Equity %	4.68%	4.17%	5.28%	5.46%	4.20%	5.33%
Debt to Equity	0.38	0.63	0.42	0.49	0.58	0.59

CONTACT INFORMATION:

Phone: 801 253-1600 Fax: 801 253-1652
Toll-Free: 800-356-3748
Address: 1600 W. Merit Pkwy., South Jordan, UT 84095 United States

STOCK TICKER/OTHER:

Stock Ticker: MMSI
Exchange: NAS
Employees: 4,150
Fiscal Year Ends: 12/31
Parent Company:

SALARIES/BONUSES:

Top Exec. Salary: $1,412,308 Bonus: $400,000
Second Exec. Salary: $515,385 Bonus: $202,000

OTHER THOUGHTS:

Estimated Female Officers or Directors: 2
Hot Spot for Advancement for Women/Minorities:

Sales, profits and employees may be estimates. Financial information, benefits and other data can change quickly and may vary from those stated here.

Metropolitan Health Networks Inc

www.metcare.com

NAIC Code: 524,114

TYPES OF BUSINESS:

Provider Service Network
Disease Management

BRANDS/DIVISIONS/AFFILIATES:

Humana Inc
MetCare of Plantation
MetCare of Palm Coast
MetCare of Stuart
MetCare of Boca Raton
MetCare of West Palm Beach
Humana Physicians Group of Daytona
MetCare of Orange City

CONTACTS: *Note: Officers with more than one job title may be intentionally listed here more than once.*

Joe Jasser, Pres.
Maria A. Xirau, Sr. VP-Medical Oper.-South Florida
Richard Bell, Medical Dir.-Central Florida
Barry Stone, Associate Medical Dir.-South & Coastal Florida
Gerald Leichman, Associate Medical Dir.-South Florida
Kevin McAdams, Sr. VP-Oper.-Central & Coastal Florida

GROWTH PLANS/SPECIAL FEATURES:

Metropolitan Health Networks, Inc. (MetCare), a subsidiary of Humana, Inc., provides and arranges for medical care for senior patients throughout five Florida counties. These counties include Broward, MetCare of Plantation; Flagler, MetCare of Palm Coast; Martin, MetCare of Stuart; Palm Beach, MetCare of Boca Raton, MetCare of Delray Beach, MetCare of Everglades, MetCare of Jupiter, MetCare of North Palm Beach, MetCare of Wellington and MetCare of West Palm Beach; and Volusia, Humana Physicians Group of Daytona, MetCare of DeLand, MetCare of New Smyrna Beach, MetCare of Orange City, MetCare of Ormond, MetCare of Port Orange and MetCare of South Daytona. MetCare aims to treat the whole person, within the context of the natural aging process. The firm works together as a team with physicians, nurses, care coordinators and the patients to create individualized plans to meet specific needs. Senior-focused primary care: listens to questions and concerns, explains care and treatments, provides advocacy with specialists/hospitals/Medicare, provides reminders of preventative screenings and tests, as well as any additional support when needed. Health resources offered by the firm include becoming motivated to be healthy, the effects of sugar, serving/portion sizes, medication adherence, importance of vaccinations, effects of osteoporosis, blood pressure information, as well as facts on colorectal cancer.

Employee benefits include three tiered health insurance, dental and vision plans; supplemental health benefits; short- and long-term disability; life insurance; a 401(k); and education assistance.

FINANCIAL DATA: *Note: Data for latest year may not have been available at press time.*

In U.S. $	2017	2016	2015	2014	2013	2012
Revenue	735,000,000	700,000,000	670,000,000	656,000,000	800,000,000	773,073,333
R&D Expense						
Operating Income						
Operating Margin %						
SGA Expense						
Net Income						
Operating Cash Flow						
Capital Expenditure						
EBITDA						
Return on Assets %						
Return on Equity %						
Debt to Equity						

CONTACT INFORMATION:

Phone: 561-241-0025 Fax: 561-241-3883
Toll-Free:
Address: 2900 North Military Trail, Ste. 201, Boca Raton, FL 33431 United States

STOCK TICKER/OTHER:

Stock Ticker: Subsidiary
Employees: 1,140
Parent Company: Humana Inc
Exchange:
Fiscal Year Ends: 12/31

SALARIES/BONUSES:

Top Exec. Salary: $ Bonus: $
Second Exec. Salary: $ Bonus: $

OTHER THOUGHTS:

Estimated Female Officers or Directors: 3
Hot Spot for Advancement for Women/Minorities: Y

Mettler-Toledo International Inc

www.mt.com

NAIC Code: 334,516

TYPES OF BUSINESS:

Manufacturing-Laboratory Equipment
Product Inspections
Manufacturing-Industrial Weighing Equipment
Manufacturing-Retail Weighing Equipment
Software

BRANDS/DIVISIONS/AFFILIATES:

Rainin
Biotix

CONTACTS: *Note: Officers with more than one job title may be intentionally listed here more than once.*

Olivier Filliol, CEO
Shawn Vadala, CFO
Robert Spoerry, Chairman of the Board
William Donnelly, Executive VP
Thomas Caratsch, Other Corporate Officer
Marc De La Gueroniere, Other Corporate Officer
Christian Magloth, Other Corporate Officer
Waldemar Rauch, Other Corporate Officer
Michael Heidingsfelder, Other Corporate Officer
Simon Kirk, Other Corporate Officer

GROWTH PLANS/SPECIAL FEATURES:

Mettler-Toledo International is a provider of precision instruments and services. The firm serves customers on a global scale, with 31% of 2017 net sales deriving from Europe, 39% from North and South America, and 30% from Asia and other countries. The company's primary products are laboratory instruments and industrial instruments. Laboratory instruments include laboratory balances that have a range from three-hundred millionths of a gram to 64 kilograms; pipettes, sold under the Rainin and Biotix brand names, which are used in pharmaceutical, biotech and academic settings; and titrators, which measure the chemical composition of samples and are used in research laboratories as well as the pharmaceutical and food and beverage industries. The company also manufactures thermal analysis units, automated lap reactors and other laboratory products such as pH meters. In addition, Mettler-Toledo offers laboratory software to analyze data from its instrumentation. The firm's industrial instruments include vehicle scale systems that can handle weights up to 500 tons, are usable with both trucks and railcars and provide accurate measurements in extreme environmental conditions. It provides product inspections and industrial scales/balances that can handle loads from a few grams to several thousand pounds for applications ranging from chemical production to weighing mail and packages. The company also produces industrial terminals and software to help automatically collect and archive data. In addition to laboratory and industrial instruments, Mettler-Toledo offers retail weighing solutions including stand-alone scales and balances with pricing and printing functions; and networks that integrate backroom, counter, self-service and checkout weighing functions.

FINANCIAL DATA: *Note: Data for latest year may not have been available at press time.*

In U.S. $	2017	2016	2015	2014	2013	2012
Revenue	2,725,053,000	2,508,257,000	2,395,447,000	2,485,983,000	2,378,972,000	2,341,528,000
R&D Expense	129,265,000	119,968,000	119,076,000	123,297,000	116,346,000	112,530,000
Operating Income	613,913,000	546,945,000	501,156,000	477,686,000	448,353,000	423,142,000
Operating Margin %	22.52%	21.80%	20.92%	19.21%	18.84%	18.07%
SGA Expense	787,464,000	732,622,000	700,810,000	728,582,000	692,788,000	684,026,000
Net Income	375,972,000	384,370,000	352,820,000	338,241,000	306,094,000	290,847,000
Operating Cash Flow	516,325,000	443,078,000	426,868,000	418,912,000	345,928,000	327,704,000
Capital Expenditure	127,426,000	123,957,000	82,506,000	89,388,000	82,349,000	95,588,000
EBITDA	683,136,000	601,014,000	554,913,000	532,343,000	484,724,000	460,143,000
Return on Assets %	15.94%	18.36%	17.52%	16.25%	14.33%	13.46%
Return on Equity %	76.55%	75.70%	54.27%	40.88%	34.73%	36.16%
Debt to Equity	1.75	2.01	0.99	0.46	0.42	0.41

CONTACT INFORMATION:

Phone: 614 438-4511 Fax:
Toll-Free:
Address: 1900 Polaris Pkwy., Columbus, OH 43240-4035 United States

STOCK TICKER/OTHER:

Stock Ticker: MTD
Employees: 14,200
Parent Company:
Exchange: NYS
Fiscal Year Ends: 12/31

SALARIES/BONUSES:

Top Exec. Salary: $851,642 Bonus: $
Second Exec. Salary: $318,056 Bonus: $

OTHER THOUGHTS:

Estimated Female Officers or Directors:
Hot Spot for Advancement for Women/Minorities:

MiMedx Group Inc

www.mimedx.com

NAIC Code: 325,414

TYPES OF BUSINESS:

Implants, Surgical, Manufacturing

BRANDS/DIVISIONS/AFFILIATES:

AmnioFix
EpiFix
OrthoFlo
AmnioFill
AmminoCord
EpiCord

CONTACTS:

Note: Officers with more than one job title may be intentionally listed here more than once.

David Coles, CEO
Edward Borkowski, CFO
Charles Evans, Chairman of the Board
Alexandra Haden, General Counsel

GROWTH PLANS/SPECIAL FEATURES:

MiMedx Group, Inc. is an integrated developer, processor and marketer of patent protected and proprietary regenerative biomaterial products and bioimplants. These bio products are processed from human amniotic membrane and other birth tissues, as well as human skin and bone. Regenerative biomaterials are the framework that provide physician's products and tissues to help the body heal itself. MiMedx's biomaterial platform technologies include AmnioFix, EpiFix, OrthoFlo, AmnioFill, AmminoCord and EpiCord. AmnioFix and EpiFix are tissue technologies process from human amniotic membrane derived from donated placentas. Human amniotic membrane is then processed using the company's proprietary PURION process, which produces a safe and effective implant. OrthoFlo is a unique human tissue allograft derived from amniotic fluid, donated by mothers delivering healthy babies by scheduled Caesarean section. It is for homologous use to protect & cushion, provide lubrication and reduce inflammation. AmnioFill is a minimally manipulated, non-viable cellular tissue matrix allograft that contains multiple extracellular matrix proteins, growth factors, cytokines, and other specialty proteins present in placental tissue to help enhance healing. AmminoCord and EpiCord are minimally manipulated, dehydrated, non-viable cellular umbilical cord allografts for homologous use that provide protective environments for the healing process and provide a connective tissue matrix to replace or supplement damaged or inadequate integumental tissue. MiMedx has supplied more than 500,000 allografts for the application in the wound care, burn, surgical, orthopedic, spine, sports medicine, ophthalmic and dental sectors of healthcare.In October 2018, the firm completed the previously communicated divestiture of the Company's subsidiary, Stability Biologics LLC (Stability Inc.), back to the former stockholders of Stability Inc.

FINANCIAL DATA:

Note: Data for latest year may not have been available at press time.

In U.S. $	2017	2016	2015	2014	2013	2012
Revenue		245,015,000	187,296,000	118,223,000	59,180,740	27,053,770
R&D Expense		12,038,000	8,413,000	7,050,000	4,843,457	2,884,546
Operating Income		18,446,000	24,364,000	7,100,000	-2,270,465	-1,989,838
Operating Margin %		7.52%	13.00%	6.00%	-3.83%	-7.35%
SGA Expense		179,997,000	133,384,000	90,480,000	46,225,660	20,970,690
Net Income		11,974,000	29,446,000	6,220,000	-4,111,853	-7,662,376
Operating Cash Flow		25,828,000	18,807,000	16,802,000	-285,477	-3,384,831
Capital Expenditure		7,111,000	6,678,000	3,152,000	3,025,414	582,931
EBITDA		23,906,000	27,096,000	9,225,000	-579,248	-5,223,876
Return on Assets %		7.27%	24.02%	6.41%	-6.86%	-24.60%
Return on Equity %		9.93%	29.84%	7.63%	-8.78%	-48.03%
Debt to Equity						0.20

CONTACT INFORMATION:

Phone: 770-651-9100 Fax:
Toll-Free: 888-543-1917
Address: 1775 West Oak Commons Court, NE Marietta, GA 30062 United States

STOCK TICKER/OTHER:

Stock Ticker: MDXG
Employees: 690
Parent Company:
Exchange: NAS
Fiscal Year Ends: 12/31

SALARIES/BONUSES:

Top Exec. Salary: $602,904 Bonus: $
Second Exec. Salary: $502,170 Bonus: $

OTHER THOUGHTS:

Estimated Female Officers or Directors:
Hot Spot for Advancement for Women/Minorities:

Mindray Medical International Limited

www.mindray.com

NAIC Code: 339,100

TYPES OF BUSINESS:

Medical/Dental/Surgical Equipment & Supplies, Manufacturing

BRANDS/DIVISIONS/AFFILIATES:

Excelsior Union Limited
ZONARE

CONTACTS: *Note: Officers with more than one job title may be intentionally listed here more than once.*

Li Xiting, Co-CEO
Wang Jianxin, COO
Li Xiting, Pres.
Fannie Lin Fan, General Counsel
Cheng Minghe, Chief Strategic Officer
Cheng Minghe, Co-CEO
David Gibson, Pres., Mindray DS USA, Inc.

GROWTH PLANS/SPECIAL FEATURES:

Mindray Medical International Limited (Mindray) is a developer, manufacturer and marketer of medical devices in China, with a significant, growing presence outside of China. Mindray offers products in seven categories. Patient monitoring systems include high acuity, mid/low acuity, transport, vital signs, telemetry and central stations and veterinary. Interoperability products include connectivity solutions, such as gateways; and integration solutions, including protocol interfaces, data management, paging interfaces, third-party integrators and certification solutions. Supplies and accessories include monitoring products such as blood pressure cuffs, electrocardiogram (ECG) lead wires, SpO2 (peripheral capillary oxygen saturation-an estimate of the amount of oxygen in the blood) sensors, temperature probes, CO2 cannula; and anesthesia products such as breathing circuits, face masks, CO2 gas sampling lines/filters and laryngeal mask airway devices. Ultrasound systems such as ZONARE branded products, hand carried products, cart-based products, touchscreens and veterinary ultrasound systems. Anesthesia systems include delivery systems and consumables. Diagnostic products include chemistry analyzers, hematology analyzers and veterinary diagnostic systems. Last, Mindray certified refurbished products include patient monitoring systems, anesthesia systems and ultrasound systems. Mindray's products are used in emergency departments, critical care units, step-down units/telemetry, perioperative care and ambulatory surgery centers. The firm comprises more than 40 subsidiaries with branch offices in 32 countries throughout North and Latin America, Europe, Africa and Asia-Pacific, as well as 31 branch offices in China. Mindray is privately- and wholly-owned by Excelsior Union Limited.

FINANCIAL DATA: *Note: Data for latest year may not have been available at press time.*

In U.S. $	2017	2016	2015	2014	2013	2012
Revenue	1,433,250,000	1,365,000,000	1,300,000,000	1,322,813,952	1,213,986,944	1,060,054,016
R&D Expense						
Operating Income						
Operating Margin %						
SGA Expense						
Net Income				193,292,000	224,754,000	180,208,992
Operating Cash Flow						
Capital Expenditure						
EBITDA						
Return on Assets %						
Return on Equity %						
Debt to Equity						

CONTACT INFORMATION:

Phone: 86 75526582888 Fax: 86 75526582500
Toll-Free:
Address: Keji 12th Rd. S., Mindray Bldg., Shenzhen, Guangdong 518057 China

STOCK TICKER/OTHER:

Stock Ticker: Private
Exchange:
Employees: 8,300
Fiscal Year Ends: 12/31
Parent Company: Excelsior Union Limited

SALARIES/BONUSES:

Top Exec. Salary: $ Bonus: $
Second Exec. Salary: $ Bonus: $

OTHER THOUGHTS:

Estimated Female Officers or Directors: 1
Hot Spot for Advancement for Women/Minorities:

MinuteClinic LLC

www.minuteclinic.com

NAIC Code: 621,498

TYPES OF BUSINESS:

Health Clinics
In-Store Clinics

BRANDS/DIVISIONS/AFFILIATES:

CVS Health Corporation
CVS Pharmacy

CONTACTS:

Note: Officers with more than one job title may be intentionally listed here more than once.

Sharon Vitti, Sr. VP
Nancy Gagliano, Chief Medical Officer
Meredith Dixon, VP-Oper.
Chris Crisafulli, Dir.-Finance
Paulette Thabault, Chief Nurse Practitioner Officer

GROWTH PLANS/SPECIAL FEATURES:

MinuteClinic, LLC, a wholly-owned subsidiary of CVS Health Corporation, is a chain of quick service healthcare clinics located in grocery stores, pharmacies and other stores. The clinics are open seven-days-a-week and are staffed by certified nurse practitioners (CNPs) who can diagnose and prescribe medications on-site with an average visit time of approximately 15 minutes. The company staffs clinics with CNPs able to treat common health problems such as ear infections, allergies and strep throat. The clinics can also administer vaccines, treat a variety of skin conditions, and offers biometric screening services to facilitate early interventions for patients with undiagnosed diabetes, hypertension and high cholesterol. Additional services include ear wax removal, motion sickness prevention, pregnancy testing, suture removal, sprain examination, tuberculosis testing and wound care. Seriously ill patients are referred to a family doctor, area doctors or a larger clinic or hospital. No appointments are needed to see a CNP, and patients can shop in the store while waiting to be seen. Treatments range from $30 to $229.99, generally less than seeing a doctor, and MinuteClinic accepts most major forms of insurance. More than 1,100 clinics are located within CVS Pharmacy and select Target stores across 33 states nationwide.

The firm offers employees medical, dental, vision, prescription, life, travel and disability coverage; an employee assistance program; paid time off; education reimbursement; and a flexible spending account.

FINANCIAL DATA:

Note: Data for latest year may not have been available at press time.

In U.S. $	2017	2016	2015	2014	2013	2012
Revenue						
R&D Expense						
Operating Income						
Operating Margin %						
SGA Expense						
Net Income						
Operating Cash Flow						
Capital Expenditure						
EBITDA						
Return on Assets %						
Return on Equity %						
Debt to Equity						

CONTACT INFORMATION:

Phone: Fax:
Toll-Free: 866-389-2727
Address: One CVS Dr., Woonsocket, RI 02895 United States

STOCK TICKER/OTHER:

Stock Ticker: Subsidiary
Employees:
Parent Company: CVS Health Corporation
Exchange:
Fiscal Year Ends:

SALARIES/BONUSES:

Top Exec. Salary: $ Bonus: $
Second Exec. Salary: $ Bonus: $

OTHER THOUGHTS:

Estimated Female Officers or Directors: 6
Hot Spot for Advancement for Women/Minorities: Y

Misonix Inc

www.misonix.com

NAIC Code: 339,100

TYPES OF BUSINESS:

Ultrasonic Medical Devices

BRANDS/DIVISIONS/AFFILIATES:

SonicOne
Bone Scalpel
SonaStar

CONTACTS:

Note: Officers with more than one job title may be intentionally listed here more than once.

Joseph Dwyer, CFO
Stavros Vizirgianakis, Director
Robert Ludecker, Senior VP, Divisional
Joseph Brennan, Vice President, Divisional
John Salerno, Vice President, Divisional
Christopher Wright, Vice President, Divisional
Daniel Voic, Vice President, Divisional

GROWTH PLANS/SPECIAL FEATURES:

Misonix, Inc. designs, manufactures and markets minimally invasive ultrasonic medical devices. These medical devices include the SonicOne wound cleansing and debridement system, used on soft and hard tissue related to ulcers, eschar infections and necrotic bone; the BoneScalpel bone dissection, sculpting and removal tool, used on small bone and spinal tissue; and the SonaStar ultrasonic aspiration device for tumor tissue removal, bone debulking and other sculpting and removal processes in neurosurgery and general surgery applications. Clinical specialties served include spine surgery, skull-based surgery (cranio-maxillo-facial), neurosurgery, orthopedic surgery, plastic surgery, as well as wound, burn and vascular surgery. In October 2017, Misonix entered into a license and exclusive manufacturing agreement with the Chinese firm Hunan Xing Hang Rui Kang Bio-Technologies Co., Ltd., under which Misonix has licensed certain manufacturing and distribution rights to its SonaStar product line in China, Hong Kong and Macau in exchange for payments totaling a minimum of $11 million.

FINANCIAL DATA:

Note: Data for latest year may not have been available at press time.

In U.S. $	2017	2016	2015	2014	2013	2012
Revenue	27,269,960	23,113,190	22,204,580	17,060,440	14,827,230	
R&D Expense	1,837,497	1,670,347	1,592,923	1,711,751	1,496,058	
Operating Income	-6,601,086	-5,829,388	-1,714,939	-2,548,964	-5,318,772	
Operating Margin %	-24.20%	-25.22%	-7.72%	-14.94%	-35.87%	
SGA Expense	23,816,110	19,661,000	15,046,320	11,963,780	11,222,690	
Net Income	-1,681,179	-1,172,146	5,571,171	1,393,299	-2,670,965	
Operating Cash Flow	-1,272,658	-316,240	2,388,454	700,056	-470,263	
Capital Expenditure	714,815	604,560	450,067	201,515	615,961	
EBITDA	-5,534,242	-4,177,416	3,959,396	2,135,678	-2,136,499	
Return on Assets %	-5.50%	-4.32%	24.23%	7.55%	-14.97%	
Return on Equity %	-6.39%	-4.86%	27.78%	9.24%	-18.19%	
Debt to Equity						

CONTACT INFORMATION:

Phone: 631 694-9555 Fax: 631 694-9412
Toll-Free: 800-694-9612
Address: 1938 New Highway, Farmingdale, NY 11735 United States

STOCK TICKER/OTHER:

Stock Ticker: MSON
Exchange: NAS
Employees: 92
Fiscal Year Ends: 06/30
Parent Company:

SALARIES/BONUSES:

Top Exec. Salary: $383,250 Bonus: $
Second Exec. Salary: $271,817 Bonus: $82,500

OTHER THOUGHTS:

Estimated Female Officers or Directors:
Hot Spot for Advancement for Women/Minorities:

Molina Healthcare Inc

www.molinahealthcare.com

NAIC Code: 524,114

TYPES OF BUSINESS:

HMO-Low Income Patients
Medicaid HMO
SCHIP HMO

BRANDS/DIVISIONS/AFFILIATES:

Molina Medicaid Solutions

CONTACTS:

Note: Officers with more than one job title may be intentionally listed here more than once.

Joseph White, CFO
Dale Wolf, Chairman of the Board
Ronna Romney, Director
Mark Keim, Executive VP, Divisional
Pamela Sedmak, Executive VP, Divisional
Jeff Barlow, Other Executive Officer
Joseph Zubretsky, President

GROWTH PLANS/SPECIAL FEATURES:

Molina Healthcare, Inc. is a multi-stage, managed care organization participating in government-sponsored health care programs for low-income persons, such as the Medicaid program and Children's Health Insurance Program (CHIP, including Perinatal). The company also focuses on a small number of persons who are dually eligible under the Medicaid and Medicare programs. Molina operates in two segments: health plans and Molina Medicaid Solutions. Health plans consists of operational health plans in 12 states and Puerto Rico and Molina's direct delivery business. The health plans, serving approximately 4.5 million, are operated by the firm's wholly-owned subsidiaries in those states, each of which is licensed as a health maintenance organization (HMO). Molina Medicaid Solutions provides design, development, implementation and business process outsourcing (BPO) solutions to state governments for their Medicaid management information systems (MMIS). MMIS is a core tool used to support the administration of state Medicaid and other health care entitlement programs. Molina Medicaid currently holds MMIS contracts in Idaho, Louisiana, Maine, New Jersey, West Virginia and the U.S. Virgin Islands; and also holds a contract to provide pharmacy rebate administration services for the Florida Medicaid program.

Molina offers employees medical, dental and vision plans; life insurance; disability; employee assistance; flexible spending accounts; 401(k); and an employee stock purchase plan.

FINANCIAL DATA:

Note: Data for latest year may not have been available at press time.

In U.S. $	2017	2016	2015	2014	2013	2012
Revenue	19,813,000,000	17,744,000,000	14,160,000,000	9,658,508,000	6,582,044,000	6,023,575,000
R&D Expense						
Operating Income	79,000,000	268,000,000	369,000,000	184,824,000	129,670,000	30,285,000
Operating Margin %	.39%	1.51%	2.60%	1.91%	1.97%	.50%
SGA Expense	1,594,000,000	1,393,000,000	1,146,000,000	764,693,000	665,996,000	532,627,000
Net Income	-512,000,000	52,000,000	143,000,000	62,223,000	52,929,000	9,790,000
Operating Cash Flow	804,000,000	673,000,000	1,125,000,000	1,060,257,000	190,083,000	347,784,000
Capital Expenditure	86,000,000	176,000,000	132,000,000	114,934,000	98,049,000	78,145,000
EBITDA	-316,000,000	488,000,000	514,000,000	326,519,000	227,083,000	114,598,000
Return on Assets %	-6.43%	.74%	2.58%	1.66%	2.14%	.54%
Return on Equity %	-34.29%	3.24%	11.13%	6.53%	6.31%	1.27%
Debt to Equity	1.13	0.71	0.74	0.89	0.67	0.33

CONTACT INFORMATION:

Phone: 562 435-3666 Fax: 562 499-0790
Toll-Free: 888-562-5442
Address: 200 Oceangate, Ste. 100, Long Beach, CA 90802 United States

STOCK TICKER/OTHER:

Stock Ticker: MOH
Employees: 21,000
Parent Company:
Exchange: NYS
Fiscal Year Ends: 12/31

SALARIES/BONUSES:

Top Exec. Salary: $175,000 Bonus: $4,000,000
Second Exec. Salary: $1,248,167 Bonus: $

OTHER THOUGHTS:

Estimated Female Officers or Directors: 2
Hot Spot for Advancement for Women/Minorities: Y

Molnlycke Health Care AB

www.molnlycke.com

NAIC Code: 339,100

TYPES OF BUSINESS:

Single-Use Surgical & Wound Care Products Manufacturing
Supply Chain & Logistics Management Consulting
Operating Room Staffing

BRANDS/DIVISIONS/AFFILIATES:

Investor AB
Safetac
SastoMed GmbH

CONTACTS: *Note: Officers with more than one job title may be intentionally listed here more than once.*

Richard Twomey, CEO
Eric De Kesel, Exec. VP-Oper.
Stefan Fristedt, CFO
Martin Lexa, Exec. VP-Human Resources & Communications
Rob Bennsion, Exec. VP-Legal, Regulatory & Quality Affairs
Maarten van Beek, Exec. VP-Corp. Comm.
Phil Cooper, Pres., Wound Care Div.
Eric De Kesel, Pres., Surgical Div.
Gunnar Brock, Chmn.
Anders Klinton, Sr. VP-Supply Chain

GROWTH PLANS/SPECIAL FEATURES:

Molnlycke Health Care AB designs and supplies products and solutions for use in wound treatment, pressure ulcer prevention and surgery. Wound management products and solutions cover the continuum of care, from hospital to care in home settings, with foam, film and fiber dressings, as well as negative pressure therapy options. These products are designed to secure ideal wound conditions for effective healing. This division's proprietary Safetac technology is a silicone adhesive layer that enables dressings to be removed with less pain and without damaging the skin. Pressure ulcer prevention products and solutions aim to stop needless patient suffering and unnecessary costs via prophylactic dressings, skin care products and devices that help clinicians turn and re-position patients. This division also provides supporting educational and consultancy services. Surgical solutions include procedure trays that include everything a surgical team needs, as well as the preparation of surgical instruments and related components. For example, laparoscopy specialists perform procedures such as cholecystectomy, appendectomy and hernia repair, and can choose from a full range of trocars, monopolar instruments and essential tray components, all of which Molnlycke provides. Molnlycke Health Care is present in more than 100 countries, and comprises 16 manufacturing sites located in nine countries across Europe, North America and Asia. The firm is majority-owned (99%) by Swedish investment company, Investor AB. In July 2018, Molnlycke acquired German wound care products company, SastoMed GmbH.

FINANCIAL DATA: *Note: Data for latest year may not have been available at press time.*

In U.S. $	2017	2016	2015	2014	2013	2012
Revenue	1,730,910,000	1,714,483,842	1,516,865,132	898,207,638	1,500,000,000	1,478,740,000
R&D Expense						
Operating Income						
Operating Margin %						
SGA Expense						
Net Income						
Operating Cash Flow						
Capital Expenditure						
EBITDA						
Return on Assets %						
Return on Equity %						
Debt to Equity						

CONTACT INFORMATION:

Phone: 46-31-722-30-00 Fax: 46-31-722-34-00
Toll-Free:
Address: Gamlestadsvaegen 3C, Gothenburg, SE-402 52 Sweden

STOCK TICKER/OTHER:

Stock Ticker: Private
Exchange:
Employees: 7,541
Fiscal Year Ends: 12/31
Parent Company: Investor AB

SALARIES/BONUSES:

Top Exec. Salary: $ Bonus: $
Second Exec. Salary: $ Bonus: $

OTHER THOUGHTS:

Estimated Female Officers or Directors: 1
Hot Spot for Advancement for Women/Minorities:

Moore Medical LLC

www.mooremedical.com

NAIC Code: 423,450

TYPES OF BUSINESS:

Distribution-Assorted Health Care Products

BRANDS/DIVISIONS/AFFILIATES:

McKesson Corporation

CONTACTS:

Note: Officers with more than one job title may be intentionally listed here more than once.

Linda M. Autore, CEO
Rick Frey, Pres.
Ryan G. Stefanski, Mgr.-Vendor Promotions

GROWTH PLANS/SPECIAL FEATURES:

Moore Medical, LLC, a subsidiary of McKesson Corporation, is an internet-enabled, multi-channel, specialty direct marketer and distributor of medical, surgical and pharmaceutical products to nearly 120,000 health care practices and facilities in non-hospital settings nationwide. The company's customers include physicians, emergency medical technicians, educational institutions, correctional institutions, municipalities, occupational healthcare professionals and other specialty practice communities. Moore Medical markets to and serves its customers through direct mail, industry-specialized telephone support staff, field sales representatives and the Internet. The firm purchases products primarily from manufacturers and other distributors and does not manufacture or assemble any products, with the exception of medical and first-aid kits. The largest product suppliers for Moore Medical are 3M, Bayer, GlaxoSmithKline, Johnson & Johnson, Kendall Healthcare Products Co., Microflex, Wyeth-Ayerst Labs, Graham Medical Products and Welch Allyn. Moore Medical has distribution centers located in Bolingbrook, Illinois; New Britain, Connecticut; Visalia, California; and Jacksonville, Florida as well as remote telesales and customer service centers in Farmington, Connecticut; Scottsdale, Arizona and Columbia, South Carolina.

FINANCIAL DATA:

Note: Data for latest year may not have been available at press time.

In U.S. $	2017	2016	2015	2014	2013	2012
Revenue						
R&D Expense						
Operating Income						
Operating Margin %						
SGA Expense						
Net Income						
Operating Cash Flow						
Capital Expenditure						
EBITDA						
Return on Assets %						
Return on Equity %						
Debt to Equity						

CONTACT INFORMATION:

Phone: 860-826-3600 Fax: 800-944-6667
Toll-Free: 800-234-1464
Address: 1690 New Britain Ave., Farmington, CT 06032 United States

STOCK TICKER/OTHER:

Stock Ticker: Subsidiary
Exchange:
Employees:
Fiscal Year Ends: 03/31
Parent Company: McKesson Corporation

SALARIES/BONUSES:

Top Exec. Salary: $ Bonus: $
Second Exec. Salary: $ Bonus: $

OTHER THOUGHTS:

Estimated Female Officers or Directors: 1
Hot Spot for Advancement for Women/Minorities:

MRI Interventions Inc

www.mriinterventions.com

NAIC Code: 339,100

TYPES OF BUSINESS:

Medical Device Manufacturing
MRI-Guided Surgical Equipment

BRANDS/DIVISIONS/AFFILIATES:

ClearPoint
ClearTrace
SmartFrame

CONTACTS:
Note: Officers with more than one job title may be intentionally listed here more than once.

Harold Hurwitz, CFO
Kimble Jenkins, Chairman of the Board
Peter Piferi, COO
Francis Grillo, President
Oscar Thomas, Secretary
Robert Korn, Vice President, Divisional
Wendelin Maners, Vice President, Divisional

GROWTH PLANS/SPECIAL FEATURES:

MRI Interventions, Inc. is a medical device company that develops and commercializes platforms for performing minimally invasive surgical procedures in the brain and heart. The procedures are performed under direct, intra-procedural magnetic resonance imaging (MRI) guidance. Currently, the company has two product platforms: its ClearPoint and ClearTrace systems. MRI's ClearPoint system is in commercial use in the U.S., and is used to perform minimally invasive surgical procedures in the brain. The system is used in procedures such as biopsies and the insertion of catheters and electrodes, and is intended to be used with both 1.5T (tesla) and 3T MRI scanners. ClearPoint includes disposables such as the company's SmartFrame trajectory device; and software, which guides the physician in surgical planning, device alignment, navigation to the target and procedure monitoring. The ClearTrace system is still in development and will be used to perform minimally invasive surgical procedures in the heart. ClearTrace is similar to traditional catheter-based cardiac interventions performed in a fluoroscopy suite (Cath Lab or EP Lab), but with two distinctions. First, ClearTrace will provide a continuous, high resolution, four dimensional imaging environment (the fourth being time), which will include detailed visualization of cardiac tissue, along with the cardiac catheters used to deliver the therapy. Second, the system will eliminate all radiation exposure for both the patient and the physician from the X-ray utilized in current procedures. Both systems are designed to work in a hospital's existing MRI suite. The firm has both license and collaborative agreements for its products with Brainlab AG, Siemens AG, Boston Scientific Corporation and The Johns Hopkins University.

FINANCIAL DATA:
Note: Data for latest year may not have been available at press time.

In U.S. $	2017	2016	2015	2014	2013	2012
Revenue	7,379,525	5,749,454	4,594,192	3,604,482	3,930,575	5,058,235
R&D Expense						
Operating Income						
Operating Margin %						
SGA Expense						
Net Income			-8,449,246	-4,524,732	-7,086,274	-5,707,136
Operating Cash Flow						
Capital Expenditure						
EBITDA						
Return on Assets %						
Return on Equity %						
Debt to Equity						

CONTACT INFORMATION:

Phone: 949-900-6833 Fax: 949-900-6834
Toll-Free:
Address: 5 Musick, Irvine, CA 92618 United States

STOCK TICKER/OTHER:

Stock Ticker: MRIC
Employees: 25
Parent Company:
Exchange: OTC
Fiscal Year Ends: 12/31

SALARIES/BONUSES:

Top Exec. Salary: $ Bonus: $
Second Exec. Salary: $ Bonus: $

OTHER THOUGHTS:

Estimated Female Officers or Directors: 1
Hot Spot for Advancement for Women/Minorities:

MSA Safety Inc

www.msasafety.com

NAIC Code: 339,100

TYPES OF BUSINESS:

Equipment/Supplies-Manufacturer
Safety & Health Equipment
Personal Protective Products
Respiratory Protective Equipment
Combat Helmets
Thermal Imaging Cameras
Security Sensors & Systems

BRANDS/DIVISIONS/AFFILIATES:

CONTACTS:

Note: Officers with more than one job title may be intentionally listed here more than once.

Nishan Vartanian, CEO
Markus Weber, Chief Information Officer
William Lambert, Director
Douglas McClaine, Other Executive Officer
Kerry Bove, Other Executive Officer
Paul Uhler, Other Executive Officer
Roberta Herman, Other Executive Officer
Bob Leenen, President, Divisional
Gavan Duff, Vice President, Subsidiary
Steven Blanco, Vice President
Kenneth Krause, Vice President

GROWTH PLANS/SPECIAL FEATURES:

MSA Safety, Inc. develops, manufactures and supplies safety and health equipment. The firm divides its product offerings by the geographic areas of its customers: Americas, International and Corporate. The company's safety products are used by workers in fire service, homeland security, the military, construction services and other industries. Customers include industrial and military end-users, distributors and retail consumers. MSA's principle product offerings fall under five categories: respiratory protection; industrial head protection; portable and fixed gas detection instruments; fixed gas and flame detection; and fall protection. The company produces numerous respiratory systems, such as self-contained breathing apparatuses (SCBA); escape hoods, which allow workers to escape from dangerous gases; and air-purifying respirators, such as military full face gas masks, half-mask respirators, respirators and pollen masks. Hand-held thermal imaging cameras are used by firefighters to see victims through dense smoke and to detect a fire's source. Industrial head protection is used in work environments with hazards such as dust, metal fragments, chemicals, extreme glare, optical radiation and items dropped from above. The company produces industrial hard hats; fire helmets; protective eyewear and face shields; and hearing protection products. MSA's portable and fixed gas detection products include single- and multiple-gas hand-held detectors, multi-point permanently installed gas detectors and flame and open-path infrared gas detectors. MSA's fall protection equipment includes confined space equipment, harnesses, fall arrest equipment, and lifelines.

MSA offers its employees life, medical, dental and vision coverage; flexible spending accounts; a disability program; retirement plan; tuition reimbursement; adoption reimbursement; and a bonus system.

FINANCIAL DATA:

Note: Data for latest year may not have been available at press time.

In U.S. $	2017	2016	2015	2014	2013	2012
Revenue	1,196,809,000	1,149,530,000	1,130,783,000	1,133,885,000	1,112,058,000	1,168,904,000
R&D Expense	50,061,000	46,847,000	48,630,000	48,247,000	45,858,000	40,900,000
Operating Income	64,855,000	171,362,000	138,039,000	143,204,000	141,585,000	141,150,000
Operating Margin %	5.41%	14.90%	12.20%	12.62%	12.73%	12.07%
SGA Expense	297,801,000	306,144,000	315,270,000	322,797,000	309,206,000	321,234,000
Net Income	26,027,000	91,936,000	70,807,000	88,506,000	88,247,000	90,637,000
Operating Cash Flow	230,336,000	134,894,000	55,254,000	107,031,000	110,781,000	150,476,000
Capital Expenditure	23,725,000	25,523,000	36,241,000	33,583,000	36,517,000	32,209,000
EBITDA	83,012,000	203,595,000	153,564,000	166,967,000	161,574,000	177,353,000
Return on Assets %	1.71%	6.61%	5.26%	7.08%	7.52%	8.05%
Return on Equity %	4.53%	17.22%	13.57%	16.19%	17.26%	20.17%
Debt to Equity	0.75	0.65	0.89	0.46	0.46	0.59

CONTACT INFORMATION:

Phone: 724 776-8600 Fax:
Toll-Free: 800-672-2222
Address: 1000 Cranberry Woods Dr., Pittsburgh, PA 16066 United States

STOCK TICKER/OTHER:

Stock Ticker: MSA
Employees: 4,300
Parent Company:
Exchange: NYS
Fiscal Year Ends: 12/31

SALARIES/BONUSES:

Top Exec. Salary: $829,899 Bonus: $
Second Exec. Salary: $452,399 Bonus: $

OTHER THOUGHTS:

Estimated Female Officers or Directors: 3
Hot Spot for Advancement for Women/Minorities: Y

MultiPlan Inc

www.multiplan.com

NAIC Code: 524,298

TYPES OF BUSINESS:

Medical Cost Evaluation Services

BRANDS/DIVISIONS/AFFILIATES:

Hellman & Friedman LLC

CONTACTS:

Note: Officers with more than one job title may be intentionally listed here more than once.

Mark Taback, CEO
David Redmond, CFO
Dale White, Exec. VP-Sales

GROWTH PLANS/SPECIAL FEATURES:

MultiPlan, Inc. provides technology-enabled health care cost management solutions. The firm's solutions deliver a single electronic gateway to a comprehensive set of claim cost management solutions that help control the financial risks associated with medical bills, while helping providers more effectively control reimbursements. Electronic claims are compared against cost savings mechanisms in a specific order, consistent with the requirements of contracts and benefit plans. The process also avoids errors and delays that often result when claims are routed from vendor to vendor. MultiPlan has approximately 900,000 healthcare providers under contract, and more than 60 million consumers who access its network products. As a result, 40 million claims are reduced through the firm's network and non-network solutions every year. The company's health care management solutions serve insurers, health plans, third party administrators, self-funded employers, HMOs, PPOs and other entities that pay medical bills in commercial healthcare, government, workers' compensation and auto medical markets. Solutions include primary networks, complementary network, specialty networks, non-networks and network management services, as well as a network of facilities offering contracted savings on various organ and stem cell transplant procedures. MultiPlan is owned by Hellman & Friedman, LLC.

MultiPlan offers its employees medical, dental and vision insurance; 401(k); life insurance plans; short- and long-term disability; paid time off; tuition reimbursement; flexible spending account; and employee assistance programs.

FINANCIAL DATA:

Note: Data for latest year may not have been available at press time.

In U.S. $	2017	2016	2015	2014	2013	2012
Revenue						
R&D Expense						
Operating Income						
Operating Margin %						
SGA Expense						
Net Income						
Operating Cash Flow						
Capital Expenditure						
EBITDA						
Return on Assets %						
Return on Equity %						
Debt to Equity						

CONTACT INFORMATION:

Phone: 212-780-2000 Fax: 212-780-0420
Toll-Free: 800-677-1098
Address: 115 Fifth Ave., New York, NY 10003 United States

STOCK TICKER/OTHER:

Stock Ticker: Private
Employees: 2,000
Parent Company: Hellman & Friedman LLC
Exchange:
Fiscal Year Ends:

SALARIES/BONUSES:

Top Exec. Salary: $ Bonus: $
Second Exec. Salary: $ Bonus: $

OTHER THOUGHTS:

Estimated Female Officers or Directors:
Hot Spot for Advancement for Women/Minorities:

Mylan NV

www.mylan.com

NAIC Code: 325,412

TYPES OF BUSINESS:

Drugs-Generic
Generic Pharmaceuticals
Active Pharmaceutical Ingredients

BRANDS/DIVISIONS/AFFILIATES:

EipPen
Perforomist

CONTACTS: *Note: Officers with more than one job title may be intentionally listed here more than once.*

Heather Bresch, CEO
Rajiv Malik, Pres.
John Sheehan, CFO
Ken Parks, CFO
Anthony Mauro, Chief Commercial Officer
C. Todd, Director Emeritus
Rajiv Malik, Director
Rodney Piatt, Director
Anthony Mauro, President, Geographical
Joseph Haggerty, Secretary
Robert J. Coury, Chmn.

GROWTH PLANS/SPECIAL FEATURES:

Mylan N.V. develops, licenses, manufactures, distributes and markets generic/branded pharmaceutical products, specialty pharmaceuticals and active pharmaceutical ingredients (APIs). The firm offers one of the industry's broadest product portfolios, including more than 7,500 marketed products around the world, to customers in more than 165 countries and territories. Mylan reports its results in three segments on a geographic basis as follows: North America, Europe and Rest of World. The North America segment, representing 42% of net sales for 2017, is primarily made up of the operations in the U.S. and Canada. The Europe segment, 34%, is made up of operations in approximately 35 countries within the region. The Rest of World segment, 24%, is primarily made up of Mylan's own operations in approximately 30 countries, as well as through partners and distributors in 90 additional emerging markets. This division's key markets include Japan, Australia, China, Brazil, Russia, India, South Africa and certain markets in the Middle East and Southeast Asia. A significant portion of the firm's revenue is through the sale of the EpiPen Auto-Injector, the number one dispensed epinephrine auto-injector in the world. The EpiPen is used for the treatment of severe allergic reactions and has been sold in the U.S. and internationally since the mid-1980s. Another key product by the company is the Perforomist inhalation solution, a long-acting beta2-adrenergic agonist indicated for long-term, twice-daily administration in the maintenance treatment of bronchoconstriction in chronic obstructive pulmonary disorder patients. Mylan owns 12 manufacturing and distribution facilities in the U.S., including Puerto Rico. Outside the U.S. and Puerto Rico, the firm utilizes production and distribution facilities in 11 countries, including key facilities in India, Australia, Japan, Ireland, Hungary and France.

FINANCIAL DATA: *Note: Data for latest year may not have been available at press time.*

In U.S. $	2017	2016	2015	2014	2013	2012
Revenue	11,907,700,000	11,076,900,000	9,429,300,000	7,719,600,000	6,909,143,000	6,796,110,000
R&D Expense	783,300,000	826,800,000	671,900,000	581,800,000	507,823,000	401,341,000
Operating Income	1,424,000,000	1,374,100,000	1,363,500,000	1,400,500,000	1,120,891,000	1,106,216,000
Operating Margin %	11.95%	12.40%	14.46%	18.14%	16.22%	16.27%
SGA Expense	2,575,800,000	2,496,100,000	2,180,700,000	1,625,700,000	1,411,629,000	1,400,747,000
Net Income	696,000,000	480,000,000	847,600,000	929,400,000	623,711,000	640,850,000
Operating Cash Flow	2,064,800,000	2,047,200,000	2,008,500,000	1,014,800,000	1,106,563,000	949,018,000
Capital Expenditure	896,200,000	750,600,000	871,700,000	754,400,000	334,580,000	305,325,000
EBITDA	3,243,400,000	2,099,500,000	2,286,900,000	1,874,300,000	1,576,673,000	1,659,382,000
Return on Assets %	1.97%	1.68%	4.44%	5.97%	4.59%	5.44%
Return on Equity %	5.69%	4.59%	13.01%	29.99%	19.85%	18.75%
Debt to Equity	0.96	1.36	0.64	1.76	2.57	1.59

CONTACT INFORMATION:

Phone: 44 01707853000 Fax: 44 01707261803
Toll-Free:
Address: Bldg. 4, Trident Place, Mosquito Way, Hatfield, Hertfordshire AL10 9UL United Kingdom

STOCK TICKER/OTHER:

Stock Ticker: MYL
Employees: 35,000
Parent Company:
Exchange: NAS
Fiscal Year Ends: 12/31

SALARIES/BONUSES:

Top Exec. Salary: $1,300,000 Bonus: $
Second Exec. Salary: $1,000,000 Bonus: $

OTHER THOUGHTS:

Estimated Female Officers or Directors: 3
Hot Spot for Advancement for Women/Minorities: Y

National Dentex Corporation

www.nationaldentex.com

NAIC Code: 339,100

TYPES OF BUSINESS:

Dental Prosthetic Appliances
Dental Laboratories

BRANDS/DIVISIONS/AFFILIATES:

GDC Holdings Inc
GeoDigm Corporation
nSequence

CONTACTS: *Note: Officers with more than one job title may be intentionally listed here more than once.*

Steven E. Casper, CEO
Steven E. Casper, Pres.
Corey M. Benish, Chief Strategy Officer

GROWTH PLANS/SPECIAL FEATURES:

National Dentex Corporation (NDX) designs, manufactures, markets and sells dental restoration products and related appliances. NDX products offer a full spectrum of innovative restorative solutions such as crowns, bridges, dentures, partial dentures, implants, abutments, bite guards, retainers, bleaching trays, sleep apnea treatments, retainers and maintainers, and more. Services include consultation and digital transformation offerings for practices, including dental programs, data plans and equipment. NDX comprises a major dental lab network with more than 30 labs. These labs include local dental labs, which build partnerships locally in order to provide consultative, high-quality products and services to local dental practices; national dental labs, providing a range of restoration products to dentists throughout the U.S.; aesthetic dental labs, which employs artisans and craftsmen that leverage the latest advancements in dentistry to support demanding dental practices; and advanced technology labs, which offer cutting-edge surgical guides and digital preparation services such as the nSequence guided prosthesis, which combines a proprietary 3D digital workflow with patient-specific surgical guides for implant restoration procedures. NDX operates as a subsidiary of GeoDigm Corporation, itself a subsidiary of GDC Holdings, Inc.

The company offers its employees medical and dental insurance, educational assistance, dependent care flexible spending accounts, a 401(k) and life insurance.

FINANCIAL DATA: *Note: Data for latest year may not have been available at press time.*

In U.S. $	2017	2016	2015	2014	2013	2012
Revenue						
R&D Expense						
Operating Income						
Operating Margin %						
SGA Expense						
Net Income						
Operating Cash Flow						
Capital Expenditure						
EBITDA						
Return on Assets %						
Return on Equity %						
Debt to Equity						

CONTACT INFORMATION:

Phone: 877-942-5871 Fax:
Toll-Free: 800-678-4140
Address: 11601 Kew Gardens, Ste. 200, Palm Beach Gardens, FL 33410 United States

STOCK TICKER/OTHER:

Stock Ticker: Subsidiary
Employees:
Parent Company: GDC Holdings Inc
Exchange:
Fiscal Year Ends: 12/31

SALARIES/BONUSES:

Top Exec. Salary: $ Bonus: $
Second Exec. Salary: $ Bonus: $

OTHER THOUGHTS:

Estimated Female Officers or Directors: 1
Hot Spot for Advancement for Women/Minorities:

National HealthCare Corporation

www.nhccare.com

NAIC Code: 623,110

TYPES OF BUSINESS:

Nursing Care Facilities
Rehabilitative Services
Medical Specialty Units
Pharmacy Operations
Assisted Living Projects
Managed Care Contracts
Nutritional Support Services
Real Estate

BRANDS/DIVISIONS/AFFILIATES:

Caris Healthcare LP

CONTACTS: *Note: Officers with more than one job title may be intentionally listed here more than once.*

Brian Kidd, Chief Accounting Officer
B. Anderson Flatt, Chief Information Officer
Mike Ussery, COO
Stephen Flatt, Director
Robert Adams, Director
John Lines, General Counsel
Julia Powell, Other Executive Officer
Leroy McIntosh, Senior VP, Divisional
Jeffrey Smith, Senior VP

GROWTH PLANS/SPECIAL FEATURES:

National HealthCare Corporation (NHC) operates long-term healthcare centers and home healthcare programs in 10 states. NHC's health services include long-term healthcare centers, rehabilitative services, medical specialty units, pharmacy operations, assisted living projects, managed care contracts, hospice programs and homecare programs. As of August 2018, the firm services approximately 76 skilled nursing facilities (9,597 beds) which include 68 centers with 8,682 beds that are leased or owned and eight facilities with 915 beds that are managed for others. NHC also operates or manages 24 assisted living centers that have a total of 1,132 units; five independent living centers that consist of 475 retirement apartments; and 36 homecare programs licensed in four states (Tennessee, South Carolina, Missouri and Florida). The company's care centers provide in-patient skilled and intermediate nursing care services and in-patient and out-patient rehabilitation services. Its centers also provide rehabilitative care, including physical, occupational and speech therapies. Skilled nursing care consists of 24-hour nursing service by registered or licensed practical nurses and intermediate nursing care by non-licensed personnel. Most of the company's retirement centers are constructed adjacent to NHC's healthcare properties. It operates specialized care units such as Alzheimer's disease care units, sub-acute nursing units and a number of in-house pharmacies. In addition, NHC has a partnership agreement and a 75.1% non-controlling ownership interest in Caris Healthcare, LP, which specializes in hospice care services in NHC-owned healthcare centers and in other settings. Caris provides care to more than 1,000 patients each day in 29 locations within Georgia, Missouri, South Carolina, Tennessee and Virginia. Apart from its healthcare services, NHC is engaged in management, accounting and financial services; nutritional support services; advisory services; and insurance services.

FINANCIAL DATA: *Note: Data for latest year may not have been available at press time.*

In U.S. $	2017	2016	2015	2014	2013	2012
Revenue	966,996,000	926,638,000	906,622,000	871,683,000	788,957,000	761,262,000
R&D Expense						
Operating Income	59,000,000	64,483,000	69,734,000	70,176,000	72,412,000	66,490,000
Operating Margin %	6.10%	6.95%	7.69%	8.05%	9.17%	8.73%
SGA Expense	612,410,000	589,299,000	572,702,000	39,731,000	39,449,000	39,355,000
Net Income	56,205,000	50,538,000	53,143,000	53,369,000	64,613,000	57,957,000
Operating Cash Flow	94,466,000	90,882,000	73,963,000	75,694,000	102,348,000	64,693,000
Capital Expenditure	32,347,000	62,601,000	58,416,000	53,298,000	43,438,000	22,003,000
EBITDA	122,091,000	123,171,000	124,996,000	121,742,000	131,054,000	121,527,000
Return on Assets %	5.14%	4.73%	4.37%	4.35%	5.88%	5.51%
Return on Equity %	8.19%	7.77%	7.75%	8.26%	11.11%	10.59%
Debt to Equity	0.17	0.21	0.23	0.07	0.01	0.02

CONTACT INFORMATION:

Phone: 615 890-2020 Fax: 615 890-0123
Toll-Free:
Address: 100 Vine St., Murfreesboro, TN 37130 United States

STOCK TICKER/OTHER:

Stock Ticker: NHC
Employees: 14,450
Parent Company:
Exchange: ASE
Fiscal Year Ends: 12/31

SALARIES/BONUSES:

Top Exec. Salary: $144,528 Bonus: $860,000
Second Exec. Salary: $335,893 Bonus: $249,000

OTHER THOUGHTS:

Estimated Female Officers or Directors: 2
Hot Spot for Advancement for Women/Minorities: Y

National Healthcare Group Pte Ltd

corp.nhg.com.sg

NAIC Code: 622,110

TYPES OF BUSINESS:

General Medical and Surgical Hospitals
Psychiatric and Substance Abuse Hospitals
Medical and Diagnostic Laboratories
Medical School
College
Esthetician (i.e., Skin Care) Services
Pharmacies and Drug Stores

BRANDS/DIVISIONS/AFFILIATES:

Tan Tock Seng Hospital
Khoo Teck Puat
Institute of Mental Health
National Healthcare Group Polyclinics
National Skin Centre
NHG College
Primary Care Academy
Admiralty Medical Centre

CONTACTS: *Note: Officers with more than one job title may be intentionally listed here more than once.*

Philip Choo, CEO
Lim Yee Juan, CFO
Olivia Tay, Chief Human Resources Officer
Ho Khai Leng, CIO
Kay Kuok, Chmn.

GROWTH PLANS/SPECIAL FEATURES:

National Healthcare Group Pte. Ltd. (NHG), based in Singapore, is a group of health care institutions composed of multiple divisions. The Tan Tock Seng Hospital is Singapore's second largest acute care general hospital with over 1,500 beds. Khoo Teck Puat Hospital is a 590-bed general and acute care hospital. Yishun Community Hospital is a 428-bed hospital that provides intermediate care for recuperating patients who do not require intensive care services. The Institute of Mental Health is a 2,000-bed acute tertiary psychiatric hospital that offers a comprehensive range of psychiatric, rehabilitative and counselling services for children, adolescents, adults and the elderly. The National Healthcare Group Polyclinics, the primary health care arm of the NHG, has nine polyclinics that serve a significant proportion of the population in the central, northern and western parts of Singapore. The National Skin Centre is an outpatient specialist dermatological center that cares for about 1,000 patients daily. NHG College, with programs in the fields of leadership, clinical education, health care and risk management, develops the talent for NHG. NHG Diagnostics provides laboratory and radiography services in primary health care, with an extensive network of tele-radiology and professional service for imaging centers. NHG Pharmacy manages the pharmacy and retail pharmacies of NHG's nine polyclinics. Primary Care Academy provides the training needs and skills upgrading of primary care doctors, nurses, allied health professionals and ancillary staff in Singapore and the region. Johns Hopkins Singapore International Medical Centre, located in Tan Tock Hospital, provides outpatient diagnostic and consultation services, screening programs, expert second opinions and inpatient care focusing on treatment of various cancers. Admiralty Medical Centre provides specialized outpatient consultations, day surgery procedures and endoscopies.

FINANCIAL DATA: *Note: Data for latest year may not have been available at press time.*

In U.S. $	2017	2016	2015	2014	2013	2012
Revenue	1,601,250,000	1,525,000,000	1,498,089,174	1,374,743,402		
R&D Expense						
Operating Income						
Operating Margin %						
SGA Expense						
Net Income						
Operating Cash Flow						
Capital Expenditure						
EBITDA						
Return on Assets %						
Return on Equity %						
Debt to Equity						

CONTACT INFORMATION:

Phone: 65-6496-6000 Fax: 65-6496-6870
Toll-Free:
Address: 3 Fusionopolis Link #03-08, Nexus@one-north, Singapore, 138543 Singapore

STOCK TICKER/OTHER:

Stock Ticker: Government-Owned
Employees: 12,500
Parent Company:
Exchange:
Fiscal Year Ends: 03/31

SALARIES/BONUSES:

Top Exec. Salary: $ Bonus: $
Second Exec. Salary: $ Bonus: $

OTHER THOUGHTS:

Estimated Female Officers or Directors:
Hot Spot for Advancement for Women/Minorities:

National Home Health Care Corp

www.nhhc.net

NAIC Code: 621,610

TYPES OF BUSINESS:

Home Health Care Services
Disease Management Services
Physical, Occupational & Speech Therapies
Staffing Services
Medical Social Services
Mental Health Services

BRANDS/DIVISIONS/AFFILIATES:

Blue Wolf Capital Partners LLC
Allen Health Care Services
New England Home Care Inc
Accredited Health Services Inc
Medical Resources Home Health Corp

CONTACTS: *Note: Officers with more than one job title may be intentionally listed here more than once.*

G. Scott Herman, CEO
Steven Fialkow, Pres.
Steven Fialkow, Corp. Sec.
R. Scott Gasset, Chief Bus. Dev. & Strategic Officer
Robert P. Heller, VP-Finance

GROWTH PLANS/SPECIAL FEATURES:

National Home Health Care Corp. (NHHC) is a provider of home health care services. NHHC provides home health care services including monitoring, interventions and medication administration by registered nurses; technical procedures and medical dressing changes by licensed practical nurses; muscle strengthening and restoration of range of motion by physical and occupational therapists; communication and oral skill restoration by speech pathologists; acute and chronic illness assistance by medical social workers; personal care such as bathing assistance by home health aides; and private duty services such as continuous hourly nursing care and sitter services. The company has four principal operating subsidiaries: Allen Health Care Services (in New York); New England Home Care, Inc. (Connecticut); Accredited Health Services, Inc. (New Jersey); and Medical Resources Home Health Corp. (Massachusetts). Allen Health Care Services provides registered nurses, personal care aides, home health aides and homemakers. New England Home Care provides full-service home health care 24 hours a day, seven days a week. The company also offers specialty services such as adult/geriatric, pediatric, post-acute rehabilitation and behavioral health. Accredited Health Services and Medical Resources Home Health Corp. provide home health care to seniors and disabled individuals. NHHC is owned by private equity firm, Blue Wolf Capital Partners, LLC. In April 2018, NHHC announced that parent Wolf Capital was going to partner with Kelso & Company to merge NHHC, Great Lakes Caring and Jordan Health Services, forming one of the largest providers of home-based care in the U.S.

FINANCIAL DATA: *Note: Data for latest year may not have been available at press time.*

In U.S. $	2017	2016	2015	2014	2013	2012
Revenue						
R&D Expense						
Operating Income						
Operating Margin %						
SGA Expense						
Net Income						
Operating Cash Flow						
Capital Expenditure						
EBITDA						
Return on Assets %						
Return on Equity %						
Debt to Equity						

CONTACT INFORMATION:

Phone: Fax: 860-613-3304
Toll-Free: 800-286-6300
Address: 136 Berlin Rd., Cromwell, CT 06416 United States

STOCK TICKER/OTHER:

Stock Ticker: Private Exchange:
Employees: 4,600 Fiscal Year Ends: 07/31
Parent Company: Blue Wolf Capital Partners LLC

SALARIES/BONUSES:

Top Exec. Salary: $ Bonus: $
Second Exec. Salary: $ Bonus: $

OTHER THOUGHTS:

Estimated Female Officers or Directors:
Hot Spot for Advancement for Women/Minorities:

National University Health System (NUHS)

www.nuhs.edu.sg

NAIC Code: 622,110

TYPES OF BUSINESS:

General Medical and Surgical Hospitals
Medical School
Dental School
Colleges, Universities and Professional Schools

BRANDS/DIVISIONS/AFFILIATES:

National University of Singapore
MOH Holdings Pte Ltd
National University Hospital
Ng Teng Fong General Hospital
Jurong Community Hospital
Alexandra Hospital
National University Cancer Institute
NUS Faculty of Dentistry

CONTACTS: *Note: Officers with more than one job title may be intentionally listed here more than once.*

Tan Chorh Chuan, Chmn.

GROWTH PLANS/SPECIAL FEATURES:

National University Health System (NUHS) is an integrated academic health system and regional health organization in Singapore. The firm was established as a joint venture between the National University of Singapore and MOH Holdings Pte Ltd. Its hospitals include National University Hospital, Ng Teng Fong General Hospital, Jurong Community Hospital and Alexandra Hospital. NUH is a 1,200-bed tertiary hospital; Ng Teng and Jurong Community are an integrated healthcare development delivering patient-centered services in a seamless manner; and Alexandra offers integrated continuum care via programs, health informatics and technology in collaboration with NUHS and community partners. National specialty centers include: National University Cancer Institute, which offers cancer care and management; National University Heart Centre, which offers cardiology, cardiothoracic and vascular surgery services for patients with heart disease; and National University Centre for Oral Health, which will be completed in 2019, and will offer oral health services to elderly patients and those with special needs. Other facilities include the National University Polyclinics (clinics), and Jurong Medical Centre (medical center). Last, academic health sciences institutions include NUS Yong Loo Lin School of Medicine, NUS Faculty of Dentistry, and NUS Saw Swee Hock School of Public Health.

FINANCIAL DATA: *Note: Data for latest year may not have been available at press time.*

In U.S. $	2017	2016	2015	2014	2013	2012
Revenue						
R&D Expense						
Operating Income						
Operating Margin %						
SGA Expense						
Net Income						
Operating Cash Flow						
Capital Expenditure						
EBITDA						
Return on Assets %						
Return on Equity %						
Debt to Equity						

CONTACT INFORMATION:

Phone: 65-6779-5555 Fax: 65-6775-0913
Toll-Free:
Address: 1E Kent Ridge Rd., Singapore, 119228 Singapore

STOCK TICKER/OTHER:

Stock Ticker: Joint Venture Exchange:
Employees: 9,000 Fiscal Year Ends:
Parent Company: National University of Singapore

SALARIES/BONUSES:

Top Exec. Salary: $ Bonus: $
Second Exec. Salary: $ Bonus: $

OTHER THOUGHTS:

Estimated Female Officers or Directors:
Hot Spot for Advancement for Women/Minorities:

Natus Medical Incorporated

www.natus.com

NAIC Code: 339,100

TYPES OF BUSINESS:

Medical Diagnostics Manufacturer
Newborn Care Products

BRANDS/DIVISIONS/AFFILIATES:

Aurical
ICS
Madsen

CONTACTS:

Note: Officers with more than one job title may be intentionally listed here more than once.

Carsten Buhl, CEO, Divisional
James Hawkins, CEO
Jonathan Kennedy, CFO
Robert Gunst, Chairman of the Board
William Moore, Co-Founder
Austin Noll, General Manager, Divisional
Leslie McDonnell, General Manager, Divisional
D. Chung, Vice President, Divisional

GROWTH PLANS/SPECIAL FEATURES:

Natus Medical Incorporated is a provider of health care products used for the screening, detection, treatment, monitoring and tracking of common medical ailments in newborns. These ailments are associated with newborn care, hearing impairment, neurological dysfunction, epilepsy, sleep disorders and balance and mobility disorders. Natus divides its products into three categories: neurology, newborn care and otometrics. The neurology segment is made up of five lines of products: electroencephalography equipment and supplies used to monitor and visually display the electrical activity generated by nerve cells in the brain and other key physiological signals for diagnosis and monitoring of neurological disorders; electromyography equipment and supplies used to measure electrical activity in the nerves, muscles, brain and spinal cord; polysomnography equipment and supplies used to measure a variety of respiratory and physiologic function to assist in the diagnosis and monitoring of sleep disorders; intraoperative monitoring products and supplies used to assist surgeons and neurophysiologists in preserving the functional integrity of a patient's nervous system before and after surgery; and transcranial doppler ultrasound technology, which assists clinicians in evaluating the integrity of blood flow in the brain. The newborn care segment offers newborn hearing screening as well as newborn brain injury products to diagnose brain injury, monitor drug therapies and treat the injury. Last, the otometrics category includes products and services such as computer-based audiological, otoneurologic and vestibular instrumentation and sound rooms for hearing and balance care professionals worldwide. Its global brands of otometric products include Aurical, ICS and Madsen. In late-2017, Natus acquired certain neurosurgery business assets from Integra LifeSciences, including a monitoring product line, a manufacturing facility and the U.S. rights relating to Integra's fixed pressure shunts and to Codman's DURAFORM dual graft implant, catheters and collection systems.

FINANCIAL DATA:

Note: Data for latest year may not have been available at press time.

In U.S. $	2017	2016	2015	2014	2013	2012
Revenue	500,970,000	381,892,000	375,865,000	355,834,000	344,112,000	292,280,000
R&D Expense	51,822,000	33,443,000	30,434,000	31,788,000	32,073,000	29,966,000
Operating Income	9,631,000	56,796,000	55,618,000	45,851,000	34,279,000	5,254,000
Operating Margin %	1.92%	14.87%	14.79%	12.88%	9.96%	1.79%
SGA Expense	200,590,000	135,711,000	134,038,000	136,748,000	135,679,000	128,248,000
Net Income	-20,293,000	42,594,000	37,924,000	32,478,000	22,878,000	3,883,000
Operating Cash Flow	19,726,000	72,687,000	36,852,000	42,143,000	36,797,000	19,392,000
Capital Expenditure	4,066,000	3,396,000	5,194,000	5,720,000	3,700,000	7,340,000
EBITDA	40,329,000	72,212,000	68,748,000	57,610,000	46,086,000	17,523,000
Return on Assets %	-2.98%	7.54%	8.29%	7.54%	5.59%	1.09%
Return on Equity %	-4.83%	10.54%	10.20%	9.85%	7.95%	1.47%
Debt to Equity	0.36	0.33			0.08	0.04

CONTACT INFORMATION:

Phone: 925-223-6700 Fax:
Toll-Free: 800-255-3901
Address: 6701 Knoll Center Pkwy., Ste. 120, Pleasanton, CA 94566 United States

STOCK TICKER/OTHER:

Stock Ticker: BABY
Employees: 1,160
Parent Company:
Exchange: NAS
Fiscal Year Ends: 12/31

SALARIES/BONUSES:

Top Exec. Salary: $750,000 Bonus: $
Second Exec. Salary: $440,000 Bonus: $

OTHER THOUGHTS:

Estimated Female Officers or Directors: 1
Hot Spot for Advancement for Women/Minorities:

Netcare Limited

www.netcareinvestor.co.za

NAIC Code: 622,110

TYPES OF BUSINESS:

General Medical and Surgical Hospitals

BRANDS/DIVISIONS/AFFILIATES:

Medicross
Netcare 911
National Renal Care
Akeso
Tsepong

CONTACTS:
Note: Officers with more than one job title may be intentionally listed here more than once.

Richard Friedland, CEO
Keith Gibson, CFO
Duncan Empey, Dir.-Medical
Lynelle Bagwandeen, General Counsel
Melanie Da Costa, Dir.-Strategy & Health Policy
Kerishnie Naiker, Dir.-Comm.
Craig Lovelace, CFO-U.K.
Jacques du Plessis, Managing Dir.-Hospitals
Elaine Young, Managing Dir.-Hospitals, U.K.
Tumi Nkosi, Dir.-Bus. Dev. & Corp. Affairs
Charmaine Pailman, Managing Dir.-Primary Care
Thevendrie Brewer, Chmn.
Stephen Collier, CEO-U.K.

GROWTH PLANS/SPECIAL FEATURES:

Netcare Limited is a holding company that operates through subsidiaries to invest in and support healthcare systems throughout South Africa. The firm also invests in innovative and advanced medical technologies and related solutions. Netcare operates the largest private hospital, primary healthcare, emergency medical services and renal care networks in South Africa. Together, the group offers primary health care, sub-acute care, day surgery, occupational health and employee wellness services through Medicross. It offers emergency medical services through Netcare 911; renal dialysis through National Renal Care; and mental health and psychiatric services through Akeso. Netcare also provides private training for personnel engaged in emergency medical and nursing services. As of August 2018, Netcare's network comprised 54 hospitals, 10 cancer care centers, 63 renal dialysis units with 860 dialysis stations, 95 primary healthcare centers, 79 Netcare 911 emergency sites, 12 mental health/psychiatric clinics, seven training campuses and more. Majority-owned Tsepong, based in Lesotho, is engaged in a public private partnership (PPP) with the national government. Tsepong provides clinical services in a 425-bed hospital, and provides primary health care services at three filter clinics and a gateway clinic. It also manages these facilities.

FINANCIAL DATA:
Note: Data for latest year may not have been available at press time.

In U.S. $	2017	2016	2015	2014	2013	2012
Revenue						
R&D Expense						
Operating Income						
Operating Margin %						
SGA Expense						
Net Income						
Operating Cash Flow						
Capital Expenditure						
EBITDA						
Return on Assets %						
Return on Equity %						
Debt to Equity						

CONTACT INFORMATION:

Phone: 27 113010000 Fax: 27 113010499
Toll-Free:
Address: 76 Maude St., Corner West St., Sandown, Sandton 2196 South Africa

STOCK TICKER/OTHER:

Stock Ticker: NWKHY
Employees: 30,056
Parent Company:
Exchange: PINX
Fiscal Year Ends: 09/30

SALARIES/BONUSES:

Top Exec. Salary: $ Bonus: $
Second Exec. Salary: $ Bonus: $

OTHER THOUGHTS:

Estimated Female Officers or Directors: 7
Hot Spot for Advancement for Women/Minorities: Y

New York City Health and Hospitals Corporation

www.nyc.gov/html/hhc

NAIC Code: 622,110

TYPES OF BUSINESS:

General Medical and Surgical Hospitals
Community Health Clinics
HMO
Long-Term Care Facilities
Home Health Care
Correctional Facility Health Services

BRANDS/DIVISIONS/AFFILIATES:

MetroPlus
OneCity Health

CONTACTS:

Note: Officers with more than one job title may be intentionally listed here more than once.

Mitchell Katz, CEO
Alan D. Aviles, Pres.
John Ulberg, CFO
Ana Marengo, Sr. VP-Mktg. & Communications
Ross Wilson, Sr. VP-Quality
Kevin Lynch, CIO
Salvatore J. Russo, Corp. General Counsel
LaRay Brown, Sr. VP-Corp. Planning & Community Health
Ana Marengo, Sr. VP-Corp. Comm.
Marlene Zurack, Sr. VP-Finance
Tamiru Mammo, Chief of Staff
Caroline M. Jacobs, Sr. VP-Safety & Human Dev.
Joanna Omi, Sr. VP-Organizational Innovation & Effectiveness
Lynda D. Curtis, Sr. VP-South Manhattan Health Care Network
Gordon J. Campbell, Chmn.

GROWTH PLANS/SPECIAL FEATURES:

New York City Health and Hospitals Corporation (HHC) provides health care to all five boroughs of New York. The company operates 11 acute care hospitals, as well as primary and preventative care facilities. Services offered by the group include child health, adolescent health, alcohol/drug dependency, asthma care, bariatric, behavioral/mental health, burn, cancer, cardiology, colon cancer screening, dental, diabetes, flu vaccination, geriatric, HIV/AIDS, HPV vaccine, language/translation, mammograms, neonatal intensive care, obstetrics/gynecology, palliative care, Parkinson's Disease, pediatrics, quit smoking, rehab, sexual response assault teams, sickle cell disease, sleep disorder labs, stroke prevention/care, telehealth initiatives, trauma centers, vision care, women's health and environmental health. If it is difficult for patients to leave home due to age, chronic condition or other, HHC provides health care services to patients at their homes to residents of Manhattan, Queens, Brooklyn and the Bronx. In addition, MetroPlus is HHC's health plan that offers low to no-cost health insurance to eligible people living in Manhattan, Brooklyn, Queens, Staten Island and the Bronx. OneCity Health is the NYC Health + Hospitals-sponsored performing provider system (PPS), designed to reduce avoidable and unnecessary hospital stays. OneCity Health comprises hundreds of health care providers and community-based organizations who work together to keep their communities healthy. HHC's long-term care facilities provide 24-hour care for its patients.

FINANCIAL DATA:

Note: Data for latest year may not have been available at press time.

In U.S. $	2017	2016	2015	2014	2013	2012
Revenue	7,293,634,000	7,682,559,000	6,457,731,000	6,389,047,000	7,469,345,389	7,113,154,000
R&D Expense						
Operating Income						
Operating Margin %						
SGA Expense						
Net Income		40,145,000	-58,062,000	-92,680,000	-76,809,112	-433,938,000
Operating Cash Flow						
Capital Expenditure						
EBITDA						
Return on Assets %						
Return on Equity %						
Debt to Equity						

CONTACT INFORMATION:

Phone: 212-788-3321 Fax: 212-788-0040
Toll-Free:
Address: 125 Worth St., New York, NY 10013 United States

STOCK TICKER/OTHER:

Stock Ticker: Nonprofit
Employees: 34,891
Parent Company:
Exchange:
Fiscal Year Ends: 06/30

SALARIES/BONUSES:

Top Exec. Salary: $ Bonus: $
Second Exec. Salary: $ Bonus: $

OTHER THOUGHTS:

Estimated Female Officers or Directors: 6
Hot Spot for Advancement for Women/Minorities: Y

New York Health Care Inc

NAIC Code: 621,610

www.nyhc.com

TYPES OF BUSINESS:

Home Health Care Services
Home Health Care
Prenatal and Postnatal Care
Dementia and Alzheimer's
Infusion Therapy

BRANDS/DIVISIONS/AFFILIATES:

CONTACTS:

Note: Officers with more than one job title may be intentionally listed here more than once.

Murry Englard, CEO
Glen Persaud, Dir.-Human Resources

GROWTH PLANS/SPECIAL FEATURES:

New York Health Care, Inc. (NYHC) is a health care company that delivers home healthcare services to all ages, including the elderly. The firm provides companionship services, pediatric nurses, home health aides, licensed practical nurses, geriatric care and infusion therapy nurses. The company's services include medication reminders, meal preparation, light housekeeping, household organization and tasks, accompaniment to medical appointments/family gatherings/senior centers, socialization, pre- and post-surgery transportation, mental cueing, safety supervision, and more. Baby nurses assist with breastfeeding/lactation support, prenatal/postnatal care, nighttime feedings, promoting healthy feeding habits and sleep environments, bathing and dressing the newborn, sterilization of nursery items and supporting parents with regards to infant care. NYHC uses music to encourage social interaction, brain stimulation, communication and verbal expression for patients with dementia or Alzheimer's. NYHC brings assistance to the client's home, senior residences and assisted living facilities as well as to hospitals. In addition, the firm is approved by the New York State Department of Health to provide consumer directed personal assistance services (CDPAP), a statewide Medicaid program that offers an alternative way of receiving home care services where the consumer has more control over who provides their care and how it is provided. The firm covers Brooklyn, Bronx, Queens, Manhattan, Staten Island, Nassau, Suffolk, Westchester, Rockland and Orange Counties.

FINANCIAL DATA:

Note: Data for latest year may not have been available at press time.

In U.S. $	2017	2016	2015	2014	2013	2012
Revenue						
R&D Expense						
Operating Income						
Operating Margin %						
SGA Expense						
Net Income						
Operating Cash Flow						
Capital Expenditure						
EBITDA						
Return on Assets %						
Return on Equity %						
Debt to Equity						

CONTACT INFORMATION:

Phone: 718-375-6700 Fax: 718-375-1555
Toll-Free: 888-978-6942
Address: 33 West Hawthorne Ave, 3/Fl, Valley Stream, NY 11581 United States

STOCK TICKER/OTHER:

Stock Ticker: BBAL
Employees: 1,460
Parent Company:
Exchange: PINX
Fiscal Year Ends: 12/31

SALARIES/BONUSES:

Top Exec. Salary: $ Bonus: $
Second Exec. Salary: $ Bonus: $

OTHER THOUGHTS:

Estimated Female Officers or Directors:
Hot Spot for Advancement for Women/Minorities:

NewYork-Presbyterian Healthcare System

www.nyp.org/

NAIC Code: 622,110

TYPES OF BUSINESS:

General Medical and Surgical Hospitals
Nursing Homes
Rehabilitation Centers

BRANDS/DIVISIONS/AFFILIATES:

NewYork-Presbyterian Hospital
NewYork-Presbyterian/Weill Cornell Medical Center
NewYork-Presbyterian/The Allen Hospital
NewYork-Presbyterian/Lower Manhattan Hospital
NewYork-Presbyterian/Westchester Division
NewYork-Presbyterian/Lawrence Hospital
NewYork-Presbyterian/Hudson Valley Hospital
NewYork-Presbyterian/Queens

CONTACTS: *Note: Officers with more than one job title may be intentionally listed here more than once.*

Steven J. Corwin, CEO
Laura L. Forese, Exec. VP
Phyllis R. Lantos, Exec. VP
Kimlee Roldan-Sanchez, Chief Admin. Officer
Gary J. Zuar, Sr. VP-Finance
Wilhelmina Manzano, Chief Nursing Officer
Eric Vorenkamp, VP-Insurance
Eliot J. Lazar, Chief Quality & Patient Safety Officer
Lori MacDonald, VP-Internal Audit & Corp. Compliance
Frank A. Bennack, Chmn.

GROWTH PLANS/SPECIAL FEATURES:

NewYork-Presbyterian Healthcare System is a comprehensive, integrated academic health care delivery system. The organization collaborates with two renowned medical schools, Weill Cornell Medicine and Columbia University College of Physicians and Surgeons, to provide medical education, groundbreaking research, as well as patient-centered clinical care. NewYork-Presbyterian is organized into four divisions: hospital, regional hospital network, physician's services and community/population health. The hospital division comprises NewYork-Presbyterian Hospital, an academic center committed to patient care, research, education and community services. The hospital serves more than 2 million visits annually. This division comprises seven campuses: NewYork-Presbyterian/Columbia University Medical Center, NewYork-Presbyterian/Weill Cornell Medical Center, NewYork-Presbyterian/The Allen Hospital, NewYork-Presbyterian/Lawrence Hospital, NewYork-Presbyterian/Morgan Stanley Children's Hospital, NewYork-Presbyterian/Lower Manhattan Hospital and NewYork-Presbyterian/Westchester Division. The regional hospital network division comprises regional hospitals in the New York metropolitan region: NewYork-Presbyterian/Brooklyn Methodist Hospital, NewYork-Presbyterian/Hudson Valley Hospital and NewYork-Presbyterian/Queens. The physician's services division connects medical experts with patients in their communities in order to expand coordinated healthcare delivery across the region. This segment includes the NewYork-Presbyterian medical groups in Westchester, Queens and Brooklyn in collaboration with Weill Cornell and ColumbiaDoctors. Last, the community/population health division comprises ambulatory care network sites and community healthcare initiatives.

FINANCIAL DATA: *Note: Data for latest year may not have been available at press time.*

In U.S. $	2017	2016	2015	2014	2013	2012
Revenue	5,600,000,000	5,200,000,000	4,800,000,000	4,500,000,000	4,264,510,000	3,880,000,000
R&D Expense						
Operating Income						
Operating Margin %						
SGA Expense						
Net Income			303,171,000	378,392,000	356,108,000	325,900,000
Operating Cash Flow						
Capital Expenditure						
EBITDA						
Return on Assets %						
Return on Equity %						
Debt to Equity						

CONTACT INFORMATION:

Phone: 646-962-2357 Fax: 212-746-8235
Toll-Free: 877-697-9355
Address: 520 E. 70th St., New York, NY 10021 United States

STOCK TICKER/OTHER:

Stock Ticker: Nonprofit
Employees: 24,586
Parent Company:
Exchange:
Fiscal Year Ends: 12/31

SALARIES/BONUSES:

Top Exec. Salary: $ Bonus: $
Second Exec. Salary: $ Bonus: $

OTHER THOUGHTS:

Estimated Female Officers or Directors: 5
Hot Spot for Advancement for Women/Minorities: Y

NMI Health Inc

nmihealth.com

NAIC Code: 339,100

TYPES OF BUSINESS:

Medical Equipment-Anti-Contamination
Facemasks
Nanotechnology
Anti-Microbial Fabrics

BRANDS/DIVISIONS/AFFILIATES:

SilverCare Plus
X-Static

CONTACTS:

Note: Officers with more than one job title may be intentionally listed here more than once.

Edward J. Suydam, CEO
Edward J. Suydam, Pres.
Michael J. Marx, CFO
Marc L. Khan, Chief Medical Officer

GROWTH PLANS/SPECIAL FEATURES:

NMI Health, Inc. is a healthcare product development and distribution company providing innovative infection prevention medical textiles and fabrics to a variety of healthcare-related markets. The firm has evolved from a specialty filter producer that developed a state-of-the-art air filtration technology for removing infectious bacteria and viruses in air flow systems into a provider of innovative infection prevention products and solutions. Hospital associated infections, also known as nosocomial infections, are the fourth leading cause of death in the U.S., behind cancer, heart disease and strokes. Nosocomial infections first appear between 48 hours and four days after a patient is admitted to a health care facility, and normally occur in the urinary tract, a surgical site, the lungs or bloodstream. Soft surfaces fabrics play an important role in the transmission of bacteria in the health care setting, causing recontamination during frequent contact. Laundering alone is not effective at addressing this challenge because fabrics begin to re-contaminate immediately after use. NMI's SilverCare Plus antimicrobial performance fabrics are specifically designed to reduce both soft surface contamination and lateral transmission of bacteria from and between patients, visitors and health care personnel. SilverCare Plus with X-Static eliminates 99.9% of bacteria directly on the fabric, providing ongoing, comprehensive and proactive anti-microbial performance. NMI's products include medical scrubs, lab coats, patient gowns, privacy curtains, bed sheets and blankets.

FINANCIAL DATA:

Note: Data for latest year may not have been available at press time.

In U.S. $	2017	2016	2015	2014	2013	2012
Revenue	588,000	560,000	544,506	454,513	235,291	454,513
R&D Expense						
Operating Income						
Operating Margin %						
SGA Expense						
Net Income				-831,119	-425,930	-831,119
Operating Cash Flow						
Capital Expenditure						
EBITDA						
Return on Assets %						
Return on Equity %						
Debt to Equity						

CONTACT INFORMATION:

Phone: 914-760-7857 Fax: 845-223-1882
Toll-Free:
Address: 50 W. Liberty, Ste. 880, Reno, NV 89501 United States

STOCK TICKER/OTHER:

Stock Ticker: Private
Employees: 4
Parent Company:
Exchange:
Fiscal Year Ends: 12/31

SALARIES/BONUSES:

Top Exec. Salary: $ Bonus: $
Second Exec. Salary: $ Bonus: $

OTHER THOUGHTS:

Estimated Female Officers or Directors:
Hot Spot for Advancement for Women/Minorities:

Nobel Biocare Holding AG

www.nobelbiocare.com

NAIC Code: 339,100

TYPES OF BUSINESS:

Dental Equipment and Supplies Manufacturing

BRANDS/DIVISIONS/AFFILIATES:

Danaher Corporation
NobelActive
NobelParallel CC
NobelReplace
Branemark System
NobelZygoma
NobelProcera
creos

CONTACTS: *Note: Officers with more than one job title may be intentionally listed here more than once.*

Hans Geiselhoringer, Pres.
Victor Nieto, VP-Global Operations
Howard Yu, CFO
Rikke Tengberg, VP-Human Resources
Hans Geiselhoringer, Exec. VP-Research, Products & Dev.
Jorg von Manger-Koenig, Sr. VP-Legal & Compliance
Frank Mengis, Sr. VP-Global Oper.
Petra Rumpf, Exec. VP-Corp. Dev.
Melker Nilsson, Exec. VP-Global Customer & Sales Dev.
Philip Bernard Whitehead, Chmn.

GROWTH PLANS/SPECIAL FEATURES:

Nobel Biocare Holding AG is a global dental medical devices group. The firm provides innovative restorative and aesthetic dental solutions including dental implant systems, prosthetics, computer-aided design and computer-aided manufacturing (CAD/CAM) systems. It also offers treatment planning, guided surgery solutions and biomaterials. Implant systems include NobelActive, which provides stability even in compromised bone situations; NobelParallel CC, providing a conical connection that offers flexibility; NobelReplace, which comprises a tapered dental implant body with a tight sealed connection; Nobel Speedy, designed for under-preparation and bicortical anchorage; Branemark System, comprising lengths from 7 to 52.5 millimeters; and NobelZygoma, comprising zygomatic (malar bone/cheek bone) prosthetic flexibility. Prosthetic solutions include CAD/CAM with NobelProcera, as well as prefabricated abutments, screws and crowns, fixed implant restorations, fixed-removable implant restorations and bridges. Other restorative solutions for guided bone and tissue regeneration include creos xenoprotect re-absorbable porcine collagen membrane, which provides handling properties and barrier function; creos allo.gain bone particulates for bone grafting purposes; creos allo.gain dbm putty, which is a pure allograft without any filler or inert carrier; and creos allo.protect, a re-absorbable pericardium membrane that provides a barrier during the healing process. Headquartered in Switzerland, the firm has global locations in the Americas, Asia Pacific, Europe, the Middle East and Africa. Nobel Biocare is owned by Danaher Corporation, a global science and technology innovator.

FINANCIAL DATA: *Note: Data for latest year may not have been available at press time.*

In U.S. $	2017	2016	2015	2014	2013	2012
Revenue						
R&D Expense						
Operating Income						
Operating Margin %						
SGA Expense						
Net Income						
Operating Cash Flow						
Capital Expenditure						
EBITDA						
Return on Assets %						
Return on Equity %						
Debt to Equity						

CONTACT INFORMATION:

Phone: 41 432114200 Fax: 41 432114242
Toll-Free:
Address: Balz Zimmermann-Strasse 7, Balsberg, Kloten CH-8302 Switzerland

STOCK TICKER/OTHER:

Stock Ticker: NBHGF
Employees: 2,487
Parent Company: Danaher Corporation
Exchange: PINX
Fiscal Year Ends: 12/31

SALARIES/BONUSES:

Top Exec. Salary: $ Bonus: $
Second Exec. Salary: $ Bonus: $

OTHER THOUGHTS:

Estimated Female Officers or Directors: 2
Hot Spot for Advancement for Women/Minorities:

Nobilis Health Corp

www.nobilishealth.com/

NAIC Code: 621,999

TYPES OF BUSINESS:

Healthcare Development and Management

BRANDS/DIVISIONS/AFFILIATES:

North American Spine
Migraine Treatment Centers of America
MIRI Women's Health
Onward Orthopedics
NueStep
Clarity Vein & Vascular
Hamilton Vein and Vascular
Elite Sinus Spine and Ortho LLC

CONTACTS: *Note: Officers with more than one job title may be intentionally listed here more than once.*

Harry Fleming, CEO
P. Young, CFO
Marcos Rodriguez, Chief Accounting Officer
Patrick Yoder, Other Executive Officer
Marissa Arreola, Other Executive Officer
Kenneth Efird, President

GROWTH PLANS/SPECIAL FEATURES:

Nobilis Health Corp. is a health care development and management company. The firm owns and operates more than 30 facilities located in Texas and Arizona, including Dallas, Houston, Austin, El Paso and San Antonio, Scottsdale and Phoenix, Arizona. These facilities include hospitals, ambulatory surgical centers and multi-specialty clinics. Nobilis comprises a physician partnership and patient retention strategy that maximizes return on investment, minimizes risk and reduces per-brand marketing costs. Marketing nine independent brands, Nobilis Health utilizes its proprietary, direct-to-consumer marketing technology to acquire and retain patients, with a focus on a specified set of procedures performed at its centers by local physicians. Nobilis markets nine brands and has partnered with specialized, board-certified, fellowship-trained surgeons who focus on minimally-invasive surgery. Brands of the company include: North American Spine, which offers back and neck surgeries; Migraine Treatment Centers of America, which offers a non-pharmaceutical surgical implant for the relief of chronic migraine pain; Evolve, a bariatric surgery brand to treat obesity; MIRI Women's Health, which offers surgeries for gynecological conditions and offers second opinions for those seeking an alternative to traditional hysterectomies; Onward Orthopedics, which treats non-spine joint issues for patients of all ages and types; NueStep, which provides minimally-invasive relief of foot and ankle pain due to nerve entrapment and other podiatric issues; Clarity Vein & Vascular, offering surgical treatment of painful and/or unsightly vascular conditions; Arizona Vein & Vascular Center, treating venous conditions and disorders; and Hamilton Vein and Vascular, which diagnosis and treats vein disorders. In November 2017, Nobilis Health acquired a 50.1% interest in Elite Sinus Spine and Ortho, LLC, which manages three ambulatory surgical centers in Houston, Texas.

FINANCIAL DATA: *Note: Data for latest year may not have been available at press time.*

In U.S. $	2017	2016	2015	2014	2013	2012
Revenue	299,717,000	285,744,000	229,216,000	84,029,000	31,128,000	20,897,000
R&D Expense						
Operating Income	22,309,000	10,038,000	31,650,000	20,833,000	4,676,000	5,357,000
Operating Margin %	7.44%	3.51%	13.80%	24.79%	15.02%	25.63%
SGA Expense	263,403,000	267,259,000	189,322,000	61,352,000	20,400,000	10,711,000
Net Income	3,797,000	6,449,000	50,840,000	6,720,000	1,416,000	1,199,000
Operating Cash Flow	26,390,000	1,559,000	6,715,000	4,013,000	3,488,000	4,764,000
Capital Expenditure	5,152,000	5,541,000	4,380,000	2,023,000	1,180,000	283,000
EBITDA	40,891,000	24,420,000	47,021,000	22,476,000	5,407,000	6,207,000
Return on Assets %	1.03%	2.35%	29.08%	10.32%	7.97%	10.52%
Return on Equity %	2.58%	4.78%	58.89%	23.36%	17.82%	33.65%
Debt to Equity	0.83	0.54	0.27	0.24	0.01	0.36

CONTACT INFORMATION:

Phone: 713 355-8614 Fax: 713 355-8615
Toll-Free:
Address: 11700 Katy Freeway, Ste. 300, Houston, TX 77079 United States

STOCK TICKER/OTHER:

Stock Ticker: HLTH
Employees: 900
Parent Company:
Exchange: ASE
Fiscal Year Ends: 12/31

SALARIES/BONUSES:

Top Exec. Salary: $549,038 Bonus: $
Second Exec. Salary: $395,000 Bonus: $

OTHER THOUGHTS:

Estimated Female Officers or Directors:
Hot Spot for Advancement for Women/Minorities:

Nordion (Canada) Inc

www.nordion.com/

NAIC Code: 339,100

TYPES OF BUSINESS:

Drug Discovery & Development Services
Medical Isotopes
Imaging Agents
Sterilization Products
Irradiation Systems
Health Care Product Distribution

BRANDS/DIVISIONS/AFFILIATES:

Sotera Health LLC

CONTACTS: *Note: Officers with more than one job title may be intentionally listed here more than once.*

Kevin Brooks, Pres.
Les Hockey, CFO
Leslee Tape, VP-Human Resources
Grant Gardiner, Corp. Sec.
Tamra Benjamin, VP-Public & Gov't Rel.
Jill Chitra, Sr. VP-Quality & Regulatory Affairs
Christopher Ashwood, Sr. VP-Corp. Svcs.
Tom Burnett, Gen. Mgr.-Medical Isotopes

GROWTH PLANS/SPECIAL FEATURES:

Nordion (Canada), Inc. is a global biotechnology firm providing products used for the prevention, diagnosis and treatment of disease. Nordion focuses on the development and manufacture of technologies for use in medical imaging, radiotherapeutics and radiopharmaceuticals as well as sterilization technologies for medical products and food safety. Its operations are divided into two divisions: medical isotopes and gamma technologies. The medical isotopes division supplies medical isotopes used in the diagnosis and treatment of diseases, while also offering specific treatments for various cancers, including liver cancer and non-Hodgkin's lymphoma. The gamma technologies segment's products include primarily the isotope cobalt-60, using gamma radiation to ensure the destruction of harmful micro-organisms that can reside in food and on medical equipment. Nordion manufactures state-of-the-art cobalt irradiation systems, as well as gamma irradiation systems. The firm has built 120 large-scale irradiation facilities worldwide, which are still in operation. Nordion's customers include a broad range of manufacturers of medical products such as pharmaceutical manufacturers, biotechnology companies, manufacturers of medical supplies and devices, plus academic and government institutions. Nordian is a subsidiary of Sotera Health, LLC. In April 2018, parent Sotera announced an agreement to sell Nordion's medical isotopes segment to BWX Technologies, Inc. That same month, Nordion announced plans to develop a new research reactor-based source of molybdenum 99 (Mo-99) in collaboration with General Atomics and the University of Missouri Research Reactor.

FINANCIAL DATA: *Note: Data for latest year may not have been available at press time.*

In U.S. $	2017	2016	2015	2014	2013	2012
Revenue	12,075,000	11,500,000	11,000,000	10,000,000	9,000,000	8,700,000
R&D Expense						
Operating Income						
Operating Margin %						
SGA Expense						
Net Income						
Operating Cash Flow						
Capital Expenditure						
EBITDA						
Return on Assets %						
Return on Equity %						
Debt to Equity						

CONTACT INFORMATION:

Phone: 613 592-2790 Fax: 613 592-6937
Toll-Free:
Address: 447 March Rd., Ottawa, ON K2K 1X8 Canada

STOCK TICKER/OTHER:

Stock Ticker: Subsidiary
Exchange:
Employees: 350
Fiscal Year Ends: 10/31
Parent Company: Sotera Health LLC

SALARIES/BONUSES:

Top Exec. Salary: $ Bonus: $
Second Exec. Salary: $ Bonus: $

OTHER THOUGHTS:

Estimated Female Officers or Directors: 4
Hot Spot for Advancement for Women/Minorities: Y

Novanta Inc

NAIC Code: 334,510

www.gsig.com

TYPES OF BUSINESS:

Equipment-Laser Systems
Motion Control Components
Lasers-Dermatology & Ophthalmology
Printed Circuit Board Spindles
Encoders
Thermal Printers

BRANDS/DIVISIONS/AFFILIATES:

World of Medicine GmbH
Laster Quantum Limited
ThingMagic

CONTACTS: *Note: Officers with more than one job title may be intentionally listed here more than once.*

Matthijs Glastra, CEO
Robert Buckley, CFO
Stephen Bershad, Chairman of the Board
Peter Chang, Chief Accounting Officer
Brian Young, Other Executive Officer

GROWTH PLANS/SPECIAL FEATURES:

Novanta, Inc. designs, develops, manufactures and sells precision photonic and motion control components and subsystems to original equipment manufacturers (OEMs) in the medical and advanced industrial markets. Novanta's business consists of three segments: photonics, vision and precision motion. The photonics segment produces photonics-based solutions such as CO2 laser sources and laser scanning and laser beam delivery products, to customers worldwide. This division serves highly-demanding applications such as industrial material processing, metrology, medical and life science imaging, and medical laser procedures. Photonics manufacturing facilities are located in Massachusetts, Washington, Arizona, the U.K. and China. The vision segment produces a wide range of medical-grade technologies, including visualization solutions, imaging informatics products, optical data collection and machine vision technologies, radio frequency identification (RFID) technologies, thermal printers, light and color measurement instrumentation and embedded touch screen solutions. Vision manufacturing facilities are located in New York and California. The precision motion segment produces optical encoders, precision motor and motion control technology, air bearing spindles and precision machined components. Precision motion manufacturing facilities are located in Massachusetts, California, the U.K. and China. Many of Novanta's manufacturing facilities are ISO 9001 certified, and the majority of its products manufactured for the medical market are manufactured under the ISO 13485 certification. During 2017, Novanta acquired: World of Medicine GmbH, a provider of medical insufflators, pumps and related disposables for OEMs; an additional 35% of Laster Quantum Limited (for a total 76% share), a U.K.-based provider of solid state continuous wave lasers, femtosecond lasers and optical light engines to OEMs; and ThingMagic, a Massachusetts-based provider of ultra-high frequency radio frequency identification modules and finished RFID readers to OEMs.

FINANCIAL DATA: *Note: Data for latest year may not have been available at press time.*

In U.S. $	2017	2016	2015	2014	2013	2012
Revenue	521,290,000	384,758,000	373,598,000	364,706,000	341,612,000	271,498,000
R&D Expense	41,673,000	32,002,000	31,043,000	28,954,000	26,352,000	22,393,000
Operating Income	64,737,000	40,508,000	37,187,000	26,571,000	24,378,000	23,849,000
Operating Margin %	12.41%	10.52%	9.95%	7.28%	7.13%	8.78%
SGA Expense	102,025,000	81,691,000	82,049,000	84,380,000	81,449,000	65,584,000
Net Income	60,051,000	22,003,000	35,615,000	-24,252,000	7,309,000	19,538,000
Operating Cash Flow	63,378,000	47,788,000	33,416,000	42,289,000	49,200,000	28,430,000
Capital Expenditure	9,094,000	12,442,000	5,552,000	5,415,000	4,988,000	4,308,000
EBITDA	95,495,000	60,865,000	56,301,000	50,368,000	44,585,000	27,998,000
Return on Assets %	6.90%	5.22%	8.74%	-6.23%	2.04%	5.69%
Return on Equity %	13.95%	8.73%	15.63%	-10.71%	3.11%	8.94%
Debt to Equity	0.74	0.27	0.39	0.55	0.26	0.18

CONTACT INFORMATION:

Phone: 781 266-5700 Fax: 613 592-7549
Toll-Free: 800-342-3757
Address: 125 Middlesex Turnpike, Bedford, MA 01730 United States

STOCK TICKER/OTHER:

Stock Ticker: NOVT
Exchange: NAS
Employees: 1,269
Fiscal Year Ends: 12/31
Parent Company:

SALARIES/BONUSES:

Top Exec. Salary: $511,254 Bonus: $
Second Exec. Salary: $404,279 Bonus: $

OTHER THOUGHTS:

Estimated Female Officers or Directors: 1
Hot Spot for Advancement for Women/Minorities:

Novartis AG

www.novartis.com

NAIC Code: 325,412

TYPES OF BUSINESS:

Drugs-Diversified
Therapeutic Drug Discovery
Therapeutic Drug Manufacturing
Generic Drugs
Over-the-Counter Drugs
Ophthalmic Products
Nutritional Products
Veterinary Products

BRANDS/DIVISIONS/AFFILIATES:

Sandoz
Alcon
Novartis Institutes for BioMedical Research
Global Drug Development
Novartis Technical Operations
Novartis Business Services

CONTACTS: *Note: Officers with more than one job title may be intentionally listed here more than once.*

Vasant Narasimhan, CEO
Harry Kirsch, CFO
Steffen Lang, Global Dir.-Technical Operations
Steven Baert, Head-Human Resources
Mark C. Fishman, Pres., Novartis Institute for Biomedical Research
Bertrand Bodson, Chief Digital Officer
Peter Kornicker, Chief Compliance Officer
Felix Ehrat, General Counsel
Paul van Arkel, Head-Corp. Strategy & External Affairs
Michele Galen, Head-Comm.
Kevin Buehler, Head-Alcon
David Epstein, Head-Novartis Pharmaceuticals
George Gunn, Head-Novartis Animal Health
Jeffrey George, Head-Sandoz Div.
Joerg Reinhardt, Chmn.

GROWTH PLANS/SPECIAL FEATURES:

Novartis AG researches, develops and manufactures pharmaceuticals, as well as a large number of consumer and animal healthcare products. The company has a diverse portfolio, operating through three primary divisions: innovative medicines, which develops, manufactures, distributes and sells innovative patent-protected prescription medicines; Sandoz, which develops, manufactures, distributes and sells generic pharmaceuticals and biosimilars; and Alcon, which develops, manufactures, distributes and sells surgical and vision care products. Each of these divisions are supported by the following cross-divisional organizational units: Novartis Institutes for BioMedical Research, Global Drug Development, Novartis Technical Operations (NTO) and Novartis Business Services (NBS). Novartis Institutes for BioMedical Research is the innovation engine of Novartis. It supports the innovative medicines division and collaborates with the Sandoz division. Global Drug Development oversees all drug development activities for the innovative medicines division and biosimilars portfolio. NTO centralizes management of Novartis' manufacturing operations across the innovative medicines and Sandoz divisions. NBS delivers integrated solutions to all Novartis divisions and units worldwide. Headquartered in Switzerland, the company's products are sold in approximately 155 countries worldwide. In March 2018, Novartis agreed to sell its 36.5% stake in GlaxoSmithKline plc's consumer healthcare joint venture, to GlaxoSmithKline for $13 billion. That April, Novartis agreed to acquire AveXis, Inc., a U.S.-based gene-therapy company, for $8.7 billion.

FINANCIAL DATA: *Note: Data for latest year may not have been available at press time.*

In U.S. $	2017	2016	2015	2014	2013	2012
Revenue	50,135,000,000	49,436,000,000	50,387,000,000	53,634,000,000	58,831,000,000	57,561,000,000
R&D Expense	8,972,000,000	9,039,000,000	8,935,000,000	9,086,000,000	9,852,000,000	9,332,000,000
Operating Income	8,629,000,000	8,268,000,000	8,977,000,000	11,089,000,000	10,910,000,000	11,511,000,000
Operating Margin %	17.21%	16.72%	17.81%	20.67%	18.54%	19.99%
SGA Expense	14,997,000,000	14,192,000,000	14,247,000,000	14,993,000,000	17,609,000,000	17,290,000,000
Net Income	7,703,000,000	6,712,000,000	17,783,000,000	10,210,000,000	9,175,000,000	9,505,000,000
Operating Cash Flow	12,621,000,000	11,475,000,000	11,897,000,000	13,897,000,000	13,174,000,000	14,194,000,000
Capital Expenditure	2,746,000,000	2,879,000,000	3,505,000,000	3,404,000,000	3,571,000,000	3,068,000,000
EBITDA	15,852,000,000	14,567,000,000	14,260,000,000	17,658,000,000	16,343,000,000	16,887,000,000
Return on Assets %	5.85%	5.12%	13.84%	8.11%	7.32%	7.86%
Return on Equity %	10.33%	8.83%	24.06%	14.07%	12.79%	14.08%
Debt to Equity	0.31	0.23	0.21	0.19	0.15	0.19

CONTACT INFORMATION:

Phone: 41 613241111 Fax: 41 613248001
Toll-Free:
Address: Lichtstrasse 35, Basel, 4056 Switzerland

STOCK TICKER/OTHER:

Stock Ticker: NVS
Employees: 118,393
Parent Company:
Exchange: NYS
Fiscal Year Ends: 12/31

SALARIES/BONUSES:

Top Exec. Salary: $2,164,948 Bonus: $2,029,639
Second Exec. Salary: $1,120,000 Bonus: $873,600

OTHER THOUGHTS:

Estimated Female Officers or Directors: 4
Hot Spot for Advancement for Women/Minorities: Y

Novo-Nordisk AS

www.novonordisk.com

NAIC Code: 325,412

TYPES OF BUSINESS:

Drugs-Diabetes
Hormone Replacement Therapy
Growth Hormone Drugs
Hemophilia Drugs
Insulin Delivery Systems
Educational & Training Services

BRANDS/DIVISIONS/AFFILIATES:

Tresiba
Xultophy
Ryzodeg
Fiasp

CONTACTS: *Note: Officers with more than one job title may be intentionally listed here more than once.*

Lars Jorgensen, CEO
Kare Schulz, Pres.
Jesper Brandgaard, CFO
Mads Krogsgaard Thomsen, Chief Science Officer
Helge Lund, Chmn.

GROWTH PLANS/SPECIAL FEATURES:

Novo Nordisk AS is a global healthcare company engaged in the discovery, development, manufacturing and marketing pharmaceutical products. As a leader in diabetes care, it has one of the broadest diabetes product portfolios in the industry, including new generation insulins, a full portfolio of modern insulins as well as a human once-daily GLP-1 analog. In addition, Novo Nordisk has a leading position within hemophilia care, growth hormone therapy and hormone replacement therapy. Operations are divided into two segments: diabetes and obesity care, and biopharmaceuticals. The diabetes and obesity care segment covers insulin, GLP-1 (glucagon-like peptide), other protein-related products (such as glucagon, protein-related delivery systems and needles) and oral antidiabetic drugs. The biopharmaceuticals segment covers the therapy areas of hemophilia care, growth hormone therapy and hormone replacement therapy. Novo products include: Tresiba (insulin degludec) is a once-daily new-generation insulin launched in more than 50 countries, including the U.S.; Xultophy, a once-daily single-injection combination of insulin degludec (Tresiba) and liraglutide (Victoza), which is marketed in 18 countries, including the U.S.; Ryzodeg, a soluble formulation of insulin degludec and insulin aspart, which is marketed in 18 countries; and Fiasp, a fast-acting insulin aspart, launched in 17 countries and was due to launch in the U.S. during 2018. The major production facilities owned by Novo Nordisk are located in Denmark, and internationally in the U.S., France, China and Brazil. Active pharmaceutical ingredient (API) production is located in Denmark, primarily in Kalundorg, with secondary locations in Hillerod and Gentofte, although two API production sites in the U.S. are currently being established, and expected to commence operation in 2020. Construction of a new facility in Hillerod, Denmark, for producing medicines for the treatment of diabetes and obesity is expected to commence operation in 2019.

FINANCIAL DATA: *Note: Data for latest year may not have been available at press time.*

In U.S. $	2017	2016	2015	2014	2013	2012
Revenue	17,409,300,000	17,422,400,000	16,821,850,000	13,841,590,000	13,025,800,000	12,161,390,000
R&D Expense	2,184,268,000	2,269,837,000	2,120,987,000	2,144,990,000	1,828,744,000	1,698,442,000
Operating Income	7,632,156,000	7,548,769,000	7,706,503,000	5,376,035,000	4,908,601,000	4,593,914,000
Operating Margin %	43.83%	43.32%	45.81%	38.83%	37.68%	37.77%
SGA Expense	5,006,951,000	5,040,462,000	5,013,965,000	4,170,901,000	4,190,851,000	3,874,137,000
Net Income	5,943,066,000	5,911,114,000	5,433,393,000	4,127,415,000	3,925,260,000	3,340,461,000
Operating Cash Flow	6,416,579,000	7,530,377,000	5,967,537,000	4,939,618,000	4,043,405,000	3,462,346,000
Capital Expenditure	1,347,905,000	1,288,521,000	998,460,000	675,667,200	567,965,700	564,536,700
EBITDA	8,097,408,000	7,957,754,000	7,249,044,000	5,855,782,000	5,516,468,000	5,013,654,000
Return on Assets %	38.15%	40.06%	41.28%	35.93%	37.03%	32.87%
Return on Equity %	80.20%	82.23%	79.89%	63.91%	60.53%	54.89%
Debt to Equity						

CONTACT INFORMATION:

Phone: 45 44448888 Fax: 45 44490555
Toll-Free:
Address: Novo Alle, BagsvÃ¦rd, 2880 Denmark

STOCK TICKER/OTHER:

Stock Ticker: NVO
Exchange: NYS
Employees: 42,500
Fiscal Year Ends: 12/31
Parent Company:

SALARIES/BONUSES:

Top Exec. Salary: $4,900,000 Bonus: $1,700,000
Second Exec. Salary: $1,854,773 Bonus: $935,180

OTHER THOUGHTS:

Estimated Female Officers or Directors: 3
Hot Spot for Advancement for Women/Minorities: Y

NuVasive Inc

www.nuvasive.com

NAIC Code: 339,100

TYPES OF BUSINESS:

Medical Equipment Development
Spinal Surgery Equipment

BRANDS/DIVISIONS/AFFILIATES:

Maximum Access Surgery (MAS)
NVM5
Intra-Operative Monitoring
MaXcess
FormaGraft
Osteocel Plus
SpheRx
Pulse

CONTACTS: *Note: Officers with more than one job title may be intentionally listed here more than once.*

Gregory Lucier, CEO
Jereme Sylvain, Controller
Peter Leddy, Executive VP, Divisional
Skip Kiil, Executive VP, Divisional
Stephen Rozow, Executive VP, Divisional
Carol Cox, Executive VP, Divisional
Matthew Link, Executive VP, Divisional
Rajesh Asarpota, Executive VP
Joan Stafslien, Executive VP

GROWTH PLANS/SPECIAL FEATURES:

NuVasive, Inc. designs, develops and markets minimally invasive products for the surgical treatment of spine disorders. Its principle products include the Maximum Access Surgery (MAS) minimally disruptive surgical platform, which combines three categories of solutions that collectively minimize soft tissue disruption during spine fusion surgery: NVM5, Intra-Operative Monitoring (IOM) and MaXcess. NVM5 is a proprietary, software-driven intraoperative nerve avoidance system. It allows surgeons to perform fusion surgery through a process NuVasive calls the eXtreme Lateral Interbody Fusion (XLIF), meaning the surgeon enters the body from the side rather than front or back. The system is compatible with numerous existing surgical instruments, meaning surgeons can use the products to augment machines they are already comfortable with. IOM provides insight into the nervous system which is analyzed in real time by healthcare professionals for the interpretation of intra-operative information. MaXcess is a unique tri-blade system that combines instrumentation and specialized implants that provide maximum surgical spinal access while disrupting soft tissue as little as possible. The firm's line of biologics includes the FormaGraft synthetic collagen product, used to provide a scaffold for bone growth; and Osteocel Plus, an allograft (meaning not derived from the patient's own body) mesenchymal stem cell (MSC) matrix, a bone graft substitute. Specialized implants designed to function with the MAS platform are used for interbody disc height restoration to facilitate fusion and stabilization of the spine, and have been developed to be delivered through the MaXcess system, which minimizes the invasiveness of implant procedures. Its products include SpheRx and Armada pedicle screw systems. In July 2018, NuVasive announced that its Pulse surgical automation platform received 510(k) clearance from the U.S. FDA. The Pulse platform addresses spine technology and clinical requirements across all spine procedures.

Employee benefits include medical insurance, a stock purchase program and paid holiday/sick leave.

FINANCIAL DATA: *Note: Data for latest year may not have been available at press time.*

In U.S. $	2017	2016	2015	2014	2013	2012
Revenue	1,029,520,000	962,072,000	811,113,000	762,415,000	685,173,000	620,255,000
R&D Expense	50,425,000	47,999,000	35,851,000	37,986,000	32,209,000	35,296,000
Operating Income	117,848,000	80,217,000	97,257,000	58,852,000	33,090,000	46,704,000
Operating Margin %	11.44%	8.33%	11.99%	7.71%	4.82%	7.52%
SGA Expense	539,913,000	533,624,000	464,530,000	469,648,000	420,064,000	372,416,000
Net Income	83,006,000	37,147,000	66,291,000	-16,720,000	7,902,000	3,144,000
Operating Cash Flow	178,979,000	156,295,000	88,727,000	115,548,000	97,439,000	130,082,000
Capital Expenditure	112,491,000	94,290,000	107,792,000	58,424,000	47,597,000	41,189,000
EBITDA	233,422,000	207,941,000	207,012,000	82,538,000	100,052,000	90,875,000
Return on Assets %	5.17%	2.59%	5.03%	-1.32%	.67%	.27%
Return on Equity %	11.13%	5.34%	9.93%	-2.70%	1.39%	.60%
Debt to Equity	0.73	0.81	0.54	0.56	0.58	0.61

CONTACT INFORMATION:

Phone: 858 909-1800 Fax:
Toll-Free: 800-475-9131
Address: 7475 Lusk Blvd., San Diego, CA 92121 United States

STOCK TICKER/OTHER:

Stock Ticker: NUVA
Employees: 1,500
Parent Company:
Exchange: NAS
Fiscal Year Ends: 12/31

SALARIES/BONUSES:

Top Exec. Salary: $257,808 Bonus: $800,000
Second Exec. Salary: $833,649 Bonus: $

OTHER THOUGHTS:

Estimated Female Officers or Directors: 1
Hot Spot for Advancement for Women/Minorities:

NxStage Medical Inc

www.nxstage.com

NAIC Code: 325,413

TYPES OF BUSINESS:

Diagnostic and Other Electromedical Equipment Manufacturing

BRANDS/DIVISIONS/AFFILIATES:

System One
NxStage Kidney Care

CONTACTS: *Note: Officers with more than one job title may be intentionally listed here more than once.*

Jeffrey Burbank, CEO
Matthew Towse, CFO
Robert Funari, Director
Joseph Turk, President
Winifred Swan, Senior VP

GROWTH PLANS/SPECIAL FEATURES:

NxStage Medical, Inc. is a medical device company which develops, manufactures and markets products for the treatment of kidney failure, fluid overload and related blood treatments and procedures. Its primary product, System One, delivers the therapeutic flexibility and clinical benefits associated with traditional dialysis machines in a smaller, portable, easy-to-use form which can be used by health care professionals and trained lay users in patient homes, as well as more traditional care settings such as hospitals and dialysis clinics. System One is well-suited for home hemodialysis and a range of dialysis therapies including more frequent, or daily, dialysis. System One is cleared by the U.S. FDA for home hemodialysis, home nocturnal hemodialysis, as well as hospital and clinic-based dialysis. NxStage also sells needles and blood tubing sets mainly to dialysis clinics for the treatment of End Stage Renal Disease (ESRD). The company has three reporting segments: System One, in-center and services. Within the System One segment, the company sells the System One and related products in the home and critical care markets. The home market consists of dialysis centers that provide treatment options for patients that have ESRD, while the critical care market consisting of hospitals or facilities that treat patients with sudden loss of kidney function. NxStage sells essentially the same System One cyclers and disposables within each market. The in-center segment sells blood tubing sets and needles to dialysis clinics. The services segment provides dialysis services to patients at the firm's NxStage Kidney Care dialysis centers. NxStage's international network of affiliates and distribution partners provide treatment for patients in over 21 countries. In July 2018, NxStage agreed to sell its bloodlines business, which operates under the Medisystems name.

The firm offers employees medical, dental, vision, disability, life and AD&D insurance; flexible spending accounts; 401(k); and various assistance programs.

FINANCIAL DATA: *Note: Data for latest year may not have been available at press time.*

In U.S. $	2017	2016	2015	2014	2013	2012
Revenue	393,941,000	366,378,000	336,123,000	301,501,000	263,429,000	242,132,000
R&D Expense	39,608,000	31,032,000	26,237,000	22,635,000	18,887,000	17,111,000
Operating Income	-13,851,000	-4,285,000	-14,629,000	-22,187,000	-17,798,000	-11,206,000
Operating Margin %	-3.51%	-1.16%	-4.35%	-7.35%	-6.75%	-4.62%
SGA Expense	142,531,000	125,238,000	119,863,000	115,455,000	101,414,000	86,903,000
Net Income	-13,992,000	-4,771,000	-15,342,000	-23,946,000	-18,561,000	-15,153,000
Operating Cash Flow	4,802,000	4,587,000	10,542,000	-20,273,000	-10,141,000	6,241,000
Capital Expenditure	9,194,000	8,848,000	11,537,000	20,097,000	16,246,000	7,694,000
EBITDA	19,903,000	28,352,000	16,647,000	5,500,000	6,653,000	12,319,000
Return on Assets %	-4.50%	-1.52%	-4.97%	-7.76%	-5.99%	-5.02%
Return on Equity %	-6.98%	-2.42%	-8.02%	-12.44%	-9.47%	-8.68%
Debt to Equity	0.05	0.05	0.06	0.06		

CONTACT INFORMATION:

Phone: 978 687-4700 Fax: 978 687-4809
Toll-Free:
Address: 350 Merrimack St., Lawrence, MA 01843 United States

STOCK TICKER/OTHER:

Stock Ticker: NXTM
Exchange: NAS
Employees: 3,400
Fiscal Year Ends: 12/31
Parent Company:

SALARIES/BONUSES:

Top Exec. Salary: $638,281 Bonus: $
Second Exec. Salary: $408,500 Bonus: $

OTHER THOUGHTS:

Estimated Female Officers or Directors: 2
Hot Spot for Advancement for Women/Minorities:

OhioHealth Corporation

www.ohiohealth.com

NAIC Code: 622,110

TYPES OF BUSINESS:

General Medical and Surgical Hospitals
Health Insurance
Home Health Care
Hospice Services
Long-Term Care
Surgery Centers
Rehabilitation Services

BRANDS/DIVISIONS/AFFILIATES:

WorkHealth
OhioHealth Listens
OhioHealth Physician Group
OhioHealth Research and Innovation Institute
Doctors Hospital
Hardin Memorial Hospital
O'Bleness Hospital
Riverside Methodist Hospital

CONTACTS: *Note: Officers with more than one job title may be intentionally listed here more than once.*

David Blom, CEO
Michael W. Louge, COO
David Blom, Pres.
Vinson M. Yates, CFO
Sue Jablonski, Sr. VP-Mktg. & Communications
Johnni Beckel, Sr. VP-Human Resources
Bruce Vanderhoff, Chief Medical Officer
Jim Weeast, Sr. VP
Frank Pandora, II, General Counsel
Michael Bernstein, Chief Strategy Officer
Sue Jablonski, Chief Comm. Officer
Cheryl Herbert, Sr. VP-Clinical Support Services
Hugh Thornhill, Pres., Medical Specialty Foundation
Steve Garlock, Sr. VP-Cancer Services
Karen Morrison, Sr. VP-External Affairs
James Newbrough, Pres., HomeReach
John P. McConnell, Chmn.

GROWTH PLANS/SPECIAL FEATURES:

OhioHealth Corporation, founded in 1891, is a not-for-profit, faith-based health system that serves 47 Ohio counties. The system comprises nearly 30,000 associates, physicians and volunteers, along with a network of 11 hospitals and more than 200 ambulatory sites. OhioHealth provides hospice, home health, medical equipment and other health services. Just a few of OhioHealth's hospitals include Doctors Hospital, Grady Memorial Hospital, Hardin Memorial Hospital, Mansfield Hospital, O'Bleness Hospital, Riverside Methodist Hospital and Shelby Hospital. Health care services and programs of the firm include surgical weight management, cancer, ear/nose/throat, endoscopy, interventional radiology, maternity, palliative care, robotic surgery, sports medicine, blood conservation, eICU, hospice, laboratory services, orthopedics, pastoral care, senior health, breast health, diabetes, emergency and trauma care, heart and vascular, limb reconstruction and preservation, pain management and sleep disorders. In addition to its hospitals, OhioHealth comprises: WorkHealth, a workers' compensation and rehabilitation services provider; OhioHealth Listens, an online community of volunteer patient and their family members focused on providing feedback on strategies, protocols and practices related to the patient experience at OhioHealth; and OhioHealth Physician Group, a group of physicians, advanced practice providers and associates committed to improving the health of those served by OhioHealth, providing convenient access to patient-centered care. The OhioHealth Research and Innovation Institute supports research conducted throughout its hospital system, including clinical studies in various therapeutic areas.

OhioHealth offers employees medical, dental, vision, life, disability and AD&D insurance; flexible spending accounts; adoption assistance; child care centers; concierge services; vendor discounts; a credit union membership; an employee assistance program; a discount stock purchase plan; tuition reimbursement; a 403(b)/401(k) plan; and a pension plan.

FINANCIAL DATA: *Note: Data for latest year may not have been available at press time.*

In U.S. $	2017	2016	2015	2014	2013	2012
Revenue	3,768,067,800	3,588,636,000	3,284,881,000	2,770,000,000	2,528,529,000	2,371,600,000
R&D Expense						
Operating Income						
Operating Margin %						
SGA Expense						
Net Income		231,665,000	274,875,000	185,000,000	215,177,000	229,157,000
Operating Cash Flow						
Capital Expenditure						
EBITDA						
Return on Assets %						
Return on Equity %						
Debt to Equity						

CONTACT INFORMATION:

Phone: 614-544-4455 Fax:
Toll-Free:
Address: 180 E. Broad St., Columbus, OH 43215 United States

STOCK TICKER/OTHER:

Stock Ticker: Nonprofit
Exchange:
Employees: 29,000
Fiscal Year Ends: 06/30
Parent Company:

SALARIES/BONUSES:

Top Exec. Salary: $ Bonus: $
Second Exec. Salary: $ Bonus: $

OTHER THOUGHTS:

Estimated Female Officers or Directors: 3
Hot Spot for Advancement for Women/Minorities: Y

Olympus Corporation

NAIC Code: 339,100

www.olympus-global.com

TYPES OF BUSINESS:

Medical Equipment Manufacturing
Imaging Equipment
Communication Equipment
Endoscopy Equipment

BRANDS/DIVISIONS/AFFILIATES:

Image Stream Medical Inc

CONTACTS: *Note: Officers with more than one job title may be intentionally listed here more than once.*

Hiroyuki Sasa, Pres.
Akihiro Taguchi, Sr. Exec. Managing Officer
Haruo Ogawa, Exec. Managing Officer
Toshiaki Gomi, Exec. Managing Officer
Yasushi Sakai, Exec. Managing Officer

GROWTH PLANS/SPECIAL FEATURES:

Olympus Corporation manufactures and sells precision machinery and instruments. It operates four businesses: medical, scientific solutions, imaging and others. The medical business, which derives nearly 80% of the firm's annual revenue, works with healthcare professionals in order to provide medical technology and precision manufacturing, with a focus on early detection of diseases and minimally-invasive procedures. Its offerings include: endoscopes such as video imaging systems, gastrointestinal/colono/duodeno/broncho endoscopes, ultrasound systems, capsule endoscopy systems, cleaning/sterilization systems, medical information systems, therapeutic peripherals and ancillary products; endosurgery products for gastroenterological surgery, thoracic surgery, urology, gynecology, orthopedic surgery, neurosurgery, anesthesiology and otolaryngology, therapeutic and surgical equipment; and endotherapy products. The scientific solutions business engages in research and development in regards to healthcare, life science and industrial fields. Its products and solutions include biological microscope systems, industrial microscope systems, remote visual inspection products and non-destructive testing systems. The imaging business creates digital cameras, with each of its interchangeable lens cameras (the OM-D series and the PEN series) comprising advanced mirror-less optics. This division's other products include compact digital cameras, digital camera accessories, lens barrel units, optical components, digital audio recorders, binoculars and related software and applications. In June 2017, the firm acquired Image Stream Medical, Inc., a healthcare systems integrator based in Massachusetts, USA. In April 2018, Olympus agreed to acquire the lithotripsy system design and production technology from Cybersonics, Inc., which offers innovative solutions for medical and surgical procedures.

FINANCIAL DATA: *Note: Data for latest year may not have been available at press time.*

In U.S. $	2017	2016	2015	2014	2013	2012
Revenue						
R&D Expense						
Operating Income						
Operating Margin %						
SGA Expense						
Net Income						
Operating Cash Flow						
Capital Expenditure						
EBITDA						
Return on Assets %						
Return on Equity %						
Debt to Equity						

CONTACT INFORMATION:

Phone: 81 333402111 Fax:
Toll-Free:
Address: 3-1 Nishi-Shinjuku 2-chome, Shinjuku Monolith, Tokyo, 163-0914 Japan

STOCK TICKER/OTHER:

Stock Ticker: OCPNY
Exchange: PINX
Employees: 37,444
Fiscal Year Ends: 03/31
Parent Company:

SALARIES/BONUSES:

Top Exec. Salary: $ Bonus: $
Second Exec. Salary: $ Bonus: $

OTHER THOUGHTS:

Estimated Female Officers or Directors:
Hot Spot for Advancement for Women/Minorities:

Omnicare Inc

www.omnicare.com

NAIC Code: 446,110

TYPES OF BUSINESS:

Specialty Pharmacies
Infusion Therapy
Consulting Services
Pharmaceutical Research
Medical Records Services
Billing Services
Pharmaceutical Distribution

BRANDS/DIVISIONS/AFFILIATES:

CVS Health Corporation

GROWTH PLANS/SPECIAL FEATURES:

Omnicare, Inc. is a leading healthcare services company specializing in the management of complex pharmaceutical care. The company operates in two segments: post-acute care and senior living care. The post-acute care segment delivers more than 70 million prescriptions annually to skilled nursing facility customers nationwide. Its services include 24/7/365 access, cost containment programs, advanced digital tools, daily delivery, medication reviews, specialized packaging and compliance management. The senior living care segment builds consultative partnerships with senior assisted living facilities in order to provide support to members within those communities. Its services are the same as those listed for post-acute care. For independent living communities, this segment offers a broad range of industry-leading capabilities to serve the healthcare needs of the residents and help businesses and communities manage health in affordable and effective ways. These solutions include pharmacy care team support, hand-delivery of residents' medications and always-on savings for products used on a daily basis. Omnicare operates as a wholly-owned subsidiary of CVS Health Corporation.

Employees receive medical, dental, vision, prescription, disability, AD&D and life insurance; an employee assistance program; flexible spending accounts; and a wellness plan.

CONTACTS: *Note: Officers with more than one job title may be intentionally listed here more than once.*

Nitin Sahney, CEO
Robert Kraft, CFO
Alexander Kayne, General Counsel
Kirsten Marriner, Other Executive Officer
David Hileman, Senior VP, Divisional
Amit Jain, Senior VP, Divisional

FINANCIAL DATA: *Note: Data for latest year may not have been available at press time.*

In U.S. $	2017	2016	2015	2014	2013	2012
Revenue	6,990,000,000	6,800,000,000	6,630,000,000	6,417,614,848	6,013,398,016	6,160,388,096
R&D Expense						
Operating Income						
Operating Margin %						
SGA Expense						
Net Income				144,527,008	-43,432,000	194,874,000
Operating Cash Flow						
Capital Expenditure						
EBITDA						
Return on Assets %						
Return on Equity %						
Debt to Equity						

CONTACT INFORMATION:

Phone: 513-719-2600 Fax:
Toll-Free: 800-990-6664
Address: 201 E. Fourth St., 900 Omnicare Ctr.,, Cincinnati, OH 45202 United States

STOCK TICKER/OTHER:

Stock Ticker: Subsidiary
Employees: 12,451
Parent Company: CVS Health Corporation
Exchange:
Fiscal Year Ends: 12/31

SALARIES/BONUSES:

Top Exec. Salary: $ Bonus: $
Second Exec. Salary: $ Bonus: $

OTHER THOUGHTS:

Estimated Female Officers or Directors: 3
Hot Spot for Advancement for Women/Minorities: Y

Opto Circuits (India) Ltd

NAIC Code: 339,100

www.optoindia.com

TYPES OF BUSINESS:

Medical Electronics

BRANDS/DIVISIONS/AFFILIATES:

Criticare Systems
Mediaid
Unetixs Vascular
Eurocor
Cardiac Science
Powerheart
Freeway

CONTACTS: *Note: Officers with more than one job title may be intentionally listed here more than once.*

Vinod Ramnani, Managing Dir.
Jayesh Patel, Dir.-Eng.
Thomas Dietker, Dir.-Mergers & Acquisitions
Usha Ramnani, Exec. Dir.

GROWTH PLANS/SPECIAL FEATURES:

Opto Circuits (India) Ltd. (OCI) is a multinational medical device company headquartered in Bengaluru, India. The firm designs, develops, manufactures, markets and distributes medical products used by health care establishments in more than 150 countries. Opto Circuits specializes in vital signs monitoring, emergency cardiac care, vascular treatments and sensing technologies. Its products are U.S. FDA listed and CE marked, with some brands marketed as Criticare Systems, Mediaid, Unetixs Vascular, Eurocor and Cardiac Science. Criticare Systems specializes in monitoring systems and accessories used in anesthesia, critical care, medical transport and outpatient care settings. Mediaid specializes in pulse oximeters, vital signs monitors, oximeter sensors, thermometers, ECG, infusion and syringe pumps, oxygen sensors, oxygen analyzers and monitors, blood pressure cuffs and veterinary products. Unetixs Vascular offers technically advanced, non-invasive vascular diagnostic systems for hospital or mobile services. Eurocor provides interventional physicians with innovative coronary stent technologies and special cardiovascular and endovascular devices, manufactured in Europe. Eurocor's products are indicated for minimally invasive cardiovascular and peripheral surgery and comply with biological and biomechanical principles to offer highly flexible, adaptable solutions. Its Freeway brand of shunt balloon catheters are marketed globally for arteriorvenous (AV) access to help patients with end-stage renal disease. Cardiac Science designs, manufactures and markets Powerheart automated external defibrillators (AEDs) and related services that facilitate successful deployments in order to combat sudden cardiac arrest (SCA). Powerheart G5 is the first FDA-cleared AED to combine fully-automatic shock delivery, dual-language functionality, variable escalating energy and fast shock times to help save a sudden cardiac arrest victim's life.

FINANCIAL DATA: *Note: Data for latest year may not have been available at press time.*

In U.S. $	2017	2016	2015	2014	2013	2012
Revenue	33,832,700	51,994,830	181,709,275	220,603,861	231,200,000	394,000,000
R&D Expense						
Operating Income						
Operating Margin %						
SGA Expense						
Net Income	-78,316,700	-292,625	-30,213,672	1,370,876	14,900,000	62,400,000
Operating Cash Flow						
Capital Expenditure						
EBITDA						
Return on Assets %						
Return on Equity %						
Debt to Equity						

CONTACT INFORMATION:

Phone: 91-80-2852 1040 Fax: 91-80-2852-1094
Toll-Free:
Address: 83 Wipro Ave., Electronic City, Bengaluru, Kamataka, 560 100 India

STOCK TICKER/OTHER:

Stock Ticker: 532391
Employees: 1,840
Parent Company:
Exchange: Bombay
Fiscal Year Ends: 03/31

SALARIES/BONUSES:

Top Exec. Salary: $ Bonus: $
Second Exec. Salary: $ Bonus: $

OTHER THOUGHTS:

Estimated Female Officers or Directors:
Hot Spot for Advancement for Women/Minorities:

Optos plc

www.optos.com

NAIC Code: 334,510

TYPES OF BUSINESS:

Electromedical and Electrotherapeutic Apparatus Manufacturing

BRANDS/DIVISIONS/AFFILIATES:

Nikon Corporation
optomap
Daytona
California

CONTACTS:

Note: Officers with more than one job title may be intentionally listed here more than once.

Robert Kennedy, CEO
Quinn Lyzun, Deputy CEO

GROWTH PLANS/SPECIAL FEATURES:

Optos plc is a retinal imaging company. The firm is primarily engaged in the design, development, manufacture and marketing of medical devices delivering retinal examinations at customer sites. Its proprietary optomap medical devices produce ultra-widefield (UWF), high resolution digital images of approximately 82% of the retina in a single capture. An optomap image provides clinical information that facilitates the early detection, management and effective treatment of disorders and diseases evidenced in the retina such as retinal detachments and tears, glaucoma, diabetic retinopathy and age-related macular degeneration. The firm's Daytona and California products represent ultra-widefield retinal imaging technology and have been converted to desktop models. The ergonomic body of both devices is designed to increase patient comfort and to correctly position the eye for image capture. Color, red-free and autofluorescence (AF) are included in both devices. California features fluorescein angiography as well as Optos' UWF imaging modality, indocyanine green angiography used for imaging the choroidal vasculature for the diagnosis, management and treatment of certain eye conditions such as neovascular age-related macular degeneration. Optos operates primarily in the U.K., and has additional operations in North America and continental Europe, addressing markets such as Germany, Switzerland, Norway, Sweden, Spain and France. Optos is a wholly-owned subsidiary of Nikon Corporation.

FINANCIAL DATA:

Note: Data for latest year may not have been available at press time.

In U.S. $	2017	2016	2015	2014	2013	2012
Revenue	102,900,000	122,900,000		168,900,000	158,200,000	193,200,000
R&D Expense						
Operating Income						
Operating Margin %						
SGA Expense						
Net Income	25,100,000	5,800,000		8,500,000	6,400,000	17,600,000
Operating Cash Flow						
Capital Expenditure						
EBITDA						
Return on Assets %						
Return on Equity %						
Debt to Equity						

CONTACT INFORMATION:

Phone: 44 1383843300 Fax:
Toll-Free:
Address: Queensferry House, Enterprise Way, Dunfermline, Scotland KY11 8GR United Kingdom

STOCK TICKER/OTHER:

Stock Ticker: Subsidiary
Employees: 391
Parent Company: Nikon Corporation
Exchange:
Fiscal Year Ends: 03/31

SALARIES/BONUSES:

Top Exec. Salary: $ Bonus: $
Second Exec. Salary: $ Bonus: $

OTHER THOUGHTS:

Estimated Female Officers or Directors:
Hot Spot for Advancement for Women/Minorities:

Organogenesis Inc

NAIC Code: 325,414

www.organogenesis.com

TYPES OF BUSINESS:

Tissue Replacement Products
Wound Dressing Products
Regenerative Medicine

BRANDS/DIVISIONS/AFFILIATES:

NanoMatrix Inc
Apligraf
Dermagraft
PuraPly

CONTACTS:

Note: Officers with more than one job title may be intentionally listed here more than once.

Gary S. Gillheeney, Sr., CEO
Patrick Bilbo, COO
Geoff MacKay, Pres.
Tim M. Cunningham, CFO
Brian Grow, Chief Commercial Officer
Thomas L. Pearl, VP-Human Resources
Dolores Baksh, Dir.-Research & Development
Phillip Nolan, VP-Mfg. Oper.
Erik Ostrowski, VP-Finance
Dario Eklund, VP-Bio-Surgery & Oral Regeneration
Zorina Pitkin, VP-Quality Systems
Patrick Bilbo, VP-Regulatory
Milka Bedikian, VP-Global Mktg. & Bioactive Wound Healing
Michael Catarina, Dir.-Enterprise Mgmt.
Zorina Pitkin, VP-Quality Systems

GROWTH PLANS/SPECIAL FEATURES:

Organogenesis, Inc. is a regenerative medicine firm that designs, develops and manufactures products containing living cells or natural connective tissue. It specializes in bio-active wound healing and oral regeneration. The firm's bio-active wound healing products include FDA-approved Apligraf, which is designed for the treatment of venous leg ulcers and diabetic foot ulcers; and Dermagraft, which is FDA-approved for the treatment of diabetic foot ulcers. Apligraf is a living cell-based product that is commercially available. The two layers of Apligraf make it effective in speeding up wound healing and achieving healing in wounds previously unresponsive to treatment. Dermagraft helps restore the comprised diabetic foot ulcer dermal bed in order to facilitate healing by providing a substrate over which the patient's own epithelial cells can migrate to close the wound. In addition, Organogenesis' PuraPly wound-healing product is the first and only purified collagen matrix plus PHMB (polyhexamethylene biguanide) antimicrobial that supports healing across a variety of wound types. PuraPly's purified Type 1 collagen matrix creates a durable, biocompatible scaffold, as well as an effective barrier against a wide range of microorganisms. The company's subsidiary, NanoMatrix, Inc. utilizes electrospinning to create designer scaffolds for the purposes of regenerative medicine. The firm's corporate headquarters is based in Massachusetts, USA, with Organogenesis Switzerland GmbH, based in Switzerland, serving the European market.

FINANCIAL DATA:

Note: Data for latest year may not have been available at press time.

In U.S. $	2017	2016	2015	2014	2013	2012
Revenue	477,750,000	455,000,000	418,500,000	400,000,000	380,000,000	362,164,992
R&D Expense						
Operating Income						
Operating Margin %						
SGA Expense						
Net Income						
Operating Cash Flow						
Capital Expenditure						
EBITDA						
Return on Assets %						
Return on Equity %						
Debt to Equity						

CONTACT INFORMATION:

Phone: 781-575-0775 Fax: 781-575-1570
Toll-Free:
Address: 85 Dan Rd., Canton, MA 02021 United States

STOCK TICKER/OTHER:

Stock Ticker: Private
Employees: 600
Parent Company:
Exchange:
Fiscal Year Ends: 12/31

SALARIES/BONUSES:

Top Exec. Salary: $ Bonus: $
Second Exec. Salary: $ Bonus: $

OTHER THOUGHTS:

Estimated Female Officers or Directors: 4
Hot Spot for Advancement for Women/Minorities: Y

ORPEA Groupe

www.orpea.biz

NAIC Code: 623,110

TYPES OF BUSINESS:

Nursing Care Facilities (Skilled Nursing Facilities)
Dependency Care

BRANDS/DIVISIONS/AFFILIATES:

CONTACTS:
Note: Officers with more than one job title may be intentionally listed here more than once.

Yves le Masne, CEO
Jean-Claude Brdenk, COO

GROWTH PLANS/SPECIAL FEATURES:

ORPEA Groupe is a leading European operator in dependency care. The France-based company specializes in various types of long- and short-term care in relation to physical and mental dependency, including diminished autonomy due to age, rehabilitation and post-acute care, and mental health disorders. Care facilities for those with diminished autonomy primarily take place in nursing homes, but can also include assisted living facilities, retirement homes, post-acute care facilities, rehabilitation facilities and psychiatric care facilities. In addition, ORPEA provides home care services for people with diminished autonomy. The firm's post-acute care and rehabilitation facilities provide medical care and rehabilitation services following surgery or an acute episode of a chronic illness. Psychiatric care facilities care for people with mental health issues, admitted on a voluntary basis, and include those with mood disorders (depression, bipolar disorder), anxiety disorders (obsessive compulsive behavior, panic attacks, anxiety, social phobia), addictions, eating disorders and post-traumatic stress disorder. Home care services include cleaning, ironing, gardening, moral support, supervision, personal hygiene assistance, meal assistance, help in walking or help with car travel. In France, there are more than 345 ORPEA facilities, more than 45 facilities in Spain, 15 facilities in Italy, 34 facilities in Switzerland, 60 facilities in Belgium, more than 80 facilities in Austria, 165 facilities in Germany, more than 15 facilities in Czech Republic and more than 15 in Poland.

FINANCIAL DATA:
Note: Data for latest year may not have been available at press time.

In U.S. $	2017	2016	2015	2014	2013	2012
Revenue						
R&D Expense						
Operating Income						
Operating Margin %						
SGA Expense						
Net Income						
Operating Cash Flow						
Capital Expenditure						
EBITDA						
Return on Assets %						
Return on Equity %						
Debt to Equity						

CONTACT INFORMATION:

Phone: 33 147757807 Fax:
Toll-Free:
Address: 52, Quai De Dion Bouton, Puteaux Cedex, 92 813 France

STOCK TICKER/OTHER:

Stock Ticker: ORPEF
Employees: 8,777
Parent Company:
Exchange: PINX
Fiscal Year Ends:

SALARIES/BONUSES:

Top Exec. Salary: $ Bonus: $
Second Exec. Salary: $ Bonus: $

OTHER THOUGHTS:

Estimated Female Officers or Directors:
Hot Spot for Advancement for Women/Minorities:

Orthofix International NV

NAIC Code: 339,100

www.orthofix.com

TYPES OF BUSINESS:

Medical Equipment-Orthopedic
Bone Reconstruction Equipment
Orthopedic Fixation Devices

BRANDS/DIVISIONS/AFFILIATES:

Orthofix
ProCallus
Xcaliber
SpinalStim
CervicalStim
PhysioStim
Trinity Evolution
Spinal Kinetics

CONTACTS: *Note: Officers with more than one job title may be intentionally listed here more than once.*

Brad Mason, Pres.
Ronald Matricaria, Chairman of the Board
Kimberley Elting, Other Executive Officer
Michael Finegan, Other Executive Officer
Raymond Fujikawa, President, Divisional
Robert Goodwin, President, Divisional
Bradley Niemann, President, Divisional
Davide Bianchi, President, Divisional
Ronald Matricaria, Chmn.

GROWTH PLANS/SPECIAL FEATURES:

Orthofix International NV (OFIX) designs, manufactures and distributes medical equipment used principally by musculoskeletal medical specialists. The firm serves more than 50 countries. The company has multiple trademarked products including Orthofix, ProCallus, XCaliber, SpinalStim, CervicalStim, PhysioStim, Trinity Evolution and VeroNail. These products are designed to address the lifelong bone-and-joint health needs of patients of all ages, helping them achieve a more active and mobile lifestyle. Orthofix divides its business into four segments: BioStim, biologics, extremity fixation and spine fixation. BioStim manufactures and provides support services for several market leading devices that enhance bone fusion and utilize the firm's patented pulsed electromagnetic (PEMF) technology. Biologics provides regenerative products that enable physicians to treat spinal and orthopedic conditions. Extremity fixation offers products that are unrelated to the spine and are used in fracture repair, deformity correction and bone reconstruction. Spine fixation created implant products used in spinal surgeries. In 2017, 43% of sales were attributed to the BioStim segment, 14% to biologics, 24% to extremity fixation and 19% to spine fixation. Orthofix directly distributes its products in the U.S., the U.K., Italy, the U.K., Germany, France and Brazil. Other international markets utilize independent distributors. The firm also has administrative and training facilities in the U.S., the U.K., Brazil, France and Germany. Manufacturing facilities are limited to the U.S. and Italy. In May 2018, Orthofix acquired California-based Spinal Kinetics, along with its M6 cervical disc implant, for $105 million.

FINANCIAL DATA: *Note: Data for latest year may not have been available at press time.*

In U.S. $	2017	2016	2015	2014	2013	2012
Revenue	433,823,000	409,788,000	396,489,000	402,277,000	400,534,000	462,320,000
R&D Expense	29,700,000	28,803,000	26,389,000	24,994,000	26,768,000	28,577,000
Operating Income	38,328,000	35,436,000	9,255,000	17,136,000	14,106,000	90,983,000
Operating Margin %	8.83%	8.64%	2.33%	4.25%	3.52%	19.67%
SGA Expense	272,758,000	257,696,000	274,320,000	258,951,000	254,673,000	254,170,000
Net Income	6,223,000	3,056,000	-2,809,000	-8,537,000	-25,515,000	51,295,000
Operating Cash Flow	53,341,000	44,707,000	43,224,000	50,958,000	66,881,000	11,206,000
Capital Expenditure	16,948,000	18,334,000	27,899,000	18,525,000	29,678,000	28,774,000
EBITDA	58,452,000	56,277,000	30,178,000	40,014,000	36,765,000	111,244,000
Return on Assets %	1.60%	.79%	-.70%	-2.09%	-5.50%	8.55%
Return on Equity %	2.22%	1.10%	-.95%	-2.79%	-7.19%	14.36%
Debt to Equity					0.06	0.05

CONTACT INFORMATION:

Phone: 39 045 67 19 000 Fax: 39 045 67 19 380
Toll-Free:
Address: Via delle Nazioni 9, Bussolengo Verona, 37012 Italy

STOCK TICKER/OTHER:

Stock Ticker: OFIX
Employees: 938
Parent Company:
Exchange: NAS
Fiscal Year Ends: 12/31

SALARIES/BONUSES:

Top Exec. Salary: $705,576 Bonus: $
Second Exec. Salary: $401,972 Bonus: $

OTHER THOUGHTS:

Estimated Female Officers or Directors: 2
Hot Spot for Advancement for Women/Minorities:

Owens & Minor Inc

www.owens-minor.com

NAIC Code: 423,450

TYPES OF BUSINESS:

Distribution-Medical & Surgical Equipment
Supply Chain Management

BRANDS/DIVISIONS/AFFILIATES:

CONTACTS:

Note: Officers with more than one job title may be intentionally listed here more than once.

P. Phipps, CEO
Robert Snead, CFO
Michael Lowry, Chief Accounting Officer
Erika Davis, Chief Administrative Officer
Stephen Olive, Chief Information Officer
Nicholas Pace, Executive VP
Christopher Lowery, President, Divisional
Stuart Morris-Hipkins, President, Divisional
Geoffrey Marlatt, Senior VP, Divisional
Charles Colpo, Senior VP, Divisional

GROWTH PLANS/SPECIAL FEATURES:

Owens & Minor, Inc., founded in 1882, is a leading healthcare logistics company that connects the world of medical products to the point of care. The company provides vital supply chain assistance to the providers of health care services and the manufacturers of health care products, supplies and devices in the U.S. and Europe. Owens & Minor's service portfolio covers procurement, inventory management, delivery and sourcing for the healthcare market. It serves customers ranging from hospitals, integrated healthcare systems, group purchasing organizations and the U.S. federal government to manufacturers of life-science and medical devices and supplies, including pharmaceuticals in Europe. The firm's operations are divided into three segments: domestic, international and proprietary products. The domestic segment includes all functions in the U.S. relating to the role as a healthcare services company, providing distribution and logistics services to healthcare providers and manufacturers. The international segment provides contract logistics services to the pharmaceutical, biotechnology and medical device industries. This division's warehousing and transportation offerings include storage, controlled-substance handling, cold-chain, emergency and export delivery, inventory management and pick/pack services, as well as order-to-cash, re-labeling and returns management. Last, the proprietary products segment provides product-related solutions, which help manufacturers and healthcare providers source, assemble and deliver procedure kits to the point-of-care. This division's facilities in the U.S. and Ireland offer the combining of instruments and supplies into kits and trays, which serve a wide number of surgical specialties, including robotics, orthopedics, cardiology, cath labs, gastric, laproscopic and labor and delivery. It also offers minor procedure kits. In May 2018, Owens & Minor acquired the surgical and infection prevention business of Halyard Health, Inc. for approximately $710 million.

Owens & Minor offers its employees educational assistance; incentive pay; flexible benefit plans; and medical, dental, vision, life and disability insurance.

FINANCIAL DATA:

Note: Data for latest year may not have been available at press time.

In U.S. $	2017	2016	2015	2014	2013	2012
Revenue	9,318,275,000	9,723,431,000	9,772,946,000	9,440,182,000	9,071,532,000	8,908,145,000
R&D Expense						
Operating Income	149,958,000	224,274,000	228,763,000	202,337,000	210,527,000	206,917,000
Operating Margin %	1.60%	2.30%	2.34%	2.14%	2.32%	2.32%
SGA Expense	1,016,978,000	970,424,000	933,596,000	926,977,000	863,656,000	682,595,000
Net Income	72,793,000	108,787,000	103,409,000	66,503,000	110,882,000	109,003,000
Operating Cash Flow	56,774,000	186,934,000	269,597,000	-3,761,000	140,554,000	218,506,000
Capital Expenditure	50,737,000	30,121,000	36,616,000	70,808,000	60,129,000	38,963,000
EBITDA	209,401,000	279,667,000	294,745,000	265,744,000	261,113,000	246,521,000
Return on Assets %	2.35%	3.91%	3.71%	2.60%	4.86%	5.21%
Return on Equity %	7.26%	11.02%	10.33%	6.54%	11.03%	11.45%
Debt to Equity	0.88	0.58	0.57	0.61	0.20	0.22

CONTACT INFORMATION:

Phone: 804 723-7000 Fax: 804 270-7281
Toll-Free:
Address: 9120 Lockwood Blvd., Mechanicsville, VA 23116 United States

STOCK TICKER/OTHER:

Stock Ticker: OMI Exchange: NYS
Employees: 7,900 Fiscal Year Ends: 12/31
Parent Company:

SALARIES/BONUSES:

Top Exec. Salary: $922,500 Bonus: $
Second Exec. Salary: $653,162 Bonus: $

OTHER THOUGHTS:

Estimated Female Officers or Directors: 4
Hot Spot for Advancement for Women/Minorities: Y

Par Pharmaceutical Companies Inc

www.parpharm.com

NAIC Code: 325,412

TYPES OF BUSINESS:

Drugs-Generic & Branded
Pharmaceutical Intermediates

BRANDS/DIVISIONS/AFFILIATES:

Endo International plc

CONTACTS:

Note: Officers with more than one job title may be intentionally listed here more than once.

Paul V. Campanelli Paul V. Campanelli, Pres.
Thomas J. Haughey, Pres.
Suketu Sanghvi, VP-Formulation Dev.
Robert Polke, Sr. VP-Manufacturing
Chad Gassert, VP-Bus. Dev. & Licensing
Allison Wey, VP-Corp. Affairs
Allison Wey, VP-Investor Rel.
Michael Altamuro Michael Altamuro, VP-Mktg. & Bus. Analytics
Joseph Barbarite, Sr. VP-Quality & Compliance
Michelle Bonomi-Huvala, VP-Regulatory Affairs

GROWTH PLANS/SPECIAL FEATURES:

Par Pharmaceutical Companies, Inc. develops, manufactures and markets generic pharmaceuticals. The company offers differentiated specialty dosage and sterile injectable drug products and is advancing a research & development pipeline of potential new products. Generic pharmaceuticals are carefully manufactured formulations of the original patented brand name products in order to make healthcare more affordable. Par Pharmaceutical's products include a range of prescription and over-the-counter products comprised of tablets, capsules, liquids, suspensions, creams and ointments. Therapeutic categories include antihypertensives, analgesics, antibiotics, cough/cold, antidepressants, antipsychotics, among others. The company manufactures and distributes drugs at various dosage strengths, some of which are manufactured by themselves and some by other companies. Par Pharmaceutical operates as a subsidiary of Endo International plc, and has offices in New York, California, Michigan and Alabama, in the U.S., as well as in Chennai, India. The company's facilities comprise more than 1 million square feet of manufacturing and packing space, including over 200,000 square feet of quality control and R&D labs and 518,000 square feet for distribution purposes. During 2017, the firm received FDA approval for its ephedrine sulfate injection, a drug administered parenterally as a pressor agent to address clinically-important hypotension in surgical environments.

FINANCIAL DATA:

Note: Data for latest year may not have been available at press time.

In U.S. $	2017	2016	2015	2014	2013	2012
Revenue	3,885,000,000	3,700,000,000	3,660,964,160	1,308,621,000	1,097,467,000	1,085,888,000
R&D Expense						
Operating Income						
Operating Margin %						
SGA Expense						
Net Income			-897,195,000	-105,517,000	-105,871,000	-32,545,000
Operating Cash Flow						
Capital Expenditure						
EBITDA						
Return on Assets %						
Return on Equity %						
Debt to Equity						

CONTACT INFORMATION:

Phone: 845-573-5500 Fax: 845-425-7907
Toll-Free:
Address: One Ram Ridge Rd., Chestnut Ridge, NY 10977 United States

STOCK TICKER/OTHER:

Stock Ticker: Subsidiary
Exchange:
Employees: 3,700
Fiscal Year Ends: 12/31
Parent Company: Endo International plc

SALARIES/BONUSES:

Top Exec. Salary: $ Bonus: $
Second Exec. Salary: $ Bonus: $

OTHER THOUGHTS:

Estimated Female Officers or Directors: 3
Hot Spot for Advancement for Women/Minorities: Y

Partners HealthCare

www.partners.org

NAIC Code: 622,110

TYPES OF BUSINESS:

General Medical and Surgical Hospitals
Home & Long-Term Care
Medical Schools
Private Practices
Teaching Hospitals
Mental Health Hospitals

BRANDS/DIVISIONS/AFFILIATES:

Massachusetts General Hospital
Brigham & Women's Hospital
Cooley Dickinson Hospital
BWH Brookside
Massachusetts Eye and Ear
North Shore Medical Center
Partners HealthCare at Home
Partners eCare

CONTACTS: *Note: Officers with more than one job title may be intentionally listed here more than once.*

David Torchiana, CEO
Gary L. Gottlieb, Pres.
Peter K. Markell, CFO
Elizabeth Mort, Sr. Medical Dir.
Peter K. Markell, Exec. VP-Admin.
Brent L. Henry, General Counsel
Lynne J. Eickholt, Chief Strategy Officer
Sara Andrews, Chief Dev. Officer
Rich Copp, VP-Comm.
Peter K. Markell, Exec. VP-Finance
David E.Storto, VP-Non-Acute Care Svcs.
Peter R. Brown, Chief of Staff
Kathryn E. West, VP-Real Estate & Facility
Tejal K. Gandhi, Chief Quality & Safety Officer
Scott M. Sperling, Chmn.

GROWTH PLANS/SPECIAL FEATURES:

Partners HealthCare is one of the largest healthcare systems in Massachusetts. The firm was founded as the umbrella corporation for Massachusetts General Hospital and Brigham & Women's Hospital. It has since grown to include academic medical centers, community and specialty hospitals, a managed care organization, a physician network, community health centers, home health, long-term care services and more. Member hospitals and organizations in the network include Brigham and Women's Falkner Hospital, Cooley Dickinson Hospital, Martha's Vineyard Hospital, Massachusetts Eye and Ear, McLean Hospital, MGH Institute of Health Professions, Nantucket Cottage Hospital, Neighborhood Health Plan, Newton-Wellesley Hospital, North Shore Medical Center, Partners Community Physicians Organization, Partners HealthCare at Home, Spaulding Rehabilitation Network and Wentworth-Douglass Hospital. Community Health Centers include BWH Brookside, BWH Southern Jamaica Plain, MGH Charlestown, MGH Chelsea and MGH Revere. Partners HealthCare programs include The Partners HealthCare Asthma Center, Partners HealthCare Connected Health, Partners HealthCare Personalized Medicine, Partners HealthCare Online Specialty Consultations, Partners Innovation, Mongan Institute for Health Policy and Partners Urgent Care. The firm collaborates with the Center for Integration of Medicine and Innovative Technology, Dana-Farber/Partners CancerCare, Harvard Clinical Research Institute and Ragon Institute of MGH, MIT and Harvard. Partners HealthCare unites its network of approximately 70,000 clinicians and staff across system through Partners eCare platform, to improve patient quality, safety and efficiency.

The company offers employees medical, dental, vision and life coverage; spending accounts; child care; tuition reimbursement; prescription drug coverage; a retiree medical savings account; and work/life resources.

FINANCIAL DATA: *Note: Data for latest year may not have been available at press time.*

In U.S. $	2017	2016	2015	2014	2013	2012
Revenue	13,125,000,000	12,500,000,000	11,665,645,000	10,906,053,000	10,346,039,000	8,981,337,000
R&D Expense						
Operating Income						
Operating Margin %						
SGA Expense						
Net Income		-108,000,000	-91,989,000	119,845,000	600,009,000	352,335,000
Operating Cash Flow						
Capital Expenditure						
EBITDA						
Return on Assets %						
Return on Equity %						
Debt to Equity						

CONTACT INFORMATION:

Phone: 617-278-1000 Fax:
Toll-Free:
Address: 800 Boylston St., 11/Fl, Boston, MA 02199 United States

STOCK TICKER/OTHER:

Stock Ticker: Nonprofit
Employees: 68,000
Parent Company:
Exchange:
Fiscal Year Ends: 09/30

SALARIES/BONUSES:

Top Exec. Salary: $ Bonus: $
Second Exec. Salary: $ Bonus: $

OTHER THOUGHTS:

Estimated Female Officers or Directors: 11
Hot Spot for Advancement for Women/Minorities: Y

Patterson Companies Inc

NAIC Code: 423,450

www.pattersoncompanies.com

TYPES OF BUSINESS:

Dental Products & Related Services
Veterinary Products
Non-Wheelchair Assistive Products

BRANDS/DIVISIONS/AFFILIATES:

Patterson Dental Supply Inc
Animal Health International Inc

CONTACTS:

Note: Officers with more than one job title may be intentionally listed here more than once.

Mark Walchirk, CEO
Donald Zurbay, CFO
Dennis Goedken, CFO
John Buck, Director
Andrea Frohning, Other Executive Officer
Kevin Pohlman, President, Divisional
Les Korsh, Vice President

GROWTH PLANS/SPECIAL FEATURES:

Patterson Companies, Inc. is a value-added specialty distributor serving the U.S. and Canadian dental supply markets and the U.S., Canadian and U.K. animal health supply markets. The company operates through these two segments: dental supply and animal health. The dental supply segment comprises subsidiary Patterson Dental Supply, Inc., which is one of the largest distributors of dental products in North America, offering full-service, value-added supplies to approximately 100,000 dentists, dental laboratories, institutions and other healthcare professionals. The division provides consumable products, including X-ray film, restorative materials, hand instruments and sterilization products; basic and advanced technology dental equipment; practice management and clinical software; patient education systems; and office forms and stationery. Patterson Dental also offers related services including dental equipment installation, maintenance and repair, dental office design and equipment financing. The animal health segment comprises subsidiary Animal Health International, Inc., which distributes biologicals, pharmaceuticals, parasticides, supplies and equipment to the animal health supply market. This market is engaged in beef and dairy cattle, poultry and swine, and other food-producing animals. It also includes the companion animal supply market, which primarily consists of dogs, cats and horses. This segment offers over 100,000 stock-keeping units (SKUs) sources from over 3,000 manufacturers to its customers, including many proprietary branded products, which provide a competitive edge in relation to price as well as to customer loyalty.

Employee benefits include medical, dental and vision coverage; flexible spending accounts; short- and long-term disability; life and accident insurance; a 401(k); employee stock purchase and ownership plans; education and employee assistance; and employee discounts.

FINANCIAL DATA:

Note: Data for latest year may not have been available at press time.

In U.S. $	2017	2016	2015	2014	2013	2012
Revenue	5,593,127,000	5,386,703,000	4,375,020,000	4,063,715,000	3,637,212,000	
R&D Expense						
Operating Income	287,928,000	347,713,000	373,427,000	345,756,000	354,455,000	
Operating Margin %	5.14%	6.45%	8.53%	8.50%	9.74%	
SGA Expense						
Net Income	170,893,000	187,184,000	223,261,000	200,612,000	210,272,000	
Operating Cash Flow	162,719,000	156,329,000	262,691,000	195,836,000	299,195,000	
Capital Expenditure	47,019,000	79,354,000	62,945,000	40,387,000	21,983,000	
EBITDA	377,759,000	434,141,000	427,694,000	398,611,000	403,516,000	
Return on Assets %	4.86%	5.78%	7.68%	7.23%	7.75%	
Return on Equity %	12.05%	12.66%	14.95%	13.99%	15.18%	
Debt to Equity	0.71	0.70	0.47	0.49	0.51	

CONTACT INFORMATION:

Phone: 651 686-1600 Fax: 651 686-9331
Toll-Free: 800-328-5536
Address: 1031 Mendota Heights Rd., St. Paul, MN 55120 United States

STOCK TICKER/OTHER:

Stock Ticker: PDCO Exchange: NAS
Employees: 7,500 Fiscal Year Ends: 04/30
Parent Company:

SALARIES/BONUSES:

Top Exec. Salary: $820,005 Bonus: $
Second Exec. Salary: $544,774 Bonus: $116,021

OTHER THOUGHTS:

Estimated Female Officers or Directors: 4
Hot Spot for Advancement for Women/Minorities: Y

Pediatric Services of America Inc

www.psahealthcare.com

NAIC Code: 621,610

TYPES OF BUSINESS:

Pediatric Health Care & Related Services
Case Management Services
Private Duty Nursing
Prescribed Pediatric Extended Care

BRANDS/DIVISIONS/AFFILIATES:

Aveanna Healthcare LLC
PSA Healthcare

GROWTH PLANS/SPECIAL FEATURES:

Pediatric Services of America, Inc., operating as PSA Healthcare, provides home healthcare and related services for medically-fragile patients. The company operates through a network of 78 company-owned branch offices located in 16 U.S. states. PSA used to provide services primarily to infants and children, but has been providing more and more adult home care services in addition to maintaining its national focus on medically-complex children. The firm's broad range of services include in-home private duty nursing such as in-home aide, respite care, school nurse services, therapies and rehabilitation. PSA offers 24/7 clinical support and supervision services, and maintains a family-centered approach. During 2017, Services of America was acquired by Aveanna Healthcare, LLC, a leading pediatric home health care company in the U.S.

CONTACTS: *Note: Officers with more than one job title may be intentionally listed here more than once.*

Tony Strange, CEO
Jim McCurry, Pres.
Debbie Lewis, VP-Oper. Dev.

FINANCIAL DATA: *Note: Data for latest year may not have been available at press time.*

In U.S. $	2017	2016	2015	2014	2013	2012
Revenue						
R&D Expense						
Operating Income						
Operating Margin %						
SGA Expense						
Net Income						
Operating Cash Flow						
Capital Expenditure						
EBITDA						
Return on Assets %						
Return on Equity %						
Debt to Equity						

CONTACT INFORMATION:

Phone: 770-441-1580 Fax:
Toll-Free:
Address: 400 Interstate North Parkway, SE, Ste. 1600, Atlanta, GA 30339 United States

STOCK TICKER/OTHER:

Stock Ticker: Subsidiary
Employees: 4,100
Parent Company: Aveanna Healthcare LLC
Exchange:
Fiscal Year Ends: 09/30

SALARIES/BONUSES:

Top Exec. Salary: $ Bonus: $
Second Exec. Salary: $ Bonus: $

OTHER THOUGHTS:

Estimated Female Officers or Directors: 3
Hot Spot for Advancement for Women/Minorities: Y

Sales, profits and employees may be estimates. Financial information, benefits and other data can change quickly and may vary from those stated here.

PerkinElmer Inc

NAIC Code: 325,413

www.perkinelmer.com

TYPES OF BUSINESS:

Diagnostic Systems
Mechanical Components
Optoelectronics
Pharmaceutical Manufacturing
Life Science Systems
Environmental Safety Equipment

BRANDS/DIVISIONS/AFFILIATES:

Aanalyst
AxION
Glutomatic
OilExpress
Supra-clean
DELFIA
NeoGram
EnLite

CONTACTS: *Note: Officers with more than one job title may be intentionally listed here more than once.*

Robert Friel, CEO
Andrew Okun, Chief Accounting Officer
James Corbett, Executive VP
Joel Goldberg, General Counsel
Deborah Butters, Other Executive Officer
Prahlad Singh, President, Divisional
Daniel Tereau, Senior VP, Divisional
Tajinder Vohra, Senior VP, Divisional
Frank Wilson, Senior VP

GROWTH PLANS/SPECIAL FEATURES:

PerkinElmer, Inc. provides technology, services and solutions for the diagnostics, food, environmental, industrial, life sciences research and laboratory services markets. The company operates through two segments: discovery and analytical solutions, and diagnostics. The discovery and analytical solutions segment comprises a portfolio of technologies that help life sciences researchers better understand diseases and develop treatments. This division also helps the ability to detect, monitor and manage contaminants and toxic chemicals impacting the environment and food supply. Just a few of the many product, services and application solutions developed by this segment include: gas chromatographs, mass spectrometers, sample-handling equipment, advanced liquid chromatography systems, analyzers, quantitative pathology research solutions, radiometric detection solutions, screening systems and plate readers. The diagnostics segment offers instruments, reagents, assay platforms and software to hospitals, medical labs, clinicians and medical research professionals. This division focuses on reproductive health, emerging market diagnostics and applied genomics. Products, services and application solutions include screening platforms, in vitro diagnostic kits, blood analyzing kits, informatics data management, X-ray detectors, umbilical cord blood banking services, automated liquid handling platforms, next-generation sequencing automation and nucleic acid quantitation and automated small-scale purification. Brand names include AAnalyst, AxION, Glutomatic, OilExpress, Supra-clean, DELFIA, NeoGram, Vectra and EnLite. PerkinElmer is headquartered in Waltham, Massachusetts, and markets its products and services in more than 150 countries. In May 2018, the firm acquired Shanghai Spectrum Instruments Co., Ltd., a manufacturer of analytical instruments in China.

FINANCIAL DATA: *Note: Data for latest year may not have been available at press time.*

In U.S. $	2017	2016	2015	2014	2013	2012
Revenue	2,256,982,000	2,115,517,000	2,262,359,000	2,237,219,000	2,166,232,000	2,115,205,000
R&D Expense	139,404,000	124,278,000	125,928,000	121,141,000	133,023,000	132,639,000
Operating Income	317,460,000	288,190,000	299,724,000	224,132,000	258,101,000	197,833,000
Operating Margin %	14.06%	13.62%	13.24%	10.01%	11.91%	9.35%
SGA Expense	616,167,000	600,885,000	598,848,000	659,335,000	585,850,000	632,734,000
Net Income	292,633,000	234,299,000	212,425,000	157,778,000	167,212,000	69,940,000
Operating Cash Flow	288,453,000	350,615,000	287,098,000	281,597,000	158,591,000	152,170,000
Capital Expenditure	39,089,000	31,702,000	29,632,000	29,072,000	38,991,000	42,408,000
EBITDA	445,658,000	385,568,000	394,019,000	322,609,000	331,727,000	223,239,000
Return on Assets %	5.64%	5.55%	5.11%	3.90%	4.26%	1.80%
Return on Equity %	12.56%	10.98%	10.23%	7.81%	8.50%	3.69%
Debt to Equity	0.71	0.48	0.47	0.51	0.46	0.48

CONTACT INFORMATION:

Phone: 781 663-6900 Fax:
Toll-Free: 800-762-4000
Address: 940 Winter St., Waltham, MA 02451 United States

STOCK TICKER/OTHER:

Stock Ticker: PKI
Employees: 8,000
Parent Company:
Exchange: NYS
Fiscal Year Ends: 01/31

SALARIES/BONUSES:

Top Exec. Salary: $1,063,200 Bonus: $
Second Exec. Salary: $538,692 Bonus: $

OTHER THOUGHTS:

Estimated Female Officers or Directors: 1
Hot Spot for Advancement for Women/Minorities: Y

Pfizer Inc

NAIC Code: 325,412

www.pfizer.com

TYPES OF BUSINESS:

Pharmaceuticals
Infusion Technologies

BRANDS/DIVISIONS/AFFILIATES:

Prevnar 13
Xeljanz
Eliquis
Lyrica
Enbrel
Lipitor
Premarin
Celebrex

CONTACTS: *Note: Officers with more than one job title may be intentionally listed here more than once.*

Ian Read, CEO
John Young, President, Divisional
Frank DAmelio, CFO
Loretta Cangialosi, Chief Accounting Officer
Freda Lewis-Hall, Chief Medical Officer
Rady Johnson, Chief Risk Officer
Albert Bourla, COO
Charles Hill, Executive VP, Divisional
Sally Susman, Executive VP, Divisional
Laurie Olson, Executive VP, Divisional
Douglas Lankler, Executive VP
Alexander Mackenzie, Executive VP
Margaret Madden, Other Executive Officer
Angela Hwang, President, Divisional
Mikael Dolsten, President, Divisional
Kirsten Lund-Jurgensen, President, Divisional
Mikael Dolsten, President, Divisional

GROWTH PLANS/SPECIAL FEATURES:

Pfizer, Inc. is a research-based, global pharmaceutical company that discovers, develops, manufactures and markets healthcare products. Pfizer operates in two business segments: innovative health and essential health. The innovative health segment focuses on developing and commercializing novel, value-creating medicines and vaccines that significantly improve patients' lives, as well as products for consumer healthcare. Key therapeutic areas within this division include internal medicine, vaccines, oncology, inflammation/immunology, rare diseases and consumer healthcare. Leading brands within this segment include Prevnar 13, Xeljanz, Eliquis, Lyrica, Enbrel, Ibrance, Xtandi and several over-the-counter (OTC) consumer products. The essential health segment comprises legacy brands that have lost or will soon lose market exclusivity in both developed and emerging markets. These branded products include generics, generic sterile injectable products and biosimilars. This division also includes a research and development organization, as well as the company's manufacturing business. Brands within this segment include Lipitor, Premarin, Norvasc, Lyrica (within Europe, Russia, Turkey, Israel and Central Asia countries), Celebrex, Viagra and Inflectra/Remsima, as well as several sterile injectable products.

FINANCIAL DATA: *Note: Data for latest year may not have been available at press time.*

In U.S. $	2017	2016	2015	2014	2013	2012
Revenue	52,546,000,000	52,824,000,000	48,851,000,000	49,605,000,000	51,584,000,000	58,986,000,000
R&D Expense	7,657,000,000	7,872,000,000	7,690,000,000	8,393,000,000	6,678,000,000	7,870,000,000
Operating Income	14,107,000,000	13,730,000,000	12,976,000,000	13,499,000,000	16,366,000,000	17,991,000,000
Operating Margin %	26.84%	25.99%	26.56%	27.21%	31.72%	30.50%
SGA Expense	14,784,000,000	14,837,000,000	14,809,000,000	14,097,000,000	14,355,000,000	16,616,000,000
Net Income	21,308,000,000	7,215,000,000	6,960,000,000	9,135,000,000	22,003,000,000	14,570,000,000
Operating Cash Flow	16,470,000,000	15,901,000,000	14,512,000,000	16,883,000,000	17,765,000,000	17,054,000,000
Capital Expenditure	2,217,000,000	1,999,000,000	1,496,000,000	1,583,000,000	1,465,000,000	1,327,000,000
EBITDA	19,844,000,000	15,294,000,000	15,321,000,000	19,137,000,000	23,540,000,000	21,215,000,000
Return on Assets %	12.40%	4.25%	4.13%	5.35%	12.29%	7.79%
Return on Equity %	32.57%	11.61%	10.23%	12.38%	27.93%	17.83%
Debt to Equity	0.47	0.52	0.44	0.44	0.39	0.38

CONTACT INFORMATION:

Phone: 212 733-2323 Fax: 212 573-7851
Toll-Free:
Address: 235 E. 42nd St., New York, NY 10017 United States

STOCK TICKER/OTHER:

Stock Ticker: PFE
Employees: 96,500
Parent Company:
Exchange: NYS
Fiscal Year Ends: 12/31

SALARIES/BONUSES:

Top Exec. Salary: $1,956,750 Bonus: $
Second Exec. Salary: $1,356,750 Bonus: $

OTHER THOUGHTS:

Estimated Female Officers or Directors: 7
Hot Spot for Advancement for Women/Minorities: Y

Pharmaceutical Product Development LLC

www.ppdi.com

NAIC Code: 541,711

TYPES OF BUSINESS:

Contract Research
Drug Discovery & Development Services
Clinical Data Consulting Services
Medical Marketing & Information Support Services
Drug Discovery Services
Medical Device Development

BRANDS/DIVISIONS/AFFILIATES:

Carlyle Group (The)
Hellman & Friedman

CONTACTS:

Note: Officers with more than one job title may be intentionally listed here more than once.

David Simmons, CEO
Christine A. Dingivan, Chief Medical Officer
B. Judd Hartman, General Counsel
William W. Richardson, Sr. VP-Global Bus. Dev.
Randy Buckwalter, Head-Media
Luke Heagle, Head-Investor Rel.
Lee E. Babiss, Chief Science Officer
David Johnston, Exec. VP-Global Lab Svcs.
David Simmons, Chmn.
Paul Colvin, Exec. VP-Global Clinical Dev.

GROWTH PLANS/SPECIAL FEATURES:

Pharmaceutical Product Development, LLC (PPD), jointly owned by The Carlyle Group and Hellman & Friedman, provides drug discovery and development services to pharmaceutical, biotechnology, medical device, academic and government organizations. PPD's services are divided into seven segments: early development, which offers a range of early development services, phase 1 clinical trial services and non-clinical consulting; clinical development, which helps advance drug research and development for products; PPD Laboratories, which provides comprehensive lab services; post-approval, which provides post-approval studies and late-stage clinical trials management; PPD Consulting, which acts as a consulting partner that assists companies with their biopharmaceutical product's success from pre-clinical through post-approval; functional service partnerships, provides customizable outsourcing solutions, including full-time equivalent models, units-based contracts and geographical-aligned agreements; and technology/innovation/performance, which helps companies deliver life-changing medicines, cutting-edge technologies, real-time analytics and customized training. Therapeutic areas of studies include cardiovascular, critical care, dermatology, dental pain research, endocrine and metabolics, gastroenterology, hemotology and oncology, immunology, infectious diseases, neuroscience, ophthalmology, respiratory and urology. PPD is headquartered in North Carolina, USA, with nearly 90 additional offices spanning 47 countries.

FINANCIAL DATA:

Note: Data for latest year may not have been available at press time.

In U.S. $	2017	2016	2015	2014	2013	2012
Revenue	1,350,000,000	1,300,000,000	1,200,000,000	1,222,000,000	1,023,100,000	749,100,032
R&D Expense						
Operating Income						
Operating Margin %						
SGA Expense						
Net Income						
Operating Cash Flow						
Capital Expenditure						
EBITDA						
Return on Assets %						
Return on Equity %						
Debt to Equity						

CONTACT INFORMATION:

Phone: 910-251-0081 Fax: 910-762-5820
Toll-Free:
Address: 929 N. Front St., Wilmington, NC 28401-3331 United States

STOCK TICKER/OTHER:

Stock Ticker: Private
Employees: 20,000
Parent Company: Carlyle Group (The)
Exchange:
Fiscal Year Ends: 12/31

SALARIES/BONUSES:

Top Exec. Salary: $ Bonus: $
Second Exec. Salary: $ Bonus: $

OTHER THOUGHTS:

Estimated Female Officers or Directors: 2
Hot Spot for Advancement for Women/Minorities:

PharMerica Corporation

www.pharmerica.com

NAIC Code: 446,110

TYPES OF BUSINESS:

Specialty Pharmacy Operations
Healthcare Pharmacy Management

BRANDS/DIVISIONS/AFFILIATES:

KKR & Co LP
Walgreens Boots Alliance Inc

CONTACTS: *Note: Officers with more than one job title may be intentionally listed here more than once.*

Gregory Weishar, CEO
Suresh Vishnubhatla, VP-Operations
Robert Dries, CFO
Robert E. Dries, CFO
Suresh Vishnubhatla, Executive VP, Divisional
Thomas Caneris, General Counsel
Robert McKay, Senior VP, Divisional

GROWTH PLANS/SPECIAL FEATURES:

PharMerica Corporation provides pharmacy management services for skilled nursing facilities, long-term care facilities, assisted living facilities, hospitals and other institutional care settings. PharMerica collaborates with its clients to develop products and services that help them provide quality care, control costs and remain regulatory compliant. The company's solutions include account management and comprehensive reporting and analytics tools. Its services include multiple packaging and dispensing options (from blister packs to multi-dose packs), on-site IV services, online ordering, admission and discharge services, as well as on-site access to emergency, time-sensitive and first dose medications. PharMerica also provides implementation teams that focus exclusively on transitioning new nursing facility customers to its pharmacy service. These teams offer ongoing education and training services. PharMerica itself comprises more than 100 long-term care pharmacies in over 45 U.S. states, including Hawaii. In December 2017, PharMerica became a joint venture of KKR & Co. LP and Walgreens Boots Alliance, Inc. in a $1.4 billion deal. The JV subsequently ceased from being publicly-traded.

FINANCIAL DATA: *Note: Data for latest year may not have been available at press time.*

In U.S. $	2017	2016	2015	2014	2013	2012
Revenue	2,140,000,000	2,091,100,032	2,028,499,968	1,894,499,968	1,757,900,032	1,832,600,064
R&D Expense						
Operating Income						
Operating Margin %						
SGA Expense						
Net Income		21,600,000	35,100,000	6,800,000	18,900,000	22,900,000
Operating Cash Flow						
Capital Expenditure						
EBITDA						
Return on Assets %						
Return on Equity %						
Debt to Equity						

CONTACT INFORMATION:

Phone: 502 627-7000 Fax: 813 318-6459
Toll-Free: 866-209-2178
Address: 1901 Campus Pl., Louisville, KY 40299 United States

STOCK TICKER/OTHER:

Stock Ticker: Joint Venture
Employees: 5,700
Parent Company:
Exchange: NYS
Fiscal Year Ends: 12/31

SALARIES/BONUSES:

Top Exec. Salary: $ Bonus: $
Second Exec. Salary: $ Bonus: $

OTHER THOUGHTS:

Estimated Female Officers or Directors:
Hot Spot for Advancement for Women/Minorities:

Philips Healthcare

www.healthcare.philips.com

NAIC Code: 334,510

TYPES OF BUSINESS:

Manufacturing-Medical Equipment
Diagnostic & Treatment Equipment
Imaging Equipment
Equipment Repair & Maintenance
Healthcare Consulting

BRANDS/DIVISIONS/AFFILIATES:

Koninklijke Philips NV
Philips HealthSuite Digital Platforms
Remote Diagnostic Technologies
NightBalance

CONTACTS: *Note: Officers with more than one job title may be intentionally listed here more than once.*

Frans van Houten, CEO-Koninklijke Philips
Eric Silfen, Chief Medical Officer
Clement Revetti, Chief Legal Officer
Michael Dreher, Global Head-Oper. & Customer Svcs.
Diego Olego, Chief Strategy & Innovation Officer
Rachel Bloom-Baglin, Media Contact-Global
Frans van Houten, CEO-Royal Philips Electronics NV
Steve Laczynski, Pres., Americas
Desmond Thio, Pres., China
Brent Shafer, CEO-Home Health Care Solutions
Arjen Radder, Pres., Asia Pacific

GROWTH PLANS/SPECIAL FEATURES:

Philips Healthcare, a subsidiary of Koninklijke Philips NV, manufactures medical diagnostic and treatment solutions, distributing its products to more than 100 countries worldwide. The company operates in four business segments: personal health, diagnosis and treatment, connected care and health informatics, and HealthTech. The personal health business delivers integrated, connected solutions that support healthier lifestyles and those living with chronic disease. This segment's products focus on the following: health and wellness, in regards to mother and child care and oral care; personal care, in regards to beauty and male grooming; domestic appliance, in regards to kitchen appliances, coffee, air, garment care and floor care; and sleep/respiratory care, in regards to related drug and treatment solutions/remedies. The diagnosis and treatment segment offers precision medicine and least-invasive treatment and therapies primarily via smart devices, software and services. These products and services include diagnostic imaging devices, image-guided therapy devices and solutions, and ultrasound products. The connected care and health informatics segment aims to improve patient outcomes, increase efficiency and drive toward value-based care via patient monitoring and clinical informatics systems and solutions, within and outside the hospital. Last, the HealthTech segment is engaged in innovation and strategy for the collaboration between medical-related businesses and the markets they serve. The Philips HealthSuite Digital Platforms are common digital frameworks that connect consumers, patients and healthcare providers in a cloud-based connected health ecosystem of devices, apps and tools. During 2018, Philips Healthcare acquired Remote Diagnostic Technologies, a U.K.-based innovator of advanced solutions for the pre-hospital market; NightBalance, a digital health scale-up company based in the Netherlands; and agreed to acquire EPD Solutions, an innovator in image-guided procedures for cardiac arrhythmias.

FINANCIAL DATA: *Note: Data for latest year may not have been available at press time.*

In U.S. $	2017	2016	2015	2014	2013	2012
Revenue	21,298,000,000	20,196,679,771	14,406,749,346	12,100,715,917	12,574,865,989	13,632,240,000
R&D Expense						
Operating Income						
Operating Margin %						
SGA Expense						
Net Income	2,240,000,000	1,570,860,000	697,041,000	748,736,000	976,696,340	1,805,250,000
Operating Cash Flow						
Capital Expenditure						
EBITDA						
Return on Assets %						
Return on Equity %						
Debt to Equity						

CONTACT INFORMATION:

Phone: 978-659-3000 Fax:
Toll-Free: 800-722-9377
Address: 3000 Minuteman Rd., Andover, MA 01810 United States

STOCK TICKER/OTHER:

Stock Ticker: Subsidiary
Exchange:
Employees: 73,951
Fiscal Year Ends: 12/31
Parent Company: Koninklijke Philips NV

SALARIES/BONUSES:

Top Exec. Salary: $ Bonus: $
Second Exec. Salary: $ Bonus: $

OTHER THOUGHTS:

Estimated Female Officers or Directors: 2
Hot Spot for Advancement for Women/Minorities:

Philips Respironics Inc

www.respironics.com/

NAIC Code: 339,100

TYPES OF BUSINESS:

Equipment/Supplies-Respiratory Devices

BRANDS/DIVISIONS/AFFILIATES:

Koninklijke Philips NV
Dream

CONTACTS: *Note: Officers with more than one job title may be intentionally listed here more than once.*

John Frank, Managing Dir.
Mir Taha Farooq, Dir.-Sales & Mktg.
Deborah DiSanzo, CEO-Philips Health Care

GROWTH PLANS/SPECIAL FEATURES:

Philips Respironics, Inc., a subsidiary of Koninklijke Philips NV, is a leading developer, manufacturer and marketer of medical devices for the treatment of patients suffering from sleep and respiratory disorders. The company's products are grouped into two categories: sleep therapy and respiratory care. Sleep therapy devices are an effective way to help patients adopt sleep apnea therapy for the long term. They are designed for engagement with and connectivity to extended care teams for the rediscovery of restful sleep, dreams and a sense of normalcy. Sleep apnea products include the Dream line, which comprises a suite of sleep apnea therapy technology with personalized tools to keep therapy on track; interface masks, a portfolio of advanced mask designs including full-face, minimal-contact, pillows and pediatric masks; patient compliance management, which take an active role in sleep apnea therapy and helps providers manage sleep-disordered breathing patients easily and efficiently; sleep diagnostics, offering home sleep testing and in-lab sleep diagnostics in order for doctors to then choose from a line of diagnostic sensors, titration devices and software through which to diagnose their patients; and sleep therapy systems, which are designed to provide exceptional therapy and enhance patient comfort. The respiratory disorders segment works with care providers to support a patient-centered and COPD (chronic obstructive pulmonary disease) management approach. Products include oxygen, with both stationary and portable oxygen therapy options; respiratory drug delivery, offering a line of sturdy and easy-to-use respiratory drug delivery products to help patients monitor their condition and take their medication; ventilation, offering lightweight, easy-to-use ventilators which provide invasive and non-invasive ventilator support for a wide range of adult and pediatric patients; pulse oximetry, offering a range of lightweight yet exceptional battery life pulse oximetry systems; and airway clearance devices, providing non-invasive secretion clearance for use in hospital and at home.

FINANCIAL DATA: *Note: Data for latest year may not have been available at press time.*

In U.S. $	2017	2016	2015	2014	2013	2012
Revenue						
R&D Expense						
Operating Income						
Operating Margin %						
SGA Expense						
Net Income						
Operating Cash Flow						
Capital Expenditure						
EBITDA						
Return on Assets %						
Return on Equity %						
Debt to Equity						

CONTACT INFORMATION:

Phone: 724-387-5200 Fax: 724-387-5010
Toll-Free:
Address: 1010 Murry Ridge Ln., Murrysville, PA 15668-8525 United States

STOCK TICKER/OTHER:

Stock Ticker: Subsidiary
Employees:
Parent Company: Koninklijke Philips NV
Exchange:
Fiscal Year Ends:

SALARIES/BONUSES:

Top Exec. Salary: $ Bonus: $
Second Exec. Salary: $ Bonus: $

OTHER THOUGHTS:

Estimated Female Officers or Directors: 1
Hot Spot for Advancement for Women/Minorities:

Ping An Healthcare and Technology Co Ltd

www.pahtg.com/en/

NAIC Code: 519,130

TYPES OF BUSINESS:

Health Care Internet Portals
Healthcare Consultation

BRANDS/DIVISIONS/AFFILIATES:

CONTACTS:

Note: Officers with more than one job title may be intentionally listed here more than once.

Tao Wang, CEO
Xue Bai, COO
Edwin Morris, CFO
Qi Wang, CTO
Tao Wang, Chmn.

GROWTH PLANS/SPECIAL FEATURES:

Ping An Healthcare and Technology Co., Ltd. operates an online and mobile healthcare platform, offering related consultations. The platform offers information about medical and wellness services such as family doctor services, consumer healthcare services, beauty care, medical insurance, pharmacies and health management. It connects consumers and patients with healthcare resources and enables them to retrieve information, obtain advice and book and manage appointments. Its nationwide network covers approximately 3,100 hospitals, 1,100 checkup centers, 500 dental clinics and 7,500 pharmacy outlets. As of December 31, 2017, there were nearly 193 million registered users, and the platform averages 370,000 daily online consultations. Consultation services include referrals, second opinions and appointment booking through the platform's AI-assisted in-house medical team and external doctors. Hospital partners may also provide consultation services through the system. In addition, Ping An Healthcare and Technology offers annual health membership programs to individuals and corporations in China. Health-related products can be purchased through the online or mobile platform, with more than 175,000 stock-keeping units to choose from. Ping An's mission is to build a global healthcare ecosystem that promotes healthy living via technology.

FINANCIAL DATA:

Note: Data for latest year may not have been available at press time.

In U.S. $	2017	2016	2015	2014	2013	2012
Revenue	286,825,000	86,483,900	42,984,100			
R&D Expense						
Operating Income						
Operating Margin %						
SGA Expense						
Net Income	93,970,600	36,550,600	17,101,200			
Operating Cash Flow						
Capital Expenditure						
EBITDA						
Return on Assets %						
Return on Equity %						
Debt to Equity						

CONTACT INFORMATION:

Phone: Fax: 86 21 3863 3719
Toll-Free:
Address: 16-19/Fl, Block B, No. 166, Kaibin Rd., Ping An Bldg., Shanghai, China

STOCK TICKER/OTHER:

Stock Ticker: 1833
Employees:
Parent Company:
Exchange: Hong Kong
Fiscal Year Ends:

SALARIES/BONUSES:

Top Exec. Salary: $ Bonus: $
Second Exec. Salary: $ Bonus: $

OTHER THOUGHTS:

Estimated Female Officers or Directors:
Hot Spot for Advancement for Women/Minorities:

Precision Optics Corporation

www.poci.com

NAIC Code: 334,510

TYPES OF BUSINESS:

Endoscopic Equipment, Electromedical (e.g., Bronchoscopes, Colonoscopes, Cystoscopes), Manufacturing
Optical Systems

BRANDS/DIVISIONS/AFFILIATES:

CONTACTS:
Note: Officers with more than one job title may be intentionally listed here more than once.

Joseph Forkey, CEO
Jack Dreimiller, CFO
Richard Forkey, Director

GROWTH PLANS/SPECIAL FEATURES:

Precision Optics Corporation provides state-of-the-art optics and optical systems for medical, biomedical and industrial applications, and has been in business since 1982. The company develops and manufactures its advanced optical instruments primarily for the medical industry, but also for the military and industrial industries to a minimal extent. Medical instrumentation lines include traditional endoscopes and endocouplers as well as other custom imaging and illumination products for use in minimally-invasive surgical procedures. Precision Optics' research and development division has developed next-generation capabilities for designing and manufacturing 3D endoscopes, very small Microprecision lenses and enhancing imaging systems for minimally-invasive surgery purposes, all of which are commercialized. The firm's expertise includes the design, development and manufacturing of optical and mechanical-optical components, sub-assemblies and systems such as lenses, prisms, thin film coatings, optical assemblies, sinuscopes, arthroscopes, laparoscopes, stereo-endoscopes, beamsplitters, endocouplers, camera adapters and fiber optic assemblies. Precision Optics' 100,000-square-foot manufacturing site in central Massachusetts has the capacity to meet the needs of its customers, whether small businesses or large corporations.

FINANCIAL DATA:
Note: Data for latest year may not have been available at press time.

In U.S. $	2017	2016	2015	2014	2013	2012
Revenue						
R&D Expense						
Operating Income						
Operating Margin %						
SGA Expense						
Net Income						
Operating Cash Flow						
Capital Expenditure						
EBITDA						
Return on Assets %						
Return on Equity %						
Debt to Equity						

CONTACT INFORMATION:

Phone: 978 630-1800 Fax: 978 630-1487
Toll-Free:
Address: 22 East Broadway, Gardner, MA 01440 United States

STOCK TICKER/OTHER:

Stock Ticker: PEYE
Employees: 27
Parent Company:
Exchange: PINX
Fiscal Year Ends: 06/30

SALARIES/BONUSES:

Top Exec. Salary: $195,000 Bonus: $
Second Exec. Salary: $120,000 Bonus: $

OTHER THOUGHTS:

Estimated Female Officers or Directors:
Hot Spot for Advancement for Women/Minorities:

Precision Therapeutics Inc

NAIC Code: 339,100

www.precisiontherapeutics.com

TYPES OF BUSINESS:

Surgical Appliance and Supplies Manufacturing

BRANDS/DIVISIONS/AFFILIATES:

Skyline Medical Inc
STREAMWAY System
TumorGenesis Inc
Helomics Holding Corporation

CONTACTS: *Note: Officers with more than one job title may be intentionally listed here more than once.*

Bob Myers, CFO
David Johnson, COO
Carl Schwartz, Director
Thomas McGoldrick, Director

GROWTH PLANS/SPECIAL FEATURES:

Precision Therapeutics, Inc., formerly Skyline Medical Inc., is a medical device company that manufactures an environmentally conscientious system for the collection and disposal of infectious fluids that result from surgical procedures and post-operative care. The firm's primary product is the STREAMWAY System. The STREAMWAY System is a wall mounted fully automated system that disposes of an unlimited amount of suctioned fluid providing uninterrupted performance for surgeons while virtually eliminating healthcare workers' exposure to potentially infectious fluids found in the surgical environment. The system also provides a way to dispose of ascetic fluid with no evac bottles, suction canisters, transport or risk of exposure. In addition to the STREAMWAY System, Skyline also manufactures and sells two disposable products required for system operation: a bifurcated single procedure filter with tissue trap and a single use bottle of cleaning solution. Both items are used on a single procedure basis and must be discarded after use. The firm markets and distributes its products to medical facilities where bodily and irrigation fluids produced during surgical procedures must be contained, measured, documented and disposed. In January 2018, Skyline Medical announced that effective the following February it was changing its name to Precision Therapeutics. The following February, the firm formed subsidiary TumorGenesis, Inc., to develop the next generation of patient derived tumor models for precision cancer therapy and drug development. That June, Precision Therapeutics agreed to acquire the remaining 75% of Helomics Holding Corporation to give it complete ownership.

FINANCIAL DATA: *Note: Data for latest year may not have been available at press time.*

In U.S. $	2017	2016	2015	2014	2013	2012
Revenue	654,836	456,495	654,354	951,559	468,125	188,772
R&D Expense						
Operating Income	-7,746,593	-6,526,011	-4,399,643	-6,467,448	-8,927,381	-7,159,690
Operating Margin %	-1182.98%	-1429.59%	-672.36%	-679.66%	-1907.05%	-3792.77%
SGA Expense	8,253,384	5,642,769	4,750,015	7,033,684	9,205,799	7,219,922
Net Income	-7,746,593	-6,526,014	-4,790,530	-6,833,568	-9,406,304	-7,422,155
Operating Cash Flow	-4,459,750	-4,381,440	-7,487,293	-3,371,413	-3,855,166	-1,184,165
Capital Expenditure	55,272	44,747	60,565	121,237	216,116	
EBITDA	-7,675,031	-6,443,655	-4,321,077	-6,392,809	-8,621,040	-7,161,727
Return on Assets %	-240.88%	-154.64%	-146.64%	-914.55%	-1953.53%	-1819.60%
Return on Equity %	-429.46%	-260.17%				
Debt to Equity						

CONTACT INFORMATION:

Phone: 651-389-4800 Fax:
Toll-Free:
Address: 2915 Commers Dr., Ste. 900, Eagan, MN 55121 United States

STOCK TICKER/OTHER:

Stock Ticker: AIPT
Exchange: NAS
Employees: 12
Fiscal Year Ends: 12/31
Parent Company:

SALARIES/BONUSES:

Top Exec. Salary: $149,053 Bonus: $36,000
Second Exec. Salary: $131,234 Bonus: $33,000

OTHER THOUGHTS:

Estimated Female Officers or Directors:
Hot Spot for Advancement for Women/Minorities:

Premera Blue Cross

www.premera.com

NAIC Code: 524,114

TYPES OF BUSINESS:

Insurance-Medical & Health, HMOs & PPOs
Dental Insurance
Long-Term Care Insurance

BRANDS/DIVISIONS/AFFILIATES:

Blue Cross Blue Shield Association

CONTACTS:

Note: Officers with more than one job title may be intentionally listed here more than once.

Jeff Roe, CEO
Jim Messina, COO
H. R. Brereton (Gubby) Barlow, Pres.
David Braza, CFO
Roki Chauhan, Chief Medical Officer
Mark Gregory, CIO
John Pierce, General Counsel
Kirsten (Kacey) Kemp, Sr. VP-Oper.
Brian Ancell, Exec. VP-Strategic Dev. & Health Care Svcs.
Yoram (Yori) Milo, Chief Legal Public Policy Officer
Richard Maturi, Sr. VP-Health Care Delivery Systems
Jeff Roe, Sr. VP-Employer & Individual Markets

GROWTH PLANS/SPECIAL FEATURES:

Premera Blue Cross is a nonprofit Blue Cross Blue Shield Association licensed health insurance provider for Washington and Alaska. Through a network of 38,000 healthcare providers, the firm serves more than 2 million members. Premera health plans include preferred provider organization (PPO) plans, exclusive provider organization (EPO) plans, Medicare supplemental, indemnity coverage, dental and long-term care. Premera also offers a collection of products that allow business customers to tailor health plans with features from health maintenance organizations (HMOs), PPOs or managed indemnity plans. Employers then decide which doctor and hospital network to support along with options for out-of-network coverage, deductibles, co-pays and pharmacy benefits. The company's estimator tool provides patients with an estimate of their out of pocket costs based on their specific benefits package.

The firm offers employees medical and dental coverage, a health savings account, life insurance, disability insurance, a flexible spending account, a 401(k) plan, a pension plan, an education assistance program and an employee assistance program.

FINANCIAL DATA:

Note: Data for latest year may not have been available at press time.

In U.S. $	2017	2016	2015	2014	2013	2012
Revenue	4,704,835,800	4,480,796,000	4,286,797,000	3,835,243,000	3,361,800,000	3,344,800,000
R&D Expense						
Operating Income						
Operating Margin %						
SGA Expense						
Net Income		69,873,000	-19,880,000	66,277,000	130,500,000	98,200,000
Operating Cash Flow						
Capital Expenditure						
EBITDA						
Return on Assets %						
Return on Equity %						
Debt to Equity						

CONTACT INFORMATION:

Phone: 425-918-4000 Fax:
Toll-Free: 800-722-1471
Address: 7001 220th SW, Bldg. 1, Mountlake Terrace, WA 98043 United States

STOCK TICKER/OTHER:

Stock Ticker: Nonprofit Exchange:
Employees: 3,250 Fiscal Year Ends: 12/31
Parent Company: Blue Cross Blue Shield Association

SALARIES/BONUSES:

Top Exec. Salary: $ Bonus: $
Second Exec. Salary: $ Bonus: $

OTHER THOUGHTS:

Estimated Female Officers or Directors: 3
Hot Spot for Advancement for Women/Minorities: Y

Premier Inc

NAIC Code: 561,110

www.premierinc.com

TYPES OF BUSINESS:

Management Services
Supply Chain Management
Health Care Consulting
Insurance Services
IT Services
Labor Performance Services

BRANDS/DIVISIONS/AFFILIATES:

PremierConnect

CONTACTS:

Note: Officers with more than one job title may be intentionally listed here more than once.

Susan DeVore, CEO
Kelly Rakowski, Senior VP, Divisional
Craig McKasson, CFO
Richard Statuto, Chairman of the Board
Leigh Anderson, Chief Information Officer
Michael Alkire, COO
Terry Shaw, Director
David Klatsky, General Counsel
Durral Gilbert, President, Divisional
David Hargraves, Senior VP, Divisional
Kelli Price, Senior VP, Divisional
Mike Moloney, Vice President, Divisional

GROWTH PLANS/SPECIAL FEATURES:

Premier, Inc. is primarily a medical supply chain management and healthcare consulting company. Premier is a member-owned healthcare alliance of hospitals, health systems and other healthcare organizations located in the U.S., as well as stockholders. Together with its subsidiaries and affiliates, Premier is a leading healthcare improvement company that unites approximately 3,900 U.S. hospitals and health systems and approximately 150,000 other providers and organizations to transform healthcare. It accomplishes this via integrated data and analytics, collaborative services, supply chain solutions and advisory services. The firm delivers a comprehensive technology-enabled platform that offers critical supply chain services, clinical, financial, operational and population health software-as-a-service (SaaS) informatics products, advisory services and performance improvement collaborative programs. Premier operates through two business segments: supply chain services, which assists its group purchasing organization (GPO) members in managing their non-labor expense categories through a combination of products, services and technologies, serving acute and alternate sites, specialty pharmacy offerings and direct sourcing activities; and performance services, which provides information technology analytics and workflow automation and advisory services. The firm's PremierConnect technology platform infrastructure allows members to analyze data through detailed standard and ad-hoc analyses, benchmarking, interactive dashboards, mobile access and custom report services.

Premier offers its employees medical, dental and vision coverage; business travel insurance; tuition reimbursement; flexible spending accounts; and an employee assistance program.

FINANCIAL DATA:

Note: Data for latest year may not have been available at press time.

In U.S. $	2017	2016	2015	2014	2013	2012
Revenue	1,454,673,000	1,162,594,000	1,007,029,000	910,549,000	869,290,000	
R&D Expense	3,107,000	2,925,000	2,937,000	3,389,000	9,370,000	
Operating Income	317,720,000	265,948,000	266,042,000	302,052,000	372,667,000	
Operating Margin %	21.84%	22.87%	26.41%	33.17%	42.87%	
SGA Expense	405,471,000	403,611,000	332,004,000	294,421,000	248,301,000	
Net Income	113,425,000	41,614,000	38,743,000	28,332,000	7,376,000	
Operating Cash Flow	392,247,000	371,470,000	364,058,000	368,122,000	375,180,000	
Capital Expenditure	71,372,000	76,990,000	70,734,000	55,740,000	42,427,000	
EBITDA	424,931,000	350,104,000	320,364,000	341,875,000	401,887,000	
Return on Assets %	3.49%	48.34%	-62.32%	-294.02%	1.27%	
Return on Equity %					9.32%	
Debt to Equity					0.28	

CONTACT INFORMATION:

Phone: 704-357-0022 Fax: 704-357-6611
Toll-Free: 877-777-1552
Address: 13034 Ballantyne Corporate Pl., Charlotte, NC 28277 United States

STOCK TICKER/OTHER:

Stock Ticker: PINC
Employees: 2,400
Parent Company:
Exchange: NAS
Fiscal Year Ends: 06/30

SALARIES/BONUSES:

Top Exec. Salary: $977,838 Bonus: $
Second Exec. Salary: $797,531 Bonus: $

OTHER THOUGHTS:

Estimated Female Officers or Directors: 5
Hot Spot for Advancement for Women/Minorities: Y

Prime Healthcare Services Inc

www.primehealthcare.com

NAIC Code: 622,110

TYPES OF BUSINESS:

General Medical and Surgical Hospitals

BRANDS/DIVISIONS/AFFILIATES:

Prime A Investments LLC
Prime Healthcare Foundation (The)

CONTACTS:

Note: Officers with more than one job title may be intentionally listed here more than once.

Prem Reddy, CEO
Mike Sarian, Pres.-Operations
Mike Healther, CFO
Elizabeth Nikels, VP-Mktg. & Communications
Arti Dhuper, VP-Human Resources
Will Conaway, CIO
Prem Reddy, Chmn.

GROWTH PLANS/SPECIAL FEATURES:

Prime Healthcare Services, Inc. owns and operates 45 acute care hospitals in 14 U.S. states with more than 8,000 patient beds. Of the 45 hospitals, 15 are not-for-profit. The firm's hospitals provide a full range of both inpatient and outpatient services, including general acute care, emergency room, general and specialty surgery, intensive/critical care, obstetrics, behavioral health, rehabilitation and diagnostic services. Prime Healthcare is the largest for-profit operator of hospitals in the state of California, based on the number of facilities, and is one of the Top 5 largest for-profit hospital systems in the nation. The firm is a physician-founded and physician-driven health system with doctors and clinicians leading the organization at every level. The majority of Prime Healthcare's hospitals have contractual agreements with the major managed care providers: Aetna, Blue Cross, Health Net and United Healthcare. The Prime Healthcare Foundation, a 501(c)3 public charity, is dedicated to improving access to health care and increasing educational opportunities in health care. The foundation owns and operates 15 hospitals in California, Texas, Ohio, Pennsylvania and Georgia. Many of these were acquired in or near bankruptcy and donated to the Foundation debt-free. Prime Healthcare is a subsidiary of Prime A. Investments, LLC., which owns and operates real estate properties.

FINANCIAL DATA:

Note: Data for latest year may not have been available at press time.

In U.S. $	2017	2016	2015	2014	2013	2012
Revenue						
R&D Expense						
Operating Income						
Operating Margin %						
SGA Expense						
Net Income						
Operating Cash Flow						
Capital Expenditure						
EBITDA						
Return on Assets %						
Return on Equity %						
Debt to Equity						

CONTACT INFORMATION:

Phone: 909-235-4400 Fax:
Toll-Free:
Address: 3300 E. Guasti Rd., Ontario, CA 91761 United States

STOCK TICKER/OTHER:

Stock Ticker: Nonprofit
Employees: 40,000
Parent Company: Prime A Investments LLC
Exchange:
Fiscal Year Ends:

SALARIES/BONUSES:

Top Exec. Salary: $ Bonus: $
Second Exec. Salary: $ Bonus: $

OTHER THOUGHTS:

Estimated Female Officers or Directors:
Hot Spot for Advancement for Women/Minorities:

Profarma Distribuidora de Produtos Farmaceuticos SA

www.profarma.com.br

NAIC Code: 424,210

TYPES OF BUSINESS:

Wholesale Pharmaceuticals Distribution
Health Care & Cosmetics Distribution

BRANDS/DIVISIONS/AFFILIATES:

Profarma Specialty
Drogasmil
Farmalife
Rosario
Tamoio

CONTACTS:

Note: Officers with more than one job title may be intentionally listed here more than once.

Sammy Birmarcker, CEO
Maximiliano Guimaraes Fischer, CFO
Manoel Birmarcker, VP

GROWTH PLANS/SPECIAL FEATURES:

Profarma Distribuidora de Produtos Farmaceuticos SA is among the largest wholesale distributors of pharmaceutical products in Brazil. The company distributes medicines, personal care products and cosmetics to over 37,000 drugstores in 3,800 cities, reaching nearly 96% of the Brazilian market. Profarma'a delivery network includes nine distribution centers in Bahia, Goias, Minas Gerais, Paraiba, Parana, Pernambuco, Rio de Janeiro, Rio Grande do Sul and Sao Paulo. In many of Brazil's major cities, orders can be delivered in a matter of hours and most shipments arrive within one day. Profarma maintains an electronic ordering system to facilitate transactions and order tracking. The company operates through three segments: pharma distribution, specialties and retail. Pharma distribution derives approximately 70% of sales revenue and comprises the wholesale operations, selling medicines and health and beauty products to pharmaceutical retailers. Specialties derives 15% of sales revenue and comprises Profarma's hospital, dermatological products, vaccines and special medications through joint venture, Profarma Specialty. Retail derives approximately 15% of sales revenue and comprises the Drogasmil, Farmalife, Rosario and Tamoio retail chains, which together have 225 stores throughout the midwest of Brazil. This division is the sixth-largest pharmaceutical retail chain in the country.

FINANCIAL DATA:

Note: Data for latest year may not have been available at press time.

In U.S. $	2017	2016	2015	2014	2013	2012
Revenue	1,443,000,000	1,302,987,332	1,073,391,133	864,726,002	870,209,271	810,774,229
R&D Expense						
Operating Income						
Operating Margin %						
SGA Expense						
Net Income	-34,006,400	-15,631,386	-6,762,967	-13,051,073	5,019,643	10,290,269
Operating Cash Flow						
Capital Expenditure						
EBITDA						
Return on Assets %						
Return on Equity %						
Debt to Equity						

CONTACT INFORMATION:

Phone: 55-21-4009-0200 Fax: 55-21-2491-4082
Toll-Free:
Address: Av. Ayrton Senna, 2150 Bl. P, 3/Fl, Rio de Janeiro, RJ 22775-900 Brazil

STOCK TICKER/OTHER:

Stock Ticker: PFRM3
Employees: 2,700
Parent Company:
Exchange: Sao Paulo
Fiscal Year Ends: 12/31

SALARIES/BONUSES:

Top Exec. Salary: $ Bonus: $
Second Exec. Salary: $ Bonus: $

OTHER THOUGHTS:

Estimated Female Officers or Directors:
Hot Spot for Advancement for Women/Minorities:

Protech Home Medical Corp

www.protechhomemedical.com

NAIC Code: 621,999

TYPES OF BUSINESS:

In-Home Patient Monitoring

BRANDS/DIVISIONS/AFFILIATES:

Patient Home Monitoring Corp

CONTACTS:

Note: Officers with more than one job title may be intentionally listed here more than once.

Greg Crawford, CEO
Jerry Kirm, VP-Operations
Hardik Mehta, CFO
W. Zehnder, Other Corporate Officer
Mark Miles, VP-IT
Mike Moore, President
Greg Crawford, Chmn.

GROWTH PLANS/SPECIAL FEATURES:

Protech Home Medical Corp. (formerly Patient Home Monitoring Corp.) is a healthcare services company with operations in the U.S. Protech provides in-home monitoring and disease management services for patients. The firm's primary line of service includes providing in-home monitoring equipment, supplies and services to patients who take prescription blood thinners such as Coumadin (warfarin). Other products and services include oxygen therapy, INR (international normalized ratio) self-testing, daily and ambulatory aids, power mobility options, home ventilation, sleep apnea and PAP (positive airway pressure) treatments. The company seeks to expand its offerings in regards to the management of several chronic disease states, with a focus on patients with heart or pulmonary disease, sleep disorders, reduced mobility and other chronic health conditions. During 2018, Patient Home Monitoring Corp. changed its corporate name to Protech Home Medical Corp. as a reflection of its new focus and strategy to utilize disruptive technology for advancing organic growth and increasing market share.

FINANCIAL DATA:

Note: Data for latest year may not have been available at press time.

In U.S. $	2017	2016	2015	2014	2013	2012
Revenue	58,745,380	107,110,800	55,157,330	16,301,230	3,058,263	3,000,814
R&D Expense						
Operating Income	-9,916,923	-31,236,920	9,825,762	2,312,187	614,716	445,556
Operating Margin %	-16.88%	-29.16%	17.81%	14.18%	20.10%	14.84%
SGA Expense	39,658,460	61,707,690	23,726,640	8,145,283	1,387,098	1,574,200
Net Income	-18,276,150	-58,021,540	-18,923,320	-1,203,378	-1,958,765	-415,202
Operating Cash Flow	-4,667,693	-4,511,539	-2,458,854	-1,004,917	170,071	-849,607
Capital Expenditure	2,330,000	2,973,846	5,761,186	1,034,096	72,492	559,164
EBITDA	-7,581,539	-42,690,000	-7,820,988	858,303	-1,416,596	-93,542
Return on Assets %	-17.35%	-41.89%	-19.37%	-6.33%	-44.83%	-21.67%
Return on Equity %	-22.74%	-51.02%	-25.91%	-20.48%	-222.91%	-51.22%
Debt to Equity	0.10	0.06	0.03		0.50	0.44

CONTACT INFORMATION:

Phone: 859-300-6455 Fax:
Toll-Free:
Address: 1019 Town Dr., Wilder, KY 41076 United States

STOCK TICKER/OTHER:

Stock Ticker: PHM
Employees: 47
Parent Company:
Exchange: TSX
Fiscal Year Ends: 09/30

SALARIES/BONUSES:

Top Exec. Salary: $ Bonus: $
Second Exec. Salary: $ Bonus: $

OTHER THOUGHTS:

Estimated Female Officers or Directors:
Hot Spot for Advancement for Women/Minorities:

Proteus Digital Health Inc

www.proteus.com

NAIC Code: 334,510

TYPES OF BUSINESS:

Electromedical and Electrotherapeutic Apparatus Manufacturing
Ingestible Sensor
Digital medicines

BRANDS/DIVISIONS/AFFILIATES:

CONTACTS:

Note: Officers with more than one job title may be intentionally listed here more than once.

Andrew M. Thompson, CEO
Uneek Mehra, CFO

GROWTH PLANS/SPECIAL FEATURES:

Proteus Digital Health, Inc. is a creator of digital medicine. Digital medicine therapy includes drugs that communicate when taken, wearable sensors that capture physiologic response, applications that support patient self-care and physician decision making, as well as data analytics to serve the needs of doctors and health systems. The goal of Proteus' digital medicines is to empower patients and their families, enable physicians and health systems to more effectively manage risk and ensure that outcomes are reliably achieved. Proteus has received FDA market clearance in the U.S. and a CE mark in Europe for wearable and ingestible sensor devices. The company has more than 450 issued patents, is headquartered in Redwood City, California, and is privately-held by investors that include Carlyle, Essex Woodlands, Kaiser Permanente, Medtronic, Novartis, Otsuka, PepsiCo and ON Semiconductor. In April 2018, Proteus announced that together with its collaborators, the company had developed a pipeline of 31 digital medicines for mental health, cardiovascular and metabolic conditions, infectious diseases and oncology.

FINANCIAL DATA:

Note: Data for latest year may not have been available at press time.

In U.S. $	2017	2016	2015	2014	2013	2012
Revenue						
R&D Expense						
Operating Income						
Operating Margin %						
SGA Expense						
Net Income						
Operating Cash Flow						
Capital Expenditure						
EBITDA						
Return on Assets %						
Return on Equity %						
Debt to Equity						

CONTACT INFORMATION:

Phone: 650-632-4031 Fax: 650-632-4071
Toll-Free:
Address: 2600 Bridge Parkway, Redwood City, CA 94065 United States

STOCK TICKER/OTHER:

Stock Ticker: Private
Employees:
Parent Company:
Exchange:
Fiscal Year Ends:

SALARIES/BONUSES:

Top Exec. Salary: $ Bonus: $
Second Exec. Salary: $ Bonus: $

OTHER THOUGHTS:

Estimated Female Officers or Directors:
Hot Spot for Advancement for Women/Minorities:

Providence St Joseph Health

www.psjhealth.org

NAIC Code: 622,110

TYPES OF BUSINESS:

General Medical and Surgical Hospitals
Assisted Living Facilities
Low Income Living Facilities
Counseling

BRANDS/DIVISIONS/AFFILIATES:

Providence Health & Services
St. Joseph Health
Covenant Health
Facey Medical Foundation
Hoag Memorial Presbyterian
Kadlec
Pacific Medical Centers
Institute for Mental Health and Wellness

CONTACTS: *Note: Officers with more than one job title may be intentionally listed here more than once.*

Rod Hochman, CEO
Mike Butler, Pres.-Operations
Venkat Bhamidipati, CFO
Myron Berdischewsky, Chief Medical & Quality Officer
Cindy Strauss, Sr. VP
David Brown, VP-Strategy & Bus. Dev.
Deborah Burton, VP
Jack Friedman, Sr. VP-Accountable Care & Payor Relations
Joel Gilbertson, VP-Gov't. & Public Affairs
John O. Mudd, Sr. VP-Mission leadership
Dave Hunter, VP-Supply Chain Mgmt.

GROWTH PLANS/SPECIAL FEATURES:

Providence St. Joseph Health comprises 55 hospitals, 829 clinics, 25,000 physicians, supportive housing facilities and 119,000 caregivers with the goal of improving the health of the communities it serves, especially the poor and the vulnerable. The faith-based firm provides a comprehensive range of services across Alaska, California, Montana, New Mexico, Oregon, Texas and Washington. The Providence St. Joseph Health family includes: Providence Health & Services (Alaska, Washington, Montana, Oregon and California), St. Joseph Health (California and Texas), Covenant Health (Texas), Facey Medical Group (California), Hoag Memorial Presbyterian (California), Kadlec (Washington), Pacific Medical Centers (Washington), as well as Swedish Health Services (Washington). The company established the Institute for Mental Health and Wellness to provide effective mental health services for those who struggle with mental health stigmatization, diagnosis and treatment. The funds derived by the foundation support research and startup operations regarding mental health awareness, diagnosis and treatment.

FINANCIAL DATA: *Note: Data for latest year may not have been available at press time.*

In U.S. $	2017	2016	2015	2014	2013	2012
Revenue	23,163,000,000	18,878,000,000	14,434,000,000	12,261,825,000	11,099,009,000	10,608,249,000
R&D Expense						
Operating Income						
Operating Margin %						
SGA Expense						
Net Income	780,000,000	5,231,000,000	77,000,000	771,422,000	253,270,000	1,216,516,000
Operating Cash Flow						
Capital Expenditure						
EBITDA						
Return on Assets %						
Return on Equity %						
Debt to Equity						

CONTACT INFORMATION:

Phone: 425-525-3355 Fax:
Toll-Free:
Address: 1801 Lind Avenue SW, Renton, WA 98057 United States

STOCK TICKER/OTHER:

Stock Ticker: Nonprofit
Employees: 100,000
Parent Company:
Exchange:
Fiscal Year Ends: 12/31

SALARIES/BONUSES:

Top Exec. Salary: $ Bonus: $
Second Exec. Salary: $ Bonus: $

OTHER THOUGHTS:

Estimated Female Officers or Directors: 5
Hot Spot for Advancement for Women/Minorities: Y

Quality Systems Inc

www.qsii.com

NAIC Code: 511210D

TYPES OF BUSINESS:

Computer Software, Healthcare & Biotechnology

BRANDS/DIVISIONS/AFFILIATES:

NextGen Healthcare Information Systems
NextGen Office
NextGen Mobile Health Solution
NextGen Population Health Informed Analytics
NextGen Managed Cloud Services
NextGen Financial Suite
NextGen Connected Health Solutions
NextGen Managed Cloud Services

CONTACTS: *Note: Officers with more than one job title may be intentionally listed here more than once.*

John Frantz, CEO
James Arnold, CFO
Sheldon Razin, Chairman Emeritus
David Metcalfe, Chief Technology Officer
Scott Bostick, COO
Jeffrey Margolis, Director
Craig Barbarosh, Director
Jeffrey Linton, Executive VP

GROWTH PLANS/SPECIAL FEATURES:

Quality Systems, Inc. provides software, services and analytics solutions to the ambulatory care market. The company, along with its NextGen Healthcare Information Systems subsidiary, develops and markets software and services that automate certain aspects of practice management and electronic health records (EHR). Quality Systems' clients range from large multi-specialty to small specialty practices and include networks of practices such as physician hospital organizations (PHOs), management service organizations (MSOs), independent physician associations (IPAs), accountable care organizations (ACOs), ambulatory care centers (ACCs) and community health centers (CHCs). The firm's NextGen Healthcare line of solutions are built on an integrated platform that enable clients to target clinical and financial outcomes concurrently with improved physician and patient engagement. They begin with a clinical and financial core that can be deployed on premise and in the cloud. Clients have control over how platform capabilities are implemented to drive their desired outcomes. Its open web-based application program interfaces (APIs) and drive secure the exchange of health and patient data with connected health solutions. The platform's primary products include: NextGen Enterprise EHR, which stores and maintains clinical patient information and offers a workflow module, prescription management, automatic document and letter generation and much more; NextGen Enterprise PM, an integrated practice management (PM) offering that is scalable; and NextGen Office, a cloud-based EHR and PM solution for physicians and medical billing services. Other products include the NextGen Mobile Health Solution, NextGen Population Health Informed Analytics, NextGen Population Health Performance Management, NextGen Connected Health Solutions, NextGen Managed Cloud Services, NextGen Financial Suite and NextGen Contract Audit & Recovery Service, among others. In January 2018, Quality Systems acquired Inforth Technologies for its specialty-focused clinical content.

FINANCIAL DATA: *Note: Data for latest year may not have been available at press time.*

In U.S. $	2017	2016	2015	2014	2013	2012
Revenue	509,624,000	492,476,992	490,224,992	444,667,008	460,228,992	429,835,008
R&D Expense						
Operating Income						
Operating Margin %						
SGA Expense						
Net Income	18,241,000	5,657,000	27,332,000	15,680,000	42,724,000	75,657,000
Operating Cash Flow						
Capital Expenditure						
EBITDA						
Return on Assets %						
Return on Equity %						
Debt to Equity						

CONTACT INFORMATION:

Phone: 949 255-2600 Fax:
Toll-Free: 800-888-7955
Address: 18111 Von Karman, Ste. 800, Irvine, CA 92612 United States

STOCK TICKER/OTHER:

Stock Ticker: QSII Exchange: NAS
Employees: 2,791 Fiscal Year Ends: 02/28
Parent Company:

SALARIES/BONUSES:

Top Exec. Salary: $ Bonus: $
Second Exec. Salary: $ Bonus: $

OTHER THOUGHTS:

Estimated Female Officers or Directors:
Hot Spot for Advancement for Women/Minorities:

Quest Diagnostics Inc

www.questdiagnostics.com

NAIC Code: 621,511

TYPES OF BUSINESS:

Services-Testing & Diagnostics
Clinical Laboratory Testing
Clinical Trials Testing
Esoteric Testing Laboratories

BRANDS/DIVISIONS/AFFILIATES:

Nichols Institute
Athena Diagnostics
Med Fusion
Cleveland HeartLab

CONTACTS: *Note: Officers with more than one job title may be intentionally listed here more than once.*

Stephen Rusckowski, CEO
Mark Guinan, CFO
James Davis, Executive VP, Divisional
Michael Prevoznik, General Counsel
Jon Cohen, Other Corporate Officer
Catherine Doherty, Other Corporate Officer
Everett Cunningham, Senior VP, Divisional
Carrie Eglinton Manner, Senior VP, Divisional
Robert Klug, Vice President

GROWTH PLANS/SPECIAL FEATURES:

Quest Diagnostics, Inc. is a U.S. clinical laboratory testing company, offering diagnostic testing and related services to the health care industry. The firm's operations consist of routine, esoteric and clinical trials testing. Quest operates through its national network of over 2,200 patient service centers, principal laboratories in several major metropolitan areas, rapid-response laboratories, outpatient anatomic pathology centers, hospital-based laboratories and esoteric testing laboratories on both coasts. Routine tests measure various important bodily health parameters. Tests in this category include blood cholesterol level tests, complete blood cell counts, urinalyses, pregnancy and prenatal tests, substance-abuse tests and allergy tests such. The company also provides cancer diagnostics, including anatomic pathology services in the U.S. Gene-based and other esoteric tests require more sophisticated technology and highly skilled personnel. Quest's esoteric testing laboratories, comprising the Nichols Institute, Med Fusion, Cleveland HeartLab and Athena Diagnostics, are among the leading esoteric clinical testing laboratories in the world. Esoteric tests involve endocrinology, genetics, immunology, microbiology, oncology, serology, endocrinology, hematology and toxicology. Clinical trial testing primarily involves assessing the safety and efficacy of new drugs to meet FDA requirements. The company has clinical trials testing centers in the U.S. and the U.K., and provides clinical trials testing in Argentina, Brazil, China and Singapore through affiliated laboratories. Additionally, Quest provides risk management services to the life insurance industry in the U.S. and Canada as well as many other countries.

The firm offers employees medical, dental and life insurance; employee assistance program; and flexible spending accounts.

FINANCIAL DATA: *Note: Data for latest year may not have been available at press time.*

In U.S. $	2017	2016	2015	2014	2013	2012
Revenue	7,709,000,000	7,515,000,000	7,493,000,000	7,435,000,000	7,146,000,000	7,382,562,000
R&D Expense						
Operating Income	1,165,000,000	1,159,000,000	1,065,000,000	983,000,000	1,001,000,000	1,200,797,000
Operating Margin %	15.11%	15.42%	14.21%	13.22%	14.00%	16.26%
SGA Expense	1,750,000,000	1,681,000,000	1,679,000,000	1,728,000,000	1,704,000,000	1,745,200,000
Net Income	772,000,000	645,000,000	709,000,000	556,000,000	849,000,000	555,721,000
Operating Cash Flow	1,175,000,000	1,069,000,000	810,000,000	938,000,000	652,000,000	1,187,168,000
Capital Expenditure	252,000,000	293,000,000	263,000,000	308,000,000	231,000,000	182,234,000
EBITDA	1,453,000,000	1,479,000,000	1,561,000,000	1,330,000,000	1,793,000,000	1,522,679,000
Return on Assets %	7.46%	6.40%	7.11%	5.88%	9.28%	5.94%
Return on Equity %	16.10%	13.78%	15.71%	13.43%	20.86%	14.08%
Debt to Equity	0.76	0.80	0.74	0.75	0.79	0.80

CONTACT INFORMATION:

Phone: 973 520-2700 Fax:
Toll-Free: 800-222-0446
Address: 3 Giralda Farms, Madison, NJ 07940 United States

STOCK TICKER/OTHER:

Stock Ticker: DGX
Employees: 43,000
Parent Company:
Exchange: NYS
Fiscal Year Ends: 12/31

SALARIES/BONUSES:

Top Exec. Salary: $1,100,000 Bonus: $
Second Exec. Salary: $590,000 Bonus: $

OTHER THOUGHTS:

Estimated Female Officers or Directors: 3
Hot Spot for Advancement for Women/Minorities: Y

Quidel Corporation

www.quidel.com

NAIC Code: 325,413

TYPES OF BUSINESS:

Rapid Diagnosis Products
Point-of-Care Diagnostic Tests
Research Products

BRANDS/DIVISIONS/AFFILIATES:

QuickVue
MicroVue
QuickVue+
ELVIS
Amplivue
Solana
Virena
Thyretain

CONTACTS: *Note: Officers with more than one job title may be intentionally listed here more than once.*

Douglas Bryant, CEO
Randall Steward, CFO
Kenneth Buechler, Chairman of the Board
Robert Bujarski, General Counsel
Ratan Borkar, Senior VP, Divisional
Werner Kroll, Senior VP, Divisional
Michael Abney, Senior VP, Divisional
Edward Russell, Senior VP, Divisional

GROWTH PLANS/SPECIAL FEATURES:

Quidel Corporation develops, manufactures and markets rapid diagnostic products at the professional point-of-care level for infectious diseases, women's health and gastrointestinal diseases. The firm's products detect and manage medical conditions and illnesses such as infectious diseases, pregnancy, general health screening, oncology, autoimmune disorders and osteoporosis. Quidel sells its products to professionals for use in physician offices, hospitals, clinical laboratories, reference laboratories, leading universities, retail clinics and wellness screening centers. Brand names include QuickVue, QuickVue+, Quidel, MicroVue, FreshCells, D3, FastPoint, Super E-Mix, ELVIS, ELVIRA, Sofia, AmpliVue, Solana, Virena, Lyra and Thyretain. The company markets its products in the U.S. through a network of national and regional distributors, supported by a direct sales force. Three of its distributors, McKesson Corporation, Cardinal Health, Inc. and Fisher Scientific, are top market leaders. Internationally, the company sells and markets primarily in Japan, Europe and the Middle East through exclusive distributor agreements. The firm has two manufacturing operations in San Diego, California and Athens, Ohio. The San Diego facility is dedicated to tissue culture, cell culture, protein purification and immunochemistry; and the Athens facility consists of cell culturing and dispensing, as well as laboratories devoted to tissue culture for the production of monoclonal antibodies. In October 2017, Quidel acquired the Triage MeterPro cardiovascular and toxicology business, and B-type Naturietic Peptide assay business run on Beckman Coulter analyzers from Alere, Inc. In February 2018, Quidel announced plans to establish a Business Service Centre in Galway, Ireland to support its expanding international business.

The company offers employees medical, dental, vision and life insurance; flexible spending and employee assistance programs; tuition reimbursement; and 401(k) and stock purchase plans.

FINANCIAL DATA: *Note: Data for latest year may not have been available at press time.*

In U.S. $	2017	2016	2015	2014	2013	2012
Revenue	277,743,000	191,603,000	196,129,000	182,615,000	175,410,000	155,741,000
R&D Expense	33,644,000	38,672,000	35,514,000	37,913,000	34,186,000	27,716,000
Operating Income	26,058,000	-4,439,000	2,738,000	-5,650,000	5,990,000	8,846,000
Operating Margin %	9.38%	-2.31%	1.39%	-3.09%	3.41%	5.67%
SGA Expense	96,440,000	74,883,000	77,333,000	67,344,000	60,087,000	50,959,000
Net Income	-8,165,000	-13,808,000	-6,079,000	-7,074,000	7,390,000	4,993,000
Operating Cash Flow	27,709,000	11,815,000	36,309,000	35,686,000	25,682,000	19,633,000
Capital Expenditure	17,510,000	11,909,000	17,032,000	11,241,000	22,501,000	27,722,000
EBITDA	56,820,000	18,357,000	26,124,000	22,715,000	28,905,000	32,118,000
Return on Assets %	-1.23%	-3.47%	-1.41%	-1.95%	2.87%	1.91%
Return on Equity %	-3.81%	-6.58%	-2.62%	-3.01%	3.48%	2.59%
Debt to Equity	1.66	0.73	0.67	0.59	0.02	0.05

CONTACT INFORMATION:

Phone: 858 552-1100 Fax:
Toll-Free: 800-874-1517
Address: 12544 High Bluiff Dr. Ste. 200, San Diego, CA 92130 United States

STOCK TICKER/OTHER:

Stock Ticker: QDEL
Employees: 627
Parent Company:
Exchange: NAS
Fiscal Year Ends: 12/31

SALARIES/BONUSES:

Top Exec. Salary: $574,846 Bonus: $
Second Exec. Salary: $375,058 Bonus: $

OTHER THOUGHTS:

Estimated Female Officers or Directors: 1
Hot Spot for Advancement for Women/Minorities:

RadNet Inc

www.radnet.com

NAIC Code: 621,512

TYPES OF BUSINESS:

Diagnostic Imaging Centers
Medical Imaging Centers

BRANDS/DIVISIONS/AFFILIATES:

RadNet Management Inc
Beverly Radiology Medical Group III

CONTACTS:

Note: Officers with more than one job title may be intentionally listed here more than once.

Howard Berger, CEO
Mark Stolper, CFO
Norman Hames, COO, Divisional
Stephen Forthuber, COO, Divisional
John Crues, Director
Mital Patel, Executive VP, Divisional
Jeffrey Linden, Executive VP
Michael Murdock, Executive VP

GROWTH PLANS/SPECIAL FEATURES:

RadNet, Inc. operates a network of nearly 300 diagnostic imaging centers in six states. These centers, which are located in California, Maryland, Florida, Delaware, New Jersey and New York, perform millions of procedures annually and specialize in medical imaging services and general diagnostic radiology. The facilities are usually located near RadNet's multi-modality sites to help accommodate overflow in target demographic areas. Some of the firm's most common imaging procedures are X-ray, fluoroscopy, endoscopy and modalities such as CT scans and digital image processing. The centers also offer open MRI, allowing studies with patients not typically compatible with conventional MRI, such as pediatric, claustrophobic or obese patients. Patients are generally referred to the centers by their treating physicians and may be affiliated with an IPA, HMO, PPO or similar organization. RadNet Management, Inc. manages the centers. It supplies the equipment as well as non-medical operational, management, financial and administrative services for the centers, with the medical services provided by affiliates such as Beverly Radiology Medical Group III (BRMG). The company derives most of its revenues from commercial insurance payers (59%, as of fiscal 2017-2018), 12% from managed care capitated payers, 20% from Medicare and 3% from Medicaid. During 2017, the firm sold five centers in the state of Rhode Island, divesting all of its holdings in the state. In April 2018, RadNet acquired five imaging centers in Fresno, California, which were operated by Sierra Imaging Associates, Women's Imaging Specialists in Healthcare and Valley Metabolic Imaging.

FINANCIAL DATA:

Note: Data for latest year may not have been available at press time.

In U.S. $	2017	2016	2015	2014	2013	2012
Revenue	922,186,000	884,535,000	809,628,000	717,569,000	702,986,000	647,153,000
R&D Expense						
Operating Income	51,192,000	39,247,000	39,983,000	54,418,000	44,635,000	45,684,000
Operating Margin %	5.55%	4.43%	4.93%	7.58%	6.34%	7.05%
SGA Expense	1,821,000	2,877,000	745,000	1,241,000	806,000	736,000
Net Income	53,000	7,230,000	7,709,000	1,376,000	2,120,000	64,517,000
Operating Cash Flow	142,225,000	91,641,000	67,037,000	61,004,000	66,422,000	75,269,000
Capital Expenditure	88,948,000	65,892,000	133,756,000	51,168,000	55,846,000	89,941,000
EBITDA	133,804,000	122,501,000	116,940,000	105,637,000	110,567,000	109,424,000
Return on Assets %		.85%	.97%	.18%	.29%	9.67%
Return on Equity %	.09%	17.83%	40.63%	52.10%		
Debt to Equity	9.34	12.62	18.65	106.77		

CONTACT INFORMATION:

Phone: 310 478-7808 Fax: 310 478-5810
Toll-Free:
Address: 1510 Cotner Ave., Los Angeles, CA 90025 United States

STOCK TICKER/OTHER:

Stock Ticker: RDNT
Employees: 7,285
Parent Company:
Exchange: NAS
Fiscal Year Ends: 12/31

SALARIES/BONUSES:

Top Exec. Salary: $700,000 Bonus: $1,200,000
Second Exec. Salary: $525,000 Bonus: $262,500

OTHER THOUGHTS:

Estimated Female Officers or Directors:
Hot Spot for Advancement for Women/Minorities:

Ramsay Health Care Limited

www.ramsayhealth.com.au

NAIC Code: 622,110

TYPES OF BUSINESS:

General Medical and Surgical Hospitals

BRANDS/DIVISIONS/AFFILIATES:

Masada Private Hospital
Ramsay Health Care (Victoria) Pty Ltd
New Farm Clinic
St Leonards Clinic

CONTACTS:
Note: Officers with more than one job title may be intentionally listed here more than once.

Craig R. McNally, Managing Dir.
Bruce R. Soden, Dir.-Finance
John D. C. OGrady, General Counsel
Paul Fitzmaurice, Dir.-Oper.
Craig McNally, Dir.-Global Strategy & European Oper.
Bruce Soden, Dir.-Finance
Danny Sims, Dir.-Hospital Oper., Australia & Indonesia
Jill Watts, Dir.-U.K. Oper.
Michael S Siddle, Deputy Chmn.
Michael S. Siddle, Chmn.
Damien Michon, Dir.-French Oper.

GROWTH PLANS/SPECIAL FEATURES:

Ramsay Health Care Limited is a global hospital group operating 235 hospitals and day surgery facilities across Australia, the U.K., France, Indonesia and Malaysia. Ramsay Health caters to a broad range of healthcare needs, from day surgery procedures to highly complex surgery as well as psychiatric care and rehabilitation. With approximately 25,000 beds, the company employs over 60,000 staff and treats more than 3 million patients each year. Ramsay's rehabilitation unit, Masada Private Hospital, located in Australia is comprised of 30 private rooms, patient recreation areas, clinician support areas and a gymnasium. Ramsay Health Care (Victoria) Pty Ltd. is a psychiatric facility that provides inpatient and outpatient psychiatric care services. It also offers clinical services such as addiction services, and symptom management for adolescents with a range of psychiatric conditions (mood disturbance, anxiety disorders and psychosis). Ramsay's New Farm Clinic is a designated private mental healthcare facility with three inpatient programs: elderly assessment, eating disorders and mood disorders. In early-2018, Ramsay began business at its new St. Leonards Clinic in Sydney, a mental health hospital with 112 single rooms, day service and on-site consulting suites. The clinic replaced The Northside Clinic in Greenwich, which opened in 1973.

Ramsay Health offers employees opportunities to work around Australia, flexible career paths which encourage nurses to become effective managers, employee benefit programs and flexible salary packaging to suit individual needs.

FINANCIAL DATA: *Note: Data for latest year may not have been available at press time.*

In U.S. $	2017	2016	2015	2014	2013	2012
Revenue	6,271,475,200	6,257,324,544	5,296,322,048	3,552,325,632	2,991,363,328	2,870,361,088
R&D Expense						
Operating Income						
Operating Margin %						
SGA Expense						
Net Income	353,796,672	325,829,952	278,973,952	219,796,672	192,767,008	176,631,680
Operating Cash Flow						
Capital Expenditure						
EBITDA						
Return on Assets %						
Return on Equity %						
Debt to Equity						

CONTACT INFORMATION:

Phone: 61-2-9433-3444 Fax: 61-2-9433-3460
Toll-Free:
Address: Level 8, 154 Pacific Hwy., St Leonards, NSW 2065 Australia

STOCK TICKER/OTHER:

Stock Ticker: RMSYF
Exchange: PINX
Employees: 60,000
Fiscal Year Ends: 06/30
Parent Company:

SALARIES/BONUSES:

Top Exec. Salary: $ Bonus: $
Second Exec. Salary: $ Bonus: $

OTHER THOUGHTS:

Estimated Female Officers or Directors: 1
Hot Spot for Advancement for Women/Minorities:

RCCH HealthCare Partners

rcchhealth.com

NAIC Code: 622,110

TYPES OF BUSINESS:

General Medical and Surgical Hospitals

BRANDS/DIVISIONS/AFFILIATES:

Billings Clinic
Medical University of South Carolina
Baylor Scott & White (Texas)
University of Alabama-Birmingham
James Cancer Center Network (The)
UW Medicine
Apollo Global Management LLC

CONTACTS: *Note: Officers with more than one job title may be intentionally listed here more than once.*

Martin Rash, CEO
Rob Jay, Pres.
Mike Browder, Exec. VP
Martin Rash, Chmn.

GROWTH PLANS/SPECIAL FEATURES:

RCCH HealthCare Partners provides hospital and healthcare services to non-urban communities throughout the U.S. The company comprises 17 regional health systems in 12 states, including Alabama, Arizona, Arkansas, Idaho, Iowa, Montana, Ohio, Oklahoma, Oregon, South Carolina, Texas and Washington. RCCH has more than 2,000 affiliated physicians and mid-level providers. The organization operates through partnerships and joint ventures such as Billings Clinic, Medical University of South Carolina (MUSC Health), Baylor Scott & White (Texas), University of Alabama-Birmingham, The James Cancer Center Network (Ohio State University) and UW Medicine. RCCH is owned by certain funds managed by affiliates of Apollo Global Management, LLC. In July 2018, the firm announced an agreement to merge with and into LifePoint Health, Inc., a leading healthcare provider in the U.S.

FINANCIAL DATA: *Note: Data for latest year may not have been available at press time.*

In U.S. $	2017	2016	2015	2014	2013	2012
Revenue	2,300,000,000	1,800,000,000	1,700,000,000	750,000,000	722,300,000	718,200,000
R&D Expense						
Operating Income						
Operating Margin %						
SGA Expense						
Net Income						
Operating Cash Flow						
Capital Expenditure						
EBITDA						
Return on Assets %						
Return on Equity %						
Debt to Equity						

CONTACT INFORMATION:

Phone: 615-764-3000 Fax: 615-764-3030
Toll-Free:
Address: 103 Continental Place, Ste 200, Brentwood, TN 37027 United States

STOCK TICKER/OTHER:

Stock Ticker: Private Exchange:
Employees: 13,120 Fiscal Year Ends:
Parent Company: Apollo Global Management LLC

SALARIES/BONUSES:

Top Exec. Salary: $ Bonus: $
Second Exec. Salary: $ Bonus: $

OTHER THOUGHTS:

Estimated Female Officers or Directors:
Hot Spot for Advancement for Women/Minorities:

Regeneron Pharmaceuticals Inc

www.regeneron.com

NAIC Code: 325,412

TYPES OF BUSINESS:

Drugs-Diversified
Protein-Based Drugs
Small-Molecule Drugs
Genetics & Transgenic Mouse Technologies

BRANDS/DIVISIONS/AFFILIATES:

Arcalyst
Praluent
EYLEA
Dupixent
ZALTRAP
VelociGene
VelociMou
VelocImmune

CONTACTS:

Note: Officers with more than one job title may be intentionally listed here more than once.

Leonard Schleifer, CEO
Robert Landry, CFO
P. Vagelos, Chairman of the Board
George Yancopoulos, Chief Scientific Officer
Neil Stahl, Executive VP, Divisional
Robert Terifay, Executive VP, Divisional
Daniel Van Plew, Executive VP
Joseph Larosa, General Counsel
Marion McCourt, Senior VP, Divisional
Christopher Fenimore, Vice President

GROWTH PLANS/SPECIAL FEATURES:

Regeneron Pharmaceuticals, Inc. is a biopharmaceutical company that discovers, develops, manufactures and commercializes pharmaceutical drugs for the treatment of serious medical conditions. Regeneron's marketed products include: Arcalyst (rilonacept), a therapy for the treatment of cryopyrin-associated periodic syndromes (CAPS), a rare, inherited inflammatory condition; Praluent (alirocumab) injection, an adjunct to diet and maximally-tolerated statin therapy for adults who require additional lowering of LDL cholesterol; EYLEA (aflibercept), an injection treatment for neovascular age-related macular degeneration patients; Dupixent (dupilumab), an injection for the treatment of adult patients with moderate-to-severe atopic dermatitis; and ZALTRAP (ziv-aflibercept), an injection for treatment, in combination with 5-fluorouracil, leucovorin, irinotecan, of patients with metastatic colorectal cancer. Regeneron's proprietary technologies include VelociGene, VelociMouse and VelocImmune. The VelociGene technology allows precise DNA manipulation and gene staining, helping to identify where a particular gene is active in the body. VelociMouse technology allows for the direct and immediate generation of genetically altered mice from embryonic stem cells, avoiding the lengthy process involved in generating and breeding knock-out mice from chimeras. VelocImmune is a novel mouse technology platform for producing fully human monoclonal antibodies. Additionally, VelociMab technologies allow rapid screenings of therapeutic antibodies and eliminates the need for slower development techniques; VelociT produces fully-human therapeutic T-cell receptors against tumor and viral antigens; and VelociHum is an immunodeficient mouse platform that can be used to accurately test human therapeutics against human immune cells and to study human tumor models. The firm has 15 product candidates in clinical development, all of which were generated using VelocImmune technology.

Regeneron employee benefits include medical, dental, vision, prescription, life, AD&D and short- and long-term disability coverage; and various employee assistance programs.

FINANCIAL DATA:

Note: Data for latest year may not have been available at press time.

In U.S. $	2017	2016	2015	2014	2013	2012
Revenue	5,872,227,000	4,860,427,000	4,103,728,000	2,819,557,000	2,104,745,000	1,378,477,000
R&D Expense	2,075,142,000	2,052,295,000	1,620,577,000	1,271,353,000	859,947,000	625,554,000
Operating Income	2,079,591,000	1,330,741,000	1,251,916,000	838,431,000	760,028,000	457,713,000
Operating Margin %	35.41%	27.37%	30.50%	29.73%	36.11%	33.20%
SGA Expense	1,320,433,000	1,177,697,000	838,526,000	504,755,000	329,415,000	210,755,000
Net Income	1,198,511,000	895,522,000	636,056,000	348,074,000	424,362,000	750,269,000
Operating Cash Flow	1,307,112,000	1,473,396,000	1,330,780,000	743,157,000	583,648,000	-74,615,000
Capital Expenditure	272,626,000	511,941,000	677,933,000	333,006,000	156,323,000	49,337,000
EBITDA	2,249,097,000	1,441,755,000	1,314,247,000	865,805,000	801,001,000	496,665,000
Return on Assets %	15.23%	14.23%	13.41%	10.20%	16.86%	44.08%
Return on Equity %	22.62%	22.10%	20.52%	15.48%	26.54%	86.68%
Debt to Equity	0.11	0.07	0.09	0.18	0.25	0.36

CONTACT INFORMATION:

Phone: 914 347-7000 Fax:
Toll-Free:
Address: 777 Old Saw Mill River Rd., Tarrytown, NY 10591 United States

STOCK TICKER/OTHER:

Stock Ticker: REGN
Employees: 5,400
Parent Company:
Exchange: NAS
Fiscal Year Ends: 12/31

SALARIES/BONUSES:

Top Exec. Salary: $1,285,500 Bonus: $
Second Exec. Salary: $1,092,700 Bonus: $

OTHER THOUGHTS:

Estimated Female Officers or Directors:
Hot Spot for Advancement for Women/Minorities:

Regional Health Properties Inc

www.regionalhealthproperties.com

NAIC Code: 623,311

TYPES OF BUSINESS:

Continuing Care Retirement Communities
Assisted Living Facilities for the Elderly

BRANDS/DIVISIONS/AFFILIATES:

GROWTH PLANS/SPECIAL FEATURES:

Regional Health Properties, Inc. is a self-managed real estate investment company that invests primarily in real estate purposed for long-term care and senior living. Through its subsidiaries, the company's business mainly consists of leasing and subleasing such facilities to third-party tenants, which operate them. As of August 2018, Regional Health owned, leased or managed for third parties 30 facilities located in the Southeast portion of the U.S., including Alabama, Georgia, North Carolina, Oklahoma and South Carolina. Services provided by the facilities include skilled nursing, assisted living, social services, various therapy services and other rehabilitative and healthcare services for both long-term and short-stay patients and residents.

CONTACTS: *Note: Officers with more than one job title may be intentionally listed here more than once.*

Brent Morrison, Interim CEO
E. Clinton Cain, Interim CFO
William McBride, Director

FINANCIAL DATA: *Note: Data for latest year may not have been available at press time.*

In U.S. $	2017	2016	2015	2014	2013	2012
Revenue	25,148,000	27,337,000	18,400,000	193,314,000	222,847,000	201,658,000
R&D Expense						
Operating Income	5,138,000	4,255,000	-7,641,000	1,323,000	695,000	1,909,000
Operating Margin %	20.43%	15.56%	-41.52%	.68%	.31%	.94%
SGA Expense	13,171,000	16,408,000	16,302,000	25,257,000	28,600,000	24,737,000
Net Income	-985,000	-7,462,000	-23,518,000	-13,599,000	-12,567,000	-6,884,000
Operating Cash Flow	5,145,000	-3,409,000	-17,806,000	-5,292,000	5,061,000	1,527,000
Capital Expenditure	2,221,000	1,500,000	1,799,000	3,457,000	4,490,000	5,777,000
EBITDA	10,006,000	9,551,000	-296,000	8,623,000	8,635,000	8,714,000
Return on Assets %	-7.60%	-10.15%	-15.04%	-7.41%	-6.13%	-3.57%
Return on Equity %				-226.09%	-185.71%	-61.04%
Debt to Equity				20.25	15.09	22.10

CONTACT INFORMATION:

Phone: 678 869-5116 Fax:
Toll-Free:
Address: 454 Satellite Boulevard NW, Ste. 100, Suwanee, GA 30024-7191 United States

STOCK TICKER/OTHER:

Stock Ticker: RHE
Employees: 19
Parent Company:
Exchange: ASE
Fiscal Year Ends: 12/31

SALARIES/BONUSES:

Top Exec. Salary: $300,000 Bonus: $50,000
Second Exec. Salary: $187,500 Bonus: $

OTHER THOUGHTS:

Estimated Female Officers or Directors:
Hot Spot for Advancement for Women/Minorities:

ResCare Inc

NAIC Code: 623,210

www.rescare.com

TYPES OF BUSINESS:

Residential Intellectual and Developmental Disability Facilities
Job Corps Training Services
Employment Training Services
Home Care Services

BRANDS/DIVISIONS/AFFILIATES:

Onex Corporation
Rest Assured Telecare
BrightSpring Health Services

CONTACTS: *Note: Officers with more than one job title may be intentionally listed here more than once.*

Jon Rousseau, CEO
Ralph G. Gronefeld, Jr., Pres.
Steven S. Reed, Chief Legal Officer
Nel Taylor, Chief Comm. Officer
Michael Hough, Exec. VP-Workforce Svcs.

GROWTH PLANS/SPECIAL FEATURES:

ResCare, Inc. is a diversified health and human services provider in the U.S. The company operates in six segments. The residential services segment offers support services to adults and youths with intellectual, cognitive and other developmental disabilities in community home settings. The homecare services segment primarily offers periodic in-home care services to the elderly and persons with disabilities. Its services include daily visitation, meal preparation, housekeeping and transportation as well as live-in care and telecare. The workforce services segment operates in more than 350 locations, which offer job training and placement programs to assist welfare recipients and disadvantaged job seekers in finding employment and improving their careers prospects. The pharmacy services segment is a limited, closed-door pharmacy focused on serving individuals with cognitive, intellectual and developmental disabilities who are receiving support and services from ResCare or other private providers. This division also offers clinical support including seminars, conferences, webinars, email education and even individualized educational support. The host homes/foster care segment partners with people in the community who open their homes to individuals with intellectual, developmental and physical disabilities. These individuals reside with providers of host homes, enjoying a family environment and opportunities to become part of the community. This division assists families via foster care and adoption services, parent education and counseling solutions, child care and disability determination services. Last, Rest Assured Telecare is a proprietary platform offering a full suite of home 24/7 monitoring services and solutions including real-time telecommunication interactions to avoid adverse events, improve health outcomes and lower health costs. ResCare is owned by private equity firm Onex Corporation. In mid-August 2018, ResCare announced it was changing its name to BrightSpring Health Services to reflect its evolving platform of innovative solutions for improving health outcomes and lower costs for complex populations and payer systems.

FINANCIAL DATA: *Note: Data for latest year may not have been available at press time.*

In U.S. $	2017	2016	2015	2014	2013	2012
Revenue	1,875,000,000	1,825,000,000	1,800,000,000	1,645,000,000	1,616,633,000	1,599,100,000
R&D Expense						
Operating Income						
Operating Margin %						
SGA Expense						
Net Income						
Operating Cash Flow						
Capital Expenditure						
EBITDA						
Return on Assets %						
Return on Equity %						
Debt to Equity						

CONTACT INFORMATION:

Phone: 502-394-2100 Fax: 502-394-2206
Toll-Free: 800-866-0860
Address: 9901 Linn Station Rd., Louisville, KY 40223 United States

STOCK TICKER/OTHER:

Stock Ticker: Private
Employees: 30,000
Parent Company: Onex Corporation
Exchange:
Fiscal Year Ends: 12/31

SALARIES/BONUSES:

Top Exec. Salary: $ Bonus: $
Second Exec. Salary: $ Bonus: $

OTHER THOUGHTS:

Estimated Female Officers or Directors: 1
Hot Spot for Advancement for Women/Minorities: Y

ResMed Inc

www.resmed.com

NAIC Code: 334,510

TYPES OF BUSINESS:

Sleep Disordered Breathing Medical Equipment
Diagnosis & Treatment Products

BRANDS/DIVISIONS/AFFILIATES:

AirSense 10
S9
AirCurve 10

CONTACTS:

Note: Officers with more than one job title may be intentionally listed here more than once.

Michael Farrell, CEO
Brett Sandercock, CFO
Peter Farrell, Chairman of the Board
David Pendarvis, Chief Administrative Officer
Rajwant Sodhi, Chief Technology Officer
Robert Douglas, COO
James Hollingshead, President, Divisional
Richie McHale, President, Divisional

GROWTH PLANS/SPECIAL FEATURES:

ResMed, Inc. is an Australian-founded company that develops, manufactures and distributes medical equipment and cloud-based software applications for treating, diagnosing and managing sleep disordered breathing (SDB) and other respiratory disorders. SDB includes obstructive sleep apnea (OSA) and other related respiratory disorders that occur during sleep. The company was originally founded to commercialize a continuous positive airway pressure (CPAP) treatment for OSA, which delivers pressurized air, typically through a nasal mask, to prevent collapse of the upper airway during sleep. Since the introduction of nasal CPAP, the firm has developed a number of innovative products for SDB, including mask systems, headgear, airflow generators, diagnostic products and other accessories. The firm's CPAP include AirSense 10 Elite and AirSense 10 CPAP. Its variable positive airway pressure (VPAP) products include the S9 family: VPAP ST-A and COPD (chronic obstructive pulmonary disease; and the AirCurve 10 family: S, V Auto, ST, ASV and CS. Other product categories include automatic positive airway pressure (APAP) products, diagnostic products and data/patient management products. The company's business strategy includes expanding into new clinical applications by seeking to identify new uses for its technologies, as well as increasing consumer awareness of little-known conditions. The firm sells products in over 120 countries through wholly-owned subsidiaries and independent distributors. Through various subsidiaries, ResMed owns approximately 1,127 issued U.S. patents (including approximately 430 design patents) and approximately 2,083 issued foreign patents. In May 2018, ResMed agreed to acquire HEALTHCAREfirst, a cloud-based software and services provider for home health and hospice agencies. That July, ResMed and Verily agreed to form a joint venture to develop software solutions that enable healthcare providers to more efficiently identify, diagnose, treat and manage individuals with sleep apnea and other breathing-related sleep disorders.

FINANCIAL DATA:

Note: Data for latest year may not have been available at press time.

In U.S. $	2017	2016	2015	2014	2013	2012
Revenue	2,066,737,000	1,838,713,000	1,678,912,000	1,554,973,000	1,514,457,000	
R&D Expense	144,467,000	118,651,000	114,865,000	118,226,000	120,124,000	
Operating Income	456,732,000	435,866,000	409,236,000	411,413,000	354,824,000	
Operating Margin %	22.09%	23.70%	24.37%	26.45%	23.42%	
SGA Expense	553,968,000	488,057,000	478,627,000	450,414,000	430,802,000	
Net Income	342,284,000	352,409,000	352,886,000	345,273,000	307,133,000	
Operating Cash Flow	414,053,000	547,933,000	383,180,000	391,268,000	402,823,000	
Capital Expenditure	71,476,000	67,829,000	71,944,000	81,156,000	71,782,000	
EBITDA	559,136,000	537,621,000	514,750,000	510,661,000	469,786,000	
Return on Assets %	10.17%	12.94%	15.52%	15.10%	14.12%	
Return on Equity %	18.72%	21.47%	21.09%	20.49%	19.08%	
Debt to Equity	0.55	0.51	0.18	0.17		

CONTACT INFORMATION:

Phone: 858 836-5000 Fax: 858 746-2900
Toll-Free: 800-424-0737
Address: 9001 Spectrum Ctr. Blvd., San Diego, CA 92123 United States

STOCK TICKER/OTHER:

Stock Ticker: RMD
Employees: 5,940
Parent Company:
Exchange: NYS
Fiscal Year Ends: 06/30

SALARIES/BONUSES:

Top Exec. Salary: $890,160 Bonus: $
Second Exec. Salary: $746,345 Bonus: $

OTHER THOUGHTS:

Estimated Female Officers or Directors: 2
Hot Spot for Advancement for Women/Minorities:

Rhon Klinikum AG

en.rhoen-klinikum-ag.com/

NAIC Code: 622,110

TYPES OF BUSINESS:

General Medical and Surgical Hospitals

BRANDS/DIVISIONS/AFFILIATES:

Rhon-Klinikum Campus Bad Neustadt
Klinikum Frankfurt (Oder)
University Hospital Giessen
University Hospital Marburg
Zentralklinik Bad Berka

CONTACTS: *Note: Officers with more than one job title may be intentionally listed here more than once.*

Stephan Holzinger, CEO
Gunther K. Weiss, COO
Bernd Griewing, CMO
Esther Walter, Head-Press & Public Relations
Martin L. Hansis, Head-Quality Mgmt.
Franz Mlynek, Head-Major Investments Division
Stephan Holzinger, Chmn.

GROWTH PLANS/SPECIAL FEATURES:

Rhon-Klinikum AG is a Germany-based company that along with its subsidiaries, builds and acquires acute-care hospitals of all categories. In addition to rehabilitation hospitals, it is focused on outpatient, day clinical and base care facilities. The company owns and operates hospital clinics in four locations, with a total of 5,300 beds. Rhon-Klinikum Campus Bad Neustadt comprises six clinics directly linked at this one location, and includes: the Cardiovascular Clinic, the Frankenklinik for the Rehabilitation of Cardiovascular Patients, the Clinic for Hand Surgery, the Neurological Clinic, the Psychosomatic Clinic and the Saaletalklinik, as well as two additional addiction therapy facilities. Klinikum Frankfurt (Oder) is a hospital with specialized medical services, 773 inpatient beds. Approximately 35,000 inpatients and more than 44,000 outpatients are treated annually from Frankfurt (Oder), which includes 21 clinics, six institutions and psychiatric outpatient institutions, as well as three-day clinics. University Hospital Giessen and Marburg offers medical services, modern diagnostics and comprehensive therapy at the highest international standard. It is a full-service hospital covering the whole range of modern medicine from ophthalmology to trauma surgery to dentistry. This hospital comprises 80 clinics and institutions at the dual locations of Giessen and Marburg, and is Germany's third-largest university hospital. Last, Zentralklinik Bad Berka is an academic teaching hospital, as well as a hospital with a nationwide service mission. Each year, the team of doctors, nurses and medical assistants treat thousands of patients from all over Germany, Europe and several non-European countries in a total of 20 clinics and specialist departments. Services are provided to patients with thoracic, pulmonary and vascular diseases, tumors, neurological conditions, as well as diseases of the spinal column, joints and heart.

FINANCIAL DATA: *Note: Data for latest year may not have been available at press time.*

In U.S. $	2017	2016	2015	2014	2013	2012
Revenue	1,632,700,000	1,411,279,598	1,439,218,866	1,691,479,176	3,819,000,000	3,630,000,000
R&D Expense						
Operating Income						
Operating Margin %						
SGA Expense						
Net Income	44,005,900	70,345,739	97,749,655	2,020,467	109,800,000	114,200,000
Operating Cash Flow						
Capital Expenditure						
EBITDA						
Return on Assets %						
Return on Equity %						
Debt to Equity						

CONTACT INFORMATION:

Phone: 49 9771 65-0 Fax: 49 9771 97 46 7
Toll-Free:
Address: Salzburger Leite 1, Bad Neustadt/Saale, 97616 Germany

STOCK TICKER/OTHER:

Stock Ticker: RHK Exchange: Xetra
Employees: 16,688 Fiscal Year Ends: 12/31
Parent Company:

SALARIES/BONUSES:

Top Exec. Salary: $ Bonus: $
Second Exec. Salary: $ Bonus: $

OTHER THOUGHTS:

Estimated Female Officers or Directors:
Hot Spot for Advancement for Women/Minorities:

Rite Aid Corporation

www.riteaid.com

NAIC Code: 446,110

TYPES OF BUSINESS:

Drug Stores

BRANDS/DIVISIONS/AFFILIATES:

Riteaid.com
Rite Aid
GNC

CONTACTS: *Note: Officers with more than one job title may be intentionally listed here more than once.*

John Standley, CEO
Darren Karst, CFO
Matthew Schroeder, Chief Accounting Officer
Kermit Crawford, COO
David Abelman, Executive VP, Divisional
Bryan Everett, Executive VP, Divisional
Jocelyn Konrad, Executive VP, Divisional
Bill Renz, Senior VP, Divisional
Ted Williams, Vice President, Divisional
Nate Newcomer, Vice President, Divisional

GROWTH PLANS/SPECIAL FEATURES:

Rite Aid Corporation is a U.S.-based retail drugstore company which operates over 2,500 drug stores in 19 states (as of August 2018). Rite Aid stores primarily market prescription drugs, which accounted for 65.9% of fiscal 2018 total drugstore sales. Other marketed merchandise, which accounted for the remaining 34.1% of sales, includes non-prescription medications, health and beauty aids, personal care items, cosmetics, household items, beverages, convenience foods, greeting cards and seasonal merchandise. In addition to its marketed products, the firm offers an automated refill option for customers with ongoing prescriptions; and it also makes prescription refill reminder phone calls. Customers can order prescription refills through the company's eCommerce site Riteaid.com. The firm's average store size is approximately 13,600 square feet. Its larger stores are located in the western U.S. Rite Aid offers approximately 3,000 products under the Rite Aid private brand. The company maintains a strategic alliance with GNC, which enables Rite Aid to sell GNC branded and co-branded products. Rite Aid operates more than 2,300 GNC store-within-Rite Aid-stores. Approximately 60% of Rite Aid's stores are freestanding, 53% include a drive-through pharmacy, and 59% include a GNC store-within-Rite Aid-store. A majority of stores also include one-hour photo shops. In March 2018, Rite Aid completed its sale of 1,932 stores and three distribution centers to Walgreens Boots Alliance for $4.2 billion. That August, Rite Aid announced that it mutually agreed with Albertsons Companies, Inc. to terminate their previously-announced merger agreement.

The company offers its employees health, dental, vision and prescription plans; vision discount plan; basic and supplemental life and AD&D insurances; flexible spending accounts; bereavement leave; employee assistance; 401(k); stock purchase plan; and more.

FINANCIAL DATA: *Note: Data for latest year may not have been available at press time.*

In U.S. $	2017	2016	2015	2014	2013	2012
Revenue	32,845,070,000	30,736,660,000	26,528,380,000	25,526,410,000		26,121,220,000
R&D Expense						
Operating Income	531,706,000	812,909,000	881,090,000	762,572,000		261,924,000
Operating Margin %	1.61%	2.64%	3.32%	2.98%		1.00%
SGA Expense	7,242,359,000	7,013,346,000	6,695,642,000	6,561,162,000		6,531,411,000
Net Income	4,053,000	165,465,000	2,109,173,000	249,414,000		-368,571,000
Operating Cash Flow	225,863,000	997,402,000	648,959,000	702,046,000		266,537,000
Capital Expenditure	481,111,000	669,995,000	539,386,000	421,223,000		250,137,000
EBITDA	1,048,667,000	1,237,190,000	1,241,060,000	1,078,550,000		577,580,000
Return on Assets %	.03%	1.64%	26.68%	3.07%		-5.07%
Return on Equity %	.67%	51.83%				
Debt to Equity	11.89	11.98	97.17			

CONTACT INFORMATION:

Phone: 717 761-2633 Fax: 717 975-5905
Toll-Free: 800-748-3243
Address: 30 Hunter Lane, Camp Hill, PA 17011 United States

STOCK TICKER/OTHER:

Stock Ticker: RAD
Employees: 90,000
Parent Company:
Exchange: NYS
Fiscal Year Ends: 02/28

SALARIES/BONUSES:

Top Exec. Salary: $1,184,500 Bonus: $
Second Exec. Salary: $927,000 Bonus: $

OTHER THOUGHTS:

Estimated Female Officers or Directors: 3
Hot Spot for Advancement for Women/Minorities: Y

Roche Holding AG

www.roche.com

NAIC Code: 325,412

TYPES OF BUSINESS:

Pharmaceuticals Manufacturing
Antibiotics
Diagnostics
Cancer Drugs
Virology Products
HIV/AIDS Treatments
Transplant Drugs

BRANDS/DIVISIONS/AFFILIATES:

F Hoffmann-La Roche Ltd
Genentech Inc
Chugai Pharmaceutical Co Ltd
Flatiron Health
Ignyta Inc

CONTACTS: *Note: Officers with more than one job title may be intentionally listed here more than once.*

Severin Schwan, CEO
Alan Hippe, CFO
Cristina A. Wilbur, Head-Human Resources
John C. Reed, Head-Roche Pharmaceutical Research & Early Dev.
Alan Hippe, CIO
Gottlieb Keller, General Counsel
Daniel ODay, COO-Pharmaceuticals
Stephen Feldhaus, Head-Comm.
Richard Scheller, Head-Genentech Research & Early Dev.
Roland Diggelmann, COO-Diagnostics
Sophie Kornowski-Bonnet, Head-Roche Partnering
Christoph Franz, Chmn.
Osamu Nagayama, CEO

GROWTH PLANS/SPECIAL FEATURES:

Roche Holding AG, also referred to as F. Hoffmann-La Roche Ltd. and based in Switzerland, is a world-leading healthcare and biotechnology company. The firm occupies an industry-leading position in the global diagnostics market and ranks as one of the top producers of pharmaceuticals, with recognition in the areas of oncology, autoimmune disease and metabolic disorder treatments, virology and transplantation medicine. The company's operations currently extend to over 100 countries, with additional alliances and research and development agreements with corporate and institutional partners furthering Roche's collective reach. It operates in two divisions: pharmaceuticals, which generates the majority of the firm's annual sales; and diagnostics. The pharmaceuticals division focuses on translating science into breakthrough medicines for patients, with research at Roche and wholly-owned Genentech, Inc. in the U.S., as well as Chugai Pharmaceutical Co., Ltd. in Japan. This segment has more than 150 worldwide partners engaged in clinical development, manufacturing and commercial operations, with a focus on oncology, immunology, ophthalmology, infectious diseases and neuroscience. More than half of the compounds in this division's product pipeline are biopharmaceuticals. The diagnostics division performs blood, tissue and other types of patient samples, as well as in vitro diagnostics for the purpose of obtaining information in relation to improved disease management and patient care. Diagnostic services and solutions provide prevention, screening, diagnosis, prognosis, stratification, treatment and monitoring capabilities in regard to diseases. In April 2018, the firm acquired Flatiron Health, specializing in U.S. cancer data analytics. Earlier that year, Roche acquired an additional stake of Ignyta, Inc., for a total 84.71% holding. Ignyta develops precisely-targeted therapeutics guided by diagnostic tests to patients with cancer.

FINANCIAL DATA: *Note: Data for latest year may not have been available at press time.*

In U.S. $	2017	2016	2015	2014	2013	2012
Revenue						
R&D Expense						
Operating Income						
Operating Margin %						
SGA Expense						
Net Income						
Operating Cash Flow						
Capital Expenditure						
EBITDA						
Return on Assets %						
Return on Equity %						
Debt to Equity						

CONTACT INFORMATION:

Phone: 41-61-688-1111 Fax: 41-61-691-9391
Toll-Free:
Address: Grenzacherstrasse 124, Basel, 4070 Switzerland

STOCK TICKER/OTHER:

Stock Ticker: RHHBY
Employees: 80,080
Parent Company:
Exchange: PINX
Fiscal Year Ends: 12/31

SALARIES/BONUSES:

Top Exec. Salary: $ Bonus: $
Second Exec. Salary: $ Bonus: $

OTHER THOUGHTS:

Estimated Female Officers or Directors: 4
Hot Spot for Advancement for Women/Minorities: Y

SafeGuard Health Enterprises Inc

www.metlife.com/individual/insurance/dental-insurance/safeguard.html

NAIC Code: 524,114

TYPES OF BUSINESS:

HMO/PPO
Vision Insurance Products
Administrative Services
Dental & Vision Benefit Plans
Employee Assistance Programs

BRANDS/DIVISIONS/AFFILIATES:

MetLife Inc
SafeGuard Health Plans Inc
SafeHealth Life Insurance Company

GROWTH PLANS/SPECIAL FEATURES:

SafeGuard Health Enterprises, Inc., a wholly-owned subsidiary of MetLife, Inc. (Metropolitan Life Insurance Company), provides dental and vision benefit plans (including HMO, PPO and indemnity plans) to government and private sector employers, associations and individuals. The company also offers scheduled benefit plans, administrative services and employee assistance programs. Subsidiaries include SafeGuard Health Plans, Inc. and SafeHealth life Insurance Company. SafeGuard Health Plans, Inc. provides dental benefits, as well as vision benefits for California-based VHMOs (vision health maintenance organizations). SafeHealth Life Insurance Company provides vision benefits for VPPOs (vision preferred provider organizations). Individual dentist HMO plans are available in California, Florida and Texas only through SafeGuard Health Plans, Inc.

CONTACTS: *Note: Officers with more than one job title may be intentionally listed here more than once.*

Steven A. Kandarian, CEO-MetLife
William J. Wheeler, Pres., The Americas-Metlife, Inc.
Ricardo A. Anzaldua, General Counsel-Metlife, Inc.

FINANCIAL DATA: *Note: Data for latest year may not have been available at press time.*

In U.S. $	2017	2016	2015	2014	2013	2012
Revenue						
R&D Expense						
Operating Income						
Operating Margin %						
SGA Expense						
Net Income						
Operating Cash Flow						
Capital Expenditure						
EBITDA						
Return on Assets %						
Return on Equity %						
Debt to Equity						

CONTACT INFORMATION:

Phone: 949-425-4300 Fax: 949-425-4586
Toll-Free: 800-880-1800
Address: 95 Enterprise, Ste. 100, Aliso Viejo, CA 92656 United States

STOCK TICKER/OTHER:

Stock Ticker: Subsidiary Exchange:
Employees: 360 Fiscal Year Ends: 12/31
Parent Company: Metropolitan Life Insurance Company

SALARIES/BONUSES:

Top Exec. Salary: $ Bonus: $
Second Exec. Salary: $ Bonus: $

OTHER THOUGHTS:

Estimated Female Officers or Directors:
Hot Spot for Advancement for Women/Minorities:

Safilo Group SpA

www.safilo.com

NAIC Code: 339,100

TYPES OF BUSINESS:

Ophthalmic Goods Manufacturing

BRANDS/DIVISIONS/AFFILIATES:

Carrera
Polaroid
Safilo
Smith
Oxydo

CONTACTS:
Note: Officers with more than one job title may be intentionally listed here more than once.

Angelo Trocchia, CEO
Gerd Graehsler, CFO
Luca Fuso, Head-Licensed Brand Div.
Marco Pessi, General Counsel
Massimo Lisot, Dir.-Bus. Dev.
Ross Brownlee, Head-Americas
Eugenio Razelli, Chmn.
Massimo Renon, Head-EMEA
Maurizio Roman, Global Supply Chain, Logistics & Prod. Officer

GROWTH PLANS/SPECIAL FEATURES:

Safilo Group SpA is an eyewear manufacturer that produces and distributes sunglasses, optical frames and sports eyewear worldwide. The company's in-house brands are: Carrera, Polaroid, Safilo, Smith and Oxydo. Licensed brands include Banana Republic, Boss, Celine, Dior, Fendi, Fossil, Gucci, Jack Spade, Jimmy Choo, Juicy Couture, Kate Spade, MaxMara, Hugo Boss, Bobbi Brown, Pierre Cardin, Marc Jacobs, Swatch, Elie Saab, Havaianas, Max & Co., Liz Claiborne, Saks Fifth Avenue and Tommy Hilfiger. Safilio's global havaianas eyewear license agreement with Brazilian company, Alpargatas, runs up to 2021; and its collaboration agreement with Swatch, runs into 2021. The firm's products are divided into three market ranges: high-end, mid-range and lower-end. Sunglasses are responsible for most of the firm's revenue, with prescription frames coming in second and sport and accessory items deriving nearly 10% of sales. Safilo has seven owned global distribution plants and more than 30 subsidiaries in seven regions, and three primary distribution centers, reaching nearly 100,000 retail stores worldwide.

FINANCIAL DATA:
Note: Data for latest year may not have been available at press time.

In U.S. $	2017	2016	2015	2014	2013	2012
Revenue						
R&D Expense						
Operating Income						
Operating Margin %						
SGA Expense						
Net Income						
Operating Cash Flow						
Capital Expenditure						
EBITDA						
Return on Assets %						
Return on Equity %						
Debt to Equity						

CONTACT INFORMATION:

Phone: 39 496985111 Fax: 39 496985380
Toll-Free:
Address: Settima Strada n. 15, Padova, 35 129 Italy

STOCK TICKER/OTHER:

Stock Ticker: SAFLY
Exchange: PINX
Employees: 7,109
Fiscal Year Ends: 12/31
Parent Company:

SALARIES/BONUSES:

Top Exec. Salary: $ Bonus: $
Second Exec. Salary: $ Bonus: $

OTHER THOUGHTS:

Estimated Female Officers or Directors: 1
Hot Spot for Advancement for Women/Minorities:

Sanofi Genzyme

www.sanofigenzyme.com

NAIC Code: 325,412

TYPES OF BUSINESS:

Pharmaceuticals Discovery & Development
Genetic Disease Treatments
Surgical Products
Diagnostic Products
Genetic Testing Services
Oncology Products
Biomaterials
Medical Devices

BRANDS/DIVISIONS/AFFILIATES:

Sanofi SA
Aldurazyme
Caprelsa
Dupixent
Eloxatin
Kevzara
Taxotere
Zaltrap

CONTACTS: *Note: Officers with more than one job title may be intentionally listed here more than once.*

Bill Sibold, Managing Dir.
Robin Swartz, Head-Bus. Oper.
David Meeker, Pres.
Philippe Sauvage, CFO
Bo Piela, Dir.-Communications
Deb Shapiro, Head-Human Resources
Richard J. Gregory, Head-R&D
William Aitchison, Head-Global Mfg.
Tracey L. Quarles, General Counsel
Charles Thyne, Head-Global Quality, Industrial Oper.
G. Andre Turenne, Head- Strategy & Bus. Dev.
Caren P. Arnstein, Head-Corp. Comm.
Ron C. Branning, Chief Quality Officer
Nicholas Grund, Sr. VP-Asia Pacific & Canada
Carlo Incerti, Head-Global Medical Affairs
Yoshi Nakamura, Pres., Japan-Asia Pacific
Robin Kenselaar, Head-EMEA

GROWTH PLANS/SPECIAL FEATURES:

Sanofi Genzyme is the specialty care global business unit of Sanofi SA, with a focus on rare diseases, multiple sclerosis, immunology and oncology. The rare diseases segment develops therapeutic products to treat patients suffering from genetic and other chronic debilitating diseases, including lysosomal storage disorders (LSDs) and endocrinology. More than 7,000 different rare disease collectively affect over 350 million people worldwide. The multiple sclerosis (MS) segment works to deliver scientific advances and novel therapeutic options to the more than 2.3 million people affected by MS worldwide. MS is a chronic disease caused when the body's immune system attacks the central nervous system, damaging the myelin sheath, the protective layer covering the nerves that carry signals between the brain and spinal cord and the rest of the body. This division offers both oral and infusion treatment options. The immunology segment researches and develops new therapeutic candidates that may have a significant impact on people affected by immune system disorders, including atopic dermatitis, rheumatoid arthritis, asthma, nasal polyposis and eosinophilic esophagitis. Last, the oncology segment builds on Sanofi Genzyme's established legacy in cancer treatment by researching potential new options to offer in this area of medicine. This division is building a pipeline of future therapies in immune-oncology, in which a patient's immune system is used to fight cancer cells. Sanofi Genzyme's product portfolio includes: Aldurazyme, Aubagio, Caprelsa, Cerdelga, Cerezyme, Clolar, Dupixent, Elitek, Eloxatin, Fabrazyme, Jevtana, Kevzara, Lemtrada, Lumizyme, Mozobil, Taxotere, Thymoglobulin, Thyrogen and Zaltrap.

Employees of the company receive benefits including medical, dental, vision, life and disability coverage; college tuition savings plans; a 401(k); and work and life assistance benefits.

FINANCIAL DATA: *Note: Data for latest year may not have been available at press time.*

In U.S. $	2017	2016	2015	2014	2013	2012
Revenue	6,796,680,000	5,287,820,000	4,097,534,726	3,923,570,000		
R&D Expense						
Operating Income						
Operating Margin %						
SGA Expense						
Net Income						
Operating Cash Flow						
Capital Expenditure						
EBITDA						
Return on Assets %						
Return on Equity %						
Debt to Equity						

CONTACT INFORMATION:

Phone: 617-252-7500 Fax: 617-252-7600
Toll-Free:
Address: 500 Kendall St., Cambridge, MA 02142 United States

STOCK TICKER/OTHER:

Stock Ticker: Subsidiary
Exchange:
Employees: 13,500
Fiscal Year Ends: 12/31
Parent Company: Sanofi SA

SALARIES/BONUSES:

Top Exec. Salary: $ Bonus: $
Second Exec. Salary: $ Bonus: $

OTHER THOUGHTS:

Estimated Female Officers or Directors: 4
Hot Spot for Advancement for Women/Minorities: Y

Sanofi SA

en.sanofi.com

NAIC Code: 325,412

TYPES OF BUSINESS:

Pharmaceuticals Development & Manufacturing
Over-the-Counter Drugs
Cardiovascular Drugs
CNS Drugs
Oncology Drugs
Diabetes Drugs
Generics
Vaccines

BRANDS/DIVISIONS/AFFILIATES:

Sanofi Pasteur
Cerezyme
Aubagio
Jevtana
Dupixent
Lantus
Praluent
Bioverativ Inc

CONTACTS: *Note: Officers with more than one job title may be intentionally listed here more than once.*

Olivier Brandicourt, CEO
Elias Zerhouni, Pres., Global R&D
Karen Linehan, General Counsel
David-Alexandre Gros, Chief Strategy Officer
David Meeker, CEO-Genzyme
Olivier Charmeil, Sr. VP-Vaccines
Philippe Luscan, Exec. VP-Global Industrial Affairs
Serge Weinberg, Chmn.
Peter Guenter, Exec. VP-Global Commercial Oper.

GROWTH PLANS/SPECIAL FEATURES:

Sanofi SA is an international pharmaceutical group engaged in the research, development, manufacturing and marketing of healthcare products. It operates in three primary segments: pharmaceuticals, consumer healthcare and vaccines. The most important pharmaceutical products marketed by Sanofi include: rare diseases, comprising a portfolio of enzyme replacement therapies, including Cerezyme for Gaucher disease and Myozyme for Pompe disease, among others; multiple sclerosis, including Aubagio, a once-daily oral immunomodulator and Lemtrada, a monoclonal antibody; oncology, including Jevtana, for patients with prostate cancer and Taxotere, for several types of cancer, among others; immunology, including Dupixent, for adults with moderate-to-severe atopic dermatitis and Kevzara, for adults with severe rheumatoid arthritis; diabetes, including Lantus, a long-acting human insulin analog and Amaryl, an oral once-daily sulfonylurea, among others; and cardiovascular diseases, including Praluent, a cholesterol-lowering drug and Multaq, an anti-arrhythmic drug. The consumer healthcare segment is supported by four strategic categories: allergy cough and cold, pain, digestive, and nutritionals. Last, the vaccines segment operates through Sanofi Pasteur, which sells leading vaccines in five areas: pediatric vaccines, influenza vaccines, adult and adolescent booster vaccines, meningitis vaccines, and travel and endemic vaccines. During early-2018, the firm acquired Bioverativ, Inc., a biotechnology company focused on therapies for hemophilia and other rare blood disorders; agreed to acquire Ablynx NV, a biopharmaceutical company engaged in the discovery and development of Nanobodies.

FINANCIAL DATA: *Note: Data for latest year may not have been available at press time.*

In U.S. $	2017	2016	2015	2014	2013	2012
Revenue	42,102,570,000	40,362,840,000	40,540,760,000	39,666,240,000	38,732,410,000	41,815,330,000
R&D Expense	6,363,531,000	6,014,653,000	5,909,989,000	5,609,955,000	5,547,156,000	5,723,921,000
Operating Income	8,374,230,000	8,755,669,000	8,295,151,000	7,943,947,000	7,534,597,000	9,055,704,000
Operating Margin %	19.89%	21.69%	20.46%	20.02%	19.45%	21.65%
SGA Expense	11,696,710,000	11,031,520,000	10,910,570,000	10,590,770,000	10,003,490,000	10,404,700,000
Net Income	9,808,118,000	5,476,218,000	4,985,464,000	5,105,245,000	4,322,596,000	5,776,253,000
Operating Cash Flow	8,581,231,000	9,115,014,000	10,373,300,000	8,942,900,000	8,086,987,000	9,502,267,000
Capital Expenditure	2,274,683,000	2,422,375,000	3,223,631,000	1,810,676,000	1,625,770,000	1,874,637,000
EBITDA	11,205,950,000	11,516,450,000	11,719,970,000	11,760,670,000	12,540,990,000	13,184,090,000
Return on Assets %	8.24%	4.54%	4.29%	4.53%	3.78%	4.95%
Return on Equity %	14.58%	8.14%	7.50%	7.76%	6.50%	8.74%
Debt to Equity	0.24	0.29	0.22	0.23	0.18	0.18

CONTACT INFORMATION:

Phone: 33-1-53-77-40-00 Fax:
Toll-Free:
Address: 54, rue La Boetie, Paris, 75008 France

STOCK TICKER/OTHER:

Stock Ticker: SNY
Exchange: NYS
Employees: 1,068,529
Fiscal Year Ends: 12/31
Parent Company:

SALARIES/BONUSES:

Top Exec. Salary: $1,200,000 Bonus: $
Second Exec. Salary: $700,000 Bonus: $

OTHER THOUGHTS:

Estimated Female Officers or Directors: 6
Hot Spot for Advancement for Women/Minorities: Y

Sartorius Stedim Biotech SA

www.sartorius-stedim.com

NAIC Code: 423,450

TYPES OF BUSINESS:

Medical, Dental, and Hospital Equipment and Supplies Merchant Wholesalers

BRANDS/DIVISIONS/AFFILIATES:

Satorius AG

CONTACTS:

Note: Officers with more than one job title may be intentionally listed here more than once.

Volker Nievel, Dir.-Operations
Rainer Lehmann, Dir.-Finance & IT
Gerry MacKay, Dir.-Mktg. & Sales
Jorg Pfirrmann, Head-General Admin.
Joachim Kreuzburg, Head-Legal & Compliance
Joachim Kreuzburg, Head-Oper.
Joachim Kreuzburg, Head-Communications
Jorg Pfirrmann, Head-Finance
Joachin Kreuzburg, Chmn.

GROWTH PLANS/SPECIAL FEATURES:

Sartorius Stedim Biotech SA is a provider of equipment and services for the development, quality assurance and production processes of the biopharmaceutical industry. The company's services are divided into two segments: lab products and services and bioprocess solutions. The lab products and services division focuses on high-value laboratory instruments, such as lab balances, pipettes and laboratory water purification systems. It also offers the widest range of consumables, such as laboratory filters and pipette tips. In the bioprocess solutions division, the firm's portfolio of products, technologies and services cover wide areas of the biopharmaceutical process chain ranging from fermentation, cell cultivation, filtration and purification to media storage and transportation. The company's key customers are from the biotech, pharma and food industries as well as from public research institutes and laboratories. Sartorius maintains 50 sites in more than 30 countries, 19 of which are production facilities, and the remainder comprising sales, commercial agencies and R&D sites in Europe, North America and Asia. Sales (for 2017) by region include 43% derived by EMEA (Europe, the Middle East and Africa), 32% by the Americas and 25% by Asia/Pacific. Sartorius Stedim operates as a subsidiary of Satorius AG.

FINANCIAL DATA:

Note: Data for latest year may not have been available at press time.

In U.S. $	2017	2016	2015	2014	2013	2012
Revenue						
R&D Expense						
Operating Income						
Operating Margin %						
SGA Expense						
Net Income						
Operating Cash Flow						
Capital Expenditure						
EBITDA						
Return on Assets %						
Return on Equity %						
Debt to Equity						

CONTACT INFORMATION:

Phone: 33 442845600 Fax: 33 442845619
Toll-Free:
Address: Avenue de Jouques ZI des Paluds, Aubagne, 13781 France

STOCK TICKER/OTHER:

Stock Ticker: SDMHF
Exchange: PINX
Employees: 4,991
Fiscal Year Ends: 12/31
Parent Company: Satorius AG

SALARIES/BONUSES:

Top Exec. Salary: $ Bonus: $
Second Exec. Salary: $ Bonus: $

OTHER THOUGHTS:

Estimated Female Officers or Directors:
Hot Spot for Advancement for Women/Minorities:

Semler Scientific Inc

www.semlerscientific.com

NAIC Code: 334,510

TYPES OF BUSINESS:

Electromedical and Electrotherapeutic Apparatus Manufacturing

BRANDS/DIVISIONS/AFFILIATES:

QuantaFlo
WellChec

CONTACTS:

Note: Officers with more than one job title may be intentionally listed here more than once.

Douglas Murphy-Chutorian, CEO
Daniel Conger, CFO

GROWTH PLANS/SPECIAL FEATURES:

Semler Scientific, Inc. is an emerging growth company providing technology solutions to improve the clinical effectiveness and efficiency of healthcare insurers and physician groups. The firm develops, manufactures and markets innovative proprietary products and services that assist our customers in evaluating and treating chronic diseases. Currently, Semler has only one FDA patent on the market, QuantaFlo. QuantaFlo is the combination of four proprietary peripheral arterial disease (PAD) tests. QuantaFlo is a four-minute in-office blood flow test that healthcare providers can use to determine blood flow measurements as part of their examinations of a patient's vascular condition, including assessments of patients who have vascular disease. A second product provided by Semler is the WellChec. WellChec is a multi-test service platform that more comprehensively evaluates patients for chronic disease. When QuataFlo and WellChec are used in tandem the firm believes that it positions itself to provide valuable information to insurance companies and physician customers, which in turn permits them to guide patient care and close the gap between the cost of patient care and compensation for providing that care.

FINANCIAL DATA:

Note: Data for latest year may not have been available at press time.

In U.S. $	2017	2016	2015	2014	2013	2012
Revenue						
R&D Expense						
Operating Income						
Operating Margin %						
SGA Expense						
Net Income						
Operating Cash Flow						
Capital Expenditure						
EBITDA						
Return on Assets %						
Return on Equity %						
Debt to Equity						

CONTACT INFORMATION:

Phone: 408-627-4557 Fax:
Toll-Free: 877-774-4211
Address: 2330 NW Everett St., Portland, OR 97210 United States

STOCK TICKER/OTHER:

Stock Ticker: SMLR
Employees: 29
Parent Company:
Exchange: PINX
Fiscal Year Ends: 12/31

SALARIES/BONUSES:

Top Exec. Salary: $367,500 Bonus: $305,906
Second Exec. Salary: $169,386 Bonus: $33,877

OTHER THOUGHTS:

Estimated Female Officers or Directors:
Hot Spot for Advancement for Women/Minorities:

Sentara Healthcare

www.sentara.com

NAIC Code: 622,110

TYPES OF BUSINESS:

General Medical and Surgical Hospitals
Health Insurance
Primary Care Practices
Home Health Care
Air Medical Transport
Rehabilitation Services
Physical Therapy Services
Organ Transplants

BRANDS/DIVISIONS/AFFILIATES:

Sentara Norfolk General
Sentara Leigh
Sentara Virginia Beach General
Sentara CarePlex
Sentara Obici
Orthopedic Hospital at Sentara Leigh
Sentara Williamsburgh Regional Medical Center
Sentara Medical Group

CONTACTS: *Note: Officers with more than one job title may be intentionally listed here more than once.*

Howard Kern, CEO
Michael Gentry, COO
Howard Kern, Pres.
Robert A. Broermann, CFO
Becky Sawyer, Sr. VP-Human Resources
Michael Reagin, CIO
Vicky G. Gray, VP-System Dev.
Elwood Boone, Pres., Sentara Virginia Beach General Hospital
Michael V. Gentry, VP-Southside
Henry Harris, Chmn.
Ray Darcey, Pres., Sentara Enterprises

GROWTH PLANS/SPECIAL FEATURES:

Sentara Healthcare is a nonprofit health care provider in Virginia and North Carolina. The firm's system includes advanced imaging centers, nursing and assisted-living centers, outpatient campuses, physical therapy and rehabilitation services, a home health and hospice agency, a 3,800-provider medical staff and four medical groups. Hospitals include Sentara Norfolk General, Sentara Leigh, Sentara Virginia Beach General, Sentara Princess Anne, Sentara CarePlex, Sentara Obici, Sentara Albemarle Medical Center, Orthopaedic Hospital at Sentara CarePlex, Orthopedic Hospital at Sentara Leigh, Sentara Heart, Hospital for Extended Recovery and Sentara Williamsburg Regional Medical Center. The company also extends health insurance to 445,000 people through Optima Health, Sentara's award-winning health plan. Its air transport system, Nightingale, is an air ambulance service in southeastern Virginia. The firm operates the region's comprehensive solid organ transplant center, which conducts organ transplants, including heart transplants. Long-term life assistance, provided through the Life Care division, includes an adult day care center, the Mobile Meals program and a program for all-inclusive care for the elderly (PACE). Sentara Medical Group, a division of Sentara, provides family and internal medicine to Southeastern Virginia and Northeastern North Carolina.

FINANCIAL DATA: *Note: Data for latest year may not have been available at press time.*

In U.S. $	2017	2016	2015	2014	2013	2012
Revenue	5,337,579,450	5,083,409,000	4,833,912,000	4,694,379,000	4,298,726,000	4,068,228,000
R&D Expense						
Operating Income						
Operating Margin %						
SGA Expense						
Net Income		358,984,000	211,520,000	273,357,000	221,780,000	263,798,000
Operating Cash Flow						
Capital Expenditure						
EBITDA						
Return on Assets %						
Return on Equity %						
Debt to Equity						

CONTACT INFORMATION:

Phone: 757-455-7540 Fax: 757-455-7964
Toll-Free: 800-736-8272
Address: 6015 Poplar Hall Dr., Norfolk, VA 23502 United States

STOCK TICKER/OTHER:

Stock Ticker: Nonprofit
Employees: 28,000
Parent Company:
Exchange:
Fiscal Year Ends: 04/30

SALARIES/BONUSES:

Top Exec. Salary: $ Bonus: $
Second Exec. Salary: $ Bonus: $

OTHER THOUGHTS:

Estimated Female Officers or Directors: 6
Hot Spot for Advancement for Women/Minorities: Y

Shandong Weigao Group Medical Polymer Co Ltd

www.weigaogroup.com

NAIC Code: 339,100

TYPES OF BUSINESS:

Surgical and Medical Instrument Manufacturing

BRANDS/DIVISIONS/AFFILIATES:

CONTACTS:
Note: Officers with more than one job title may be intentionally listed here more than once.

Long Jing, Managing Dir.
Wu Xue Geng, CFO
Wang Yi, Deputy General Manager
Hua Wei Zhang, Chmn.

GROWTH PLANS/SPECIAL FEATURES:

Shandong Weigao Group Medical Polymer Co., Ltd. is a Chinese firm principally engaged in the research, production and sale of medical supplies, orthopedic materials and heart stents. The company's sales network is made up of customer liaison centers, sales offices and more than 170 municipal representative offices. Products are sold to thousands of healthcare organizations and distributors, such as hospitals, blood stations and trading companies. Weigao Group's products are organized in seven categories: single use infusion sets, blood collection sets and stations, syringes, trauma and spinal orthopedic products, hemodialysis products, operation room consumables and sterilization supply center products. These products include pressure extension tubes, catheters, infusion needles, blood transfusion pressure products, blood bags, blood cell separator systems, temperature equipment and supplies, femoral supplies, metal bone screws and plates, blood dialyzers, hemodialysis liquid concentrates, disposable laryngeal masks, medical foam, nasal oxygen cannulas, wound dressings, medical drying cupboards, steam sterilizers and automatic pulse vacuum sterilizers. Products are designed and manufactured according to the standards of International Organization for Standardization and the China Quality Certification Center for Medical Devices. Weigao Group has an international reach with products exported to 30 countries.

FINANCIAL DATA:
Note: Data for latest year may not have been available at press time.

In U.S. $	2017	2016	2015	2014	2013	2012
Revenue						
R&D Expense						
Operating Income						
Operating Margin %						
SGA Expense						
Net Income						
Operating Cash Flow						
Capital Expenditure						
EBITDA						
Return on Assets %						
Return on Equity %						
Debt to Equity						

CONTACT INFORMATION:

Phone: 86-631-5621999 Fax: 0631-5621999
Toll-Free:
Address: No. 18 Xinshan Rd., Weihai, 264210 China

STOCK TICKER/OTHER:

Stock Ticker: SHWGY Exchange: PINX
Employees: 7,866 Fiscal Year Ends: 12/31
Parent Company:

SALARIES/BONUSES:

Top Exec. Salary: $ Bonus: $
Second Exec. Salary: $ Bonus: $

OTHER THOUGHTS:

Estimated Female Officers or Directors:
Hot Spot for Advancement for Women/Minorities:

Shanghai RAAS Blood Products Co Ltd

www.raas-corp.com

NAIC Code: 325,414

TYPES OF BUSINESS:

Biological Product (except Diagnostic) Manufacturing
Plasma-derived Production

BRANDS/DIVISIONS/AFFILIATES:

Tonrol Bio-Pharmaceutical Co Ltd

CONTACTS: *Note: Officers with more than one job title may be intentionally listed here more than once.*

Chen Jie, Pres.

GROWTH PLANS/SPECIAL FEATURES:

Shanghai RAAS Blood Products Co., Ltd. was founded in 1988, and is a leading blood products company throughout China and Asia. The firm's products include human albumin, human immunoglobulin, coagulation factors and more, of which have been registered in nearly 20 countries. Shanghai RAAS is one of the few domestic manufacturers able to export its blood products. The company has 35 plasma collection stations (including some under construction), which comprise a total annual production capacity of 900 tons. More than 30 million vials of products have been used, and without any virus contamination or adverse reaction reported (as of August 2018). Shanghai RAAS' research and development activities primarily focus on plasma-derived products and recombinant protein such as coagulation factors. The firm utilizes advanced biological engineering and processing technologies to increase the yield and quality of its blood products. Subsidiary Tonrol Bio-Pharmaceutical Co., Ltd. specializes in product development, production and marketing. Tonrol currently has 14 plasma stations (two under construction), and eight main products made to more than 30 specifications.

FINANCIAL DATA: *Note: Data for latest year may not have been available at press time.*

In U.S. $	2017	2016	2015	2014	2013	2012
Revenue	296,000,000	334,747,000	310,182,000	214,469,000	81,184,600	104,918,000
R&D Expense						
Operating Income						
Operating Margin %						
SGA Expense						
Net Income	127,744,000	237,494,000	228,082,000	83,018,500	23,310,500	35,447,500
Operating Cash Flow						
Capital Expenditure						
EBITDA						
Return on Assets %						
Return on Equity %						
Debt to Equity						

CONTACT INFORMATION:

Phone: 86-21-22130888 Fax: 86-21-37515875
Toll-Free:
Address: 2009 Wangyuan Rd., Fengxian Dist., Shanghai, Shanghai 201401 China

STOCK TICKER/OTHER:

Stock Ticker: 2253
Employees:
Parent Company:
Exchange: Shenzhen
Fiscal Year Ends:

SALARIES/BONUSES:

Top Exec. Salary: $ Bonus: $
Second Exec. Salary: $ Bonus: $

OTHER THOUGHTS:

Estimated Female Officers or Directors:
Hot Spot for Advancement for Women/Minorities:

Shire Plc

NAIC Code: 325,412

www.shire.com

TYPES OF BUSINESS:

Drugs-Diversified
Drug Delivery Technology
Small-Molecule Drugs

BRANDS/DIVISIONS/AFFILIATES:

Vyvanse
Intuniv
Equasym XL
Pentasa
Replagal
Fosrenol
Carbatrol
Xagrid

CONTACTS: *Note: Officers with more than one job title may be intentionally listed here more than once.*

Flemming Ornskov, CEO
Jeffrey Poulton, CFO
Tatjana May, General Counsel
Susan Kilsby, Chmn.

GROWTH PLANS/SPECIAL FEATURES:

Shire Plc is an international specialty pharmaceutical company. The firm focuses on specialty pharmaceuticals, regenerative medicine and human genetic therapies (HGT). Its specialty medicines aim toward the treatment of behavioral health and gastro intestinal conditions including attention deficit hyperactivity disorder (ADHD) and ulcerative colitis. Shire's products for the treatment of ADHD include Vyvanse, a pro-drug stimulant; Intuniv, an alpha-2A receptor agonist; Equasym XL, for the treatment of neuroscience conditions; and Adderall XR, an extended release treatment that uses MICROTROL drug delivery technology. The firm's treatments for GI diseases include Pentasa controlled release capsules for the treatment of patients with mild to moderately active ulcerative colitis; and Lialda and Mezavant for the induction of remission in patients with ulcerative colitis. Shire's HGT products include Replagal, a treatment for Fabry disease; Elaprase, a treatment for Hunter syndrome; VPRIV, for treatment of Gaucher Disease; and Firazyr, a peptide-based therapeutic developed for the symptomatic treatment of acute attacks of HAE (hereditary angioedema), a debilitating genetic disease. The firm also offers Fosrenol, a phosphate binder for use in chronic kidney disease patients; Carbatrol, an anti-convulsant for individuals with epilepsy; Reminyl for the symptomatic treatment of mild to moderately severe dementia; and Xagrid, which is used for the reduction of elevated platelet counts in at-risk essential thrombocythemia patients. The firm markets products throughout the world, including its major markets in North America, Europe, Latin America and Asia Pacific. In May 2018, the firm agreed to be acquired by Takeda Pharmaceutical Co. Ltd., a Japanese pharmaceuticals company, for Â£40 billion ($62.4 billion). The deal, which is expected to close in the first half of 2019, would be one of the biggest deals ever in the pharmaceuticals industry

Shire offers employees health, dental and vision insurance; flexible spending accounts; life and AD&D insurance; disability benefits; employee assistance and stock programs; and a 401(k) plan.

FINANCIAL DATA: *Note: Data for latest year may not have been available at press time.*

In U.S. $	2017	2016	2015	2014	2013	2012
Revenue	15,160,600,000	11,396,600,000	6,416,700,000	6,022,100,000	4,934,300,000	4,681,200,000
R&D Expense	1,763,300,000	1,439,800,000	1,564,000,000	1,067,500,000	933,400,000	965,500,000
Operating Income	3,397,200,000	1,951,700,000	1,542,500,000	1,949,500,000	1,678,800,000	956,300,000
Operating Margin %	22.40%	17.12%	24.03%	32.37%	34.02%	20.42%
SGA Expense	3,530,900,000	3,015,200,000	2,341,200,000	2,025,800,000	1,651,300,000	2,114,000,000
Net Income	4,271,500,000	327,400,000	1,303,400,000	3,405,500,000	665,100,000	745,400,000
Operating Cash Flow	4,256,700,000	2,658,900,000	2,337,000,000	4,228,400,000	1,463,000,000	1,382,900,000
Capital Expenditure	798,800,000	648,700,000	114,700,000	77,000,000	157,000,000	193,100,000
EBITDA	4,749,300,000	2,547,500,000	2,064,600,000	3,774,300,000	2,056,100,000	1,258,200,000
Return on Assets %	6.33%	.78%	8.61%	31.02%	8.50%	13.05%
Return on Equity %	13.11%	1.68%	14.09%	48.54%	14.49%	25.44%
Debt to Equity	0.46	0.68				0.28

CONTACT INFORMATION:

Phone: 353 14297700 Fax: 353 14297701
Toll-Free:
Address: Miesian Plz., Blocks 2&3, 50-58 Baggot St., Dublin 2, DO2 Y754 Ireland

STOCK TICKER/OTHER:

Stock Ticker: SHPG Exchange: NAS
Employees: 23,044 Fiscal Year Ends: 12/31
Parent Company:

SALARIES/BONUSES:

Top Exec. Salary: $2,202,074 Bonus: $1,828,272
Second Exec. Salary: $788,332 Bonus: $587,050

OTHER THOUGHTS:

Estimated Female Officers or Directors: 3
Hot Spot for Advancement for Women/Minorities: Y

SHL Telemedicine Ltd

www.shl-telemedicine.com

NAIC Code: 511210D

TYPES OF BUSINESS:

Computer Software, Healthcare & Biotechnology
Personal Telemedicine Systems
Medical Call Center Services
Cardiac Testing Services
Remote Cardiac Monitoring
Ambulance Services
Outpatient Diagnostic Imaging

BRANDS/DIVISIONS/AFFILIATES:

smartheart
CardioSen'C
CardioB
CCM
TeleWeight
TelePress
TeleBreather
TelePulse Oximeter

CONTACTS: *Note: Officers with more than one job title may be intentionally listed here more than once.*

Yoav Rubenstein, CEO
Yossi Vadnagra, CFO
Arie Roth, Chief Medical Dir.
Yoni Dagan, Chief Technology Officer
Irit Alroy, CTO
Yoav Rubinstein, Head-Global Bus. Dev.
Yariv Alroy, Co-CEO
Georg F. von Oppen, Managing Dir.-SHL Telemedicine, Germany
Erez Nachtomy, Exec. VP

GROWTH PLANS/SPECIAL FEATURES:

SHL Telemedicine Ltd. develops and markets personal telemedicine systems that transmit medical data from an individual to a medical call and provides medical call center services to patients. The company, headquartered in Tel Aviv, Israel, focuses on providing personal telemedicine services related to heart ailments in markets such as the Netherlands, Germany and Italy. SHL monitors patient's health and wellbeing in order to reduce the need for emergency intervention and hospitalization. The company's goal is to increase its users' chances of survival if a heart attack strikes, and to generally improve their quality of life following a medical event. SHL has developed a full hospital-grade ECG (electrocardiogram) device to enter the smartphone era, allowing users to travel the world while their smartphones send ECGs from distant business and holiday destinations to their physician, cardiologist or telemedicine center for evaluation. Products include the smartheart mobile ECG device; the CardioSen'C cellular-digital ECG transmitter device; the CardioB for easy handling; the CardioBeeper 12/12 handheld ECG transmitter; the CCM (central communication module), which transmits medical data to the company's telemedicine centers from a variety of medical monitoring devices developed by SHL; the TeleWeight, a trans-telephonic weight monitoring device; the TelePress, a remote blood pressure monitoring device; the TeleBreather, a remote, electronic, hand-held device that tests how well the user's lungs are working; and the TelePulse Oximeter, a small electronic, hand-held diagnostic devices to measure the saturation level of oxygen in the user's blood, and also measures pulse rate.

FINANCIAL DATA: *Note: Data for latest year may not have been available at press time.*

In U.S. $	2017	2016	2015	2014	2013	2012
Revenue	37,378,000	40,548,000	34,581,000	39,976,000	29,674,000	26,938,000
R&D Expense		3,555,000	2,690,000	2,492,000	2,206,000	1,449,000
Operating Income	4,567,000	-4,448,000	-12,005,000	1,149,000	-5,394,000	-5,654,000
Operating Margin %	12.21%	-10.96%	-34.71%	2.87%	-18.17%	-20.98%
SGA Expense	2,477,000	18,500,000	18,846,000	18,623,000	19,128,000	18,510,000
Net Income	2,408,000	-11,096,000	-16,635,000	829,000	2,232,000	-7,304,000
Operating Cash Flow	11,844,000	-429,000	3,980,000	-3,117,000	2,815,000	1,626,000
Capital Expenditure	1,602,000	1,814,000	2,750,000	4,279,000	4,078,000	4,432,000
EBITDA	8,650,000	-579,000	-8,842,000	7,225,000	-567,000	-1,383,000
Return on Assets %	3.75%	-16.18%	-19.97%	.82%	2.14%	-7.02%
Return on Equity %	9.08%	-33.41%	-31.99%	1.27%	3.43%	-11.45%
Debt to Equity	0.05	0.40	0.22	0.21	0.26	0.32

CONTACT INFORMATION:

Phone: 972 35612212 Fax: 972 36242414
Toll-Free:
Address: Yigal Alon 90, Tel Aviv, 67891 Israel

STOCK TICKER/OTHER:

Stock Ticker: SMDCF
Employees: 448
Parent Company:
Exchange: GREY
Fiscal Year Ends: 12/31

SALARIES/BONUSES:

Top Exec. Salary: $ Bonus: $
Second Exec. Salary: $ Bonus: $

OTHER THOUGHTS:

Estimated Female Officers or Directors: 3
Hot Spot for Advancement for Women/Minorities: Y

Siemens AG

www.siemens.com

NAIC Code: 334,513

TYPES OF BUSINESS:

Industrial Control Manufacturing
Energy & Power Plant Systems & Consulting
Medical & Health Care Services & Equipment
Lighting & Optical Systems
Automation Systems
Transportation & Logistics Systems

BRANDS/DIVISIONS/AFFILIATES:

Siemens Healthineers AG
Siemens Wind Power
Siemens Real Estate
Fast Track Diagnostics
Enlighted Inc

CONTACTS: *Note: Officers with more than one job title may be intentionally listed here more than once.*

Joe Kaeser, CEO
Joe Kaeser, Pres.
Klaus Helmrich, CTO
Peter Y. Solmssen, Head-Corp. Legal & Compliance
Joe Kaeser, Head-Controlling
Roland Busch, CEO-Infrastructure & Cities Sector
Hermann Requardt, CEO-Health Care Sector
Michael Suess, CEO-Energy Sector
Siegfried Russwurm, CEO-Industry Sector
Jim Hagemenn Snabe, Chmn.
Barbara Kux, Chief Sustainability Officer

GROWTH PLANS/SPECIAL FEATURES:

Siemens AG is engaged in electrification, automation and digitalization. Its businesses are grouped into 11 divisions. Building technologies offers fire protection, security, building automation, heating, ventilation and air conditioning (HVAC) and energy management products and services in relation to environmentally-friendly buildings and infrastructure. Digital factory offers seamlessly-integrated hardware, software and technology-based services that supports manufacturing companies worldwide in enhancing the flexibility and efficiency of their manufacturing processes. Energy management supplies products, systems, solutions and services for the economical, reliable and intelligent transmission and distribution of electrical power. Financial services provides business-to-business financial solutions worldwide, and supports customer investments with project and structured financing as well as leasing and equipment finance. Mobility offers integrated products, solutions and services concerning the transportation of people and goods by rail and road. Power and gas provides products and solutions for the oil and gas, power and industrial markets. Power generation offers products and services for ensuring reliable rotating power equipment within the utility, oil and gas, and industrial processing sectors worldwide. Process industries and drives provides innovative, integrated technology across the entire lifecycle in relation to products, processes and plants. Siemens Healthineers AG supplies medical infrastructure, and develops and markets medical imaging, laboratory diagnostics and clinical IT products and solutions. Last, Siemens Wind Power supplies environmentally-friendly renewable energy solutions. Siemens Healthineers and Siemens Wind Power are separately-managed businesses. In addition, Siemens Real Estate manages the company's global real estate holdings. In December 2017, Siemens acquired medical technology company Fast Track Diagnostics. In May 2018, it acquired Enlighted, Inc., a provider of smart Internet of Things (IoT) systems.

FINANCIAL DATA: *Note: Data for latest year may not have been available at press time.*

In U.S. $	2017	2016	2015	2014	2013	2012
Revenue						
R&D Expense						
Operating Income						
Operating Margin %						
SGA Expense						
Net Income						
Operating Cash Flow						
Capital Expenditure						
EBITDA						
Return on Assets %						
Return on Equity %						
Debt to Equity						

CONTACT INFORMATION:

Phone: 49 8963633032 Fax: 49 8932825
Toll-Free:
Address: Wittelsbacherplatz 2, Munich, 80333 Germany

STOCK TICKER/OTHER:

Stock Ticker: SIEGY
Exchange: PINX
Employees: 372,000
Fiscal Year Ends: 09/30
Parent Company:

SALARIES/BONUSES:

Top Exec. Salary: $2,325,852 Bonus: $1,581,463
Second Exec. Salary: $1,581,532 Bonus: $640,493

OTHER THOUGHTS:

Estimated Female Officers or Directors: 5
Hot Spot for Advancement for Women/Minorities: Y

Siemens Healthineers

www.healthcare.siemens.com

NAIC Code: 339,100

TYPES OF BUSINESS:

Medical Equipment Manufacturing
Information Systems
Management Consulting
Diagnostic Tests
Healthcare Consulting

BRANDS/DIVISIONS/AFFILIATES:

Siemens AG
Medicalis Corporation
Fast Track Diagnostics

CONTACTS: *Note: Officers with more than one job title may be intentionally listed here more than once.*

Bernd Montag, CEO
Michael Reitermann, COO
Jochen Schmitz, CFO
J. Marc Overhage, Chief Medical Informatics Officer
Michael Long, Sr. VP-Exec. & Customer Rel.
Brenna Quinn, Sr. VP-Solutions Dev.
Carlos Arglebe, VP-Quality Mgmt.
Gail Latimer, VP
Hartmut Schaper, Sr. VP-Health Svcs., Int'l

GROWTH PLANS/SPECIAL FEATURES:

Siemens Healthineers, a business segment of Siemens AG, is one of the largest suppliers to the healthcare industry. Siemens Healthcare and its subsidiaries offer innovative medical technologies, healthcare information systems, management consulting and support services. The company operates in three business divisions: imaging, diagnostics and advanced therapies. The imaging business comprises computed tomography, magnetic resonance, molecular imaging, X-ray products, syngo software and ultrasound. The diagnostic business comprises clinical chemistry/immunoassay, hemostasis/hematology, blood gas, urinalysis, molecular virology, liquid biopsy, automation and IT. Last, the advanced therapies business comprises angio systems, mobile C-arms, hybrid operating roomss and imaging for radiation oncology. During 2017, the firm acquired Medicalis Corporation, a provider of software solutions for diagnostic imaging; and acquired Fast Track Diagnostics, a Luxembourg-based supplier of molecular diagnostic tests.

FINANCIAL DATA: *Note: Data for latest year may not have been available at press time.*

In U.S. $	2017	2016	2015	2014	2013	2012
Revenue	16,043,730,000	15,754,160,000	15,043,610,000			
R&D Expense	1,457,146,000	1,331,550,000	1,226,887,000			
Operating Income	2,663,100,000	2,461,914,000	2,282,824,000			
Operating Margin %	16.59%	15.62%	15.17%			
SGA Expense	2,584,022,000	2,565,415,000	2,452,611,000			
Net Income	1,659,495,000	1,524,596,000	1,485,056,000			
Operating Cash Flow	2,296,779,000	2,150,250,000	2,210,722,000			
Capital Expenditure	541,923,500	493,080,600	414,001,600			
EBITDA	3,352,716,000	3,168,973,000	2,972,439,000			
Return on Assets %	7.00%	6.59%	6.56%			
Return on Equity %	50.89%	43.24%	34.61%			
Debt to Equity						

CONTACT INFORMATION:

Phone: 49-69-797-6602 Fax:
Toll-Free:
Address: Henkestrasse 127, Erlangen, D-91052 Germany

STOCK TICKER/OTHER:

Stock Ticker: SEMHF
Employees: 48,000
Parent Company: Siemens AG
Exchange: GREY
Fiscal Year Ends: 09/30

SALARIES/BONUSES:

Top Exec. Salary: $ Bonus: $
Second Exec. Salary: $ Bonus: $

OTHER THOUGHTS:

Estimated Female Officers or Directors: 3
Hot Spot for Advancement for Women/Minorities: Y

Sigma Healthcare Limited

sigmahealthcare.com.au

NAIC Code: 424,210

TYPES OF BUSINESS:

Drugs and Druggists' Sundries Merchant Wholesalers

BRANDS/DIVISIONS/AFFILIATES:

Amcal
Guardian
PharmaSave
Chemist King
Discount Drug Stores
Central Healthcare Services (CHS)

CONTACTS: *Note: Officers with more than one job title may be intentionally listed here more than once.*

Mark Hooper, CEO
Richard Church, Gen. Mgr-Operations
Iona MacPherson, CFO
Paula Jeffs, Dir.-Human Resources
Scott Jones, Gen. Mgr.-Merch.
Sue Morgan, General Counsel
Vincent Gualtieri, Gen. Mgr.-Wholesale Sales
Michael Robertson, Gen. Mgr.-Retail Oper.
Richard Church, Gen. Mgr.-Logistics
Claire Pallot, Gen. Mgr.-Multi Channel
Brain Jamieson, Chmn.
Alan O Hara, Gen. Mgr.-Supply Chain & Transformation

GROWTH PLANS/SPECIAL FEATURES:

Sigma Healthcare Limited is an Australian wholesaler, manufacturer and retailer of pharmaceuticals. The company's pharmacy network is comprised of more than 1,200 branded and independent stores, including the Amcal, Guardian, PharmaSave, Chemist King and Discount Drug Stores retail brand names. These stores provide pharmaceuticals, health and well-being items, as well as beauty products. Sigma maintains long-term alliances with independent pharmacy support groups, enabling the company to offer its solutions to suit any pharmacy, including large format branded pharmacies as well as independent community pharmacies. The firm also distributes to hospital pharmacies and health facilities through wholly-owned Central Healthcare Services, which is branded as CHS. Sigma's supply and logistics division maintains a network of 15 distribution centers, serving more than 4,000 pharmacies nationwide with over 15,000 products lines daily via deliveries by road, sea and air.

The firm offers its employees an employee share plan and product discounts.

FINANCIAL DATA: *Note: Data for latest year may not have been available at press time.*

In U.S. $	2017	2016	2015	2014	2013	2012
Revenue	3,347,451,904	2,661,216,256	2,406,870,016	2,272,496,384	2,247,366,400	2,179,389,952
R&D Expense						
Operating Income						
Operating Margin %						
SGA Expense						
Net Income	40,270,772	38,239,972	39,959,564	40,537,308	14,148,986	37,232,896
Operating Cash Flow						
Capital Expenditure						
EBITDA						
Return on Assets %						
Return on Equity %						
Debt to Equity						

CONTACT INFORMATION:

Phone: 61-03-92159215 Fax: 61-03-92159188
Toll-Free:
Address: 3 Myer Pl., Rowville, VIC 3178 Australia

STOCK TICKER/OTHER:

Stock Ticker: SHTPY Exchange: PINX
Employees: 156 Fiscal Year Ends: 01/31
Parent Company:

SALARIES/BONUSES:

Top Exec. Salary: $ Bonus: $
Second Exec. Salary: $ Bonus: $

OTHER THOUGHTS:

Estimated Female Officers or Directors: 4
Hot Spot for Advancement for Women/Minorities: Y

Simcere Pharmaceutical Group

www.simcere.com

NAIC Code: 325,412

TYPES OF BUSINESS:

Branded Generic Pharmaceuticals
Drug Research

BRANDS/DIVISIONS/AFFILIATES:

Bicun
Zailin
Endostar
Yingtaiqing
Iremod
AnQi
Jiebaisu
Simcere Innovation Center

CONTACTS: *Note: Officers with more than one job title may be intentionally listed here more than once.*

Jinsheng Ren, CEO
Honggang Feng, Pres.
Yushan Wan, VP-Finance
Baoxing Zha, VP-Mktg.
Xiaojin Yin, Sr. VP-R&D
Haibo Qian, VP
Jie Liu DElia, Corp. VP-Bus. Dev.
Jie Liu DElia, Corp. VP-Corp. Communications
Jindong Zhou, Exec. VP
Quanfu Feng, VP
Jialun Tian, VP-Hospital Sales
Jinsheng Ren, Chmn.
Jie Liu DElia, Pres., Simcrere of America

GROWTH PLANS/SPECIAL FEATURES:

Simcere Pharmaceutical Group is a Chinese manufacturer and supplier of branded generic pharmaceuticals. The company manufactures and sells more than 50 pharmaceutical products and is the exclusive distributor of additional pharmaceutical products marketed under the firm's brand name. Simcere also has approval from the Chinese FDA to manufacture and sell hundreds of other products. These products are used for treatment of a wide range of diseases, including cancer, cerebrovascular and cardiovascular diseases, infections, arthritis, diarrhea, allergies, respiratory conditions and urinary conditions. Simcere's products include: Bicun, an anti-stroke medication and the first synthetic-free radical scavenger sold in China; Zailin, a generic amoxicillin granule antibiotic; Endostar, a recombinant human endostatin injection to eradicate tumors; Yingtaiqing, a generic diclofenac sodium sustained-release capsule for inflammation and pain relief; Iremod, a disease modifying anti-rheumatic drug; AnQi, an amoxicillin tablet for infections; BiCun, an edaravone injection for improving neurological symptoms and functional disorders caused by acute cerebral infarction; Antine, for various kinds of rheumatic pain for soft tissues; Sinofuan, an anti-cancer sustained-release fluorouracil implant; and Jiebaisu, a nedaplatin injection. Simcere has filed more than 315 patent applications, of which 123 have been approved so far. The company has successfully developed more than 50 new drugs, with 20 innovative drugs and several generic drugs under development. In March 2018, the firm established Simcere Innovation Center, which is currently building offices in Shanghai, China and Boston, Massachusetts (USA), to integrate Simcere's R&D resources and attract international professionals for the purpose of seizing opportunities for global innovation and to build a sustainable development engine for the company.

FINANCIAL DATA: *Note: Data for latest year may not have been available at press time.*

In U.S. $	2017	2016	2015	2014	2013	2012
Revenue	546,000,000	520,000,000				
R&D Expense						
Operating Income						
Operating Margin %						
SGA Expense						
Net Income						
Operating Cash Flow						
Capital Expenditure						
EBITDA						
Return on Assets %						
Return on Equity %						
Debt to Equity						

CONTACT INFORMATION:

Phone: 86 2525566666 Fax: 86 2585472579
Toll-Free:
Address: No. 699-18 Xuanwu Ave., Nanjing, Jiangsu 210042 China

STOCK TICKER/OTHER:

Stock Ticker: Subsidiary
Employees: 14,000
Parent Company: Simcere Holding Limited
Exchange:
Fiscal Year Ends: 12/31

SALARIES/BONUSES:

Top Exec. Salary: $ Bonus: $
Second Exec. Salary: $ Bonus: $

OTHER THOUGHTS:

Estimated Female Officers or Directors: 1
Hot Spot for Advancement for Women/Minorities:

Sinopharm Group Co Ltd

www.sinopharmholding.com

NAIC Code: 424,210

TYPES OF BUSINESS:

Drugs and Druggists Sundries Merchant Wholesalers

BRANDS/DIVISIONS/AFFILIATES:

China National Pharmaceutical Group Corporation
Shanghai Fosun Pharmaceutical

CONTACTS: *Note: Officers with more than one job title may be intentionally listed here more than once.*

Yulin Wei, CEO
Zhiming Li, Pres.
Li Zhiming, Chief Legal Officer
Zhang Jian, Head-Auditing
Ma Wanjun, VP
Lu Jun, VP
Shi Jinming, VP
Liu Wei, Joint Sec.

GROWTH PLANS/SPECIAL FEATURES:

Sinopharm Group Co., Ltd. is China's largest pharmaceuticals and healthcare products distributor and a leading provider of supply chain services. The company is jointly-owned by China National Pharmaceutical Group Corporation and Shanghai Fosun Pharmaceutical. The company has more than 300 wholly-owned subsidiaries, comprising a business and distribution network covering 31 provinces, municipalities and autonomous regions. In addition, the group manages retail pharmacy chains. It is a licensed distributor of narcotic drugs in China, and has held a majority of the market share. Operations of the group are divided into pharmaceutical distribution, medicine retail business and medicine and chemical regent production. Its products are supported through research and development centers, manufacturing facilities, traditional Chinese medicine plantations and marketing and distribution networks. Operations are conducted internationally as well, with locations in Africa, France, Germany, Hong Kong, the U.S. and Vietnam.

FINANCIAL DATA: *Note: Data for latest year may not have been available at press time.*

In U.S. $	2017	2016	2015	2014	2013	2012
Revenue						
R&D Expense						
Operating Income						
Operating Margin %						
SGA Expense						
Net Income						
Operating Cash Flow						
Capital Expenditure						
EBITDA						
Return on Assets %						
Return on Equity %						
Debt to Equity						

CONTACT INFORMATION:

Phone: 86-21-23052666 Fax: 86-21-23052888
Toll-Free:
Address: 1001 Zhongshan Rd. West, Shanghai, Shanghai 200051 China

STOCK TICKER/OTHER:

Stock Ticker: SHTDF
Exchange: PINX
Employees: 61,694
Fiscal Year Ends: 12/31
Parent Company:

SALARIES/BONUSES:

Top Exec. Salary: $ Bonus: $
Second Exec. Salary: $ Bonus: $

OTHER THOUGHTS:

Estimated Female Officers or Directors:
Hot Spot for Advancement for Women/Minorities:

Smile Brands Inc

www.smilebrands.com

NAIC Code: 621,210

TYPES OF BUSINESS:

Dental Practice Management

BRANDS/DIVISIONS/AFFILIATES:

Gryphon Investors
ConsumerHealth Inc
Bright Now! Dental
Monarch Dental
Castle Dental
Johnson Family Dental
AXIOM Implant Specialty Dentistry
Whitney Ranch Dental

CONTACTS: *Note: Officers with more than one job title may be intentionally listed here more than once.*

Steven Bilt, CEO
Brad Schmidt, CFO
Jody Martin, CMO
Tanisha J. Wicker, Sr. VP-Human Resources
George Suda, CIO
Neal Crowley, General Counsel
Dennis R. Fratt, Sr. VP-Oper. Svcs. Group
William P. McCarthy, Sr. VP-Real Estate & Facility Dev.
Stephen R. Ashlock, VP-Specialty Svcs.
Jeff Hamill, VP-West
Steve Laudicino, VP-East
Fred Ward, VP-Central
Brian Stern, Sr. VP-Patient Experience

GROWTH PLANS/SPECIAL FEATURES:

Smile Brands, Inc. provides business support services to dental offices throughout the U.S. The group supports the practices of independent dentists by managing the administrative, financial, marketing and information services aspects of their practices. Its brands include Bright Now! Dental, Monarch Dental, Castle Dental, Newport Dental, Los Gatos Dental Specialists, OneSmile Dental, A+ Dental Care, Grant Road Dental, Johnson Family Dental, Premier Private Practice Dental Group, AXIOM Implant Specialty Dentistry, Maddison Ave. Dental, Perfect Smile Dental, Summerlin Dental and Whitney Ranch Dental. These branded offices are located in Arizona, Arkansas, California, Colorado, Florida, Indiana, Maryland, Nevada, Ohio, Oregon, Pennsylvania, Tennessee, Texas, Utah, Virginia and Washington. In addition, wholly-owned subsidiary ConsumerHealth, Inc. operates as a staff-model dental health service plan licensed by the state of California under the provisions of the California Knox-Keene Health Care Service Plan Act of 1975. ConsumerHealth is a mixed-model plan that provides dental services to its enrollees through its individual, group and Medicaid product lines, as well as through agreements to service group enrollees of other dental plans. The subsidiary owns and operates 14 staff-model dental facilities in California, and employs or contracts directly with each of the dentists, specialists and hygienists that work at ConsumerHealth facilities. Smile Brands' primary equity sponsor is Gryphon Investors, a leading middle-market private equity firm based in San Francisco, California. Gryphon focuses on investing in physician-centric healthcare businesses.

Smile Brands offers employees health, dental, vision, group life, AD&D and short/long-term disability insurance plans, flexible spending accounts, supplemental medical plans, a 401(k) plan and other types of voluntary insurances.

FINANCIAL DATA: *Note: Data for latest year may not have been available at press time.*

In U.S. $	2017	2016	2015	2014	2013	2012
Revenue	483,000,000	460,000,000	459,000,000	456,000,000	455,000,000	451,000,000
R&D Expense						
Operating Income						
Operating Margin %						
SGA Expense						
Net Income						
Operating Cash Flow						
Capital Expenditure						
EBITDA						
Return on Assets %						
Return on Equity %						
Debt to Equity						

CONTACT INFORMATION:

Phone: 714-668-1300 Fax: 714-428-1300
Toll-Free:
Address: 100 Spectrum Center Drive, Ste. 1500, Irvine, CA 92618 United States

STOCK TICKER/OTHER:

Stock Ticker: Private
Employees: 1,300
Parent Company: Gryphon Investors
Exchange:
Fiscal Year Ends: 12/31

SALARIES/BONUSES:

Top Exec. Salary: $ Bonus: $
Second Exec. Salary: $ Bonus: $

OTHER THOUGHTS:

Estimated Female Officers or Directors: 2
Hot Spot for Advancement for Women/Minorities: Y

Smith & Nephew plc

NAIC Code: 339,113

www.smith-nephew.com

TYPES OF BUSINESS:

Implants, Surgical, Manufacturing
Reconstructive Joint Implants
Arthroscopic Enabling Technologies
Wound Management Products

BRANDS/DIVISIONS/AFFILIATES:

Rotation Medical Inc

CONTACTS:

Note: Officers with more than one job title may be intentionally listed here more than once.

Namal Nawana, CEO
Graham Baker, CFO
Brad Cannon, CMO
Elga Lohler, Chief Human Resources Officer
Ros Rivaz, CTO
Jack Campo, Chief Legal Officer
Gordon Howe, Pres., Global Oper.
Cyrille Petit, Chief Corp. Dev. Officer
Phil Cowdy, Head-Corp. Affairs
Phil Cowdy, Head-Corp. Affairs & Strategic Planning
Mike Frazzette, Pres., Advanced Surgical Devices
Arjun Rajaratnam, Chief Compliance Officer
Roberto Quarta, Chmn.
Francisco Canal Vega, Pres., Latin America

GROWTH PLANS/SPECIAL FEATURES:

Smith & Nephew plc develops and markets advanced medical technology devices for healthcare professionals. The company organizes its business into four business units: orthopedics reconstruction, advanced wound management, sports medicine and trauma & extremities. The orthopedics reconstruction segment is comprised of joint replacement systems for knees, hip and shoulders as well as ancillary products, like bone cement used in reconstructive surgery. The advanced wound management unit supplies products for chronic and acute wounds. Chronic wounds, such as pressure, leg or diabetic foot ulcers, are generally difficult to heal; and acute wounds, such as burns and post-operative wounds, are generally life threatening, with potential scarring and infection. Many products for this segment target wounds associated with older populations. The sports medicine segment offers minimally invasive surgery techniques, with a focus on the surgery of joints, including knee, shoulder and hip; fixation systems and specialized devices for damaged tissue repair; and radiofrequency wands, mechanical blades as well as fluid management equipment for surgical access. The trauma & extremities segment includes internal and external fixation devices and orthobiological materials used in the stabilization of severe fractures and deformity correction procedures. In December 2017, Smith & Nephew acquired tissue regeneration developer Rotation Medical, Inc.

FINANCIAL DATA:

Note: Data for latest year may not have been available at press time.

In U.S. $	2017	2016	2015	2014	2013	2012
Revenue	4,765,000,000	4,669,000,000	4,634,000,000	4,617,000,000	4,351,000,000	4,137,000,000
R&D Expense	223,000,000	230,000,000	222,000,000	235,000,000	231,000,000	171,000,000
Operating Income	934,000,000	801,000,000	628,000,000	749,000,000	810,000,000	906,000,000
Operating Margin %	19.60%	17.15%	13.55%	16.22%	18.61%	21.89%
SGA Expense	2,360,000,000	2,366,000,000	2,641,000,000	2,471,000,000	2,210,000,000	2,050,000,000
Net Income	767,000,000	784,000,000	410,000,000	501,000,000	556,000,000	729,000,000
Operating Cash Flow	1,090,000,000	849,000,000	1,030,000,000	683,000,000	867,000,000	902,000,000
Capital Expenditure	376,000,000	392,000,000	358,000,000	375,000,000	340,000,000	265,000,000
EBITDA	1,388,000,000	1,584,000,000	1,112,000,000	1,186,000,000	1,184,000,000	1,484,000,000
Return on Assets %	10.08%	10.80%	5.66%	7.63%	9.70%	14.03%
Return on Equity %	17.83%	19.78%	10.24%	12.39%	14.02%	20.61%
Debt to Equity	0.30	0.39	0.36	0.41	0.08	0.11

CONTACT INFORMATION:

Phone: 44 2074017646 Fax: 44 2079303353
Toll-Free:
Address: 15 Adam St., London, WC2N 6LA United Kingdom

STOCK TICKER/OTHER:

Stock Ticker: SNN
Employees: 16,737
Parent Company:
Exchange: NYS
Fiscal Year Ends: 12/31

SALARIES/BONUSES:

Top Exec. Salary: $1,330,347 Bonus: $1,208,911
Second Exec. Salary: $547,273 Bonus: $683,797

OTHER THOUGHTS:

Estimated Female Officers or Directors: 6
Hot Spot for Advancement for Women/Minorities: Y

Smiths Group plc

www.smiths.com

NAIC Code: 339,100

TYPES OF BUSINESS:

Machinery, Manufacturing
Medical Devices, Manufacturing

BRANDS/DIVISIONS/AFFILIATES:

Smiths Detection
Smiths Medical
Smiths Interconnect
John Crane
Flex-Tek
Morpho Detection LLC

CONTACTS: *Note: Officers with more than one job title may be intentionally listed here more than once.*

Andrew Reynolds Smith, CEO
John Francis Shipsey, CFO
Sheena Mackay, Dir.-Human Resources
George Buckley, Chmn.

GROWTH PLANS/SPECIAL FEATURES:

Smiths Group plc is a global technology company with five main divisions: Smiths Detection, Smiths Medical, Smiths Interconnect, John Crane and Flex-Tek. Smiths Detection provides security equipment for the detection and identification of explosives, chemical and biological agents, weapons, narcotics and contraband. This equipment is used by military forces, airport security, customs officers and emergency services. Smiths Medical is a provider of specialist medical devices and equipment, which include airway management, pain management, needle safety, temperature monitoring, infusion systems, vascular access and in-vitro fertilization. Smiths Interconnect manufactures electronic components and sub-systems such as millimeter wave components and antennas, fiber optic and coaxial cables, industrial surge protectors and wireless technology products. John Crane provides products and services to the oil and gas, power generation, chemicals, pharmaceutical, pulp and paper and mining industries. Flex-Tek provides components such as flexible hose and ducting for heating and conveying gas, liquid and airborne solids to the aerospace, medical, industrial, construction and domestic appliance industries. Smiths Group has operations in more than 50 countries, and its products and services reach approximately 200 countries and territories. During 2017, the firm sold Interconnect's microwave telecoms business; completed the acquisition of Morpho Detection, LLC; and sold Morpho's explosive trace detection business to OSI Systems, Inc. for $75.5 million. In early-2018, Smiths Group sold John Crane's bearings business; and agreed to acquire Seebach GmbH, a provider of highly-engineered filtration solutions.

FINANCIAL DATA: *Note: Data for latest year may not have been available at press time.*

In U.S. $	2017	2016	2015	2014	2013	2012
Revenue						
R&D Expense						
Operating Income						
Operating Margin %						
SGA Expense						
Net Income						
Operating Cash Flow						
Capital Expenditure						
EBITDA						
Return on Assets %						
Return on Equity %						
Debt to Equity						

CONTACT INFORMATION:

Phone: 44 2078085500 Fax: 44 2078085544
Toll-Free:
Address: 4/Fl, 11-12 St. James's Square, London, SW1Y 4LB United Kingdom

STOCK TICKER/OTHER:

Stock Ticker: SMGKF
Exchange: PINX
Employees: 22,000
Fiscal Year Ends: 07/31
Parent Company:

SALARIES/BONUSES:

Top Exec. Salary: $1,017,546 Bonus: $1,753,310
Second Exec. Salary: $528,341 Bonus: $750,114

OTHER THOUGHTS:

Estimated Female Officers or Directors:
Hot Spot for Advancement for Women/Minorities: Y

Sonic Healthcare Limited

NAIC Code: 621,511

www.sonichealthcare.com.au

TYPES OF BUSINESS:

Medical Laboratories

BRANDS/DIVISIONS/AFFILIATES:

Sonic Clinical Services
IPN Medical Centres
Sonic HealthPlus
Australian Skin Cancer Clinics

CONTACTS:
Note: Officers with more than one job title may be intentionally listed here more than once.

Colin Goldschmidt, CEO
Christopher Wilks, CFO
Mark Compton, Chmn.

GROWTH PLANS/SPECIAL FEATURES:

Sonic Healthcare Limited is an international medical diagnostics company, offering laboratory and diagnostic imaging services to the medical community and their patients. The firm's services are categorized into three groups: laboratory medicine/pathology, diagnostic imaging/radiology and Sonic Clinical Services. The laboratory medicine/pathology group is the largest laboratory medicine company in Australia, Germany, the U.K. and Switzerland. It also has a significant presence in the U.S., and divisions in the U.K., Belgium, Ireland and New Zealand. This group's laboratories are staffed by more than 500 specialist pathologists and thousands of medical scientists and technicians. The diagnostic imaging group comprises more than 100 radiology centers in Australia, performing millions of examinations annually via 180 specialist radiologists and nuclear physicians. Last, Sonic Clinical Services is the primary care division of Sonic Healthcare, and offers general practice services and after hours general practitioner services as well as occupational health services, remote health services, community and home nursing services. Its activities also include primary care research programs, health assessment technologies, hospital avoidance programs, clinical trials and chronic disease management programs. Brands within Sonic Clinical Services include IPN Medical Centres, Sonic HealthPlus and Australian Skin Cancer Clinics. It provides national healthcare services and solutions throughout Australia, including metropolitan, regional and rural locations.

FINANCIAL DATA:
Note: Data for latest year may not have been available at press time.

In U.S. $	2017	2016	2015	2014	2013	2012
Revenue	3,656,819,200	3,579,816,960	2,996,450,048	2,789,427,712	2,478,373,376	2,381,581,056
R&D Expense						
Operating Income						
Operating Margin %						
SGA Expense						
Net Income	309,531,840	326,609,280	251,590,432	278,570,176	242,400,880	228,651,232
Operating Cash Flow						
Capital Expenditure						
EBITDA						
Return on Assets %						
Return on Equity %						
Debt to Equity						

CONTACT INFORMATION:

Phone: 61 298555444 Fax: 61 298785066
Toll-Free:
Address: 14 Giffnock Ave, Macquarie Park, NSW 2113 Australia

STOCK TICKER/OTHER:

Stock Ticker: SKHCF Exchange: PINX
Employees: Fiscal Year Ends: 06/30
Parent Company:

SALARIES/BONUSES:

Top Exec. Salary: $ Bonus: $
Second Exec. Salary: $ Bonus: $

OTHER THOUGHTS:

Estimated Female Officers or Directors: 2
Hot Spot for Advancement for Women/Minorities:

Sonova Holding AG

www.sonova.com

NAIC Code: 334,510

TYPES OF BUSINESS:

Auditory Devices & Hearing Aids

BRANDS/DIVISIONS/AFFILIATES:

Phonak
Hansaton
Unitron
Advanced Bionics
AudioNova Group

CONTACTS: *Note: Officers with more than one job title may be intentionally listed here more than once.*

Arnd Kaldowski, CEO
Hans Mehl, VP-Operations
Hartwig Grevener, CFO
Hans Mehl, VP-Oper.
Paul Thompson, VP-Corp. Dev.
Ignacio Martinez, VP-Intl Sales
Hansjurg Emch, VP-Medical
Alexander Zschokke, VP-Channel Solutions
Robert F. Spoerry, Chmn.

GROWTH PLANS/SPECIAL FEATURES:

Sonova Holding AG develops and markets medical devices for the hearing-impaired. Based in Switzerland, Sonova is a leading producer of hearing healthcare solutions, wireless communication systems and products for hearing protection. The company, which operates four major subsidiaries in over 90 countries, is divided into two segments: hearing aids and cochlear implants. The hearing aids segment consists of a global brand portfolio: Phonak, Hansaton and Unitron. Phonak has been in business for more than 70 years, and offers innovative, state-of-the-art hearing systems and wireless devices. Hansaton is a unique hearing aid manufacturer with a tradition of creating innovative solutions that focus on giving the joy of life back to people with hearing loss. Unitron partners with hearing care professionals to support in-clinic success via patient experience with products, services and resources. The cochlear implants segment is represented by the Advanced Bionics brand. Advanced Bionics is North America's leading producer of cochlear inner-ear implants, which are neurostimulation devices that offer those suffering from severe hearing loss and deafness the ability to hear. Advanced Bionics develops cutting-edge cochlear implant technology designed to help children and adults enjoy clear, high-resolution sound, optimal speech understanding in noisy settings and quality music experience. In addition, Sonova's AudioNova Group expands its European presence, and is a service network of hearing care providers dedicated to delivering service and technology solutions for people with hearing loss. The firm aims to continually improve information, education, screening, counseling and support for customers. It operates under brands such as Audium, AuditionSante, Boots Hearingcare, Connect Hearing, Fiebing, Geers, Hansaton, Lapperre, Lindacher, Schoonenberg, Triton and Vitakustik.

Sonova offers its employees wellness programs, access to health classes and access to childcare.

FINANCIAL DATA: *Note: Data for latest year may not have been available at press time.*

In U.S. $	2017	2016	2015	2014	2013	2012
Revenue	2,409,844,224	2,084,206,080	2,047,142,784	1,962,873,344	1,805,898,752	1,629,445,376
R&D Expense						
Operating Income						
Operating Margin %						
SGA Expense						
Net Income	351,240,832	339,022,848	362,126,912	342,849,408	111,574,176	248,223,040
Operating Cash Flow						
Capital Expenditure						
EBITDA						
Return on Assets %						
Return on Equity %						
Debt to Equity						

CONTACT INFORMATION:

Phone: 41 589283333 Fax: 41 589283399
Toll-Free:
Address: Laubisrutistrasse 28, Stafa, 8712 Switzerland

STOCK TICKER/OTHER:

Stock Ticker: SONVF
Exchange: PINX
Employees: 14,242
Fiscal Year Ends: 03/31
Parent Company:

SALARIES/BONUSES:

Top Exec. Salary: $ Bonus: $
Second Exec. Salary: $ Bonus: $

OTHER THOUGHTS:

Estimated Female Officers or Directors: 2
Hot Spot for Advancement for Women/Minorities:

Span America Medical Systems Inc

www.spanamerica.com

NAIC Code: 339,100

TYPES OF BUSINESS:

Supplies-Therapeutic Mattresses
Polyurethane Foam Products
Wound Management Products
Skin Care
Bed Frames

BRANDS/DIVISIONS/AFFILIATES:

Savaria Corporation
MC Healthcare Products
Geo-Matt
PressureGuard
Span-Aids
Isch-Dish
Selan

CONTACTS: *Note: Officers with more than one job title may be intentionally listed here more than once.*

James Ferguson, Pres.
Erick C. Herlong, VP-Operations
Thomas Henrion, Chairman of the Board
Richard C. Coggins, CFO
Clyde Shew, VP-Mktg. & Sales
Richard Coggins, Director
Clyde Shew, Vice President, Divisional
Erick Herlong, Vice President, Divisional
James Teague, Vice President, Divisional
William Darby, Vice President, Divisional
Mark Sitter, Vice President, Divisional
Robert Ackley, Vice President, Divisional
James OReagan, Vice President, Divisional

GROWTH PLANS/SPECIAL FEATURES:

Span-America Medical Systems, Inc. manufactures and distributes polyurethane foam products for the medical and custom products markets. These products include polyurethane foam mattress overlays for powered and non-powered therapeutic replacement mattresses; medical bed frames and patient positioning and seating products all for pressure management; and patient comfort and positioning. Span-America markets its products to acute care hospitals, long-term care facilities and home health care providers, primarily in North America. The company produces various foam mattress overlays, including convoluted foam pads and its patented Geo-Matt overlay. The Geo-Matt design includes individual foam cells cut to exacting tolerances on computer-controlled equipment to create a clinically effective mattress surface. These products provide patients with greater comfort and treat patients who have or are susceptible to developing pressure ulcers. Span-America's overlay products are mattress pads rather than complete mattresses and are marketed as less expensive alternatives to more complex replacement mattresses. Span-America's more complex non-powered replacement mattresses include the PressureGuard line, which combines a polyurethane foam shell and static air cylinders. Through subsidiary M.C. Healthcare Products, the firm manufactures medical bed frames and related products for the long-term care industry. The company's specialty line of positioners is sold primarily under the trademark Span-Aids and consists of items that aid in relieving the basic patient positioning, problems of elevation, immobilization, muscle contracture, foot drop and foot or leg rotation. The company offers Isch-Dish patient seating products that address principal areas of care and wound healing. Span-America also markets Selan skin care creams. Span-America operates as an indirect, wholly-owned subsidiary of Savaria Corporation.

FINANCIAL DATA: *Note: Data for latest year may not have been available at press time.*

In U.S. $	2017	2016	2015	2014	2013	2012
Revenue	71,008,526	67,627,168	64,314,996	55,857,376	73,833,552	76,146,424
R&D Expense						
Operating Income						
Operating Margin %						
SGA Expense						
Net Income		4,247,331	3,993,398	2,590,767	5,067,417	5,214,973
Operating Cash Flow						
Capital Expenditure						
EBITDA						
Return on Assets %						
Return on Equity %						
Debt to Equity						

CONTACT INFORMATION:

Phone: 864 288-8877 Fax: 864 288-8692
Toll-Free: 800-888-6752
Address: 70 Commerce Ctr., Greenville, SC 29615 United States

STOCK TICKER/OTHER:

Stock Ticker: Subsidiary
Exchange:
Employees: 260
Fiscal Year Ends: 10/31
Parent Company: Savaria Corporation

SALARIES/BONUSES:

Top Exec. Salary: $ Bonus: $
Second Exec. Salary: $ Bonus: $

OTHER THOUGHTS:

Estimated Female Officers or Directors: 2
Hot Spot for Advancement for Women/Minorities:

Specialty Laboratories Inc

www.specialtylabs.com

NAIC Code: 621,511

TYPES OF BUSINESS:

Clinical Laboratory Tests
Assays

BRANDS/DIVISIONS/AFFILIATES:

Quest Diagnositcs Inc

CONTACTS: *Note: Officers with more than one job title may be intentionally listed here more than once.*

Steve Rusckowski, CEO-Quest
Stephen H. Rusckowski, CEO

GROWTH PLANS/SPECIAL FEATURES:

Specialty Laboratories, Inc., a subsidiary of Quest Diagnostics, Inc., operates a research-based clinical laboratory, predominantly focused on developing and performing esoteric clinical laboratory tests, referred to as assays. The laboratory, Quest Diagnostics Nichols Institute of Valencia, California, offers a comprehensive menu of thousands of assays, many of which it developed through internal research and development efforts, that are used to diagnose, evaluate and monitor patients in the areas of endocrinology, genetics, infectious diseases, neurology, pediatrics, urology, allergy and immunology, cardiology and coagulation, hepatology, microbiology, oncology, rheumatology, women's health, dermatopathology, gastroenterology, nephrology, pathology and toxicology. Some of the company's assays include evaluations for H1N1, SARS, vitamin D deficiency, potassium and chlorine levels, protein chemistry and the ovarian cancer marker HE4. In addition, Specialty Labs owns proprietary information technology that accelerates and automates test ordering and results reporting with customers. The company's primary customers are hospitals, independent clinical laboratories and physicians.

The firm offers employees health and dental plans, a 401(k) plan, a stock purchase plan (through Quest Diagnostics), short- and long-term disability plans, flexible spending accounts, an employee assistance program and an education reimbursement program.

FINANCIAL DATA: *Note: Data for latest year may not have been available at press time.*

In U.S. $	2017	2016	2015	2014	2013	2012
Revenue	388,500,000	370,000,000	368,000,000	355,000,000	350,000,000	334,973,536
R&D Expense						
Operating Income						
Operating Margin %						
SGA Expense						
Net Income						
Operating Cash Flow						
Capital Expenditure						
EBITDA						
Return on Assets %						
Return on Equity %						
Debt to Equity						

CONTACT INFORMATION:

Phone: 661-799-6543 Fax: 661-799-6634
Toll-Free: 800-421-7110
Address: 27027 Tourney Rd., Valencia, CA 91355 United States

STOCK TICKER/OTHER:

Stock Ticker: Subsidiary
Exchange:
Employees: 4,349
Fiscal Year Ends: 12/31
Parent Company: Quest Diagnostics Inc

SALARIES/BONUSES:

Top Exec. Salary: $ Bonus: $
Second Exec. Salary: $ Bonus: $

OTHER THOUGHTS:

Estimated Female Officers or Directors: 1
Hot Spot for Advancement for Women/Minorities:

Spectrum Health

www.spectrumhealth.org

NAIC Code: 622,110

TYPES OF BUSINESS:

General Medical and Surgical Hospitals
Trauma Center
Neonatal Center
Burn Center
Poison Center
HMO
Long-Term Care
Children's Hospital

BRANDS/DIVISIONS/AFFILIATES:

Priority Health

CONTACTS:

Note: Officers with more than one job title may be intentionally listed here more than once.

Tina Freese Decker, CEO

GROWTH PLANS/SPECIAL FEATURES:

Spectrum Health is one of the largest health systems in western Michigan. The firm's not-for-profit system of care is dedicated to improving the health of families and individuals. As of fiscal 2017, Spectrum's organization includes 12 hospitals, 180 ambulatory sites, 115 acute care hospitals, more than 1,600 independent physicians, 2,200 active volunteers and its nationally-recognized health plan, Priority Health. Spectrum Health provides inpatient and outpatient services throughout Michigan and facilities are located in cities such as Grand Rapids, Holland, Zeeland, Belding, Reed City, Fremont, Kentwood, Rockford, Cutlerville, Greenville, Wyoming, Big Rapids, Canadian Lakes, East Grand Rapids, Allendale, Hastings, Lake Odessa, Grand Blanc, Grand Haven, Coopersville, Stanwood, Evart and many more. The organization is also West Michigan's largest provider of post-acute care including skilled nursing, long-term acute, home and residential care. Spectrum Health's services include insurance, wellness products, state-of-the-art technology and medical treatments. Major services offered by the firm include cancer, continuing care, diabetes, endocrinology, digestive disease, heart and vascular, neurosciences, orthopaedics, pediatrics, rehabilitation, transplant and women's health.

Employees of the company receive benefits including medical, dental, vision, life, disability and AD&D coverage; flexible spending accounts; retirement plans; employee assistance services; tuition assistance; and paid time off.

FINANCIAL DATA:

Note: Data for latest year may not have been available at press time.

In U.S. $	2017	2016	2015	2014	2013	2012
Revenue	5,681,000,000	5,220,515,000	4,625,176,000	4,107,828,000	3,937,360,000	3,849,984,000
R&D Expense						
Operating Income						
Operating Margin %						
SGA Expense						
Net Income	282,000,000	212,044,000	367,311,000	147,747,000	212,257,000	144,114,000
Operating Cash Flow						
Capital Expenditure						
EBITDA						
Return on Assets %						
Return on Equity %						
Debt to Equity						

CONTACT INFORMATION:

Phone: 616-391-1774 Fax: 616-391-2780
Toll-Free: 866-989-7999
Address: 100 Michigan St. NE, Grand Rapids, MI 49503 United States

STOCK TICKER/OTHER:

Stock Ticker: Nonprofit
Exchange:
Employees: 23,000
Fiscal Year Ends: 06/30
Parent Company:

SALARIES/BONUSES:

Top Exec. Salary: $ Bonus: $
Second Exec. Salary: $ Bonus: $

OTHER THOUGHTS:

Estimated Female Officers or Directors:
Hot Spot for Advancement for Women/Minorities:

SSM Health

www.ssmhealth.com

NAIC Code: 622,110

TYPES OF BUSINESS:

General Medical and Surgical Hospitals
Nursing Homes
HMO
Hospice Services

BRANDS/DIVISIONS/AFFILIATES:

SSM Health St Mary's Hospital
SSM Health Good Samaritan Hospital
SSM Health at Home
SSM Health St Francis Hospital
SSM Health Cardinal Glennon Children's Hospital
Bone and Joint Hospital at St Anthony
SSM Health St Clare Hospital
Columbus Community Hospital

CONTACTS: *Note: Officers with more than one job title may be intentionally listed here more than once.*

Laura Kaiser, CEO/Pres.
Maggie Fowler, Chief Nursing Officer
Chris Howard, Pres., Hospital Oper.
Paula J. Friedman, Sr. VP-Strategic Dev.
Dixie L. Platt, Sr. VP-Comm., Public Policy & External Rel.
Gaurov Dayal, Pres., Finance, Integration & Home Care Delivery
Michael Panicola, Sr. VP-Missions & Organizational Ethics
Kris A. Zimmer, Sr. VP-Finance

GROWTH PLANS/SPECIAL FEATURES:

SSM Health is a Catholic not-for-profit health system serving the comprehensive health needs of communities throughout the Midwest. The organization includes 24 hospitals, more than 300 physician offices and other outpatient care sites, 10 post-acute facilities, comprehensive home care and hospice services, a pharmacy benefit company, an insurance company, a technology company and an Accountable Care Organization. Its locations include Illinois, Missouri, Oklahoma and Wisconsin. SSM has been active for more than 125 years. The company has more than 5,370 licensed beds at its owned sites. During fiscal 2017-2018, it admitted over 178,000 in-patients and had approximately 1.6 million outpatient visits. SSM maintains nearly 10,000 medical staff who provide a range of services from rehabilitation, pediatrics and home health to hospice, residential and skilled nursing care. The company's health-related businesses include information and support services such as materials management and home care. The firm's facilities include SSM Health St. Mary's Hospital, SSM Health Good Samaritan Hospital, SSM Health at Home, SSM Health St. Francis Hospital, SSM Health Cardinal Glennon Children's Hospital, Bone and Joint Hospital at St. Anthony, SSM Health St. Clare Hospital and Columbus Community Hospital. In August 2018, SSM announced that it was in discussions to sell several Missouri health facilities in Jefferson City, Mexico (in Audrain County) and Maryville, as well as outpatient, home care, hospice and medical group locations throughout the region.

SSM Health Care offers its employees paid time off, tuition reimbursement or loan payment reimbursement, adoption reimbursement, a medical plan contribution discount, flex care, dependent care coverage, a 403(b) retirement plan, a 401(a) retirement match plan, a pension plan and a phased retirement plan.

FINANCIAL DATA: *Note: Data for latest year may not have been available at press time.*

In U.S. $	2017	2016	2015	2014	2013	2012
Revenue	6,497,006,000	6,109,171,000	5,459,303,000	4,895,736,000	3,814,638,000	3,327,152,000
R&D Expense						
Operating Income						
Operating Margin %						
SGA Expense						
Net Income	242,974,000	98,718,000	209,932,000	146,479,000	126,662,000	58,163,000
Operating Cash Flow						
Capital Expenditure						
EBITDA						
Return on Assets %						
Return on Equity %						
Debt to Equity						

CONTACT INFORMATION:

Phone: 314-994-7800 Fax: 314-994-7900
Toll-Free:
Address: 10101 Woodfield Lane, St. Louis, MO 63132 United States

STOCK TICKER/OTHER:

Stock Ticker: Nonprofit
Employees: 29,500
Parent Company:
Exchange:
Fiscal Year Ends: 12/31

SALARIES/BONUSES:

Top Exec. Salary: $ Bonus: $
Second Exec. Salary: $ Bonus: $

OTHER THOUGHTS:

Estimated Female Officers or Directors: 4
Hot Spot for Advancement for Women/Minorities: Y

St Jude Children's Research Hospital

www.stjude.org

NAIC Code: 622,310

TYPES OF BUSINESS:

Children's Hospitals-Specialty
Pediatric Cancer Research & Treatment

BRANDS/DIVISIONS/AFFILIATES:

American Lebanese Syrian Associated Charities
International Outreach Program
Cure4Kids
Pediatric Cancer Genome Project

CONTACTS: *Note: Officers with more than one job title may be intentionally listed here more than once.*

James R. Downing, CEO
Pat Keel, CFO
James Downing, Scientific Dir.
Keith Perry, CIO
Robyn Diaz, Interim Chief Legal Officer
Mary Anna Quinn, Sr. VP-Support Oper.
Kimberly Ovitt, Sr. VP
Pam Dotson, Chief Nursing Officer
Richard J. Gilbertson, Exec. VP
Larry E. Kun, Exec. VP

GROWTH PLANS/SPECIAL FEATURES:

St. Jude Children's Research Hospital, founded in 1962, is one of the world's premier centers for research and treatment of pediatric cancers and other catastrophic diseases. St. Jude's fundraising arm, ALSAC (American Lebanese Syrian Associated Charities) covers the cost of treatment not covered by insurance and all costs of treatment for those who have no insurance, including lodging, travel and food. St. Jude has also developed groundbreaking treatments that have dramatically increased survival rates for brain tumors, solid tumors, Hodgkin disease, non-Hodgkin lymphoma and many other catastrophic diseases. The hospital pioneered a treatment for acute lymphoblastic leukemia, the most common form of childhood leukemia, dramatically raising the cure rate from less than 20% in 1962 to over 80% today. Current research at the hospital is focused on work in bone-marrow transplantation, gene therapy, biochemistry of cancerous cells, radiation treatment, blood diseases, hereditary diseases and the psychological effects of catastrophic illnesses. St. Jude operates the International Outreach Program, a program that provides developing countries with the resources and technology to better treat catastrophic childhood diseases. The hospital also maintains Cure4Kids, a medical education and collaboration website for doctors, scientists and healthcare workers who treat children with such diseases. In recent years, St. Jude became the first pediatric cancer center to become a National Cancer Institute (NCI) Comprehensive Cancer Center. Current research efforts include the St. Jude Children's Research Hospital-Washington University Pediatric Cancer Genome Project, a project to sequence and compare the normal and cancer genomes of hundreds of children with cancer. By comparing the complete genomes from cancerous and normal cells for more than 800 patients, the project has successfully pinpointed the genetic factors behind some of the toughest pediatric cancers and is now using multiple approaches to analyze cancer genomes even further.

FINANCIAL DATA: *Note: Data for latest year may not have been available at press time.*

In U.S. $	2017	2016	2015	2014	2013	2012
Revenue	1,971,606,000	1,383,231,000	1,299,851,000	1,586,578,000	1,291,397,000	978,978,000
R&D Expense						
Operating Income						
Operating Margin %						
SGA Expense						
Net Income	693,962,000	203,636,000	196,346,000	589,177,000	355,646,000	78,125,000
Operating Cash Flow						
Capital Expenditure						
EBITDA						
Return on Assets %						
Return on Equity %						
Debt to Equity						

CONTACT INFORMATION:

Phone: 901-595-3300 Fax:
Toll-Free: 800-822-6344
Address: 262 Danny Thomas Place, Memphis, TN 38105 United States

STOCK TICKER/OTHER:

Stock Ticker: Nonprofit
Exchange:
Employees: 4,929
Fiscal Year Ends: 06/30
Parent Company:

SALARIES/BONUSES:

Top Exec. Salary: $ Bonus: $
Second Exec. Salary: $ Bonus: $

OTHER THOUGHTS:

Estimated Female Officers or Directors: 7
Hot Spot for Advancement for Women/Minorities: Y

STAAR Surgical Company

www.staar.com

NAIC Code: 339,100

TYPES OF BUSINESS:

Equipment-Ophthalmic Surgery
Intraocular Lenses

BRANDS/DIVISIONS/AFFILIATES:

STAAR Surgical AG
STAAR Japan Inc
Collamer
Visian
CentraFLOW

CONTACTS: *Note: Officers with more than one job title may be intentionally listed here more than once.*

Caren Mason, CEO
Deborah Andrews, CFO
Louis Silverman, Chairman of the Board
Keith Holliday, Chief Technology Officer
Samuel Gesten, Other Executive Officer
Hans-Martin Blickensdoerfer, Senior VP, Divisional

GROWTH PLANS/SPECIAL FEATURES:

STAAR Surgical Company develops, produces and markets medical devices used to improve or correct vision in patients with refractive conditions, cataracts and glaucoma. STAAR maintains operational and administrative facilities in the U.S., Switzerland and Japan, and sells its products in more than 75 countries. The company's main product line consists of one-piece and three-piece foldable silicone and Collamer intraocular lenses (IOLs) used after cataract extraction. The lens is folded and implanted into the eye behind the iris and in front of the natural lens using minimally invasive techniques. This procedure is performed with topical anesthesia on an outpatient basis, with visual recovery within one to 24 hours. The firm's Monrovia, California manufacturing facility produces the Visian implantable Collamer lens (ICL) product family, the Collamer IOL product family, preloaded silicone IOLs and injector systems. The Aliso Viejo, California manufacturing facility produces the raw material for Collamer lenses (both IOLs and ICLs) and utilizes its proprietary CentraFLOW technology, offering a central port for fluid flow and therefore eliminating the need for an iridotomy or iridectomy. In Switzerland, STAAR operates an administrative and distribution facility in Nidau via wholly-owned STAAR Surgical AG. This facility also comprises manufacturing capabilities for the company's ICL products and related devices. In Japan, STAAR operates administrative and distribution facilities in Japan via wholly-owned STAAR Japan, Inc. Final packaging of silicone preloaded IOL injectors and final inspection of its acrylic preloaded IOL injectors are performed at these facilities.

FINANCIAL DATA: *Note: Data for latest year may not have been available at press time.*

In U.S. $	2017	2016	2015	2014	2013	2012
Revenue	90,611,000	82,432,000	77,123,000	74,987,000	72,215,000	72,215,000
R&D Expense	19,116,000	20,294,000	14,761,000	12,363,000	6,708,000	6,708,000
Operating Income	-3,631,000	-12,655,000	-5,337,000	-8,027,000	700,000	700,000
Operating Margin %	-4.00%	-15.35%	-6.92%	-10.70%	.96%	.96%
SGA Expense	48,795,000	50,730,000	43,299,000	44,360,000	42,901,000	42,698,000
Net Income	-2,139,000	-12,129,000	-6,533,000	-8,392,000	398,000	398,000
Operating Cash Flow	2,853,000	1,049,000	-2,162,000	-7,951,000	3,355,000	3,355,000
Capital Expenditure	1,046,000	3,205,000	2,045,000	4,054,000	3,448,000	3,448,000
EBITDA	1,170,000	-9,437,000	-3,076,000	-6,031,000	3,435,000	3,435,000
Return on Assets %	-3.20%	-18.89%	-10.72%	-13.88%	.64%	.71%
Return on Equity %	-5.29%	-31.60%	-17.20%	-22.09%	1.02%	1.16%
Debt to Equity	0.01	0.03		0.01		

CONTACT INFORMATION:

Phone: 626 303-7902 Fax: 626 303-2962
Toll-Free: 800-352-7842
Address: 1911 Walker Ave., Monrovia, CA 91016 United States

STOCK TICKER/OTHER:

Stock Ticker: STAA
Exchange: NAS
Employees: 336
Fiscal Year Ends: 12/31
Parent Company:

SALARIES/BONUSES:

Top Exec. Salary: $562,800 Bonus: $308,763
Second Exec. Salary: $352,214 Bonus: $115,939

OTHER THOUGHTS:

Estimated Female Officers or Directors: 1
Hot Spot for Advancement for Women/Minorities:

Stericycle Inc

NAIC Code: 562,112

www.stericycle.com

TYPES OF BUSINESS:

Medical Waste Treatment

BRANDS/DIVISIONS/AFFILIATES:

Bio-Systems
Steri-Safe
Shred-it

CONTACTS:

Note: Officers with more than one job title may be intentionally listed here more than once.

Charles Alutto, CEO
Dan Ginnetti, Chief Accounting Officer
Richard Hoffman, Chief Accounting Officer
Robert Murley, Director
Robert Guice, Executive VP, Divisional
Joseph Arnold, Executive VP
Kurt Rogers, Executive VP
Brenda Frank, Executive VP
Ruth-Ellen Abdulmassih, Executive VP

GROWTH PLANS/SPECIAL FEATURES:

Stericycle, Inc. is engaged in the business of medical waste disposal. Through its national networks of 256 processing facilities, 325 transfer sites, 110 warehouse/parking facilities, 75 customer service or administration offices, 22 communication centers and two landfills, the firm serves the U.S. and 21 other countries. In order to dispose of medical waste, Stericycle utilizes various technologies, including autoclaving, an electro-thermal-deactivation system (ETD), chemical treatment and incineration. While Stericycle's customers are mainly hospitals, clinics, acute care facilities and dental offices, it also handles disposal of expired or surplus products from pharmacies and pharmaceutical manufacturers. The company generally provides its customers with its own waste containers, such as the plastic Bio-Systems containers, to avoid needle sticks and leakages. After treatment, the residual ash is passed on to a third-party landfill and the containers are returned to customers. Stericycle utilizes its own branded methodologies, which include Steri-Safe, a compliance program designed to familiarize clients with regulatory policies, mail-back programs, product recalls, returns and onsite waste disposal services. The company serves more than 1 million customers worldwide, including large-quantity generators such as hospitals, blood banks and pharmaceutical manufacturers; and small-quantity generators such as outpatient clinics, medical and dental offices, long-term and sub-acute care facilities and retail pharmacies. In addition, Stericycle owns Shred-it, a global leader in secure information destruction. Documents are cross-cut shredded and then baled to be sold as office paper for recycling.

The company offers its employees medical, dental, vision, life, AD&D, long-term care, auto and home insurance; flexible spending accounts; an employee assistance program; tuition reimbursement; short- and long-term disability; a prepaid legal program; a 401(k) plan; an employee stock purchase plan; and paid vacation, holidays and funeral leave.

FINANCIAL DATA:

Note: Data for latest year may not have been available at press time.

In U.S. $	2017	2016	2015	2014	2013	2012
Revenue	3,580,700,000	3,562,342,000	2,985,908,000	2,555,601,000	2,142,807,000	1,913,149,000
R&D Expense						
Operating Income	-7,600,000	433,775,000	487,612,000	556,336,000	535,619,000	468,836,000
Operating Margin %	- .21%	12.17%	16.33%	21.76%	24.99%	24.50%
SGA Expense	1,470,100,000	904,179,000	712,803,000	489,937,000	390,610,000	356,817,000
Net Income	42,400,000	206,359,000	267,046,000	326,456,000	311,372,000	267,996,000
Operating Cash Flow	508,600,000	547,249,000	390,328,000	448,500,000	403,467,000	387,448,000
Capital Expenditure	143,000,000	136,160,000	114,761,000	86,496,000	73,109,000	65,236,000
EBITDA	235,600,000	678,478,000	615,817,000	658,326,000	621,397,000	545,154,000
Return on Assets %	.33%	2.53%	4.47%	7.88%	8.38%	7.97%
Return on Equity %	.82%	6.43%	11.11%	17.91%	18.91%	19.56%
Debt to Equity	0.90	1.02	1.11	0.80	0.73	0.82

CONTACT INFORMATION:

Phone: 847 367-5910 Fax: 847 367-9493
Toll-Free: 800-643-0240
Address: 28161 N. Keith Dr., Lake Forest, IL 60045 United States

STOCK TICKER/OTHER:

Stock Ticker: SRCL
Exchange: NAS
Employees: 25,000
Fiscal Year Ends: 12/31
Parent Company:

SALARIES/BONUSES:

Top Exec. Salary: $1,000,000 Bonus: $
Second Exec. Salary: $550,000 Bonus: $

OTHER THOUGHTS:

Estimated Female Officers or Directors:
Hot Spot for Advancement for Women/Minorities:

STERIS plc

www.steris.com

NAIC Code: 339,100

TYPES OF BUSINESS:

Healthcare Products & Related Services
Life Sciences Products
Sterilization Services
Defense-Related Decontamination Systems

BRANDS/DIVISIONS/AFFILIATES:

CONTACTS: *Note: Officers with more than one job title may be intentionally listed here more than once.*

Walter M. Rosebrough Jr., CEO
John Wareham, Chairman of the Board
Michael J. Tokich, CFO
Michiel de Zwaan, VP-Human Resources
J. Zangerle, General Counsel
Kathleen Bardwell, Other Executive Officer
Walter Rosebrough, President
Sudhir Pahwa, Senior VP, Divisinal
Gulam Khan, Senior VP, Divisional
Daniel Carestio, Senior VP, Divisional
Adrian Coward, Senior VP, Divisional
Suzanne Forsythe, Vice President, Divisional

GROWTH PLANS/SPECIAL FEATURES:

STERIS plc is a provider of infection prevention and other procedural products and services. The company offers a mix of innovative capital equipment products such as sterilizers and surgical tables, and connectivity solutions such as operating room (OR) integration; consumable products such as detergents and skin care products, gastrointestinal endoscopy accessories and barrier product solutions; and other services such as equipment installation and maintenance, microbial reduction of medical devices, instrument and scope repair, laboratory testing services and off-site reprocessing. STERIS operates in four business segments: healthcare products, healthcare specialty services, life sciences and applied sterilization technologies. The healthcare products segment offers infection prevention and procedural solutions for healthcare providers worldwide. Healthcare specialty services provides a range of specialty services for healthcare providers, including hospital sterilization services and instrumentation/scope repairs. The life sciences segment offers capital equipment and consumable products, as well as equipment maintenance and specialty services for pharmaceutical manufacturers and research facilities. The applied sterilization technologies segment offers contract sterilization and laboratory services for medical device and pharmaceutical customers, among others.

STERIS offers its employees medical, dental, vision and prescription options; life, short- and long-term insurance; flexible spending accounts; 401(k); employee and travel assistance; business travel accident insurance; and tuition reimbursement.

FINANCIAL DATA: *Note: Data for latest year may not have been available at press time.*

In U.S. $	2017	2016	2015	2014	2013	2012
Revenue	2,612,756,000	2,238,764,000	1,850,263,000	1,622,252,000	1,501,902,000	
R&D Expense	59,397,000	56,664,000	54,139,000	48,641,000	41,305,000	
Operating Income	286,166,000	212,107,000	226,820,000	220,011,000	242,264,000	
Operating Margin %	10.95%	9.47%	12.25%	13.56%	16.13%	
SGA Expense	680,069,000	626,710,000	493,342,000	380,970,000	337,694,000	
Net Income	109,965,000	110,763,000	135,064,000	129,442,000	159,977,000	
Operating Cash Flow	424,086,000	254,675,000	246,040,000	209,631,000	227,815,000	
Capital Expenditure	172,901,000	126,407,000	85,255,000	86,367,000	87,412,000	
EBITDA	417,308,000	358,332,000	319,548,000	282,795,000	311,808,000	
Return on Assets %	2.14%	2.97%	6.77%	7.09%	10.10%	
Return on Equity %	3.77%	5.41%	12.80%	13.05%	18.11%	
Debt to Equity	0.52	0.51	0.58	0.47	0.52	

CONTACT INFORMATION:

Phone: 44-116-276-8636 Fax:
Toll-Free:
Address: Rutherford House, Stephensons Way, Chaddesden, Derby DE21 6LY United Kingdom

STOCK TICKER/OTHER:

Stock Ticker: STE
Employees: 12,000
Parent Company:
Exchange: NYS
Fiscal Year Ends: 03/31

SALARIES/BONUSES:

Top Exec. Salary: $859,616 Bonus: $
Second Exec. Salary: $472,308 Bonus: $

OTHER THOUGHTS:

Estimated Female Officers or Directors: 2
Hot Spot for Advancement for Women/Minorities: Y

Steward Health Care System LLC

www.steward.org

NAIC Code: 622,110

TYPES OF BUSINESS:

General Medical and Surgical Hospitals
Hospice & Home Health Care Services
Private College
Charitable Organizations

BRANDS/DIVISIONS/AFFILIATES:

Cerberus Capital Management LP
Carney Hospital
Nashoba Valley Medical Center
Sebastian River Medical Center
Northside Medical Center
Easton Hospital
Steward Health Care Network
Home Choice

CONTACTS: *Note: Officers with more than one job title may be intentionally listed here more than once.*

Ralph de la Torre, CEO
John Polanowicz, COO
John Doyle, CFO
Brian Carty, CMO
Patrick Lombardo, Exec. VP-Human Resources
Justine Carr, Chief Medical Officer
Julie Berry, CIO
Stuart Grief, Chief Admin. Officer
Joseph Maher, Jr., General Counsel
Michael G. Callum, Pres., Steward Medical Group
Mark Girard, Pres., Steward Health Care Network
Robert Guyon, Exec. VP
Karen Murray, Chief Compliance Officer
Ralph de la Toree, Chmn.

GROWTH PLANS/SPECIAL FEATURES:

Steward Health Care System, LLC is the largest private for-profit hospital operator in the U.S. The company operates 38 community hospitals in the U.S., as well as the country of Malta. Steward Health's network includes more than 25 urgent care centers, 42 preferred skilled nursing facilities and 40,000 health care professionals serving approximately 150 communities. Hospitals in the system include, but are not limited to, Carney Hospital, Nashoba Valley Medical Center, Sebastian River Medical Center, Northside Regional Medical Center and Easton Hospital. In addition to these facilities, the firm provides care to more than 2 million patients annually through its Steward Health Care Network, which is comprised of both primary care physicians and a range of specialists committed to keeping patients healthy and helping them avoid costly hospital visits. The network operates across 10 states. Other services include behavioral health services, a center for advanced cardiac surgery, centers for cancer care, centers for weight control, home care and hospice services, MAKOplasty services (knee and hip replacement) and maternity services. Home Choice is Steward Health's managed risk platform, covering more than 530,000 members in Arizona and Utah. The platform comprises health insurance plans, a management services organization and accountable care networks enabled by an integrated care model. Steward Health is owned by Cerberus Capital Management, LP. In September 2017, the firm acquired and merged with IASIS Healthcare, LLC, making Steward the largest private for-profit hospital operator in the U.S.

FINANCIAL DATA: *Note: Data for latest year may not have been available at press time.*

In U.S. $	2017	2016	2015	2014	2013	2012
Revenue	1,785,000,000	1,700,000,000	1,650,000,000	1,610,000,000	1,600,000,000	1,550,000,000
R&D Expense						
Operating Income						
Operating Margin %						
SGA Expense						
Net Income						
Operating Cash Flow						
Capital Expenditure						
EBITDA						
Return on Assets %						
Return on Equity %						
Debt to Equity						

CONTACT INFORMATION:

Phone: 469-341-8800 Fax:
Toll-Free:
Address: 500 Boylston St., Boston, MA 02116 United States

STOCK TICKER/OTHER:

Stock Ticker: Private Exchange:
Employees: 40,000 Fiscal Year Ends:
Parent Company: Cerberus Capital Management LP

SALARIES/BONUSES:

Top Exec. Salary: $ Bonus: $
Second Exec. Salary: $ Bonus: $

OTHER THOUGHTS:

Estimated Female Officers or Directors: 4
Hot Spot for Advancement for Women/Minorities: Y

Stryker Corporation

www.stryker.com

NAIC Code: 339,100

TYPES OF BUSINESS:

Equipment-Orthopedic Implants
Powered Surgical Instruments
Endoscopic Systems
Patient Care & Handling Equipment
Imaging Software
Small Bone Innovations

BRANDS/DIVISIONS/AFFILIATES:

Entellus Medical Inc

CONTACTS:

Note: Officers with more than one job title may be intentionally listed here more than once.

Kevin Lobo, CEO
Glenn Boehnlein, CFO
William Berry, Chief Accounting Officer
Bijoy Sagar, Chief Information Officer
Michael Hutchinson, General Counsel
M. Fink, Other Executive Officer
Graham McLean, President, Divisional
Timothy Scannell, President, Divisional
David Floyd, President, Divisional
Lonny Carpenter, President, Divisional
Katherine Owen, Vice President, Divisional
Yin Becker, Vice President, Divisional

GROWTH PLANS/SPECIAL FEATURES:

Stryker Corporation develops, manufactures and markets innovative products and services that help improve patient and hospital outcomes. The firm's products are sold in over 85 countries through company-owned subsidiaries and branches, as well as by third-party dealers and distributors. Stryker's products include implants used in joint replacement and trauma surgeries, surgical equipment, surgical navigation systems, endoscopic systems, communications systems, patient handling equipment, emergency medical equipment, intensive care disposable products, neurosurgical devices, spinal devices, neurovascular devices and other products used in a variety of medical specialties. These products are segregated within the three business segments of: MedSurg, deriving 45% of 2017 net sales; orthopedics, 38%; and neurotechnology and spine, 17%. Stryker owns approximately 2,674 U.S. patents and approximately 3,886 international patents. In February 2018, Stryker acquired Entellus Medical, Inc., a global medical technology company whose products are designed for the minimally-invasive treatment of various ear, nose and throat disease states. That June, the firm agreed to acquire SafeAir AG, a Swiss medical device company focused on the design, development and manufacture of innovative surgical smoke evacuation solutions.

Stryker offers employees health insurance, retirement programs, tuition reimbursement and wellness programs.

FINANCIAL DATA:

Note: Data for latest year may not have been available at press time.

In U.S. $	2017	2016	2015	2014	2013	2012
Revenue	12,444,000,000	11,325,000,000	9,946,000,000	9,675,000,000	9,021,000,000	8,657,000,000
R&D Expense	787,000,000	715,000,000	625,000,000	614,000,000	536,000,000	471,000,000
Operating Income	2,463,000,000	2,324,000,000	2,157,000,000	2,007,000,000	1,304,000,000	1,816,000,000
Operating Margin %	19.79%	20.52%	21.68%	20.74%	14.45%	20.97%
SGA Expense	4,552,000,000	4,137,000,000	3,610,000,000	3,575,000,000	4,066,000,000	3,466,000,000
Net Income	1,020,000,000	1,647,000,000	1,439,000,000	515,000,000	1,006,000,000	1,298,000,000
Operating Cash Flow	1,559,000,000	1,812,000,000	899,000,000	1,782,000,000	1,886,000,000	1,657,000,000
Capital Expenditure	598,000,000	490,000,000	270,000,000	233,000,000	195,000,000	210,000,000
EBITDA	3,105,000,000	2,870,000,000	2,554,000,000	2,385,000,000	1,611,000,000	2,093,000,000
Return on Assets %	4.78%	8.97%	8.47%	3.07%	6.95%	10.13%
Return on Equity %	10.45%	18.23%	16.82%	5.83%	11.40%	15.94%
Debt to Equity	0.66	0.70	0.38	0.37	0.30	0.20

CONTACT INFORMATION:

Phone: 269 385-2600 Fax: 269 385-1062
Toll-Free:
Address: 2825 Airview Blvd., Kalamazoo, MI 49002 United States

STOCK TICKER/OTHER:

Stock Ticker: SYK
Employees: 33,000
Parent Company:
Exchange: NYS
Fiscal Year Ends: 12/31

SALARIES/BONUSES:

Top Exec. Salary: $1,163,333 Bonus: $
Second Exec. Salary: $631,667 Bonus: $

OTHER THOUGHTS:

Estimated Female Officers or Directors: 7
Hot Spot for Advancement for Women/Minorities: Y

Sun Pharmaceutical Industries Ltd

www.sunpharma.com

NAIC Code: 325,412

TYPES OF BUSINESS:

Pharmaceuticals, Manufacturing
Generic Drug Manufacturer

BRANDS/DIVISIONS/AFFILIATES:

Ranbaxy Inc
OOO Sun Pharmaceutical Industries Ltd
Rexcel Egypt LLC
SPIL De Mexico SA de CV
Sun Global Canada Pty Ltd
Taro Pharmaceuticals Industries Ltd
Vidyut Investments Limited

CONTACTS: *Note: Officers with more than one job title may be intentionally listed here more than once.*

Dilip Shanghvi, Managing Dir.
Sunil R. Ajmera, Company Sec.
Mira Desai, Contact-Investor Rel.
Dilip S. Shanghvi, Managing Dir.
Israel Makov, Chmn.

GROWTH PLANS/SPECIAL FEATURES:

Sun Pharmaceutical Industries Ltd. (SPIL) is an India-based specialty pharmaceuticals company manufacturing pharmaceuticals and active pharmaceutical ingredients (APIs). It manufactures and markets a number of pharmaceutical formulations as generics, branded generics, specialty and over-the-counter products, anti-retrovirals, active pharmaceutical ingredients (APIs) and intermediates in India, the U.S. and elsewhere. Its products are manufactured in the full range of dosage forms, including tablets, capsules, injectables, ointments, creams and liquids. The company also manufactures specialty APIs such as controlled substances, steroids, peptides and anti-cancers. SPIL maintains over 45 manufacturing sites, including 10 locations in North America. The firm has placed special emphasis on growing its business in the U.S. generics market through targeted product development and strategic acquisitions. SPIL holds over 2,600 registered and marketed products in more than 40 markets around the world. In India, the company is also involved in developing medications for various specialized therapy areas, with particular focus on psychiatry, neurology, oncology, cardiology, diabetology, gastroenterology and orthopedics. The firm's research and design facilities focus on generic process and formulation research as well as developing complex delivery systems. SPIL reports its earnings in three segments: India branded drugs, USA generics and APIs. Subsidiaries include Ranbaxy, Inc.; OOO Sun Pharmaceutical Industries Ltd.; Rexcel Egypt, LLC; SPIL De Mexico SA de CV; Sun Global Canada Pty. Ltd.; Taro Pharmaceuticals Industries Ltd.; and Vidyut Investments Limited.

FINANCIAL DATA: *Note: Data for latest year may not have been available at press time.*

In U.S. $	2017	2016	2015	2014	2013	2012
Revenue						
R&D Expense						
Operating Income						
Operating Margin %						
SGA Expense						
Net Income						
Operating Cash Flow						
Capital Expenditure						
EBITDA						
Return on Assets %						
Return on Equity %						
Debt to Equity						

CONTACT INFORMATION:

Phone: 91-22-43244324 Fax: 91-22-43244343
Toll-Free:
Address: Sun House, CTS No. 201 B/1 Western Express Highway, Mumbai, Mumbai 400 063 India

STOCK TICKER/OTHER:

Stock Ticker: SMPQY
Employees: 30,000
Parent Company:
Exchange: PINX
Fiscal Year Ends: 03/31

SALARIES/BONUSES:

Top Exec. Salary: $ Bonus: $
Second Exec. Salary: $ Bonus: $

OTHER THOUGHTS:

Estimated Female Officers or Directors: 1
Hot Spot for Advancement for Women/Minorities:

Sunrise Medical GmbH

www.sunrisemedical.com

NAIC Code: 339,100

TYPES OF BUSINESS:

Medical Supplies-Wheelchairs
Home Respiratory Devices
Ambulatory & Bath Safety Aids
Therapeutic Mattresses & Support Surfaces
Patient-Room Beds & Furnishings
Speech Communication Devices

BRANDS/DIVISIONS/AFFILIATES:

Nordic Capital
Breezy
Quickie
Sopur
RGK
Jay
Whitmyer
Sunrise Medical Education

CONTACTS: *Note: Officers with more than one job title may be intentionally listed here more than once.*

Johan Ek, Acting CEO
Randi Binstock, VP-Bus. Dev.

GROWTH PLANS/SPECIAL FEATURES:

Sunrise Medical GmbH designs, manufactures and markets wheelchairs and other medical products that address the recovery, rehabilitation and respiratory needs of patients in institutional and home care settings. The company's family of products is comprised of many brands in the home care industry. Its products include custom, manual and power wheelchairs and related seating systems; ambulatory, bathing and lifting products; healthcare beds; and furniture and therapeutic mattresses. Sunrise's broad range of wheelchairs includes the Breezy line, a multipurpose line; Quickie line, designed for all purposes, including the playing of sports such as tennis and basketball; the Sopur line of manual wheelchairs with adaptive capabilities including clampable handbikes, sport handbikes and toile/shower wheelchairs; the Zippie Wheelchair line, which is designed for children; and the RGK line, which are custom-made wheelchairs to meet specific desires and needs. Sunrise also manufactures the Sterling line of electromobile eScooters, and the Gemino line of lightweight rollators. The firm's Jay line consists of cushions designed to increase comfort including the Fusion cushion which combines J2's skin protection capabilities with J3's stability; flow fluid and contoured base cushions; cushions with fluid or air inserts for skin protection; flow fluid and memory foam cushions; cushions for kids; contoured and water-resistant cushions; and gel cushions for mild to moderate cushion needs. In addition, the Whitmyer brand offers wheelchair headrests. The Sunrise Medical Education department conducts seminars around the country that provide technical and clinical information for respiratory therapists, nurses, physicians and physical therapists. In addition, the firm customizes its products to meet the needs of the consumer. The company has sales organization and distributors in over 130 countries, and is privately-owned by Nordic Capital.

FINANCIAL DATA: *Note: Data for latest year may not have been available at press time.*

In U.S. $	2017	2016	2015	2014	2013	2012
Revenue	570,465,000	530,000,000	501,461,100	477,582,000		
R&D Expense						
Operating Income						
Operating Margin %						
SGA Expense						
Net Income						
Operating Cash Flow						
Capital Expenditure						
EBITDA						
Return on Assets %						
Return on Equity %						
Debt to Equity						

CONTACT INFORMATION:

Phone: 49072539800 Fax: 4,907,253,980,222
Toll-Free: 800-333-4000
Address: Kahlbachring 2-4, Malsch, 69254 Germany

STOCK TICKER/OTHER:

Stock Ticker: Private
Employees: 2,180
Parent Company: Nordic Capital
Exchange:
Fiscal Year Ends: 06/30

SALARIES/BONUSES:

Top Exec. Salary: $ Bonus: $
Second Exec. Salary: $ Bonus: $

OTHER THOUGHTS:

Estimated Female Officers or Directors: 1
Hot Spot for Advancement for Women/Minorities:

Sunrise Senior Living LLC

www.sunriseseniorliving.com

NAIC Code: 623,310

TYPES OF BUSINESS:

Assisted Living Facilities
Assisted Living Centers
Independent Living Centers
Nursing Homes

BRANDS/DIVISIONS/AFFILIATES:

Welltower Inc
CareConnect

CONTACTS:

Note: Officers with more than one job title may be intentionally listed here more than once.

Chris Winkle, CEO
Edward Burnett, CFO
Jeff Fischer, Sr. VP-Oper.
Farinaz Tehrani, General Counsel
Paul J. Klaassen, Chmn.

GROWTH PLANS/SPECIAL FEATURES:

Sunrise Senior Living, LLC is an international provider of senior living services. The firm operates more than 230 communities located throughout the U.S., Canada and the U.K., with a total unit capacity of over 30,000. Sunrise offers services tailored to the unique needs of each of its residents, typically in apartment-like assisted or independent living environments. Upon move-in, the company assists the resident in developing an individualized service plan, including selection of resident accommodations and the appropriate level of care. Services provided range from basic care, consisting of assistance with activities of daily living, to reminiscence care, which consists of programs and services to help cognitively impaired residents such as those with Alzheimer's or dementia. Sunrise's CareConnect electronic health record system helps to support the firm's focus on providing quality resident care and services. The firm targets sites for development located in major metropolitan areas and their surrounding suburban communities, considering factors such as population, age demographics and estimated level of market demand. Sunrise is a subsidiary of Welltower, Inc., a real estate investment trust that primarily invests in assisted living facilities and other forms of housing and medical facilities for senior citizens.

The firm offers employees medical, prescription drug, dental and vision plans; health care and dependent care flexible spending accounts; wellness programs; tuition assistance; and short- and long-term disability coverage.

FINANCIAL DATA:

Note: Data for latest year may not have been available at press time.

In U.S. $	2017	2016	2015	2014	2013	2012
Revenue	1,650,000,000	1,625,000,000	1,600,000,000	1,456,200,000	1,342,000,000	1,315,882,667
R&D Expense						
Operating Income						
Operating Margin %						
SGA Expense						
Net Income						
Operating Cash Flow						
Capital Expenditure						
EBITDA						
Return on Assets %						
Return on Equity %						
Debt to Equity						

CONTACT INFORMATION:

Phone: 703 273-7500 Fax: 703 744-1628
Toll-Free:
Address: 7902 Westpark Dr., McLean, VA 22102 United States

STOCK TICKER/OTHER:

Stock Ticker: Subsidiary
Exchange:
Employees: 10,000
Fiscal Year Ends: 12/31
Parent Company: Welltower Inc

SALARIES/BONUSES:

Top Exec. Salary: $ Bonus: $
Second Exec. Salary: $ Bonus: $

OTHER THOUGHTS:

Estimated Female Officers or Directors: 1
Hot Spot for Advancement for Women/Minorities: Y

Supreme Products Co Ltd

www.supremeproducts.co.th

NAIC Code: 339,100

TYPES OF BUSINESS:

Medical Equipment Distribution
Medical Equipment Manufacturing

BRANDS/DIVISIONS/AFFILIATES:

CONTACTS:

Note: Officers with more than one job title may be intentionally listed here more than once.

Kamthorn Kanchanawatee, Managing Dir.
Chan Jangbenjarong, Pres.

GROWTH PLANS/SPECIAL FEATURES:

Supreme Products Co., Ltd. manufactures, distributes and imports medical equipment in Thailand. The company offers a variety of product suites or centers, many of which have overlapping products. Aesthetic products include varicose vein laser removal systems and light-based acne treatments. Ambulance products include oxygen tanks, defibrillators, sphygmomanometers (blood pressure cuffs) and stethoscopes. Basic medical equipment includes otoscopes, stethoscopes, transilluminators, vital signs monitors, lighting and baumanometers. Birthing room products include pulse oximeters (blood-oxygen meters). Eye care and LASIK (laser-assisted in situ keratomileusis) products include general eye exam machines as well as eye surgery equipment such as laser scalpels. Filmless radiography products include digital X-ray, bone densitometry and mammography machines. Heart products include cardio-pulmonary exercise testing equipment, ultrasound equipment and pulmonary function testing. Hi-tech imaging products include computed tomography (CT), magnetic resonance imaging (MRI) and positron emission tomography (PET) scanners. ICU/CCU (intensive care unit/critical care unit) products include ventilators, hyper- and hypothermia systems, portable patient monitors and data receiving stations. Medical check-up products include weighing scales and ergometers, which measure the amount of work done during exercise. Neonatal ICU and infant care products include incubators. Oncology products include radiotherapy and light induced fluorescence endoscopy (for early-stage cancer detection) machines. Operating room (OR) renovation ambulatory surgical products include anesthetic agents and surgical tables. Urology products include extracorporeal shock wave lithotripsy systems, used to treat kidney stones. Last, women's health center products include ultrasound and mammography machines. In addition, Supreme is engaged in manufacturing robotic drug dispensing systems. Some of Supreme's products are manufactured by third-parties.

FINANCIAL DATA:

Note: Data for latest year may not have been available at press time.

In U.S. $	2017	2016	2015	2014	2013	2012
Revenue						
R&D Expense						
Operating Income						
Operating Margin %						
SGA Expense						
Net Income						
Operating Cash Flow						
Capital Expenditure						
EBITDA						
Return on Assets %						
Return on Equity %						
Debt to Equity						

CONTACT INFORMATION:

Phone: 66-2434-0040 Fax: 66-2433-3971
Toll-Free:
Address: 449 & 451 Somdejphapinklao Rd., Bangyeekhan, Bangkok, 10700 Thailand

STOCK TICKER/OTHER:

Stock Ticker: Private
Exchange:
Employees: 500
Fiscal Year Ends: 06/30
Parent Company:

SALARIES/BONUSES:

Top Exec. Salary: $ Bonus: $
Second Exec. Salary: $ Bonus: $

OTHER THOUGHTS:

Estimated Female Officers or Directors: 2
Hot Spot for Advancement for Women/Minorities:

Surgery Partners Inc

NAIC Code: 621,493

www.surgerypartners.com

TYPES OF BUSINESS:

Freestanding Ambulatory Surgical and Emergency Centers
Eye-Care Services
Laser Vision Correction
Corrective Lenses Labs
Eye-Care Products Distribution
Purchasing and Supply Chain Services
Marketing Services

BRANDS/DIVISIONS/AFFILIATES:

Bain Capital LP
Tampa Pain Relief Center Inc

CONTACTS: *Note: Officers with more than one job title may be intentionally listed here more than once.*

Wayne Deveydt, CEO
R. David Kretschmer, CFO
Dennis Dean, Chief Accounting Officer
Bryan Fisher, COO, Divisional
T. Devin O'Reilly, Director
Thomas Cowhey, Executive VP
Angela Justice, Other Executive Officer
Anthony Taparo, President, Divisional
Brandan Lingle, President, Divisional
George Goodwin, President, Divisional
Ronald Zelhof, Senior VP, Divisional
Jennifer Baldock, Senior VP

GROWTH PLANS/SPECIAL FEATURES:

Surgery Partners, Inc. is a health care services company. The firm owns or operates, primarily in partnership with physicians, a portfolio of more than 180 facilities, including ambulatory surgical centers (ASCs), surgical hospitals, a diagnostic laboratory, multi-specialty physician practices and urgent care facilities across 32 U.S. states. Surgery Partners operates three primary segments: surgical facility services, ancillary services and optical services. The surgical facility services segment consists of the company's ASCs and surgical hospitals, and includes its anesthesia services. The surgical facilities provide non-emergency surgical procedures across many specialties, including gastroenterology, general surgery, ophthalmology, orthopedics and pain management, among many others. The ancillary services segment consists of the firm's diagnostic laboratory ad multi-specialty physician practices. These physician practices included Surgery Partners' owned and operated practices pursuant to long-term management service agreements. The optical services segment consists of an optical laboratory and an optical products group purchasing organization. The optical lab manufactures eyewear, and the optical products purchasing organization negotiates volume-buying discounts with optical product manufacturers. In addition, Surgery Partners' multi-specialty physician practice employs two models in connection with its network of physician practices: in Florida, the firm owns and operates Tampa Pain Relief Center, Inc., which has businesses throughout the state; and in states other than Florida, the firm operates physician practices pursuant to long-term management service agreements with separate professional corporations that are wholly-owned by physicians. The company's eight urgent care facilities treat injuries or illnesses requiring immediate care, but not serious enough to require an emergency room visit. In August 2017, Bain Capital LP acquired Surgery Partners from HIG Capital, LLC.

FINANCIAL DATA: *Note: Data for latest year may not have been available at press time.*

In U.S. $	2017	2016	2015	2014	2013	2012
Revenue		1,145,438,000	959,891,000	403,289,000	284,599,000	260,215,000
R&D Expense						
Operating Income		200,233,000	176,450,000	93,089,000	70,868,000	61,325,000
Operating Margin %		17.48%	18.38%	23.08%	24.90%	23.56%
SGA Expense		60,246,000	55,992,000	31,452,000	26,339,000	25,263,000
Net Income		9,453,000	1,429,000	-65,897,000	-9,062,000	1,916,000
Operating Cash Flow		125,239,000	84,481,000	21,949,000	49,078,000	46,377,000
Capital Expenditure		39,109,000	33,439,000	7,736,000	4,150,000	4,694,000
EBITDA		239,784,000	210,995,000	108,150,000	82,531,000	72,533,000
Return on Assets %		.42%	.07%	-5.64%	-1.90%	
Return on Equity %		334.67%				
Debt to Equity		146.16				

CONTACT INFORMATION:

Phone: 615-234-5900 Fax: 615-234-5998
Toll-Free:
Address: 310 Seven Springs Way, Ste. 500, Brentwood, TN 37027 United States

STOCK TICKER/OTHER:

Stock Ticker: SGRY
Employees: 6,000
Parent Company: Bain Capital LP
Exchange: NAS
Fiscal Year Ends: 12/31

SALARIES/BONUSES:

Top Exec. Salary: $422,955 Bonus: $225,000
Second Exec. Salary: $316,946 Bonus: $247,500

OTHER THOUGHTS:

Estimated Female Officers or Directors: 2
Hot Spot for Advancement for Women/Minorities:

Surgical Care Affiliates Inc

www.scasurgery.com

NAIC Code: 622,110

TYPES OF BUSINESS:

Surgery Centers

BRANDS/DIVISIONS/AFFILIATES:

UnitedHealth Group Inc

CONTACTS:

Note: Officers with more than one job title may be intentionally listed here more than once.

Michael Lucey, CEO
Bill Linder, VP-Operations
Tom De Weerdt, CFO
Richard Sharff, Executive VP
Joseph Clark, Executive VP

GROWTH PLANS/SPECIAL FEATURES:

Surgical Care Affiliates, Inc. (SCA) provides inpatient and outpatient surgery throughout the U.S. The company owns than 210 ambulatory surgery centers, surgical hospitals and hospital surgery departments. SCA builds strategic relationships with medical partners in order to acquire, develop and optimize facilities in alignment with customer needs. SCA has partnerships with approximately 8,500 physicians who perform 1 million procedures in SCA facilities each year. SCA also offers management services and solutions such as clinical systems, operating systems and financial systems. Clinical systems include clinical toolkits and checklists, clinical training and detailed clinical variance analysis. Operating systems offer schedule efficiency, supply chain management and benchmarking. Financial systems offer precise case costing and related analytics. Together, the facilities and management solutions offer patients easy scheduling, convenient access, short wait times and billing transparency. On average, patients pay approximately 45% less than they would if they had the identical procedure performed at a hospital. These savings are reflected in patients' co-pays and co-insurance. Physicians are provided advanced clinical systems, health system partnership capabilities, market development, analytics and more. Health plans can improve quality, access and cost by organizing their member surgeons into a new market, and optimize site of service, implant selection and utilization. And health systems can capture additional inpatient and outpatient market share and develop low-cost venue surgical care. During 2017, SCA was acquired by UnitedHealth Group, Inc. for $2.3 billion. UnitedHealth subsequently combined Optum's primary and urgent care delivery services business with and into SCA. SCA ceased from being publicly traded.

FINANCIAL DATA:

Note: Data for latest year may not have been available at press time.

In U.S. $	2017	2016	2015	2014	2013	2012
Revenue	2,000,000,000	1,281,405,056	1,051,489,984	864,736,000	802,035,008	750,140,992
R&D Expense						
Operating Income						
Operating Margin %						
SGA Expense						
Net Income		35,447,000	115,321,000	31,980,000	-51,344,000	-20,010,000
Operating Cash Flow						
Capital Expenditure						
EBITDA						
Return on Assets %						
Return on Equity %						
Debt to Equity						

CONTACT INFORMATION:

Phone: 847 236-0921 Fax:
Toll-Free:
Address: 520 Lake Cook Rd., Ste. 400, Deerfield, IL 60015 United States

STOCK TICKER/OTHER:

Stock Ticker: Subsidiary Exchange:
Employees: 7,500 Fiscal Year Ends: 12/31
Parent Company: UnitedHealth Group Inc

SALARIES/BONUSES:

Top Exec. Salary: $ Bonus: $
Second Exec. Salary: $ Bonus: $

OTHER THOUGHTS:

Estimated Female Officers or Directors:
Hot Spot for Advancement for Women/Minorities:

Sutter Health Inc

www.sutterhealth.org

NAIC Code: 622,110

TYPES OF BUSINESS:

General Medical and Surgical Hospitals
Neonatal Care
Pregnancy & Birth
Training Programs
Medical Research Facilities
Home Health Services
Hospice Networks
Long-Term Care

BRANDS/DIVISIONS/AFFILIATES:

Memorial
Sutter
Kahi Mohala
Alta Bates
Eden
Menlo Park Surgical
California Pacific
Sutter Health Plus

CONTACTS: *Note: Officers with more than one job title may be intentionally listed here more than once.*

Sarah Krevans, CEO

GROWTH PLANS/SPECIAL FEATURES:

Sutter Health, Inc. is one of the nation's largest nonprofit healthcare systems. Through its affiliates, the firm serves more than 100 Northern California communities via 5,500 physicians, which are members of the Sutter medical network. Sutter Health operates approximately 24 hospitals, 36 ambulatory surgery centers, six cardiac centers, nine cancer centers, five acute rehabilitation centers, seven behavioral health centers, five trauma centers, nine neonatal intensive care units (ICUs) and 33 urgent care centers. The company's hospitals are branded under the Memorial, Sutter, Kahi Mohala, Alta Bates, Eden, Menlo Park Surgical, California Pacific and Novato Community names. Many of the hospitals operate charitable foundations. Sutter Health is a regional leader in labor and delivery, neonatology and pediatrics services, as well as orthopedics, bariatric, cosmetic, diabetes, heart and vascular, mental health, sleep disorders, transplant services and cancer care services. The company was one of the first health networks in its area to implement eICU (electronic ICU) centers, which allow enhanced comprehensive and consistent monitoring of ICU patients by feeding monitoring data to a central location. Sutter Health Plus is an HMO that offers affordably-priced health plans to individuals and employer groups.

FINANCIAL DATA: *Note: Data for latest year may not have been available at press time.*

In U.S. $	2017	2016	2015	2014	2013	2012
Revenue	12,444,000,000	11,873,000,000	10,998,000,000	10,161,000,000	9,600,000,000	9,560,000,000
R&D Expense						
Operating Income						
Operating Margin %						
SGA Expense						
Net Income	958,000,000	622,000,000	145,000,000	458,000,000	358,000,000	549,000,000
Operating Cash Flow						
Capital Expenditure						
EBITDA						
Return on Assets %						
Return on Equity %						
Debt to Equity						

CONTACT INFORMATION:

Phone: 916-733-8800 Fax:
Toll-Free:
Address: 2200 River Plaza Dr., Sacramento, CA 95833 United States

STOCK TICKER/OTHER:

Stock Ticker: Nonprofit
Exchange:
Employees: 67,000
Fiscal Year Ends: 12/31
Parent Company:

SALARIES/BONUSES:

Top Exec. Salary: $ Bonus: $
Second Exec. Salary: $ Bonus: $

OTHER THOUGHTS:

Estimated Female Officers or Directors: 3
Hot Spot for Advancement for Women/Minorities: Y

Suven Life Sciences Limited

www.suven.com

NAIC Code: 325,412

TYPES OF BUSINESS:

Drug Discovery & Development
Manufacturing & Packing Support
Contract Research
Regulatory Support

BRANDS/DIVISIONS/AFFILIATES:

Formulation Development Center

CONTACTS: *Note: Officers with more than one job title may be intentionally listed here more than once.*

Venkat Jasti, CEO
K. Hanumantha Rao, Sec.
Kalyani Jasti, Pres., U.S. Oper.

GROWTH PLANS/SPECIAL FEATURES:

Suven Life Sciences Limited is an India-based developer and manufacturer of bio-pharmaceutical drugs. The company operates contract research and development support in three business segments: drug discovery research (DDR), contract research and manufacturing services (CRAMS) and Formulation Development Center (FDC). DDR collaborates in medicinal, process and analytical chemistry; in-vitro screening; and phase I bioanalysis to optimize a product candidate for clinical trials. CRAMS offers support services for companies developing new chemical entities (NCE), especially in the areas of clinical trials and commercial manufacturing. FDC provides drug discovery and development support services and contract pharmaceutical services. It comprises formulation development laboratories, process development laboratories, packaging and testing laboratories, as well as stability chambers and warehousing. Suven's current research and development discovery pipeline includes: products to treat neurodegenerative disease, including cognition, Alzheimer's and Schizophrenia; products to treat sleep disorders; and products to treat pain, major depressive disorder and psychiatric disorders. Based in India, Suven has an international office in New Jersey, USA.

FINANCIAL DATA: *Note: Data for latest year may not have been available at press time.*

In U.S. $	2017	2016	2015	2014	2013	2012
Revenue	87,139,900	77,889,165	78,186,338	79,300,000	83,800,000	42,400,000
R&D Expense						
Operating Income						
Operating Margin %						
SGA Expense						
Net Income	19,024,100	10,018,370	16,324,759	16,600,000	23,700,000	5,100,000
Operating Cash Flow						
Capital Expenditure						
EBITDA						
Return on Assets %						
Return on Equity %						
Debt to Equity						

CONTACT INFORMATION:

Phone: 91-40-2354-1142 Fax: 91-40-2354-1152
Toll-Free:
Address: 6/Fl. Serene Chambers, Rd. No. 5, Ave. 7, Banjara Hills, Hyderabad, 500 034 India

STOCK TICKER/OTHER:

Stock Ticker: SUVEN
Employees: 1,072
Parent Company:
Exchange: Bombay
Fiscal Year Ends: 03/31

SALARIES/BONUSES:

Top Exec. Salary: $ Bonus: $
Second Exec. Salary: $ Bonus: $

OTHER THOUGHTS:

Estimated Female Officers or Directors: 2
Hot Spot for Advancement for Women/Minorities:

Suzuken Co Ltd

www.suzuken.co.jp

NAIC Code: 424,210

TYPES OF BUSINESS:

Drugs and Druggists' Sundries Merchant Wholesalers
Pharmaceutical Manufacture
Pharmaceutical Distribution
Healthcare Marketing
Medical Equipment
Nursing Care
Medical Food

BRANDS/DIVISIONS/AFFILIATES:

Sanwa Kagaku Kenkyusho Co Ltd
Pfercos Co Ltd
S-mile Inc
Sanki Wellbe Co Ltd
S-Care Mate Co Ltd
JIT Co Ltd
Life Medicom Co Ltd
Galenus Co Ltd

CONTACTS: *Note: Officers with more than one job title may be intentionally listed here more than once.*

Hiromi Miyata, Pres.
Yoshiki Bessho, Chmn.

GROWTH PLANS/SPECIAL FEATURES:

Suzuken Co., Ltd. is engaged in the pharmaceutical business in Japan. The company's businesses include pharmaceutical manufacturing, medical equipment manufacturing, pharmaceutical distribution, dispensing, distribution and logistics, as well as nursing care and other healthcare-related services. Suzuken manufactures proprietary and contract pharmaceuticals at its factories located in Fukushima and Kumamoto. The firm offers comprehensive support in the orphan disease, investigational drug and pharmaceutical manufacturer distribution domains. It also conducts marketing support for pharmaceutical manufacturers. Subsidiary Sanwa Kagaku Kenkyusho Co., Ltd. researches, develops, manufactures and sells pharmaceuticals, diagnostic agents, medical food products, nursing care food products and health care products. The firm also conducts contract manufacturing of pharmaceuticals. Medical equipment manufactured and sold by Suzuken include electrocardiographs and stethoscopes. The company also develops related medical materials and health promotion equipment for general consumers. Suzuken is also engaged in, and supports, home medical care, in which pharmacists visit the homes of patients or the elderly and give guidance on drug management and drug administration. This involves pharmacies being equipped with a sterile dispensary capable of preparing injections or infusions necessary for home medical care, and which can be used by other pharmacies. Subsidiaries Pfercos Co., Ltd. and S-mile, Inc. are responsible for the company's insurance pharmacy business, with more than 300 pharmacy clients across 20 prefectures. Subsidiary Sanki Wellbe Co., Ltd. and S-Care Mate Co., Ltd. provide tailored nursing care to elderly in the Chugoku, Kanto and Chubu regions. This nursing care division also provides drug management guidance and support to nursing care facilities. Other healthcare-related businesses include: JIT Co., Ltd., which develops and operates product control in medical institutions; Life Medicom Co., Ltd. develops publication and public relation activities in regards to medical care and health; and Galenus Co., Ltd. sells medical food, nursing care food and functional food products.

FINANCIAL DATA: *Note: Data for latest year may not have been available at press time.*

In U.S. $	2017	2016	2015	2014	2013	2012
Revenue	19,124,940,000	20,034,200,000	17,709,840,000	17,875,710,000	17,034,800,000	
R&D Expense						
Operating Income	168,243,100	253,947,100	119,052,300	160,411,800	101,393,600	
Operating Margin %						
SGA Expense						
Net Income	191,584,200	260,384,800	170,113,300	192,834,000	129,023,600	
Operating Cash Flow	242,879,000	183,932,800	424,465,000	-369,124,200	485,578,100	
Capital Expenditure	115,590,700	147,599,300	148,057,900	103,398,700	108,217,900	
EBITDA	396,286,600	512,497,800	370,994,400	429,140,400	320,194,200	
Return on Assets %						
Return on Equity %						
Debt to Equity						

CONTACT INFORMATION:

Phone: 81 529612331 Fax:
Toll-Free:
Address: 8 Higashi Kataha-machi, Nagoya, 461-8701 Japan

STOCK TICKER/OTHER:

Stock Ticker: SZUKF Exchange: GREY
Employees: 19,459 Fiscal Year Ends:
Parent Company:

SALARIES/BONUSES:

Top Exec. Salary: $ Bonus: $
Second Exec. Salary: $ Bonus: $

OTHER THOUGHTS:

Estimated Female Officers or Directors:
Hot Spot for Advancement for Women/Minorities:

Symmetry Surgical Inc

www.symmetrysurgical.com

NAIC Code: 339,100

TYPES OF BUSINESS:

Surgical and Medical Instrument Manufacturing

BRANDS/DIVISIONS/AFFILIATES:

RoundTable Healthcare Partners LP
Bookwalter
RapidClean
Classic
Microsect
Olsen
Flash Pak
Vesolock

CONTACTS: *Note: Officers with more than one job title may be intentionally listed here more than once.*

Brian J. Straeb, Pres.
Ronda Harris, Chief Accounting Officer
Thomas Sullivan, Director
Craig Reynolds, Director

GROWTH PLANS/SPECIAL FEATURES:

Symmetry Surgical, Inc. is a global marketer and distributor of medical devices with some limited manufacturing focused on the general surgery market. The firm offers over 20,000 products and sells primarily to hospitals and surgical centers in the U.S., as well as to countries worldwide through direct representatives, dealers and distributors. Symmetry's current product portfolio includes a broad range of reusable stainless steel and titanium, hand-held general and specialty surgical instruments; single use and disposable instruments; electro-surgery instruments; retractor systems; ligation clips and appliers; and containers and sterilization devices sold directly to hospitals and other sites of care. The company reports its revenue in two segments: Symmetry Surgical Branded Products and Alliance Partners Products. Symmetry Surgical Branded Products include surgical instruments such as retractor instruments/systems, electro-surgery instruments, ligation clips and appliers, containers and sterilization devices and general and specialty instruments. These products comprise Symmetry's owned brands and are distributed globally. Alliance Partners Products consist of complementary products offered by other manufacturers which Symmetry Surgical distributes, primarily in markets within the U.S. This includes complementary general surgery instruments used in surgical lighting, laparoscopic surgery and accessories. Products in this category are products offered for sale in the firm's capacity as a distributor and the firm does not own the underlying intellectual property. Symmetry Surgical offers products under the brands Bookwalter, RapidClean, Classic, Microsect, Olsen, Secto, Magna-Free, Greenberg, Flash Pak, Rhoton and Vesolock, among many others. Symmetry is privately-held by RoundTable Healthcare Partners LP. In July 2018, Symmetry agreed to acquire the electrosurgical business and related intellectual property, inclusive of the Bovie brand, from Bovie Medical Corporation for $97 million. The transaction was expected to close by year's end.

FINANCIAL DATA: *Note: Data for latest year may not have been available at press time.*

In U.S. $	2017	2016	2015	2014	2013	2012
Revenue	90,300,000	86,000,000	84,527,000	81,782,000	88,947,000	107,005,000
R&D Expense						
Operating Income						
Operating Margin %						
SGA Expense						
Net Income			1,200,000	-35,775,000	-12,185,000	9,121,000
Operating Cash Flow						
Capital Expenditure						
EBITDA						
Return on Assets %						
Return on Equity %						
Debt to Equity						

CONTACT INFORMATION:

Phone: 800 251-3000 Fax: 800 342-3272
Toll-Free:
Address: 3034 Owen Dr., Antioch, TN 30713 United States

STOCK TICKER/OTHER:

Stock Ticker: Private
Employees: 189
Parent Company: RoundTable Healthcare Partners LP
Exchange:
Fiscal Year Ends: 12/31

SALARIES/BONUSES:

Top Exec. Salary: $ Bonus: $
Second Exec. Salary: $ Bonus: $

OTHER THOUGHTS:

Estimated Female Officers or Directors:
Hot Spot for Advancement for Women/Minorities:

Take Care Health Systems LLC

www.takecarehealth.com

NAIC Code: 621,498

TYPES OF BUSINESS:

Health Clinics
In-Store Clinics

BRANDS/DIVISIONS/AFFILIATES:

Wallgreens Boots Alliance Inc
Healthcare Clinic

CONTACTS:
Note: Officers with more than one job title may be intentionally listed here more than once.

Stefano Pessina, CEO-Walgreens
Gregory D. Wasson, Pres.

GROWTH PLANS/SPECIAL FEATURES:

Take Care Health Systems, LLC, a wholly-owned subsidiary of Walgreens Boots Alliance, Inc., operates the Healthcare Clinic nurse-practitioner-based system, a chain of quick service healthcare clinics. The clinics are open seven days a week and offer walk-in and appointment treatment from certified nurse practitioners. The clinic accepts most insurance carriers, and out-of-pocket costs typically range from $5 to $220. The firm offers prevention and wellness services, treatment services and monitoring and management services. Prevention and wellness services include vaccinations, physicals and health screenings and testing. Treatment services addresses minor illnesses, aches, pains and injuries, such as joint pain, pink eye, bronchitis and jellyfish stings as well as skin conditions including shingles, ringworm and eczema. The firm's monitoring and management services track chronic conditions including high cholesterol, thyroid conditions, diabetes, asthma, osteoporosis and minor depression. The segment also provides medication renewal, breathing treatments, injection services and EpiPen refills. Take Care currently has over 400 clinics in Walgreens stores nationwide. Within the company's clinics, advanced information systems manage patient records, collect information about symptoms during consultations and provide suggestions about diagnoses. When a prescription is issued, it is automatically sent to the in-store pharmacy or to the drug store of the patient's choice.

FINANCIAL DATA:
Note: Data for latest year may not have been available at press time.

In U.S. $	2017	2016	2015	2014	2013	2012
Revenue						
R&D Expense						
Operating Income						
Operating Margin %						
SGA Expense						
Net Income						
Operating Cash Flow						
Capital Expenditure						
EBITDA						
Return on Assets %						
Return on Equity %						
Debt to Equity						

CONTACT INFORMATION:

Phone: 484-351-3200 Fax: 484-351-3800
Toll-Free: 866-825-3227
Address: 161 Washington St., 8 Tower Bridge, Ste. 1400, Conshohocken, PA 19428 United States

STOCK TICKER/OTHER:

Stock Ticker: Subsidiary Exchange:
Employees: Fiscal Year Ends:
Parent Company: Walgreens Boots Alliance Inc

SALARIES/BONUSES:

Top Exec. Salary: $ Bonus: $
Second Exec. Salary: $ Bonus: $

OTHER THOUGHTS:

Estimated Female Officers or Directors:
Hot Spot for Advancement for Women/Minorities: Y

Takeda Oncology

www.takedaoncology.com

NAIC Code: 325,412

TYPES OF BUSINESS:

Pharmaceuticals Discovery & Development
Gene-Based Drug Discovery Platform
Small-Molecule Drugs

BRANDS/DIVISIONS/AFFILIATES:

Takeda Pharmaceutical Company Ltd
ADCETRIS
ALUNBRIG
iCLUSIG
MEPACT
NINLARO
VECTIBIX
VELCADE

CONTACTS: *Note: Officers with more than one job title may be intentionally listed here more than once.*

Christophe Bianchi, Pres.
Karen Ferrante, Head-R&D Site
Laurie Bartlett Keating, General Counsel
Kyle Kuvalanka, VP-Bus. Dev. & Corp. Strategy
Lisa Adler, VP-Corp. Comm.
Todd Shegog, Sr. VP-Finance
Christophe Bianchi, Exec. VP

GROWTH PLANS/SPECIAL FEATURES:

Takeda Oncology, formerly Millennium Pharmaceuticals, Inc., is a fully-integrated biopharmaceutical company. The firm is a wholly-owned subsidiary of Takeda Pharmaceutical Company Limited, operating Takeda's oncology business division. Millennium is organized to discover, develop and deliver best-in-class oncology therapies for patients worldwide. Its medicines include ADCETRIS, ALUNBRIG, iCLUSIG, MEPACT, NINLARO, VECTIBIX and VELCADE. ADCETRIS (brentuximab vedotin) is approved in more than 65 countries, and indicated for treatment of patients with classical Hodgkin lymphoma and systemic anaplastic large cell lymphoma. ALUNBRIG (birgatinib) is for patients with anaplastic lymphoma kinase (ALK)-positive metastatic non-small cell lung cancer. iCLUSIG (ponatinib) for patients with chronic/accelerated myeloid leukemia or positive acute lymphoblastic leukemia (Ph+ ALL). MEPACT (mifamurtide) is approved in the European Union and several other countries, but not the U.S., and for patients with high-grade resectable non-metastatic osteosarcoma after macroscopically complete surgical resection. NINLARO (ixazomib) is approved in the U.S., and is an oral medicine for the treatment of people with multiple myeloma who have received at least one prior therapy. VECTIBIX (panitumumab) is approved in more than 40 countries, including the U.S. and the EU, and is an epidermal growth factor receptor antagonist indicated for the treatment of wild-type KRAS metastatic colorectal cancer. VELCADE (bortezomib) is approved in more than 90 countries, including the U.S. and the EU, and is an injection that is a type of chemotherapy for the treatment of multiple myeloma and relapsed mantle cell lymphoma in a class of medicines called proteasome inhibitors. Current developments include seven programs in phase 3, 13 in phase 2 and 19 in phase 1. Millennium's oncology division includes hubs in seven countries: the U.S., Japan, the U.K., Germany, France, Brazil and Indonesia.

Millennium offers employees medical, dental, vision, life and disability insurance; 401(k), profit sharing bonuses and incentives plans; and various employee assistance programs.

FINANCIAL DATA: *Note: Data for latest year may not have been available at press time.*

In U.S. $	2017	2016	2015	2014	2013	2012
Revenue	1,050,000,000	1,000,000,000	960,000,000			
R&D Expense						
Operating Income						
Operating Margin %						
SGA Expense						
Net Income						
Operating Cash Flow						
Capital Expenditure						
EBITDA						
Return on Assets %						
Return on Equity %						
Debt to Equity						

CONTACT INFORMATION:

Phone: 617-679-7000 Fax: 617-374-7788
Toll-Free: 800-390-5663
Address: 40 Landsdowne St., Cambridge, MA 02139 United States

STOCK TICKER/OTHER:

Stock Ticker: Subsidiary Exchange:
Employees: 1,225 Fiscal Year Ends: 03/31
Parent Company: Takeda Pharmaceutical Company Limited

SALARIES/BONUSES:

Top Exec. Salary: $ Bonus: $
Second Exec. Salary: $ Bonus: $

OTHER THOUGHTS:

Estimated Female Officers or Directors:
Hot Spot for Advancement for Women/Minorities: Y

Takeda Pharmaceutical Company Limited

www.takeda.com

NAIC Code: 325,412

TYPES OF BUSINESS:

Pharmaceuticals Discovery & Development
Over-the-Counter Drugs
Vitamins

BRANDS/DIVISIONS/AFFILIATES:

Lansoprazole
Pantoprazole
Bortezomib
Ixazomib
Vortioxetine
Alogliptin Benzoate
Azilsartan
Febuxostat

CONTACTS: *Note: Officers with more than one job title may be intentionally listed here more than once.*

Christophe Weber, CEO
Costa Saroukos, CFO
David Osborne, Global Human Resources Officer
Tadataka Yamada, Chief Medical & Scientific Officer
Nancy Joseph-Ridge, Gen. Mgr.-Pharmaceutical Dev. Div.
Toyoji Yoshida, Managing Dir.-Internal Control & Special Missions
Shinji Honda, Sr. VP-Corp. Strategy
Frank Morich, Chief Commercial Officer
Trevor Smith, CEO-Takeda Pharmaceuticals Europe Ltd.
Masato Iwasaki, Sr. VP-Pharmaceutical Mktg. Div.
Haruhiko Hirate, Sr. VP
Anna Protopapas, Exec. VP-Global Bus. Dev.
Yasuchika Hasegawa, Chmn.
Frank Morich, CEO-Takeda Pharmaceuticals Intl

GROWTH PLANS/SPECIAL FEATURES:

Takeda Pharmaceutical Company Limited, based in Japan, is an international research-based global pharmaceuticals company. It operates research and development facilities in eight countries, and production facilities in 18 countries. Takeda discovers, develops, manufactures and markets pharmaceutical products, which are grouped into five categories: gastrointestinal, oncology, central nervous system (CNS), cardiovascular and metabolic, and others. Gastrointestinal products include Lansoprazole, for peptic ulcers; Dexlansoprazole, for acid reflux disease; Lubiprostone, for chronic idiopathic constipation and opioid-induced constipation; Pantoprazole, for gastric acid-related disorders; Vonoprazan, for acid-related diseases; and Vedolizumab, for ulcerative colitis and Crohn's disease. Oncology products include Bortezomib, for multiple myeloma; Leuprorelin Acetate, for prostate/breast cancer and endometriosis; Brentuximab Vedotin, for malignant lymphoma; and Ixazomib, for multiple myeloma. CNS' Vortioxetine is a treatment for major depressive disorder. Cardiovascular and metabolic products include Alogliptin Benzoate, for Type-2 diabetes; and Azilsartan, for hypertension. Other products include Febuxostat and Colchicine, each for hyperuricemia and gout. In early-2018, Takeda agreed to acquire TiGenix, a European cell therapy company. In May 2018, the firm agreed to acquire Shire Plc, an Irish pharmaceuticals company, for Â£40 billion ($62.4 billion). The deal, which is expected to close in the first half of 2019, would be one of the biggest deals ever in the pharmaceuticals industry.

FINANCIAL DATA: *Note: Data for latest year may not have been available at press time.*

In U.S. $	2017	2016	2015	2014	2013	2012
Revenue						
R&D Expense						
Operating Income						
Operating Margin %						
SGA Expense						
Net Income						
Operating Cash Flow						
Capital Expenditure						
EBITDA						
Return on Assets %						
Return on Equity %						
Debt to Equity						

CONTACT INFORMATION:

Phone: 81 33278-2111 Fax: 81 33278-2880
Toll-Free:
Address: 1-1, Nihonbashi-Honcho 2-Chome, Chuo-ku, Tokyo, 103-0023 Japan

STOCK TICKER/OTHER:

Stock Ticker: TKPYY
Employees: 27,230
Parent Company:
Exchange: PINX
Fiscal Year Ends: 03/31

SALARIES/BONUSES:

Top Exec. Salary: $ Bonus: $
Second Exec. Salary: $ Bonus: $

OTHER THOUGHTS:

Estimated Female Officers or Directors: 3
Hot Spot for Advancement for Women/Minorities: Y

Tandem Diabetes Care Inc

www.tandemdiabetes.com

NAIC Code: 334,510

TYPES OF BUSINESS:

Electromedical and Electrotherapeutic Apparatus Manufacturing

BRANDS/DIVISIONS/AFFILIATES:

the t:slim X2 Insulin Delivery System
t:flex Insulin Delivery System

CONTACTS: *Note: Officers with more than one job title may be intentionally listed here more than once.*

Leigh Vosseller, CFO
Susan Morrison, Chief Administrative Officer
John Sheridan, COO
Dick Allen, Director
Kim Blickenstaff, Director
David Berger, Executive VP
Brian Hansen, Executive VP

GROWTH PLANS/SPECIAL FEATURES:

Tandem Diabetes Care, Inc. is a medical device company with an innovative approach to the design, development and commercialization of a family of products for people with insulin-dependent diabetes. The firm's manufacturing and sales activities primarily focus on its flagship product, the t:slim X2 Insulin Delivery System (t:slim X2), based on a proprietary technology platform. The simple-to-use t:slim X2 is the smallest durable insulin pump available, and the only pump currently available that is capable of remote feature updates. Tandem has commercially launched five insulin pumps since inception, all of which have been developed using its proprietary technology platform. Two of these pumps have featured continuous glucose monitoring technology (CGM). Since the launch of its first product in August 2012, the firm has shipped nearly 68,000 pumps to customers in the U.S. Tandem plans to begin commercialization of t:slim X2 in select geographies outside the U.S., including Canada, during 2018. In 2017, t:slim X2 represented approximately 95% of new pump shipments of the firm. In addition to the t:slim X2, the firm continues to offer the t:flex Insulin Delivery System for people with greater insulin needs. In September 2017, Tandem commenced commercial sales of t:slim X2 integrated with the Dexcom G5 Mobile CGM system, manufactured by Dexcom, and discontinued new sales of t:slim G4.

FINANCIAL DATA: *Note: Data for latest year may not have been available at press time.*

In U.S. $	2017	2016	2015	2014	2013	2012
Revenue	107,601,000	84,248,000	72,850,000	49,722,000	29,006,640	2,474,698
R&D Expense	20,661,000	18,809,000	16,963,000	15,791,000	11,079,200	9,009,030
Operating Income	-62,944,000	-78,051,000	-69,004,000	-75,664,000	-49,434,000	-33,048,160
Operating Margin %	-58.49%	-92.64%	-94.72%	-152.17%	-170.42%	-1335.44%
SGA Expense	86,377,000	82,834,000	78,621,000	75,121,000	44,521,200	22,690,880
Net Income	-73,033,000	-83,447,000	-72,418,000	-79,524,000	-63,138,850	-33,015,080
Operating Cash Flow	-66,136,000	-61,173,000	-58,764,000	-61,378,000	-47,756,650	-33,471,170
Capital Expenditure	5,718,000	8,930,000	5,838,000	4,579,000	6,009,772	5,529,010
EBITDA	-54,818,000	-72,266,000	-63,838,000	-71,163,000	-55,262,220	-28,457,640
Return on Assets %	-70.31%	-70.26%	-62.54%	-59.19%	-62.50%	-122.74%
Return on Equity %		-290.04%	-122.70%	-93.49%		
Debt to Equity			0.46	0.53	0.25	

CONTACT INFORMATION:

Phone: 858 366-6900 Fax:
Toll-Free:
Address: 11075 Roselle St., San Diego, CA 92121 United States

STOCK TICKER/OTHER:

Stock Ticker: TNDM
Employees: 591
Parent Company:
Exchange: NAS
Fiscal Year Ends: 12/31

SALARIES/BONUSES:

Top Exec. Salary: $583,495 Bonus: $
Second Exec. Salary: $389,423 Bonus: $164,813

OTHER THOUGHTS:

Estimated Female Officers or Directors:
Hot Spot for Advancement for Women/Minorities:

Team Health Holdings Inc

www.teamhealth.com

NAIC Code: 621,111

TYPES OF BUSINESS:

Physicians and Hospital Staff Services
Hospital Administrative Services
Pediatrics
Radiology & Teleradiology Services
Urgent Care

BRANDS/DIVISIONS/AFFILIATES:

Blackstone Group LP (The)
TEAMHealth
X32 Healthcare
Emergency Medicine Consultants Ltd

CONTACTS: *Note: Officers with more than one job title may be intentionally listed here more than once.*

Leif M. Murphy, CEO
Michael Wiechart, COO
H. Massingale, Chairman of the Board
David Jones, CFO
Oliver Rogers, Executive VP
Steven Clifton, Executive VP
Leif Murphy, President
Lynn Massingale, Chmn.

GROWTH PLANS/SPECIAL FEATURES:

Team Health Holdings, Inc. is a physician-led company offering outsourced integrated care services. This 20,000-clinician-strong healthcare provider offers outsources staffing, administrative support and management services across the full continuum of care under the TEAMHealth brand name. Practice areas include emergency medicine, anesthesiology, hospital medicine, hospital medicine subspecialties, ambulatory care, post-acute care and behavioral health. Team Health's staff include residents, physicians, medical directors and advanced practice clinicians. Team Health is privately-held private The Blackstone Group LP. During January-July 2018, Team Health acquired the following: X32 Healthcare, an emergency department performance improvement consulting practice; Emergency Medicine Consultants Ltd., which provides emergency medicine staffing for healthcare facilities; the clinical operations of EmergiNet, which provides emergency medicine staffing for Piedmont Henry Hospital and Piedmont Rockdale Hospital, in Georgia; and the clinical operations of Premier Medical P.C., which provides emergency care to patients at St. Vincent's East, in Birmingham, Alabama.

FINANCIAL DATA: *Note: Data for latest year may not have been available at press time.*

In U.S. $	2017	2016	2015	2014	2013	2012
Revenue	4,200,000,000	3,900,000,000	3,597,246,976	2,819,642,880	2,383,595,008	2,069,022,976
R&D Expense						
Operating Income						
Operating Margin %						
SGA Expense						
Net Income			82,711,000	97,738,000	87,409,000	63,772,000
Operating Cash Flow						
Capital Expenditure						
EBITDA						
Return on Assets %						
Return on Equity %						
Debt to Equity						

CONTACT INFORMATION:

Phone: 865 693-1000 Fax:
Toll-Free: 800-818-1498
Address: 265 Brookview Ctr. Way, Ste. 400, Knoxville, TN 37919 United States

STOCK TICKER/OTHER:

Stock Ticker: Private Exchange:
Employees: 20,000 Fiscal Year Ends: 12/31
Parent Company: Blackstone Group LP (The)

SALARIES/BONUSES:

Top Exec. Salary: $ Bonus: $
Second Exec. Salary: $ Bonus: $

OTHER THOUGHTS:

Estimated Female Officers or Directors: 3
Hot Spot for Advancement for Women/Minorities: Y

Teleflex Incorporated

www.teleflex.com

NAIC Code: 339,100

TYPES OF BUSINESS:

Medical Equipment & Supplies, Manufacturing
General & Specialized Surgical Products
Hospital Products & Equipment

BRANDS/DIVISIONS/AFFILIATES:

NeoTract Inc
UroLift System

CONTACTS: *Note: Officers with more than one job title may be intentionally listed here more than once.*

Thomas Powell, CFO
Benson Smith, Chairman of the Board
Liam Kelly, President
Thomas Kennedy, Senior VP, Divisional
Karen Boylan, Vice President, Divisional
Cameron Hicks, Vice President, Divisional
John Deren, Vice President
James Leyden, Vice President

GROWTH PLANS/SPECIAL FEATURES:

Teleflex Incorporated manufactures specialty engineered products for the medical industry, specializing in services for vascular access, respiratory care, general and regional anesthesia, cardiac care, urology and surgery. The company is a world-leading provider of medical devices, with global manufacturing sites and selling to more than 130 countries. Teleflex operates through seven segments: vascular North America (NA), interventional NA, anesthesia North America, surgical NA, EMEA, Asia and OEM. Vascular NA's products facilitate a variety of critical care therapies, including the administration of intravenous medications, the measurement of blood pressure and taking blood samples through a single puncture site, all under the Arrow brand. Interventional NA's products include vascular solutions for treating coronary and peripheral vascular diseases, and include various catheters, guide extensions, micro-introducers for arterial and venous catheterization procedures, catheter turning control torque, bone access systems, de-clotting systems and low-profile hybrid ports. Anesthesia North America comprises airway management and pain management products as well as pre-hospital emergency applications. Surgical NA products include ligation clips and closures, percutaneous surgical systems, appliers and sutures and access ports. The EMEA (Europe, the Middle East and Africa), Asia and OEM (original equipment manufacturer) segments design, manufacture and distribute medical devices primarily used in critical care, surgical applications and cardiac care. Products offered by the Asia segment are primarily used in acute care settings for diagnostic, therapeutic and surgical procedures. The OEM segment also designs, manufactures and supplies devices and instruments for other medical device manufacturers, with products including catheters, sheath/dilator sets, sutures, fibers and bioresorbable resins. In October 2017, Teleflex acquired NeoTract, Inc., a medical device company that developed and commercialized the UroLift System, a minimally-invasive medical device for treating lower urinary tract symptoms due to benign prostatic hyperplasia.

Teleflex offers employees comprehensive medical, dental and vision benefits, retirement plans and employee assistance programs.

FINANCIAL DATA: *Note: Data for latest year may not have been available at press time.*

In U.S. $	2017	2016	2015	2014	2013	2012
Revenue	2,146,303,000	1,868,027,000	1,809,690,000	1,839,832,000	1,696,271,000	1,551,009,000
R&D Expense	84,770,000	58,579,000	52,119,000	61,040,000	65,045,000	56,278,000
Operating Income	387,069,000	374,313,000	323,302,000	302,731,000	271,713,000	237,458,000
Operating Margin %	18.03%	20.03%	17.86%	16.45%	16.01%	15.30%
SGA Expense	699,963,000	563,308,000	568,982,000	578,657,000	502,187,000	454,489,000
Net Income	152,530,000	237,377,000	244,863,000	187,679,000	150,881,000	-190,057,000
Operating Cash Flow	419,885,000	408,480,000	300,810,000	286,565,000	226,544,000	186,054,000
Capital Expenditure	70,903,000	53,135,000	61,448,000	67,571,000	63,580,000	65,394,000
EBITDA	522,720,000	418,572,000	414,362,000	396,701,000	325,611,000	-15,336,000
Return on Assets %	3.02%	6.11%	6.23%	4.58%	3.79%	-4.96%
Return on Equity %	6.67%	11.44%	12.49%	9.81%	8.17%	-10.11%
Debt to Equity	0.88	0.39	0.32	0.36	0.48	0.54

CONTACT INFORMATION:

Phone: 610-225-6800 Fax:
Toll-Free:
Address: 550 East Swedesford Rd., Ste 400, Wayne, PA 19087 United States

STOCK TICKER/OTHER:

Stock Ticker: TFX Exchange: NYS
Employees: 12,600 Fiscal Year Ends: 12/31
Parent Company:

SALARIES/BONUSES:

Top Exec. Salary: $939,681 Bonus: $
Second Exec. Salary: $616,777 Bonus: $

OTHER THOUGHTS:

Estimated Female Officers or Directors: 2
Hot Spot for Advancement for Women/Minorities:

Tenet Healthcare Corporation

www.tenethealth.com

NAIC Code: 622,110

TYPES OF BUSINESS:

General Medical and Surgical Hospitals
Specialty Care Facilities
Outpatient Centers
Diagnostic Imaging Centers
Rural Health Care Clinics
HMOs

BRANDS/DIVISIONS/AFFILIATES:

Conifer Holdings Inc
United Surgical Partners International

CONTACTS: *Note: Officers with more than one job title may be intentionally listed here more than once.*

Daniel Cancelmi, CFO
Ronald Rittenmeyer, Chairman of the Board
R. Ramsey, Chief Accounting Officer
Audrey Andrews, General Counsel
Paul Castanon, Other Corporate Officer
J. Evans, President, Divisional
Keith Pitts, Vice Chairman

GROWTH PLANS/SPECIAL FEATURES:

Tenet Healthcare Corporation specializes in the provision of health care services, primarily through the operation of general hospitals. The company operates 68 hospitals, 21 short-stay surgical hospitals, 470 outpatient centers, nine facilities in the U.K. via subsidiaries, partnerships and joint ventures. Subsidiary Conifer Holdings, Inc. provides health care business process services in the areas of revenue cycle management, technology-enabled performance and health management to health systems, individual hospitals, physician practices, self-insured organizations and health plans. Each of the company's general hospitals offers acute care services, operating and recovery rooms, radiology services, respiratory therapy services, clinical laboratories and pharmacies. In addition, most offer intensive care, critical care or coronary care units, physical therapy, as well as orthopedic, oncology and outpatient services. Some of the hospitals also offer tertiary care services such as open-heart surgery, neonatal intensive care and neuroscience. Along with hospitals, Tenet's subsidiaries operate three academic medical centers, two children's hospitals, two specialty hospitals and one critical access hospital, for a combined total of 19,141 licensed beds, serving primarily urban and suburban communities in 12 states. Within the January-July 2018 time period, Tenet had purchased the remaining 15% interest in United Surgical Partners International from Welsh, Carson, Anderson & Stowe, increasing its ownership to 95%, with Baylor Scott and White Health owning the remaining 5%. The firm also sold its Philadelphia-area acute care hospitals, its MacNeal Hospital in Chicago, its minority interest in Baylor Scott & White Medical Center, and its Des Peres Hospital in St. Louis.

The company offers its employees medical, dental and vision insurance; life and AD&D insurance; a 401(k) plan; an employee stock purchase plan; and credit union membership.

FINANCIAL DATA: *Note: Data for latest year may not have been available at press time.*

In U.S. $	2017	2016	2015	2014	2013	2012
Revenue	19,179,000,000	19,621,000,000	18,634,000,000	16,615,000,000	11,102,000,000	9,119,000,000
R&D Expense						
Operating Income	1,389,000,000	1,432,000,000	1,380,000,000	1,103,000,000	797,000,000	773,000,000
Operating Margin %	7.24%	7.29%	7.40%	6.63%	7.17%	8.47%
SGA Expense	12,359,000,000	12,480,000,000	11,974,000,000	10,653,000,000	7,155,000,000	5,809,000,000
Net Income	-704,000,000	-192,000,000	-140,000,000	12,000,000	-134,000,000	152,000,000
Operating Cash Flow	1,200,000,000	558,000,000	1,026,000,000	687,000,000	589,000,000	593,000,000
Capital Expenditure	707,000,000	875,000,000	842,000,000	933,000,000	691,000,000	508,000,000
EBITDA	1,797,000,000	2,077,000,000	1,853,000,000	1,750,000,000	861,000,000	1,176,000,000
Return on Assets %	-2.92%	-.79%	-.66%	.06%	-1.06%	1.61%
Return on Equity %	-521.48%	-34.65%	-20.86%	1.70%	-14.12%	12.63%
Debt to Equity		36.12	20.81	17.96	14.15	4.51

CONTACT INFORMATION:

Phone: 469-893-2200 Fax:
Toll-Free:
Address: 1445 Ross Ave., Ste. 1400, Dallas, TX 75202 United States

STOCK TICKER/OTHER:

Stock Ticker: THC
Employees: 131,610
Parent Company:
Exchange: NYS
Fiscal Year Ends: 12/31

SALARIES/BONUSES:

Top Exec. Salary: $925,000 Bonus: $300,000
Second Exec. Salary: $1,059,231 Bonus: $

OTHER THOUGHTS:

Estimated Female Officers or Directors: 5
Hot Spot for Advancement for Women/Minorities: Y

Terumo Corporation

www.terumo.co.jp

NAIC Code: 339,100

TYPES OF BUSINESS:

Surgical Appliance and Supplies Manufacturing
Medical Device Manufacturer
Medical Device Distributor

BRANDS/DIVISIONS/AFFILIATES:

Terumo Medical Corporation
Terumo Europe NV
Terumo Cardiovascular Systems Corporation
Terumo BCT Inc
MicroVention Inc
Vascutek Inc

CONTACTS: *Note: Officers with more than one job title may be intentionally listed here more than once.*

David Perez, Pres.
Antoinette Gawin, VP

GROWTH PLANS/SPECIAL FEATURES:

Terumo Corporation develops, manufactures and distributes medical devices and services worldwide. The firm operates in three business segments: cardiac and vascular, general hospital and blood management. The cardiac and vascular business derives 55% of the company's annual revenue and specializes in endovascular intervention and cardiovascular surgery. Endovascular intervention utilizes catheters, which are thin tubular devices inserted into the patient's blood vessel to perform diagnostic and/or therapeutic procedures. Cardiovascular surgery utilizes cardiopulmonary bypass systems, artificial vascular grafts, introducer sheaths, guidewires and radial artery compression devices. Other products produced by this division include stents, imaging systems, intravascular ultrasound systems, drug-elutable beads and more. The general hospital business produces infusion systems, closed anti-cancer drug infusion systems, blood glucose monitoring systems, digital blood pressure monitors, thermometers, pulse oximeters, body composition monitors, adhesion barriers, pain management drugs, peritoneal dialysis devices, dialysis fluids, fall prevention products, oral care products, urine test strips, IV solutions, pre-filled syringes and condensed liquid nutritional supplements. Last, the blood management business is a global leader in blood component and cellular technologies, and offers a combination of apheresis collections, manual and automated whole blood processing, and therapeutic apheresis and cell processing technologies. This segment maintains blood centers, blood donation rooms and blood processing centers. It also produces medical devices for blood transfusion. Terumo's global locations are spread across North and South America, Europe, the Middle East, Africa, China, Asia and Japan. Subsidiaries of the firm include Terumo Medical Corporation; Terumo Europe NV; Terumo Cardiovascular Systems Corporation; Terumo BCT Inc., MicroVention, Inc.; and Vascutek, Inc.

FINANCIAL DATA: *Note: Data for latest year may not have been available at press time.*

In U.S. $	2017	2016	2015	2014	2013	2012
Revenue						
R&D Expense						
Operating Income						
Operating Margin %						
SGA Expense						
Net Income						
Operating Cash Flow						
Capital Expenditure						
EBITDA						
Return on Assets %						
Return on Equity %						
Debt to Equity						

CONTACT INFORMATION:

Phone: 81 333748111 Fax:
Toll-Free:
Address: 2-44-1, Hatagaya Shibuya-ku, Tokyo, 151-0072 Japan

STOCK TICKER/OTHER:

Stock Ticker: TRUMY Exchange: PINX
Employees: 23,319 Fiscal Year Ends: 03/31
Parent Company:

SALARIES/BONUSES:

Top Exec. Salary: $ Bonus: $
Second Exec. Salary: $ Bonus: $

OTHER THOUGHTS:

Estimated Female Officers or Directors:
Hot Spot for Advancement for Women/Minorities:

Teva Pharmaceutical Industries Limited

www.tevapharm.com

NAIC Code: 325,412

TYPES OF BUSINESS:

Drugs-Generic
Active Pharmaceutical Ingredients

BRANDS/DIVISIONS/AFFILIATES:

PGT Healthcare

CONTACTS: *Note: Officers with more than one job title may be intentionally listed here more than once.*

Kare Schultz, CEO
Michael McClellan, CFO
Mark Sabag, Exec. VP-Human Resources
Michael Hayden, Chief Scientific Officer
Richard S. Egosi, Chief Legal Officer
Erez Israeli, Chief Bus. Process Officer
Iris Beck-Codner, Chief Comm. Officer
Kevin Mannix, VP-Investor Rel.
Sol J. Barer, Chmn.
Itzhak Krinsky, Chmn.-Teva Japan & South Korea

GROWTH PLANS/SPECIAL FEATURES:

Teva Pharmaceutical Industries Limited, based in Israel, is a pharmaceutical company that produces, distributes and sells pharmaceutical products internationally. The firm comprises three regions: North America, Europe and growth markets--each of which manages Teva's entire product portfolio, including generics, specialty medicines and over-the-counter (OTC) medicines. Teva develops, manufactures and sells generic medicines in a variety of dosage forms, including tablets, capsules, injectables, inhalants, liquids, ointments and creams. The generics division also offers a broad range of basic chemical entities, as well as specialized product families such as sterile products, hormones, narcotics, high-potency drugs and cytotoxic substances. The specialty medicines business focuses on delivering innovative solutions to patients and providers via medicines, devices and services in key regions and markets worldwide. These solutions include Teva's core therapeutic areas of central nervous system (CNS) and respiratory medicines. CNS includes multiple sclerosis, neurodegenerative disorders, movement disorders and pain care; and respiratory medicines focus on asthma and chronic obstructive pulmonary disease (COPD). This division also has specialty products in oncology and other areas. Last, the OTC division manufactures and markets more than 200 consumer healthcare brands, including OTC medicines and vitamins, minerals and food supplements in more than 70 countries worldwide. OTC operates through joint venture, PGT Healthcare, with Teva owning 51% and Proctor & Gamble owning 49%. In late-2017, the firm sold Plan B One-Step and other women's health products, including Take Action, Aftera and Next Choice One Dose, to Foundation Consumer Healthcare for $675 million; and sold Paragard, a copper releasing intrauterine contraceptive, to CooperSurgical for $1.1 billion. In February 2018, Teva sold a portfolio of products within its global women's health business across contraception, fertility, menopause and osteoporosis for $703 million to CVC Capital Partners; this portfolio is marketed and sold outside the U.S.

FINANCIAL DATA: *Note: Data for latest year may not have been available at press time.*

In U.S. $	2017	2016	2015	2014	2013	2012
Revenue	22,385,000,000	21,903,000,000	19,652,000,000	20,272,000,000	20,314,000,000	
R&D Expense	1,848,000,000	2,111,000,000	1,525,000,000	1,488,000,000	1,427,000,000	
Operating Income	4,013,000,000	4,652,000,000	5,114,000,000	4,490,000,000	3,961,000,000	
Operating Margin %	15.59%	21.23%	22.81%	22.14%	19.49%	
SGA Expense	4,986,000,000	5,096,000,000	4,717,000,000	5,078,000,000	5,319,000,000	
Net Income	-16,265,000,000	329,000,000	1,588,000,000	3,055,000,000	1,269,000,000	
Operating Cash Flow	3,507,000,000	5,225,000,000	5,542,000,000	5,127,000,000	3,237,000,000	
Capital Expenditure	874,000,000	901,000,000	772,000,000	929,000,000	1,031,000,000	
EBITDA	-15,392,000,000	2,894,000,000	3,930,000,000	5,446,000,000	3,206,000,000	
Return on Assets %	-20.21%	.09%	3.12%	6.50%	2.58%	
Return on Equity %	-76.07%	.24%	6.31%	13.31%	5.59%	
Debt to Equity	2.10	1.09	0.31	0.36	0.46	

CONTACT INFORMATION:

Phone: 972 392-67267 Fax: 972 392-34050
Toll-Free:
Address: 5 Basel St., Petach Tikva, 49131 Israel

STOCK TICKER/OTHER:

Stock Ticker: TEVA
Employees: 57,000
Parent Company:
Exchange: NYS
Fiscal Year Ends: 12/31

SALARIES/BONUSES:

Top Exec. Salary: $696,346 Bonus: $900,000
Second Exec. Salary: $1,534,467 Bonus: $

OTHER THOUGHTS:

Estimated Female Officers or Directors: 4
Hot Spot for Advancement for Women/Minorities: Y

Texas Health Resources

www.texashealth.org

NAIC Code: 622,110

TYPES OF BUSINESS:

General Medical and Surgical Hospitals
Medical Research
Retirement Community

BRANDS/DIVISIONS/AFFILIATES:

Texas Health Research and Education Institute

CONTACTS:

Note: Officers with more than one job title may be intentionally listed here more than once.

Barclay E. Berdan, CEO
Jeffrey L. Canose, COO
Ronald R. Long, CFO
Michelle Kirby, Exec. VP-Chief People Officer
Joey Sudomir, Sr. VP-CIO
Jonathan Scholl, Chief Strategy Officer
Oscar L. Amparan, Exec. VP-Southeast Zone Operations Leader
Harold Berenzweig, Exec. VP-Southwest Zone Clinical Leader
Mark C. Lester, Exec. VP-Southeast Zone Clinical Leader
Joan Clark, Chief Nurse Exec.

GROWTH PLANS/SPECIAL FEATURES:

Texas Health Resources (THR) is one of the largest faith-based, non-profit healthcare delivery systems in the U.S. The firm serves more than 7 million people in the Dallas-Ft. Worth area through three hospital systems. The company has 29 acute-care, transitional, rehabilitation and short-stay hospitals, with more than 3,900 hospital beds that are overseen by more than 6,000 physicians. These hospitals are owned, operated or joint-ventured with THR. In addition, the firm's network includes 20 outpatient facilities and more than 250 other community access points, such as doctors' offices and clinics. The company's Texas Health Research and Education Institute (THRE) subsidiary is a non-profit research institute responsible for the research and education activities across THR's acute-care and short-stay hospitals. THRE works individually with THR physicians and staff to foster and support research interests, meet education needs and provide support via medical libraries. In May 2018, THR announced plans to invest $300 million in the Fort Worth campus, expanding the hospital to a nine-story patient bed tower and modernizing surgical services. The project is expected to be complete in 2021.

The firm offers employees health, dental and vision insurance; flexible spending accounts; an employee assistance program; a 401(k) plan; tuition reimbursement; adoption assistance; and life, disability and AD&D insurance.

FINANCIAL DATA:

Note: Data for latest year may not have been available at press time.

In U.S. $	2017	2016	2015	2014	2013	2012
Revenue	4,746,000,000	4,520,000,000	4,260,792,000	4,064,395,000	3,846,247,000	3,703,828,000
R&D Expense						
Operating Income						
Operating Margin %						
SGA Expense						
Net Income			310,300,000	589,306,000	767,728,000	
Operating Cash Flow						
Capital Expenditure						
EBITDA						
Return on Assets %						
Return on Equity %						
Debt to Equity						

CONTACT INFORMATION:

Phone: 682-236-7900 Fax:
Toll-Free: 877-847-9355
Address: 612 E. Lamar Blvd., Arlington, TX 76011 United States

STOCK TICKER/OTHER:

Stock Ticker: Nonprofit
Exchange:
Employees: 24,460
Fiscal Year Ends: 12/31
Parent Company:

SALARIES/BONUSES:

Top Exec. Salary: $ Bonus: $
Second Exec. Salary: $ Bonus: $

OTHER THOUGHTS:

Estimated Female Officers or Directors: 4
Hot Spot for Advancement for Women/Minorities: Y

Theragenics Corporation

www.theragenics.com

NAIC Code: 339,100

TYPES OF BUSINESS:

Medical Devices
Surgical Products

BRANDS/DIVISIONS/AFFILIATES:

Juniper Investment Company
CP Medical Corporation
Galt Medical Corporation
NeedleTech Products Inc
TheraSeed
AgX100

CONTACTS: *Note: Officers with more than one job title may be intentionally listed here more than once.*

Francis J. Tarallo, CEO
M. Christine Jacobs, Pres.
Francis J. Tarallo, Treasurer

GROWTH PLANS/SPECIAL FEATURES:

Theragenics Corporation is a medical device company serving the cancer treatment and surgical markets. The company operates in two segments: the brachytherapy seed business and the surgical products business. The brachytherapy seed business segment produces and markets TheraSeed, the firm's premier palladium-103 prostate cancer treatment device; and AgX100, an iodine-based therapy seed. TheraSeed is an implant the size of a grain of rice that is used primarily in treating localized prostate cancer with a one-time, minimally invasive procedure. The implant emits radiation within the immediate prostate area, killing the tumor while sparing surrounding organs from significant radiation exposure. Physicians, hospitals and other health care providers, primarily located in the U.S., utilize the TheraSeed device. AgX100 works similarly to Theraseed, but has a 60-day half-life instead of a 17-day half-life, meaning it expends half of its radioactive energy in the first two months of implantation. The surgical products business segment consists of wound closure, vascular access and specialty needle products. Wound closure products include sutures, needles and other surgical products with applications in, among other areas, urology, veterinary medicine, cardiology, orthopedics, plastic surgery and dental surgery. Vascular access products include introducers, guidewires and related products. Specialty needles include coaxial, biopsy, spinal and disposable veress needles; and access trocars. The surgical products business sells its devices and components primarily to original equipment manufacturers (OEMs) and a network of distributors. The firm's wholly-owned subsidiaries CP Medical Corporation, Galt Medical Corporation and NeedleTech Products, Inc. comprise the surgical products business. Theragenics is privately-owned by Juniper Investment Company.

The company offers employees medical, dental and life insurance; short- and long-term disability coverage; 401(k) and an employee stock purchase plan.

FINANCIAL DATA: *Note: Data for latest year may not have been available at press time.*

In U.S. $	2017	2016	2015	2014	2013	2012
Revenue						
R&D Expense						
Operating Income						
Operating Margin %						
SGA Expense						
Net Income						
Operating Cash Flow						
Capital Expenditure						
EBITDA						
Return on Assets %						
Return on Equity %						
Debt to Equity						

CONTACT INFORMATION:

Phone: 770 271-0233 Fax: 770 271-1954
Toll-Free:
Address: 5203 Bristol Industrial Way, Buford, GA 30518 United States

STOCK TICKER/OTHER:

Stock Ticker: Private
Exchange:
Employees: 535
Fiscal Year Ends: 12/31
Parent Company: Juniper Investment Company

SALARIES/BONUSES:

Top Exec. Salary: $ Bonus: $
Second Exec. Salary: $ Bonus: $

OTHER THOUGHTS:

Estimated Female Officers or Directors: 3
Hot Spot for Advancement for Women/Minorities: Y

Thermo Fisher Scientific Inc

www.thermofisher.com

NAIC Code: 423,450

TYPES OF BUSINESS:

Laboratory Equipment & Supplies Distribution
Contract Manufacturing
Equipment Calibration & Repair
Clinical Trial Services
Laboratory Workstations
Clinical Consumables
Diagnostic Reagents
Custom Chemical Synthesis

BRANDS/DIVISIONS/AFFILIATES:

Thermo Scientific
Applied Biosystems
Invitrogen
Fisher Scientific
Unity Lab Services
Patheon NV

CONTACTS: *Note: Officers with more than one job title may be intentionally listed here more than once.*

Marc Casper, CEO
Jim Manzi, Chairman of the Board
Mark Stevenson, COO
Michael Boxer, General Counsel
Michel Lagarde, President, Divisional
Patrick Durbin, President, Divisional
Gregory Herrema, President, Divisional
Stephen Williamson, Senior VP
Peter Hornstra, Vice President

GROWTH PLANS/SPECIAL FEATURES:

Thermo Fisher Scientific, Inc. is a distributor of products and services principally to the scientific-research and clinical laboratory markets. The firm serves over 400,000 customers including biotechnology and pharmaceutical companies; colleges and universities; medical-research institutions; hospitals; reference, quality control, process-control and research and development labs in various industries; and government agencies. It operates in four segments: life sciences solutions, analytical instruments, specialty diagnostics and laboratory products and services. Life sciences solutions provides a portfolio of reagents, instruments and consumables used in biological and medical research, discover and production of new drugs and vaccines. This division also provides diagnosis of disease. Analytical instruments provides a broad offering of instruments, consumables, software and services used for a range of applications in the laboratory, on the production line and in the field. These products are used by customers in pharmaceutical, biotechnology, academic, government, environmental, research, industrial markets, as well as clinical laboratories. Specialty diagnostics offers a range of diagnostic test kits, reagents, culture media, instruments and associated products in order to serve customers in healthcare, clinical, pharmaceutical, industrial and food safety laboratories. Laboratory products and services offers everything needed for the laboratory to enable customers to focus on core activities and become more efficient, productive and cost-effective. This segment's products are used primarily for drug discovery and development, as well as for life science research in order to advance the prevention and cure of diseases and enhance quality of life. The company's five primary brands include Thermo Scientific, Applied Biosystems, Invitrogen, Fisher Scientific and Unity Lab Services. In 2017, the firm acquired Patheon NV. In June 2018, Thermo Fisher opened a precision medicine science center in Cambridge, Massachusetts.

Employee benefits include tuition reimbursement, retirement plans and training & development opportunities. Benefits vary by country.

FINANCIAL DATA: *Note: Data for latest year may not have been available at press time.*

In U.S. $	2017	2016	2015	2014	2013	2012
Revenue	20,918,000,000	18,274,100,000	16,965,400,000	16,889,600,000	13,090,300,000	12,509,900,000
R&D Expense	888,000,000	754,800,000	692,300,000	691,100,000	395,500,000	376,400,000
Operating Income	3,065,000,000	2,638,400,000	2,451,500,000	1,904,800,000	1,687,300,000	1,564,200,000
Operating Margin %	14.65%	14.43%	14.45%	11.27%	12.88%	12.50%
SGA Expense	5,492,000,000	4,975,900,000	4,612,100,000	4,896,100,000	3,446,300,000	3,354,900,000
Net Income	2,225,000,000	2,021,800,000	1,975,400,000	1,894,400,000	1,273,300,000	1,177,900,000
Operating Cash Flow	4,005,000,000	3,156,300,000	2,816,900,000	2,619,600,000	2,010,700,000	2,039,500,000
Capital Expenditure	508,000,000	444,400,000	422,900,000	427,600,000	282,400,000	315,100,000
EBITDA	5,054,000,000	4,251,500,000	4,039,500,000	4,251,900,000	2,581,500,000	2,494,700,000
Return on Assets %	4.33%	4.65%	4.71%	5.07%	4.29%	4.34%
Return on Equity %	9.47%	9.42%	9.42%	10.12%	7.87%	7.72%
Debt to Equity	0.74	0.71	0.53	0.60	0.56	0.45

CONTACT INFORMATION:

Phone: 781 622-1000 Fax: 781 933-4476
Toll-Free: 800-678-5599
Address: 168 Third Ave., Waltham, MA 02451 United States

STOCK TICKER/OTHER:

Stock Ticker: TMO
Employees: 55,000
Parent Company:
Exchange: NYS
Fiscal Year Ends: 12/31

SALARIES/BONUSES:

Top Exec. Salary: $1,425,000 Bonus: $
Second Exec. Salary: $922,212 Bonus: $

OTHER THOUGHTS:

Estimated Female Officers or Directors: 1
Hot Spot for Advancement for Women/Minorities: Y

Thomas Jefferson University Hospitals Inc hospitals.jefferson.edu

NAIC Code: 622,110

TYPES OF BUSINESS:

General Medical and Surgical Hospitals

BRANDS/DIVISIONS/AFFILIATES:

Thomas Jefferson University

CONTACTS:

Note: Officers with more than one job title may be intentionally listed here more than once.

Stephen K. Klasko, CEO
Peter L. DeAngelis, Jr., Exec. VP
Stephen P. Crane, Chmn.

GROWTH PLANS/SPECIAL FEATURES:

Thomas Jefferson University Hospitals, Inc. is one of the leading healthcare providers in the Philadelphia area. Its extensive care network maintains offices throughout Pennsylvania, New Jersey and Delaware. The firm is recognized in 11 different specialty areas: orthopedics; cancer; ear, nose and throat; gastroenterology and gastrointestinal surgery; nephrology; neurology and neurosurgery; ophthalmology; diabetes and endocrinology; geriatrics; cardiology and heart surgery; urology. Thomas Jefferson University Hospitals have more than 950 licensed acute care beds throughout its primary locations. The organization comprises hospitals, outpatient centers and urgent care centers. The hospital partners with Thomas Jefferson University to be a leading innovator in the medical field.

The firm offers its employees medical, dental, vision, life and AD&D insurance; adoption assistance; access to a credit union; dependent life insurance; flexible spending accounts; GlobalFit program; a prepaid legal plan; wellness program; long-term disability and care insurance; prescription drug coverage; retirement plans; savings bonds, transportation benefits; travel accident insurance; and tuition assistance.

FINANCIAL DATA:

Note: Data for latest year may not have been available at press time.

In U.S. $	2017	2016	2015	2014	2013	2012
Revenue						
R&D Expense						
Operating Income						
Operating Margin %						
SGA Expense						
Net Income						
Operating Cash Flow						
Capital Expenditure						
EBITDA						
Return on Assets %						
Return on Equity %						
Debt to Equity						

CONTACT INFORMATION:

Phone: 215-955-6000 Fax:
Toll-Free:
Address: 111 South 11th St., Philadelphia, PA 19107 United States

STOCK TICKER/OTHER:

Stock Ticker: Nonprofit
Employees: 9,500
Parent Company:
Exchange:
Fiscal Year Ends:

SALARIES/BONUSES:

Top Exec. Salary: $ Bonus: $
Second Exec. Salary: $ Bonus: $

OTHER THOUGHTS:

Estimated Female Officers or Directors:
Hot Spot for Advancement for Women/Minorities:

Thoratec Corporation

www.thoratec.com

NAIC Code: 339,100

TYPES OF BUSINESS:

Medical Equipment-Ventricular Assistance Devices
Medical Equipment-Ventricular Assistance Devices
Circulatory Support Products
Vascular Graft Products

BRANDS/DIVISIONS/AFFILIATES:

Abbott Laboratories
Thoratec Paracorporeal Ventricular Assist Device
Thoratec Implantable Ventricular Assist Device
HeartMate
Thoratec HeartMate PHP
CentriMag Acute Circulatory System
PediVAS

CONTACTS: *Note: Officers with more than one job title may be intentionally listed here more than once.*

D. Keith Grossman, CEO
Taylor Harris, CFO
Neil Meyer, Other Corporate Officer
Niamh Pellegrini, President, Geographical
David Lehman, Secretary
Vasant Padmanabhan, Senior VP, Divisional

GROWTH PLANS/SPECIAL FEATURES:

Thoratec Corporation is a global manufacturer of mechanical circulatory support products for the treatment of heart failure. Thoratec's primary cardiovascular product lines are its ventricular assist devices (VADs), which may be placed inside or outside the body; can be used for left, right or biventricular support; and are suitable for patients of varying sizes and ages. VADs consist of FDA-approved and CE Mark-approved products: the Thoratec Paracorporeal Ventricular Assist Device, the Thoratec Implantable Ventricular Assist Device, and the HeartMate line of left ventricular assist systems (LVAS). Commercially available in Europe only, Thoratec HeartMate PHP (percutaneous heart pump) is designed to provide hemodynamic left ventricular support. Thoratec also markets the CentriMag Acute Circulatory System for acute circulatory support, PediMag and PediVAS pediatric surgical support systems and PVAD external pulsatile devices. Collectively, the firm's mechanical circulatory support devices are FDA-approved for bridge-to-transplant, long-term support for patients suffering from advanced-stage heart failure who are not eligible for heart transplantation, post-cardiotomy myocardial recovery and support during cardiac surgery. Thoratec estimates that doctors have implanted more than 20,000 of its devices, primarily for patients awaiting a heart transplant or those who require permanent support. Headquartered in Pleasanton, California, Thoratec has facilities in Massachusetts, California and Michigan, domestically, as well as in the U.K and Switzerland, internationally. Thoratec operates as a wholly-owned subsidiary of Abbott Laboratories.

FINANCIAL DATA: *Note: Data for latest year may not have been available at press time.*

In U.S. $	2017	2016	2015	2014	2013	2012
Revenue	550,200,000	524,000,000	514,800,000	477,560,000	502,820,992	491,654,016
R&D Expense						
Operating Income						
Operating Margin %						
SGA Expense						
Net Income				50,391,000	73,326,000	56,163,000
Operating Cash Flow						
Capital Expenditure						
EBITDA						
Return on Assets %						
Return on Equity %						
Debt to Equity						

CONTACT INFORMATION:

Phone: 925 847-8600 Fax: 925 847-8574
Toll-Free: 800-456-1477
Address: 6035 Stoneridge Dr., Pleasanton, CA 94588 United States

STOCK TICKER/OTHER:

Stock Ticker: Subsidiary
Exchange:
Employees: 1,000
Fiscal Year Ends: 12/31
Parent Company: Abbott Laboratories

SALARIES/BONUSES:

Top Exec. Salary: $ Bonus: $
Second Exec. Salary: $ Bonus: $

OTHER THOUGHTS:

Estimated Female Officers or Directors:
Hot Spot for Advancement for Women/Minorities:

Tivity Health Inc

www.tivityhealth.com/

NAIC Code: 524298A

TYPES OF BUSINESS:

Disease Management Programs
Ambulatory Surgery Centers
Arthritis Care
Osteoporosis Care
Cardiac Disease Management Services
Respiratory Disease Management Services
Online Disease Management
Outsourced Diabetes Treatment Programs

BRANDS/DIVISIONS/AFFILIATES:

SilverSneakers
Prime
WholeHealth Living

CONTACTS: *Note: Officers with more than one job title may be intentionally listed here more than once.*

Donato Tramuto, CEO
Adam Holland, CFO
Kevin Wills, Chairman of the Board
Glenn Hargreaves, Chief Accounting Officer
Mary Flipse, Other Executive Officer

GROWTH PLANS/SPECIAL FEATURES:

Tivity Health, Inc. provides fitness and health improvement programs targeted for people aged 50 and older. The company offers three programs: SilverSneakers fitness, Prime fitness and WholeHealth Living. SilverSneakers is a senior fitness program offered to members of Medicare Advantage, Medicare Supplement and group retiree plans. Prime fitness is a fitness facility program provided through commercial health plans, employers and insurance exchanges. Tivity's national network of fitness centers delivers both SilverSneakers and Prime fitness, and encompass about 16,000 locations as well as 1,000 alternative locations that provide classes outside of traditional fitness centers. The WholeHealth Living program is primarily sold to commercial health plans. Its network includes over 80,000 complementary, alternative and physical medicine practitioners to serve individuals through health plans and employers who seek health services such as physical therapy, occupational therapy, speech therapy, chiropractic care, acupuncture and more. Tivity's primary customers include Humana, Inc. and United Healthcare, Inc., each of which comprised more than 10% (and together comprised about 38%) of 2017 revenues.

FINANCIAL DATA: *Note: Data for latest year may not have been available at press time.*

In U.S. $	2017	2016	2015	2014	2013	2012
Revenue	556,942,000	500,998,000	770,598,000	742,183,000	663,285,000	677,170,000
R&D Expense						
Operating Income	123,619,000	100,315,000	16,692,000	7,433,000	1,902,000	30,668,000
Operating Margin %	22.19%	20.02%	2.16%	1.00%	.28%	4.52%
SGA Expense	34,361,000	39,478,000	68,142,000	83,092,000	61,205,000	60,888,000
Net Income	63,715,000	-129,111,000	-30,947,000	-5,561,000	-8,541,000	8,024,000
Operating Cash Flow	105,276,000	37,902,000	60,960,000	52,098,000	71,528,000	40,698,000
Capital Expenditure	5,910,000	14,474,000	34,730,000	42,991,000	41,346,000	48,912,000
EBITDA	123,753,000	126,674,000	33,094,000	60,811,000	54,693,000	80,629,000
Return on Assets %	10.79%	-20.46%	-4.04%	-.71%	-1.14%	1.10%
Return on Equity %	27.62%	-55.03%	-10.58%	-1.83%	-2.93%	2.94%
Debt to Equity		0.86	0.75	0.75	0.78	0.99

CONTACT INFORMATION:

Phone: 615 614-4929 Fax: 615 665-7697
Toll-Free: 800-869-5311
Address: 701 Cool Springs Blvd., Franklin, TN 37067 United States

STOCK TICKER/OTHER:

Stock Ticker: TVTY
Employees: 500
Parent Company:
Exchange: NAS
Fiscal Year Ends: 12/31

SALARIES/BONUSES:

Top Exec. Salary: $850,000 Bonus: $
Second Exec. Salary: $354,288 Bonus: $

OTHER THOUGHTS:

Estimated Female Officers or Directors: 1
Hot Spot for Advancement for Women/Minorities:

TLC Vision Corporation

www.tlcvision.com

NAIC Code: 621,493

TYPES OF BUSINESS:

Eye Clinics
Laser Vision Correction Services
Blood Filtration Equipment
Management Software & Systems

BRANDS/DIVISIONS/AFFILIATES:

Charlesbank Capital Partners LLC
HIG Capital LLC
TLC Laser Eye Centers
Sightpath Medical LLC
TruVision Health LLC

CONTACTS:
Note: Officers with more than one job title may be intentionally listed here more than once.

George Neal, CEO
Jonathan Compton, Dir.-Taxation
Ellen-Jo E. Plass, Pres

GROWTH PLANS/SPECIAL FEATURES:

TLC Vision Corporation provides eye care services, primarily laser refractive surgery. This surgery involves using an excimer laser to treat common refractive vision disorders such as myopia (nearsightedness), hyperopia (farsightedness) and astigmatism by reshaping the cornea of the eye. The majority of the company's excimer lasers are manufactured by VISX, which is a subsidiary of Abbott Medical Optics, itself a subsidiary of Johnson & Johnson. TLC physicians use excimer lasers to perform refractive, cataract and optometric surgery. The vast majority of procedures performed at the company's TLC Laser Eye Centers are LASIK (laser-assisted-in-situ keratomileusis) treatments. Also, through its Sightpath Medical, LLC subsidiary, the company furnishes hospitals and other facilities with mobile or fixed-site access to cataract surgery equipment, supplies and technicians. TruVision Health, LLC is a managed care contractor for elective healthcare services. TLC Vision is owned by private equity firms Charlesbank Capital Partners, LLC and H.I.G. Capital, LLC.

FINANCIAL DATA:
Note: Data for latest year may not have been available at press time.

In U.S. $	2017	2016	2015	2014	2013	2012
Revenue	210,000,000	200,000,000	200,000,000	230,200,000	250,000,000	240,000,000
R&D Expense						
Operating Income						
Operating Margin %						
SGA Expense						
Net Income						
Operating Cash Flow						
Capital Expenditure						
EBITDA						
Return on Assets %						
Return on Equity %						
Debt to Equity						

CONTACT INFORMATION:

Phone: 905-602-2020 Fax: 905-602-2025
Toll-Free: 800-852-1033
Address: 5280 Solar Dr., Ste. 300, Mississauga, ON L4W 5M8 Canada

STOCK TICKER/OTHER:

Stock Ticker: Private
Exchange:
Employees: 800
Fiscal Year Ends: 12/31
Parent Company: Charlesbank Capital Partners LLC

SALARIES/BONUSES:

Top Exec. Salary: $ Bonus: $
Second Exec. Salary: $ Bonus: $

OTHER THOUGHTS:

Estimated Female Officers or Directors: 2
Hot Spot for Advancement for Women/Minorities:

Toho Holdings Co Ltd

www.tohohd.co.jp/

NAIC Code: 424,210

TYPES OF BUSINESS:

Drugs and Druggists' Sundries Merchant Wholesalers
Pharmaceuticals

BRANDS/DIVISIONS/AFFILIATES:

Kyoso Mirai Group
Kyosomirai Pharma Co Ltd
Toho Pharmaceutical Co Ltd
PharmaCluster Co Ltd
Tokyo Research Center of Clinical Pharmacology

CONTACTS: *Note: Officers with more than one job title may be intentionally listed here more than once.*

Katsuya Kato, Pres.
Norio Hamada, Chmn.

GROWTH PLANS/SPECIAL FEATURES:

Toho Holdings Co., Ltd. is a Japan-based company engaged in the manufacture, wholesale, sale and dispensing of pharmaceuticals. Subsidiary Kyosomirai Pharma Co., Ltd. manufactures and sells prescription pharmaceuticals, with a focus on generic drugs. Kyosomirai also manufactures prescription pharmaceuticals for third-parties on a contract basis. Toho Pharmaceutical Co., Ltd. is a pharmaceutical wholesaling company, which distributes the sale of pharmaceutical products to retailers, medical institutions and other related customers. The company offers a fully-automated logistics system and utilizes advanced robot technology for picking and loading, all of which result in a shipment accuracy of 99.99%. PharmaCluster Co., Ltd. is a dispensing pharmacy management company serving home and retail pharmacies engaged in the healthcare sector. In addition, Tokyo Research Center of Clinical Pharmacology Co., Ltd. is a site management organization owned by Toho Holdings that assists certain medical institutions with clinical trials under contract. Toho Holdings is part of the Kyoso Mirai Group of companies.

FINANCIAL DATA: *Note: Data for latest year may not have been available at press time.*

In U.S. $	2017	2016	2015	2014	2013	2012
Revenue	11,062,800,000	11,632,600,000	9,713,370,000	11,569,900,000	12,098,900,000	
R&D Expense						
Operating Income						
Operating Margin %						
SGA Expense						
Net Income	127,833,000	193,548,000	113,127,000	101,215,000	122,287,000	
Operating Cash Flow						
Capital Expenditure						
EBITDA						
Return on Assets %						
Return on Equity %						
Debt to Equity						

CONTACT INFORMATION:

Phone: 81 334197811 Fax: 81 334146042
Toll-Free:
Address: 5-2-1, Daizawa, Setagaya-ku, Tokyo, 155-8655 Japan

STOCK TICKER/OTHER:

Stock Ticker: 8129
Employees:
Parent Company: Kyoso Mirai Group
Exchange: Tokyo
Fiscal Year Ends: 03/31

SALARIES/BONUSES:

Top Exec. Salary: $ Bonus: $
Second Exec. Salary: $ Bonus: $

OTHER THOUGHTS:

Estimated Female Officers or Directors:
Hot Spot for Advancement for Women/Minorities:

TransEnterix Inc

www.transenterix.com

NAIC Code: 334,510

TYPES OF BUSINESS:

Electromedical and Electrotherapeutic Apparatus Manufacturing

BRANDS/DIVISIONS/AFFILIATES:

Senhance Surgical System

CONTACTS: *Note: Officers with more than one job title may be intentionally listed here more than once.*

Todd Pope, CEO
Joseph Slattery, CFO
Paul Laviolette, Chairman of the Board
Anthony Fernando, COO

GROWTH PLANS/SPECIAL FEATURES:

TransEnterix, Inc. is a medical device company that is pioneering the use of robotics to improve minimally invasive surgery by addressing the clinical challenges associated with current laparoscopic and robotic options. The firm is focused on the commercialization and further development of the Senhance Surgical System (Senhance System), which digitizes laparoscopic minimally invasive surgery. The Senhance System is a multi-port robotic surgery system which allows multiple robotic arms to control instruments and a camera. The Senhance System features advanced technology that gives surgeons haptic feedback and the ability to move the camera via eye movement. The system replicates laparoscopic motion that is familiar to experienced surgeons and integrates three-dimensional high definition (3DHD) vision technology. The Senhance System also offers responsible economics to hospitals by offering robotic technology with reusable instruments thereby reducing additional costs per surgery when compared to laparoscopy. In December 2017, the firm announced that it had entered into an agreement with Great Belief International Limited (GBIL) to advance the SurgiBot System, a single-port, robotically enhanced laparoscopic surgical platform, towards global commercialization, the agreement transfers ownership of the SurgiBot System assets to GBIL.

FINANCIAL DATA: *Note: Data for latest year may not have been available at press time.*

In U.S. $	2017	2016	2015	2014	2013	2012
Revenue	7,111,000	1,519,000		401,000	1,431,000	35,000
R&D Expense	21,989,000	29,273,000	29,669,000	27,944,000	12,700,000	2,916,000
Operating Income	-59,274,000	-55,754,000	-42,540,000	-36,609,000	-22,243,000	-6,655,000
Operating Margin %	-833.55%	-3670.44%		-9129.42%	-1554.36%	-19014.28%
SGA Expense	29,811,000	19,964,000	10,686,000	7,971,000	6,164,000	3,392,000
Net Income	-144,796,000	-119,980,000	-46,948,000	-37,652,000	-28,358,000	-6,724,000
Operating Cash Flow	-39,795,000	-52,386,000	-38,509,000	-33,228,000	-21,236,000	-6,939,000
Capital Expenditure	1,991,000	1,361,000	1,234,000	2,174,000	1,377,000	29,000
EBITDA	-48,930,000	-46,845,000	-39,107,000	-35,299,000	-20,760,000	-6,502,000
Return on Assets %	-67.89%	-56.48%	-24.46%	-29.89%	-47.60%	-394.02%
Return on Equity %	-97.59%	-81.30%	-31.39%	-33.20%	-53.87%	
Debt to Equity	0.04	0.04	0.07	0.07	0.04	

CONTACT INFORMATION:

Phone: 919 765-8400 Fax: 919 765-8459
Toll-Free:
Address: 635 Davis Drive, Morrisville, NC 27560 United States

STOCK TICKER/OTHER:

Stock Ticker: TRXC
Exchange: ASE
Employees: 104
Fiscal Year Ends: 12/31
Parent Company:

SALARIES/BONUSES:

Top Exec. Salary: $466,796 Bonus: $
Second Exec. Salary: $334,184 Bonus: $

OTHER THOUGHTS:

Estimated Female Officers or Directors:
Hot Spot for Advancement for Women/Minorities:

Trinity Health

www.trinity-health.org

NAIC Code: 622,110

TYPES OF BUSINESS:

General Medical and Surgical Hospitals
Assisted Living Facilities
Hospice Programs
Senior Housing Communities
Management & Consulting Services

BRANDS/DIVISIONS/AFFILIATES:

Senior Emergency Departments

CONTACTS:

Note: Officers with more than one job title may be intentionally listed here more than once.

Richard J. Gilfillan, CEO
Michael A. Slubowski, Pres.
Benjamin R. Carter, CFO
Edmund F. Hodge, Chief Human Resource Officer
P. Terrence O'Rourke, Exec. VP-Clinical Transformation
Benjamin R. Carter, Exec. VP-Finance
James Bosscher, Chief Investment Officer
Paul Conlon, Sr. VP-Clinical Quality & Patient Safety
Rebecca Havlisch, Chief Nursing Officer
Louis Fierens, Sr. VP-Supply Chain & Capital Projects Mgmt.

GROWTH PLANS/SPECIAL FEATURES:

Trinity Health is one of the nation's largest multi-institutional Catholic health care delivery systems, serving patients and communities in 22 states. Trinity Health operates 94 hospitals and 122 continuing care facilities, which include home care, hospice, PACE (explained below) and senior living facilities. The organization returns approximately $1 billion to its communities annually in the form of charity care and other community benefits programs. Trinity Health is known for its focus on the country's aging population, and is the innovator of Senior Emergency Departments, the largest non-profit provider of home healthcare services in the nation. The firm is a leading provider of PACE, which stands for Program of All-inclusive Care for the Elderly. Other services offered by the company include a military and veterans health program, research activities and supply chain management solutions.

The firm offers employees health and dental coverage, short- and long-term disability, paid time-off, life insurance, flexible spending accounts, 403(b) and 401(k) plans, tuition reimbursement and professional education as well as adoption assistance.

FINANCIAL DATA:

Note: Data for latest year may not have been available at press time.

In U.S. $	2017	2016	2015	2014	2013	2012
Revenue	17,627,845,000	16,339,047,000	14,388,150,000	13,600,000,000	13,293,723,000	12,480,453,000
R&D Expense						
Operating Income						
Operating Margin %						
SGA Expense						
Net Income	1,336,823,000	89,803,000	671,630,000	951,405,000	666,439,000	492,910,000
Operating Cash Flow						
Capital Expenditure						
EBITDA						
Return on Assets %						
Return on Equity %						
Debt to Equity						

CONTACT INFORMATION:

Phone: 734-343-1000 Fax:
Toll-Free:
Address: 20555 Victor Parkway, Livonia, MI 48152-7018 United States

STOCK TICKER/OTHER:

Stock Ticker: Nonprofit
Employees: 97,000
Parent Company:
Exchange:
Fiscal Year Ends: 06/30

SALARIES/BONUSES:

Top Exec. Salary: $ Bonus: $
Second Exec. Salary: $ Bonus: $

OTHER THOUGHTS:

Estimated Female Officers or Directors: 4
Hot Spot for Advancement for Women/Minorities: Y

Trustmark Companies

www.trustmarkins.com

NAIC Code: 524,113

TYPES OF BUSINESS:

Life Insurance
Health Insurance
Employee Benefits Management

BRANDS/DIVISIONS/AFFILIATES:

CoreSource
Starmark
HealthFitness Corporation

CONTACTS: *Note: Officers with more than one job title may be intentionally listed here more than once.*

Joseph L. Pray, CEO
Phil Goss, CFO
Jim Coleman, CMO
Krsitin Zelkowitz, Chief Human Resources Officer
Bradley Bodell, CIO

GROWTH PLANS/SPECIAL FEATURES:

Trustmark Companies offer health and life insurance and benefits administration services to employer groups through three major operating subsidiaries. These subsidiaries include CoreSource, Starmark and HealthFitness Corporation. CoreSource is one of the nation's largest employee benefit administrators, managing health care for over 1.1 million people across the U.S. It serves self-insured employers with claims administration, case management, provider network development, information management, fraud detection, COBRA administration and prescription-drug benefit administration. Starmark serves the health and life insurance needs of employers for smaller businesses with 2 to 99 employees. HealthFitness offers onsite and web-based workplace programs that help improve employee health and fitness. HealthFitness programs include medical screenings, risk assessment, corporate fitness, health management and coaching. In total, Trustmark Companies has over 2 million covered plan participants.

FINANCIAL DATA: *Note: Data for latest year may not have been available at press time.*

In U.S. $	2017	2016	2015	2014	2013	2012
Revenue	842,777,548	863,274,682	882,683,041	917,505,556	947,327,068	932,700,000
R&D Expense						
Operating Income						
Operating Margin %						
SGA Expense						
Net Income	24,801,418	18,966,519	8,645,781	11,716,081	29,017,258	
Operating Cash Flow						
Capital Expenditure						
EBITDA						
Return on Assets %						
Return on Equity %						
Debt to Equity						

CONTACT INFORMATION:

Phone: 847-615-1500 Fax: 847-615-3910
Toll-Free:
Address: 400 Field Dr., Lake Forest, IL 60045 United States

STOCK TICKER/OTHER:

Stock Ticker: Mutual Company Exchange:
Employees: 4,150 Fiscal Year Ends: 12/31
Parent Company:

SALARIES/BONUSES:

Top Exec. Salary: $ Bonus: $
Second Exec. Salary: $ Bonus: $

OTHER THOUGHTS:

Estimated Female Officers or Directors:
Hot Spot for Advancement for Women/Minorities: Y

Tufts Associated Health Plans Inc

www.tuftshealthplan.com

NAIC Code: 524,114

TYPES OF BUSINESS:

Insurance-Medical & Health, HMOs & PPOs
Administrative Services

BRANDS/DIVISIONS/AFFILIATES:

ConnectorCare

CONTACTS: *Note: Officers with more than one job title may be intentionally listed here more than once.*

Thomas A. Croswell, CEO
Tricia Trebina, COO
James Roosevelt, Jr., Pres.
Maurice Hebert, CFO
Marc Backon, Pres.-Commercial Products
Lydia Greene, Sr. VP-Chief Human Resources
Paul Kasuba, Chief Medical Officer
Patty Blake, Sr. VP-Senior Products
Lois Dehis Cornell, General Counsel
Tricia Trebino, Sr. VP-Oper.
Brian P. Pagliaro, Sr. VP-Client Svcs.
Tracey Carter, Chief Actuary
Marc Spooner, Sr. VP- Health Care Svcs.
Christina Severin, Sr. VP-Tufts Health Plan

GROWTH PLANS/SPECIAL FEATURES:

Tufts Associated Health Plans, Inc. was founded in 1979, and is a not-for-profit health maintenance organization. Tufts offers a broad array of health care coverage options to individuals and employer groups across the life span, regardless of age or circumstance. These products and services include HMO (health maintenance organization) and PPO (preferred provider organization) plans to national, tiered and limited network plans, including commercial, Medicare and Medicaid coverage. For individuals and small groups, Tufts offers two plans: direct, offering low-cost ConnectorCare plans and federal premium tax credits to those who qualify; and premier, offering access to Tuft's standard network. Direct and premier have different networks of doctors, meaning some doctors may be in one network and not the other Tufts also offers an EPO (exclusive provider organization) plan, which is a self-insured version of its HMO plan; a POS (point of service) plan, which is a combination of its traditional HMO model with out-of-network coverage; an HMO coinsurance option for HMO plans with or without a deductible; and an HMO choice co-pay, which is a high-quality managed care plan that is simple to administer. Tufts comprises a national PPO for multi-state employers with 100 or more employees. Its tiered network plans give employers maximum value while encouraging members to choose providers based on cost and quality measures and have lower out-of-pocket costs. The firm's online marketplace allows employers to offer a variety of healthcare benefits to its employees.

The firm offers employees a 401(k) plan; medical, vision, life, disability and dental insurance; employee discounts; flexible spending accounts; adoption assistance; domestic partners insurance; an onsite clinic; an employee referral program; an employee assistance program; a recognition program; vacation; and educational reimbursement.

FINANCIAL DATA: *Note: Data for latest year may not have been available at press time.*

In U.S. $	2017	2016	2015	2014	2013	2012
Revenue	4,700,000,000	4,600,000,000	4,300,000,000	4,200,000,000	4,000,000,000	3,900,000,000
R&D Expense						
Operating Income						
Operating Margin %						
SGA Expense						
Net Income	59,400,000	3,000,000	26,100,000	59,100,000	70,300,000	103,400,000
Operating Cash Flow						
Capital Expenditure						
EBITDA						
Return on Assets %						
Return on Equity %						
Debt to Equity						

CONTACT INFORMATION:

Phone: 617-972-9400 Fax:
Toll-Free:
Address: 705 Mount Auburn St., Watertown, MA 02472 United States

STOCK TICKER/OTHER:

Stock Ticker: Private
Employees: 2,750
Parent Company:
Exchange:
Fiscal Year Ends: 12/31

SALARIES/BONUSES:

Top Exec. Salary: $ Bonus: $
Second Exec. Salary: $ Bonus: $

OTHER THOUGHTS:

Estimated Female Officers or Directors: 5
Hot Spot for Advancement for Women/Minorities: Y

United Surgical Partners International Inc www.unitedsurgical.com

NAIC Code: 621,493

TYPES OF BUSINESS:

Outpatient Surgical Facility Management

BRANDS/DIVISIONS/AFFILIATES:

Tenet Healthcare Corporation

CONTACTS:
Note: Officers with more than one job title may be intentionally listed here more than once.

William H. Wilcox, CEO
Brett P. Brodnax, Pres.
Jason Cagle, CFO
Sandi Karrmann, Chief Human Resources Officer
David Zarin, Sr. VP-Medical Affairs
David Bordofske, CIO
John J. Wellik, Sr. VP-Admin
Jason B. Cagle, General Counsel
Jonathan R. Bond, Sr. VP-Oper.
Brett P. Brodnax, Chief Dev. Officer
Kristin Blewett, Sr. VP-Comm.
Philip A. Spencer, Sr. VP-Bus. Dev.
Monica Cintado, Sr. VP-Dev.
William H. Wilcox, Chmn.

GROWTH PLANS/SPECIAL FEATURES:

United Surgical Partners International, Inc. (USPI) is an ambulatory surgery provider in the U.S. The company's network owns and operates more than 270 ambulatory surgery facilities, 101 urgent care centers and 24 imaging centers, serving 2.5 million patients annually. USPI also pursues strategic relationships with nonprofit hospitals and healthcare systems by allowing them to outsource their non-emergency surgical procedures to the company's facilities. USPI's partners deliver ambulatory solutions in USPI facilities throughout the country, and its more than 9,000 physician partners provide patient care. Therefore, USPI provides the infrastructure and support these partners need to perform their work and duties. USPI operates as a subsidiary of Tenet Healthcare Corporation, a diversified healthcare services company.

The company offers employees a comprehensive benefits package, paid time off, seven holiday paid days per year, a 401(k) plan and education assistance.

FINANCIAL DATA:
Note: Data for latest year may not have been available at press time.

In U.S. $	2017	2016	2015	2014	2013	2012
Revenue	710,000,000	680,000,000	660,000,000	640,824,000	616,231,000	540,235,000
R&D Expense						
Operating Income						
Operating Margin %						
SGA Expense						
Net Income			138,128,000	127,060,000	127,060,000	103,484,000
Operating Cash Flow						
Capital Expenditure						
EBITDA						
Return on Assets %						
Return on Equity %						
Debt to Equity						

CONTACT INFORMATION:

Phone: 972-713-3500 Fax: 972-713-3550
Toll-Free:
Address: 15305 Dallas Pkwy., Ste. 1600, Addison, TX 75001 United States

STOCK TICKER/OTHER:

Stock Ticker: Subsidiary Exchange:
Employees: 6,700 Fiscal Year Ends: 12/31
Parent Company: Tenet Healthcare Corporation

SALARIES/BONUSES:

Top Exec. Salary: $ Bonus: $
Second Exec. Salary: $ Bonus: $

OTHER THOUGHTS:

Estimated Female Officers or Directors: 3
Hot Spot for Advancement for Women/Minorities: Y

UnitedHealth Group Inc

NAIC Code: 524,114

www.unitedhealthgroup.com

TYPES OF BUSINESS:

Medical Insurance
Wellness Plans
Dental & Vision Insurance
Health Information Technology
Physician Practice Groups
Pharmacy Benefits Management
PBM

BRANDS/DIVISIONS/AFFILIATES:

United Healthcare
OptumHealth
OptumInsight
OptumRX
United Healthcare Employer & Individual
DaVita Medical Group
UnitedHealthcare Community & State
Surgical Care Affiliates, Inc.

CONTACTS: *Note: Officers with more than one job title may be intentionally listed here more than once.*

Steven Nelson, CEO, Subsidiary
Larry Renfro, CEO, Subsidiary
David Wichmann, CEO
John Rex, CFO
Stephen Hemsley, Chairman of the Board
Tom Roos, Chief Accounting Officer
D. Wilson, Executive VP, Divisional
Marianne Short, Executive VP

GROWTH PLANS/SPECIAL FEATURES:

UnitedHealth Group, Inc. is a diversified health and insurance firm that serves over 75 million people worldwide. The company provides individuals with access to health care services and resources through approximately 1.2 million physicians and other care providers and 6,500 hospitals across the U.S. The company has four operating segments: UnitedHealthcare, which includes United Healthcare Employer & Individual, UnitedHealthcare Medicare & Retirement and UnitedHealthcare Community & State; OptumHealth; OptumInsight; and OptumRX. The United Healthcare segment provides consumer-oriented health benefit plans and services for large national employers, public sector employers, mid-sized employers, small businesses and individuals nationwide; health and well-being services for individuals age 50 and older; and network-based health services for beneficiaries of government-sponsored health care programs. The OptumHealth segment is engaged in care services, behavioral solutions, specialty benefits and financial services in fields such as dental, vision, disability, therapy and stop-loss coverage. The OptumInsight segment provides technology, operational and consulting services to participants in the health care industry. The OptumRX segment offers a comprehensive suite of integrated pharmacy benefit management (PBM) services to more than 66 million people through over 67,000 retail network pharmacies as well as mail order service facilities. In December 2017, the firm announced that it would purchase 280 clinics, the Davita Medical Group, from DaVita Inc., bringing 280 clinics along with related physicians and other health care employees totaling 2,200 people.

The company offers its employees medical, vision, dental, life and disability insurance; flexible spending accounts; an employee assistance program; a 401(k); adoption assistance; and tuition reimbursement.

FINANCIAL DATA: *Note: Data for latest year may not have been available at press time.*

In U.S. $	2017	2016	2015	2014	2013	2012
Revenue	200,136,000,000	184,012,000,000	156,397,000,000	129,695,000,000	121,744,000,000	109,938,000,000
R&D Expense						
Operating Income	14,186,000,000	12,102,000,000	10,311,000,000	9,495,000,000	8,878,000,000	8,574,000,000
Operating Margin %	7.56%	6.99%	7.01%	7.87%	7.85%	8.36%
SGA Expense	29,557,000,000	28,401,000,000	24,312,000,000	21,681,000,000	19,362,000,000	17,306,000,000
Net Income	10,558,000,000	7,017,000,000	5,813,000,000	5,619,000,000	5,625,000,000	5,526,000,000
Operating Cash Flow	13,596,000,000	9,795,000,000	9,740,000,000	8,051,000,000	6,991,000,000	7,155,000,000
Capital Expenditure	2,023,000,000	1,705,000,000	1,556,000,000	1,525,000,000	1,307,000,000	1,070,000,000
EBITDA	17,454,000,000	14,985,000,000	12,714,000,000	11,752,000,000	10,998,000,000	10,563,000,000
Return on Assets %	8.06%	5.99%	5.87%	6.67%	6.91%	7.42%
Return on Equity %	24.53%	19.46%	17.53%	17.39%	17.76%	18.58%
Debt to Equity	0.60	0.67	0.75	0.49	0.46	0.45

CONTACT INFORMATION:

Phone: 952 936-1300 Fax: 952 936-0044
Toll-Free: 800-328-5979
Address: 9900 Bren Rd. E., Minnetonka, MN 55343 United States

STOCK TICKER/OTHER:

Stock Ticker: UNH Exchange: NYS
Employees: 230,000 Fiscal Year Ends: 12/31
Parent Company:

SALARIES/BONUSES:

Top Exec. Salary: $1,206,538 Bonus: $
Second Exec. Salary: $1,162,308 Bonus: $

OTHER THOUGHTS:

Estimated Female Officers or Directors: 4
Hot Spot for Advancement for Women/Minorities: Y

UnitedHealthcare Community & State

www.uhccommunityandstate.com

NAIC Code: 524,114

TYPES OF BUSINESS:

Insurance-Medical & Health, HMOs & PPOs

BRANDS/DIVISIONS/AFFILIATES:

UnitedHealth Group Inc

CONTACTS:

Note: Officers with more than one job title may be intentionally listed here more than once.

Heather Cianfrocco, CEO
Rashmita Mistry, COO
Jean Benson, CFO
Steven Cragle, CMO
Amy Adlington, VP-Human Resources
Kevin Smith, Chief Medical Officer
Bill Hagan, West Region Pres.
Jim Donovan, Sr. VP-Bus. Dev.
John Cosgriff, Chief of Staff
Bror Hultgren, Central Region Pres.
Steve Meeker, Southwest Region Pres.
Heather Cianfrocco, Northeast Region Pres.

GROWTH PLANS/SPECIAL FEATURES:

UnitedHealthcare Community & State (UHCS), a division of UnitedHealth Group, Inc., is a health benefits company. UHCS provides diversified solutions to the economically disadvantaged, the medically underserved and those without the benefit of employer-funded health care coverage. The company helps states and communities serve the impoverished via clinical care, prevention initiatives, food delivery, transportation and educational programs. Products offered include temporary assistance for needy families (TANF), children's health insurance program (CHIP), ABD programs (aged, blind and disabled), long-term services/support, dual special needs plans and more. UHCS participates in programs in 25 U.S. states, as well as in Washington D.C., and serves more than 6 million beneficiaries.

Employee benefits include medical, vision and dental coverage; flexible spending accounts; life insurance; short- and long-term disability; an employee stock purchase plan; 401(k); an employee assistance program; volunteer support; tuition reimbursement; and adoption assistance.

FINANCIAL DATA:

Note: Data for latest year may not have been available at press time.

In U.S. $	2017	2016	2015	2014	2013	2012
Revenue	31,000,000,000	29,500,000,000	29,000,000,000	23,600,000,000	12,500,000,000	14,000,000,000
R&D Expense						
Operating Income						
Operating Margin %						
SGA Expense						
Net Income						
Operating Cash Flow						
Capital Expenditure						
EBITDA						
Return on Assets %						
Return on Equity %						
Debt to Equity						

CONTACT INFORMATION:

Phone: 703-506-3555 Fax: 703-506-3556
Toll-Free:
Address: 8045 Leesburg Pike, 6/Fl, Vienna, VA 22182 United States

STOCK TICKER/OTHER:

Stock Ticker: Subsidiary
Exchange:
Employees: 3,535
Fiscal Year Ends: 12/31
Parent Company: UnitedHealth Group Inc

SALARIES/BONUSES:

Top Exec. Salary: $ Bonus: $
Second Exec. Salary: $ Bonus: $

OTHER THOUGHTS:

Estimated Female Officers or Directors: 3
Hot Spot for Advancement for Women/Minorities: Y

UnitedHealthcare National Accounts www.uhc.com/employer/national-accounts

NAIC Code: 524,292

TYPES OF BUSINESS:

Employee Benefits Management
Electronic Billing & Payment Systems
Consulting Services

BRANDS/DIVISIONS/AFFILIATES:

UnitedHealth Group Inc
Bridge2Health

CONTACTS:
Note: Officers with more than one job title may be intentionally listed here more than once.

Elizabeth Winsor, CEO
Alison Richards, Sr. VP-Strategic Initiatives
Steve Burdick, Sr. VP-Specialty Client Group
Tom Elliott, Sr. VP-Client Rel.
John Ryan, Sr. VP
John Cravero, Sr. VP-Nat'l Client Oper.
Shawn Mobley, Sr. VP-Client Dev.

GROWTH PLANS/SPECIAL FEATURES:

UnitedHealthcare National Accounts, a subsidiary of UnitedHealth Group, Inc., provides healthcare benefits management, as well as a variety of services such as administration, consulting, technology and outsourcing. The company is one of the few in the health benefits industry to focus on large employers, specializing in solutions for clients with more than 3,000 employees in multiple locations. The firm offers UnitedHealth products under the following categories: medical solutions, offering network solutions to meet the needs of all employers, including PPO, premium tiered plans, Centers of Excellence for complex and common conditions, ACO product, narrow network products and more; consumer-driven health plans, in which employers can choose between funding options to help employees pay for and manage their healthcare expenses; health, wellness and behavioral health solutions; pharmacy benefits management; ancillary and specialty benefits, including dental, vision, critical illness and accident insurance; Bridge2Health, the firm's integrated approach to employee benefits; and retiree solutions. UnitedHealthcare National Accounts' services include digital access via online tools and mobile apps for viewing/printing ID cards, researching benefits, finding providers, comparing price points, reviewing/paying claims and engaging in wellness programs.

The firm offers employees medical, vision and dental coverage; spending accounts, including a flexible spending account, dependent care account and commuter reimbursement account; life insurance; tuition reimbursement; and an adoption assistance plan.

FINANCIAL DATA:
Note: Data for latest year may not have been available at press time.

In U.S. $	2017	2016	2015	2014	2013	2012
Revenue						
R&D Expense						
Operating Income						
Operating Margin %						
SGA Expense						
Net Income						
Operating Cash Flow						
Capital Expenditure						
EBITDA						
Return on Assets %						
Return on Equity %						
Debt to Equity						

CONTACT INFORMATION:

Phone: 860-702-5000 Fax: 860-702-9830
Toll-Free: 800-328-5979
Address: 185 Asylum St., Hartford, CT 06103 United States

STOCK TICKER/OTHER:

Stock Ticker: Subsidiary
Exchange:
Employees: 3,000
Fiscal Year Ends: 12/31
Parent Company: UnitedHealth Group Inc

SALARIES/BONUSES:

Top Exec. Salary: $ Bonus: $
Second Exec. Salary: $ Bonus: $

OTHER THOUGHTS:

Estimated Female Officers or Directors: 3
Hot Spot for Advancement for Women/Minorities: Y

Universal Health Services Inc

www.uhsinc.com

NAIC Code: 622,110

TYPES OF BUSINESS:

General Medical and Surgical Hospitals
Radiation Oncology Centers
Behavioral Health Hospitals
Surgical Hospitals
Administrative Services
Physician Recruitment
Facilities Planning

BRANDS/DIVISIONS/AFFILIATES:

Danshell Group (The)

CONTACTS: *Note: Officers with more than one job title may be intentionally listed here more than once.*

Alan Miller, CEO
Steve Filton, CFO
Marc Miller, Director
Marvin Pember, Executive VP
Debra Osteen, Executive VP

GROWTH PLANS/SPECIAL FEATURES:

Universal Health Services, Inc. (UHS) owns and operates through its subsidiaries acute care hospitals, outpatient facilities and behavioral healthcare facilities. UHS owns and/or operates 326 inpatient acute care and behavioral health facilities and 32 outpatient and other facilities located in the U.S., the U.K., Puerto Rico and the U.S. Virgin Islands. Among the acute care facilities in the U.S., 26 are inpatient acute care hospitals, four are free-standing emergency departments, four are outpatient surgery/cancer care centers and one is a surgical hospital. Among the behavioral healthcare facilities: the U.S. comprises 188 inpatient and 20 outpatient facilities; the U.K. comprises 108 inpatient and two outpatient facilities; and Puerto Rico and U.S. Virgin Islands comprise four inpatient and one outpatient facilities. In July 2018, UHS acquired The Danshell Group, adding 25 facilities with a total 288 beds in the U.K. for learning disability and autism services.

The company offers its employees medical, dental, vision, life, AD&D and disability insurance; coverage availability for blended families; family and caregiving support; wellness support; a savings plan; an employee stock purchase plan; and flexible spending accounts.

FINANCIAL DATA: *Note: Data for latest year may not have been available at press time.*

In U.S. $	2017	2016	2015	2014	2013	2012
Revenue	10,409,870,000	9,766,210,000	9,043,451,000	8,065,326,000	7,283,822,000	6,961,400,000
R&D Expense						
Operating Income	1,280,178,000	1,276,072,000	1,243,580,000	1,071,574,000	954,439,000	941,713,000
Operating Margin %	12.29%	13.06%	13.75%	13.28%	13.10%	13.52%
SGA Expense	103,127,000	97,324,000	94,973,000	93,993,000	97,758,000	94,885,000
Net Income	752,303,000	702,409,000	680,528,000	545,343,000	510,733,000	443,446,000
Operating Cash Flow	1,182,581,000	1,288,474,000	1,020,898,000	1,035,876,000	884,241,000	815,271,000
Capital Expenditure	557,506,000	519,939,000	379,321,000	391,150,000	358,493,000	363,192,000
EBITDA	1,716,807,000	1,681,473,000	1,640,952,000	1,405,003,000	1,317,607,000	1,203,621,000
Return on Assets %	7.13%	7.03%	7.31%	6.30%	6.18%	5.58%
Return on Equity %	15.79%	15.98%	17.03%	15.60%	17.11%	17.68%
Debt to Equity	0.70	0.88	0.79	0.85	0.98	1.37

CONTACT INFORMATION:

Phone: 610 768-3300 Fax: 610 768-3336
Toll-Free:
Address: 367 S. Gulph Rd., King Of Prussia, PA 19406 United States

STOCK TICKER/OTHER:

Stock Ticker: UHS Exchange: NYS
Employees: 62,230 Fiscal Year Ends: 12/31
Parent Company:

SALARIES/BONUSES:

Top Exec. Salary: $1,635,063 Bonus: $
Second Exec. Salary: $752,216 Bonus: $

OTHER THOUGHTS:

Estimated Female Officers or Directors: 2
Hot Spot for Advancement for Women/Minorities: Y

Universal Hospital Services Inc

www.uhs.com

NAIC Code: 532,490

TYPES OF BUSINESS:

Medical Equipment Rental and Services
Technical & Professional Services
Medical Equipment Sales & Remarketing

BRANDS/DIVISIONS/AFFILIATES:

UHS Holdco Inc
Agiliti Inc

CONTACTS:

Note: Officers with more than one job title may be intentionally listed here more than once.

Tom Leonard, CEO
Kevin Ketzel, Pres.
Jim Pekarek, CFO
Daniel Lucas, VP-Prod. Dev. & Mktg.
Lee Pulju, General Counsel
Timothy Kuck, Exec. VP-Bus. Dev. & Strategy
Susan Wolf, VP-Finance
Phil Zelle, VP-Oper., East Region
Debbie Norman, VP-Oper., West Region
Steve Heintze, Sr. VP-Specialty Sales

GROWTH PLANS/SPECIAL FEATURES:

Universal Hospital Services, Inc. (UHS) is a nationwide provider of health care technology management and service solutions. UHS owns or manages more than 800,000 units of medical equipment for approximately 7,000 national, regional and local acute care hospitals and alternate site providers throughout the U.S. The company has delivered medical equipment management and service solutions for nearly 80 years, all of which help clients reduce costs, increase operating efficiencies, improve caregiver satisfaction and support optimal patient outcomes. UHS' services include equipment management, medical equipment rental, clinical engineering, on-site management, surgical services and manufacture services. Medical equipment covers the fields of bariatrics, beds, therapy surfaces, critical care, early mobility, fall prevention, infusion therapy, maternal/infant care, patient monitoring, respiratory therapy, safe patient handling, surgical lasers, surgical equipment and wound care management. UHS is privately-held by UHS Holdco, Inc. In August 2018, parent UHS Holdco agreed to merge UHS with Federal Street Acquisition Corp. (FSAC) pursuant to forming a new, publicly-traded company called Agiliti, Inc.

FINANCIAL DATA:

Note: Data for latest year may not have been available at press time.

In U.S. $	2017	2016	2015	2014	2013	2012
Revenue	514,783,000	479,501,000	448,681,000	436,664,000	428,440,000	415,326,000
R&D Expense						
Operating Income						
Operating Margin %						
SGA Expense						
Net Income	8,828,000	-13,760,000	-28,648,000	-66,517,000	-43,037,000	-35,198,000
Operating Cash Flow						
Capital Expenditure						
EBITDA						
Return on Assets %						
Return on Equity %						
Debt to Equity						

CONTACT INFORMATION:

Phone: 952-893-3200 Fax: 952-893-0704
Toll-Free: 800-847-7368
Address: 6625 W. 78th St., Ste. 300, Minneapolis, MN 55439 United States

STOCK TICKER/OTHER:

Stock Ticker: Private
Employees: 2,892
Parent Company: UHS Holdco Inc
Exchange:
Fiscal Year Ends: 12/31

SALARIES/BONUSES:

Top Exec. Salary: $ Bonus: $
Second Exec. Salary: $ Bonus: $

OTHER THOUGHTS:

Estimated Female Officers or Directors: 3
Hot Spot for Advancement for Women/Minorities: Y

UPMC

www.upmc.com

NAIC Code: 622,110

TYPES OF BUSINESS:

General Medical and Surgical Hospitals

BRANDS/DIVISIONS/AFFILIATES:

UPMC Cancer Center
UPMC International
UPMC Enterprises

CONTACTS: *Note: Officers with more than one job title may be intentionally listed here more than once.*

Jeffrey Romoff, CEO

GROWTH PLANS/SPECIAL FEATURES:

UPMC (University of Pittsburgh Medical Center) is a non-profit healthcare provider and insurer, and is engaged in inventing new models of cost-effective, patient-centered care. UPMC operates more than 35 academic, community and specialty hospitals; 600 doctor's offices and outpatient sites; and offers an array of rehabilitation, retirement and long-term care facilities. The firm is organized into four major operating units: provider services, insurance services, UPMC International and UPMC Enterprises. The provider services unit includes regional hospitals; specialty service lines such as transplantation, women's health, behavioral health, pediatrics, UPMC Cancer Centers and rehabilitation; in-home care and retirement living options; and contract services, including pharmacy and clinical laboratories. The insurance services unit offers health insurance to companies and their employees as well as recipients of government programs such as Medicare and Medical Assistance; integrated workers' compensation and disability services; and coverage for behavioral health services to Medical Assistance beneficiaries in most Pennsylvania counties. UPMC International offers advisory services, infrastructure consultation and clinical management in the following countries: China, offering pathology consultation and healthcare collaboration services; Colombia, offering adult and pediatric oncology center consultation; Ireland, offering cancer center consultation; Italy, offering transplantation, radiotherapy, biotechnology and preventative medicine center advisory and consultation; Japan, offering education in primary care and family medicine; Kazakhstan, offering oncology center consultation; Lithuania, offering oncology services; Singapore, offering transplantation and clinical management services; and the U.K., offering IT and cancer care services. Last, UPMC Enterprises utilizes science and technology to solve healthcare challenges, striving to make it more efficient, affordable and personalized.

FINANCIAL DATA: *Note: Data for latest year may not have been available at press time.*

In U.S. $	2017	2016	2015	2014	2013	2012
Revenue	15,643,000,000	13,500,000,000	12,000,000,000	11,415,912,000	10,188,439,000	10,600,000,000
R&D Expense						
Operating Income						
Operating Margin %						
SGA Expense						
Net Income	245,000,000	215,000,000	416,809,000	463,460,000	359,390,000	
Operating Cash Flow						
Capital Expenditure						
EBITDA						
Return on Assets %						
Return on Equity %						
Debt to Equity						

CONTACT INFORMATION:

Phone: 877-986-9812 Fax:
Toll-Free: 800-533-8762
Address: 200 Lathrop St., Pittsburgh, PA 15213 United States

STOCK TICKER/OTHER:

Stock Ticker: Nonprofit
Exchange:
Employees: 80,000
Fiscal Year Ends:
Parent Company:

SALARIES/BONUSES:

Top Exec. Salary: $ Bonus: $
Second Exec. Salary: $ Bonus: $

OTHER THOUGHTS:

Estimated Female Officers or Directors:
Hot Spot for Advancement for Women/Minorities:

Urgent Care MSO LLC (MedExpress)

www.medexpress.com

NAIC Code: 621,493

TYPES OF BUSINESS:

Urgent Medical Care Centers and Clinics (except Hospitals), Freestanding

BRANDS/DIVISIONS/AFFILIATES:

UnitedHealth Group Inc
Optum
MedExpress
MedExpress Walk-In Care

CONTACTS: *Note: Officers with more than one job title may be intentionally listed here more than once.*

Frank Alderman, CEO
Robert Hiser, CIO

GROWTH PLANS/SPECIAL FEATURES:

Urgent Care MSO LLC (MedExpress) is a management services company which provides management services on behalf of private office practices operating urgent and walk-in care centers under the MedExpress name. In Delaware, Med Express is referred to as MedExpress Walk-In Care. These centers offer 12 hours a day, every day. The firm accepts most insurance, but insurance is not required to receive affordable healthcare. It collaborates with other local healthcare providers to ensure best possible outcomes for patients and families. Patient services and treatment are categorized into four groups: illness, injury, wellness and prevention, and work-related services. The illness group includes allergies, cold/flu, ear infection, lab work, TB testing, IVs, EKGs, Lyme Disease, respiratory illness, skin ailments and strep throat. The injury group includes bites and stings, broken bones, burns, cuts and scrapes, frostbite, heat exhaustion, strains and sprains and X-rays. The wellness and prevention group includes camp, school and sports physicals; flu shots; immunizations; and vaccinations. Last, the work-related group provides work-related services and treatments; at-work or on-site services; injury care; and workers' compensation. MedExpress has more than 200 medical centers in 17 U.S. states. Urgent Care MSO is an Optum company, which itself is a division of UnitedHealth Group, Inc.

FINANCIAL DATA: *Note: Data for latest year may not have been available at press time.*

In U.S. $	2017	2016	2015	2014	2013	2012
Revenue						
R&D Expense						
Operating Income						
Operating Margin %						
SGA Expense						
Net Income						
Operating Cash Flow						
Capital Expenditure						
EBITDA						
Return on Assets %						
Return on Equity %						
Debt to Equity						

CONTACT INFORMATION:

Phone: 304-225-2500 Fax: 304-225-2576
Toll-Free:
Address: 1751 Earl Core Rd., Morgantown, WV 26505 United States

STOCK TICKER/OTHER:

Stock Ticker: Private Exchange:
Employees: Fiscal Year Ends:
Parent Company: UnitedHealth Group Inc

SALARIES/BONUSES:

Top Exec. Salary: $ Bonus: $
Second Exec. Salary: $ Bonus: $

OTHER THOUGHTS:

Estimated Female Officers or Directors:
Hot Spot for Advancement for Women/Minorities:

US NeuroSurgical Inc

www.usneuro.com

NAIC Code: 621,493

TYPES OF BUSINESS:

Neurological Surgery Centers (Gamma Knife)
Radiation Treatment

BRANDS/DIVISIONS/AFFILIATES:

US NeuroSurgical Holdings Inc
USN Corona Inc
Corona Gamma Knife LLC
NeuroPartners LLC
Medical Oncology Partners LLC
United Oncology Medical Associates of Florida LLC

CONTACTS: *Note: Officers with more than one job title may be intentionally listed here more than once.*

Alan Gold, CEO
Susan Greenwald, Vice President

GROWTH PLANS/SPECIAL FEATURES:

U.S. NeuroSurgical, Inc. owns and operates stereotactic radiosurgery centers, utilizing the Leksell PERFEXION gamma knife (radiation) technology. The company currently owns and operates a gamma knife center on the premises of New York University Medical Center (NYU) in New York, New York, as well as a center at San Antonio Regional Hospital (SARH) in Upland, California. U.S. NeuroSurgical's business strategy is to provide cost-effective approaches that allow hospitals, physicians and patients access to gamma knife treatment on a cost-per-treatment basis. U.S. NeuroSurgical's business model is to own, or hold an interest in, the gamma knife units, and charge the medical facility, where the unit is housed and maintained, based on utilization. Its main target market is medical centers in major health care catchment areas that have physicians experienced with and dedicated to the use of the gamma knife. Wholly-owned subsidiary USN Corona, Inc. holds investments in Corona Gamma Knife, LLC and NeuroPartners, LLC, both of which develop and manage the gamma knife center at SARH. USN Corona is a part owner of Medical Oncology Partners, LLC, which wholly-owns United Oncology Medical Associates of Florida, LLC. U.S. NeuroSurgical itself operates as a wholly-owned subsidiary of U.S. NeuroSurgical Holdings, Inc.

FINANCIAL DATA: *Note: Data for latest year may not have been available at press time.*

In U.S. $	2017	2016	2015	2014	2013	2012
Revenue	3,414,000	3,212,000	2,971,000	2,607,000		1,956,000
R&D Expense						
Operating Income						
Operating Margin %						
SGA Expense						
Net Income	538,000	536,000	396,000	561,000	-667,000	729,000
Operating Cash Flow						
Capital Expenditure						
EBITDA						
Return on Assets %						
Return on Equity %						
Debt to Equity						

CONTACT INFORMATION:

Phone: 301 208-8998 Fax: 301 208-3254
Toll-Free:
Address: 2400 Research Blvd., Rockville, MD 20850 United States

STOCK TICKER/OTHER:

Stock Ticker: USNU Exchange: PINX
Employees: 3 Fiscal Year Ends: 12/31
Parent Company: US NeuroSurgical Holdings Inc

SALARIES/BONUSES:

Top Exec. Salary: $ Bonus: $
Second Exec. Salary: $ Bonus: $

OTHER THOUGHTS:

Estimated Female Officers or Directors:
Hot Spot for Advancement for Women/Minorities:

US Oncology Inc

NAIC Code: 621,111

www.usoncology.com

TYPES OF BUSINESS:

Oncologists' offices
Oncology Pharmaceutical Services
Outpatient Cancer Center Operations
Research & Development Services

BRANDS/DIVISIONS/AFFILIATES:

McKesson Corporation
US Oncology Network (The)
iKnowMed
Oncology Portal
US Oncology Research Network

CONTACTS: *Note: Officers with more than one job title may be intentionally listed here more than once.*

Claire Crye, Mgr.-Public Rel.
Lucy Langer, Chmn.

GROWTH PLANS/SPECIAL FEATURES:

U.S. Oncology, Inc., operating as The US Oncology Network, is a cancer management company which provides management services under long-term agreements to oncology practices. Part of McKesson Corporation's specialty health segment, the firm provides support services for cancer patients and doctors through hundreds of affiliated sites across the county. More than 995,000 patients are treate annually through the network. The company has nearly 1,400 affiliated physicians in all aspects of diagnosis and outpatient treatment of cancer, including medical oncology, radiation, gynecologic oncology, stem cell transplantation, diagnostic radiology and clinical research. The company also assists in a number of aspects in the conducting of clinical trials, including protocol development, data coordination, institutional review, board coordination and contract review/negotiation. The firm has two primary technology product offerings: iKnowMed and the Oncology Portal. iKnowMed is an internet-based electronic medical record system designed specifically for oncologists. The company's Oncology Portal is an online community for the discussion of patient care, research discoveries and the latest industry updates. The company also operates US Oncology Research Network (USOR). USOR is one of the nation's largest research networks specializing in Phase I-Phase IV oncology clinical trials. In August 2018, U.S. Oncology and Novocure announced that they were collaborating on PANOVA-3, a phase 3 trial testing the efficacy of tumor treating fields combined with nab-paclitaxel and gemcitabine in patients with unresectable, locally-advanced pancreatic cancer. The U.S. Oncology Network would be opening 10 clinical trial sites enrolling patients in Novocure's PANOVA-3 trial.

FINANCIAL DATA: *Note: Data for latest year may not have been available at press time.*

In U.S. $	2017	2016	2015	2014	2013	2012
Revenue						
R&D Expense						
Operating Income						
Operating Margin %						
SGA Expense						
Net Income						
Operating Cash Flow						
Capital Expenditure						
EBITDA						
Return on Assets %						
Return on Equity %						
Debt to Equity						

CONTACT INFORMATION:

Phone: 281-863-1000 Fax:
Toll-Free: 800-381-2637
Address: 10101 Woodloch Forest, The Woodlands, TX 77380 United States

STOCK TICKER/OTHER:

Stock Ticker: Subsidiary
Employees: 9,600
Parent Company: McKesson Corporation
Exchange:
Fiscal Year Ends: 12/31

SALARIES/BONUSES:

Top Exec. Salary: $ Bonus: $
Second Exec. Salary: $ Bonus: $

OTHER THOUGHTS:

Estimated Female Officers or Directors:
Hot Spot for Advancement for Women/Minorities:

US Physical Therapy Inc

corporate.usph.com

NAIC Code: 621,340

TYPES OF BUSINESS:

Occupational & Physical Therapy Clinics

BRANDS/DIVISIONS/AFFILIATES:

CONTACTS:

Note: Officers with more than one job title may be intentionally listed here more than once.

Christopher Reading, CEO
Lawrence McAfee, CFO
Jerald Pullins, Chairman of the Board
Glenn McDowell, COO, Divisional
Graham Reeve, COO, Geographical
Jon Bates, Vice President

GROWTH PLANS/SPECIAL FEATURES:

U.S. Physical Therapy, Inc. (UPT) is a holding company engaged in the operation of outpatient physical therapy and occupational therapy clinics. These clinics provide pre- and post-operative care/treatment of orthopedic-related disorders, sports-injuries, preventive care, rehabilitation of injured workers and neurological-related injuries. UPT operates through subsidiary clinic partnerships, in which it generally owns a 1% general partnership interest and a 49% through 94% limited partnership interest. The managing therapists of the clinics own the remaining limited partnership interest in the majority of the clinics. UPT also operates some clinics through wholly-owned subsidiaries under profit sharing arrangements with therapists. There are approximately 580 outpatient physical and occupational therapy clinics located throughout the U.S. Each clinic's staff typically includes one or more licensed physical or occupational therapists along with assistants, aides, exercise physiologists and athletic trainers. The clinics initially perform an evaluation of each patient, which is then followed by a treatment plan specific to the injury as prescribed by the patient's physician. The treatment plan may include procedures such as ultrasound, electrical stimulation, therapeutic exercise, hot packs, iontophoresis, daily life skills management and home exercise programs. A clinic's business primarily comes from referrals by local physicians. UPT also manages more than 30 physical therapy practices for third parties. In May 2018, UPT acquired a majority interest (65%) in an undisclosed provider of industrial injury prevention services, which performs its services through industrial sports medicine professionals in over 450 client facilities across 26 U.S. states.

Employee benefits include medical, dental and vision coverage; life & AD&D insurance; short- and long-term disability; flexible benefit plans; a 401(k); and educational assistance.

FINANCIAL DATA:

Note: Data for latest year may not have been available at press time.

In U.S. $	2017	2016	2015	2014	2013	2012
Revenue	414,051,000	356,546,000	331,302,000	305,074,000	264,058,000	252,088,000
R&D Expense						
Operating Income	54,728,000	49,533,000	47,294,000	45,768,000	38,770,000	37,803,000
Operating Margin %	13.21%	13.89%	14.27%	15.00%	14.68%	14.99%
SGA Expense	35,889,000	32,479,000	31,067,000	30,399,000	25,931,000	24,782,000
Net Income	22,256,000	20,551,000	22,279,000	20,853,000	12,723,000	17,933,000
Operating Cash Flow	56,526,000	51,050,000	41,243,000	45,194,000	44,795,000	39,249,000
Capital Expenditure	7,095,000	8,260,000	6,263,000	5,167,000	4,637,000	4,234,000
EBITDA	64,526,000	58,405,000	55,327,000	52,526,000	44,339,000	43,096,000
Return on Assets %	5.77%	6.51%	8.49%	8.89%	6.42%	10.70%
Return on Equity %	11.34%	11.73%	14.41%	15.18%	10.36%	15.98%
Debt to Equity	0.27	0.26	0.29	0.23	0.31	0.14

CONTACT INFORMATION:

Phone: 713 297-7000 Fax: 713 297-7090
Toll-Free: 800-580-6285
Address: 1300 W. Sam Houston Pkwy. S., Ste. 300, Houston, TX 77042 United States

STOCK TICKER/OTHER:

Stock Ticker: USPH
Employees: 3,800
Parent Company:
Exchange: NYS
Fiscal Year Ends: 12/31

SALARIES/BONUSES:

Top Exec. Salary: $720,458 Bonus: $
Second Exec. Salary: $468,794 Bonus: $

OTHER THOUGHTS:

Estimated Female Officers or Directors:
Hot Spot for Advancement for Women/Minorities:

USMD Health System

www.usmdinc.com

NAIC Code: 622,110

TYPES OF BUSINESS:

Hospitals

BRANDS/DIVISIONS/AFFILIATES:

WellMed Medical Management Inc
USMD Hospital at Arlington
USMD Hospital at Fort Worth
USMD Urology Associates of North Texas
USMD Medical Clinic of North Texas
USMD Prostate Cancer Center

CONTACTS: *Note: Officers with more than one job title may be intentionally listed here more than once.*

Richard C. Jonston, CEO
James Berend, CFO
Josh Hardy, CFO
Tim Smith, CIO
Chris Carr, Executive VP
Richard Johnston, Executive VP

GROWTH PLANS/SPECIAL FEATURES:

USMD Health System comprises two hospitals and more than 50 primary care and specialty clinics serving the Dallas-Fort Worth metropolitan area. USMD Hospital at Arlington's services include surgery, robotic surgery, bariatrics, oncology, men's services and women's services. Since October 2003, this hospital's surgeons have performed more than 4,500 robot-assisted surgeries. USMD Hospital at Fort Worth's services include both adult surgery and pediatric surgery. USMD Urology Associates of North Texas is comprised of 40 physicians and 20 locations throughout Dallas and Fort Worth, and is one of the nation's largest fully-integrated urology practices. USMD Medical Clinic of North Texas is a physicians' group with more than 40 clinics offering medical care in the areas of family medicine, internal medicine, obstetrics, gynecology, pediatrics, allergy, immunology, cardiology, gastroenterology, general surgery, geriatrics, infectious disease, interventional pain management, medical oncology, neurology, physical medicine, rehabilitation, psychotherapy, podiatry, rheumatology, sports medicine, travel medicine and diabetes education. Last, USMD Prostate Cancer Center offers a comprehensive approach to prostate cancer treatment and management. The center's treatment options are utilized for all types and stages of prostate cancer, including nerve-sparing robotic radical prostatectomy, cryotherapy, radiation therapy and robotic radiosurgery. Over 6,000 robotic prostatectomy surgeries have been performed by the center, which also has one of the largest cryotherapy programs in the world. USMD Health Systems operates as a wholly-owned subsidiary of WellMed Medical Management, Inc.

FINANCIAL DATA: *Note: Data for latest year may not have been available at press time.*

In U.S. $	2017	2016	2015	2014	2013	2012
Revenue	351,750,000	335,000,000	325,152,992	294,764,992	234,727,008	105,702,000
R&D Expense						
Operating Income						
Operating Margin %						
SGA Expense						
Net Income			-1,616,000	-32,400,000	979,000	2,100,000
Operating Cash Flow						
Capital Expenditure						
EBITDA						
Return on Assets %						
Return on Equity %						
Debt to Equity						

CONTACT INFORMATION:

Phone: 214 493-4000 Fax:
Toll-Free:
Address: 6333 N. State Hwy. 161, Ste. 200, Irving, TX 75038 United States

STOCK TICKER/OTHER:

Stock Ticker: Subsidiary
Exchange:
Employees: 1,470
Fiscal Year Ends:
Parent Company: WellMed Medical Management Inc

SALARIES/BONUSES:

Top Exec. Salary: $ Bonus: $
Second Exec. Salary: $ Bonus: $

OTHER THOUGHTS:

Estimated Female Officers or Directors:
Hot Spot for Advancement for Women/Minorities:

Utah Medical Products Inc

www.utahmed.com

NAIC Code: 339,100

TYPES OF BUSINESS:

Equipment-Obstetrics & Gynecology
Disposable Products
Electrosurgical Systems
Neonatal Intensive Care Equipment
Blood Pressure Management

BRANDS/DIVISIONS/AFFILIATES:

Utah Medical Products Ltd
Columbia Medical Inc
Abcorp Inc
Femcare Holdings Ltd
Utah Medical Products Canada Ltd
Femcare Canada
INTRAN PLUS
DELTRAN

CONTACTS: *Note: Officers with more than one job title may be intentionally listed here more than once.*

Kevin Cornwell, CEO
Brian Koopman, Controller

GROWTH PLANS/SPECIAL FEATURES:

Utah Medical Products, Inc. (UTMD), produces medical devices that are predominantly proprietary, disposable and for hospital use. Products of the firm are divided into four categories: labor and delivery/obstetrics (LDO), neonatal intensive care (NIC), gynecology/urology/electrosurgery (GUE) and blood pressure monitoring (BPM). LDO products consist of electronic fetal monitoring systems, vacuum-assisted delivery systems and obstetrical tools. Brand names within this category includes INTRAN PLUS intrauterine pressure catheters, AROM-COT pronged finger cover and CORDGUARD clamping system. NIC brands and products include the DISPOSA-HOOD infant respiratory hood that administers oxygen and flushes carbon dioxide while maintaining a neutral thermal environment; DELTRAN blood pressure monitoring system; GESCO and UMBILI-CATH biocompatible silicone catheters; ENFit catheter connectors and oral syringes; URI-CATH pre-assembled, closed urinary drainage system; MYELO-NATE lumbar sampling kit for obtaining cerebral spinal fluid samples; and HEMO-NATE disposable filter that removes microaggregates from stored blood prior to transfusion into a neonate. GUE products include the LETZ loop excision system; EPITOME electrosurgical scalpel; FILSHIE CLIP system; PATHFINDER PLUS endoscopic irrigation device; Add-a-Cath easy suprapubic introduction; LIBERTY device for incontinence in women; EndoCurette endometrial tissue sampling; and LUMIN gynecological laparoscopic tool. BPM includes the DELTRAN disposable pressure transducer used to convert physiological pressure into an electrical signal displayed on electronic monitoring equipment. Subsidiaries include Utah Medical Products Ltd.; Columbia Medical, Inc.; Abcorp, Inc.; Femcare Holdings Ltd.; and Utah Medical Products Canada Ltd. (dba Femcare Canada).

UTMD offers full-time employees medical, dental and vision; life insurance; AD&D; short- and long-term disability; stock options; unemployment insurance; worker's compensation insurance; 401(k) with company matching funds; and bonus plans for all employee classifications.

FINANCIAL DATA: *Note: Data for latest year may not have been available at press time.*

In U.S. $	2017	2016	2015	2014	2013	2012
Revenue	41,414,000	39,298,000	40,157,000	41,278,000	40,493,000	41,552,000
R&D Expense	447,000	475,000	522,000	460,000	491,000	563,000
Operating Income	19,011,000	16,187,000	15,651,000	16,202,000	14,828,000	15,196,000
Operating Margin %	45.90%	41.19%	38.97%	39.25%	36.61%	36.57%
SGA Expense	6,937,000	7,028,000	8,012,000	8,321,000	8,954,000	9,547,000
Net Income	8,505,000	12,128,000	11,843,000	11,378,000	11,406,000	10,169,000
Operating Cash Flow	16,908,000	14,528,000	13,801,000	15,387,000	12,309,000	13,563,000
Capital Expenditure	1,597,000	3,302,000	246,000	1,132,000	344,000	255,000
EBITDA	21,855,000	19,255,000	18,757,000	19,457,000	18,109,000	18,455,000
Return on Assets %	10.04%	15.57%	14.78%	14.06%	14.47%	13.26%
Return on Equity %	11.54%	17.46%	17.64%	18.18%	20.44%	22.17%
Debt to Equity				0.01	0.08	0.17

CONTACT INFORMATION:

Phone: 801 566-1200 Fax: 801 566-2062
Toll-Free: 866-754-9789
Address: 7043 S. 300 W., Midvale, UT 84047 United States

STOCK TICKER/OTHER:

Stock Ticker: UTMD
Employees: 173
Parent Company:
Exchange: NAS
Fiscal Year Ends: 12/31

SALARIES/BONUSES:

Top Exec. Salary: $156,000 Bonus: $
Second Exec. Salary: $118,507 Bonus: $

OTHER THOUGHTS:

Estimated Female Officers or Directors: 1
Hot Spot for Advancement for Women/Minorities:

Sales, profits and employees may be estimates. Financial information, benefits and other data can change quickly and may vary from those stated here.

Valeritas Inc

NAIC Code: 339,100

www.valeritas.com

TYPES OF BUSINESS:

Surgical and Medical Instrument Manufacturing

BRANDS/DIVISIONS/AFFILIATES:

V-Go Disposable Insulin Delivery Device
V-Go PreFill
V-Go SIM
V-Go Link

CONTACTS: *Note: Officers with more than one job title may be intentionally listed here more than once.*

John Timberlake, CEO
Geoffrey Jenkins, Exec. VP-Oper.
Erick Lucera, Exec. VP
Hokan Lars Ojert, VP-Sales
Dave Lewis, VP-Mktg.
Peter Devlin, Chmn.

GROWTH PLANS/SPECIAL FEATURES:

Valeritas, Inc. is a commercial-stage medical technology company focused on developing innovative technologies to improve the health and quality of life of people with Type 2 diabetes. The firm is the producer of the V-Go Disposable Insulin Delivery Device (V-Go). V-Go is a small, discreet and easy-to-use disposable insulin delivery device that a patient adheres to his or her skin every 24 hours. V-Go enables patients to closely mimic the body's normal physiologic pattern of insulin delivery throughout the day and to manage their diabetes with insulin without the need to plan a daily routine around multiple daily injections. Currently, Valeritas is developing three next-generation single-use disposable V-Go devices: V-Go PreFill, which would allow the company to sell V-Go along with the insulin in one commercial product, featuring a pre-filled insulin cartridge that the patient can snap into the V-Go device, eliminating the insulin-filling process; V-Go SIM, which features a one-way communication to smart devices such as phones and tablets through radio frequency (RF)/Bluetooth technology; and V-Go Link, which provides real-time tracking information of basal and bolus dosing utilization, allowing patients and their health care professionals to have a deeper understanding of their current dosing habits.

FINANCIAL DATA: *Note: Data for latest year may not have been available at press time.*

In U.S. $	2017	2016	2015	2014	2013	2012
Revenue	20,450,000	19,500,000	18,097,000	13,493,000	6,166,000	555,000
R&D Expense						
Operating Income						
Operating Margin %						
SGA Expense						
Net Income	-49,301,000	-46,367,000	-103,811,000	-65,572,000	-87,597,000	-52,547,000
Operating Cash Flow						
Capital Expenditure						
EBITDA						
Return on Assets %						
Return on Equity %						
Debt to Equity						

CONTACT INFORMATION:

Phone: 908 927-9920 Fax: 908 927-9927
Toll-Free:
Address: 750 Route 202 South, Ste. 600, Bridgewater, NJ 08807 United States

STOCK TICKER/OTHER:

Stock Ticker: VLRX
Employees: 103
Parent Company:
Exchange:
Fiscal Year Ends: 12/31

SALARIES/BONUSES:

Top Exec. Salary: $ Bonus: $
Second Exec. Salary: $ Bonus: $

OTHER THOUGHTS:

Estimated Female Officers or Directors:
Hot Spot for Advancement for Women/Minorities:

Varian Medical Systems Inc

www.varian.com

NAIC Code: 334,510

TYPES OF BUSINESS:

Radiation Oncology Systems
X-Ray Equipment
Software Systems
Security & Inspection Products

BRANDS/DIVISIONS/AFFILIATES:

humediQ Global GmbH
IDENTIFY

CONTACTS:

Note: Officers with more than one job title may be intentionally listed here more than once.

Dow Wilson, CEO
Gary Bischoping, CFO
R. Eckert, Chairman of the Board
Magnus Momsen, Chief Accounting Officer
Timothy Guertin, Director
John Kuo, General Counsel
Kolleen Kennedy, President, Divisional

GROWTH PLANS/SPECIAL FEATURES:

Varian Medical Systems, Inc. designs, manufactures, sells and services hardware and software products for treating cancer. These systems treat cancer with conventional radiotherapy as well as with advanced treatment such as fixed field intensity-modulated radiation therapy, image-guided radiation therapy, volumetric modulated arc therapy, stereotactic radiosurgery, stereotactic body radiotherapy and brachytherapy. Varian's software solutions also include informatics software for information management, clinical knowledge exchange, patient care management, practice management and decision-making support for comprehensive cancer clinics, radiotherapy centers and medical oncology practices. Its hardware products include linear accelerators, brachytherapy afterloaders, treatment simulation and verification equipment and accessories. Varian has sales and support offices worldwide, including North America, Europe, the Middle East, India, Africa, Latin America and Asia Pacific. In August 2018, Varian acquired humediQ Global GmbH, the manufacturer of IDENTIFY, an automated patient identification, positioning and motion management system for radiation therapy.

Varian offers employees medical, life, AD&D, disability, dental and vision plans; a 401(k); educational reimbursement; an employee assistance program; and a stock purchase plan.

FINANCIAL DATA:

Note: Data for latest year may not have been available at press time.

In U.S. $	2017	2016	2015	2014	2013	2012
Revenue	2,668,200,000	3,217,800,000	3,099,111,000	3,049,800,000	2,942,897,000	2,807,015,000
R&D Expense	210,000,000	253,500,000	245,211,000	234,840,000	208,208,000	185,742,000
Operating Income	393,300,000	567,700,000	548,967,000	596,285,000	608,890,000	594,074,000
Operating Margin %	14.74%	17.64%	17.71%	19.55%	20.69%	21.16%
SGA Expense	552,300,000	540,100,000	488,514,000	470,550,000	432,589,000	416,520,000
Net Income	249,600,000	402,300,000	411,485,000	403,703,000	438,248,000	427,049,000
Operating Cash Flow	399,100,000	356,300,000	469,556,000	448,986,000	455,185,000	492,775,000
Capital Expenditure	59,100,000	80,400,000	91,384,000	89,649,000	76,277,000	61,103,000
EBITDA	432,400,000	648,000,000	631,117,000	644,126,000	679,071,000	660,325,000
Return on Assets %	7.13%	10.84%	11.82%	11.82%	13.80%	15.88%
Return on Equity %	15.42%	23.30%	24.72%	24.24%	27.18%	31.01%
Debt to Equity		0.16	0.19	0.23	0.26	

CONTACT INFORMATION:

Phone: 650 493-4000 Fax:
Toll-Free: 800-544-4636
Address: 3100 Hansen Way, Palo Alto, CA 94304 United States

STOCK TICKER/OTHER:

Stock Ticker: VAR
Employees: 7,800
Parent Company:
Exchange: NYS
Fiscal Year Ends: 09/30

SALARIES/BONUSES:

Top Exec. Salary: $1,000,000 Bonus: $
Second Exec. Salary: $664,936 Bonus: $

OTHER THOUGHTS:

Estimated Female Officers or Directors: 6
Hot Spot for Advancement for Women/Minorities: Y

VCA Inc

NAIC Code: 541,940

www.vca.com

TYPES OF BUSINESS:

Animal Health Care Services
Veterinary Diagnostic Laboratories
Full-Service Animal Hospitals
Veterinary Equipment
Ultrasound Imaging

BRANDS/DIVISIONS/AFFILIATES:

Mars Inc

CONTACTS: *Note: Officers with more than one job title may be intentionally listed here more than once.*

Robert Antin, CEO
Arthur J. Antin, COO
Tomas W. Fuller, CFO
Josh Drake, President, Subsidiary
Robert Antin, Chmn.

GROWTH PLANS/SPECIAL FEATURES:

VCA, Inc. is a leading animal health care company operating in the U.S. and Canada. The firm provides services and diagnostic testing to support veterinary care, and sells diagnostic equipment and other medical technology products to the veterinary market. VCA's hospitals offer a full range of general medical and surgical services for companion animals, as well as specialized treatments, including advanced diagnostic services, internal medicine, oncology, ophthalmology, dermatology and cardiology. In addition, the company provides pharmaceutical products and performs a variety of pet wellness programs such as health examinations, diagnostic testing, routine vaccinations, spaying, neutering and dental care. VCA's network of more than 800 animal hospitals provides service to over 8 million patients annually. Dog day care and boarding services are also offered at more than 130 locations. In September 2017, VCA was acquired by Mars, Inc. for $9.1 billion. VCA operates as a distinct and separate business unit within Mars' Petcare segment.

FINANCIAL DATA: *Note: Data for latest year may not have been available at press time.*

In U.S. $	2017	2016	2015	2014	2013	2012
Revenue	2,700,000,000	2,516,863,000	2,133,675,008	1,918,482,944	1,803,368,960	1,699,641,984
R&D Expense						
Operating Income						
Operating Margin %						
SGA Expense						
Net Income		209,196,000	211,048,992	135,438,000	137,511,008	45,551,000
Operating Cash Flow						
Capital Expenditure						
EBITDA						
Return on Assets %						
Return on Equity %						
Debt to Equity						

CONTACT INFORMATION:

Phone: 310 571-6500 Fax: 310 571-6700
Toll-Free: 800-966-1822
Address: 12401 W. Olympic Blvd., Los Angeles, CA 90064 United States

STOCK TICKER/OTHER:

Stock Ticker: Subsidiary
Exchange:
Employees: 11,500
Fiscal Year Ends: 12/31
Parent Company: Mars Inc

SALARIES/BONUSES:

Top Exec. Salary: $ Bonus: $
Second Exec. Salary: $ Bonus: $

OTHER THOUGHTS:

Estimated Female Officers or Directors:
Hot Spot for Advancement for Women/Minorities:

Vision Service Plan

www.vsp.com

NAIC Code: 524,114

TYPES OF BUSINESS:

Insurance-Supplemental & Specialty Health
Vision Insurance
Optical Frames
Laboratory Products & Materials, Optometry

BRANDS/DIVISIONS/AFFILIATES:

VSP Vision Care
Marchon Eyewear
Altair
VSP Optics
Eyefinity

CONTACTS: *Note: Officers with more than one job title may be intentionally listed here more than once.*

Michael J. Guyette, Pres.
Matthew Alpert, Sec.
Gordon W. Jennings, Treas.
Claudio Gottardi, Pres./CEO-Marchon Eyewear Inc.
Jim McGrann, Pres., VSP Vision Care
Steve Baker, Pres., Eyefinity
Daniel Mannen, Chmn.

GROWTH PLANS/SPECIAL FEATURES:

Vision Service Plan (VSP) is a vision care health insurance company operating in the U.S., Canada, Australia, Ireland and the U.K. VSP serves its members via private practice doctors in both rural and metropolitan areas. The firm's network consists of 39,000 doctor partners as well as more than 88 million Vision Care members worldwide. VSP's five providers include VSP Vision Care, Marchon Eyewear, Altair Eyewear, VSP Optics Group and Eyefinity Practice Solutions. VSP Vision Care is a national not-for-profit vision benefits and services company. Marchon is one of the largest global designers, manufacturers and distributors of fashionable and technologically-advanced eyewear and sunwear. Altair provides independent eye care professionals with eyewear products and business solutions to help deliver quality patient care. VSP Optics combines ophthalmic technology and lab services to create custom lens solutions for individual customers. Last, Eyefinity offers integrated products and services to streamline everyday processes to help eye care facilities succeed. Its products and solutions include practice management software; electronic health record (EHR) solutions for federal stimulus payments; desktop and cloud-based solutions for single and multi-location practices; website hosting with a customizable e-Commerce platform; online transaction services for claim filing, frame and lens purchasing and lab ordering; and business consulting services.

FINANCIAL DATA: *Note: Data for latest year may not have been available at press time.*

In U.S. $	2017	2016	2015	2014	2013	2012
Revenue						
R&D Expense						
Operating Income						
Operating Margin %						
SGA Expense						
Net Income						
Operating Cash Flow						
Capital Expenditure						
EBITDA						
Return on Assets %						
Return on Equity %						
Debt to Equity						

CONTACT INFORMATION:

Phone: 916-851-5000 Fax: 916-851-4858
Toll-Free: 800-852-7600
Address: 3333 Quality Dr., Rancho Cordova, CA 95670 United States

STOCK TICKER/OTHER:

Stock Ticker: Private
Employees:
Parent Company:
Exchange:
Fiscal Year Ends: 12/31

SALARIES/BONUSES:

Top Exec. Salary: $ Bonus: $
Second Exec. Salary: $ Bonus: $

OTHER THOUGHTS:

Estimated Female Officers or Directors: 1
Hot Spot for Advancement for Women/Minorities: Y

Vizient Inc

www.vizientinc.com

NAIC Code: 561,400

TYPES OF BUSINESS:

Group Buying Programs for Medical Supplies
Consulting to Hospitals and Health Care Services
Supply Chain Management
E-Commerce Services
Health Services Resource Management
Health Care Analytics

BRANDS/DIVISIONS/AFFILIATES:

CONTACTS: *Note: Officers with more than one job title may be intentionally listed here more than once.*

Byron Jobe, CEO
David F. Ertel, CFO
Colleen Risk, Chief People Officer
Jill Witter, General Counsel
Pete Allen, Area Sr. VP-Sourcing Oper.
Larry McComber, Sr. VP-Strategic Svcs.
Kyle Pyron, VP-Corp. Comm.
Mike Woodhouse, VP-Financial Svcs. & Supplier Audit
Cathy Denning, Sr. VP-Sourcing Oper.
David Berry, VP
Mike Clemens, VP-Sourcing Oper., Capital, Construction & Imaging

GROWTH PLANS/SPECIAL FEATURES:

Vizient, Inc. is the nation's largest member-owned health care services company. Backed by network-based insights in clinical, operational and supply chain performance, Vizient empowers its members to deliver exceptional, cost-effective care. The firm's innovative solutions leverage analytics and engages consultants in an effort to solve its member's most pressing issues, with focus areas including patient experience, elimination of avoidable practice variation, physician alignment and engagement, service line optimization, quality outcomes, patient safety, care redesign and scale/cost efficiencies. Vizient members are not-for-profit health care organizations of all types and sizes, from academic medical centers to acute and non-acute community providers. Membership provides access to the many ways Vizient optimizes each interaction along the continuum of patient care. Within Vizient, more than 10 national groups for senior leaders, numerous performance improvement peer-to-peer networks and a hospital engagement network all provide opportunities to solve common challenges with fellow members. Suppliers are part of the Vizient portfolio as well. Suppliers deliver critical tools and technology for exceptional, cost-effective care, including medications and supplies, as well as cutting-edge medical devices. Vizient offices are located in Dallas, Atlanta, Baton Rouge, Boston, Charlotte, Chicago, Indianapolis, Kansas City, Los Angeles, Minneapolis, Oklahoma City, Philadelphia, Seattle, San Francisco and Washington, D.C.

Vizient offers its employees medical, dental and vision insurance; 401(k); paid time off; adoption reimbursement; tuition assistance; and fitness options.

FINANCIAL DATA: *Note: Data for latest year may not have been available at press time.*

In U.S. $	2017	2016	2015	2014	2013	2012
Revenue						
R&D Expense						
Operating Income						
Operating Margin %						
SGA Expense						
Net Income						
Operating Cash Flow						
Capital Expenditure						
EBITDA						
Return on Assets %						
Return on Equity %						
Debt to Equity						

CONTACT INFORMATION:

Phone: 972-830-0000 Fax:
Toll-Free: 800-842-5146
Address: 290 E. John Carpenter Fwy, Irving, TX 75062 United States

STOCK TICKER/OTHER:

Stock Ticker: Private
Exchange:
Employees:
Fiscal Year Ends: 12/31
Parent Company:

SALARIES/BONUSES:

Top Exec. Salary: $ Bonus: $
Second Exec. Salary: $ Bonus: $

OTHER THOUGHTS:

Estimated Female Officers or Directors: 3
Hot Spot for Advancement for Women/Minorities: Y

Walgreens Boots Alliance Inc

www.walgreens.com

NAIC Code: 446,110

TYPES OF BUSINESS:

Drug Stores
Mail-Order Pharmacy Services
Pharmacy Benefit Management
Health Care Center Management
Online Pharmacy Services
Photo Printing Services
Specialty Pharmacy Services
Home Infusion Services

BRANDS/DIVISIONS/AFFILIATES:

Alliance Healthcare
Walgreens
Duane Reade
Boots
No7
Botanics
Sleek MakeUP
Soap & Glory

CONTACTS: *Note: Officers with more than one job title may be intentionally listed here more than once.*

Stefano Pessina, CEO
George Fairweather, CFO
James Skinner, Chairman of the Board
Kimberly Scardino, Chief Accounting Officer
Marco Pagni, Chief Administrative Officer
Alexander Gourlay, Co-COO
Ornella Barra, Co-COO
Kathleen Wilson-Thompson, Executive VP
Ken Murphy, Executive VP

GROWTH PLANS/SPECIAL FEATURES:

Walgreens Boots Alliance, Inc. is a global pharmacy-led health and wellbeing enterprise, with more than 13,200 stores worldwide. The company's pharmaceutical wholesale and distribution network is comprised of more than 390 distribution centers delivering to over 230,000 pharmacies, doctors, health centers and hospitals on an annual basis. The firm operates through three business segments: retail pharmacy USA, retail pharmacy international and pharmaceutical wholesale. Retail pharmacy USA oversees pharmacy-led health and beauty retail businesses in 50 states, the District of Columbia, Puerto Rico and the U.S. Virgin Islands. It operates more than 9,800 retail stores, and fills over 760 million prescriptions (including immunizations) annually. The retail pharmacy international segment oversees pharmacy-led health & beauty retail businesses in eight countries, operating more than 4,720 retail stores across the U.K., Thailand, Norway, Ireland, The Netherlands, Mexico and Chile. The pharmaceutical wholesale segment operates primarily under the Alliance Healthcare brand, and supplies medicines and other healthcare products to more than 110,000 pharmacies, doctors, health centers and hospitals from 289 distribution centers in 11 countries, primarily located in Europe. Walgreens' portfolio of retail and business global brands include Walgreens, Duane Reade, Boots and Alliance Healthcare, as well as global health & beauty product brands such as No7, Botanics, Sleek MakeUP, Liz Earl and Soap & Glory. During 2017, Walgreens agreed to purchase 1,932 stores Rite Aid stores in the U.S., as well as three distribution centers and related inventory for $4.3 billion. Ownership of these stores were expected to be transferred in phases and complete during 2018. In mid-2018, Walgreens sold a 30% stake in Guangzhou Pharmaceuticals Corporation (retaining a 20% stake); and agreed to acquire a 40% stake in Sinopharm Holding GuoDa Drugstores Co., Ltd., based in China.

Walgreens offers medical, prescription, dental, life and accident insurance; and profit sharing and stock purchase plans.

FINANCIAL DATA: *Note: Data for latest year may not have been available at press time.*

In U.S. $	2017	2016	2015	2014	2013	2012
Revenue	118,214,000,000	117,351,000,000	103,444,000,000	76,392,000,000	72,217,000,000	71,633,000,000
R&D Expense						
Operating Income	5,422,000,000	5,964,000,000	4,353,000,000	3,577,000,000	3,576,000,000	3,464,000,000
Operating Margin %	4.58%	5.08%	4.20%	4.68%	4.95%	4.83%
SGA Expense	23,740,000,000	23,910,000,000	22,571,000,000	17,992,000,000	17,543,000,000	16,878,000,000
Net Income	4,078,000,000	4,173,000,000	4,220,000,000	1,932,000,000	2,450,000,000	2,127,000,000
Operating Cash Flow	7,251,000,000	7,847,000,000	5,664,000,000	3,893,000,000	4,301,000,000	4,431,000,000
Capital Expenditure	1,351,000,000	1,325,000,000	1,251,000,000	1,106,000,000	1,212,000,000	1,550,000,000
EBITDA	7,076,000,000	7,682,000,000	6,095,000,000	4,893,000,000	4,859,000,000	4,630,000,000
Return on Assets %	5.88%	5.89%	7.96%	5.31%	7.10%	6.98%
Return on Equity %	14.22%	13.74%	16.44%	9.68%	13.00%	12.85%
Debt to Equity	0.46	0.62	0.43	0.18	0.23	0.22

CONTACT INFORMATION:

Phone: 847 315-2500 Fax: 847 914-2804
Toll-Free: 800-925-4733
Address: 108 Wilmot Rd., Deerfield, IL 60015 United States

STOCK TICKER/OTHER:

Stock Ticker: WBA Exchange: NAS
Employees: 345,000 Fiscal Year Ends: 08/31
Parent Company:

SALARIES/BONUSES:

Top Exec. Salary: $891,406 Bonus: $
Second Exec. Salary: $891,406 Bonus: $

OTHER THOUGHTS:

Estimated Female Officers or Directors: 7
Hot Spot for Advancement for Women/Minorities: Y

WebMD Health Corp

www.webmd.com

NAIC Code: 519,130

TYPES OF BUSINESS:

Health Care Internet Portals
Content Licensing

BRANDS/DIVISIONS/AFFILIATES:

KKR & Co Inc
Internet Brands Inc
WebMD Health Network
Medscape
MedicineNet.com
eMedicineHealth.com
RxList.com
WebMD.boots.com

CONTACTS: *Note: Officers with more than one job title may be intentionally listed here more than once.*

Steven L. Zatz, CEO
Martin Wygod, Chairman of the Board
Blake DeSimone, CFO
Kathleen Tourjee, VP-Human Resources
Michael Glick, Executive VP
Douglas Wamsley, Executive VP
Steven Zatz, President

GROWTH PLANS/SPECIAL FEATURES:

WebMD Health Corp. provides health information services to consumers, physicians, health care professionals, employers and health plan providers via the internet. Additionally, the company provides personalized telephonic, online or onsite health coaching and condition management services. The firm's public online service, WebMD Health Network, offers WebMD Health, its primary public portal; and Medscape from WebMD, a public portal for physicians and healthcare professionals. WebMD Health provides health and wellness articles and features decision-support services to help consumers make informed decisions about healthcare providers, health risks and treatment options. Available information and interactive tools include detailed data on specific diseases or conditions, physician location and individual healthcare data storage. Medscape from WebMD assists physicians and health care professionals in improving clinical knowledge with original content such as daily news, commentary, conference coverage and continuing medical education. Additional websites in the WebMD Health Network include MedicineNet.com, eMedicineHealth.com, RxList.com and WebMD.boots.com. The firm generates revenue from its public offerings primarily through advertising sales and sponsorships. Additionally, the company generates revenue through the sale of advertising in its WebMD Magazine consumer publication, distributed free of charge to physicians for use in their office waiting rooms; and is also available online through iOS app. Revenue is also generated from the private side through content and technology licensed to employers and health plans, either directly or through distributors. Private portals offered by WebMD enable employees and health plan members to learn about benefits, providers and treatment decisions, customized to a user's health insurance plan. During 2017, WebMD was acquired by KKR & Co., Inc.'s Internet Brands, Inc. subsidiary, and subsequently ceased from being publicly traded.

FINANCIAL DATA: *Note: Data for latest year may not have been available at press time.*

In U.S. $	2017	2016	2015	2014	2013	2012
Revenue	740,298,321	705,046,016	636,398,976	580,449,024	515,292,992	469,865,984
R&D Expense						
Operating Income						
Operating Margin %						
SGA Expense						
Net Income		91,304,000	64,024,000	42,063,000	15,116,000	-20,344,000
Operating Cash Flow						
Capital Expenditure						
EBITDA						
Return on Assets %						
Return on Equity %						
Debt to Equity						

CONTACT INFORMATION:

Phone: 212-624-3700 Fax:
Toll-Free:
Address: 395 Hudson St., New York, NY 10011 United States

STOCK TICKER/OTHER:

Stock Ticker: Subsidiary
Employees: 1,815
Parent Company: KKR & Co Inc
Exchange:
Fiscal Year Ends: 12/31

SALARIES/BONUSES:

Top Exec. Salary: $ Bonus: $
Second Exec. Salary: $ Bonus: $

OTHER THOUGHTS:

Estimated Female Officers or Directors: 1
Hot Spot for Advancement for Women/Minorities: Y

Weight Watchers International Inc

www.weightwatchers.com

NAIC Code: 812,191

TYPES OF BUSINESS:

Weight Management Programs
Franchising
Branded Diet Products

BRANDS/DIVISIONS/AFFILIATES:

Beyond the Scale
Freestyle
SmartPoint
WeightWatchers.com
Weight Watchers eTools

CONTACTS: *Note: Officers with more than one job title may be intentionally listed here more than once.*

Mindy Grossman, CEO
Nicholas Hotchkin, CFO
Raymond Debbane, Chairman of the Board
Michael Colosi, General Counsel
Corinne Pollier-Bousquet, President, Geographical
Stacey Mowbray, President, Geographical

GROWTH PLANS/SPECIAL FEATURES:

Weight Watchers International, Inc. (WWI) is a global weight management services provider operating through a network of company-owned and franchised operations. The firm has four operating segments: North America, United Kingdom, Continental Europe and other. Each reporting segment provides similar products and services through various offerings. North America consists of WWI's U.S. and Canada company-owned operations; United Kingdom consists of company-owned operations in the U.K.; Continental Europe consists of WWI's Germany, Switzerland, France, Spain, Belgium, Netherlands and Sweden company-owned operations; and other includes Australia, New Zealand, Mexico and Brazil company-owned operations. WWI also has franchise operations in the U.S. and certain other countries. Revenues from North America, United Kingdom, Continental Europe and other include 69.7%, 7.6%, 18.3% and 4.4% in fiscal 2017, respectively. WWI's Beyond the Scale and Freestyle weight management plans were developed from a combination of advancements in scientific research and customer insights. These plans go beyond a singular focus on weight loss and encompass a holistic approach toward a healthier body and mind, which results in a happier life. The weight loss strategy gives each food a SmartPoint value determined by a proprietary formula based on the food's calories, saturated fat, sugar and protein content. The formula takes into account how these nutrients are processed by the body as well as their impact on satiety. Customers following the SmartPoint system can eat any food as long as the point value of their total food consumption stays within their personalized point budget. Online subscriptions via WeightWatechers.com, include the SmartPoint tracking system, SmartPoint calculators, foods lists, weight tracker, progress charts, nutritional guideline information, fitness workouts and videos, recipes and food databases, recipe builders, meal ideas and restaurant guides. These online features are labeled as Weight Watchers eTools.

FINANCIAL DATA: *Note: Data for latest year may not have been available at press time.*

In U.S. $	2017	2016	2015	2014	2013	2012
Revenue	1,306,911,000	1,164,902,000	1,164,419,000	1,479,916,000	1,724,123,000	1,826,812,000
R&D Expense						
Operating Income	280,628,000	200,811,000	168,058,000	299,314,000	460,757,000	510,805,000
Operating Margin %	21.47%	17.23%	14.43%	20.22%	26.72%	27.96%
SGA Expense	412,021,000	384,690,000	406,029,000	503,237,000	540,355,000	571,981,000
Net Income	163,514,000	67,699,000	32,945,000	98,647,000	204,725,000	257,426,000
Operating Cash Flow	222,274,000	119,044,000	54,815,000	231,619,000	323,516,000	349,391,000
Capital Expenditure	40,648,000	34,341,000	36,259,000	51,686,000	61,934,000	78,733,000
EBITDA	308,744,000	251,920,000	230,628,000	329,825,000	483,377,000	544,138,000
Return on Assets %	12.99%	5.02%	2.24%	6.74%	15.58%	21.99%
Return on Equity %						
Debt to Equity						

CONTACT INFORMATION:

Phone: 212 589-2700 Fax:
Toll-Free:
Address: 675 Avenue of the Americas, 6/Fl, New York, NY 10010 United States

STOCK TICKER/OTHER:

Stock Ticker: WTW
Employees: 18,000
Parent Company:
Exchange: NYS
Fiscal Year Ends: 12/31

SALARIES/BONUSES:

Top Exec. Salary: $555,966 Bonus: $200,000
Second Exec. Salary: $544,615 Bonus: $

OTHER THOUGHTS:

Estimated Female Officers or Directors: 1
Hot Spot for Advancement for Women/Minorities: Y

Welch Allyn Inc

NAIC Code: 339,100

www.welchallyn.com

TYPES OF BUSINESS:

Equipment-Mobile Patient Monitoring Systems
Cardiac Defibrillators
Diagnostic and Therapeutic Devices
Precision Lamps
Image-Based Data Collection Systems
Remote Imaging Services
Equipment Sales and Rentals

BRANDS/DIVISIONS/AFFILIATES:

Hill-Rom Holdings Inc

CONTACTS: *Note: Officers with more than one job title may be intentionally listed here more than once.*

Alton Shader, Pres.
Valerie Finarty, VP-Operations
Steve Meyer, Pres.
Healther McClanahan, VP-Finance
Richard Marritt, CMO
Nicole Hulik, Dir.-Human Resources
Mike Ehrhart, Exec. VP-Prod. Dev.
Gregory Porter, General Counsel
Darrell Clapper, Exec. VP-Global Oper.
Jon Soderberg, Exec. VP-Corp. Dev.
Joseph Hennigan, Exec. VP-Finance
John Tierney, Sr. VP-Americas
Hisham Hout, Sr. VP-Europe & Middle East
Darrell Clapper, Exec. VP-Supply Chain Mgmt.

GROWTH PLANS/SPECIAL FEATURES:

Welch Allyn, Inc., founded in 1915, is a manufacturer of products in five categories: physical assessment, vital signs monitoring, diagnostic cardiopulmonary, software and services, and thermometry. The firm manufactures products for eye, ear, nose and throat applications; stethoscopes; blood pressure management products; cardiopulmonary products; thermometry products; patient monitors and systems; defibrillation products; lighting products; women's health products; endoscopy products; weight management products; veterinary health products; and replacement parts. Welch Allyn's products are sold to physician offices, hospitals, emergency medical service providers, dental care providers, veterinarians, medical students, optometry students, veterinary students and the U.S. government. The firm operates through offices worldwide, including North America, Latin America, Europe, the Middle East, Africa, Asia and the Pacific Rim. The company engages in partnership programs for the goal of researching, developing and marketing innovative products. Welch Allyn is wholly-owned by Hill-Rom Holdings, Inc., a global medical technology company.

The firm offers employees an annual company performance bonus; access to a fitness center; wellness programs; AD&D, disability, medical, dental and vision insurance; medical and dependent care flexible spending accounts; and life insurance.

FINANCIAL DATA: *Note: Data for latest year may not have been available at press time.*

In U.S. $	2017	2016	2015	2014	2013	2012
Revenue	753,900,000	718,000,000	715,000,000	700,560,000	650,000,000	500,000,000
R&D Expense						
Operating Income						
Operating Margin %						
SGA Expense						
Net Income						
Operating Cash Flow						
Capital Expenditure						
EBITDA						
Return on Assets %						
Return on Equity %						
Debt to Equity						

CONTACT INFORMATION:

Phone: 315-685-4100 Fax: 315-685-4091
Toll-Free: 800-535-6663
Address: 4341 State St. Rd., Skaneateles Falls, NY 13153 United States

STOCK TICKER/OTHER:

Stock Ticker: Subsidiary
Employees: 2,500
Parent Company: Hill-Rom Holdings Inc
Exchange:
Fiscal Year Ends: 12/31

SALARIES/BONUSES:

Top Exec. Salary: $ Bonus: $
Second Exec. Salary: $ Bonus: $

OTHER THOUGHTS:

Estimated Female Officers or Directors: 1
Hot Spot for Advancement for Women/Minorities: Y

WellCare Health Plans Inc

www.wellcare.com

NAIC Code: 524,114

TYPES OF BUSINESS:

Insurance-Medical & Health, HMOs & PPOs

BRANDS/DIVISIONS/AFFILIATES:

WellCare
Ohana
Easy Choice
Staywell
Care1st
Harmony
Missouri Care

CONTACTS:
Note: Officers with more than one job title may be intentionally listed here more than once.

Kenneth Burdick, CEO
Andrew Asher, CFO
Michael Meyer, Chief Accounting Officer
Darren Ghanayem, Chief Information Officer
Mark Leenay, Chief Medical Officer
Christian Michalik, Director
Michael Polen, Executive VP, Divisional
Michael Radu, Executive VP, Divisional
Kelly Munson, Executive VP, Divisional
Anat Hakim, General Counsel
Timothy Trodden, Other Executive Officer
Rhonda Mims, Other Executive Officer
Michael Yount, Other Executive Officer

GROWTH PLANS/SPECIAL FEATURES:

WellCare Health Plans, Inc. manages government-sponsored healthcare programs with a focus on Medicaid and Medicare programs. The firm offers a variety of managed care health plans for families, children and the aged, blind and disabled, as well as prescription drug plans. The company has served health plans and prescription drug plans for approximately 4.4 million members (as of August 2018). WellCare's Medicare plans have been offered under the WellCare name, except for its Hawaii and California coordinated care plans (CCPs), which are under the names Ohana and Easy Choice, respectively. For Medicaid plans, the brands depend on the state and consist of: Staywell, Care1st, Ohana, Harmony, Missouri Care and WellCare. In May 2018, WellCare agreed to acquire three Meridian companies, collectively for $2.5 billion. They include: Meridian Health Plan of Michigan, Inc.; Meridian Health Plan of Illinois, Inc.; and MeridianRx. The transaction was expected to close by year's end.

WellCare offers employees several family benefit plans, wellness plans, dental and vision, prescription drug coverage, life insurance, AD&D, disability, 401(k), flexible spending accounts, tuition reimbursement and an employee assistance plan.

FINANCIAL DATA:
Note: Data for latest year may not have been available at press time.

In U.S. $	2017	2016	2015	2014	2013	2012
Revenue	17,007,200,000	14,237,100,000	13,890,200,000	12,959,900,000	9,527,900,000	7,409,032,000
R&D Expense						
Operating Income	537,500,000	588,600,000	384,200,000	211,800,000	293,000,000	300,561,000
Operating Margin %	2.89%	4.13%	2.76%	1.63%	3.07%	4.05%
SGA Expense	1,484,700,000	1,133,100,000	1,132,900,000	1,018,800,000	856,500,000	690,842,000
Net Income	373,700,000	242,100,000	118,600,000	63,700,000	175,300,000	184,728,000
Operating Cash Flow	1,050,000,000	748,300,000	712,600,000	299,300,000	178,900,000	-30,739,000
Capital Expenditure	128,400,000	105,300,000	137,000,000	74,800,000	62,000,000	61,268,000
EBITDA	631,800,000	676,200,000	462,900,000	277,100,000	334,300,000	332,092,000
Return on Assets %	5.14%	4.26%	2.44%	1.60%	5.72%	7.15%
Return on Equity %	16.92%	12.98%	7.13%	4.09%	12.34%	15.14%
Debt to Equity	0.48	0.49	0.52	0.56	0.39	0.09

CONTACT INFORMATION:

Phone: 813 290-6200 Fax:
Toll-Free: 800-795-3432
Address: 8725 Henderson Rd., Renaissance 1, Tampa, FL 33634 United States

STOCK TICKER/OTHER:

Stock Ticker: WCG
Exchange: NYS
Employees: 7,400
Fiscal Year Ends: 12/31
Parent Company:

SALARIES/BONUSES:

Top Exec. Salary: $1,169,231 Bonus: $
Second Exec. Salary: $633,846 Bonus: $

OTHER THOUGHTS:

Estimated Female Officers or Directors: 3
Hot Spot for Advancement for Women/Minorities: Y

Welltok Inc

welltok.com

NAIC Code: 511210D

TYPES OF BUSINESS:

Computer Software, Healthcare and Biotechnology

BRANDS/DIVISIONS/AFFILIATES:

CafeWell
EngageME
Opportunity Analysis
SmartReach

CONTACTS: *Note: Officers with more than one job title may be intentionally listed here more than once.*

Jeff Margolis, CEO
Rob Scavo, Pres.
Chris Power, Sr. VP
Michelle Snyder, CMO
Chaz Hinkle, Chief People Officer
Jeff Margolis, Chmn.

GROWTH PLANS/SPECIAL FEATURES:

Welltok, Inc. designs and develops a technology that drives engagement through a combination of social, incentive and personalization technologies in the healthcare industry. Its mission is to help every consumer achieve optimal health potential by connecting payers, health systems, care organizations and other population health managers with their members and reward them for healthy physical, emotional and financial behaviors. Welltok's CafeWell platform guides consumers toward optimal health through personalized programs, resources and incentives. CafeWell's key features include: a personal health itinerary, comprising a set of activities, resources and content designed for each individual consumer; a rewards program; an organized ecosystem with in-house curated content of connect partner programs and the individual's personal programs; coaching, via group video sessions, blogs and personal messaging; concierge, an on-demand, 24/7 artificial intelligent chatbot to guide consumers through benefits in a simplified manner; and an administration module for gaining program insight and managing platform configurations from a central location. EngageME is a communication platform for providing a positive engagement experience across the entire organization, enabling total visibility into the population as a whole as well as into individual members. Opportunity Analysis is designed to predict, manage and optimize program engagement for a deep understanding of the population's engagement preferences as well as related health risks and costs. Last, SmartReach provides analytics-driven insights and targeted multi-channel outreach for maximizing resources, lowering costs, boosting plan ratings and improving member experiences and outcomes. Just a few of Welltok's many investors include: Bessemer Venture Partners, Emergence Capital, Georgian Partners, InterWest Partners, Miramar Venture Partners and New Enterprise Associates. In April 2018, Welltok announced that it raised $75 million in a Series E2 funding round with participation from new and existing investors. New investors include Future Fund Management Agency, Ziff Davis, NF Trinity Capital (Hong Kong) Limited and ITOCHU Corporation.

FINANCIAL DATA: *Note: Data for latest year may not have been available at press time.*

In U.S. $	2017	2016	2015	2014	2013	2012
Revenue	68,800,000	625,000,000				
R&D Expense						
Operating Income						
Operating Margin %						
SGA Expense						
Net Income						
Operating Cash Flow						
Capital Expenditure						
EBITDA						
Return on Assets %						
Return on Equity %						
Debt to Equity						

CONTACT INFORMATION:

Phone: 720-222-9490 Fax:
Toll-Free: 888-935-5865
Address: 1515 Arapahoe St., Tower 3, Ste. 700, Denver, CO 80202 United States

STOCK TICKER/OTHER:

Stock Ticker: Private
Employees: 443
Parent Company:
Exchange:
Fiscal Year Ends:

SALARIES/BONUSES:

Top Exec. Salary: $ Bonus: $
Second Exec. Salary: $ Bonus: $

OTHER THOUGHTS:

Estimated Female Officers or Directors:
Hot Spot for Advancement for Women/Minorities:

William Demant Holding Group

www.demant.com

NAIC Code: 334,510

TYPES OF BUSINESS:

Human Hearing Assistance Technology
Hearing Aids
Diagnostic Instruments
Personal Communications Technology

BRANDS/DIVISIONS/AFFILIATES:

Oticon
Bernafon
Sonic
Phonic Ear
FrontRow
Interacoustics
Maico
Micromedical

CONTACTS: *Note: Officers with more than one job title may be intentionally listed here more than once.*

Soren Nielsen, CEO
Niels Jacobsen, Pres.
Rene Schneider, CFO
Niels B. Christiansen, Chmn.

GROWTH PLANS/SPECIAL FEATURES:

William Demant Holding Group is a Danish holding company that oversees the operations of several subsidiaries engaged in the development and manufacturing of hearing devices, hearing implants and diagnostic instruments in over 130 countries. The hearing devices division derives 87% of the firm's total revenue, and includes the Oticon, Bernafon and Sonic brands of devices. Oticon is a leading manufacturer of hearing care solutions such as hearing aids and fitting systems; Bernafon develops quality hearing systems via Swiss engineering and technology; and Sonic is a U.S.-based manufacturer of hearing instruments renowned for superior sound processing, noise reduction, directional capabilities and award-winning design. Other brands in this division include Phonic Ear and FrontRow. The hearing implants division (4%) is comprised of Oticon Medical, which develops bone anchored hearing systems and implant solutions such as cochlear implants that help overcome several to total bilateral (second degree) hearing loss. The diagnostic instruments division (9%) includes the Maico, Interacoustics, Amplivox, Grason-Stadler, MedRx and Micromedical brands which develop, manufacture and distribute audiometers for hearing measurement, as well as other instruments used by audiologists and ear-nose-and-throat specialists.

FINANCIAL DATA: *Note: Data for latest year may not have been available at press time.*

In U.S. $	2017	2016	2015	2014	2013	2012
Revenue						
R&D Expense						
Operating Income						
Operating Margin %						
SGA Expense						
Net Income						
Operating Cash Flow						
Capital Expenditure						
EBITDA						
Return on Assets %						
Return on Equity %						
Debt to Equity						

CONTACT INFORMATION:

Phone: 45 39177300 Fax: 45 39278900
Toll-Free:
Address: Kongebakken 9, Smorum, 2765 Denmark

STOCK TICKER/OTHER:

Stock Ticker: WILYY Exchange: PINX
Employees: 13,280 Fiscal Year Ends: 12/31
Parent Company:

SALARIES/BONUSES:

Top Exec. Salary: $ Bonus: $
Second Exec. Salary: $ Bonus: $

OTHER THOUGHTS:

Estimated Female Officers or Directors: 1
Hot Spot for Advancement for Women/Minorities:

Wright Medical Group NV

www.wmt.com

NAIC Code: 339,100

TYPES OF BUSINESS:

Orthopedic Implants
Reconstructive Joint Devices
Biologics Materials

BRANDS/DIVISIONS/AFFILIATES:

CHARLOTTE
DARCO
INBONE
PRO-TOE
SALVATION
EVOLVE
GRAFTJACKET
FUSIONFLEX

CONTACTS: *Note: Officers with more than one job title may be intentionally listed here more than once.*

Robert J. Palmisano, CEO
Barry J. Regan, Sr. VP-Operations
Lance A. Berry, CFO
Julie D. Dewey, Sr. VP-CCO
Andrew C. Morton, Sr. VP-Human Resources
Kevin OBoyle, Director
James Lightman, General Counsel
William Griffin, General Manager, Divisional
Julie Tracy, Other Executive Officer
Jonathan Porter, Other Executive Officer
Kevin Cordell, President, Divisional
Peter Cooke, President, Divisional
Robert Palmisano, President
Robert Burrows, Senior VP, Divisional
Jennifer Walker, Senior VP, Divisional
Gregory Morrison, Senior VP, Divisional
Lance Berry, Senior VP
David D. Stevens, Chmn.

GROWTH PLANS/SPECIAL FEATURES:

Wright Medical Group NV is a global medical device company focused on extremities and biologics products. The firm is a recognized leader of surgical solutions for the upper extremities (shoulder, elbow, wrist and hand), lower extremities (foot and ankle) and biologics markets, three of the fastest growing segments in orthopedics. Wright Medical markets its products in over 50 countries worldwide. Foot and ankle hardware include the CHARLOTTE system, which comprises the CLAW compression plate designed for corrective foot surgeries; the DARCO plating system designed as implants to incorporate fixed angle, locking screw technology into a fixation set for foot surgery; INBONE ankle systems; trauma devices such as plates, pins, nails and screws to help stabilize fractures; PRO-TOE hammertoe fixation systems; TENFUSE nail allograft; BIOFOAM wedge system for corrective osteotomies of the foot; VALOR fusion nail systems; SALVATION limb salvage products; and BIOARCH subtalar arthroereisis implant; and the Swanson line of toe joint replacement products. Upper extremity hardware includes EVOLVE radial head replacement prosthesis for the elbow; MICRONAIL intramedullary fracture repair systems; and RAYHACK precision cutting guides and plates for shortening procedures. Biologics include the GRAFTJACKET soft tissue graft for augmentation of tendon and ligament repairs; PRO-DENSE injectable graft of calcium sulfate and calcium phosphate; OSTEOSET synthetic bone graft substitute; MIIG injectable graft; FUSIONFLEX demineralized moldable scaffold; CANCELLO-PURE bone wedges; ALLOPURE allograft bone wedges; and ALLOMATRIX injectable putty. In June 2018, Wright Medical received premarket approval from the U.S. Food and Drug Administration for its AUGMENT injectable bone graft product.

FINANCIAL DATA: *Note: Data for latest year may not have been available at press time.*

In U.S. $	2017	2016	2015	2014	2013	2012
Revenue	744,989,000	690,362,000	415,461,000	344,953,000	310,959,000	277,520,000
R&D Expense	50,115,000	50,514,000	39,855,000	24,139,000	22,387,000	22,524,000
Operating Income	-19,691,000	-122,958,000	-189,969,000	-11,880,000	-15,196,000	-11,091,000
Operating Margin %	-2.64%	-17.81%	-45.72%	-3.44%	-4.88%	-3.99%
SGA Expense	525,222,000	541,558,000	429,398,000	237,158,000	206,851,000	170,447,000
Net Income	-202,598,000	-432,373,000	-298,701,000	-29,471,000	-36,426,000	-21,744,000
Operating Cash Flow	-184,810,000	37,824,000	-195,870,000	1,008,000	24,982,000	14,431,000
Capital Expenditure	65,573,000	54,944,000	43,748,000	32,328,000	37,565,000	24,700,000
EBITDA	65,537,000	-36,996,000	-143,566,000	18,061,000	9,745,000	1,286,000
Return on Assets %	-9.16%	-19.74%	-21.73%	-4.32%	-5.35%	-3.72%
Return on Equity %	-31.76%	-49.64%	-38.94%	-5.86%	-7.57%	-5.19%
Debt to Equity	1.42	1.13	0.54	0.14	0.12	0.26

CONTACT INFORMATION:

Phone: 44-845-8334435 Fax:
Toll-Free:
Address: Fraser House 56 Kingston Rd., Middlesex, TW18 4NL United Kingdom

STOCK TICKER/OTHER:

Stock Ticker: WMGI
Employees: 2,394
Parent Company:
Exchange: NAS
Fiscal Year Ends: 12/31

SALARIES/BONUSES:

Top Exec. Salary: $945,792 Bonus: $
Second Exec. Salary: $115,962 Bonus: $452,183

OTHER THOUGHTS:

Estimated Female Officers or Directors: 4
Hot Spot for Advancement for Women/Minorities: Y

Young Innovations Inc

www.ydnt.com

NAIC Code: 339,100

TYPES OF BUSINESS:

Dental Instruments
Home Dental Care Products-Toothbrushes
Ultrasonic Systems
X-Ray Machines & Related Supplies

BRANDS/DIVISIONS/AFFILIATES:

Jordan Company LP (The)
Linden Capital Partners
Young
Denticator
Obtura Spartan Endodontics
HealthSonics
MyDent International Enterprises Corporation
Promident LLC (Johnson-Promident)

CONTACTS: *Note: Officers with more than one job title may be intentionally listed here more than once.*

Dave Sproat, CEO
Dale Carroll, VP-Operations
Christopher Roth, CFO
Dave Misiak, VP-Mktg. & Sales
Mark Peluse, VP-Human Resources
Julia A. Carter, VP-Finance

GROWTH PLANS/SPECIAL FEATURES:

Young Innovations, Inc. manufactures and distributes products and equipment used to facilitate the practice of dentistry and to promote oral health. Founded in the early 1900s as Young Dental, the company's portfolio of brands is designed to deliver innovative solutions to dental professionals and their patients. These brands include: the Young line of prophylactic angle, fluoride varnish and hygiene handpieces; the Denticator line of angles, handpieces, cups, toothbrushes and toothpaste; the Panoramic line of panoramic X-ray machines; the Athena Champion line of dental handpieces, replacement turbines, dental burs, lubricants and related parts and accessories; the Plak Smacker line of toothbrushes, floss kits, infection control products, hygiene gloves and more; the Biotrol line of dental infection control products; the Obtura Spartan Endodontics line of infection control products, backfill devices, ultrasonics, heat source devices, rotary files and endodontic surgery products; the HealthSonics line of cleaners, solutions and asepsis products; the Microbrush line of applicators, moisture control and matrix systems for restorative dentistry; the Oral-B line of toothbrushes, prophylaxis pastes, fluoride, trays, topical treatments, detection tablets and angles; the Opti-Cide3 line of sanitizers; the Zooby line of pediatric angles, toothpastes, fluorides, exam gloves, bibs and face masks; the American Eagle Instruments line of dental instruments and diagnostics; the Defend (by Mydent International) line of face masks, shields, gloves, disinfectants, sterilization products, impression materials, mixing tips, disposables, barrier products, instruments and more; and the Johnson-Promident line of handpieces, rotary instruments, curing lights, sonic scalers, endodontic products, lubricants, cleaners, polishing equipment, scaling equipment and related parts and accessories. In late-2017, The Jordan Company LP purchased a controlling interest in Young Innovations, with Linden Capital Partners retaining a minority share. During 2018, Young Innovations acquired Mydent International Enterprises Corporation as well as Promident, LLC (Johnson-Promident).

FINANCIAL DATA: *Note: Data for latest year may not have been available at press time.*

In U.S. $	2017	2016	2015	2014	2013	2012
Revenue						
R&D Expense						
Operating Income						
Operating Margin %						
SGA Expense						
Net Income						
Operating Cash Flow						
Capital Expenditure						
EBITDA						
Return on Assets %						
Return on Equity %						
Debt to Equity						

CONTACT INFORMATION:

Phone: 847-458-5400 Fax:
Toll-Free:
Address: 2260 Wendt St, Algonquin, IL 60102 United States

STOCK TICKER/OTHER:

Stock Ticker: Private Exchange:
Employees: 371 Fiscal Year Ends: 12/31
Parent Company: Jordan Company LP (The)

SALARIES/BONUSES:

Top Exec. Salary: $ Bonus: $
Second Exec. Salary: $ Bonus: $

OTHER THOUGHTS:

Estimated Female Officers or Directors: 1
Hot Spot for Advancement for Women/Minorities:

Yuhan Corporation

eng.yuhan.co.kr/Main

NAIC Code: 325,412

TYPES OF BUSINESS:

Pharmaceuticals
Traditional Foods
Cleaning Products
Fine Chemicals

BRANDS/DIVISIONS/AFFILIATES:

Yuhan Chemical Inc
Yuhan Medica Corporation
Yuhan-Clorox Co Ltd
Gujarat Themis Biosyn Ltd
Yuhan Research Institute

CONTACTS: *Note: Officers with more than one job title may be intentionally listed here more than once.*

Jung Hee Lee, CEO
Chris C.K. Sa, Dir.-New Prod. Dev.
Chris C.K. Sa, Dir.-Bus. Dev.
Yoon-Saerb Kim, Co-CEO
Do Hwan Oh, Managing Dir.

GROWTH PLANS/SPECIAL FEATURES:

Yuhan Corporation is a pharmaceuticals company that develops drugs for diabetes, viral and fungus infection, osteoporosis, arthritis, cancer and hepatitis C. Yuhan's first fully-developed drug, Revanex, an anti-ulcer agent for gastrointestinal diseases, is one of the first new drugs ever developed in Korea. The firm conducts its research through the Yuhan Research Institute. Yuhan's drug discovery laboratory engages in new drug development including combinatorial chemistry, molecular design, high-throughput screening and joint development programs. Its biotech laboratory research ranges from genetically-engineered pharmaceuticals to home test kits and hospital diagnosis kits. The lab has developed new veterinary medicines, home pregnancy test kits and prostate cancer diagnosis kits. The pharmaceuticals development lab mainly researches novel drug delivery systems, including nano-particle and nano-emulsion production techniques, and seeks to improve existing drugs. The process development lab researches active pharmaceutical ingredient production methods and conducts contract manufacturing of custom pharmaceutical materials. The drug evaluation lab conducts pre-clinical trials and studies new drug candidates. The pharmaceuticals analysis lab develops analysis systems and equipment, analyzing areas such as drug stability, protein structure and clinical samples. It also studies the physical and chemical properties of drugs and verifies the viability of proposed analysis techniques. Subsidiary Yuhan Chemical, Inc. has designed plants that produce pharmaceutical ingredients meeting cGMP (current good manufacturing practice) standards, while subsidiary Yuhan Medica Corporation produces third-party owned pharmaceutical products and is expanding its traditional food business. Joint venture (with Clorox) Yuhan-Clorox Co. Ltd. produces hygienic, disinfectant and plumbing relief products. Joint venture Gujarat Themis Biosyn Ltd., based in India, produces and markets finished products such as Rifampicin and Rifa-S antibiotics, which are used to treat various bacterial infections.

FINANCIAL DATA: *Note: Data for latest year may not have been available at press time.*

In U.S. $	2017	2016	2015	2014	2013	2012
Revenue	1,056,920,000	1,094,810,000	1,011,809,783	861,600,000	906,500,000	745,900,000
R&D Expense						
Operating Income						
Operating Margin %						
SGA Expense						
Net Income	117,988,000	133,619,000	112,980,182	77,000,000	83,100,000	77,600,000
Operating Cash Flow						
Capital Expenditure						
EBITDA						
Return on Assets %						
Return on Equity %						
Debt to Equity						

CONTACT INFORMATION:

Phone: 82-2-828-0181 Fax: 82-2-828-0050
Toll-Free:
Address: 74, Noryangjin-ro, dongjak-gu, Seoul, South Korea

STOCK TICKER/OTHER:

Stock Ticker: 100 Exchange: Seoul
Employees: 1,700 Fiscal Year Ends: 12/31
Parent Company:

SALARIES/BONUSES:

Top Exec. Salary: $ Bonus: $
Second Exec. Salary: $ Bonus: $

OTHER THOUGHTS:

Estimated Female Officers or Directors:
Hot Spot for Advancement for Women/Minorities:

Yunnan Baiyao Group Co Ltd

www.yunnanbaiyao.com.cn

NAIC Code: 325,411

TYPES OF BUSINESS:

Medicinal and Botanical Manufacturing

BRANDS/DIVISIONS/AFFILIATES:

GROWTH PLANS/SPECIAL FEATURES:

Yunnan Baiyao Group Co., Ltd. manufactures and sells Chinese pharmaceutical products in China and internationally. The company's pharmaceutical products include powders, tablets, capsules and liquids. Other related items address wound care, blood circulation, swelling reduction, injuries, muscle relaxers, colds, flu and rheumatic and respiratory issues. Many of Yunnan's products are categorized into traditional Chinese medicines, but also into raw medicine materials. Consumer products include shampoo, toothpaste, acne care, deodorant, face masks, eye care, sanitary products, disinfectants, first aid kits and much more. Yunnan operates several subsidiaries engaged in pharmaceuticals, consumer health products and biotechnology. Products are sold in both domestic and overseas markets, with domestic being primary.

CONTACTS: *Note: Officers with more than one job title may be intentionally listed here more than once.*

Minghui Wang, Chmn.

FINANCIAL DATA: *Note: Data for latest year may not have been available at press time.*

In U.S. $	2017	2016	2015	2014	2013	2012
Revenue	3,733,430,000	3,224,890,000	3,178,980,000	3,042,490,000	2,574,110,000	
R&D Expense						
Operating Income						
Operating Margin %						
SGA Expense						
Net Income	480,991,000	421,755,000	426,914,000	407,248,000	379,623,000	
Operating Cash Flow						
Capital Expenditure						
EBITDA						
Return on Assets %						
Return on Equity %						
Debt to Equity						

CONTACT INFORMATION:

Phone: 86-87-1832-4198 Fax: 86-87-1832-3863

Toll-Free:

Address: 222 Er'huan Xi Rd., Kunming, Yunnan China

STOCK TICKER/OTHER:

Stock Ticker: 538 Exchange: Shenzhen

Employees: 8,300 Fiscal Year Ends:

Parent Company:

SALARIES/BONUSES:

Top Exec. Salary: $ Bonus: $

Second Exec. Salary: $ Bonus: $

OTHER THOUGHTS:

Estimated Female Officers or Directors:

Hot Spot for Advancement for Women/Minorities:

Zimmer Biomet Holdings Inc

www.zimmerbiomet.com/

NAIC Code: 339,100

TYPES OF BUSINESS:

Orthopedic Supplies
Human Bone Joint Replacement Systems
Orthopedic Support Devices
Operating Room Supplies
Powered Surgical Instruments
Dental Implants

BRANDS/DIVISIONS/AFFILIATES:

Persona
Zimmer
Transposal
JuggerKnot
3i T3
Timberline
SternaLock
Sidus

CONTACTS: *Note: Officers with more than one job title may be intentionally listed here more than once.*

Bryan Hanson, CEO
Larry Glasscock, Director
Daniel Florin, Executive VP
Daniel Williamson, President, Divisional
Aure Bruneau, President, Divisional
David Nolan, President, Divisional
Robert Delp, President, Geographical
Sang Yi, President, Geographical
Katarzyna Mazur-Hofsaess, President, Geographical
Chad Phipps, Senior VP
Tony Collins, Vice President

GROWTH PLANS/SPECIAL FEATURES:

Zimmer Biomet Holdings, Inc. designs, manufactures and markets musculoskeletal products for the healthcare industry. These include orthopedic reconstructive products; sports medicine, biologics, extremities and trauma products; spine, bone healing, craniomaxillofacial and thoracic products; dental implants; and related surgical products. Zimmer Biomet collaborates with healthcare professionals worldwide to advance the pace of innovation. The company's products and solutions help treat patients suffering from disorders of, or injuries to bones, joints or supporting soft tissues. Knee products include the Persona, NexGen, Vanguard and Oxford branded systems. Hip products include the Zimmer, Taperloc, Arcos, Continuum and G7 branded systems. Surgical, sports medicine, biologics, foot and ankle, extremities and trauma products include the Transposal and Transposal Ultra fluid waste management systems, automatic tourniquet systems, JuggerKnot soft anchor system, Gel-One cross-linked hyaluronate, Zimmer Trabecular Metal reverse shoulder system, Comprehensive shoulder system and Zimmer Natural Nail system. Dental products include the Tapered Screw-Vent and 3i T3 implant systems. Spine and craniomaxillofacial and thoracic products include the Polaris spinal system, Timberline lateral fusion system, Mobi-C cervical disc, SternaLock closure and fixation systems brand lines. Other products include PALACOS bone cement and SinalPak fusion stimulator. During 2018, Zimmer obtained: FDA clearance of the Comprehensive augmented baseplate for shoulder reconstruction; FDA clearance, as well as the first surgical case utilizing the Persona Trabecular Metal Tibia; and FDA clearance of the Sidus stem-free shoulder system (which became available in the U.S. in 2018).

FINANCIAL DATA: *Note: Data for latest year may not have been available at press time.*

In U.S. $	2017	2016	2015	2014	2013	2012
Revenue	7,824,100,000	7,683,900,000	5,997,800,000	4,673,300,000	4,623,400,000	4,471,700,000
R&D Expense	369,900,000	365,600,000	268,800,000	192,800,000	205,000,000	225,600,000
Operating Income	1,328,600,000	1,071,600,000	914,300,000	1,153,200,000	1,112,400,000	1,189,100,000
Operating Margin %	16.98%	13.94%	15.24%	24.67%	24.06%	26.59%
SGA Expense	3,378,500,000	3,299,000,000	2,667,500,000	2,050,000,000	1,966,900,000	1,912,300,000
Net Income	1,813,800,000	305,900,000	147,000,000	720,100,000	761,000,000	755,000,000
Operating Cash Flow	1,582,300,000	1,632,200,000	816,700,000	1,052,800,000	963,100,000	1,151,900,000
Capital Expenditure	493,000,000	530,200,000	434,100,000	342,300,000	292,900,000	264,500,000
EBITDA	1,854,800,000	1,796,800,000	1,152,200,000	1,382,800,000	1,409,700,000	1,426,100,000
Return on Assets %	6.89%	1.13%	.79%	7.49%	8.18%	8.61%
Return on Equity %	16.94%	3.12%	1.79%	11.23%	12.51%	13.28%
Debt to Equity	0.75	1.10	1.16	0.21	0.26	0.29

CONTACT INFORMATION:

Phone: 574-267-6639 Fax: 574-267-8137
Toll-Free: 800-613-6131
Address: 345 East Main St., Warsaw, IN 46580 United States

STOCK TICKER/OTHER:

Stock Ticker: ZBH Exchange: NYS
Employees: 18,500 Fiscal Year Ends: 05/31
Parent Company:

SALARIES/BONUSES:

Top Exec. Salary: $820,597 Bonus: $100,000
Second Exec. Salary: $706,338 Bonus: $

OTHER THOUGHTS:

Estimated Female Officers or Directors: 3
Hot Spot for Advancement for Women/Minorities: Y

Zoll Medical Corporation

www.zoll.com

NAIC Code: 339,100

TYPES OF BUSINESS:

Cardiac Resuscitation Devices
Disposable Electrodes
Intravascular Temperature Management
Information Management

BRANDS/DIVISIONS/AFFILIATES:

Asahi Kasei Corporation
Zoll
731
RescueNet
ZOLL LifeVest

CONTACTS: *Note: Officers with more than one job title may be intentionally listed here more than once.*

Jonathan A. Rennert, CEO
Jonathan A. Rennert, Pres.
E. Jane Wilson, VP-R&D
A. Ernest Whiton, VP-Admin.
Aaron M. Grossman, General Counsel
John P. Bergeron, Treas.
Steven K. Flora, Sr. VP-North American Sales
Ward M. Hamilton, Sr.VP
Richard A. Packer, Chmn.
Alex N. Moghadam, VP-Int'l Oper.

GROWTH PLANS/SPECIAL FEATURES:

Zoll Medical Corporation, an Asahi Kasei Corporation company, develops and markets medical devices and software solutions that assist in emergency care. Its products include defibrillation, monitoring, circulation, CPR feedback, data management, fluid resuscitation and therapeutic temperature management devices. Market sectors that use Zoll products and technologies include emergency medical services (EMS), fire departments, hospitals, public safety, alternate care, military and government and homeland security. Products and technologies include: automated external defibrillators (AEDs), providing treatment for sudden cardiac arrest (SCA), and include real-time cardiopulmonary resuscitation feedback on the depth and rate of chest compressions; the 731 family of portable ventilators, for environments ranging from the emergency department to military operations, and provide therapies to ventilate and support infants through adults. Additional products include temperature management systems, which provide power and control to rapidly and safely manage the core body temperature of critically-ill or surgical patients; intrathoracic pressure regulation (IPR) therapy, which creates a vacuum inside the chest cavity that enhances circulation, increases blood pressure and lowers intracranial pressure; and the RescueNet suite of patient data management, which helps medical professionals manage information such as vital signs, end-tidal CO2 trends and CPR performance. ZOLL LifeVest is a wearable defibrillator worn by patients at risk for SCA, providing protection during their changing activity condition and while permanent SCA risk has not been established.

FINANCIAL DATA: *Note: Data for latest year may not have been available at press time.*

In U.S. $	2017	2016	2015	2014	2013	2012
Revenue	997,500,000	950,000,000	900,000,000			
R&D Expense						
Operating Income						
Operating Margin %						
SGA Expense						
Net Income						
Operating Cash Flow						
Capital Expenditure						
EBITDA						
Return on Assets %						
Return on Equity %						
Debt to Equity						

CONTACT INFORMATION:

Phone: 978-421-9655 Fax: 978-421-0025
Toll-Free: 800-348-9011
Address: 269 Mill Rd., Chelmsford, MA 01824 United States

STOCK TICKER/OTHER:

Stock Ticker: Subsidiary
Exchange:
Employees: 4,000
Fiscal Year Ends: 09/30
Parent Company: Asahi Kasei Corporation

SALARIES/BONUSES:

Top Exec. Salary: $ Bonus: $
Second Exec. Salary: $ Bonus: $

OTHER THOUGHTS:

Estimated Female Officers or Directors:
Hot Spot for Advancement for Women/Minorities:

ADDITIONAL INDEXES

CONTENTS:

INDEX OF FIRMS NOTED AS HOT SPOTS FOR ADVANCEMENT FOR WOMEN & MINORITIES

New York City Health and Hospitals Corporation
NewYork-Presbyterian Healthcare System
Nordion (Canada) Inc
Novartis AG
Novo-Nordisk AS
OhioHealth Corporation
Omnicare Inc
Organogenesis Inc
Owens & Minor Inc
Par Pharmaceutical Companies Inc
Partners HealthCare
Patterson Companies Inc
Pediatric Services of America Inc
PerkinElmer Inc
Pfizer Inc
Premera Blue Cross
Premier Inc
Providence St Joseph Health
Quest Diagnostics Inc
ResCare Inc
Rite Aid Corporation
Roche Holding AG
Sanofi Genzyme
Sanofi SA
Sentara Healthcare
Shire Plc
SHL Telemedicine Ltd
Siemens AG
Siemens Healthineers
Sigma Healthcare Limited
Smile Brands Inc
Smith & Nephew plc
Smiths Group plc
SSM Health
St Jude Children's Research Hospital
STERIS plc
Steward Health Care System LLC
Stryker Corporation
Sunrise Senior Living LLC
Sutter Health Inc
Take Care Health Systems LLC
Takeda Oncology
Takeda Pharmaceutical Company Limited
Team Health Holdings Inc
Tenet Healthcare Corporation
Teva Pharmaceutical Industries Limited
Texas Health Resources
Theragenics Corporation
Thermo Fisher Scientific Inc
Trinity Health
Trustmark Companies
Tufts Associated Health Plans Inc
United Surgical Partners International Inc
UnitedHealth Group Inc
UnitedHealthcare Community & State
UnitedHealthcare National Accounts
Universal Health Services Inc
Universal Hospital Services Inc
Varian Medical Systems Inc
Vision Service Plan
Vizient Inc
Walgreens Boots Alliance Inc
WebMD Health Corp
Weight Watchers International Inc
Welch Allyn Inc
WellCare Health Plans Inc
Wright Medical Group NV
Zimmer Biomet Holdings Inc

INDEX OF SUBSIDIARIES, BRAND NAMES AND AFFILIATIONS

INDEX OF SUBSIDIARIES, BRAND NAMES AND AFFILIATIONS, CONT.

INDEX OF SUBSIDIARIES, BRAND NAMES AND AFFILIATIONS, CONT.

INDEX OF SUBSIDIARIES, BRAND NAMES AND AFFILIATIONS, CONT.

INDEX OF SUBSIDIARIES, BRAND NAMES AND AFFILIATIONS, CONT.

INDEX OF SUBSIDIARIES, BRAND NAMES AND AFFILIATIONS, CONT.

INDEX OF SUBSIDIARIES, BRAND NAMES AND AFFILIATIONS, CONT.

INDEX OF SUBSIDIARIES, BRAND NAMES AND AFFILIATIONS, CONT.

INDEX OF SUBSIDIARIES, BRAND NAMES AND AFFILIATIONS, CONT.

INDEX OF SUBSIDIARIES, BRAND NAMES AND AFFILIATIONS, CONT.

INDEX OF SUBSIDIARIES, BRAND NAMES AND AFFILIATIONS, CONT.

INDEX OF SUBSIDIARIES, BRAND NAMES AND AFFILIATIONS, CONT.

INDEX OF SUBSIDIARIES, BRAND NAMES AND AFFILIATIONS, CONT.

INDEX OF SUBSIDIARIES, BRAND NAMES AND AFFILIATIONS, CONT.

INDEX OF SUBSIDIARIES, BRAND NAMES AND AFFILIATIONS, CONT.

INDEX OF SUBSIDIARIES, BRAND NAMES AND AFFILIATIONS, CONT.

INDEX OF SUBSIDIARIES, BRAND NAMES AND AFFILIATIONS, CONT.

A Short HealthCare Industry Glossary

3DCRT: Three-dimensional conformal radiotherapy (3DCRT) is a method of radiation therapy whereby PET CAT and other imaging technologies are used to more precisely map tumors or tissues to be treated with radiation. The intent is to better focus the radiation and limit damage to surrounding tissues. (Also, see "Image Guided Radiation Therapy (IGRT).")

510(k): An application filed with the FDA for a new medical device to show that the apparatus is "substantially equivalent" to one that is already marketed.

Abbreviated New Drug Application (ANDA): An application filed with the FDA showing that a substance is the same as an existing, previously approved drug (i.e., a generic version).

Absorption, Distribution, Metabolism and Excretion (ADME): In clinical trials, the bodily processes studied to determine the extent and duration of systemic exposure to a drug.

ACA: See "Affordable Care Act (ACA)."

Accountable Care Organization (ACO): A network of health care providers, including hospitals and primary and specialty care physicians, that provides care and services. The intent is to create large health systems featuring virtually all possible types of specialties and care. The intent is to modernize health care delivery, foster care via teams of doctors, improve communications and efficiency, and make better use of resources such as digital patient records.

Accountable Health Plan: See "Accountable Care Organization (ACO)."

ACO: See "Accountable Care Organization (ACO)."

Adaptive Trial Design: A process in which drug trials are altered or improved in response to trial progression. Recent discoveries may be introduced, and trials may proceed despite the fact that the drugs involved may be successful in only a small number of patients that share specific variables such as DNA defects.

ADME: See "Absorption, Distribution, Metabolism and Excretion (ADME)."

Adverse Event (AE): In clinical trials, a condition not observed at baseline or worsened if present at baseline. Sometimes called Treatment Emergent Signs and Symptoms (TESS).

AE: See "Adverse Event (AE)."

Affordable Care Act (ACA): Short for Patient Protection and Affordable Care Act. Sometimes called Obamacare. Federal Regulations established in March 2010 that greatly expand government oversight of the availability of health care insurance, including Medicaid, Medicare and private insurance. The act also expands regulation of medical practices and pricing.

Alternate Site Care: Health care that was previously provided in general hospitals, but is now offered in less costly, alternate sites. Examples of alternate care include home IV therapy, outpatient surgery centers, rehabilitation units within nursing homes and free-standing centers providing dialysis, radiation therapy and imaging.

ANDA: See "Abbreviated New Drug Application (ANDA)."

Angiogenesis: Blood vessel formation, typically in the growth of malignant tissue.

Angioplasty: The re-opening of a blood vessel by non-surgical techniques such as balloon dilation or laser, or through surgery.

Antibody: A protein produced by white blood cells in response to a foreign substance. Each antibody can bind only to one specific antigen. See "Antigen."

Antigen: A foreign substance that causes the immune system to create an antibody. See "Antibody."

APAC: Asia Pacific Advisory Committee. A multi-country committee representing the Asia and Pacific region.

Apoptosis: A normal cellular process leading to the termination of a cell's life.

Applied Research: The application of compounds, processes, materials or other items discovered during basic research to practical uses. The goal is to move discoveries along to the final development phase.

Arthroscopy: The examination of the interior of a joint using a type of endoscope that is inserted into the joint through a small incision. See "Endoscope."

Assay: A laboratory test to identify and/or measure the amount of a particular substance in a sample. Types of assays include endpoint assays, in which a single measurement is made at a fixed time; kinetic assays, in which increasing amounts of a product are formed with time and are monitored at multiple points; microbiological assays, which measure the concentration of antimicrobials in biological material; and immunological assays, in which analysis or measurement is based on antigen-antibody reactions.

Baby Boomer: Generally refers to people born from 1946 to 1964. In the U.S., the initial number of Baby Boomers totaled about 78 million. The term evolved to describe the children of soldiers and war industry workers who were involved in World War II and who began forming families after the war's end. In 2011, the oldest Baby Boomers began reaching the traditional retirement age of 65.

Baseline: A set of data used in clinical studies, or other types of research, for control or comparison.

Basic Research: Attempts to discover compounds, materials, processes or other items that may be largely or entirely new and/or unique. Basic research may start with a theoretical concept that has yet to be proven. The goal is to create discoveries that can be moved along to applied research. Basic research is sometimes referred to as "blue sky" research.

Behavioral Health: The assessment and treatment of mental health and/or substance abuse disorders. Substance abuse includes alcohol and other drugs.

Big Pharma: The top tier of pharmaceutical companies in terms of sales and profits (e.g., Pfizer, Merck, Johnson & Johnson).

Bioavailability: In pharmaceuticals, the rate and extent to which a drug is absorbed or is otherwise available to the treatment site in the body.

Bioequivalence: In pharmaceuticals, the demonstration that a drug's rate and extent of absorption are not significantly different from those of an existing drug that is already approved by the FDA. This is the basis upon which generic and brand name drugs are compared.

Biogenerics: Genetic versions of drugs that have been created via biotechnology. Also, see "Follow-on Biologics."

Bioinformatics: Research, development or application of computational tools and approaches for expanding the use of biological, medical, behavioral or health data, including those to acquire, store, organize, archive, analyze or visualize such data. Bioinformatics is often applied to the study of genetic data. It applies principles of information sciences and technologies to make vast, diverse and complex life sciences data more understandable and useful.

Biologics: Drugs that are synthesized from living organisms. That is, drugs created using biotechnology, sometimes referred to as biopharmaceuticals. Specifically, biologics may be any virus, therapeutic serum, toxin, antitoxin, vaccine, blood, blood component or derivative, allergenic or analogous product, or arsphenamine or one of its derivatives used for the prevention, treatment or cure of disease. Also, see "Biologics License Application (BLA)," "Follow-on Biologics," and "Biopharmaceuticals."

Biologics License Application (BLA): An application to be submitted to the FDA when a firm wants to obtain permission to market a novel, new biological drug product. Specifically, these are drugs created through the use of biotechnology. It was formerly known as Product License Application (PLA). Also see "Biologics."

Biopharmaceuticals: That portion of the pharmaceutical industry focused on the use of biotechnology to create new drugs. A biopharmaceutical can be any biological compound that is intended to be used as a therapeutic drug, including recombinant proteins, monoclonal and polyclonal antibodies, antisense oligonucleotides, therapeutic genes, and recombinant and DNA vaccines. Also, see "Biologics."

Biosimilar: See "Follow-on Biologics."

Biotechnology: A set of powerful tools that employ living organisms (or parts of organisms) to make or modify products, improve plants or animals (including humans) or develop microorganisms for specific uses. Biotechnology is most commonly thought of to include the development of human medical therapies and processes using recombinant DNA, cell fusion, other genetic techniques and bioremediation.

BLA: See "Biologics License Application (BLA)."

BPO: See "Business Process Outsourcing (BPO)."

Brachytherapy: A method of internal radiation therapy whereby tiny containers of radioactive material, sometimes referred to as "seeds," are implanted directly in contact with tissue that is afflicted with cancerous tumors. It is a common method of treating prostate cancer and is sometimes used for the treatment of breast cancer. These seeds are never removed from the body. They typically have a radioactive half-life of six months. Eventually, they emit virtually no radiation at all.

Brand: A marketing strategy that places a focus on the brand name of a product, service or firm in order to increase the brand's market share, increase sales, establish credibility, improve satisfaction, raise the profile of the firm and increase profits. Also, see "Brand."

Branding: A marketing strategy that places a focus on the brand name of a product, service or firm in order to increase the brand's market share, increase sales, establish credibility, improve satisfaction, raise the profile of the firm and increase profits. Also, see "Brand."

B-to-B, or B2B: See "Business-to-Business."

B-to-C, or B2C: See "Business-to-Consumer."

B-to-E, or B2E: See "Business-to-Employee."

B-to-G, or B2G: See "Business-to-Government."

Business Process Outsourcing (BPO): The process of hiring another company to handle business activities. BPO is one of the fastest-growing segments in the offshoring sector. Services include human resources management, billing and purchasing and call centers, as well as many types of customer service or marketing activities, depending on the industry involved. Also, see "Knowledge Process Outsourcing (KPO)" and Business Transformation Outsourcing (BTO)."

Business Transformation Outsourcing (BTO): A segment within outsourcing in which the client company revamps its business processes with the goal of transforming its business by following a collaborative approach with its outsourced services provider.

Business-to-Business: An organization focused on selling products, services or data to commercial customers rather than individual consumers. Also known as B2B.

Business-to-Consumer: An organization focused on selling products, services or data to individual consumers rather than commercial customers. Also known as B2C.

Business-to-Employee: A corporate communications system, such as an intranet, aimed at conveying information from a company to its employees. Also known as B2E.

Business-to-Government: An organization focused on selling products, services or data to government units rather than commercial businesses or consumers. Also known as B2G.

CANDA: See "Computer-Assisted New Drug Application (CANDA)."

Capex: Capital expenditures.

Capitation: A method of contracting for health services in which care providers, such as physicians, receive a fixed, per-patient fee each year, rather than a payment for each office visit and each procedure. Also see "Fee-For-Service" and "Value-Based Reimbursement."

Captive Offshoring: Used to describe a company-owned offshore operation. For example, Microsoft owns and operates significant captive offshore research and development centers in China and elsewhere that are offshore from Microsoft's U.S. home base. Also see "Offshoring."

Carcinogen: A substance capable of causing cancer. A suspected carcinogen is a substance that may cause cancer in humans or animals but for which the evidence is not conclusive.

Cardiac Catheterization Laboratory: Facilities offering special diagnostic procedures for cardiac patients, including the introduction of a catheter into the interior of the heart by way of a vein or artery or by direct needle puncture. Procedures must be performed in a laboratory or a special procedure room.

Cardiac Intensive Care Services: Services provided in a unit staffed with specially trained nursing personnel and containing monitoring and specialized support or treatment equipment for patients who (because of heart seizure, open-heart surgery or other life-threatening conditions) require intensified, comprehensive observation and care. May include myocardial infarction care, pulmonary care, and heart transplant units.

Case Report Form (CRF): In clinical trials, a standard document used by clinicians to record and report subject data pertinent to the study protocol.

CAT Scan: See "Computed Tomography (CT)."

Catheter: A tubular instrument used to add or withdraw fluids. Heart or cardiac catheterization involves the passage of flexible catheters into the great vessels and chambers of the heart. IV catheters add intravenous fluids to the veins. Foley catheters withdraw fluid from the bladder. Significant recent advances in technology allow administration of powerful drug and diagnostic therapies via catheters.

CBER: See "Center for Biologics Evaluation and Research (CBER)."

CDC: See "Centers for Disease Control and Prevention (CDC)."

CDER: See "Center for Drug Evaluation and Research (CDER)."

CDRH: See "Center for Devices and Radiological Health (CDRH)."

Center for Biologics Evaluation and Research (CBER): The branch of the FDA responsible for the regulation of biological products, including blood, vaccines, therapeutics and related drugs and devices, to ensure purity, potency, safety, availability and effectiveness. www.fda.gov/cber

Center for Devices and Radiological Health (CDRH): The branch of the FDA responsible for the regulation of medical devices. www.fda.gov/cdrh

Center for Drug Evaluation and Research (CDER): The branch of the FDA responsible for the regulation of drug products. www.fda.gov/cder

Centers for Disease Control and Prevention (CDC): The federal agency charged with protecting the public health of the nation by providing leadership and direction in the prevention and control of diseases and other preventable conditions and responding to public health emergencies. Headquartered in Atlanta, it was established as an operating health agency within the U.S. Public Health Service on July 1, 1973. See www.cdc.gov.

Centers for Medicare and Medicaid Services (CMS): A federal agency responsible for administering Medicare and monitoring the states' operations of Medicaid. See www.cms.hhs.gov.

Chemotherapy: The treatment of cancer using anticancer drugs, often conducted in association with radiation therapy. See "Radiation Therapy."

Chromosome: A structure in the nucleus of a cell that contains genes. Chromosomes are found in pairs.

Class I Device: An FDA classification of medical devices for which general controls are sufficient to ensure safety and efficacy.

Class II Device: An FDA classification of medical devices for which performance standards and special controls are sufficient to ensure safety and efficacy.

Class III Device: An FDA classification of medical devices for which pre-market approval is required to ensure safety and efficacy, unless the device is substantially equivalent to a currently marketed device. See "510 K."

Clinical Research Associate (CRA): An individual responsible for monitoring clinical trial data to ensure compliance with study protocol and FDA GCP regulations.

Clinical Trial: See "Phase I Clinical Trials," along with definitions for Phase II, Phase III and Phase IV.

Clone: A group of identical genes, cells or organisms derived from one ancestor. A clone is an identical copy. "Dolly" the sheep is a famous case of a clone of an animal. Also see "Cloning (Reproductive)" and "Cloning (Therapeutic)."

Cloning (Reproductive): A method of reproducing an exact copy of an animal or, potentially, an exact copy of a human being. A scientist removes the nucleus from a donor's unfertilized egg, inserts a nucleus from the animal to be copied and then stimulates the nucleus to begin dividing to form an embryo. In the case of a mammal, such as a human, the embryo would then be implanted in the uterus of a host female. Also see "Cloning (Therapeutic)."

Cloning (Therapeutic): A method of reproducing exact copies of cells needed for research or for the development of replacement tissue or organs. A scientist removes the nucleus from a donor's unfertilized egg, inserts a nucleus from the animal whose cells are to be copied and then stimulates the nucleus to begin dividing to form an embryo. However, the embryo is never allowed to grow to any significant stage of development. Instead, it is allowed to grow for a few hours or days, and stem cells are then removed from it for use in regenerating tissue. Also see "Cloning (Reproductive)."

CMS: See "Centers for Medicare and Medicaid Services (CMS)."

COBRA: See "Consolidated Omnibus Budget Reconciliation Act (COBRA)."

Code of Federal Regulations (CFR): A codification of the general and permanent rules published in the Federal Register by the executive departments and agencies of the Federal Government. The code is divided into 50 titles that represent broad areas subject to federal regulation. Title 21 of the CFR covers FDA regulations.

Coinsurance (Co-insurance): A practice in some medical coverage plans, homeowners insurance, Medicare and other types of insurance coverage whereby the beneficiary is required to pay a set percentage of costs in certain circumstances. For example, the covered party may be required to pay 20% of costs.

Committee for Veterinary Medicinal Products (CVMP): A committee that is a veterinary equivalent of the CPMP (see "Committee on Proprietary Medicinal Products (CPMP)") in the EU. See "European Union (EU)."

Committee on Proprietary Medicinal Products (CPMP): A committee, composed of two people from each EU Member State (see "European Union (EU)"), that is responsible for the scientific evaluation and assessment of marketing applications for medicinal products in the EU. The CPMP is the major body involved in the harmonization of pharmaceutical regulations within the EU and receives administrative support from the European Medicines Evaluation Agency. See "European Medicines Evaluation Agency (EMEA)."

Compounding Pharmacy: Compounding pharmacies are those that combine or alter drugs in order to meet a physician's prescription requirements. Examples include altering the contents of a pill so that it becomes a drinkable formula, modifying chemotherapy drugs to meet a specific patient'sneeds or adding flavoring to a medicine to make it more acceptable to a child.

Computed Tomography (CT): An imaging method that uses x-rays to create cross-sectional pictures of the body. The technique is frequently referred to as a "CAT Scan." A patient lies on a narrow platform while the machine's x-ray beam rotates around him or her. Small detectors inside the scanner measure the amount of x-rays that make it through the part of the body being studied. A computer takes this information and uses it to create several individual images, called slices. These images can be stored, viewed on a monitor, or printed on film. Three-dimensional models of organs can be created by stacking the individual slices together. The newest machines are capable of operating at 256 slice levels, creating very high resolution images in a short period of time.

Computer-Assisted New Drug Application (CANDA): An electronic submission of a new drug application (NDA) to the FDA.

Concierge Care: A medical practice in which patients typically receive enhanced access to physicians by paying a monthly or annual retainer fee. Services may include same-day or next-day appointments and after-hours access to physicians via pagers, cellphone or email.

Consolidated Omnibus Budget Reconciliation Act (COBRA): A federal law that requires employers to offer uninterrupted health care coverage to certain employees and their beneficiaries whose group coverage has been terminated.

Continuing Care Retirement Communities (CCRCs): Communities that provide coordinated housing and health-related services to older individuals under an agreement which may last as little as one year or as long as the life of the individual.

Continuity of Care: A systematic approach to a patient's care through the patient's continuous relationship with a team of health care providers, led by the primary care physician. In order to facilitate this approach, all of the patient's care providers must have real time access to the patient's health records, which is one of the goals of Electronic Health Records (EHRs) and Electronic Health Interchanges (EMIs). See "Electronic Health Record (EHR)."

Contract Research Organization (CRO): An independent organization that contracts with a client to conduct part of the work on a study or research project. For example, drug and medical device makers frequently outsource clinical trials and other research work to CROs.

Coordinator: In clinical trials, the person at an investigative site who handles the administrative responsibilities of the trial, acts as a liaison between the investigative site and the sponsor, and reviews data and records during a monitoring visit.

Copayment (Co-payment): An amount that is commonly required to be paid by the patient under health care plans including Medicare. For example, the patient may be required to pay $20 toward the cost of a doctor's office visit, or $15 toward the cost of a prescription drug.

COSTART: In medical and drug product development, a dictionary of adverse events and body systems used for coding and classifying adverse events.

CPMP: See "Committee on Proprietary Medicinal Products (CPMP)."

CRA: See "Clinical Research Associate (CRA)."

CRF: See "Case Report Form (CRF)."

CRM: See "Customer Relationship Management (CRM)."

CRT: Conformal radiotherapy. See "3DCRT."

Cryoablation: A technology based on the use of extremely cold temperatures delivered via a catheter or other device to treat tissues. It is an accepted method of treating cancer of the prostate. It also has applications in the prevention of heart arrhythmia.

Cryosurgery: See "Cryoablation."

CT: See "Computed Tomography (CT)."

Current Procedural Terminology (CPT): The most widely accepted medical nomenclature used to report medical procedures and services under public and private health insurance programs. CPT is also used for administrative management purposes, such as claims processing and developing guidelines for medical care review.

Customer Relationship Management (CRM): Refers to the automation, via sophisticated software, of business processes involving existing and prospective customers. CRM may cover aspects such as sales (contact management and contact history), marketing (campaign management and telemarketing) and customer service (call center history and field service history). Well known providers of CRM software include Salesforce, which delivers via a Software as a Service model (see "Software as a Service (Saas)"), Microsoft and Oracle.

CVMP: See "Committee for Veterinary Medicinal Products (CVMP)."

Data and Safety Monitoring Board (DSMB): See "Data Monitoring Board (DMB)."

Data Monitoring Board (DMB): A committee that monitors the progress of a clinical trial and carefully observes the safety data.

Deductible (Insurance Deductible): The initial amount of a loss that must be paid by the insurance policy holder. For example, a typical automobile policy deductible is $500, which means that the first $500 of any loss must be paid by the policy holder before the insurance company will pay for a portion above $500.

Defibrillator: In medicine, an instrument used externally (as electrodes on the chest) or implanted (as a small device similar in size to a pacemaker) that delivers an electric shock to return the heart to its normal rhythm.

Demand Chain: A similar concept to a supply chain, but with an emphasis on the end user.

Demographics: The breakdown of the population into statistical categories such as age, income, education and sex.

Deoxyribonucleic Acid (DNA): The carrier of the genetic information that cells need to replicate and to produce proteins.

Development: The phase of research and development (R&D) in which researchers attempt to create new products from the results of discoveries and applications created during basic and applied research.

Device: In medical products, an instrument, apparatus, implement, machine, contrivance, implant, in vitro reagent or other similar or related article, including any component, part or accessory, that 1) is recognized in the official National Formulary or United States Pharmacopoeia or any supplement to them, 2) is intended for use in the diagnosis of disease or other conditions, or in the cure, mitigation, treatment or prevention of disease, in man or animals or 3) is intended to affect the structure of the body of man or animals and does not achieve any of its principal intended purposes through chemical action within or on the body of man or animals and is not dependent upon being metabolized for the achievement of any of its principal intended purposes.

Diagnostic Radioisotope Facility: A medical facility in which radioactive isotopes (radiopharmaceuticals) are used as tracers or indicators to detect an abnormal condition or disease in the body.

Dialysis: An artificial blood-filtering process used to clean the blood of patients with malfunctioning kidneys.

Dietary Supplements Sold as Food: Legal diet aids that do not require licensing under medical regulations. Typically, dietary supplements sold as food are offered in powder, tablet, pill or capsule form.

Direct Primary Care: A physicians' business model whereby patients pay a monthly fee for unlimited access to their doctors. Additional enhanced services, such as preventative care and email access to doctors, are often added in a comprehensive package. An important reason enabling direct primary care firms to offer reasonable rates is the fact that the patient pays directly, so there is no overhead involved in dealing with insurance companies.

Disease Management: The use of programs that closely monitor the condition of a patient on a regular basis while educating and motivating that person about lifestyle and treatment alternatives that will reduce the impacts of certain conditions.

Distributor: An individual or business involved in marketing, warehousing and/or shipping of products manufactured by others to a specific group of end users. Distributors do not sell to the general public. In order to develop a competitive advantage, distributors often focus on serving one industry or one set of niche clients. For example, within the medical industry, there are major distributors that focus on providing pharmaceuticals, surgical supplies or dental supplies to clinics and hospitals.

DMB: See "Data Monitoring Board (DMB)."

DNA: See "Deoxyribonucleic Acid (DNA)."

DNA Chip: A revolutionary tool used to identify mutations in genes like BRCA1 and BRCA2. The chip, which consists of a small glass plate encased in plastic, is manufactured using a process similar to the one used to make computer microchips. On the surface, each chip contains synthetic single-stranded DNA sequences identical to a normal gene.

Doctor of Nursing Practice (DNP): A designation for a nurse who has completed rigorous educational, clinical and testing requirements in order to achieve doctoral-level nurse status, with an emphasis on clinical competence. This is a step beyond a Nurse Practitioner. A Doctor of Nursing Practice may use the DrNP designation after their names, or begin their names with "Dr." as a title, but they do not have the same status as MDs. In many states in the U.S., DNPs will be able to write prescriptions and operate independent health clinics, but regulations may vary from state to state, and they will not have all of the authority enjoyed by MDs. Many top schools of nursing also offer Ph.D. programs for nurses, typically with an emphasis on preparing them to be professors of nursing and educational leaders. Also, see "Nurse Practitioner."

Dosimetry: The accurate measurement of doses of radiation as used in medical treatment and imaging. The sources of such radiation may be x-ray, radiation therapy used for cancer treatment or other types of radiation.

Drug Utilization Review: A quantitative assessment of patient drug use and physicians' patterns of prescribing drugs in an effort to determine the usefulness of drug therapy.

DSMB: See "Data and Safety Monitoring Board (DSMB)."

EBRT: See "External Beam Radiation Therapy (EBRT)."

Echo Boomers: See "Generation Y."

Ecology: The study of relationships among all living organisms and the environment, especially the totality or pattern of interactions; a view that includes all plant and animal species and their unique contributions to a particular habitat.

E-Commerce: The use of online, Internet-based sales methods. The phrase is used to describe both business-to-consumer and business-to-business sales.

EEG: See "Electroencephalography (EEG)."

Efficacy: A drug or medical product's ability to effectively produce beneficial results within a patient.

EFGCP: See "European Forum for Good Clinical Practices (EFGCP)."

EHR: See "Electronic Health Record (EHR)."

ELA: See "Establishment License Application (ELA)."

Electroencephalography (EEG): Measures electrical activity in the brain.

Electronic Data Interchange (EDI): An accepted standard format for the exchange of data between various companies' networks. EDI allows for the transfer of e-mail as well as orders, invoices and other files from one company to another.

Electronic Health Record (EHR): An electronic record of patient health care information which can be updated by all of a patient's care providers from any location. Information may include patient demographics, details regarding progress and care, medications, vital signs, past medical history, immunizations, laboratory data and radiology reports. The EHR automates and streamlines workflow throughout the care spectrum.

Electroporation: A health care technology that uses short pulses of electric current (DC) to create openings (pores) in the membranes of cancerous cells, thus leading to death of the cells. It has potential as a treatment for prostate cancer. In the laboratory, it is a means of introducing foreign proteins or DNA into living cells.

EMEA: The region comprised of Europe, the Middle East and Africa.

Employee Assistance Program (EAP): A program designed to help employees, employers and family members find solutions to workplace and personal problems.

EMR: Electronic Medical Record. See "Electronic Health Record (EHR)."

Endoscope: A tiny, flexible tube-shaped instrument with a fiber optic light and a video camera lens at the end. It is inserted into the body through a natural body opening or a small incision, and has both diagnostic and therapeutic capabilities. Laparoscopic surgery is conducted in a minimally invasive manner using the endoscope to enable the surgeon to see the tissue being operated on. Such surgery is often conducted through an incision as small as one or two centimeters in length. Consequently, patients tend to heal very quickly after such surgery.

Enterprise Resource Planning (ERP): An integrated information system that helps manage all aspects of a business, including accounting, ordering and human resources, typically across all locations of a major corporation or organization. ERP is considered to be a critical tool for management of large organizations. Suppliers of ERP tools include SAP and Oracle.

Enzyme: A protein that acts as a catalyst, affecting the chemical reactions in cells.

ERP: See "Enterprise Resource Planning (ERP)."

Establishment License Application (ELA): Required for the approval of a biologic (see "Biologics"). It permits a specific facility to manufacture a biological product for commercial purposes. Compare to "Product License Agreement (PLA)."

ESWL: See "Extracorporeal Shock Wave Lithotripter (ESWL)."

Etiology: The study of the causes or origins of diseases.

EU: See "European Union (EU)."

EU Competence: The jurisdiction in which the European Union (EU) can take legal action.

European Community (EC): See "European Union (EU)."

European Forum for Good Clinical Practices (EFGCP): The organization dedicated to finding common ground in Europe on the implementation of Good Clinical Practices. See "Good Clinical Practices (GCP)." www.efgcp.org

European Medicines Evaluation Agency (EMEA): The European agency responsible for supervising and coordinating applications for marketing medicinal products in the European Union (see "European Union (EU)" and "Committee on Proprietary Medicinal Products (CPMP)"). The EMEA is headquartered in the U.K. www.eudraportal.eudra.org

European Union (EU): A consolidation of European countries (member states) functioning as one body to facilitate trade. Previously known as the European Community (EC). The EU has a unified currency, the Euro. See europa.eu.int.

Exclusive Provider Organization: Technically the same as an HMO, with the exception that the organization provides coverage only for services from contracted providers. See "Health Maintenance Organization (HMO)."

External Beam Radiation Therapy (EBRT): The application of radiation to a patient via external sources, such as X-ray, gamma ray or proton beam, in order to kill cancerous cells and shrink tumors.

Extracorporeal Shock Wave Lithotripter (ESWL): A medical device used for treating stones in the kidney or urethra. The device disintegrates kidney stones noninvasively through the transmission of acoustic shock waves directed at the stones.

FASB: See "Financial Accounting Standards Board (FASB)."

FD&C Act: See "Federal Food Drug and Cosmetic Act (FD&C Act)."

FDA: See "Food and Drug Administration (FDA)."

Federal Food, Drug and Cosmetic Act (FD&C Act): A set of laws passed by the U.S. Congress, which controls, among other things, residues in food and feed.

Fee-For-Service: Payment to health care providers, such as physicians, calculated for each service provided, such as an office visit, MRI, blood test or other procedure. The more services that a patient receives, the higher the bill. Also, see "Capitation" and "Value-Based Reimbursement" for discussions of alternatives to Fee-For-Service.

Fee-For-Service Equivalency: The amount of reimbursement for treatment of patients via a capitation payment schedule compared to a fee-for-service reimbursement. See "Capitation" and "Fee-For-Service."

Financial Accounting Standards Board (FASB): An independent organization that establishes the Generally Accepted Accounting Principles (GAAP).

Fissure: A long narrow crack or opening.

Follow-on Biologics: A term used to describe generic versions of drugs that have been created using biotechnology. Because biotech drugs ("biologics") are made from living cells, a generic version of a drug probably won't be biochemically identical to the original branded version of the drug. Consequently, they are described as "follow-on" biologics to set them apart. Since these drugs won't be exactly the same as the originals, there are concerns that they may not be as safe or effective unless they go through clinical trials for proof of quality. In Europe, these drugs are referred to as "biosimilars." See "Biologics."

Food and Drug Administration (FDA): The U.S. government agency responsible for the enforcement of the Federal Food, Drug and Cosmetic Act, ensuring industry compliance with laws regulating products in commerce. The FDA's mission is to protect the public from harm and encourage technological advances that hold the promise of benefiting society. www.fda.gov

Formulary: A preferred list of drug products that typically limits the number of drugs available within a therapeutic class for purposes of drug purchasing, dispensing and/or reimbursement. A government body, third-party insurer or health plan, or an institution may compile a formulary. Some institutions or health plans develop closed (i.e. restricted) formularies where only those drug products listed can be dispensed in that institution or reimbursed by the health plan. Other formularies may have no restrictions (open formulary) or may have certain restrictions such as higher patient cost-sharing requirements for off-formulary drugs.

Functional Imaging: The uses of PET scan, MRI and other advanced imaging technology to see how an area of the body is functioning and responding. For example, brain activity can be viewed, and the reaction of cancer tumors to therapies can be judged using functional imaging.

GAAP: See "Generally Accepted Accounting Principles (GAAP)."

Gamma Knife: A unique type of radiation therapy with tissue-sparing properties. It involves focusing low-dose gamma radiation on a tumor, while exposing only a small amount of healthy, nearby tissue to radiation. It is often used to treat certain brain cancers.

Gated Benefit Plans: Health insurance plans that require holders to pass general health tests such as screenings for diabetes, thyroid problems and the presence of nicotine to qualify for higher levels of coverage. To keep coverage, holders must have annual physicals and procedures such as mammograms and colonoscopies if over age 50.

GCP: See "Good Clinical Practices (GCP)."

GDP: See "Gross Domestic Product (GDP)."

Gene: A working subunit of DNA; the carrier of inheritable traits.

Gene Chip: See "DNA Chip."

Gene Therapy: A type of treatment based on first identifying the fact that a patient has a specific gene mutation related to a specific disease, followed by the introduction of healthy genes into the patient's body with the goal of altering or replacing the defective genes. This is the Holy Grail of the biotechnology industry, as it offers the potential to cure otherwise incurable diseases. It has also proven to be extremely difficult to carry out without significant side effects. A major commercial hurdle was passed in late 2012, when the European Medicines Agency (EMA) approved a gene therapy to treat a rare lipoprotein lipase (LPL) deficiency. The therapy, called Glybera and developed by Dutch biotech company uniQure, was the first approved gene therapy drug in the Western world.

Generally Accepted Accounting Principles (GAAP): A set of accounting standards administered by the Financial Accounting Standards Board (FASB) and enforced by the U.S. Security and Exchange Commission (SEC). GAAP is primarily used in the U.S.

Generation M: A very loosely defined term that is sometimes used to refer to young people who have grown up in the digital age. "M" may refer to any or all of media-saturated, mobile or multi-tasking. The term was most notably used in a Kaiser Family Foundation report published in 2005, "Generation M: Media in the Lives of 8-18 year olds." Also, see "Generation Y" and "Generation Z."

Generation X: A loosely-defined and variously-used term that describes people born between approximately 1965 and 1980, but other time frames are recited. Generation X is often referred to as a group influential in defining tastes in consumer goods, entertainment and/or political and social matters.

Generation Y: Refers to people born between approximately 1982 and 2002. In the U.S., they number more than 90 million, making them the largest generation segment in the nation's history. They are also known as Echo Boomers, Millenials or the Millenial Generation. These are children of the Baby Boom generation who will be filling the work force as Baby Boomers retire.

Generation Z: Some people refer to Generation Z as people born after 1991. Others use the beginning date of 2001, or refer to the era of 1994 to 2004. Members of Generation Z are considered to be natural and rapid adopters of the latest technologies.

Genetic Code: The sequence of nucleotides, determining the sequence of amino acids in protein synthesis.

Genetically Modified (GM) Foods: Food crops that are bioengineered to resist herbicides, diseases or insects; have higher nutritional value than non-engineered plants; produce a higher yield per acre; and/or last longer on the shelf. Additional traits may include resistance to temperature and moisture extremes. Agricultural animals also may be genetically modified organisms.

Genetically Modified Organism (GMO): An organism that has undergone genome modification by the insertion of a foreign gene. The genetic material of a GMO is not found through mating or natural recombination.

Genetics: The study of the process of heredity.

Genome: A genome is an organism's complete set of DNA, including all of its genes. Each genome contains all of the information needed to build and maintain that organism. In humans, a copy of the entire genome—more than 3 billion DNA base pairs—is contained in all cells that have a nucleus.

Genomics: The study of genes, their role in diseases and our ability to manipulate them.

GI Generation: Generally considered to be Americans who were born between 1901 and 1924. They made up the bulk of people who entered the U.S. Armed Forces during World War II. "GI" stands for Government Issue, a reference to the equipment issued to members of the military.

Globalization: The increased mobility of goods, services, labor, technology and capital throughout the world. Although globalization is not a new development, its pace has increased with the advent of new technologies.

GLP: See "Good Laboratory Practices (GLP)."

GM: See "Genetically-Modified (GM) Foods."

GMO: See "Genetically Modified Organism (GMO)."

GMP: See "Good Manufacturing Practices (GMP)."

Good Clinical Practices (GCP): FDA regulations and guidelines that define the responsibilities of the key figures involved in a clinical trial, including the sponsor, the investigator, the monitor and the Institutional Review Board. See "Institutional Review Board (IRB)."

Good Laboratory Practices (GLP): A collection of regulations and guidelines to be used in laboratories where research is conducted on drugs, biologics or devices that are intended for submission to the FDA.

Good Manufacturing Practices (GMP): A collection of regulations and guidelines to be used in manufacturing drugs, biologics and medical devices.

Gross Domestic Product (GDP): The total value of a nation's output, income and expenditures produced with a nation's physical borders.

Gross National Product (GNP): A country's total output of goods and services from all forms of economic activity measured at market prices for one calendar year. It differs from Gross Domestic Product (GDP) in that GNP includes income from investments made in foreign nations.

Group Practice Without Walls: A "quasi" group formed when a hospital sponsors or provides capital to physicians for the establishment of a practice to share administrative expenses while remaining independent practitioners.

Health Indemnity Insurance: Provides traditional insurance coverage, after a deductible, for specified health care needs. Typically, the patient can go to any physician or any hospital, and there is no aspect of managed care involved.

Health Information Exchange: A electronic network for health care providers that enables easy access to patients' health care records.

Health Maintenance Organization (HMO): An insurance entity that provides managed health care services. An HMO functions as a form of health care insurance which is sold on a group basis. The HMO contracts with doctors, hospitals, labs and other medical facilities for low rates in exchange for high volume. For the patient, only visits to professionals within the HMO network are covered in the highest possible amount by the HMO. The patient selects a primary care physician who is approved by the HMO. For care, the patient first visits the primary care physician who may refer the patient to a specialist on an as-needed basis. Also see "Managed Care" and "Preferred Provider Organization (PPO)."

Health Reimbursement Account (HRA): A form of health care coverage plan provided to employees by their employer. Under an HRA, the employer places a given amount of money into a special account each year for the employee to spend on health care. The employer also provides a high-deductible health coverage plan. The employee elects when and how to spend the money in the account on health care. Because of the high deductible, the employee's share of the monthly premium tends to be much lower than under an HMO or PPO, but the employee faces the burden of paying the high deductible when necessary. Unspent funds in the account can roll over from year to year so that the account grows, but the employee loses the fund balance when leaving the employer.

Health Savings Account (HSA): A plan that combines a tax-free savings and investment account (somewhat similar to a 401k) with a high-deductible health coverage plan. The intent is to give the consumer more incentive to control health care costs by reducing unnecessary care while shopping for the best prices. The consumer contributes pre-tax dollars annually to a savings account (up to $2,850 for an individual or $5,650 for a family, as of 2007). The employer may or may not match part of that contribution. The account may be invested in stocks, bonds or mutual funds. It grows tax-free, but the money may be spent only on health care. Unspent money stays in the account at the end of each year. The consumer must purchase an insurance policy or health care plan with an annual deductible of at least $1,000 for individuals or $2,000 for families.

HESC: See "Human Embryonic Stem Cell (HESC)."

HHS: See "U.S. Department of Health and Human Services (HHS)."

HIE: See "Health Information Exchange."

HIFU: See "High Intensity Focused Ultrasound (HIFU)."

High Intensity Focused Ultrasound (HIFU): A method of using sound waves to produce a focused amount of high heat in tumors or tissues in order to destroy them through thermoablation. Target temperature is about 70 to 90 degrees Centigrade (158 to 194 degrees Fahrenheit). This is a noninvasive treatment that is already in wide use in Europe, Asia and Canada for treatment of particular conditions, particularly cancer of the prostate. Late stage clinical trials were being conducted in the U.S. as of 2007. Several additional uses are being studied, including treatment of cancer of the kidney.

HIPAA: The Health Insurance Portability and Accountability Act of 1996, which demands that all billing and patient data must be exchanged electronically between care givers and insurance payers. A major focus of HIPAA requirements is the protection of patient data privacy.

HMO: See "Health Maintenance Organization (HMO)."

Home Care Agencies: Home health agencies, home care aid organizations and hospices.

Human Embryonic Stem Cell (HESC): See "Stem Cells."

Human Resources Outsourcing (HRO): Refers to the practice of hiring an outsourced services provider to manage an organization's day-to-day human resources needs.

ICD9: International Classification of Diseases - Version 9. A government coding system used for classifying diseases and diagnoses.

IFRS: See "International Financials Reporting Standards (IFRS)."

IGRT: See "Image Guided Radiation Therapy (IGRT)."

Image Guided Radiation Therapy (IGRT): A radiation technique that takes advantage of sophisticated imaging technologies in order to best target radiation therapy. Prostate cancer is often treated with IGRT. To treat that disease, tiny metal markers are implanted in the prostate using an outpatient procedure. The IGRT equipment is then able to locate the position of the prostate exactly by determining the location of the markers in real time. Varian is a leading manufacturer of IGRT equipment. The technology is similar to IMRT, but better enables radiation technicians to use ultrasound, CT or X-ray images to line up the radiation beam with the intended target. Also, see "Intensity Modulated Radiation Therapy (IMRT)."

Imaging: In medicine, the viewing of the body's organs through external, high-tech means. This reduces the need for broad exploratory surgery. These advances, along with new types of surgical instruments, have made minimally invasive surgery possible. Imaging includes MRI (magnetic resonance imaging), CT (computed tomography or CAT scan), MEG (magnetoencephalography), improved x-ray technology, mammography, ultrasound and angiography.

Imaging Contrast Agent: A molecule or molecular complex that increases the intensity of the signal detected by an imaging technique, including MRI and ultrasound. An MRI contrast agent, for example, might contain gadolinium attached to a targeting antibody. The antibody would bind to a specific target, a metastatic melanoma cell for example, while the gadolinium would increase the magnetic signal detected by the MRI scanner.

Immunoassay: An immunological assay. Types include agglutination, complement-fixation, precipitation, immunodiffusion and electrophoretic assays. Each type of assay utilizes either a particular type of antibody or a specific support medium (such as a gel) to determine the amount of antigen present.

Immunotherapy: A biotech related therapy that based on a strategy to stimulate and/or suppress the immune system in order to help the body fight cancer, infection, and other diseases. Some types of immunotherapy only target certain cells of the immune system. Others affect the immune system in a general way. Types of immunotherapy include cytokines, vaccines and certain monoclonal antibodies. Advancements in genetic sequencing and analysis are aiding significant advances in immunotherapy.

IMRT: See "Intensity Modulated Radiation Therapy (IMRT)."

In Vitro: Laboratory experiments conducted in the test tube, or otherwise, without using live animals and/or humans.

In Vivo: Laboratory experiments conducted with live animals and/or humans.

IND: See "Investigational New Drug Application (IND)."

Independent Practice Organization (IPO): A legal entity that holds managed care contracts. The IPO then contracts with physicians, often in solo practice, to provide care either on a fee-for-services or capitated basis. The purpose of an IPO is to assist solo physicians in obtaining managed care contracts, while allowing them to maintain their own private practices. (Sometimes referred to as Independent Practice Association.)

Indication: Refers to a specific disease, illness or condition for which a drug is approved as a treatment. Typically, a new drug is first approved for one indication. Then, an application to the FDA is later made for approval of additional indications.

Induced Pluripotent State Cell (IPSC): A human stem cell produced without human cloning or the use of human embryos or eggs. Adult cells are drawn from a skin biopsy and treated with four reprogramming factors, rendering cells that can produce all human cell types and grow indefinitely.

Industry Code: A descriptive code assigned to any company in order to group it with firms that operate in similar businesses. Common industry codes include the NAICS (North American Industrial Classification System) and the SIC (Standard Industrial Classification), both of which are standards widely used in America, as well as the International Standard Industrial Classification of all Economic Activities (ISIC), the Standard International Trade Classification established by the United Nations (SITC) and the General Industrial Classification of Economic Activities within the European Communities (NACE).

Information Technology (IT): The systems, including hardware and software, that move and store voice, video and data via computers and telecommunications.

Informed Consent: Must be obtained in writing from people who agree to be clinical trial subjects prior to their enrollment in the study. The document must explain the risks associated with the study and treatment and describe alternative therapy available to the patient. A copy of the document must also be provided to the patient.

Infusion Therapy: The introduction of fluid other than blood into a vein. See "Intravenous Therapy."

Initial Public Offering (IPO): A company's first effort to sell its stock to investors (the public). Investors in an up-trending market eagerly seek stocks offered in many IPOs because the stocks of newly public companies that seem to have great promise may appreciate very rapidly in price, reaping great profits for those who were able to get the stock at the first offering. In the United States, IPOs are regulated by the SEC (U.S. Securities Exchange Commission) and by the state-level regulatory agencies of the states in which the IPO shares are offered.

Institutional Review Board (IRB): A group of individuals usually found in medical institutions that is responsible for reviewing protocols for ethical consideration (to ensure the rights of the patients). An IRB also evaluates the benefit-to-risk ratio of a new drug to see that the risk is acceptable for patient exposure. Responsibilities of an IRB are defined in FDA regulations.

Intellectual Property (IP): The exclusive ownership of original concepts, ideas, designs, engineering plans or other assets that are protected by law. Examples include items covered by trademarks, copyrights and patents. Items such as software, engineering plans, fashion designs and architectural designs, as well as games, books, songs and other entertainment items are among the many things that may be considered to be intellectual property. (Also, see "Patent.")

Intensity Modulated Radiation Therapy (IMRT): A radiation technology that enables the technician to apply narrowly focused radiation directly toward cancerous tumors. IMRT helps to limit the amount of damage to surrounding tissues. The process includes using multiple beams (typically from seven to 12) aimed at the tumor from various directions. The beams meet at the tumor to administer the desired dosage. Breaking the dose down into multiple beams lessens the level of radiation that healthy tissues are exposed to. The point at which the beams join can be shaped to conform to the exact size, shape and location of the tumor, thus further sparing healthy tissue. Advanced imaging, such as CT, is used to provide precise guidance to the tumor's location. Also see "Image Guided Radiation Therapy (IMRT)."

International Financials Reporting Standards (IFRS): A set of accounting standards established by the International Accounting Standards Board (IASB) for the preparation of public financial statements. IFRS has been adopted by much of the world, including the European Union, Russia and Singapore.

Intravenous Therapy: The introduction of fluid other than blood into a vein. See "Infusion Therapy."

Investigational New Device Exemption (IDE): A document that must be filed with the FDA prior to initiating clinical trials of medical devices considered to pose a significant risk to human subjects.

Investigational New Drug Application (IND): A document that must be filed with the FDA prior to initiating clinical trials of drugs or biologics.

Investigator: In clinical trials, a clinician who agrees to supervise the use of an investigational drug, device or biologic in humans. Responsibilities of the investigator, as defined in FDA regulations, include administering the drug, observing and testing the patient, collecting data and monitoring the care and welfare of the patient.

Iontophoresis: The transfer of ions of medicine through the skin using a local electric current.

IP: See "Intellectual Property (IP)."

IPO: In health care, see "Independent Practice Organization (IPO)."

IRB: See "Institutional Review Board (IRB)."

IRE: Irreversible Electroporation. See "Electroporation."

ISO 9000, 9001, 9002, 9003: Standards set by the International Organization for Standardization. ISO 9000, 9001, 9002 and 9003 are the highest quality certifications awarded to organizations that meet exacting standards in their operating practices and procedures.

IT: See "Information Technology (IT)."

IT-Enabled Services (ITES): The portion of the Information Technology industry focused on providing business services, such as call centers, insurance claims processing and medical records transcription, by utilizing the power of IT, especially the Internet. Most ITES functions are considered to be back-office procedures. Also, see "Business Process Outsourcing (BPO)."

ITES: See "IT-Enabled Services (ITES)."

Just-in-Time (JIT) Delivery: Refers to a supply chain practice whereby manufacturers receive components on or just before the time that they are needed on the assembly line, rather than bearing the cost of maintaining several days' or weeks' supply in a warehouse. This adds greatly to the cost-effectiveness of a manufacturing plant and puts the burden of warehousing and timely delivery on the supplier of the components.

Knowledge Process Outsourcing (KPO): The use of outsourced and/or offshore workers to perform business tasks that require judgment and analysis. Examples include such professional tasks as patent research, legal research, architecture, design, engineering, market research, scientific research, accounting and tax return preparation. Also, see "Business Process Outsourcing (BPO)."

LAC: An acronym for Latin America and the Caribbean.

Laparoscope: See "Endoscope."

Laparoscopic Surgery: See "Endoscope."

LDCs: See "Least Developed Countries (LDCs)."

Least Developed Countries (LDCs): Nations determined by the U.N. Economic and Social Council to be the poorest and weakest members of the international community. There are currently 50 LDCs, of which 34 are in Africa, 15 are in Asia Pacific and the remaining one (Haiti) is in Latin America. The top 10 on the LDC list, in descending order from top to 10th, are Afghanistan, Angola, Bangladesh, Benin, Bhutan, Burkina Faso, Burundi, Cambodia, Cape Verde and the Central African Republic. Sixteen of the LDCs are also Landlocked Least Developed Countries (LLDCs) which present them with additional difficulties often due to the high cost of transporting trade goods. Eleven of the LDCs are Small Island Developing States (SIDS), which are often at risk of extreme weather phenomenon (hurricanes, typhoons, Tsunami); have fragile ecosystems; are often dependent on foreign energy sources; can have high disease rates for HIV/AIDS and malaria; and can have poor market access and trade terms.

Licensed Practical Nurse (LPN): A nurse who has completed a practical nursing program and is licensed to provide basic patient care under the supervision of a registered nurse or physician. Also known as a Licensed Vocational Nurse (LVN).

Ligand: Any atom or molecule attached to a central atom in a complex compound.

Lithotripsy: See "Extracorporeal Shock Wave Lithotripter (ESWL)."

LOHAS: Lifestyles of Health and Sustainability. A marketing term that refers to consumers who choose to purchase and/or live with items that are natural, organic, less polluting, etc. Such consumers may also prefer products powered by alternative energy, such as hybrid cars.

Low-Calorie: Refers to foods with 40 or fewer calories per serving.

Low-Cholesterol: Refers to foods with 20 or fewer milligrams of cholesterol and two or fewer grams of saturated fat per serving.

Low-Fat: Refers to foods with three or fewer grams of fat per serving.

Low-Sodium: Refers to foods with 140 or fewer milligrams of sodium per serving.

Magnetic Resonance Imaging (MRI): The use of a uniform magnetic field and radio frequencies to study tissues and structures of the body. This procedure enables the visualization of biochemical activity of the cell in vivo without the use of ionizing radiation, radioisotopic substances or high-frequency sound.

Magnetoencephalography (MEG): A newer technology derived from both MRI and electroencephalography (EEG). Like EEG, MEG registers brain patterns, but whereas EEG measures electrical activity in the brain, MEG measures magnetic waves, primarily in the cerebral cortex of the brain.

Managed Care: A system of prepaid medical plans providing comprehensive coverage to voluntarily enrolled members. Managed health care typically covers professional fees, hospital services, diagnostic services, emergency services, limited mental services, medical treatment for drug or alcohol abuse, home health services and preventive health care. The most common systems in managed care are HMOs (Health Maintenance Organizations) and PPOs (Preferred Provider Organizations), but there are other variations on these models. The word "managed" is used to describe this type of coverage because the total cost and extent of a patient's care is carefully managed and controlled by the group's administrators. Part of this management includes limiting the patient's choice to physicians, hospitals and labs that have agreed to provide reduced fees in exchange for high volume. Patients who receive care outside of this network will receive lesser reimbursement from the managed care provider. Also see "Health Maintenance Organization (HMO)," "Preferred Provider Organization (PPO)" and "Utilization Management."

Management Services Organization (MSO): A corporation, owned by a hospital or a physician/hospital joint venture, that provides management services to one or more medical group practices. The MSO purchases the tangible assets of the practices and leases them back as part of a full-service management agreement, under which the MSO employs all non-physician staff and provides all supplies and administrative systems for a fee.

Manufacturing Resource Planning (MRP II): A methodology that supports effective planning with regard to all resources of a manufacturing company, linking MRP with sales and operations planning, production planning and master production scheduling.

Market Segmentation: The division of a consumer market into specific groups of buyers based on demographic factors.

Medicaid: A federally supported and state-administered assistance program providing medical care for certain low-income individuals and other citizens. Medicaid was initially envisioned as a safety net for the poor. Today, in addition to meeting many of the health needs of low income households, the majority of Medicaid funds go to seniors and the seriously disabled to pay for nursing home care.

Medical Device: See "Device."

Medical Home: A physician practice model that is designed to be something of a collaborative partnership between patient, family and primary care physician. The medical home calls on outside specialists when they are needed as part of this team. The medical home is intended to foster communication and understanding, while maintaining a continuous record of all of a patient's medical history.

Medical Savings Account (MSA): See "Health Savings Account (HSA)."

Medical Tourism: The practice of patients in countries such as the U.S., Canada and the U.K. seeking inexpensive medical care in foreign countries.

Medicare: A U.S. government program that pays hospitals, physicians and other medical providers for serving patients aged 65 years and older, certain disabled people and most people with end-stage renal disease (ESRD). Medicare consists of two basic programs: Part A covers hospice care, home health care, skilled nursing care and inpatient hospital stays. Part B covers doctors' fees, outpatient care, X-rays, medical equipment and other fees not covered by Part A. Medicare Part C is designed to expand the types of private plans that beneficiaries may choose from, such as PPOs, and allows for the use of medical savings accounts. Prescription coverage was recently added as Medicare Part D.

MEG: See "Magnetoencephalography (MEG)."

Millenials: See "Generation Y."

Minimally Invasive Surgery: The use of very small incisions and advanced instruments that may be viewed through microscopes or video. Includes laparoscopy, endoscopy, electrosurgery and cryosurgery. This practice promotes rapid healing.

Minimally-Invasive Surgery: See "Endoscope."

Molecular Imaging: An emerging field in which advanced biology on the molecular level is combined with noninvasive imaging to determine the presence of certain proteins and other important genetic material.

Monoclonal Antibodies (mAb, Human Monoclonal Antibody): Antibodies that have been cloned from a single antibody and massed produced as a therapy or diagnostic test. An example is an antibody specific to a certain protein found in cancer cells.

NAICS: North American Industrial Classification System. See "Industry Code."

Nanotechnology: The science of designing, building or utilizing unique structures that are smaller than 100 nanometers (a nanometer is one billionth of a meter). This involves microscopic structures that are no larger than the width of some cell membranes.

National Drug Code (NDC): An identifying drug number maintained by the FDA.

National Institutes of Health (NIH): A branch of the U.S. Public Health Service that conducts biomedical research. www.nih.gov

NCE: See "New Chemical Entity (NCE)."

NDA: See "New Drug Application (NDA)."

Neonatal Intensive Care Services (NICU): A unit that must be separate from the newborn nursery. It provides intensive care to all sick infants, including those with very low birth weights (less than 1500 grams). The NICU can provide mechanical ventilation, neonatal surgery and special care for the sickest infants.

New Chemical Entity (NCE): See "New Molecular Entity (NME)."

New Drug Application (NDA): An application requesting FDA approval, after completion of the all-important Phase III Clinical Trials, to market a new drug for human use in the U.S. The drug may contain chemical compounds that were previously approved by the FDA as distinct molecular entities suitable for use in drug trials (NMEs). See "New Molecular Entity (NME)."

New Molecular Entity (NME): Defined by the FDA as a medication containing chemical compound that has never before been approved for marketing in any form in the U.S. An NME is sometimes referred to as a New Chemical Entity (NCE). Also, see "New Drug Application (NDA)."

NIH: See "National Institutes of Health (NIH)."

Nonclinical Studies: In vitro (laboratory) or in vivo (animal) pharmacology, toxicology and pharmacokinetic studies that support the testing of a product in humans. Usually at least two species are evaluated prior to Phase I clinical trials. Nonclinical studies continue throughout all phases of research to evaluate long-term safety issues.

Nurse Practitioner: A registered nurse (RN) who has completed advanced training and licensing. Nurse practitioners may work independent of a physician, or sometimes with a physician's light supervision. They provide direct examination, diagnosis and treatment of patients, and in many states they may write prescriptions and operate clinics. Also, see "Doctor of Nursing Practice (DNP)."

ODM: See "Original Design Manufacturer (ODM)."

OECD: See "Organisation for Economic Co-operation and Development (OECD)."

OEM: See "Original Equipment Manufacturer (OEM)."

Offshoring: The rapidly growing tendency among U.S., Japanese and Western European firms to send knowledge-based and manufacturing work overseas. The intent is to take advantage of lower wages and operating costs in such nations as China, India, Hungary and Russia. The choice of a nation for offshore work may be influenced by such factors as language and education of the local workforce, transportation systems or natural resources. For example, China and India are graduating high numbers of skilled engineers and scientists from their universities. Also, some nations are noted for large numbers of workers skilled in the English language, such as the Philippines and India. Also see "Captive Offshoring" and "Outsourcing."

Oncology: The diagnosis, study and treatment of cancer.

Onshoring: The opposite of "offshoring." Providing or maintaining manufacturing or services within or nearby a company's domestic location. Sometimes referred to as reshoring.

Open Access: Typically found in an IPA HMO, this arrangement allows members to consult specialists without obtaining a referral from another doctor.

Organisation for Economic Co-operation and Development (OECD): A group of more than 30 nations that are strongly committed to the market economy and democracy. Some of the OECD members include Japan, the U.S., Spain, Germany, Australia, Korea, the U.K., Canada and Mexico. Although not members, Estonia, Israel and Russia are invited to member talks; and Brazil, China, India, Indonesia and South Africa have enhanced engagement policies with the OECD. The Organisation provides statistics, as well as social and economic data; and researches social changes, including patterns in evolving fiscal policy, agriculture, technology, trade, the environment and other areas. It publishes over 250 titles annually; publishes a corporate magazine, the OECD Observer; has radio and TV studios; and has centers in Tokyo, Washington, D.C., Berlin and Mexico City that distributed the Organisation's work and organizes events.

Original Design Manufacturer (ODM): A contract manufacturer that offers complete, end-to-end design, engineering and manufacturing services. ODMs design and build products, such as consumer electronics, that client companies can then brand and sell as their own. For example, a large percentage of laptop computers, cell phones and PDAs are made by ODMs. Also see "Original Equipment Manufacturer (OEM)" and "Contract Manufacturing."

Original Equipment Manufacturer (OEM): 1) A company that manufactures a component (or a completed product) for sale to a customer that will integrate the component into a final product. The OEM's customer will put its own brand name on the end product and distribute or resell it to end users. 2) A firm that buys a component and then incorporates it into a final product, or buys a completed product and then resells it under the firm's own brand name. This usage is most often found in the computer industry, where OEM is sometimes used as a verb. Also see "Original Design Manufacturer (ODM)" and "Contract Manufacturing."

Orphan Drug: A drug or biologic designated by the FDA as providing therapeutic benefit for a rare disease affecting less than 200,000 people in the U.S. Companies that market orphan drugs are granted a period of market exclusivity in return for the limited commercial potential of the drug.

Orthodontics: A specialized branch of dentistry that restores the teeth to proper alignment and function. There are several different types of appliances used in orthodontics, braces being one of the most common.

OTC: See "Over-the-Counter Drugs (OTC)."

Outsourcing: The hiring of an outside company to perform a task otherwise performed internally by the company, generally with the goal of lowering costs and/or streamlining work flow. Outsourcing contracts are generally several years in length. Companies that hire outsourced services providers often prefer to focus on their core strengths while sending more routine tasks outside for others to perform. Typical outsourced services include the running of human resources departments, telephone call centers and computer departments. When outsourcing is performed overseas, it may be referred to as offshoring. Also see "Offshoring."

Over-the-Counter Drugs (OTC): FDA-regulated products that do not require a physician's prescription. Some examples are aspirin, sunscreen, nasal spray and sunglasses.

Panomics: The individual combination of factors including genes, proteins and molecular pathways, that fuel the growth of malignant cells.

Paramedical: A person trained to assist medical professionals and supplement physicians and nurses in their activities in order to give emergency medical treatment.

Patent: An intellectual property right granted by a national government to an inventor to exclude others from making, using, offering for sale, or selling the invention throughout that nation or importing the invention into the nation for a limited time in exchange for public disclosure of the invention when the patent is granted. In addition to national patenting agencies, such as the United States Patent and Trademark Office, and regional organizations such as the European Patent Office, there is a cooperative international patent organization, the World Intellectual Property Organization, or WIPO, established by the United Nations.

Pathogen: Any microorganism (e.g., fungus, virus, bacteria or parasite) that causes a disease.

Patient Protection and Affordable Care Act (PPACA): See "Affordable Care Act."

PCMH: Patient Centered Medical Home. See "Medical Home."

PCR: See "Polymerase Chain Reaction (PCR)."

Peer Review: The process used by the scientific community, whereby review of a paper, project or report is obtained through comments of independent colleagues in the same field.

PET (Imaging): See "Positron Emission Tomography (PET)."

Pharmacodynamics (PD): The study of reactions between drugs and living systems. It can be thought of as the study of what a drug does to the body.

Pharmacoeconomics: The study of the costs and benefits associated with various drug treatments.

Pharmacogenetics: The investigation of the different reactions of human beings to drugs and the underlying genetic predispositions. The differences in reaction are mainly caused by mutations in certain enzymes responsible for drug metabolization. As a result, the degradation of the active substance can lead to harmful by-products, or the drug might have no effect at all.

Pharmacokinetics (PK): The study of the processes of bodily absorption, distribution, metabolism and excretion of compounds and medicines. It can be thought of as the study of what the body does to a drug. See "Absorption, Distribution, Metabolism and Excretion (ADME)."

Pharmacology: The science of drugs, their characteristics and their interactions with living organisms.

Pharmacy Benefit Manager (PBM): An organization that provides administrative services in processing and analyzing prescription claims for pharmacy benefit and coverage programs. Many PBMs also operate mail order pharmacies or have arrangements to include prescription availability through mail order pharmacies.

Phase I Clinical Trials: Studies in this phase include initial introduction of an investigational drug into humans. These studies are closely monitored and are usually conducted in healthy volunteers. Phase I trials are conducted after the completion of extensive nonclinical or pre-clinical trials not involving humans. Phase I studies include the determination of clinical pharmacology, bioavailability, drug interactions and side effects associated with increasing doses of the drug.

Phase II Clinical Trials: Include randomized, masked, controlled clinical studies conducted to evaluate the effectiveness of a drug for a particular indication(s). During Phase II trials, the minimum effective dose and dosing intervals should be determined.

Phase III Clinical Trials: Consist of controlled and uncontrolled trials that are performed after preliminary evidence of effectiveness of a drug has been established. They are conducted to document the safety and efficacy of the drug, as well as to determine adequate directions (labeling) for use by the physician. A specific patient population needs to be clearly identified from the results of these studies. Trials during Phase III are conducted using a large number of patients to determine the frequency of adverse events and to obtain data regarding intolerance.

Phase IV Clinical Trials: Conducted after approval of a drug has been obtained to gather data supporting new or revised labeling, marketing or advertising claims.

Physician-Hospital Organization (PHO), Closed: A PHO that restricts physician membership to those practitioners who meet criteria for cost effectiveness and/or high quality.

Physician-Hospital Organization (PHO), Open: A joint venture between the hospital and all members of the medical staff who wish to participate. The PHO can act as a unified agent in managed care contracting, own a managed care plan, own and operate ambulatory care centers or ancillary services projects, or provide administrative services to physician members.

Pivotal Studies: In clinical trials, a Phase III trial that is designed specifically to support approval of a product. These studies are well-controlled (usually by placebo) and are generally designed with input from the FDA so that they will provide data that is adequate to support approval of the product. Two pivotal studies are required for drug product approval, but usually only one study is required for biologics.

PMA: See "Pre-Market Approval (PMA)."

Point-of-Service Plan (POS): A managed care plan in which member patients may go outside of the network to be attended by their preferred physicians, but pay a higher deductible if they so choose. Routine care is provided by a primary care physician who also provides referrals to in-network specialists.

Polymerase Chain Reaction (PCR): In molecular biology, PCR is a technique used to reproduce or amplify small, selected sections of DNA or RNA for analysis. It enables researchers to create multiple copies of a given sequence.

Positron Emission Tomography (PET): Positron Emission Tomography (often referred to as a PET scan) is a nuclear medicine imaging technology that uses computers and radioactive (positron emitting) isotopes, which are created in a cyclotron or generator, to produce composite pictures of the brain and heart at work. PET scanning produces sectional images depicting metabolic activity or blood flow rather than anatomy.

Post-Marketing Surveillance: The FDA's ongoing safety monitoring of marketed drugs.

PPACA: Patient Protection and Affordable Care Act. See: "Affordable Care Act."

Pre-Boomer: A term occasionally used to describe people who were born between 1935 and 1945. They are somewhat older than Baby Boomers (born between 1946 and 1962). Also see "Baby Boomer."

Precision Medicine: The use of genomic, epigenomic, and other data to define individual patterns of disease within a patient, potentially leading to better individual treatment, particularly through drugs targeted at specific gene mutations.

Preclinical Studies: See "Nonclinical Studies."

Preferred Provider Organization (PPO): Insurance entities that provide "managed health care" services. A PPO is a modified version of the HMO model. Generally, patients who are members of PPOs have more flexibility in the personal choice of physicians than do members of HMOs. Patients pay higher premiums than HMOs because of this flexibility. Patients are encouraged to visit physicians who are part of the PPO's system, but may also receive very good reimbursement for visiting physicians who are "out-of-network." Also see "Health Maintenance Organization (HMO)" and "Managed Care."

Pre-Market Approval (PMA): Required for the approval of a new medical device or a device that is to be used for life-sustaining or life-supporting purposes, is implanted in the human body or presents potential risk of illness or injury.

Premium (Insurance Premium): An insurance premium is the monthly or yearly fee charged for coverage by the insurance underwriter.

Primary Care Network: A group of primary care physicians who pool their resources to share the financial risk of providing care to their patients who are covered by a particular health plan.

Private Fee For Service (PFFS): Insurance provided under Medicare, in which private companies offer Centers for Medicare and Medicaid Services approved plans that allow patients to choose their own doctors and hospitals. PFFS plans provide beneficiaries with all of their Medicare benefits plus any additional benefits the company chooses to provide. Services generally require a co-payment plus, in certain cases, up to 35% of a Medicare-approved amount.

Product License Agreement (PLA): See "Biologics License Application (BLA)."

Proton Beam Radiation Therapy (PBRT): The use of a highly advanced technology to deliver external beam radiation therapy (EBRT) to a patient in order to kill cancerous cells and shrink tumors. While traditional radiation therapies rely on photons delivered by X-rays or gamma rays, Proton Beam Radiation Therapy relies on a particle accelerator to create and deliver protons. Protons are high-energy particles that carry a charge. By varying the velocity of the particles at the time that they enter the body, physicists are able to control the exact spot within the body where the radiation is released. The higher the velocity, the deeper within the body the radiation begins to take effect. With traditional radiation (based on photons rather than protons), there is a significant entry dose of radiation that can be harmful to healthy tissues. Proton beam therapy has the ability to better focus the radiation on the exact place of the tumor, significantly cutting down on side effects and damage to surrounding tissues. There are only a handful of proton beam centers in the world.

Provider Service Network (PSN): An insurance entity, owned by hospitals and physicians, that provides managed health care services.

PSN: See "Provider Service Network (PSN)."

Psychiatry: A branch of medicine concerned with the study, treatment and prevention of mental, emotional and behavioral disorders. Psychiatrists are doctors and can treat patients using drugs and other physical methods.

Psychology: The scientific study of human behavior and mental processes. Psychologists treat patients using therapeutic methods, including counseling or group work.

Public Health Service (PHS): May stand for the Public Health Service Act, a law passed by the U.S. Congress in 1944. PHS also may stand for the Public Health Service itself, a U.S. government agency established by an act of Congress in July 1798, originally authorizing hospitals for the care of American merchant seamen. Today, the Public Health Service sets national health policy; conducts medical and biomedical research; sponsors programs for disease control and mental health; and enforces laws to assure the safety and efficacy of drugs, foods, cosmetics and medical devices. The FDA (Food and Drug Administration) is part of the Public Health Service, as are the Centers for Disease Control and Prevention (CDC).

Public-Private Partnership (PPP, or P3): Partnerships that involve government agencies with private companies in the construction, operation and/or funding of publicly-needed buildings and infrastructure, such as toll roads, airports, waterworks, sewage plants or power plants.

QOL: See "Quality of Life (QOL)."

Quality of Life (QOL): In medicine, an endpoint of therapeutic assessment used to adjust measures of effectiveness for clinical decision-making. Typically, QOL endpoints measure the improvement of a patient's day-to-day living as a result of specific therapy.

Quantified Self: An evolving concept that refers to the use of electronic devices and electronic communications to gather, record and transmit personal information. An extreme practice of quantified self would be a person who uses a wearable, digital camera to record his surroundings 24/7, and who blogs, tweets or posts to social media his daily activities on a continuous basis. The most practical application of quantified self will most likely be in mobile health, (the personal health Internet). Examples include the wearing of wireless heart monitors, sleep monitors or pedometers that record daily health and exercise data in order to manage health problems or improve fitness.

R&D: Research and development. Also see "Applied Research" and "Basic Research."

Radiation Therapy: Radiation therapy is frequently used to destroy cancerous cells. This branch of medicine is concerned with radioactive substances and the usage of various techniques of imaging, for the diagnosis and treatment of disease. Services can include megavoltage radiation therapy, radioactive implants, stereotactic radiosurgery, therapeutic radioisotope services, or the use of x-rays, gamma rays and other radiation sources.

Radio Frequency Ablation (RFA): The use of focused radiowaves to produce high levels of heat within tumors in order to kill cancer. It is typically applied via needles that have been placed in the tumor, using ultrasound or other imaging techniques to insure correct placement. It is often used in the treatment of cancer of the kidney.

Radio Frequency Identification (RFID): A technology that applies a special microchip-enabled tag to an individual item or piece of merchandise or inventory. RFID technology enables wireless, computerized tracking of that inventory item as it moves through the supply chain from factory to transport to warehouse to retail store or end user. Also known as radio tags.

Radioisotope: An object that has varying properties that allows it to penetrate other objects at different rates. For example, a sheet of paper can stop an alpha particle, a beta particle can penetrate tissues in the body and a gamma ray can penetrate concrete. The varying penetration capabilities allow radioisotopes to be used in different ways. (Also called radioactive isotope or radionuclide.)

Radiotherapy: The use of doses of high-energy radiation to kill cancer cells and shrink tumors. Radiation may be applied externally, through external beam radiation therapy, or internally through small radioactive implants. Sources of radiation may include X-ray, gamma ray or proton beams.

Radiowave Therapy: See "Radio Frequency Ablation (RFA)."

Registered Nurse (RN): A graduate of an accredited school of nursing who has been registered and licensed to practice by a state authority. A registered nurse (RN) typically has received more formal education than an LPN (licensed practical nurse) or LVN (licensed vocational nurse). An RN often has received a 4-year college degree leading to the bachelors in science-nursing (BSN).

RFID: See "Radio Frequency Identification (RFID)."

Ribonucleic Acid (RNA): A macromolecule found in the nucleus and cytoplasm of cells; vital in protein synthesis.

RNA: See "Ribonucleic Acid (RNA)."

Safe Medical Devices Act (SMDA): An act that amends the Food, Drug and Cosmetic Act to impose additional regulations on medical devices. The act became law in 1990.

SIC: Standard Industrial Classification. See "Industry Code."

Silent Generation: Generally considered to be people born between 1925 and 1945, although the dates vary. Most of the Silent Generation were born during the Great Depression, through the end of World War II.

Single Nucleotide Polymorphisms (SNPs): Stable mutations consisting of a change at a single base in a DNA molecule. SNPs can be detected by HTP analyses, such as gene chips, and they are then mapped by DNA sequencing. They are the most common type of genetic variation.

SMDA: See "Safe Medical Devices Act (SMDA)."

SNP: See "Single-Nucleotide Polymorphisms (SNPs)."

SPECT: Single Photon Emission Computerized Tomography. A nuclear medicine imaging technology that combines existing technology of gamma camera imaging with computed tomographic (CT) imaging technology to provide a more precise and clear image.

Sponsor: The individual or company that assumes responsibility for the investigation of a new drug, including compliance with the FD&C Act and regulations. The sponsor may be an individual, partnership, corporation or governmental agency and may be a manufacturer, scientific institution or investigator regularly and lawfully engaged in the investigation of new drugs. The sponsor assumes most of the legal and financial responsibility of the clinical trial.

Stem Cells: Cells found in human bone marrow, the blood stream and the umbilical cord that can be replicated indefinitely and can turn into any type of mature blood cell, including platelets, white blood cells or red blood cells. Also referred to as pluripotent cells.

Stereotactic Body Radiation Therapy (SBRT): See "Stereotactic Radiotherapy."

Stereotactic Radiotherapy: The use of precise three dimensional positioning while delivering a high dose of radiation to a tumor. It is often used to treat brain tumors. The procedure involves the bolting of a metallic frame, like a halo, to the patient's head to prevent any movement and to enhance delivery of radiation.

Study Coordinator: See "Coordinator."

Subsidiary, Wholly-Owned: A company that is wholly controlled by another company through stock ownership.

Summary Plan Description: A description of an employee's entire benefit package as required by self-funded plans.

Supply Chain: The complete set of suppliers of goods and services required for a company to operate its business. For example, a manufacturer's supply chain may include providers of raw materials, components, custom-made parts and packaging materials.

Taste Masking: The creation of a barrier between a drug molecule and taste receptors so the drug is easier to take. It masks bitter or unpleasant tastes.

TESS: See "Adverse Event (AE)."

Third-Party Administrator: An independent person or organization that administers the group plan's benefits and claims and administration for self-insured companies.

Tomotherapy: A relatively new method of radiation treatment that combines the use of very sophisticated computer-controlled radiation beam collimation with an on-board computed tomography (CT) scanner to image the treatment site. The intent is to create an enhanced level of accuracy in beam delivery.

Trial Coordinator: See "Coordinator."

U.S. Department of Health and Human Services (HHS): This agency has more than 300 major programs related to human health and welfare, the largest of which is Medicare. See www.hhs.gov

Ultrashort Pulse Laser (USP): A technology that utilizes ultrafast lasers that pulse on and off at almost immeasurable speed. Scientists estimate that USP flashes once every femtosecond, which is a billionth of a millionth of a second. USP destroys atoms by knocking out electrons, which causes no rise in temperature in surrounding atoms as is associated with traditional lasers. Potential applications include vastly improved laser surgery, scanning for explosives, gemstone verification and processing donated human tissue for transplantation.

Ultrasound: The use of acoustic waves above the range of 20,000 cycles per second to visualize internal body structures. Frequently used to observe a fetus.

Unitized Pricing: Pricing for insurance coverage in which employees pay per person as opposed to choosing between individual and family coverage.

Utility Patent: A utility patent may be granted by the U.S. Patent and Trademark Office to anyone who invents or discovers any new, useful, and non-obvious process, machine, article of manufacture, or composition of matter, or any new and useful improvement thereof.

Utilization Management: A system in which utilization case managers (frequently registered nurses with several years of hospital experience) are assigned to each patient who receives hospitalization or extended treatment. These case managers constantly review the amount of care being provided to the patient in question, frequently resulting in significant cost savings. Also see "Managed Care."

Validation of Data: The procedure carried out to ensure that the data contained in a final clinical trial report match the original observations.

Value Added Tax (VAT): A tax that imposes a levy on businesses at every stage of manufacturing based on the value it adds to a product. Each business in the supply chain pays its own VAT and is subsequently repaid by the next link down the chain; hence, a VAT is ultimately paid by the consumer, being the last link in the supply chain, making it comparable to a sales tax. Generally, VAT only applies to goods bought for consumption within a given country; export goods are exempt from VAT, and purchasers from other countries taking goods back home may apply for a VAT refund.

Value-Based Reimbursement: A method of payment from health care insurers to care providers. In value-based reimbursement, as opposed to fee-for-service, physicians and hospitals may be paid recurring fees for improving patients' health, reducing trips to the emergency room and other wellness-enhancing measures, with the goal of reducing the overall cost of care. Also see "Fee-For-Service."

Vegan: A person whose diet includes only plant products and excludes all forms of animal products, including meat, fish, poultry, eggs, dairy, gelatin and honey.

Vegetarian:

Vendor: Any firm, such as a manufacturer or distributor, from which a retailer obtains merchandise.

Videolaseroscopy: A procedure using an endoscope equipped with a laser that is being used in minimally-invasive surgery to excise and or cauterize damaged tissue in the abdomen and lungs.

World Health Organization (WHO): A United Nations agency that assists governments in strengthening health services, furnishing technical assistance and aid in emergencies, working on the prevention and control of epidemics and promoting cooperation among different countries to improve nutrition, housing, sanitation, recreation and other aspects of environmental hygiene. Any country that is a member of the United Nations may become a member of the WHO by accepting its constitution. The WHO currently has 191 member states.

World Trade Organization (WTO): One of the only globally active international organizations dealing with the trade rules between nations. Its goal is to assist the free flow of trade goods, ensuring a smooth, predictable supply of goods to help raise the quality of life of member citizens. Members form consensus decisions that are then ratified by their respective parliaments. The WTO's conflict resolution process generally emphasizes interpreting existing commitments and agreements, and discovers how to ensure trade policies to conform to those agreements, with the ultimate aim of avoiding military or political conflict.

WTO: See "World Trade Organization (WTO)."

Xenotransplantation: The science of transplanting organs such as kidneys, hearts or livers into humans from other mammals, such as pigs or other agricultural animals grown with specific traits for this purpose.

Zoonosis: An animal disease that can be transferred to man.

Zootechnical Feed Additives: Medicines, such as growth promoters and antibiotics, which are incorporated as additives into feed.

Lightning Source UK Ltd.
Milton Keynes UK
UKHW05f2133051018
330013UK00003B/24/P